Tools & Techniques
of
ESTATE
PLANNING

13 EDITION

LEIMBERG
KASNER
KANDELL
MILLER
ROSENBLOOM
LEVY
POLACEK

5081 Olympic Boulevard
Erlanger, KY 41018

.NUCO.com

The
**National
Underwriter**
Company
A Unit of Highline Media LLC

11/04

ISBN 0-87218-652-0

Library of Congress Control Number: 2004107518

THE NATIONAL UNDERWRITER COMPANY

Copyright © 1977, 1979, 1980, 1982, 1983, 1985,
1987, 1989, 1990, 1992, 1995, 1998, 2001, 2004

The National Underwriter Company
P.O. Box 14367
Cincinnati, OH 45250-0367

Thirteenth Edition

Printed in the United States of America

DEDICATION

To our wives, parents, children,
and grandchildren and others
whom we love,
who have taught us —
and from whom
we will learn so much more.
And to our friend and co-author,
Herbert L. Levy,
whom we deeply miss.

ABOUT THE AUTHORS

Stephan R. Leimberg

Stephan R. Leimberg is CEO of LISI, Leimberg Information Services, Inc., a provider of e-mail/internet news and commentary for professionals on recent cases, rulings, and legislation; CEO of Leimberg and LeClair, Inc., an estate and financial planning software company; and President of Leimberg Associates, Inc., a publishing and software company in Bryn Mawr, Pennsylvania.

Leimberg is the author of numerous books on estate, financial, and employee benefit and retirement planning and a nationally known speaker. Leimberg is the creator and principal author of the entire eight book *Tools and Techniques* series including *The Tools and Techniques of Estate Planning, The Tools and Techniques of Financial Planning, The Tools and Techniques of Employee Benefit and Retirement Planning, The Tools and Techniques of Life Insurance Planning, The Tools and Techniques of Charitable Planning, The Tools and Techniques of Income Tax Planning, The Tools and Techniques of Investment Planning, and The Tools and Techniques of Risk Management*. Leimberg is co-author, with noted attorney Howard Zaritsky, *Tax Planning with Life Insurance, The New, New Book of Trusts* with attorneys Charles K. Plotnick and Daniel Evans, and *How to Settle an Estate* with Charles K. Plotnick.

Leimberg is creator or co-creator of many software packages for the financial services professional including *NumberCruncher* (estate planning), *IRS Factors Calculator* (actuarial computations), *Financial Analyzer II, Estate Planning Quickview* (Estate Planning Flow Charts), *Toward a Zero Estate Tax* (PowerPoint Estate Planning Client Seminar), *Gifts That Give, Gifts That Give Back* (Powerpoint Client Charitable Planning Seminar), and Long-Term Care (Powerpoint Client Seminar).

A nationally known speaker, Professor Leimberg has addressed the Miami (Heckerling) Estate Planning Institute, the NYU Tax Institute, the Notre Dame Law School and Duke University Law School's Estate Planning Conference, The American Bar Association Planning Techniques for Large Estate and Sophisticated Planning Techniques courses of study, the National Association of Estate Planners and Councils, and the AICPA's National Estate Planning Forum. Leimberg has also spoken to the Federal Bureau of Investigation, and the National Aeronautics and Space Administration.

Leimberg was named 1998 Edward N. Polisher Lecturer of the Dickinson School of Law, and was awarded the Excellence in Writing Award of the American Bar Association's Probate and Property Section. He has been honored as Estate Planner of the Year by the Montgomery County Estate Planning Council and as Distinguished Estate Planner by the Philadelphia Estate Planning Council. He is also recipient of the President's Cup of the Philadelphia Life Underwriters, a two time Boris Todorovitch Lecturer, and the first Ben Feldman Lecturer.

Jerry A. Kasner

Jerry A. Kasner is holder of the California Bar Institute's Joanne M. Garvey Award for lifetime achievement as a tax lawyer and teacher, a retired Professor of Law at Santa Clara University. He has also been an Adjunct Professor of Law in the Graduate Tax Program at the University of San Diego and a Lecturer in the Graduate Estate Planning Program at the University of Miami (Florida). Professor Kasner is an attorney and a Certified Public Accountant in California. He is an Academic Fellow in the American College of Trusts and Estate Counsel. He is also presently acting as a consultant to the California Law Revision Commission.

Professor Kasner is the author of *Post Mortem Estate Planning* and the co-author of *After Death Tax Planning*. His articles have appeared in *Journal of Taxation, Taxation for Accountants, Community Property Journal, The Practical Lawyer, Tax Ideas*, Phi-Net, and various other publications. He has also written course materials for the AICPA, California Continuing Education of the Bar, California Society of CPAs, and the College for Financial Planning.

He has appeared at numerous conferences for legal, accounting and other estate planning professionals throughout the country, including the New York University Tax Institute, the University of Miami Estate Planning Institute, the Southern California Tax and Estate Planning Forum, the Notre Dame Estate Planning Institute, AICPA Estate and Financial Planning Conferences, American College/CCH Financial Planning Conferences, *Trusts and Estates* Estate Planning Conference, and the IAFP Annual Conference.

Stephen N. Kandell

Stephen N. Kandell is a CLU and is Estate and Business Specialist for First Union Corporation located in Philadelphia, Pennsylvania. Prior to that, Mr. Kandell was self-employed working in the estate and business insurance field. While self-employed, he was also an Estate & Business Analysis Consultant for Consolidated Brokerage Services, Inc., a full-scale brokerage firm located in Cranford, New Jersey. Previous to that, he was employed by several major life insurance companies both in their home offices and field offices. He graduated cum laude from City College of New York (B.B.A.) and completed his legal training at New York University School of Law, where he received both his J.D. and LL.M. degrees.

Mr. Kandell has written several articles in the estate planning, income taxation and life insurance planning fields. In addition, he has lectured before various legal, banking, insurance, and financial services groups throughout the United States as well as abroad.

Ralph Gano Miller

Ralph Gano Miller is a member of the California Bar and a cum laude graduate of Stanford University with a BA and Masters Degree in Business Administration. He is a summa cum laude graduate of the University of San Diego Law School.

Mr. Miller is a CPA and author of numerous law review and journal articles on various estate planning tools and techniques. He is the author of the estate planning Primer and co-authored the Tax Planning Handbook for Educators on income tax, as well as the Handbook of Estate Planning. He was the designer of ViewPlan's Estate Forecast Model software, and edited ViewPlan's quarterly newsletter, the ViewPlanner. He has served as a member of the Board of Regents of the University of San Diego Law School, and as a professor of federal income taxation and gift and estate taxation at the California Western Law School.

He was a founding member of the Independent Board of Trustees of the California Western University Law School. He was an instructor of the Advanced Estate Planning Course of the CLU program for many years and has spoken at many tax institutes, including the New York University and University of Southern California Tax Institutes.

He is a member of the American Bar Association Sections on Taxation and Real Property, Probate and Trust Law and served as Chairman of the Administrative Law Section.

Mr. Miller has served as Chairman, Section of Taxation, of the San Diego County Bar Association's Section on Taxation and Real Property, Probate and Trust Law. He served as President of the Southern California Estate Planning Council.

He is past Chairman of the Taxation Advisory Commission, Board of Legal Specialization for the State Bar of California, and is a certified specialist in tax law in California. He also served as a member of the Board of Legal Specialization.

Mr. Miller is the Chairman of Miller, Ewald & Monson, a Professional Law Corporation in San Diego, California.

Morey S. Rosenbloom

Morey S. Rosenbloom is a partner in the Philadelphia law firm of Blank, Rome, Comisky & McCauley and serves as chairman of the Tax and Fiduciary Department. Mr. Rosenbloom was formerly a principal in CMS Companies, a Philadelphia based merchant banking firm. He graduated from Temple University School of Law and served as a legal assistant to the then Chief Justice, John C. Bell, of the Supreme Court of the Commonwealth of Pennsylvania.

Mr. Rosenbloom is an adjunct professor of law at the Law School at Temple University and has been an instructor of the American College Advanced Estate Planning Course. He has served as the Chairman of the Real Property, Probate and Trust Law Section of the Pennsylvania Bar Association. Mr. Rosenbloom is a fellow of the American College of Trust and Estate Counsel and recent recipient of the "Distinguished Service Award" given by the Philadelphia Planning Council.

He has lectured at numerous seminars on the topic of estate and business planning to various legal, banking, insurance and estate planning groups throughout the country.

Mr. Rosenbloom has co-authored many publications and articles, including *Practical Will Drafting*, *Computing The Federal Estate Tax*, *The Wait and See Buy-Sell*, and *Funding Corporate Buy-Sell Agreements With Life Insurance*.

Herbert L. Levy

Herbert L. Levy was, before his death in December 1982, in the private practice of law in Allentown, Pa. He graduated from City University of New York (B.S. in accounting, 1964), St. John's University School of Law (J.D. 1966) and New York University School of Law (LL.M. in taxation, 1967) where he served as Tax Editor of the N.Y.U. *Tax Law Review.*

He was co-author of *Introduction to Estates and Trusts Practice in the Commonwealth of Pennsylvania* (7 editions).

Mr. Levy instructed the American College's Advanced Estate Planning Course and was a frequent lecturer on estate planning and taxation.

Timothy C. Polacek

Timothy C. Polacek is a partner in the San Diego law firm of Miller, Monson, Peshel, Polacek & Hoshaw, practicing in the areas of tax, business and estate planning. He also heads the firm's business valuation practice, which includes appraisal work for closely-held businesses and discount valuations for investment entities. He holds a degree in Business Administration from the University of San Diego, graduating summa

cum laude. He also received his J.D. from the University of San Diego.

Mr. Polacek is a member of the California Bar. He has written numerous articles on the use of family limited partnerships for wealth preservation and frequently speaks to other professionals on business planning and valuation.

ACKNOWLEDGMENTS

We wish to thank attorney Charles K. Plotnik for his chapters on selection of an executor, trustee, and attorney and a probate primer for the could be executor.

NumberCruncher software illustrations throughout the book are courtesy of Leimberg and LeClair, Inc. (610-924-0515).

Special thanks to William J. Wagner, J.D., LL.M., CLU, of the National Underwriter staff who was the major technical editor of this 13th edition. Bill, along with the following staff, does much more than merely "polish up" a fine job; he and his associates proof voluminous copy, meticulously check each point for

accuracy, and assure an up-to-the-last-minute update before *Tools and Techniques* goes to press. Thank you, Deborah A. Miner, J.D., CLU, ChFC; April A. Caudill, J.D., CLU, ChFC; Joseph F. Stenken, J.D., CLU, ChFC; Sonya E. King, J.D., LL.M.; and John H. Fenton, J.D., M.S.B.A., for your help.

Most importantly, the authors would like to acknowledge you, our loyal readers, who have kept *Tools and Techniques* one of the most widely read professional books on estate planning ever. Many of you have had every one of the previous twelve editions on your shelves. To you, and to those of you for whom the 13th is the first, we want you to know how very much we continue to appreciate your trust.

PREFACE TO THE 13TH EDITION

In 1975, my friend and co-author, the late Herbert Levy, and I wrote the first version of this book. Its objective was to provide concise, accurate, objective information but even more importantly to be the quickest possible way for a busy practicing professional to gain an overview and practical working knowledge of the various tools and techniques of estate planning. Not just education but rather time effective education for immediate performance! With tax law changing almost annually and with massive revising occurring before every major political change in power, those goals are more important now than ever.

You, our reader, may be an attorney, a CPA, trust officer, CLU, ChFC, CFP, a newcomer in the field of estate planning, a student at a graduate or law school, or even a person seeking to plan your own estate. You all have one thing in common: Your world is moving at a pace faster than you ever believed possible and your time is more precious than ever. You need to be able to quickly grasp - and be able to share with others - the pros and cons of the various tools and techniques and understand which tool or technique (or more likely which combination of tools and techniques) will provide you or your client or your client's family with the most financial security at the least possible cost.

This 13th Edition will be of great help to you in learning complex information and issues - and equally as important - communicating those ideas in a manner that is both understandable and which conveys the urgency and significance of action. It will also be of great aid in understanding the only thing on earth more complex than tax law, the individuals you serve. A superb knowledge of tax law is less than worthless if you do not also appreciate and take into consideration the human dynamics of each case. Throughout the book, you will find reminders of the importance of the human aspects of the estate planning profession.

Clients want six things that planners often fail to adequately consider or provide: They want CCCFAA, control, certainty, compassion, flexibility, assurance that they have done the "right thing," and an avoidance of aggravation (and audit). As you read each of the many topics in this resource, consider the extent to which a given tool or technique will cost - or enhance the client's control over property or the lives of others. Think carefully about how likely it is that the client will actually carry out and actually be able to accomplish his or her goals using your suggestions. Have you listened - really listened - to the client and client's family with care? Have you heard, not only their words, but also their hopes and fears? Will the tool or technique lock the client or the client's family into a box or have you built

sufficient options, escape hatches, and other ways to change into your plan? Have (can) you assure(d) the client that all of the proper steps have been taken and he or she has done what is needed to be done? And finally, will your plan quietly accomplish its objectives or will it make the client (in)famous? In other words, at what cost in paperwork, audits, or litigation will success come? My point is that a good estate plan is more than just a proper tax blend of the tools and techniques you'll find in the pages that follow.

Ethical consciousness and moral backbone is more important than ever in the post-Enron era. It is essential that you continually distinguish between a strictly legalistic view of ethics (i.e., a mere avoidance of legal violations or the appearance of a conflict of interest) and a pro-active constant awareness and practice of the highest possible standards. You must decide - as you practice day by day - how you can best use your moral imagination, and consider the ethical efficacy as well as legitimacy of your suggestions, and strive for much more than moral mediocrity.

This 13th Edition of TOOLS AND TECHNIQUES OF ESTATE PLANNING further updates and expands our coverage of a number of relatively new tools. One of these is a list of URLs, addresses of web pages of government, individuals, and commercial organizations that provide information on estate planning topics. These lists are linked to literally hundreds of other sites that provide even more information. As you search, keep "bookmarks" of those places that are most helpful for comprehensive and current information.

My co-authors and I urge you to continue to use all the resources at your command - and to acquire the resources you need to practice optimally - to gain knowledge. But with your new found knowledge, gain wisdom - and build a core of ethical strength to apply the information you learn to properly and compassionately help others - not as a "high priest of knowledge" but rather as a caring human being and counselor.

We hope you will enjoy and profit from this completely updated text. We have fully incorporated all the most recent legislative changes, as well as hundreds of recent cases and rulings, since the publication of the 12th Edition. More importantly, you will find our opinions as to IRS trends and warnings as to future potential IRS attacks and suggestions as to how to avoid them. Let us know if this 13th Edition succeeds in helping you help others and how we can improve and expand the information in this resource.

Stephan R. Leimberg

INTRODUCTION AND BIBLIOGRAPHY

Estate planning is a fascinating subject. No two problems are ever quite the same and no perfect answers or well-established rules exist to solve problems. Estate planning is not merely planning to save or reduce taxes during lifetime or at death; it is far more complex because a person and his or her relationship with property and other people is involved.

There is no easy way to learn estate planning. The field is vast, increasingly complex, and covers not only income, estate, and gift tax law but requires the practitioner to assimilate and incorporate many facets of corporate, probate, estate, trust, and securities law as well.

The essential concern is to ascertain all the facts, whether they may seem material or relevant at the time, and place them in context with the clients(s) desires and objectives and the beneficiaries' needs and circumstances. From those facts and goals, one must then recognize and clearly state the problems.

Then the real challenge begins: finding or creating the appropriate solutions.

A good library of up-to-date texts, tapes, and articles is essential. The following is a list of some of the books and information sources we have found useful: (It is extremely important to check with the publisher to see if the version you are purchasing or using is the most recent version and if it encompasses all of the recent major tax law changes.)

Abbin, et al, *Tax Economics of Charitable Giving* (New York, NY: RIA Group, 2003), 800-950-1216.

Abbin, Carlson, Vorsatz, *Income Taxation and Fiduciaries and Beneficiaries* (Chicago, IL: CCH, 2003), 800-775-5730.

Adler, *Rules of the Road: A Guide to the Law of Charities in the United States* (Washington, DC: Council on Foundations, 1999), 888-239-5221.

Baldwin, *The Lawyer's Guide to Insurance* (Chicago, IL: ABA, 1999), 800-285-2221.

Bittker and Eustice, *Federal Income Taxation of Corporations and Shareholders* (Student Edition) (New York, NY: RIA Group, 2002), 800-950-1216.

Blattmachr, *Income Taxation of Estates and Trusts* (New York, NY: PLI, 1995), 800-260-4754.

Bureau of National Affairs, *Tax Management Income, Estates, Gifts and Trusts Portfolios* (Washington, DC: BNA 2004).

Brody, *The Irrevocable Life Insurance Trust* (Chicago, IL: ABA, 1999) 800-285-2221.

Brody and Richey, *Comprehensive Deferred Compensation* (Cincinnati, OH: National Underwriter Company, 1997), 800-543-0874.

Brody and Weinberg, *The Insured Stock Purchase Agreement* (Chicago, IL: ABA, 1997), 800-285-2221.

Casner and Pennell, *Estate Planning*, (Chicago, IL: CCH, 2003), 800-248-3248.

Catherall and Feld, *Estate and Gift Tax Digest* (New York, NY: RIA Group, 2003), 800-950-3055.

Choate, *Life and Death Planning for Retirement Benefits* (Boston, MA: Ataxplan Publications, 2003), 800-247-6553.

Commerce Clearing House, Inc., *Federal Tax Articles*, (Chicago, IL: CCH, 2003), 800-248-3248.

Commerce Clearing House, Inc., *Financial and Estate Planning Reporter*, (Chicago, IL: CCH, 2000), 800-248-3248.

Commerce Clearing House, Inc., *Inheritance Estate and Gift Tax Reporter*, (Chicago, IL: CCH, 2003), 800-248-3248.

Commito, *Comprehensive Buy-Sell* (Cincinnati, OH: National Underwriter Company, 1998), 800-543-0874.

Commito, *Working with LLCs and FLPs* (Cincinnati, OH: National Underwriter Company, 2000), 800-543-0874.

Cunningham, *Drifting Limited Liability Company Operating Agreements* (New York, NY: Aspen, 2004), 800-638-8437.

Donner and Finmann, *Planning for Retirement Distributions* (New York, NY: Aspen, 2003), 800-638-8437.

Eber, *A CPA's Guide to Today's Hottest Device in Estate Planning: The Family Limited Partnership* (New York, NY: AICPA, 2000).

Esperti and Peterson, *The Encyclopedia of Estate and Wealth Strategies and The Journal of MultiDisciplinary Practice* (The Academy of Multidisciplinary Practice), 800-741-4358.

Etkind, *The ESOP Handbook* (Leimberg Associates, Inc.), 610-924-0515.

Ferguson, Freeland and Ascher, *Federal Income Taxation of Estates, Trusts and Beneficiaries*, (Chicago, IL: CCH, 2004).

Fithian, *Values-Based Estate Planning – A Step-by-Step Approach to Wealth Transfers for Professional Advisors* (New York, NY: John Wiley, 2000), 800-879-4539.

Gallagher and Ratner, *Federal Income Taxation of Life Insurance* (Chicago, IL: ABA, 1999), 800-285-2221.

Giamarco and Mittra, *Estate Planning with Insurance* (Troy, MI: Cox Hodgman & Giamarco), 248-528-2200.

Grassi, *A Practical Guide for Drafting Irrevocable Life Insurance Trusts* (Philadelphia, PA: ALI-ABA, 2003), 800-253-6397.

Hendrickson, *Interstate and International Estate Planning*, (New York, NY: Practicing Law Institute, 1968).

Jordan and Quynn, *Planned Giving for Small Nonprofits* (New York, NY: Wiley, 2002), 800-225-5945.

Kahn and Colson, *Federal Taxation of Estates and Trusts*, ALI-ABA.

Kasner, *Post Mortem Tax Planning*, (Boston, MA: WG&L, 1998), 800-950-3055, and *Guide to Practical Estate Planning* (Ft. Worth, TX: Practitioner's Publishing Co., 1994-2001), 800-323-8724.

Keebler, *Stretch IRA Advisor's Reference Guide* (Clearwater, FL: Wealth Advisory Group, 2001), 727-462-0404, and *The Professional's Guide to the Roth IRA: Implementing the 2001 Tax Act* (New York, NY: AICPA, 2001).

Klein and Bahls, *S Corporations and Life Insurance* (Chicago, IL: ABA, 2000), 800-285-2221.

Leimberg, *The Cutting Edge*, Leimberg Associates, Inc.

Leimberg and Doyle, *The Tools and Techniques of Life Insurance Planning*, (Cincinnati, OH: National Underwriter Company, 1999), 800-543-0874.

Leimberg et al, *The Tools and Techniques of Charitable Planning*, (Cincinnati, OH: National Underwriter Company, 2001), 800-543-0874.

Leimberg et al, *The Tools and Techniques of Income Tax Planning*, (Cincinnati, OH: National Underwriter Company, 2004), 800-543-0874.

Leimberg and McFadden, *The Tools and Techniques of Employee Benefit and Retirement Planning*, (Cincinnati, OH: National Underwriter Company, 2003), 800-543-0874.

Leimberg, Plotnick, Miller, and Evans, *The New, New Book of Trusts*, Leimberg Associates, Inc.

Leimberg, Rosenbloom and Yohlin, *The Corporate Buy-Sell Handbook*, Leimberg Associates, Inc.

Leimberg and Zaritsky, *Tax Planning with Life Insurance*, (New York, NY: RIA Group, 2003), 800-950-1216.

Manning, Rosenbloom, and Halperin, *Manning on Estate Planning* (New York, NY: PLI, 1995), 800-260-4754.

McCoy and Miree, *Family Foundation Handbook*, Chicago, IL: CCH, 2004), 800-234-1660.

McGovern and Kurtz, *Wills, Trusts and Estates*, (Eagan, MN: West Group, 2004), 800-328-9352.

Mertens, *Law of Federal Gift and Estate Taxation* (New York, NY: Lofit Publications, Inc., 1959).

Mertens, *Law of Federal Income Taxation* (Chicago, IL: Callahan and Co., 1934-35).

Mezzullo, *An Estate Planner's Guide to Family Business Entities*, (Chicago, IL: ABA, 2003), 800-285-2221.

Mezzullo, *An Estate Planner's Guide to Buy-Sell Agreements for the Closely-Held Business*, (Chicago, IL: ABA, 2003), 800-285-2221.

Mezzullo, An *Estate Planner's Guide to Life Insurance*, (Chicago, IL: ABA, 2000), 800-285-2221.

National Underwriter Company, *Tax Facts on Insurance & Employee Benefits* (*Tax Facts 1*) and *Tax Facts on Investments* (*Tax Facts 2*) (Cincinnati, OH: National Underwriter Company, 2004), 800-543-0874.

Nossaman and Wyatt, *Trust Administration and Taxation* (New York, NY: Matthew Bender and Co., 1966).

Plotnick and Leimberg, *How to Settle an Estate* (New York, NY: Plume, 2002).

Rabkin and Johnson, *Current Legal Forms With Tax Analysis* (New York, NY: Matthew Bender and Co., 1948).

Rabkin and Johnson, *Federal Income, Gift and Estate Taxation* (New York, NY: Matthew Bender and Co., 1942).

Slavutin, *Guide to Life Insurance Strategies* (Ft. Worth, TX: PIA, 1997-98), 800-323-8724.

Schlesinger & Howard, *Pre-Mortem Estate Planning Checklist* (Philadelphia, PA: ALI-ABA, 2003), 800-253-6397.

Stephens, Maxfield, Lind and Calfee, *Federal Estate and Gift Taxation* (New York, NY: RIA Group, 2002), 800-950-1216.

Stocker, Rikoon, Champine, and Racanelli, *Stocker and Rikoon on Drawing Wills and Trusts* (New York, NY: PLI, 1999), 800-260-4754.

Wagner, *Ultimate Trust Resource* (including Trust Calculator) (Cincinnati, OH: National Underwriter Company, 2004 Supp.), 800-543-0874.

Warren and Surrey, *Federal Estate and Gift Taxation* (Brooklyn, NY: Foundation Press, 1960).

Weisz, *Supertrust IV* (Plymouth Meeting, PA: Wisestone Financial Publishing, 1991).

Westfall and Mair, *Estate Planning Law and Taxation* (New York, NY: RIA Group, 2001), 800-950-1216.

Wynn, *Split-Dollar Life Insurance* (Chicago, IL: ABA, 1991), 800-285-2221.

Zaritsky, *Structuring Buy-Sell Agreements* (New York, NY: Thomson Publishing, 1999), 800-950-1216.

Zaritsky, *Tax Planning for Family Wealth Transfers* (Boston, MA: WG&L, 1997), 800-950-1216.

We highly recommend tax services such as Research Institute of America, Commerce Clearing House, and Tax Management. These services are most useful. The Advanced Sales Reference Service, published by The National Underwriter Company, has a strong following within the life insurance community. Additionally, journals such as the *Journal of Taxation, Tax Law Review, Taxes, Taxation for Lawyers, Estate Planning, Taxation for Accountants, Trusts and Estates, The Practical Tax Lawyer,* and *The Journal of the Society of Financial Service Professionals* are highly useful.

Two of the best tools for "Keeping Current" are a quarterly cassette service of the same name available from the Society of Financial Service Professionals, and the e-mail commentary service, LISI, at www.leimberg services.com that provides almost daily information on recent cases, rulings, and legislation.

A service that specializes in the taxation and uses of life insurance in business and estate planning is *Think About It*, a monthly newsletter by Leimberg Associates, Inc. used extensively by life underwriters associations and insurance companies throughout the country.

Keep in mind that TOOLS AND TECHNIQUES is a survey text. It is not meant to be a detailed examination of any one particular area. We have tried to design the text to give you enough familiarity with an area so that when doing research, you will have an initial understanding of that area.

We strongly recommend the *Advanced Sales Reference Service*, referred to earlier. References to "ASRS" appearing immediately above the "Chapter Endnotes" are to this service.

CONTENTS

Part 6: Life Insurance

Part 7: Charitable Giving

Part 8: Intrafamily and Other Business Transfers Techniques

Part 9: Planning for Employee Benefits and Retirement

Part 10: Incapacity Planning

Part 11: Valuation Issues

Appendices

Part 1:

THE PURPOSE AND PRACTICE
OF ESTATE PLANNING

Chapter 1

OVERVIEW OF ESTATE PLANNING

Often, in order to encourage cooperation and full disclosure of pertinent data, it is necessary or helpful to explain to a client what estate planning is, who should be concerned with estate planning, how the federal estate tax laws work, and the mistakes that are commonly made because of a lack of proper planning.

WHAT IS ESTATE PLANNING?

Estate planning is the process of planning the accumulation, conservation, and distribution of an estate in the manner that most efficiently and effectively accomplishes your personal tax and nontax objectives. Every estate is planned – either by the individual or by the state and federal governments.

"Controlled estate planning" is a systematic process for uncovering problems and providing solutions in clients' L.I.V.E.S. Planners should use this L.I.V.E.S. acronym to illustrate the seven major areas of estate planning and emphasize the significance and urgency of action to solve them:

1. Lack of liquidity: Insufficient cash to pay administrative costs, taxes and other estate settlement expenses. A lack of liquidity can trigger a forced sale and result in the loss of an estate's most precious assets at pennies on the dollar.

2. Improper disposition of assets: When the wrong asset goes at the wrong time to the wrong person in the wrong manner, the result is often disaster. For example, picture the proceeds of $100,000 of group insurance or a $500,000 pension plan being paid to a 21 year old child.

3. Inflation (need to diversify and "inflation-proof" portfolio): Many individuals have placed all their financial eggs in one basket or have not considered the diminished and diminishing purchasing power of life insurance adequate only four or five years ago. The ravages of inflation and risk of placing all of a client's family financial security in one investment (or business) must be factored into the estate plan.

4. Inadequate income or capital at retirement/death/disability: Planners and clients often forget that cash demands for survivors' food, clothing, shelter, and schooling often will exhaust the funds that would otherwise be available for estate liquidity needs–and vice versa.

5. Value–need to stabilize and maximize value of business and other assets: Clients who own businesses should build key employee protection into their plans, establish "golden handcuffs" to retain key employees and attract new ones, and use their businesses to solve personal financial problems.

6. Excessive transfer costs: Simply put, many clients' families will pay a severe–and needless price–for the inaction of senior family members. The difference between an "I love you–all to my spouse" will and the use of a well designed bypass and marital trust combination can sometimes be measured in almost a quarter of a million dollars of senseless federal estate tax payments.

7. Special problems: Clients must not overlook the extreme importance of planning for the spouse or child who can not, should not, or does not want to handle a family business or large investment portfolio, or for a handicapped spouse or child. Satisfying the desire to give back to, enrich, and support charity is also often a strong planning need.

A possible addition to the list above is "Flexibility" which may now be required in some estates to deal with the estate tax and generation-skipping transfer tax changes made by EGTRRA 2001. The Act increases the effective exemptions and reduces the top tax rates in the years 2002 to 2009. It also repeals both taxes (but not the gift tax) for one year in 2010. The uncertainty created by these changes argues for providing as much flexibility as possible in planning. This may be arranged in some cases by appointing a trust protector who has powers, usually subject to court approval, to change the terms of the trust.

WHO NEEDS ESTATE PLANNING?

More sophisticated planning than a simple will is indicated for:

1. Individuals with estates exceeding the unified credit equivalent ($1.5 million in 2004 and scheduled to increase to $3,500,000 by 2009, with repeal of the estate tax for one year in 2010).

2. Individuals in combined state and federal income tax brackets in excess of 15 percent.

3. People with:

   a. Children who are minors.

   b. Children (or spouses or other dependents) who are exceptionally artistic or intellectually gifted.

   c. Children (or spouses or other dependents) who are retarded, emotionally disturbed, or physically handicapped.

   d. Spouses (or children or other dependents) who can't or don't want to handle money, securities or a business.

   e. Closely held business interests.

   f. Property in more than one state or persons who often move from state to state.

   g. Charitable objectives.

   h. Special property such as fine art, a coin, gun, or stamp collection.

   i. Pets that are particularly important to them.

4. Nonresident aliens, resident aliens, aliens about to move to the U.S., individuals considering expatriation, and U.S. citizens with property interests in foreign countries.

THE TEN MOST COMMON ESTATE PLANNING MISTAKES

(And How to Avoid Them)[1]

[*Editor's Note:* While the following is addressed to clients, financial services professionals should be on the lookout for these common mistakes and periodically review clients' plans accordingly.]

This entire commentary is devoted to the types of problems that can cost you and your family tens of thousands of dollars and unbelievable heartache. Since only a fool learns from his own mistakes, this commentary is dedicated to the wise man (and woman) who can profit from the lessons so many have expensively learned the hard way.

Here are ten areas of common (and serious) mistakes that can be easily solved with the assistance of a financial services professional. Have you made one or more of these mistakes? If you haven't checked, how do you know?

Mistake 1: Improper Use of Jointly-Held Property

If used excessively or used by the wrong parties (especially by unmarried individuals) the otherwise "poor man's will" becomes a poor will for an otherwise good man or woman. In short, jointly held property can become a nightmare of unexpected tax and nontax problems including:

A. When property is titled jointly, there is the potential for both federal and state gift tax.

B. There is the possibility of double federal estate taxation; if the joint ownership is between individuals other than spouses, the entire property will be taxed in the estate of the first spouse to die – except to the extent the survivor can prove contribution to the property. Then, whatever the survivor receives and does not consume or give away will be included (and taxed a second time) in the survivor's gross estate.

C. Once jointly owned property with right of survivorship has passed to the survivor, the provisions of the decedent's will are ineffective. This means the property is left outright to the survivor who is then without the benefit of management protection or investment advice.

D. The surviving spouse can give away or at death leave the formerly jointly owned property to anyone she wants regardless of the desires of the deceased spouse. In other words, holding property jointly equates to a total loss of control since the surviving spouse can ignore the decedent's wishes as to the ultimate disposition of the property. This loss of control can be especially horrendous when the joint owners are not related.

E. Since the jointly held property passes directly to the survivor (who then could possibly squander, gamble, give away, or lose the property to creditors), the decedent's executor could be faced with a lack of adequate cash to pay estate taxes and other settlement expenses.

F. A well drawn estate plan is designed to avoid double taxation – often by passing at least a portion of the estate into a CEBT (Credit Equivalent Bypass Trust). In this manner up to $1,500,000 in 2004 (this amount is scheduled to increase to $3,500,000 in 2009) can be sheltered from federal estate tax at both the first decedent's death and then again (since the surviving spouse has only an income interest) escape estate tax at the death of the surviving spouse. But holding property in joint tenancy thwarts that objective. Instead of going to a bypass trust to avoid a second tax, the property goes directly to the survivor and will be taxed at the survivor's death. So the unified credit exemption equivalent of the first spouse to die is wasted.

Mistake 2: Improperly Arranged Life Insurance

A. The proceeds of life insurance are often payable to a beneficiary at the wrong time (before that person is emotionally or physically or legally capable of handling it) or in the wrong manner (outright instead of being paid over a period of years or paid into trust).

B. There is inadequate insurance on the life of the key person in a family (the "breadwinner") or the key person in a corporation (the "rainmaker").

C. Often, no contingent (backup) beneficiary has been named. The "Rule of Two" should be applied here: In any dispositive document there should be – for every name in the document – at least two backups.

D. The proceeds of the policy are includable in the gross estate of the insured because the policy was purchased by the insured and then transferred within three years of the insured's death. The solution is to have the ultimate beneficiary, acting without direction from the insured and using her (or its) own money, purchase and own the insurance from its inception. That party should also be named beneficiary.

E. When the policyowner of a policy on the life of another names a third party as beneficiary, at the death of the insured, the proceeds are treated as a gift to the beneficiary from the policy owner. For example, if a wife purchases a policy on her husband's life but names her children as beneficiaries, at the husband's death she is making a gift in the amount of the proceeds to the children.

F. If a corporation names someone other than itself (or its creditor) as the beneficiary of insurance on the life of a key employee, when the proceeds are paid, the IRS will argue that the proceeds are not income tax free and should be treated as either dividends if paid to or on behalf of a shareholder or compensation if paid to an employee who is not a shareholder (assuming the premiums were never reported as income or there was no split dollar agreement or no "Table 2001" income reported). Worse yet, if the insured owned more than 50 percent of the corporation's stock, he is deemed to have incidents of ownership (that means federal estate tax inclusion of the proceeds) in the policy on his life. So, for example, the same $1,000,000 proceeds could be taxed as a dividend for income tax purposes (as much as $150,000 of income tax in 2004) and also be taxed as an asset in the estate for estate tax purposes (depending on the year of death, as much as $480,000 of estate tax in 2004).

G. Whenever life insurance is paid to the insured's estate, it is needlessly subjected to the claims of the insured's creditors and in many states unnecessarily subjected to state inheritance tax costs. Probate costs are increased without reason and the proceeds are then subjected to the potential for an attack on the will or an election against the will.

H. If a life insurance policy – or any interest in a life insurance policy – is transferred for any kind of valuable consideration in money or money's worth, the proceeds may lose their income tax free status. For example, if a child buys the $1,000,000 term insurance policy owned on her father's life from his corporation or business partner, when she receives the proceeds, the entire $1,000,000 could be subjected to ordinary income tax (as much as $350,000 in 2004).

I. Where a husband is required by a divorce decree or separation agreement to purchase or maintain insurance on his life, he will receive no income tax deduction for premium payments if he owns the policy – even if his ex-wife is named as irrevocable beneficiary. No alimony deduction is allowed on the cash values in a policy the husband is required to transfer to his ex-wife under a divorce decree. The safest way to assure a deduction is for the husband to increase his tax deductible alimony and for the ex-wife to purchase new insurance on his life, which she owns and on which she is the beneficiary. It is extremely important for each spouse recently divorced to immediately review his own life, health and disability insurance situation.

Mistake 3: Lack of Liquidity

A. Most people don't have the slightest idea of how much it will cost to settle their estates or how quickly the taxes and other expenses must be paid. Worse yet, they don't realize that a forced (fire) sale of their most precious assets, highest income producing property, or loss of control of their family business will result from an insufficiency of cash. (If you haven't checked, how do you know your executor will have enough cash to avoid a forced sale?)

B. Liquidity demands have increased significantly in the last few years and should be revisited by those who have not done a "what if …" hypothetical probate. Among the expenses that demand cash from the estate's executor are:

1. Federal Estate Taxes

2. State Death Taxes

3. Federal Income Taxes (including taxes on pension distributions)

4. State Income Taxes (including taxes on pension distributions)

5. Probate and Administration Costs

6. Payment of Maturing Debts

7. Maintenance and Welfare of Family

8. Payment of Specific Cash Bequests

9. Funds to Continue Operation of Family Business, Meet Payroll and Inventory Costs, Recruit Replacement Personnel, and Pay for Mistakes While New Management is Learning the Business

10. Generation-Skipping Transfer Tax (top estate tax rate)

Most larger estates will be subjected to almost all of these taxes and costs.

Mistake 4: Choice of the Wrong Executor

A. Naming the wrong people to administer the estate can be disastrous. The person who administers the estate must – with dispatch – often without compensation, with great personal financial risk, and without conflict of interest:

1. Collect all assets

2. Pay all obligations

3. Distribute the remaining assets to beneficiaries

Although this three step process seems simple, in reality these tasks are highly complex, time consuming, and in some cases technically demanding. Is the named executor capable?

B. Selection of a beneficiary as an executor can result in a conflict of interest. That person may be forced to choose between his interest and that of the other beneficiaries. This problem can be solved by adding an independent third party such as a bank trust department to serve alone or together with a family member.

C. Selection of a business associate may result in a conflict of interest. If the executor's job is to decide whether or not to sell the business interest or the task is to obtain the highest possible sales price, the executor will be responsible for the course of action that will best serve the beneficiaries' interests. Yet that may be diametrically opposed to his own. He may be selling himself out of a job or demanding a higher price for the business than he is willing to pay.

D. Sometimes the selected executor has neither the time nor the inclination to devote to the sometimes long and drawn out process of estate administration. Does the executor even live in the state of the testator?

E. The appointment of executors who do not know or get along well with the family members they are to serve sometimes results in chaos.

Mistake 5: Will Errors

A. One of the greatest mistakes is dying without a valid will. This results in "intestacy" which is another way of saying that the state will force its own will upon the heirs it chooses.

B. Too many wills have not been updated. A will should be reviewed at least:

1. At the birth, adoption, or death of a child

2. Upon the marriage, divorce, or separation of anyone named in the will

3. Upon every major tax law change

4. Upon a move of the testator to a new state

5. On a significant change in income or wealth of either the testator or a beneficiary

6. On any major change in the needs, circumstances, or objectives of the testator or the beneficiaries

Mistake 6: Leaving Everything to Your Spouse

A. Far too many people feel that there will be no federal estate tax because of the unlimited estate tax marital deduction and so they leave their entire estates to their spouses. But upon the death of the surviving spouse, everything that he received (assuming it has not been consumed or given away) is then piled on top of the assets that spouse owns. It is then that the "second death wallop" occurs with federal estate tax starting on taxable amounts in excess of $1,500,000 in 2004 (increasing slowly and scheduled to reach $3,500,000 by 2009). The solution can be simple: The establishment of a CEBT (credit equivalent bypass trust). Up to $1,500,000 of assets in 2004 (increasing as noted above) can be left to a trust that provides income to the surviving spouse as well as other financial security but will not be taxed in his estate no matter when he dies or no matter how large trust funds grow. The balance of the estate can go in trust or outright to the surviving spouse. If that amount together with the surviving spouse's own assets doesn't exceed the unified credit equivalent for the year of death plus any allowable exclusion, this portion will also pass estate tax free when the surviving spouse dies.

B. Some individuals leave huge amounts outright to a surviving spouse, amounts that they themselves have never managed (few people have ever managed huge amounts at one time let alone managed spouses at any time). Often the survivor doesn't have the slightest training or experience in handling and

investing a large stock portfolio, real estate holdings, or running a family business.

Mistake 7: Improper Disposition of Assets

A. An improper disposition of assets occurs whenever the wrong asset goes to the wrong person in the wrong manner or at the wrong time. Leaving an entire estate to a surviving spouse or leaving a large or complex estate outright to a spouse unprepared or unwilling to handle it is a good example. Leaving a sizeable estate outright to a teenager is another.

B. "Equal but inequitable" distributions are common. If an estate is divided equally among four children who have drastically different income or capital needs, an equal distribution can be very unfair. Consider, for example, four children, the oldest of which is a brilliant and financially successful medical doctor and the youngest of which has serious learning disabilities and is still in junior high school. Think of a family with a physically handicapped child and three healthy children with no physical problems. Obviously, their needs and circumstances are not the same. Should each child receive an equal share? The proper solution may be a "sprinkle" provision in a trust that empowers the trustee to provide extra income or principal to a child that needs more in a given year.

C. Obvious examples of improper dispositions include the gift of a high powered sports car to a child, or to a senior citizen who no longer drives. "That can't happen in my estate," many people would be tempted to say. But upon the death of a primary beneficiary at the same time or soon after the testator, quite often there is no secondary beneficiary, or the second beneficiary who is named shouldn't receive the asset in the same manner as the primary beneficiary. The solution is to consider a trust or custodial arrangements and to provide in the will or other dispositive instruments for young children and legally incompetent people. Consider also the importance of a well considered "common disaster" or "simultaneous death" provision so that the asset avoids needless second probates and double inheritance taxes and goes to the right person in the right manner.

Mistake 8: Failure to Stabilize and Maximize Value

A. Many business owners have not stabilized the value of their businesses in the event of the disability or death of key personnel. What economic "shock absorbers" have been put in place to cushion the blow caused if a key employee was lured away by competition at the wrong time? Who will pay for the fixed expenses of the practice or business if the key employee is not there to generate income? Key employee life and disability insurance coupled with good business overhead coverage will certainly help.

B. Buy-sell agreements are essential to a business that is to survive the death of one of its owners. Yet many businesses have no such agreement. Or the agreement isn't in writing. Or the price (or price setting mechanism) doesn't reflect the current value of the business. Or the agreement isn't properly funded. So there is no guarantee that the heirs will receive the price they are entitled to – or no assurance that the surviving owners will have the cash they need to buy out the heirs (especially the dissident ones who want to tell them how to run their company).

C. Wills, trusts, life insurance contracts, HR-10 (Keogh) plans, IRAs, tax deferred annuities, without "backup" beneficiaries mean that money that could otherwise pass outside of the probate estate may instead be subjected unnecessarily to such costs and risks. The value of all those instruments and wealth transfer tools can be enhanced at no cost by merely naming secondary beneficiaries.

Mistake 9: Lack of Adequate Records

A. It can drive your executor crazy – and cost thousands of dollars of expenses – if estate and financial documents are hard to find. Take out a safe deposit box. Tell your executor where it is and make sure your executor has or can get the key and has access to it. Put all your important documents in that box. Each year, put an updated list of the names and phone numbers of advisors your family can count on in the box. Check with your attorney on the rules that apply at death: some safe deposit boxes are "frozen" (the state requires that the bank seal the box from entry until the inheritance tax examiner can inventory the contents) and there can be lengthy delays in getting to the papers in the box.

B. It is possible for an executor to obtain new copies of old income tax returns from the IRS – but why put the executor to the trouble and expense? Be sure to keep tax returns and records at least six years. (If carryover basis ever actually becomes effective, it may be important to retain tax returns and other papers pertaining to basis indefinitely.)

C. Many survivors have never been told what the decedent's goals were, what assets they can rely on for income or capital needs, or how best to utilize the available resources. Most widows or surviving children never had a meaningful discussion with the decedent about their financial security if…

Mistake 10: Lack of a "Master Strategy" Game Plan

A. Do it yourself estate and financial planning is the closest thing to do it yourself brain surgery. Few people can do it successfully. Yet, even do it yourself planning – from taking courses or reading books or listening to radio shows on the subject – is sometimes preferable to no planning. Actually, an intelligent layman can learn and do quite a bit if the time is taken at least once a year to quantify in dollar terms financial needs and objectives ("here's what we must have and here's what we'd like to have"), current financial status (here's where we are), and a game plan for getting to the goal in the most efficient and effective way. Using the right team of CPA, attorney, life insurance agent, trust officer, and other financial services professionals to conduct an annual "Financial Firedrill" to help formulate and execute that plan can make all the difference.

The Bottom Line

A key principle in estate planning is that *you can't eliminate the big mistakes in your estate plan until you've identified them.* Every family (and single person) – every year – should stage a "financial firedrill." Become informed. Educate yourself now. Educate your survivors – before they *are* the survivors! Teach them how to handle money and make decisions. Show them, by example, how to read the bottom line on where their financial security stands.

A "financial firedrill" means that, with the assistance of competent financial services professionals, you annually measure your needs. Establish an order of priorities and then develop and put into effect plans to make certain that you are on target to meet your financial security needs.

OPTIONAL CHECKLIST FOR DISCUSSION

One or more of the following checklists can be given to a client to review and fill out prior to meeting with the planner or it can be reviewed and processed with the client. In addition, a planner may want to use these checklists to review potential estate planning issues to be considered. (Ralph Gano Miller uses these checklists in his California law practice to help his clients prepare for the interview.)

ASRS: Sec. 51

CHAPTER ENDNOTES

1. By Stephan R. Leimberg, Copyright 2001, by Stephan R. Leimberg.

RALPH GANO MILLER   CLIENT_____
MILLER, MONSON, PESCHEL, POLACEK & HOSHAW
A Professional Law Corporation

OPTIONAL CHECKLIST FOR DISCUSSION

As an option in preparing for our meeting, you may wish to review the following, which covers many of the specific areas of potential benefit and some of the unique problems that relate to various circumstances in which clients find themselves. By reviewing the list and checking off those items that relate to your circumstances, we will be able to focus more clearly on your particular concerns at our estate planning conference. This will also provide you an opportunity to consider beforehand the matters that will come under discussion.

Please do not delay your meeting because of the fact that you have not had a chance to review the checklist, since there will be an opportunity in our discussions to cover any area in which you have an interest.

Checklist Index

CHECKLISTS FOR VARIOUS CIRCUMSTANCES

Please recognize that the comments in this checklist are necessarily incomplete and that many important areas of potential benefit and detriment have not been covered. Therefore, you should not take any actions on the basis of the material in these lists without consulting with one of the attorneys in our office or with some other attorney.

[Some editing of the checklist has been done for this book.]

1. HOW TO USE THE CHECKLISTS

To save you time, you will probably wish to review only those aspects of the checklist that actually relate to your circumstances, since some aspects are redundant. Using the list of topics below, check the ones that relate to your circumstances, or to areas in which you might be interested (such as incorporating a business which presently might be held as a sole proprietorship).

In every case, you will wish to review either Checklist A or B (depending on your marital status). In addition, as an example, if you have an incorporated business or professional practice, you may wish to review the following additional areas:

Owners of Private Corporations

Professionals

Once you have determined the topics you wish to review, you can then turn to the appropriate page for each topic as shown below and check off the individual items of interest that are listed under that topic. Please also use the check-off boxes at the bottom of each page of the checklists to indicate those pages that you wish to review at our conference.

In reviewing specific areas of potential benefit or problems, please note that those which relate to non-tax matters (N), estate, gift or generation-skipping tax (E) or income or payroll tax (I) are indicated by the letter next to the check-off box to provide an easier means of identifying those areas which are of special interest to you.

The references to chapters after the heading of each item are to chapters of the [13th edition of *The Tools and Techniques of Estate Planning*].

Checklist Index

CHECKLISTS FOR VARIOUS CIRCUMSTANCES

CHECKLIST FOR VARIOUS CIRCUMSTANCES

A. ALL HUSBANDS AND WIVES WITH SOME ESTATE

AREAS OF POSSIBLE BENEFIT

[ ]N*   (1)   Avoidance of Probate: Use of a trust to both avoid the cost of probate and to eliminate the very substantial delays and restrictions of probate can be a benefit to even a very small estate. Although this course of planning is usually very beneficial, it may not apply if there are many potential liabilities of the decedent (e.g., a physician, engineer, or attorney with no malpractice coverage or coverage which may be inadequate) that might be "scraped off" through the probate creditors-claim process. For some professionals or businesses, the unavailability of adequate malpractice coverage is probably the only strong argument for not avoiding probate. However, even for these persons, an intervivos trust will provide a means of keeping "safe from creditors" assets such as insurance and retirement plan proceeds from being mixed with other assets in a probate estate. For most estates, avoidance of probate (and conservatorship) is a major benefit to consider.

[ ]N   (2)   Providing Assistance with Asset Management: Use of a trust may also provide financial planning assistance to a child or a spouse who is not experienced in handling funds and also delay distribution of trust principal until the beneficiary gains more experience in managing assets. Outright gifts to a child (which usually will be held by a court appointed guardian), being distributed at age 18 or 21, may also destroy planning for college. This problem may be avoided by a trust to provide for education and living expenses and distribution of the proceeds at later dates (e.g., one-third each at ages 25, 30 and 35).

[ ]N   (3)   Broad Durable Power of Attorney: Like most states, California permits one to give to another person a power of attorney which will be valid even if the person giving it becomes incompetent. This can aid greatly in the proper use of funds and avoid a conservatorship of the estate in some situations for a period of time. However, some people are unwilling to give someone else a power to deal broadly with their assets.

[ ]N   (4)   Limited Durable Power of Attorney: Some people prefer to give someone else only the power to transfer to a trust created by the grantor of the power property owned by the grantor. With this power, if the grantor is in a coma or otherwise unable to act, the holder of the power can shift the ownership of the grantor's assets to a revocable trust (previously created by the grantor) in order to avoid their being subject to probate at the grantor's death.

[ ]N   (5)   Health Care Power of Attorney: California also allows one to designate a person who will have the power to make health care decisions, often permitting the avoidance of a conservatorship of the person. This document also allows one to indicate their wishes as to being placed in a rest home (as opposed to staying in their own home). It also provides a means of giving instructions as to any donation of body parts after death.

[ ]N   (6)   "Pull the Plug" Directive: Those persons who want to do so may have a directive created, strictly adhering to state requirements, which may direct a physician to not sustain their life when there is no reasonable expectation that they may regain the use of their faculties.

[ ]N   (7)   Clarification of Property Rights Through Property Agreement: The actual ownership of property acquired before and during marriage is usually of importance, and often can be difficult to trace for either estate or income tax purposes or for marital rights purposes. A brief agreement can set forth and even change the form of title of their assets. This can be particularly important for people living in a community property state in order to receive a new stepped-up income tax basis (at one spouse's death) on both halves of property that they considered community property but which was titled as joint tenancy property.

---

*   The letters N, I or E after each check-off box indicates whether the specific item is more related to non-tax matters (N), income or payroll tax (I) or estate gift or generation-skipping tax (E).

[ ]N   (8)   <u>Provision of Liquidity Through Insurance</u> (Chapter 30): Where liquidity is important, it can be provided by life insurance, something that has become a "better buy" item in recent years.

[ ]E   (9)   <u>Full Use of Unified Credit</u> (Chapter 15): Since every citizen or resident has the unified credit available to offset either gift tax (credit protects up to $1 million of gifts after 2001) during his or her lifetime or estate tax (credit protects portion of estate ranging from $1,500,000 in 2004 to $3,500,000 in 2009) at death (see also Chapter 22), most estate planning for married couples since 1981 has been focused on the maximum use of the credit at the death of the first spouse to die so that, at the death of the second spouse, certain assets that have been already taxed and set aside (nearly always in a trust) will not be subject to tax again at the survivor's death.

[ ]E   (10)   <u>Measured Use of The Marital Deduction</u> (Chapter 24): Property left to a surviving spouse or to a marital deduction trust that qualifies for the marital deduction will not be subject to tax at the death of the first spouse. A great bulk of estate planning for spouses calls for a measured amount of property to be taxed so as to result in a tax equal to the remaining unified credit, with the balance of the property subject to the marital deduction and thus, deferred as to estate tax until survivor's death. The property that has been taxed (with the tax offset by the unified credit) can escape taxation at the death of the surviving spouse.

With proper planning, the surviving spouse may have all of the assets available without any reduction for taxes to be paid to the federal government (i.e., having a zero net estate tax to pay) and thus have a more financially secure position for the remainder of her or his life. However this approach can result in more overall estate taxes for the spousal unit than might be the case if some estate tax were paid at the first spouse's death. Use of the qualified terminable interest property (QTIP) concept of obtaining the marital deduction can be flexible so as to permit payment of none, some or all of the estate tax due at the first death, to be decided after the first spouse's death.

[ ]E   (11)   <u>Use of Gift Tax Annual Exclusion</u> (Chapter 22): Outright gifts and other gifts qualifying as "present interests" with values up to $11,000 (as indexed for inflation in 2004) can be made to each person in the world each year without creating any taxable gifts.

Where financial security permits, a program of annual gifts of $11,000-or-less can greatly reduce the amount of tax to be paid at the death of anyone. Currently, such gifts may be made even a few minutes before death and thus may also be a part of death-bed tax planning.

[ ]E   (12)   <u>Taxable Gifts of Appreciating Property</u> (Chapter 22): Where financial security permits, gifts made now of property which is expected to increase in value can be good planning even though a gift tax results.

Use of the unified credit to offset such gift tax will essentially reduce the amount of credit left available for offsetting estate tax at death. However, giving an asset now that is worth $100,000 is much better than having that same asset included in one's estate if it is then expected to be worth $500,000.

If the gift is community property, it is divided between the two spouses. Where the property given is separate property, the availability of "gift splitting" (Chapter 22) permits the same result.

[ ]E   (13)   <u>Sales to Next Generation of Appreciating Property</u>: Future appreciation in a property may be avoided by a sale of the entire property to the persons who would otherwise inherit it. The potential estate tax benefits here must be weighed against the income taxes paid by the seller that would have never been paid if the property were retained until death.

[ ]E   (14)   <u>Gifts of Insurance</u>: A transfer of insurance, either outright or through the use of non-revocable trusts, may be an example of a gift with a high potential for appreciation since, for gift tax purposes, the gift is measured only by the value of the property at the time of the gift (usually the "interpolated terminal reserve value," approximately the same as the cash surrender value of the policy). Regardless of the gift value, the entire face amount of the policy will be paid over to the donee(s) at the insured's death. Besides being extremely effective in transferring values

without significant transfer tax, such planning can often be done without any significant impairment of the financial security of the donor(s).

[ ]E (15) <u>Private Annuities</u> (Chapter 36): The monthly Section 7520 rate (120% of the mid-term applicable federal rate) applies for valuing such annuities.

[ ]E (16) <u>Sales of Remainder Interests in Property</u>: This is generally no longer feasible due to IRC Section 2702. There are, however, some quite technical transactions that may be undertaken to accomplish this.

[ ]E (17) <u>Split Interest Purchases of Property</u> (Chapter 38): Generally, less feasible than previously due to IRC Section 2702.

[ ]E (18) <u>Freezing Values of Assets</u> (Chapter 58): Partnership "freezes" and corporate arrangements with different classes of stock can in many circumstances shift the increase in value from one generation to the next; but such transactions are now generally subject to IRC Section 2701.

[ ]E/N (19) <u>Use of Generation-Skipping Trusts</u> (Chapter 18): Although the generation-skipping tax restricts what had been almost an open field for delaying tax through successive generations, it still leaves some very significant areas of benefit that should be considered.

Up to $1,500,000 (in 2004) per donor ($3,000,000 for a married couple with proper planning) can benefit the children and go to their children (the grandchildren of the donors) without any tax at the death of each child or his spouse or anyone else in his generation. EGTRRA 2001 increases this amount in steps to $3,500,000 in 2009 and repeals the tax for one year in 2010. All larger estates should consider the possible use of this planning technique, including its use in relation to property that may be inherited by the client.

Apart from the estate tax benefits, this type of trust can also provide lifetime financial assistance and a measure of security to a child who is not "money wise."

[ ]E (20) <u>Qualified Family-Owned Business</u> (Chapter 42): An estate tax deduction may be available if a substantial part of the estate consists of a family-owned business. This deduction is not available for decedents dying in 2004 to 2010.

[ ]I (21) <u>Grantor Retained Income Trusts (GRITs)</u> (Chapter 26): Another technique used to reduce the transfer tax impact of a gift involves creating a trust which retains for the donor the right to the income from the gifted property for a certain number of years. Generally, grantor retained annuity trusts (GRATs) and grantor retained unitrusts (GRUTs) will be used instead of GRITs due to IRC Section 2702.

[ ]I/E (22) <u>Charitable Remainder Trusts</u> (Chapter 33): In circumstances where one has an asset with a very low income tax basis that does not produce satisfactory income (or if another reason exists to dispose of it), it is possible to avoid tax on the gain on sale by creating a trust which will ultimately go to a charity, transferring the asset to the trust and having the trust sell it. The original owner(s) may retain a payment stream from the newly invested sales proceeds, which have not been reduced by any income taxes. Insurance on the donor(s) may often be a basis for replacing the value of the assets which otherwise would have gone to the children of the donor(s).

POTENTIAL PROBLEMS

[ ]N (1) <u>Possible Estate Liabilities</u>: To the extent that the decedent has a large amount of potential liabilities (e.g., an anesthesiologist, a civil engineer, a tax shelter attorney who has neglected to carry professional liability insurance, or a businessman who has found himself saddled with large debts), probate may be of some benefit in that most states provide a creditors claim period which cuts off liabilities to those creditors that do not file their claims in the proper way within that period. Similar procedures are available in some states for trusts.

Differences in state laws affect this, but there are some circumstances where most, if not all, of the assets, should be subjected to probate in order to "cleanse" them of potential liabilities of the decedent. The availability of adequate professional or business liability insurance is a factor to be considered in determining whether to have assets (other than insurance or retirement fund benefits) be probated.

[ ]N   (2)   Diversion of Assets to Replacement Spouse: Children are often unintentionally deprived of security and benefits where assets are held in joint tenancy with a surviving spouse or left outright to a surviving spouse and that surviving spouse remarries. Without a trust to protect the children, there is no way to be certain that the children will receive any benefits, particularly if the survivor remarries and is subject to pressure to prove his or her love and devotion to a new spouse by joint tenancy ownership or a new will.

[ ]N   (3)   Distributions to Children at Early Ages: An estate built with great care and effort may be wasted, with little or no real benefit to the next generation, by leaving the property outright to a child who has no experience or ability in managing the assets. Early distributions also usually have a very adverse effect on educational planning.

[ ]N   (4)   Loss of Mental Capacity: If no trust has been created to hold the assets and provide a successor trustee to manage the assets, or where no one has been given a broad durable power of attorney, incapacity may cause serious disruption of a business and also disrupt payment of normal expenses of living. In this circumstance, a relatively cumbersome and expensive court conservatorship of the estate is the only way to provide some management for the assets.

[ ]N   (5)   Spouse's and Children's Ignorance of Estate Affairs: Failure to provide information as to the existence and/ or location of assets may seriously disrupt the process of garnering the estate assets and properly managing them.

[ ]N   (6)   Lack of Liquidity: Although liquidity may not be required with current planning techniques at the first spouse's death for estate tax, it may well be required for other purposes, particularly if the decedent was in business or farming. Further, for larger estates, at the death of the second spouse, there may be a need to either have cash liquidity or liquidate many of the estate assets at a loss in order to pay death taxes.

Although it is possible to have a zero estate tax liability at the death of the first-to-die spouse, there are circumstances where it may be beneficial to have funds available at the first death to pay estate taxes on assets at that time and avoid the increase in value which may take place during the lifetime of the surviving spouse. Where other liquidity may not be available, insurance on one or both of the spouses (or the survivor of them) may be the best answer.

[ ]E   (7)   <u>Having an Estate Plan Which Does Not Qualify For the Unlimited Marital Deduction</u> (Chapter 24): Many pre-1982 estate plans now result in payment of substantial federal estate tax at the death of the first spouse to die. The "totally tax-free transfer to a surviving spouse" simply doesn't happen under many pre-1982 estate plans, including some plans which use trusts to reduce estate taxes.

[ ]E   (8)   <u>Loss of Unified Credit</u>: (Chapter 24): The most frequently encountered estate "problem" for married couples is that of the first spouse to die leaving all assets outright to a surviving spouse.

A deduction is available for estate tax purposes as to any assets left to a surviving spouse. Thus, the decedent leaving all assets to a surviving spouse has no tax to pay (since all the tax will be deferred until the survivor's death) and thus, loses the advantage of the unified credit to reduce the overall estate and gift taxes on the estates of the two spouses. This is true regardless of whether the decedent had separate property or community property. See Chapter 24 for a description of the use of a trust to create sufficient tax and take advantage of the unified credit so that the property in that trust, taxed at the first spouse's death and segregated until the survivor's death, can avoid tax at the survivor's death.

[ ]E/N   (9)   <u>Generation-Skipping Transfer Tax</u> (Chapter 18): Trusts with grandchildren and lower generations as beneficiaries may be subject to generation-skipping transfer tax. Also, direct gifts to grandchildren can trigger not only death taxes but also generation-skipping taxes, and should be evaluated.

[ ]E   (10)   <u>State Inheritance Taxes</u>: Not all state laws follow the federal tax rules allowing a total marital deduction for gifts to surviving spouses. Planning must also consider the applicable laws of the state since such inheritance taxes can be significant.

California, Florida, Nevada and a number of other states have no inheritance or other death tax that would cause a higher overall death tax. Some states do have a "pick-up" tax that takes advantage of the federal credit for state death taxes and lets them share some of the federal estate tax.

[ ]E   (11)   <u>Gifts with Retained Interests</u> (Chapter 15): Where the donor retains an interest in a property (either technically as by retaining a life estate in property deeded to someone else or practically as by continuing to live in and make use of a house given to someone else), the property will be brought back into the donor's estate for estate tax purposes. Proper planning, e.g., paying full market rent on the residence given away but continuing to be used, can avoid any adverse results in some situations.

[ ]E   (12)   <u>Custodianship Gifts</u> (Chapter 23): A typical example of a retained right is the donor who makes a gift to a child and appoints himself or herself as the custodian of the gift until the child reaches maturity. Such gifts will be brought back into the taxable estate of the donor if he or she is the custodian of the gift.

[ ]E   (13)   <u>State Gift Taxes</u>: As with inheritance taxes, state gift tax laws often differ from federal laws, and some states have lower or no amounts of gifts which are excluded from gift tax and there may well be no marital deduction available for certain gifts in certain states. State gift taxes can be very substantial. Most states (including California, Florida, and Nevada) have no gift taxes.

[ ]E   (14)   <u>Accidental Gifts</u>: Although planned giving can be a most effective way of reducing transfer taxes, care should be taken to not create unintended taxable gifts.

Except as between husband and wife, nearly every creation of a co-ownership with any other person (e.g., putting a stock or piece of real property in joint tenancy with someone) creates a taxable gift. Obtaining competent tax advice is the only way to avoid such gifts.

Interest-free loans or below-market-rate loans are a potential area for unintended taxable gifts (Chapter 37).

[ ]E   (15)   <u>Insurance Gifts Within Three Years of Death</u> (Chapter 30): Gifts with three years of death are generally not brought back into the taxable estate, except with regard to gifts of insurance and certain other gifts. Thus, either direct or indirect gifts of insurance within that period can result in the taxability of the insurance proceeds in the donor's estate. Community property rules may often present unique problems in identifying the donor of insurance (Chapter 30).

[ ]E   (16)   <u>Lack of a Qualifying Marriage</u>: The increasing frequency of absence of a formal marriage makes this a very real danger for couples who in other times would have married. Depending on state law, either a formal or a common law marriage can qualify for the marital deduction, but there must be a "marriage." Documentation for a marriage or a divorce in foreign countries must be examined by a competent attorney. California and several other states do not recognize "common law" marriages (those based on people living together).

[ ]E/I   (17)   <u>Failure to be Aware of Law Changes</u>: Although laws sometimes change in regard to wills and trusts, the changes are much more frequent with regard to estate, gift, and income taxes. Ignorance of such changes can have very adverse effects on an estate plan. Estate plans should be reviewed regularly with competent counsel.

[ ]E/I (18) <u>Property Tax Reassessment at Death</u>: Where state law (e.g., Proposition 13 in California) has prevented valuation increases for property tax purposes, death can lift the barrier to such increases in valuation and also to tax increases. Some exceptions to such increases often exist and estate planning must be done with property tax matters in mind.

[ ]E/I (19) <u>Retirement Plan Beneficiary Designation Forms</u>: Where benefits built up in a qualified retirement plan are planned to be transmitted at death, this is accomplished not by one's will or trust but by using a beneficiary designation form created for such a purpose. In those circumstances where there is a gift to anyone other than the surviving spouse of a participant (perhaps a gift over to a trust in the event the spouse does not survive or disclaims the gift), great care must be taken to see that the laws created by the Retirement Equity Act of 1984 are not violated. This law generally restricts all transfers of benefit from a qualified plan other than in the form of annuity payments. Further, any spouse of at least one year has an immediate right to half of the value in the plan to be left to her or him in the form of an annuity. Beneficiary designation forms must be carefully reviewed to spot any violations of this law.

[ ]E/I (20) <u>Possible Retirement Plan Control By Will</u>: A California court has surprisingly said that regardless of retirement plan rules and possible preemption of state law by federal law, an interest in a retirement plan may be controlled by one's will. Many other states follow California law. Therefore, until this matter is resolved, it may be necessary to have one's will reference and confirm the effect of plan beneficiary designation forms. Otherwise, planning for proper direction of such plan proceeds may be frustrated.

CHECKLIST FOR VARIOUS CIRCUMSTANCES

B. <u>SINGLE PERSONS</u>

AREAS OF POSSIBLE BENEFIT

(1)   <u>Implications for the Single Client</u>: With the exception of a marital deduction, all the potential benefits described in the checklist for "Husbands and Wives" are available to a single person. This group includes persons who have never married, those who have had an annulment or divorce and also survivors of marriage, both with and without children. However, the marital deduction is available only to the extent that there is an existing spouse who receives a lifetime gift or assets transmitted at death.

With the possible exception of the annuity (discussed below), there are few unique estate planning benefits available for a single person, although income taxation rules may from time to time give some advantage to a single person as compared to one who is married.

[ ]N   (2)   <u>Use of Annuities</u>: For those persons who truly have no financial responsibility for anyone else, the purchase of commercial annuities may have some application in increasing the cash available each month during the person's lifetime. However, the need for protection of purchasing power from inflation often argues against putting the majority of one's assets into such investments. Certain annuities provide some degree of protection from inflation.

[ ]I   (3)   <u>Use of Charitable Remainder Trusts</u> (Chapter 33): Where the single person has no need for concern over leaving assets to children or other persons, consideration should be given to obtaining a current income tax deduction by giving to a charity the right to use property after the single person's death. Although the flexibility of sale and/or consumption of the asset is lost, the income is retained and income tax lessened because of the deduction. Gain on sale of assets placed in the trust can escape taxation if placed in such a trust.

POTENTIAL PROBLEMS

(1)   <u>Implications for the Single Client</u>: All the potential problems with regard to the above "All Husbands and Wives With Some Estate" apply to the single person. The exception is that there is no accidental loss of unified credit by leaving all the assets to a surviving spouse since the marital deduction does not apply to a single person.

[ ]N   (2)   <u>Difficulty in Finding Conservator of Person or Estate</u>: For those single persons who have no children, it is often much more difficult to find someone in whom they have enough confidence to make decisions regarding their person and all their assets when the single person is no longer able to make such decisions well.

[ ]N   (3)   <u>The Lee Marvin Syndrome</u>: Unmarried persons who have a live-in companion but no written agreement as to ownership of property or rights to income have a substantial exposure to lawsuits that may drastically reduce assets that would otherwise go to the beneficiaries of their estate plan. A written property agreement can solve this problem.

[ ]N   (4)   <u>Heirs' Lack of Knowledge of Estate</u>: Assets of a single person are frequently never all found since the executor, often an unrelated person and often a corporate fiduciary, may never have been given information as to the existence or location of assets.

[ ]N   (5)   <u>Single Parent Finding Guardian For Children</u>: Failure to direct some thought and effort toward the often difficult question of finding a suitable guardian for the children of a single parent often results in not only not finding a suitable guardian but also often causes the single parent to delay having a will or trust drafted.

[ ]E   (6)   <u>No Easy Way to Defer Estate Taxes</u> (Chapter 24): Without a valid surviving spouse, estate taxes must be faced and the single person's estate must be prepared to bear the brunt of such taxes.

CHECKLIST FOR VARIOUS CIRCUMSTANCES

C. PERSONS WITH POTENTIAL INHERITANCE

AREAS OF POSSIBLE BENEFIT

[ ]N   (1)   <u>Avoidance of Probate And/Or Conservatorships for Parents</u>: Probate of a parent's estate and particularly that of the surviving parent, puts the burden of such delays and costs directly on the client. Use of an intervivos trust will permit the avoidance of such a probate. It also permits the avoidance of what may be an expensive and cumbersome conservatorship (or guardianship) proceeding where the parent is not managing assets well. A trust that is contained in one's will does not avoid probate at the death of the owner of the property.

[ ]E   (2)   <u>Generation-Skipping Trust</u> (Chapter 18): Where the client has an expectation of an inheritance, there should be a discussion of the possibility of receiving such inheritance in the form of a trust which typically gives the client (as trustee) the control over all the benefits from the assets to be inherited, but also permits the avoidance of the generation-skipping transfer tax and the estate tax.

POTENTIAL PROBLEMS

[ ]N   (1)   <u>Reduction of Parental Control Over Children</u>: Direct gifts to clients' children from the clients' parents may often interfere significantly with parental control, particularly as to education of the client's children. Use of a trust may avoid this problem and still provide the benefit the grandparents' desire.

[ ]N   (2)   <u>Dissipation of Estate by Parent's New Spouse</u>: Where the parent leaves all assets to a new spouse with the intent that she or he will leave it to the children of the prior marriage, the children often never receive any of the assets. Use of a trust by the parent to control the assets would avoid this problem. Often such a trust can be best created before the death of either parent.

[ ]E   (3)   <u>Loss of Generation-Skipping Exemption</u> (Chapter 18): There is an exemption from generation-skipping transfer tax for $1,500,000 (in 2004) per donor, or $3,000,000 for a couple. EGTRRA 2001 increases the exemption in steps to $3,500,000 in 2009 and repeals the GST tax for one year in 2010. However, without proper planning, the exemption of both parents and particularly that of the first parent to die can be lost. This is a very important aspect if generation-skipping for an inheritance is planned.

[ ]E   (4)   <u>Accidental Application of Generation-Skipping Transfer Tax</u>: Planning in which the parent of the client plans to benefit both the client and the client's children may often unwittingly cause application of the generation-skipping tax, resulting in a tax at the death of the client on assets which will go on to benefit the next generation. Under some circumstances, the generation-skipping tax may apply and the estate tax unified credit of the child is wasted.

CHECKLIST FOR VARIOUS CIRCUMSTANCES

D. PERSONS MOVING FROM OTHER STATES OR COUNTRIES

AREAS OF POSSIBLE BENEFIT

[ ]E (1) <u>Gifts to Permit Both Spouses to Use Unified Credit</u>: Where one spouse has more property (because of state laws or inheritance) than the other spouse, gifts to the spouse with the smaller estate should be considered in order to be certain that such spouse has sufficient estate to take advantage of the full amount of the unified credit and/ or generation-skipping exemption. Where the spouse with the larger amount of assets is unwilling to make outright gifts to the other spouse, consideration may be given to having the other spouse purchase and continue to own life insurance on his or her life in an amount which will take advantage of the opportunity to pass assets tax free because of the unified credit.

  If the gift is of real property or some other asset that may be subject to the laws of another state, care must be taken to determine if that state imposes gift taxes on transfers between spouses.

[ ]E (2) <u>Change of Residence to Avoid State Death Taxes</u>: Since many states (e.g., Florida, Nevada, California, etc.) have no additional death taxes beyond the amount allowed as a credit for federal estate tax purposes, changing one's residence to one of those states may avoid significant death taxes.

[ ]E (3) <u>Possibility of Nonresidents Making Gifts Before Becoming Residents</u>: In some circumstances, nonresidents (e.g., an exile from San Salvador temporarily living in the U.S. but who is as yet not a U.S. citizen or resident) may be able to make gifts without being subject to U.S. gift taxes. In some such cases, planning may include gifts to family members made before becoming a resident of the U.S.

[ ]I (4) <u>Ownership Change to Community Property</u> (Chapter 19, How Basis is Determined): Where one spouse has separate property (e.g., acquired through earnings in a separate property state or from inheritance) that has increased in value, consideration should be given to changing that property to community property. If the property is left as separate property and the non-owning spouse dies, the property will retain its present income tax basis. If the property is changed to community property, in a properly conceived estate plan, it is possible that the death of either spouse will provide the survivor with a new and increased income tax basis for the property equal to the fair market value of the property at the time of the death of the first spouse to die.

POTENTIAL PROBLEMS

[ ]N (1) <u>Ancillary Probate</u>: If a person retains ownership of real property in another state, there will probably have to be two probates, one for the state of residence and another for the state in which the retained real property is located. Use of a trust to hold such out-of-state property can usually avoid this costly and cumbersome circumstance.

[ ]N (2) <u>State Law Differences for Execution and Administration of Wills and Trusts</u>: A will drafted in one state may not be valid to transfer real property or certain other assets located in another state since the formalities required of such a document and the rules for inheritance, qualification of executors, etc., are controlled by the law of each state. The will must be examined by an attorney in the state in which the clients are currently residents.

[ ]N (3) <u>Surviving Spouse's Rights Differ From State to State</u>: State laws also differ as to what rights the spouses have in property acquired during marriage (e.g., community property spouses each having a half interest in earnings during the marriage), rights in separate property at the death of a spouse, and also intestacy rules (which operate in the absence of a valid will). All of these differences may be magnified in comparing the laws of different states.

[ ]N   (4)   <u>Real Property in Other States Usually Subject to that State's Laws</u>: Even though the residence of the owners was considered in drafting their wills, laws of the location of the property will usually apply – including the aspect of the validity of the form of the will, rights of surviving spouses and the rules of intestacy.

[ ]N   (5)   <u>Foreign Residents</u>: For those persons who have previously lived in or who are currently residents of or perhaps even have property in other countries, there must be an examination of the law of the other country to see if a will must be drafted in accordance with its laws in order to be effective as to assets in that country.

[ ]E   (6)   <u>Accidental Gifts Prior to 1982</u> (Chapter 22): Transfers of ownership between husband and wife prior to 1982 may very well have resulted in taxable gifts for federal estate tax purposes and for a state's gift tax purposes even though no gift was intended. Putting separate property (e.g., which was inherited or which was earned in a separate property state) of one spouse into co-ownership with the other in many cases resulted in taxable gift, and ERTA did not wipe out such prior gift tax liabilities. Such transfers should be reviewed to determine if any gift tax liability exists or if any steps should be taken to currently record the circumstances that argued against the transaction having been considered a gift.

[ ]E   (7)   <u>Possibility of Two State Death Taxes Applying</u>: By having indicia of residence (e.g., drivers license, lodge membership, income tax filings, etc.) in two or more states, it is possible to be subject to state death tax in each state.

[ ]E   (8)   <u>Different U.S. Estate and Gift Tax Rules for Nonresidents</u> (Chapter 20): Foreign citizens who are not U.S. residents do not have all of the estate tax benefits of U.S. citizens in relation to federal estate and gift tax and also often with regard to state gift and death taxes. Such noncitizens with significant assets must have their estate plans prepared by an attorney who is aware of the impact of such differences on estate planning.

[ ]E   (9)   <u>Special Trust Required to Obtain Marital Deduction For Transfer To Noncitizens</u>: The benefit of the marital deduction for transfers to spouses who are not U.S. citizens is lost unless the transferred property is held in a qualified domestic trust (QDOT). A QDOT must have a trustee that is a citizen of, or a corporation created in, the United States. This rule will invalidate any prior estate plan involving noncitizens that is not amended to comply with these rules.

CHECKLIST FOR VARIOUS CIRCUMSTANCES

E. OWNERS OF PRIVATE CORPORATIONS

AREAS OF POSSIBLE BENEFIT

[ ]N   (1)   <u>Shield Against Corporate Liabilities</u> (Chapter 47): Wherever the business activity has some potential financial dangers, a business operated through a properly organized and operated corporation with sufficient capital may protect the other assets of a client.

[ ]N   (2)   <u>Pooling of Capital for Business</u> (Chapter 47): Issuance of shares to various persons permits the pooling of capital and thus raising of more funds than would otherwise be available to any individual proprietor for the capital needs of a business activity.

[ ]N   (3)   <u>Maintaining Value of Business – Buy and Sell Agreement</u> (Chapter 40): Often the most important aspect of estate planning is preserving the values built up in the private corporation. Executing a proper buy and sell agreement may be an effective way of doing this in many situations that involve private corporations.

[ ]N   (4)   <u>Capitalization to Permit Retention of Control</u>: In circumstances where gifts of stock to family members are contemplated, consideration might be given early to issuance of both voting and nonvoting stock.

[ ]N   (5)   <u>Use of a Voting Trust to Permit Retention of Control</u>: Where issuance of nonvoting stock is not practical, the possibility of maintaining control is feasible in some circumstances by the use of a voting trust.

[ ]E   (6)   <u>Early Gifts of Stock Within Family</u>: Where it is likely the corporation will appreciate in value, gifts of stock at an early stage of the corporation's growth may permit the transfer of a much larger part of the future value without there being any significant gift tax consequences. The effect of IRC Section 2701 on such transfers must be considered (Chapter 58).

[ ]E   (7)   <u>Capitalization to Permit Easier Corporate Freeze – A Lost Planning Tool</u>: When an increase in the value of a corporation is a very significant possibility, consideration was previously given early to issuance of both preferred stock (which can be recovered by the corporation at stated prices) and common stock (to be given to the next generation) which will not have such restrictions, and thus will have the major potential for increase in value. The effect of IRC Section 2701 on such transfers must be considered (Chapter 58).

[ ]E   (8)   <u>Corporation or Partnership May Qualify More Assets for Estate Tax Deferral</u> (Chapter 16): All of the "business assets" in a going business corporation may qualify at a client's death to meet the minimum percentage limits in order to achieve deferral of the related estate tax over a period of as long as 14 years and with some of the tax bearing interest at a very low rate. Although the value of "passive assets" held by the business do not qualify for deferral, holding assets in a corporation or partnership may still result in a larger amount qualifying for deferral of tax than if such assets were owned by an individual proprietor.

[ ]I   (9)   <u>Retaining Rights at Original Incorporation of Business</u> (Chapter 47): As opposed to putting all the assets of a business into the corporation in exchange for stock, when forming a corporation consideration should be given to taking back a note in place of some of the stock so that some money or other assets can be later drawn out of the corporation against such note without recognition of income tax.

[ ]I   (10)   <u>Fringe Benefit Planning</u>: The following are some of the most typically used fringe benefit planning techniques:

      (a)   group term life insurance (Chapter 30)

      (b)   medical reimbursement plans (Chapter 54)

(c)   disability insurance deductibility

(d)   cafeteria plans

(e)   split-dollar insurance coverage (Chapter 30)

(f)   education costs

(g)   financial counseling

(h)   prepaid group legal services

(i)   dependent care assistance

(j)   auto and travel costs

[ ]I   (11) <u>Use of High Profile Qualified Retirement Plans</u> (Chapters 49, 50, 52): Pension and profit sharing plans, both for corporations and for individual proprietors and partners, are recognized by tax experts as probably the most effective tax shelter for those persons in a business or profession.

[ ]I   (12) <u>Use of Dividends Received Deduction</u>: When investment of corporate funds is considered, the deduction afforded corporations of 80% (70% in some circumstances) of any dividends received should be taken into consideration.

[ ]I   (13) <u>Use of Corporation's Initial Low Income Tax Rate</u> (Chapter 47): Tax rates as low as 15% for income tax purposes makes the corporation a very useful tool for building capital for some businesses or professions. However, "personal service corporations" (e.g., most of those that practice law, medicine, or consulting using shareholders as employees) do not have the advantage of the lower corporate tax rate. Thus, all income of such corporations will be taxed at the 35% rate.

[ ]I   (14) <u>Electing S Corporation Status</u> (Chapter 46): Where circumstances warrant, the corporation may be shifted to being taxed like a partnership through election into "S" status, thus having the income taxed at the shareholder's own individual rate. The ability to make this election is subject to a number of important rules. Relative tax brackets of corporations and shareholders should be considered.

Since stock of S corporations cannot be held for a significant period of time in most trusts without revocation of the S election, the existence of a possible future addition of such a corporation in one's estate must be brought to the attention of the estate planner. It is possible to draft trusts that can continue to hold S corporation stock without revocation of the "S" election.

[ ]I   (15) <u>Shifting Income to Low Tax Bracket Family Members</u> (Chapter 46): The S corporation election described above also permits the shifting of income to other family members by giving them ownership of stock. Relative tax brackets of each should be considered. Income of children under age 14 is generally taxed at the parent's marginal tax rate.

[ ]I   (16) <u>Using an ESOP to Defer or Avoid Gain on Sale</u> (Chapter 49): The deferral of gain is permitted on a sale of the corporation stock in certain circumstances by the use of an employee stock ownership plan (ESPOP) as the buyer and the reinvestment of sale proceeds in domestic stock on the open market. This is a potentially important benefit for many clients.

[ ]I   (17) <u>Using an ESOP to Redeem Stock With Pretax Dollars</u> (Chapter 49): The installation of an ESOP can provide the means in some circumstances to redeem stock by making deductible cash contributions to a qualified plan to

build up a fund for the purchase. In some circumstances this can also provide for acquisition of the stock in conjunction with a bank loan and the repayment of that loan with tax deductible funds contributed to the ESOP.

[ ]I   (18)   <u>Noncash Deductions Through Use of ESOP</u> (Chapter 49): Where taxable income may be high and cash resources low, the installation of the ESOP can provide for cash-free deductions by having the corporation issue stock to the ESOP. However, this planning also shifts some stock ownership to the employees of the corporation.

[ ]I   (19)   <u>Lifetime Stock Redemptions to Remove Cash</u>: Where some shareholders are not related, it may be possible to redeem stock of certain shareholders with the recognition of gain as a sale instead of dividend treatment. This will permit treatment as long-term capital gains.

[ ]I   (20)   <u>Avoiding Tax on Underlying Gains</u>: Even though the corporation may contain assets (e.g., unrecognized receivables, appreciated inventory, fixed assets which have been depreciated, etc.) that would normally produce income to the corporation when sold, under many circumstances all of the assets may be sold together through a sale of the corporation's stock, and thus a gain avoided at the corporation's level until the asset is sold or converted to cash. The selling shareholder, however, recognizes the gain that may exist with regard to his stock. However, item (28) below regarding the loss of the General Utilities doctrine should be reviewed.

[ ]I   (21)   <u>Stock Redemption at Death to Pay Death Taxes</u> (Chapter 41): Special rules permit redemption of stock under IRC Section 303 in an amount equal to the total of both federal and state death taxes without having the redemption treated as a dividend.

[ ]I   (22)   <u>Total Stock Redemption at Death of Community Property Shareholder</u> (Chapter 19 - Basis): By holding property in community property form, the death of one spouse gives the surviving spouse an income tax basis in both halves of the stock equal to the then fair market value. The corporation can then be liquidated and no gain is recognized at the shareholder level.

However, corporations that have not elected S corporation status under certain specific rules are required to recognize any gain inherent in the assets upon liquidation (e.g., a building worth $100,000 with a cost basis to the corporation of only $30,000), as noted also in item (27) below.

[ ]I   (23)   <u>Shifting of Income Between Tax Years</u> (Chapter 47): By having a fiscal year of the corporation that overlaps the owner-employee's usual December 31st taxable year (e.g., having a January 31st year end for the corporation), it is possible to shift income from one year to the next. Holding back salary payments during the year and making them in January of the succeeding year may shift income from one taxable year of the owner-employee to his next taxable year, without creating any taxable income for the corporation. Generally, this is not available for S corporations and personal service corporations.

[ ]I   (24)   <u>$50,000 Borrowable From Qualified Retirement Plan</u> (Chapter 52): The amount of money that can be borrowed by a participant from a corporate qualified plan is generally limited to $50,000.

[ ]I   (25)   <u>Full Deduction for California Income Tax Purposes of Plan Contributions</u>: Several states restrict the deduction allowed for contributions allowed to noncorporate retirement plans (Keogh plans). Some states, like California, have conformed to federal law and permit a full deduction. However, this can be an important reason for using a corporation in those states that have income tax rules that restrict such deductions.

[ ]I   (26)   <u>Rollover of Qualified Plan Account to IRA on Retirement or Death of Spouse</u> (Chapter 51): Recognition of income tax can be avoided by a "terminating" qualified retirement plan participant or spouse of a deceased participant by transferring – under certain conditions – the plan proceeds to an individual retirement account (IRA). Because such a transfer could have other ramifications, this should be carefully considered.

[ ]I   (27)   <u>Loss of the General Utilities Doctrine</u>: Liquidation of corporations other than S corporations will result in recognizing a tax at the corporate level on the excess of the value of any assets over the corporation's income tax basis

in them. E.g., a real property owned by the corporation with a corporate tax basis (cost less depreciation) of $20,000 but which is worth $100,000 at time of liquidation, will result in a corporate tax on the $80,000 difference. Even some S corporations can recognize all or part of this corporate gain upon liquidation under the "built in gain" rules. Thus, a taxable gain can be recognized at both the corporate and shareholder levels upon liquidation of a corporation.

POTENTIAL PROBLEMS

[ ]N   (1)   <u>Wrong Choice of Form of Buy-and-Sell Agreement</u> (Chapter 40): Whether you use a stock redemption agreement or a cross purchase agreement depends on several factors which should be reviewed with a competent advisor to avoid loss of potential benefits.

[ ]N   (2)   <u>Buy-In Problems Created by High Stock Values</u>: Where future shareholders may not have much capital and where the corporation has accumulated a great deal of fair market value, many qualified prospective co-shareholders may be preempted from buying into the corporation. An example of this might be a large medical radiology group that over the years has accumulated in the operating corporation a very large amount of value related to accounts receivable and to the radiology equipment used in the practice. For a bright young doctor, it may simply cost too much to consider buying into such a corporation.

[ ]N   (3)   <u>Cash Problems in Redeeming Shares</u>: The same problem as described above of accumulating too much in the way of asset values in a corporation may make the redemption of shares a very difficult problem.

[ ]N   (4)   <u>Piercing of Corporate Veil by Creditors</u> (Chapter 47): Inadequate capitalization or failure to follow corporate procedures may result in a corporation failing to provide a shield for shareholders as to any liability for corporate debts.

[ ]N   (5)   <u>Securities Law Problems</u> (Chapter 47): Failure to observe legal requirements in creating a corporation may cause adverse civil results and even criminal penalties. The incorporation should be done by an experienced and competent attorney.

[ ]E   (6)   <u>Corporate Owned Insurance on Life of Majority Shareholder</u> (Chapter 30): Ownership by the corporation of insurance on the majority shareholder may result in that insurance being included in the taxable estate of the client-shareholder.

[ ]E   (7)   <u>Stock Valuation Problems</u> (Chapter 57): The various methods approved by the courts for valuation of corporations should be reviewed with a competent tax attorney in determining the value which estate tax authorities will place on the corporate stock. The client may be unpleasantly surprised to learn of the high value that will be assigned to a corporate ownership.

[ ]E   (8)   <u>Loss of Estate Tax Exclusion of Pension and Profit-Sharing Benefits</u> (Chapter 52): Except for some unusual circumstances, the exclusion previously available for values in qualified corporate retirement plans (as well as those of partnerships and individual proprietors) is no longer allowed. Many estate plans require important revisions because of this change in the law.

[ ]I   (9)   <u>Double Taxation of Dividends</u>: (Chapter 47): Where a corporation accumulates earnings, it pays income tax on them (unless it has elected to be taxed as an S corporation). However, when the dividends are paid to the shareholder, the corporation receives no deduction or offset against taxable income but the shareholder is subject to income tax on the dividends received. For this reason, very few large dividends are paid to shareholders of privately owned C corporations.

[ ]I   (10)   <u>Real Property Owned by Corporation</u>: In many planning circumstances where the business activity itself is in a corporation, the ownership of the building in which the business is carried on is maintained outside the corporation. Failure to do this may cause recognition of gain at both corporate and individual levels, in those

circumstances where either the business or the real property are to be sold separately or where C corporations (and even some S corporations) liquidate.

[ ]I   (11)   <u>Corporation Ignored as Sham by Taxing Authorities</u> (Chapter 47): Failure to observe the requirements for corporate meetings, salary arrangements, separation of ownership as between shareholder and corporation, etc., may result in all the corporate income being taxed to the individual shareholders.

[ ]I   (12)   <u>Possible Dividend Treatment for Payments or Benefits to Shareholder</u> (Chapter 47): Certain salary payments and other payments to or for the benefit of shareholders (e.g., personal use of a corporate auto) may be challenged by the IRS and denied as deductions to the corporation on the basis that they are "dividends."

[ ]I   (13)   <u>Special IRS Scrutiny For Corporate Partners</u> (Chapter 47): The IRS has a tool to use against those corporations that are partners of a partnership, e.g., medical or legal "incorporated partnerships." Corporations in this situation should review IRC Section 269A with competent tax counsel to see if changes in the form of business or practice should be considered.

[ ]I   (14)   <u>Limitation on Accumulation of Corporate Earnings</u> (Chapter 47): Accumulation of corporate earnings beyond $250,000 ($150,000 for service corporations in many professional areas) may result in an additional tax equal to 15% (in 2004). Avoidance of such tax on such accumulations requires a showing that the earnings are required to be retained for the "reasonable needs of the business."

[ ]I   (15)   <u>Extra Tax on "Incorporated Pocketbooks"</u> (Chapter 47): Where 60% of the corporate income is from rents, royalties, dividends, interest and certain personal service income (with some very significant exceptions), a large extra income tax may apply.

[ ]I   (16)   <u>No/Low Interest Loans From Corporation</u> (Chapter 37): Income is recognized as a dividend where a corporate owner has a loan from his corporation at no interest or at a rate lower than market. Since it is a dividend, the corporation gets no deduction.

[ ]I   (17)   <u>Payroll Taxes</u>: Income received as salary by a shareholder-employee is subject to social security tax paid by both the corporation and the employee. There is currently a special income tax deduction of 50% of the self-employment tax. Payment of rent or dividends is not subject to this tax or to any state payroll taxes.

[ ]I   (18)   <u>Possible Second Tax on Liquidations</u>: For C corporation liquidations, the corporation will be taxed to the extent that any assets have a value in excess of the corporation's basis in them (e.g., a building with $100,000 which has a tax basis of only $30,000). Certain S corporations can avoid this corporate level of tax, which is in addition to the tax on the shareholder to the extent that the net proceeds from the liquidation exceed his or her basis in the corporate stock.

CHECKLIST FOR VARIOUS CIRCUMSTANCES

F. INDIVIDUAL PROPRIETORS

AREAS OF POSSIBLE BENEFIT

[ ]N (1) <u>No Corporate Creation or Operation Costs</u>: The individual proprietorship is the simplest form of doing business and avoids legal fees for incorporation as well as those for subsequent annual meetings, etc.

[ ]I (2) <u>Only One Level of Income Taxation</u>: By avoiding the corporation, one avoids the taxation of income at the corporate level and its subsequent second taxation where the payment to the shareholder is deemed to be a dividend, as opposed to being an expense deductible to the corporation (e.g., salary). One also avoids the corporate tax (which is in addition to the shareholder tax) on appreciation at the time of the sale of the business (followed by a liquidation).

[ ]I (3) <u>Assets Removable From Business Without Tax</u>: Unlike the corporation or certain partnership circumstances, the individual proprietorship allows the taxpayer to remove assets or add assets without the recognition of any gain for income tax purposes.

[ ]I (4) <u>Avoidance of Social Security Tax for Family Employees</u>: Payments of salary to spouses or children permits shifting of income from an individual proprietor to other persons in the family without payment of social security taxes. This is becoming more important as social security taxes are increasing.

[ ]I (5) <u>Payroll Taxes</u>: There is a special income tax deduction of 50% of the self-employment tax.

[ ]I (6) <u>Ability to Produce Losses Which Can Offset Salary or Other Taxable Income</u>: Where the business is actively pursued by the owner (and thus is not a "passive" activity) and produces a tax loss, the amount of the loss can be used to reduce the amount of ordinary taxable income. However, if the taxpayer does not materially participate in an active business or the activity is considered passive, then any loss will be considered a passive loss and can only offset passive income. Passive income does not include portfolio income (e.g., interest, dividends). The allowance of passive losses is generally deferred until there is passive income to offset it. Tax shelters are the target of the passive loss rules. Material participation by the individual is now required in order to have the loss be currently applied to offset other income of the individual.

POTENTIAL PROBLEMS

[ ]N (1) <u>Lack of Shield Against Liabilities</u> (Chapter 47): Unlike a corporation, the individual proprietor is liable for all debts of the business.

[ ]N (2) <u>More Difficult to Give Some of Business and Retain Control</u>: Unlike a corporate circumstance, it is very difficult to give interests in the individual proprietorship without having to deal with the possibility of some control shifting to the donee.

[ ]I (3) <u>All Inherent Gain in Assets Recognized on Sale of Business</u>: Sale of an individual proprietorship will result in the recognition of gain taxed as ordinary income with regard to sale of accounts receivable, inventory and other assets which have a value in excess of income tax basis.

[ ]I (4) <u>Lack of Corporate Fringe Benefits</u>: The various corporate fringe benefits described above for corporations generally do not apply to an individual proprietorship.

[ ]I (5) <u>Low Keogh Plan Deduction Limit For Some State Income Taxes</u>: Some states permit only a small income tax deduction for contributions to Keogh plans. Some states, e.g., California, permit the full deduction for such contributions.

[ ]I   (6)   <u>All Income Taxable at Individual Rates</u>: None of the income developed by an individual proprietorship will be taxed at the often lower corporate rates or on the tax return of other family members.

[ ]I   (7)   <u>No Use of ESOP Available</u>: Unlike the corporation, the sale of an individual proprietorship may not have the gain deferred by sale to an ESOP and investment in corporate common stock.

[ ]I   (8)   <u>No Shifting of Income Between Tax Years</u>: All of the income earned in a taxable year will be subject to tax in that year as opposed to the circumstances of a corporation with a fiscal year different from that of its shareholder-employee.

[ ]I   (9)   <u>All Business Earnings Subject to Self-Employment Tax</u>: Unlike the corporation, where retained income may be subject only to income tax and not social security tax, earnings of an individual proprietor business are generally subject to both income tax and self-employment tax.

[ ]N   (10)   <u>No Pooling of Capital For Business Purposes</u> (Chapter 47): Since no other persons may be involved in the proprietorship, the individual may supply only his own or borrowed funds.

[ ]N   (11)   <u>Difficult to Create Market-At-Death For Business</u> (Chapter 40): Although buy-and-sell agreements may, under unusual circumstances, be created for individual proprietorships, the lack of a partner or other shareholders as a potential ready buyer is a disadvantage in creating a market for the business.

[ ]E   (12)   <u>Fewer Assets May Qualify For Estate Tax Deferral</u> (Chapter 16): In determining whether or not an estate meets the percentage requirements necessary to qualify for deferral of a portion of the estate tax, only those assets of an individual proprietorship which can be shown to relate directly to the business may be included in determining such percentages.

[ ]I   (13)   <u>No Shifting of Income to Children</u>: Unlike a partnership or an S corporation, the individual proprietorship income cannot be shifted to other persons but children can be hired as employees and paid a deductible salary if they perform needed tasks. Income in excess of $1,600 (in 2004) shifted to children under age 14 will be taxed at their parents' top marginal rate.

[ ]I   (14)   <u>No Operation of Individual Proprietorship In a Trust</u>: Unlike almost all other assets, there is a significant danger in holding and operating an individual proprietor business in a trust. The danger is that the IRS may be able to tax the entire trust as if it were a corporation, a very bad result! Therefore, any business operated in trusts, including revocable intervivos family planning trusts, should be operated through a corporation or a partnership, which type of entity can be operated through the trust without this danger.

CHECKLIST FOR VARIOUS CIRCUMSTANCES

G. PARTNERS AND MEMBERS OF LLCS

AREAS OF POSSIBLE BENEFIT

[ ]N   (1)   <u>Pooling of Capital for Business</u>: Like a corporation, the assets of more than one person may be combined to meet the capital needs of the business.

[ ]N   (2)   <u>Market For Business – Buy-and-Sell Agreement</u> (Chapter 40): The existence of partners or members often creates a market for business interests which does not exist for an individual proprietorship.

[ ]N   (3)   <u>Protection From Liability Available Through Limited Partnerships and LLCs (Chapters 43, 44)</u>: Although the general partner(s) will always be liable for all debts and other liabilities of the partnership, a limited partnership may be created which will limit both the liability and control of a limited partner. In the case of an LLC, all members will be isolated from personal liability.

[ ]E   (4)   <u>Reduced Value of Certain Partnerships and LLCs For Estate Tax Purposes</u> (Chapter 43): The family partnership was a vehicle often used for attempting to "freeze" the value of real property and other assets including business interests; but such transactions are now generally subject to IRC Section 2701 (Chapter 58).

However, certain partnerships and LLCs which have restrictions on withdrawal of assets after the death of a partner or member can still be a very effective vehicle for reducing value of a partner's or member's interest in a partnership or LLC (but see discussion of IRC Sections 2701 and 2704 (Chapter 58) and 2703 (Chapter 40).

[ ]I   (5)   <u>Some Removal of Assets From Business or Even Liquidation Without Tax</u>: Unlike a corporation, under proper circumstances, assets may sometimes be removed from a partnership or LLC, or the partnership or LLC may be liquidated without the recognition of any gain for income tax purposes. Gain may be recognized without competent advice.

[ ]I   (6)   <u>Only One Level of Income Tax</u>: Like an individual proprietorship, there is no double taxation of income (at both the corporate and an individual level). This benefit is really often a detriment where lower corporate income tax rates might otherwise apply (e.g., the 15% corporate rate for the first $50,000 of income each year for corporations which are not "personal service corporations").

[ ]I   (7)   <u>Some Shifting of Income to Other Family Members</u> (Chapter 43): By observing the relevant rules, some income may be shifted to other family members by giving interests in the ownership of the partnership or LLC.

[ ]I   (8)   <u>Special Allocations of Income Between Partners or Members May be Possible</u> (Chapter 43): With a partnership or LLC agreement drafted by an attorney with experience in dealing with such "special allocations," it may be possible to allocate income and even income tax deductions among the partners or members in such a way as to optimize income tax planning.

[ ]I   (9)   <u>Losses May Be Available to Offset Personal Income</u>: Like an individual proprietorship, losses from active general partnerships flow through to the taxpayer and may offset personal income, e.g., salary, interest, etc. However, losses from passive activities and activities in which the partner does not materially participate can only offset passive income. Passive income does not include portfolio income (e.g., interest, dividends).

POTENTIAL PROBLEMS

(1-10) The numbered items listed for the potential problems of individual proprietors also apply to partnerships and LLCs:

[ ]N (11) <u>Possible Liability For Actions of Partners</u>: Certain actions of a partner in relation to a general partnership may result in liability for all the other partners.

[ ]I (12) <u>Tax Due on Certain Removals of Assets From Business</u>: Certain assets, e.g., accounts receivable which have not been taken into income or highly appreciated inventory, may result in the recognition of income if withdrawn from the partnership or LLC under some circumstances.

[ ]I (13) <u>Greater Tax Shelter Audit Potential</u>: Because the partnership has been used so frequently for tax shelters, the IRS now seems to view all partnerships and LLCs with more suspicion.

[ ]I (14) <u>Disposition of Certain Partnership or LLC Interests May Trigger Recognition of Gain</u>: Where the income tax basis of the partner or member has been significantly reduced (as by depreciation expense), it may become impossible to even give away a partnership or LLC interest without the recognition of a large amount of gain.

[ ]I (15) <u>Accidental Loss of Right to Partnership or LLC Deductions</u>: In an attempt to deal with certain sophisticated tax shelter partnerships, rules may be imposed on all partnerships or LLCs which may cause a partner's or member's share of expense to be capitalized as opposed to being available to offset income.

[ ]I (16) <u>Passive Limited Partnerships</u>: The deduction of "passive losses" is generally disallowed. If the limited partner does not materially participate, losses from the limited partnership generally cannot be taken currently but must be deferred until there is "passive income" (which excludes dividends, interest and certain other income) against which the passive loss can be offset.

[ ]I (17) <u>Inactive General Partners Not Allowed Current Partnership Loss Deductions</u>: In focusing on "passive income" as a likely way to deal with tax shelters, the passive loss rules require that there be "material participation" in the activity in order for even a general partner to currently deduct the loss from the partnership. A lower standard of "active participation" is required for real estate rental activity.

[ ]I (18) <u>Avoiding Corporate Classification</u>: In structuring both limited partnerships and LLCs, care must be taken to avoid at least two of the four corporate characteristics – limited liability, free transferability of interest, continuity of life, and centralized management.

CHECKLIST FOR VARIOUS CIRCUMSTANCES

H. BUSINESS PERSONS IN GENERAL

AREAS OF POSSIBLE BENEFIT

[ ]N (1) <u>Creating and Maintaining Market For Business</u> (Chapter 40): Whether the business is in a corporate, partnership, LLC, or individual proprietorship form, planning can be done to create a market for the business whether that may be by creating a buy-and-sell agreement or whether it is accumulating information on other prospective purchasers of the business.

[ ]E (2) <u>Sharing of Name Goodwill Within Family</u> (Chapter 22): It may be possible to bestow benefits onto family members by permitting the use of a business name without the actual recognition of a gift or the application of a gift tax.

[ ]E (3) <u>Personal Financial Guarantees For Family Members</u> (Chapter 22): Like the use of a family name, personal financial guarantees may currently permit the bestowing of real benefits on a family member or other person without the actual recognition of a gift or the application of a gift tax (but beware of continuing expansion of the *Dickman* deemed gift theory).

[ ]E (4) <u>Special Use (Low) Valuation For Estate Tax</u> (Chapter 57): Unlike investments in cash, securities or investment real property, certain assets involved in a business (such as real property used for business) or farming may be subject to special rules which will permit use of lower values for estate tax purposes.

[ ]E (5) <u>Deferral and Installment Payments For Estate Tax</u> (Chapter 16): Again, unlike investments in cash, securities or investment real property, investment of the assets in an active business may permit the payment of related estate tax over a period as long as 14 years and at a very low interest rate for a portion of the tax.

[ ]E (6) <u>Qualified Family-Owned Business</u> (Chapter 42): An estate tax deduction may be available if a substantial part of the estate consists of a family-owned business. The deduction is not available from 2004 to 2010.

POTENTIAL PROBLEMS

[ ]N (1) <u>Heirs Ignorant of Market For Business</u> (Chapter 40): Preservation of estate values argues strongly for communicating to one's spouse and heirs any plans for the business and especially potential markets for the sale of the business.

[ ]N (2) <u>Lack of Instruction to Heirs as to Disposition or Continuation of Business</u>: Often only the family member active in the business knows whether it should be continued or sold upon his death. Failure to communicate to other family members on this point may result in a tragically wrong decision as to the disposition or continuation of the business.

[ ]N (3) <u>Lack of Successor Management</u> (Chapter 40): Existence of a buy-and-sell agreement may provide for some successor management that otherwise would not be available for the business. The universal dislike for thinking of one's own death often results in no planning in this important area for maintenance of the value of the business.

[ ]N (4) <u>Lack of Cash Reserves at Owner's Death</u> (Chapter 30): Failure to provide for cash availability (e.g., through insurance) at the death of the person on whom the business depends often results in the complete collapse of the business.

CHECKLIST FOR VARIOUS CIRCUMSTANCES

I. RANCHER OR FARMER

AREAS OF POSSIBLE BENEFIT

[ ]E   (1)   <u>Special Use (Low) Valuation For Estate Tax</u> (Chapter 57): Ranches and farms actually worked by the client are subject to very favorable rules for valuation as farm land rather than their value for use as shopping centers, subdivisions, etc.

[ ]E   (2)   <u>Deferral and Installment Payments For Estate Tax</u> (Chapter 16): Ranchers and farmers are particularly favored in the application of rules for the deferral of tax and payment (at low interest rates) over a period as long as 14 years.

[ ]I   (3)   <u>No Income Recognized Until Sale of Product</u>: Special cash basis rules for farmers permit the reaping of crops without the recognition of the income until the time the crops are actually sold and value received by the seller.

[ ]I   (4)   <u>Some Greater Flexibility For Cash Deduction</u>: Although some restrictions have been placed on the deductibility of farm payments, the farmer generally has more flexibility in this regard than the average business man.

[ ]I   (5)   <u>Avoidance of Income Tax at Death on Some Products</u>: Certain crops and livestock may receive a new income tax basis at death so as to prevent any recognition of gain upon their being sold.

POTENTIAL PROBLEMS

[ ]N   (1)   <u>Liquidity Problems of Land Ownership</u> (Chapter 30): Typically, a farmer or rancher has the greatest need for estate tax liquidity (often in the form of insurance) since so much of the total value of the farm is in the form of land that may not be readily saleable without destroying the farm as a viable unit.

[ ]N   (2)   <u>Loss of Political Power</u>: Because efficiency of operation and a number of other factors have drastically reduced the number of farmers in relation to the rest of the nation, the formerly very impressive political power of the American farmer or rancher has deteriorated greatly. This fact, combined with increasing free world trade in agriculture, has resulted in reductions in income received from certain areas of farming.

[ ]E   (3)   <u>Loss of Deferral of Estate Tax</u> (Chapters 16): Changing the farm operation to a cash rent basis can cause loss of this particularly important estate tax benefit.

CHECKLIST FOR VARIOUS CIRCUMSTANCES

J. PROFESSIONALS

General Comment: Usually the term "professional" is applied to those persons who have met certain educational goals and who usually perform services for others (e.g., architects, dentists, doctors, engineers, lawyers, etc.).

Although many of these people work for large companies as employees, a large proportion work essentially for themselves, as individual proprietors, partners and in corporate form. Thus, the professional should review the appropriate checklists for Individual Proprietorships, Partners and LLCs, or Owners of Private Corporations, or perhaps that of the Corporate Executive where the category may be appropriate (usually thought of as applying to highly paid employees of large corporations).

Over the years, many professionals have incorporated for income tax benefit reasons. While some of incentives for such incorporations have been removed, there are many benefits of incorporation still available and the professional who is not yet incorporated should review the possible benefits and detriments listed in the checklist for Owners of Private Corporations to determine if his estate might be improved by incorporating.

Below are listed some specific areas of possible benefit or problems which generally apply to professionals, regardless of the form in which they practice their profession:

AREAS OF POSSIBLE BENEFIT

[ ]N (1) Cost Savings Available From Professional Groups: Frequently, membership in professional groups may provide medical or insurance coverage at lower rates than are generally available.

[ ]N (2) Market For Business/Practice Enhanced by Professional Group: Some groups provide special services for retirees or estates of deceased members in finding a purchaser for the practice or business. Although professional goodwill may often die with a practitioner, in many cases such services can be very beneficial.

POTENTIAL PROBLEMS

[ ]N (1) Licensing Limitation on Marketability of Business or Practice: Most states limit the practice of many professions only to those persons who are licensed by the state. Upon the death of someone practicing one of these professions, there is only the limited market of state licensees to whom the practice or business may be transferred. Such restrictions on marketability obviously will reduce the value that will be received from such a sale.

[ ]N (2) Licensing Restrictions on Transfers to Family Members: The same license restrictions typically often prevent shifting the value of the business or profession to the next generation over a period of years.

[ ]N (3) Personal Liability Even Where Corporate Form Used: Except for those professionals who perform work for the benefit of large corporations as opposed to benefiting the public, there is always some personal exposure of a professional who performs services for another person or entity. Although a sufficiently capitalized and properly operated corporation can shield the owner-employee from liability caused by the acts of other persons, each individual is still liable for his or her own acts regardless of the fact that the business may be carried on in a corporate form.

[ ]I (4) No Low Corporate Tax Rates: For most professionals who use the corporate form, there will be the disadvantage that income left in the corporation cannot be taxed at only 15% or 25% rates for lower levels of income. A personal service corporation is taxed at a flat 35% rate.

CHECKLIST FOR VARIOUS CIRCUMSTANCES

K. <u>CORPORATE EXECUTIVES</u>

AREAS OF POSSIBLE BENEFIT

[ ]N   (1)   <u>Sick Pay - Disability Pay</u>: Executives working for large corporations whose welfare and profitability does not depend solely on their efforts have a very real benefit in the contract provisions usually available for continuation of pay regardless of whether they may be sick or disabled. Agreements to spread compensation over future years often produce income tax benefits for the employee. Typically, this is available in and feasible for large corporations where the lack of current deductibility for such future payments is not the significant problem that it is for the smaller, private corporations.

[ ]I   (2)   <u>Income Tax Benefits Allowed to All Corporate Employees</u> (Chapter 47): The various possible benefits described in the Owners of Private Corporations check-list are all available to the extent that the corporation is willing to tailor its decisions to benefit the corporate executive. Often the cost of including other employees of a large corporation may limit flexibility in benefits available to executives but they may still be very substantial.

[ ]I   (3)   <u>"Non-Qualified" Deferred Compensation</u> (Chapter 48): The stability and good financial position of many large corporations permit many executives to enter, reasonably worry-free, into agreements which defer some portion of their compensation to future years (usually after a planned retirement date) when income tax can be expected to have less impact. Additionally, many such arrangements provide the equivalent of accumulation of "effective interest" (in the form of increase of the compensation based on how long it is deferred) that is not taxed until it is received.

[ ]I   (4)   <u>Incentive Stock Options</u>: Incentive stock options may both defer taxation and shift such benefits from ordinary income rates to capital gain rates. Strict rules must be adhered to in issuing such options.

[ ]I   (5)   <u>Regular and Restricted Stock Options</u>: Although they may not qualify for the special tax benefits afforded incentive stock options, options to buy stock of a very successful business may be very valuable. By having certain restrictions on such options, in some instances the amount of gain recognized may be substantially reduced without a proportionate reduction in real value to the corporate employee.

[ ]I   (6)   <u>"Phantom Stock" Plans</u>: Contracts can provide both current income based upon the equivalent of ownership of stock and also future payment for equity which would be equal to the amount to which stock might have appreciated.

[ ]I   (7)   <u>Education</u>: Any company employee can receive tax-free, under many circumstances, education which is related to the business and designed to improve existing skills or to qualify a person for an existing job even though these expenses are all paid for and deducted by the employer company.

[ ]I   (8)   <u>Professional and Business Club Dues</u>: Like education, if these are really related to the business, they may be received tax-free by an individual and can be deducted by the corporation. However, greater scrutiny is being directed at such benefits.

[ ]I   (9)   <u>Death Benefits</u>: Some large companies also have practices of making payments that may be considered gifts to the employees. However, the IRS frequently does not quietly accept the concept of seeing a deductible expense result in no taxable income to the employee.

[ ]I   (10)   <u>Expense Accounts</u>: Like the private corporation, travel and entertainment expenses paid for by the employee may be reimbursed to the executive tax-free (50% not deductible by the corporation in some cases), to the extent that it may be shown that they are required for a company to carry out its business. More strict substantiation of such expenses has been required in recent years.

[ ]I   (11)   <u>Company Lodging</u>: A long line of cases show that there may be a reasonable deduction for the corporation to provide an employee with tax-free lodging where it is in the best interests of the company that he live on the corporate premises or close to such premises. Each case must be examined on its own merits.

[ ]I   (12)   <u>Additional Executive "Perks" and Benefits</u>: Many other additional executive perquisites are frequently offered, including housing aid, company cars, country club dues, tickets for various performances, sabbatical leaves, and similar niceties. However, the possibility of receiving significant benefits without the recognition of income has been greatly restricted. Some benefits may well end up as a basis for income recognition by the recipients.

POTENTIAL PROBLEMS

[ ]N   (1)   <u>Possibility of Being Lulled into a False Sense of Security and High Spending Habits</u>: Since most of us prefer to ignore unpleasant things, many executives who have relied upon retirement based on time spent with the employer have not felt it necessary to put aside funds for retirement and often find that a change in corporate structure may cut off their plans for relying on corporate funding for retirement.

[ ]N   (2)   <u>Non-Diversification of Assets Through Investment in Company Stock</u>: Often executives show their loyalty and find some job leverage by investing all of their available funds in stock of the employer corporations. This may be increased by the existence of an employer "stock savings plan" which invests in stock of the employer. Employees of some companies have done well with such circumstances, but many others would have done much better to diversify their asset holdings.

[ ]N   (3)   <u>Directing Available Cash Into Tax Shelters With Little/No Real Value</u>: Where the executive feels frustrated that all of his earnings are taxable as ordinary income and that he has no "tax benefits," he often succumbs to the thought of reducing current income tax by putting his or her cash into "tax shelters." With the exception of certain investments in real property and occasionally oil programs on a diversified basis, most such "investments" do not produce real assets which provide security for retirement or for the family in the event of death of the executive.

Further, most tax shelters will not be effective in providing current deductions against salary income. An exception is "actively" managed real property producing losses up to $25,000. Even this exemption is phased out as the taxpayer's adjusted gross income increases from $100,000 to $150,000, at which level no rental property losses are allowed regardless of how actively the properties are managed by the taxpayer.

[ ]E   (4)   <u>Forced Migrancy Can Cause Asset Title Problems</u>: Company mandated moves between separate property and community property states can cause accidental gifts between spouses (generally, not taxable for federal tax purposes) and confusion with title which should be reviewed with competent tax counsel.

[ ]I   (5)   <u>Loss of Deduction For Unreimbursed Travel and Entertainment Expenses</u>: Substantiation of all such expenses is generally required. For the executive who plans to deduct on his own return such expenses which are not reimbursed by his employer, if he has a tax return preparer do his return, the preparer will require a written certificate from the executive that adequate records exist. Further, such deductions are permitted only to the extent that they, together with other "miscellaneous" deductions, exceed 2% of adjusted gross income.

[ ]I   (6)   <u>Recognition of Income From "Perks" and Discounts</u>: The scope of benefits that can be received tax free by the employee has been greatly restricted. Those benefits that create no additional cost for the employer, like filling empty airline seats with employees or their relatives, may continue to be tax-free (in a more scrutinized form), but those that actually cost the employer are now subjected to rules that reduce benefits usually afforded tax free to executives.

[ ]I   (7)   <u>"Golden Parachute" Excise Tax</u>: Where there are payments or property transfers that are contingent on a change in ownership or control of a corporation or its assets, or large payments (over certain salary limits), a 20% excise tax is imposed on the recipient - in addition to income tax!

CHECKLIST FOR VARIOUS CIRCUMSTANCES

L. PERSONS PLANNING FOR RETIREMENT

AREAS OF POSSIBLE BENEFIT

[ ]N/I (1) <u>Build Up of Assets in a Qualified Plan</u> (Chapter 52): Using the income-tax-free provisions of a qualified retirement plan permits a much more rapid build up of assets to provide financial security for retirement than would the same amount paid out as additional current salary.

[ ]N (2) <u>Receipt of Social Security Payments Before Actual Retirement</u>: Although the relatively vague social security (SS) eligibility rules may sometimes prevent it, some persons upon reaching age 62 or 65 have shifted their earnings to future years (e.g., to age 70 when earnings do not inhibit SS payments) by deferred compensation arrangements with employers or by shifting income to a corporation or pension plan in order to be able to draw the social security benefits for which they paid over past years.

[ ]I (3) <u>Stretching Qualified Plan Benefits Over Retirement Period</u> (Chapter 52): Where the plan rules permit, electing to receive plan benefits over a period of time may often provide a larger total retirement benefit by postponing the recognition of income tax until payments are received, and thus permitting a large amount of such benefits still in the plan to continue tax-free production of income for future payments to the retired employee. Generally payment from such plans must start on the later of April 1 of the year after the participant reaches age 70½ or retires.

[ ]I (4) <u>Qualifying for "Lump Sum Averaging" for Qualified Plan Payments</u> (Chapter 52): Some plans may require a "lump sum" distribution of plan assets. Meeting certain requirements can permit the availability of certain rules of income taxation which, for smaller and medium size plan benefits which are paid out as "lump sums," can result in lower income taxes than otherwise would result. Very strict rules must be observed.

[ ]I (5) <u>Use of Deferred Compensation Program to Reduce Income Taxes</u>: Where the employer makes it feasible and one's financial stability and budget permits, shifting some current compensation to future years after retirement may both reduce income tax overall and also, under some circumstances, permit an employee who does not retire at 65 to begin to receive Social Security (SS) payments. Local SS offices are looking more closely at such arrangements, however.

[ ]I (6) <u>Use of Corporation to Receive Income Produced After Retirement</u>: Many employers, particularly those with significant pension benefits, may permit an employee to "retire" and to stay on as a consultant without significant employee benefits. Using a corporation to provide such consulting services may often reduce income tax and sometimes make social security payments currently available. Social Security offices actively seek to restrict such practices.

POTENTIAL PROBLEMS

[ ]N (1) <u>Loss of Insurance or Medical Benefits Previously Provided by Employment</u>: Failure to review company insurance programs may result in loss of life insurance or medical coverage which might have been assumed before retirement by the employee at lower group rates not usually available to individuals.

[ ]N (2) <u>Failure to Create Estate For Retirement</u>: Although this problem may not be solvable in some circumstances, it can be avoided in many circumstances with good planning and will power.

[ ]N (3) <u>Stagnation of Physical and Mental Abilities</u>: Studies consistently show that continued mental abilities and physical capacities can be maintained where activity is continued as opposed to cessation of physical and mental

effort upon retirement. Planning for continued activity in an area where one has the opportunity to find satisfaction will not only improve financial circumstances but also lead to a longer and fuller life.

[ ]I   (4)   Failure to Qualify Lump Sum Retirement Plan Benefit for "Lump Sum Averaging": Failure to follow strict rules (e.g., permitting only one "averaging" after age 59½) can cause retirement benefit payments to be taxed at regular ordinary income tax rates.

[ ]I   (5)   Requiring Sale of Company Stock Held in Retirement Plan: Lack of good tax advice can lose a tax benefit to those persons who are retiring from employment which included a qualified retirement plan which, in the retiree's account, contained stock contributed by the employer or purchased by the plan. Correct treatment will permit the acquisition of such stock and taxation only at the price at which it was acquired by the plan. Sale of the stock by the plan before distribution will result in loss of the benefit.

CHECKLIST FOR VARIOUS CIRCUMSTANCES

M. <u>PERSONS PLANNING FOR MARRIAGE</u>

AREAS OF POSSIBLE BENEFIT

[ ]N (1) <u>Entering Into Premarital Agreement Clarifying Title Holding</u>: Hindsight clearly shows the advantage to both parties of facing the question of property rights and laying out in a clear agreement any understandings with regard to change of ownership of property. Listing the property belonging to each person at the beginning of the marriage has much merit and little real detriment.

[ ]N (2) <u>Entering Into Premarital Agreement Clarifying Ownership of Earnings and Retirement Plan Rights</u>: Not only should the separate property or community property rights of each party in the earnings of either party be clarified before the marriage but, particularly where there may be retirement plans, the separate property aspects of such retirement rights generated before the marriage should be clarified. The increasing importance of private retirement plan rights to many people argues for maintaining them as separate property until it is certain that the new marriage will be a stable one.

[ ]N (3) <u>Executing New Will After or In Contemplation of Marriage</u>: By executing a will which recognizes either an impending marriage or one that has just occurred, the new spouse will not be in the position of being a "pretermitted heir" and thus the testamentary scheme will not be disrupted by the laws of intestacy which favor such "pretermitted heirs."

[ ]N (4) <u>Use of Trust to Avoid Probate as to Prenuptial Agreement Assets</u>: Where a spouse-to-be has been given certain rights, e.g., a life estate, in specific assets in place of other marital rights, it may serve the purposes of both avoiding probate and avoiding future creditors of the donor by placing that asset or set of assets into an irrevocable trust.

[ ]E (5) <u>Ability to Defer Estate Tax With Marital Deduction</u> (Chapter 24): The existence of a formal marriage permits the deferral of estate tax by an arrangement which benefits the new spouse at least during her or his lifetime. A QTIP trust will permit the assets to avoid taxation at the death of the owning spouse as long as the income is paid to the new spouse. At the new spouse's death, the assets can thereafter go to the children of the prior marriage or to anyone else. This may often permit a business, which could not currently provide the funds for estate tax without causing its collapse, to mature and be in a position where cash reserves may be developed for payment of estate tax at the death of the second spouse and thus preserving the asset for the children of the first marriage.

Obviously, for the presently single person who wants to provide a benefit for a "live-in partner," marriage can provide a totally estate tax-free transition at his or her death.

[ ]E (6) <u>The Ability to Make Tax-Free Gifts by Deferral Until Marriage</u>: Gifts in large amounts which would produce a gift tax if given to a "friend" or "live-in partner" can be transferred totally free of gift tax if given to a person with whom there has been a formal marriage.

[ ]E (7) <u>Creating Estate Tax Deductible Liability in Place of Marital Right of Spouse</u>: In some states, the amount that would be automatically given under state laws to a spouse would not result in any deduction for estate tax purposes. Many such rights can be replaced with a clear liability which, when reduced to a proper contract, may result in a deductible liability for the estate of the deceased spouse.

POTENTIAL PROBLEMS

[ ]N (1) <u>Ineffective Termination of Prior Marriages</u>: In order for the marital deduction to be available, there must be a real marriage. The failure to properly terminate a prior marriage will prevent a subsequent marriage from being effective.

[ ]N   (2)   <u>Lack of New Estate Plan</u>: Failure to execute a will or trust which recognizes the new marriage may give the new spouse rights, as a pretermitted heir, which divert assets from the children of a prior marriage. For example, in California, half of the separate property of a wife will go to her new husband as a pretermitted heir if he is not recognized in her will, and thus the child of the wife from a former marriage will receive only half of the assets of the mother.

[ ]N   (3)   <u>Failure to Recognize the Possible Automatic Payments "to Spouse"</u>: Many company death benefits, salary continuation rights and pension benefits may be paid automatically "to the spouse of the employee" where there has been a failure to properly designate the employee's intended objects of his bounty (e.g., his mother or his children from a former marriage).

[ ]E   (4)   <u>Making Significant Gifts Before Marriage</u> (Chapter 22): The marital deduction does not apply to gifts made other than to spouses. Gifts made before marriage can use the $11,000 (as indexed in 2004) gift tax annual exclusion, but the excess is subject to gift tax.

[ ]N   (5)   <u>Failure to Deal With Rights in Retirement Plans</u>: Where either or both of the spouses have rights that have been built up in retirement plans, failure to deal with such rights by a written agreement may have a very bad result in the event of a divorce or a death.

[ ]E   (6)   <u>Automatic Right of New Spouse to Half of Retirement Plan Benefits</u>: Upon one year of marriage, the participant's spouse receives the equivalent of the right to half of the pension benefits. Without a specific manner of written approval of the new spouse, the participant cannot direct all of his plan benefit to the children of his prior marriage or to anyone else! Without the prescribed form of written approval from the new spouse, existing designation of persons other than the spouse are invalid as to the spouse's half! This is very important for persons about to marry.

CHECKLIST FOR VARIOUS CIRCUMSTANCES

N. PERSONS PLANNING FOR SEPARATION OR DIVORCE

POSSIBLE AREAS OF BENEFIT

[ ]N   (1)   <u>Use of Alimony and/or Child Support Trust to Insure Payment</u>: Putting assets into a separate irrevocable trust, at the time of the divorce, may insure actual payment of such amounts as compared to the possible results of leaving the assets in the hands of the other spouse.

[ ]N   (2)   <u>Use of Insurance Trust to Insure Premium Payment</u> (Chapter 31): Life insurance may be a most important asset in many instances, and both the ability of the other spouse to cancel the policy and the failure of the other spouse to make premium payments can be avoided by placing into an irrevocable trust both the policy and assets which will produce income to make the premium payments.

[ ]I   (3)   <u>Avoiding Income Tax and Changing Beneficiary Designation on Division of Pension Plan Benefits</u> (Chapter 52): Proper planning and a tolerant employer can result in the division of retirement benefits upon divorce without the often premature recognition of income tax caused by the actual distribution of such assets.

Now, under current law, a properly drafted qualified domestic relations order (QDRO) can provide for such segregation and the ability of the divorced spouse who was not a plan participant to have a new and changed provision for beneficiary arrangements in the event of death prior to distribution of the assets from the qualified retirement plan.

[ ]I   (4)   <u>Arranging Deductibility of Some Legal Costs</u>: Certain aspects of a divorce, e.g., advice in regard to taxation, may be deductible. Identifying these amounts and limiting other areas of cost may result in significant income tax savings.

[ ]I   (5)   <u>Qualifying Alimony For Deductibility</u>: Requirements for deductibility of alimony should be reviewed and observed in arranging alimony payments so that the desired deductibility can be provided. Where there is only a single income earner, such deductibility can result in an overall larger amount available to both persons after income taxes.

[ ]I   (6)   <u>Providing For Children as Income Tax Exemptions</u>: The rules provide a definite means of shifting such exemptions in the manner the parties desire. Such rules must be observed closely in the child support agreement and they may even be drafted in such a way as to help enforce child support payments.

[ ]I   (7)   <u>Contribution to IRA Based on Alimony Receipt</u> (Chapter 51): Amounts received that qualify for alimony may be the basis for a deductible payment into an IRA.

POTENTIAL PROBLEMS

[ ]N   (1)   <u>Failure to Change Estate Plan</u>: Although divorce may effectively revoke a will as to spousal benefits, divorce does not necessarily change the effect of a will or trust in some circumstances, and estate plans should be reviewed and perhaps revised in contemplation of or promptly after any divorce or separation in order to carry out the intentions of the client.

[ ]N   (2)   <u>Loss of Medical Plan Coverage</u>: Where one spouse's employment provides medical plan benefits for both spouses and possibly for children, most divorce or legal separation circumstances will terminate such protection for the non-employed family members where the employee works for a small company. However, COBRA requires that employers of 20 or more employees must provide, at 2% over cost, coverage for dependents of terminated employees where there has been a separation or divorce.

[ ]N (3) <u>Loss of Life Insurance Coverage</u>: As with the employer provided medical plan coverage described above, divorce or legal separation often destroys possible life insurance protection previously afforded.

[ ]I (4) <u>Recognition of Income Tax on Retirement Plan Division</u> (Chapter 52): Division of retirement plan rights, which result in distribution of the assets to the participant or the spouse, will result in current income tax, a circumstance that may well be avoided by seeking an arrangement for division of the retirement benefits or other available means of preventing receipt and current income tax recognition. Actions that are not founded on good tax advice can result in the unnecessary recognition of gain. A properly drawn qualified domestic relations order (QDRO) can shift benefits to a non-participant spouse without forcing recognition of income tax. Even where assets are distributed from a qualified plan to the spouse of the participant, income tax may be deferred by reinvesting such distribution in an individual retirement account (IRA) within 60 days of its receipt.

Chapter 2

DATA GATHERING AND ANALYSIS

There is no question that the most important skill of an estate or financial planner is the ability to understand who the client is, where that client stands in relation to the objectives (realized or subconscious) he may have, and what things have to be done to move the client closer to the realization of these goals. Knowledge of the client, the objects of the client's bounty, the client's property, and the relation of each to the others is essential to the estate or financial planner in utilizing this skill.

An ability to gather accurate, comprehensive, and useful information is most efficiently developed through the use of a data gathering system. Each question in the pages that follow is designed to help the attorney, the CPA, the trust officer, the financial planner, or life insurance agent obtain comprehensive and useful information in a logical, orderly manner.

The reason for some questions will be apparent, the justification for others will be less obvious but equally important. Not every question should be asked of every client or prospective client. Nor are the forms and questions meant to be used "as is" in every case. They are meant only as a starting place, to be adapted to suit each professional's needs and method of operation. Some will use only a few pages; others will ask almost every question and use almost every page. It is important to recognize that the data gathering and worksheet forms in TOOLS AND TECHNIQUES must be used carefully and selectively, and modified to both the needs of the planner and the circumstances of the client.

FORMS

Sample Information Request Letter

Many estate planners and conservationists prefer to obtain as much knowledge as possible about a potential client before their initial interview. This saves the time of all concerned. If handled properly, pre-interview data gathering helps prepare both the client and the estate planner for the interview and involves the client in the planning process.

The sample information request letter reiterates the "when and where" of the first meeting. A controllable atmosphere, such as the professional's office, is usually a much better location for data gathering than a client's home or office.

The client is asked to complete as much of the data gathering form as possible in advance of the first meeting and mail it back to the planner. Note that these are simple "non-threatening" questions, but are necessary for a multiplicity of reasons.

Data Gathering Forms

Page 46 – The Cover Page

There is a reason for every page and every line of the data gathering forms. A client notes immediately that his file is considered personal and confidential. The client also notes that it will probably take a number of interviews to complete the initial process and then the case will be reviewed at specified times. The use of the forms indicates to the client that the planner has an organized, systematic and professional approach to estate planning.

Pages 47-48 – Family Information

Here, the client is asked to print or type information about family members. Note that Question 7 is designed to list not only the names and addresses of children but also their spouse's names, as well as the names and ages of any grandchildren.

Supplementary pages may have to be added where the client or his children have large families. It may also be helpful, where grandchildren are no longer living with their parents, to list their addresses and, if appropriate, the names of their spouses. Whenever possible, obtain social security and telephone numbers.

Often a client will be providing financial support for individuals outside his immediate family. Their names and relationship, as well as their addresses, are essential if the client wishes to provide for them either during or after his death. Likewise, clients will often want to provide financial assistance to a charitable organization. Formal names, addresses, and other vital information about such charities should be stated on this page (or on attached supplementary pages).

Page 49

A simple stick diagram of the client's family, his parent's family, and spouse's parent's family is an invaluable tool when Seniors, Juniors, and third and fourth generation children have the same names. Such a diagram also helps to understand who's who if your client has been divorced, remarried, and has children by both marriages.

Pages 50-51 – Advisors

Here, a client is forced to think about who has been, or has to be, selected to care for both the person and the property of children (or grandchildren) who are minors. A client must also select an individual or corporate fiduciary (or more than one of each or combination of both) to serve as a personal representative after his death. Alternates for both primary guardian(s) and executor(s) are essential as backups in the event the primary is ineligible, incapacitated, or for any other reason fails to qualify or ceases to act.

It is important that each member of the estate planning team locate other members of the team and inform them of progress and problems in planning the client's estate. Cooperation between the members of the team will assure the client of the best possible coordination of planning.

Page 52 – Checklist of Documents

This list outlines the key documents that are of use to the estate planner. In various situations special documents such as contracts, leases, or other agreements should be added. But generally, those shown will provide adequate information for the first interview.

Pages 53-61 – Alternative Form for Community Property Residents

Here, an alternative data gathering form, which will be particularly useful to residents of community property states, can be found. Community property planners (and common law planners who have had clients move to or from community property states) should notice a number of questions in the forms pertaining to "changes of state of residence during marriage." Problems of the peripatetic client are becoming more acute every day. The final page of the alternative forms dealing with inheritance tax information will be particularly useful in community property states.

SAMPLE INFORMATION REQUEST LETTER

Dr. Allen A. Murphy
6061 Kathleen Drive
Bala Cynwood, PA 19010

Dear Dr. Murphy:

I'm looking forward to meeting with you and your wife on Wednesday, June 16, at 2 p.m. in my office.

As I promised on the phone, I have enclosed the first several pages of a comprehensive data form we'll be using in creating an estate conservation plan. Please complete as much as you can and mail it to me in the enclosed envelope.

Also enclosed you will find a list of documents we will need. I would appreciate if you would send me photocopies of the documents in advance of our meeting or, if you prefer, you can bring them with you on Wednesday. (We can probably save a great deal of time if I can study these papers in advance of our meeting.)

Please feel free to call me if you have any questions.

Sincerely yours,

Charles McClu

CMcC/dl
Enc.

PERSONAL AND CONFIDENTIAL FILE

of

Dr. Allen A. Murphy

Initial Interview: _5/6/2004_

Interviewer: _Charles McClu_

Date of subsequent interviews or review:

PLEASE COMPLETE (print or type) AND RETURN IN THE ENCLOSED ENVELOPE:

			Birthdate	Soc. Sec. No.
1.	Full name	_Dr. Allen Albert Murphy_	_9/11/1962_	_158-43-0865_
2.	Nicknames	_Al_		
3.	Spouses's name	_Stephanie Louise Murphy_	_1/1/1964_	_158-20-3621_
4.	Nicknames	_Stephie_		

5. Home address: _6061 Kathleen Drive_   Home phone: _353-5424_

Bala Cynwood

_PA 19010_

6. Business
address: _2700 Bryn Mawr Avenue_   Bus. phone: _525-9500_

Philadelphia

_PA 19101_

7. Children (and Spouses)

	Address	Phone	Birthdate
a. _Kathleen_	_same as above_	_see above_	_7/6/1987_
b. _Christopher_	_"_	_"_	_9/1/1989_
c. _Charles_	_"_	_"_	_11/15/1991_
d. _Lawrence_	_"_	_"_	_6/2/1993_

Names and Ages of Grandchildren

a.	b.	c.	d.

8.	Parent's Names	Address	Age	Phone Number
Yours:	a. *Deceased*			
	b. *Deceased*			
Your Spouse's	a. *William Lamont*	*872 W. Overbrook St.*	*67*	*566-1276*
	b. *Mary Lamont*	*same as above*	*66*	*566-1276*

9. Dependents (other than children)/Relationship

William Lamont/Father-in-Law	*see above*	*67*	*"*
Mary Lamont/Mother-in-Law	*see above*	*66*	*"*

10. Beneficiaries (other than those listed above):

11. Please sketch a family tree showing any brothers and sisters:

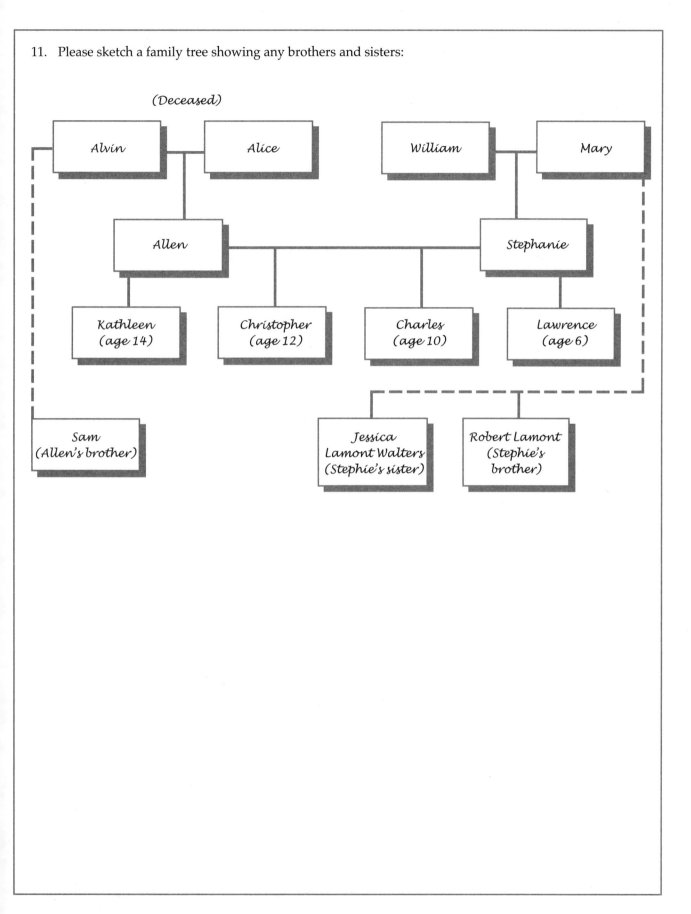

Advisors

12. Guardians for children primary:　　　　　　　　　Address　　　　　Phone Number
George and Jessica Walters　　　　_767 Fawnhill Road_　　_353-5353_
(Guardian of Person)　　　　　　　　　　　_Radnor_
　　　　　　　　　　　　　　　　　　　　　_PA 19008_

Sam Cohen (close friend)　　　　　_868 Knox Drive_　　_353-5126_
(Guardian of Property)　　　　　　　　　_Radnor_
　　　　　　　　　　　　　　　　　　　　　_PA 19008_

13. Guardians for children alternate:
Robert and Louise Lamont　　　　_121 Peyton Place_　　_609-522-8707_
(Guardian of Person)　　　　　　　　　_N. Wildwood_
　　　　　　　　　　　　　　　　　　　　　_N.J. 19808_

Stephen and Evelyn Toll　　　　　_222 Fayette Lane_　　_609-522-7604_
(Guardian of Property)　　　　　　　　　_Wildwood_
　　　　　　　　　　　　　　　　　　　　　_N.J.　19807_

14. Executors primary:
Allen (Stephie's will)

Stephie (Allen's will)

15. Executors alternate:
Sam Cohen　　　　　　　　　　　　　_see above_

Sam Cohen　　　　　　　　　　　　　_see above_

16. Accountant:
Frank Vallei, CPA　　　　　　　　_#1 Bala Avenue_　　_664-3874_
　　　　　　　　　　　　　　　　　　　　　Bala Cynwood
　　　　　　　　　　　　　　　　　　　　　_PA　19010_

		Address	Phone Number
17.	Attorney - personal:	1401 Walnut Street	568-5700
	Robert P. Krauss	Philadelphia	
		PA 19102	
	Attorney - business:		
	Robert P. Krauss	see above	"
18.	Banker/Trust Officer		
	Allen Gart (Vice-Pres. and	Girand Trust Co.	568-4858
	Senior Trust Officer)	Girand Plaza	
		Philadelphia, PA 19101	
19.	Insurance advisor:		
20.	Investment advisor/broker:		
	Donald Rahill/Bob Eclair	New builder & Co.	567-6000
		121 Roths child Bldg.	
		Philadelphia, PA 19010	
21.	Other information not listed above:		

Allen's doctor - Dr. Alton Blake

CHECKLIST OF DOCUMENTS TO BRING TO INTERVIEW

Present Wills   _____

Personal Income Tax Returns: Last 3 Years (federal and state)   _____

Business Tax Returns: Last 3 Years (include P&L and balance sheets)   _____

Life/Health/Disability Insurance Policies   _____

Employee Benefit Plan Descriptions (Pension, Profit Sharing, Group Insurance, etc.)   _____

Business Buy-Sell Agreements and Employment Contracts   _____

Pre or Post-Nuptual Agreements and Divorce Decrees/Property Settlements   _____

Trust Documents — created by you or by others for your (or your family's) benefit   _____

Gift Tax Returns   _____

Homeowner's Policy and Personal Property Floaters   _____

Deeds to Real Estate   _____

Other documents to bring   _____   _____

                             _____   _____

                             _____   _____

RALPH GANO MILLER   Client _____

INFORMATION AND DOCUMENTS
FOR ESTATE PLANNING

PLEASE BRING WITH YOU COPIES OF:

Present Wills, if any

Deeds to real property (for title purposes) and any information regarding title to property, cost and present fair market value.

Manner of title holding of any stock (how the ownership appears on the certificates) and value of each stock.

Last three years' income tax returns.

Any available financial statements.

Copies of any gift tax returns filed.

If you feel appropriate, photos or a snapshot of yourself and spouse.

IF IN BUSINESS:

Any partnership agreements.

Any corporate minute books.

Any buy-and-sell agreements.

Last three years' income tax returns (partnership or corporation).

FILLING OUT INFORMATION SHEETS

It is most helpful (as well as cost-saving for you) if you can fill out the attached forms and bring them with you when you come in. However, please do not delay your appointment for lack of answers to the questions, since we can often assist you with troublesome items at the conference.

RALPH GANO MILLER   PAGE 1

CONFIDENTIAL DATA FOR

_____

FAMILY INFORMATION

Full Legal Name	Relation	Birthdate	H&W - Birthplace Children-Addresses
_____	Husband	__/__/__	_____
_____	Wife	__/__/__	_____
_____	Child	__/__/__ Phone _____	Add. _____
_____	Child	__/__/__ Phone _____	_____ Add. _____
_____	Child	__/__/__ Phone _____	_____ Add. _____
_____	Child	__/__/__ Phone _____	_____ Add. _____
_____	Child	__/__/__ Phone _____	_____ Add. _____
			_____

Other Dependents (Describe) _____

Adopted Children?   ( ) Yes   ( ) No   Who? _____

Marriage Date _____ Where? _____

Previous marriages for either spouse? ( ) Yes ( ) No If Yes, list on back dates of Marriage term and full name of prior spouse(s) and nature of termination, (e.g. divorce, death).

Residence Address _____ Years there _____ Phone _____

Previous Residence Address _____ Years there _____

Any changes of State of residence during marriage?   ( ) Yes   ( ) No   If Yes, give dates on back — Year you came to California _____

Husband's Parents, brothers and sisters	Age	Name and age of spouse (for bro. or sis.)	City and State of residence	Health	Estimated Net Worth
*(F) _____	____	_____	_____	____	_____
*(M) _____	____	_____	_____	____	_____
*( ) _____	____	_____	_____	____	_____
*( ) _____	____	_____	_____	____	_____
*( ) _____	____	_____	_____	____	_____
Wife's Parents, etc.					
*(F) _____	____	_____	_____	____	_____
*(M) _____	____	_____	_____	____	_____
*( ) _____	____	_____	_____	____	_____
*( ) _____	____	_____	_____	____	_____
*( ) _____	____	_____	_____	____	_____

*(F) - Father; (M) - Mother, (B) - Brother, (S) - Sister

RALPH GANO MILLER   Page 2

MISCELLANEOUS INFORMATION

Husband's Occupation _____

Husband's Employer _____

Address _____ Phone _____

Number of Years _____ Title _____ Dept. _____

Husband's Previous Occupation _____

Wife's Occupation _____

Wife's Employer _____

Address _____ Phone _____

Husband's Social Security Number _____ Wife's _____

Employer ID Number (for corporation or partnership, if any) _____

If you own your own business, do you have information on prospective purchasers in the event of your death or on other aspects of disposition of the business? If yes, who knows the location of this information? _____

_____

Has Social Security status been reviewed lately: ( ) Yes ( ) No.

Armed Service: _____ Branch _____ Serial No. _____

    Current Status _____ Disability _____

Husband and wife both U.S. Citizens?   ( ) Yes ( ) No.   If not, describe: _____

_____

Life Insurance Agent _____

Casualty Insurance Agent _____

Accountant _____

Investment Advisor _____

Personal Physician _____

Business Associates _____

Safe Deposit Box No. _____ Location _____

    In whose names? _____

Is there a homestead filed on your home? ( ) Yes ( ) No

RALPH GANO MILLER

PLANNING INFORMATION

Do you have a pre or post-nuptial agreement? ( ) Yes ( ) No.   If so, bring in.

Have either of you created a living trust?   ( ) Yes ( ) No.   If yes:

    Who created?   ( ) Husband   ( ) Wife   ( ) Both

    Who is the Trustee? _____

    Who are the beneficiaries? _____

Have you ever made a gift under the Uniform Gift to Minors Act?( ) Yes ( ) No

    If Yes, Who is the custodian? _____

    Who are the donees? _____

    What was given? _____

Have either of you ever made gifts in excess of $10,000 to any person (including your spouse) in any one year?
If so, describe. _____

_____

Are you or any member of your immediate family beneficiaries of a trust?

    ( ) Yes ( ) No _____If so, who? _____

Do either of you expect to receive gifts or inheritances? ( ) Yes ( ) No.

    If so, Who? _____ How much? _____

    From Whom? _____

Describe any health problems or special needs of individual family members: _____

_____

What is your estimate of the emotional maturity of your children? _____

_____

_____

Compare, in terms of your own priorities, the importance of adequate funds in order to do the following (indicate ranking by first, second, etc.):

    Enjoy a comfortable retirement   _____

    Take care of selves and family during a period of long term disability   _____

    Provide College educations for all children   _____

    Take care of family in the event of your death   _____

    Any others that are important to you (specify)

    _____   _____

    _____   _____

    _____   _____

RALPH GANO MILLER   Page 4

PLANNING INFORMATION - CONTINUED

If your children are minors (under age 18), please indicate your first and second choices of guardian for the children if something should happen to the two of you:

First Choice   _____

Relationship   _____

Address   _____

City, State   _____

                 _____

Second Choice   _____

Relationship   _____

Address   _____

City, State   _____

                 _____

Which Bank or other corporate fiduciary might you wish to name as Executor or Trustee under your documents (recognizing that such institution may well be named only in an alternate capacity) _____

_____

If your immediate family (e.g. spouse, children, grandchildren, etc.) were all to be deceased, to whom would you wish your property to pass (for example, you might want to have it go one-half to the heirs of each of you, or to a charity or charities, etc.): _____

_____

For older clients, would you want to designate a conservator of your person and estate in the event of your inability to manage your property? If so, who? _____

_____

Do you have any preference as to funeral and/or burial arrangements, or wish to place a limit on costs? If so, please fill out the following:

Religious Services, if any _____

Disposition of Body (e.g. specify burial or cremation, any preference for undertaking arrangements, particularly if you have made any such arrangements, and with whom)_____

_____

_____

Location of Interment _____

Limitation on Overall Cost (e.g., not to exceed $____) _____

_____

RALPH GANO MILLER

SUPPLEMENTAL SCHEDULE "I"
LIFE INSURANCE

Company	Policy #	Issue Date	Owner*	Type**	Primary Beneficiary	Secondary Beneficiary, if any	Amount of Premium	Cash Value	Amount of Loan	Face Amount
On Life of Husband:										
On Life of Wife:										

* Unless otherwise indicated, insurance is usually owned by the insured; ownership by a spouse or someone else may sometimes reduce death taxes and therefore your agent may have arranged for an ownership other than by the insured

** e.g., Whole Life, Term, Endowment, Annuity, etc.

HEALTH INSURANCE

DISABILITY INCOME

DISABILITY INCOME POLICY NUMBERS						
NAME OF INSURANCE COMPANY						
INSURED						
OWNER OF POLICY						
TYPE OF CONTINUANCE OR RENEWAL PROVISION						
DEFINITION OF DISABILITY						
MONTHLY DISABILITY INCOME						
ACCIDENT						
SICKNESS						
PARTIAL DISABILITY						
ACCIDENT						
SICKNESS						
WAITING PERIOD						
ACCIDENT						
SICKNESS						
BENEFIT PERIOD						
ACCIDENT						
SICKNESS						
SUPPLEMENTARY BENEFITS						

MEDICAL EXPENSE

MEDICAL EXPENSE POLICY NUMBERS						
NAME OF INSURANCE COMPANY OR SERVICE TYPE PLAN						
INSURED						
OWNER OF POLICY						
TYPE OF CONTINUANCE OR RENEWAL PROVISIONS						
TERMINATION DATE FOR CHILD COVERAGE						
BASIC HOSPITAL						
ROOM RATE						
NO. OF DAYS						
HOSPITAL EXTRAS						
OTHER BENEFITS						
SURGICAL						
MAXIMUM						
TYPE OF SCHEDULE						
MAJOR MEDICAL						
DEDUCTIBLE						
COINSURANCE						
INSIDE LIMITS						
OVERALL MAXIMUM						

RALPH GANO MILLER

INHERITANCE TAX INFOMATION

1. Did either of you own any real or personal property at date of marriage?
    If Yes, list below and attach real property tax bill for year of marriage, if available.

    General Description of each asset   Approximate market value at mar.

    _____
    _____
    _____

2. Husband's occupation at date of marriage _____
    Husband's net worth at date of marriage _____
    Wife's occupation at date of marriage _____
    Wife's net worth at date of marriage _____

3. If either of you have received any real or personal property after date of marriage by gift, bequest,
    devise or joint tenancy survivorship, list:

General Description of Each Asset	Full name and relation-ship of person rec'd from	Date rec'd	Approx. value on date rec'd

    If California Inheritance Tax determination was made, Name of Estate _____
    _____ Court Case No. (if any) _____ County _____

    If Received by Gift, State of residence of donor*s) at date of gift: _____
    _____

4. Have any assets listed under 1 or 3 been transferred to anyone else (including spouse)?
    If Yes, for any such assets sold, give:

Asset	Date of Sale	Proceeds Received	Subsequent disp. of proceeds

    For any such assets transferred without full consideration, give:

Asset	Date of Transfer	Names & addresses of persons transferred to	Consideration if any

5. States in which you have resided   Combined net worth upon taking up
    after marriage, including California   residence in each state (all assets, including cash)

    _____

6. Does net worth at date of last arrival in California include any separate property of either of you? If Yes, state source and value: _____
_____

7. Trace subsequent disposition of combined net worth of spouses after last arrival in California_____
_____
_____
_____
_____

8. Did either of you receive damages or a settlement for personal injury after September 11, 1957? If Yes, show dates, amounts received and subsequent disposition: _____

9. Have you ever obtained a legal separation (separate maintenance) or an interlocutory divorce? If Yes, attach copy of decree and any property settlement agreement _____
Date of reconciliation _____

10. Give on attachment any additional information bearing upon the separate or community status of your property.

ANNUAL REVIEW CHECKLIST

Below you will find a number of questions. A positive answer to any of them may indicate a need to review your estate plan. Check the appropriate boxes and return to me.

Specific Bequests

☐ I would like to make specific bequests to individuals not presently included in my plans - or delete the names of one or more persons (or charities) currently named.

☐ I would like to change the amounts of some of the bequests I have made.

Changes in Valuation

☐ The value of my estate has changed more than 20 percent in the last two years.

Special Provisions for Children

☐ My health (my spouse's or children's health) has deteriorated substantially in the last year.

Newly Born or Adopted Children

☐ A child (grandchild) has been born (or adopted) since our last review.

Handicapped or Incompetent Children

☐ A child (grandchild or other dependent) has become handicapped or seriously injured since our last review.

Status of Family Marriages

☐ A member of the family has become divorced or separated since our last review.

Cancellation of Loans to Children
and Equalization of Inheritance

☐ I would like to discharge an obligation owned to me by cancelling the loan in my will.

☐ I would like to provide a clause to equalize any gifts made in the past (or to be made in the future) to certain children (grandchildren).

Life Insurance

☐ I have added (or dropped) more than $100,000 of life insurance since our last review.

☐ I have (or would like to) changed a beneficiary designation on an existing policy.

☐ I feel I may need more life insurance but I don't know how much to purchase or what type to consider.

Gifts to Minors

☐ I would like to make substantial gifts to minor children (grandchildren).

Gifts to Charities

☐ I would like to add (delete) one or more charitable beneficiaries.

☐ I would like to change the amount of my bequest to certain charities.

Business Interests

☐ I have entered into a stock (partnership) buy-sell agreement since our last review.

☐ My business situation has changed significantly since our last review.

Guardian, Executors and Trustees

☐ I would like to name a particular person as advisor to my executor and trustees.

☐ I would like to reconsider the designation of the guardians, executors, and trustees I have named.

Other

☐ I would like to review my estate plans for the following reasons.

☐ I'd like to know how the latest tax law affects my estate plan.

CHECKLIST OF INFORMATION TO KEEP IN SAFE DEPOSIT BOX

The following information or materials should be kept in your safe deposit box:

☐ (1) Birth certificates
☐ (2) Marriage certificates (including artifacts or documentation from any prior marriages or divorces)
☐ (3) Your will (and spouse's will) and trust agreements
☐ (4) Listing of life insurance policies or certificates
☐ (5) Your Social Security numbers

☐ (6) Military discharge papers
☐ (7) Bonds, stocks, and other securities
☐ (8) Real estate deeds
☐ (9) Business (Buy-Sell) Agreement
☐ (10) Automobile titles and insurance policies
☐ (11) Property insurance policies
☐ (12) Additional:

LIST number of all checking and savings accounts including bank addresses and location of safe deposit boxes:

_____ _____ _____

_____ _____ _____

LIST name, address, and phone number of fire and life insurance agent:

_____ _____ _____

_____ _____ _____

LIST name, address, and phone number of accountant:

_____ _____ _____

LIST name, address, and phone number of (current or past) employer. State date when you retired if applicable. Include employee benefits booklets:

_____ _____ _____

_____ _____ _____

LIST all debts owed to *and* owed by you:

_____ _____ _____

_____ _____ _____

LIST the names, addresses, telephone numbers and birth dates of your children and other beneficiaries (including charitable beneficiaries):

_____ _____ _____

_____ _____ _____

_____ _____ _____

Chapter 3

DEATH–SENSITIZATION FOR THE ESTATE PLANNER

It is no wonder that CLUs, CPAs, trust officers, and attorneys involved in the estate planning process spend so much time in tax planning and relatively minimal effort on "people" planning; pitifully little formal thought has been given – in or out of the classroom – to the human factor in the estate planning process. It is fascinating that the subject of life – and death – appears so seldom in the curriculum of estate planning courses given in law schools, in insurance training classes, or in estate planning seminars and workshops.

Isn't it ironic that death, the very reason for the estate planner's existence, the "biological center of the personal service involved," is hardly ever discussed in texts on estate planning?

This commentary pertains to the psychological rather than the tax aspects of death, and is meant to serve as a compilation of some of the things the estate planner – both as a professional member of a human services team and as a person – should know about death and dying. Although the thoughts and words below have been synthesized from the works of a number of scholars, a special debt is owed to Dr. Elizabeth Kubler-Ross (On Death and Dying) and Thomas L. Shaffer (Death, Property, and Lawyers). The former is a psychiatrist and social scientist of extraordinary skill and sensitivity, whose books are based on the results of hundreds of actual interviews with dying patients and their families; the latter, a former dean of Notre Dame Law School, has written the most comprehensive text available to the estate planning professional on the subject of death.

WHY SHOULD THE ESTATE PLANNER THINK ABOUT DEATH AND DYING?

Reduction of Client's Anxiety

Many professionals, even those highly learned in the law, associate estate planning merely with dispositive and tax goals. A young attorney specializing in estate planning was introduced to a well-known and highly respected probate judge by one of the attorney's clients. The client spoke admiringly of the young man's talents as an estate planner and when the judge asked, "Young man, are you really that good?" the attorney quipped, "I guess I must be – it seems that once I draw a will, my clients seem to live forever." The judge retorted, "Well then how do you know what you are doing will work?" Although the judge's retort was clever, perhaps he missed the point. A client does not have to die for the estate planning process to be successful. Estate planning can and should be an end in itself.

One of the most important goals of the estate planning process is the reduction of fear and anxiety about death. That, in fact, is what the estate planning experience (from the client's viewpoint) should be about, a personal reconciliation to death.

Properly handled, the estate planning experience can be one of great psychological satisfaction. In fact, that peace of mind is the only payoff the client himself receives from making a will. After all, will the client, by making a will, avoid family fights? Will the client, by a complex scheme of wills and trusts, save taxes? Just what is it the client wants out of the estate planning process?

Estate planning, in its broadest sense, presents an opportunity for a significant, growing, healthy encounter with one's own death. "Death is resented, perhaps, because the event itself cannot be controlled. Yet through planning, even though he cannot abolish death, the client can frustrate it by removing the worst consequences of its surprise."

Melville, in *Moby Dick*, wrote about the constructive nature and therapeutic effect on death anxiety of the will-making process:

> It may seem strange that of all men sailors should be tinkering at their last wills and testaments…. After the ceremony was concluded upon the present occasion, I felt all the easier; a stone was rolled away from my heart. Besides, all the days I should now live would be as good as the days that Lazarus lived…. I survived myself.

Free Client's Energy to Life–Related Matters

A second reason that the planning experience is an end unto itself is the relationship between death and life.

Worrying about death and its consequences is emotionally expensive. Society's taboos regarding death generate delusions that in turn siphon off energy from the task of living. If the client spends energy maintaining the denial of mortality, that much less strength is available to be used in meaningful living.

An individual's values in life are affected strongly by the way he has (or has not) dealt with death and dying. Philosophers, psychiatrists, and religious scholars stress that death should be dealt with before it is imminent, because only by giving meaning to death can one give meaning to life. They explain that a human's mortality is a good thing, that only by the limited scope of one's time can existence be dramatic and intense. What is important is how (rather than how long) we live and that we maximize the creative possibilities of life.

How can an openness (between the professional and a client) about death enhance the client's ability to live well? By helping the client come to terms with death, and by helping him create an atmosphere in which he would be willing to die, it is easier for the client to learn to see his life in relationship with others in a clearer perspective and to make his lifetime interpersonal relationships more meaningful. In other words, we can show our client that rather than repress his fears of death he should "use as an antidote for death an extensive love of life." Estate planning, then, is to reduce our client's anxiety about death and free his emotional energies for life-oriented activities.

As practitioners in people-serving professions, our efforts have consequences beyond property distribution, beyond tax savings, and even beyond the financial security of our client's survivors. What we do affects not only those who survive the client, but also the client himself. A great deal of our efforts must be directed toward the psychological satisfaction of our client.

Additional Psychological Factors Encouraging Testamentary Process

What other factors concern an individual enough for him to pay money to have a will and trust drawn? Why does he purchase life insurance and reduce his current spendable income to pay premiums? Why does he make inter vivos gifts?

Basically, there are four additional reasons. One is that structuring the future and providing support for survivors is a moral imperative. (Just as it would be immoral to neglect predeath support duties, so would it be immoral to neglect postdeath obligations.)

A second powerful impetus is guilt. Many clients feel that money or other property will somehow make up for neglect. They attempt to pay back a wife or children in property for the time they were too busy at the office to take with their family.

Security devices such as wills, trusts, and life insurance provide a client with a means of doing something to stabilize the future of his family and rob death of its ability to threaten him with his own hungry children.

Perhaps the most powerful reason for the testamentary process is the step it enables a person to take toward immortality. Some have called this the concept of "postself." Essentially, it recognizes that individuals engage in cognitive and emotional maneuverings in the present so they can survive, continue to live, and have a measure of impact and influence after the event of their physical deaths.

The Estate Planner's Responsibility by Definition or Default

Why must the estate planner (in addition to other human services teams) be involved with the subjects of death and dying? Possibly the responsibility is his by definition – or perhaps the burden rests upon him by default. Social taboos have caused the dismissal of the subject of death from the public mind. This in turn shifts the weight to those of us who are forced by our relationship with clients to deal with their feelings about death and dying. Regardless of the reason, as advisors we must recognize that our clients – even those in the prime of life – have thoughts and reactions to death; and an essential part of the estate planning process relates to a healthy resolution of those feelings.

Resolution of Professional's Own Anxieties Necessary to His Utility

It is impossible for the estate planner to help his client until his own feelings and anxieties about death are first resolved. Not until the professional knows and can deal with his own fears and thoughts concerning death can he properly construct policies and priorities based on the needs and desires of his client – rather than his own defenses.

There are many thoughts embedded in the minds and hearts of clients that beg to be shared with another human being. But we often close off the openness necessary to the flow of such information because we are unwilling to talk directly about death. A discussion of death – even the very word – is kept to a bare minimum or surrounded with euphemisms by the attorney or trust officer in the will-making process or the insurance agent in the sales interview.

The feelings of the professional, however, do not go unnoticed or without effect. His values and attitudes are communicated (both verbally and nonverbally) to a client regardless of whether the estate planner intends such message or not. His annoyance, impatience, lack of interest, or personal anxiety affects his clients more than he realizes. Our method of handling our own feelings sometimes conveys that we cannot, do not want to, and are unwilling to listen to those of others.

Rewards of Openness to the Estate Planner and Client

Substantial rewards are available to both the estate planner and his client who are willing to talk about death and dying long before it happens. A healthy and strong individual is less frightened and better able to deal with the interpersonal and financial implications of death "when it is still miles away than when it is right in front of the door." It is also easier for the client's family to discuss such matters in times of relative health and well being. Appropriate arrangements for children and others are more rationally made while the head of the household is still functioning. (The value of such predeath conversations seems obvious – yet we often postpone such talks to serve our own defenses rather than the best interests of the client and his family.)

The rewards to the estate planner are abundant. If we are strong enough to examine our own reactions more closely and take an honest look at ourselves, our own growth and maturity is nurtured. When we learn to listen, we reduce the powerlessness (and often frustration and anger) of those toward whom we profess to offer human caring.

WHY THE WORD "DEATH" IS UNSPOKEN

When the topic of death is raised – or when the professional must deal with a dying client – his concerns about his own mortality are raised toward consciousness. His childhood feeling about separation and death are reawakened. Talking about one's own death is even more sensitive and more terrible. Because it is an unknown, death is associated with a bad act, a frightening happening. We deny death by discussing it – if at all – in euphemistic

language. Much of this extends from the societal taboo concerning the recognition of man's mortality.

The problem, of course, is not uniquely reserved to the estate planner. The medical profession offers a good example of the reluctance of other professionals to meet the problem. For instance, the physician often prefers not telling a patient he has cancer. And unless the patient is persistent, the doctor might disregard the patient's questions. Even those questions intuitively perceived as a "real wish to know" are often ignored: "No one wants to know he is dying." Professionals have difficulty stating a diagnosis to a patient. They tend to use a staccato, impersonal, medical textbook style.

THE ESTATE PLANNING INTERVIEW – AN OPPORTUNITY TO TOUCH, TO FEEL, TO HELP

Coming to Grips with Life and Death

The estate planning interview is perhaps the first time in a client's life when he will be confronted with his property, his beloved ones, his mortality, and the relationship of each to the others. The impact of death must be discussed and met head on. He must recognize and internalize the possibility of unexpected sudden death and, in some cases, eventuality of rapidly approaching certain death. He must come face to face with the effects of the orphaning of his children, the potential for family strife, the problems inherent in projects left unfinished, and the psychological and financial burdens of liabilities outstanding. Additionally, the estate planning interview is an opportunity to come to grips with and eliminate the uncertainty involved in the mysterious machinery of probate.

The Process of Human Counseling

This reduction in tension and anxiety does not just happen: it must be part of a carefully thought out process on the part of the estate planner. The hoped-for result will not occur if the experts, the CPA, the CFP, the CLU, the ChFC, the attorney, or the trust officer, think of the estate planning interview as a mental tug-of-war involving on the one side the estate planner, who knows or makes up the rules, and on the other the client, who becomes willing to accept those rules by dependence on the estate planner. This psychology can only result in an arrangement that the client will probably not understand or even want. How could he if he has not "bought into" the ultimate plan?

What must the professional do to involve the client and turn what might otherwise be a cold, impersonal gathering of data into an opportunity for human counseling? It is not so difficult a task for the estate planner to identify issues or face problems. What the estate planner needs to learn is how to face a face.

Listen to the client. Study not only what the client (and his family) says, but also what he does not say. Try to understand what the client's body language (the shrug of a shoulder, the positioning of the hands, the apparent physical tension on the face, the lifting of the eyebrows, or the fleeting frown) really means. Summarize what you have been told and reflect accurately on what you have seen, felt, and heard.

Be sensitive to the client's world. Accept his feelings and try to understand them. Communicate honestly – and humanly. Be open, involved, and willing to enter the client's world. The professional must want to be personally helpful. To do this he must be tuned in not only to the client's feelings but also to his own.

Objectives of the Estate Planning Interview

The goal of the estate planner should be to help his client come to his own realizations and conclusions. To accomplish this, he must find out how the client feels about life and death – and the values and relationships that death will affect or destroy. So he must search for feelings and attitudes as well as information. The failure of an estate planner is more often a failure of perception than a restricted range of information, an incomplete understanding of "people facts" rather than "fact facts."

More specifically, the estate planner must understand his client's system of needs, his modes of expressing or revealing himself, his ideas about life, and his feelings and practices relating to his family and his career. There must also be an appreciation of the client's feelings about property, security, health and, perhaps most importantly, an ability to contemplate all of these things in relation to each other.

The Role of Property in the Testamentary Process

It is extremely important that the estate planner have an understanding of the roles of property in the testamentary process: "Our clients' thoughts and emotions are deeper, more puzzling realities than taxation or legal rhetoric." Clients are people, complex, and worthy of behavioral examination.

At its simplest level, a client's thoughts about his property could be considered mere statements on a ledger. But on higher levels, property is both an expression and an extension of a client himself, a part of the way he defines himself. (This is clearly seen when a person is stripped of his possessions. He is attacked at the deepest layers of his personality; there is less man left since something of himself has been taken away from him. The first day of basic training in the army, incarceration as a prisoner of war, and even routine hospital check-ins serve as examples of the loss of identity that is coupled with the loss that comes when clothing and other material possessions are taken away.)

The items on a person's desk, perhaps mementos of difficult business careers, are not significant for their economic values but are important because – like other property – they are an idiom of the owner's personality.

If we accept the premise that property represents and immortalizes a person, then when a person makes a gift (inter vivos or testamentary) he is really giving part of himself. He is giving his own nature and substance, since the property he gives is not inert but has the life and personification of the giver. His attitude toward giving, therefore, expresses the relationships between the people he loves and the things – the wealth and objects – he owns.

Property is used in the exercise of power, love, guilt, remorse, hope, and resignation. A person's needs, feelings, thoughts, and actions grow and attach in different manners to different kinds of properties. A home, for example, represents a protective attachment to a person's family. A business may represent the continuation or perhaps completion of a personal project (goal-striving behavior).

The estate planner should incorporate the role of personification of property in the estate planning process. He should understand that clients – in drawing wills – are interested as much in values and identifications in their property as they are in taxes. They are interested in the people they love.

WHAT IS DEATH AND WHAT DOES IT MEAN?

Death – Multifaceted Meanings and Effects

In the most general sense, death is the continuing and constantly accelerating process that begins the moment we are born. Perhaps that definition should set the stage for how we live: "We can realize that we might die at any moment and yet live as though we were never going to die."

Death attaches to each individual's soul, psyche, relationships, and property – but does so in different ways for different people. The meanings of the word "death" fluctuate, therefore, from person to person:

To some, death is the bringer of financial distress: With the extreme treatment and costs of hospitalization, financial burdens are added. Little luxuries at first and necessities later on may not be afforded any more. The immense sums that such treatment and hospitalization cost in recent years have forced many patients to sell the only possessions they had; they were unable to keep a house which they built for their old age, unable to send a child through college, and unable, perhaps, to make many dreams come true.

Death to many conjures up images of loss of dignity and independence. Guilt, anxiety, and fear color perceptions of dying. Death is frightening because it is uncertain, because it will sever important relationships (especially relationships that involve mutual obligations), and because it will cause experience to cease.

Social scientists, physicians, and philosophers have looked upon death as part of life. They have asked, if one is not able to die, is he really able to live?: "We die as we have lived. Death belongs to life as birth does. The walk is in the raising of the foot as in the laying of it down." Others have said, "death is an important interface – part of a larger process which is somehow related to what it is to be human."

Dying – How It Colors Perceptions of Death

We know much more about dying than we do about death. As estate planners, we are sometimes confronted with a client who has been told he has a limited time to live or who may even be on his deathbed. What are the feelings some of these people might experience? Some have said that dying is partially reliving the past, partially preoccupation with the illness, and partially just going on living. And death? Some say it is very much like rest: "In the end a dying man needs to die like a sleepy man needs to sleep."

Do dying and death represent failure? To many, they do. To others, the thoughts of dying and death generate fear of losing time, physical decay, the cessation of

thought, and irreversibility, and the loss of pleasure. Still others view the process of dying as a deprivation, a threat, a punishment, and a devouring of their persons.

People who are dying experience a tremendous range of problems – from the purely practical (such as transportation to and from the hospital) to the deeply internal emotional experience, such as dealing with intense sadness, anger, and guilt. Perhaps worst of all is the loneliness: "He was ... interrupted, left dangling, perhaps to die alone.... It was the isolation, the exclusion we had forced upon him. We could not be with him – we could not even hear him." The vast change in life-styles makes dying alien and lonely, mechanical and dehumanizing.

Interaction between the Estate Planner and the Dying Client

There are a number of tools and techniques in use where members of the estate planning team are aware that death is impending:

Unlike the normal estate planning situation, however, deathbed estate planning by definition usually precludes detailed research and requires immediate decisions. The estate planner is likely to propose technically sound recommendations that may be personally unacceptable to the client and his family. They may not even be willing to listen to recommendations. Sometimes, the client or his family will make requests that are technically unsound or even illegal. These must, of course, be delicately rejected.

How much can be accomplished depends on a number of variables. Three of the most important are the client's state of mind, the emotional involvement of near relatives, and the relationship between the estate planner and the client.

If the client is physically, mentally, and emotionally able to assist, his cooperation can vastly increase the effectiveness of predeath planning. But, as will be further explained below, some persons lose all interest when they learn death is near. Often the client has been kept ignorant of the gravity of his situation by a well-intentioned physician or family member. This at least complicates, if not totally frustrates, the estate planner's ability to render meaningful service.

Family members are sometimes more emotionally crippled by the impending loss they will suffer than is the client himself. His spouse, children, or other close relatives may be incapable of making logical decisions or taking pragmatic action. The special taboos against mentioning a will or "getting things in order" have kept even estate planning specialists from being of much help when faced with their own dying parents.

A close relationship between the estate planner and the client gives the advisor perspective and insight into the client's personal objectives and his family's potential problems. Even more important, the advisor's role must be to provide emotional ballast, to objectively help his client and his client's family arrange a list of priorities and implementation procedures.

THE DYING CLIENT –
EXPRESSIONS OF GRIEF

It is important for the estate planner to understand how grief is expressed by both the dying client and his survivors. How these individuals come to terms with impending death and move through the various stages of grief is thought to be strongly influenced by a person's basic personality. The leading authority feels there are essentially five stages through which a person goes: denial, anger, bargaining, depression, and acceptance. (These stages can occur in any order at any time.)

Denial is a temporary defense. In the young there is the typical "It can't happen to me" reaction. Denial serves as a healthy way of dealing with the uncomfortable and painful fact of impending death.

An expression of anger, which can be directed without reason at doctors, friends, relatives, or estate planning advisors, is thought to vary in intensity with the dying client's early life experiences. It is yet another means of expressing powerful emotional trauma.

Bargaining ("Let me live one more year and I'll be good to my children, donate money to my religious organization, etc.") is an attempt on an emotional level to postpone what is inevitable on the intellectual and physical levels.

Depression is a reaction that is a common response to the actual loss of health or use of part of the body. It is a preparatory measure to the impending loss of life.

Acceptance is often (but not always) the final stage. At this point the dying client is void of feelings and expresses an increased desire and need for sleep. The dying person's family often needs more help, support, and understanding than the client.

Another authority suggests that the stages of grief are

(1) shock

(2) disorganization

(3) expression of volatile emotions

(4) guilt

(5) feelings of loss and loneliness

(6) periods of relief and reestablishment

Feelings expressed by a dying professor included panic (he was terrified that he had lost control of his fate, decisions were made without his knowledge or consent, and he gradually found himself passively accepting the decisions), anger (he felt dehumanized, an object instead of a person), the need to talk (he wanted to share his feelings and vent his frustrations), and deep depressions (he had feelings of guilt and inadequacy as a husband and father).

WHAT THE ESTATE PLANNER
CAN DO FOR THE DYING CLIENT

Although the estate planning process should give all clients a feeling of control, a sense of usefulness, and the satisfaction of completing unfinished business, this goal is particularly important in the case of a client who has been told – because of a particular medical condition such as cancer or a failing heart – that he or she has only a limited time to live.

The Importance of Providing
the Client with Control

What should occur in the estate planning process is a series of experiences that result in change through (the client's) choice. The professional can increase the client's dignity by empowering him with as much control as possible. But it is not enough to give the dying client a voice; he must also be given a listener. Only then can he be an active participant in decision making. Psychiatrists have found that hopelessness and depression are precipitated when individuals cannot (or perceive they cannot) act on their environment. Any actions the estate planner can take to bring the dying client into the problem-solving process will help relieve the client's feelings of helplessness and increase the quality of his remaining life.

A word of warning, however, is in order. Even for the healthy client, "the testamentary experience is death-confronting, novel, and taboo-defying." For the dying client, such experience could possibly be overwhelming. Obviously, a great deal of discretion must be exercised by all the parties involved.

Helping the Client to Feel Useful by Encouraging the Completion of Unfinished Business

By presenting the estate planning process as an unfinished project, the client is given a developmental task with which he is involved. He is given value and a meaningful tie to life. This final stage – even though quite possibly limited in terms of absolute time – may be relatively as important as all previous tasks in life.

Family, as well as members of the estate planning team, must interface with the dying person and his environment. They must help the client maintain his autonomy and dignity by encouraging him to participate – and thus help him to face death in his own way. This conceptualization allows family members to help the dying person complete his unfinished business in a meaningful way that will benefit all concerned.

"Death ceases to be an absurd and intolerable scandal only when a person knows he has given meaning to his life." So the estate planner confronted with someone dying must do what he can do to give that person the sense of pride, a feeling of worth, and a knowledge he has resolved much of his unfinished business.

Development of a Support System of Advisors

The dying person and his survivors need large doses of supportive intervention that can best be accomplished by knowing the dying person's previous history of reactions to stress.

The nature of the client's response to grief will be largely determined by the quality of his lifetime personal relationships, and the use he makes of the defense mechanisms such as denial or anger and the retraction of his ego. Start where the client is – let him face impending death, denial, or acceptance, whichever he selects. Do not force him to behave according to your preconceptions or hustle him along a preplanned course.

In dealing with the dying client (or his family) proceed at the rate determined by the client's receptivity. Sense where the client is emotionally:

Set your pace at the rate at which they are able to understand. Do the correct thing financially even if it may provoke angry confrontations at some subsequent date…. The widow will generally be more rational and receptive to good advice in approximately six to nine months after the death. Do not make brisk unexplained conclusions or assertions. Do not be provoked into anger. Be deliberate, correct, and extremely open and proper. Diplomacy, patience, genuineness, and warmth are essential. Take the time to be empathetic, to listen attentively, to have unconditional positive regard…. If you find yourself becoming very angry or acting abruptly, it is best to consider why this is so and excuse yourself from the ongoing exchange until you have better composure.

Strengthen the coping mechanisms whether they are made of denial or acceptance. Reduce anxiety and fear. Help the family to understand the feelings of the dying individual and help the family with their feelings.

Perhaps the most meaningful service is the opportunity the estate planner has to allow his client to share his feelings before death and to work through those feelings, rational or irrational.

The dying need reassurance they will not be left alone. If we, as estate planners, have the courage not to desert them, they offer us a gift in return – help in completing our own unfinished business.

EFFECT OF DEATH ON THE SURVIVORS

A breadwinner's death results in drastic changes in the life of the family. These include loss of security and an end to the survivors' dependence on the decedent. Survivors will be required to take over many of the decedent's roles and tasks, accept a strange new schedule, and shoulder what are sometimes actually (and are almost always perceived as) harsh and awesome new responsibilities. Especially for widows, this often means a sudden involvement in business and financial affairs.

In every substantial estate, the widow (if there is one) has major roles to perform. Yet in most situations she lacks even a modicum of previous exposure or training to function efficiently in handling legal, business, probate or taxation problems. Quite often she has never balanced a checkbook, let alone handled an $800,000 estate. She has not been shown how to do things which will be her certain responsibility. Nor has she been taught to avoid acts that she should not even attempt.

Ironically, at the very time the widow is first involved in these matters, she is in the worst possible frame of mind. She is depressed, unhappy and insecure, and her entire social life has changed. After the few days when her friends, relatives and close family are there to comfort her, they will return to their normal lives. The widow is left – alone and lonely. Confronting her with strange and complex legal duties is like throwing her into a pitch-black room. She loses all sense of direction, does not know where the light switch is and is afraid to move because all sorts of risks and impediments are there in the darkness.

How does the widow feel? One widow said, "I feel like one of those spiraled shells washed up on the beach. Poke a straw through the twisting tunnels inside and nothing is there – no flesh, no life. Whatever lived there has dried up and gone!"

And, although the male pronoun is commonly used to designate the breadwinner/decedent, it is quite often the *man* who survives. Studies show that a widower faces even more serious emotional problems than many widows face. Men seldom have a support system to hold them up – and *keep* them up.

The word "widow" is appropriate – it comes from Sanskrit and it means "empty." The shock of that emptiness is always immediately felt. Another widow said, "It took me some time to grasp the meaning of what happened. The word 'death' didn't mean anything to me. All I thought of was that it would be impossible for Marty to be here one day and gone the next. It was as if the earth had just opened up and swallowed him. My shock turned to panic; I felt lost. I didn't want to see or talk to anyone. The thought of going to bed frightened me because I would always wake up in the middle of the night trying to stifle a scream. I couldn't believe Marty was dead."

Years ago, we had the benefit of a socially accepted collection of rites and ceremonies to help survivors make the transition. In some societies, these rites were performed for weeks or even months after an individual's death. But today, we do not often have elaborate wakes, mourning clothes or annual remembrances. Many of society's rules, rites and ceremonies of the past are gone. And so survivors are not really sure how to cope with death – they have to make their own decisions at to what to do and how to react. This uncertainty produces anxiety.

Survivors experience guilt for what they did or did not do in life to or for the deceased, or simply embarrassment for having lived while the deceased died. Survivors may feel guilty because the death of the deceased has relieved them from heavy, emotionally and financially draining burdens. ("If he'd die already, the financial nightmare would end.")

At the same time, the bereaved may feel anger at being deserted and left to face life's problems. A young daughter, speaking of her father who had just died, told us, "I felt as though he didn't have the right to die. I wasn't ready for him to die."

Perhaps the most difficult of all emotions that survivors must overcome is a deep sense of loneliness and resentment at being left alone. There are 10 million widows in our country – one out of every 6 women over age 21. A study of over 1,700 widows showed that loneliness is the single most serious problem of widowhood. One of those widows said, "It's funny, but it's love and companionship that you miss. You don't get someone out of your system so easily after 26 years …Being lonesome is a big void that can't be filled."

The second most serious problem of widowhood is the financial pressure of raising children without a father.

So besides their emotional problems, families are likely to have financial problems, or at least concern as to how they will pay current bills and continue to get along after the breadwinner's death. One widow said, "After my husband died, there was the emotional shock. The pain was so deep – so consuming – it seemed unendurable. But I learned to live with it. The economic shock was something else. It didn't strike as fast or hit as furious. It's the sort of thing you don't even notice at first. But after a while, the shock of your economic plight begins to creep into your consciousness like some black, oozing reality that you can't believe or escape. It's true … money can't compensate two children for the loss of their father; money can't reach out in the night and caress you; money can't come home at night with a briefcase, a twinkle and a hug; but money can give you some peace of mind." And so survivors must be concerned, among other things, with the need for money – because, to the extent the decedent did not provide it, his survivors have the problem of raising it – or doing without it. This in turn creates incredible psychological pressures.

Bereavement is not a commonplace occurrence in our lifetimes. The whirlwind shock of sudden change is a crisis with which many family members feel particularly unable to cope. Quite often a real, and almost always a perceived, imbalance exists between the difficulty and importance of the problems and the resources available to deal with them. Obviously, professional psychiatric and psychological help may be required.

Survivors must release their ties with the deceased. They must adjust to their new environment and form new relationships. The family must allow mourning to occur, relinquish the memory of the deceased as a force in family affairs and activities, and realign themselves in terms of readjusting responsibilities and needs.

It is particularly important that all (both children and adults) who are touched by the death of the decedent be given an opportunity to adequately work out their feelings about the event. You can expect problems to occur when a person of any age is unable to express grief or tries to hold back natural responses. Symptoms of the morbid and abnormal reactions that tend to occur when there is an unnatural delay include:

- exhausting overactivity

- symptoms similar to those manifested in the last illness of the deceased, or the outbreak of other psychosomatic illnesses such as asthma or colitis (this is a combination of normal mourning and the "It should have been me" feeling)

- furious (and usually unreasonable) hostility toward specific persons (often including the estate's executor)

- agitated and acute depression (sometimes leading to suicidal thoughts)

- extreme and prolonged difficulty in sleeping

- preoccupation with the image of the deceased (you may find dozens of pictures of the deceased suddenly appear throughout the house)

- difficulty in continuing normal social interaction and a withdrawal of interest in the outside world

ABOUT THE WILL AND PROBATE – WHAT THEY MEAN TO THE SURVIVORS

The will and the probate process itself fulfill important functions in the process of emotional repair known as mourning. The will is the last communication of the deceased. It has unique emotional meanings because in it the decedent states many of his feelings about the bereaved. Of course, the decedent's thoughts are usually not implicit in the words used. But in terms of *who* receives property, *how* that property is to be received, and *when* it will be received, the testator has expressed approval (or disapproval), gratitude (or revenge), and confidence (or a lack of confidence). Likewise, the terms of a will may emphasize that the testator recognized one child's need or another child's deservingness. Or the testator may have favored a blood relative over someone who is loved but is not related (or vice versa).

It is important to recognize that what the testator meant to say when his will was written may not be how it is taken by the beneficiaries. A devoted but less needy son who gets less than a proportionate part of his father's estate may resent the injustice of being left less than his less worthy brother.

CHOICE OF EXECUTOR – WHAT IT MEANS

A person is selected as an executor because of the testator's trust and confidence in that person. They may have had a close or very deep emotional relationship.

A bereaved executor, in performing his or her duties, facilitates the process of coming to terms with the testator's death. By carrying out the wishes of the deceased the executor is retaining and strengthening his or her relationship with the deceased, but at the same time, while going through the stages of the probate process, the executor is gradually "letting go."

Of course, the opposite is true in some situations. For instance, assume a widow had always been dependent on her husband for every decision. If the couple's son or a bank is named as executor, the sense of helplessness precipitated by the loss of her husband is increased by the lack of control she continues to experience. Her helplessness may generate fear and distrust. The result may be that every move the executor makes may be questioned or viewed with suspicion.

WHAT CAN – AND SHOULD – THE EXECUTOR DO?

One of the positive results of the estate planning process is to give survivors a feeling of control, a sense of usefulness and the satisfaction of completing the decedent's (and their own) unfinished business. Increase the family members' dignity by empowering them with as much control as possible. Keep in mind that it is not enough to give survivors a voice; one must also give them a listener. Only then can they be active participants in the decision-making process. Hopelessness and depression are precipitated and exacerbated when individuals cannot (or perceive they cannot) act on their environment.

Any steps taken to bring all family members into the decision-making process will relieve their feelings of helplessness. The death of a loved one will be experienced as less absurd, and may become more tolerable, if the family knows that the life of the deceased had meaning.

Accumulating an estate, buying life insurance, preparing the will and trust are all like buying a car, filling it with gas, and expecting that a wife or child who has never been in a car can get in and drive that vehicle in heavy traffic. We cannot, of course, make survivors into mechanics, but we can help them learn where the steering wheel is, how to make the car go, how to put on the brakes and how to read road signs. The more that can be done to explain what comes next and how the family can take the wheel, the better off they will be.

SUMMARY

As a member of the estate planning team, you must be extremely conscious of the trauma of the bereaved. Understanding the five stages of grief experienced by a dying person (denial, anger, bargaining, depression and acceptance) will help you understand what survivors experience. Every person will react to death differently than others. How the bereaved react is largely dependent on their relationship with the deceased, their emotional and financial dependence, the energy and time they

have devoted to the deceased, and how many other important relationships they may have.

Death often results in drastic life-style changes. These are coupled with various physical symptoms of grief that can be normally anticipated, as well as abnormal reactions that occur when the mourning process is delayed or repressed.

Probate is an important part of the "letting go" process; it is also a means of completing the unfinished business of the deceased and at the same time a beginning of the family's taking control.

If the estate planner can serve as a neutral outsider who is not himself emotionally overinvolved, he can be of great assistance in listening to the client's family's concerns, their wishes, and needs.

Any steps an estate planner takes to bring the survivors into the probate process and give them control will help relieve their feelings of helplessness and help them readjust.

Other Resources:

- Alexandra Armstrong and Mary R. Donahue, *On Your Own* (Chicago, IL: Dearborn, 2000).

- Lynn Caine, *Widow* (New York, NY: Morrow, 1974).

- Charles K. Plotnick and Stephan R. Leimberg, *How to Settle an Estate* (New York, NY: Plume Books, 2002).

- "Before I Die" at http://www.thirteen.org/bid/.

Chapter 4

THE UNAUTHORIZED PRACTICE OF LAW

It is sometimes difficult to draw the boundaries of professional responsibility in an area as complex and sophisticated as estate planning. Special skills and learning are necessary prerequisites not only to the attorney but also to a CPA, CFP, ChFC, CLU, trust officer, or other individual serving a client in an advisory capacity.

Yet it is clear that regardless of how knowledgeable an advisor is, only the attorney may practice law. The practice of law is regulated and limited for a number of reasons:

First, the public needs and deserves protection against advice by self-styled advisors who have been neither trained nor examined (nor licensed) by recognized educational or governmental authorities.

Second, many non-lawyers who are highly skilled in specific areas such as tax law may lack the broader viewpoint and depth provided by a good law school.

Third, the lawyer-client relationship is one of confidentiality, relative objectivity, and impartiality. Even the most ethical sales person, service provider, or trust officer cannot claim complete objectivity; his job is to sell a given investment, contract, service, or the use of a particular financial institution. This does not imply that the CFP, CLU, ChFC, or trust officer or CPA does not have highly important tasks to perform as a member of the estate planning team. On the contrary, it is often that individual who motivates the client to take action – and follows through to make sure the plan is implemented.

Were this the only responsibility and utility of those members, their positions on the "team" would be secure. But, in reality, each of those individuals can perform a function that serves as a valuable complement to the attorney's task. In fact, the attorney should not be "practicing" life insurance, providing trust services, or replacing the accountant. The very idea of an estate planning team implies that each member serves the client with his own special and essential skills. When any member of the team usurps the province of the other, it is the client who loses. Stated in a more positive manner, the client is best served if the non-attorney and attorney work together to formulate, implement,

qualify, and maintain a plan which suits the client's needs and objectives.

Returning to the topic of the unauthorized practice of law, the central issue must be: What is it? Clearly, the preparation of instruments and contracts by which legal rights are secured constitutes an invasion of the attorney's province. So, the non-attorney who drafts a will or a trust for a client is patently guilty of the unauthorized practice of law. But what of the person who reviews a will or trust and advises clients as to the desirability in their circumstances of specific clauses or instruments? Does every discussion of a legal principle constitute unauthorized practice? Is the recognized subject matter expert excused from the proscription against unauthorized practice? What if no fee is charged for the rendering of advice? Does long-time custom and tradition offer a valid reason for practice by non-lawyers?

A working knowledge of the tax law is essential to professionals in the life insurance, trust, and accounting disciplines. Generally, the protection of the public can be achieved without hampering or unduly burdening professionals with impractical and technical restrictions that have no reasonable justification. To say that non-attorneys cannot discuss any pertinent legal principles with a client would be so unrealistic and narrow as to be absurd.

But what can be safely discussed – and what cannot? Essentially, where a statute or legal interpretation has become so well known and settled that no further legal issue is involved, there should be no problem in suggesting its simple application on a general basis. This is known as the "general-specific" test; no violation arises from the sharing of legal knowledge that is either generally informatory or, if specific, is so obvious as to be common knowledge. It is only when legal rules (which are general in nature) are applied to specific factual situations that the line is crossed. Providing advice involving the application of legal principles to a specific situation is clearly the "practice of law" under the "general-specific" test.

A second criterion is known as the "complexity" theory. This theory states that the non-attorney should not answer "difficult" or "complex" questions of law. One court stated that "practicing as an attorney...is the giving of advice or the rendition of any sort of service...when the giving of such advice or the rendition of such service requires the use of any degree of legal knowledge or skill."

But perhaps the court should have gone beyond the questions of difficulty or complexity of subject matter into the issue of whether legal judgment was exercised by the non-attorney and relied on by the client. When basic legal principles are applied to specific and actual facts or the resolution of controversial or uncertain questions of law is required in an actual case, the practice of law is involved.

No safety can be found in an argument that the non-lawyer is both a specialist and an acknowledged expert in the field. The rationale for this seemingly harsh stand is that the interest of the public is not protected by narrow specialization of a person who lacks the broad perspective and orientation of a licensed attorney. That dimension of skill and knowledge comes only from a thorough understanding of legal concepts, processes, and the interaction of all the branches of law. In other words, the rules may have been learned by the non-lawyer but often the full meaning and import of the rule and its components – and the impact of that rule on other seemingly unrelated rules – may not be fully understood by even a highly competent specialist who is not also a licensed attorney.

Charging fees for legal advice seems important only where such fees were charged. Most courts have had little trouble finding violations where clients relied on advice or were provided with legal services regardless of whether or not fees were charged. Likewise, practices of the past provide little defense in the present. Recent decisions indicate that even custom and tradition long acquiesced in by the Bar does not make proscribed activities any less the practice of law.

Almost everyone agrees that the actual drafting of a will or trust or the preparation of the instruments and contracts by which legal rights are secured is the practice of law. The odds are very high that he who drafts such documents is practicing law.

Beyond this point, however, (and in the minds of some, even at this point) things become hazy. Each state has the right to decide – independently from all other states – what is meant by the "unauthorized practice of law."

Review the following fact patterns and ask, "Will this constitute the unauthorized practice of law?"

- The planner reviews a will or trust and advises a client that – in this particular circumstance –

that document will (or will not) have specific legal implications or that the instrument in question is "right" or "not right" for the client.

- After analyzing client information, the planner decides on the type of trust arrangement the client should have and selects the specific provisions that should be inserted into the plan documents.

- The planner makes "bottom line recommendations" as to which trust provisions would be most suitable to a client's needs.

- The planner drafts amendments to an existing trust.

- The planner does the initial draft of a power of attorney, but submits it for review, approval, and adoption by the client's lawyers.

- The planner gives advice regarding the impact of tax and other laws on an irrevocable trust.

If these actions are the unauthorized practice of law, is the client denied the benefit of receiving advice from accountants, actuaries, CFPs, CLUs, ChFCs, or trust officers who are experts in their fields? Would prohibiting such actions by these experts amount to a questionable restraint on interdisciplinary competition? Is it not only possible, but also highly likely, that the non-attorney expert is better suited than the attorney in matters such as product choice and design? Would thwarting the non-attorney from performing these vital roles significantly increase the cost of estate planning? In some states these are still open questions. As a practical matter, practitioners should avoid most problems by working closely with the client's attorney at the earliest opportunity.

This book is not designed to help the non-lawyer eliminate the need for an attorney. To the contrary, it is a text designed for all the members of the estate planning team to help delineate the large number of alternative solutions to general problem areas. Definitive solutions, i.e., the choice of which specific tools or techniques to use in a given case or the decisions as to how they should be used must be considered only by the client, together with his attorney. Likewise, the drafting or adopting of instruments needed to execute the techniques or utilize the tools discussed in this book is exclusively the province of the lawyer.

Every member of the estate planning team is obligated to be aware of these tools and techniques, to understand their limitations as well as their problem-solving potential, and to be knowledgeable enough to discuss them in general terms with clients and their other advisors.

Chapter 5

ETHICS

WHY ETHICS?

Ethics are standards of an aspirational and inspirational nature reflecting commitments to model standards of exemplary professional conduct.[1] Every major profession[2] has adopted some form of "near law," a Code, Canon, or set of guidelines as to what the profession expects of its members.[3] This discussion is meant to provide a checklist for the practitioner in the estate planning field.[4] It is not intended to be anything more than what its title implies, a "practical guideline," a self-monitoring device to help estate planners.

Why do professional organizations need such codes of conduct? Why do estate planners need a practical code of ethics?

First, ethics are a means of creating standards by which conduct can be measured both by the member and by the group itself. Second, ethics serve as a way to acknowledge an obligation to society, to the professional group, and to the client. Third, ethics assure the profession will be governed by high standards. Fourth, ethics are a means of examining priorities and building a tradition based on integrity.

A fifth reason for ethics is as a limitation on power. It is the "power of the experts" that ethics are meant to control: the attorney, accountant, trust officer, life insurance agent, and other members of the estate planning team all know things the client does not.[5] This special knowledge gives the professional Kafka-like power over a layman who must put great faith and trust in (and take great risk in the accuracy and appropriateness of) what he is told. The client cannot possibly know the full extent of the problems, possibilities, and consequences without the assistance of the planner.

The preparation of an estate plan vests in the planner enormous power for another reason: the planner is a person in whom the client places a great trust and confidence. It is this potential abuse of power that ethics are designed to prevent or limit.

The premise upon which practical ethics must be based is that power must be exercised in the interest of those for whose benefit it was entrusted rather than abused for the self-aggrandizement of the planner. The limitations and restrictions on the planner must not, however, be so great as to be so unenforceable, unrealistic, and impractical as to be counter productive. Practical ethics, therefore, must strike a balance. The questions that follow are designed to help do just that:

HONESTY: Has the planner engaged in any business or professional activity that involved an act (or omission) of a dishonest, deceitful, or fraudulent nature?

Has the planner used his license, degree, or designation to attribute to himself a depth or scope of knowledge, skills, and professional capabilities he does not, in fact, possess?

Has the planner been fair and honest in dealings with the IRS and in fostering confidence in the system?[6]

COMPETENCY: Does the planner have the requisite legal knowledge, practical skill, and has he exercised thoroughness?

Has the planner undertaken a role that entails responsibilities in addition to those inherent to the profession – and if so – is he properly trained and equipped (and willing and otherwise able) to perform them in a competent and efficient manner?[7]

Has the planner done the proper preparation? In other words, is he qualified to perform the services requested and does he know enough to perform any services required beyond those requested?

What has the planner done to understand the specific facts and circumstances of the client, the client's family, other beneficiaries, and their needs and objectives?

Does the planner keep abreast of changing economic and legislative conditions that may affect the client's plan?[8]

REPRESENTATION: Has the planner established the boundaries of his relationship so that the client knows what he will or will not do? Has the planner specified those limits in writing for all parties concerned?

Has the planner – in any way – denied the client the benefit of the knowledge and skill of another professional who could assist in serving the client?[9]

DILIGENCE: Did the planner do what was required in a reasonably prompt manner?

If the planner is responsible for preparing IRS forms, documents, affidavits, or other papers for the client, did he do so in a timely manner?

Did the planner advise a client promptly of any noncompliance, error, or omission having to do with a state or federal tax return or other document the client was required by law to complete?

COMMUNICATION: Did the planner return phone calls or answer letters promptly? Did he keep the client (and other professionals) informed on a regular basis of economic and legal changes that may affect the client's plans?

CONFIDENTIALITY: Did the planner keep client information confidential (except to the extent specifically authorized by the client to disclose it)?[10]

FEES: Did the planner charge fees that were reasonable and fair in light of the situation?[11] (Was the fee based on (1) the amount of work performed or the number of hours it took to do the work, (2) the difficulty and judgment involved in the problems that had to be solved, (3) the importance of the problem, and (4) his professional expertise, skill, and standing?)

Did the planner communicate, in writing, the formula by which fees or other charges would be based?

Has the planner billed, only after performing services in a satisfactory manner?

Has the planner refunded any advance fee that has not been fully earned?

CONFLICT OF INTEREST: Did the planner inform the parties he is representing of their respective rights and the pros and cons of the proposed action (or inaction) on each party?

Did the planner draft an instrument giving him or a member of his family an interest in the client's estate (assuming he is not a member of the client's family)?[12]

Has the planner written himself (or his partner) into the will as attorney for the estate and also as executor?

Has the planner used the special knowledge he has to the detriment of the client in any way?

Does the planner represent two parties who have or are likely to have conflicting interests?[13] (This problem is known as "simultaneous representation.") If so, is the planner satisfied that he can perform adequately and did he make full disclosure to, and obtain consent from, the parties?[14]

Has the planner, in any way, allowed the pursuit of financial gain or any other personal benefit to interfere with the exercise of sound professional judgment and skills?[15]

Has the planner made full disclosure of any obvious conflicts of interest in writing to the client?

Has the planner drawn an instrument that exonerates him from liability that may be incurred in another role (such as the attorney who may also serve as executor)?[16]

DISCLOSURE: Has the planner (or his associates, partners, or employer), in any other way, breached his duty of loyalty to the client by failing to disclose information?

Has the planner withheld information from another professional or governmental official that it is important and appropriate for that person to know?

Has the planner misrepresented the benefits, costs, or limitations of any estate planning tool or technique or failed to fully explain the advantages and disadvantages of viable alternatives?[17]

DIRECT CONTACT: Has the planner obtained information directly from the client or was it obtained second or third hand from another party or advisor acting as a conduit?[18]

COURTESY: Has the planner's courtesy extended not only to the client, but also to the other professionals who seek to serve that person?[19]

PUBLIC REGARD: Has the planner followed the laws applicable to his business and professional activities?[20]

Has the planner done what he can to raise the level of integrity and professionalism and avoided activities that detract from the opinion the public has of his profession?

Has the planner impaired the reputation of another practitioner?

Has the planner competed unfairly?

Has the planner used his degree or designation in less than a responsible or dignified or appropriate manner?

Does the planner avoid associating with those who are not ethical?

Has the planner provided the public with useful and objective information concerning potential problems, possible solutions, and impartial advisory opinions?

Has the planner attempted – in all dealings with the public – to avoid the appearance of impropriety?

MENTORING: Has the planner helped others enter the profession? Has he helped them attain and retain competence?

Has the planner encouraged and assisted others in obtaining higher levels of professional competence?

It is not enough to NOT advocate, sanction, participate in, or carry out an unethical act. Professional ethics require more than merely NOT doing the things you should not do. It forbids condoning the unethical act of another and requires taking positive action to do the things that should be done.

Ethics are a reminder that the estate planner is more of a counselor than an advocate, more of an advisor than a scholar. Ethics reinforce the importance of the role of all the members of the estate planning team as intermediaries and protectors who look out for the overall best interests of the family unit in recommending a course of action.

Ethics do not demand absolute, unreasoning, and undivided loyalty to a single client nor does it demand saint-like perfection in any other area. But ethics has its (generally quite affordable) price – professional honesty, integrity, and competence compatible with the realities of modern practice. In fact, the increased pride and

respect gained from others (and ourselves) is well worth the price. Can any planner afford not to pay it?

CHAPTER ENDNOTES

1. See *Code of Professional Ethics of the American Institute for Property and Liability Underwriters.*

2. See "For the Long Term — Professional Ethics and The Life Underwriter," *Life Association News*, December 1985, for an excellent discussion on that subject. Dr. Clarence C. Walton, the author of that article, states that among the characteristics of a mature professional are:

   A. Primary commitment to the interest of the client,

   B. Possession of expert knowledge,

   C. Self regulation, and

   D. Awareness of the long term consequences of his or her action

   Dr. Walton provides excellent guidelines for organizations that sincerely wish to promote and enforce a code of ethics.

3. Information on the Code of conduct for your profession should be obtained by writing to the appropriate national organization to which you belong. Attorneys should write to Information Officer, Office of Professional Ethics, American Bar Association, Chicago, Ill., for information on the ABA's Model Rules of Professional Conduct.

4. Attorneys working in this field will find excellent guidance from "Ethical Issues In Estate Practice" printed as part of the ESTATE PRACTICE UPDATE of the Pennsylvania Bar Institute, 104 South Street, Harrisburg, Pa. 17108.

5. See "Estate Planners: Where Do Your Ethics Lie?," *Trusts and Estates*.

6. The duties of a professional to the IRS are spelled out in IRS circular 230 which embraces, under a uniform standard, many of the traditional ethical and professional standards common to national professional organizations. See "Regulations within the IRS," *Trusts and Estates*, April 1990, p. 30.

7. See "Draft Statement of Principles Comes not a Moment too Soon," *Trusts and Estates*, December 1988, p. 12. For instance, a competent attorney may serve in other fiduciary roles such as an executor or trustee. One competent to handle the role of attorney may not have the training or skill (or time) to serve as an executor or trustee.

8. *The Code of Professional Responsibility of the Society of Financial Service Professionals* states, "A member shall continually improve his/her professional knowledge, skill, and competence." Furthermore, application of that rule "requires, at a minimum, meeting the applicable continuing education standards set by state licensing authorities, the Society of Financial Service Professionals, the American College, the CFP Board of Standards, and any other entity with appropriate authority over the member's license(s) or other credentials."

9. For instance, by making an unfair comparison between a person who has a license, degree, or designation, and one who does not.

   In an excellent *Trusts and Estates* article entitled, "ETHICS," the author, Frederic G. Corneel, poses a situation in which an insurance agent suggested to a consumer that he buy a very large amount of life insurance and adopt an estate plan including a revocable insurance trust. At the customer's request, the agent recommends a lawyer. The client tells the lawyer about his estate and the amount of insurance recommended to him. In the lawyer's opinion the amount of insurance is very much in excess of what is needed.

What should the lawyer do? Corneel answers that the lawyer must, of course, be guided by what he believes to be in the best interest of the client. But then he adds, "The other point for the lawyer to keep in mind is that he may well be mistaken in his evaluation of how much insurance is necessary or that, this may be a question of business, personal, or investment preference which the client is just as capable of making as the lawyer himself.

Corneel then states that "before giving his opinion to the client, however, the lawyer would be well advised to speak first with the insurance agent. The agent may have information or thought to bear on the problem that the lawyer has not considered and that might well affect his view on the matter. This is not only in the lawyer's interest, who by a simple telephone call may be kept from making a fool of himself, but it is in the interest of the client not to become the battlefield of a war among experts unless the war is unavoidable."

10. *The Code of Professional Responsibility of the Society of Financial Service Professionals* states, "A member shall respect the confidentiality of any information entrusted to, or obtained in the course of, the member's business or professional activities."

11. An excellent guide to the factors which affect attorney's fees in estate administration can be found in "Attorney's Fees in Estate Administration," *The Chase Review*, January 1990 (Chase Private Banking Group, 1211 Avenue of the Americas, New York, New York 10036).

12. See "Legal Ramifications of Unethical Estate Planning Practices," *Trusts and Estates*, October 1985, p. 47 for court response to situations in which (a) an attorney made himself legatee or devisee, (b) the attorney named himself or his partner as executor or trustee with powers to confer upon himself many of the benefits of ownership, (c) the attorney contrived to assure himself professional employment (together with a rather generous fee arrangement) representing the fiduciary in connection with the probate of a will or the administration of a trust.

13. It is quite common for a planner to work with several members of the same family. In planning, conflicts of interests may arise over (a) the exercise of tax elections or options, (b) the interpretation of a clause in a will or trust or other document, or (c) the exercise or non-exercise of discretionary authority by a fiduciary. The attorney represents multiple clients when providing advice for both spouses, parent and child, or testator and beneficiary. An excellent discussion of these conflicts can be found in the January 1990 issue of *The Chase Review*. See also "Conflicts of Interest in Estate Planning and Administration," *Trusts and Estates*, June 1984, p. 18.

14. QTIP planning presents inevitable conflicts of interest that demand full disclosure. For instance, "Is a QTIP trust contrary to the wishes or needs of a spouse who wants to obtain greater control of her spouse's property on his death?" "Is a large inter vivos intraspousal gift contrary to the interests of a wealthy spouse if some day in the future divorce occurs?"

The solution to multiple representation is, as mentioned in the body of this discussion, a "plain English" explanation of the meaning and personal impact of the planners' suggestions.

15. *Code of Professional Ethics of The American Institute for Property and Liability Underwriters, Inc.*

16. For instance, instruments should not include exculpatory provisions that would relieve the draftsperson of malpractice or malfeasance liability unless the instrument is reviewed by independent counsel for the instrument's creator.

17. Each professional must ask himself three questions:

A. What are the pros and cons of the viable alternatives?

B. Which alternatives offer the client and client's family or other intended beneficiaries the greatest financial security and the least overall cost?

C. What if the client does nothing?

Then these three issues must be shared with the client's other advisors and with the client.

18. Only through direct relations can a professional be sure that he has all of the relevant facts including an understanding of the client's objectives and fears and can make sure both parties fully understand each other.

19. *The Code of Professional Responsibility of the Society of Financial Service Professionals* states, "A member shall establish and maintain dignified and honorable relationships with those he/she serves, with fellow practitioners, and with members of other professions."

20. *The Code of Professional Responsibility of the Society of Financial Service Professionals* states, "A member has the duty to know and abide by the local, state, and national laws and regulations and all legal limitations pertaining to the member's professional activities."

Chapter 6

MALPRACTICE IN ESTATE PLANNING

"You have a malpractice case if there is no reasonable explanation for a terrible result."[1]

More technically stated, when a professional breaches the duty owed to another party and the other party is injured as a result of that breach, there is malpractice.[2]

Errors in estate planning and estate tax constitute the third most common type of legal malpractice.[3]

Reducing the risk of a malpractice suit and enhancing available defenses is the subject of this discussion.

"TARGET OF OPPORTUNITY" – WHY ME?

Those professionals wise enough to know that malpractice is a disease that may attack anyone will not ask the question, "Why Me?" Instead, they will ask, "When?" Malpractice claims are made uncomfortably often against those who – out of ignorance, arrogance, or incompetence – thought it could not happen to them. Suits are also brought against those estate planners with fine reputations who honestly thought they had done everything right. It is a dangerous misconception to think that only those who are clearly sloppy and unethical encounter malpractice claims.[4]

Mere good faith and honest intent will not protect the practitioner who has caused a client loss. It may be true that an estate planner will not be held liable for the failure to foresee the ultimate resolution of a debatable point of law or for an error in judgment if he acts in good faith and in an honest belief that his advice and acts are well founded and in the best interest of his client.[5] But such an estate planner can still be sued and still incur most of the costs of someone who in fact is guilty of malpractice.

Who are likely "targets of opportunity"?

DEEP POCKETS. When clients sue, they sue everyone in sight. But the bulk of the litigation effort is understandably against those from whom recovery is most likely. Your firm's appearance of success is a magnet. Furthermore, "judges and juries alike may be inclined to assess the loss of the poor helpless individual

against the large, seemingly impersonal institution that manages billions of dollars every day."[6] This problem is particularly evident where the defendant is a trust, insurance company, or large law firm.

INSURANCE. Certainly one contributing factor is the common knowledge that professionals carry insurance for malpractice. Almost all professionals in the financial services field carry one or more high limit insurance coverages. Some plaintiffs feel they are not suing the professional; they are suing the insurer.

TOUTED EXPERIENCE, SKILL, AND KNOW-LEDGE. In general, professionals who obtain or retain clients by holding themselves out as possessing a higher level of skill than other practitioners will be held to that higher level. If an advisor's business card says, "Estate Planner" or "Tax Specialist" or he has an advanced degree or a CFP, CLU, ChFC or otherwise advertises greater expertise or skill than an ordinary practitioner, he is expected to exercise that expertise or skill.[7]

IMPERSONAL. It is far easier to sue a party perceived as a "giant institution guided by computers rather than people" than to sue a long time advisor who has served with warmth, openness, compassion and has provided substantial personal attention in a respectful manner. This public image of banks, insurance companies, large law firms, and other institutions as impersonal money machines can best be changed from the top down by an insistence on courtesy and attention to the client from everyone in the firm.

BIG GUY vs LITTLE GUY. There is a feeling in this country, right or wrong, that the "Big Guys" are using their weight to beat up on the "Little Guys." So when the little guy gets into the judicial system, a jury may feel sympathetic and tend to punish the big guy with an angry vengeance.

FRUSTRATION WITH THE LAW(S). The potential for malpractice increases in proportion to both the complexity, speed of change, and labyrinthine interrelationship of various federal and state corporate, tax, probate, and securities laws – and clients' confusion and frustration. From the estate planner's point of view, the combination is a nightmare. If the planner feels this way, think of how angry clients must be when told that last year's law is now out and all the time, money, and emotional energy must be invested all over again.[8]

SIMPLE LIABILITY vs. COMPOUND LIABILITY

One author who both sues and defends members of estate planning teams said, "There are basically two types of malpractice liability: Simple and Compound (may be read "expensive" and "grossly expensive")."[9]

Simple liability is for simple errors in judgment or simple negligence. These mistakes are expensive but are part of the (reducible) costs of doing business. Missing a tax deadline or miscomputing a liquidity need would be examples of simple liability.

Compound liability is for gross breach of fiduciary duty, self-dealing, active concealment, fraud, oppression, and gross negligence. The author stated that "Gross negligence is usually accompanied by a fatal dose of institutional arrogance, an always fatal disease for which there is no known cure."[10] Lack of respect and common courtesy often turn what could otherwise have been a minor incident into a major, expensive legal battle.

TO WHOM IS ONE LIABLE?

This question is not always as easy to answer as it sounds. The simple answer is one is liable to those who employ you. The general rule is that a duty is only to the person with whom contracted, your client.

But one may also be liable to others as well.[11] For example, an insurance agent may have created an agency relationship with the purchaser of a life insurance policy. This would make him or her the agent of the insurance company for some purposes and agent of the client for others.

An advisor is not liable – even for an act of negligence – to someone to whom he owes no duty.[12] The legal term is "privity." But the defense that there is no privity, no duty to an injured party, can easily be forfeited and is currently being eroded in the courts.[13] For instance, if you advise the president of a family-owned corporation improperly about the appropriateness of a stock redemption plan and one is established because of reliance on your advice, unexpected dividend taxes upon the purchase by the corporation of its stock could be claimed by another family member shareholder.

This six-pronged test may be used to determine privity[14]:

1. To what extent is the transaction intended to benefit the third person?

2. Can harm to that third person be foreseen?

3. How likely is it that the third person will suffer real injury?

4. How close is the connection between the advisor's conduct and the injury that the third party could suffer?

5. How "morally wrong" is the advisor's action?

6. Would future harm to this or some other client be served by finding privity here?

At least one state will grant "standing" (the right to sue) to a narrow class of third party beneficiaries where it is clear that the client intended to benefit that party and the client is unable to enforce the contract.[15] Generally, for a third party to collect, written evidence must show that the client's intent was frustrated and the beneficiary's loss was a direct result of the planner's negligence.

WHAT CAN GET THE ADVISOR INTO TROUBLE?

IF ONE SAYS HE KNOWS, HE'D BETTER. Estate planning is too complex to be a sideline. Failure to exercise reasonable care and skill in performing duties for a person induced to rely on an advisor because of his professed skills, knowledge, or experience ("John Jones, Estate Planner") can result in liability for loss incurred.[16] Failure to exercise the degree of expertise that one professes to possess coupled with inducing reliance on that assertion to achieve a sale or sell a service creates a duty to act properly.[17] If one holds himself out as an expert and directly or indirectly promises to provide a product or service to serve a specific purpose or accomplish a particular objective, he assumes the liability for the achievement of that purpose or objective.[18] The skill, knowledge, diligence, and care used must equal or exceed that standard ordinarily exercised by others in the same profession.[19] In short, if one calls himself a professional (or by action or inaction allow others to rely on him as such), he must assume the responsibilities and duties generally associated with such a status – or be held liable for the client's loss.

NOT KNOWING WHO THE CLIENT IS. Interview both spouses (separately if appropriate). If there is marital discord or if this is a second marriage, consider recommending separate counsel. If "the couple" is perceived as the client, both should be treated accordingly. Do not talk down to or ignore the younger, or female, or less wealthy spouse – or to some other member of the family. Develop and maintain good relationships with all the members of the client's family to the extent appropriate.

There are many cases where the planner never or seldom meets the client. For instance, assume a will was prepared for a husband and wife on the instructions of the husband. If the planner never met the wife, how can it be argued that she has been properly represented by counsel or that she understood what she signed? The situation is a "lack of informed consent" case in the making.

When a spouse chooses not to read documentation or does not want to listen to complicated tax law, that same problem exists even though caused by his or her own inaction. The solution is to commit both parties – in the engagement letter – to read documents prepared for them within a specified time and to encourage them to seek independent counsel of their choice should either feel that is appropriate.

IF ONE SAYS HE WILL, HE'D BETTER. An advisor should never create false expectations by making promises he has no intention of keeping or by promising results he does not know he can deliver. He may be held liable to the beneficiaries of an estate if he promises to keep them informed of significant developments and then does not.[20] He has an obligation to substantially finish the task he has begun for a client, decline the appointment, or with the client's consent, accept the employment and associate a lawyer who is competent. He must also prepare adequately for, and give appropriate attention to, the work he has accepted.

OVERNIGHT EXPRESS. Clients often want insurance issued and wills drawn almost overnight – at the very time when they are about to leave on an extended vacation or business trip. This means there is insufficient time to collect, analyze, and act upon complete asset information. Deathbed planning is more of the same only worse. One should refuse to be rushed (but be prepared to work quickly).

HOW DOES ONE STAY OUT OF TROUBLE?

HIRING – AND FIRING – THE CLIENT. The advisor should ask why the client has chosen him. It is flattering to think that one has been selected because of one's expertise or reputation, but the reason may be because another practitioner decided not to represent the client. One should obtain as much information about the client's background with other professionals as possible before agreeing to work with the client. The first interview should be considered a primary opportunity to screen and qualify the client. Perhaps the potential client should be discarded if he seems to be a perfectionist, unrealistic, hurried, angry, overly optimistic, overly fee-conscious, or if he wants services one is not positive he can provide cost effectively.[21] One should beware of clients who are wealthy but in constant cash flow difficulty, seem immature, refuse to accept responsibility for their own actions, or appear constantly ambivalent.[22] These personality types are likely to present a future litigation problem.

Trust your instincts. One should turn down a client who requests something that is not quite right. If a client has outgrown the advisor's capacity, he should either recommend another firm or bring a specialist in to work with the client. If the advisor feels the client cannot be trusted, he should refuse to work with the client.

RISK-TAKING PROPENSITY. One of the biggest causes of claims is that the professional misjudges or never considers or does not reevaluate the risk-taking propensity of the client and the client's beneficiaries as their circumstances change. The solution is constant communication.

EXPERTISE BOUNDARIES. The advisor should do only those things he is competent (and licensed) to do – and do those things competently. Should a life insurance agent review a will or trust? Should an attorney or accountant judge the adequacy or appropriateness of a client's life insurance portfolio? Should a trust company review documents? Should a financial planner serve as trustee?[23]

Document examination exposure is real. Should one disclaim any liability for review of document viability or efficacy? Incompetent, inconsistent, and informal review is a formula for disaster. If the task is undertaken, it should be done by a person with the appropriate training, expertise, and time to do the job competently and enthusiastically. "You assume an obligation to your client to undertake reasonable research in an effort to ascertain relevant legal principles and to make an informed decision as to a course of action based on an intelligent assessment of the problem."[24]

Furthermore, the estate planner has a duty to either avoid involving a client in "murky" areas of the law if there are viable alternative tools or techniques that are available or to inform the client of the risks and let the client make the decision.[25]

Lack of specialized investment knowledge on the part of the planner or fiduciary often results in investment problems. Numerous trust funds are managed by individuals who adopt a passive and simplistic approach. The need for professional investment management and the complexity of modern portfolio theory is ignored or overlooked and too little time is spent in making investment decisions or addressing overall investment policy and asset allocation.[26]

RESOURCE LIMITS. The advisor should not accept engagements that will require resources beyond what he can cost effectively deliver. For example, if his operation does not have the backup personnel to properly service a high number of clients, he should not agree to do estate conservation for a firm's top 100 executives.

OUTSIDE EXPERTS. An advisor should seek help before it is needed. When appropriate, he should recommend that another professional be used, either in his place or together with him. If the advisor makes a specific recommendation, he may be held liable for the actions of that professional. One way to protect himself is by giving out the names of at least three qualified professionals (make sure the criteria for "qualified" extends beyond mere reputation), or stay involved with the representation.

THE "ENGAGEMENT LETTER"

The engagement letter is the first and primary step in insulating oneself from a successful malpractice suit. An engagement letter should be obtained in every client relationship at the first possible time. The letter spells out the extent and limits of the services to be performed. The following are critical elements of such a letter:

- Scope of services and description of work product;

- Period of time covered;

- Responsibilities undertaken;

- Responsibilities the client is expected to assume;

- Fee arrangements -- amount, terms, and frequency of billing;

- Arrangements for update and extension of service;

- List of parties represented – and exclusion of those not represented;

- Intended use and potential distribution (or restriction) of the advisor's work product[27]; and

- Client's acceptance signature and date.

PUT IT (ALL) IN WRITING

Protecting one's self means meticulous record keeping starting at the onset of the relationship. Changes in risk-taking propensity or attitude of the client or his family, comments at meetings, phone conversations, and other special instructions should be noted. The advisor's files should clearly reflect and support his recollection of events and should be dictated and transcribed as soon as possible after the occurrence (or preferably contemporaneous with the events). The more complete and organized the files, the more likely the judge, jury, or board of arbitrators will consider the advisor's word persuasive (assuming, of course, the files corroborate what he is now saying).

Whenever possible, quote the client's exact words.[28] This is particularly important whenever a client – or one of his other advisors – decides to pursue an aggressive tax policy or take an investment risk (and doubly important if one has advised against that course of action). For instance, if an attorney tells a client that the business does not need all of the life insurance the agent is suggesting, the agent should attempt to take down as accurately as possible the exact words of the attorney. The attorney should do the same.

Contemporaneous and near verbatim notes should also be taken if the client asks that the advisor not do a service (or anything) he would normally do or if the client asks him to attempt a service that he ordinarily would not do. For instance, if the client asks a trust officer not to review a will and trust that the bank will be handling, the trust officer should memorialize the request (and probably treat the request with suspicion).

Detailed notes are particularly important if the client seems uncooperative or unwilling to provide the information or documents (or access to personally interview a family member) that are necessary to do the job properly.

FEES. Fees should not be set at levels that will require cutting corners or operating at a loss for this engagement. The fee must be large enough to justify internally the time that should be invested in a case — or the case should be turned down. Fees should include the costs that will be incurred to meet high ethical standards and avoid malpractice by implementation of systematic quality control and other appropriate courses of action.

A fee dispute which results in litigation with a client may trigger a malpractice case. The solution is to secure a written agreement as to fees and billing procedures at the onset of the relationship with the client. One should think carefully about the wisdom of suing the client and the likelihood and expense of a malpractice lawsuit by the client. It is wise to communicate the basis or rate of fee or other method of compensation to a new client in writing before or as soon as possible after the relationship begins. The client should be billed periodically and provided detailed information of the services rendered and the time invested.

DATA FORMS. Many times the error or omission of the estate planner is due to an incomplete or incorrect understanding of the facts. The advisor should obtain comprehensive and accurate data by developing a data gathering system. Some planners feel they can gather data without forms or checklists but inevitably forget to ask questions such as, "Are both you and your spouse U.S. citizens?" or "Have you named yourself the custodian of a Uniform Transfers to Minors Account for gifts you made to your children?" One must be sure to confirm with the client the facts gathered – before acting upon them.

The advisor should verify property ownership and dispositive arrangements from the documents themselves. It is astounding how often otherwise competent attorneys draft wills and trusts that do not match the way property is owned. The forms should match the facts. It is necessary to check wills, divorce agreements, retirement and employee benefit documents rather than rely on the client's memory. Current life insurance policy information should be confirmed by writing to the insurer.

REPRESENTATION AS TO PRODUCTS. When the planner is recommending investments or insurance and, particularly if the planner is receiving a commission based on the sale, there must be a clear writing, acknowledged by the client signing, to the effect of avoiding any basis for unreasonable reliance.

With the sale of mutual funds, the warning language in the typical prospectus is worth adding to the writing to be signed by the client (e.g., that past performance is not recognized as a basis for future results, etc.).

With insurance products, there should be written recognition that all pages of the proposal have been read and understood. It would be very helpful to have the client sign the part that shows the guaranteed figures.

A significant potential problem is the rate of variable life insurance products where the return based on past performance is quite high. When or if the market turns down and the earnings evaporate, the client will only recall the high returns and will be looking for someone to blame for the disappointing results of increased premiums or lower cash value or face amount of coverage.

Some planners are reluctant to risk the possibility that the client may not go forward with the recommended action if the planner makes a point of the possible negative aspects of the transaction. However, the planner's long term reputation and success, as well as freedom from future claims, argue strongly for "getting it in writing" at the time of the decision of the client to go forward.

LIMITS OF THE RELATIONSHIP

The client's instructions must be followed – correctly. This entails first truly understanding what those instructions are. Then it requires a written memorandum (preferably signed by the client). Meticulous records of all conversations should be made. If investments are or will be involved in the relationship, an investment policy should document agreed-upon investment objectives, risk parameters, return targets, volatility tolerance, and asset allocation ranges.

A written consent should be obtained for actions outside the scope of the relationship as contained in the engagement letter.

RECORDS AND SYSTEMS

THE RIGHT STUFF. The advisor should keep research documents that indicate decisions were made in a methodical and logical manner and that a deliberate investigation preceded and supported each suggestion. Documents which illustrate the tax law as it existed at the time tax decisions were made should be retained.[29] Memos to the file, prepared contemporaneously with conversations with a client and decision making, are highly useful in establishing the background and intent at the time an action was taken. Controversial decisions should be made only with the informed knowledge and written consent of the client. Any oral advice should also be documented immediately.

The advisor needs to develop and use a presentation system that will prove that regular discussions covering all of the important areas of estate planning with a client took place.[30] A checklist should be incorporated into that system in order to demonstrate that these issues have been discussed with the client and reflect the client's circumstances and objectives.

A retrieval system should be established to locate documents or plans that need updating for specific changes. For example, all estate planning clients should have been contacted to review wills and trusts drawn prior to September 13, 1981 because of the change to the unlimited marital deduction. Yet each year dozens of cases and rulings occur because the documents were never updated. Were the clients ever informed by their advisors of the need for a document review?

TRIGGER SYSTEM. A checklist of follow-up procedures should be developed so time-sensitive responsibilities will be met by the appropriate parties and unreasonable delays in the preparation and implementation of the plan can be avoided. Set deadlines, establish priorities, and specify responsibilities. Create a "tickler file (docketing system) to meet all deadlines, statutes of limitations, and filing and payment deadlines. Set up a centralized system to personally remind the party responsible for action and review at given times or events. Incorporate into the system a series of client reminders (e.g., "It's been three years since your will was reviewed…" or "Major new tax law changes suggest we should review your estate plan as soon as possible").

QUALITY CONTROL

An advisor is responsible for the errors or omissions of his partners, associates, and employees. Quality control is therefore not a luxury. It is a business necessity.

UNDERSTANDING OF ETHICAL ISSUES. According to an article on malpractice, written by a Commissioner of the Texas Board of Legal Specialization, almost half the candidates who sat for the certification in Texas in Estate Planning and Probate Law demonstrated "a profound lack of knowledge of ethical problems that often lead to professional liability claims."[31] One should discuss with colleagues the danger when a breach of

ethics is coupled with an angry or disgruntled client or family member.

WHO IS THE QUARTERBACK? In any operation larger than a one-person firm, it is essential that the activities of the entire staff are coordinated by a "quarterback" who accepts responsibility. This person must be sure that all staff members are kept informed and that there is a logical and automatic flow of necessary information, that no tasks have been overlooked, and that no efforts are duplicated. He must also be sure that information received by staff members is properly recorded and relayed to him and to the central file on each client. For instance, consider the lawsuit potential if the beneficiary of an estate dies within nine months of the original decedent and the same trust company serves as executor of both estates. If significant taxes could be saved by a timely disclaimer but two separate individuals are assigned to the two estates and they do not communicate with each other, the lost opportunity when the timely disclaimer period expires could turn into a lawsuit.

There should also be a quarterback for the estate planning team. All members of that team are negligent if they do not come to an agreement as to who is to do what and when each task is to be done. Liability occurs when essential tasks fall through the cracks.

INDEPENDENT REVIEW. An effective method of quality control is to have final products be reviewed by a well-qualified associate before it is shared with a client.

REVIEW OF STAFF COMPETENCE, EXPERIENCE, QUALIFICATION. Estate planning, almost by definition, requires the input of many professionals. Most planners not only must cooperate with other planners outside their offices but must also rely on paralegal and associates within their offices. Few full-blown estate plans contain no issues other than federal or estate death taxes and quite often the planner seeks advice from others on his staff. Staff members must be currently competent, and they must be well trained in and conform to standardized office procedures, policies, and proper file management techniques. Appropriate supervision for all levels of staff should be built in. Continuing education should be part of any firm's ongoing business plan.

EXTERNAL COMMUNICATIONS

Almost every authority who speaks and every article that is written on malpractice states that many lawsuits could probably have been avoided by a simple solution: "Communicate, Communicate, Communicate!"[32]

Many, or even most, of the grievance complaints and malpractice actions can be headed off if the advisor will:

MAKE IT CLEAR AND MAKE IT OFTEN. The estate planner should avoid technical jargon. He should not assume lay persons understand what he means by such terms as "a marital trust," a "durable power of attorney," or "a unified credit." He can use word pictures, graphs, flow charts, or diagrams to illustrate his points – and give the clients copies to take home.[33]

He should continually inform clients of all actions he and his staff have taken (or not taken); forward to clients copies of documents sent to other professionals; provide the client with periodic written reports even if a particular report merely explains why no progress has been made since the last report; and confirm in writing all transactions, expenses, fees, income, or other events of importance.

He should inform the client of any changes in the relationship or responsibilities of the parties; make sure reports are understandable; and use graphs, charts, and checklists to show the progress he has made.

He should confirm through a series of scheduled meetings among the client and other advisors objectives, responsibilities, and timetables.

A newsletter is a good way to keep in touch with clients on a regular basis.

The advisor should schedule regular reviews and give special emphasis to contacting clients from whom he has not heard or had contact with in a given period of time; and document his attempt to contact those who do not respond.

He should keep copies of all correspondence and conversations with other members of the estate planning team working with the client.

He should study the client's verbal and body language to be sure he is understood and encourage the client to call or write to him after the meeting to ask questions if "he has not made himself understood."

AVOID CASUAL OR INFORMAL ADVICE. The advisor should not give advice at cocktail parties or other social events.[34] Liability can be imposed even though you have not charged a fee for your services if a client relies on information you have provided.

CALLING BACK – PROMPTLY. A careful advisor will return telephone calls promptly. If this is impossible, his secretary or an associate should do so for him so the client does not feel ignored.

AVOIDING "HEEL COOLING." A planner should not keep clients waiting on the phone or in his office. He should be sure he receives messages promptly – and accurately. He should not allow a phone call to interrupt a meeting with a client. It is a good idea to reward staff members for being extra polite. In short, give the client respect and common courtesy.

AVOIDING (OR NEUTRALIZING) PROBLEMS

CONFLICTS WITH EXISTING CLIENTS.[35] The duty of loyalty requires any estate planner to be extremely cautious about serving a client in more than one capacity. For instance, the client of an attorney or CPA may want that person to serve as an executor or trustee – while at the same time desiring that person to continue to provide planning advice and other services to various family members. Can the advice be disinterested and objective? Can the professional ethically charge fees for both services? Can those fees honestly be set at "arm's length"?

Corporate fiduciaries are particularly susceptible. For instance, could the banking side of an institution, as a lender, acquire and share non-public information about a borrower company with the trust department that, as an investor for its trust accounts, is considering making investments in the same company?[36] (Use of non-public information to make investment decisions might subject a corporate fiduciary to a violation of the SEC's Rule 10b-5.[37])

Although there is no legal prohibition against representing more than one client in a single transaction, estate planners should be particularly alert for situations in which there is an obvious or potential difference in their interests. For instance, in establishing a buy-sell agreement, a stock redemption plan may favor younger shareholders with lower percentages of ownership at the expense of older shareholders who own a larger percentage of the company's stock. Likewise, a defined benefit plan typically favors older, long service employees while profit-sharing and defined contribution pension plans usually are to the benefit of younger employees.

Another conflict of interest problem that often occurs where more than one person is represented is the disclosure of confidential information. Can an estate planner freely tell a wife what her husband has disclosed? Can a planner share information from one shareholder with others? The planner needs to inform all parties that information may not be privileged or confidential as to other members of the group unless specific direction is given.

Some conflicts of interest are unavoidable but must be recognized. For instance, consider the family that requests estate planning advice as a unit but who, as individuals, have different needs and desires. What should be done in a marital situation where a husband calls and requests a QTIP trust as opposed to the classic general power of appointment marital trust? What happens when there are children of a prior marriage and the client wants to make lifetime gifts to them? What if a client is ill or infirm in some way and is or becomes dependent on someone else for basic needs? How will the "undue influence issue" be handled? What are the planner's responsibilities and duties when a child, a charitable development officer, or another professional brings the case to him? What if that person also pays his fee?

Any possible conflicts of interest should be disclosed – in writing – to the client as quickly as possible or the planner should withdraw without disclosure if confidential information is involved. Recognition of disclosure and acceptance of its consequent risks should be acknowledged in any instrument signed by the client.

The planner should avoid or treat extremely carefully any financial involvement in a client's business or in a business venture.

CONFLICTS WITH FUTURE CLIENTS. Will acceptance of this client create a conflict for more desirable work with another client in the future?[38]

RED FLAG PROCEDURES. It is important for the planner to train himself and his staff to recognize "red flags." A procedure for identifying problems and quickly dealing with them is essential.

DEALING WITH PROBLEMS. The planner must routinely review and deal with problems promptly. If a problem occurs, he must call or write the client immediately and explain the problem and the potential consequences and alternatives. If a client is angry or dissatisfied, he ought to take immediate action – talk to the client and resolve the problem. He cannot safely assume the problem will go away or that the client will forget it.

THE PROBLEM TEAM. A good idea is to create a "Problem Team" in the firm that meets immediately every time the potential for a dissatisfied client is recognized. That team should not only review the file in the case in point but also any other procedures, activities, omissions, or oversights which may trigger future problems that could develop into litigation.

EARLY ACTIVE REMEDIAL CONCILIATORY EFFORTS. The quicker an attempt is made to resolve the problem to the client's satisfaction, the less likely there will be litigation. Providing a large apology might avoid writing a small check. Writing a small check might avoid defending a large lawsuit. One litigation attorney put it this way: "The good will that can be generated by such an act and accompanying attitudes might be much cheaper and better in the long run than paying expensive attorneys for years of litigation with an uncertain outcome."[39] Sometimes, assigning a new person to speak to the client will serve to quell the objection.

ABOUT YOUR MALPRACTICE INSURANCE

SUFFICIENT LEVELS OF COVERAGE. The first step in evaluating your current insurance is to see if you have enough insurance to cover any likely risk. But this is only a first step.

"CLAIMS MADE" POLICIES. Most malpractice coverage is sold on a "claims made" basis. This means the policy only covers claims that are first asserted and reported to the insurer within the policy year.

"PRIOR ACTS" COVERAGE. The cause of action alleging estate planning malpractice typically does not occur until years after the estate planning documents are signed. If the policy has a "prior acts" coverage, it covers a claim asserted during a policy year in which the negligence giving rise to the claim occurred in some prior year.[40] If a policy lacks or excludes prior acts or limits prior acts coverage, it is likely that there will be a "coverage gap." There will be no coverage under the policy in effect when the alleged negligence occurred because the claim was not made in that policy year. The current policy will not cover the alleged negligence because negligence alleged to have occurred before the present policy year is excluded or omitted from the coverage.

THE "TAIL." A tail is an extended reporting option somewhat related to prior acts coverage. If one purchases a tail, he is permitted (usually at the end of each policy year or earlier if the policy is canceled during the term) to convert "claims made" coverage to "occurrence" coverage for any negligence allegedly committed – but not yet reported – up to the end of that policy year. The extended reporting of claims option available through a tail is expensive. The premium is a multiple of the regular annual premium. Tails should be considered by retiring planners who will no longer keep their full malpractice coverage in force or by attorneys who are forced to switch malpractice insurance carriers because of a cancellation or a refusal of a carrier to renew coverage (typically due to claims made) if the new carrier refuses to provide prior acts coverage. Tails are "cut off" after some period of time unless the tail is unlimited. Under an unlimited tail, the insurer remains liable for negligence occurring before the policy period expires regardless of when the claim is asserted.

THE DEDUCTIBLE. Most estate planners opt for a higher deductible in order to reduce the premium outlay. But one should check to see if the legal costs he would incur in a malpractice suit apply against his share of the deductible. Does the deductible apply "per claim" or "per policy year"? Where there is more than one claim in a given policy year, a per claim deductible becomes a hidden cost: a second deductible must be satisfied in the event of a second claim within a year. A per year deductible means the deductible amount need be paid only once in a given year regardless of the number of claims. Because when it rains, it pours, a per claim provision might prove quite costly.

SETTLEMENT. Some policies give the insurer the right to limit its exposure through a provision entitled, "Settlement." This means the insurer can force a settlement with the plaintiff (regardless of the insured's wishes) because of the cost. Some settlement provisions state that if one does not wish to settle under specified terms, the insurer will limit its payment to the amount specified in a settlement agreement at which point all other exposure (including defense cost) becomes the insured's obligation. Why might an insured not want to settle – even though economically it might make sense? The psychological cost of admitting wrongdoing or malpractice – coupled with the loss in reputation – are strong reasons why he may want to maintain the right to say "NO" to a settlement. One should be sure that right does not expose him to a loss of coverage above the limits in the proposed settlement.

DUTY TO DEFEND vs. DUTY TO INDEMNIFY. A "duty to defend" policy requires the insurer to appoint defense counsel and pay that attorney's fees as billed. An "indemnification" policy allows the insured to select counsel but he must fund his defense unless he can reach an interim fee agreement.[41] The insured will not be reimbursed for defense costs until the case is concluded. Obviously, interim funding can be a problem.

DEFINITION OF "DAMAGES." The way covered damages is defined is crucial. One may be exposed to fines, penalties, punitive, or even treble, damages. Check with the insurance agent to clarify how broadly or narrowly the policy construes the term "damages."

INNOCENT PARTNER COVERAGE. Does the policy provide coverage for the defalcations of another member of the firm? One is liable for his partner's embezzlement even if he has not benefited by it. The insurer will deny a claim based on your partner's fraud and/or criminal activity unless there is "innocent partner" coverage.

OTHER KEY PROVISIONS. A malpractice policy ideally will provide coverage for the defense costs if it is claimed the insured is guilty of intentional conduct (even though the policy does not indemnify the costs of the intentional conduct). Does the policy cover libel or slander or defense of RICO claims?

INSURER'S STABILITY. It is important to check the financial stability of the insurer and to be sure the insurer has a solid reputation for integrity and responsiveness. It is worth finding out if the insurer itself has been involved in litigation with its own insureds. The lowest premium will not compensate you for the aggravation and other costs of suing the carrier to get it to defend properly a malpractice case.

HANDLING A CLAIM. A detailed discussion of malpractice claims procedures is beyond the scope of this chapter. However, the following steps will help in the defense of a malpractice suit:

1. Notify the insurer immediately no matter how small the suit is.

2. Once the insured has been notified formally that he is being sued, say as little as necessary to the suing client.

3. Secure all work product immediately.

4. Inform the entire staff of the problem and the action game plan.

5. Do whatever is necessary to assist in the defense of the case.

THE TOTAL COST

The frequency of malpractice actions can be expected to increase. No profession in the estate planning team will escape unscathed.[42]

DIRECT COSTS. Malpractice premiums are in the highest classification – along with corporate securities work – for a very good reason. The dollars at risk are big.

LOSS OF REPUTATION. The cost of a malpractice suit cannot be measured merely in terms of the court judgment or out-of-court settlement or the cost of attorneys. The cost to a professional's reputation (win or loose) may be staggering. For instance, it would be difficult to attract new partners or new associates if one has been successfully sued for malpractice.

LOSS OF STANDING WITH PEERS. Estate planning is a process based partially on knowledge and largely on trust. A malpractice suit calls into question competence which in turn destroys confidence, not only of current and potentially future clients but also the confidence of other members of the planning team with whom one must deal.

THE PSYCHOLOGICAL TRAUMA. An estate planner who becomes a defendant in a lawsuit must deal with the incredible pressure and emotional trauma of being sued.[43] Often, the planner (and perhaps office associates, partners, and friends) will see the action taken by the client as an attack on his professional ability, integrity, or judgment. This cannot help the practitioner's morale and will probably result in adverse fallout on other projects. This psychological strain is compounded by time; the legal process is typically long and drawn out over a period of years even if the claim is unfounded.

HIDDEN ECONOMIC COSTS. Colleagues from whom the practitioner received referrals and the general public may hear about the lawsuit. This will cause almost certain financial damage. The planner is required to participate in his own defense whether or not he is adequately insured. This, in turn, translates into dozens or sometimes hundreds of unbillable hours gathering facts and records and recreating the facts, giving depositions, briefing defense attorneys, and testifying at trial.

CUT AND RUN? If it appears a matter cannot be resolved by the procedures discussed above, consider "discharging the client." Obviously, this is a last resort but it should not be overlooked in a "heads they win – tails we lose situation."

SUMMARY

Creating and maintaining a successful estate planning practice requires a methodical systematic approach to risk management. Planners are vulnerable to litigation no matter how careful they are. But the risk of a claim and the potential for a successful claim can be substantially reduced through continuing a vigorous and systematized policy of internal and external positive communication, common sense courtesy, quality control, and a strong emphasis on high quality continuing education of every member of the firm.

A planner should check that he has:

- Established and improved client relationships.

- Controlled the management of client relationships.

- Improved office practices.

- Identified problem areas.

- Corrected problems before they occur.

Looking at everything in this discussion positively, the "action suggestions" described here can also be thought of not only as defensive but as the blueprint for a vigorous office organizing and client market building campaign.

CHAPTER ENDNOTES

1. Attorney Jack Olendar of Washington, D.C. quoted in "Avoiding Malpractice Suits: Some Sound Advice," *Trusts and Estates*, April 1990, p. 18. Another good rule of thumb mentioned in this same well written article is that "we have a true and grievous malpractice claim" where the facts and results would "surprise and dismay the average trust and estate lawyer."

2. Legal malpractice consists of three elements: (a) a duty, (b) a breach of duty, and (c) resulting damages.

3. "How Estate Planners Can Cope with the Increasing Risk of Malpractice Claims," *Estate Planning*, May 1985.

4. See "Avoiding Malpractice Suits: Some Sound Advice," *Trusts and Estates*, April 1990, p. 12.

5. This is called the "best judgment" or "good faith" defense.

6. "Corporate Fiduciaries Face Special Liability Problems," *Trusts and Estates*, December 1988, p. 29.

7. *Killey Trust*, 457 Pa. 474 (1974). Large corporate planners such as banks and trust companies will likely be held to a higher level of competence than others because of their access to information and expertise.

   On the other hand, the sophistication, education, and expertise of the client is not a defense. See *Blankenheim v. E.F. Hutton and Co. Inc.*, HOO4920 (Calif. Ct. App. 2/15/90), which held that the relationship between a stockbroker and his customer is fiduciary in nature, imposing on the former the duty to act in the highest good faith toward his customer. The court held that the plaintiff's concession that they were experts in the accounting and taxation area and any experience the plaintiff may have acquired following his investment was irrelevant to reliance on the broker's representations at the time of the sale.

8. Consider, for example, that the estate planner must consider the provisions of federal (and perhaps state) securities laws if the client holds more than 10 percent of a covered class of equity securities. Did you know that a malpractice claim might be converted into an unfair trade practice claim in order to gain the advantage of a longer statute of limitations? In one case the attorney drafted a trust that failed to qualify for the marital deduction. This action was barred by a 3-year statute of limitations. So the plaintiff also sued for a violation of the state's Unfair Trade Practice Act which had a much longer statute of limitations and allowed a suit by "any person who purchases or leases goods, services, or property." The estate successfully alleged that the draftsman had engaged in an unfair and deceptive act and practice by holding himself out as an attorney reasonably skilled in the preparation and drafting of last wills and testaments and in his ability to comply with the decedent's wishes and to minimize the tax obligations of her estate.

9. "Protecting the Corporate Fiduciary's Tender Backside," *Trusts and Estates*, February 1988, p. 63.

10. Adjectives which might characterize "institutional arrogance" include unreasonable, unknowledgeable, intransigent, implacable, belligerent, and rude.

11. See "Court Decisions Reinforce the Idea that an Insurance Agent Who Holds Himself Out to Have Great Expertise will be Bound to the Exercise of It," *Trusts and Estates*, October 1988, p. 55.

12. See *Bell v. Manning*, 613 S. W.2d 335.

13. *Lucas v. Hamm*, 15 Cal. Rptr. 821 (1961).

14. The California Supreme Court used this test in *Biakanja v. Irving*, 320 P.2d 16 (1958).

   Although there is a trend toward relaxing the requirement of privity, New York and Texas are staunch supporters of the rule. See *Victor v. Goldman*, 344 N.Y.S.2d 672 (1973) and *Dickey v. Jansen*, 731 S.W.2d 581 (1987).

15. Pennsylvania Supreme Court in *Guy v. Liederbach*, 459 A.2d 744 (1983).

16. See *Bogley v. Middletown Tavern, Inc.*, 421 A.2d 444 (1984). Of course, the knee jerk defense is, "The insurance was purchased in an arm's length transaction involving no confidential or fiduciary relationship between the insured and the agent." This tact might work if the agent never professed to be anything other than a salesperson. See *Lazovick v. Sun Life Ins. Co. of America*, 586 F. Supp. 918 (E.D. Pa. 1984).

17. See *Anderson v. Knox*, 297 F.2d 702 (9th Cir. 1961), cert. den., 370 U.S. 915 (1962); *Gediman v. Anheuser Busch, Inc.*, 299 F.2d 537 (2d Cir. 1962).

18. See *Wright Body Works v. Columbus Interstate Insurance*, 210 S.E. 2d 801 (1974).

19. *State Farm Life v. Fort Wayne National Bank*, 474 N.E. 2d 524 (Ind. 1985).

20. *Morales v. Field*, DeGoff, Huppert and MacGown, 99 Cal. Appl 3d 307.

21. See "Does This Prospect Mean Trouble?," *Practical Financial Planning*, October/November 1988, p. 23.

22. See "Reducing the Risk of Estate Planning Malpractice," BNA, *Tax Management Estates, Gifts, and Trusts Journal*, March/April 1984, p. 36.

23. See "How Not to be a Trustee," *Financial Planning*, May 1990, p. 69.

24. *Horne v. Peckham*, 97 Cal. App. 3d 404 (1979).

25. Where there is reasonable doubt among well informed practitioners, there should be no liability. But this assumes a diligent quest for answers was made. Failure to research an issue or fully understand the facts will result in a denial of the "unsettled law" defense. See *Martin v. Burns*, 429 P.2d 660 (1967).

26. See "Steps to Protect the Fiduciary from Liability for Investment Decisions," *Estate Planning*, July/August, 1989, p. 228.

27. In "Taming the Liability Monster," *L&H Perspective*, V. 15, No. 1/1989, p. 38, the author states that "A nightmare for the professional is reliance by unknown third parties on their work product." Where might this nightmare be more real than in estate planning where a great deal of it is done specifically for others? (Of course, it is the planner's responsibility to know who those third party beneficiaries are and what circumstances and needs and desires they may have).

28. As one attorney was interviewing a couple, he would pause from time to time to "capsulize" their thoughts into a dictaphone. Before he did, he would remind them each time, "Be sure to stop me if this isn't exactly what you want or if I've misunderstood what you've just said."

29. You may have to prove that, at the time you were making the decision, the available information was much different than it is at the time litigation occurs. See "How to Manage a Growing Tax Practice," *The Practical Accountant*, May 1990, p. 27.

30. See "Avoiding and Handling Malpractice Claims against Estate Planners," *Estate Planning*, September/October 1989, p. 267.

31. See "Avoiding Malpractice Suits: Some Sound Advice," *Trusts and Estates*, April 1990, p. 12.

32. See "Coping with Administrative Problems: There's More to Life and Death than Taxes," 21 *U. of Miami Institute on Estate Planning*, Chapter 17 (1987).

33. Some attorneys use commercially written brochures to make their points or to give clients something to take home that will help them understand more complex concepts.

34. See *Newton Estate*, TC Memo 1990-208, for an example of the damage a well intended but offhand remark can do. The executor's reliance on the statement of an attorney as to the filing deadline did not constitute reasonable cause for the filing delay where the attorney admittedly had not been retained to render advice on federal estate tax matters, was not paid any fee for the advice, did not normally practice in that area of the law, and had advised the executor to verify any information with a tax practitioner. The "offhand remark" may not result in a malpractice case for this attorney – but it certainly would not result in a love affair with the client either.

35. Consider an index which includes data on clients and other parties to transactions with which the firm is involved. Include a procedure through which the system automatically updates the files to add the names of new family members, business associates, or others related to the client.

36. "Corporate Fiduciaries Face Special Liability Problems," *Trusts and Estates*, December 1988, p. 29.

37. The classic solution is a corporate policy that restricts or limits the information flow between the banking and the trust departments.

38. Obtain a "Waiver of Conflict" letter with respect to one-time consulting arrangements. Obtain advance written consent to

future simultaneous adverse representation on any matter not substantially related to the matter undertaken for a new client.

39. "Protecting the Corporate Fiduciary's Tender Backside," *Trusts and Estates*, February 1988, p. 72.

40. See "About Your Malpractice," *Lawyer's Digest*, May 1988, p. 11.

41. "How the Accountant/Financial Planner can Reduce Exposure to Liability Claims," *The Practical Accountant*, February 1990, p. 15.

42. See "Taming the Liability Monster," *L&H Perspective*, Vol. 15/No. 1, 1989, p. 37.

43. See "Strategies to Avoid Malpractice," *Practical Financial Planning*, April/May 1989, p. 29.

Part 2:

OWNERSHIP AND
TRANSFER OF PROPERTY

Chapter 7

OWNERSHIP AND TRANSFER OF PROPERTY[1]

In order to plan an estate, it is necessary to know the ways in which property is owned and how property is transferred. The way in which property can be transferred can be dependent on the form of ownership. In addition, property transfers can involve gifts, contracts, wills, intestate succession, and trusts. There may even be certain limitations on how a person can transfer property. Forms of ownership and transfer of property are discussed broadly below. Gifts, wills, and trusts are discussed in even greater detail in other chapters.

OWNERSHIP OF PROPERTY

There are various ways in which property can be owned. In general, property is owned outright, as tenants in common, as joint tenants with rights of survivorship, or as community property.

Outright Ownership

Outright ownership is often as simple as: John owns an automobile, or Mary owns a diamond necklace. John and Mary are generally free to do whatever they want with their property. Of course, if John borrowed money to purchase the automobile, the lender generally has the right to recovery of any outstanding loan upon a transfer of the automobile. In this situation, although John may generally be free to use the automobile as he pleases, John can really transfer only the value of the automobile in excess of the loan.

Life Estate / Remainder

Sometimes outright ownership can be split into a life estate and a remainder. A person with a life estate is generally free to use the property or income from the property for life. The person with the remainder interest receives the property when the person with the life estate dies. For example, Mike owns a house. When Mike dies, Mike leaves the house so that his sister, Sally, can live in the house for her life. Sally has a life estate. When Sally dies, the property will pass to Mike's nephew, Bob. Bob has a remainder interest.

Tenancy in Common

A tenancy in common is a form of co-ownership of property. Tenants in common own an undivided right to possess property. Each tenant is generally free to transfer his interest in the property as he wishes.

Joint Tenancy with Right of Survivorship

Another form of co-ownership of property is a joint tenancy with right of survivorship. Joint tenants also have an undivided right to the enjoyment of property. However, when a joint tenant dies, that person's interest in the property passes to the remaining joint tenant or joint tenants. While a joint tenant is alive, a joint tenant can generally sever the joint tenancy or transfer his interest to another.

For example, Dad leaves a vacation home to his three children, Tom, Ann, and Rita, as joint tenants with right of survivorship. Ann dies first. The vacation home is then owned by Tom and Rita as joint tenants. Tom dies next. Rita succeeds to outright ownership of the vacation home.

Tenancy by the Entirety

In some states, a joint tenancy with right of survivorship between spouses is called a tenancy by the entirety. When one spouse dies, the jointly owned property passes to the surviving spouse. However, while both spouses are alive and married to each other, one spouse cannot terminate a tenancy by the entirety without the consent of the other spouse.

Community Property

Ten states have a form of ownership between spouses called community property. Those states are Alaska, Arizona, California, Idaho, Louisiana, Nevada, New Mexico, Texas, Washington, and Wisconsin.

In a community property state, each spouse owns a one-half interest in property acquired while the spouses are married. Each spouse is generally free to transfer his one-half interest in the property at death as he wishes. However, while both spouses are alive and married to each other, one spouse cannot dispose of the community property without the consent of the other spouse.

Community property can be important even if a couple does not currently live in a community property state. Community property generally remains community property even when the spouses move to a noncommunity property state.

Certain property is noncommunity property even if a couple live in a community property state. Property that a spouse acquired prior to marriage remains the separate property of that spouse. Also, property acquired individually by one spouse by gift or inheritance during marriage is also the separate property of that spouse. Additionally, property acquired by a couple prior to moving to a community property state would generally remain noncommunity property.

Spouses are generally free to make agreements regarding community property. For example, the spouses can agree that what would otherwise be community property is not community property.

TRANSFERS OF PROPERTY

Lifetime

During lifetime, a person can generally transfer interests the person owns by gift, either outright or in trust. See Chapter 22 regarding gifts.

At Death

At death, property generally passes by contract, form of ownership, will, or intestate succession. Property passes by intestate succession when a person dies without a will. There are some limitations on how a person can pass property.

Examples of property passing by contract generally include life insurance and annuity proceeds, and retirement benefits. At the death of the insured or participant, life insurance and annuity proceeds and retirement benefits pass to the person who has been named beneficiary on the beneficiary designation form. If a beneficiary is not named, the property will generally pass to the owner's estate and be disposed of in the owner's will or by intestate succession.

Property owned jointly with right of survivorship passes to the survivor or survivors when a joint tenant dies.

If the property owned by a decedent does not pass automatically by contract or form of ownership, it will pass to the decedent's estate. If the decedent has a will, the property would then pass as provided in the will. Otherwise, the property will pass as provided by state law under the rules for intestate succession.

Wills

A will is a legal instrument by which a person leaves certain instructions for after death. A will is generally used to dispose of a decedent's property. However, a will can also provide for other matters, such as the naming of an executor, or a guardian for minor children.

A will must be executed with certain formalities. A will is generally a written document and must be signed by the person creating the will at the end of the document. The person creating the will is often called a testator.

The will must also generally be signed by witnesses who attest to the capacity of the testator to make a will. Two witnesses are required in most states. It may be desirable to have three witnesses. The third witness can serve as a backup witness, even if only two witnesses are required.

A person must have the capacity to make a will at the time that the will is executed. Capacity means that the testator must (1) be of legal age, (2) understand the extent of his property, (3) understand the natural objects of his bounty, and (4) understand the nature of his dispositions.

The legal age to make a will is 18 in many, but not all, states.

Understanding the extent of his property means the testator knows in general that he owns a home in Ohio and a home in Florida, two life insurance policies, retirement benefits, two bank accounts, three mutual funds, household possessions, etc.

The natural objects of the testator's bounty might include, for example, a spouse and three children.

The testator must also understand the nature of his dispositions. For example, that his spouse Mary gets the house, his brother Tom gets $10,000, his sister Janet gets the antique ring, his estranged son Mike gets nothing, and Mary gets everything else.

A will does not take effect until the testator dies. The testator is generally free to revoke or change his will up until his death.

A will can provide three types of legacies: a specific legacy, a general legacy, and a residual legacy.

A specific legacy disposes of a specific piece or pieces of property. For example, the will might leave "all personal and household effects to my wife Rachel." Or the will might leave "my 1962 Corvette to my niece Heather." If the property that is the subject of a specific bequest does not exist at the testator's death, the legatee receives nothing. For example, if the Corvette does not exist at the testator's death, Heather gets nothing.

A general legacy disposes of a certain amount or value of property. For example, the will might leave "$10,000 to my nephew Ralph." If there is $10,000 of property remaining after specific legacies have been satisfied, Ralph will get $10,000 even if property must be sold.

A residual legacy disposes of all property that has not been disposed of through specific and general legacies. In other words, a residual legacy disposes of everything that is left after all other legacies have been satisfied.

A legatee is a person who receives a legacy from the testator.

Frequently, the residual legatee is a primary beneficiary. For example, the residual legatee might be the testator's spouse. The testator should take into consideration that the residual legatee may get nothing if the estate should shrink and the specific and general legacies wipe out the estate.

If a specific or general legatee is not alive at the time of the testator's death, the specific or general legacy lapses and passes to the residual legatee. However, some states provide that a specific or general legacy for certain persons related to the testator does not lapse but rather goes to descendants of the legatee. If the testator does not wish this result, the testator can provide a legacy "if he survives me."

The testator can provide by will which legacies are to bear the burden of death taxes. Such a provision can substantially affect the amount received by any legatee. In the absence of such a provision, most states would apportion the death taxes among all legacies. A few states would charge the death taxes to the residuary estate.

A will should periodically be reviewed. Questions such as the following should be asked:

- Does the testator still live in the same state?

- Does the testator own real estate in another state?

- Is the testator still married to the same person?

- Does the testator wish to change any beneficiaries?

- Does the testator have any new relatives, such as a newborn child? Have any beneficiaries died?

- Has state law on wills changed? Have tax laws changed?

At the testator's death, the will must be offered for probate. The probate court will establish the validity of the will and oversee its enforcement.

For more on wills, see Chapter 8 and Chapter 9.

Limitations

There are certain limitations on how a decedent may dispose of his property at death.

Under state law, a surviving spouse is generally given a right to elect to take against the will. Such a right allows the spouse to receive a statutory share of the decedent's estate, even if the decedent provided otherwise. The statutory share is often equal to the fraction of the decedent's estate that the spouse would receive under the rules for intestate succession, discussed later. Thus, a surviving spouse is usually entitled to at least a third or a half of the decedent's estate.

The spouse's right to elect against the will can be waived by agreement during lifetime. For example, the right to elect might be waived in an antenuptial agreement.

In some states, a surviving spouse might be given a homestead right. Such a right would generally permit the surviving spouse to live in the family home during such spouse's lifetime. In some states, children might also be given homestead rights.

In most states, an allowance is provided to the surviving spouse and children for a period of time after the decedent's death. The period might be for six months or a year. The allowance is designed to provide support for the family until the estate is administered.

In many states, exemptions are provided for certain property. For example, the surviving spouse and children might be entitled to certain household furnishings or clothes.

In most states, a child born or adopted after the execution of a will is entitled to share in the estate if provision is not otherwise made for the child. In some states, a child alive at the time of the execution of the will who is omitted from the will is entitled to share in the estate unless it appears the omission was intentional.

A few states provide that a will executed before marriage is revoked upon marriage. A few states provide that such a will is revoked unless other provisions are made for the new spouse. Conversely, most states provide that provisions in a will for a former spouse are revoked upon divorce.

A few states restrict the amount that may go to charity if a decedent is survived by a spouse or child.

Intestate Succession

If a decedent does not have a will, property generally will pass as provided by state law under the rules for intestate succession. The rules for intestate succession essentially make a will for the decedent. They do this by prescribing that property will pass in certain proportions to persons who are of certain relationships to the decedent.

As described previously, some property owned by a decedent passes automatically by contract or form of ownership rather than by will or intestate succession.

The rules for intestate succession vary widely from state to state.

Typically, a spouse with children would receive either (1) some dollar amount plus a fraction of the estate, or (2) some fraction of the estate. The fraction received by the spouse is often one-third or one-half of the estate. The children would receive the balance of the estate.

Where there is a spouse but no children, the spouse takes all in many states. In some other states, the spouse might be given a fraction of the estate (as above), but the parents or brother and sisters of the deceased would take the balance.

Trusts

A trust is a fiduciary relationship in which property is held by one (or more) person(s) for the benefit of one (or more) person(s). The person creating the trust is generally called a settlor, trustor, or grantor. The grantor typically executes a trust document and transfers property to the person who will be responsible for administering the terms of the trust, who is called a trustee. The person for whose benefit the trustee administers the trust is called a beneficiary. The property held in trust is often called the trust corpus or res.

State law controls the creation, operation, and termination of a trust. Common law is generally controlling except to the extent that a state has enacted a statute dealing with a particular aspect of trusts. The trust may generally have any terms except to the extent that a term is illegal or against public policy.

Theoretically, the law of any state with which the trust has contact could apply. Such states could include the state where the grantor resided upon creation of the trust, where the trustee is located or resides, where trust property is located (especially with regard to real estate), or where the beneficiaries reside. The grantor may specify in the trust document the state whose laws are to be applied to the operation and termination of the trust.

Usually, the beneficiaries of the trust are the grantor and/or members of the grantor's family. Having a charity as a beneficiary is also very common.

A trust may provide for management of property, accumulation or distributions of income to beneficiaries, distributions of trust corpus to beneficiaries, withdrawal powers in beneficiaries, and other powers of appointment.

Trusts arising at death (testamentary trusts) are subject to probate at the grantor's death. On the other hand, trusts created during lifetime (inter vivos trusts) are generally not subject to probate.

Trusts created during lifetime are either revocable or irrevocable; a trust created at death is irrevocable. A revocable trust is a trust in which the grantor retains the right to revoke the trust; upon revocation, property in the trust would be returned to the grantor. A trust that is not revocable is irrevocable.

There are many income, gift, estate, and generation-skipping transfer tax implications to trusts (see Chapters 15 to 19, in general, regarding taxes). In fact, many of the popular trusts, such as those discussed in Chapter 24 (marital trusts and credit shelter bypass trusts), Chapter 31 (irrevocable life insurance trusts), Chapter 26 (grantor trusts), and Chapter 33 (charitable trusts and wealth replacement trusts), are designed and utilized, at least in part, to obtain favorable tax treatment.

A revocable trust is taxable to the grantor for income tax purposes. The grantor is not treated as making a gift upon transfer of property to a revocable trust; however, a revocable trust is includable in the grantor's estate at death. See Chapter 28 regarding revocable trusts.

The grantor of an irrevocable trust generally makes a gift upon transfer of property to an irrevocable trust. Whether the grantor is taxable upon trust income or whether the irrevocable trust is includable in the grantor's estate generally depends on what interests the grantor has in the irrevocable trust.

Rule Against Perpetuities

Interests of a beneficiary in a trust must generally vest within the period allowed for in the rule against perpetuities. For example, all members of a class must generally be ascertainable immediately or within the period allowed for in the rule against perpetuities. And a beneficiary must generally be born within the period allowed for in the rule against perpetuities.

The common law version of the rule against perpetuities generally provides that interests in property must vest no later than a life in being plus 21 years (plus a gestation period, if necessary). Interests that did not vest within the rule against perpetuities at the creation of a trust would be void. Many states have a version of the common law rule against perpetuities (sometimes codified). Other states have adopted a "wait and see"' approach; that is, an interest is only void if the interest actually fails to vest within the perpetuities period. The Uniform Statutory Rule Against Perpetuities (1990) (some version of which is in effect in approximately one-half the states) provides that a nonvested interest is invalid unless (1) as of the date of the creation of the trust, the interest is certain to vest or terminate within a period measured by a life in being plus 21 years (plus a gestation period, if necessary), or (2) the interest either vests or terminates within 90 years of its creation. Some states have eliminated the rule against perpetuities.

Trusts should be drafted so as to comply with the rule against perpetuities (if applicable). A clause may also be inserted that provides that any interest must vest within the time provided by the rule against perpetuities.

Spendthrift Provisions

In a broad sense, a spendthrift provision is a provision in a trust in which the grantor attempts to provide funds to a beneficiary while limiting the ability of the beneficiary to squander the funds or creditors of the beneficiary from reaching the funds. Spendthrift provisions might include any of the following: (1) prohibition of beneficiary transferring the beneficiary's interest; (2) forfeiture of beneficiary's interest if beneficiary attempts to transfer interest; (3) distributions of income or principal to a beneficiary limited to support of the beneficiary (possibly, limited to distributions on behalf of beneficiary for support rather than distributions directly to beneficiary); (4) distributions to a beneficiary at the trustee's discretion; or (5) prohibition against creditors reaching beneficiary's interest.

There is a considerable amount of diversity among the states as to when a creditor of a beneficiary can reach the beneficiary's trust interest. Unless the trust document or state law provides otherwise, a creditor of a beneficiary can generally reach the beneficiary's trust interest.

State laws generally attempt to restrict the ability of a grantor to prevent creditors from reaching a beneficiary's interest in one of the following ways: (1) no restriction, creditor can reach trust interest; (2) creditor can reach amount not needed by beneficiary for support; (3) creditor can reach amount above some dollar amount; or (4) creditor cannot reach trust property.

ASRS: Sec. 46-50

CHAPTER ENDNOTES

1. This chapter is derived from *Estate Planning* and *The Ultimate Trust Resource*, both written by William J. Wagner and published by The National Underwriter Company.

Chapter 8

WILLS

WHAT IS IT?

A will is the legal expression or declaration of an individual's wishes as to the disposition of his property after death. Revocable during the individual's lifetime, a will is not operative until death and is applicable to the situation as it exists at the testator's death.

WHEN IS THE USE OF SUCH A DEVICE INDICATED?

1. The most important reason for creating a will is to provide the testator (in some jurisdictions, "testatrix" is the feminine form; either form means the one who makes or executes the "will and testament") with an opportunity to control the passing of his or her property and thereby to avoid "intestacy." Without a will the decedent's assets will pass by the laws of intestate succession of the state in which the decedent resides or in which his property is located.

    The principle of the intestate succession laws is to distribute the decedent's property as the government believes the decedent would have wanted had a will been executed.

    Typically, the rules for distribution of separate property are as follows:

    A. Should the decedent die intestate with a spouse but no children, the spouse takes the entire estate.

    B. If a spouse and children survive, each takes some portion of the estate.

    C. If only the decedent's children survive, they take the entire estate.

    D. If no spouse or children survive, the estate goes to the decedent's parents, and if they do not survive, then to the decedent's siblings or their heirs.

    E. The next level of intestate takers is the decedent's grandparents and their heirs (the aunts, uncles, and cousins of decedent).

    F. If none of the decedent's heirs survive, the next takers are the issue of the decedent's pre-deceased spouse.

    G. If none of the above survive, the estate goes to the next of kin.

    H. The state is the final taker.

    While the rules above are typical, the laws in a particular state may have some variation. The above rules generally apply in the ten community property states (Alaska, Arizona, California, Idaho, Louisiana, Nevada, New Mexico, Texas, Washington, and Wisconsin) as to separate property; but if the property is held as community property, even where there are children, all community property goes to the surviving spouse in the absence of a will.

    Louisiana has unique rules that limit what a decedent may do with property, in some circumstances forcing the transfer of property to a certain person (usually the surviving spouse) regardless of the terms of the will.

    Be certain to remember that real property in a particular state is subject to the rules of that state. Therefore, for example, a will dealing with oil interests or other interests in land located in Louisiana is subject to the laws of Louisiana, even though the testator is a resident of New Jersey.

2. As described above, without a valid will the decedent's property goes to his or her relatives as provided by statute. By making a will, a person can pass property in a different manner than that provided by statute. With a will, property generally can be left to one or more relatives, of any degree, or friends or charities to the exclusion of others.

    However, many states have laws that require the spouse and/or children to take some share of the estate. Property can be willed to non-relatives such as friends or charities, subject to rules in certain states that require some rights to pass to the spouse or children.

3. In a will, the testator can name the "personal representative" of the estate. A person or institution can be named to act as executor (in some states, "executrix" is used as a feminine form) and be appointed to carry out the directions in the will and to dispose of the property according to the testamentary provisions.

   The named personal representative may often be a relative or close friend. But, if the estate is large or complicated, the testator should consider appointing either a professional or an institution accustomed to dealing with assets and with the sometimes complicated rules of probate.

   The will may provide that the executor need not be bonded, which can save money for the estate, but which gives up some protection. If there is no valid will or if no executor is named or if the named executor for any reason fails to qualify or ceases to act, the court will appoint an "administrator" (in some states, "administratrix" is used as a feminine form) to administer the estate.

4. A will can set out the terms of a trust in which the named trustee can manage assets on behalf of the beneficiaries for many years after the death of the testator. This may be especially appropriate in order to manage assets for the benefit of the testator's minor children. Such a trust is referred to as a "testamentary" trust since it is created through the decedent's last will and testament and comes into being at the probate of the will.

   The terms of a testamentary trust are very important. Sometimes people have such trusts terminate when a child reaches age 18 or 21. Such an early distribution, at a time before the child has had the experience of handling large sums of money, often results in the child's not going to college and also losing all of the inheritance.

5. When there are minor children, the will can nominate a guardian of both the "person" and the "estate" of each child. A "guardian of the person" generally provides for the custody and care of the child. A "guardian of the estate" manages the child's assets. State laws generally require a court to give significant weight to such a nomination by a parent who has custody of a child. Without such a provision, the court names the guardian upon the death of the parent(s) based on available information and often depending on who volunteers.

6. A will allows the testator to make alternative provisions in case some of the heirs predecease him or her. For instance, if a child dies, the testator may want to leave that share to the child's siblings, or perhaps to the child's issue.

7. Some types of property are not affected by the provisions in a will. Assets held in joint tenancy or tenancy by the entirety pass by right of survivorship to the remaining joint tenant(s). Policies of life insurance, IRAs, and certain other assets pass by contract to the person(s) named in beneficiary designations.

8. Even where an individual has a living trust which holds most of the individual's assets in order to avoid probate, it is still very important to have a will which will "pour over" into the previously established trust any assets which were not already transferred to the trust.

9. The majority of states provide that if a spouse or child is not named in a will, such a person is deemed to be a "pretermitted heir." Regardless of what the will says, such person will take the share of the estate that would be given to that person under the state's rules of intestacy. Thus, it is wise to mention all such persons in the will so that they cannot claim to be pretermitted heirs left out of the will only because they were overlooked by the testator.

10. A will affords the testator the opportunity to minimize estate taxes (discussed below) and other transfer costs and provide who is to bear the burden of such costs.

WHAT ARE THE REQUIREMENTS?

1. The general rule is that any person 18 or more years of age who is of sound mind may make a will.[1] While this is the general rule, a few states have a different minimum age requirement.

2. The law ordinarily requires less mental capacity to make a will than to make a contract. An individual can make a will even if sick, elderly, weak, or of low mental capacity. In general, most states require that the testator know (1) the nature and extent of his property and (2) the natural objects of his bounty.

3. Except where a "holographic will" (one written entirely in the testator's handwriting) or an oral ("nuncupative") will is allowed, wills must meet

certain legal requirements. Typically, an attested will must be in writing, signed by the testator (or in the testator's name by some other person in the testator's presence and at his direction), and must be witnessed by at least two persons.[2] Some states still require three witnesses while at least one, Pennsylvania, requires no witnesses at the time the will is signed.

4. Approximately half of the states recognize a holographic or handwritten will.[3] A will which is not effective under other provisions may be effective as a holographic will, whether or not witnessed, if it is dated and the signature and the material provisions are in the handwriting of the testator.[4] In some states, having printed or typed material on the holographic will can invalidate it.

5. Less than half of the states recognize oral (nuncupative) wills. This is a will declared or dictated by the testator during the last illness, before a sufficient number of witnesses, and later reduced to writing. In some states such wills are valid only under certain circumstances. For instance, they may be valid only to transfer a limited amount of personal property.[5]

HOW DOES ONE CHOOSE THE TERMS OF A WILL?

John Lee is preparing for his retirement and has decided to "get his affairs in order." He knows that without a will, his spouse and his children will each receive a portion of his estate. Since John's wife is a wealthy woman in her own right, as the recipient of the estate of her parents, John would rather leave his assets to the children. The children are not experienced in dealing with assets and his wife deals well with assets.

John has three children. The youngest has been estranged from the family for many years. John makes a will leaving all of his assets in a trust for the benefit of his two other children, one-half to each. He names his eldest child as executor of the estate and the second child as the successor executor. John's wife was named as the trustee of the trust for the two older children.

John realizes that certain of his assets, his life insurance and his IRA account, will not pass by his will. He has named his two eldest children as equal beneficiaries of those assets. To avoid his wife and estranged child taking intestate shares as pretermitted heirs, his will names them but leaves nothing to them.

John has made his decisions on the basis of need and degree of positive feelings he has for each beneficiary. His exclusion of his wife does not indicate a lack of feeling for her (a fact he may wish to communicate in the will) but a recognition that she does not need his assets for her security and also that adding more to her estate would increase the share which would ultimately be paid in death taxes.

By leaving the funds for the two older children in trust with his wife as trustee, he has provided good management to protect the trust assets for the children. The trust terms also provide John's wife with latitude as to the distribution of the assets as between the children and how and when they will receive the assets. Thus, John has not deprived his wife of some continuing parental control.

Although some people would "always leave things equally to the children," John has recognized the estrangement of the one child and has made the difficult but perhaps logical decision to leave the assets to the children who are still close to the family. In making such decisions, there is simply no "right way" that can always be applied to distributing assets; the decisions must be made on the basis of what is important to each testator and the circumstances of the persons and organizations he wishes to benefit.

HOW IS A WILL CHANGED OR REVOKED?

A will may be changed by writing a separate document which is not intended to be a new will but which is meant to change a provision of an existing will. Such a document is called a "codicil."

A new will, to the extent that it does not state that it is revoking all prior wills, may often merely change the terms of an existing will. In other words, the unrevoked prior will(s) remain valid to the extent not inconsistent with a later will. For this reason, it is good practice to make clear in a will that it is intended to revoke all prior wills, if that is the testator's goal.

Generally, a codicil must be signed with the same formalities as a will in order to be valid.

Revocation of a will also may occur by destroying a will or defacing it with the intent to revoke. Sometimes the issue of the testator's intent (e.g., if the will is burned together with other papers or trash, was there an intention to revoke the will?) will result in expensive litigation. A specific statement of revocation in a new will (or writing

"Revoked" across an old will and signing and dating that revocation) often may achieve the testator's goals more effectively.

Certain circumstances will cause the revocation of a will without any action on the part of the testator. Examples of this include revocation by marriage and revocation by divorce. Particular state law must be checked.

WHAT ARE THE DEATH TAX IMPLICATIONS?

At death, federal estate taxes are imposed on property that is transferred to the beneficiaries. However, each U.S. resident has a unified credit that eliminates the estate tax on the first $1,500,000 (in 2004, increasing gradually to $3,500,000 in 2009) in estate assets. EGTRRA 2001 repeals the estate tax for one year in 2010. The unified credit exemption equivalent (or applicable exclusion amount) returns to $1,000,000 after 2010.

While most states have abolished their state death taxes (except for a "credit estate tax," i.e., an estate tax sufficient to absorb the credit allowed against the federal estate tax for state death taxes actually paid) many do still have death taxes. Such a state death tax may be due even though there is no federal estate tax to pay.

If the decedent's assets are valued in excess of the unified credit exemption equivalent above, federal estate tax (discussed in Chapter 15) will be owed unless a deduction can be taken. The most common deductions are the marital deduction (discussed in Chapter 24, Trust-Marital Deduction and Bypass) and the charitable deduction (discussed in Chapter 32, Charitable Contribution).

Other deductions generally available include the following:

A. Debts of the decedent;

B. Administration expenses;

C. Casualty losses to estate assets;

D. Funeral expenses; and

E. Family-owned business deduction (see Chapter 42).

If a married individual wishes to minimize taxes at his death, he should be certain to have a will that provides for all assets in excess of the unified credit exemption equivalent above to pass to his spouse or to a trust for the benefit of the spouse, so a marital deduction can be taken for those assets. The taxable estate will thus be reduced to the value that can be "sheltered" by the decedent's unified credit.

However, if all of the assets are left to a spouse, there will be a 100% marital deduction and no assets will be available to take advantage of the unified credit (which is a "use it or lose it" benefit). The result will be that all of the assets will be taxed at the death of the surviving spouse and the unified credit of the first-to-die spouse will be wasted. This is reviewed in more detail in Chapter 24, relating to the marital deduction.

Generally, unless the will provides otherwise, estate taxes are apportioned among all beneficiaries of the estate (although in a few states death taxes are paid from the residue).[6] Alternatively, the testator may want to provide that taxes should be paid from the residue (assets not specifically disposed of elsewhere in the will) so that the recipients of specific gifts will not be responsible for the tax on the gift(s) they receive.

For example, if the will provides for taxes to be paid from the residue, Susie, the distributee of the decedent's Rolls Royce, will not have to make an out of pocket payment for her share of estate taxes, providing that there are sufficient assets in the estate residue to pay such taxes.

WHAT ARE THE INCOME TAX IMPLICATIONS?

For income tax purposes a probate estate is a separate taxable entity. A federal fiduciary income tax return (Form 1041), and often a state income tax return, must be filed annually during the period of administration if sufficient income ($600 or more for the federal return) is received during a 12 month period, or if the trust has a beneficiary who is a non-resident alien.

No income tax is recognized solely as the result of a death. As a matter of fact, there may be a tax benefit at death, since most of the assets in the decedent's gross estate receive a new income tax basis equal to the fair market value of each asset at the time of the decedent's death. Assuming the asset increased in value or is worth more than its basis in the decedent's hands during lifetime, it receives a "step-up" in basis. The taxable gain inherent in the asset disappears. Thus, an asset could be sold immediately after death and there would be no income tax to pay. For example, assume, 20 years before his death, a client purchased stock for $20 a share. If it was valued in his estate at $80 a share, that $80 would become the new basis for purposes of determining gain if his beneficiary sold it. If the stock were worth less than its basis, the basis would be stepped down.

One exception to this rule is any asset that would have been taxed as income had the decedent lived long enough to receive it. Unpaid fees due to a doctor or lawyer who reports his income on a cash basis, or notes resulting from the sale of property reported on the installment method would be examples of these. These assets are generally termed "income in respect of decedent" and they retain whatever income tax basis the testator had in them.

For decedents dying in 2010, along with repeal of the estate tax for one year, a modified carryover basis regime replaces the step-up in basis, (i.e., a step-up in basis is allowed, but only on the value of the estate below specified levels).

ISSUES AND IMPLICATIONS IN COMMUNITY PROPERTY STATES

Assets held as community property are owned equally by the spouses. At death, each spouse has testamentary power of distribution over his half of the community assets. Thus there is no certainty that the survivor will receive the decedent's one-half share of the community assets, but the absence of a will generally will produce that result.[7]

In common law (non-community property) states, the surviving spouse may sometimes be protected against disinheritance through laws of forced shares, dower, or curtesy.

In a community property state, the will of the deceased spouse may affect the survivor's half of the community property. For example, the decedent's will may purport to give all of the community property assets (the shares of both husband and wife) to a trust for the benefit of the surviving spouse and the children. If so, the survivor must elect whether to take under the will (thus assenting to the decedent's disposition of the survivor's one-half community property interest) or to take his one-half of the community property outright (denying the decedent's power to dispose of the survivor's community property interest).

QUESTIONS AND ANSWERS

Question – All of the client's assets are held in joint tenancy or in a manner in which a beneficiary is designated (e.g., IRAs). Does the client need a will?

Answer – While the assets currently owned by the client will pass to the survivors or beneficiaries without probate, at some time the client may acquire additional assets that are titled in another manner. Also, the named joint tenant(s) or beneficiary(ies) might predecease the client. A will is always valuable to prevent against intestacy.

Question – Is it difficult to change a will as circumstances change?

Answer – A will can be amended or revoked at any time during the lifetime of the testator. It is possible to revoke a will in full and to create a new will, or to revoke only a portion of the will and add new provisions by means of a codicil. The will itself can provide for changing circumstances by making provisions for successor beneficiaries and/or executors in the event of the death of any named beneficiaries and/or executors.

Question – When should a will be updated?

Answer – Generally, a will should be reviewed at more or less regular intervals. Most specifically a will should be reviewed:

(1) When there are significant changes in the value of property that is intended to be distributed.

(2) Where the testator has moved from one state to another.

(3) Where there have been changes in family circumstances such as births, deaths, marriages, divorces.

(4) Where the personal representative, guardian or trustee can no longer serve as originally expected.

(5) Where federal or state tax laws change.

(6) Where changes in business ventures occur.

(7) Where disposition or other objectives change.

This list is not all encompassing but is representative of some of the major changes to cause a will review and possible change.

Question – Can the imposition of estate taxes at death be avoided by having assets pass outside the will?

Answer – The gross estate includes all assets owned by the decedent at death. This includes assets held in the decedent's name, assets transferred to a revocable trust by the decedent, the decedent's interest in joint tenancy assets, proceeds of life insurance from policies owned by the decedent, and the value of most retirement plans (IRAs, for example). Even assets outside the United States are subject to federal estate tax for a U.S. citizen. Unless a will employs tax avoidance devices such as the marital or charitable deductions, the will really has no effect on the amount of estate tax that is owed.

However, some state death taxes are inheritance taxes, which vary the amount of deduction and tax rate based upon the relationship of the recipient to the testator. To the extent that the will provides a different distribution of property than would an intestacy, the amount of inheritance tax to be paid may be changed. The other form of death tax, called an estate tax, is a tax based in general on the total value of the assets in the estate, rather than how much is inherited by each person and the relationship of that person to the testator. Two areas where even estate taxes are affected by who is the recipient of a bequest or devise include gifts made to spouses (which may result in a marital deduction) and transfers to charities (which may qualify for a charitable deduction).

Question – Does a client with a modest estate need a will?

Answer – There are many reasons almost every adult should have a will. Even though an estate is modest, it can be important to name a guardian for both the person and the estate of the client's children. A client may have very strong feelings that a close friend is the best person to care for the children and if those wishes are not expressed, the children may end up in the custody of relatives or others who would not have been chosen to deal with the children and/or their assets. In some cases, a client may wish to leave the personal custody of a child to one person and leave the management of the child's assets to another.

Question – Suppose a client planned to avoid probate by putting assets in a revocable intervivos trust (a "living trust"). Can the client change the disposition of assets in the trust by changing his will?

Answer – As long as the client has actually placed the assets in the intervivos trust, his will will not have any effect on these assets unless the trust provides for amendment or exercise of a power of appointment to be made by a will. When a living trust is used, generally the will is only a "pour-over will" which directs to the trust any assets not already placed in the trust. The revocable trust can be changed by a written amendment in the form set out in the trust for such changes.

In order to avoid the question of whether the trust terms are to be changed or a power of appointment exercised inadvertently by a will, the majority of planners provide that changes in a trust can be made only by an instrument in writing other than a will.

Question – Can probate be avoided through an intervivos trust?

Answer – Yes, but only if the title of assets has been transferred from the client's name to that of the trustee of the trust. Failure to make the transfers will leave assets subject to a will and subject to the costs and delays of going through a probate in order to get into the trust.

Question – Is it expensive to have assets subject to probate?

Answer – Probate fees vary from state to state. In some states, they can be as high as a flat 5% of all probate property – plus additional fees for "extraordinary work" (preparing tax returns, some sales of property, fighting will contests, etc.). Both the executor and the attorney for the estate are entitled to a fee for their services.

Question – Assume a trust is desired to protect a client's children. Will it cost more to use a testamentary trust included as part of his will or more if an "intervivos trust" is used as a separate instrument?

Answer – There are at least three cost aspects to consider. One is the cost of going through probate, which is required for a testamentary trust but which can be avoided if assets are transferred before death to an intervivos trust. A different aspect is that some states require regular accounting to be made to the court by testamentary trusts, giving possibly better supervision but resulting in added attorney fees and court costs for each accounting. Lastly, the legal fees for drafting an intervivos trust may be greater since its use requires two documents (the trust and a "pour-over" will) and often some documentation to transfer title of assets.

Question – Is there any benefit to having property go through probate as opposed to having assets transferred to an intervivos trust prior to death?

Answer – Going through probate involves stricter supervision of the management and disposition of assets. To the extent that a client is concerned that the trustee who administers the trust may not carry out the trust terms in exactly the manner desired, the probate procedure may have some substantial benefit.

Another benefit of probate is that it has a "cut-off period" for creditors. As part of the probate process, a notice of the death is given to all creditors.[8] After notice, creditors have a specified period of time in which to file their claims and those creditors who do not make their claims within that time are thereafter cut off. With an intervivos trust, generally these claims are not cut off. For example, suppose a doctor were to die and a malpractice claim developed ten months after his death. That claim might well be cut off by a proper probate, but it would not be cut off with regard to any assets held in an intervivos trust at his death. Those assets have not gone through the "cleansing action" of probate. Some states, such as California, have a similar termination of creditors' rights for assets held in intervivos trusts.

Question – Under what circumstances can a will be challenged or contested when offered for probate?

Answer – A will can be contested by an interested or aggrieved party on many different grounds. Among the most common causes for contesting are:

(1) The testator lacked sufficient mental capacity.

(2) The testator was unduly influenced at the time the will was drafted.

(3) The will was not executed according to the statutory formalities.

(4) The will offered for probate has been revoked.

(5) The will offered for probate was a forgery.

Question – What things should an estate planner examine in reviewing a will?

Answer – See "How to Review a Will: A Checklist for the Estate and Financial Planner" in Chapter 9.

ASRS, Sec. 50

CHAPTER ENDNOTES

1. Uniform Probate Code §2-501.
2. Uniform Probate Code §2-502.
3. Dan E. McConaughey, *Wills*, 18 (1984).
4. Uniform Probate Code §2-502(b).
5. Dan E. McConaughey, *Wills*, 22 (1984).
6. Uniform Probate Code §3-916.
7. Robert J. Lynn, *Introduction to Estate Planning*, 2nd Ed., 23 (1978).
8. Known or ascertainable creditors usually receive direct notice. Unknown creditors usually are notified by publication. The United States Supreme Court has struck down as unconstitutional an Oklahoma statute that bars claims presented more than two months after notice by publication. The court held that such notice does not necessarily satisfy the requirement of due process, that if a creditor's identity is known or reasonably ascertainable, the creditor must receive actual notice. *Tulsa Prof. Collection Serv., Inc. v. Pope*, 485 US 478 (1988), rev'g and remanding 733 P.2d 396.

Chapter 9

HOW TO REVIEW A WILL:
A CHECKLIST FOR THE ESTATE AND FINANCIAL PLANNER

[*Editor's Note*: A version of this article under the title "How to Review a Will" appeared in the magazine *Financial Planning* in two parts, April and May, 1988. The checklist has been updated in this book.]

INTRODUCTION

A will is the legal document that specifies how a person wants to dispose of the real and personal property he owns in his own name at the time of his death. Most mentally competent adults have the legal capacity to draw a will. But few persons are knowledgeable enough to do so properly. Only an attorney should draft a will and even most attorneys should not attempt to draw their own.

Despite this, every member of the estate planning team, including the financial planner, should know how to review a will.

First, it is necessary to coordinate the will properly with other dispositive documents such as employee benefit plans. For example, if the will is not synchronized with an executive's pension, group insurance, and 401(k) or other retirement plan, there is no way to minimize overall death taxes and provide for a smooth and efficient estate administration.

Second, it is impossible to know if there will be appropriate liquidity unless the will and its various dispositive schemes are examined.

Third, wills become outdated and tax laws change (for instance, a marital deduction provision in a will drafted before September 13, 1981, may not qualify for the unlimited marital deduction; TRA '97 increased the unified credit in a series of steps and introduced a family-owned business exclusion; and EGTRRA 2001 introduced a slow but steady increase in the unified credit, a gradual reduction in the top estate tax rates, and a repeal of the estate tax for one year in 2010). The circumstances, needs, and desires of the parties are always in flux. The attorney who drafted the will may

have died and it may have been many years since the will was revised or reviewed by either the client or attorney.

Every professional in the estate planning team must therefore be able to examine a will and spot – in general terms at least – what's wrong.

"What's wrong" with a given will is more often a question of what has been omitted or what has changed or what are the present objectives of the client than what has been improperly drafted. "What's wrong" is even more often the failure of the draftsman to match the facts of the case or the circumstances or desires of the parties with the documents. "What's wrong" may be something the accountant, for instance, knows that no other professional knows. "What's wrong" may be that the will has not been updated for years and no longer addresses the current circumstances or client goals or latest tax law. "What's wrong" may be that a will alone– without a trust or the use of other tools or techniques–is inadequate or does not maximize the possibility to accomplish the client's objectives with greater certainty and lesser cost.

The following is a (by no means complete) checklist designed to give each member of the estate planning team the tools needed to examine a will:

INTRODUCTORY CLAUSE

Start with the introductory ("exordium") clause, which should be the first paragraph in the will. The purpose of this preamble is to

(1) identify the testator, the person disposing of property at death;

(2) establish domicile, the county that will have legal jurisdiction for purposes of determining the validity of the will and interpreting will provisions, for purposes of state inheritance taxation (technically, what is said in a will about the testator's domicile is not dispositive but is

evidence which will usually be considered even if subordinated to proof of facts to the contrary);

(3) declare that the document in question is intended to dispose of the testator's property at death and no matter how many wills have been written in the past, this is meant to be the last will; and

(4) revoke all prior wills. This is designed to nullify old and forgotten wills – and "codicils" (legally effective modifications of existing wills).

An example of this introductory clause is:

I, Edward Grieg, a resident of and domiciled in the city of Bryn Mawr in Montgomery County, Pennsylvania, declare this to be my last will. I revoke all wills and codicils made prior to this will.

Planners should check:

(1) Is the spelling of the client's name correct? Has the client's full name been used?

(2) Is the client "A/K/A" ("also known as"), i.e., is there some other name by which the client is known and should that name be listed?

(3) Is the domicile correct? For tax or other planning purposes, would it make sense to begin to document a different domicile? Will the will meet all the statutory requirements of the stated domicile? If the client spends a great deal of time in more than one residence, could the address mentioned in the will trigger a "double domicile" problem (e.g., where more than one state claims the decedent was a domiciliary of the state and therefore has the right to impose an inheritance tax)?

(4) Is there a reason prior wills and codicils should not be revoked? Instead of a new will, should the present document be a codicil making a small change but otherwise ratifying an existing will? For instance, if there is a potential for an attack on this will on the grounds of mental incompetency, fraud, or undue influence, a prior will providing a similar disposition will help prove the mental capacity of the testator and may discourage would-be contestants from attacking the current will. Conversely, if a beneficiary has been deleted, a new will should be drawn rather than a codicil to avoid the mention of the eliminated beneficiary.

After the introductory clause, the will can take either of two directions. It can (1) describe the steps that take place in administering the testator's estate (such as payment of debts and taxes and then payment of legacies) or it can (2) dispose of legacies first and describe obligations later. We will take the former approach in formulating this checklist.

DEBTS CLAUSE

The next clause usually pertains to the payment of debts, expenses, and costs. The purposes of this clause are:

(1) To state the source from which each debt will be paid. (This is an extremely important point because of the death tax implications. For instance, if a surviving spouse rather than some other beneficiary must pay debts, to that extent the marital deduction will be decreased and taxes may be increased. Furthermore, if the burden falls on the wrong person(s), the testator's goals may not be met.)

(2) To establish as debts items that might not otherwise be considered the testator's obligations.

An example of the payment of debts clause is:

I direct all of my debts (including any expenses of my last illness) and my funeral expenses be paid.

Planners should check:

(1) Does the testator have any rights to property held in the trust of another person (a so-called "power of appointment") and, if so, what effect does the debts clause have on that property? Does it expose that property to the claims of creditors?

(2) Will the beneficiaries receive more or less than the client intended when the will was drawn because of the operation of this provision? Has the size of the debt changed since the will was drawn? What will be the federal and state death tax impact of the clause?

(3) What is the effect of the Equal Rights Amendment in the state of domicile? In some states the will of a married woman should contain a direction to pay debts and taxes.

Otherwise, the burden of her funeral and medical expenses will be placed on her surviving husband – thus barring a deduction for payment of those expenses by her estate.

(4) Did the will provide detailed funeral arrangements? Most authorities feel this is inadvisable since the will may not be found or may not be accessible in sufficient time after the testator's death. Should such provisions be placed in a "Letter of Instructions," an informal and nonlegal list of requests, suggestions, and recommendations that should not be placed in the will?

(5) Does the client intend that "payment of debts" include the mortgage on property left to a specific individual? In some states, absent an express direction to the contrary, when specific property is left to an individual (a "specific bequest"), any debt on that property will not be paid off. In other states, such a clause will require the executor to satisfy the mortgage. Does the named beneficiary of a life insurance policy that has been pledged as the collateral for a loan have the right to have the loan paid off because of the "pay my [just] debts" clause? The planner must check state law. In at least one state the answer depends on who the lender is. The result, absent specific direction to the contrary, is one way if the lender is the insurance company (the beneficiary takes only the net proceeds) and another (the beneficiary is entitled to have the estate pay off the debt out of other estate assets) if the creditor is an independent lending institution.

TAX CLAUSE

The clause pertaining to the payment of death taxes can either be stated next or appear after the provisions disposing of property.

The purpose of the tax clause is to establish the source for the payment of the federal estate tax, the state inheritance and estate tax, and any federal or state generation-skipping transfer tax.

This is an example of a tax clause:

I direct that all inheritance, estate, transfer, succession, legacy and other death taxes upon property required to be included in my taxable estate whether or not

passing under this Will [except (1) transfer taxes levied pursuant to the provisions of Chapter 13 of the Internal Revenue Code of 1986, relating to "generation-skipping transfers," or any similar state law, and (2) taxes on property held in trust under the Will (or any revocable trust) of my spouse], and any interest and penalties thereon, shall be charged against and paid from my residuary estate passing under Article *FOURTH* of Part I of this my Will.

Planners should check:

(1) State "apportionment" statutes. If there is no tax clause in the will or if it does not adequately address the payment of a particular death tax, state law will allocate the burden of taxes among the beneficiaries. Many states require beneficiaries to pay a share of estate taxes unless the will provides otherwise. The result is often an inappropriate or unintended reduction of the shares of certain beneficiaries or adverse tax consequences. (For example, there may be a spiraling reduction of the estate tax marital deduction. The deduction is allowed only for the net amount passing to the surviving spouse. If that amount is reduced by an estate tax burden, the tax increases – further reducing the amount passing to the spouse, etc.) An "anti-apportionment" tax clause may be the solution. For instance, suppose you wanted a child to receive $100,000 of your client's $2,000,000 estate free and clear. Without special provision, that child would be forced to pay his share of taxes, or 1/20 of the total federal and state death taxes. With a special tax clause, the child will receive the entire $100,000.

(2) Does the client expect or want property passing outside the probate estate to pay its share of tax if it in fact generates tax? For instance, assume $1,000,000 of pension proceeds (or life insurance) is payable to the client's two oldest children and $1,000,000 of cash is payable to the client's two youngest children. Who is to pay the tax on the $2,000,000? What if the $1,000,000 of pension proceeds (or life insurance) is state inheritance tax exempt but the cash is not? Unless the will provides to the contrary, estate taxes must be paid by recipients of property passing outside the will. The will should specify who pays taxes on both probate and nonprobate property.

(3) Assume a sizable amount of property will pass through a revocable living trust. Is the tax clause

in that instrument coordinated with the tax clause in the will or are they incompatible? What if assets under the will are to "pour over" into a previously funded trust which itself will generate significant estate taxes. Is there (should there be) a will provision calling upon the trust to help the estate pay taxes? Does the trust have a provision recognizing and empowering a "call" on its assets to pay the probate estate's taxes?

(4) Who is to pay the tax on a generation-skipping transfer? Absent a contrary direction, the taxes will probably be payable from the assets of the fund subject to the tax. Some draftsmen specifically provide that such taxes are not to be imposed on the "skip person's" estate.

(5) Assume the facts indicate that very large taxable gifts have been made by the client. The taxable portion of these gifts – to the extent not included in the client's gross estate – will be considered "adjusted taxable gifts." They will increase the rate of federal estate tax payable on the taxable estate remaining. Will an unexpectedly high burden be placed on the assets remaining because of these prior gifts and should the tax clause take such gifts into account in apportioning the tax burden?

(6) Should certain beneficiaries be insulated from tax for either tax reasons or to accomplish the dispositive goals of the client or better meet the needs of the beneficiaries? For example, should a child to whom property has been given be exempted by the will from paying the estate tax on that property?

TANGIBLE PERSONAL PROPERTY CLAUSE

A clause pertaining to the disposition of tangible personal property is often next. The purposes of this clause are:

(1) to provide for who will receive personal property and the terms under which they will receive it; and

(2) to make special dispositions among the persons and the organizations of the testator's choice.

An example of the tangible personal property dispositive clause is:

I give to my daughter, Eva Grieg, all of my clothing, household furnishings, jewelry, automobiles, books,

pictures, and all other articles of tangible personal property owned by me at the date of my death. If my daughter, Eva Grieg, does not survive me, I give the property mentioned above in equal shares to my grandchildren, Gretta and Gail Grieg or the survivor who is alive at the date of my death.

or

I give the Philadelphia Museum of Art my painting of "Helga" by Andrew Wyeth.

Planners should check:

(1) Does (or should) the client make specific bequests of all "intimate" items such as a watch or ring? Absent such provisions, if personal property has been left to several individuals, the result is often needless expense in determining who gets what or reducing the estate to cash (not to mention the potential for bitter intrafamily fights). If specific bequests have been made, has each item been described in enough detail so that there will be no confusion as to which diamond ring the testator meant? (Use the same description as is found in the insurance policy covering the loss or theft of the item).

(2) Has provision been made in case the item specifically left to a beneficiary is not owned by the decedent at death? For instance, what if one ring is sold and the proceeds are used to purchase a second. Does the named beneficiary receive the second ring?

(3) If the item specifically bequeathed has been lost, stolen, etc. and the loss has been covered by insurance, would the client want the named beneficiary to receive the insurance? In many states the bequest of an item of personal property does not – absent specific direction to the contrary – also pass the insurance covering the item.

(4) Does the client intend to pass – under the category of personal property – cash in a safe deposit box, travelers' checks, and cash found in his home or on his person? Does the client know that cash on deposit is typically not considered tangible personal property?

(5) If the client has property in many different places, consider allowing the executor – at the expense of the estate – to take possession of the property "as and where is" (a provision which will permit

the beneficiary to receive the property free of delivery costs and protect the fiduciary and beneficiaries during administration from the risk that specific assets will be lost).

(6) The phrase "personal effects" may not encompass items of household use or even a car. Consider specific mention of items of tangible personal property.

(7) Is there a "catchall" phrase that passes the residue of tangible personalty? The phrase, "all other tangible personal property" should dispose of any residual property.

(8) Should the will confirm that certain property such as household furnishings, silverware, etc. belongs to someone else?

(9) Does this clause dispose of property by referring to an instrument outside the will? This "incorporation by reference" is not recommended since it often leads to litigation.

(10) The use of the term "contents" should be avoided. Personal property should not be described by its location.

General checkup of legacies:

(1) Has property been left outright to a minor who is legally incapable of handling it or to a person under a physical, mental, or emotional handicap who does not have the physical or intellectual capacity?

(2) Are all beneficiaries named alive? Are there "backup" beneficiaries (at least two) for each beneficiary? Are they the beneficiaries the client currently desires?

(3) Are any of the gifts conditioned on events or circumstances that are impossible, "against public policy," or in violation of the Constitution? For example, a bequest would be invalidated by the courts if it were made on the condition that the recipient first divorce her spouse.

(4) Are there gifts to "my issue" (which would unintentionally disinherit an adopted person)?

(5) Do gifts to charities meet state law requirements? Has the charity's full legal (corporate) name and address been stated? (The popular name is often

different from the full legal name). Have you checked the IRS's "Cumulative List of Organizations" or obtained assurances from the charity itself to make sure the gift to the charity will qualify for a tax deduction? Has the client named a backup charity? Check to be sure the will specifies that taxes are to be paid from the portion of the residue not passing to charity. Otherwise, what should be a tax-free bequest must bear its portion of the total taxes. That reduces the charity's share and therefore increases taxes. This in turn creates a new cycle of problems.

(6) If someone is intentionally omitted, have you checked state law to see if such an omission is permissible? Are there defamatory statements in the will concerning an heir? (At the probate of the will, such statements may become libelous and expose the client's estate to an action for damages.)

(7) Does the will make so many specific bequests of cash that the residuary estate doesn't have enough left to pay estate taxes? Keep in mind that the IRS can attach the assets of any beneficiary for the unpaid estate tax. Check to be sure the executor will have a sufficient reserve of funds for paying estate tax and all the bequests to residuary beneficiaries.

(8) Note that a tangible personal property clause should nearly always be used where the residue of the estate will be paid to a trust. Few clients want trusts involved in handling personal effects such as jewelry, or household furniture, antiques, or cars.

DEVISES OF REAL ESTATE CLAUSE

The next clause pertains to "devises," testamentary grants of real property. The purposes of the devises clause are:

(1) to specify which real estate is to be disposed of under the will and to dispose of that real estate, and

(2) to handle the problems where the property has been sold or destroyed prior to the testator's death.

An example of a devise is:

I leave my residence located at 207 Rawles Run Lane, Bryn Mawr, Pa. to my daughter, Larrissa

Grieg. If, at the time of my death, I am no longer using the property at 207 Rawles Run Lane as my residence, then this devise is to be void and of no effect; however, if I own any other real estate which I am using as my residence at that time, then, in such an event, I devise such other real estate to my daughter, Larrissa Grieg. If my daughter, Larrissa Grieg, does not survive me, this devise shall lapse and such real estate shall become part of my residuary estate.

SPECIFIC BEQUESTS OF INTANGIBLES AND CASH

After disposing of tangible personal property and real estate, the will may then cover specific gifts of intangibles (property where the item itself is evidence of value) such as gifts of cash or accounts receivable. An example of a gift of an intangible asset is:

I give 100 shares of Rohm and Haas stock to my niece, Danielle Green.

or

I give the sum of Five Thousand ($5,000) dollars to my sister, Sara Black, if she survives me.

Planners should check:

(1) Has provision been made in the event the primary beneficiary does not survive the decedent?

(2) Does the will spell out what gift, if any, is made if the decedent does not possess, at the time of death, the stock mentioned in the will? What if the stock had been sold but new stock was purchased with the proceeds? What if there was a stock split and only a specified number of shares were given?

RESIDUARY CLAUSE

The next clause is called the "residuary clause." The purposes of the residuary clause are to:

(1) transfer all assets not disposed of up to this point,

(2) (in some cases) provide a mechanism for "pouring over" assets from the will to a

previously established (inter vivos) trust (if a pourover is made, it is important to review the trust as carefully as the will itself), and

(3) provide for an alternative disposition in case the primary beneficiary has died or the trust to which probate assets (assets passing under a valid will or by intestacy) were to be poured over was for some reason invalid, previously revoked, or never came into existence.

An example of a residuary clause is:

All the rest, residue, and remainder of the property that I own at the date of my death, real and personal, tangible or intangible, regardless of where it is situated, I leave to my daughter, Larrissa Grieg. But if Larrissa Grieg does not survive me, then I leave the said property in equal shares to my grandchildren, Ronald Reimus and Reginald Reimus or to the survivor of them.

Planners should check:

(1) Has a spouse been disinherited? If so, is the client aware of the "elective rights" (rights to a portion of the probate estate and perhaps certain other property owned by the decedent at death regardless of what the will provides) the surviving spouse has even if the will is valid? (It may be possible to control the surviving spouse to some degree by inserting a provision at least as attractive as the spouse's intestate share or by a provision reducing or eliminating the share of a person in whom the spouse is interested if he exercises his right of election. An alternative is a pre- or post-nuptial agreement).

(2) Has the client, inadvertently, exercised a "power of appointment" (a right to direct the disposition of property in a trust established by someone else)? In some states, a residuary clause automatically exercises a general power of appointment unless the trust requires that it must be specifically referred to in order to make a valid exercise or unless the will itself states that no exercise is intended.

(3) Is there a disposition to a young adult, minor, or a person legally, mentally, or emotionally incompetent that should be made in trust? Is there provision for the executor to retain the property during the minority of such a person or to use income or principal for that person's

benefit? Has the right person been named as the custodian of a child's property and are there backups in case that person is unwilling or unable to serve?

(4) Is there a default provision in case a trust into which the residue was to have poured is for any reason revoked or never came into existence?

(5) If a child dies, will that child's share pass to the parties desired by the client?

(6) Does the will address the possibility of the birth of a child to the client (it's never too late)?

(7) Has the client, in lieu of leaving his residuary estate outright to his spouse, created a marital deduction formula disposition through a so-called formula clause?

Marital deduction formula clauses are very important to review and analyze. They are often found in the wills of clients who own assets of at least the unified credit equivalent ($1,500,000 in 2004, scheduled to increase to $3,500,000 by 2009). Such clauses typically divide the client's estate into two parts, one "marital" and the other "nonmarital." The marital portion passes property to the client's surviving spouse as part of the marital deduction and may contain an outright or trust disposition. The nonmarital portion is designed to set aside property exempted from federal estate tax by reason of the client's available unified credit and passes property to persons other than the surviving spouse (or to a credit equivalent "bypass trust" for the benefit of the surviving spouse that will not be included in the spouse's estate on his death).

Particular care must be taken not to inadvertently over pack the bypass trust and pay less than expected or desired into the marital trust. This underfunding of the marital trust could easily occur due to increases in the unified credit exemption equivalent.

The language used in the formula typically takes the form of a fixed sum (a "pecuniary marital deduction") or a fraction of the client's residuary estate (a "fractional share marital deduction"). The formula clause (especially if it is a pecuniary one) will also have to contain a provision for funding the marital deduction when assets are distributed to it.

If the marital deduction clause directs that the property is to be held in trust, the surviving spouse must generally be entitled to all of the trust's net income in each year

and no other person may be interested in the income or principal during the survivor's lifetime.

Any planner who regularly reviews client wills should familiarize himself with marital deduction requirements, or, at least, direct inquiries to persons who have expertise in this area.

POWERS CLAUSE

The next clause is often one pertaining to the powers of the executor (and trustee if the will establishes a "testamentary trust," a trust created at the testator's death under the will). The purposes of the powers clause are to:

(1) give the executor (and trustee) specific power and authority over and above those provided by state law to enable the executor to conserve and manage the property, and

(2) limit, where desired and appropriate, the executor's power and authority (for instance, the client may not want the executor to make certain investments), and

(3) provide authority to continue a business (or handle other property with special management or investment problems) and the special flexibility necessary to accomplish that objective, and

(4) protect the executor against suit by other beneficiaries by specifying the powers necessary to accomplish the executor's role.

An (abbreviated) example of a powers clause is:

I authorize my executor (as well as any substitute executor) in his, her, or its discretion, with respect to all property, real and personal, in addition to the powers conferred by law, to:

1. retain assets

2. purchase investments

3. hold cash

4. vote and grant proxies

5. sell, exchange, or dispose of

6. distribute in cash or in kind

7. delegate to agents

8. assign or compromise claims

9. borrow funds

10. lease, manage, develop real estate

11. abandon property

12. make certain tax elections

13. receive and use employee benefits

Planners should check:

(1) Are there any assets or problems in this case which require special powers to fulfill the desires of the client or provide the executor with sufficient flexibility? (Beware of "boilerplate" clauses). Are there powers that should be added? Are there "standard" powers that should be removed or modified.

(2) Will any power adversely affect the estate tax marital deduction? For instance, a marital deduction trust, under IRC Sections 2056(b)(5) or 2056(b)(7), must provide that the surviving spouse receive all income at least annually. Consider the impact of a power allowing the trustee under a testamentary trust to retain nonincome producing property. Unless the will/trust also contains a provision allowing the surviving spouse to demand that the trust assets be sold or made income producing, the marital deduction may be lost. Will such a power thwart other objectives of the testator? For instance, what if the unproductive property was stock in a family corporation? A sale of such stock would raise income but could cause the loss of family control of the corporation.

The draftsman might consider including a "savings clause" that would nullify any power, duty, or discretionary authority that might jeopardize the marital deduction.

(3) Will any of the powers granted cause a conflict of interest? For instance, if the executor is a bank, discretionary authority to invest in its own securities or common trust funds will cause a conflict that must be specifically "forgiven" by the will (assuming the client wants to do so). Is the executor a business partner or co-

shareholder of the insured? What problems might they create?

(4) Is there specific authority for the executor to make distribution "in kind" (as opposed to selling estate assets and making the distribution in cash)? In some states absent specified power to do so, the executor may have no choice: the distribution must be made in cash.

APPOINTMENT OF FIDUCIARIES CLAUSE

The appointment of the executor, trustee of any testamentary trust, and guardian of any minor child, often comes toward the end of the will.

The purposes of the fiduciary appointment clause are:

(1) to name the individual(s) or corporate fiduciary or combinations of individual(s) and fiduciaries who will administer the testator's estate and any trust that the will creates;

(2) to give the executor the appropriate power to act on behalf of the estate and carry out the terms of the will;

(3) to specify if and how the executor is to be compensated;

(4) state whether or not the executor is to post bond;

(5) to specify the authority of and decision making process for co-executors; and

(6) to name guardian(s) and successor guardian(s) of any minor child of the testator.

An example of the appointment clause is:

I appoint my nephew, Farnsworth Dowlrimple III, as the executor under this will. If for any reason he fails to qualify or ceases to act, I appoint the Left Bank and Trust of Overflow, Pa. as my executor. I confer upon my executor all the powers enumerated in clause _____ above. No executor shall be required to furnish any bond or other security in any jurisdiction. I direct that my nephew, Farnsworth, shall receive no compensation for his services as Executor and that the Left Bank and Trust of Overflow, Pa. be entitled to be compensated for its services as executor in accordance with its regularly adopted schedule of compensation in effect and applicable at the time of the performance of such services.

Planners should check:

(1) Does the client trust the individual who is currently named as executor and backup executor? Is that individual or corporate fiduciary legally qualified to act as executor? (Has the attorney who drew the will been named as executor? Typically, absent special circumstances, this raises a number of ethical questions and raises the spectre of a conflict of interest.)

(2) Should the executor's bond be waived?

(3) Is the executor named willing to serve? (How recently has the client checked?)

(4) Is the guardian for minors willing to act? Is he able to act? Is that person suitable?

(5) Is a prolonged estate (or trust) administration anticipated? If so, consider giving executors (trustees) the power to appoint successors by filing an instrument with the probate or other appropriate court.

TESTATOR'S SIGNING CLAUSE

The next to the last clause in a will is typically the testator's signing or "testimonium" provision. The purposes of the testimonium clause are

(1) to establish that the document is intended to be the testator's last will,

(2) to meet statutory requirements that require the testator's signature at the logical conclusion of the will, and

(3) to state the date on which the will was signed.

An example of a testimonium clause is:

In witness of the above, I subscribe my name, this 11th day of October 2004 at Bryn Mawr, Pennsylvania to this, my last will, which consists of 13 pages (each of which I have initialed at the bottom).

Planners should check:

(1) Is the will signed by the testator at its logical end? Is each page numbered? Is the page count correct?

(2) Are there duplicate or triplicate signed wills in existence? If the testator was given a signed duplicate which is not found at his death, it is possible that a presumption will arise that the testator destroyed it with the intention of revoking it. The potential for litigation is therefore increased significantly. The better practice is for only one original to be executed.

ATTESTATION CLAUSE

The final clause in a will is the "attestation" provision. The purposes of the attestation (often called the witness) clause are to:

(1) witness the testator's signing,

(2) comply with statutory requirements,

(3) underline the testamentary character of the document, and

(4) comply with state law requirements in cases where the testator signed by a mark (such as an "X") or where, at the testator's direction and on his behalf, the will was signed by someone else (as would be the case where the testator was physically incapable of signing but mentally competent).

An example of an attestation clause is:

This will was signed by Edward Grieg, the testator, and declared to be his last will in our presence. We, at his request and in his presence and in the presence of each other, state that we witnessed his signing and declaration and at his request we have signed our names as witnesses this 11th day of October 2004.

Planners should check:

(1) Are there three witnesses to the testator's signing? Although most states require less, three witnesses will comply with the most stringent probate requirements of any state and as a practical matter provide stronger evidence of the competence and testamentary intent of the testator.

(2) Were any of the witnesses beneficiaries under the will? This is inadvisable for at least two reasons: First, the witnesses may become incompetent to testify as to the execution or

validity of the will. Second, witnesses who are also beneficiaries may be prevented from receiving bequests under the will.

(3) Are the addresses of the witnesses stated? Although addresses may not be legally required, they make it easier to locate and identify witnesses when needed.

(4) Is the will "self proving"? I.e., in some states a notarized affidavit attached to the will signed by the witnesses (and in some states, the testator, also) that describes the circumstances of the execution of the will may permit the will to be admitted to probate without the requirement that the witnesses be found or appear before the court in the probate proceeding.

OTHER CLAUSES

There are, of course, many other clauses that should be considered in reviewing a will. Some additional points for the planner to check are:

(1) Is the federal estate tax marital deduction important? If so, consider that the Uniform Simultaneous Death Act, which applies in most states, presumes that the testator survives in the event of a simultaneous death involving the testator and a beneficiary. This would cause a loss of the estate tax marital deduction unless the will superseded state law by providing a "common disaster" clause. This provision makes the presumption that the testator's spouse is deemed to have survived.

(2) Does the will consider the possibility that one or more beneficiaries will disclaim? The will should state who would receive property if the named beneficiary renounces his interest. The transfer is then treated as if the decedent had left property directly to the ultimate recipient.

(3) Have the provisions in the will been coordinated with other dispositive instruments? For instance, is the will coordinated with all trusts, with employee benefit plans, buy-sell agreements, and life insurance beneficiary designations?

(4) Are the problems of minors, incompetents, and other beneficiaries with special needs or circumstances properly addressed in the will? In other words, is the right asset going to the right person at the right time and in the right manner?

Has the client considered the financial burden that may be placed on the guardians of minor children, and have appropriate financial provisions been made so that they can afford to raise both the client's children and their own? (Some may want to set up a special life insurance funded trust that, if necessary, can provide to the guardians needed dollars, but, if not, will go to the client's children later in life.)

(5) Is the client's spouse's will coordinated with the client's will?

(6) Is there a "spendthrift clause" to provide protection against the claims of creditors?

SUMMARY

Although only an attorney should draft a will, every member of the estate planning team should make it a practice to review a client's will on a regular basis. The nonattorney's role in the will review process should be thought of not as a replacement for or as a means of "second guessing" the attorney, but rather as a source of additional strength in the planning process. The estate planner can provide in that regard a valuable resource to ascertain how the client's total dispositive plan can most effectively and efficiently meet the current needs, circumstances, and goals of both the client and the client's beneficiaries.

Chapter 10

POWER OF APPOINTMENT

WHAT IS IT?

A power of appointment is a right given in a will, trust, or other instrument by one person (the donor) to another (the donee or powerholder) allowing the donee to name the recipient (appointee) of the donor's property at some future time. Thus, it is the right to dispose of someone else's property and is, therefore, a way to give someone other than the testator or grantor a right to "complete" the provisions of the latter's will or trust. This authority over the disposition of property can provide substantial flexibility in an estate plan, help accomplish the donor's dispositive objectives, and serve as an important tax-saving tool.

WHEN IS THE USE OF SUCH A DEVICE INDICATED?

1. When an estate owner would like someone other than himself to make decisions concerning his property. A power of appointment is a means of providing for an interested, intelligent and informed person who will likely be living and capable of making a wise choice of (a) who should receive trust property, (b) how much income or principal should be allocated to any given individual, and (c) when principal or income should be paid out. Often, delegation of decision-making through a power of appointment is a way to avoid family conflict or confrontation by placing the decision-making responsibility in the hands of an objective (or outside-the-family) party.

2. When the estate owner does not know what the future needs of his intended beneficiaries will be–or even who or how many beneficiaries he will have. This is particularly important when a trust has many beneficiaries and their needs and circumstances are likely to vary. The power of appointment makes it possible to postpone the time of decision as to the ultimate disposition of property until a date when all the relevant facts affecting that decision are known.

3. When the estate owner desires to qualify assets for the marital deduction but would like to provide both asset management through a trust and have some right to designate who will receive the property (a gift over to third parties such as children) if the spouse does not exercise the power. (If the estate owner's primary objective is to be sure children or someone other than the surviving spouse receives the principal, rather than a power of appointment, he should consider a qualifying terminable interest property (QTIP) trust, a trust that provides the surviving spouse with income for life and then passes principal to the designated remainder persons. This topic is covered in more detail in Chapter 24.)

4. When the assets in trust would otherwise be subjected to the generation-skipping transfer tax upon a taxable termination of the trust. A grant of a power of appointment, while causing inclusion of the assets in the powerholder's estate, can result in a lower tax to be paid because estate taxes are imposed at graduated rates and the generation-skipping tax is imposed as a flat tax at the highest estate tax rate.

WHAT ARE THE REQUIREMENTS?

There are no required or "magic" words or phrases for creating a power of appointment. In fact, it is possible to create such a power without even using the word *appoint*. The courts examine whether the words used in the will or trust manifest an intent to create a power. Thus, a power to invade or consume trust corpus is a power of appointment. So, too, is the power to affect the beneficial enjoyment of a trust by altering, amending, revoking or terminating the trust.[1]

A donee might exercise a power by will with specific language such as:

> Under the will of my deceased husband, Alan, I have, as to certain property, a power of appointment by will; I, now, in the exercise of that power, appoint the property subject to such power as follows: (Then the exercise of the power would follow.)

Another way to exercise the power (assuming a specific reference to that power is not required for its exercise) would be for the donee to mention powers as part of a general devise or bequest.

> I bequeath and devise all the residue of my property, real and personal, including any property over which I may have a power of appointment, to _____ .

In many states such a general reference to powers of appointment is construed as being sufficient to include that property and in some states the residuary clause need not even refer to powers of appointment to exercise a general power of appointment.

Because of the possibility of confusion and the unintended exercise of a power by the residuary clause in the will of a donee of a power which is exercisable by will, many draftsmen require that the power be exercised by "an instrument other than a will." In this fashion, the donee cannot, intentionally or unintentionally, exercise the power by a will, but instead, must use a separate document.

A *release* of a power is a formal statement that the donee is giving up the power. A *lapse* is the termination of a power without exercise. Either a release or a lapse may result in inclusion in a donee's estate for federal estate tax purposes, under the same conditions as an exercise; if the donee's property was transferred directly from the donee of a power of appointment to the recipient, would it be includable in the donee's estate? If yes, property subject to the power will be similarly included.

For purposes of trust law, a power of appointment is "general" if there are no restrictions on the donee's choice of appointees. Where there are certain restrictions, then the power is termed a "limited" or "special" power.

A separate categorization of powers of appointment exists with regard to federal estate tax. Regardless of whether there are other restrictions on the possible appointees of the power, the power will be termed a "general" power for purposes of federal estate tax law if it can be appointed in favor of any one or more of the group consisting of the holder of the power, his estate, creditors or estate's creditors. A power that can be appointed to satisfy a legal obligation of the powerholder is treated as exercisable in favor of the powerholder.[2]

The property owner must decide upon the person to whom the power is to be given (the "donee" or "powerholder"). This person can be anyone who has, under local law, the legal capacity to execute the instrument that must be employed to use the power. For example, if the donor specified that the donee must exercise the power by will, the donee must be old enough to execute a valid will. However, the donee need not necessarily have attained that age at the time of creation of the power.

Once a donee has been selected, that person must follow–precisely–the manner of exercising the power of appointment that the donor specified. This means that if the donor provided the donee with a power to be exercised during lifetime, it cannot be exercised by will (since a will takes effect after death). If the donor had not stated how the power is to be exercised, the donee can use any normal method by which the property subject to the power could be transferred. Therefore, real property could be appointed by deed and stock certificates by endorsement.

In some states, a power of appointment will automatically be exercised–regardless of whether or not the donee has referred to the power–by the residuary clause ("all the rest, residue, and remainder I give") in the donee's will (unless the donee has stated a contrary intent).[3] In many states, if the donee does not exercise the power, the property subject to appointment does not pass to the donee's intestate successors (the donee does not technically own the property for property law purposes, even if he holds a general power of appointment under federal tax law); therefore, it will pass according to the donor's desires if they were expressed in a "gift over," also known as a provision in default of appointment.

HOW IT IS DONE – EXAMPLES

Alan Ferry would like to provide his wife with a power of appointment. He might do this by providing in his will language similar to the following:

> Upon the death of my said wife, or, if she shall not survive me, then upon my death, to pay over the principal to such persons (including, but not limited to, my said wife or her estate), and/or corporations, in such estates, interests, and proportions and in such manner, without any restriction or limitation whatsoever, as my said wife may, if she survives me, appoint by making specific reference to this power in and by her last will duly admitted to probate; or, in default of such appointment, then to divide the principal of the trust, as it shall then exist, into as many equal shares as I shall have children then living and deceased children of mine who shall be survived by issue then living.

This provision would give the wife a "general" power of appointment for purposes of the law of trusts. Additionally, it is a general power for estate tax purposes since it is one in which the donee, Alan's wife, has the power to pass on an interest to anyone including herself or her estate, her creditors, or the creditors of her estate. The example illustrates a "testamentary" power, a power exercisable only by will at the donee's death. If Alan's wife predeceases Alan or dies without effectively exercising her power to appoint, the principal goes to the "takers in default" (of exercise), Alan's children.

Suppose Alan wanted to be sure that his property would be kept intact within his family. He could limit the class to whom his wife could appoint by giving her a limited or "special" power. He might use language such as:

> Upon my wife's death, such property shall be distributed to such of my issue and spouses of my issue as she shall appoint by an instrument other than a will making specific reference to this power; and if she shall make no effective appointment, then in equal shares to my children, the issue of any such child who is not then living to take their parent's share, per stirpes. Provided further, that in no event may my wife make any such appointment to herself, her estate, her creditors or the creditors of her estate, or to satisfy any of her legal obligations.

Here, the power is a "special" (or limited) power for trust purposes, and is also not a "general power" for estate tax purposes.

However, if the wife were given the power by her husband to appoint the property to any descendants of the donor's grandfather or the spouses of such descendants, the power would be "special" for trust law purposes, but would be a "general" power for estate tax purposes (since, as a spouse of a descendant of the husband's grandfather, she could include herself within the group of appointees and appoint the property to herself).

For most planning purposes, the categorization for estate and gift tax law purposes is more important and that categorization will be used exclusively in the balance of this discussion.

The distinction between a general and a special power has very important tax ramifications that are discussed below.

WHAT ARE THE TAX IMPLICATIONS?

1. The place to start is to classify powers of appointment for federal income, estate, gift, and generation-skipping transfer tax consequences in the following categories:

a. A general power of appointment, which for federal gift, estate, and generation-skipping transfer tax purposes grants the holder the power to appoint the assets to the powerholder, the estate of the powerholder, or creditors of either the powerholder or the powerholder's estate, or in satisfaction of the powerholder's legal obligation.

If a power of appointment is "general," the exercise, release, or lapse of the power will be considered a transfer of the property by the powerholder for gift, estate, and generation-skipping transfer tax purposes. If this occurs during life, the result is a taxable gift. If at death, the property is subject to estate tax. Such transfers could also be subject to generation-skipping transfer tax.

An exception to this rule is a de minimis power of appointment that lapses annually. For example, if the powerholder has the power to appoint $11,000 from a trust each year to any person and the power lapses at the end of the year, the lapse of such a power is a taxable gift only to the extent the value of the lapsed transfer exceeds the greater of $5,000 or 5% of the value of the trust property. So, if the trust has assets with a net value of $1,000,000 in this example, none of the amount of each year's lapse would be considered a taxable gift [$1,000,000 x 5% = $50,000].

Another exception to this rule is a power exercisable only with the consent of the creator of the power or a person who has a substantial adverse interest in the exercise of the power, generally another beneficiary who will lose something if the power is exercised.

EGTRRA 2001 repeals the estate tax and the generation-skipping transfer tax for one year in 2010. Along with repeal of the estate tax, a modified carryover basis replaces a step-up in basis for property acquired from a decedent dying in 2010. For purposes of the modified carryover rules, a decedent is not treated as the owner of property by reason of a power of appointment. Therefore, a step-up in basis cannot be allocated to property subject to a power of appointment of a powerholder who dies in 2010.

b. A special power to appoint to anyone in the world other than the powerholder, the estate of the powerholder, or creditors of either the powerholder or the powerholder's estate, or in satisfaction of a legal obligation of the powerholder. The exercise, release, or lapse of this power, as broad as it sounds, is still not a general power and will usually have no adverse tax consequences.

c. A special power to appoint property to or for the benefit of the powerholder that is limited by so-called "ascertainable standards." These are standards relating to the health, education, maintenance, or support (HEMS) of the powerholder. The exercise, lapse, or release of this power has no tax consequences.

d. A power exercisable by the powerholder, acting alone, to vest corpus or income of a trust in the powerholder. This causes the powerholder to be treated as the owner of all or part of the trust for federal income tax purposes.

2. The mere existence of a general power of appointment (as considered for federal estate tax purposes) will cause property subject to it to be includable in a donee's estate. (A power granted in a will is generally considered to be created at the testator's death.[4] A power granted in an inter vivos instrument is considered created on the date the agreement becomes effective, usually the date it is executed.)

3. If a general power is exercised or released by a disposition that, if it were a transfer of property owned by the powerholder, would be includable in the powerholder's gross estate under the lifetime transfer rules, the property subject to the power will be includable. For example, where a beneficiary of a trust exercised a power to amend a trust by requiring mandatory payment of trust income to himself during his life instead of discretionary payments as provided by the trust, the trust property was included in his gross estate, being in the nature of a transfer of property with a retained life income interest.[5]

4. A release or lapse of a general power is treated the same as if the powerholder gave property he could have taken personally (or disposed of to the beneficiary of his choice) to the takers in default. For this reason, a release or lapse of a general power may be subject to gift taxation.[6] A qualified disclaimer of a general power of appointment (perhaps to avoid the tax on generation-skipping transfers) will probably also avoid the gift tax problem.

5. Neither the mere existence of a special power of appointment nor the exercise, release, or lapse of such a right will cause inclusion in the powerholder's gross estate.

6. No gift tax is imposed by the exercise, release, or lapse of a special power of appointment.

ISSUES AND IMPLICATIONS IN COMMUNITY PROPERTY STATES

Since community property excludes property received by inheritance or gift, it would be very unusual for any property received (or given away by permitting a lapse) to be a community property right initially.

However, a community property agreement (some states require it to be in writing) which was all-inclusive, purporting to have both spouses hold as community property all assets they owned, can have the effect, in some states, of creating a gift by transmuting separate property into community property and thus resulting in a gift of one-half of the value from one spouse to the other. If the agreement can be interpreted as including rights of one spouse under a power of appointment, then the right may become community property, resulting in a gift equal to one-half the value of the right at the time of entering into the agreement. Because of the unlimited marital deduction, no federal gift tax would be triggered.

The more common problem encountered is to have the permitted appointee of the property ask to have the property transferred under the exercise of the power titled in the name of his spouse and himself, as community property, thus creating a gift to the appointee's spouse of one-half the value of the property when the spouse receives her one-half community interest in what was intended to be the sole property of the permitted appointee under the power. As was mentioned above, the unlimited marital deduction would eliminate any gift tax exposure under federal tax law. However, state gift tax law should be examined to see if any state gift tax would be caused by such an event.

Where the holder of a "limited" or "special" power has freedom to choose, among the permitted appointees of a power (e.g., where the power includes "the issue of grantor and spouses of such issue"), then the power may be exercised to give each spouse an undivided interest without any gift involvement. The property could, under these circumstances, be appointed to the spouses as community property, joint tenants or tenants in common (each as to one-half), without any gift being recognized.

QUESTIONS AND ANSWERS

Question – How does the rule against perpetuities affect powers?

Answer – The common law rule against perpetuities states the principle that no interest in property is effective unless it *must* vest, if at all, not later than 21 years (plus, if applicable a gestation period) after some life or lives in being at the time an interest is created. In other words, the measuring period under the rule against perpetuities relates back to the creation of the power. (Some states, such as Pennsylvania, use "wait and see" rules. The interest will be valid *unless* it does not *actually* vest within the appropriate period.) In many states, if the powerholder *could*, in any fashion, make an appointment of the property under the donor's terms beyond the time period permitted by the rule, the power is void. (The test is whether the power, by its terms, *will* be exercised within the allowable time period allowed by the rule.)

Question – Is a power to consume, invade, or appropriate property for the benefit of the powerholder a general power for federal estate tax purposes if it is limited to an ascertainable standard relating to the health, education, support, or maintenance (HEMS) of the powerholder-decedent?

Answer – No. This makes such provisions extremely useful estate planning techniques for providing financial flexibility without consequent tax burden.[7] The power over income or corpus or both must be reasonably measurable in terms of the powerholder's needs for health, education, or support (or any combination of these needs). Maintenance and support mean the same thing, are relative terms, and are not limited to bare necessities. In other words the maintenance and support of an individual who has a $100,000 a year standard of living will be very different than someone who is accustomed to a $700,000 a year standard.

Proper wording is essential; if the holder of a power can use property for his "comfort, welfare, or happiness," the power is general and will cause the property interest to be subject to federal taxation.[8]

Question – Is property includable in a beneficiary's estate if an independent trustee has a discretionary right to make distributions to that person?

Answer – Where the donor gives an independent trustee discretionary authority to invade principal to meet a beneficiary's reasonable needs, that power will not cause property to be includable in the beneficiary's estate.[9] This is yet another way to provide additional security without adverse tax effects.

Question – Is property includable in a powerholder-decedent's estate where there is a requirement that the powerholder of a general power of appointment must give notice to the trustee before the exercise takes effect?

Answer – Whether or not the notice has been given before death and whether or not the power has actually been exercised, inclusion will result. The mere existence of a general power created after 1942 will cause inclusion of the property subject to the power.

Question – What is a "5 or 5 power"?

Answer – This is a very commonly used and highly valuable technique to provide flexibility and financial security for a beneficiary with little or no tax consequence. There is a de minimis rule (a rule that says, in essence, that for administrative reasons the tax law will ignore small amounts) that provides property subject to a general power will be included in a powerholder-decedent's estate (or considered a taxable gift) only to the extent that the property that could have been appointed by the exercise of the power the powerholder allowed to lapse exceeds the greater of (a) $5,000 or (b) 5% of the total value of the fund subject to the power as valued at the time of the lapse.[10]

Stated another way, to the extent that a lapse of a general power within a calendar year exceeds the greater of (a) $5,000 or (b) 5% of the assets subject to the power, the *excess* is treated as a release of a general power and taxed accordingly. The excess may be treated as a gift subject to gift tax or as a transfer that may be subject to estate tax. To make certain that the limits set forth above are not breached, the right of invasion must be made noncumulative.

Example: Brian Gordon was the income beneficiary of a trust with assets of $200,000. The value of the trust remained constant. Brian was also given a noncumulative power (which he did not exercise and which therefore lapsed each year) to withdraw $10,000 of principal a year. On Brian's death, only the $10,000 subject to the power at the time of his death is included in his gross estate. The power that lapsed in prior years can be ignored because the amount that could be appointed each year did not exceed the greater of $5,000 or 5% of the corpus of $200,000.

Jamie Gordon was the income beneficiary of a trust with assets of $80,000. She also had a noncumulative power (which she did not exercise) to withdraw $10,000 of principal a year. At the expiration of each year, Jamie is deemed to have released a general power to the extent of $5,000 (i.e., a $10,000 lapse minus the greater of $5,000 or 5% of $80,000 [$4,000]).

Assume that Jamie died in the sixth year of the trust's existence and that the value of the trust assets remained constant at $80,000. Each $5,000 released by Jamie constituted one-sixteenth (5,000/80,000) of the value of the trust assets. Therefore, Jamie's gross estate would include $35,000 on account of this trust. The $35,000 consists of $10,000 on account of the power held by the decedent at the time of her death and $25,000 (i.e., five-sixteenths of the $80,000 value of trust assets equals $25,000) on account of the lapse of the power in each of the five prior years. Each year's lapse is included in the decedent's gross estate to the extent of one-sixteenth of the value of the trust assets because it had the effect of a transfer with a retained life estate.

In addition to the inclusion for estate tax purposes, the failures to exercise the power would result in gifts to the remainder persons of the trust, with the reduction each year by the then value of Jamie's life estate in the lapsed amounts. The relative value of the life estate and remainder interest can be obtained from the government valuation tables in Appendix B.

While the lapse of a "5 or 5 power" may have no estate or gift tax consequences, the same is not true for income taxes. IRC section 678(a)(2) provides that a nongrantor (e.g., the powerholder) is "treated as the owner of any portion of a trust with respect to which … such person has previously partially released or otherwise modified such a power and after the release or modification retains such control as would, within the principles of [IRC] sections 671 to 677, inclusive, subject a grantor of a trust to treatment as the owner thereof" (e.g., a retained income interest in the transferred interest). Thus, if a trust beneficiary has a "5 or 5 power" (e.g., a Crummey withdrawal right limited to the greater of $5,000 or 5% of the trust corpus) and fails to exercise the power in a given year, that powerholder becomes the grantor of that portion of the trust over which the power lapsed.[11]

As such, if the power is allowed to lapse in multiple years, the powerholder-beneficiary becomes the grantor of an ever-increasing portion of the trust assets and will be taxed on the income accordingly.

This discrepancy between the income tax treatment of the trust and the estate and gift tax consequences of the beneficiary's lapse can, however, be useful. First, trusts reach the higher income tax rates much sooner than do individuals.[12] Therefore, taxation of the powerholder-beneficiary rather than the trust can save taxes. In addition, if the beneficiary is treated as the owner of the entire trust for income tax purposes (e.g., all amounts contributed to the trust were subject to the income beneficiary's withdrawal power), the trust can qualify as an eligible shareholder of an S corporation under IRC section 1361(c)(2)(A)(i) even if the trust is not eligible under other provisions.[13]

Question – Is the creation of a special power to appoint trust property to lineal descendants of the transferor or powerholder generally a good estate planning technique?

Answer – Most estate planners consider this special power to be an excellent planning technique. Since the appointees are someone other than the powerholder, his estate, creditors, etc., it is a special power, and has no tax consequences to the powerholder. A note of caution, however – if the powerholder has an obligation to support permissible appointees, and the appointment could satisfy that support obligation, it might be classified as a general power. As a result, such a power should not be given to parents permitting them to use it to support their minor children. Or, a specific restriction, barring the powerholder from appointing the assets to satisfy his legal obligations, should be included in the grant of the power.

One reason such a power is so useful is that it permits someone, generally the surviving spouse, to alter the plan of ultimate distribution to take into consideration varying needs of the children and issue. If one adult child is very successful, and another is not, the appointment can be used to alter otherwise equal distributions to them.

An important use of this power is to permit planning for the generation-skipping transfer tax. The powerholder could "skip" generations where the property would otherwise be distributed to children, and shift it to grandchildren. If the property in question is exempt from generation-skipping transfer tax for reasons discussed in Chapter 18, this may be very beneficial. For example, if a child has accumulated a taxable estate of his own, the power can be exercised so that assets to which the donor's (the grantor of the power) generation-skipping exemption had been allocated can pass, in trust, for that child's lifetime (thus allowing that child the use and benefit of the assets) and pass free of estate taxes to grandchildren at the child's death.

Question – Can a special (limited) power cause gift tax problems?

Answer – Yes. When an income beneficiary of a trust who also holds a special power of appointment exercises that power during lifetime and in doing so terminates his life interest, there may be a taxable gift. The amount of the gift is the present value of the income interest forfeited by the life tenant-donor. Life income beneficiaries should therefore be careful in exercising a lifetime special power because the IRS will argue that, to the extent the exercise terminates the income interest and that interest goes to someone else, a transfer subject to gift tax has been made.[14]

Question – What is a "hanging power" and is it viable?

Answer – A "hanging power" creates a cumulative power in the beneficiary to appoint any lapsed property in excess of $5,000 per year by will at death.[15] The hanging power thus avoids a lapse of the excess amount by permitting the holder to exercise it in the future. If the trust is not terminated when the beneficiary dies, then the beneficiary is in possession of the power at death. Property subject to that power is therefore includable in the powerholder's estate for federal estate tax purposes. If the trust terminates before the powerholder dies, there is no adverse estate tax result (although there may be gift

tax consequences if unused withdrawal powers exceed a 5 or 5 limitation in the year of termination).

Under this hanging power approach, the withdrawal power – up to the 5 or 5 limitation – lapses in any given year. The excess withdrawal power is carried over to future years. In future years the carried-over withdrawals are lapsed to the extent of the 5 or 5 ceiling.

The following illustrates this strategy:

Year	Gift	Withdrawal Powers	Lapses
2001	$10,000	$10,000	$5,000
2002	11,000	16,000	5,000
2003	-0-	11,000	5,000
2004	-0-	6,000	5,000
2005	-0-	1,000	1,000
2006	-0-	-0-	-0-

There are a number of unresolved problems in using hanging powers. First, if the gifts continue over a number of years, the total withdrawal potential could be sizable, and a beneficiary might be tempted to make a withdrawal of the total amount available. Second, the cumulative, unused withdrawals are includable in the estate for estate tax purposes. Third, if life insurance is used, premiums are paid throughout the life of the policy, and the cumulative withdrawals may continue to increase. This can be ameliorated using a vanishing premium approach.

A private letter ruling held that the hanging power used by a taxpayer was not valid because it was the type of adjustment clause that was "contrary to public policy."[16] Experts don't totally agree that this spells the end of the hanging power, but suggest caution is advised.

ASRS: Sec. 46, ¶70; Sec. 54, ¶44.3(i); Sec. 55. ¶57.5(e); Sec. 58

CHAPTER ENDNOTES

1.   Treas. Reg. §20.2041-1(b)(1).

2.   IRC Sec. 2041; Treas. Reg. §20.2041-1(c)(1).

3.   Casner, *Estate Planning*, 695, Note 16 (3rd ed. 1961, 1977 Supp.).

4.   Treas. Regs. §§20.2041-1(e), 25.2514-1(e).

5.   IRC Sec. 2041(a)(2); Treas. Reg. §20.2041-3(d)(1). See also *Est. of Gartland*, 34 TC 867 (1960), aff'd 293 F.2d 575 (7th Cir.), cert. den. 368 U.S. 954.

6.   IRC Secs. 2514(a), 2514(b).

7. IRC Sec. 2041(b)(1)(A).

8. Treas. Regs. §§20.2041-1(c)(2), 25.2514-1(c)(2). See also Rev. Rul. 77-60, 1977-1 CB 282.

9. *Est. of Council*, 65 TC 594 (1975).

10. Treas. Regs. §§20.2041-3(d)(3), 25.2514-3(c)(4).

11 Let. Ruls. 9625031, 9810008, 199942037.

12. IRC Sec. 1.

13. Let. Ruls. 9625031, 199942037.

14. *Est. of Regester v. Comm.*, 83 TC 1 (1984).

15. Let. Rul. 8229097.

16. Let. Rul. 8901004.

Chapter 11

DISCLAIMERS

WHAT IS IT?

A disclaimer (or renunciation) is an unqualified refusal by a potential beneficiary to accept benefits given through a testamentary or lifetime transfer of property. Most often, a disclaimer refers to the refusal by a potential beneficiary to accept a bequest under the terms of a will or trust.

For federal tax purposes, the disclaimant is regarded as never having received the property (that is, for tax purposes it's as if he predeceased the transferor). As a result of this consequence, no transfer is considered to have been made *by the disclaimant* for federal gift, estate, or generation-skipping transfer tax purposes.[1]

The requirements of federal law will apply, for federal estate, gift, and generation-skipping transfer tax purposes even if local law does not characterize the refusal as a disclaimer. For these federal tax purposes, the time limits prescribed for a qualified disclaimer should also supersede any time period prescribed by local law. To be fully effective for both state and federal purposes, the disclaimer must also comply with the applicable state law, and may have to meet separate rules for state gift or state death taxes.

However, even though a disclaimer that meets the federal requirements does not also have to meet the state requirements, the effect of the disclaimer must be that the disclaimant must not receive the property or accept benefits from the property, which must pass to some other person, or the surviving spouse. The result is that for a disclaimer to be recognized, it must shift the property rights under state law as well as federal law. In other words, if the disclaimer has no effect under state law, and the disclaimant is treated as the owner of the property, the disclaimer is also ineffective for federal purposes.

WHEN IS THE USE OF SUCH A DEVICE INDICATED?

1. When an individual with children and a large estate in his own right is left a bequest by another individual and this bequest would compound his potential estate tax problem, a disclaimer may be an appropriate estate planning tool. He may wish to disclaim the bequest in favor of the next recipients under the will or trust, very often his children. By making the disclaimer, the disclaimed property will not be included in the parent's estate at his death.

2. Where an individual who is in a high income tax bracket is left a bequest "if he is living otherwise to his children" (who are in lower income tax brackets), a disclaimer can shift the income taxation to the children's lower brackets (assuming they are age 14 or older) if they are the next recipients of the gift under the will or trust.

3. Where an individual wishes to make a tax free gift to the person who would be the next recipient under the will or trust, he can disclaim the property.

4. When property is left to a spouse who doesn't need or want it, she could disclaim the portion she doesn't want and avoid a needless double taxation.

5. As a corollary to the last situation, where the value of the property left to the spouse creates a marital deduction which reduces the decedent's taxable estate below the amount offset by the decedent's unified credit, a disclaimer by the surviving spouse can be used to increase the decedent's estate to an amount which will be fully offset by the unified credit, and keep the property out of the estate of the surviving spouse. Refer to the extended discussion in Chapter 24.

6. Where the bequest to the surviving spouse is not sufficient to take advantage of the optimum marital deduction, a disclaimer by other beneficiaries in favor of the surviving spouse may be used to qualify a transfer for the marital deduction. This planning option takes on even greater importance because of the increasing unified credit exemption equivalents created by the Economic Growth and Tax Relief Act of 2001. Refer to the discussion of marital deduction planning in Chapter 24.

7. Where there is a trust with an interest passing to charity that does not meet the requirements for a

charitable deduction discussed in Chapter 33, a disclaimer by other beneficiaries may be used to qualify the trust interest for the deduction.

WHAT ARE THE REQUIREMENTS?[2]

1. There must be an irrevocable and unqualified refusal to accept an interest in property.

2. The refusal must be in writing.

3. The writing must be received by the transferor, his legal representative, or the holder of legal title to the property.

4. The refusal must be received no later than nine months after the day on which the transfer creating the interest is made or, if later, nine months after the day on which the donee or beneficiary attains the age of 21.

5. The disclaimer must be made prior to acceptance of the interest or any of its benefits. A beneficiary and his counsel should exercise extreme caution in their approach to an inheritance, as seemingly inconsequential, and often unintended, actions can constitute "acceptance" of the gift, thereby precluding a disclaimer.[3]

6. The interest must pass either to the spouse of the decedent or to a person other than the disclaimant without any direction on the part of the disclaimant. (A valid disclaimer by a surviving spouse may be made even though the interest passes to a trust in which she has an income interest.)

7. The interest disclaimed should be an entire interest, but can be an undivided fractional part of the proposed gift. Since it is often difficult to identify within nine (9) months the exact amount of an inheritance, the amount of a disclaimer can be calculated pursuant to the terms of a formula.

8. As a corollary to the last situation, where the potential disclaimant is entitled to receive an annuity or unitrust payment from a charitable remainder trust, discussed in Chapter 33, and does not need the payment, a disclaimer of that interest will allow the transferor a 100% charitable deduction instead of a deduction limited to the value of the charitable remainder.

9. The beneficiary of a gift or bequest who is insolvent or in bankruptcy may disclaim the gift or bequest to avoid claims of creditors. However, local law must be consulted to assure this will be effective.

HOW IT IS DONE – EXAMPLES

1. Doug Koch, a wealthy client, has four children. An aunt of his just died and, under the terms of her will, named Mr. Koch as recipient of her entire estate if he is alive. If he is deceased when she dies, Mr. Koch's four children are named equally as contingent heirs. Mr. Koch has adequate assets and income to live comfortably, and does not need additional property to compound his already high potential estate tax. By filing in writing an effective "qualified disclaimer" within nine months of his aunt's death, Mr. Koch will be deemed to have predeceased his aunt for both federal gift and estate tax purposes and his interest in her estate would be distributed to his children under the terms of her will without any federal gift, estate, or GST tax liability to him.

    However, if Doug had consulted his estate planner before taking action, the planner might have brought about Doug's reconsideration of his proposed disclaimer by an explanation along these lines: If Doug makes a qualified disclaimer, then for federal transfer tax purposes, his interest in his aunt's estate will be treated as if the interest had never been distributed to him. That means her estate will be distributed to whomever local law says will take upon Doug's disclaimer. *If* the distributees are Doug's children (or others in their generation or younger), Doug's disclaimer will have created a direct skip transfer(s) from his aunt to his children. The transfer(s) may or may not attract the GST tax, depending upon how much property is involved and on the extent to which the aunt's GST exemption ($1,500,000 in 2004) is allocated to the transfer(s). If the aunt's estate is in the 48% federal estate tax bracket in 2004, the estate tax and the GST tax combined could virtually confiscate the property otherwise going to Doug's children.

2. Mr. Ed Radosh specifically leaves $100,000 to his son with a gift over to his favorite charity if his son disclaims. His son can decide after his father's death whether to accept the bequest and donate the bequest to charity if he wishes and receive an income tax deduction, or if it would be more beneficial to disclaim the property in favor of the charity and have the estate receive the charitable deduction.

3. Mr. Jules Einhorn thought that at his death his wife would have ample funds and his son very little.

Therefore, he left most of his property to his son with a contingent gift to his wife in the event his son predeceased him. At the time of Mr. Einhorn's death the son was financially well off, but the mother was in more difficult financial straits. By disclaiming his share and permitting the wife to take, the son not only allowed a better distribution of assets but also may have qualified Mr. Einhorn's estate for a marital deduction due to the transfer of the assets to the surviving spouse. This could result in a substantial saving on federal estate taxes. She could then make gift tax-free transfers to her son using the annual gift tax exclusion and the unified credit.

4. The combined estates of Mr. and Mrs. Smith are worth approximately $750,000. They each intend to leave their share of the estate to the other, or if both are deceased, in trust for their minor children. Since the total value of their estates is less than the unified credit exemption equivalent ($1,500,000 in 2004), there is no estate tax consequence. However, the estate has a substantial growth potential.

The Smiths should consider the use of a disclaimer trust. This is a trust that will only function in the event the surviving spouse (or his or her estate representative) disclaims the bequest under the will or trust. The trust may be for the benefit of the spouse and the children, or the children only. If, at the death of the first spouse, the combined estates of the deceased and surviving spouses would exceed the unified credit exemption equivalent ($1,500,000 in 2004), then the surviving spouse can disclaim into the trust to take advantage of all or part of the unified credit exemption equivalent of the estate of the deceased spouse. When the surviving spouse dies, the trust created by the disclaimer will bypass his or her taxable estate.

WHAT ARE THE TAX IMPLICATIONS?

1. A disclaimer of a property interest or a power is not treated as a gift for gift tax purposes.[4]

2. A disclaimed interest in property is not considered to be a transfer by a disclaimant/decedent for estate tax purposes and will not be included in his estate at death as a transfer with a retained life estate.[5]

3. If property is disclaimed by a person in favor of a surviving spouse or charity, the marital or charitable deduction will be permitted, provided the property would otherwise qualify for these deductions.[6]

4. Any income received on disclaimed property will be chargeable to the person in whose favor the property was disclaimed.

IMPLICATIONS AND ISSUES IN COMMUNITY PROPERTY STATES

Please refer to the background information on Community Property contained in Chapter 7. A qualified disclaimer is taken into account for purposes of the marital deduction. In either a separate property or a community property state, a disclaimer can be expected initially to qualify the estate for the marital deduction or to increase or decrease the deduction if the surviving spouse gains or loses because of the disclaimer.

The availability of the unlimited marital deduction, which applies to both separate and community property, alleviates concerns for future planning in this area. However, different rules apply to the disposition of separate and community property by will in community property states and therefore it is still important to carefully characterize all of the property interests held by a decedent and his or her spouse to determine if under community property rules a disclaimer is desired or required.

Where the entire community property is subjected to probate (both the decedent's one-half interest and the surviving spouse's one-half interest) upon the death of only one spouse, the surviving spouse should exercise caution to disclaim only the community property interest of the decedent. A disclaimer of both halves would probably result in a taxable gift to the individual who takes as the result of the disclaimers. As mentioned in Chapter 7, several types of problems can arise when attempting to determine whether specific property is to be characterized as community, quasi-community or separate.

QUESTIONS AND ANSWERS

Question – Can a beneficiary of a life insurance policy disclaim his interest in the proceeds?

Answer – Yes, such an interest may be disclaimed within nine months of the decedent's death. However, if the beneficiary was an irrevocable beneficiary, the disclaimer most likely must be made within nine months of the beneficiary designation.

Question – Can an interest in jointly held property be disclaimed?

Answer – Yes, if made within nine months of the creation of the gift and before any of the property or its benefits have been accepted by the disclaimant. However, with respect to a disclaimer of joint property that passes by right of survivorship, the nine month period generally starts with the date of death of the first joint tenant regardless of whether either tenant could have partitioned the property under state law while both tenants were living.[7]

Question – Can an individual after attaining age 21 disclaim property if he has received an interest in the property during his minority?

Answer – The law indicates that an individual can make a "qualified disclaimer" after attaining age 21, if the disclaimer is made within nine months after reaching age 21 and if the other requirements of the law are met. However, the law does not allow a "qualified disclaimer" if benefits have been received from the property prior to the disclaimer.

A beneficiary who is under 21 years of age has until 9 months after his 21st birthday in which to make a qualified disclaimer of his interest in property. Any actions taken with regard to an interest in property by a beneficiary or a custodian prior to the beneficiary's 21st birthday will not be an acceptance by the beneficiary of the interest. For example, a minor who receives dividends on stock prior to the age of 21 will not be deemed to have made an acceptance, assuming he did not accept dividends after attaining age 21. This rule holds even with respect to a gift under the Uniform Gifts to Minors Act or the Uniform Transfers to Minors Act where under either Act custodianship ends and the property is delivered to the donee when he attains age 18.[8]

Question – If a testator dies leaving a trust with income payable to his wife for her lifetime and remainder payable to his children, can the children disclaim their remainder interest after their mother's death?

Answer – Not unless the mother died within nine months of the testator since the disclaimer must be made within nine months of the testator's death since this is when the gift was complete. The children would have to disclaim within this period or, if later, within 9 months of the date the child reaches age 21. Note that the answer here is the same even if the children must survive their mother to receive the bequest.

Question – Is a disclaimer valid where a surviving spouse refuses to accept all or a portion of an interest in property passing from a decedent, and, as a result of that refusal, the property passes to a trust in which that spouse has an income interest [such as the typical family (nonmarital "B") trust]?

Answer – A disclaimer will be valid where a spouse refuses an interest in property even if, as a result of that disclaimer, he or she receives an income interest (as long as that income interest does not result from the surviving spouse's direction). Also, the spouse must not have the power after the disclaimer, as trustee or otherwise, to direct the distribution of the trust assets to other beneficiaries.

This "Blank Check" postmortem marital deduction planning tool means an estate owner doesn't have to decide how much of his estate should go to a surviving spouse by will. His will can allow that decision to be made by the survivor when more facts are known. All the estate owner's property could be left to the surviving spouse with a provision that any part of the bequest that is disclaimed will be placed in the nonmarital ("bypass") trust. This planning may–in some cases–be preferable to a specific marital formula bequest.

Question – What are some of the other things one considers about the use of a disclaimer?

Answer – Some of the factors to be considered are:

1. If a disclaiming beneficiary is indebted to the estate, the instrument should specify whether the debt may be set off against the alternative takers (who might be the disclaimant's children).[9]

2. A disclaimer of a power may extinguish it; hence, it may be desirable to designate an alternative donee of the power.[10]

3. A disclaimer of a legacy may result in the disclaimed legacy passing to the disclaimant's issue under an anti-lapse statute.[11]

4. A disclaimer could cause a premature "closing" of a class of beneficiaries.[12]

5. It is generally desirable to express a partial disclaimer in the form of a fraction or percentage. A partial disclaimer may be valid only if it represents an "undivided portion of an

interest."[13] However, the disclaimer regulations do permit a beneficiary to disclaim specific assets in a trust, if as a result of that disclaimer, the assets in question will be allocated to another trust or to beneficiaries other than the trust.

6. To guard against the possibility that the disclaimed property may not pass to someone other than the disclaimant (unless it is to a surviving spouse), an alternative taker should be provided for. Further, the statutory schedule may not coincide with the settlor's intent.

7. The instrument should indicate whether a disclaimer accelerates future interests.[14]

Question – What is the effect of a disclaimer if federal requirements are met but state disclaimer laws are not?

Answer – State law is important because it governs property rights, and how and under what conditions and to whom property will pass. It is possible that a person could make a valid disclaimer under federal law–say within the nine month statutory period– which would not meet a shorter period required for an effective disclaimer of property rights under state law. Federal law provides that the disclaimer can be effective if the property passes as the result of the disclaimer to the party who would have received it if the disclaimer had been effective under state law.

Question – What is the problem, if any, in disclaiming life insurance proceeds?

Answer – If a life insurance policy names a spouse but no secondary beneficiary, a disclaimer could result in the policy proceeds falling into the estate of the insured. This would expose the proceeds to creditors, additional probate fees, will provisions, and in many states unnecessary estate inheritance taxes. If the disclaiming spouse is the beneficiary under the will, a further renunciation would be necessary because the insurance proceeds would fall into the probate estate because of the first disclaimer. Planners should examine beneficiary designations and coordinate life insurance (or pension plan) proceeds so that a single renunciation will accomplish the intended objectives.

Question – Is it possible to disclaim some but not all of a beneficiary's interest in a trust?

Answer – It is possible to disclaim separately different income or corpus interests in a trust, and it is permissible to disclaim a specific dollar amount of a gift or inheritance. Certain disclaimers will be effective for federal estate and gift tax purposes even if not recognized under local law (provided that, under local law the interest is transferred to another person as the result of attempting the disclaimer without any direction on the part of the disclaimant.)

Mandatory actions by the disclaimant that are required under local law merely to divest ownership of the property in the disclaimant and vest it in another person will not disqualify the disclaimer. In the case of a beneficiary of an interest in property who is under 21 years of age, any actions taken with regard to the interest by the beneficiary or a custodian prior to the beneficiary's 21st birthday will not be considered an acceptance of the interest by the beneficiary. In case of disclaimers of less than an entire interest, each interest or power with respect to property that is separately created by the transferor is generally treated as a separate interest. This means that a client can make a qualified disclaimer of one interest in corpus while retaining another interest.

Question – Assume the surviving spouse is entitled to survivor's benefits under a qualified pension or profit sharing plan. Can he disclaim all or any part of those benefits?

Answer – The IRS has recently ruled that such disclaimers are effective. This planning device can be extremely important in view of the requirements that such plans provide survivor annuities, discussed in Chapter 52. Where the retirement plan benefit is most of the value in the estate, the mandatory payment to a surviving spouse may deprive the decedent's estate of the full value of the unified credit. A disclaimer can be used to shift at least part of the benefit away from the surviving spouse to take full advantage of the decedent's credit, and keep that part of the benefit out of the estate of the surviving spouse.

Question – Can the trustee of a trust disclaim powers held as a trustee, such as the power to make distributions to the trustee as a beneficiary?

Answer – Although the cases and rulings are not entirely clear on this issue, the cautious answer is that a qualified disclaimer can be made only by the beneficiary or donee, not the trustee. For example, if the trustee has the power to make distributions to himself or herself and wants to avoid the tax consequences of such a power, the trustee should disclaim the right to *receive* the distributions, not the right to make them. The trustee would then be disclaiming as a beneficiary, not as a trustee.

ASRS: Sec. 54, ¶44.3(m); Sec. 55, ¶57.5(f)

CHAPTER ENDNOTES

1. IRC Sec. 2518(a). However, it is possible for a disclaimer to create a generation-skipping transfer (GST) *by someone other than the disclaimant*. This result can occur because under GST tax law a "direct skip" transfer (i.e., a transfer to or for an individual two or more generations younger than the transferor) is a GST subject to the GST tax (if it is also subject to federal estate or gift tax). IRC Secs. 2612(c), 2613(a). The first example under HOW IT IS DONE–EXAMPLES illustrates how a disclaimer can create such a GST.

2. IRC Sec. 2518(b).

3. See *Est. of Engelman*, 121 TC 54 (2002).

4. IRC Sec. 2518(a).

5. See *Brown v. Routzahn*, 63 F.2d 914 (6th Cir.), cert. denied 290 U.S. 641 (1933).

6. IRC Secs. 2056(d)(2), 2055(a).

7. Treas. Reg. §25.2518-2(c)(4).

8. Treas. Regs. §§25.2518-2(d)(3), 25.2518-2(d)(4), Example (11).

9. *Matter of Colacci*, 549 P.2d 1096 (Colo. App. 1976).

10. Schwartz, "Effective Use of Disclaimers," 19 B.C. Law Rev. 551 (1978).

11. *Brannan v. Ely*, 157 Md. 100, 145 Atl. 361 (1929); *Thompson v. Thornton*, 197 Mass. 273, 83 N.E. 880 (1908).

12. See Schwartz, *Future Interests & Estate Planning*, §11.4 (Supp. 1978).

13. Schwartz "Effective Use of Disclaimers," 19 B.C. Law Rev. 551, 567, 573 (1978).

14. Schwartz *Future Interests & Estate Planning*, §§11.5-11.9 (Supp. 1978).

Chapter 12

SELECTION OF EXECUTOR, TRUSTEE, AND ATTORNEY

[Editor's Note: The pages appearing below, "How to Select an Executor, Trustee, and Attorney," by Stephan R. Leimberg and Charles K. Plotnick, are reproduced with the publisher's permission from *How to Settle an Estate*, by Plotnick and Leimberg (New York: Plume Book, 2001). The authors are grateful for the significant assistance of Lawrence Brody, Esq., of Bryan, Cave in St. Louis, Missouri.]

INTRODUCTION

Selecting the people to carry out the provisions of an estate plan is one of the most important and difficult tasks involved in the estate planning process. This chapter concerns three of the most essential parties in the estate planning process: the executor, the trustee, and the attorney. It will establish practical guidelines in the selection process from the point of view of the person who ultimately must make those choices, the client.

It is impossible to make a proper selection of any member of the estate planning team without understanding–in general terms–what it is that the individual should be doing and how that person interacts with others who have important roles to fulfill. For this reason, you'll find a brief discussion of the duties of the executor, trustee, and estate's attorney before the attributes and selection criteria of each are covered.

PART I–SELECTING AN EXECUTOR

Duties of the Executor

An executor is the person (and/or institution) named in a valid will to serve as the personal representative of a testator when his or her will is being probated. In bygone years, this person was referred to as the "executor" if male and "executrix" if female but now is commonly referred to as the executor or personal representative regardless of gender.

When death occurs, the executor must locate and probate the decedent's will (prove that it was the decedent's will and that it in fact was his or her last

will). The executor must then collect the decedent's property; pay debts, taxes, and expanses; and distribute any remaining assets to the beneficiaries specified in the decedent's will.

An executor's responsibilities typically last from nine months to two or three years. In rare instances (such as when there is a contest of a will or the estate remains open for tax or other reasons) the executor's duties continue for a period of years.

Attributes of a Good Executor

When choosing an executor, the major attributes to consider are:

1. Sensitivity.

2. Competence.

3. An understanding of the needs and appreciation of the circumstances of the beneficiaries.

4. Knowing of the nature, value, and extent of the decedent's assets.

5. Experience in the administration of estates.

6. Business and investment experience.

7. Familiarity with the decedent's business.

8. Ability to serve.

9. Willingness to serve.

10. Geographic proximity to the estate's beneficiaries and the estate's assets.

11. Lack of any conflict of interest.

12. Integrity and loyalty.

Sensitivity. Although the intangible attribute of "caring" both about the people involved and the performance of one's duties cannot be accurately or objectively measured, this single quality is perhaps the most important of all the factors in the selection process. It is always possible for the personal representative, if lacking knowledge in certain areas, to learn more about the subject or hire others with expertise.

The highest preference should be given to the identification of an individual who is willing and able to give concerned personal attention and extra effort to the psychological as well as financial needs and individual circumstances of the beneficiaries. Often this individual will be the beneficiary with the largest share of the estate and almost always will be a close relative or friend of the decedent.

Competence. Competence encompasses both the legal ability to serve and the intellectual and emotional capacity to serve effectively.

Legal capacity entails U.S. citizenship in some jurisdictions and the satisfaction of state law requirements such as (*a*) age (21 or 18 in most states), (*b*) mental competency (generally, the same required to be a testator or in some states a higher capacity, the ability to contract), and (*c*) domicile (some states require that the executor be a domiciliary of the state in which the will is probated while others allow executors from other states but may require that an out-of-state executor post a bond).

Intellectual capacity in a general sense does not require that the executor be completely aware of all the decedent's personal affairs or the intricacy of the decedent's business. What is necessary is that the person selected has the ability to analyze the situation as quickly as possible under the circumstances, determine what facets of the estate administration can be handled within the bounds of the executor's personal knowledge and capabilities, and then secure the appropriate professional assistance in these areas in which the executor knows he or she lacks experience. In other words, the executor must have the ability to organize both facts and people and understand and follow through with what must be done.

Emotional capacity involves the ability to make a multitude of important decisions. Often these decisions (e.g., the selection of and negotiations with the estate's attorney and tax elections) must be made within a relatively short time span and yet may have tremendous financial significance to the estate and its beneficiaries. An intelligent individual capable of making quick, well-considered decisions will more than make up for an initial lack of experience.

An understanding of the needs and circumstances of the beneficiaries. Personal knowledge of the beneficiaries, their ages, health conditions, income requirements, strengths, weaknesses, and eccentricities is extremely helpful to an executor. One child, for instance, may need immediate and continuing medical care, while another may be a highly successful surgeon. An elderly parent may need cash to meet the daily necessities of life or be so wealthy that a delay in the distribution of assets from a deceased child may have no adverse effect.

Knowledge of the nature, value, and extent of the decedent's assets. If an executor is familiar with the specific assets that comprise the estate, that information can be of great use in performing each of the most essential of his or her duties. For example, if one of the principal assets of the estate is a business in which the executor was active in the management, the advantage to the estate of that experience and continuity could be quickly translated into dollars.

Many individuals invest in or amass collectibles for pleasure. An executor with expertise in this area would know how to safeguard, transport, insure, have appraised, and sell such items far more readily than an executor with no particular knowledge of the subject matter. This is particularly true with respect to large collections of art, precious gems, stamps, coins, and many other similar items.

One of the most troublesome responsibilities of an executor is also one that must be started early in the estate administration process-the discovery and assembly of all the decedent's assets. An executor who is privy to the extent of the estate and knows the location of all of the assets or the names of those persons who can help in this key part of the estate's probate will have great advantage. This should simplify the tasks and enable the executor to realize a great deal more from those assets. Prior familiarity is of considerable benefit if the decedent's assets were varied and located in different states or overseas.

Experience at administering an estate. Although death is a common occurrence, few individuals have experience in being executors. Obviously, if an individual has probated at least one or two estates, he or she is an ideal candidate. Note that this criterion emphasizes one of the major strengths of a corporate fiduciary vis-à-vis an individual. Few if any individuals have probated as many estates as a bank or trust company specializing in estate planning and administration. In ultra large or highly complex estates this consideration should be given high priority.

Business and investment experience and familiarity with the testator's investments and business. Intelligence and emotional maturity may not be enough to handle successfully the administration of an estate. The brightest spouse or most intelligent child may lack the business or investment experience to handle a large corporation or a sizable stock and bond portfolio. The experience-tested executor clearly will have an edge in a case where significant business or investment decisions will have to be made.

Professional executors such as banks and trust companies are in the business of collecting, managing, and investing securities. They typically have separate departments to handle, analyze, and evaluate securities, supervise and sell real estate, and run businesses. To a lesser degree, professional advisors and associates (even friendly competitors in rare cases) who knew the operation of the decedent's business can provide invaluable service to the estate.

Obviously, a buy-sell agreement can incredibly simplify the task of an executor where a business interest comprises the bulk of an individual's estate. But where there is no such agreement, the executor must-at least temporarily-assume whatever role the decedent had in the business.

Depending on the circumstances and nature of the business, it could be either continued or terminated. But without knowledge of the details of the business or expertise in the specific area involved, the executor or administrator would obviously be working under a considerable handicap. Even a professional executor such as a bank or trust company may not have the requisite expertise if the decedent's business was in a specialized or personalized area in which particular or unique knowledge was necessary to survive in the marketplace.

Clearly, the executor who has an in-depth understanding of the inner workings of the decedent's business or profession has a tremendous edge over the neophyte. But although there is no substitute for experience, intelligent individuals who have the ability to obtain the necessary information and experience as well as the time and inclination to administer the estate can usually do a credible and often an outstanding job, if they are willing to put time and effort into the performance of their duties.

Consider also that individuals or banks with strong investment or business expertise can be named as coexecutors or can be hired on an hourly or annual retainer basis by the estate's executor. Certainly, any executor without extensive investment knowledge should secure the services of skilled advisors and investment personnel where appropriate. An executor who does nothing-to the detriment of the estate's beneficiaries-is just as liable to surcharge as the executor who makes a mistake of commission. So it is essential for a nonprofessional executor to secure competent advice when dealing with an estate largely composed of securities.

Ability and willingness to serve. It is extremely important in selecting a personal representative to consider the ability of the chosen person (or persons) to serve. The duties and responsibilities of an executor can amount to considerable time and effort, ranging from dozens of hours to hundreds and even thousands of hours. The decedent's heirs suffer the consequences if the designated executor is unable or unwilling to perform the necessary tasks.

Most laymen are under the impression that to name someone the executor of an estate is to bestow upon them a great honor. To the extent the term *executor* carries with it the ultimate in trust, this impression is justified. But with that honor, the personal representative must accept an awesome measure of responsibility and potential liability.

An executor is considered a *fiduciary*. This means a potential lawsuit by beneficiaries for breach of confidentiality, conflicts of interest, failure to exercise due care or diligence or prudence, failure to properly preserve or protect estate assets, failure to file timely and proper tax returns or maintain adequate records, and the breach of the duty to make all major discretionary decisions personally and not to delegate such decisions. This responsibility and potential personal liability may drastically reduce the willingness of the nominee to accept the position. (For this reason, no one can be forced to accept the position of executor. And for that reason every will should provide at least one, and preferably more than one, backup executor in case the one named fails to qualify or ceases to act.)

Geographic proximity to the estate's assets and beneficiaries. Testators should consider, when selecting an executor, the physical distance the executor may have to travel and the time the executor may have to spend away from home. For example, New York state law may allow a son who lives in California to be the executor of his father's estate-but will the son be able to take the time away from his own job (not to mention his family) to serve properly? What expenses will be incurred out of the son's pocket or what nonreimbursable income will be lost by the son because he must be handling an estate on the opposite end of the continent? Quite often, the executor's fee or the size of the estate will be insufficient to economically justify the executor's expenditure of time. In such instances it may be preferable to appoint a local executor-perhaps a bank or a trust company-and to have the distant relative serve as an unofficial advisor to the executor or as a coexecutor.

Lack of conflict of interest. An otherwise logical choice of a particular individual or individuals may fail to consider potential conflicts of interest. For example, an older child may well be qualified to manage her father's affairs. But will a conflict arise between the personal interest of that older child and a surviving parent or younger siblings? Such problems can easily occur when the executor makes decisions on where to take certain deductions or other tax-oriented elections. This problem can be even worse if the relatives are stepparents or stepchildren.

The problem of a potential conflict of interest is particularly acute where a business associate is named as executor. It is imperative to consider in advance of such a nomination the effect that the associate's handling of the business ("to sell or not to sell," and if so, to whom and at what price?) will have on the testator's personal heirs. What if the most likely purchaser is the associate himself? How can the heirs be assured they have received a fair price for the business interest? Or how can they know the right decision was to sell rather than to retain the business? How do they know he did not pay himself an exorbitant salary (as well as an exorbitant executor's fee)? It is inevitable that doubt will linger when a partner or coshareholder is named as executor, regardless of how careful that person is to make decisions impartially and in the best interest of the beneficiaries.

Another area in which a conflict of interest can easily occur is where a client names the attorney who drafted the will as executor. In our opinion an attorney who unilaterally names himself or his law partner as attorney-without the knowledge or express direction of the client-has committed a breach of ethics and has clearly acted improperly.

If the attorney who drew the will is named as executor, then, technically, he or she is not an employee or agent of the beneficiaries. That means they have no power to fire him as executor if he doesn't answer phone calls or if letters requesting information about the estate go unanswered. It will be difficult for beneficiaries to challenge his actions or lack of actions. If that person hires himself or his business partner as the estate's attorney, beneficiaries have little right to question the

legality. Who, aside from the court upon final audit of the estate, can question the fee that such an executor pays himself as attorney? The appointment of attorney as executor reduces the checks and balances desirable in the probate of an estate and-aside from the other issues of competency, ability, and willingness to take the time away from the practice of law to do a proper job-creates inevitable conflict of interest.

There are, of course, exceptions to the general rule that the attorney who draws the will should not be named as the estate's executor. For instance, if the attorney is a close relative of the testator or the natural object of his bounty, it is proper and in most cases appropriate for that attorney to be named as executor. If the attorney is the one individual most familiar with the decedent's assets, family, and business, then the attorney may be a logical choice, but in this case it may be best to name the attorney as coexecutor with a family member.

The very possibility of a conflict of interest may put the potential executor in an uncomfortable and even dangerous situation. In many cases such an individual will injure his own interest in the attempt to bend over backwards to avoid the appearance of impropriety. Nevertheless, he will always be conscious of the likelihood of second guessing by beneficiaries if they feel the apportionment of profits or proceeds was inadequate. Such an individual should, in many cases, properly and promptly refuse to serve as executor.

One possible solution to a potential conflict of interest is to name a business associate as an advisor or as coexecutor with a bank and to name some third coexecutor so there could not be a tie vote. In fact, wherever there is any potential for a conflict of interest a professional fiduciary should be considered. Impartiality is one of the major strengths of having a bank or trust company serve as executor.

Integrity and loyalty. These are among the duties owed by a fiduciary to the beneficiaries of the estate. But it is as essential that the testator have absolute trust in the honesty and loyalty of the executor for reasons that go beyond the obvious legal or ethical implications; an important part of the estate planning process is the peace of mind an individual obtains in knowing that his or her affairs are in order and that the financial security he has paid for during his lifetime will serve those he loves and wants to benefit in the years beyond his lifetime. For these reasons, it is essential that the testator have absolute trust that his will will be carried out as he intended to the best of the executor's ability.

Fees. Although fees are not among the listed attributes of a good executor, they are an important consideration in the selection process. The amount of fee a personal representative is entitled to may be determined by (1) the statutory law of the state where the estate is probated, (2) local county rules or customs governing what the personal representative is entitled to charge to services rendered to the estate, or (3) in the case of professional executors such as banks or trust companies, an advertised fixed and scheduled fee (for a large estate the scheduled fee may possibly be lowered by negotiation, in which an attorney specializing in estate administration can be invaluable), or (4) provisions in the will or in separate contractual agreements between the testator and the nominated executor.

An executor is entitled to reasonable compensation for services rendered. Fees should not be determined solely on the basis of the monetary amount of the decedent's probate assets but should take into account the nature of the executor's tasks, the time spent, the complexity of the problems and decisions that have to be made, the professional background and competence of the executor, and the ultimate results and benefits obtained for the heirs.

There are valid tax and nontax reasons why an executor who is a relative or friend of the testator may or may not accept a fee. Although the selection process should encompass the likely course of action the executor will take in this regard, it is important that this factor not override or take the place of the other selection criteria.

In many cases testators expect that family members named as executors will charge no fees but that professional fiduciaries will. Although in many situations this assumption will be correct, this selection criterion should be tempered by considering the mistakes the nonprofessional may make that the professional would not and the opportunities the nonprofessional may miss that the professional would not.

Summary. The choice of executor(s) and backups (there should always be at least one and preferably two backups) is complicated by a combination of family, personal, tax, and nontax considerations both tangible and intangible. All of these must be considered and balanced, for the executor's tasks and responsibilities are often complex and their successful and prompt completion is always-from the heirs' viewpoint-crucial.

PART II–SELECTING A TRUSTEE

Duties of the Trustee

A trustee is the person (and/or institution) named in a trust agreement to carry out the objectives and follow the terms of the trust. A trustee can be an individual (professional or nonprofessional) or a corporate fiduciary. It is also possible and common to appoint both individual and corporate trustees for reasons that will be discussed below.

It is useful in enumerating the duties and listing the attributes of a good trustee to consider the typical objectives that a trust is designed to accomplish. These goals include the following actions:

1. Reduce or eliminate income or estate or generation-skipping transfer taxes at the federal or state level.

2. Reduce or eliminate probate costs.

3. Provide a vehicle that will serve as a receptacle for both probate and nonprobate assets and facilitate attainment of other estate planning objectives through unified administration.

4. Provide for minor children in a manner more flexible and custom-tailored to the grantor's desires than the Uniform Gifts or Uniform Transfers to Minors Acts allow.

5. Provide for recipients who are legally of majority age but who lack the emotional or intellectual maturity or physical capacity or technical training to handle large sums of money or an investment portfolio or a family business.

6. Provide for individuals who have the capacity to handle large sums of money or an investment portfolio or a family business but choose not to make the necessary investment decisions or deal with the constant problems or devote the degree of attention required.

7. Postpone full ownership of trust assets until the beneficiaries of the trust have attained ages specified by the grantor or until events specified by the grantor have occurred.

8. Enable the investment of an asset that does not lend itself to fragmentation. This often occurs

where the grantor desires to spread the beneficial ownership among a number of individuals. Life insurance policies and real estate are just two examples of assets that are difficult to split up or are worth substantially more if held together.

9. Limit the parties who can obtain the assets and achieve particular dispositive objectives. For instance, where family control of a business or a specific asset is important, the grantor will want to limit the class of beneficiaries and prevent recipients from disposing of property to persons outside the family. A common example is the desire to protect assets from the consequence of an unsuccessful marriage.

The duties of the trustee may therefore include the satisfaction of a number of tax and nontax objectives that include but are not limited to the investment, management, and protection of trust assets and compliance with the dispositive intentions of the grantor.

To a great extent the selection process and decision criteria for selecting a trustee will follow the same pattern as in choosing an executor; premium will be placed on many of the same attributes. But there are several significant distinctions.

Unlike the role of the executor, which is typically concluded within a year or two, the trustee's responsibilities commonly last for at least one generation and often last beyond two or three generations. This fact should have a significant effect on the choice of trustee or on the decision to name both cotrustees and successor trustees (or to provide a mechanism for their appointment by a resigning trustee or by the beneficiaries).

A second distinguishing factor is that the choice of trustee, unlike the selection of the executor, is tax sensitive. In other words, there will be situations in which tax consequences will vary widely (results ranging from success to tax disaster) according to whether the grantor, the grantor's spouse, the beneficiaries, the grantor's business associates, the grantor's professional advisors, or a totally independent third party is named as trustee.

The decision is further complicated by a multiplicity of personal, family, business, investment, and nontax considerations-which must all be weighed by the grantor and the attorney drafting the trust. Quite often, a trade-off between flexibility and tax-saving objectives will be required. And even with the aid of skilled counsel, some compromise may be necessary.

Attributes of a Good Trustee

When selecting a trustee, the major attributes to consider are:

1. Availability.

2. Impartiality and lack of conflict of interest.

3. Financial security.

4. Investment sophistication, policy, and track record.

5. Business sophistication.

6. Accounting and tax-planning expertise.

7. Recordkeeping and reporting ability.

8. Knowledge of and sensitivity to beneficiaries and their circumstances.

9. Fees.

10. Tax-neutral impact.

11. Decision-making abilities.

12. Competence.

13. Standard to which trustee will be held.

14. Integrity.

15. Flexibility to meet changing circumstances.

16. Willingness to serve throughout the term of the trust.

17. Experience as a trustee.

18. Neutral state law impact.

Availability. This criterion has two aspects, permanency and proximity. Corporate trustees are often considered because they possess one attribute that individuals (even individuals who are professional trustees) do not possess-perpetual existence, at least in the sense that a bank (or its successor) is likely to be in business during the entire term of the trust even if it lasts for generations, whereas individuals, even professional trustees, may with unpredictable frequency retire or make a career change or die or become disabled. Although banks may take holidays, they never take vacations. So to some extent it can be said that corporate fiduciaries have an availability advantage over individuals.

This perpetual-existence theory must be considered in perspective; only change lasts forever. The real issue is whether the trustee will be able to serve effectively long enough. The briefly considered answer to this question would still seem to give unparalleled advantage to a bank, especially when the possible senility or emotional instability or physical disability of an individual trustee is considered. It is particularly difficult to protect beneficiaries against these human frailties, since there is no automatic retirement mechanism for super-annuated or mildly incompetent trustees.

But consider that with change in personnel at senior management, professional, and clerical levels, even if the same legal entity is involved, both the personalities and the principles on which money is managed and invested may have changed so drastically as to constitute a new entity for all practical purposes. Surely, in the time span of a trust running for two or more generations, turnover in most banks will effect a drastic if not revolutionary change in people dealing with and policies affecting trust beneficiaries. The bank that was so friendly and competent (perhaps because its senior management gave great priority to trust business in the years in which the trust was established) may be cold and less than satisfactory to a second generation of beneficiaries.

Availability must also be considered in geographic terms. An individual trustee is likely-over a long period of time-to move from the city in which the trust or its beneficiary is located. Of course, although banks generally remain and in fact are becoming regional in scope, since beneficiaries often move (or perhaps did not live in the same city or state or country as the grantor to begin with), dealing with the bank selected by the grantor may no longer be convenient. Consider provisions giving beneficiaries the power to change from one corporate fiduciary to another. (See discussion below of removal and replacement of trustees.)

Impartiality and absence of a conflict of interest. How will the trustee react when faced with a choice that favors him at the expense of other beneficiaries-or favors others at his expense? What are the intrafamily implications of those choices? For instance, will he alienate one family member by (even properly) denying a distribution, or ingratiate himself to another by being liberal in his policy of making distributions? Can he say no to one child and yes to another without causing a never-ending family feud? A trustee who is also a family member may

be forced by conscience or by duty to make choices injurious to the harmony of family relationships.

Will the trustee (such as the grantor's spouse) be subject to the influence of one or more children (or a second spouse or lover) to make distributions that may not be in the best interest of other beneficiaries? Is the family member-trustee easily persuaded or likely to show favoritism? The remarriage of a spouse or child who is named as trustee may result in less than impartial decisions-especially where the trustee has been given discretionary powers over trust income or principal-even if the new spouse is not included in the class of possible recipients.

A child/trustee may take on the role of a parent to his or her remaining parent or siblings. This may be positive, but is also may result in an attempt to control the lives of family members through the family finances as if that person were a parent rather than a child.

An independent professional trustee is not subject to such problems. Since the choice between no and yes may be one of the most important duties of a trustee, this ability of a professional trustee to be objective and impartial should be given high preference in the decision-making process.

Conflict of interest can occur even where there is no issue of impartiality. For example, assume that grantor names his attorney as trustee. The attorney/trustee would most likely be objective and impartial as between the conflicting interests of family members. But consider these questions:

- Once the grantor has died, who will negotiate with the attorney to ensure that fees are reasonable?

- Who could fire the attorney (or trustee) if services were not performed properly or in a timely manner?

- Can the attorney remain impartial as a trustee if he represents the business of one of the beneficiaries?

- Is it appropriate for an accountant serving as trustee to continue in the dual capacity if he also represents a business owned by the trust?

- What if there is an argument between the attorney/trustee and the grantor (or the trust's beneficiaries) that is entirely personal or is on the attorney/client level and has nothing to do with the relationship he has as a trustee?

- Is it possible for an attorney/trustee to fairly represent the beneficiaries, the grantor, or cotrustees in a trust-related situation?

- Will the attorney or accountant be willing to allocate appropriate time to the trust or will at the same time that the person is concentrating on obtaining and servicing professional clients (especially if the fees for serving as trustee are substantially lower than that charged in the professional's practice)?

Conflict of interest problems would plague a business associate or partner who was named trustee. For instance, if the trust held stock in one or more businesses in which the trustee was an officer or shareholder, his salary, or his stock interest would be affected by his actions taken as a trustee. What if the trustee was the art dealer for the trust of an artist who trusted him and had the highest degree of respect for the dealer's integrity, judgment, and marketing expertise? Assume the trust's assets consisted mainly of the artist's paintings. The dealer/trustee would be bound to obtain the highest price possible when selling trust assets. But as a dealer, he would want to pay the lowest possible price. Would it be appropriate to continue as trustee under those circumstances? It is risky to name anyone who is likely to buy or lease assets from or sell or lease assets to the trust or have any other dealings with trust property.

Some of these impartiality and conflict-of-interest problems can be overcome or minimized if anticipated in advance. But in most cases, if such problems can occur, they will. Often, the problem is not that an unethical transaction has occurred or an improper decision has been made. Rather, it is that the parties are uncomfortable merely because the beneficiaries know it could happen and the trustee knows the beneficiaries may distrust, second-guess, or sue him merely because they suspect a conflict of interest could have occurred or might occur.

Financial security. This refers to the security of the funds entrusted to the trustee and the "depth of the trustee's pockets" in the event of a successful malfeasance or misfeasance suit by beneficiaries. A nonprofessional trustee will not have an internal audit staff to review the acts of the person administering the trust. This lack of a system of checks and balances is one of the major shortcomings of an individual nonprofessional trustee. Conversely, banks and trust companies are audited both internally and (usually by the state) exter-

nally. All investments made by a corporate fiduciary must be approved by a trust investment committee, and the portfolio, which is typically diversified, is reviewed frequently.

If sued, will the fiduciary be available to answer for and be able to pay damages for a wrongful act? The answer is likely to be "no" with respect to an individual trustee but "yes" with respect to a corporate fiduciary. For example, in the event of an embezzlement or some other impropriety or breach of trust, the odds of a recovery from a bank or trust company are significantly higher than from an individual trustee merely because of the relative sizes of the fiduciary's own assets. Banks serving as trustees are required to meet minimum amounts of capitalization requirements.

An individual trustee can acquire physical security for trust assets by hiring safe deposit and other facilities. Banks and trust companies have such protection on site but of course build charges for their use into their fees.

Investment sophistication, track record, and investment policy. The trustee's ability to successfully invest and reinvest trust funds is one of the more important attributes to consider in the selection process. In this regard, many professional and even nonprofessional individuals have proved more astute or competent than their corporate counterparts. In some cases the grantor's opinion of a spouse or child as "financially inept" has proved to be an incorrect perception.

But the highly computerized and experienced investment departments of banks and professional individual fiduciaries do have an advantage over anyone who is not a professional investor. A further advantage of the professional trustee is that trust assets can be invested in a bank's common trust funds, which increases the safety of trust investments through diversity.

The ultimate decision in this category should not be made until the various track records are compared. The performance of commercial trust departments has varied considerably from bank to bank and from the investments returns of other investment managers.

Investment policy is an important consideration in the selection process. Corporate fiduciaries tend to be conservative. This may be either attractive or a drawback depending on how aggressive the grantor's own style or personal objectives are.

The investment decisions of an ultraconservative trustee may not be suited to the beneficiaries' risk-taking propensities or their growth and income objectives. But this in turn may be more in keeping with the grantor's long-range goals of restraining the lifestyle of income and principal recipients.

So the ultimate decision is not between professional and nonprofessional or between individual and corporate fiduciary; it must be made on the basis of the type of investment policy the grantor of the trust desires and the particular trustee that will come closest to matching that policy.

Business sophistication. Where one or more businesses are held in the trust, it is extremely important that the trustee have expertise in running that type of business. Even if the trustee should and will sell it, knowing when and how best to dispose of it is a very important skill. If the business is large or large relative to other trust assets, or if it is a specialized or personal service type of business, this may mean that a family member, business associate, professional advisor, or even a former competitor may have to be considered in spite of impartiality issues or potential conflicts of interest.

Typically, corporate fiduciaries do not continue businesses left in trust. The business is quickly sold and the proceeds are reinvested. In most cases that will be the appropriate course of action, since few banks have enough of the right type of personnel to continue the success of a growing business, and a failing business should usually be liquidated as quickly as possible. Nonprofessional individual fiduciaries rarely have the time to run a business even if they have the expertise and experience.

Accounting and tax planning expertise. Corporate fiduciaries have a definite advantage over nonprofessional individual trustees when considering the myriad accounting procedures, tax compliance, and tax planning opportunities that must be handled by a trustee. The level of sophistication, expertise, and experience that should be applied over the lifetime of any trust is one that few nonprofessionals can provide. This means that most family members will simply be incapable of fully understanding all of the problems that must be avoided and the availability and implications of the tax and property law elections that must be weighed. Even knowledgeable attorneys and accountants do not have the requisite practical day-to-day experience unless they practice solely in this field.

It is possible and in many cases appropriate for a trustee to hire agents for advice and assistance. Most trustees will communicate regularly with outside attorneys and accountants. But planning policy and decisions must be made by the trustee; these are among the duties that cannot be delegated. Thus, the trustee must have a working knowledge of the accounting laws and both federal and state tax laws (income, estate, gift, and generation-skipping). Will an untrained trustee know whom to call or if the advice received is both legally correct and practical? Will a nonprofessional understand the interplay between tax, trust, and property law well enough to interpret provisions in the trust and adequately inform beneficiaries about the tax and other legal effects of various choices?

Recordkeeping and reporting ability. A trust is a long-term arrangement under which accountings must be made periodically over many years to a number of parties that may include the grantor, the beneficiaries, the appropriate federal and state taxing authorities, and the supervising court. This requires regular statements of the receipts, disbursements, and assets of the trust in an intelligible form, and careful long-term record storage.

Knowledge of and sensitivity to beneficiaries and their circumstances. In some cases an understanding of the family involved and their special needs or desires and how they relate to the grantor's objectives should properly take priority over many of the other objectives on this list. If the financial encouragement of a handicapped child, for example, is not provided through the trust, the trust may fail in its purpose regardless of how much tax it saves or how closely the trustee meets both the letter of the law and the terms of the trust itself. *Sensitivity* here is therefore used interchangeably with *flexibility*. If flexibility in dealings with trust beneficiaries and a high degree of personal sensitivity are primary considerations, a nonprofessional trustee is indicated.

Fees. Corporate and other professional fiduciaries charge a fee for their services. Usually, this fee is based on a percentage of the income and principal of the trust. A distribution fee equal to a percentage of the principal disbursed from the trust is also often charged (upon termination or otherwise). Although this fee is typically set according to a standard schedule of fees, it may be possible to negotiate the fee in the case of a trust with a large amount of assets. This may be an amount agreed on or may be a flat hourly charge. Where trust assets consist solely of unfunded life insurance trusts, unimproved real estate, or closely held stock, the nonprofessional may be the best choice for a trustee. Likewise, trusts with assets of less than $200,000 in value are often discouraged from using corporate fiduciaries because of the fees.

Many individuals name their spouses or relatives or close friends or even trust beneficiaries because they will serve as a personal favor or as an accommodation and will not charge a fee to act as a trustee. This may be an economic necessity where the value of trust assets is small and payment of the minimum fees to the corporate fiduciary would significantly reduce the income and principal of the trust. But in most cases, the fee saved by using a nonprofessional amounts to a false economy.

There is a further aspect with respect to fees and the selection of a trustee; in selecting a relative who is also a beneficiary, will the fees charged be understood by and acceptable to other beneficiaries, or will such fees-even if reasonable for the services performed-be resented and cause conflict?

Tax-neutral impact. A revocable trust has a neutral impact on taxes at both federal and state levels. As long as the grantor has reserved the right to revoke the trust at any time, in most situations he will be treated as if he had not established a trust and had remained as the outright owner of the property in the trust. So with respect to a revocable trust, it does not matter for tax purposes who is selected as trustee. For example, the grantor will be taxed on the income of a revocable trust whether he names himself, his spouse, a beneficiary, a friend, a business associate, a professional whom he employs, or an independent corporate or other professional fiduciary.

But if one of the major reasons for establishing an irrevocable trust is to save taxes (federal and state income, estate, or generation-skipping transfer), the identity of the trustee is a very tax-sensitive decision: Inclusion of the trust's assets in income (or in the gross estate or in the generation-skipping tax base) will result if the wrong party is selected as trustee. The potential for adverse tax results increases significantly when the trustee is given discretionary powers over the income or principal of the trust if the trustee or a cotrustee is the grantor, his or her spouse, a family member (or some combination of them), or if one or more of these people becomes a trustee under a successor provision in the trust.

Consequently, the adverse tax consequences can be avoided very simply by providing that these individuals may not become a trustee or by specifying that if such a person is a trustee, he or she may not participate in a decision that will result in the to-be-avoided tax result. For example, a surviving spouse/trustee would be prohibited from exercising a broad discretionary power over principal in her own favor if the objective of the trust was to prevent inclusion of assets in her estate. But it is obvious that favorable tax results are obtained at the cost of a loss of flexibility.

The following commentary summarizes the major income and estate tax consequences of powers held by various parties. It emphasizes that before naming the grantor or anyone with an interest in the trust as trustee, consideration must be given to these implications.

I.   Powers to affect beneficial enjoyment.

A.   Power to distribute income to the grantor or the grantor's spouse.

1.   Grantor as trustee.

a. Grantor taxed on the income of the trust since the grantor will be treated as the owner of trust assets.

b. Assets in the trust includable in the grantor's gross estate.

2.   Nonadverse party as trustee.

a. Grantor taxed on the income of the trust.

b. Assets in the trust not includable in the grantor's gross estate.

3.   Adverse party as trustee.

a. Grantor not taxed on trust income.

b. Assets in the trust not includable in grantor's gross estate.

B.   Power to distribute income to beneficiaries other than the grantor or the grantor's spouse without the restriction of an ascertainable standard.

1.   Grantor as trustee.

a. Grantor taxed on the income of the trust since the grantor will be treated as the owner of the trust.

b. Assets in the trust includable in the gross estate of the grantor if the power can be exercised by the grantor alone or with any other party (adverse or not).

2.   Nonadverse party as trustee.

a. Grantor taxed on the income of the trust since the grantor will be treated as the owner of the trust (unless the power is limited to withholding distributions temporarily during legal disability).

b. Assets in the trust not includable in the estate of the grantor unless the grantor has retained the right to substitute himself as trustee.

3. Independent party as trustee.

a. Grantor not taxed on the income of the trust.

b. Assets in the trust will generally not be includable in the grantor's gross estate unless the grantor can substitute himself as beneficiary.

C. Power-subject to an ascertainable standard-to distribute income to beneficiaries other than the grantor or the grantor's spouse.

1. Grantor as trustee.

a. Grantor taxed on the income of the trust since the grantor will be taxed as the owner of the trust (unless the power can be exercised only with the consent of an adverse party).

b. Assets in the trust will generally not be includable in the grantor's gross estate since the power can only be exercised pursuant to ascertainable standards.

2. Person other than the grantor (or the grantor's spouse) as trustee.

a. Grantor not taxed on the income of the trust.

b. Assets in the trust will generally not be includable in the grantor's estate unless the grantor can substitute himself as trustee.

D. Power-subject to an ascertainable standard-to distribute principal to a beneficiary or class of beneficiaries.

1. Grantor as trustee.

a. Grantor not taxed on the income of the trust.

b. Assets in the trust will generally not be included in the grantor's estate because exercise of the power is limited by an ascertainable standard.

2. Person other than grantor as trustee.

a. Assets in the trust will generally not be included in the grantor's estate because exercise of the power is limited by an ascertainable standard.

E. Power to distribute principal to a current income beneficiary.

1. Grantor as trustee.

a. Grantor not taxable on the income of the trust.

b. Assets in the trust will be includable in the grantor's gross estate unless the power is limited by an ascertainable standard.

2. Person other than grantor as trustee.

a. Grantor not taxable on the income of the trust.

b. Assets in the trust will not be includable in the grantor's gross estate unless the grantor can substitute himself as trustee.

F. Power to distribute or accumulate income for a current income beneficiary.

1. Grantor as trustee.

a. Income of the trust not taxable to the grantor.

b. Assets in the trust will be includable in the grantor's estate unless the power can be exercised only pursuant to an ascertainable standard.

2. Person other than grantor as trustee.

a. Income of the trust not taxable to the grantor.

b. Assets in the trust will not be includable in the grantor's estate unless the power can be exercised without an ascertainable standard and the grantor can substitute himself as the trustee.

G. Power to make mandatory distributions of income or principal to specified beneficiaries other than the grantor or the grantor's spouse.

   1. Grantor as trustee.

      a. Income of the trust not taxable to the grantor unless trust income is used to discharge his legal obligations.

      b. Assets in the trust will not be included in the grantor's gross estate because the grantor has retained no power to affect beneficial enjoyment of trust property.

   2. Person other than grantor as trustee.

      a. Income of the trust not taxable to the grantor unless trust income is used to discharge his legal obligations.

      b. Assets in the trust not includable in the grantor's gross estate.

II. Administrative powers.

A. Power to allocate receipts between principal and income.

   1. Grantor as trustee.

      a. Grantor not taxable on the income of the trust.

      b. Assets of the trust will not be includable in the grantor's estate unless the power can be exercised by the grantor in a nonfiduciary capacity either alone or in conjunction with another person.

   2. Person other than grantor as trustee.

      a. Grantor not taxable on the income of the trust.

      b. Assets of the trust will not be includable in the grantor's estate.

B. Power to use trust income to pay premiums on insurance insuring the life of the grantor or the grantor's spouse.

   1. Grantor as trustee.

      a. Grantor is taxable on the income of the trust to extent the income is or may be used for the payment of life insurance premiums without the consent of an adverse party.

      b. Assets of the trust will not be includable in the grantor's gross estate assuming the trust both owns and is beneficiary of the policy proceeds.

   2. Nonadverse party as trustee.

      a. Grantor will be taxed on the income of the trust.

      b. Assets of the trust will not be includable in the gross estate of the grantor.

   3. Adverse party as trustee.

      a. Grantor will not be taxed on income of the trust.

      b. Assets of the trust will not be includable in the gross estate of the grantor.

C. Power to purchase, exchange, or otherwise deal with trust assets for less than adequate consideration.

   1. Grantor as trustee.

      a. Grantor will be taxed on income of the trust if he or a nonadverse party (or both) can exercise the power without the consent of an adverse party.

      b. Assets of the trust will be includable in the gross estate of the grantor.

   2. Nonadverse party as trustee.

      a. Grantor will be taxable on trust income if the nonadverse party can exercise the power without the consent of an adverse party.

      b. Assets in the trust will not be includable in the estate of the grantor unless the grantor can substitute himself as trustee.

3. Adverse party as trustee.

a. Grantor not taxed on the income of the trust.

b. Assets in the trust will not be includable in the estate of the grantor unless the grantor can substitute himself as trustee.

D. Power to borrow trust income or principal without adequate interest or adequate security.

1. Grantor as trustee.

a. Grantor taxed on trust income if trust property can be loaned to grantor without adequate interest or security (income will not be taxed to grantor if approval of adverse party needed).

b. Assets in trust will be includable in grantor's gross estate.

2. Person other than grantor as trustee.

a. Grantor not taxed on trust income if person other than grantor is trustee and that person has the power to make loans to anyone.

b. Assets will not be included in grantor's gross estate unless he can substitute himself as trustee.

E. Power to vote the securities of a controlled corporation.

1. Grantor as trustee.

a. Grantor taxed on income of trust if (1) power can be exercised in a nonfiduciary capacity and (2) the stockholdings of the grantor and the trust are significant from the viewpoint of control.

b. Assets in the trust must be included in the grantor's gross estate.

2. Person other than grantor as trustee.

a. Grantor taxed on trust income if power to vote securities held by person with nonadverse interest in a nonfiduciary capacity without consent of person in

fiduciary capacity, assuming stock holdings of grantor and trust are significant from the viewpoint of control.

b. Assets in the trust will not be included in the grantor's estate unless he has retained the power to substitute himself as trustee.

F. Power to reacquire trust principal by substituting property of equal value.

1. Grantor as trustee.

a. Grantor will be taxed on trust income if the power can be exercised by anyone in a nonfiduciary capacity without the consent of a person in a fiduciary capacity.

b. Assets in the trust will be includable in the gross estate of the grantor.

2. Persons other than the grantor as trustee.

a. Grantor will be taxed on trust income if the power can be exercised by anyone in a nonfiduciary capacity without the consent of a person in a fiduciary capacity.

b. Assets in the trust will not be includable in the grantor's gross estate unless he can substitute himself as trustee.

III. Powers over principal.

A. Power to revoke the trust and revest the principal in the grantor or in grantor's spouse.

1. Grantor as trustee.

a. Grantor taxed on trust income unless power can be exercised only with consent of adverse party.

b. Assets in trust includable in grantor's gross estate if power exercisable only by grantor alone or with any person whether or not adverse (unless the power can be exercised only with consent of all persons with a vested or contingent interest in the estate).

2. Nonadverse party as trustee.

a. Grantor taxed on trust income unless power can be exercised only with consent of adverse party.

b. Assets in trust not includable in grantor's estate unless power is exercisable by trustee and grantor can substitute himself as trustee.

3. Adverse party as trustee.

a. Grantor not taxed on trust income.

b. Assets in trust not includable in grantor's gross estate.

B. Power to terminate trust and distribute principal to beneficiaries.

1. Grantor as trustee.

a. Grantor not taxed on trust income if principal can be paid out only to income beneficiaries in same proportion as they currently receive income, or if principal can be paid out only with the approval of an adverse party.

b. Assets in the trust are includable in the grantor's gross estate if the grantor can exercise the power alone or with any other person whether or not adverse.

2. Adverse party as trustee.

a. Grantor not taxed on trust income.

b. Assets in trust not includable unless power exercisable by trustee and grantor can substitute himself as trustee.

3. Nonadverse party as trustee.

a. Grantor taxed on trust income unless approval of adverse party required or unless payment must be made to current income beneficiaries in proportion to income receipts.

b. Assets in trust not includable unless power exercisable by trustee and grantor can substitute himself as trustee.

4. Independent Trustee.

a. Grantor not taxed on trust income if half or more of trustees are independent.

b. Assets in trust not includable unless power exercisable by trustee and grantor can substitute himself as trustee.

IV. Powers to discharge legal obligations.

A. Power to discharge support obligation.

1. Grantor as trustee.

a. Grantor not taxable on trust income merely because of the existence of the power unless he has the power in a nonfiduciary capacity or the power is to support his or her spouse. But the grantor will be taxed on the income to the extent it in fact is used to discharge the grantor's support obligation.

b. Assets in the trust will be includable in the grantor's estate if trust income may be used to discharge the grantor's legal obligation.

2. Persons other than grantor as trustee.

a. Grantor not taxable on income unless it is in fact used to discharge the grantor's legal obligation.

b. Assets in the trust will not be included unless the grantor could substitute himself for the trustee.

Decision-making ability. The trustee selected must be able to make many decisions, some of great significance, over an extended period of time. This entails the need for emotional maturity and wisdom as well as knowledge.

Competence. A trustee must have the legal capacity to contract. This precludes the appointment of a minor or an incompetent adult. In many states a nonresident individual can act as a trustee (although as a practical matter, geographical considerations often contraindicate selecting a person who lives a considerable distance from the beneficiaries of the trust). Some states bar nonresident corporations from serving as trustees.

Skill to which trustees will be held. A trustee will be hold to a high degree of skill and care. Under the "prudent person" rule, a trustee must use the same degree of care and skill that a person of ordinary prudence would exercise in dealing with his own property.

The Uniform Probate Code, adopted by many states, places a higher standard on professional trustees by providing that if the trustee has greater skill than that of a person of ordinary prudence, he is under a duty to exercise such skill.

Integrity. Honesty and loyalty are the watchwords of trusts. Vast sums of money and other assets are entrusted to fiduciaries who must exercise a high degree of care over trust property and act consistently on behalf of trust beneficiaries.

Flexibility to meet changing circumstances. Change in tax law and in the circumstances and goals of each of the beneficiaries is the only certainty. Since a trust is a mechanism specifically designed to meet that change, the trustee must be willing and able to change as well.

Willingness to serve throughout the term of the trust. An individual trustee could easily lose interest through the long years and even generations a trust may last. Corporate fiduciaries are more likely than individuals to continue for the full term.

Experience as a trustee. This is the most rare of all characteristics. Obviously, past experience in administering a trust is invaluable. Through experience, the fiduciary is more likely to appreciate the broad and complex multiplicity of laws involved, know who to call on for assistance, avoid many mistakes, and more efficiently administer and execute the terms of the trust.

Neutral state law impact. State trust laws must be considered in selecting a trustee. If state law trust requirements are not met, the trust will be invalid and provide none of any intended tax benefits. This is because federal laws's recognition of a trust as a separate tax entity presupposes validity of the trust under state law.

When a beneficiary is named as trustee, the Doctrine of Merger must be considered. This doctrine holds that the trust as a separate entity ceases to exist when the legal title to the property held by the trustee is identical to the beneficial interest held by the beneficiary. For instance, if the grantor's son is both the sole trustee and sole beneficiary, the trust will cease to exist.

Cotrustees

After considering each of the desirable characteristics of a good trustee, it will become obvious to most grantors that it is impossible to select a trustee that has all of the advantages and none of the disadvantages. Many grantors therefore attempt to obtain the strengths of both the corporate and the nonprofessional trustee by naming a cotrustee. Often, one or more family members and a corporate fiduciary are selected.

Combining the positive aspects of more than one trustee has a cost; certain drawbacks or issues must be considered. For instance, if two trustees are selected, what is the procedure if they do not agree on a given issue? If three or more are selected, will the majority rule? What responsibility does a dissenting trustee have for an action (or nonaction) taken by the majority?

Removal and Succession of Trustees

As part of the selection process itself, a grantor should think about the removal of current trustees and the appointment of successor trustees (typically, at least two should be named). The trust instrument itself should consider issues such as the following:

- Who, if anyone, should be given the power to remove trustees?

- Should such a power be given to the grantor, the beneficiaries, the trustee(s), or an outside party?

- How narrow or broad should a removal power be (i.e., under what circumstances should someone be able to remove a trustee)?

- How often may a removal power be exercised?

- How will succession be determined?

- What restrictions will be placed on the successor trustee?

- What are the various tax consequences of allowing the grantor or the beneficiaries to remove a trustee and without restriction appoint a new one?

Summary. The selection of a trustee is a most difficult one because of the longevity of most trusts, the complexity of the tax and other laws with which the trustee must comply, and the sensitivity a trustee must have to both the grantor's objectives and the beneficiary's needs and desires. For these reasons, one or more cotrustees (almost always professionals) is indicated where the terms of the trust are complex or the estate is large.

PART III–SELECTING AN ATTORNEY

Duties of the Attorney

The duties of the attorney will depend on the client's stage in the estate planning cycle-accumulation, conservation, or distribution. In actuality it is sometimes difficult to know where one stage ends and another begins. Clearly, the attorney must be aware in each stage of the implications of what is done at that stage for the other two stages-and of the consequences to the client and his beneficiaries. For instance, it may be easier and less expensive in the planning stage of the cycle to draft a simple will than a series of more complex trusts. But the client's family may have fared better in the later stages had the attorney done a more extensive estate plan.

An estate planning attorney must gather data regarding the client and his family or other potential beneficiaries and their circumstances; the client's sources of wealth, income, liabilities, and expenses; and the client's financial goals and fears. The attorney must then assemble this data and relate each of these objective facts and subjective feelings to each other and be able to ascertain the client's current position and the extent of his weaknesses in the following areas:

1. Liquidity: Will the client during his lifetime and his executor at his death be able to pay taxes and other expenses without the need for a forced sale?

2. Disposition of assets: Are they going to the right person at the right time in the right manner?

3. Adequacy of capital and income: Does the client have enough capital and income in the event of death or disability, or at retirement, or for special family needs such as the care of a handicapped child, or for charitable bequests?

4. Stability and maximization of value: Has the client first put a floor under and then maximized the value of the assets he currently owns? For instance, the value of a business without adequate liability or fire insurance coverage has not been stabilized; the value of a partnership without a fully funded buy-sell plan has not been maximized.

5. Excessive transfer costs: Is the client paying too much in income taxes, or will the client's estate pay an unnecessary amount of estate or other death taxes or transfer costs?

6. Special needs: Does the client have special needs or desires that must be met, such as making gifts to a charity, supporting a poor relative, or protecting a spendthrift spouse?

An estate planning attorney must not only understand these problems and their solutions but also be able to communicate them to the client in a manner that will allow the client to make informed decisions.

Often the attorney must organize the entire estate planning team. Always the attorney should work with the client and the client's other professional advisors in establishing an order of priorities and responsibilities and make sure each aspect of the plan is completed in a timely manner.

Only the attorney can draft the appropriate documents. These range in complexity and length from a simple durable power of attorney, which may run four or five pages, to the recapitalization of the client's business and the complete restructuring of the nature of the client's estate plan, which may take hundreds of drafted pages.

Attributes of a Good Attorney

Many of the same attributes important in the selection of an executor or trustee are also of key importance in the search for an attorney. For example, an attorney with business experience who is also familiar with the client's business can be invaluable. The major attributes that should be considered in the selection of an estate planning (or administration) attorney are competence, compassion, clarity, and affordability.

Competence. The level of competence necessary depends to a great extent on the nature and extent of the client's wealth and the complexity of the client's situation. Most general practitioners are competent to draft a power of attorney or simple will. This may be all that is necessary in smaller estates where all the parties involved including the beneficiaries are self-sufficient adults and there are no unusual assets, objectives, or problems.

But once the estate reaches the size at which federal estate taxes may be imposed, or if the client or any of the client's beneficiaries are under a legal, physical, mental, or emotional disability, or if there is any unusual fact pattern, it is best to find a attorney who specializes in estate planning and administration. The question is how do you find an attorney in the estate planning field, and then how do you ascertain his or her competence? Some of the ways to locate attorneys practicing in the estate planning field are discussed below.

1. Call the county or city estate planning council. Ask for a copy of the membership directory. This should contain lists of not only attorneys but also CPAs, CFPs, CLUs and ChFCs, trust officers, and other key members of the estate planning team. This list, of course, does not ensure any specific level of competence, but most estate planning councils require peer nomination for entrance, and membership fees help eliminate those who do not spend substantial time in the practice of estate planning. More important, estate planning councils make continuing education and in-depth seminars available to their members. The best attorneys active in the estate planning and administration field tend to be members of an estate planning council.

2. Many states now certify attorneys in selective areas of practice. Texas, for example, examines an attorney through a rigorous additional state bar-administered examination in the estate planning area. Attorneys who have earned the right to specialize in estate planning through certification will usually signify that in their telephone book listing and on their business cards and stationery.

3. Trust officers are excellent sources for finding attorneys active in estate planning. Visit three or four banks with large trust offices. Ask for the two or three most competent attorneys. If the same name is mentioned favorably by more than one trust officer, he or she might be a good choice. CLUs, ChFCs, CFPs, and CPAs are also excellent sources for the names of competent attorneys who specialize in estate planning.

4. Attorneys who specialize in estate planning often lecture at business meetings or adult education courses. After attending one or two sessions, a person should find it easy to tell if the attorney can communicate complex legal matter effectively.

5. Practicing attorneys who teach estate planning in law schools, in the tax masters' programs at business schools, and especially those who have taught the American College's estate planning courses for several years are excellent candidates.

6. Some attorneys write in professional journals such as *Taxation for Accountants, the Practical Lawyer, Estate Planning Magazine, The Journal of The Society of Financial Service Professionals, Trusts and Estates Magazine, The Practical Accountant,* or the *Journal of Accountancy*. Some write regular newspaper columns or do radio talk shows on estate planning.

7. Attorneys with an LLM (masters) in taxation generally have higher than average expertise in the estate planning area.

8. Friends and business associates may be able to provide referrals.

9. Bar association referral services and local law schools with tax masters programs are also good sources of estate planning attorneys.

Compassion. The single most important distinction between a truly good estate planning attorney and the average practitioner is not a superior knowledge of the tax law, nor is it the sense of combativeness that makes winners out of litigation attorneys: it is an attitude of being counselor rather than advocate. The estate planning attorney will be keenly sensitive to the importance of the client's business, for instance, not only as figures on a ledger sheet but also as a personification of the client and as part of a goal-striving behavior. Such an attorney will be extremely conscious of the circumstances, needs, hopes, and fears of the client and of his intended beneficiaries.

Clarity. An estate planning attorney must be able to communicate. Often, the attorney will captain the estate planning team. This means he or she must be able to request information from other professionals, explain to them what each member of the estate planning team is doing and what remains to be done. The attorney must also be able to communicate clearly with non-professionals, such as the client or the client's family, the nature and extent of problems the client may not have known existed.

Clarity encompasses not only transferring information but also the urgency of deciding and then acting. The estate planning attorney must be able to convey the importance of the client's doing certain things (such as signing a will, obtaining adequate amounts of life or disability insurance, or establishing a buy-sell agreement) now!

Affordability. Malpractice premiums for estate planning and administration attorneys are among the highest in the profession. This is indicative of the complexity of the practice and of the potential for making expensive mistakes. The point is, selecting the right attorney is a cost-saving factor. The lowest fee may be far from the least expensive.

Clients should demand a written and signed statement of the attorney's hourly fee or an estimate of the overall cost for planning or administering the estate-before allowing work to begin.

There is one more important consideration involving the relationship of an attorney to the estate of a deceased person. In most cases the attorney who drafted a will or trust or other estate planning document should be employed to help execute it. That attorney will probably know the client and his intentions better than anyone else. But if the personal representative of a deceased person is not satisfied with the deceased person's attorney or if the decedent gave no indication of his or her choice of attorney for the estate, the personal representative should, in practically every instance, make his or her own independent selection of an attorney qualified in the area of administering the decedent's estate.

Since the executor has the full responsibility if something goes wrong, the executor has the right and responsibility to personally select the estate's attorney-regardless of which attorney drew the decedent's will. In fact, a number of states protect that right with specific legislation.

Summary. The selection of an attorney who specializes in estate planning should focus primarily on identifying someone who has competence, compassion, the ability to communicate clearly with other professionals and with clients, and who is willing to work at a price that is in line with a client's means.

Chapter 13

PROBATE[1]

Any adult could be an executor. But few of us would want to be if we knew the awesome, complex, and time-consuming responsibilities and potential liabilities the task entails.

GENERAL ROLE OF AN EXECUTOR

When a person dies, the law requires that his property must be collected. After debts, taxes, and expenses are paid, the remaining assets are distributed to whoever is entitled to that property. That distribution is determined by the person's will or the intestate laws of the state. It is the executor's or administrator's responsibility to collect the assets, to pay the death taxes, debts, and expenses of the decedent (the person who died), and to make the appropriate distribution of any remaining assets. The entire process by which these tasks are accomplished (with the guidance and supervision of the court system) is called "probate." The court that oversees the process is called the probate or orphans' or surrogates' court.

DISTINCTION BETWEEN EXECUTOR AND ADMINISTRATOR

An "executor" is the person appointed in the will of the decedent. In some jurisdictions, the person named as executor in the will has limited or no authority to act until his appointment is approved by the appropriate court. If the decedent left no will, if the will is invalid for some reason, or if the named executor is unable or unwilling to serve, then either the surviving spouse or another relative of the decedent, or one or more of the persons entitled to his or her estate, may be appointed as the "personal representative." In some jurisdictions, a creditor or any other "person" may be appointed if no one of higher priority is able or willing to serve. If not named in the will, the personal representative is called the "administrator" of the estate.

It is the executor or administrator (a female appointee is sometimes referred to as "executrix" or "administratrix") who will probate the decedent's will. In its most narrow sense, the term "probate" means to prove that the will was the decedent's, and that the will being offered is the "last will" of the decedent. In its broader sense, "probate" refers to the entire process of administering the will, including gathering the decedent's assets, paying the decedent's debts, and distributing the remaining assets to the beneficiaries.

FUNERAL ARRANGEMENTS

Typically, the funeral will take place before the executor has been appointed. So the executor's only legal duty with respect to the funeral will be to pay the bill if it is reasonable.

APPOINTMENT OF THE PERSONAL REPRESENTATIVE

Even before the appointment of a personal representative of a decedent's estate, a determination has to be made as to where the deceased person was domiciled. A person's domicile is his permanent and principal home, the place to which he always intends to return. The difference between domicile and residence is that your residence is where you happen to be living. Domicile requires not only your presence, but also an intention to make it your permanent home.

The will must then be recorded in the office of the local register of wills of the county in which the decedent was domiciled (often the clerk of the county court). The register of wills (or the appropriate court of jurisdiction) will issue either "letters of administration" to the administrator or "letters testamentary" to the executor. These "letters" are proof of the legal authority of the personal representative to collect and deal with the assets of the decedent's estate. (In some jurisdictions to make things simpler, the register of wills gives the executor "short certificates," brief documents evidencing the fact that you are the executor or administrator of the decedent's estate.)

The executor or administrator assumes title to the decedent's property and acts on behalf of the estate.

EMPLOYMENT OF THE ATTORNEY FOR THE ESTATE

An executor is entitled to use any qualified attorney he or she would like. The term "qualified attorney" is stressed because of the complexity of handling an estate. Generally, an executor may use any attorney he feels is competent – even if the decedent named a different attorney in his will.

For both state law and federal tax purposes, the executor or administrator must keep informed as to exactly how the estate is being administered. He can't just close his eyes and shift all the responsibility to the attorney. In one case, a court held an administratrix responsible for the actions of her attorney where she had surrendered all her duties to the attorney and exercised no effective supervision whatsoever over his activities. The court felt that she did not exercise that degree of care, prudence, circumspection, and foresight that a prudent person would employ in matters of her own.

COLLECTING THE ASSETS

After the executor is appointed, the first thing he should do is to get together with the members of the decedent's family, assuming that they are the decedent's beneficiaries, and make sure that he has a clear understanding of the size and nature of the decedent's estate. The second step, if the size, nature, and complexity of the estate warrant, is to hire competent counsel. Once appropriate counsel has been employed the executor should take specific steps to safeguard and collect the decedent's assets as quickly as possible.

It is extremely important that the executor take every possible measure to make certain that he has a complete inventory of all of the decedent's assets. In this regard, he should review the decedent's past income tax returns, cancelled checks, and mail to determine if there are any purchases, accounts, securities, or other assets of which the executor is not otherwise aware.

Prior income tax returns, for example, might list interest from bank accounts or dividends from securities of which the executor has no knowledge. From this information, the executor can trace the present location of the assets and determine whether those assets were still owned by the decedent at the time of his death. In addition, the executor must try to collect all outstanding claims that the decedent had against others at his death. In one case, a court even held the executor responsible for failing to make a claim that the estate

was the beneficiary of – and therefore entitled to – monies from another state.

The executor should advertise the fact that he has been appointed executor so that creditors or other persons who might have an interest in the decedent's estate will have public notice of his death and thus have time to present any claims against the estate to the executor. In many jurisdictions, publication of notice in a newspaper is required. The public notice also gives creditors warning that claims must be made before a certain date or else the claims will be barred. If notice of one's appointment as executor is advertised, and the prescribed period of time elapses from the first date of publication, then the executor files his final account with the court. Only after that time elapses and the executor has accounted for what came into the estate, what went out, and what he paid to the beneficiaries, can the executor be discharged of all responsibility for handling the estate.

There is no special order in which the executor must collect the decedent's assets, but it is usually logical to file the appropriate claim form to collect the decedent's life insurance as soon as possible. There are also forms for collecting social security and veterans' administration benefits. Sometimes unpaid salary, as well as other fringe benefits, must be collected. Arrange to have the decedent's safe-deposit box opened and make a list of its contents.

It is important for the executor to open an estate checking account and a savings account. The executor can then take all the liquid assets and pass them through the checking account and savings account, if appropriate, in order to have an accurate accounting of the assets collected and bills paid.

The executor should give notice of the decedent's death to the banks where the decedent had his accounts. He should obtain from the banks letters giving the exact values of the accounts on the date of death, the dates that the accounts were opened, and the exact names on the accounts.

All securities in the decedent's name should be assembled, and the executor should maintain close contact with the decedent's broker to be certain that he has an accurate record of all the securities that the decedent owned, or had an interest in, at the time of his death. There are certain forms the executor must obtain to transfer title to stocks or bonds. The executor must also determine the value of the securities on the decedent's date of death according to the valuation method prescribed by the Internal Revenue Service.

If the decedent held real estate in his own name, the executor must be certain that the property is protected, that appropriate amounts of insurance are obtained or maintained, and that adequate safeguards are instituted to maintain the security of the property. If it is decided that the property should be sold, the executor is responsible for making sure that the sale is conducted properly and a fair price is received. Even if the executor makes a completely innocent mistake, it could cost him money. For example, one executor mistakenly obligated an estate to two real estate commissions. As a result, the court held that the executor was personally responsible for the amount of the overpayment.

It is also necessary for the executor to have court approval for the sale of real estate unless that power is specifically given to him in the will. In another case, the court found that even where the will gave the executor all the powers set forth in the general statutes of the state, which included the power to sell any property of the decedent without court approval, the executor still did not have the right to sell real estate without court approval.

As assets are collected, they should also be valued. This means an appraisal must be made of the real property and of any personal property that the decedent owned, such as jewelry, clothing, automobiles, and household furniture and effects. And, of course, a value has to be placed on any business interest of the decedent. In some jurisdictions, all assets other than cash or cash equivalents must be appraised by court-appointed appraisers. In one recent case, the court felt that because the executor erred in calculating the value of the decedent's shares in a corporation, and thereby obtained a sales price below the value of the shares, the executor should be surcharged.

HANDLING THE BUSINESS

Where the executor finds a business among the decedent's assets, particular attention must be given to the books of the business. He should examine prior tax returns and take whatever action is necessary to ensure that the business is being run as efficiently as possible. A determination will have to be made as to whether the business should be continued or liquidated. In this regard, the executor can be guided by the decedent's instructions in his will, by the wishes of the family, or by whatever professional guidance the executor can obtain. If the decedent had any business agreements, such as a buy-sell agreement with a surviving partner, or with a surviving shareholder if the business is incorporated, or

with the corporation itself, then the executor must comply with the provisions of the agreement.

Very serious problems can arise in trying to conserve the value of a decedent's business or real estate. If the decedent's business was a sole proprietorship, then it terminates on his death. A partnership also terminates, in effect, unless the proper predeath agreements have been made, such as buy-sell agreements that would enable the surviving partner or partners to continue the business. If the business is closed for any period of time following the decedent's death, its value as a going concern is greatly diminished. An interruption of the normal flow of business will result in the loss of customers and a large drop in the value for which the business might be sold. If the assets of the business are perishable, or have a time value, then the executor faces the problem of taking immediate action or having these business assets dissipated.

Unfortunately, the executor can be held personally responsible for negligence in the management of a decedent's business. In fact, the results in most cases where businesses are continued without court authorization are generally unfavorable to the personal representatives. The court in one such case held that the personal representative did not have the unqualified right to perpetuate a decedent's enterprise without approval of the court, and that any loss to the estate suffered by continuation of the business fell upon the representative.

INVESTING AND PROTECTING THE ASSETS

The executor should take steps to ascertain that the assets are properly invested, so that there will be no possibility of the executor's being held responsible for dissipating the assets or allowing their value to decrease unreasonably. In investing these assets, an executor is required to exercise the same degree of judgment that a reasonable person would exercise in the management of his own estate. In one case, the executrix held an estate balance of approximately $6,000 in a noninterest-bearing checking account for 3 years because of the need for ready cash and liquidity of funds. The court, however, felt that it would have been more prudent to invest the money and not permit it to remain idle. The executrix was consequently charged for failing to invest the funds.

Protection of assets is another responsibility of an executor, who must make certain that silverware, jewelry, and art objects are protected and insured, so that he will not be held responsible in the event of loss by theft, fire, or other unforeseen calamity.

The executor must try to obtain a fair price if he sells the assets. For example, the executor of the estate of a prominent painter sold paintings to an art dealer, and the dealer later resold the paintings at prices ranging from six to ten times what the dealer paid the estate for them. The court held the executor responsible for the loss to the estate.

What does an executor do when property is not in the decedent's name alone, but the decedent owns it jointly with his wife, or another family member, or even a business associate? Whenever property is held in joint names, the applicable state law will determine whether the decedent's interest in the property will be included as part of his estate to be administered by the executor or whether, in fact, the property will pass directly to the remaining joint owner or owners. For example, in most states, property owned jointly by husband and wife is owned as a joint tenancy with the right of survivorship (sometimes know as "tenancy by the entirety"). The right of survivorship means that upon the death of one of these joint owners the survivor owns all property rights to the exclusion of the executor.

However, property is sometimes owned by several persons "in common." In this situation, each person has an undivided right to a certain percentage of the property. Where the decedent owned a tenancy in common, the executor will represent the decedent's interests in his or her proportionate share of the property. In some cases, questions can be raised as to what exactly the decedent's interest is, and these cases require extreme caution on the part of the executor. There is also the problem of the responsibility for the taxes due on the decedent's interest in his share of the jointly held property.

PAYMENT OF TAXES, DEBTS, AND EXPENSES

A decedent's assets must often be converted into cash in order to pay expenses, debts, and taxes. Since no two decedents own exactly the same property, no two estates will be handled in an identical manner. There is very little demand for some of the personal property that people own. Therefore it is hard to realize cash from many of these assets. Of course, assets such as the proceeds of life insurance, certificates of deposits, and Treasury bills may be available to take care of the estate's liabilities. Listed securities can also be quickly converted to cash, but the market value at the time that funds are needed might preclude their sale at that time.

Assets such as real estate and business interests are not readily convertible into cash, and it might take months, or even years in the case of business interests, to realize cash from these assets. Therefore the executor has to analyze the assets of the estate after they have been assembled, determine what amounts of cash will be needed to cover the debts, expenses, and taxes of the estate, and then develop a plan to make the necessary funds available when required.

Typical debts that the decedent might have outstanding at his death include outstanding loans, credit card balances, and day-to-day bills such as household bills, telephone, electric, gasoline, department store charges, and past taxes.

Common expenses are the costs of administering the estate. These include probate costs, legal fees, executor's or administrator's fees, fees for appraisers, costs included in selling real estate and personal property, costs arising on account of the decedent's last illness, and the costs involved in winding up the executor's business.

Numerous categories of taxes must be paid in the process of settling an estate. In many estates the executor must pay two categories of death taxes – state inheritance and estate taxes, and the federal estate tax. In addition, the executor is also responsible for the payment of unpaid income taxes, both federal and state, and any state personal property and real estate taxes that might be due on the personal and real property in the decedent's name.

State death taxes are typically paid by the executor out of the estate's assets. (Technically, with respect to an inheritance tax, the person receiving the property is taxed on his right to receive such assets. An estate tax taxes the right to transfer property.) The amount of any inheritance tax, which is on the transfer itself, usually depends on the relationship of the beneficiary or receiver of the property to the decedent. For example, in Pennsylvania property left to children, grandchildren, parents, or anyone in the family line is taxed to the recipient at the rate of 6 percent, while property left to all other beneficiaries is taxed at 15 percent. There are exceptions for certain types of property held jointly by husband and wife for which no tax is due. There are also specific exemptions, such as for the proceeds of life insurance paid to a named beneficiary, for charitable bequests, and for real estate located outside of the taxing state.

Where a decedent owns real estate located in a state different from that of his domicile at the time of death, the state in which the real estate is located has the right to tax the property. This often leads to problems, especially in those cases where two states are trying to tax the same property.

A federal estate tax return must be filed if the decedent's net assets exceed a specified amount at the time of his or her death. (It is important to remember that the decedent's estate for federal estate tax purposes may be different from the decedent's estate for state death tax purposes.)

Tax returns must, of course, accompany tax payments. The federal estate tax return is a long and highly complex form, requiring a great deal of time both in assembling the necessary information and in preparing the return. There are important questions that must be answered by the executor as well as available options that can result in considerable tax savings to the estate, and with which the executor must be familiar. Before listing the assets on the return, the executor must first decide on the value of the assets at the time of death. For cash or listed securities, the value of the asset is fixed. However, in determining the value of a business interest or of real estate, it is first necessary to have the properties in question appraised. Appropriate parallels should then be drawn between similar assets, so that a valuation can be arrived at that will keep taxes to a minimum, but will also be acceptable to the government as a fair representation of the market value of the properties as of the date of the decedent's death.

For estate tax purposes, the executor has the choice of using the value of property as of the date of death or selecting the alternate valuation date value. This simply means valuing the assets in the estate at a date 6 months following the decedent's death. Alternate valuation would be advantageous in the event that the value of the property had fallen during that period, and this is a very important decision on the part of the executor.

There are also certain types of closely held business property and farm property that may qualify for specific tax advantages because of the nature of the property. The estate may also qualify for a deduction if a significant portion of the estate consists of a family-owned business interest. The executor should be aware of these special elections as well as other important valuation rules and should use them to the best advantage of the estate and its beneficiaries.

Another very important tax-saving device is the marital deduction. Under law prior to 1981, the estate of a decedent received a deduction for any property left to the decedent's spouse in a qualified manner in an amount equal to the greater of one-half of the decedent's adjusted gross estate or $250,000. Under current law, it is now possible to transfer an unlimited amount of money and/or property to a surviving spouse who is a U.S. citizen, outright or in trust, and not pay any federal estate tax. It is even possible to provide that the surviving spouse will receive only the income from that property, with the remainder passing at death to some third party, such as the couple's children. (Under prior law, this would have caused a loss of the marital deduction.) Prompt action on the part of the executor, though, is essential if this enhanced flexibility is to be secured. Still other choices and elections must be made by executors to fully maximize the almost unlimited tax-saving potential of current law.

Federal estate taxes are due 9 months from the date of death. There are serious penalties if the return is not filed promptly or if an extension is not obtained within a specified time period. In certain circumstances, there are options available to an executor that will extend the time period for the payment of all or a portion of the federal estate tax. If the estate qualifies, no payment of the tax is required for 4 years (although interest at an extremely favorable rate is payable during this time). The executor can then pay the tax due (plus interest) in up to ten annual installments. This can stretch out the payments for up to 14 years.

The executor is responsible for knowing all of these dates and taking advantage of all options and elections. Courts have held that where the untimely filing of federal estate tax returns resulted in a loss to the estate, the executor was personally responsible. There are many cases where beneficiaries have attempted to surcharge executors for their failure to take advantage of tax saving and expense-saving opportunities.

In many cases there are other taxes to be paid and other forms to be filed. For example, income taxes have to be paid on the income that the decedent earned prior to his death. Tax also has to be paid on the income generated from the assets in the estate. Options are available to the executor in regard to the timing of the estate's income tax return, and the executor should make this determination after a thorough review of the entire tax picture of the decedent, the estate, and the beneficiaries.

There is also a federal (and in some cases a state) gift tax, the returns for which would have been filed by the decedent in most cases. The executor should review any transfers made by the decedent prior to his death and make a determination as to whether any gift taxes are due. If so, the appropriate gift tax returns should be filed. Thus an executor has to be aware of the recent changes in the gift tax laws as well as the changes in the state and income tax provisions.

DISTRIBUTING REMAINING ASSETS

Once an executor has assembled the decedent's assets and paid appropriate debts, expenses, and taxes, he must distribute any remaining assets according to the decedent's will or under state intestacy laws. In the case of a very small estate where the spouse might be the executor and sole beneficiary, distribution can be accomplished by turning the property over to the beneficiary and accepting a "receipt and release" to the executor of any liability to the beneficiary. However, while this is certainly the most expedient and inexpensive way of concluding an estate, the executor may remain liable for any unpaid debts and for outstanding taxes and may be responsible for any number of other problems that might arise.

If the executor wishes to be formally discharged from his duties, responsibilities, and liabilities, then it is necessary to prepare a final account of administration. Unpaid creditors and beneficiaries are given notice of the filing of the account. In the event that there are charitable gifts in the will, the notice must be sent to the attorney general or other appropriate official appointed to protect the interests of the charities. On the date of the audit, those persons having any objections appear and are given the right to a further hearing, if necessary, to present their position to the court. When the court is satisfied that all of the procedures in handling the estate have been complied with, then the account is approved, a formal schedule of distribution is presented and approved, and the executor distributes the assets to the beneficiaries and is discharged from his responsibilities. When trusts have been established in the decedent's will, assets are transferred from the executor to the trusts so that these trusts can be immediately implemented if assets have not already been so transferred.

Complications in making distribution often occur because the people mentioned in the decedent's will are not all available to take distribution, or assets that are supposed to pass to named beneficiaries are not in the decedent's estate at the time of his death, or are there in different form. For example, if a decedent leaves his estate equally to his two brothers, and subsequent to the writing of the will but prior to his death the two brothers die, with one leaving two children and the other survived solely by his wife, how should the executor distribute the proceeds? The answer would depend upon an interpretation of the decedent's will, or the law of the state of domicile, or perhaps a combination of both.

Further complications arise when a decedent has bequeathed specific assets that are no longer in his estate at the time of his death. For example, bequests of "all my money in my savings account at XYZ Bank to my brother" and "all of my stock certificates to my sister" would be complicated if, before his death, the decedent had closed out his bank account and used part of the funds to purchase securities and part to purchase an automobile. In any event, if the executor made distribution in any contested situation without court approval, the executor could be held personally responsible if it was later determined that the distribution was improper.

Of course, the executor must make distribution promptly, unlike the tardy executrix who one court felt unreasonably and intentionally withheld distribution of the funds to her sisters, under the will of their mother, and was charged with interest at the legal rate during the period of the delay.

SUMMARY

Being an executor is a serious business. In addition to having to understand incredibly complex state and federal tax laws, the executor must also be accountable to the decedent's family, beneficiaries if they are not members of the decedent's family, creditors, business associates, various branches of government for the myriad of taxes for which the executor is responsible, and finally to the court for the proper performance of the executor's duties. It is for these reasons that the use of a corporate fiduciary should be considered (as sole or coexecutor) by every estate owner.

ASRS: Sec. 50

CHAPTER ENDNOTE

1.   Copyright 2004 by Charles K. Plotnick and Stephan R. Leimberg.

Chapter 14

EXECUTOR'S PRIMARY DUTIES

An executor's duties have previously been discussed in conjunction with selecting an executor for an estate (see Chapter 12). In addition, an executor's duties with regard to probate of an estate have been discussed in Chapter 13. Here, these and other duties have been summarized in a checklist of an executor's primary duties. These duties have been generally divided into estate duties, income tax duties, estate tax duties, and other duties.

While it is generally useful for an executor to review the checklist after a decedent dies, it is probably also useful to review the checklist while an individual is still alive. The estate or financial planner and the individual can then address some of the issues while the individual is alive and provide some guidance to the executor. In addition, some actions might be made while the individual is alive to facilitate the availability of information or records needed after death. See also Chapter 21 on post-mortem elections.

CHECKLIST OF EXECUTOR'S PRIMARY DUTIES

Estate Duties [Chapters 12, 13]

1. Probate of will.

2. Advertise Grant of Letters.

3. Open estate checking and savings accounts.

4. Write to banks for date of death value.

5. Value securities.

6. Appraisal of real property and personal property.

7. Obtain 3 years of U.S. individual income tax returns and 3 years of cancelled checks.

8. Obtain 5 years financials on business interest plus all relevant agreements.

9. Obtain copies of all U.S. gift tax returns filed by decedent.

10. Obtain evidence of all debts of decedent and costs of administering estate.

11. File personal property tax returns – due February 15 of each year estate in administration.

12. Determine if the estate subject to ancillary administration.

13. Determine if administration expenses and losses should be claimed as an income or estate tax deduction.

14. File inventory – check local state law for requirements and due date.

15. Apply for tax waivers.

16. File account or prepare informal family agreement.

17. Prepare audit notices and statement of proposed distribution / obtain waiver of accounting.

18. File schedule of distribution if applicable.

Income Tax Duties [Chapter 19]

1. File Form 56 – Notice of Fiduciary Relationship.

2. Determine if any of decedent's medical expenses unpaid at death.

3. Determine if the estate has received after death income taxable under IRC Section 691.

4. Consider requesting prompt assessment of decedent's U.S. income taxes.

5. File final U.S. and state individual income tax return (IRS Form 1040) – due April 15 of the year after the year in which death occurs and gift tax returns – due by time estate tax return due [Chapter 17].

6. Apply for U.S. I.D. number if estate will file U.S. income tax returns.

7. File U.S. Fiduciary Income Tax Return (Form 1041) – choice of fiscal year.

Estate Tax Duties [Chapter 15]

1. Prepayment of state inheritance tax – check state law to determine if permissible and advantages and if so, the applicable deadlines.

2. Obtain alternate valuation date values for federal estate tax return [Chapter 57].

3. Consider election to take deduction (repealed in 2004) for family-owned business interest under IRC Section 2057 [Chapter 42].

4. Consider election of extension of time to pay U.S. estate or generation-skipping transfer tax (IRC Sections 6161 or 6166) – must be filed on or before due date of U.S. estate tax returns including extensions [Chapter 16].

5. Consider election to defer payment of inheritance tax on remainder interests – where permitted, determine deadline for election.

6. Consider election for special valuation of farm or business real estate under IRC Section 2032A – must be made with timely filed U.S. estate tax return [Chapter 57].

7. Elect (or do not elect) to qualify certain terminable interest property for marital deduction [Chapter 24].

8. Ascertain if credit for tax on prior transfers is allowable.

9. File state inheritance or estate tax return and federal estate tax return – federal due within 9 months of death – extensions may be requested – check local state law for due date and possible extensions.

10. Consider requesting prompt assessment of U.S. estate tax return.

Other Duties

1. Inventory of safe deposit box.

2. Claim for life insurance benefits – obtain Form 712 from insurance company

   a. Consider mode of payment.

3. Claim for pension and profit-sharing benefits.

   a. Consider mode of payment.

   b. Obtain copies of plan, IRS approval and beneficiary designation.

4. Apply for lump sum Social Security benefits and V.A. benefits.

5. Consider redemption under IRC Section 303 [Chapter 41].

Part 3:

TAXES

Chapter 15

ESTATE TAX

The federal estate tax is a tax on the transfer of property when a person dies. It is measured by the value of the property rights that are shifted from the decedent to others; that is, it is a tax on the right to transfer property or an interest in property, rather than a tax on the right to receive property – the basic characteristic of an inheritance tax.

It is important to recognize that the estate tax is not limited to property actually transferred by the decedent at death. To thwart tax avoidance schemes, the tax is levied on certain lifetime transfers that in essence are tantamount to testamentary dispositions and on transfers over which the decedent retained certain interests or powers.

EGTRRA 2001 repeals the estate tax for one year in 2010.

GENERAL

Basically, the federal estate tax is computed in five stages:

(1) The *gross estate* is the total of all property in which the decedent had an interest and that is required to be included in the estate. A conservation easement exclusion may be available.

(2) The *adjusted gross estate* is determined by subtracting allowable funeral and administration expenses (as well as certain debts, taxes, and losses) from the gross estate. The calculation of the adjusted gross estate is primarily for the purpose of determining whether or not IRC Section 303 redemption and/or IRC Section 6166 installment payout tests can be met.

(3) The *taxable estate* is determined by subtracting from the adjusted gross estate any allowable marital deduction or charitable deduction. A deduction for either a qualified family-owned business interest or for state death taxes may also be available (other deductions).

(4) The *federal estate tax payable before credits* (or tentative tax) is determined as follows: (a) the *tentative tax base* (or contribution base) is calculated by adding to the taxable estate any "adjusted taxable gifts" (essentially, this means the taxable portion of post-1976 gifts that were not already included in the decedent's gross estate); (b) the tax rate schedule is then applied to determine the tentative tax; (c) the aggregate amount of gift tax which would have been payable with respect to gifts made by the decedent after 1976 if the tax rate schedule (IRC Sec. 2001(c)) as in effect at the decedent's death had been applicable at the time of such gift is then subtracted from the tentative tax to arrive at the estate tax payable before credits.

(5) To determine *federal estate tax*, the estate tax payable before credits is reduced, dollar-for-dollar, by subtracting the amount of any allowable:

(a) unified credit

(b) state death tax credit

(c) credit for pre-1977 gift tax

(d) credit for tax paid on prior transfers (or previously taxed property credit)

(e) credit for foreign death taxes

The resulting federal estate tax is imposed on the decedent's estate and is usually payable by the decedent's executor on the date the return is due (i.e., within nine months of the decedent's death).

Each stage mentioned above will now be examined in more detail. The form at Figure 15.1 may be useful in following the flow of dollars from the gross estate to the net federal estate tax payable. References to the applicable line of such form will be made throughout the text. Section references in the headings are to Internal Revenue Code sections.

Figure 15.1

	FEDERAL ESTATE TAX WORKSHEET		
1	Year of Death		_____
2	Gross Estate (before exclusions)		$_____
3	- Conservation Easement Exclusion		($_____)
4	Gross Estate		$_____
5	- Funeral and Administration Expenses Deduction	$_____	
6	- Debts and Taxes Deduction	$_____	
7	- Losses Deduction	$_____	
8	- Subtotal: 5 to 7		($_____)
9	Adjusted Gross Estate		$_____
10	- Marital Deduction	$_____	
11	- Charitable Deduction	$_____	
12	- Other Deductions	$_____	
13	- Subtotal: 10 to 12		($_____)
14	Taxable Estate		$_____
15	+ Adjusted Taxable Gifts		$_____
16	Computation Base		$_____
17	Tax on Computation Base		$_____
18	- Gift Tax on Adjusted Taxable Gifts		($_____)
19	Tentative Tax		$_____
20	- Unified Credit	$_____	
21	- State Death Tax Credit	$_____	
22	- Pre-1977 Gift Tax Credit	$_____	
23	- Previously Taxed Property Credit	$_____	
24	- Foreign Death Tax Credit	$_____	
25	- Total Credits		($_____)
26	Federal Estate Tax		$_____

Source: *Advanced Sales Reference Service* (a National Underwriter Company publication).

ASCERTAINING THE GROSS ESTATE (LINES 2 – 4)

The total of the value of the following (as of the appropriate valuation date) equals the gross estate before exclusions (Line 2) for federal estate tax purposes:

(1) property owned outright;

(2) certain property transferred gratuitously within three years of death and gift taxes paid on all gifts made within three years of death;

(3) certain lifetime transfers where the decedent retained the income or control over the income from the property transferred;

(4) certain gratuitous lifetime transfers where the transferee's possession or enjoyment of the property is conditioned on surviving the decedent;

(5) gratuitous lifetime transfers over which the decedent retained the right to alter, amend, or revoke the gift;

(6) annuities or similar arrangements purchased by the decedent and payable for life to both the annuitant and to a specified survivor (joint and survivor annuities);

(7) certain jointly held property where another party will obtain the decedent's interest at death by survivorship;

(8) general powers of appointment (a power so broad that it approaches actual ownership of the property subject to the power);

(9) life insurance in which the decedent possessed incidents of ownership (economic benefits in the policy) or which was payable to or for the benefit of the decedent's estate;

(10) QTIP in the estate of the surviving spouse.

The gross estate before exclusions is reduced by any qualified conservation easement exclusion (Line 3) to produce the gross estate (Line 4).

(1) Property Owned Outright (§2033)

All property owned by an individual at the time of death valued on the applicable valuation date is includable in the computation of the gross estate. This section of the tax law causes property to be includable if (a) it was beneficially owned by the decedent at the time of his death and (b) it was transferred at death by the decedent's will or by state intestacy laws. But because the tax is levied on the transmission of property at death, the measure of that inclusion is the extent to which the property interest passes from the decedent to an heir, legatee, or devisee. Regardless of how much the decedent owned during lifetime, property interests are includable only to the extent such rights are passed on to some other party at the estate owner's death.

All types of property owned by a decedent outright at death, whether real or personal property (both tangible and intangible) are includable. This means that intangible personal property such as stocks, bonds, mortgages, notes, and other amounts payable to the decedent are includable in the gross estate, as well as tangible personal property such as a decedent's jewelry and other personal effects.

However, decedent must possess more than the bare legal title to property before it can be includable in the estate. For example, if under state law the decedent was the trustee of property or was a "strawman" owner and had no beneficial interest in the property, no part of such property would be includable in the estate. So if the president of a corporation signed as owner of a life insurance policy on his life but all premiums were paid by the corporation, the policy was carried and treated as a corporate asset on its books, and the corporation was named beneficiary, the proceeds should not be includable as insurance in his estate (he would be considered a mere nominal owner).

Furthermore, the decedent's gross estate will include the value of his share of certain property held in concert with others. For instance, if an individual holds property as a tenant in common with another person, the decedent's share will be includable as property owned at death. Similarly, the value of the decedent's share of community property will be included in his estate.

It is important to note that, except for QTIP property in the estate of the surviving spouse, no inclusion is required for property in which the decedent's interest was obtained from someone else and was limited to lifetime enjoyment; i.e., an interest that terminated at the decedent's death and that the decedent had no right to transmit at death will not be included. So if Brett gives Eric the right to live in Brett's home in Miami for as long as Eric lives (and nothing more), the value of that home will not be includable in Eric's estate. On the other hand, if Brett had given Eric's wife, Pat, the house in Miami for her lifetime and the remainder to Eric, and Eric dies before Pat, Eric's gross estate will include the value of his remainder interest, since it does not terminate at his death. An interest will be includable even if it is limited, contingent, or extremely remote as long as it does not end when the decedent dies. (Of course, the contingency or remoteness of the interest will affect its valuation.)

The right to future income earned but not received prior to a decedent's death is a property interest that will be includable in the decedent's estate. Future income rights include bonuses, rents, dividends, interest payments and the decedent's share of any post-death partnership profits earned but not yet paid at death. The right of a life insurance agent to receive renewal commissions is a prime example of entitlement to future income. Such rights, as of the date of death or the alternate valuation date, whichever is applicable, are generally considered property owned outright and must be included in the decedent's gross estate. The income tax term for such right is "income in respect of a decedent" and a special income tax deduction to the extent of the estate tax attributable to the "income in respect of a decedent" is allowed under IRC Section 691.

(2) Certain Property Transferred Gratuitously Within Three Years of Death (§2035)

The general rule is that gifts (transfers for less than full and adequate consideration in money or money's worth) made within 3 years of death are not, with certain exceptions, includable regardless of the size of the gift or the manner in which it is made. There are two major classes of exemptions:

The first class of exceptions to that general rule is a transfer of an interest in property which is included in the value of the gross estate under IRC section 2036 (transfer with retained life estate), 2037 (transfer taking effect at death), 2038 (revocable transfer), 2042 (life insurance) or would have been included under any of such sections if such interest had been retained by the decedent. For example, inclusion is still required to the extent the transfer by the insured within 3 years of death was "with respect to a life insurance policy."

When testing to see if a decedent's estate qualifies for an IRC Section 303 stock redemption, an IRC section 6166 installment payout of estate tax, or special use valuation under IRC Section 2032A (the second class of exceptions), property given away within 3 years of death may be brought back into the gross estate. Even though, for purposes of computing the estate tax, a transfer within 3 years of death would not be brought back, it would be "brought back" in to see if the decedent's estate would qualify under the 303 (or 6166 or 2032A) tests. In qualifying for the IRC Section 6166 election, the "more than 35% of adjusted gross estate" requirement (see Chapter 16) is met only if the estate meets such requirement both with and without application of the three-year inclusion rule of IRC Section 2035.

(3) Gratuitous Lifetime Transfers Where the Decedent Retained the Income or Control over the Income (§2036)

If an estate owner, during lifetime, transferred property as a gift, the value of that property will be includable in the donor's gross estate if the donor retained, for the donor's life (or for a period incapable of being determined without referring to the date of the donor's death or for a period that does not in fact end before the donor's death):

(a) a life estate;

(b) the possession, enjoyment, or right to income from the property; or

(c) the right to specify who will possess or enjoy either the property itself or the income it produces.

Example: Carolyn transfers stock in Texas Electric Company to a trust. She provides that the income from the trust is payable to herself for life and that the corpus will then pass to her daughter. The Texas Electric Company stock would be includable in Carolyn's estate, since she has retained a life estate.

The rationale for including this type of lifetime transfer is that the right to enjoy or control property or designate who will receive the property or its income is characteristic of ownership. Therefore, a transfer subject to this type of retained right is–to an important degree–

essentially an incomplete disposition. Since the donee's possession or enjoyment of the property cannot begin until the decedent dies and "transfers" the retained interest, the donor will continue to be treated as owning the property.

(4) Gratuitous Lifetime Transfers Conditioned On Surviving the Decedent (§2037)

Property must be included in a decedent's gross estate if the lifetime gift the decedent made is contingent on the donee surviving the decedent. If the donee can obtain possession or enjoyment through ownership only by being alive at the time the donor dies, and the donor retained a significant (more than 5% chance) right to regain the property personally (either while living or through the right to dispose of it by will or intestacy at death), the value of the property transferred (not the value of the interest retained) will be includable. This is often called the "But if...back to" section. Why? Because it will not be operative unless the transferring document provides wording to the effect of: *"But if the donee does not survive the donor, the property comes back to the donor."*

The right to regain the property is called a "reversionary interest." To cause inclusion, the actuarial value of the transferor's reversionary interest must be significant. Stated more precisely, the right to regain the property (or the right to dispose of it) must be worth actuarially more than 5 percent of the property's value.

Example: During his lifetime, Stuart transferred property to his wife, Mona, for her lifetime. Upon Mona's death, the property was to return to Stuart if he was living. If he was not living, the property was to go to Stuart's daughter, Ellen. Stuart dies before Mona. Stuart's daughter can obtain the possession or enjoyment of the property only if she survives Stuart. If she is not alive at the time Stuart dies, neither she nor her heirs will receive any interest in the property. Stuart retained a reversionary interest under the original transfer. If Stuart's reversion is worth more than five percent (5%) of the value of the property he placed in trust, the value of the remainder interest will be includable in Stuart's estate. Such a transfer is includable because it is considered to be, in substance, a substitute for disposing of the property by will.

(5) Gratuitous Lifetime Transfers in Which the Decedent Retained the Right to Alter, Amend, or Revoke the Gift (§2038)

If the decedent made a transfer of property during lifetime but retained a power (alone or together with others) to alter, amend, revoke, or terminate the gift, the value of property subject to that power (not the entire value of the transfer of property) will be included in the gross estate.

The courts have interpreted this provision broadly and the mere power retained by the donor to vary the timing of when a beneficiary will receive an interest (even if the beneficiary cannot forfeit the interest) will cause inclusion. Furthermore, if the donor has retained any of such forbidden powers, inclusion is required even if the donor holds those powers in his capacity as trustee and cannot regain the property or personally benefit from it in any way. (The capacity in which the power is held is irrelevant.) The provision is so broad that the mere retention and possession of such power is all that is required; the donor-decedent does not have to have the physical or mental capacity to use it.

(6) Annuities or Similar Arrangements Purchased by the Decedent and Payable for Life to Both the Annuitant and Specified Survivor (§2039)

If there is an annuity (or similar payment) payable as a result of the recipient's surviving the decedent and if the payment is made under a contract that also provided the decedent with a payment (or a right to a payment) for life (or for a period which did not in fact end before death or for a period which cannot be ascertained without referring to death), the value of that income right is includable in the decedent's gross estate. The value of the survivorship interest in a commercial annuity is the amount that the same insurance company would charge for a single annuity on the survivor at the time of the first annuitant's death. The value of a survivorship private annuity is determined using government valuation tables. For example, Steve purchased a private annuity that would pay him $20,000 a year for life and upon his death would pay his wife, Jayne, $10,000 a year for as long as she lives. If Steve died before Jayne, the present value of future annuity payments to Jayne would be includable in his gross estate. Using the government valuation tables reproduced in Appendix B (Table S), if Jayne were age 55 when Steve died and a 5.0 percent Section 7520 rate was applicable, the annuity would have a present value at that time of $131,173.

This inclusion provision applies not only to commercial joint and survivor annuities but also to certain other types of payments made under a contract or agreement to the survivor(s) of the decedent.

The general rule stated above is subject to three qualifications. First, contracts (such as a life annuity) that provide payments to the decedent and end at death are not subject to this provision since they are not capable of "death time" transmission; i.e., there is no transferable interest.

Second, to the extent the survivor or anyone other than the decedent furnished part of the original purchase price, that portion of the survivor's annuity will not be included in the decedent's gross estate. So if the survivor paid one-third of the initial premium, only two-thirds of the value of survivor's income interest would be includable. If the decedent's employer furnished all or part of the purchase price, that contribution is treated as if it were made by the decedent.

Where the death proceeds of a life insurance policy are taken under a settlement option, they are considered life insurance proceeds rather than an annuity and are not taxed according to annuity rules.

(7) Jointly Held Property Where Another Party Will Obtain the Decedent's Interest at Decedent's Death by Survivorship (§2040)

There are two rules that affect the estate taxation of property held jointly with the right of survivorship. The first is the "50-50 rule." It provides that only 50 percent of certain property titled and held jointly by the decedent and spouse with rights of survivorship, or as tenants by the entirety, will be includable in the decedent's estate–regardless of the size of his contribution (in fact, even if contribution of more than half can be proven by the survivor, this rule must be used).

Example: If Stan and his wife, Shelley, purchase 100 shares of AT&T for $50,000 and hold the property as joint tenants with rights of survivorship, even if the entire contribution was made by Stan from his salary, only 50% will be included in his estate. If the stock is worth $120,000 at that time, $60,000 will be included in his estate.

This 50-50 rule applies to both real and personal property regardless of how it was acquired or when it was purchased. But it can be used only in the case of a joint tenancy between spouses (and only between spouses) or a tenancy by the entirety (and if the joint interest was created after 1976).

The "percentage-of-contribution rule" (also known as the "consideration-furnished rule") is the second rule that affects the estate taxation of property held jointly with the right of survivorship and is used where the 50-50 rule does not apply. Essentially, this provision measures the estate tax includability of jointly held property with survivorship rights by referring to the portion of the purchase price attributable to the decedent's contribution.

Actually, the rule is that jointly held property is includable in the estate of the first joint owner to die, except to the extent the survivor can prove contribution (out of funds other than those acquired by gift from the decedent). So if the survivor can prove contribution of one-third of the original purchase price, only two-thirds of the value of the jointly held property will be includable in the decedent's estate. If the survivor can prove contribution of two-thirds of the original purchase price, only one-third would be includable in the decedent's estate.

Assume Stan and his son Bill purchased 200 shares of stock for $100,000. Bill contributes $60,000. At Bill's death, 60 percent of the value of the stock at that time is includable in Bill's estate. If the stock has an estate tax value of $120,000, $72,000 (.60 x $120,000) would be includable.

(8) General Powers of Appointment (§2041)

When a power of appointment (the right to say who is to receive property in trust) is so extensive that it approaches actual ownership of the affected property, property subject to the power will be includable in the gross estate of the person who holds the power. Such property will be includable in a decedent's gross estate regardless of whether the power could be exercised at death or only during lifetime. In general, a general power of appointment is a power to appoint to the powerholder, the powerholder's estate, or the creditors of either.

Inclusion of property over which a decedent held a general power of appointment will be required in certain circumstances even if the power is "released" (formally given up) or in some cases if the power is allowed to "lapse" (fails through the lack of use).

Likewise, the lifetime exercise or release of a general power is often treated as if the decedent made a lifetime transfer of the property subject to the power. So if the exercise (or release) is made within three years of the decedent's death, it will (to the extent that a gift tax return was required to be filed) be brought back into the computation of the gross estate.

(9) Life Insurance in Which the Decedent Possessed Incidents of Ownership or Which Was Payable to or for the Benefit of the Decedent's Estate (§2042)

If a decedent dies possessing any incidents of ownership in a life insurance policy on his life, regardless of the identity of the beneficiary, the proceeds will be includable in the decedent's gross estate. The term "incidents of ownership" refers to the right to benefit from the policy (or to decide who is to enjoy the benefit) in an economic sense. For example, if an insured had the right to name a policy beneficiary, surrender a policy, or borrow its cash value, the insured would be enjoying the economic benefits of a policy.

Almost any meaningful ownership attribute in the policy held by the decedent will cause the entire proceeds to be includable in the gross estate. This is true regardless of how the decedent obtained the ownership rights or whether the use of such powers could directly or indirectly benefit the decedent. Mere possession of the ownership right at death (not the capacity to utilize the power) is all that is required to cause inclusion.

A decedent's gross estate will also include the proceeds of any policy payable to his executor or for the benefit of the decedent's estate–whether or not the decedent had retained any incidents of ownership in the policy at death. Therefore naming the insured's estate or executor either the direct or indirect beneficiary (such as naming a trustee beneficiary and requiring the use of trust assets to satisfy estate obligations) will cause inclusion of the proceeds–even if the insured possessed none of the incidents of ownership in the policy.

Corporate owned life insurance is includable in a decedent's estate if he owned more than 50 percent of the corporation's stock at his death, but only to the extent it is payable to a party other than the corporation or its creditors. Assume Chuck Heikenen owned 60 percent of the CH Corporation. The corporation owned a $1,000,000 policy on Chuck's life. If the $1,000,000 were payable to the corporation, it would push up the value per share of the stock included in

Chuck's estate. But if the $1,000,000 were payable to Chuck's brother, the entire $1,000,000 would be includable. (The IRS would probably also claim that the distribution constituted either a dividend or deferred compensation and apply income tax to the distribution as well.)

For more on life insurance, see Chapters 30 and 31.

(10) Assets That Have Qualified for QTIP (Qualified Terminable Interest Property) Treatment and Must Be Included in the Surviving Spouse's Estate (§2044)

If a marital deduction (either gift or estate tax) was allowed for the transfer of property in which the decedent had a qualifying income for life, such property must be included in the decedent's gross estate. For instance, if a $1,000,000 deduction was allowed at Sam's death to his estate for property left to his wife, Sadie, at Sadie's death the value of such property at the time of her death will be included in her estate.

So if an election to have qualified terminable interest property qualify for the estate tax marital deduction (or the gift tax marital deduction) is made, the value of that property at the surviving spouse's death will be included in the estate of the surviving spouse – unless that spouse made a lifetime transfer of his "qualifying income interest for life" (which would have resulted in a gift subject to gift tax).

For more on QTIPs, see Chapter 24.

Qualified Conservation Easement Exclusion (Line 3)

An estate tax exclusion is provided for qualified conservation easements under IRC Section 2031(c). The exclusion is available for the lesser of (1) the applicable percentage of the value of land subject to the qualified conservation easement, reduced by the amount of any charitable deduction for the easement under IRC Section 2055(f), or (2) the exclusion limitation.

The applicable percentage is equal to 40 percent reduced (but not below zero) by two percentage points for every percentage point (or fraction thereof) by which the value of the conservation easement is less than 30 percent of the value of the land (determined without regard to the easement and reduced by any development right). The exclusion limitation is $500,000.

The land subject to the conservation easement must generally (1) on the date of the decedent's death be located within the U.S. or its possessions; and (2) be owned by decedent or members of decedent's family at all times during the 3 year period ending at decedent's death.

This exclusion is discussed in detail in Chapter 34.

Valuation

The Date Assets Are Valued. Generally, federal estate taxes are based on the fair market value of the transferred property as of (a) the date the decedent died, or (b) an "alternate valuation date," six months after the date of the decedent's death. (This optional valuation date is designed to alleviate hardship where there is a sudden and sharp decline in the value of the estate's assets). The executor can choose either date but must value all assets using the chosen date. The election must be made at the time a timely return is filed. Generally this means within nine months of the decedent's death but could be longer if the time to file is extended by the IRS.

If property is distributed, sold, exchanged or otherwise disposed of within six months after the decedent's death and the alternate valuation date is elected, the asset disposed of will be valued as of the disposition date. Certain types of property diminish in value as time goes on; for example, the present value of an annuity reduces each time a payment is made. Any such property interest (where the value is affected by the mere passing of time) is valued as of the date the decedent died (even if the alternate valuation date is selected). An adjustment to the value of such asset is then made for any difference in value due to factors other than the mere lapse of time.

The alternate valuation election is available only in those situations in which such an election will result in a reduction of the federal gross estate size *and* in a reduction of federal estate tax liability. In other words, both the total property value in the gross estate and the federal estate tax liability must be reduced below the date of death values in order for the alternate valuation date to be elected.

This provision prevents a "no cost" step-up in basis and thwarts the executor who might intentionally value property high in order to obtain a higher income tax basis, while knowing there would be no additional estate tax to pay because of the unlimited marital deduction or because the unified credit would absorb any estate tax otherwise payable.

Valuation is discussed in detail in Chapter 57.

DETERMINING THE ADJUSTED GROSS ESTATE (LINE 9)

Once the gross estate is calculated, certain deductions are allowed in arriving at the adjusted gross estate.

Deductions allowed fall into three categories:

(1) funeral and administrative expenses;

(2) debts (including certain taxes); and

(3) casualty and theft losses.

Funeral expenses, subject to certain limitations, are deductible (see line 5). Such expenses would include interment, burial lot or vault, grave marker, perpetual care of the gravesite, and transportation of the person bringing the body to the place of burial. Deductions are generally limited to a "reasonable" amount.

Administrative expenses encompass those costs of administering property that are includable in the decedent's gross estate. Essentially this means the expenses incurred in the collection and preservation of probate assets, in the payment of estate debts, and in the distributing of probate assets to estate beneficiaries. Such expenses include court costs, accounting fees, appraisers' fees, brokerage costs, executors' commissions, and attorneys' fees. These vary widely from location to location and depend on the size of the estate and the complexity of the administration problems involved.

Deductions cannot exceed the amount allowed by the laws of the jurisdiction under which the estate is being administered.

Certain administration costs may be deducted from either the federal estate tax return (Form 706) or from the estate's income tax return (Form 1041). The estate's executor has the option of electing either one (but not both).

Generally, the executor will elect to deduct attorneys' fees and executors' commissions from the return in which the tax rates are higher. This will result in an overall tax saving, but note that a deduction on the income tax return, as opposed to the estate tax return, or vice versa, may result in favoring one beneficiary or group of beneficiaries over another.

Bona fide debts, including mortgages and other liens, that were (a) personal obligations of the decedent at the time of death (together with any interest accrued to the date of death), and (b) founded on adequate and full consideration in money or money's worth are deductible (line 6). Mortgages are deductible if the decedent was personally liable and the full value of the property was includable in the estate. But if the decedent had no personal liability for the payment of the underlying debt and the creditor would look only to encumbered property for payment, the mortgage would result in a reduction in the value of the property subject to the mortgage.

In the case of community property, only those claims and expenses that were the decedent's personal obligations are deductible in full. This means an allocation of claims and expenses must be made. Since only one-half of the total community property is includable, only half of any obligation attributable to community property is deductible.

Certain taxes unpaid at the time of the decedent's death are considered debts. Three common deductible taxes are:

(1) income taxes unpaid but reportable for some tax period prior to the decedent's death;

(2) gift taxes that were not paid on gifts the decedent made sometime prior to death; and

(3) property taxes that accrued but remained unpaid at the time of the decedent's death.

Casualty and theft losses incurred by the estate are deductible if the loss arose from fire, storm, shipwreck (or other casualty), or theft (line 7).

To be deductible, the loss must have occurred during the time the estate was in the process of settlement and before it was closed. Such deductions are limited in two respects: the deduction is reduced (1) to the extent that insurance or any other compensation is available to offset the loss, and (2) to the extent that a loss is reflected in the alternate valuation (an executor can elect to value assets in the estate either on the date of death or at the alternate date).

At the executor's option, losses may be deducted from either the estate tax return or the estate's income tax return. Typically, they will be taken on the return that produces the highest deduction.

DETERMINATION OF TAXABLE ESTATE (LINE 14)

The adjusted gross estate may be reduced by (1) a marital deduction, (2) a charitable deduction, (3) a family-owned business deduction, and (4) a state death tax deduction.

A marital deduction (line 10) is allowed for property that (a) is included in the decedent's gross estate, and (b) passes at the decedent's death to a surviving spouse, (c) "in a qualifying manner" (in a manner that gives the surviving spouse control and enjoyment essentially tantamount to outright ownership or that meets the requirements of qualified terminable interest property (QTIP), as defined below).

The maximum amount allowable as a marital deduction for federal estate tax purposes is the net value of the property passing to the surviving spouse in a qualifying manner. Otherwise, there is no limit to the marital deduction. An individual could conceivably transfer his entire estate to his spouse estate tax free.

Under prior law most "terminable interests" (where the surviving spouse's interest would cease upon the occurrence or nonoccurrence of a particular event and the children or some other party would receive the marital property) would not qualify for the marital deduction.

Most terminable interests can qualify for the marital deduction if the executor makes the appropriate QTIP election in a timely manner. A qualifying terminable interest is one which (a) passes from the decedent, (b) gives the surviving spouse a lifetime income payable at least annually, and (c) the decedent's executor makes an irrevocable election on his estate tax return by listing the property on Schedule M (the marital deduction schedule) of the return.

The election is really the price of qualifying what under prior law would not have qualified. For instance, an individual can now provide, "income to my wife for life. At her death the principal goes to my children." The election would obligate the wife's estate to pay the appropriate estate tax on the interest as if she were the ultimate recipient instead of the children. In other words,

the value of the principal is included in the estate of the life tenant. (Her executor is, however, entitled to recover from the person who receives the principal the share of estate taxes generated in her estate by the inclusion of that property–unless in her will she chooses to exonerate that individual.)

The marital deduction is discussed in more detail in Chapter 24.

A charitable deduction (line 11) is allowed for the fair market value of any type of gift to a "qualified charity" at a decedent's death. The deduction is limited to the net value of the property includable in the gross estate that is transferred to the charity. In other words, a decedent could conceivably leave his entire estate to charity and receive a deduction for the entire amount. The charitable deduction is discussed in more detail in Chapters 32 and 33.

Up to $675,000 of qualified family-owned business interests (line 12, other deductions) may be deducted from the gross estate under IRC Section 2057. However, EGTRRA 2001 repeals the deduction for 2004 to 2010. In general, 50 percent of the value of the adjusted gross estate must consist of family-owned business interests. Similar to the requirements for special use valuation, (1) for at least 5 of the 8 years ending on decedent's death, the business interests must have been owned by decedent or members of decedent's family, and decedent or members of decedent's family must have materially participated in the business, and (2) for 10 years after decedent's death (or until the earlier death of the qualified heir), such business interests must be owned by members of decedent's family, and members of decedent's family must materially participate in the business. Additional tax, plus interest thereon, is due if the ownership or material participation requirements are not met after decedent's death. This deduction is discussed in detail in Chapter 42.

A deduction for state death taxes (line 12, other deductions) replaces the state death tax credit (see below) from 2005 to 2009.

ESTATE TAX PAYABLE BEFORE CREDITS (LINE 19)

Once the taxable estate (Line 14) is found, adjusted taxable gifts (line 15) are added to arrive at the tentative tax base (or contribution base, line 16). Adjusted taxable gifts are defined as the taxable portion of all post-1976 gifts. A gift is taxable to the extent it exceeds the sum of any allowable (a) gift tax annual exclusion, (b) gift tax exclusion for qualified transfers for educational or medical expenses, (c) gift tax marital deduction (similar to the estate tax marital deduction but for lifetime gifts to a spouse), and (d) gift tax charitable deduction. Gifts that for any reason have already been includable in a decedent's gross estate (i.e., a gift with a retained life estate) are not considered adjusted taxable gifts.

Adding adjusted taxable gifts to the taxable estate makes the estate tax computation part of a unified transfer tax calculation. The process uses a cumulative approach, with "death time" dispositions merely being the last in a series of gratuitous transfers. The net effect of adding in adjusted taxable gifts is to subject the taxable estate at death to rates that are higher than if the computation did not consider lifetime gifts.

When adjusted taxable gifts are combined with the taxable estate, the result is the contribution base, the amount upon which the tax rates are based.

At this point, the tax on the contribution base (line 17) is computed by applying the appropriate rates (see the Gift and Estate Tax Rate Schedules in Appendix A) to the contribution base. Different tax rate schedules apply depending on the year of death (Line 1). These rates are "progressive." The tax on a contribution base of $1,000 is $180. On $100,000, the tax is $23,800. On $1 million, the tax is $345,800.

The advantage of the graduated rates is lost to estates in excess of $10,000,000. This is accomplished in the following manner: The gift and estate tax liability for taxable transfers in excess of $10,000,000 is increased by imposing an additional 5 percent add-on tax on the excess of (a) the taxable transfer over (b) $10,000,000. EGTRRA 2001 repeals this additional 5 percent add-on tax for 2002 to 2010. Where applicable, this additional tax is reflected in the Gift and Estate Tax Rate Schedules in Appendix A.

The five percent rate adjustment does not affect the maximum federal estate tax rate for purposes of computing the generation-skipping transfer tax (GST tax). Thus, the GST tax rate is 55% in 2001, and in 2011 and later. See Chapter 18.

Since the taxable portion of gifts made after 1976 have already been added back in as adjusted taxable gifts, the gift tax generated (or that would have been generated) by such gifts is subtracted at this point (line 18).

DETERMINING THE FEDERAL ESTATE TAX PAYABLE

Certain tax credits are allowed as a dollar-for-dollar reduction of the estate tax. These credits are (a) the unified credit (line 20), (b) the state death tax credit (line 21), (c) the credit for pre-1977 gift tax (line 22), (d) the credit for taxes on prior transfers (line 23), and (c) the credit for foreign death taxes (line 24).

A unified credit is allowed against the estate tax otherwise payable ($555,800 in 2004 to 2005; $780,000 in 2006 to 2008; $1,445,800 in 2009; and $345,800 in 2011 and thereafter). See the Unified Credit tables in Appendix A. The term "unified credit" was adopted because that credit is used as an offset against gift as well as estate taxes. [Note, however, that the unified credit for gift tax purposes is only $345,800 in years after 2001.] However, to the extent the unified credit has been used against gift taxes, the credit available against the estate tax is, in effect, lowered. No refund is available if the credit exceeds the estate tax.

The required computation process has the effect of reducing the credit by requiring the "add back" of adjusted taxable gifts. In other words, although the unified credit in the example below does not appear to be reduced by $1,800 (the tax on a $10,000 gift which was not paid only because the decedent used $1,800 of credit), the effect is the same because of the adding back of the $10,000 worth of adjusted taxable gifts. Stated another way, adding back $10,000 of adjusted taxable gifts "restores" the $1,800 of unified credit.

Example: Assume a widow died in 2004 with a $1,600,000 taxable estate. In 1977 she made only one taxable gift of $10,000 (after utilizing the annual exclusion). The widow paid no gift tax because $1,800 of her unified credit was applied to offset the $1,800 gift tax liability. These facts resulted in the following estate tax liability (ignoring other tax credits):

Taxable Estate	$1,600,000
Adjusted taxable gifts	10,000
Total	$1,610,000
Tax on $1,610,000	605,300
Less: gift taxes paid on lifetime transfers	-0-
Less: unified credit	555,8000
Tax due	$ 49,500

The second credit allowed against the estate tax is for any death taxes paid to a state because of property includable in the decedent's gross estate. This includes estate, inheritance, legacy, or succession taxes. The maximum credit allowable is the lower of (a) the death tax actually paid to the state, or (b) the ceiling amount provided in the maximum credit table in Appendix A. Note that the IRS table used to calculate the state death tax credit is based on the taxable estate (line 14) rather than the contribution base (line 16). EGTRRA 2001 reduces the state death tax credit ceiling amount by 25% in 2002, 50% in 2003, and 75% in 2004, and replaces the credit with a deduction (see above) for 2005 to 2009. See the Maximum Credit Table for State Death Taxes in Appendix A.

A third credit is available for gift tax paid on gifts made before 1977 where the property is included in the donor's gross estate because of retained strings in the gifted property.

A credit for foreign death taxes is intended to prevent double taxation. It is allowed for death taxes paid to a foreign country or a United States possession on property that is (a) included in the decedent's gross estate, and (b) situated (and subject to tax) in that country or possession. The credit is available only to United States citizens or resident aliens.

Finally, where a prior decedent (the transferor) transferred property (which was taxed at death) to the decedent and the property is includable in the present decedent's estate, a credit will be allowed for all or part of the estate tax paid by the transferor's estate on the transferred property. The present decedent must have received the property prior to death. The transferor must have died within ten years before or two years after the present decedent.

As long as the property was includable in the transferor's estate and passed from the transferor to the present decedent, the method of transfer is irrelevant; it can be by will, by intestacy, by election against the will, by lifetime gift, as life insurance proceeds, or as joint property with right of survivorship.

Interestingly enough, the law arbitrarily assumes that property that was in the transferor's estate and that was transferred to the present decedent is subject to double taxation (and is therefore entitled to the credit). There is no requirement that the property actually be in existence at the present decedent's death or if in existence subject to federal estate tax at that time.

The credit is the lower of:

(1) the federal estate tax attributable to the transferred property in the transferor's estate, or

(2) the federal estate tax attributable to the transferred property in the estate of the present decedent.

The credit is reduced by 20 percent increments every two years, and at the end of ten years after the transferor's death no credit is allowable. For example, between years two and four only 80 percent of the credit is allowable.

EXAMPLE

Mary Green died in 2004. Her gross estate was $1,750,000. During her lifetime, she made one $10,000 taxable gift that was protected by the unified credit. Her estate had funeral and administration expenses of $35,000, and debts of $25,000. Figure 15.2 illustrates calculation of her federal estate tax.

For examples of estate tax planning calculations with marital trusts and bypass trusts, see Chapter 24.

PAYMENT OF THE ESTATE TAX

As mentioned above, the estate tax is due at the time the return is to be filed nine months after the decedent's death. A return must be filed if the gross estate exceeds the "exemption equivalent" (applicable exclusion) provided by the estate tax unified credit ($1,500,000 in 2004 to 2005; $2,000,000 in 2006 to 2008; $3,500,000 in 2009; and $1,000,000 in 2011 and thereafter: see the Estate Tax Unified Credit table in Appendix A). This threshold amount is lowered by the total of any adjusted taxable gifts (which have not been included in the gross estate). Therefore, in some estates filing will be required even if the taxable estate is far less than the exemption equivalent.

The "reasonable cause" extension. As stated previously, the tax is due 9 months from the date of the decedent's death. But an executor or administrator can request that the IRS grant an extension of time for paying the tax–up to 12 months from the date fixed for the payment–if there is reasonable cause. Furthermore, the IRS could, at its discretion, upon the executor's showing of reasonable cause, grant a series of exten-

Figure 15.2

	FEDERAL ESTATE TAX WORKSHEET		
1	Year of Death		2004
2	Gross Estate (before exclusions)		$1,750,000
3	- Conservation Easement Exclusion		$0
4	Gross Estate		$1,750,000
5	- Funeral and Administration Expenses Deduction	$35,000	
6	- Debts and Taxes Deduction	$25,000	
7	- Losses Deduction	$0	
8	- Subtotal: 5 to 7		($60,000)
9	Adjusted Gross Estate		$1,690,000
10	- Marital Deduction	$0	
11	- Charitable Deduction	$0	
12	- Other Deductions	$0	
13	- Subtotal: 10 to 12		$0
14	Taxable Estate		$1,690,000
15	+ Adjusted Taxable Gifts		$10,000
16	Computation Base		$1,700,000
17	Tax on Computation Base		$645,800
18	- Gift Tax on Adjusted Taxable Gifts		$0
19	Tentative Tax		$645,800
20	- Unified Credit	$555,800	
21	- State Death Tax Credit	$19,320	
22	- Pre-1977 Gift Tax Credit	$0	
23	- Previously Taxed Property Credit	$0	
24	- Foreign Death Tax Credit	$0	
25	- Total Credits		($575,120)
26	Federal Estate Tax		$70,680

Source: *Advanced Sales Reference Service* (a National Underwriter Company publication).

sions which–in total–could run as long as 10 years from the due date of the original return. There is no definition of reasonable cause in the Internal Revenue Code or regulations. However, the regulations give illustrative examples of situations where reasonable cause will be found:

(a) a substantial portion of the estate consists of rights to receive future payments such as annuities, accounts receivable, or renewal commissions and the estate cannot borrow against these assets without incurring substantial loss;

(b) the gross estate is unascertainable at the time the tax is normally due because the estate has a claim to substantial assets that cannot be collected without litigation; or

(c) an estate does not have sufficient funds to pay claims against the estate (including estate taxes when due) and at the same time provide a reasonable allowance during the period of administration for decedent's surviving spouse and dependent children because the executor, despite reasonable efforts, cannot convert assets in his possession into cash.

The "up to 14-year closely held business interest" extension: Under IRC Section 6166, an executor may elect to pay estate tax attributable to a closely held business in 14 annual installments if the interest in the closely held business exceeds 35 percent of the adjusted gross estate. This very attractive extension is explained in detail in Chapter 16.

ASRS: Sec. 54

Chapter 16

EXTENSIONS OF TIME TO PAY ESTATE TAX

WHAT IS IT?

Generally, the federal estate tax is payable in full within nine months of the date of death.[1] (EGTRRA 2001 repeals the estate tax for one year for decedents dying in 2010.) The Internal Revenue Code does provide relief under certain circumstances by allowing an executor to pay the federal estate taxes attributable to the decedent's business over a period of years.

If the requirements of IRC Section 6166 are met, the executor in his discretion may elect to pay the federal estate tax (and generation-skipping transfer tax) attributable to the decedent's interest in a closely held business in installments over a period of up to 14 years. During the first four years the executor pays only interest on the unpaid tax. Then, in equal annual increments over as many as ten additional years, the executor pays off the principal of the unpaid tax (together with interest on the unpaid balance).

Section 6166 permits a four year deferral of tax followed by a maximum ten year payout of the tax. Interest with respect to the deferral is payable at 2% on the tax generated by the first $1,140,000 (as indexed for 2004) of business value and at 45% of the regular underpayment rate on the balance.

Section 6166 is available for any estate that qualifies under the rules of the Internal Revenue Code, regardless of the position of the Internal Revenue Service. However, if the estate does not qualify for the Section 6166 extension, it still may be possible to obtain some extension under an alternative IRC Section 6161, which is discretionary with the IRS.

Under Section 6161, the IRS may extend the period for payment of tax for a period up to ten years beyond the due date of the estate tax return if the IRS finds that there is "reasonable cause" to grant such an extension.

Under IRC Section 6159, the IRS may permit the installment payment of taxes where the IRS believes it will facilitate payment of such taxes.

Under IRC Section 6163, estate tax attributable to reversionary and remainder interests in property can be deferred until after preceding interests in the property terminate.

WHEN IS THE USE OF SUCH A DEVICE INDICATED?

1. When the estate has insufficient liquidity to pay the estate taxes when due without selling assets at a substantial loss.

2. Where the estate can earn a greater after-tax rate of return than it spends in interest for the deferral privilege.

3. Where future profits or cash flow from the decedent's business can be used to pay all or part of the deferred tax.

WHAT ARE THE REQUIREMENTS?

A. Section 6159

Section 6159 provides that the IRS is authorized to enter into written agreements with taxpayers to pay taxes in installments where the IRS determines that such an agreement will facilitate payment of such taxes. Such an agreement may be modified or terminated by the IRS if (1) information provided by the taxpayer was inaccurate or incomplete, (2) the IRS believes that collection of such tax is in jeopardy, (3) the IRS determines that the financial condition of the taxpayer has changed (in which case 30 days notice to the taxpayer is required, including the reason for such change), (4) the taxpayer fails to make a timely installment payment (or to timely pay any other tax), or (5) the taxpayer fails to provide a financial update as requested by the IRS. Interest is payable on such installments at the regular underpayment rate.

B. Section 6161

1. The IRS may extend the time for payment of the tax shown on the return for a period of up to ten

years beyond the due date of the return, upon a showing of "reasonable cause" for the granting of the extension.

2. "Reasonable cause" for the extension is not expressly defined. Each case is examined on an independent factual basis. However, there are certain guidelines used to establish the presence of reasonable cause. These include: (a) inability to marshal assets to pay the estate tax when otherwise due; (b) an estate comprised in substantial part of assets consisting of rights to receive payments in the future, with the estate having insufficient present cash to pay the estate tax and an inability to borrow against these assets except on unreasonable terms; (c) the assets cannot be collected without litigation; or, (d) there are not sufficient funds available, after the exercise of due diligence, with which to pay the tax in a timely fashion.

3. Interest is payable on such deferred taxes at the regular underpayment rate.

C. Section 6163

If a reversionary or remainder interest in property is includable in the gross estate, the executor can elect to defer payment of the estate tax attributable to the reversionary or remainder interest until nine months after the termination of any precedent interests in the property. In addition, the IRS may extend the payment of such tax for a reasonable period of up to an additional three years for reasonable cause.

D. Section 6166

1. The gross estate must include an interest classified as a "closely held" business, the value of which *exceeds* 35% of the adjusted gross estate. In the case of an estate in which the decedent made a gift of property within three years of death, the estate is treated as meeting the more than 35% requirement only if the estate meets such requirement both with and without the application of the three-year inclusion rule of IRC section 2035 (see Chapter 15 regarding the estate tax).[2]

2. Aggregation of various business interests of the decedent is allowed for purposes of meeting the percentage requirement, provided the decedent owned at least 20% of the total value of each, and each activity otherwise qualifies as a closely held trade or business.

3. The amount of federal estate or generation-skipping transfer tax that may be deferred (i.e., paid in installments) is only that amount of value attributable to the value of the closely held trade or business. The balance of the estate tax or GST tax must be paid at the regular payment date.

4. Generally, if the estate qualifies under Section 6166 and an election is made, the first installment of principal is due not later than five years and nine months from the date of death. (This deferral period is not available to certain lending and finance businesses that qualify for installment payments under IRC Sec. 6166(b)(10), as added by EGTRRA 2001.) Each succeeding installment is to be paid within one year after the previous installment.

   With the exception of lending and finance businesses and holding companies, which are limited to installment payments stretched out over only five years, the maximum number of principal installments which may be paid under this provision is 10, thus generally allowing for payment over a 14-year period (four years of interest only, up to 10 more years of principal and interest).

   During the 4-year period immediately following death, interest only payments are to be made, with interest being at a beneficial 2% rate in relation to the tax on the first $1,140,000 in value of the closely held business (see "How It Is Done," below) and at 45% of the regular underpayment rate on the balance. The underpayment rate varies quarterly and is available at www.nationalunderwriter.com/taxfactsfx. Interest calculated using these special rates is not deductible for estate or income tax purposes.

5. To qualify as an interest in a "closely held" business, the interest can be in a sole proprietorship, a partnership, or a corporation. A partnership interest will qualify if 20% or more of the total capital interest in the partnership is included in the gross estate, or if the partnership has 45 or fewer partners. Stock in a corporation qualifies if 20% or more in value of the voting stock is included in determining the gross estate of the decedent, or the corporation has 45 or fewer shareholders. (The number of allowable partners or shareholders was 15 for decedents dying prior to 2002.)

   For purposes of the "45 or fewer owners" test, a partnership interest or corporate stock held by another partnership or corporation or by an estate or trust will be treated as if owned proportionately by shareholders, partners, or beneficiaries (the rule applies in the case of trusts only if a beneficiary has a present interest). A partnership interest or stock held by a member of the decedent's family is considered to be owned by the decedent for purposes of the "45 or fewer owners" test. (But if this attribution is necessary to qualify for Section 6166, the 4 year deferral of tax and the special 2% interest rate are forfeited.)

6. In addition, as interpreted by the Service, the definition of a "trade or business" is not as broad in scope as under many other provisions of the Internal Revenue Code. The business must be "actively" carried on and require a "management" function, rather than being of a nature where the taxpayer merely supervises his investment (such as an apartment house), and the investment is the actual capital producing factor.[3]

7. Only *active* business assets are considered for purposes of the "more than 35% of adjusted gross estate" test. Only active business assets can be considered in determining the value of the business interest that qualifies for the deferral. This "active asset" rule, which denies installment payment for passive assets, applies to all corporations and partnerships. (It does not apply, however, for purposes of determining whether or not an acceleration of the tax will be required.)

8. The IRS is now enforcing its right to demand a bond of up to twice the value of the deferred estate tax. This bond is difficult (some say impossible) to obtain and relatively expensive.

HOW IT IS DONE–AN EXAMPLE OF SECTION 6166

Dr. Andrea Apter died in 2004 when the value of her closely held business, a computer center, was $2,400,000. Her gross estate was $3,900,000. Administrative costs, debts, and expenses totaled $300,000. Federal estate taxes totaled $933,300. Qualification for Section 6166 is determined as follows.

Section 6166 (up to 14 year) Installment Payout

(1) Estate Tax Value of closely held
     business included in gross estate $2,400,000
(2) Adjusted Gross Estate $3,600,000
(3) 35% x Adjusted Gross Estate $1,260,000

Line 1 exceeds Line 3; estate qualifies

Since the estate qualifies for Section 6166 deferral, the executor can elect to pay that portion of estate taxes attributable to the inclusion of the farm or other closely held business in installments over up to 14 years (first four years, no tax due, only interest–up to next 10 years equal annual installments of tax and declining interest on unpaid balance).

Two or more businesses may be aggregated if the decedent held 20% or more interest in each such business.

In this example, the decedent's estate could utilize a Section 6166 installment payout. The deferral amount would be computed according to the following formula: (Assume the net estate and GST tax payable after credits is $933,300.)

Computing Section 6166 Deferral Limitation

$$\text{Net Estate and GST Tax (after credits)} \quad \times \quad \frac{\text{Value of Includable Closely Held Business Interest}}{\text{Adjusted Gross Estate}}$$

$$\$933,300 \quad \times \quad \frac{\$2,400,000}{\$3,600,000} \quad = \quad \$625,311$$

Therefore, $307,989 of tax ($933,300 - $625,311) must be paid immediately.

IRC section 6601(j) places an overall limitation on the portion of the tax deferred under Section 6166 that qualifies for the 2% interest rate, calculated as follows.

Section 6601(j) 2% Interest Limitation

(1) $1,000,000 as indexed $1,140,000
(2) Unified Credit Equivalent $1,500,000
(3) Sum of (1) and (2) $2,640,000
(4) Estate Tax (disregard credits) on (2) $1,088,000
(5) Unified Credit .... ($555,800)
(6) Section 6601(j) 2% Interest Limitation $532,200

The Section 6601(j) 2% interest limitation must be calculated for the year of death (2004 in this example), using the then current $1,140,000 as indexed, Unified Credit Equivalent, estate tax rates, and Unified Credit.

The portion of tax deferrable at 2% interest is equal to $532,200, or the lesser of the estate tax deferrable under Section 6166 ($625,311) or the Section 6601(j) limitation ($532,200). The balance of the tax deferrable under Section 6166, $93,111 ($625,311 - $532,200), is deferrable at 45% of the regular underpayment rate. The interest is not deductible for estate or income tax purposes.

Figure 16.1

	SECTION 6166 PAYMENT SCHEDULE*						

Year	Tax 2%	Interest 2%	Tax 2.25%	Interest 2.25%	Tax Payment	Interest Payment	Total Payment
1	$532,200	$ 10,751	$93,111	$ 2,119	$ -	$ 12,870	$ 12,870
2	532,200	10,751	93,111	2,119	-	12,870	12,870
3	532,200	10,751	93,111	2,119	-	12,870	12,870
4	532,200	10,751	93,111	2,119	-	12,870	12,870
5	532,200	10,751	93,111	2,119	62,531	12,870	75,401
6	478,980	9,676	83,800	1,907	62,531	11,583	74,114
7	425,760	8,601	74,489	1,695	62,531	10,296	72,827
8	372,540	7,526	65,178	1,483	62,531	9,009	71,540
9	319,320	6,451	55,867	1,271	62,531	7,722	70,253
10	266,100	5,375	46,556	1,059	62,531	6,435	68,966
11	212,880	4,300	37,244	847	62,531	5,148	67,679
12	159,660	3,225	27,933	636	62,531	3,861	66,392
13	106,440	2,150	18,622	424	62,531	2,574	65,105
14	53,220	1,075	9,311	212	62,531	1,287	63,818
Totals		$ 102,133		$ 20,127	$ 625,311	$ 122,261	$ 747,572

* Maximum estate tax deferrable at 2% for decedents dying in 2004 is $532,200. Interest at 45% of the underpayment rate is projected at 2.25 percent (45% x 5%). Interest is compounded daily. Underpayment interest rate changes quarterly.

Figure 16.1 shows a projected Section 6166 payment schedule based upon this example. An executor may wish to evaluate whether the projected interest expense from deferral will be less than the rate of return available for alternative utilizations of capital.

WHAT ARE THE TAX IMPLICATIONS?

1. Interest is payable on the tax which is not paid by the due date of the return.[4] Tax deferrable under IRC Sections 6159, 6161, or 6163 is deferred at the regular underpayment rate. The regular underpayment rate is redetermined quarterly so as to be three percentage points over the short-term federal rate. The interest owed is compounded daily.

   Under IRC section 6166, a special 2% interest rate is allowed. This rate is limited to the estate tax attributable to the first $1,140,000 (in 2004) of farm or other closely held business property (generally, a maximum tax of $532,200 in 2004; see "How It Is Done," above).[5] Amounts of estate tax attributable to value in excess of the $1,140,000 amount bear interest at 45% of the regular underpayment rate.

2. Interest for tax deferred under Section 6166 using the special 2% and 45% of the regular underpayment rate rates cannot be deducted for estate or income tax purposes. Otherwise, the interest charged for the deferred tax is a deductible administration expense for estate tax purposes. Alternatively, the interest paid each year can be deducted by the executor as an income tax deduction on the estate's income tax return.

3. Note that now the IRS almost always requires the estate post a bond of as much as twice the amount of the estate tax to be deferred. This may make the use of Section 6166 difficult and much more expensive.

IMPLICATIONS AND ISSUES IN COMMUNITY PROPERTY STATES

In general, for purposes of the definition of an interest in a closely held trade or business under Section 6166, in regard to the 45 owner test of the allowable number of shareholders or partners, the husband and wife are treated as one partner or shareholder if the interest is owned as community property. This also applies if the form of ownership is as joint tenants, tenants by the entirety, or tenants in common.

QUESTIONS AND ANSWERS

Question – Is a bond required of the executor?

Answer – The IRS, in almost every case, deems a bond necessary. It is requiring the executor to post a bond for the payment of the tax. The amount is up to twice the amount of the tax for which an extension is granted.

The executor is also liable–personally–for payment of the tax. He can only be discharged if (a) he pays the tax due or (b) furnishes a bond or security for unpaid (but not yet due) taxes.

Question – Is there an alternative to the requirement that the executor post bond?

Answer – The executor can make an election–under Section 6166–to accept an IRS lien in lieu of the executor's personal liability or bond.[6]

The requirements of the lien (which serves to discharge the executor from personal liability and eliminate the requirement of a bond) are:

(1) The executor–and all parties who have an interest in the property subject to the lien–must file an agreement consenting to the lien.

(2) A person must be designated as agent for the persons who consented to the lien and the estate's beneficiaries.[7]

(3) The Service may require additional lien property if the value of the original property is–or falls below–the total of (a) unpaid taxes and (b) aggregate interest owed.

Question – Once the installment payout period begins, can the IRS terminate it?

Answer – The deferred tax is accelerated (i.e., becomes due immediately) in three situations:

(1) when all or a significant portion of the business is disposed of or liquidated;

(2) interest or installment payments are not made within six months of the due date; or

(3) if the estate has undistributed net income (there may be an acceleration to that extent).

Question – Why shouldn't an advisor suggest that a client use a Section 6166 installment payout as an alternative to life insurance?

Answer – First, Section 6166 cannot be relied upon. The mathematical percentage test may be failed or the firm may be considered an unqualified company. The executor may not be able to post the required bond or may determine the cost of such a bond is exorbitant or unaffordable by the estate. The alternative to a bond is a lien, which itself may be impractical or unacceptable to the estate.

Second, Section 6166 does not "create" assets–the right to make installment payments merely postpones the necessity of paying a certain portion of the total estate tax. Interest *added* to the tax may increase the total cost substantially.

Where will the money to pay both tax and interest come from? If it comes from the business, it probably will be in the form of a dividend. In any event, *the dollars to make the deferred payments have to come from somewhere–and they will be after-tax (expensive) dollars.*

Third, only a portion of the Federal taxes can be deferred in most cases.

Where will the executor find the cash to pay

(a) administrative expenses?

(b) debts?

(c) the remaining portion of Federal estate taxes?

(d) state death taxes?

(e) income taxes?

(f) pecuniary bequests?

Fourth, with certain exceptions, successors in interest cannot dispose of the business–or a major portion of it–without triggering an acceleration ("pay it now").

Fifth, the executor may remain personally liable for unpaid taxes during the entire deferral period (or the successors-in-interest have to tie their hands with a special tax lien to assure the IRS that payment will be made).

Sixth, final distribution to beneficiaries may be delayed over an extended period of time. Most beneficiaries will not want to wait for 14 years to receive their full share of the inheritance.

Seventh, since all beneficiaries must sign the elective agreement to discharge the executor from personal liability, guardians may have to be appointed for minors and otherwise incompetent beneficiaries. Such guardians may refuse to sign such an exoneration.

Question – Is there any danger of losing the right to have an extension of time if the estate, as it appears on the estate tax return as filed, qualifies for an extension?

Answer – Yes. The values of the various assets in the estate can be changed upon audit by IRS. It is the ultimately determined values that will control. It is possible that the estate will not meet the Section 6166 requirements after the IRS increases the value of assets other than the decedent's business.

Question – How is the election made under Section 6166?

Answer – Notice of election under Section 6166 must be filed on or before the due date (including any extensions) of the U.S. Estate Tax Return[8] (Form 706). No special form of notice is required and a letter addressed to the IRS setting forth the identity of the taxpayer, the amount of tax to be deferred, the identity of the closely held business and the computation of qualification under the applicable section will suffice.

Question – What if, based upon the value set forth on the U.S. Estate Tax Return, the decedent's interest in the closely held business does not qualify under Section 6166, but it is possible that after examination by the IRS such interest will qualify?

Answer – If the estate does not qualify for a payout of federal estate taxes on the values returned or if the estate does qualify, but no tax is due on the values returned, the executor can file a "protective election." The "protective election" would set forth the information required under Revenue Ruling 74-499 (see also Revenue Ruling 76-51).

Question – In determining the "at least 20%" requirement of Section 6166 for the aggregation of two or more closely held businesses, or whether 20% or more of the value of a closely held business is included in the gross estate, can the executor elect to have interests of family members considered as owned by the decedents?

Answer – Yes. The interest of family members can, if elected by the executors, be considered as owned by the decedent in determining the "at least 20%" requirements for qualification under Section 6166.[9] This election is applicable only to a capital interest in a partnership and to stock that is "not readily tradable." If this election is made by the executor, the five year deferral provision of Section 6166 is not available and the payout must be spread over a period not to exceed ten years. In addition, the 2% special rate is not available.

Question – Can holding company stock qualify for installment payout of estate taxes under Section 6166?

Answer – "Yes, but." Only the portion of stock of a holding company (not that of operating subsidiaries) that directly or indirectly owns stock in a closely held active trade or business (so called "business company") will be treated as stock in the active company and may therefore qualify.[10] To qualify, the "45 or fewer shareholders" or the "20% or more" test and the "more than 35%" test must be met.

The ability to pay out federal estate taxes attributable to holding company stock may come at some cost. The executor must agree to forego both the deferral of principal payments and the special 2% interest rate (and the holding company is only entitled to make installment payments over five years rather than 10 years). This adds to the cost of the payout in two important ways: first, the time value of money works against the estate since much more money (the principal of the unpaid estate tax) must be paid much more quickly. Second, the special 2% rate is not available.

Question – Can rental activities ever be classified as active businesses to meet the requirements of Section 6166?

Answer – Although the estate will face an uphill battle on this issue, the IRS has ruled that the decedent's rental activities may be classified as closely held businesses for purposes of Section 6166. These rulings only apply where the decedent took an active role in managing the rental properties, and generally involve such activities as negotiating leases, supervising repairs and maintenance, and dealing directly with tenants.

ASRS: Sec. 54, ¶44.7

CHAPTER ENDNOTES

1. IRC Secs. 6151(a), 6075(a).

2. IRC Sec. 2035(d)(4).

3. Treas. Reg. §20.6166-2(c); Rev. Rul. 75-365, 1975-2 CB 471; Rev. Rul. 75-366, 1975-2 CB 472; Rev. Rul. 75-367, 1975-2 CB 472.

4. IRC Secs. 6601(a), 6621.

5. IRC Sec. 6601(j).

6. IRC Sec. 6324A.

7. IRC Sec. 6324A(c).

8. Rev. Rul. 74-499, 1974-2 CB 397.

9. IRC Secs. 6166(b)(1)(B)(i), 6166(b)(7), 6166(b)(8), 6166(b)(9), 6166(g)(1), 6166(g)(2).

10. IRC Sec. 6166(b)(8).

Chapter 17

GIFT TAX

This chapter will present an overview of the federal gift tax law and basic planning considerations in the following order:

1. Purpose, Nature, and Scope of Gift Tax Law

2. Advantages of Lifetime Gifts

3. Technical Definition of a Gift

4. Gratuitous Transfers That Are Not Gifts

5. Exempt Gifts

6. Requirements for a Completed Gift

7. Valuation of Property for Gift Tax Purposes

8. Computing the Tax on Gifts

9. Reporting of Gifts and Payment of the Tax

10. Relationship of the Gift Tax System to the Income Tax System

11. Determination of the Basis of Gift Property

12. Relationship of the Gift Tax System to the Estate Tax System

13. Factors to Consider in Selecting Appropriate Subject of a Gift

(1) PURPOSE, NATURE, AND SCOPE OF GIFT TAX LAW

Purpose

If an individual could give away his entire estate during lifetime without the imposition of any tax, a rational person would arrange affairs so that at death nothing would be subject to the federal estate tax. Likewise, if a person could, freely and without tax cost, give income-producing securities or other property to mem-

bers of his family, the burden of income taxes could be shifted back and forth at will to lower brackets, and income taxes would be saved.

The federal gift tax was designed to discourage taxpayers from making such inter vivos (lifetime) transfers and, to the extent that this objective was not met, to compensate the government for the loss of estate and income tax revenues.

Nature

The gift tax is an excise tax, a tax levied not directly on the subject of the gift itself or on the right to receive the property, but rather on the right of an individual to transfer money or other property to another. (The tax is imposed only on transfers by individuals, but certain transfers involving corporations are treated as indirect transfers by corporate stockholders.)

The gift tax is based on the value of the property transferred.

The gift tax is computed on a progressive schedule based on cumulative lifetime gifts. In other words, the tax rates are applied to total lifetime taxable gifts (all gifts less the exclusions and deductions described in Section 8) rather than only to taxable gifts made in the current calendar year.

Scope

The regulations summarize the comprehensive scope of the gift tax law by stating that "all transactions whereby property or interests are gratuitously passed or conferred upon another, regardless of the means or device employed; constitute gifts subject to tax." Almost any transfer or shifting of property or an interest in property can subject the donor (the person transferring the property or shifting the interest) to potential gift tax liability to the extent that the transfer is not supported by adequate and full consideration in money or money's worth, i.e., to the extent that the transfer is gratuitous.

Direct and indirect gifts, gifts made outright and gifts in trust (of both real and personal property) can be the subject of a taxable gift. The gift tax is imposed on the shifting of property rights, regardless of whether the property is tangible or intangible. It can be applied even if the property transferred (such as a municipal bond) is exempt from federal income or other taxes.

The broad definition includes transfers of life insurance, partnership interests, royalty rights, and gifts of checks or notes of third parties. Even the forgiving of a note or cancellation of a debt may constitute a gift.

Almost any party can be the donee (recipient) of a gift subject to tax. The donee can be an individual, partnership, corporation, foundation, trust, or other "person." (A gift to a corporation is typically considered a gift to the other shareholders in proportion to their proprietary interest. Similarly, a gift to a trust is usually considered to be a gift to the beneficiary[ies] in proportion to their interest.)

In fact, a gift can be subject to the tax (assuming the gift is complete) even if the identity of the donee is not known at the date of the transfer and cannot be ascertained.

(2) ADVANTAGES OF LIFETIME GIFTS

Nontax–Oriented Advantages

Individuals give property away during their lifetimes for many reasons. Although a detailed discussion of the nontax motivations for lifetime giving is beyond the scope of this chapter, some of the reasons include (a) privacy that would be impossible to obtain through a testamentary gift, (b) potential reduction of probate and administrative costs, (c) protection from the claims of creditors, (d) the vicarious enjoyment of seeing the donee use and enjoy the gift, (e) the corresponding opportunity for the donor to see how well or how poorly the donee manages the business or other property, and (f) provision for the education, support, and financial well-being of the donee.

Tax–Oriented Advantages

The unification of the estate and gift tax systems attempted to impose the same tax burden on transfers made during life as at death. The disparity of treatment between lifetime and "deathtime" transfers was minimized through the adoption of a single unified estate and gift tax rate schedule. Both lifetime and "deathtime" gifts are subject to the same rate schedule and are taxed cumulatively, so that gifts made during lifetime push up the rate at which gifts made at death will be taxed.

EGTRRA 2001 increases the amount protected by the estate tax unified credit in steps to $3,500,000 in 2009. It also repeals the estate tax for one year in 2010. On the other hand, the amount protected by the gift tax unified credit is only $1,000,000 in years after 2001 and the gift tax is not repealed. Thus, the estate and gift tax are not quite as unified as before. In addition, EGTRRA 2001 reduces the top estate and gift tax rates over 2001 to 2010. In 2011, the estate and gift tax revert to as they existed prior to EGTRRA 2001. See the gift and estate tax tables in Appendix A.

These changes can work to the disadvantage of gifts that are greater than the amount protected by the gift tax unified credit in some circumstances. For example, does it make sense to make a gift and pay gift tax in one year: If the tax rate would be lower if the gift is made in a later year? If the estate tax is reduced or eliminated by the estate tax unified credit or repeal of the estate tax in the year of death?

Although at first glance it seemed that unification eliminated the advantage of inter vivos gifts, there are still some significant advantages.

First, an individual can give up to $11,000 (in 2004) gift tax free every year to each of an unlimited number of donees. This means that a person desiring to make $11,000 gifts to each of his four children and four grandchildren could give a total of $88,000 each year without gift tax liability. (This $11,000 gift tax annual exclusion is described in greater detail in Section 8.)

An individual's spouse can also give such gifts. Thus, a married couple can transfer gift tax free up to $22,000 (in 2004) per year of money or other property, multiplied by an unlimited number of donees. In the example above, the donor and spouse together could give up to $176,000 annually on a gift tax-free basis. In fact, one spouse can make the entire gift if the other spouse consents; the transaction can then be treated as if both spouses made gifts. This is known as "gift splitting." Split-gift provisions are also covered in Section 8.

Gift tax free transfers can translate into significant federal estate tax savings. Consider the estate tax savings potential if the amount given to the donees over the life expectancy of the donor is invested (in life insurance, annuities, mutual funds, etc.). Figure 17.1 illus-

Figure 17.1

ESTATE TAX OR GST TAX ADVANTAGE OF THE GIFT TAX ANNUAL EXCLUSION*	
DONOR'S AGE	40
DONEES' ANNUAL AFTER-TAX RETURN ON GIFTS	4.00%
AMOUNT OF UNUSED ANNUAL EXCLUSION (with gift splitting between husband and wife).	$22,000
NUMBER OF DONEES	5
DONOR'S LIFE EXPECTANCY (YEARS)	42.5
TOTAL AMOUNT OF GIFTS ($22,000/year/donee x 5 donees x 43 years)	$4,730,000
DONOR'S PROJECTED ESTATE TAX BRACKET	48.00%
POTENTIAL ESTATE TAX SAVINGS	$2,270,400
PROJECTED VALUE OF GIFTS AT LIFE EXPECTANCY (43 years)	$12,101,312
POTENTIAL ESTATE TAX SAVINGS IF ANNUAL GIFTS INVESTED BY DONEES AT COMPOUND INTEREST	$5,808,654

*Illustration courtesy of NumberCruncher Software

trates the potential estate or generation-skipping transfer tax savings possible if a 40-year-old donor split gifts to five donees over his life expectancy.

A second tax incentive for making an inter vivos as opposed to testamentary ("deathtime") gift is that if a gift is made more than 3 years prior to a decedent's death, the amount of any gift tax paid on the transfer is not brought back into the computation of the gross estate. In the case of a sizable gift, avoidance of the "gross up rule" can result in meaningful tax savings. ("Gross up rule" means that all gift tax payable on taxable gifts made within 3 years of death are included in calculating the value of the gross estate even if the gift itself is not added back.) For example, if an individual makes a $2 million taxable gift in 2004, the $780,800 gift tax payable on that transfer will not be brought back into the estate tax computation if the gift was made more than 3 years before the donor's death. This example ignores any credits or annual exclusion applicable to the gift.

Third, any appreciation accruing between the time of the gift and the date of the donor's death escapes estate taxation. This may result in a considerable estate tax (as well as probate and inheritance tax) saving. If a father gives his daughter stock worth $100,000 and it grows to $600,000 by the date of the father's death, only the $100,000 value of the stock at the time of the gift enters into the estate tax computation. The $500,000 of appreciation does not enter into the computation of an "adjusted taxable gift" and thus does not push up the decedent's marginal estate tax bracket.

An excellent way of making use of this advantage is a gift of life insurance to an adult beneficiary or to an irrevocable trust for adult or minor beneficiaries more than 3 years prior to the insured's death. A $1,000,000 death benefit could be removed from a donor's estate at the cost of only the gift tax on the value of the policy at the time of the transfer (in the case of a whole life policy, usually roughly equivalent to the policy cash value plus unearned premiums at the date of the gift). If the insured lives for more than 3 years after the transfer and the premiums are present interest gifts of $11,000 (based on annual exclusion in 2004) a year or less, there would be no estate tax inclusion and none of the "appreciation" (the difference between the death benefit payable and the adjusted taxable gift if any at the time the policy was transferred) would be in the insured's estate.

Fourth, there are often strong income tax incentives for making an inter vivos gift. This advantage derives from moving taxable income from a high-bracket donor to a lower-bracket donee age 14 or over. For example, shifting $10,000 of annual income through the transfer of income-producing securities, real estate, or other property results in an immediate and annually recurring $2,000 savings if the property is given by a 40 percent bracket parent to a child in a 20 percent state and federal combined income tax bracket. Actually, since the property, and not just income from the property, is transferred, the income tax savings can be even greater after compounding. The year-in year-out income tax savings may far exceed the estate tax savings, as Figure 17.2 illustrates.

Fifth, gifts of the proper type of assets more than 3 years prior to death may enable a decedent's estate to meet the mathematical tests for an IRC Section 303 stock redemption, an IRC Section 6166 installment payout of taxes, and the IRC Section 2032A special-use valuation of farms and certain other business real property.

Figure 17.2

ADVANTAGE OF INCOME SHIFTING - CHILD 14 OR OLDER		
Investment $100,000		
Rate of Return 10%		
Parent's Tax Rate 40%		
Parent's After Tax Rate of Return 6%		
Child's Tax Rate 20%		
Child's After Tax Rate of Return 8%		

	Accumulated Value		Advantage
Years	Parent (6%)	Child (8%)	of Gift
5	$26,765	$29,387	$2,622
10	$35,817	$43,178	$7,362
15	$47,931	$63,443	$15,512
20	$64,143	$93,219	$29,076

Sixth, no gift taxes have to be paid until the transferor makes *taxable* gifts in excess of the gift tax unified credit exemption equivalent ($1,000,000 after 2001). Only taxable gifts in excess of a donor's unused exemption equivalent will cause a loss of income and/or capital because of gift taxes paid.

(3) TECHNICAL DEFINITION OF A GIFT

Elements of a Gift

Under common law, a gift is defined simply as a voluntary transfer without any consideration. But for tax law purposes, neither the statutes nor the regulations specifically define what is meant by the term "gift." However, the regulations dealing with the valuation of gifts provide that

> Value of property transferred
>
> minus
>
> Consideration received
>
> equals
>
> Gift

in cases where property is transferred for less than adequate and full consideration in money or money's worth.

Note that this definition focuses on whether the property was transferred for adequate and full consideration in money or the equivalent of money, rather than turning on whether the transferor intended to make a gift. This is because Congress did not want to force the IRS to have to prove something as intangible and subjective as the state of mind of the transferor. This does not negate the importance of donative intent, but, instead of probing the transferor's actual state of mind, an examination is made of the objective facts of the transfer and the circumstances in which it was made.

Certain factors are examined by courts to determine if there was an "intent" to make a gift:

(1) Was the donor competent to make a gift?

(2) Was the donee capable of accepting the gift?

(3) Was there a clear and unmistakable intention on the part of the donor to absolutely, irrevocably, and currently divest himself of dominion and control over the gift property?

Assuming that these three objective criteria are met, three other elements must be present. There must be

(1) an irrevocable transfer of the present legal title to the donee so that the donor no longer had dominion and control over the property in question;

(2) a delivery to the donee of the subject matter of the gift (or the most effective way to command dominion and control of the gift); and

(3) acceptance of the gift by the donee.

Although all these requirements must be met before a gift is subject to tax, the essence of these tests can be distilled into the following factors (state law is examined to determine the presence or absence of these elements):

(1) There must be an "intention" by the donor to make a gift.

(2) The donor must deliver the subject matter of the gift.

(3) The donee must accept the gift.

Adequate and Full Consideration in Money or Money's Worth Defined

Sufficiency of Consideration Test

Since the measure of a gift is the difference between the value of the property transferred and the consideration received by the transferor, a $100,000 building that is transferred from a mother to her daughter for $100,000 in cash clearly does not constitute a gift. However, the mere fact that consideration has been given does not pull a transaction out of the gift tax orbit; to be exempt from the tax the consideration received by the transferor must be equal in value to the property transferred. This is known as the "sufficiency of consideration test." If the daughter in the example above had paid $60,000, the excess value of the building, $40,000, would not be removed from the scope of the gift tax. To escape the gift tax, there must be "adequate and full consideration" equal in value to the property transferred.

Effect of Moral, Past, or Nonbeneficial Consideration

Consideration is not "in money or money's worth" when the consideration is moral consideration, past consideration, or consideration in the form of a detriment to the transferee that does not benefit the transferor. The classic example is the case where a man transferred $100,000 to a widow when she promised to marry him. (Upon remarriage she would forfeit a $100,000 interest in a trust established for her by her deceased husband; the $100,000 from her fiance was to compensate her for the loss.) The Supreme Court held that the widow's promise to marry her fiance was not sufficient consideration because it was incapable of being valued in money or money's worth. Nor was her forfeiture of $100,000 in the trust sufficient consideration, since, although the widow did in fact give up something of value, the benefit of that value did not go to the transferor, her fiance.

Consideration in Marital Rights and Support Rights Situations

Two issues often arise in connection with the consideration question: (1) Does the relinquishment of marital rights constitute consideration in money or money's worth? (2) Does the relinquishment of support rights constitute consideration in money or money's worth?

The Internal Revenue Code is specific in the case of certain property settlements. It provides that transfers of property or property interests made under the terms of a written agreement between spouses in settlement of marital or property rights are deemed to be for an adequate and full consideration. Such transfers are therefore exempt from the gift tax, whether or not the agreement is supported by a divorce decree, if the spouses enter into a final decree of divorce within 2 years after entering the agreement. So, for example, if a husband agrees to give his wife $10,000 as a lump-sum settlement on divorce in exchange for her release of all marital rights she may have in his estate, the $10,000 transfer is not subject to the gift tax if the stated requirements above are met. But even in a case where the 2-year requirement was not met, a taxpayer has successfully argued that the transfer was not made voluntarily and was therefore not a gift.

A spouse's relinquishment of the right to support constitutes consideration that can be measured in money or money's worth. Likewise, a transfer in satisfaction of the transferor's minor children's right to support is made for money's worth. (But most transfers to (or for the benefit of) adult children are generally treated as gifts unless, for some reason, state law requires the transferor to support that child.)

Transfers Pursuant to Compromises or Court Orders

Consideration is an important factor where a transfer is made pursuant to compromises of bona fide disputes or court orders. Such transfers are not considered taxable gifts because they are deemed to be made for adequate and full consideration. For example, if a mother and daughter are in litigation and the daughter is claiming a large sum of money, a compromise payment by the mother to the daughter is not a gift. However, in an intrafamily situation in which the court is not convinced that a bona fide arm's length adversary proceeding was present, the gift tax will be imposed. For example, in a case where a widow "settled" with a son who threatened to "break" his father's will, the gift tax was levied.

Likewise, the gift tax can be applied even in the case of a transfer made pursuant to (or approved by) a court decree if there is not an adversary proceeding. For instance, if an incompetent's property were transferred to his mother, the transfer would be a gift even though it was approved by court decree (assuming the incompetent had no legal duty to care for the parent).

Types of Gifts

Direct Gifts

Cash or tangible personal property is the subject of most transfers that can be reached by the gift tax law. Generally, delivery of the property itself effectuates the gift. In the case of corporate stock, a gift occurs when endorsed certificates are delivered to the donee or his agent or the change in ownership is delivered to the corporation or its transfer agent. Real property is typically given by the delivery of an executed deed.

If a person purchases a U.S. savings bond but has the bond registered in someone else's name and delivers the bond to that person, a gift has been made. If the bonds are titled jointly between the purchaser and another, no gift occurs until the other person has cashed in the bond or has the bond reissued in his name only. See Section 6, "Requirements for a Completed Gift."

Income that will be earned in the future can constitute a gift presently subject to tax. For example, an author can give his right to future royalties to his daughter. Such a gift is valued according to its present value; i.e., the gift is not considered to be a series of year-by-year gifts valued as the income is paid, but rather a single gift valued on the date the right to future income is assigned. Current valuation will be made even if, for some reason, the payments are reduced substantially or even if they cease. No adjustment is required or allowed if the actual income paid to the donee is more or less than the valuation.

Forgiving a debt constitutes a gift in nonbusiness situations. For example, if a father lends his son $100,000 and later cancels the note, the forgiveness constitutes a $100,000 gift. However, if the father lends the son $100,000 and the initial agreement is that the loan is repayable immediately upon the father's demand, no gift is made.

Some forgiveness of indebtedness, however, constitutes income to the benefited party. If a creditor tore up a debtor's note in return for services rendered by the debtor, the result would be the same as if the creditor compensated the debtor for the services rendered and then the debtor used the cash to satisfy the debt. The debtor realizes income and does not receive a gift.

Payments in excess of one's obligations can be gifts. Clearly a person does not make a gift when he pays his bills. Therefore when a person pays bills or purchases food or clothing for his wife or minor children, he is not making gifts. Courts have allowed considerable latitude in this area. But if a father gives his minor daughter a $50,000 ring, the IRS may claim the transfer goes beyond his obligation of support. Payments made in behalf of adult children are often considered gifts. For example, if a father pays his adult son's living expenses and mortgage payments, or gives an adult child a monthly allowance, the transfer is a gift subject to tax.

In another situation, the taxpayer, pursuant to an agreement incorporated in a divorce decree, created two trusts for the support of his minor children. He put a substantial amount of money in the trusts, which provided that after the children reached 21 they were to receive the corpus. The court measured the economic value of the father's support obligation and held that the excess of the trust corpus over that value was a taxable gift. Only the portion of the transfer required to support the children during their minority was not subject to the gift tax.

Indirect Gifts

Indirect gifts, such as the payment of someone else's expenses, are subject to the gift tax. For instance, if a person makes payments on an adult son's car or pays premiums on a life insurance policy his wife owns on his life, such payments are gifts.

The shifting of property rights alone can trigger gift tax consequences. In one case, an employee gave up his vested rights to employer contributions in a profit-sharing plan. He was deemed to have made a gift to the remaining participants in the plan. Similarly, an employee who has a vested right to an annuity is making a gift if he irrevocably chooses to take a lesser annuity coupled with an agreement that payments will be continued to his designated beneficiary. No gift occurs until the time the employee's selection of the survivor annuity becomes irrevocable.

Third-party transfers may be the medium for a taxable gift. For example, if a father gives his son $100,000 in consideration of his son's promise to provide a lifetime income to the father's sister, the father has made an indirect gift to his sister. Furthermore, if the cost of providing a lifetime annuity for the sister is less than $100,000, the father also has made a gift to his son.

The creation of a family partnership may involve an indirect gift. The mere creation or existence of a family partnership (which is often useful in shifting and spreading income among family members and in reducing estate taxes) does not, per se, mean a gift has been made. But if the value of the services of some family member partners is nil or minimal and earnings are primarily due to assets other than those contributed by the partners in question, the creation of the partnership (or the contribution by another partner of assets) may constitute a gift.

At the other extreme, in cases where new partners are to contribute valuable services in exchange for their share of the partnership's earnings and where the business does not contain a significant amount of capital assets, the formation of a family partnership does not constitute a gift.

Transfers by and to corporations are often forms of indirect gifts. Technically, the gift tax is not imposed upon corporations. But transfers by or to a corporation are often considered to be made by or to corporate stockholders. The regulations state that if a corporation makes a transfer to an individual for inadequate consideration, the difference between the value of the money or other property transferred and the consideration paid is a gift to the transferee from the corporation's stockholders. For example, a gratuitous transfer of property by a family-owned corporation to the father of the shareholders of a corporation could be treated as a gift from the children to their father.

Generally, a transfer to a corporation for inadequate consideration is a gift from the transferor to the corporation's other shareholders. For example, a transfer of $120,000 by a father to a corporation owned equally by him and his three children is treated as a gift of $30,000 from the father to each of the three children. (The amount of such a gift is computed after subtracting the percentage of the gift equal to the percentage of the transferor's ownership.)

A double danger lies in corporate gifts. The IRS may argue that (1) in reality the corporation made a distribution taxable as a dividend to its stockholders and (2) that the shareholders in turn made a gift to the recipient of the transfer. Since any distribution from a corporation to a shareholder generally constitutes a dividend to the extent of corporate earnings and profits, the IRS could claim that a transfer was first a constructive dividend to the shareholders and then a constructive gift by them to the donee. For example, if a family-owned corporation sold property with a fair market value of $450,000 for $350,000 to the son of its shareholders, the transaction could be considered a $100,000 constructive dividend to the shareholder-parents, followed by a $100,000 constructive gift by them to their son.

Life insurance or life insurance premiums can be the subject of an indirect gift in three types of situations: (1) the purchase of a policy for another person's benefit, (2) the assignment of an existing policy, and (3) payment of premiums. (The first two of these three situations are discussed directly below. Premium payments are discussed in Section 7.)

If an insured purchases a policy on his life and

(1) names a beneficiary(ies) other than his estate, and

(2) does not retain the right to regain the policy or the proceeds or revest the economic benefits of the policy (i.e., retains no reversionary interest in himself or his estate); and

(3) does not retain the power to change the beneficiaries or their proportionate interests (i.e., makes the beneficiary designation irrevocable)

he has made a gift measurable by the cost of the policy. All three of these requirements must be met, however, before the insured will be deemed to have made a taxable gift.

If an insured makes an absolute assignment of a policy or in some other way relinquishes all his rights and powers in a previously issued policy, a gift is made. It is measurable by the replacement cost (in the case of a whole life policy generally equal to the interpolated terminal reserve plus unearned premium at the date of the gift).

This can lead to an insidious tax trap. Assume a wife owns a policy on the life of her husband. She names her children as revocable beneficiaries. At the death of the husband, the IRS could argue that the wife has made a constructive gift to the children. In this example, the gift is equal to the entire amount of the death proceeds. It is as if the wife received the proceeds to which she was entitled and then gave that money to her children.

An extension of this reasoning, which was actually (and successfully) applied by the IRS, is a case where the owner of policies on the life of her husband placed the policies in trust for the benefit of her children. Because she reserved the right to revoke the trust at anytime before her husband died, she had not made a completed gift until his death. It was not until his death that she relinquished all her powers over the policy. When the husband died, the trust became irrevocable, and therefore the gift became complete. The value of the gift was the full value of the death proceeds, rather than the replacement value of the policy when it was placed in trust.

(4) GRATUITOUS TRANSFERS THAT ARE NOT GIFTS

A number of common situations do not attract the gift tax because they do not involve gifts in the tax sense. These situations fall into three basic categories: (A) where property or an interest in property has not been transferred, (B) certain transfers in the ordinary course of business, and (C) sham gifts.

The Requirement That Property or an Interest in Property Be Transferred

(1) Gratuitous Services Rendered

The gift tax is imposed only on the transfer of "property" or "an interest in property." Although the term "property" is given the broadest possible meaning, it does not include services that are rendered gratuitously. Regardless of how valuable the services one person renders for the benefit of another person, those services do not constitute the transfer of property rights and do not, therefore, fall within the scope of the gift tax.

Difficult questions often arise in this area. For example, if an executor performs the multiplicity of services required in the course of the administration of a large and complex estate, the services are clearly of economic benefit to the estate's beneficiaries. Yet since services are just that, they do not constitute a transfer of property rights. If the executor formally waives the fee (within 6 months of appointment as executor) or fails to claim the fees or commissions by the time of filing and indicates through action (or inaction) that he intends to serve without charge, no property has been transferred.

Conversely, once fees are taken (or if the fees are deducted on an estate, inheritance, or income tax return), the executor has received taxable income. If he then chooses not to (or neglects to) actually receive that money and it goes to the estate's beneficiaries, he is making an indirect (and possibly taxable) gift to those individuals.

(2) Interest-Free Loans

Does the right to use property (such as money) at no charge constitute a gift of property? Yes, interest-free and below market rate loans are treated as taxable gifts. A gift tax is imposed on the value of the right to use the borrowed money, the so-called "foregone interest" (see Chapter 37), generally the going rate of interest the money could earn in the given situation. (By this reasoning, giving someone the use of real estate or other property, such as a vacation home or car, at little or no rent would seem to be a gift, but the IRS has been focusing on property interest transfers rather than permitted-use cases.)

(3) Disclaimers (Renunciations)

Generally, a potential donee is deemed to have accepted a valuable gift unless he expressly refuses it. But in some cases an intended donee may decide (for whatever reason) that he does not want or does not need the gift. If he disclaims the right to the gift (refuses to take it), it will usually go to someone else as the result of that renunciation.

By disclaiming, the intended transferee is in effect making a transfer to the new recipient subject to the gift tax unless the disclaimer meets certain rules.

A disclaimer that meets those rules is called a "qualified disclaimer" and is treated for gift tax purposes as if the property interest went directly from the original transferor to the person who receives it because of the disclaimer. In other words, the disclaimant is treated as if he made no transfer of property or an interest in property to the person to whom the interest passes because of the disclaimer. This makes the qualified disclaimer an important estate-planning tool.

There are a number of requirements for a qualified disclaimer of gifted property:

(1) The refusal must be in writing.

(2) The writing must be received by the transferor, his legal representative, or the holder of the legal title to the property no later than 9 months after the later of (a) the date on which the transfer creating the interest is made or (b) the date the person disclaiming reaches age 21.

(3) The person disclaiming must not have accepted the interest or any of its benefits.

(4) Because of the refusal, someone other than the person disclaiming receives the property interest. The person making the disclaimer cannot in any way influence who is to be the recipient of the disclaimer.

Disclaimers are discussed in detail in Chapter 11.

(4) Promise to Make a Gift

Although income that will be earned in the future can be the subject of a gift, the promise to make a gift in the future is not taxable even if the promise is enforceable. This is because a mere promise to make a transfer in the future is not itself a transfer. The IRS agrees, as long as the gift cannot be valued. But if the promise is enforceable under state law, the IRS will attempt to subject it to the gift tax when it becomes capable of valuation.

Transfers in the Ordinary Course of Business

(1) Compensation for Personal Services

Situations often arise in business settings that purport to be gifts from corporate employers to individuals. The IRS often claims that such transfers are, in fact, compensation for personal services rather than gifts. The IRS argues that the property transfers constitute income to the transferee rather than a gift by the transferor. In these cases, the focus changes to the effect on the transferee: Has the transferee received taxable income or has he received a tax-free gift?

A payment may be taken out of the normal gift tax rules (and thus be considered taxable income to the recipient) by the regulations, which state that "the gift tax is *not* applicable to…ordinary business transactions." An ordinary business transaction, defined as a sale, exchange, or other transfer of property (a transaction which is bona fide, at arm's length, and free from donative intent) made in the ordinary course of business, will be considered as if made for an adequate and full consideration in money or money's worth.

A situation will be considered an ordinary business transaction and not be classified as a tax-free gift to the recipient if it is "free from donative intent." This means that donative intent becomes quite important. The taxpayer-recipient, of course, would like to have the transaction considered an income tax-free gift. The IRS would reap larger revenues if the transfer were considered compensation and therefore were taxable income.

When will a payment be considered a tax-free gift to the recipient (the donor must still pay any gift taxes) rather than taxable income? A gift is deemed to have been made if the donor's dominant reason for making the transfer was detached and disinterested generosity (for example where an employer makes flood relief payments to his employees because of a feeling of affection, charity, or similar impulses) rather than consideration for past, present, or future services of the recipient employees.

A transfer is not a gift if the primary impetus for the payment is (a) the constraining force of any legal or moral duty, or (b) anticipated benefit of an economic nature.

Among the factors typically studied in examining the donor's intent are:

(1) the duration and value of the employee's services;

(2) the manner in which the employer determined the amount of the reputed gift; and

(3) the way the employer treated the payments in corporate books and on tax returns, i.e., was the payment deducted as a business expense? (The corporation's characterization of payment is often persuasive where the corporation makes a payment or series of payments to the widow of a deceased employee. The employer generally prefers to have such payments taxed as compensation to the employee's survivors so that the corporation can deduct payments as compensation for past services of the employee.)

In one case, a business friend gave the taxpayer a car after the taxpayer had furnished him with the names of potential customers. The car was not a gift but was intended as payment for past services as well as an inducement for the taxpayer to supply additional names in the future. In another case, however, the employer had made a payment of $20,000 to a retiring executive when he resigned. After examining the employer's esteem and kindliness, and the appreciation of the retiring officer, the court stated that the transfer was a non(income) taxable gift. Another court, in a similar case, came to the same conclusion when it found payments were made "from generosity or charity rather than from the incentive of anticipated economic benefit."

This type of issue, gift or compensation, is settled on a case-by-case basis after an analysis of the circumstances evidencing motive or intent. Usually the intrafamily transfer will be considered a gift, even if the recipient rendered past services. Transfers to persons outside the family will usually be considered compensation.

(2) Bad Bargains

A bad bargain is another "ordinary course of business" situation; a sale, exchange, or other property transfer made in the ordinary course of business is treated as if it were made in return for adequate and full consideration in money or money's worth. This assumes the transaction is (a) bona fide, (b) at arm's length, and (c) not donative in intent.

There are a number of court-decided examples of "bad bargains" that have not resulted in gift tax treatment. In one case, certain senior executive shareholders sold stock to junior executives at less than fair market value pursuant to a plan arranged to give the younger executives a larger stake in business profits. The court noted that the transfers were for less than adequate consideration, but stated that "the pertinent inquiry for gift tax purposes is whether the transaction is a genuine business transaction, as distinguished, for example, from the marital or family type of transaction." Bad bargains, sales for less than adequate money's worth, are made every day in the business world for one reason or another; but no one would think for a minute that any gift is involved, even in the broadest sense of the term "gift."

Another example of a "no-gift" situation would be where a group of businessmen convey real estate to an unrelated business corporation with the expectation of doing business with that corporation sometime in the future.

But the "ordinary course of business" exception has its limits; no protection from the gift tax law would be afforded where the transferor's motive was to pass on the family fortune to the following generation. In one case a father transferred property to his children at a price below the fair market value. In return, he received noninterest-bearing notes, rather than cash, and he continued to make certain payments with respect to the property on the children's behalf. The court found these actions showed that, in reality, he was not dealing with his children at arm's length. It is possible that the same result could occur if the father employed the son at a wage of $50,000 a year, but the son rendered services worth only $20,000 a year. The IRS could claim that the $30,000 difference constituted a gift.

Sham Gifts

It is often advantageous for income or estate tax purposes to characterize a transaction as a gift. The taxpayer's goal is to shift the burden of income taxes from a high- to a relatively lower-bracket relative age 14 or older. But if the transfer has no real economic significance other than the hoped-for tax savings, it will be disregarded for tax purposes; i.e., if the transaction does

not have meaning apart from its tax sense, it will not be considered a gift by the IRS or by the courts and will therefore not shift the incidence of taxation. For example, a well-known golfer contracted with a motion picture company to make a series of pictures depicting his form and golf style. In return, the golfer was to receive a lump sum of $120,000 plus a 50 percent royalty on the earnings of the picture. But before any pictures were made, he sold his father the right to his services for $1. The father, in turn, transferred the rights to the contract to a trust for his son's three children. The court held that the entire series of transactions had no tax effect and that the income was completely taxable to the golfer.

Assignments of income

Assignment of income questions are among the most common, and also confusing, in the tax law, because they often involve inconsistent property, gift, and income tax results. For example, a person could agree to give his son one-half of every dollar he earned in the following year. The agreement might be effective for property law purposes, and the son could have an enforceable legal right to half his father's income. Gift tax law might also recognize the transfer of a property right, and the present value of a father's future income could be subject to the gift tax. Yet, for income tax purposes, the father would remain liable for taxes on the entire earnings.

A general agent for a life insurance company assigned renewal commissions to his wife. The wife had a property law right to the commissions. The present worth of the renewals the wife would receive was treated as a gift. Yet, the general agent was subject to income tax on the commissions as they were paid. In a similar case, a doctor transferred the right to accounts receivable from his practice to a trust for his daughter. Again, the court held that as the trustee received payments from the doctor's patients, those sums were taxable to the doctor even though he had made an irrevocable and taxable gift to the trust.

Gifts of income from property meet a similar fate. For example, if a person assigns the right to next year's rent from a building to her daughter or next year's dividends from specified stock to her grandson, the transfers will be effective for property law purposes and will generate gift taxes. But the income will be taxable to the donor for income tax purposes.

Gifts of property, however, produce a more satisfactory result to the donors; if the tree (property) is given away, the fruit (income) it bears will be taxable to the tree's new owner. Thus, if the donor in the examples above had given the building and the stock, gifts equal to the value of those properties would be made; and the income produced by those assets would be taxed to her daughter and grandson, respectively. Likewise, if stock that cost the donor $1,000 is transferred to a donee at a time when it is worth $2,500 and is later sold by the donee for $3,000, the donee takes the donor's cost ($1,000) as his basis, and is taxed on the gain ($2,000).

(5) EXEMPT GIFTS

A few types of gratuitous transfers are statutorily exempted from the gift tax. A qualified disclaimer, described above, is a good example. Certain transfers of property between spouses in divorce and separation situations are further examples.

Tuition paid to an educational institution for the education or training of an individual is exempt from the gift tax regardless of the amount paid or the relationship of the parties; no family ties must exist for this unlimited exclusion to apply. This means parents, grandparents, or even friends can pay private school or college tuition for an individual without fear of incurring a gift tax.

Still another exempt transfer is the payment of medical care. A donor, any donor, can pay for the medical care of a donee without making a gift. This allows children or other relatives or friends to pay the medical expenses of needy individuals (or anyone else) without worrying about incurring a gift tax.

(6) REQUIREMENTS FOR A COMPLETED GIFT

A completed transfer is necessary before the gift tax can be applied. The phrase "completed transfer" implies that the subject of the gift has been put beyond the donor's recall, i.e., that he has irrevocably parted with dominion and control over the gift. There would be no completed gift if the donor had the power to change the disposition of the gift and thus alter the identity of the donee(s) or amount of the gift. More technically stated, if the donor can (alone or in conjunction with a party who does not have a substantial amount to lose by the revocation) revoke the gift, it is not complete.

Parting with dominion and control is a good test of completeness, but in a number of cases it is difficult to ascertain just when that event occurs. Some of the more common problem areas are (a) incomplete delivery

situations, (b) cancellation of notes, and (c) incomplete transfers to trusts.

When Delivery is Complete

Incomplete delivery situations involve transfers where certain technical details have been omitted or a stage in the process has been left uncompleted. For example, no gift is made at the moment the donor gives the donee a personal check or note; the transfer of a personal check is not complete and taxable until it is paid (or certified or accepted) by the drawee or it is negotiated for value to a third person. For instance, if a check is mailed in December, received in late December, but not cashed until January of the following year, no gift is made until that later year. This is because, typically, the maker of a check is under no legal obligation to honor the check until it is cashed (presented for payment or negotiated to a third person for value). Likewise, a gift of a negotiable note is not complete until it is paid.

An individual on his deathbed will sometimes make a gift *causa mortis* (in anticipation of his imminent death) and then quite unexpectedly recover. Assuming that the facts indicate (1) the transfer was made in anticipation of death from a specific illness and that (2) the gift was contingent on the occurrence of the donor's death, neither the original conveyance nor the return of the property to the donor is subject to the gift tax if the transferor recovers and the transferee returns the property. A gift *causa mortis* is therefore incomplete as long as the donor is alive but becomes complete at the donor's death.

A gift of stock is completed on the date the stock was transferred or the date endorsed certificates are delivered to the donee (or his agent) or to the corporation (or its transfer agent).

Transfer of U.S. government bonds is governed by federal rather than state law. Even if state law requirements for a valid gift are met, for tax purposes no completed gift has been made until the registration is changed in accordance with federal regulations. For example, if a grandmother purchases a U.S. savings bond that is registered as payable to her and to her two children as co-owners, no gift is made to the grandchildren until one of them surrenders the bond for cash.

The creation of a joint bank account (checking or savings) constitutes a common example of an incomplete transfer. Typically, the person making a deposit can withdraw all of the funds or any portion of them. Therefore, the donor has retained a power to revoke the gift and it is not complete. When the donee makes a withdrawal of funds from the account (and thereby eliminates the donor's dominion and control), a gift of the funds occurs.

A similar situation occurs in the case of a joint brokerage account; the creation and contribution to a joint brokerage account held in "street name" is not a gift until the joint owner makes a withdrawal for his personal benefit. At that time, the donee acquires indefeasible rights and the donor parts irrevocably with the funds. Conversely, if a person calls her broker and says, "Buy 100 shares of Texas Oil and Gas and title them in joint names, mine and my husband's, with rights of survivorship," the purchase constitutes a gift to her husband. He has acquired rights that he did not have before to a portion of the stock. (No gift tax would be due in this case, due to the unlimited gift tax marital deduction described below.)

Totten trusts (bank savings accounts where the donor makes a deposit for the donee (Joanne Q. Donor in trust for James P. Donee) and retains possession of the savings book) are, typically, revocable transfers. Here again, because the donor can recover the entire amount deposited, no gift occurs until the donee makes a withdrawal of funds.

Some property cannot conveniently be delivered to the intended donee; farm property is a good example. Where it would be difficult or impossible to make physical delivery of the gift, a gift will usually be considered completed where the delivery is as complete as possible. In one case, a father owned cattle he wished to give his minor children. The court held that the gift was complete when he branded the livestock with each child's initials even though he kept the cattle with others he owned. The court held that the father was acting as the natural guardian of the children and had done everything necessary to make a completed gift.

Real estate is transferred by executing a deed in favor of the donee. But if the donor retains the deed, does not record it, makes no attempt to inform the donee of the transfer, and continues to treat the property as his own, no transfer occurs.

Cancellation of Notes

In many cases, a transfer of property will be made and then the transferor will take back installment notes from the transferee. The transaction will be treated as a

sale for income tax purposes. However, if the transferor forgives the notes, the forgiveness would be a gift.

Cancellation of notes is a frequently used technique for two reasons. First, it provides a simple means of giving gifts to a number of donees of property that is not readily divisible. Second, by forgiving the notes over a period of years, the donor could maximize the use of the $11,000 (in 2004) annual exclusion and unified credit discussed below in Section 8. A good example is a situation where the donor deeds real estate to her sons and takes back notes payable serially on an annual basis. Each son is required to pay his mother $11,000 per year. But when the notes become due, the donor marks the note "cancelled by gift." The gift would occur in the year each note was cancelled, as long as there is no preestablished and predetermined plan for the donor to forgive notes on a systematic basis in future years.

Note that although the annual exclusion would eliminate the gift tax consequences, in this example there is an income tax liability since the donor is actually selling the real estate to her sons. The difference between the donor's basis (cost plus or minus appropriate adjustments) and the amount she'll realize on the sale is taxable (under the installment sales rules since the notes are payable over more than one tax year).

Incomplete Gifts in Trust

Donors will sometimes transfer property to a trust, but retain the right to revoke the transfer. When property is transferred to such a revocable trust, that transfer is not a completed gift. Only when the donor relinquishes all his retained control over the transferred property (i.e., when the trust becomes irrevocable) is a completed gift made.

Tax liability is measured by the value at the moment the gift becomes complete, rather than at the time of the transfer. This can have harsh tax consequences. For example, if the donor retains the power to alter the interests of the trust beneficiaries, even if he cannot exercise any powers for his own benefit, the transfer is not complete.

Assume, for instance, that the donor transfers stock to a trust for his two children and three grandchildren. The income of the trust is payable to the donor's children for as long as they live. Then, the remainder is payable to his grandchildren or their estates. If the donor retains the power to vary the amount of income his children will receive or to reach into corpus to enhance their security, the gift is incomplete. But the gift will be complete when the donor relinquishes control. If that happens when the stock has substantially increased in value, as is often the case, the gift tax payable by the donor may also substantially increase.

GRATs (grantor retained annuity trusts) and GRUTs (grantor retained unitrusts) are based on the fact that gift tax liability is measured by the property's value at the moment the gift becomes complete. By making a gift to an irrevocable nonreversionary trust, but reserving an annuity or unitrust interest for a specified period of years, an individual reduces the value of the gift. (See Chapter 26 regarding GRATs and GRUTs.)

When the property is ultimately transferred, many years after the grantor contributed the property to the trust, it may have appreciated significantly. In essence, this "leverages" the unified credit, since the date of transfer value is typically much greater than the value of trust assets at the inception of the trust.

(7) VALUATION OF PROPERTY FOR GIFT TAX PURPOSES

Valuation is the first step in the gift tax computation process. Only after the property is valued can the annual exclusion and various deductions be applied in arriving at the amount of the taxable gift and the ultimate gift tax. (See Chapter 57 regarding "Valuation Planning.")

The value of the property on the date the gift becomes complete is the amount of the gift. Value, for gift tax purposes, is defined as "the price at which the property would change hands between a willing buyer and a willing seller, neither being under any compulsion to buy or to sell, and both having reasonable knowledge of relevant facts."

Although the provisions of the gift tax law on valuation parallels the estate tax law in many respects, there is one major difference: property transferred during lifetime is valued for gift tax purposes on the date the gift is made. No alternate valuation is allowed.

There are certain valuation problems unique to the gift tax law. These include problems associated with (1) indebtedness with respect to transferred property, (2) restrictions on the use or disposition of property, (3) transfers of large blocks of stock, (4) valuation of mutual fund shares, and (5) valuation of life insurance and annuity contracts.

Indebtedness with Respect to Transferred Property

Generally, when the subject of a gift is encumbered or otherwise subject to an obligation, only the net value of the gift, the value of the property less the amount of the obligation, is subject to the gift tax. Under this rule, which assumes the donor is *not* personally liable for the debt, the amount of the gift is the donor's equity in the property.

However, if the donor is personally liable for the indebtedness that is secured by a mortgage on the gift property, a different result occurs. In this case, the amount of the gift may be the entire value of the property, unreduced by the debt. The reason for the difference is that where a solvent donor makes a gift subject to a debt and the creditor proceeds against the pledged property, the donee is, in effect, paying the donor's personal debt. In some cases, this makes the donee a creditor of the donor. If the donee can then collect from the donor the amount he has paid to the donor's creditor, the donee has received the entire value of the gift rather than merely the equity.

Example: Assume the donor transfers a $100,000 building subject to a $40,000 mortgage on which he is personally liable. If the donor's creditors collect the $40,000 by proceeding against the pledged building and the donee is subrogated to that creditor's rights against the donor-debtor (i.e., the donee now stands in the shoes of the creditor), the donee can collect an additional $40,000 from the donor.

A third possibility is that the donor-debtor is personally liable for the indebtedness secured by a mortgage on the gifted property, but the donee has no right to step into the creditor's shoes and recover the debt from the donor. In this case, the amount of the gift is merely the amount of the donor's equity in the property. In the example above, that amount would be $60,000 ($100,000 fair market value minus $40,000 of indebtedness).

Where the donee has no right to proceed against the donor and recover the debt, actual facts must determine the result. If the donor, in fact, pays off the liability after transferring the mortgaged property to the donee, he is making an additional gift. But if the donee pays off the liability (or if the mortgagee forecloses), the gift was only the donor's equity.

Among the obligations that could be imposed upon a donee is a requirement that the donee pay the gift tax.

This is called a "net gift." The donor has primary liability to pay the gift tax, and the donee is only secondarily liable. The donor could expressly, or by implication, require the donee to pay the donor's gift tax liability. If the donee is required to pay the gift tax imposed on the transfer (or if the tax is payable out of the transferred property), the value of the donated property must be reduced by the amount of the gift tax. But the gift tax computation is based on the value of the property transferred. Obviously, the two figures, the net amount transferred and the tax payable on the transfer, are interdependent. Fortunately, there is a revenue ruling formula for making the computation.

An example of the net gift calculation follows.

TRUE TAX ON NET GIFT

Year	2004
Tentative Taxable Gift	$1,100,000
Gift Tax on $1,100,000	$386,800
Unified Credit	$345,800
Tentative Tax [$386,800 - $345,800]	$41,000
Tax Rate	41%
True Tax [$41,000 ÷ (1 + .41)]	$29,078
Net Gift [$1,000,000 - $29,078]	$970,922

It is important to note that, for income tax purposes, there are court cases that state that the donor must recognize gain where the donee pays the tax or where payment is made from the gifted property. Gain is realized by the donor for income tax purposes to the extent the gift tax paid by the donee exceeds the donor's basis for the property. It is as if the donor sold the property for an amount equal to the gift tax, realized a gain, and then gave the remaining value of the gift property to the donee.

Restrictions on the Use or Disposition of Property

Value is affected by restrictions placed on the donee's use or ability to dispose of the property received. The general rule is that most restrictive agreements do not fix the value of such property but often have a persuasive effect on price. For example, a donor gives stock to his daughter subject to an agreement between the corporation and its shareholders. Under that agreement, the corporation is entitled to purchase those shares at their book value, $30 per share, upon the retirement or death of the stockholder.

Does the existence of a restrictive agreement fix the value of the shares at book value? After all, in the

example, no buyer would pay more than $30 a share while the restriction is operative. But if the stock has "use values" other than sale values (for example, if the stock paid dividends of $10 a year) it may have a fair market value in excess of $30. On one hand, the corporation's option right to purchase the stock at $30 a share limits the fair market value, but on the other hand "use values," such as the right to receive dividends, increase the fair market value.

How much the use values increase the fair market value is largely dependent on how much time is likely to pass before the corporation has an opportunity to exercise its option and on the probability of the corporation's exercising its option at that time.

In the example above, a court would probably state that the existence of a restrictive agreement would not fix the purchase price, since the circumstances requiring purchase (retirement or death) do not exist at the date of the gift. But the existence of the agreement itself is likely to have a depressing effect on the market value of the stock and result in a discounted gift tax value. (However, see discussion of IRC Section 2703 in Chapter 40 and IRC Section 2704 in Chapter 58 regarding restrictions that may be disregarded when valuing property.)

Transfers of Large Blocks of Stock

Another principle that applies, to some degree, to both lifetime and "deathtime" gifts is the so-called blockage rule. The blockage rule is not based on forced sale value. Instead, it attempts to value gifts of large blocks of stock based on the price the property would bring if the stock were liquidated in a reasonable time in some way outside the usual marketing channels. The marketability (and therefore the value) of a massive number of shares of stock may have a lower value than the current per share market value of the same stock, because of the depressive effect if the block is dumped on the market all at once. The utility of blockage evaluation is diminished, and may be inapplicable, when a large block is divided among a number of donees or when gifts are spread over a number of tax years.

Valuation of Mutual Fund Shares

Mutual fund shares are valued at their net asset value, the price of the fund net of any "load" charge.

Valuation of Life Insurance and Annuity Contracts

When a life insurance policy is the subject of a gift, the value is the policy's replacement value: the cost of similar or comparable policies issued by the same company.

If the policy is transferred immediately (within the first year) after its purchase, the gift is equal in value to the gross premium paid to the insurer.

If the policy is paid up at the time it is assigned (or is a single-premium policy), the amount of the gift is the amount of premium the issuing company would charge for the same type of single-premium policy of equal face amount on the insured's life, based on the insured's age at the transfer date. (Impaired health of the insured is not considered by the regulations, but it is possible that the IRS would argue that the adverse health of the insured at the time of the gift may affect valuation.)

If the policy is in a premium-paying stage at the time it is transferred, the value of the gift is generally equal to the sum of (a) the interpolated terminal reserve, plus (b) unearned premiums on the date of the gift.

Except in the early years of most contracts, the interpolated terminal reserve is roughly equivalent to the policy's cash value. In special conditions, such as where the interpolated terminal reserve does not approximate the policy's true value (for example, if the insured donor was terminally ill and had only 1 or 2 months to live), the value of a premium-paying policy may be more than the sum of the interpolated terminal reserve plus unearned premiums as of the date of the gift. (Unearned premiums are defined as the proportionate part of the last premium paid that is attributable to the remainder of the period for which the premium was paid.)

Mr. Martin owned an ordinary life policy on his partner's life to fund a cross-purchase agreement. The policy was 9 years and 4 months old at the time of Mr. Martin's death. The gross annual premium was $2,800, and Mr. Martin died four months after the most recent "premium due" date. Assuming no accrued dividends or policy loans, the policy would be valued as follows:

Terminal reserve at end of 10th year	$14,601
Terminal reserve at end of 9th year	12,965
Increase (10th year)	$ 1,636
Portion of year between death of Mr. Martin and last preceding premium due date is $\frac{4}{12}$ ($\frac{1}{3}$) of a year.	
$\frac{1}{3}$ of increase in reserve ($\frac{1}{3}$ of $1,636)	$ 545
+	
Terminal reserve — end of 9th year	12,965
=	
Interpolated terminal reserve at date of Martin's death	13,510
+	
$\frac{2}{3}$ of gross premium	1,874
Total value of insurance policy	$15,384

The interpolated reserve method will be allowed as long as the contract is not an unusual contract and this method does not develop an amount that varies greatly from the true value of the contract.

Premiums paid by (or on behalf of) the donor after the transfers are also gifts. Therefore, when an owner of a life insurance policy irrevocably assigns that policy to another person or a trust, each premium he pays subsequent to the transfer is considered a gift to the new policy owner (or the beneficial owner[s] of the trust's assets).

Usually, the premium payor and the donor are the same. However, the IRS has stated that if an employee assigns his group life insurance policy to an irrevocable trust he had established for his family, a cash premium paid by the employer is deemed to be a gift of the amount of the premium. The deemed gift is from the employee to the beneficiaries of the trust. But (in a rather poorly considered and not widely accepted ruling) the assignment of the group term coverage itself was held not to be a taxable gift because the coverage had no ascertainable value.

In a split-dollar arrangement, an interest in a life insurance policy is often assigned to a trust. See Chapter 30, on life insurance, regarding the valuation of such interests.

(8) COMPUTING THE TAX ON GIFTS

Gift tax rates are applied to a net figure, "taxable gifts." Before the tax on a transfer is computed, certain reductions are allowed. These reductions may include

(1) "gift splitting"

(2) an annual exclusion

(3) a marital deduction

(4) a charitable deduction

Gift Splitting

The tax law permits a married donor, with the consent of the nondonor spouse, to elect to treat a gift to a third party as though each spouse has made half of the gift. The election must be made on the applicable gift tax return of the donor spouse.

Gift splitting is an artificial mechanism: even if one spouse makes the entire gift, the single transfer is treated for tax computation purposes as though each spouse made only one-half of the gift. This means that the rate of tax that each will pay is separately calculated by reference to his or her own particular prior gifts.

Furthermore, if a nondonor spouse has agreed to treat half of the donor spouse's gift as if made by the nondonor spouse, it will have a direct effect on the future gift tax and estate tax that spouse will eventually have to pay if the gift exceeds the annual exclusion. Even though such spouse did not *actually* make half the gift, it will, nevertheless, to the extent it exceeds the $11,000 (in 2004) annual exclusion, become an "adjusted taxable gift" to be added to all other gifts deemed to have been made for purposes of calculating the future gift tax bracket of the nondonor spouse and to be added to the taxable estate at the nondonor spouse's death.

Gift splitting, which applies only to gifts by a married donor to a third party and only with respect to noncommunity property, was introduced into the tax law to equate the tax treatment of common-law taxpayers with that of community-property residents. When one spouse earns a dollar in a community-property state, fifty cents is deemed to be owned by the other spouse automatically and immediately. Therefore, if the couple gave that dollar to their daughter, each spouse would be treated as having given only fifty cents.

Gift splitting places the common-law resident in the same relative position. For example, if a married individual in a common-law state gives his son a gift worth $22,000 and the requisite gift splitting election is made, for purposes of the gift tax computation that individual is considered to have given only $11,000. His spouse is treated as if she gave the other $11,000, even if, in fact, none of the gift was her property.

If the spouses elect to "split" gifts to third parties, all gifts made by either spouse during that reporting period must be split.

The privilege of gift splitting is available only with regard to gifts made while the couple is married. Therefore, gifts the couple makes before they are married may not be split even if they are later married during the same calendar year. Likewise, gifts made after the spouses are legally divorced or one spouse dies may not be split. But gifts made before one spouse dies may be split; even if that spouse dies before signing the appropriate consent or election, the deceased spouse's executor can make the appropriate election or consent.

The Annual Exclusion

Purpose of the Exclusion

A *de minimis* rule is one that is instituted primarily to avoid the bother of administrative record keeping. The gift tax annual exclusion is a classic example of such a rule. It was instituted to eliminate the need for a taxpayer to keep an account of or report numerous small gifts. Congress intended that the amount of the annual exclusion be set large enough so that no reporting would be required in the case of wedding gifts or other occasional gifts of relatively small amounts.

Effect of Gift Splitting Coupled with Exclusion

Generally, the annual exclusion allows the donor to make, tax free, up to $11,000 (in 2004) worth of gifts (other than "future-interest gifts" as they are defined below) to any number of persons each year. Since an exclusion of up to $11,000 is allowed per donee per year, the total maximum excludable amount is determined by multiplying the number of persons to whom gifts are made by $11,000. For example, if an unmarried individual makes cash gifts in 2004 of $2,000, $8,000, and $16,000 to his brother, father, and son, respectively, the $2,000 gift would be fully excludable, the entire $8,000 gift to his father would be excludable, and $11,000 of the $16,000 gift to his son would be excludable.

If the same individual is married and his spouse consents to splitting the gift, each spouse is deemed to have made one-half of the gift. This means that both spouses can maximize the use of their annual exclusions. Assuming the nondonor spouse made no gifts, the computation at Figure 17.3 shows that none of the $26,000 of gifts would be subject to tax.

Present versus Future Interest

An annual exclusion is allowed only for "present-interest gifts" and is denied to "gifts of future interests."

Figure 17.3

Donee	Amount of Gift to Donee	Treated as if Donor Gave	Exclusion	Subject to Tax	Treated as if Nondonor Spouse Gave	Exclusion	Subject to Tax
Brother	$ 2,000	$ 1,000	$ 1,000	—	$ 1,000	$ 1,000	—
Father	$ 8,000	$ 4,000	$ 4,000	—	$ 4,000	$ 4,000	—
Son	$16,000	$ 8,000	$ 8,000	—	$ 8,000	$ 8,000	—
Totals	$26,000	$13,000	$13,000	—	$13,000	$13,000	—

A present interest is one in which the donee's possession or enjoyment begins at the time the gift is made. A future interest refers to any interest or estate in which the donee's possession or enjoyment will not commence until some period of time after the gift is made. More technically, "future interest" is a legal term, and includes reversions, remainders, and other interests or estates, whether vested or contingent, and whether or not supported by a particular interest or estate, which are limited to commence in use, possession, or enjoyment at some future date or time.

An easy way to distinguish between a present interest (which qualifies for the gift tax annual exclusion) and a future interest (which does not qualify for the gift tax exclusion) is to ascertain:

> At the moment of the gift, did the donee have an immediate, unfettered, and actuarially ascertainable legal right to use, possess, or enjoy the property in question?

If the answer is "Yes," the gift is a present interest. If the answer is "No," the gift is a future interest gift.

Clearly, the outright and unrestricted gift of property to a donee (even a minor) that passes legal and equitable title qualifies as a present-interest gift.

A single gift can be split into two parts: one a present interest that qualifies for the annual exclusion and the other a future interest that does not. For example, a widowed donor creates a trust in 2004 and places income-producing property in the trust. The income is payable annually to the donor's son for life. At the son's death, the remainder is payable to the donor's grandson. The gift to the son of the right to receive income annually for life is a present-interest gift, since he has unrestricted right to its immediate use, possession, or enjoyment. Arbitrarily assuming a 5.0% Section 7520 rate, if the son

is 30 years old at the time of the gift and $100,000 is placed into the trust, the present value of that gift would be worth $86,871 ($100,000 times .86871, which is the present value of the stream of income produced by $100,000 of capital and payable annually for the life of a 30-year-old, according to tables in government regulations – see single life valuation tables in Appendix B). Of the $86,871, $11,000 (in 2004) would be excludable.

If the donor was married and the appropriate election and consent were filed, each spouse could claim an $11,000 (in 2004) exclusion, even though only the donor placed property in the trust. No exclusion is allowed with respect to the ultimate gift of the corpus to the grandson, since his possession or enjoyment may not commence for some time in the future.

Assume the donor and his spouse had provided that their son was to receive income for 10 years and then the principal was to pass to another beneficiary, a grandson. Arbitrarily assuming a 5.0% Section 7520 rate, if the donor had placed only $1,000 in the trust, the exclusion for the gift of the income interest would be $386 ($1,000 times .386087, the term certain income interest valuation factor in Appendix B). Gift splitting with a spouse would not increase the amount of the exclusion. Each spouse would be allowed a $193 exclusion.

No exclusion would be allowed for the gift of the future interest (remainder) that passes to the grandson at the end of 10 years, even though he has an interest that cannot be forfeited. This is because he does not have the right to immediate possession or enjoyment; any delay (no matter how unlikely or how short) in the absolute and immediate right of use, possession, or enjoyment is fatal to the gift tax exclusion.

Note that if the trustee in either situation above had been given the power or discretion to accumulate the income, rather than distribute it, the donor's son would not have received the unfettered and immediate use of the income, and it would be impossible to ascertain the present value of the income interest. For example, assume the trustee is directed to pay the net income to the son for as long as he lives, but is authorized to withhold payments of income during any period he deems advisable and add such payments to corpus. In this case, even the income interest would be a gift of a future interest. No annual exclusion would be allowed.

Where a trustee is required by the trust agreement to accumulate income for a time (or until the occurrence of a specified event), the income interest is a future interest.

The number and amount (or availability) of exclusions depends on the identity of the donee(s), the type of asset involved, and restrictions, if any, placed on the asset.

Summary of Rules for Ascertaining the Amount and Availability of the Gift Tax Annual Exclusion

These rules regarding the annual exclusion can be summarized as follows:

(1) In determining the number of annual exclusions to which a donor is entitled, a gift in trust is a gift to a trust's beneficiaries, and not to the trust.

(2) If the trustee is required to distribute trust income at least annually, the value of an income interest in a trust qualifies for the exclusion even if the value of the remainder interest does not.

(3) The gift of an interest that is contingent upon survivorship is a gift of a future interest. (If a gift in trust is made with income going to the grantor's son for life, then income to the grantor's daughter for life, the gift to the son will qualify but the daughter's interest will not.)

(4) A gift is one of a future interest if enjoyment depends on the exercise of a trustee's discretion. (The nature of the interest must be present as of the date of the gift and is not, for example, determined by what the trustee may subsequently do, or not do, in the exercise of a discretionary power.)

(5) A gift must have an ascertainable value to qualify for the exclusion. (The exclusion will be denied if the donor or anyone else can divert the income from the beneficiary.)

Identity of Donees

When a gift is made in trust, the beneficiaries of the trust (and not the trust itself) are considered the donees. For instance, if there are three life income beneficiaries, up to three annual exclusions could be obtained. Conversely, if five trusts were established for the same beneficiary, only one exclusion is allowed. (Technically, the actuarial value of each gift in trust to that beneficiary would be totaled. That per donee total is then added to direct gifts the donor made to that beneficiary to ascertain whether and to what extent an annual exclusion remains and is allowable for the present transfer.)

A transfer to a corporation is treated as a gift to its shareholders. However, the gift is one of a future interest.

Transfers to two or more persons as joint tenants with right of survivorship, tenants by the entireties, or tenants in common are considered multiple gifts. Each tenant is deemed to receive an amount equal to the actuarial value of his interest in the tenancy. If, for example, one person has a one-half interest in a tenancy in common, a cash gift of $6,000 to the tenancy would be treated as a $3,000 gift to that person. This would be added to other gifts made directly by the same donor to determine how much of the exclusion will be allowed. In all probability, gifts to partnerships should follow the same rules: a gift to a partnership should be treated as if made to each partner in proportion to his partnership interest.

Note that a joint gift, in which neither party can sever his interest without the other's consent, will be considered a future interest gift and will not qualify for the annual exclusion. For instance, if Herb gives Diana and Laura joint ownership in a policy on his life, and if the insurer will not allow either Diana or Laura to sever her interest without the other's consent, Herb has made a future interest gift to each daughter.

Gifts to Minors

Outright gifts to minors pose no particular qualification problem. The IRS states in a revenue ruling that "an unqualified and unrestricted gift to a minor, with or without the appointment of a guardian, is a gift of a present interest." But there are, of course, practical problems involved, especially with larger gifts. Although minors can buy, sell, and deal with some limited types of property, such as U.S. savings bonds, gifts of other types of property create difficulties. For example, some states do not give minors the legal capacity to purchase their own property, care for it, or sell or transfer it. Some states forbid the registration of securities in a minor's name, and a broker may be reluctant to deal in securities titled in a minor's name. In many states, a minor has the legal ability to disaffirm a sale of stock sold at a low price that later rises in value. Furthermore, a buyer receives no assurance of permanent title when a minor signs a real estate deed.

Legal guardianship of the minor is not a viable answer in many situations. Since guardianship laws are rigid, a guardian must generally post bond, and periodic and expensive court accounting is often required. Most importantly, a parent may not want to give a legal minor control over a large amount of cash or other property.

To minimize these and other practical problems involved with most large gifts to minors, such transfers are generally made in trust or under some type of guardianship or custodian arrangement. An incredible amount of litigation developed over whether such gifts qualified for the annual exclusion. IRC Section 2503 provides clear and precise methods of qualifying gifts to minors for the exclusion. There are three basic means of qualifying "cared-for gifts" to minors under Section 2503: (1) a Section 2503(b) trust, (2) a Section 2503(c) trust, or (3) the Uniform Gifts to Minors Act (or the Uniform Transfers to Minors Act).

Section 2503(b) Trust. To obtain an annual exclusion for gifts to a trust, an individual can establish a trust that requires that income *must* be distributed at least annually to or for use of the minor beneficiary. The trust agreement would state how income is to be used and would give the trustee no discretion as to its use. The minor would receive possession of the trust principal whenever the trust agreement specifies. A distribution does not have to be made by age 21; corpus may be held for as long as the beneficiary lives or for any shorter period of time. In fact, the principal can actually bypass the income beneficiary and go directly to the individuals whom the grantor, or even the named beneficiary, has specified. The trust agreement can also control the dispositive scheme if the minor dies before receiving trust corpus. Trust assets do not have to be paid to the minor's estate or appointees.

Mandatory payment of income to (or in behalf of) beneficiaries seems onerous, especially while the beneficiary is a minor. But such income could be deposited in a custodial account and used for the minor's benefit or left to accumulate in a custodial account until the minor reaches majority (at which time the unexpended amount would be turned over to the beneficiary).

Although the entire amount of property placed in a 2503(b) trust would be considered a gift, for exclusion purposes it would be split into two parts: income and principal. The value of the income, measured by multiplying the amount of the gift by a factor that considers both the duration over which the income interest will be paid and the discounted worth of $1 payable over the appropriate number of years, would be eligible for the annual exclusion. The balance of the gift would not qualify for the annual exclusion.

Example: Assume a donor places $10,000 into a Section 2503(b) trust that is required to pay his 10-year-old daughter all income until she reaches age 25. Assume a 5.0% Section 7520 rate. The present value of the income the daughter would receive over those 15 years is $5,190 ($10,000 x .518983, see term certain valuation tables in Appendix B). If the income were payable for her entire life, the present value would jump to almost $9,417 ($10,000 x .94171, see single life valuation tables in Appendix B).

It is important to note that, according to at least one revenue ruling, the annual exclusion would be denied for a 2503(b) trust that permits principal to be invested in nonincome-producing securities, nonincome-producing real estate, or life insurance policies (since they do not produce taxable income).

Section 2503(c) Trust. The Section 2503(b) trust described above has the advantage of not requiring distribution of principal at the minor's reaching age 21, but it does require a current (annual) distribution of income. The Section 2503(c) trust requires the distribution of income and principal when the minor reaches 21. But it does not require the trustee to distribute income currently.

Certain requirements make it possible for a donor to obtain the exclusion by a gift to a minor under Section 2503(c): the trust must provide: (1) the income and principal may be expended by or on behalf of the beneficiary; and (2) to the extent not so expended income and principal will pass to the beneficiary at 21; or (3) if the beneficiary dies prior to that time, income and principal will go to the beneficiary's estate or appointees under a general power of appointment. (The annual exclusion will not be lost merely because local law prevents a minor from exercising a general power of appointment.)

A substantial amount of flexibility can be built into the 2503(c) trust. Income that has been accumulated in the trust, as well as any principal, can be paid over to the donee when he reaches age 21. This may be indicated if the sums involved are not substantial. But the donor may want the trust to continue to age 25 or some other age. It is possible to provide continued management of the trust assets and, at the same time, avoid forfeiting the annual exclusion by giving the donee, at age 21, a right for a limited but reasonable period to require immediate distribution by giving written notice to the trustee. If the beneficiary fails to give written notice, the trust can continue automatically for whatever period the donor provided when he established the trust. Some states have lowered the age of majority from 21 to age 18 or some in between age. A trust can provide that the distribution can be made between the age of majority and age 21 without jeopardizing the Section 2503(c) exclusion. (The rule is that age 21 is the maximum, rather than the minimum, age at which the right to trust assets must be made.)

A 2503(c) trust has a number of advantages over the type of custodianship found in the Uniform Gifts to Minors Act or Uniform Transfers to Minors Act arrangements, as shown in Figure 17.4.

Uniform Gifts (Transfers) to Minors Act. The Uniform Gifts to Minors Act or the Uniform Transfers to Minors Act (reference to either Act herein is simply to the Uniform Act–see chapter 23 for background) provides an alternative to the Section 2503(c) trust. The Uniform Act is frequently utilized for smaller gifts because of its simplicity and because it offers the benefits of management, income and estate tax shifting, and the investment characteristics of a trust with little or none of the setup costs.

The Uniform Act is also indicated over a trust if the gift consists of stock in an S corporation. That's because, generally speaking, a trust (other than a voting, electing small business trust, QSST, or "grantor" trust) cannot hold S corporation stock without causing a loss of the election privilege. The result might be double taxation of corporate profits and forfeiture of the privilege of passing through profits (and losses) to shareholders. (See the discussion of QSSTs and IRC Section 687 Trusts in Chapter 46.)

The original Uniform Gifts to Minors Act was approved in 1956 and provided for gifts of money and securities to minors. In 1966, the Uniform Act was

Figure 17.4

Factor	Trust	UGMA	UTMA
Type of property	Donor can make gifts of almost any type of property	Type of property must be permitted by appropriate statute. Gift of real estate may not be permitted	Donor can make gifts of almost any type of property
Dispositive provisions	Donor can provide for disposition of trust assets if donee dies without having made disposition	Disposition must follow statutory guideline	Disposition must follow statutory guideline
Investment powers	Trustee may be given broad virtually unlimited investment powers	Custodian limited to investment powers specified by statute	Custodian limited to investment powers specified by statute
Time of distribution of assets	Trust can continue automatically even after beneficiary reaches age 21. Trustee can make distribution between state law age of majority and age 21	Custodial assets must be paid to beneficiary upon reaching statutory age	Custodial assets must be paid to beneficiary upon reaching statutory age

revised to accommodate gifts of life insurance policies and annuity contracts. Over the years between 1956 and 1984, all states adopted one or other of the Uniform Acts or variations thereof. Most states, from time to time, added to the kinds of property that could be given under the Act. In 1983, the National Conference of Commissioners on Uniform State Laws, concerned about the lack of uniformity among the states with respect to the Uniform Gifts to Minors Act, yielded to the expansive approach taken by most of the states and approved the Uniform Transfers to Minors Act.

The 1983 Act accommodates gifts, lifetime and testamentary, of any interest in property. At this writing, nearly all of the states have replaced their Uniform Gifts to Minors Act with the Uniform Transfers to Minors Act. For up to date highlights of state UGMA and UTMA provisions, see the *Advanced Sales Reference Service* (published by the National Underwriter Company) at ¶550 of section 48.

By way of example, in Pennsylvania, a state that has a variation of the Uniform Transfers to Minors Act, a custodianship gift may be made as follows:

20 Pa C.S. §5309. Manner of creating custodial property and effecting transfer
(a) **Creation of custodial property.**—Custodial property is created and a transfer is made whenever:
(1) An uncertificated security or a certificated security in registered form is either:
(i) registered in the name of the transferor, an adult other than the transferor or a trust company, followed in substance by the words: "as custodian for (name of minor) under the Pennsylvania Uniform Transfers to Minors Act"; or
(ii) delivered if in certificated form, or any document necessary for the transfer of an uncertificated security is delivered, together with any necessary endorsement to an adult other than the transferor or to a trust company as custodian, accompanied by an instrument in substantially the form set forth in subsection (b).
(2) Money is paid or delivered to a broker or financial institution for credit to an account in the name of the transferor, an adult other than the transferor or a trust company, followed in substance by the words: "as custodian for (name of minor) under the Pennsylvania Uniform Transfers to Minors Act."
(3) The ownership of a life or endowment insurance policy or annuity contract is either:
(i) registered with the issuer in the name of the transferor, an adult other than the transferor or a trust company followed in substance by the words: "as custodian for (name of minor) under the Pennsylvania Uniform Transfers to Minors Act"; or
(ii) assigned in a writing delivered to an adult other than the transferor or to a trust company whose name in the assignment is followed in substance by the words: "as custodian for (name of minor) under the Pennsylvania Uniform Transfers to Minors Act."

(4) An irrevocable exercise of a power of appointment or an irrevocable present right to future payment under a contract is the subject of a written notification delivered to the payor, issuer or other obligor that the right is transferred to the transferor, an adult other than the transferor or a trust company, whose name in the notification is followed in substance by the words: "as custodian for (name of minor) under the Pennsylvania Uniform Transfers to Minors Act."
(5) An interest in real property is recorded in the name of the transferor, an adult other than the transferor or a trust company, followed in substance by the words: "as custodian for (name of minor) under the Pennsylvania Uniform Transfers to Minors Act."
(6) A certificate of title issued by a state or the Federal Government which evidences title to tangible personal property is either:
(i) issued in the name of the transferor, an adult other than the transferor or a trust company, followed in substance by the words: "as custodian for (name of minor) under the Pennsylvania Uniform Transfers to Minors Act"; or
(ii) delivered to an adult other than the transferor or to a trust company, endorsed to that person followed in substance by the words: "as custodian for (name of minor) under the Pennsylvania Uniform Transfers to Minors Act."
(7) An interest in any property not described in paragraphs (1) through (6) is transferred to an adult other than the transferor or to a trust company by a written instrument in substantially the form set forth in subsection (b).

(b) **Form.**—An instrument in the following form satisfies the requirements of subsection (a)(1)(ii) and (7):

TRANSFER UNDER THE PENNSYLVANIA

UNIFORM TRANSFERS TO MINORS ACT

I, (name of transferor or name and representative capacity if a fiduciary), hereby transfer to (name of custodian), as custodian for (name of minor) under the Pennsylvania Uniform Transfers to Minors Act, the following: (insert a description of the custodial property sufficient to identify it).
Dated:_____

_____
(Signature)

(name of custodian) acknowledges receipt of the property described above as custodian for the minor named above under the Pennsylvania Uniform Transfers to Minors Act.
Dated:_____

_____
(Signature of custodian)

(c) **Control of Custodial Property.**—A transferor shall place the custodian in control of the custodial property as soon as practicable.

The Effect of Type of Asset

The type of asset given and restrictions placed on that asset may prevent the donor from obtaining the annual exclusion.

An outright "no strings attached" gift of life insurance will qualify for the annual exclusion. Life insurance (and annuity policies) are subject to the same basic test as any other type of property in ascertaining whether the interest created is "present or future," even though the ultimate obligation under a life insurance policy, payment of the death benefit, is to be discharged in the future. A policy does not have to have cash value at the time of the gift to make the transfer one of a present interest. But the annual exclusion would be lost if the donor prevented the donee from surrendering the policy or borrowing its cash value or limited the donee's right to policy cash values in any way.

When a life insurance policy is transferred or otherwise assigned to a trust, will the transfer of policy cash values constitute a present interest? The answer depends on the terms of the trust. Generally, the gift will be one of a future interest, since beneficiaries are not usually given an immediate right to possession or enjoyment of the policy values or other items constituting trust corpus. For example, a trust will typically provide no payments to beneficiaries unless they survive the insured. Furthermore, there is generally no actuarially sound method of making an allocation between the value of a present interest and future interest. Unless the given beneficiary's present interest can be ascertained, no exclusion is allowed. (A related attack used by the IRS is that insurance is nonincome-producing property. This concept is discussed further below.)

Premium payments will usually be considered present- or future-interest gifts depending on the classification of the policy itself; if the assignment of the policy was considered a present interest, premiums paid by the donor after the transfer will qualify for the annual exclusion. For instance, if a person makes an absolute assignment of a policy on his life to his daughter but continues to pay premiums, premiums paid subsequent to the transfer would be present-interest gifts. Conversely, if the gift of the policy was a future interest, premium payments made by the donor after the transfer may also be considered future-interest gifts.

A gift in trust of a life insurance policy or of premiums can be made a present interest by inserting a "Crummey" power (named after the major case in this area). A Crummey power gives the named individual(s) an immediate, unfettered, and actuarially ascertainable right; in short, the absolute right to withdraw a specified amount or portion of the assets contributed to the trust. This withdrawal right (essentially, a general power of appointment over a specified amount or portion of each year's contribution to the trust) makes the gift in trust of a life insurance policy or of premiums qualify for the gift tax annual exclusion.

Clearly, an outright gift of nonincome-producing property will qualify for the gift tax exclusion. Will the same property qualify if placed in a trust? The IRS uses three arguments to disallow annual exclusions:

(1) the right to income (which is the only current right given to a life beneficiary) from a gift of nonincome-producing property is a future interest since its worth is contingent upon the trustee's converting it to income-producing property;

(2) it is impossible to ascertain the value of an income interest in property that is not income-producing at the time of the gift; and

(3) if a gift tax exclusion *is* allowable, the exclusion must be limited to the actual income produced by the property (or expected to be produced) multiplied by the number of years over which the income beneficiary is expected to receive the income, discounted to its present value.

Nondividend-paying stock is a good example of property that may not qualify for the gift tax exclusion when it is placed into a trust. The IRS has been successful in a number of cases in disallowing an exclusion for gifts in trust of stock in closely held corporations paying no dividends. Gifts in trust of life insurance policies pose the same problem: a mother assigns policies on her life to a trust created to provide financial protection for her daughter. Upon the mother's death, the policy proceeds will be reinvested and the daughter will receive the net income of the trust for life. Will the mother be allowed the exclusion for the present value of her daughter's income interest? The regulations answer in the negative since the daughter will not receive income payments until her mother dies.

But even these last two types of property can qualify for the annual exclusion if the beneficiary is given the power to require the trustee to make assets in the trust income-producing. Consider, however, the potential adverse implications of that power if the beneficiary chooses to exercise it.

Gift Tax Marital Deduction

An individual who transfers property to a spouse is allowed an unlimited deduction (subject to certain conditions) known as the gift tax marital deduction.

The purpose of the gift tax marital deduction is currently to enable spouses to be treated as an economic unit.

Requirements to Qualify for Gift Tax Marital Deduction

For a gift to qualify for the gift tax marital deduction, the following conditions must be satisfied: (1) The donor's spouse must be a United States citizen at the time the gift is made. [While the marital deduction is not available for gifts to non-citizen spouses, the gift tax annual exclusion is increased to $114,000 (in 2004) for such gifts if they would otherwise qualify for the marital deduction.] (2) The recipient of the gift must be the spouse of the donor at the time the gift is made. (3) The property transferred to the donee-spouse must not be the type of terminable interest that will disqualify the gift for the marital deduction.

Most of the qualifications above are self-explanatory. The terminable interest rule for marital deduction gifts is similar to the rule employed for estate tax purposes. Essentially, the effect of these rules is that generally no marital deduction will be allowed where (a) the donee-spouse's interest in the transferred property will terminate upon the lapse of time or at the occurrence or failure of a specified contingency, (b) where the donee-spouse's interest will then pass to another person who received his interest in the property from the donor-spouse, and (c) that person did not pay the donor full and adequate consideration for that interest.

The exception is for a gift of "QTIP" assets. (In the past a gift or bequest of a terminable interest in property, one which could end for example at a spouse's death and therefore escape taxation, would not have been eligible for the gift (or estate) tax marital deduction.)

Current law now provides that if a donor spouse gives a donee spouse a "qualifying income interest for life," it will qualify for a gift (or estate) tax marital deduction. To qualify,

(1) the surviving spouse must be entitled to all the income from the property (and it must be payable annually or more frequently),

(2) no person can have a power to appoint any part of the property to any person other than the surviving spouse, and

(3) the property must be taxable at the donee-spouse's death (in the case of a bequest, the first decedent's executor makes an irrevocable election that the property remaining at the surviving spouse's death is taxable in her estate).

Also, a life estate with power of appointment in the donee spouse qualifies for the marital deduction. Marital deduction trusts are discussed in detail in Chapter 24.

Gift Tax Charitable Deduction

A donor making a transfer of property to a qualified charity may receive a charitable deduction equal to the value of the gift (to the extent not already excluded by the annual exclusion). The net effect of the charitable deduction, together with the annual exclusion, is to avoid gift tax liability on gifts to qualified charities. There is no limit on the amount that can be passed, gift tax free, to a qualified charity.

The gift tax deduction is allowed for all gifts made during the calendar year by U.S. citizens or residents if the gift is to a qualified charity. A qualified charity is defined as (a) the United States, a state, territory, or any political subdivision or the District of Columbia if the gift is to be used exclusively for public purposes; (b) certain religious, scientific, or charitable organizations; (c) certain fraternal societies, orders, or associations; (d) certain veterans' associations, organizations, or societies.

Technically the charitable deduction is limited. A charitable deduction is allowed only to the extent that each gift exceeds the annual exclusion. For example, during 2004 a single client makes total gifts of $52,000: $26,000 to his daughter and $26,000 to The American College. After taking annual exclusions, gifts qualifying for the charitable deduction would amount to $15,000 (the $26,000 gift to The American College less the $11,000 (in 2004) annual exclusion). Therefore the client's charitable deduction would be limited to $15,000. The reason for the rule is this: If the annual exclusion were already deducted, the allowance of a charitable deduction equal to the total amount of the gift would result in an extra $11,000 exclusion. The operation of these rules is illustrated below.

In certain cases a donor will transfer a remainder interest to a qualified charity. A personal beneficiary will be given all or part of the income interest in the transferred property, and the charity will receive the remainder at the termination of the income interest. Where a charitable remainder is given to a qualified charity, a gift tax deduction is allowable for the present value of that remainder interest only if at least one of the following conditions is satisfied:

(1) the transferred property was either a personal residence or a farm; or

(2) the transfer was made to a charitable remainder annuity trust; or

(3) the transfer was made to a charitable remainder unitrust; or

(4) the transfer was made to a pooled income fund.

The terms "charitable remainder annuity trust," "charitable remainder unitrust," and "pooled income fund" are defined in essentially the same manner as they are for estate and income tax purposes. They are discussed in detail in Chapter 33.

Calculating Gift Tax Payable

The process of computing the gift tax payable begins with ascertaining the amount of taxable gifts in the current reporting calendar year. In order to find the amount of taxable gifts, it is first necessary to value all gifts made. If appropriate, the gift is then "split," annual exclusions and marital and charitable deductions are applied. An example and computation format will illustrate the process.

Assume a single donor in the last month of 2004 makes certain outright gifts: $160,000 to his son, $125,000 to his daughter, $8,000 to his grandson, and $25,000 to The College For Financial Planning (a total of $318,000).

Computing Taxable Gifts

Step 1	*List* total gifts for year		$318,000
Step 2	*Subtract* one-half of gift deemed to be made by donor's spouse (split gifts)	$ 0	
	Gifts deemed to be made by donor		$318,000
Step 3	*Subtract* annual exclusion(s)	$ 41,000	
	Gifts after subtracting exclusion(s)		$277,000
Step 4	*Subtract* marital deduction	$ 0	
Step 5	*Subtract* charitable deduction	$ 14,000	
	Taxable gifts		$263,000

Note that, although there were four donees, the annual exclusion was $41,000 and did not total four times $11,000, or $44,000. This is because the annual exclusion is the lower of (a) $11,000 (in 2004) or (b) the actual net value of the property transferred. In this example the gift to the grandson was only $8,000, which limits the annual exclusion for that gift to $8,000.

A slight change in the fact pattern above will illustrate the computation where the donor is married and his spouse consented to split their gifts to third parties. In this case, only half the gifts made by the donor would be taxable to the donor (half the gifts made by the donor's spouse to third parties would also be included in computing the donor's total gifts).

A separate (and essentially identical) computation is made for the donor's spouse. That computation would show (a) the other half of the husband's gifts to third parties plus (b) half of the wife's actual gifts to third parties (since all gifts must be split if any gifts are split).

Computing Taxable Gifts

Step 1	*List* total gifts for year		$318,000
Step 2	*Subtract* one-half of gift deemed to be made by donor's spouse (split gifts)	$159,000	
	Gifts deemed to be made by donor		$159,000
Step 3	*Subtract* annual exclusion(s)	$ 37,000	
	Gifts after subtracting exclusion(s)		$122,000
Step 4	*Subtract* marital deduction	$ 0	
Step 5	*Subtract* charitable deduction	$ 1,500	
	Taxable gifts		$120,500

(The calculation on the wife's return would parallel this return.)

Note that in this example the annual exclusions were computed *after* the split and each donor's exclusions would be:

(a)	Gift to son	$11,000
(b)	Gift to daughter	11,000
(c)	Gift to grandson	4,000
(d)	Gift to The College for Financial Planning	11,000
		$37,000

The charitable deduction for each spouse would be $1,500 [($25,000 ÷ 2) - $11,000 (in 2004)].

If the married donor in the fact pattern directly above had also made an outright gift of $200,000 to his wife, the computation would be as follows:

Computing Taxable Gifts

Step 1	List total gifts for year		$518,000
Step 2	Subtract one-half of gift deemed to be made by donor's spouse (split gifts)	$159,000	
	Gifts deemed to be made by donor		$359,000
Step 3	Subtract annual exclusion(s)	$ 48,000	
	Gifts after subtracting exclusion(s)		$311,000
Step 4	Subtract marital deduction	$189,000	
Step 5	Subtract charitable deduction	$ 1,500	
	Taxable gifts		$120,500

When the total value of taxable gifts for the reporting period is found, the actual tax payable is computed using the following method:

Computing Gift Tax Payable

Step 1	Compute gift tax on all *taxable* gifts regardless of when made (use gift tax rate schedule)	$_____
Step 2	Compute gift tax on all *taxable* gifts made prior to the present year's gift(s) (use gift tax rate schedule)	$_____
Step 3	Subtract Step 2 result from Step 1 result	$_____
Step 4	Enter gift tax credit remaining	$_____
Step 5	Subtract Step 4 result from Step 3 result to obtain *gift tax payable*	$_____

For instance, a widow gives $1,400,000 to her daughter and $100,000 to The College for Financial Planning in 2004. Both transfers are present-interest gifts. If she had made no previous taxable gifts in the current or prior years or quarters, the computation would be as follows:

Computing Taxable Gifts

Step 1	List total gifts for year		$1,500,000
Step 2	Subtract one-half of gift deemed to be made by donor's spouse (split gifts)	$ 0	
	Gifts deemed to be made by donor		$1,500,000
Step 3	Subtract annual exclusion(s)	$ 22,000	
	Gifts after subtracting exclusion(s)		$1,478,000
Step 4	Subtract marital deduction	$ 0	
Step 5	Subtract charitable deduction	$ 89,000	
	Taxable gifts		$1,389,000

To find the gift tax payable on this amount, the procedure would be as follows:

Computing Gift Taxable Payable

Step 1	Compute gift tax on all *taxable* gifts regardless of when made ($1,389,000)	$508,070
Step 2	Compute gift tax on all *taxable* gifts made prior to the present gift(s)	$ 0
Step 3	Subtract Step 2 result from Step 1 result	$508,070
Step 4	Enter gift tax (unified) credit remaining (2004)	$345,800
Step 5	Subtract Step 4 result from Step 3 result to obtain *gift tax payable*	$162,270

The Step 1 entry, $508,070, is found by using the gift tax rate schedule in effect for the year of the gift (see Appendix A). Note that the current rate table is used regardless of when the earlier gifts were made.

If the donor in the example above had made $100,000 of additional taxable gifts in 2000 (a total of $1,489,000), the computation would be as follows:

Computing Gift Taxable Payable

Step 1	Compute gift tax on all *taxable* gifts regardless of when made ($1,489,000)	$551,070
Step 2	Compute gift tax on all *taxable* gifts made prior to the present gift(s)	$ 23,800
Step 3	Subtract Step 2 result from Step 1 result	$527,270
Step 4	Enter gift tax credit remaining (2004)	$322,000
Step 5	Subtract Step 4 result from Step 3 result to obtain *gift tax payable*	$205,270

This illustrates the cumulative nature of the gift tax (the $100,000 prior taxable gifts pushed the present $1,389,000 of taxable gifts into a higher bracket) and the progressive rate structure. Also, since the taxable gifts in prior years used up part of the available credit, to that extent they are not available to reduce the tax liability for the present gifts.

Credits

A unified credit can be applied against the tax on gifts made either during lifetime or at death or part can be applied against each. The gift tax credit, which provides a dollar-for-dollar reduction of the tax otherwise payable, is as follows:

Donors Making Gifts in	Receive a Credit of
1982	$ 62,800
1983	79,300
1984	96,300

Donors Making Gifts in	Receive a Credit of
1985	121,800
1986	155,800
1987-1997	192,800
1998	202,050
1999	211,300
2000-2001	220,550
2002-2009	345,800
2010	330,800
2011-	345,800

The unified credit is substantially greater for estate tax purposes than it is for gift tax purposes for 2004 to 2009 (see Appendix A). Also, EGTRRA 2001 repeals the estate tax, but not the gift tax, for one year in 2010.

(9) REPORTING OF GIFTS AND PAYMENT OF THE TAX

Split–Gifts

A return must be filed in any year in which a married couple elects to split gifts.

Future–Interest Gifts

A gift tax return is required for a gift of a future interest regardless of the amount of the gift. For example, if an individual transfers $100,000 to an irrevocable trust payable to the grantor's wife for life and then to the grantor's son, a gift tax return would be required regardless of the value of the son's remainder interest.

The term "future interest" is defined the same as for annual exclusion purposes: a gift in which the donee does not have the unrestricted right to the immediate use, possession, or enjoyment of the property or the income from the property.

Present–Interest Gifts

No gift tax return is due (if gifts are not split and no future interest gifts are made) until present-interest gifts made to one individual for the year exceed $11,000 (in 2004). When present-interest gifts made to one individual for the year exceed that limit, a return must be filed for such year even if no gift tax would be due (e.g., if gift splitting provisions eliminated the tax). For example, if a married woman gave $15,000 to her son and split the

gift, the transfer would be tax free. However, a gift tax return would be required because it exceeded the annual exclusion limit (and because the gift was split).

A gift tax return must be filed and the gift tax due, if any, on reported gifts must be paid by April 15 of the year following the year in which the taxable gifts were made. When an extension is granted for income tax return filing, the time limit for gift tax return filing is automatically extended.

Gifts to Charities

No return must be filed and no reporting is required for charitable contributions of $11,000 (in 2004) or less in value unless a noncharitable taxable gift is also made. In that case, the charitable transfer must be reported at the same time the noncharitable gift is noted on a gift tax return. If the value of the charitable transfer exceeds $11,000, the general rule is that the transfer must be reported on a gift tax return for that year unless the transfer is of the donor's entire interest in the property.

If a split-interest gift is made to a charity (where there are charitable and noncharitable donees of the same gift), the donor will not be able to claim a charitable deduction for the entire value of the transfer. In this case, the donor must file and report the transfer subject to the filing requirements discussed above. For example, if an individual establishes a charitable remainder trust with payments to his daughter for life and the remainder payable to charity at her death, a gift tax return would have to be filed.

Liability for Payment – Net Gift

The donor of the gift is primarily liable for the gift tax. However, if the donor for any reason fails to pay the tax when it falls due, the donee becomes liable to the extent of the value of the gift. This liability begins as soon as the donor fails to pay the tax when due.

If a donor makes a gift and the donee decides, voluntarily, to pay the gift tax out of the property just received, the gift tax value of the gift is the entire fair market value of the property. In other words, if the donee is not obligated by the terms of the gift to pay the gift tax but chooses to pay it anyway, he must pay a tax based on the full fair market value of the property received based on the donor's gift tax bracket.

Conversely, if the terms of the gift obligate the donee to pay the gift tax, the value of the gift (and therefore the amount of the gift tax liability) is reduced. If a gift is made subject to an express or implied condition at the time of transfer that the gift tax is to be paid by the donee or out of the property transferred, the donor is receiving consideration (taxable as income) in the amount of the gift tax to be paid by the donee.

The value of the "net gift' is measured by the fair market value of the property passing from the donor less the amount of any gift tax paid by the donee. In computing the donee's gift tax liability, the donor's unified credit must be used.

The formula used to compute the donee's tax is:

$$\text{tentative tax} \div (1 + \text{donor's gift tax rate})$$

For instance, assume a retired, 66 year old, single donor living almost entirely from the income of $4,000,000 worth of tax-free municipal bonds who made no prior gifts made a gift of property worth $1,111,000 in 2004. The gift was made to his niece on the condition that she pay the federal gift taxes. As the calculation below illustrates, the tentative tax on a tentative taxable gift of $1,100,000 ($1,111,000 - $11,000 annual exclusion) is $41,000. But the gift tax actually payable is $29,078, a difference of $11,922. The gift tax is the same as if the donor had made a taxable gift of $970,922 and paid the gift tax himself.

TRUE TAX ON NET GIFT

Year	2004
Tentative Taxable Gift	$1,100,000
Gift Tax on $1,100,000	$386,800
Unified Credit	$345,800
Tentative Tax [$386,800 - $345,800]	$41,000
Tax Rate	41%
True Tax [$41,000 ÷ (1 + .41)]	$29,078
Net Gift [$1,000,000 - $29,078]	$970,922

Note that the formula is not applicable if the gift is split between the donor and spouse, each of whom is in a different gift tax bracket because either or both have made prior taxable gifts. Quite often, however, you can determine the correct tax bracket by inspection and adjusting for the bracket differential by computing the tentative tax in the correct lower bracket. In other situations, you'll have to make trial computations using first the bracket indicated by the tentative taxable gift and then later using the next lower bracket.

Time Tax Is Due

Generally, the gift tax must be paid at the same time the return is filed. However, reasonable extensions of time for payment of the tax can be granted by the IRS, but only upon a showing of "undue hardship." This means more than inconvenience. It must appear that the party liable to pay the tax will suffer a "substantial financial loss" unless an extension is granted. (A forced sale of property at a sacrifice price would be an example of a substantial financial loss.)

(10) RELATIONSHIP OF THE GIFT TAX SYSTEM TO THE INCOME TAX SYSTEM

When the gift tax law was written, one of the principal purposes was to complement the income tax law by discouraging taxpayers from making gifts to reduce their taxable incomes. It is true that to some extent the gift tax does supplement the income tax system and there is some overlap. However, it is important to note that the tax treatment accorded a given transaction when the two taxes are applied will not necessarily be consistent.

A lack of consistency between the gift and income tax systems forces the practitioner to examine four different issues:

(1) Is the transfer one upon which the gift tax will be imposed?

(2) Will the transfer constitute a taxable exchange subject to the income tax?

(3) If the transfer was made in trust, will the income from the transferred property be taxable to the donor, or will the incidence of taxation be shifted to the recipient of the property (the trust or its beneficiaries)?

(4) If the income is taxable to the beneficiary, will it be taxable at the parent's rate or at the beneficiary's tax bracket (as it would be if (a) the income were earned income no matter what the beneficiary's age, or (b) the beneficiary were age 14 or older no matter whether the income was earned or unearned)?

In summary, the treatment of a transaction for gift tax purposes is not necessarily consistent with the income tax consequences. Therefore it is important not to place undue reliance upon the provisions and interpretations of the income tax law when determining probable results or potential interpretations of the gift tax system (or vice versa).

(11) DETERMINATION OF THE BASIS OF GIFT PROPERTY

When property is transferred from a donor to a donee and the donee later disposes of the property through a sale or other taxable disposition, gain depends on the donee's basis. In return, the donee's basis is "carried over" from the donor; i.e., the donor's cost basis for the gift property immediately prior to the gift becomes the donee's cost basis for that property.

Example: If an individual has paid $5 a share for stock and transfers it when it is worth $25, and the donee sells it when it is worth $35, the donee's cost basis for that property is the donor's $5 cost. The gain, therefore, is the difference between the amount realized by the donee, $35, and the donee's adjusted basis, $5, or $30.

An addition to basis is allowed for a portion of any gift tax paid on the transfer from the donor to the donee. The basis addition is for that portion of the tax attributable to the "appreciation" in the gift property (the excess of the property's gift tax value over the donor's adjusted basis determined immediately before the gift). This increase in basis may be added to the donee's carryover basis for the property.

Stated as a formula, the basis of gifted property is the donor's basis increased as follows:

$$\frac{\text{Net Appreciation In Value Of Gift}}{\text{Amount Of Gift}} \times \text{Gift Tax Paid}$$

This means the basis carried over from the donor is increased by only the gift tax on the net appreciation in the value of the gift. For example, an individual bought stock worth $40,000 and gave it to his daughter when it was worth $100,000. If the donor paid $18,000 in gift taxes at the time of the gift, the daughter's basis would be

a. Donor's basis plus	$40,000
b. Gift tax on "net appreciation in value" (here, the difference between the $100,000 value of the gift at the time of transfer and the donor's cost, $40,000) $\dfrac{\$60,000}{\$100,000} \times \$18,000 =$ equals	10,800
c. Daughter's basis	$50,800

However, for purpose of determining loss, if the basis of the gifted property is lower than the fair market value of the property at the time of the gift, the basis is equal to such fair market value.

(12) RELATIONSHIP OF THE GIFT TAX SYSTEM TO THE ESTATE TAX SYSTEM

The estate and gift tax system are somewhat unified. The unification correlates the estate and gift tax laws in three essential ways:

(1) Lifetime gifts and testamentary transfers are taxed by using the same tax rates (see Appendix A), rather than separate and different rates. However, EGTRRA 2001 repeals the estate tax, but not the gift tax, for one year in 2010.

(2) There is a single unified tax credit that can be applied to lifetime and "deathtime" gifts. However, the gift tax unified credit generally caps at only $345,800 for years after 2001, while the estate tax unified credit increases to as much as $1,455,800 in 2009 (see Appendix A).

(3) The estate tax imposed at death is found by adding the taxable portion of gifts made during lifetime (after 1976) to the taxable estate to arrive at the tentative tax base (any gift tax paid on post-1976 transfers can be subtracted to arrive at the estate tax liability).

For these reasons, there are many correlations between the two tax systems. Like the income tax law, however, the gift tax law is not always consistent with the estate tax law.

When a gift is made, certain issues must be considered. In spite of the lifetime transfer, will the transferred property be included among the other assets in the donor's gross estate upon his death? Will the property a donor transfers during lifetime be subjected first to a gift tax and later included in the donor's gross estate? For example, if a donor gives a policy of insurance on his life to his son, the transfer would be considered a taxable gift and if the donor dies within 3 years after making the gift, the transferred property would be includable in his gross estate.

Likewise, if the donor transfers property but retains a life interest, both gift and estate taxes will be payable. Although the gift tax paid may generally be subtracted in arriving at the estate tax liability, because of the "time value" of money (i.e., the donor's loss of the use of gift taxes paid), the net result is less favorable than a mere washout (i.e., it is in essence a prepayment of the death tax).

(13) FACTORS TO CONSIDER IN SELECTING APPROPRIATE SUBJECT OF A GIFT

Gift tax strategy must be part of a well-planned and carefully coordinated estate-planning effort. This in turn requires careful consideration as to the type of property to give. There are a number of strategies and factors that must be examined in selecting the types of property that are appropriate for gifts.

Some of the general considerations in selecting property to give include:

(1) Is the property likely to appreciate in value? Other things being equal, planners generally try to pick property that will appreciate substantially in value from the time of the transfer. The removal from the donor's estate of the appreciation in the property (as well as the income from the property) should save a meaningful amount of estate taxes.

The best type of property will have a low gift tax value and a high estate tax value. Life insurance, for example, is property with a low present value but a high appreciation potential. If held until the date the insured dies, its appreciation in value is guaranteed.

(2) Is the donee in a lower income tax bracket than the donor? Income splitting between the donor and a donee age 14 or older can be obtained by transferring high income-producing property to a family member in a lower bracket. High income-producing property is best for this purpose. High-dividend participating preferred stock in a closely held business or stock in a successful S corporation is a good example of high income-producing property.

Conversely, if the donor is in a lower bracket than the donee (for instance, if the parent who is retired makes a gift to a financially successful middle-aged child), the use of low-yield growth-type property may be indicated. Typically, gifts to children under age 14 should emphasize growth.

(3) Is the property subject to indebtedness? A gift of property subject to indebtedness that is greater than its cost to the donor may result in a taxable gain. A gift of such property causes the donor to realize capital gain on the excess of the debt over basis. For example, the gift of a building that cost the donor $10,000, appreciated to $100,000, and was mortgaged to $70,000 would result in an income tax gain to the donor on the difference between the debt outstanding at the time of the transfer and the donor's basis. In this example, the gain would be $60,000. It would be realized at the time the gift became complete.

(4) Is the gift property's cost basis above, below, or approximately the same as the property's fair market value? Income tax law forbids the recognition of a capital loss if the subject matter of the gift has a cost basis above the property's present fair market value. Neither the donor nor the donee can recognize a capital loss with respect to such property. Furthermore, if the gift property's cost basis is above present fair market value, there will be no gift tax addition to basis because that addition depends on appreciation at the time of the transfer. Since there is no appreciation, no gift tax addition would be allowed.

Conversely, if the donor's cost basis for income tax purposes is very low relative to the fair market value of the property, it might be advantageous to retain the property until death because of the "stepped-up basis" at death rules. (This is especially true if inclusion of the property will generate little or no gift tax because it will pass to a surviving spouse and qualify for a marital deduction or if the asset owner is "sheltered" by the unified credit.) The result of the stepped-up basis provision is that a portion of the future capital gain would be avoided in the event the property is later sold by the estate or heir. [EGTRRA 2001 replaces stepped-up basis with a modified carryover basis for one year for property acquired from a decedent dying in 2010.] But if the property should be sold, it may pay to transfer it first to a low-bracket age 14 or over family member by gift; that individual could then sell it and realize a lower tax. For instance, on a $10,000 gain, a father in a 35% bracket (in 2004) would pay $1,500 in tax (15% maximum capital gains rate). If, instead, he gave the stock to his college age daughter, who was in a 15% bracket, she would pay $500 in tax (5% maximum capital gains rate), a $1,000 saving.

A third possibility is that the donor's cost basis is approximately the same or only slightly below fair market value. Again, the rules providing for a gift tax addition to basis are of little help. The addition to basis is limited to gift tax allocable to appreciation in the property at the time of the gift. One further factor that should be considered is the likelihood that the donee will want or need to sell the property in the foreseeable future. If this is not likely, the income tax basis (except for depreciable property) will be relatively meaningless.

ASRS: Sec. 55.

Chapter 18

GENERATION–SKIPPING TRANSFER TAX

WHAT IS IT?

This chapter discusses the generation-skipping transfer tax and planning with generation-skipping transfers, including the use of generation-skipping trusts.

A generation-skipping transfer (GST) is any transfer of property by gift or at death, to any person who, under federal tax law, is assigned to a generation that is two or more generations below that of the transferor (i.e., one or more generations below the transferor is skipped). In the case of family members, this means, for example, that transferor's grandchildren and great nieces and nephews would be assigned two generations below the transferor. Such persons who are two or more generations below that of the transferor are defined as skip persons.

The generation-skipping transfer tax applies to generation-skipping transfers. An annual exclusion ($11,000 in 2004) and an exclusion for certain transfers for educational or medical purposes is available that reduces the amount of a generation-skipping transfer. A transferor has a GST exemption ($1,500,000 in 2004) that can be allocated to generation-skipping transfers. An inclusion ratio is calculated based on allocations of GST exemption to generation-skipping transfers. The GST tax is calculated by multiplying the GST tax rate (48% in 2004) by the amount of the GST transfer property and the inclusion ratio for such property. For GST exemptions and tax rates in other years, see Figure 18.1.

EGTRRA 2001 repeals the generation-skipping transfer tax and the estate tax for one year in 2010.

WHEN IS THE USE OF SUCH A DEVICE INDICATED?

The generation-skipping transfer was traditionally used as a device to save federal gift and estate tax by keeping property out of the taxable estates of the members of the intermediate generation. The beneficiary could be trustee, have all the income, invade the principal for needs and control the distribution of the property as long as the beneficiary did not have a general power of appointment (i.e., the power to ap- point the property to the beneficiary or the beneficiary's estate, or creditors of either). Now the generation-skipping transfer tax implications of such transfers must also be considered.

There are three levels where generation-skipping transfer techniques are useful. First, where a client stands to inherit a substantial estate from a parent and already has a substantial estate of his own, a generation-skipping trust would be set up to receive the parent's property for the benefit of the client. A generation-skipping trust would allow the client-beneficiary the use and enjoyment of the inherited property, together with protection against creditors, divorce courts or bankruptcy. The amount subject to the GST exemption will also be excluded from the beneficiary's already substantial estate. Although the client's parent may pay gift or estate tax, the client does not pay estate tax or GST tax on the exempt inherited property at death. Furthermore, no estate tax or GST tax is paid by the client's children or future issue depending on the term allowed for the trust.

Secondly, a generation-skipping trust may be used where parents wish to minimize transfer taxes in a child's estate but still give the child the use and benefit of the property, or where the parents wish to protect the property from a spendthrift child, or from being subject to loss through a child's divorce or bankruptcy. In these situations, a generation-skipping trust would be set up to provide income to the child for life, but with the principal being preserved for subsequent distribution to grandchildren. The trust can continue through the grandchildren's lives (and for great-grandchildren as well), avoiding transfer tax in each generation, subject only to the limitation on the maximum life of a trust under state law. In the case of many estates, however, the generation skip occurs as a result of the death of a member of the intermediate generation before such member receives full ownership of the gift or inheritance, as when a trust is provided for a child until he attains age 30, and that child dies before attaining age 30 leaving grandchildren surviving.

Thirdly, a client may wish to make direct transfers to a grandchild or other skip person for the beneficiary's support or enjoyment, or in order to avoid tax in the estate of the intervening generation. Gifts that immediately benefit grandchildren will generally be subject to the GST tax unless they qualify for the generation-skipping exemption or the annual exclusion.

EGTRRA 2001 repeals the generation-skipping transfer tax and the estate tax for one year in 2010.

WHAT ARE THE REQUIREMENTS?

There is no special form of generation-skipping transfer. It could simply be a gift or bequest to a skip person, or the establishment of a trust in which distributions will or may be made to a skip person. All that is really required to trigger the device is any gift or transfer of property at death that will or may benefit a skip person.

HOW IT IS DONE – AN EXAMPLE

A generation-skipping trust can be created as part of an individual's will or revocable trust, so that it comes into being only upon the transferor's death. If the transferor intends to make gifts to the generation-skipping transfer trust, the trust will be created as a separate document. In that case, the generation-skipping trust is also usually a receptacle for assets passing from the transferor at his death.

The trust instrument would provide for two trusts. The "exempt" trust would receive gifts or bequests to which the transferor's generation-skipping transfer tax exemption has or will be allocated, and this is the trust that will pass tax-free at the recipient's death. Any assets passing to the trust for which no exemption is allocated will pass to a "nonexempt" trust.

For optimal results, planners prefer to fund the exempt trust with assets with the greatest growth potential. This concept allows the maximum amount of assets to pass to future generations without transfer tax because, once the exemption is allocated to the trust, the growth is also exempt.

The exempt and nonexempt trusts are established so that they have GST tax inclusion ratios of zero and one respectively (i.e., no trust is partially exempt and partially nonexempt). When the exempt trust is established with an inclusion ration of zero, that trust maintains its 100% immunity from GST tax as long as there are no later additions of nonexempt property.

In a family intervivos trust with distributions to the survivor's trust, a bypass trust and a QTIP trust, assuming that the donors have made no taxable lifetime gifts, the person making the allocation would typically make an allocation of the GST tax exemption of the first trustor to die to the bypass trust. The bypass trust is typically funded with an amount equal to the estate tax unified credit equivalent (or applicable exclusion), $1,500,000 in 2004. Thus, $1,500,000 of the GST exemption would also be allocated to the bypass trust to make it GST exempt.

When the GST exemption was $1,120,000 in 2003, the decedent had $120,000 of exemption remaining after allocating $1,000,000 (the amount protected by the estate tax unified credit in 2003) to the bypass trust. If the remaining assets exceeded $120,000, the trust instrument would instruct the executor to split the QTIP into two separate trusts. $120,000 would be placed in an exempt QTIP trust, to which the remaining $120,000 of GST exemption would be allocated. The rest of the assets would go to the other separate QTIP trust and would be fully nonexempt. On the federal estate tax return, the executor would make a "reverse QTIP election," so that the $120,000 of property in the exempt QTIP would be treated as passing from the first spouse to die for purposes of the GST tax.) Use of the reverse QTIP election would permit the full use of the GST exemption of the first donor spouse to die without incurring any gift or estate tax at the first death.

In 2004 to 2009, the amount passing to the bypass trust, the estate tax unified credit equivalent, is equal to the GST exemption, so division of the QTIP trust may not be required. However, if the decedent made gifts or transfers during lifetime that made the amounts of estate tax unified credit and GST exemption remaining at death unequal, a reverse QTIP election may still be useful. In 2010, the estate tax and the GST tax are repealed for one year.

The trust instrument would also instruct the trustee to make any distributions of principal to the surviving spouse first from the nonexempt trust. This is because there is no GST tax on distributions to nonskip persons such as spouses. In addition the trustee would also be instructed to pay any taxes attributable to the QTIP trusts first from the nonexempt QTIP, upon the death of the surviving trustor. When the surviving spouse dies, that spouse's executor would allocate the spouse's GST exemption to other trust property that was not already exempt under the first spouse's exemption.

After the death of both donors, the exempt bypass and QTIP trusts, together with the amount of assets from the surviving spouse to which that spouse's unused GST exemption would be allocated, could be held in trust for the children for their lives, and then held in trust for the grandchildren, and then held for the great grandchildren, subject to the rule against perpetuities. There would be no tax imposed (either estate tax or GST tax) at the death of each successive generation.

The provisions of the trust for the children would provide that the trust for their benefit be divided/maintained in exempt and nonexempt trusts for GST purposes. The children are typically given the income from both the exempt and nonexempt trusts. The children are also usually given a nongeneral power of appointment over the assets of the exempt trust.

The nongeneral power of appointment allows the children the flexibility to appoint the principal of the trust in different proportions either to whomever they like or sometimes only to a specified class of beneficiaries, usually their own children or perhaps a life estate to their spouse. Since the power is not a general power of appointment, the property is not included in their estates. In addition, since the original donor's GST tax exemption was allocated to the exempt trust, when the trust passes to the grandchildren or their issue (all classified as skip persons), it is exempt from generation-skipping tax. Thus, the exempt trust passes from the parents, through the children's generation, to future generations free from estate and GST tax.

The trust instrument typically grants the children a general power of appointment over the principal of the nonexempt trust so that the nonexempt trust will be purposely included in their estate for estate tax purposes. This avoids the GST tax that would otherwise be imposed at the maximum estate tax rate (because the nonexempt trust will pass to skip persons). By having the property included in the child's estate for estate tax purposes, it is possible to take advantage of the child's estate tax unified credit and graduated tax rates. The nonexempt trust can also be drafted to allow the child to make gifts to his or her issue (or others) under the gift tax annual exclusion.

The same exempt/nonexempt structure would continue to apply to the trusts as they pass to the grantor's grandchildren, great-grandchildren, and so on, the object being to preserve the exempt trust from transfer tax at each generation level.

A limited power of appointment is often given to some nonbeneficiary (sometimes called a "trust protector") to be able to alter the trust to deal with changes in tax law or other circumstances.

WHAT ARE THE TAX IMPLICATIONS?

Generation–Skipping Transfer Tax

General Rules

A flat rate tax equal to the highest gift and estate tax rate (48 percent in 2004, see Figure 18.1) is imposed on every generation-skipping transfer.[1] EGTRRA 2001 repeals the generation-skipping transfer tax for one year in 2010. Essentially the generation-skipping transfer tax (GSTT) will affect transfers to grandchildren or others in the grandchildren's or younger generations. The tax applies to outright transfers and to transfers in trust or arrangements having substantially the same effect as a trust, such as transfers involving life estates and remainders, estates for years, and insurance and annuity contracts.[2]

Every individual is allowed to make aggregate transfers during lifetime or at death, that will be wholly exempt from the GST tax (the GST exemption is $1,500,000 in 2004, see Figure 18.1).[3]

Essentially, the GST tax rate is equal to the maximum estate tax rate at the time a *taxable distribution*, *taxable termination*, or *direct skip* is made.[4] Technically, the *applicable rate* is the maximum federal estate tax rate multiplied by a fraction called an *inclusion ratio*. This inclusion ratio is described below.

The *taxable amount*, which is the amount to be multiplied by the applicable rate mentioned in the preceding paragraph, depends on whether the transfer is considered a taxable distribution, a taxable termination, or a direct skip.

Generation Assignment

For GST purposes, all persons are assigned to a generation. In the case of related persons, this is done by reference to the ancestral chain relating back to grandparents of the transferor, except that spouses of the transferor or a descendent are always assigned to the same generation as the transferor or descendent. Unrelated persons are assigned to the transferor's generation if such person is not more than 12½ years younger than the transferor, otherwise unrelated persons are assigned to succeeding generations on the basis of 25 years for each generation (i.e., first younger generation – 12½ to 37½ years younger than transferor). Where the trans-

Figure 18.1

GENERATION-SKIPPING TRANSFER TAX		
Year	Exemption	Rate
2001	$1,060,000	55%
2002	$1,100,000	50%
2003	$1,120,000	49%
2004	$1,500,000	48%
2005	$1,500,000	47%
2006	$2,000,000	46%
2007	$2,000,000	45%
2008	$2,000,000	45%
2009	$3,500,000	45%
2010	NA	NA
2011	$1,120,000*	55%

* Plus increases for indexing for inflation after 2003.

feree is an entity (i.e., estate, trust, partnership, or corporation), individuals who own beneficial interests in the entity are assigned to generations.[5]

Where persons are initially assigned to generations under the rules just discussed, it is possible that subsequent events will result in generation reassignment. For example, upon a taxable transfer to succeeding generations of skip persons, such as grandchildren and great-grandchildren, each transfer is subject to tax, but upon each successive transfer, the transferor is assigned to a lower generation. This is to prevent the imposition of the GST tax twice on transfers to persons in the same generation.[6]

If an individual's parent who is a lineal descendant of the transferor or transferor's spouse is deceased at the time of a transfer from which the individual's interest is derived, the individual and all succeeding generations move up one generation. This predeceased parent rule also applies to collateral relatives (e.g., nephews and nieces) if the transferor had no living lineal descendants at the time of the transfer.[7]

Skip Persons

A person assigned two or more generations below the transferor is a "skip person." A trust may be a skip person if all beneficiaries holding interests in the trust are skip persons, or no person holds an interest in the trust, but no distributions could be made to "nonskip persons." If a trust is a skip person, its beneficiaries are not assigned to a generation.[8]

Solely for GSTT purposes, a person holds an "interest" in a trust or trust equivalent if he or she is entitled to receive current nondiscretionary distributions of income or corpus, or is a permissible current recipient of income or corpus and is not a qualified charity.[9]

Taxable Distribution

A taxable distribution is any distribution of income or corpus from a trust to a skip person that is not otherwise subject to estate or gift tax.[10] For instance, a distribution from a trust to a grandson of the grantor would be to a skip person. Likewise, if a mother creates a trust providing distributions of income or principal to her daughter or granddaughter at the discretion of the trustee, a distribution from that trust to the granddaughter is a taxable distribution. A distribution from one trust to a second trust would be considered a transfer to a skip person if all interests in the second trust were held by skip persons.

The taxable amount in the case of a taxable distribution is the net value of the property received by the distributee less any consideration he paid. In other words, the taxable amount is what the distributee received, reduced by (1) any expenses incurred by him in connection with the determination, collection, or refund of the GST tax, and (2) any consideration paid for the distribution. The transferee is obligated to pay the GST tax in a taxable distribution. If the trust itself pays the tax for the transferees, the payment will be treated as an additional taxable distribution.[11]

The tax levied upon a taxable distribution is *tax inclusive*. That means the amount subject to tax includes (1) the property *and* (2) the GST tax itself.

Example: If a trustee makes a taxable distribution of $10,000 of trust income to a grandchild in 2004 (assuming a trust inclusion ratio of one), the tax would be $4,800 (if paid by the grandchild). The grandchild will net only $5,200.

Taxable Termination

A taxable termination is essentially the termination by death, lapse of time, release of a power, or otherwise of an interest in property held in a trust resulting in skip persons holding all the interests in the trust. For instance, if Alan leaves a life income to his son, Sam, with a remainder to his granddaughter, Gina, the son's death terminates his life interest in trust property and it then passes to Gina, a skip person. A taxable termination occurs on the date of the son's death. A taxable termination cannot occur as long as at least one nonskip person has a present interest in the property. However, nominal interests are disregarded in determining whether a person has an interest in a trust if a significant purpose for their creation is to postpone or avoid a GST tax.[12] Furthermore, there is no taxable termination if an estate or gift tax is imposed on the nonskip individual (the son in this example) at termination.

The taxable amount in the case of a taxable termination is the value of all property involved less (1) a deduction for any expenses, debts, and taxes (other than the GST tax) generated by the property, and (2) any consideration paid by the transferee. If one or more taxable terminations with respect to the same trust occur at the same time as a result of the death of an individual, the executor may elect to value all the taxable termination property under federal estate tax alternate valuation rules. The trustee (broadly defined to mean the person in actual or constructive possession of the GST property) is responsible for the payment of the tax in a taxable termination.

The tax payable upon a taxable termination is *tax inclusive* because, as with the taxable distribution, the property subject to the transfer includes the generation-skipping tax itself.

Example: Assume $1 million is placed into an irrevocable trust for the benefit of the grantor's

daughter for life with remainder to his granddaughter. At the daughter's death in 2004, a taxable termination occurs. Assume no exemptions were claimed and the trust has an inclusion ratio of one. The tax is 48 percent of $1 million, or $480,000. It must be paid out of property passing to the granddaughter. Therefore, the granddaughter nets only $520,000.

Direct Skips

A direct skip is a transfer subject to an estate or gift tax made to a skip person.

A gift from an individual to his grandchild is a direct skip. A direct skip can also occur when an individual makes a transfer to a trust if all the beneficiaries of the trust are skip persons. Therefore, an individual who creates an irrevocable trust for the benefit of his grandchildren would be making a direct skip upon funding the trust.

The taxable amount in the case of a direct skip is the value of the property or interest in property (including the current right to receive income or corpus or power of appointment) received by the transferee, reduced by any consideration paid by the transferee. The transferor (the decedent in the case of a death time transfer or the donor in the case of a lifetime transfer) is responsible for payment of the GST tax in the case of a direct skip.

The tax in a direct skip is *tax exclusive*. In other words, the tax is paid by the transferor or the estate and the taxable amount does not include the amount of generation-skipping tax.

Example: A grandfather makes a lifetime gift of $1 million to his granddaughter in 2004. Assume no exemptions are available and the inclusion ratio is one. The grandparent must pay a generation-skipping tax of $480,000. But the tax is paid, not out of the gift, but out of additional assets of the grandparent. The grandchild will therefore net the full $1 million.

Exemptions and Exclusions

An exemption is available from the GST tax ($1,500,000 in 2004, see Figure 18.1). For a married couple, each spouse has a GST exemption. A gift subject to the GST tax which is "split" by the spouses will be treated as having been made half by each spouse, and each spouse can use some (or all) of his or her GST exemption to avoid the GST tax.[13]

Certain transfers are excluded from the definition of the term generation-skipping transfer. Transfers excluded from the definition include:

- certain transfers that, if made by gift, would qualify as gift tax free as direct payments made for the donee's educational or medical expenses.[14]

- transfers that pass gift tax free under the annual exclusion rules. Transfers in trust will not qualify for this exemption unless (1) no portion of the trust's income or principal can be distributed to or used for the benefit of anyone other than the grandchild as long as the grandchild is alive, and (2) if the grandchild dies prior to the termination of the trust, the assets of the trust must be includable in the grandchild's estate.[15]

- certain transfers that have already been subjected to the GST tax in which the transferee was in the same or lower generation as the present transferee.[16]

Unless the governing instrument directs otherwise (by specific reference to the GST tax), the GST tax is charged to the property constituting the transfer.[17]

Property subject to the GST tax must be valued as of the time of the generation-skipping transfer. However, where the tax involves a direct skip (for example, from grandparent to grandchild), if the property is included in the transferor's estate, its value for GST tax purposes is the same as its value for federal estate tax purposes, including elections for the alternate valuation date or special-use valuation.

Computing the Tax

A GST exemption (see Figure 18.1) is allowed in computing the tax actually payable. Because married individuals making a lifetime transfer can elect to treat the transfer as if made one-half by each, the exemption can be doubled. To understand how this exemption works and how the tax is actually calculated, it is first necessary to examine the "inclusion ratio."

The inclusion ratio procedure is in two parts. Compute the *applicable fraction* as follows:

1. State the portion of the GST tax exemption allocated to the trust or direct skip. $_____

2. (a) State the value of the property transferred to the trust (or involved in the direct skip). $_____

   (b) State the total of any federal estate or state death tax actually recovered from the trust attributable to such property. $_____

   (c) State the amount of any charitable deduction allowed under estate or gift tax law with respect to the property. $_____

   (d) Add (b) and (c). $_____

3. Subtract (d) from (a). $_____

4. Divide the line 1 exemption by line 3. This is the "applicable fraction." $_____

Once the applicable fraction is computed, the inclusion ratio is calculated. The inclusion ratio is 1 minus the applicable fraction (line 4).

An exception to the above computation is for a charitable lead annuity trust. The computation for transfers to such a trust after October 13, 1987 is as follows:

$$\frac{\text{GST exemption allocated to the transfer, increased by the interest rate used in computing the lead interest for the number of years of the term}}{\text{Actual value of property after the lead interest terminates}}$$

If a person allocates GST exemption equal to the remainder interest and if the trust performs as expected by the government valuation tables, the fraction would be 1/1. However, it is obviously impossible to know in advance how the trust will perform, so allocation of the GST exemption for a charitable lead annuity trust is a guessing game.

After computing the inclusion ratio, that number is multiplied by the maximum federal estate tax rate (see Figure 18.1) to arrive at the applicable rate.

The total GST tax due is determined by multiplying the taxable amount by the applicable rate.[18] (See Figure 18.2.)

Figure 18.2

		COMPUTING THE GENERATION SKIPPING TRANSFER TAX A SIMPLIFIED WORKSHEET	
Step 1	List	Value of property transferred	$4,000,000
Step 2	List	Exemption allocated to transfer	$1,000,000
Step 3	List	State & fed tax paid on transfer	$600,000
Step 4	List	Gift or estate tax charitable deductions allowed on transfer	$0
Step 5	Add	Steps 3 and 4	$600,000
Step 6	Subtract	Step 5 from Step 1	$3,400,000
Step 7	Divide	Step 2 by Step 6 This is the "applicable fraction"	0.2941
Step 8	Subtract	Step 7 from one (1) This is the "inclusion ratio"	0.7059
Step 9	Multiply	Step 8 by 55% This is the "applicable rate"	0.3882
Step 10		Assuming no growth, the GST tax is	$1,552,941

This computation assumes:

(A) Transfer of $4,000,000
(B) Federal and state death taxes of $600,000
(C) No charitable deductions
(D) $1,000,000 exemption available.

Courtesy of *NumberCruncher Software*.

A credit for state death taxes will be allowed against the GST tax if the transfer (other than a direct skip) occurs at the same time and as a result of an individual's death. The credit is the lower of (a) the amount of any GST tax actually paid to a state under its laws or (b) 5 percent of the GST tax payable to the federal government.

The worksheet at Figure 18.3, illustrates the entire process for a transfer other than a charitable lead annuity trust.

Figure 18.4 shows the impact of the GST tax when the taxable event occurs, not at the time assets are placed into the trust, but at a later date (20 years in this example).

Figure 18.3

		GENERATION SKIPPING TRANSFER TAX SIMPLIFIED WORKSHEET	
Step 1	List	Value of property transferred	_____
Step 2	List	Exemption allocated to transfer	_____
Step 3	List	State & fed tax paid on transfer	_____
Step 4	List	Gift or estate tax charitable deductions allowed on transfer	_____
Step 5	Add	Steps 3 and 4	_____
Step 6	Subtract	Step 5 from Step 1	_____
Step 7	Divide	Step 2 by Step 6 This is the "applicable fraction"	_____
Step 8	Subtract	Step 7 from one (1) This is the "inclusion ratio"	_____
Step 9	Multiply	Step 8 by GST tax rate This is the "applicable rate"	_____
Step 10	Multiply	Step 1 by Step 9	$_____

Courtesy of *Leimberg and LeClair, Inc.*

Figure 18.4

PROJECTING THE ULTIMATE GST TAX			
	Initial value of assets		$4,000,000
Less	Federal and state death taxes		$600,000
Equals	Net value of assets		$3,400,000
Input:	Assumed growth rate (net after tax)	.06	
Input:	Years until taxable event	20	

		Future Value	**GST Tax**
At	.040	$7,449,819	$2,892,020
At	.050	$9,021,212	$3,502,034
At	.060	$10,904,261	$4,233,034
At	.070	$13,156,927	$5,107,519
At	.080	$15,847,254	$6,151,904

Courtesy of *NumberCruncher Software.*

Liability for Payment of GST Tax

If the transfer is a taxable distribution, the GST tax is on the amount received by the transferee, less expenses relating to the determination of the GST tax, and the transferee pays it. If the transfer is a taxable termination or partial termination, the GST tax is on the value of the property in which the interest terminates, less expenses "attributable" to the property, and the trustee pays it. In the case of direct skips (other than a direct skip from a trust), the GST tax is on the value of the property received, and the transferor pays it.[19]

Special Provisions

There are special provisions for the following:

- QTIP property (see below)

- taxation of multiple skips

- basis adjustments (In general, basis is increased by an amount equal to the portion of the GST tax actually imposed which is attributable to the appreciation of the property transferred.[20])

- disclaimers (A disclaimer that results in property passing to a person at least two generations below that of the original transferor will result in a GST tax. For instance, assume a daughter disclaimed a bequest from her mother. As a result of that disclaimer, certain property passes to the mother's granddaughter. The GST tax would be imposed on the transfer – in addition to the federal estate tax.)

- administration

- return requirements (The GST tax return must be filed by the person liable for the payment of the generation-skipping tax. In the case of a direct skip other than a direct skip from a trust, the return must be filed on or before the due date of the applicable gift or estate tax return. In other cases, the GST tax return must be filed on or before the 15th day of the 4th month after the close of the taxable year in which the transfer occurs.)

Trusts can have multiple generation skips and each skip would be taxed. For example, a trust could be for the benefit of a child, a grandchild, and a great-grandchild. A taxable termination would occur at the death of the child and at the death of the grandchild. But if a direct skip is directly to a great grandchild, two taxes are not imposed.

IRC Section 303 can be used to make protected redemptions of stock to pay a GST tax.

IRC Section 6166, which allows for installment payments of federal estate tax, allows deferral of the tax generated under a GST because of direct skips resulting at death.

Planning for GST Tax

The generation-skipping tax may be imposed *in addition to* any estate or gift tax that may also be due because of the transfer. It appears that in many cases the total cost of making a property transfer can exceed the value of the gift.

Example 1: Assume a grandfather in a 48 percent gift tax bracket makes a gift in 2004. Assume the value of his gift is $2 million, and it is made to a trust for his grandchild. Assume he doesn't allocate any of his generation-skipping transfer tax exemption (or he has already used the exemption) and he has already used his gift tax unified credit. The generation-skipping transfer tax is $960,000 ($2,000,000 x .48). For gift tax purposes, the amount of the gift to the grandson is $2,000,000. The gift tax on the total deemed gift is $960,000 ($2,000,000 x .48). The total tax therefore is $1,920,000, which almost equals the value of the gift actually made.

Example 2: Assume a father in a 48 percent federal estate tax bracket establishes a testamentary trust in 2004 that provides, "to my son for life, then to my grandson." Assume he has already used his GST exemption (and the estate tax unified credit is disregarded.) He leaves $5 million, and the federal estate tax is $2,400,000 ($5,000,000 x .48). That leaves $2,600,000 to provide income for his son. Assume that during the son's lifetime there is no appreciation in the trust. At the son's death in 2011, a generation-skipping transfer tax is levied at 55 percent and amounts to $1,430,000 ($2,600,000 x .55). The total tax on the $5 million is therefore $3,830,000 ($2,400,000 plus $1,430,000).

Trust distributions will be subjected to the tax regardless of whether they are made from income or from corpus. Recipients of income subject to the GST tax may take an income tax deduction (similar to the IRD deduction under IRC Section 691) for the GST tax imposed on the distribution.

Allocation of the GST Exemption

Given the severity of the GST tax, probably the most important planning decision is how to allocate the GST exemption.

When all or a portion of a person's exemption is allocated to a GST in computing the applicable fraction, this has the effect of exempting from the GST tax all future appreciation on the property designated to be exempt. For example, assume a divorced man transfers $1 million in trust for his children and grandchildren. To eliminate the GST tax, he allocates $1 million of GST exemption to the trust and avoids any GST tax. All the property in that trust will always be exempt from the GST tax no matter how much it appreciates. (If asset values are rapidly increasing, the more quickly the allocation is made, the better.) But if the individual had allocated only half of his exemption, one-half of all future distributions from the trust to his grandchildren would be subject to the tax as taxable distributions, and one-half of the value of the assets remaining in the trust would be subject to the GST tax when his children die (as taxable terminations). When selecting assets that will be protected by the GST exemption, assets most likely to appreciate should be used. This is because, once assets are protected by the exemption, any growth in the value of the assets is beyond the scope of the GST tax. Therefore, it would make great sense to include life insurance on the grantor's life among these assets.

The GST exemption may be allocated by the donor (or the executor) among any property that is transferred. Once made, the election is irrevocable. Regulations specifically permit allocations of the exemption by formula without requiring taxpayers to specify a dollar amount on the gift or estate tax return.[21]

The GST exemption will be automatically allocated to a direct skip during life unless the donor elects otherwise.

Prior to 2001, a lifetime gift that was not a direct skip required the filing of a gift tax return to allocate the donor's GST exemption. EGTRRA 2001 provides that with respect to a lifetime gift to a generation-skipping trust (an indirect skip), the GST exemption will be automatically allocated to an indirect skip unless the donor elects otherwise. Elections with respect to indirect skips can be made with respect to a transfer or for all transfers to a trust. An election can also be made to treat any trust as a generation-skipping trust.[22]

For this purpose, a generation-skipping trust is generally any trust that could have a generation-skipping transfer with respect to the transferor unless the trust has certain provisions for nonskip persons. Such provisions include (1) more than 25% of the trust must be distributed to, or withdrawn by, nonskip persons prior to reaching age 46 (or a date or event prior to such birthday); (2) more than 25% of the trust must be distributed to, or withdrawn by, nonskip persons if they are living on the date of death of an individual named in the trust who is more than 10 years older than such skip persons; (3) if a nonskip person dies before a date or event described in (1) or (2), more than 25% of the trust must be distributed to such person's estate or subject to a general power of appointment by such individual; (4) the trust would be includable in the gross estate of a nonskip person (other than the transferor) if the person died immediately after the transfer; or (5) the trust is a CLAT, CLUT, CRAT, or CRUT with a nonskip remainder person.

As a general rule, the allocation of the exemption will be based on the fair market value of the property on the effective date of allocation. The effective date of allocation for direct skips during the transferor's lifetime is the date of transfer. Where a timely filed gift tax return is filed, the effective date of allocation even for skips other than direct skips is generally the date of transfer as to which the Form 709 relates. An application can be made for an extension of time to make a timely allocation of GST exemption and the Service has been quite lenient in granting such extensions. EGTRRA 2001 permits certain retroactive allocations to be made when certain nonskip beneficiaries of a trust die. Also, where late allocations are made during life, the transferor may, solely for purposes of determining the fair market value, elect to treat the allocation as having been made on the first day of the month during which the late allocation is made. However, such an election is not effective with respect to life insurance if the insured has died.[23] Where property is held in trust, the allocation must be made to the entire trust, rather than to specific trust assets.[24]

Where some GST tax exemption is allocated to gifts to pay premiums through an irrevocable life insurance trust, some practitioners suggest deliberately filing "late" so that the allocation will apply to the then reduced value of the policy rather than to the full amount of the premium. Obviously, this involves the risk of the insured dying and requiring the exemption to be allocated on the basis of the face amount of its policy. It may also require filing a gift tax return to elect out of automatic allocation.

As discussed above, taxable distributions and taxable terminations are *tax inclusive* whereas direct skips are *tax exclusive*. Since the government takes less from the donor where the transfer is tax exclusive (direct skip) an allocation to direct skips tends to be wasteful. Therefore, in order to maximize the use of one's GST tax exemption, it is preferable to allocate it whenever pos-

sible to what otherwise would be to taxable distributions and taxable terminations.

At the transferor's death, where the executor or other person making the allocation fails to allocate the exemption, it is allocated automatically according to a statutory formula. The statute allocates any unused exemption first to direct skips occurring at the individual's death on a pro rata basis, and then to any trusts from which a taxable distribution or termination could occur after the transferor's death.[25] Thus, the statutory order of allocation tends to be nonoptimal.

Split–gifts and the Reverse QTIP Election

If husband and wife elect to split a gift pursuant to IRC Section 2513, each is deemed transferor as to one-half.[26] Since each spouse has a GST exemption to allocate, this can be extremely important in planning transfers that could be subject to the tax.

Where one spouse makes a gift to the other, either during lifetime or at death, in a form that qualifies for the marital deduction, there is a danger that all or part of the available GST exemption of the transferor spouse will be lost. For example, if husband died in 2003 and left his entire estate in excess of the amount necessary to offset his available unified credit to his wife, this would have left a taxable estate of no more than $1,00,000 (see Chapter 24). Since his estate could have sheltered up to $1,120,000 in 2003 from GST tax, the result is a loss of up to $120,000 of that exemption.

However, where the transfer had been in the form of a QTIP trust, even though the transferor spouse or estate claimed the full marital deduction, an election could have been made solely for GST purposes to treat the QTIP property as if no QTIP election was made at the date of gift or death.[27] This is an "all or nothing election," i.e., the election to treat the property as if no QTIP election has been made must apply to all qualifying property in the trust. If the total value of the QTIP trust may exceed the available GST exemption, the will or trust should provide for division of the single QTIP trust into two trusts to take advantage of the reverse election.

Example: Wife's taxable estate is valued at $2 million in 2003. Her estate plan creates three trusts – a bypass trust of the estate tax unified credit equivalent (or applicable exclusion) ($1,000,000 in 2003) to offset the unified credit, one reverse QTIP trust equal in value to any unused GST exemption not otherwise applied by her executor, and a second QTIP trust for the balance of her estate. Assuming the executor applies $1,000,000 of the $1,120,000 (in 2003) GST exemption to the bypass trust, the first QTIP trust can be established with a value of $120,000, and the remaining GST exemption will be applied to it. This will leave a second QTIP trust of $880,000, which may be subject to GST tax on subsequent distributions or termination. (Of course, the husband, at his death, could allocate his GST exemption against the second QTIP trust.)

This problem will become increasingly academic because the GST exemption will equal the estate tax unified credit equivalent (applicable exclusion) amount in 2004 to 2009 and the estate tax and GST tax are repealed for one year in 2010. However, if the decedent makes gifts or transfers during lifetime that make the amounts of estate tax unified credit and GST exemption remaining at death unequal, a reverse QTIP election may still be useful.

Grantor Retained Income, Annuity, and Unitrust

The GST tax may have an impact on transfers of remainder interests in property where the transferor retains the income, use of, or payment from a trust for a term of years. The subject of grantor retained income trusts, annuity trusts, and unitrusts is covered in Chapter 26. The issue here is the GST tax consequences of such trusts where the remainder interests pass to skip persons.

It is possible to make such a transfer that is complete for gift tax purposes, but which may be includable in the transferor's taxable estate. The question is whether for GST purposes the transfer is made at the date of transfer or the date of death of the transferor. The grantor retained income trust, grantor retained annuity trust, or grantor retained unitrust is a perfect example.

In such arrangements, the GST rules postpone allocation of the exemption until there is an actual GST transfer, or the transferor dies, or the property would no longer be included in his estate.[28] The law provides that where transferred property would be includable in the transferor's taxable estate under any statute other than IRC Section 2035 if the transferor were to die immediately after the transfer, allocation of his GST exemption will be postponed during the "estate tax inclusion period," which runs until the earlier of (1) the date the property would no longer be included in the taxable estate, (2) the date there is an actual generation-skipping transfer, or (3) if neither event occurs during the transferor's lifetime, the death of the transferor. If the transfer is a direct skip, allocation is deemed to occur at the end of the estate tax inclusion period. The postponement period is only for purposes of determining the inclusion ratio, and should not affect other rules (e.g., there should be no step-up in generation for a child whose parent was alive when the transfer was made even if the parent dies before the end of the inclusion period).

Multi-Generational Planning

If the taxable transfer is to succeeding generations of skip persons (i.e., grandchildren and great-grandchildren), each transfer is subject to tax. Upon each successive taxable transfer, the transferor is assigned to a lower generation.[29] However, a transfer to a person more than two generations below the transferor is subject to only one GST tax. This may lead to the establishment of multi-generational trusts that permit distributions at least two generations below the transferor. In the case of older clients, direct skip transfers assigned at least two generations below the transferor should be considered. Compare the result where a trust provides for distributions to children for life, then grandchildren for life, remainder to great-grandchildren. There will be three taxable events – when the trust is created (estate or gift tax), when child dies (taxable termination), and when the last surviving grandchild dies (taxable termination). Allowing distributions directly to great-grandchildren while child is still alive eliminates one level of tax. Also, direct transfers to grandchildren after a child is dead eliminate one level of tax, since the grandchildren move up a generation.

Another approach to multi-generational planning is the establishment of a "dynastic" trust to take advantage of the GST exemptions of a client and spouse that is intended to continue through succeeding generations as long as the law will permit. The actual distribution of these trust assets will be postponed as long as possible, to avoid estate tax as long as possible. Such trusts could last many years, limited only by a legal limitation called the rule against perpetuities, which prohibits the establishment of trusts that last indefinitely. For example, if a trust with a present value of $2,000,000 will continue in existence at least 75 years, and grows at an annual rate of only 4%, it will increase to over $37,000,000. This kind of planning may appeal to clients who have a tradition of preserving wealth in a family through succeeding generations.

Example: Tom and Pam Monson have an estate of $2,200,000 and plan to use life insurance and leveraging to maximize the utilization of their GST tax exemptions for the benefit of their five children and their issue. The transferors make annual gifts to the trust to pay the life insurance premiums. Those annual gifts are exempt from gift tax under the annual exclusion. In addition, GST exemption is allocated to the annual gifts. The premiums are $25,000 per year for 16 years, for a total of $400,000 of premium (assume $200,000 given by each spouse). The insurance is the "survivorship" type that only pays when the survivor dies.

In this situation, although only $400,000 of GST exemption was allocated to the life insurance trust premiums, all of the $1,000,000 of insurance proceeds paid at the second spouse's death will be sheltered from generation-skipping transfer tax.

At Tom's death in 2014, his estate is divided $1,000,000 (the unified credit equivalent amount in 2014) to the bypass trust and $100,000 to the QTIP trust. Tom's executor allocates $1,000,000 of his GST exemption to the bypass trust. [GST exemptions, after inflation adjustments, are assumed to be adequate for the allocations described in this example.]

Pam's executor, at her death in 2014, allocates $1,118,000 GST exemption to the generation-skipping gift trust for the children into which the QTIP trust and the spouse's property flows ($100,000 QTIP trust plus $1,100,000 spouse's property, minus estate tax of $82,000). Tom's $1,000,000 bypass trust also flows into that trust. That trust holds the $1,000,000 life insurance policy. The end result is that $3,118,000 ends up being exempt from GST tax instead of just $2,118,000 because of the leveraging of life insurance, even assuming a zero growth rate.

If the assets were to grow in value after the allocations of exemption, the amounts going to the GST tax exempt trust for the children would be even greater. Furthermore, as the trust continues down to lower generations, assets in the trust avoiding GST and estate tax may compound even further.

Planning to Pay Estate Tax Rather than GST Tax

Almost the reverse of multi-generational planning is planning transfers to trigger federal estate tax in the estates of each succeeding generation. Any transfer from a trust other than a direct skip that is subject to estate or gift tax with respect to a person in the first generation below the grantor is exempt from GST tax. In many situations, since the GST tax is computed at the highest possible federal estate tax rate, it would be preferable to allow the property in a nonexempt trust to pass through the taxable estates of children to grandchildren, since the federal estate tax imposed on the property cannot exceed the GST tax, and in many cases, will be substantially less. This could be accomplished by giving children a general power of appointment over the trust, at least up to the amount needed to put the child in the highest estate tax bracket. While this may result in tax saving, there is always a danger the children will exercise the power and cause the property to pass to someone other than the grandchildren. A possible solution is to give the child only the power to appoint to creditors of his estate, which is a general power of appointment.

Exclusion for Nontaxable Gifts

Gifts that are not taxable by reason of the gift tax annual exclusion are also exempt from GST tax under most circumstances. The inclusion ratio for nontaxable gifts is zero. This includes gifts not subject to tax under IRC Sections 2503(b) and 2503(e), and by inference, 2503(c). However, in the case of transfers after March 31, 1988, only nontaxable gifts that are direct skips would have a zero inclusion ratio. In addition, nontaxable gifts to trusts would not have a zero inclusion unless:

1. No portion of the trust could be distributed to a person other than a single beneficiary, and

2. If that beneficiary dies before the trust terminates, the trust assets will be included in his estate.

Therefore, for purposes of the generation-skipping transfer tax, annual exclusions are not available for Crummey withdrawal powers (see Chapters 22 and 30).

To Skip or Not to Skip?

Where there is intentional planning to skip generations, the GST tax cost must be compared to the estate or gift tax cost of transferring the property to the first generation (children), who would then transfer to the second generation (grandchildren). Relative tax cost on a tax inclusive basis should be considered. Assuming a 48% (in 2004) transfer tax rate:

1. Since the gift tax is exclusive of the gift, a 48% gift tax rate amounts to a tax inclusive rate of 32.4% [48% ÷ (1 + 48%)].

2. The estate tax inclusive rate is 48%, since the tax is included in the tax base, i.e., the taxable estate.

3. The GST tax on taxable distributions and terminations is tax inclusive, since it is imposed on the transferee, and the tax inclusive rate is 48%.

4. The GST tax on direct skips is tax exclusive, resulting in a 32.4% tax inclusive rate.

5. However, the GST tax on lifetime gifts is also considered to be a taxable gift, and a gift tax will be paid on the GST tax. Similarly, if a direct skip is made at death, the GST tax will have to be paid from assets that were also subject to the federal estate tax. The total tax could equal 96% (48% + 48%) of the value of the gift.

6. On the other hand, if a lifetime direct skip gift is made, both the gift tax and GST tax paid will reduce the taxable estate of the donor (in the case of the gift tax, assuming he or she lives at least three years after the transfer).

Other Planning Considerations

As a general rule, the GST tax applies to transfers after October 22, 1986. However, lifetime transfers that were made after September 25, 1985 and were subject to gift tax are also subject to the GST tax. GST tax does not apply to any transfer from a trust that was irrevocable on September 25, 1985, so long as no additions are made after that date. Even if a trust is grandfathered for GST purposes, the trust may become tainted to the extent that there are either actual or constructive additions.

A constructive addition will occur where a general power of appointment is exercised or released, or lapses over a portion of the grandfathered trust. However a constructive addition will not occur where a nongeneral power of appointment is exercised if the exercise will not postpone or suspend the vesting, absolute ownership or power of alienation of the inter-

est for a period longer than allowed by the rule against perpetuities from the date of the creation of the trust. However, the exercise of a power of appointment that validly postpones or suspends the vesting, absolute ownership or power of alienation of an interest in property for a term of years that will not exceed 90 years (measured from the date of creation of the trust) is not considered an exercise that will extend beyond the perpetuities period.[30]

These rules create the opportunity to change the distribution of grandfathered trusts via exercise of nongeneral powers of appointment without adversely affecting its grandfathered (exempt from GST tax) status.

Since irrevocable trusts created before September 26, 1985, are completely exempt from the GST tax system (but only to the extent no additions are made to the trust from that date), it is important not to taint such trusts by adding new property to them. Not only would this create a tax where none existed, but it would also create an administrative nightmare tracking and allocating pre- and post- September 26 assets and appreciation.

Whenever possible, transfer some assets from a rich spouse to a less wealthy spouse. This is because the GST exemption is not freely transferable between spouses. But a transfer to a less wealthy spouse can double the advantage of the GST exemption since both spouses can take advantage of it. This is similar to the rationale for making transfers to a spouse in order to achieve the full benefit of both spouses' unified credits.

Greater emphasis should now be placed on protecting irrevocable life insurance trusts from the GST tax by advising clients to consider allocating a portion of the GST exemption to each transfer made to the trust. Keep in mind that the use of a portion of the GST exemption to shield, say, twenty $50,000 annual premiums protects not only that $1,000,000, but also the future trust corpus generated by the policy proceeds created by those premium payments. Leveraging the GST exemption this way (for as long as this technique lasts) may be the single most effective long run means of keeping wealth within the family.

ISSUES AND IMPLICATIONS IN COMMUNITY PROPERTY STATES

Where community property is involved, gift splitting by husbands and wives may not be necessary, nor may it be necessary for one spouse to consider a transfer to the other so that both may use their full GST exemption.

QUESTIONS AND ANSWERS

Question – The will of a client provides for a family trust that authorizes the trustee to make distributions from the trust to the spouse, children, and grandchildren of client. On the death of the spouse, the trust will be distributed to the then surviving children. However, if no children then survive, the share of such a deceased child will pass to his or her issue. Under what circumstances will trust distributions be subject to GST tax?

Answer – Distributions of trust income or principal to the spouse and children will not be subject to GST tax. The spouse is assigned to the same generation as the client, and the children to the first generation below. Thus, none of these beneficiaries are skip persons. However, any income or principal distributions to grandchildren will be subject to GST tax, since they are skip persons.

When the spouse dies, distributions of shares of the trust to children will not be subject to GST tax, since the children are not skip persons. However, any distribution of a share of the trust to the issue of a deceased child of the client will be a taxable termination subject to GST tax, since the grandchildren are skip persons.

Question – Client's will directs that his estate be distributed to a trust that will be divided into separate shares, one for each of his children living at his death, and one for the issue of any child who predeceased the client. Under what circumstances will distributions from this trust be subject to GST tax?

Answer – Under the GST rules, separate shares in a single trust are treated as separate trusts. Distributions to children from the trusts created for them are not subject to GST tax, since they are not skip persons. Distributions from the shares set aside for the issue of a child who predeceased the client are also not subject to GST tax. The reason is that the sole beneficiaries of such a share, which is treated as a separate trust, would be skip persons (i.e., grandchildren of the client). When all of the beneficiaries of a trust are skip persons, the trust itself is a skip person. Thus the transfer to the trust is a direct skip. However, the law also provides that when a transfer is a direct skip, but the skip persons are grandchildren of the transferor whose parents have predeceased, those grandchildren move up a generation. As a result, it appears they are no longer skip persons, and distributions to them should not trigger a GST tax.

Question – Under the terms of an irrevocable trust, Trustee is directed to accumulate income until beneficiary attains age 21, and cannot make corpus distributions to beneficiary until that time. For GST purposes, does the beneficiary have an "interest" in the trust?

Answer – Beneficiary has no interest in the trust until attaining age 21. This is because he is not entitled to receive any present distributions of trust income or principal. If he or she is the only beneficiary, there is no person with an interest in the trust. It appears there could be no taxable termination until the beneficiary attains age 21.

Question – Transferor creates a trust providing for an annuity payable to his granddaughter for life, remainder to charity. Assume this is a qualified charitable remainder trust (see Chapter 33). Who is treated as having an interest in the trust?

Answer – Both the granddaughter and the charity have interests in the trust, and the future interest of the charity becomes a present interest for GST tax purposes. This is a special rule that only applies to charities. The transfer to the trust cannot be a direct skip since the charity, which is assigned to the transferor's generation, has an interest. However, distributions to the granddaughter will be taxable distributions to a skip person.

Question – A family trust created under a will is a pot trust for lineal descendants, which will terminate and be distributed to then living lineal descendants when the youngest grandchild attains age 65. Assuming all children of the testator die before the youngest grandchild attains age 65, what are the GST tax consequences?

Answer – Upon the death of the last child, there is a taxable termination, since the only remaining beneficiaries of the trust, grandchildren and possibly their descendants, are skip persons. At this time, the grandchildren will be reassigned to their parent's generation, so that subsequent distributions to them will not be taxed again. But distributions to their descendants will be subject to GST tax.

Question – At date of death, the estate value of assets in decedent's estate is $2 million. The will provides that the executor is to allocate $1 million in assets to a trust based on date of death value. However, the actual value of the assets transferred to the trust at date of allocation has increased from $1 million to

$1.3 million. For purposes of computing the exclusion ratio, is the denominator of the fraction $1,000,000 or $1,300,000?

Answer – The denominator of the fraction is the pecuniary amount ($1 million in this example) only if the pecuniary payment of property must be satisfied on a basis that fairly reflects net appreciation or depreciation (between the valuation date and the date of distribution) in all of the assets from which the distribution could have been made. Otherwise the denominator of the fraction would have to be the date of distribution value ($1.3 million in this example).[31]

Question – Transferor conveyed property worth $500,000 to a generation-skipping trust in 2000 and allocated $300,000 of her exemption to it. In 2004, when that property was worth $700,000, she transferred $100,000 cash to the trust, and claimed a $100,000 exemption. What is the inclusion ratio?

Answer – The inclusion ratio is:

$$1 - \frac{\$100,000 + (60\% \times \$700,000)}{\$100,000 + \$700,000} =$$

$$1 - \frac{\$520,000}{\$800,000} = 65\%$$

The 60% represents the nontax portion of the trust before the second transfer, $300,000/$500,000.[32]

Question – Where a preexisting life insurance trust is grandfathered as a pre- September 25, 1985 trust, can gifts to cover premium payments continue without the trust being subject to GST tax?

Answer – No, additional transfers to pay life insurance premiums would be considered additions to the trust. The additions to the trust will result in inclusion of part of the trust for GST tax purposes unless the lifetime exemption is allocated to cover the portion of the trust that is not grandfathered.

ASRS: Sec. 56.

CHAPTER ENDNOTES

1. IRC Secs. 2601, 2602.
2. IRC Sec. 2652(b).
3. IRC Sec. 2631.
4. IRC Sec. 2641.
5. IRC Sec. 2651.
6. IRC Sec. 2653(a).
7. IRC Sec. 2651(e).
8. IRC Sec. 2613.
9. IRC Sec. 2652(c).
10. IRC Sec. 2612(b).
11. IRC Sec. 2621.
12. IRC Sec. 2652(c)(2); Treas. Reg. §26.2612-1(e)(2)(ii).
13. IRC Sec. 2652(a)(2).
14. IRC Sec. 2611(b).
15. IRC Sec. 2642(c).
16. IRC Sec. 2611(b).
17. IRC Sec. 2603(b).
18. IRC Sec. 2641, 2642.
19. IRC Sec. 2603.
20. IRC Sec. 2654(a).
21. Treas. Reg. §26.2632-1(d).
22. IRC Sec. 2632.
23. Treas. Reg. §26.2642-2(a)(2).
24. Treas. Reg. §26.2632-1.
25. IRC Sec. 2632(c).
26. IRC Sec. 2652(a)(2).
27. IRC Sec. 2652(a)(3).
28. IRC Sec. 2642(f).
29. IRC Sec. 2653(a).
30. Treas. Reg. §26.2601-1(b)(1)(v)(B)(2).
31. Treas. Reg. §26.2642-2(b).
32. IRC Sec. 2642(d).

Chapter 19

FEDERAL INCOME TAX ISSUES

The estate or financial planner must attain a degree of familiarity with the income taxation of estates and trusts to properly service clients. This should include familiarity with income in respect of a decedent (IRD). Only through a working knowledge of the income tax ramifications of various trust arrangements will a member of the estate planning team be able to perform properly. The estate or financial planner must also be familiar with the rules for income tax basis, especially for property transferred by gift or at death.

INCOME TAXATION OF TRUSTS AND ESTATES

General Scheme of Taxation

Trusts and estates are treated in the tax law as separate taxpayers that are required to file annual federal income tax returns. The problem that Congress faced in taxing the income of trusts or estates was whether to tax such entities in a manner similar to corporations or partnerships or to tax them as some hybrid entity.

If a trust or estate were taxed like a corporation there would be a double taxation–the trust or estate would be taxed on its income for the year, and the beneficiaries would be taxed a second time on the distribution received. Beneficiaries would be treated like shareholders who receive taxable dividends, even though the corporation's taxable income includes the same distribution. The double taxation, especially for small estates or trusts, would make this approach highly unfavorable to taxpayers.

If a trust or estate were taxed as a partnership, the trust or federal estate tax return would merely be informational. All income of the trust or estate would be taxed to the individual beneficiaries, just as partners in a partnership must report their proportionate share of the taxable income of the partnership on their own individual returns. This method would be particularly harsh in cases where the trustee has discretion to either accumulate or distribute income and chose to accumulate it, or in an estate where an executor has no duty to distribute income until the termination of the estate. If

this approach had been adopted, a beneficiary could be paying tax on amounts not yet received.

Congress adopted a hybrid approach for estates and trusts known as the "sharing" concept. The general rule is that the trust or estate will pay income tax on the amount it retains. Beneficiaries will pay the tax on the income of the trust or estate actually distributed to them. The mechanics of obtaining this result are obtained through the utilization of the distributable net income (DNI) concept. Thus, income is taxed only once.

The concept of DNI is utilized to achieve three main results. First, it ensures that the trust or estate receives a deduction for amounts distributed and provides a limit for that deduction. For example, assume that a trust earns $10,000 in income and distributes $6,000 of that income to the sole beneficiary. The trust would be taxed on the amount it retains, $4,000, and would have a special deduction of $6,000 for the amounts distributed.

Second, DNI limits the portion of distributions that is taxable to beneficiaries. If the trust in the above example distributed $12,000 to the beneficiary, the trust would be allowed to deduct $10,000, and the trust would have no tax liability. The beneficiary would be taxed on only $10,000 of the $12,000 he received.

The first $10,000 is deemed to have come from income. The balance, $2,000, is considered a tax-free distribution of trust corpus. In this case, for tax purposes, the characterization of the $12,000 and its breakdown into income and corpus are not left to the trustee. Under the "income first" rule, the trustee's classification of a distribution as "income" or "corpus" is ignored; instead, all amounts distributed are deemed to be income to the extent of DNI. For example, assume the trust had interest income of $10,000 that a trustee decided to accumulate. In the same year the trustee decided to distribute $10,000 of corpus to one of the beneficiaries. If the trustee made the distribution, the beneficiary would be deemed to have received $10,000 in income, even though in actuality the trustee might have been distributing an amount from corpus.

The third function of DNI is to ensure that the character of distributions to a beneficiary remains the same as in the hands of a trust or estate. Tax-exempt interest received by a trust and distributed to a beneficiary retains its character as tax-exempt and is exempt from ordinary income taxation to the beneficiary or heirs. Likewise, what enters the trust or estate as ordinary income remains ordinary income when received by beneficiaries or heirs. This is known as the "conduit" theory.

Income Taxation of Trusts

A trust is a tax-paying entity. The taxable income of a trust (or an estate) is computed in basically the same manner as that of an individual. However, trusts (and estates) do not have a 10% tax rate. Also, the tax brackets for trusts (and estates) are much more progressive than those for individuals (see Appendix A).

In computing tax liability, multiple trusts are treated as one trust and their incomes are aggregated if the trusts have substantially the same grantor or grantors and substantially the same primary beneficiary or beneficiaries and if a principal purpose for the existence of the trusts is the avoidance of federal income tax.

Generally, for tax purposes trusts are treated as separate entities from the grantor, the trustee, and the beneficiary. The basic question in the income taxation of trusts is, "Who will be taxed on trust income–the trust, the beneficiary, or the grantor?" Generally, the burden of taxation falls on either the trust itself or the beneficiary. But it is possible for the income of the trust to be taxed to the grantor. For this reason, trusts are categorized for income tax purposes as either a "simple" trust or a "complex" trust. Either type of trust may also be a "grantor" trust.

A "simple" trust is one in which the trust agreement requires that all trust income be distributed currently to the beneficiaries. A simple trust may not make distributions from amounts other than current income. Principal may not be distributed and no charitable gifts can be made by this type of trust; otherwise, it will be deemed a complex trust for that taxable year.

A simple trust is treated as a separate tax entity. As such, it has the same deductions an individual has, subject to certain exceptions. It also has a special deduction for income that is distributable to its beneficiaries. The net result is that a simple trust does not pay tax on income it pays out. The beneficiary of a simple trust will report the income that he receives or that is receivable by him. In other words, a simple trust acts like a funnel–a true and complete conduit for passing the trust income from the grantor to the beneficiaries.

A second type of trust is known as the "complex" trust. A complex trust is any trust which is not a simple trust, that is, a complex trust is one in which the trustee either must–or may–accumulate income. The trustee of a complex trust–unlike the trustee of a simple trust–can also distribute corpus (principal). He can also make gifts to charities.

A complex trust–like a simple trust–is a separate tax entity. It is allowed a special deduction for actual distributions of income but pays tax on any income it does not distribute. Generally, the same rules that govern complex trusts apply also to the income taxation of a decedent's estate.

A trust is not allowed a standard deduction. Further, the personal exemption is limited to $300 for a simple trust and $100 for a complex trust. (If a trust is required to distribute its income to a beneficiary, it will not lose the $300 exemption even if it distributes corpus or makes a charitable contribution in a given year and thus is considered complex for all other purposes.)

In some cases the trust itself is disregarded as a taxable entity. A grantor trust, for example, is either a simple or complex trust in which the trust is disregarded as a taxable entity. Generally, in the case of either a simple or a complex trust, the trust or its beneficiary will be taxable on the income of the trust. However, in some cases the grantor is taxed on the trust income whether or not the grantor actually receives the income.

IRC Sections 671 to 677 discussed below are known as the "grantor-trust" rules. An understanding of these rules is essential for the tax planner.

Sec. 671 –Substantial Owner Rules

When the grantor of a trust is treated as the owner of a portion of the trust corpus for income tax purposes, those items of income, deductions, and credits that are attributable to that portion of the trust are deemed to be those of the grantor. Accordingly, the grantor of the trust is deemed the recipient of trust income and is allowed a deduction to the extent there are trust expenses and/or credits. Note, however, that the grantor is owner only for income tax purposes under this rule. The estate tax exclusion must be tested under estate tax rules. (This applies to all the IRC sections covered below.)

Sec. 673–Reversionary Interest Rules

For income tax purposes (subject to a limited exemption for reversionary interests taking effect on the death of a minor lineal descendant under age 21) the grantor is treated as the owner of that portion of a trust in which the grantor or the grantor's spouse has a reversionary interest in either the corpus or the income: if, as of the date of inception of that trust or at the time of an addition to that trust, the value of the reversionary interest exceeds 5 percent of the value of the property in which the reversion is retained. Arbitrarily assuming a 6.0% Section 7520 rate, the value of the reversionary interest exceeds 5 percent of the value of a term trust if the trust runs for any period of time less than approximately 52 years.

Sec. 674–Beneficial Interest Rules

In general, where a grantor of a trust, a nonadverse party, or both can control the beneficial enjoyment of a trust, the grantor is taxed as the owner of the trust for income tax purposes. Where the grantor or nonadverse party needs consent of an adverse party to change the beneficiary's enjoyment of the trust, the grantor is not deemed the owner of the trust corpus, and the income earned from such a trust is not attributable to the grantor.

Sec. 675–Administrative Powers Rules

The retention by the grantor of certain administrative powers can cause the grantor to be deemed the owner of the corpus of the trust for income tax purposes. Powers exercisable by the grantor, or even a nonadverse party, that would cause the income to be attributable to the grantor are:

1. powers that enable the grantor to purchase, exchange, or otherwise deal with or dispose of the corpus or income of the trust for less than adequate consideration in money or money's worth;

2. powers that allow the grantor to borrow trust corpus or income without adequate interest or security;

3. powers of administration exercisable in a nonfiduciary capacity by any person without the approval or consent of any person in a fiduciary capacity. Powers of administration are such powers as the power to vote stock of a corporation in which the grantor or the trust has a significant voting interest, the power to control investment of the trust funds, and the power to reacquire the trust corpus by substituting other property of an equivalent value.

Sec. 676–Power to Revoke Rules

The grantor is treated for income tax purposes as the owner of any portion of a trust if he can revoke the trust either acting alone or with a nonadverse party (unless the power is as remote as that permitted under the Section 673 reversionary interest rules).

Sec. 677–Income for Benefit of Grantor Rules

The grantor of a trust is treated as the owner of the trust for income tax purposes if the income of the trust is or may–at the discretion of the grantor or a nonadverse party, or both–be distributed to the grantor, held or accumulated for future distribution to the grantor, or applied to the payment of premiums on life insurance policies on the life of the grantor or the grantor's spouse.

In addition, the income from property transferred in trust is taxable to the grantor of the trust where the income is distributed to the grantor's spouse, held or applied for future distribution to the grantor's spouse, or applied to the payment of premiums on life insurance policies on the life of the grantor's spouse.

Sec. 678–"Person Other than Grantor" Rules

Finally, if a person other than the grantor has the power, exercisable solely by himself, to vest the corpus or income therefrom in himself, such a person is treated as the owner of the corpus so that trust income will be taxable to that individual (unless the trust income is otherwise taxable to the grantor).

Income Taxation of Estates

Decedent's Final Return

An executor or administrator has the duty to file two different types of income tax returns for a decedent. He must file a decedent's last life return and an estate's income tax return.

A decedent-taxpayer's tax year ends with the date of his death. For example, if "X" dies on March 30, an income tax return must be filed for the short year of January 1 to March 30. The return must be filed on the regular due date, April 15th, of the following year. The amount of income and deductible expenses that must be reported depends on the deceased taxpayer's regular method of accounting.

For cash-basis taxpayers, only income actually or constructively received must be reported. Deductions can be taken only for expenses actually paid. If the decedent was on the accrual method, the return will show all income and deductions accrued through the date of death.

Income in Respect of a Decedent (Section 691 Income)

Since this is the final income tax return for the individual, if he was a cash-basis taxpayer, income that he earned but had not received by the date of his death would not be included in his final return, because he did not actually or constructively receive the item by the date of death. For example, an insurance agent's renewal commissions paid after death cannot be included in his last life return, assuming the deceased agent was a cash-basis taxpayer.

However, income that the decedent would have included in gross income if he had lived and had received it does not escape taxation. Income in respect of a decedent (IRD), such as the life insurance commissions above or installment payments received after a decedent's death, is taxed to the recipient of the payments. In other words, the estate or the beneficiary who receives income in respect of a decedent will pay tax upon it in the same manner that it would have been taxed to the decedent. If it would have been ordinary income to the decedent (had he lived), it will be ordinary income to the estate or beneficiary. What would have been return of capital to the decedent remains tax free when recovered by the estate or beneficiary. There is no step-up in basis at death (basis is discussed below) for income in respect of a decedent.

The estate or beneficiary that includes an item of income in respect of a decedent is entitled to a deduction on the same income tax return for the amount of additional federal estate tax attributable to inclusion of that item in the decedent's federal estate tax return.

Taxation of the Estate

As a taxable entity, an estate must pay tax on its income. If the income of the estate consists of dividends from stock and interest from bonds, these items will comprise the gross income of the estate. Likewise, if there is rental income, royalty income, income from the sale or exchange of property, or income from a business carried on by the executor or administrator, then the income of the estate will include those items as well.

Because an estate is considered a separate tax entity, it has not only income but also deductions. An estate may deduct reasonable amounts paid for administration costs including executor's fees, legal fees in connection with the administration of the estate, and expenses of preparing the income tax return of the estate. If the estate manages a business, it will be entitled to deduct ordinary and necessary business expenses.

Some of these expenses, such as administration expenses, may be taken on either the income tax return of the estate or as deductions from the gross estate to obtain the net estate for federal estate tax purposes. However, the same expense generally may not be taken as a deduction on both the estate income tax return and the estate tax return. In these cases, the executor would have to weigh the relative advantages and take the deduction where it would be most advantageous.

An estate is also entitled to a deduction for amounts of income distributed. An estate may take a $600 personal exemption. As previously mentioned, to the extent that the estate retains income, it will be taxed, and to the extent that the beneficiaries receive income, they are taxed.

The estate may have income and DNI available to distribute to beneficiaries. The only beneficiaries who will not pay income tax on distributions of income from estates are those who receive specific bequests under the will in three installments or less. For example, assume that the will of the decedent, Leslie Little, states "$5,000 to my favorite nephew, Al, and all the rest, residue, and remainder to my cousin, Jeffrey Little." During the first year of the administration of the estate, assets held by the executor generate $16,000 of income. The executor distributes $5,000 to Al and $11,000 to Jeffrey. Since Al's $5,000 was a specific bequest, he is not taxed. This amount is considered a distribution of estate corpus. In this case, Jeffrey would be taxed on the $11,000 he received, and the estate would be taxed on the remaining $5,000 of income.

On the other hand, if Leslie's will stated that the $5,000 bequest to Al was to be paid in five equal annual installments, and in the first year he received $1,000, he would be taxed on the $1,000 only if the payment is made out of income. Beneficiaries will be taxed also on any specific bequests that are required to be paid out of income.

As previously mentioned, the "income first" rule requires that all distributions are deemed to be paid out of income first, even if the executor, administrator, or trustee in fact distributes principal in the form of cash or property. For example, assume in the previous example that the distribution to Jeffrey consisted solely of stock. Jeffrey would still be deemed to receive income.

HOW BASIS IS DETERMINED

What Basis Is and Why It Is Important

Basis is the starting point in any computation used to determine how much gain (or loss) is incurred upon a sale of property. Gain, for example, is found by the following formula:

Amount realized - Adjusted basis = Gain

Therefore, the higher the basis, the lower the reportable gain on a sale of an asset.

Basis is also the key factor in determining the allowable depreciation deduction that may be taken on buildings and other business or investment assets that wear out over time. Again, a high basis is advantageous since depreciation (i.e., the recovery of capital over a given useful life through annual deductions) or amortization (i.e., the recovery of cost in equal annual increments) depends directly on how much capital – that is, how much investment – the taxpayer has in the property.

Basis, therefore, is generally what a person or other taxpayer "paid" for property. For instance, if property is acquired through a purchase, usually the basis of that asset is its cost. In a loose sense, basis can be thought of as the actual or constructive cost of property for tax purposes (although technically the term, basis, has broader implications).

Basis At Death

Assets owned by a decedent receive a new federal income tax basis equal to the property's fair market value for federal estate tax purposes.[1] (EGTRRA 2001 changed the rules for property acquired from a decedent dying in 2010 – see below.) When the fair market value of the asset is higher than the pre-death basis, the old basis is "stepped-up" to the fair market value. Thus, if a father bought a farm for $5,000 and it was valued at $50,000 for federal estate tax purposes when he died, and he left it to his son, the son (or the father's estate) might have to pay an estate tax, but the son could then sell the farm for its $50,000 value without having to pay any

income tax. This is because the $5,000 basis is "stepped up" to $50,000. Using the formula above, when the new adjusted basis of $50,000 is subtracted from the amount realized on the sale, $50,000, there is no gain. This concept is particularly important in buy-sell agreements where stock is purchased at a shareholder's death at a pre-arranged price or under a pre-arranged formula.

No Step-up in Basis Where Decedent Had Acquired Property by Gift Within a Year of Death If Property Is Left To Donor or Donor's Spouse

Under prior law, some owners of appreciated property transferred that property to a dying individual and had then received a step-up in basis when the property was left to them under the decedent's will or by intestacy.

Current law contains a provision intended to prevent the avoidance of income taxes on appreciated property by such transfers to dying donees. The law currently provides that if (a) the decedent had received appreciated property by gift during the 1-year period ending on the date of death, and (b) that property was acquired from the decedent by (or passes from the decedent to) the donor of that property (or to the donor's spouse), the basis of that property in the donor's hands (or in the hands of the donor's spouse) is the adjusted basis of the property in the hands of the decedent immediately before death. In short, the old trick would not work any more.

Example: Assume a daughter transferred property with a $10,000 cost and $100,000 fair market value to her mother within one year of the mother's death. Assume the mother left the property to her daughter. The mother's basis would not be stepped up. Rather, it would remain the same as it was in the mother's hands just before she died. In most cases, this means that the daughter will receive the same basis (with adjustments for any gift taxes she paid upon the gift to the mother) as she had before she made the gift.

There is a solution: If the donee-decedent lives for more than one year after receiving the gift, or if the gift is left to anyone other than the donor or the donor's spouse, the property will receive a stepped-up basis. So the property could be left to grandchildren in this example and it would receive a $100,000 basis. This could, of course, have generation-skipping transfer tax implications (see Chapter 18).

Effect of Step–up Basis Rules on Stock Redemptions and Cross Purchase Agreements

As noted in the chapter on IRC Section 303 Stock Redemptions, there are specific rules as to the non-recognition of income tax gain upon the redemption of stock to pay death taxes in certain situations.

Stock includable in the decedent's estate receives a new basis equal to its value at death (or the alternate valuation date if elected). This is usually close to the redemption value, particularly if the stock redemption is promptly carried out. Typically, no (or little) gain is recognized by the estate or other seller of the stock upon the redemption.

Overall Effect

The step-up in basis rule has an effect on all tax planning that relates to the sale of assets after death or assets that might be held until death.

There is an incentive for the owner of property with a very low income tax basis, in relation to its market value, to hold the property until death so that the estate can sell it without any income tax on the appreciation in value.

However, inflation is becoming a greater factor in planning, and the wise estate planner will take into consideration the probable future increase in value, with possible concurrent increase in death taxes (consider the implications of both the unified credit and the unlimited marital deduction), and balance this against a current sale. This is particularly appropriate to consider where the sale would be to a person who would eventually receive the property upon the owner's death.

EGTRRA 2001

EGTRRA 2001 replaces stepped-up basis with a modified carryover basis system for one year for property acquired from a decedent dying in 2010. Such property will receive a basis equal to the lesser of the adjusted basis of the decedent (plus a limited step-up amount) or the fair market value of the property on the date of the decedent's death. The executor of the decedent's estate will be allowed to increase the basis of assets being transferred by up to a total of $1.3 million. Property passing to the spouse of the decedent may be stepped-up by an additional $3 million. The step-up in basis for property acquired from a nonresident noncitizen decedent cannot exceed $60,000. However, the basis of any property cannot be stepped up above fair market value.

Clients should be urged to begin keeping accurate records now with regard to the cost of assets, including such items as purchase price, improvements, depreciation, etc. EGTRRA 2001 adds penalties for failure to file basis information returns with the IRS under the modified carryover rules for transfers at death in excess of $1.3 million and for any appreciated property acquired by the decedent as a gift, or for less than adequate consideration, within three years prior to the decedent's death. Similar information is also required with gift tax returns for 2010.

Both the decedent's and the surviving spouse's share of community property will be treated as owned by the decedent under the modified carryover rules. Therefore, each spouse's share will be eligible for an increase in basis (up to the maximum allowable amount).

Implications and Issues in Community Property States

Stepped-up basis focuses attention on the manner of holding title to property between spouses. (See EGTRRA 2001, above, for rules in 2010.)

If property is held by spouses in a community property state as the separate property of one spouse, it will all be included in the spouse's estate and will receive a new basis at death. The entire property can go to the surviving spouse under the marital deduction rules and will not be subject to tax. Thus, the entire property will get a new stepped-up basis even though it may escape estate tax entirely.

If the property is held as community property, only one-half of the property is included in the estate of the first spouse to die but, equalizing the basis with the separate property arrangement, both halves receive a new income tax basis.[2]

However, this step-up in basis does not occur if the property is held in joint-tenancy or tenancy-in-common.

Take the example of a husband and wife purchasing property using funds earned while residents of a community property state. They want to hold the property in some form of co-ownership. The cost of the property was $1,000 and, at the date-of-death of the first spouse to die, the value is $10,000.

Figure 19.1

Situation I — Property sold for $10,000 prior to death of either spouse			
Plan:	**#1** **Tenants by Entirety**	**#2** **Tenants in Common**	**#3** **Community Property**
Sales price of property	$10,000	$10,000	$10,000
Tax basis of spouses:			
Husband's half	$500	$500	$500
Wife's half	500	500	500
Total Basis	$1,000	$1,000	$1,000
	$9,000	$9,000	$9,000

Situation II — Property sold for $10,000 after death of husband			
Plan:			
Sales price of property	$10,000	$10,000	$10,000
Tax basis of spouses:			
Husband's half	$5,000	$5,000	$5,000
Wife's half	500	500	5,000
Total Basis	5,500	5,500	10,000
Taxable gain on sale	$4,500	$4,500	$-0-

The couple has three different ways to take the property in co-ownership:

1. As joint-tenancy (or tenants by the entirety);

2. As tenants in common; or

3. As community property.

Note the significant difference in income tax basis in Situation II, Figure 19.1.

Thus, with the reinstatement of the stepped-up basis rule, where property has been paid for with community property earnings or if the contribution to the acquisition was otherwise equal, it again affords a significant advantage as to federal income tax to hold such property in community property as opposed to either joint-tenancy (known as tenancy by the entirety in some states as applied to spouses) or tenancy-in-common.

As to state income tax, one must look to the basis rules of the particular community property state to determine the basis of property for that state's income tax. For example, California now follows the federal rule – that the income tax basis of community property will adjust to fair market value on the death of either spouse, but only a decedent's one-half interest in joint tenancy property will be so adjusted.

Federal income tax is generally much more important than state income tax for most returns and therefore the double step-up in federal income tax basis of property held as community property will continue to be a very important tax planning consideration.

QUESTIONS AND ANSWERS

Question – Does property receive a new income tax basis equal to fair market value when it is given away during one's lifetime?

Answer – No. In general, the donee retains the donor's basis, increased by the amount of gift tax (or a part thereof) paid with respect to the gift. (See "Computing the Tax on Gifts," section (8), Chapter 17). However, if such basis is greater than the fair market value of the property at the time of the gift, then for purposes of determining loss, upon the donee's sale of the property, the basis is such fair market value.[3] If the property is given in trust, the donee's basis is the donor's basis increased or decreased by any gain or loss the donor recognized on the transfer under the law applicable in the year of the transfer.[4] Where property is transferred between spouses, or between former spouses if the transfer is incident to the divorce, the transferee's basis is the same as the transferor's basis.[5]

Property that is given away, but for some reason is brought back into the donor's estate for death tax purposes will receive a new basis equal to the fair market value at the time of death. Thus, having a gift brought back into the estate may be good for the donee (who gets a new basis) but bad for the estate (which has to pay death taxes on a larger estate).[6]

Question – If a property is sold with the seller taking back a note and the installment basis of recognizing gain is elected, does the note receive a new basis if the seller dies owning the note?

Answer – No. The gain that is inherent in the note will still be recognized.[7] Thus, a sale of the property before death will result in the gain being recognized, either during the seller's lifetime or after his death.

Question – If, instead of selling an asset such as stock, the shareholder enters into a buy-sell agreement, does the stock receive a stepped-up basis?

Answer – Yes. In general, the stock receives a new basis if it is still held by the shareholder at death as long as there is not a binding executed contract that did not depend on death.

However, entering into a contract of sale that calls for payment of a purchase price and the delivery of an asset upon completion of the payment will generally be treated as if the stock were sold and a note taken back. Gain will still be recognized to the extent there is any payment yet to be made on the purchase of the asset.

Question – If an attorney (or other taxpayer) reporting on the cash basis for income tax purposes dies with clients owing money for services rendered, do these debts receive a stepped-up basis?

Answer – No. Such amounts, which would have been income to the decedent if he had lived, are termed "income in respect of a decedent" (IRD) and do not receive a stepped-up basis at death.[8] They will be taxed to the taxpayer's estate as income, just as they would have been if he had received them during his lifetime.

Question – Does the person's estate that receives such "income in respect of a decedent" receive any deductions for the estate tax paid on such amounts included in the estate?

Answer – Yes. There is an income-tax deduction for a portion of the estate tax paid on such amounts of "income in respect of a decedent".[9]

Question – If an estate is so small that no estate tax is payable, or if no tax is payable because of the unlimited estate tax marital deduction, does the property still receive a stepped-up basis?

Answer – Yes. Regardless of the size of the estate or whether or not a federal estate tax is payable, a stepped-up (or stepped-down if the property has decreased in value below the original cost) basis will apply. Payment of estate tax is not a condition for receiving a new income tax basis.

Question – If a personal representative elects to use the alternate valuation date (six months after death) for valuing property for estate tax purposes, does that affect the stepped-up basis rule?

Answer – Yes. If the alternate valuation date is elected for federal estate tax purposes,[10] the fair market value of the property on that six-months-after-death date will be the new income tax basis of the property.[11]

Question – How is basis adjusted in a generation-skipping transfer?

Answer – Very similarly to the basis adjustment allowed when a gift tax is paid on a transfer. The transferee's basis is increased – but not beyond the fair market value of the property transferred – by an amount equal to that portion of the GST tax imposed on the transfer generated by the potential gain in the property immediately prior to the transfer.

Basis Adjustments for Taxable Distributions or Direct Skips

Fair market value of transferred property $1,000,000
Adjusted basis before GST transfer $600,000
GST tax imposed on transfer $480,000
Net appreciation [$1,000,000 - $600,000] $400,000
Basis increase [$480,000 x ($400,000 ÷ $1,000,000)] $192,000
Transferee's basis [$600,000 + $192,000] $792,000

If the GST tax is imposed because of a taxable termination that occurs at the same time as, and as the result of, an individual's death, the property's basis is stepped up similar to the normal step-up in basis of property at death (with certain limitations).

ASRS: Sec. 53.

CHAPTER ENDNOTES

1. IRC Sec. 1014.
2. IRC Sec. 1014(b)(6).
3. IRC Secs. 1015(a), (d).
4. IRC Sec. 1015(b).
5. IRC Sec. 1015(e).
6 . IRC Secs. 1014(b)(2), (3), (9).
7. IRC Sec. 691(a)(4).
8. IRC Secs. 1014(c), 691.
9. IRC Sec. 691(c).
10. IRC Sec. 2032.
11. IRC Sec. 1014(a)(2).

Chapter 20

NON U.S. PERSONS IN THE ESTATE PLAN

WHAT IS IT?

Special planning opportunities and problems are present where at least some family members are not U.S. citizens. Techniques will depend largely on the following:

(1) The extent to which these individuals have property situated in the U.S.

(2) Whether they are classified as either resident or nonresident aliens.

(3) Whether they were U.S. citizens who have renounced their citizenship through expatriation to other nations.

(4) Whether the spouse of the client is a citizen of the U.S.

Any planning in this area will be contingent on whether or not there is a treaty with the country in question which covers tax issues. The practitioner must always determine if such treaty provisions exist.

WHEN IS THE USE OF SUCH A PLAN INDICATED?

The international or multinational plan will be required in the following situations:

1. Where the client or family member is an alien who is considered to be a resident in the U.S. The tests for determining if an alien is a U.S. resident is different for federal income tax law than it is for federal estate tax law. Under the income tax rules, the test is objective, i.e., is the alien physically present in the U.S.?[1] If so, the alien is, subject to a complex set of tests and rules, usually treated as a resident. The federal estate tax regulations define a U.S. resident as a person who, at the time of his death, is "domiciled" in the U.S. Under these regulations, a non U.S. citizen is not domiciled in the U.S. unless he intends to remain here indefinitely.[2] Thus, in the case of the estate tax, the test is a subjective test relating to the "intent" of the person. This section will focus on estate, gift, and generation-skipping transfer tax planning issues.

   If the alien is treated as a resident for estate tax purposes, it follows that the alien's lifetime transfers are subject to gift and estate taxes in essentially the same manner as U.S. citizens resident in the U.S. The basic gift tax law is that the tax applies to all transfers by any individual, whether resident or nonresident.[3] There is an exception for the transfer of intangible property by a nonresident noncitizen.[4]

2. Where the client or family member is not a citizen or resident of the U.S., but is subject to federal estate tax because his taxable estate includes property situated in the U.S.[5] Property situated in the U.S. includes any stock issued by a domestic corporation (i.e., a U.S. corporation); any property which was situated in the U.S. when it was transferred by the decedent, but which would be included in his estate under IRC sections 2035 to 2038; and debt obligations of a U.S. person, the U.S., or a state or any political subdivision thereof.[6] It does not include life insurance or certain bank deposits and debt obligations.[7]

3. Where a surviving spouse is not a U.S. citizen, regardless of such spouse's domicile. The issue is the availability of the gift or estate tax marital deduction for transfers of assets to or in trust for the spouse.[8]

4. Where the client is a U.S. citizen not residing in the U.S. The estate and gift taxes are imposed on all U.S. citizens, regardless of where they live.[9] The generation-skipping transfer tax statutes do not specifically cover this, but since the tax is triggered by a taxable transfer for gift or estate tax purposes, the same rule should apply.

WHAT ARE THE REQUIREMENTS?

Subject to the foregoing rules, the goal of estate planning for clients in this category is to minimize the impact of U.S. taxes.

1. To avoid federal income tax, an alien who does not hold a permanent U.S. visa can avoid being considered a resident by not being physically present in the U.S. for more than 30 days during the current year or for more than 182 days during the three calendar year period ending with the current year (when multiplied by the applicable multiplier, which is 1 for the current year, 1/3 for the 1ˢᵗ preceding year, and 1/6 for the 2ⁿᵈ preceding year). For example, an alien who does not hold a permanent U.S. visa can avoid being considered a resident in the current year by not being physically present in the U.S. for more than 120 days in each of the two preceding years and the current year [120 x 1 = 120; 120 x 1/3 = 40; 120 x 1/6 = 20; 120 + 40 + 20 = 180]. This of course will be impossible for most aliens who are actively engaged in business in the U.S., or maintain a home here. If, however, the alien can limit his presence in the U.S. to no more than 182 days in any year, U.S. income tax may be avoided during such year if:

    a. The alien has a tax home in a foreign country, and

    b. An annual declaration is filed with the IRS with information that shows a "closer connection" with such foreign country than with the U.S.

2. To avoid federal estate tax, the alien's estate will have to establish the alien's "intent," i.e., that the alien's permanent home is outside the U.S. For example, if the alien has a bigger or better residence in the U.S. than in the alien's home country, this will be difficult. Also, the conduct of business and investment affairs should, to the extent possible, be located outside the U.S. Obviously, the alien should avoid signing documents in which the alien is described as a U.S. resident.

3. Where it appears U.S. residency will be unavoidable for either income or transfer tax purposes, the alien should seek to make gifts of assets to non U.S. persons, such as adult children living in foreign countries, before becoming a U.S. resident. This could be done with irrevocable foreign situs trusts, and limited liability companies (LLCs) discussed in Chapter 44. Many foreign countries recognize LLCs. This may be particularly useful to reduce the size of the alien's taxable estate.

4. Whether or not the alien is deemed a resident under U.S. tax laws, foreign situs trusts may be particularly useful to mitigate tax consequences. It will be essential that such a trust be irrevocable and have an independent trustee. However, the alien could retain some powers over the trust to the extent these powers do not cause the alien to be considered the "owner" of the trust for federal income or estate tax purposes. See in particular the discussion of the Income Taxation of Estates and Trusts in Chapter 19.

5. Where the alien can avoid U.S. residency, the use of foreign situs revocable trusts and foreign corporations may be indicated.

6. Where the client is a resident or U.S. citizen, but the client's spouse is not a U.S. citizen, the planner must concentrate on the federal gift and estate tax marital deduction. In general, the gift tax marital deduction is limited to $114,000 (in 2004) per year. The estate tax marital deduction is only available if the bequest ends up in a "qualified domestic trust" (QDOT). This is a trust that meets the requirements for the marital deduction discussed in Chapter 24, but which must include a series of special provisions relating to the trustee and how the trust is administered. If such a trust is used, the decedent's estate can claim the estate tax marital deduction for transfers to it, but most distributions to the surviving spouse, as well as the value of the assets remaining in the trust at the death of the surviving spouse, will be subject to federal estate tax. Moreover, this estate tax is computed by assuming such assets are added to the estate of the predeceased spouse.

    The basis in a taxable distribution from a QDOT is computed as though the transfer was made by gift. In other words, the initial basis is carried over and increased (but not above fair market value) by the amount of tax allocable to the growth in the value of the property occurring after the first spouse's death. For example, assume property worth $1,000,000 is placed into a QDOT. It grows to $1,300,000 and is paid out to the surviving spouse and taxed at that time as a capital distribution. An upward adjustment is allowed in the recipient's hands to account for the tax paid on the $300,000 of appreciation.

7. There are also special rules relating to distributions from foreign situs trusts to U.S.

beneficiaries. For example, there is an interest charge if such a trust accumulates income and then distributes the accumulation.[10] If a "U.S. person" contributes property to a foreign situs trust that has at least one U.S. beneficiary, the trust income is taxed to the grantor.[11]

8. The unified credit and state death tax credit are allowed to the estates of those considered U.S. residents for estate tax purposes even if they are not U.S. citizens.[12]

9. *Foreign Death Tax Credit:* Foreign death taxes are often imposed on property owned by a resident noncitizen where the property is situated outside the U.S. A credit is allowed for estate, inheritance, legacy, or succession taxes paid to a foreign country (or to a U.S. possession). The foreign death tax credit is allowed to the estate of a resident alien. The credit is allowed only for taxes actually paid to the foreign country or U.S. possession.[13]

HOW IT IS DONE – AN EXAMPLE

The client is the citizen of a foreign country who is not a resident of the United States. He is considering making a substantial investment in real estate in Hawaii. If he makes this investment directly, he will be subject to federal income tax on all of the income since it is U.S. source income. Further, upon his death, the value of the real property will be subject to U.S. estate tax.

If the real property were held through a foreign corporation, there would be little if any income tax advantage, but this would afford complete protection from federal estate and gift taxes. He may also consider holding the real estate through an irrevocable foreign situs trust, which will also avoid federal estate and gift taxes, and will not avoid federal income tax. The trust may be a more flexible arrangement. Further, a combination of the corporation and trust may be considered, with a corporation holding the real estate, and the corporate stock held in the irrevocable trust.

If the property is to be held by a foreign corporation, it is important to be certain the entity will be recognized as a corporation under U.S. law. Some foreign countries have entities which may nominally be classified as corporations, but which may not be recognized as such in this country. Further, the best procedure to follow is for the alien to transfer the consideration for the purchase of the U.S. real property to the foreign corporation

in exchange for stock, and then have the corporation purchase the land. There should always be consideration for the transfer of assets to a foreign corporation.

WHAT ARE THE TAX IMPLICATIONS?

As discussed above, where a noncitizen becomes a resident of the U.S. under either the income or estate tax definitions, that person will be subject to taxes in essentially the same manner as a U.S. citizen. The critical first step is to determine whether or not the alien is a resident under either tax. If so, the domestic planning options discussed in this book are generally available.

If the alien is not a resident, then the first step is to avoid U.S. gift and estate taxes by structuring the ownership of assets to avoid direct ownership by the alien of U.S. property or business interests. From the income tax standpoint, nonresident aliens are only taxed on income from sources within the U.S. The U.S. source income rules are detailed and complex (see, in general, IRC sections 871 and following).

If the nonresident alien does own U.S. situs property, than the federal estate tax will apply under the rules discussed in IRC sections 2101 and following and the unified credit available is reduced to $13,000.

Under the Foreign Investment in Real Property Tax Act, various provisions have been added to the law to insure collection of income tax on the transfer of U.S. real property by nonresident aliens, including withholding.[14]

Under proposed regulations, property situated in the U.S. is subject to the generation-skipping transfer tax regardless of the fact the transferor is a nonresident alien. These regulations also seek to extend the tax to transfers of all property to or for the benefit of U.S. persons who are lineal descendants of the transferor, even if the transfer would not be subject to U.S. gift or estate tax. Needless to say, this proposed regulation is highly controversial.

IMPLICATIONS AND ISSUES IN COMMUNITY PROPERTY STATES

Most countries in the world, other than those that follow the English common law system, such as most of the United States, do have community property laws. It is very likely assets acquired by noncitizens are community property, and planning should proceed accordingly. In addition, if the alien is a resident in a community property state, that state may seek to impose its community property rules on assets or earnings received while domiciled in the state.

QUESTIONS AND ANSWERS

Question – What is a "controlled foreign corporation," and what is its significance?

Answer – A controlled foreign corporation is a foreign corporation in which either more than 50% of the total combined voting power of all classes of stock or more than 50% of the total value of the stock is owned by United States shareholders.[15] The net effect of such status is that any income earned by the corporation will be attributed to and taxed to any shareholders who are U.S. residents.[16] This rule will apply even if the corporate stock is owned through a revocable trust. There are complex rules and exceptions. Note that a similar rule applies to a foreign personal holding company.[17] Personal holding companies are discussed in Chapter 45.

Question – Is the partnership or LLC a viable form of entity for aliens to hold investments or business interests?

Answer – The partnership has the same advantages to aliens as to other taxpayers in avoiding two levels of taxation on its income. However, if the partnership is making U.S. investments, or carrying on a U.S. trade or business, it is subject to stringent withholding requirements. If a nonresident alien owns an interest in a partnership that is carrying on U.S. business, it appears that the partnership interest will be subject to U.S. estate tax.

Question – Is an irrevocable foreign trust a viable form of business entity for aliens to hold U.S. investments or business interests?

Answer – Such a trust may be a good planning vehicle, particularly when combined with other entities, such as the foreign corporation or partnership. Again, there are strict withholding requirements on distributions from such trusts. An important advantage of the trust is the potential avoidance of federal estate and gift tax by nonresident aliens. The trust is preferable to any form of direct ownership of U.S. real estate.

Question – A nonresident alien who spends a great deal of time in the U.S. intends to take his daughter, also a nonresident alien, on a shopping trip in this country to purchase expensive jewelry. Is this advisable?

Answer – It would be better for the parent to purchase the jewelry and be the owner, return to the foreign country, and then make a gift of it to his daughter. Otherwise, the transfer is subject to U.S. gift tax.

Question – A decedent is a nonresident alien who was an expatriate from the U.S. four years before her death. Is there any estate tax exposure?

Answer – IRC section 2107 specifically provides that if one of the principal purposes of expatriation was to avoid U.S. taxes, and citizenship is lost within 10 years of death, a tax is imposed on the decedent's estate. This would result in inclusion in the decedent's taxable estate of not only property situated in the U.S. as defined in IRC section 2104, but also stock in certain foreign corporations.

Question – A nonresident alien wishes to create a trust for the benefit of U.S. citizens. How can the alien avoid U.S. tax on the trust income?

Answer – If the trust is subject to the grantor trust rules under IRC sections 671 to 677, the grantor, not the trust or its beneficiaries, will be taxed on the trust income. This also avoids the tax on accumulations discussed above.

Question – What are the requirements of a qualified domestic trust (QDOT)?

Answer – A QDOT has certain requirements.

1. The trust must meet the same requirements for the marital deduction as a trust for the benefit of a citizen spouse (see Chapter 24). Thus, it can be a QTIP trust, a trust over which the surviving spouse has the right to all income and a general power of appointment, or an "estate" trust. In an estate trust, it is not necessary that all of the income be distributed annually to the surviving spouse, so long as all trust distributions must ultimately be made to the spouse or the spouse's estate. Such a trust is often useful where the trust assets are not income producing, such as stock in a closely held corporation. Regulations may provide for arrangements other than trusts in jurisdictions where trusts are prohibited.

2. Except as provided in regulations, at least one trustee must be an individual who is a U.S.

citizen or a domestic corporation. According to regulations, if the value of the trust assets exceeds $2 million, at least one U.S. trustee must be a bank or furnish a bond equal to 65% of the value of the trust. If the trust is worth less than $2 million, either a bond must be furnished or the trust must contain a clause that not more than 35% of its fair market value can be invested in non U.S. real property. Also, an individual U.S. trustee must have a tax home in the U.S. Tangible and intangible U.S. property must be in the U.S. or a U.S. brokerage account.

3. No distribution can be made from the trust unless the U.S. citizen or domestic corporation trustee has a right under the trust to withhold from the distribution any tax due on the distribution.

4. The executor of decedent's estate must make a QDOT election. If the qualifying trust is a QTIP, both QTIP and QDOT elections must be made.

5. No marital deduction is allowed unless the property is transferred to a QDOT, or a trust reformed to qualify as a QDOT, or it is transferred to the QDOT by a surviving spouse, or the surviving spouse becomes a citizen, or there is a treaty. There must be an actual transfer or assignment to a QDOT created by the decedent, executor, or surviving spouse.

6. An estate tax is imposed on QDOT assets on the happening of any of the following events:

    (1) When any distribution other than (a) a distribution of income to the surviving spouse or (b) a distribution to the surviving spouse on account of hardship is made prior to the surviving spouse's death;

    (2) When the surviving spouse dies. The entire value of the property in the QDOT at that time will be subject to federal estate tax;

    (3) When the QDOT fails to meet any QDOT requirement designed to assure that the IRS will collect the estate tax. The estate tax will be imposed as if the surviving spouse died on the date the trust failed the requirement; or

    (4) When the QDOT pays the tax imposed upon the first of the above triggering events,

that tax itself is considered a taxable distribution that sets off yet another tax. In other words the QDOT's payment of the estate tax on a distribution is itself a distribution subject to a further estate tax.

7. The estate tax on the QDOT is computed as follows:

    Step 1: State the amount involved in the taxable event

    Step 2: Add all previous taxable events

    Step 3: Compute the federal estate tax on the estate of the first spouse to die as if the total of #1 and #2 above were included in the decedent's gross estate

    Step 4: Compute the federal estate tax on the estate of the first spouse to die as if only the amount of the previous taxable events were included in the decedent's gross estate

    Step 5: Subtract the tax computed in step #4 from the tax computed in step #3. This is the tax imposed as a result of a current taxable event.

8. If the estate otherwise qualifies, various tax elections are available upon the death of the surviving spouse, such as stock redemptions under IRC section 303, valuation elections under IRC sections 2032 and 2032A, and deferred payment of federal estate tax under IRC section 6166. Also, a charitable deduction under IRC section 2055 may be available.

Question – What are the planning advantages of gift transfers to a noncitizen spouse?

Answer – Lifetime transfers of up to $114,000 (in 2004) per year to a noncitizen spouse qualify for the gift tax marital deduction. The noncitizen spouse could leverage this gift by purchasing life insurance on the life of the citizen spouse. Such insurance would not be included in the estate of the citizen spouse, and through the use of an irrevocable life insurance trust, discussed in Chapter 31, could be excluded from the estate of the noncitizen spouse in the event such spouse is subject to federal estate tax.

Lifetime gifts to a surviving spouse are particularly useful where the surviving spouse is a U.S. resident subject to federal gift or estate taxes. In this case, gifts of up to $1,000,000 can be used to take full advantage of the noncitizen spouse's unified credit. Even gifts in excess of that amount, given at the rate of $114,000 (in 2004) per year, can be used to take advantage of the lower estate tax brackets of the noncitizen spouse. This clearly has advantages over the use of a QDOT trust, where the trust assets will eventually be taxed at the probably higher estate tax brackets that would be used in computing the tax in the estate of the predeceased spouse.

Question – What is the impact of joint tenancy forms of title holding where one spouse is not a citizen?

Answer – Under IRC section 2040(a), the entire value of the joint tenancy property is included in the estate of the spouse who contributed to the joint tenancy. Note that IRC section 2040(b), which provides that joint tenancies between husband and wife are deemed owned 50% by each for estate tax purposes, does not apply if the surviving spouse is not a citizen.[18]

CHAPTER ENDNOTES

1. IRC Sec. 7701(b).
2. Treas. Reg. §20.0-1(b).
3. IRC Sec. 2501(a)(1).
4. IRC Sec. 2501(a)(2).
5. IRC Sec. 2103.
6. IRC Sec. 2104.
7. IRC Sec. 2105.
8. IRC Secs. 2056(d), 2056A, 2523(i).
9. IRC Secs. 2001(a), 2501(a).
10. IRC Sec. 668.
11. IRC Sec. 679.
12. IRC Secs. 2010, 2011.
13. IRC Sec. 2014.
14. IRC Secs. 897, 1445.
15. IRC Sec. 957.
16. IRC Sec. 954.
17. IRC Sec. 551.
18. IRC Sec. 2056(d)(1)(B).

Chapter 21

POST MORTEM TAX ELECTIONS

After a decedent dies, a number of tax elections or tax decisions must be made. These may include income tax elections or decisions with regard to the decedent's final return, the decedent's estate or trusts, or entities in which the decedent held an interest. Estate tax and generation-skipping transfer tax elections or decisions must also be made. Issues with regard to employee benefits may need to be addressed. Also, consideration should be given to the disclaimer of property.

The following checklist reviews a number of post mortem tax elections and tax decisions. While it is generally useful to review the checklist after a decedent dies, it is probably also useful to review the checklist while an individual is still alive. The estate or financial planner and the individual can then address the issues while the individual is alive and provide some guidance as to how the elections fit into the individual's estate plan and how the elections might be made. In addition, some actions might be made while the individual is alive to facilitate the availability of an election after death.

POST MORTEM TAX ELECTIONS CHECKLIST

Part A: Income Tax Elections

Section 1: Decedent's Final Return(s)

I. Were medical expenses of the decedent paid after death?

   A. Medical expenses incurred before death and paid by the estate during the year beginning the day after the date of death may be accrued and deducted on the decedent's income tax return for the year in which the expense was incurred. IRC Secs. 213(a), 213(c).

   B. In the alternative, the medical expense can be deducted as a debt of the decedent for federal estate tax purposes under IRC Section 2053(b).

II. Did the decedent own any U.S. Savings bonds?

   A. If the decedent had not elected to accrue and report as income interest on Series E and EE Savings bonds, the personal representative may elect to do so on the final return. IRC Sec. 454(a); Rev. Rul. 68-145, 1968-1 CB 203.

   B. If this election is not made, the accrued interest is income in respect of a decedent, and a decedent's estate could elect to accrue it on the estate's income tax return.

III. Did the decedent transfer any property before death that may be replaced under the involuntary conversion rules, or make an installment sale?

   A. If property of the decedent was involuntarily converted, i.e., it was destroyed by natural disaster, condemned, etc., the estate or successor to the decedent may be able to replace it and avoid any taxation of gain to decedent for income tax purposes under IRC Section 1033.

   B. If a decedent made an installment sale, the estate can elect out of installment reporting. IRC Sec. 453; Let. Rul. 8545052.

IV. Filing a joint return – A joint return may be filed for decedent and surviving spouse for the year of death, unless the spouse remarries before the end of the year. IRC Sec. 6013(a)(2).

Section 2: Decedent's Estate and Trusts (Chapter 19, Income Taxation of Estates and Trusts)

I. Should the estate elect a fiscal year?

II. Should the executor waive commissions?

   A. If the executor or administrator of the estate intends to waive commissions, this should be done before undertaking any duties. Rev. Rul. 64-225, 1964-2 CB 15.

   B. However, it may still be possible to waive them later if no fee was deducted for any tax purpose or claimed in any probate accounting. Rev. Rul. 66-167, 1966-1 CB 20.

III. Where should administrative expenses and casualty losses be deducted?

    A. These may be claimed either as estate tax deductions under IRC Sections 2053 or 2054 or income tax deductions under IRC Section 642.

    B. If claimed as income tax deductions, a waiver of the right to claim them as estate tax deductions must be filed. IRC Sec. 642(g); Treas. Regs. §§1.642(g)-1, 1.642(g)-2.

IV. Should the decedent's revocable trust be treated as part of the estate for income tax purposes?

    A. If so, the election must be made both by the executor, if any, of the estate and the trustee of the revocable trust not later than the due date (including extensions) of the estate's income tax return for the first taxable year.

Section 3: Partnerships in which Decedent Had Interests (Chapter 43)

I. Should the partnership elect to adjust the income tax basis of partnership assets?

    A. If an appropriate election is made under IRC Sections 754 and 743(b), the basis of a deceased partner's interest in partnership assets will be adjusted to date of death or estate tax value.

    B. Even if the election is not made, if within two years after death partnership assets are distributed "in kind" to the successor of a deceased partner, the distributee may adjust basis in the same manner as provided in IRC Section 743(b).

Section 4: Closely Held Corporations in which Decedent Had Interests (Chapters 46, 47)

I. Should the estate make or continue an S election?

II. What are considerations in planning distributions from estates to trusts and other beneficiaries?

    A. Where the executor has discretion as to funding of trusts with specific trust assets, no funding with S corporation stock should be undertaken until a determination is made as to whether the trust is a qualifying shareholder.

    B. Make certain any distributee trust is a qualified trust.

Part B: Estate Tax Elections

Section 1: Alternate Valuation Elections

I. Should the estate elect to value assets at the alternate valuation date, which is:

    A. Six months after the date or death, or

    B. The date the asset is "disposed of" by the estate. IRC Sec. 2032.

    C. However, the election is only available if it reduces the actual size of the gross estate and if the estate tax liability is reduced by the election. IRC Sec. 2032(c).

Section 2: Special Use Valuation Elections (Chapter 57)

I. Did the decedent own land used in farming or closely held business?

II. Will the family continue the use of the property and materially participate in its operation?

Section 3: Qualified Family-Owned Business Interest Deduction (Chapter 42) (not available 2004 to 2010)

I. Did the decedent own an interest in a family-owned U.S. business?

II. What is its value in relation to the total estate?

III. Will the family continue to own the business and materially participate in its operation?

Section 4: Marital Deduction Elections

I. Did the decedent employ a trust that qualifies as a QTIP?

    A. QTIP elections (Chapter 24)

II. Is the surviving spouse a noncitizen?

    A. Establishing qualified domestic trusts (Chapters 24, 20)

Section 5: Payment and Deferred Payment of Federal Estate Tax (Chapter 16)

I.   Did the decedent own an interest in a closely held business?

II. What is its value in relation to the total estate?

III. Is the closely held business interest in a corporation?

    A.   IRC Section 303 stock redemptions (Chapter 41)

Part C: Employee Benefits (Chapters 49, 50, 51, 52)

I.   Is a spousal rollover available?

II. Should designated beneficiary changes be made?

    A.   Reconfiguration of the designated beneficiary by disclaimer, cash-out, etc., is allowed if such action is taken by the end of the calendar year following the calendar year of the participant's death. Treas. Reg. §1.401(a)(9)-4.

III. Should lump sum distributions and averaging be considered?

Part D: Disclaimers (Chapter 11)

I.   Should any beneficiaries of the estate consider refusing to accept their inheritance?

Part E: Generation–Skipping Elections (Chapter 18)

I.   How should the generation-skipping transfer tax exemption be allocated?

II. Should a reverse QTIP election be made?

Part 4:

GIFTS

Chapter 22

GIFTS

WHAT IS IT?

For gift tax purposes, a gift can be broadly defined to include a sale, exchange, or other transfer of property from one person (the donor) to another (the donee) without adequate and full consideration in money or money's worth.

In addition to an outright transfer, gifts can take other forms. For example, the forgiveness of a debt, foregone interest on an intra-family interest-free or below market loan, the assignment of the benefits of an insurance policy, or the transfer of property to a trust can also be considered gifts.[1]

Gifts are a major estate planning tool because of their potential for income as well as estate tax savings and for their nontax advantages.

The gift tax computation itself is explained in detail in Chapter 17.

WHEN IS THE USE OF SUCH A DEVICE INDICATED?

1. When the donor has an asset that is likely to appreciate in value over a period of time and would like to save estate taxes on the potential growth. EGTRRA 2001 repeals the estate tax for one year in 2010.

2. When a donor would like to see the donee (an individual, charity, or other organization) benefited by a gift during the donor's life for nontax motives.

3. When the donor would like to reduce probate costs and estate administration expenses, and protect family members from the claims of the client's creditors.

4. When giving away assets other than closely held stock will make it easier to qualify for an IRC section 303 redemption of stock, an IRC section 6166 installment payout of taxes attributable to a closely held business interest, an IRC section 2032A special use valuation for certain real property used for farming or closely held business purposes, and the qualified family-owned business deduction. (This technique generally works only if the gift is made more than 3 years prior to death.)

5. When the estate owner desires to maximize the marital deduction provisions of the federal estate and gift tax law. He could give his spouse an unlimited amount of property during his lifetime and pay no federal gift tax because of the 100% gift tax marital deduction. It is important to consider any state gift tax laws as well as the federal gift tax.

6. By giving income-producing property, the donor may be able to remove from his income tax bracket the future income it produces and subject it to the lower income tax bracket of a donee. For example, a high bracket property owner may make a gift to reduce federal income tax from a bracket as high as 35% to a bracket as low as 10% in 2004.[2]

All *net unearned income* of a child who has not attained age 14 before the close of the taxable year and who has at least one parent alive at the close of the taxable year will be taxed to the child, but not at the child's tax bracket. This applies to *all* net unearned income; the *source* of the assets creating the income, the *date* the income-producing property was transferred, and the *identity* of the transferor are *irrelevant*.

The tax payable by the under age 14 child on net unearned income is essentially the additional amount of tax the parent would have had to pay if the net unearned income of the child were included in the parent's taxable income.

If parents have two or more children with unearned income to be taxed at the parent's marginal tax rate, all of the children's applicable unearned income will be added together and the tax calculated. The tax is then allocated to each child based on the child's pro rata share of unearned income.

This "kiddie tax" is calculated in three stages (numbers are as indexed for 2004):

(1) There will be no tax on the first $800 of unearned income because of the child's standard deduction. (The standard deduction offsets *un*earned income first, up to $800. Any remaining standard deduction is then available to offset earned income.)

(2) The next $800 of unearned income will be taxed to the child at the child's bracket.

(3) Unearned income in excess of the first $1,600 will be taxed to the child at the appropriate parent's rate.

A dependent child under age 14 with $1,600 of unearned income is taxed as follows:

Unearned Income	$1,600
Standard Deduction	− 800
Net Unearned Income	$ 800
Taxed at Child's Rate	x 10%
Tax	$80.00

Even for children under age 14, there is still some income shifting possible.

For children age 14 or older, unearned income will be taxed to the child at his own tax bracket.

As Figure 22.1 shows, income shifting can be very successful, where a child is age 14 or older.

WHAT ARE THE REQUIREMENTS?

1. There must be a gratuitous transfer or delivery of property.[3]

2. The property that is the subject of the gift must be accepted by the donee.[4] (Of course, when the property is of benefit to the donee, acceptance is seldom an issue.)

3. The gratuitous transfer must divest the donor of control, dominion, and title over the subject matter of the gift.[5]

HOW IT IS DONE – AN EXAMPLE

1. Caroline O'Gara is age 55, married, and owns $20,000 of dividend-paying stock. The stock yields $1,000 annually. Caroline is presently in a 28% federal income tax bracket. On the advice of her lawyer, in 2004 she gives the $20,000 of stock to her 15 year old son, James (splitting the gift with her husband). This will have the result of shifting the income tax liability from Caroline, who would have netted only $720 [$1,000 – (28% x $1,000)] from the $1,000 dividends, to James, who will net $980 [$1,000 – (10% x $200)] from the dividends, a saving of $260 ($980 – $720) yearly. [James is in a 10% federal income tax bracket, has no other income, and is entitled to a $800 standard deduction, so a 10% rate is applied only to the taxable $200 ($1,000 - $800).]

2. Gerald Carter owns an asset that is worth $100,000 today. It is anticipated that the asset will appreciate at the rate of 10% per year, i.e., in 10 years it will be worth approximately $260,000. If the property is given away now, the gift tax is computed on the $100,000 (less the annual exclusion if allowable). If the asset is not given away and it becomes part of the estate (ten years from today), the estate tax is com-

Figure 22.1

ADVANTAGE OF INCOME SHIFTING - CHILD 14 OR OLDER			

Investment			$20,000
Rate of Return			10%
Parent's Tax Rate			40%
Parent's After Tax Rate of Return			6%
Child's Tax Rate			20%
Child's After Tax Rate of Return			8%

	Accumulated Value		Advantage
Years	Parent (6%)	Child (8%)	of Gift
5	$26,765	$29,387	$2,622
10	$35,817	$43,178	$7,362
15	$47,931	$63,443	$15,512
20	$64,143	$93,219	$29,076

puted on approximately $260,000. Thus, a gift made currently removes future appreciation from the estate. EGTRRA 2001 repeals the estate tax for one year in 2010.

WHAT ARE THE TAX IMPLICATIONS?

1. A gift will remove future appreciation in the property's value from an individual's estate. EGTRRA 2001 repeals the estate tax for one year in 2010.

2. Gift tax may have to be paid if the value of the gift exceeds the annual exclusion and the gift tax unified credit exemption equivalent available to the donor.[6] A potential donor should be aware that the lifetime gift tax unified credit exemption equivalent is set at $1,000,000 after 2001. (The unified credits and exemption equivalents are shown below under QUESTIONS AND ANSWERS.) If an individual is married and his spouse consents to "split" the gift, the donor spouse can effectively have the $11,000 (in 2004) annual exclusion and the unified credit of his spouse in addition to his own.[7] A married individual can give sizable gifts to a spouse with little or no gift tax liability through the gift tax marital deduction discussed below.

3. Dividend or other income generated by the property given will be taxed to the donee rather than the donor (see the discussion above at 6 under the heading "WHEN IS THE USE OF SUCH A DEVICE INDICATED").

4. The gift tax subtracted from the tentative tax in the estate tax computation is the tax that would have been payable on post-1976 gifts if the tax rate schedule as in effect at decedent's death had been in effect at the time such gifts were made. If estate and gift tax rates at the time the gift was made and at the donor's death are the same, this deduction for gift tax "payable" is equivalent to a credit for the gift tax actually paid. (A credit is available for gift tax paid on pre-1977 gifts.) If estate and gift tax rates are lower at the time of the donor's death than when the gift was made, a donor may pay a larger tax than if no gift had been made. However, any lower tax rate at death should be balanced against the appreciation of the gift that was removed from the tax system.

    The top gift and estate tax rate is 48% in 2004. The top estate and gift tax rate is reduced in steps until it reaches 45% in 2007. The top gift tax rate reaches 35% in 2010, while the estate tax is repealed for one year in 2010. The top gift and estate tax rate is scheduled to return to 55% (along with a 5% surtax) in 2011. See tables in Appendix A.

5. The tax implications also include state gift tax where applicable, which in many instances can be greater than the federal gift tax, because of the large credit and exemptions currently available under federal gift tax law.

IMPLICATIONS AND ISSUES IN COMMUNITY PROPERTY STATES

All community property states have adopted statutes that to some degree and by different methods grant equal powers of management and control of community property to each spouse. In many states, one spouse cannot make a gift of community property without the prior written consent of the other spouse. If one spouse makes a gift of community property to a third person without the consent of the other spouse, the gift is ordinarily voidable rather than void.

The gift can be voided only at the request of the nondonor spouse. The amount of the gift that can be declared void and brought back to the community estate is generally dependent upon whether the community circumstance is still in existence. If the spouses are still married, the entire gift is returned to the community estate. However, if the community has been terminated (e.g., divorce, death), the nondonor spouse has the right to recapture only one-half of the gift. The other half is allowed to remain with the donee. Therefore, it is advisable to obtain both spouses' consent prior to the gift transfer.

In general, gifts of community property have the same benefits as gifts of separate property where the gift is to a third party. However, since each spouse actually "owns" his or her one-half interest in the property, there is no need to "split" the gift. This provides an advantage for persons with community property since each has property and each can give an amount equal to the annual exclusion ($11,000 in 2004) without filing a gift tax return.

As to gifts between spouses, a marital deduction is available for the entire amount of the gift, where one spouse gives his or her community interest in property to the other.

"Accidental gifts" (i.e., taxable gifts that were not intended to be events subject to tax) can be created by transfers of title. This is particularly true in community property states where a husband and wife have acquired property in a common law state and then moved to a community property state. An example would be where a husband and wife who have acquired assets by the husband's earnings in a common law state sell their home and other real property and move to a community property state, where they invest their cash in securities in joint tenancy or community property title. The parties have always considered their property as "belonging to both of them" and frequently do not understand that purchasing joint tenancy securities resulted in a gift of one-half the value from the husband to the wife. While the unlimited marital deduction avoids federal gift tax on such transfers, there may be state gift taxes to consider. In addition, any pre-1982 transfers may have caused taxable gifts under the pre-Economic Recovery Tax Act (ERTA) rules (which did tax interspousal transfers), and interest and penalties may well apply to those gifts. Without having filed a gift tax return for the year in question, the statute of limitations does not run and the taxes, interest, and penalty must still be faced.

Many states do not impose a gift tax where real property (as opposed to securities or other types of property) is placed in joint tenancy between a husband and wife, unless the spouses elect to have the transfer treated as a gift. However, the separate nature of the property still remains, and if the title is later changed to community property or tenancy in common, or if the property is sold and a mortgage or trust deed is taken back "as joint tenants," a gift will be triggered! This is a real danger-area for persons moving to a community property state with assets earned by one of the spouses.

In addition, some states (Texas, Louisiana, Idaho) consider the income from assets with a separate property nature to be community property. Others (Arizona, California, Nevada, New Mexico, Washington) consider such income to be the separate property of the spouse who actually "owns" the property. Thus, in the latter group of states, income that comes from an asset that one spouse had before marriage or that was given to or inherited by the spouse during marriage is the separate property of that spouse.

It is important to maintain in separate accounts the proceeds of sale of one's separate property and any separate property income. Commingling these funds can transmute them into community property of both spouses and can result in a gift, an act that may result in state gift tax being imposed even though no gift was intended, by using those commingled funds to buy something in co-ownership between the spouses.

Aside from any gift tax aspects, with the increasing frequency of divorce, it may be important for ownership reasons to be able to trace separate and community property.

QUESTIONS AND ANSWERS

Question – What annual gift tax exclusions are available to a donor?

Answer – A donor can make, gift tax free, up to $11,000 (in 2004) worth of gifts (other than "future interest" gifts) to any number of persons or parties each year.[8] The total maximum excludable amount is determined by multiplying the number of persons (or organizations) to whom gifts are made by $11,000. The $11,000 amount is adjusted for inflation, rounded to the next lowest multiple of $1,000.

If the donor is married and his or her spouse consents (by signing the donor's gift tax return) to "splitting" the gift, each spouse is deemed to have given half the gift–even though one spouse in actuality made the entire gift. This has the effect of raising the per donee exclusion to $22,000 (in 2004) per year.

An annual exclusion is allowed only for "present interest" gifts and is denied for "future interest" gifts.[9]

A present interest gift is one in which the donee's possession or enjoyment begins at the instant the gift is made. A future interest is any interest in which the donee's use, possession, or enjoyment will not begin until some period of time after the gift is made. In a nutshell, if there is any delay, no matter how short, or any possibility, no matter how remote, that the donee's legal right to use, possession, or enjoyment will not begin at the moment the gift is made, the annual exclusion is denied.

Future interests (which do not qualify for the annual exclusion) include:

(1) reversions,

(2) remainders,

(3) any other delayed interest.

A single transfer may actually be two gifts and for tax purposes have to be split into two parts. One may be a present interest that qualifies for the annual exclusion. The other gift may be a future interest that will not qualify for the annual exclusion. For instance, assume a donor put $100,000 into a trust in 2004 that provided that "all the income is to go annually to my son for ten years. The remainder is to go to my daughter at the end of that time."

The first gift, the income to the son, would be a present interest. That's because, at the moment of the gift, the son has the immediate right to the income stream for 10 years. The present value of the son's right to income, according to government valuation tables, would be the gift. Assuming a Section 7520 rate of 5%, the value of the income interest for 10 years would be $38,609 ($100,000 x .386087 term certain income factor from Appendix B). If the donor was married and his spouse consented to splitting the gift, the two annual exclusions would total $22,000. Therefore, only $16,869 ($38,609 - $22,000) of the income interest would be a taxable gift, $8,439.50 from each spouse ($16,869 ÷ 2).

The second gift, the daughter's right to the remainder of the capital at the end of ten years, would be a future interest because her right to possession would be delayed. Assuming a Section 7520 rate of 5%, the value of the remainder interest after 10 years would be $61,391 ($100,000 x .613913 term certain remainder factor from Appendix B). Each spouse's share of the remainder portion of the gift would be $30,695.50 ($61,391 ÷ 2). No annual exclusion would be allowed on this portion.

Question – What are, in summary, the requirements for the gift tax annual exclusion?

Answer – The rules regarding the annual exclusion can be summarized as follows:

(1) A gift in trust is a gift to a trust's beneficiaries for purposes of determining how many annual exclusions may be allowed.

(2) The value of an income interest in a trust qualifies for the annual exclusion if the trustee is required to distribute the income annually or more frequently–even if the value of the remainder interest does not qualify.

(3) The gift of an interest that is contingent upon survivorship is a gift of a future interest. For instance, a gift, "to my son for life, then to my daughter for life, then to my brother if he survives me" is really three gifts. The first gift (to the son) is a present interest if the trustee is given no right to accumulate income and all income must be paid at least annually. The other two gifts (to the daughter and brother) are future interest gifts.

(4) A gift is a future interest gift if the donee's enjoyment depends on the exercise of a trustee's discretion. So if a trustee has the right to accumulate income, the gift is a future interest even if the trustee never exercises the right. The nature of the gift (present or future) is ascertained as of the moment of the transfer and is not determined by what the trustee actually does.

(5) A gift must have an ascertainable value to qualify for the exclusion. If the donor or anyone can divert the income from the beneficiary or it is not reasonably possible at the time of the gift to value it, the exclusion may be denied.

Question – Just how valuable is the annual exclusion– and how is it computed?

Answer – The annual exclusion can be an extremely effective income, estate, and generation-skipping transfer tax saving device. However, EGTRRA 2001 repeals the estate tax and the generation-skipping transfer tax for one year in 2010.

The illustration at Figure 22.2 multiplies the number of donees by the amount of the annual exclusion available to be split between husband and wife and then multiplies that amount by the donor's life expectancy according to the government's table in the regulations. This result is then multiplied by the federal estate tax bracket that you have projected the donor will be in at death. The result is the potential federal estate tax savings if none of the annual gifts are invested by the donees.

The illustration then assumes the donees do invest the annual gifts at the specified rate of return (being conservative since this is an after-tax figure). The final result is the potential estate tax savings–the amount that might have gone to the federal government–if no gifts were made.

Figure 22.2

ESTATE TAX OR GST TAX ADVANTAGE OF THE GIFT TAX ANNUAL EXCLUSION*	
DONOR'S AGE	40
DONEES' ANNUAL AFTER-TAX RETURN ON GIFTS	4.00%
AMOUNT OF UNUSED ANNUAL EXCLUSION (with gift splitting between husband and wife) ...	$22,000
NUMBER OF DONEES	5
DONOR'S LIFE EXPECTANCY (YEARS)	42.5
TOTAL AMOUNT OF GIFTS ($22,000/year/donee x 5 donees x 43 years)	$4,730,000
DONOR'S PROJECTED ESTATE TAX BRACKET	48.00%
POTENTIAL ESTATE TAX SAVINGS	$2,270,400
PROJECTED VALUE OF GIFTS AT LIFE EXPECTANCY	$12,101,312
POTENTIAL ESTATE TAX SAVINGS IF ANNUAL GIFTS INVESTED BY DONEES AT COMPOUND INTEREST	$5,808,654

*Illustration courtesy of NumberCruncher Software

Question – What is the unified credit against the gift tax?

Answer – The law provides a single tax credit called the "unified" credit, which is a dollar-for-dollar reduction of any gift or estate tax due. The gift tax unified credit is roughly equivalent to an exemption of $1,000,000 after 2001.[10] (The estate tax exemption equivalent (see Appendix A) is much greater than the gift tax exemption equivalent for 2004 to 2009 and the estate tax is repealed for one year in 2010.)

	Gift Tax	
	Unified Credit	*Exemption Equivalent*
2002-2009	345,800	1,000,000
2010	330,800	1,000,000
2011	345,800	1,000,000

Example: Assume Robin Scott and her husband make a $677,000 present interest gift in 2004 to their son. The computation for *each* spouse would be as follows:

Gift (split under section 2513)	$338,500
Annual Exclusion	11,000
Net Gift	327,500
Tax on Net Gift	97,150
Unified Credit	345,800
Net Tax Due	$ 0

To the extent the credit is used during lifetime it will have the effect of reducing the credit available against the estate tax. Thus, for estate tax purposes for a death in 2004 there will be only a $333,400 ($555,800 - $97,150) credit left for each spouse (see Chapter 15, Estate Tax, for details). Of course, additional amounts of estate tax unified credit are available as the credit increases in later years.

Question – What is a "split gift"?

Answer – When a husband or wife makes a gift to a third person, it may be treated as having been made one-half by the husband and one-half by the wife. This is true even though only one spouse actually makes the gift providing the other spouse consents to the gift.[11]

This would cause the gift tax rate to be lower since the unified rates are progressive. For example: A present interest gift of $111,000 (taxable gift of $100,000) made by a single individual in 2004 would result in a gift tax of $23,800, whereas the same $111,000 gift made by a husband and his consenting wife to a third party (such as a child) would result in each being considered to have made a $44,500 taxable gift and the gift tax would be $9,280 each ($18,560 for both). The savings would be $5,240. (These examples ignore the unified credit and assume no prior taxable gifts.) A gift tax return must be filed in order to be able to split the gift. Only individuals married to each other can consent to split a gift.

It should be noted that gifts by a husband and wife of community property are *not* eligible for any gift splitting.

Question – What is the gift tax marital deduction?

Answer – In computing the amount of a taxable gift, a deduction is allowed for a gift made by a husband to his wife or vice versa. This deduction is unlimited; so one spouse could conceivably give an entire estate to the other spouse without adverse gift tax consequences.

To qualify for this deduction, the donee-spouse must be given the property outright or must have at least the right to the income from the property and a general power of appointment (essentially the right to say "who gets it") over the principal.[12] (Certain so-called "qualified terminable interest" type property that gives the spouse only a life income may also qualify. This planning technique is discussed more thoroughly in Chapter 24 on marital deduction trusts.)

Question – What is the gift tax based on?

Answer – The gift tax is based on the fair market value of the property transferred.[13]

Question – How is a life insurance policy valued for gift tax purposes?

Answer – If a policy is transferred as a gift immediately after purchase, its value for gift tax purposes is the gross premium paid by the donor.

If a person makes a gift of a previously purchased policy, and the policy is a single-premium or paid-up policy, its gift value is the single premium that the issuing company would charge currently for a comparable contract of equal face value on the life of a person who is the insured's age at the time of the gift.

If the gift is of a policy on which further premium payments are payable, its value is the "interpolated terminal reserve" (roughly equivalent to the cash value) and the value of any unearned portion of the last premium.[14] A gift of group term life is measured by the value of the unearned premium at the date of the transfer, so the ideal time to make an assignment of group term life is immediately before the next premium is due.

If the insured is now uninsurable, or exceptionally ill and old, the value of the policy may be much more than the interpolated terminal reserve value, depending on health circumstances.

Question – Who must file a gift tax return and when must it be filed?

Answer – The donor must file a gift tax return (Form 709) on or before April 15th following the close of the

calendar year in which a gift was made exceeding the annual exclusion or a split gift was elected. (An extension of time to file the income tax return automatically extends the time for filing gift tax returns.)

Rules for filing of state gift tax returns vary with the different states.

Question – When is the best time to make a gift?

Answer – Like the answer to the question "When is the best time to plant an oak tree?" the answer to this question is, "twenty years ago." The next best time is right now! The $11,000 (in 2004) per donee annual exclusion ($22,000 when a spouse consents) discussed above is noncumulative; either use it or lose it!

Generally, stocks and other assets that fluctuate widely in value should be given away when the market value for that asset is as low as possible.

However, in any decision making as to the giving of property, the financial security of the donor, both current and long-term, should be very carefully considered.

Question – What is the best type of property to give away?

Answer – That depends on the circumstances and objectives of the parties. Income-producing property can be good property to give away if the donor is in a higher income tax bracket than the donee. The advantage of this income shifting device is somewhat curtailed for children under age 14. See the discussion of the "kiddie tax" under the heading "WHEN IS THE USE OF SUCH A DEVICE INDICATED?" at number 6.

Property that is likely to grow substantially in value (e.g., life insurance, common stock, antiques and art, or real estate) is also prime property for giving since future appreciation can be removed from the estate and the gift can be made when the gift tax values (and therefore gift tax transfer costs) are lowest. However, EGTRRA 2001 repeals the estate tax for one year in 2010.

Property that has already appreciated should be given away if a sale of such property is contemplated and the donee is in a lower income tax bracket than the donor. Property with relatively low gift tax value and high estate tax value (such as life insurance) makes an excellent gift.

Generally, it is not a good idea to give away "loss property" (property that, if sold, would result in a loss) since the donee cannot use the donor's loss. The donor should sell that property, take the deduction for the loss himself, and give away the cash proceeds.

Although stock in a closely held corporation is often thought of as an ideal asset for gift purposes, care must be taken so that not too much stock is given away. The retention of too little closely held stock might cause an estate to fail the various percentage tests that may qualify it for preferential treatment, e.g., IRC Section 303 redemptions (see Chapter 41), or IRC Section 6166 installment payments of the federal estate tax (see Chapter 16), or the qualified family-owned business deduction (see Chapter 42).

Another type of property that might be given is property owned by the donor in a state other than his own state of residence, in order to avoid facing an ancillary probate at the time of the donor's death.

Be sure to consider the age, maturity, and experience of the donee in selecting the gift.

Question – Are there certain types of property that should not be given away?

Answer – It is extremely important to focus on the circumstances of the parties (particularly your client) before making a gift. Do not give away any asset if it will reduce the client's standard of living or financially (or psychologically) endanger his "comfort level." Particularly focus on the impact of the gift on the client's income and capital needs (both present and anticipated) as well as on the client's need for liquidity.

Be aware of the effect of gifts of stock or business or farm interests on qualification for favorable tax law breaks under IRC Section 303 (partial stock redemptions to pay death taxes–see Chapter 41), IRC Section 2032A (special use valuation of closely held business and farm real property–see Chapter 57), and IRC Section 6166 (extension of time to pay federal estate tax attributable to closely held business interest–see Chapter 16).

Perhaps more important than "what" to give is "how." Outright gifts should be made only after a great deal of consideration. A trust, custodial account, or some other form of property management arrangement is appropriate where:

(1) the beneficiary is unwilling or unable to invest, manage, or handle the responsibility of the gift;

(2) the beneficiaries are minors or are adults who lack the emotional or intellectual maturity, physical capacity, or technical training to handle large sums of money or securities;

(3) the donor does not want to significantly reduce the beneficiary's financial dependence on the donor;

(4) the property does not lend itself to fragmentation but the donor desires to spread beneficial ownership among a large number of people (e.g., real estate may be more valuable in some instances if it is not subdivided);

(5) the donor wants to limit the class of beneficiaries and prevent the donee from transferring the property to persons outside the donor's family;

(6) the donor wants to treat children or other relatives equally. A donor may own several parcels of property of equal value. If he gives each to different beneficiaries, one may go up and the other may go down in value. But if they are all placed into one trust and each beneficiary is given an equal share, they will all be treated equally.

(7) The donee may be subject to future creditors or divorce.

It is often recommended that small outright gifts be made over a period of time to allow beneficiaries to handle money and other assets under the guidance of the donor. Then larger amounts can be placed into trust, again during the donor's lifetime, so that the donor can watch how the trustee invests and manages the property. Lifetime gifts give the donor the opportunity to see how both the trustee and the beneficiaries handle assets and make investments. The donor can then make adjustments to his will and other estate planning vehicles accordingly.

Question – How does the donee of property compute gain or loss on that property if it is subsequently sold?

Answer – Where property is received by gift, the donee is generally required to take over the donor's basis in the property (this is often called a substituted or "carryover" basis).

In addition, carryover basis is allowed for the federal gift tax attributable to the appreciation element of the gift. The formula for computing this is:

$$\text{Gift Tax} \quad x \quad \frac{\text{Net Amount of Appreciation}}{\text{Value of Gift}}$$

For instance, assume property worth $100,000 was given by Rob Sterling to his son Aaron. Rob's basis was $40,000. Gift tax paid on the gift was $18,000. Appreciation on the gift was $60,000 ($100,000 - $40,000). The donee's basis is $50,800 [$40,000 + ($60,000/$100,000 x $18,000)].

If the donee sells property at a gain, he must pay income tax on such gain.

For purposes of determining loss, the donee's basis is the lesser of (a) the donor's basis, or (b) the fair market value of the property at the time of the gift.

Question – What is a "net gift" and what are its tax implications?

Answer – A net gift is a gift of property subject to some obligation or encumbrance. The "debt" or obligation against the property may exist before the transfer or arise at the time of the gift. Typically, a net gift results when the donee agrees, as a condition of the gift, to pay gift taxes on the transfer.

Netting the gift can be an attractive means of transferring property when a donor does not have cash on hand (and does not want to sell other property to raise cash) to pay gift taxes. A net gift is also useful when a donor wants to limit the extent of the gift to its net value.

For gift tax purposes, the gross amount of the gift is reduced by the amount of the gift tax the donee must pay. In other words, the amount of the gift tax that the donee pays reduces the value of the gift and gift tax is computed on the value of the remaining (net) amount. This means that the actual gift tax liability is lowered since the gift taxes paid reduce the value of the taxable gift. In computing the donee's gift tax liability, the donor's unified credit must be used.

The formula used to compute the donee's tax is: Tentative tax ÷ (1.00 + donor's rate of tax).

For instance, assume a retired, 66 year old, single donor living almost entirely from the income of $4,000,000 worth of tax-free municipal bonds, who made no prior gifts, made a gift of property worth $1,111,000. The gift was made to his niece on the condition that she pay the federal gift tax. In 2004, the tentative tax on a gift of $1,100,000 ($1,111,000 minus $11,000 annual exclusion) is $41,000 ($386,800 less a $348,800 unified credit). But the gift tax actually payable is $29,078 [$41,000 ÷ (1 + 41%)].

Note that the formula is not applicable if the gift is split between the donor and spouse, each of whom is in a different gift tax bracket because either or both have made prior taxable gifts. Quite often, however, you can determine the correct tax bracket by inspection and adjust for the bracket differential by computing the tentative tax in the correct lower bracket. In other situations you'll have to make trial computations using first the bracket indicated by the tentative taxable gift and then later using the next lower bracket.

If you have difficulty with making the computation, state your facts in a letter to the Commissioner of Internal Revenue (Actuarial Department), Washington, D.C.

For estate tax purposes, only the net amount of the gift will be considered in the estate tax computation as an adjusted taxable gift. The gift tax paid by the donee can be credited against the donor's estate taxes. EGTRRA 2001 repeals the estate tax for one year in 2010.

A net gift is treated for income tax purposes as a part sale/part gift transaction to the extent the donor is relieved from paying the gift tax liability. To the extent the donor is relieved of such liability he or she realizes an immediate economic benefit that is taxable.[15] Specifically, net gifts (made after March 4, 1981) will result in income tax to the donor to the extent the gift tax paid by the donee exceeds the donor's basis in the property.

Question – Can gifts made to a dying spouse cut estate taxes and boost up the basis of appreciated property?

Answer – The so-called "reverse gift" technique is still an appealing strategy where one spouse possesses most of the family wealth and the less affluent spouse is about to die. The wealthier spouse makes a gift of low basis assets to the dying spouse. This inclusion steps up the basis of the property and better utilizes the dying spouse's unified credit.

Note that if a decedent acquires appreciated property by gift within one year of decedent's death and that property passes directly or indirectly back to the donor (or to donor's spouse) from the decedent, the basis of such property is not stepped up. It remains the basis in the hands of the decedent immediately before the decedent's death.[16] But the technique will work if the decedent lives more than one year after the transfer or the property passes from the decedent to a child or some person other than the donor or the donor's spouse. EGTRRA 2001 repeals the estate tax for one year in 2010 and creates a modified carryover basis for property received from a decedent dying in 2010.

Question – What is the Crummey technique?

Answer – Typically, a gift in trust does not become immediately available to or enjoyable by beneficiaries; it is therefore a gift of a "future" rather than a "present" interest. Only present interest gifts qualify for the $11,000 (in 2004) annual exclusion allowed by the gift tax law.

Crummey (a case decided by the 9th Circuit in 1968) involved an irrevocable life insurance trust in which the beneficiaries were given the right to *demand*–each year–the lesser of (a) $4,000 or (b) the amount of the donor's transfer (usually an amount approximating the life insurance premiums necessary) to the trust. It was held that the beneficiaries' legal right to immediate use and enjoyment of the contributions to the trust made the transfers present interest gifts that qualified for the annual gift tax exclusion. (Most authorities feel that the trust should include a provision giving each beneficiary the right to demand the lesser of $5,000 or the amount of cash transferred to the trust.)

This Crummey technique is an important estate planning tool for four reasons:

First, it enables a donor to transfer money into a trust (to enable the trustee to pay life insurance premiums) gift tax free.

Second, the donor's potential estate tax is reduced by eliminating from the estate tax base the entire amount excluded under the $11,000 (in 2004)

annual exclusion. EGTRRA 2001 repeals the estate tax for one year in 2010.

Third, the technique is an ideal method of saving gift tax on gifts in trust to minors and works even if

(a) the minor beneficiary's right to demand immediate distribution of the contributed corpus is specified to be within a limited period of time, such as the calendar year of the gift to the trust,

(b) the beneficiary in fact does not withdraw the amount contributed to the trust and loses the right to withdraw it after the end of the year in which the gift is made,

(c) the minor beneficiary doesn't have a formal guardian.

Fourth, a gift in trust that qualifies for the annual exclusion by reason of a Crummey withdrawal power will also be shielded from the generation-skipping transfer tax if such power holder is given a separate share of the trust. EGTRRA 2001 repeals the generation-skipping transfer tax for one year in 2010.

The effectiveness of the Crummey gift technique and the rules regarding its use will be subject to "clarification" by case law and revenue rulings. One such clarification relates to the donee having a reasonable period of time in which to exercise the power to withdraw the funds and sufficient notice of the existence of the creation of the power.

These refinements can be dealt with by providing a reasonable period of time for exercise of the power to withdraw (e.g., 30 days) and actual notice to the donee or his or her actual guardian or legal guardian. The trust should be created (or subsequent gifts made to it) no later than November or perhaps very early December, but not in the last few days of December.

The Crummey trust gift technique is a very important aspect of estate planning (see Chapter 31).

Question – Does the purchase of property in joint names create a taxable gift?

Answer – It depends on the type of property and also the parties involved. Generally, when property is purchased with the funds of one party and the property is titled jointly, a completed gift is made. The most notable exceptions to this are the titling of property jointly between husband and wife (which because of the unlimited marital deduction is not a taxable event), and titling of joint bank accounts and United States Savings Bonds.

In the case of a joint bank account or United States Savings Bonds, a completed gift does not occur until the noncontributing joint owner draws upon the bank account or surrenders part of the bond for cash.[17]

Question – What techniques remain available to shift wealth and income to children to save taxes?

Answer – There are still many ways to shift both wealth and income and save taxes.

(1) Give a Series EE U.S. Savings Bond that will not mature until after the donee-child is age 14. No tax will be payable until the bond is redeemed. At that time the gain will be taxed at the child's relatively lower tax bracket. A child who already owns Series EE bonds and is reporting each year's interest accrual as income may elect to change to deferred reporting. However, once an election is made to change from annual reporting it may not be revoked for five years.

(2) Give growth stocks (or growth stock mutual funds) that pay little or no current dividends. The child will therefore pay no tax currently and can hold the stock until reaching age 14. Upon a sale after reaching age 14, the child will be taxed at the child's bracket.

(3) Give *deep discount* tax-free municipal bonds that mature on or after the child's 14th birthday. The bond interest will be tax free to the child and the discount (face less cost basis) will be taxed to the child at the child's bracket when the bond is redeemed at maturity.

(4) Employ your children. Pay them a reasonable salary for work they actually perform. Remember that the standard deduction for children who are dependents is the greater of (a) $800 or (b) *earned* income plus $250; but the standard deduction cannot exceed $4,850 for single individuals. [Numbers are as indexed for 2004.]

Regardless of how much is paid to the child, the business will have a deduction at its tax bracket, and the amount will be taxable to the child at the child's bracket. Furthermore, the child could establish an IRA to shelter income further.

(5) Consider the multiple advantages of a *term of years* charitable remainder trust for children over age 14 – so the income will be taxed to the child, but the grantor will receive an immediate income tax deduction.

(6) In making gifts to children consider support obligation cases such as *Braun*[18] and *Sutliff*[19]. Parents who can with ease meet the support needs of even an adult college-age child may be considered obligated to provide support. If UGMA (Uniform Gifts to Minors Act) or UTMA (Uniform Transfers to Minors Act) custodial funds or IRC Section 2503(c) trust funds are used to send a child to college, will the parent be taxed? Worse yet, do these cases mean that the custodian or the trustee violates a fiduciary duty by using such funds to pay for a college education when it's the parent's duty (thus making such funds unavailable for the very purpose for which they were intended)?

Assuming the support problems addressed above are not applicable, judicious use of an IRC Section 2503(c) trust (but not a UGMA or UTMA account) will allow significant income shifting. The trust can accumulate income while the beneficiary is under age 14 and avoid the kiddie tax. Although only the first $1,950 (in 2004) of that income (in excess of a $100 exemption) is taxed at the 15% rate, it may not be necessary to fund the trust with property generating more than $1,950 of income. This is so because the 2503(c) trust is designed to make distributions of principal and income to meet its funding objectives.

(7) Emphasis should now be placed on *convertible planning*–the use of a *value shift* followed at the appropriate time by an *income shift*. For example, a GRAT (Grantor Retained Annuity Trust–see Chapter 26) retains for a trust grantor the right to a fixed annuity for a specified number of years. At the end of that time all income and principal will go to the grantor's child (who by then will be 14 or older). None of the principal or appreciation will be in the grantor's estate if the grantor survives the trust term. (Consider a saving clause that terminates the trust in favor of the grantor if tax law is changed to provide

that a completed gift does not occur until the donor's interest is terminated.)

(8) Life insurance and annuity policies that stay within statutory guidelines (ask for written guarantee from home office) of life insurance should be particularly attractive assuming *loading* costs are relatively low and/or backended. This includes universal, variable, and traditional whole life of the single-, annual-, and limited-payment types. In the case of single premium whole life (SPWL), the entire single premium paid at purchase starts earning the declared interest rate immediately.

The cost of insurance and expenses are recovered by the insurer from the difference between the declared interest rate and the rate the insurer actually earns. If the policy is surrendered, any unrecovered expenses are deducted from the policy's cash values.

The owner can obtain cash values at any time by (1) surrender (gain over cost is taxable) or (2) loan (loan interest is probably nondeductible). Interest is charged at about the same rate credited on borrowed sums and is free of current tax. Earnings compound free of current taxation.

Unlike tax-free municipal bonds, there is no market risk and SPWL is highly liquid. A parent can purchase the product on his own life, which makes college education for the children more likely, and the parent does not have to give up control or make a gift. If the policy is a modified endowment contract, there could be adverse income taxes on both policy surrenders and policy loans.

(9) Concentrate on gift and estate tax saving devices such as the annual exclusion. Parents should consider giving $11,000 to $22,000 (as indexed for 2004) a year of non-income-producing assets to a minor's trust or custodial account; the assets could be converted into income-producing assets slowly after the child turns age 14. The fund can be self-liquidating and exhaust itself by the time the child finishes college or graduate school.

(10) If the parent's return shows a loss, will the child's return be affected by it? (The IRC is silent.)

(11) The custodial parent is often the mother, who may have less income (and therefore be in a lower tax bracket) than the father. But what about the logistics of tax return disclosure where the father is filing returns and paying tax for the children? (Suppose he doesn't want her to know how much he has put aside for the kids, and she doesn't want to reveal her income or her new husband's income. Furthermore, the filing father cannot prepare the children's returns until the mother prepares her returns.) What about multiple children from multiple marriages? Split custody?

Techniques for funding a child's education are covered in greater detail in our book, *The Tools and Techniques of Financial Planning.*

Question – Are all gifts, regardless of amount, entitled to the benefit of the graduated gift tax rates?

Answer – No. For gifts made in 2001 and gifts made after 2010, the benefit of the graduated estate and gift tax rates is phased out for large gifts (see rate tables in Appendix A).

This is accomplished by increasing the gift tax by an additional 5% for taxable amounts exceeding $10,000,000 up to the amount at which the average tax rate is 55% ($17,184,000 in 2001 and 2011). The additional 5% is imposed until the benefits of the graduated rates are recaptured.[20] The benefits of the graduated rates are, however, fully available for taxable transfers of less than $10,000,000. EGTRRA 2001 repealed the additional 5% tax for 2002 to 2010.

Question – What is a "qualified transfer"? Is it a taxable gift?

Answer – A qualified transfer means any amount paid on behalf of an individual:

(1) as tuition to an educational institution, or

(2) to any person who provides medical care with respect to such individual as payment for such medical care.[21]

A qualified transfer is not considered a gift for gift tax purposes and no gift tax return is required for these transfers.

Question – When a gift is made to a trust, how do you figure how many annual exclusions are available if the gifts are present interest gifts?

Answer – If a gift is made in trust, the donee is considered to be each beneficiary of the trust and not the trust itself. Therefore, there are as many annual exclusions as there are present interest beneficiaries. For example, Robin Scott creates an irrevocable trust for his three minor children. Each child is given an annual non-cumulative demand right to withdraw his or her pro-rata share of any contribution to the trust not to exceed $5,000. Robin contributes $15,000 to the trust. He is considered to have made a $5,000 present interest gift to each of his three children.

Question – If property is sold, are there gift tax consequences?

Answer – It depends. If the property was sold for less than adequate and full consideration, there is a gift to the extent the value of the property exceeds the value of the consideration received. An arm's length transaction among non family members is generally considered to be an exchange for adequate and full consideration. An intra family exchange may not be considered arm's length, and could result in a partial gift if not made for adequate and full consideration.

ASRS: Sec. 51; Sec. 55.

CHAPTER ENDNOTES

1. Treas. Reg. §25.2511-1(a); IRC Sec. 7872(f)(3).
2. IRC Sec. 1.
3. Treas. Reg. §25.2511-1(c).
4. Treas. Reg. §25.2511-1(c).
5. Treas. Reg. §25.2511-2(b).
6. IRC Sec. 2503(b).
7. IRC Sec. 2513.
8. IRC Sec. 2503(b).
9. IRC Reg. §25.2503-3.
10. IRC Sec. 2505.
11. Treas. Reg. §25.2513-1.
12. IRC Sec. 2523.
13. IRC Sec. 2512; Treas. Reg. §25.2512-1.
14. Treas. Reg. §25.2512-6.
15. See Rev. Rul. 75-12, 1975-1 CB 310 for examples of how to compute the net gift. *Diedrich v. Comm.*, 82-1 USTC §9419, 50 AFTR2d 82-5054 (S.Ct., 1982), aff'g 643 F.2d 499, 81-1 USTC §9249, 47 AFTR2d 81-977 (8th Cir. 1981), rev'g TC Memo 1979-441.
16. IRC Sec. 1014(e).
17. Treas. Reg. §25.2511-1(h)(4).
18 *Braun v. Comm.*, TC Memo 1984-285.
19. *Sutliff v. Sutliff*, 489 A.2d 764 (Pa. Super. Ct. 1985).
20. IRC Sec. 2001(c)(3).
21. IRC Sec. 2503(e).

Chapter 23

UNIFORM GIFTS/TRANSFERS TO MINORS ACTS

WHAT IS IT?

The Uniform Gifts to Minors Act (UGMA) provides that an adult, while he or she is alive, may make a gift of certain types of property, such as securities, money, or a life insurance (or annuity) contract to a minor by (depending upon the property) registering the property in the name of or delivering it to a custodian for the minor. The custodian may be the donor (except in the case of unregistered securities) or another adult person or trust company. Many states also allow gifts of real property, personal property and intangibles, and a few states permit transfers to custodians from other sources, such as trusts and estates, as well as lifetime gifts.

The Uniform Transfers to Minors Act (UTMA) allows any kind of property, real or personal, tangible or intangible, to be the subject of a custodial gift, and in addition permits transfers from trusts, estates, guardianships, and from other third parties indebted to a minor who does not have a conservator. Almost all of the states have replaced their UGMA laws with the more flexible UTMA.

Under both the UGMA and the UTMA, the minor immediately acquires both legal and equitable title to the subject matter of the gift held by the custodian.

Custodial gifts reduce or avoid many of the problems and expenses of outright gifts, trusts, or guardianship arrangements for minors.

WHEN IS THE USE OF SUCH A DEVICE INDICATED?

1. When a person would like to give money or property for a minor's benefit without giving it to him or her outright and without having to incur the expense of drafting a trust.

2. When a person would like to shift some of the income tax burden from his or her high tax bracket to a minor child's lower bracket.

3. When the $11,000 (in 2004) gift tax annual exclusion is desired.

4. When a parent would like to reduce his or her potential estate tax burden by shifting future appreciation in the value of an asset to a minor.

5. Where the donor does not object to the donee's receiving the property outright upon reaching the age specified in the relevant statute – generally 18 or 21, depending on state law and often on the nature of the transaction creating the custodianship. (In several states, the age for termination of at least certain custodianships can, within limits, be changed.)

WHAT ARE THE REQUIREMENTS?

1. Property must be transferred to a custodian who holds it as custodian for the minor under the relevant state's Gifts or Transfers to Minors Act.[1]

2. If there are two or more children to whom a parent wishes to make gifts, an account must be established for each child.[2]

3. Once made, a custodial gift is irrevocable.[3]

4. The property must be distributed to the child when he or she reaches the age specified in the relevant statute – generally 18 or 21.[4] (In several states, the age for termination of at least certain custodianships can, within limits, be changed.)

HOW IT IS DONE – AN EXAMPLE

Tony Arcangelo transfers his 10 shares of IBM stock to Mrs. Arcangelo as custodian for their son, Fred, by having the stock registered as follows: "Ginny Arcangelo as custodian for Fred Arcangelo under the *Pennsylvania* Uniform Transfers to Minors Act." Such a gift is a present interest gift and would therefore qualify for the gift tax annual exclusion. The future appreciation in the value of the stock, the future dividends earned by the stock, as well as the original gifted value of the stock would be out of Mr. Arcangelo's estate. Any dividend income or capital gains from sale of the stock would be taxed to Fred. (However, see tax implications below.)

WHAT ARE THE TAX IMPLICATIONS?

1. Income from any custodial property will be taxed to the minor whether distributed or not, except to the extent it is used to discharge a legal obligation of some other person. Where income produced by a custodial gift relieves an individual such as a parent of a legal obligation, the income is taxed to that person.[5] A parent's duty to support minor children varies among the states.

    If the minor is under age 14, all unearned income in excess of $1,600 (in 2004), although it will be taxed to the minor, will generally be taxed at the parents' tax bracket. The first $800 of a child's unearned income will bear no tax because of the child's standard deduction. The next $800 will be taxed to the child at the child's tax bracket and any excess will be taxed to the child at the parents' bracket. For children 14 and over, all unearned income will be taxed to them at their appropriate bracket.

2. The gift is one of a present interest and qualifies for the gift tax annual exclusion.[6] The exclusion will be allowed even though custodial property will not be distributed to the donee until age 18 or 21 (depending on the state).[7] It seems, though, that extending the custodianship beyond the donee's age 21 (which some states permit) may disqualify the gift for the annual exclusion.[8]

    Note that there is a growing trend in state divorce courts to assume that a financially well-off parent has a legal duty to send children to college, even if they are, under state law, adults. It is suggested that custodial income be accumulated until the child reaches college age. Income can then be paid out, semester by semester, in a series of unconditional checks. The child should deposit those checks in his own account and use the funds as needed. It may be that a trust or a state sponsored tuition program may be better for these purposes.

3. The value of property transferred will generally be included in the estate of a donee. So if the donee dies, assets in the custodial account will be includable in his or her estate.

4. Custodial property will be included in the estate of the donor if the donor appoints himself or herself as custodian and dies while serving in that capacity. Likewise, if the donor becomes successor custodian and then dies, the value of the property transferred will be includable in the donor's estate.[9] Further, the value of property, the income of which is used to satisfy a donor-parent's support obligations, could be included in the donor-parent's estate. A parent's duty to support minor children varies among the states.

5. State gift taxes must be considered. Most states do not have gift taxes, although nearly all have some form of estate or inheritance tax. Some of the handful of states with gift taxes have annual exclusions limited to less than the federal gift tax annual exclusion.

IMPLICATIONS AND ISSUES IN COMMUNITY PROPERTY STATES

Where community property is the subject of a gift under the Uniform Gifts to Minors Act, each spouse is considered to be the donor as to one-half the value of the property given. Thus, in the example given above, if the Arcangelos lived in a community property state, Mrs. Arcangelo would not be a good choice for custodian, because if she were to die, one-half of the gift made to Fred from their community property would be included in her estate on the basis of the rules relating to powers to alter, amend, revoke, and terminate trusts.

The same problems as discussed in Chapter 25 may arise if one spouse gives community property without the written consent of the nondonor spouse.

Typically, in community property states, a brother or sister of one of the parents may be a good choice for custodian.

QUESTIONS AND ANSWERS

Question – What types of property can be transferred to a custodian for the benefit of a minor?

Answer – In the few states that have retained the UGMA, at least money, securities (for example, stocks, bonds, evidence of indebtedness, certificates of interest or participation in an oil, gas or mining title or lease), certain life or endowment insurance policies, and certain annuity contracts may be the subject of a custodial gift. The general intention of the UTMA, on the other hand, is to allow custodial transfers of any interest in any kind of property from almost any source.[10] Because the laws of different states vary, it is important to check your own state's laws.

Question – Who may be a custodian?

Answer – Generally, the original custodian may be (depending on the transaction) the donor, an adult other than the donor, a trust company, or a bank with trust powers.[11] Because eligibility to serve as custodian is sometimes dependent upon the nature of the transaction creating the custodial property, and because the states' laws vary, it is important to check your state's statute.

Question – What use may be made of custodial property?

Answer – Under the UGMA, the custodian may use the custodial property for the support, maintenance, education, and benefit of the minor to the extent that the custodian in his or her discretion deems suitable and proper.

Under Section 14 of the UTMA, custodial property may be expended for the use and benefit of the minor, a more expansive use of custodial property than under the UGMA.

Question – May there be one custodial account for two or more minors?

Answer – No, a separate custodial account must be established for each beneficiary. Only one custodian can be appointed for each account.[12] However, any number of separate gifts may be made.

Question – Who receives the custodial property if a minor dies?

Answer – Custodial property passes to the administrator or executor of the minor's estate.[13]

Question – Where a life insurance policy on a minor's life is placed in a custodianship account, may the custodian be the beneficiary?

Answer – Under the UGMA, no. The beneficiary may be, depending upon the state, the minor, a member of the minor's family, or the minor's estate.[14] The situation under the UTMA is less clear. Generally a custodian can pay premiums on a custodial life insurance policy on the life of the minor only if the minor or the minor's estate is the sole beneficiary.[15] But some UTMA states let the custodian pay premiums on a custodial policy on the life of the minor even if the custodian is the beneficiary.[16] Otherwise the matter is unclear. Consult your state's statute.

Question – If a custodian dies before the minor is legally an adult, how is a successor custodian appointed?

Answer – Generally, if a custodian has designated a successor, that designee becomes the custodian. The revised UGMA seems to say that if the custodian has not picked a successor, an adult member of the minor's family, the minor's guardian, or a trust company will be appointed; if there is no guardian and the minor is at least 14, the minor can pick the successor – but if the minor does not pick a successor, the court (upon petition) will designate a successor; if the minor is not yet 14, the court (upon petition) will choose the successor. Under the UTMA, if the custodian has not picked a successor, the minor can pick the successor if the minor is at least 14; if the minor does not pick a successor or is less than 14, the minor's guardian will be appointed; if there is no guardian, the court (upon petition) will select a successor.[17] But the relevant state law must be checked.

Question – Must the custodian under the Uniform Gifts to Minors Act file an income tax return?

Answer – No fiduciary return is required by the custodian. This factor, as well as the fact that no trust agreement is required, makes the custodianship perhaps the least expensive and administratively the simplest method of transferring property to a minor.

Question – If an individual (an adult) purchases a life insurance policy on his or her own life, can he or she name the custodian of a minor as beneficiary?

Answer – Yes. Under the UTMA, the owner of a life insurance policy or annuity contract can name the custodian of a minor as beneficiary.[18] Some states' versions of the UGMA permit designating the custodian as beneficiary on at least some insurance policies and annuity contracts. This provides a means for a child to be beneficiary without appointing a guardian or creating a trust for the minor. State laws must be checked.

Question – Under either the UGMA or UTMA, can a custodian invest a minor's funds in life insurance?

Answer – Virtually all states that have a version of the UGMA or of the UTMA allow a donor to make custodial gifts of life insurance. However, not all states with versions of the UGMA specifically authorize the custodian to invest a minor's funds in life insurance. Particular state statutes must be checked.

Under the UTMA, the custodian can invest a minor's funds in life insurance. The custodian may invest in life insurance or endowment policies on:

(1) The life of the minor so long as the minor or the minor's estate is the sole beneficiary

(2) The life of another person in whom the minor has an insurable interest so long as the minor, the minor's estate, or the custodian is the irrevocable beneficiary[19]

State laws must be checked.

ASRS: Sec. 48.

CHAPTER ENDNOTES

1. E.g., Calif. Prob. Code Sec. 3909 (California UTMA).

2. E.g., Calif. Prob. Code Sec. 3910.

3. E.g., Calif. Prob. Code Sec. 3911(b).

4. E.g., Calif. Prob. Code Secs. 3920, 3920.5.

5. Rev. Rul. 59-357, 1959-2 CB 212; see also *Anastasio v. Comm.*, 67 TC 814 (1977) (New York UGMA), *aff'd without published opinion*, 573 F.2d 1287 (2d Cir. 1978).

6. Rev. Rul. 59-357, 1959-2 CB 212.

7. Rev. Rul. 73-287, 1973-2 CB 321.

8. See, e.g., *id.* (gifts terminating at age 18 qualify for the annual exclusion because IRC Section 2503(c) requires that property pass to the donee by at least age 21).

9. Rev. Rul. 59-357, 1959-2 CB 212; Rev. Rul. 70-348, 1970-2 CB 193; *Est of Prudowsky*, 55 TC 890 (1971), aff'd 465 F.2d. 62 (7th Cir. 1972).

10. See, e.g., the Prefatory Note to the UTMA, 8B U.L.A. 497, 499 (West 1993); UTMA Sec. 1(6) and the comment thereto, 8B U.L.A. 497, 507-508 (West 1993).

11. E.g., Calif. Prob. Code Sec. 3909.

12. E.g., Calif. Prob. Code Sec. 3910.

13. E.g., Calif. Prob. Code Sec. 3920.

14. E.g., Mich. Comp. Laws Ann. Sec. 554.454(10).

15. UTMA Sec. 12(c), 8B U.L.A. 497, 536 (West 1993).

16. See, e.g., N.C. Gen. Stat. Sec. 33A-12(c).

17. See UGMA (1966) Sec. 7, 8A U.L.A. 367, 404-405 (West 1993); UTMA Sec. 18, 8B U.L.A. 497, 548-549 (West 1993).

18. See UTMA Secs. 3, 9(a)(4), 8B U.L.A. 497, 515, 525 (West 1993).

19. UTMA Sec. 12(c), 8B U.L.A. 497, 536 (West 1993).

Part 5:

TRUSTS

Chapter 24

MARITAL DEDUCTION AND BYPASS – TRUSTS

WHAT IS IT?

The marital/non-marital trust (also commonly referred to as the "A-B trust" or more currently sometimes the "A-B-Q" trust) is an arrangement designed to give the surviving spouse full use of the family's economic wealth, while at the same time minimizing, to the extent possible, the total federal estate tax payable at the deaths of both spouses. The term "federal estate tax" as used in this chapter means the tax imposed by Chapter 11 of the Internal Revenue Code.

Married couples can usually eliminate federal estate taxes entirely at the death of the first spouse to die through a carefully considered plan capitalizing on the marital deduction coupled with the unified credit. The marital deduction is a deduction for gift or estate tax purposes for property passing to (or in a qualifying trust for) a spouse. The unified credit is a credit provided to each citizen or resident of the United States, which can be applied against either gift taxes or estate taxes.

The goal typically is to avoid "overqualification" of the estate for the marital deduction because of "underutilization" of the unified credit in the estate of the first spouse to die. The estate tax unified credit (there is no estate tax in 2010) is scheduled to increase as follows:

	Unified Credit	Applicable Credit Amount
2004-2005	555,800	1,500,000
2006-2008	780,800	2,000,000
2009	1,455,800	3,500,000
2010	NA	NA
2011	345,800	1,000,000

Current Planning Techniques

The most common arrangement for a marital/bypass trust is to place into the bypass trust an amount equal to the unified credit exemption equivalent (or applicable exclusion), because the tax on those assets will be eliminated by the unified credit. The assets in the bypass trust will not be taxed at the surviving spouse's death. The balance of the decedent's assets will go to the marital trust tax-free using the marital deduction, but those assets will be subject to estate tax at the death of the surviving spouse.

Some couples may prefer to have some tax paid at the death of the first spouse to die (since some of the taxed portion will be taxed at the lowest federal estate tax rates instead of being shifted to the surviving spouse's estate and added "on top" of the assets the survivor already owns). However, the desire to pay an "up front" tax will be the exception. Further, the surviving spouse may use up the additional assets received or give them away. The majority of "younger" couples may well decide to accept some possible penalty in estate tax rate in order to avoid tax altogether at the death of the first spouse to die. This is obviously an important decision that the estate planner must review at length with the husband and wife.

An important decision must be made as to how much of the marital deduction property should be subject to the surviving spouse's power to say where it goes at the survivor's death.

In general, the marital deduction can be obtained for property passing outright to a surviving spouse, or in a qualifying trust for the spouse. One type of trust gives the surviving spouse a right to income for life with a power to appoint the property to anyone the surviving spouse wishes. In a qualifying terminable interest property (QTIP) trust, the spouse is also given a right to income for life; however, the spouse need not be given a power of appointment over the property. Thus, with a QTIP trust, the first spouse to die can control where the property goes at the surviving spouse's death.

For estates where it is desired that *all* of the marital deduction property or *none* of it should be subject to the survivor's power of disposition at death, it will be satisfactory to have only one marital deduction or "A" Trust, since the same rules will pertain to all of the property.

However, in many estates, it may be desirable to use a QTIP trust for some or all of the estate to ensure that at least some of the marital deduction property passes to the decedent spouse's chosen beneficiaries at the surviving spouse's death. The balance of the marital deduction property would go to a separate trust (often called "Trust A") that would be controllable by the surviving spouse as to its disposition. Particularly for community property, where the survivor already owns half, it may be very helpful to obtain the marital deduction for all of the estate in excess of the unified credit equivalent (with the exempt portion going to the bypass (or "B") trust to avoid tax at the survivor's death), but to still provide that some of the deducted property will ultimately go to the children (or to the brothers or sisters of the first spouse to die if there are no children).

Thus, a formula will often provide for putting into the "B" or family trust the amount of the unified credit exemption equivalent ($1,500,000 in 2004) at the death of the first spouse. This trust can provide for income to the survivor (and if desirable, can even give to the survivor some limited power of disposition to other people and/or the power to take out each year the greater of $5,000 or 5% of the trust principal). Even so, property in this trust will generally escape taxation at the survivor's death. Obviously, the formula to achieve this is very important. Planners must be careful that the provisions for creating the bypass trust and the marital trust are appropriate in light of the changes made by EGTRRA 2001, including substantial increases in the estate tax unified credit in the years up to 2009 and repeal of the estate tax for one year in 2010.

If it is decided to have a zero estate tax at the first death, and if it is desired that the spouse have disposition powers over all or none of the other assets, all of the other assets can go to the marital or "A" trust.

However, if it is desired that the survivor have a power of disposition over only a portion of the assets, then the portion subject to the power can go into the typical marital or "A" trust, and the balance can go into a QTIP trust. Both trusts will qualify for the marital deduction and be included in the survivor's estate at death. Either or both of these trusts can provide for invasion of principal for the benefit of the survivor, but only the "A" trust will be subject to a power of disposition at the survivor's death.

In some cases, the couple may decide to also restrict the power of the surviving spouse so that some portion may only be appointed among family members. If the surviving spouse cannot appoint such property to herself or her estate, such portion would generally go into either a bypass or a QTIP trust.

Often the revocable A-B or A-B-Q trust takes the form of a life insurance trust coupled with a "pourover will." Here a revocable ("I can tear it up and forget about it") insurance trust is created during the grantor's lifetime. The trustee is named as the beneficiary of life insurance policies issued on the grantor's life. The grantor's will contains a provision to the effect that the grantor's residuary estate, what is left after payments of debts, expenses, taxes and specific bequests, is to be "poured over" into the living trust. (Think of a funnel. Life insurance passes outside of the funnel directly to the "pool of assets" at the bottom while noncontractual [probate] assets pass through the grantor's will into the top of the funnel and flow down to join the life insurance.)

The trust instrument provides that upon receiving the insurance proceeds from the insurance company and the residuary estate property from the pourover will provisions, the total principal will then be divided into two or three parts: a portion will go to the marital or "A" trust, a portion to the family or "B" trust, and if appropriate, a portion will go to the QTIP trust, which latter will qualify for the marital deduction but be distributed at the survivor's death as provided in the trust instrument (e.g., to the children).

The use of the trust can provide flexibility while achieving the long term goals of the family and minimizing death taxes.

Whether to use a revocable trust to also hold non-insurance assets is usually a question of whether or not the other assets should be subjected to the costs, delays, and publicity which usually accompany probate. Many practitioners in Northeastern states recommend the will as the instrument to dispose of most of the noninsurance assets. In Florida and on the West Coast, the trust is frequently used to control the disposition of all of the assets, with the goal of both estate tax minimization and also avoidance of probate.

WHEN IS THE USE OF SUCH A DEVICE INDICATED?

1. When it is the desire of the spouses that the survivor have full economic benefit of the family's wealth and that the aggregate death taxes payable at the deaths of both spouses be reduced. Where an individual leaves all of his property to his spouse, his estate may be "overqualified" for the marital deduction, as discussed below. Too much property may pass to the surviving spouse and thus be needlessly taxed at the surviving spouse's death. The reason for this result is that the surviving spouse has "ownership" of all of the family wealth and therefore it is taxable for federal estate tax purposes at the surviving spouse's death. If the surviving spouse merely had the "benefit" of all of the family wealth (i.e., an A-B or A-B-Q trust arrangement),

only the portion that qualified for the marital deduction at the death of the first spouse to die (or which was already owned by the surviving spouse) would be subject to federal estate taxes at the survivor's subsequent death.

In order to maximize the utility of this technique, the A-B or A-B-Q trust device can be designed to pass to the A trust or to the A and Q trusts together exactly enough property to reduce the federal estate tax in the estate of the first spouse to die to the lowest desired amount–even to zero. Any additional property subject to tax at the decedent's death and passing to the trust would automatically pass into the B (family or nonmarital) trust (portion) and escape death taxation at the death of the second spouse to die.

2. The overqualification problem referred to above results in passing more to the surviving spouse in property interests qualifying for the marital deduction than is necessary to keep the federal estate tax at the decedent's death to the minimum. Overqualification results in wasting (in whole or in part) the decedent's unified credit. For couples with estates over the amount that can have its tax "paid for" by the unified credit (e.g., $1,500,000 in 2004), wasting the unified credit of the first to die will likely result in a larger-than-necessary estate tax falling on the surviving spouse's estate at the surviving spouse's death. (An example later in the chapter illustrates the point.) A properly designed A-B or A-B-Q trust could eliminate or minimize this problem.

3. Where the couple plan to set up "generation-skipping trusts" (see Chapter 18) for the children, the exemption from generation-skipping transfer tax of the first spouse to die can be lost if the property passes outright to the surviving spouse, or in any form of marital deduction trust other than a qualified terminable interest property trust (QTIP trust).

4. Favorable state inheritance tax treatment may be obtained. Rather than giving property outright to a spouse, if property is placed in a "marital trust," even if the spouse has a general power of appointment over the assets in that trust, the laws of some states exclude such property for state death tax purposes from the estate of the holder of the power of appointment. For example, in Pennsylvania, even though a surviving spouse could reduce the property in a marital trust subject to a

general power of appointment to his own possession, it will not be subject to state inheritance tax at the death of such spouse. Thus, from a death-tax viewpoint, in some states it is preferable to leave a surviving spouse's assets in trust coupled with a general power of appointment over such assets, rather than leave the same amount outright, all other things being equal.

However, a majority of states provide for tax-free interspousal transfers but their laws parallel the federal estate tax rules to tax to the surviving spouse's estate the assets in the marital trust which avoided taxation at the first spouse's death.

5. When management of trust property is needed for the benefit of the surviving spouse or other trust beneficiaries.

6. Where it is desired to avoid probate. In addition to the tax reductions and management benefits described above, a person's estate can avoid the expense and delay of probate by transferring the title of the person's assets to a revocable inter vivos trust during the person's lifetime, which trust would also contain the death tax minimization provisions. Since the property is already transferred before the person's death, there is no need for the court to take charge and transfer the title and therefore no probate proceedings are required.

7. Where one of the spouses is a non-U.S. citizen. (See "Planning for Non-U.S. Persons," Chapter 20.)

8. Where the first spouse to die wants to be certain that his or her assets, while benefiting the survivor spouse, will eventually go to the children (or some other beneficiary) and not the husband, wife, or friend of the surviving spouse.

9. Where it is desirable to defer until the first spouse's death the decision of whether to pay some estate tax at that time in order to lower estate tax payments at the survivor's death.

WHAT ARE THE REQUIREMENTS?

Property that passes outright to the surviving spouse can qualify for the federal estate tax marital deduction. It is also possible to qualify certain types of trusts for the marital deduction. There are three types of trusts that will qualify for the marital deduction–the "power of appointment" trust, the "estate" trust, and the QTIP trust.

1. Power of Appointment Trust–Requirements

   (a) The surviving spouse must be entitled to all of the income produced by the assets of the trust (note that the law states "all of the income" not "all of the net income").

   (b) The income produced by the trust must be payable at least annually.

   (c) The surviving spouse must be given a general power of appointment (during lifetime, at death, or both) exercisable in favor of the spouse or the spouse's estate, or the creditors of the spouse or the spouse's estate.

   (d) The power must be exercisable by the surviving spouse in all events.

   (e) No person may have any power to appoint any part of the trust assets to any person other than the surviving spouse.[1]

   An estate owner can give property in trust subject to a power of appointment but require that–to exercise the power–the donee's will (or a different instrument) must make specific reference to such power. This is important because, in some states, a residuary clause will exercise a general power of appointment automatically unless there is a specific stated intention not to exercise it. In other words, absent the requirement that the donee of a power must specifically refer to it, in certain states the donee is deemed to have exercised the power in favor of his residuary legatee.

   The trust property will qualify for the marital deduction if the spouse is given the power to appoint at death (i.e., a testamentary power of appointment). The spouse does not have to be given the power to withdraw the principal during lifetime (i.e., an inter vivos power of appointment).[2]

   A trust should provide that the spouse has the right to demand that the trust be made income producing.[3]

2. Estate Trust–Requirements

   (a) The trust must provide for income to the surviving spouse for life (payable to, or accumulated for, the surviving spouse's benefit).

   (b) The remainder of the trust (both principal and any accumulated income) must be payable to the surviving spouse's estate at the surviving spouse's death.

   An estate trust falls outside the terminable interest rules because no interest passes to anyone other than the spouse and the spouse's estate.[4] This will enable the trustee to accumulate income or invest in non-income-producing property. However, accumulations will be taxed as part of the surviving spouse's estate at the surviving spouse's death along with the original corpus.

   The estate marital trust is indicated where (a) there is a need or desire to invest in non-income-producing property, (b) the survivor will not need trust assets or income during the survivor's lifetime, and (c) the property placed into the trust is not likely to appreciate substantially in value.

3. Qualified Terminable Interest Property (QTIP) Trust–Requirements

   (a) The same requirements regarding "all income to the surviving spouse and payable at least annually" apply here as they do in the power of appointment trust. Thus, the survivor must receive all of the current beneficial interest in the trust.

   (b) However, this trust need not have any power in the surviving spouse to appoint or control the disposition of the property.

   (c) There must be no power to shift any of the trust property to anyone other than the spouse during the spouse's lifetime.

   (d) The spouse must have the power to require the trustee to make the assets produce income.

   (e) The executor must elect to have the trust treated as a QTIP trust on the estate tax return by showing its value on Schedule M of the estate tax return.

   With this type of trust, the trustor can be certain that, at the death of the survivor, the property will go to the children or wherever the trustor decides (and not to the survivor's new spouse, which may be the case with the power of appointment trust or the estate trust).

4. Other General Requirements

   Assets in the marital trust must pass to or be held for the benefit of the decedent's surviving spouse–

the person who is married to the decedent at the decedent's death.[5] Although this requirement appears simple to determine, it has been the cause of extensive litigation because of the increasing frequency of divorce and persons living together without formal marriage that is now prevalent in our society.

Furthermore, the decedent's spouse must survive the decedent. In the event of a common accident (such as a plane crash) when it is impossible to ascertain who dies first, the Uniform Simultaneous Death Act (the law in most states) would raise a presumption that neither spouse survived the other and therefore, would defeat the marital deduction. The application of such act can be overcome by inserting into the documents creating the marital trust a survivorship clause that creates a presumption that, for purposes of the marital deduction, the spouse is deemed to survive if it is not possible to establish the order of deaths.[6]

HOW IT IS DONE – AN EXAMPLE

Although there are a number of ways to accomplish the same objective, the life insurance trust/pourover will combination is very popular in some parts of the country. In this arrangement, an individual establishes a trust during lifetime and names the trust as beneficiary of his insurance policies. When the grantor dies, the insurance maintained on his life is paid directly to the trust. The grantor's other assets pass through probate and are "poured over" by will into the trust. The one pourover trust is then split into two or three parts and different trusts are created; the "A" or appointment trust, a "B" or family (also called nonmarital or bypass) trust, and, in some cases, the "Q" or QTIP trust. Since the insurance is held in a trust that is controlled by the insured grantor, it is included in the insured's estate for estate tax purposes.

A – The Survivor's Property Trust or Power of Appointment Trust

The A trust, or power of appointment trust, used to be the primary vehicle for receiving the marital deduction assets before the advent of the QTIP trust, and is still used by some practitioners for that purpose. Where the QTIP trust is used for the marital deduction instead, Trust A often will hold the surviving spouse's property, particularly in community property states, in order to provide unified management of the assets under the umbrella of the estate planning trust.

Trust A would provide that all income from the trust be paid to the surviving spouse during his lifetime. Where Trust A is used as a marital deduction trust, the pourover trust in many cases would contain a funding formula to ensure that the power of appointment trust, together with any QTIP trust, would receive just enough property to reduce the federal estate tax at the death of the grantor to zero.

In some cases, such as very elderly couples with relatively large estates, the formula for trust division may be drafted so as to pay some estate tax at the first death with the property being taxed in relatively low tax brackets. If the clients wish to permit payment of some estate taxes at the first death, this is generally better arranged by having the marital deduction property pass to a QTIP trust, since a QTIP trust allows the decision as to the amount of tax to pay to be deferred until the death of the first spouse to die. At that time, the planner and the family can better assess whether the surviving spouse's financial security may be impaired by early payment of death taxes. However, with reductions in the estate and gift tax rates and increases in the estate tax unified credit from 2005 to 2009 and a repeal of the estate tax for one year in 2010, early payment of the tax may be a risky proposition.

The surviving spouse will usually be given the right to designate by will or other written instrument who will receive the corpus of the marital trust and such appointment may be made to anyone the surviving spouse chooses, including the surviving spouse's estate. The surviving spouse may also be given the right to withdraw any part of the corpus of the appointment trust during lifetime. At the surviving spouse's death, if the surviving spouse fails to exercise the power of appointment, the remaining corpus in the appointment trust will pass to the next takers under the trust.

B – The Bypass Trust

The second trust, the "B" or bypass nonmarital (family) trust is designed to receive property that is not allocated to the power of appointment trust, the estate trust, or the QTIP trust. An amount equal to the unified credit equivalent ($1,500,000 in 2004 if no taxable gifts have been made) is placed in this trust. The trustee may be directed to distribute the net income of this trust to the surviving spouse during his lifetime, or the income may be accumulated or directed to other persons in order to reduce the overall income tax effect on the family. Since the life estate terminates at the death of the surviving spouse, the surviving spouse did not create the life estate, and the surviving spouse has no "general" power of appointment over the trust property, there will be no transfer of property that is includable in the estate of the surviving spouse which is subject to the federal estate tax at death.[7] Thus, this trust "bypasses" the survivor's taxable estate and is, therefore, often called a credit equivalent bypass trust (CEBT).

The surviving spouse can be given a "limited" or "special" power of appointment under this family trust. For example, a surviving spouse might be given the right to appoint, at his death, all or any part of the assets in the family trust to a limited class of beneficiaries,[8] such as the children of the grantor. This means that the surviving spouse can distribute the assets in this trust only to the specified children, but can do so in any proportion the spouse desires. Such a power of appointment will not be classified as a "general" power and will not subject the corpus of the trust to federal estate taxes at the death of the holder, so long as the power cannot be exercised in favor of the holder of the power, his estate, his creditors, or the creditors of his estate.

The bypass trust can also provide a noncumulative right of withdrawal. Typically, this provision states that if the A and Q trusts are depleted, the surviving spouse is given the right to make limited withdrawals from the bypass or family trust. Usually, the surviving spouse is provided with a "noncumulative" (use it or lose it) right to withdraw each year the greater of (a) 5 percent of the corpus of the trust or (b) $5,000.[9] Such a power will not cause the entire corpus of the family trust to be includable in the surviving spouse's estate (although the amount subject to withdrawal in the year of the surviving spouse's death will be included in the surviving spouse's estate).

At the death of the surviving spouse, the family or bypass trust can continue to function for the benefit of the grantor's family, generally his children. The most common dispositive provision requires that the corpus of this trust be divided into separate equal trust funds for the benefit of the grantor's children, who will receive the net income currently and will have the right to demand distributions from principal at stated ages.

Often, rather than having all of the income from the family or bypass trust pass to the surviving spouse for life, a greater degree of flexibility may be obtained by utilizing a "spraying" or "sprinkle" clause. This provision authorizes the trustees (other than a trustee who is a beneficiary), at their discretion, to spray or sprinkle the net income of the bypass trust among the surviving spouse and the grantor's children or other issue (and sometimes spouses of issue) in any way the trustees determine. The trustees can thus apportion the trust's income among the beneficiaries having the greatest need.

Alternatively, since for federal income tax purposes the trust is a separate taxable entity, the trustees could be given the right to apportion the net income of the trust among the trust and the beneficiaries after giving consideration to their relative income tax brackets. Net income generated by the trust is determined substantially in accordance with the same rules applicable to individuals, with certain important differences. Although the taxable income of the trust is subject to the federal income tax, in arriving at taxable income the trust receives a deduction for distributions made or required to be made to beneficiaries during its taxable year to the extent such distributions do not exceed "distributable net income," as that term is defined.[10] By deflecting income to beneficiaries with little or no personal income, the overall income tax for the family can be reduced. However, unearned income of a child under age 14 in excess of $1,600 (in 2004) per year will be taxed at the parent's highest marginal rate (the "kiddie tax").

In addition to income tax savings, the estate tax at the survivor's death may be reduced by use of an "accumulation" provision. Instead of the nonmarital income being paid to the surviving spouse, it may be accumulated in the nonmarital trust and pass, free of estate tax, at the survivor's death. Meanwhile, the survivor has been permitted to invade the appointment trust (or the QTIP trust, if one exists) and consume some of the principal of those trusts (instead of using the income which has been accumulated in the nonmarital trust) and, thus, the appointment trust, and any QTIP trust that would be taxed at the survivor's death, would be reduced and the estate tax lowered. However, allowing large amounts of income to accumulate in the trust may result in adverse income taxation since the top federal income tax rate of 35%, which generally applies to individuals at incomes above $319,100, kicks in at the $9,550 income level for trusts (tax rate and amounts for 2004).

The "sprinkle," "spray," or "accumulation" clauses should be avoided where the bypass trust will be a recipient of stock in an S corporation. Only certain types of trusts are permitted to own S corporation stock, and a major requirement of such trusts is that the trust benefit only a single individual, and that such individual receive all the income from the trust on an annual basis.[11]

Another alternative, becoming more common in this era of divorce and remarriage, is to use the B trust as a means of benefitting persons other than the present spouse (e.g., children of a prior marriage). The trust can arrange for continued management of the trust assets for nonspousal beneficiaries, with delayed distribution, or provide for outright distribution.

Where the grantor has planned to take advantage of generation-skipping, the B trust would continue to exist during the lives of children (usually giving them some "nongeneral" powers of appointment as well as income rights) so that the property in the trust can qualify as an "exempt" trust and avoid taxation at the death of the children or grandchildren. If generation-skipping is planned, a federal estate tax return should be filed and an election made to allocate to the B trust some of the grantor's exemption from the generation-skipping transfer tax. See Chapter 18 regarding generation-skipping transfers.

Q – The QTIP Trust

When it is desired that an amount of estate in excess of the estate tax unified credit exemption equivalent (applicable exclusion) amount (which exempt amount goes to the "bypass" or family trust) should produce a marital deduction at the death of the first spouse to die, but should not be subject to a general power of appointment in the surviving spouse, a QTIP trust may be created.

By providing the opportunity for a marital deduction, placing assets in this trust can result in zero estate tax at the death of the first spouse to die to the extent that the trustee or executor elects to take the marital deduction.

All of the income of this trust must be paid, at least annually, to the surviving spouse. No provision for invasions of the trust can be made for anyone other than the surviving spouse or the marital deduction will be lost. Likewise, it would be lost if there were any condition (e.g., remarriage) or power in anyone else that could prevent the surviving spouse from receiving all the trust income for life. Additionally, the surviving spouse should be given a power to require the trustee to make all of the trust assets income producing.

The principal of this trust may usually be invaded for the benefit of the surviving spouse, but the trust terms may provide for first using up all or part of the marital or appointment trust before invading this trust.

To the extent that the trustee has elected to take a marital deduction at the first spouse's death for assets going into that trust (usually 100%), the QTIP (Q) trust will be included in the estate of the surviving spouse.[12] Thus, the marital deduction has merely deferred the tax on any assets in this trust that are not used up for the benefit of the surviving spouse.

Any assets remaining in this trust at the survivor's death will be distributed as the grantor decided, often subject to a nongeneral power in the surviving spouse as to the method of distribution among the issue of the marriage.

If generation-skipping is planned and if some of the grantor-decedent's exemption from the generation-skipping transfer (GST) tax is still available, provisions are usually made for the QTIP trust to be divided into two trusts: trust Q-E, which will contain property to which will be allocated some of the GST exemption; and trust Q-N, which will not be exempt from the GST tax and which therefore will often have different terms than trust Q-E. Use of this GST split-trust planning to allocate some of the GST exemption to part of the QTIP is accomplished by what is sometimes referred to as a "reverse QTIP election," discussed later in this chapter.

HOW DO THE MECHANICS OF THE A–B OR A–B–Q TRUST PLAN WORK?

First, an inter vivos (living) trust instrument can be drafted creating the different trusts to be used–(the A or appointment trust, the B or bypass (family) trust and, when desired, the Q, QTIP trust.) Although the terms of the trust are determined during the grantor's lifetime, it will not become operative until it is funded (until assets are placed into the trust) at the grantor's death (or prior to death if it is desired to use this living trust to avoid probate of the trust assets).

The trust is revocable because the grantor possesses the power to alter, amend, or revoke the trust until his death. Most states allow a grantor to name the trustee as beneficiary of his life insurance proceeds and obviates the need to transfer any other property to the trust during his lifetime.[13] But, if insurance is for some reason unavailable, many states recognize a trust funded with a nominal corpus such as $100, or even less.

Either as a means of shifting assets (through probate) to the trust, or as a backup provision to put into the trust any assets unintentionally not placed in the revocable trust during lifetime, the grantor will provide in his will that his probate property, after payment of settlement costs and any specific bequests or devises, will be added (poured over) to the trust. Where liquid assets may be insufficient to pay death costs and administration expenses, a useful provision in the inter vivos trust is to permit the trustee to make cash available to the estate executor through loans or the purchase of estate assets.

Alternatively, this same marital deduction arrangement can be created in a testamentary trust (i.e., one contained in the decedent's will and which will require the assets to be subject to probate).

The essential provision in the A-B or A-B-Q trust is known as the marital deduction formula. All property included in the decedent's probate estate or made payable to the inter vivos trust will be divided in accordance with the formula clause in the trust agreement. Such a clause might provide that the power of appointment, estate, and/or QTIP trust is to be funded in an amount equal to the amount necessary to reduce the federal estate tax payable to zero, or any other specified portion of the estate. The division of the marital deduction assets between the power of appointment "A" trust and the "Q" trust could be whatever the grantor desires (e.g., half of the separate property going to the "A" trust, and the other half going to the "Q" trust). In any event, the funding clause would also provide that the amount of any such marital portion should be reduced by any property includable in the estate that passes directly to the surviving spouse as a result of the grantor's death (e.g., a specific gift of personal effects, life insurance or jointly owned property).

The net balance of the trust corpus, after allocation of the marital deduction amount and after settlement costs are paid, is then allocated to the family ("B") trust.[14] Thus, the A-B/A-B-Q trust is really two or three trusts in one, administered under one trust agreement by the same trustees.

In some multi-marriage situations, the grantor-decedent may be unwilling to defer benefit (above the unified credit applicable exclusion bypass trust level) to children of a prior marriage or other persons until after the death of the present spouse. In that event, the formula may provide for paying some estate tax at the grantor-decedent's death so that assets may pass to these other beneficiaries at that time. Insurance on the grantor-decedent may be an appropriate way to insure that cash is available to pay the required tax when it is due.

Why is the A-B/A-B-Q trust arrangement such an important estate planning tool? To fully appreciate the

implications and tax savings potential, it is necessary to examine a typical estate.

A common and often unfortunate arrangement is one where the testator leaves all of his property to his spouse (either by will, by jointly owning all assets with the spouse, or a combination of the two) and therefore overqualifies for the marital deduction and wastes the unified credit available at the death of the first spouse to die. As a result, when the settlement of both estates is considered, federal estate taxes may be higher than if other arrangements were made.

Example: Philip Martin dies in 2004 and leaves his entire estate of $3,500,000 to his wife, Kaye, if living, otherwise to their son, Michael. Philip's primary objectives are to retain control of the estate during his lifetime, to provide an adequate income for his wife after his death, and to minimize his estate settlement costs. Assuming Kaye dies in 2007, and that she does not consume any of the principal of the estate, and further assuming that the value of the estate increases at the average rate of 7 percent a year, Figure 24.1 shows how much is paid in federal estate tax in each estate and how much after tax goes to Michael at Kaye's death.

A Typical Pre–1981 A–B Trust

Prior to 1981, the typical trust to avoid additional taxes over the death of a husband and wife was to pass to the surviving spouse outright or in trust an amount equal to the then marital deduction (the greater of one-half of the separate property or $250,000). This essentially resulted in equalizing the estates taxable at each death (assuming the couple's assets were acquired from the earnings of the first spouse to die), at least for larger estates. The concept of equalizing the estates is often the most economical method of minimizing the taxes over the deaths of both husband and wife where the estates of the husband and wife will be over the available equivalent exemptions. In other cases, however, the tax burden may be greater.

If Philip had a trust designed to equalize the estates (e.g., by giving to Kaye under the marital deduction one-half of his assets), Figure 24.2 shows how much would be paid in federal estate tax in each estate and how much would pass to Michael on Kaye's death (same assumptions as stated in the previous example).

Figure 24.1

	ESTATE MARITAL PLANNER All To Spouse Plan	
	Estate of First Spouse	Estate of Second Spouse
Adjusted Gross Estate (Year: 2004)	$3,500,000	$0
Year of Death	2004	2007
Adjusted Gross Estate (Growth Rate: 7%)	$3,500,000	$4,287,650
Marital Deduction	- $3,500,000	- $0
Taxable Estate	$0	$4,287,650
Adjusted Taxable Gifts	+ $0	+ $0
Computation Base	$0	$4,287,650
Tentative Federal Estate Tax	$0	$1,810,243
Gift Tax on Adj. Tax. Gifts	- $0	- $0
Unified Credit	- $555,800	- $780,800
Federal Estate Tax	$0	$1,029,443
Net Estate at Death	$0	$3,258,208
Value of Net Estate at Second Death	$0	$3,258,208
Net Total	$3,258,208	
Total Tax	$1,029,443	

Source: Trust Calculator (part of *The Ultimate Trust Resource*, a National Underwriter Company publication)

A Typical Post–1981 A–B or A–B–Q Trust to Reduce the Tax at the First Death to Zero

If Philip had wished to be certain that no federal tax were paid at his death, regardless of the size of his estate, he could have provided for an amount of marital deduction to go to Kaye which would exactly equal the amount of deduction needed to reduce his federal estate tax to zero. This is called the "zero tax marital deduction." In that event, Figure 24.3 shows the amount of federal tax that would be paid in each estate and how much would pass to Michael upon Kaye's death.

Comparison of Plans

Savings in federal estate taxes generally occur at the survivor's death. The federal estate tax payable in Philip's estate is the same in his overqualified arrangement (example 1) as it is in the Post-1981 A-B (or A-B-Q) trust arrangement (example 3)–in both cases it is $-0-. Actually, the savings in federal estate taxes occur in Kaye's estate. The trust arrangement accomplishes this because the equivalent exemption amount at Philip's death is never taxed in either estate.

The second arrangement is "optimum" for the first spouse's death (zero estate tax then, regardless of the size of the estate), but it can result in more overall tax if the spouse's estate exceeds the unified credit exemption equivalent and the spouse does not use up some of the estate or give some of it away during her lifetime.

Electing to Pay Some Tax

In some cases, there can be some tax saving by paying tax early, where property is increasing in value. For example, if an asset now worth $100,000 is projected to be worth $500,000 at the second death, it is usually much more economical to pay the tax based on the current $100,000 value than on the $500,000 it will be worth later.

The drawback to the "old A-B" arrangement (Figure 24.2) is that the tax is *forced* to be paid at the first death. However, if a QTIP trust is used, the executor will have a right to elect how much of the property over the amount sheltered by the unified credit will be subject to tax–none of it, all of it, or any amount in between! Thus, the QTIP allows you to keep your options open, and decide at death how much, if any, tax to pay. If the loss

Figure 24.2

	ESTATE MARITAL PLANNER Estate Equalizer Plan	
	Estate of First Spouse	Estate of Second Spouse
Adjusted Gross Estate (Year: 2004)	$3,500,000	$0
Year of Death	2004	2007
Adjusted Gross Estate (Growth Rate: 7%)	$3,500,000	$2,143,825
Marital Deduction	- $1,750,000	- $0
Taxable Estate	$1,750,000	$2,143,825
Adjusted Taxable Gifts	+ $0	+ $0
Computation Base	$1,750,000	$2,143,825
Tentative Federal Estate Tax	$668.300	$845,521
Gift Tax on Adj. Tax. Gifts	- $0	- $0
Unified Credit	- $555,800	- $780,800
Federal Estate Tax	$112,500	$64,721
Net Estate at Death	$1,637,500	$2,079,104
Value of Net Estate at Second Death	$2,006,008	$2,079,104
Net Total	$4,085,112	
Total Tax	$177,221	

Source: Trust Calculator (part of *The Ultimate Trust Resource*, a National Underwriter Company publication)

of the funds used to pay the taxes will not impair the survivingspouse's security, substantial saving could be realized by paying some tax early. Again, the planner will need to weigh the potential tax savings against the increasing unified credit and the possibility of repeal of the estate tax.

IMPACT OF THE REVERSE QTIP ELECTION

The generation-skipping transfer (GST) tax, discussed in Chapter 18, is having an increasing impact on the design of the QTIP trust in new estate plans. The plan must be designed in such a way as to obtain the maximum use of the GST exemption that is available to all clients. For 2004 to 2009, the generation-skipping exemption will equal the unified credit applicable exclusion, so that in a typical plan, the bypass trust will receive the unified credit applicable exclusion amount and a like amount of generation-skipping exemption will be allocated to that trust in order to shelter it from generation-skipping taxes. However, after 2010, the unified credit applicable exclusion will be $1,000,000, and the generation-skipping exemption will be $1,000,000 indexed for inflation. At that time, the gen-

eration-skipping exemption will be more than the unified credit applicable exclusion amount.

Even in 2004 to 2009, it is still possible that the GST exemption and unified credit applicable exclusion will be unequal at death. For example, a person may have made a large lifetime gift that will reduce the value of the bypass trust below his or her available generation-skipping exemption.

In such cases, the question arises of how to fully use the decedent's excess generation skipping exemption. Congress has provided that the exemption can be allocated to a QTIP trust, on the basis of what is called the "reverse QTIP election." Under that election, even though a marital deduction is claimed for a QTIP trust, the estate can elect to treat the trust, solely for GST purposes, as if it is still part of the decedent's taxable estate. In that case, the GST exemption can be allocated to it and shelter it from any future GST tax, as discussed in Chapter 18.

However, the law provides that the reverse QTIP election can only be made as to a "separate" QTIP trust. This means that if the total amount to be allocated to the QTIP trust for marital deduction purposes exceeds the

Figure 24.3

ESTATE MARITAL PLANNER Credit Shelter/Marital Deduction Plan		
	Estate of First Spouse	Estate of Second Spouse
Adjusted Gross Estate (Year: 2004)	$3,500,000	$0
Year of Death	2004	2007
Adjusted Gross Estate (Growth Rate: 7%)	$3,500,000	$2,450,086
Marital Deduction	- $2,000,000	- $0
Taxable Estate	$1,5000,000	$2,450,086
Adjusted Taxable Gifts	+ $0	+ $0
Computation Base	$1,5000,000	$2,450,086
Tentative Federal Estate Tax	$555,800	$983,339
Gift Tax on Adj. Tax. Gifts	- $0	- $0
Unified Credit	- $555,800	- $780,800
Federal Estate Tax	$0	$ 202,539
Net Estate at Death	$1,500,000	$2,247,547
Value of Net Estate at Second Death	$1,837,564	$2,247,547
Net Total $4,085,111		
Total Tax $202,539		

Source: Trust Calculator (part of *The Ultimate Trust Resource*, a National Underwriter Company publication)

GST exemption available, it will be necessary to create two QTIP trusts, one to offset the remaining GST exemption, and the other to take advantage of the remaining marital deduction.

Example: For the Philip Martin case, assume the total value of the decedent's taxable estate is $2,500,000 in 2004, and he made a previous taxable gift of $825,000. The remaining $675,000 of his unified credit applicable exclusion will be allocated to a Bypass trust; $1,825,000 to a QTIP trust. If the executor chooses to allocate $675,000 of the $1,500,000 exemption to the Bypass trust, and $825,000 to the QTIP, it will be necessary to split the one QTIP trust into two trusts, one in the amount of $825,000, and one in the amount of $1,000,000. According to private rulings, these trusts may have identical terms.

To implement this planning, most wills and trusts now contain specific provisions for dividing one QTIP trust into two shares, frequently based on a formula to reflect the amount of GST exemption the executor elects to allocate to the QTIP.

AB TRUST VERSUS ABQ TRUST

In some cases, pre-1982 trusts were amended to take advantage of the new optimum marital deduction (no tax due at first spouse's death) by merely changing the provisions allocating assets between trusts A and B so as to reflect the unlimited marital deduction and the unified credit. The result under this AB trust arrangement is that the estate of the first to die will often pass the unified credit applicable exclusion amount ($1,500,000 in 2004) to trust B and the remainder to trust A, subject to the surviving spouse's right to say where it goes at his or her death.

Figure 24.3 shows the results of this AB trust arrangement for Philip Martin's $3,500,000 estate with only $1,837,564 required to be paid to Michael at Kaye's death and $2,247,547 available for Kaye to shift at her death to Butch, her new husband, a result that Philip may not desire.

By changing the marital deduction to a QTIP marital deduction in Figure 24.3 and employing an (A)BQ trust arrangement, Philip can still provide for zero estate tax at his death, provide for Kaye during her lifetime, and still preserve the remaining estate ($4,085,111) for Michael at Kaye's death.

WHAT ARE THE TAX IMPLICATIONS?

1. For a typical revocable intervivos trust, no gift tax is payable upon creation of the trust since the grantor, at all times, has retained the right to terminate the trust.[15]

2. After death, the assets that qualify for the marital deduction (the assets actually going into the power of appointment, estate, and/or "Q" trust) are includable in the decedent's gross estate for federal estate tax purposes, but since they qualify for the marital deduction, they are not subject to estate tax.[16] In many situations the assets of these trusts will be minimal since the available credit will reduce the marital deduction amount and property passing outside the will may be sufficient to satisfy the marital deduction remaining. For example, if in 2004 the decedent's adjusted gross estate is $1,725,000, the optimum marital deduction is $225,000 ($1,725,000 less the effective exemption of $1,500,000 = $225,000). If the decedent left $350,000 worth of life insurance proceeds to his wife, she would already have received more than the maximum optimum marital deduction. It is important to remember that the marital deduction portion, which is established by formula, can be given outright to the surviving spouse instead of in trust.

3. Assets that are not used to fund the marital deduction trusts (A and Q) are, by formula, placed into the family or bypass trust. The value of these assets is includable in the grantor's estate for federal estate tax purposes, but the available unified credit will actually result in zero tax. Further, since the surviving spouse receives no more than the income (and perhaps certain limited powers of appointment) from the bypass trust and did not transfer the property to the trust, at the surviving spouse's death these assets will not be taxed again.[17]

4. During the grantor's lifetime, income produced by any of the assets transferred to a revocable inter vivos trust will be taxed to the grantor since no irrevocable gift had been made and the grantor remained the owner of trust assets and income for both estate and income tax purposes. At the grantor's death, the income produced by trust assets will be taxable to the trust or to the income beneficiary depending on whether the income is accumulated by the trust or paid out to the income beneficiary.[18]

5. In California and certain other states that have placed limits on real property tax increases, certain transfers of the real property will cause the loss of such limits. However, transfers to revocable trusts where the owner-grantor still has the beneficial ownership and control of the property will not cause a problem. It is at the owner-grantor's death, when the trust becomes irrevocable, that the property tax laws may cause an increase in property tax, a circumstance that must be anticipated and that sometimes can be avoided.

6. EGTRRA 2001 is increasing the estate tax unified credit exemption equivalent in steps from $1,000,000 in 2002 to $3,500,000 in 2009. Also, the generation-skipping transfer tax exemption equals the estate tax exemption equivalent in 2004 to 2009. Both taxes are repealed for one year in 2010. With all of these changes, drafting for bypass and marital trusts will need to be much more flexible. QTIP elections and disclaimers may also be used to help balance funding of bypass and marital trusts.

IMPLICATIONS AND ISSUES IN COMMUNITY PROPERTY STATES

Where the draftsman is dealing with community property, it should be noted that one-half of the property already belongs to the surviving spouse, and will not be subject to the "pour over" provisions of the will of the first spouse to die, unless the first spouse specifically indicates his desire to effect distribution of both halves of the community, *and* the surviving spouse acquiesces freely in that distribution.

To the extent the surviving spouse elects to retain his community half of the property outside the trust, then a problem of split ownership and management arises, with the survivor owning one-half of the assets, and the trustee of the trust owning the other half. If the surviving spouse does allow his half of the community property to pass to the trust, it would typically go into the "A" or power of appointment trust, so the survivor retains control over how the assets are distributed during lifetime or at death.

The marital deduction rules apply to community property as well as separate property states, so community property state couples may also elect to defer the payment of any federal estate tax until the survivor's death.

Where a marital deduction is used, it will reduce the tax at the first spouse's death, but it may increase the tax at the second death if the surviving spouse does not use up the marital deduction portion during his lifetime, and result in somewhat higher overall taxes for both estates. However, most couples would prefer to minimize the tax at the first spouse's death in order to leave more assets available for the survivor's support, and take the risk of having slightly higher overall taxes.

In both community and common law states, holding property in joint tenancy (tenancy by the entirety) with right of survivorship between spouses will result in the property going outright to the surviving spouse, regardless of the provisions of the decedent's will. The marital deduction provisions may be drafted to reduce the marital deduction by the value of the assets passing outside the trust and thus still result in the optimum marital deduction amount passing to the spouse, so long as the assets passing outside the will do not exceed the optimum marital deduction amount. However, holding large amounts of property in joint tenancy can defeat the trust planning to a very significant degree since such holdings can be more than the optimum marital deduction and reduce the first to die spouse's estate to less than the unified credit applicable exclusion amount (thus resulting in a portion of the unified credit being wasted).

In many instances, a couple living in a community property state may have separate property as well as community property, and both kinds of property must be considered in determining the amount that will be optimum for the marital deduction.

The laws in Louisiana are unique and particular care should be taken to obtain counsel knowledgeable in Louisiana law and general tax law if a couple settles in or has community property located in Louisiana.

In any event, it is very important for persons who have an estate plan drafted with only separate property in mind to have the plan reviewed and most probably redrafted upon becoming a resident of a community property state.

QUESTIONS AND ANSWERS

Question – What are the disadvantages of an A-B / A-B-Q trust?

Answer – First, if the trust is an inter vivos trust and is currently "funded" (properties placed in the trust during the lifetime of the grantor), then trustee's fees must be paid. This fee can often be minimized or avoided if the grantor serves as his own trustee, which is permissible in some jurisdictions, or reserves the right and obligation to administer trust assets during lifetime–unless disabled.

Second, after the death of the grantor, the surviving spouse cannot have unlimited control of, or unlimited access to, the assets that have been placed in the nonmarital trust(s). However, it is permissible to give the surviving spouse the right to invade principal, at his own discretion, to the extent of a noncumulative right to withdraw up to 5 percent of the corpus or $5,000 annually, whichever is greater.[19] If the surviving spouse is the trustee and if such spouse needs funds for his support, education, or maintenance, in addition to the income of the nonmarital trust and $5,000 or 5 percent of the trust's capital, then the trustee can be authorized to invade principal for such purposes. This use of an ascertainable standard would prevent him from being taxed on the trust property.[20]

Furthermore, the trustee (assuming the trustee was an independent party) may be given a power in its sole and absolute discretion to distribute principal to the surviving spouse for any reason satisfactory to the trustee. However, here the surviving spouse has no right to demand a distribution of principal. A further power that can be given to the surviving spouse is the right to appoint during lifetime or at death to and among a specified class of individuals (but this class must exclude the spouse, his estate, his creditors, and the creditors of his estate).[21] For example, the grantor could state that his spouse has the right to appoint by will to and among the grantor's issue, parents, or siblings. However, where the surviving spouse has a right to income from the trust property for life and a power of appointment over trust property during life, exercise of the power of appointment during life will result in a taxable gift of the spouse's life estate in any property appointed to someone else.

Question – What functions does the trustee have in the A-B / A-B-Q trust?

Answer – The trustee will hold the assets placed in the trust during the lifetime of the grantor(s) and will serve as the recipient of life insurance payable to it, as well as property "poured over" from the decedent's will. The trustee will be the legal owner of the assets of both trusts and manage the trusts in accordance with the provisions of the trust agreement. The trust agreement can be either extremely flexible or severely restrictive, depending on the objectives of the grantor.

The trustee's primary duties are twofold: (1) to manage and invest the trust corpus in such a manner as to generate income for the beneficiaries; and (2) to preserve the corpus. The Uniform Prudent Investor's Act has been adopted by many states. It contains guidelines (and requirements) for investments by a trustee. The trust instrument may in some cases modify the rules under which the trustee will make investments.

In many instances, a corporate fiduciary may be indicated, either as sole or cotrustee, if the estate is sizable or if conflicts in interest are likely to arise between individual trustees.

Question – What are the different ways to write provisions that qualify for the maximum or optimum marital deduction?

Answer – The first is for the testator to leave a specific dollar amount bequest; however, this technique is not recommended since it is impossible, in most cases, to arrive at a dollar amount that will exactly equal the desired marital deduction at the time of the grantor's death with any degree of accuracy.

The second way is use of a funding formula that is geared to the marital deduction provisions of the Internal Revenue Code. Either a pecuniary formula bequest or a fractional share bequest is the formula clause to use. A pecuniary formula bequest is used where the testator wants the spouse to receive a fixed dollar amount (a general legacy). An example of such a clause follows:

"If my wife, Deborah, survives me, I give, devise, and bequeath to my trustees (in trust "A" or trust "Q") an amount exactly sufficient–and no larger–to reduce the federal estate tax due at my death to the lowest possible amount, after taking into consideration all other property passing to my wife or which has passed to my wife and which qualifies for the marital deduction and after allowance of all applicable credits."[22]

Under this clause, the property qualifying for the marital deduction is paid to the marital ("A" and/or "Q") trusts. The remainder of the property, after satisfying the marital deduction, is bequeathed to the family trust.

Instead of a fixed amount, the testator may want to give the spouse a fractional share of the estate. Here, the sum that goes to the spouse may fluctuate after the decedent's death and, in essence, the spouse receives a share in the residue. In this case, the clause (the fractional share bequest) should read somewhat as follows:

"If my wife, Deborah, survives me, I give, devise, and bequeath to my trustees (in trust A or trust Q) the following fractional share of my residuary estate (before such estate is diminished by the payment therefrom of estate, inheritance, or death taxes):

(a) The numerator of the fraction shall be exactly sufficient–and no larger–to reduce to the lowest possible amount the federal estate tax due at my death, after taking into consideration all other property passing to my wife or which has passed to my wife and which qualifies for the marital deduction and after allowance of all applicable credits.

(b) The denominator of the fraction shall be the value of my residuary estate, before it is diminished by the payment therefrom of estate, inheritance, or death taxes."

IT IS IMPORTANT TO NOTE THAT MANY OTHER PROVISIONS ARE REQUIRED, IN ADDITION TO THE FUNDING FORMULA, IN ORDER TO OBTAIN THE MARITAL DEDUCTION.

Question – Which type of funding formula is preferable?

Answer – This depends upon the circumstances. The most important thing to look at is the type of assets the grantor owns.

If there is a probability of a substantial increase in value during the period of settlement of the trust or estate, then the pecuniary formula clause may have some benefit if it gives the residual amount (after the marital deduction) to the bypass trust. Under these circumstances, any increase in the size of the estate can be shifted to the bypass trust and thus reduce taxation at the survivor's death.

If there is a possibility that the estate may drop in value, then it may be wise to use a pecuniary formula clause that specifies the exact amount to go to the bypass trust and lets the residue go to the marital deduction trust.

In any use of a pecuniary formula clause, it is possible to recognize an income tax where assets that have increased in value since the date of death are used to satisfy distribution to a trust. In these circumstances, a gain can be recognized and taxed.

A fractional share clause avoids the problem of any recognition of income tax gain upon transfer of assets to a trust to fund a bequest. Additionally, it shifts any increase or decrease proportionately to both the marital deduction trust and the bypass trust.

Question – What are some of the advantages of an estate trust over a power of appointment trust?

Answer – Under the estate trust, it is not necessary that all of the income be paid out to the surviving spouse. Instead, some of the income can be accumulated and kept in the trust. Where there is concern for use of income and a great deal of income available, an estate trust may provide more protection for the survivor.

Additionally, the estate trust may in some cases make it easier to retain assets that are not producing income for the trust.

Question – What are the advantages of having the marital deduction pass to a QTIP trust?

Answer – Many advantages exist. One important one is giving the trustee the power to determine how much of the trust is to be taxed at the death of the first spouse to die. Under the QTIP provisions, it is possible to arrange to have additional estate tax, so that there will be a tax to pay that is larger than the unified credit. This may be helpful in having the tax paid early and therefore having this additional property out of the way of inflation for the survivor's lifetime.

A second important benefit of a QTIP trust is that the trustor can be certain that, at the death of the survivor, the property will go where the trustor wanted the property to go and not merely to the survivor's new friend or new spouse (as is the case under the power of appointment trust where the surviving spouse must be given a power to appoint the property at the survivor's death).

Where it is desirable to give the surviving spouse some control over the disposition of assets, e.g.,

among the mutual issue of the decedent and survivor, the QTIP trust permits the modification of the disposition by the survivor if the trustor wants that to happen.

Last, the QTIP trust is the only optimum marital arrangement by which the grantor's full exemption from the generation-skipping transfer tax can be preserved for the next generation, with the property still benefiting the surviving spouse during the survivor's lifetime and still have no estate tax due at the grantor's death. For deaths occurring in 2004 to 2009, this will be less important because the generation-skipping transfer tax exemption will be equal to the estate tax unified credit exemption equivalent and a reverse QTIP election may not be required.

Question – Can an A-B/A-B-Q trust be set up in an individual's will?

Answer – Yes. This is called a testamentary trust (as contrasted to an inter vivos trust). Rather than have a separate trust instrument and a separate will, the two are combined into the will document. The provisions of the testamentary trust are generally the same as the inter vivos trust provisions.

Question – Are there any drawbacks to setting up the A-B/A-B-Q trust in the will rather than as an inter vivos document?

Answer – Use of a testamentary trust will *require* a probate at the grantor's death. Often there is a delay in probating a will. If the trust were part of the will, it would not function until the will was probated. Thus, if life insurance were payable to a testamentary trust, there could be a delay in getting funds into that trust.

Some states for inheritance tax purposes will tax insurance payable to a testamentary trust as opposed to proceeds payable to an inter vivos trust. This will unnecessarily cause additional costs to the estate.

Question – In a marital deduction trust, what constitutes income that must be paid to the surviving spouse?

Answer – Traditionally, income is generally monies earned by the trust assets, such as dividends, interest, and rental income from real property, and did not include increases in capital. However, many states have adopted the Revised Uniform Principal and Income Act that allows a trustee to invest for "total return". For example, a trustee might invest in a fund that focuses on growth and yields less income than might otherwise be realized. Under the Revised Uniform Principal and Income Act, the trustee could then allocate some of that appreciation to income to make up for the smaller yield, subject to the trustee's fiduciary duty to treat the income beneficiary and the remainderpersons fairly.

ASRS: Sec. 51, ¶280.

CHAPTER ENDNOTES

1. Treas. Reg. §20.2056(b)-5.

2. Treas. Reg. §20.2056(b)-5(a)(4).

3. Treas. Reg. §20.2056(b)-5(f)(4).

4. *Comm. v. Ellis*, 252 F.2d 109 (3rd Cir. 1958), rev'g in part, 26 TC 694.

5. Treas. Reg. §20.2056(a)-1.

6. For special rules that apply when one spouse is a non-U.S. citizen, see Chapter 24.

7. Rev. Rul. 66-86, 1966-1 CB 216.

8. Treas. Reg. §20.2041-1(c).

9. IRC Sec. 2041(b)(2); Treas. Reg. §20.2041-3(d)(3).

10. IRC Secs. 651, 661.

11. Additional requirements must be met in order for a trust to be a qualified subchapter S trust, as outlined in IRC Section 1361(d).

12. IRC Sec. 2044. The property in the trust includable in the surviving spouse's estate under Section 2044 is considered property acquired from a decedent, and thus in the hands of the one to whom the property passes from the surviving spouse has a basis equal to the fair market value of the property at the date of the surviving spouse's death or alternate valuation date (see the discussion of basis in Chapter 19). IRC Secs. 1014(b)(10), 2044(c).

13. It is extremely important to check the applicable state law to be sure that merely naming a trust as life insurance beneficiary will serve as adequate corpus.

14. See Rev. Proc. 64-19, 1964-1 CB 682.

15. Treas. Regs. §§25.2511-2(b), 25.2511-2(c).

16. IRC Sec. 2056.

17. *Est. of Milner v. Comm.*, 6 TC 874 (1946).

18. IRC Secs. 641, 652, 662.

19. IRC Sec. 2041(b)(2); Treas. Reg. §20.2041-3(d)(3).

20. Treas. Reg. §20.2041-1(c)(2).

21. Treas. Reg. §20.2041-1(c)(1).

22. Certain additional provisions must be added to this "funding" formula in order to guarantee the marital deduction. See, e.g., Rev. Proc. 64-19, 1964-1 CB 682.

Chapter 25

SECTION 2503(b) AND 2503(c) TRUSTS

WHAT IS IT?

An IRC Section 2503(c) trust is a gift tax tool that enables a grantor to make a gift to a minor in trust and still obtain the gift tax annual exclusion. The use of this irrevocable funded trust for gifts to minors eliminates many of the following practical objections to outright gifts:

1. Brokers are reluctant to deal in securities owned by minors since minors may disaffirm either a purchase of stock that subsequently falls in value or a sale of stock that later rises in value.

2. Property titled in a minor's name is, to a large extent, "frozen." It is difficult to sell or exchange that property since a minor's signature on a real estate deed gives the buyer no assurance of permanent title.

3. Guardianship must be used to avoid many of the objections of an outright transfer to a minor, but a guardian must generally post bond and account periodically to a local Orphans' (sometimes called Surrogate's or Probate) Court.

Another gift tax tool that enables a grantor to make a gift to a minor in trust and still obtain the gift tax annual exclusion is the IRC Section 2503(b) trust, discussed in the question and answer section of this chapter.

WHEN IS THE USE OF SUCH A DEVICE INDICATED?

When a client wishes to make a gift to a minor child and:

1. When the client's income tax bracket is high and the minor's income tax bracket is relatively low. Significant income shifting (resulting in significant income tax savings) is possible once the child reaches age 14.

2. When the client owns an asset that is likely to appreciate substantially over a period of time and does not want the appreciation includable in his gross estate.

3. When use of the gift tax annual exclusion is desirable.

WHAT ARE THE REQUIREMENTS?

1. A gift to a minor through a Section 2503(c) trust will be considered a gift of a present interest (so the gift will qualify for the gift tax annual exclusion) if the income and principal is available for distribution to or on behalf of the beneficiary at any time prior to the time the beneficiary reaches age 21. (Regardless of when a person becomes an adult under state law, the "magic" age is still 21 for Section 2503(c) purposes.)

2. Unexpended income and principal must be distributable to the beneficiary when that individual reaches age 21.

3. If the beneficiary dies before age 21, accumulated trust income and corpus must go to the minor's estate or appointee pursuant to a general power of appointment.[1]

4. Even if the minor is legally unable to exercise a power or to execute a will because the minor is under legal age, this fact will not cause the transfer to fail to satisfy the above conditions. Furthermore, it is permissible to provide that the trust will continue beyond the donee's 21st birthday, as long as anytime after reaching age 21, the donee can obtain the property in the trust if he wishes. Thus, the trust property does not have to be forced on a trust beneficiary upon reaching age 21.[2]

WHAT ARE THE DISADVANTAGES?

1. Expenses entailed in drafting the trust.

2. Expenses involved in filing tax returns and estimated quarterly payments (cost depends on complexity of returns and time entailed).

3. A Section 2503(c) trust can have only one beneficiary; this means money can't be transferred from the fund of a child who "goes astray" to the fund of a child who "has seen the light."

4. The assets in a Section 2503(c) trust must be distributed (or made available for distribution) to the beneficiary at age 21.

5. The Section 2503(c) trust is irrevocable; the grantor must relinquish total control to obtain tax savings.

HOW IT IS DONE – AN EXAMPLE

Jeff Mandell transfers stock in his closely held corporation to three trusts for his three minor boys. Assuming the trusts qualify under Section 2503(c), the irrevocable transfer of stock annually to the trusts will be considered gifts of a present interest. This will allow Jeff to obtain the $11,000 (in 2004) gift tax annual exclusion and therefore minimize or eliminate any gift taxes.

Gifts, to the extent they qualify for the annual exclusion (without taking gift splitting into account), reduce the value of Jeff's estate and the income from any dividends paid on the stock is taxed currently either to the trusts, if accumulated, or to the children, if distributed. Such trusts are often used to start children on a life insurance program by providing the trusts with sufficient cash each year to pay premiums for the insurance on the boys' lives. Alternatively, trust income could be used to purchase nonnecessaries or be accumulated and used to help provide nonnecessaries when the children reach college age.

WHAT ARE THE TAX IMPLICATIONS?

1. If the income of the trust is distributed (or required to be distributed) each year, it is taxable to the beneficiary.[3] Otherwise, to the extent income is accumulated, it will be taxed to the trust.[4]

2. Gifts to the trust constitute a present interest. Therefore, the gift tax annual exclusion of $11,000 (in 2004) applies as long as the conditions mentioned above are met.

3. To the extent the transfers exceed or otherwise do not qualify for the gift tax annual exclusion, they may not result in estate tax savings. This is because the taxable portion of any gift is added back in the estate tax computation as an "adjusted taxable gift"

at the date of gift value (with an offset against estate tax for gift tax which would have been payable on the transfer). Nevertheless, a benefit from the gift may result because the property brought back into the computation as an adjusted taxable gift is valued as of the date of the gift. Appreciation on property from the date it is placed in trust will be removed from the grantor's gross estate.

For instance, if a single individual gives his son $211,000 worth of stock in 2004, $200,000 would, after the donor's death, be considered an adjusted taxable gift in his estate ($11,000 qualifies for the gift tax annual exclusion). That would be true even though the stock had appreciated in value to $300,000 by the time of the individual's death. The appreciation in value, $100,000 ($300,000-$200,000) would never enter the estate tax computation.

Generally, the gross estate of a decedent does not include the value of transfers made by a decedent within three years of his death.[5] However, transfers made within three years of death of interests in property that would have otherwise been included in the gross estate under IRC Sections 2036, 2037, 2038, or 2042 are included in the gross estate at their date of death values. An unfavorable aspect of the law is that a transfer of insurance by the insured within three years of death continues to be includable in the gross estate.

Further, the entire value of the Section 2503(c) trust will be includable in the grantor's estate if the grantor is the trustee at the time of his death. It may also be includable if the income from the trust is used to satisfy such grantor-parent's duty to support the beneficiary.

IMPLICATIONS AND ISSUES IN COMMUNITY PROPERTY STATES

Where community property is the subject of a gift into a Section 2503(c) trust, each spouse is considered as being the grantor of one-half, by reason of the community ownership. For that reason, it is important that neither spouse be named as the trustee or successor trustee of the trust in order to avoid the problem of having the trust property included in the grantors' estates (see second question and answer below). In some states, if one spouse transfers community real or personal property to a trust for the benefit of a third party, such spouse must obtain the written consent of the nondonor spouse prior to such transfer or the gift could be entirely set aside.

QUESTIONS AND ANSWERS

Question – If it is likely that the grantor will make only one gift and that gift will be a relatively modest amount of marketable securities and there is little likelihood that further gifts will be made in subsequent years, should a Section 2503(c) trust be used?

Answer – No. Generally, the complexities and expenses of creating such a trust contra-indicate its use for small gifts or "single shot" gifts. In this type of situation, the use of the Uniform Gifts to Minors Act (UGMA) or the Uniform Transfers to Minors Act (UTMA) might be a more appealing alternative. However, where it seems likely that additional gifts will be made in future years, and a substantial amount of valuable property will ultimately be transferred to the minor, additional flexibility is called for and indicates the use of a Section 2503(c) trust.

The type of property in question may affect which device will be used. For example, regulations provide that stock in an S corporation may be held by a custodian under the Uniform Gifts to Minors Act.[6] However, if a gift of stock in an S corporation (see Chapter 46) is made to a Section 2503(c) trust, the corporation's election may be automatically terminated, because generally a trust may not be a shareholder of an S corporation. The law does allow a trustee to be an S corporation shareholder, but only if (a) the grantor or other individual is treated for income tax purposes as the owner of the trust property under IRC Sections 671 to 678 (a so-called "grantor trust"); (b) such a grantor trust continues after the grantor's death (limited to a period of two years after death); (c) the trust receives the stock under a will (a so-called "testamentary trust" and it holds S corporation stock only up to a maximum of two years after the stock is transferred to the trust); (d) the trust was created primarily to vote stock (a so-called "voting trust"); (e) the trust is a qualified subchapter S trust (QSST) (see last question and answer); or (f) the trust is an electing small business trust (ESBT).[7]

One reason a Section 2503(c) trust is often used instead of the Uniform Gifts to Minors Act is custodianship; UGMA provides that only one person may be custodian and specifies how a successor custodian may be named. But if a trust is created, the grantor may designate a line of succession of trustees and may provide for two or even more trustees to act together.

Question – Are there any adverse tax consequences if the grantor acts as the trustee of a Section 2503(c) trust?

Answer – Yes. If the grantor acts as trustee and dies in that capacity before trust assets have been fully distributed to the beneficiary, the assets in the trust may be includable in the grantor's estate (the same result occurs if the donor appoints himself as custodian under the Uniform Gifts to Minors Act or the Uniform Transfers to Minors Act and dies while serving in that capacity before the custodianship ends). The same result occurs where the grantor (or donor) dies while serving as successor trustee (or custodian).

For example, where the grantor is appointed successor trustee upon the death of the first trustee, the corpus is taxed in the grantor-trustee's estate because of the trustee's power to "alter, amend, revoke or terminate" the trust. Even if the only power retained is the ability to advance principal to the beneficiaries from time to time in the discretion of the trustee, the grantor, as trustee, has the power to accelerate the termination date. In essence, this is the power to terminate the trust and, therefore, adverse estate tax consequences occur if the grantor is the trustee or one of the successor trustees (or the custodian in case of transfer under the Uniform Gifts to Minors Act or Uniform Transfers to Minors Act).[8]

Question – If a father places dividend-bearing securities into a Section 2503(c) trust for his minor son using an independent bank as trustee, what types of expenditures of income would cause the income to be taxed to the father?

Answer – If the income is or may be used to pay premiums on a life insurance policy on the life of either the grantor or the grantor's spouse, or if it is used for the support of a minor whom the grantor is legally obligated to support, then such income will be taxed to the grantor (father).[9] Note that the use of capital to pay premiums would not cause the grantor to be subject to income tax on trust income. Further, if the minor is under age 14, unearned income in excess of $1,600 (in 2004), while taxed to the minor, is taxed at the parent's tax bracket.

Question – In addition to giving the beneficiary the continuing right to compel distribution upon reaching 21 is there any other arrangement that can avoid a mandatory distribution of principal and income to the beneficiary at age 21?

Answer – Yes. The beneficiary can be given a right during a *limited period* of time (i.e., 30 to 60 days), starting on his 21st birthday, to compel immediate distribution of the trust corpus by giving written notice to the trustee which, if not exercised, will permit the trust to continue by its own terms. Keep in mind that a beneficiary's power to compel distribution will cause the beneficiary to be treated as the owner of the trust for income tax purposes. This power may also lead to adverse gift and estate tax consequences to the beneficiary.[10]

Question – What is an IRC Section 2503(b) trust?

Answer – A Section 2503(b) trust is one that requires a mandatory distribution of income to the trust beneficiary on an annual or more frequent basis. All or portions of gifts to such trusts will qualify as gifts of a present interest and thus are eligible for the gift tax annual exclusion. For example, arbitrarily assuming a 5.0% Section 7520 interest rate, if the trust provides income for life to the donee to be distributed at least annually and if the donee is age eleven, then based on government valuation tables (see Appendix B) the amount of the gift which will be considered as a present interest if $10,000 was put into a Section 2503(b) trust would be $9,390 (the actuarial value of an 11 year old's right to income on $10,000 paid annually for life).

In some respects a Section 2503(b) trust is more flexible than either a Section 2503(c) trust or a custodianship account because a Section 2503(b) trust does not require distribution of principal and unexpended income at age 21 or sooner. Furthermore, a Section 2503(b) trust can last for the lifetime of the beneficiary or for any lesser period of time. Also, unlike the case with a Section 2503(c) trust or a custodianship, under a Section 2503(b) trust, the principal does not ever have to be paid over to the income beneficiary. Trust principal can go to a different donee specified by the grantor of the trust or can go to a person specified by the income beneficiary.

As income is earned by a Section 2503(b) trust, it must be distributed to the trust beneficiary. However, it can be deposited in an UGMA/UTMA custodial account and used for the benefit of the minor or left to accumulate in the custodial account until the minor reaches majority. At that time, the accumulated income will be turned over to the beneficiary. Each year, as it is earned, the income of the trust will be taxed to the minor except to the

extent it has been used to discharge a support or other legal obligation of the minor's grantor-parent.

If the minor is under age 14, income will be taxed to the minor, but (with respect to unearned income in excess of $1,600, as indexed for 2004) at the parents' top bracket. If the minor is 14 or older, all income (earned and unearned) is taxed to the minor at the minor's bracket.

For gift tax purposes, the entire amount placed into such a trust is treated as a gift. The gift is divided into two portions: an income portion and a principal (remainder) portion. The income portion will qualify for the $11,000 (in 2004) annual exclusion while the balance is considered a future interest gift and will not qualify for the exclusion.[11] To protect the annual exclusion for the income portion, the trust instrument should specifically deny the power of the trustee to invest in non-income producing property.[12]

Question – Is it possible to make a gift into a trust that can retain the property for a child past age 21 and still have the entire gift qualify for the annual exclusion?

Answer – Yes; based on the *Crummey*[13] case, if the donee has an immediate, unfettered, and ascertainable legal right at the time the gift is made to take out the amount put in, then the gift will be considered a present interest gift and qualify for the gift tax annual exclusion.

Ordinarily, failing to exercise a power to take property out of a trust (where the trust goes on under some circumstances to someone else) is a gift by the donee to the extent of the value that goes to someone else. However, there is a specific exception that ignores the gift consequence to the donee where the power is to appoint (i.e., to give) to oneself no more than the greater of $5,000 or 5% of the trust corpus.[14] To come within this rule, this type of trust gives the beneficiary the right to remove only this "5 or 5" amount each year (on a non-cumulative basis). However, the $5,000 limit is less than the amount of the annual exclusion.

There may be other persons (e.g. grandparents, uncles, aunts, etc.) who would like to make gifts to the trust. It is most probable that Crummey trusts can deal with these large gift potentials, while still avoiding a gift when the donee does not exercise his power, by giving the donee a power to appoint the trust at his death to anyone other than himself (or his estate, creditors or estate creditors).[15] This will bring the non-appointment trust assets into the donee's taxable estate, but that is not usually an unacceptable condition.

Note that gifts to grandchildren may be subject to generation-skipping transfer tax. See Chapter 18.

Question – Is a Section 2503(c) trust a good receptacle for holding stock in an S corporation?

Answer – In general, a Section 2503(c) trust is not an eligible shareholder of S corporation stock unless it also qualifies as a qualified subchapter S trust (QSST) or a grantor trust under IRC Section 678.

QSST

A QSST is defined in IRC Section 1361(d) as one that:

1. Owns stock in one or more S corporations (and may hold other types of assets).

2. Can distribute income only to one individual (who must be a United States resident or United States citizen).

3. Has trust terms requiring that

    (a) there can be only one beneficiary at any given time;

    (b) if corpus is distributed during the term of the trust, it can be distributed only to the individual who is at that time the current income beneficiary;

    (c) if an income beneficiary dies, the income interest itself will end at that death or upon the earlier termination of the trust; and

    (d) if the trust ends before the income beneficiary dies, all the assets of the trust must be distributed to that income beneficiary.

4. Requires an election to be made by the income beneficiary (or the income beneficiary's legal representative) to have the QSST qualify as such. (Once that election is made, it is irrevocable and can be revoked only if the IRS consents.)

That election must be made by each income beneficiary as he or she becomes one. Separate elections must be made if the stock of more than one S corporation is held in the trust.

If the requirements described above are met, the income beneficiary of a QSST (which can be set up during the grantor's lifetime or by will) is treated as the owner of the stock. The consequence is that all items of income, gains, losses, deductions, and credits pass directly from the S corporation to the minor beneficiary.

What are the advantages of a QSST? A gift of S corporation stock can be made to a minor through the trust without incurring the disadvantages of outright ownership. (Of course, if such a gift is made to a minor, the QSST election must be made by the legal representative of the minor.) This enables an individual to split income among family members while at the same time eliminating the gift from inclusion in his gross estate. So both income shifting and wealth transfers are possible through the QSST.

Unlike a custodianship, a QSST can continue beyond age 18 (or 21) and can last as long as the grantor directed it to last. This means that if the minor dies before the trust terminates, the trust can continue for the lives of a number of successive income beneficiaries and does not have to force trust assets into the estate of the deceased income beneficiary.

Section 678 Trust

The QSST is not the only alternative to outright and UGMA or UTMA gifts. An "IRC Section 678 trust" can also be an eligible S corporation stock shareholder. The criterion for favorable tax treatment under this type of trust is that the beneficiary must have unrestricted power "exercisable solely by himself to vest the corpus or the income therefrom in himself." In other words, the beneficiary will be taxed on the income from the S corporation held by the trust if he has the right to take both income and corpus whenever he wants. There must be no restrictions on the beneficiary's right to exercise a withdrawal power. A trust can also be considered a Section 678 trust if the beneficiary has not exercised a Crummey power to withdraw and has retained certain powers under IRC Sections 671 to 677 (e.g., beneficiary is trustee who has discretionary power to distribute income, either alone or with a nonadverse party).

A Section 678 trust can be created by a parent or grandparent who transfers S corporation stock to it for the benefit of a minor. The minor would be given an unrestricted power to withdraw income or corpus for his own benefit (or a Crummey withdrawal power and another power under IRC Sections 671 to 677).

How are gifts to QSSTs and Section 678 trusts taxed for gift tax purposes? The answer is that from a gift standpoint, a contribution to either trust will be considered a completed gift. Such gifts can qualify for the gift tax annual exclusion either by meeting the requirements of Section 2503(c) or by including a Crummey withdrawal power.

Estate Tax Implications

Will the property in a QSST or Section 678 trust be includable in the estate of a beneficiary? The answer in the case of a QSST beneficiary is that if the beneficiary is given only income rights, assets remaining in the trust at the time of the beneficiary's death will not be includable in his estate.

In the case of a Section 678 trust, inclusion depends on how the trust became qualified under Section 678. If the beneficiary is given a general power of appointment (the power of withdrawal) over all or a portion of the trust, the property subject to that power at the time of the beneficiary's death will be includable in his estate. Also, if the beneficiary exercised or released the power and retained an interest in the trust (e.g., a life estate) such that had the beneficiary been the owner of the property the property would have been includable in the powerholder's estate under IRC Sections 2035 to 2038, the property is includable in the powerholder's estate. The lapse of a Crummey withdrawal power is not treated as a release of the power if the lapse does not exceed $5,000 or 5% of the property subject to the power.

The QSST and the Section 678 trust offer two ways to shift both business-generated income and wealth to minors at minimal gift tax cost.

ASRS: Sec. 51 ¶230.2(a).

CHAPTER ENDNOTES

1. Treas. Reg. §25.2503-4.
2. Rev. Rul. 74-43, 1974-1 CB 285.
3. IRC Secs. 652, 662.
4. IRC Sec. 641; Treas. Reg. §1.641(a)-2.
5. IRC Sec. 2035.
6. Treas. Reg. §1.1361-1(e)(1).
7. IRC Secs. 1361(b)(1)(B), 1361(c)(2), 1361(d), 1361(e).
8. IRC Secs. 2036, 2038; *Est. of O'Connor v. Comm.*, 54 TC 969 (1970).
9. IRC Sec. 677.
10. Rev. Rul. 74-43, 1974-1 CB 285.
11. Treas. Reg. §25.2503-3(b); *Herr v. Comm.*, 35 TC 732 (1961), aff'd. 303 F.2d 780 (3rd Cir. 1962), acq. 1968-2 CB 2. See also *Pettus v. Comm.*, 54 TC 112 (1970); *Est. of Levine v. Comm.*, 526 F.2d 717 (2nd Cir. 1976), rev'g. 63 TC 136.
12. See *Stark v. U.S.*, 345 F. Supp. 1263 (W.D. Mo. 1972), aff'd 477 F.2d 131 (8th Cir. 1973), cert den.
13. *Crummey v. Comm.*, 397 F.2d 82 (9th Cir. 1968). See Chapter 30 on Crummey trusts.
14. IRC Sec. 2514.
15. Let. Ruls. 8545076, 8517052.

Chapter 26

GRANTOR RETAINED INTEREST TRUSTS (GRAT, GRUT, QPRT)

WHAT IS IT?

A grantor retained interest trust, as its name implies, is an irrevocable trust into which the grantor places assets and retains an interest for a fixed period of years. Principal, at the end of the specified period of years, will pass to a noncharitable beneficiary, such as a child or grandchild of the grantor.

In a grantor retained annuity trust (GRAT), the grantor retains a right to payment of a fixed amount for a fixed period of years. In a grantor retained unitrust (GRUT), the grantor retains a right to payment of a fixed percentage of the value of the trust property (determined annually) for a fixed period of years.

A grantor retained income trust (GRIT), which was commonly used for income property before the adoption of IRC Section 2702, is now limited to transfers of a personal residence or certain tangible property, such as a painting, in situations where the grantor retains the use of the property during the term of the trust. In the case of the personal residence GRIT, the trust will usually be a qualified personal residence trust (QPRT).

In all of these types of trusts, the grantor is essentially making a current gift of the right to trust assets to the remainder person at a specified date in the future. If the grantor survives the term selected, significant tax as well as other transfer cost reductions may be realized with the GRAT and GRUT. However, with respect to most GRITs, a grantor will now be treated as making a gift of the entire property transferred to trust (rather than a gift of the discounted value of the remainder). A GRIT holding a personal residence (such as a QPRT) is a notable exception to this rule.

WHEN IS THE USE OF SUCH A DEVICE INDICATED?

1. A GRAT, GRUT, or QPRT is particularly useful where the client is single and has a substantial estate upon which federal estate taxes are certain to be paid. Wealthy widows or widowers, divorced individuals, or other unmarried persons can use such a trust as a "marital deduction substitute."

2. A married couple with an estate in excess of the couple's combined unified credit equivalent can use a GRAT, GRUT, or QPRT to eliminate or reduce taxes on the death of the second spouse to die. The larger and more rapidly appreciating these estates are, the more effective such a trust would be.

3. A GRAT, GRUT, or QPRT is effective where income producing property is located in more than one state and unification and probate savings are desired. The GRAT, GRUT, or QPRT would serve to transfer ownership in a manner that would avoid ancillary administration.

4. A GRAT, GRUT, or QPRT will protect assets from a will contest, public scrutiny, or an election against the will if the grantor survives the trust term.

5. A GRIT is a useful technique when a client wants to purchase certain tangible assets such as a work of art, retain the right to display it in his or her own home, and have it pass to a specified person immediately and without probate at death. (However, if the grantor is unable to establish the value of the retained interest through comparable rentals, the gift of the transferred remainder will equal 100% of the value of the transferred property).

6. A GRAT, GRUT, or QPRT can serve as an alternative to (or be used in conjunction with) a recapitalization or other freezing technique that has the added advantages of gift tax leverage and possible estate tax savings.

7. When there is a high probability that the client will outlive the trust term that is needed to obtain a low present value gift to the remainder person.

8. When the client has assets so substantial that a significant portion can be committed to a remainder person without compromising his own personal financial security.

9. When the client has a high risk tolerance and a strong incentive to achieve gift and estate tax savings (rather than taking the safer but more costly approach of making an immediate gift).

WHAT ARE THE REQUIREMENTS?

1. An irrevocable trust must be established. A GRAT or GRUT must provide that the grantor retains the right to annuity or unitrust payments for a specified number of years (there is no limit to how few or how many years, although some have suggested that a one year term might not be permissible). Payment of the greater of an annuity or unitrust amount is permissible. As noted below, the longer the specified term of the trust, the greater the value of the retained interest and therefore the lower the taxable gift the grantor is making to the ultimate beneficiaries.

2. Evidence should be obtained of the value of the assets placed in the GRAT or GRUT. It is recommended that one or more qualified appraisers value the property shortly before it is placed into trust.

3. The grantor should be given a mandatory annuity or unitrust interest. The trust should specifically provide that the trustee has no discretion to withhold payments from the grantor (or possession of the trust property from the remainder person). Payments should be made annually or more frequently.

4. The grantor should be given only the annuity or unitrust interest (or possibly a noncontingent reversion). There is no requirement that the fixed annuity amount be the same for each year. The only requirement is that the annuity paid in a given year not exceed 120% of the amount paid the prior year. In any case, the exact amounts must be specified in the trust instrument itself. The trustee should generally be specifically prohibited from making distributions in excess of the annuity or unitrust amounts. While a GRAT or GRUT can provide for payment of income in excess of the annuity or unitrust amount to the grantor, the value of the gift of a remainder interest is not reduced by the value of such an excess income provision.

5. If the asset placed into the GRIT is a home in which the grantor resides, a written lease should be entered into after the specified term expires. That lease should require the grantor to pay a fair market rental to the remainder person. Terms of the lease should be strictly enforced by the remainder person.[1]

6. While it is not a requirement, the trustee should generally be someone other than the grantor or the grantor's spouse, especially after the grantor's retained interest has ended. Retention of an interest as a trustee could lead to additional income tax

(but see Chapter 27 on Defective Trusts) or estate tax exposure.

WHAT ARE THE ADVANTAGES?

1. GRATs, GRUTs, and QPRTs work so well because GRATs, GRUTs, and QPRTs are based on two basic principles:

    a. Gift taxes are based on the value of the gift to the donee and a gift (and therefore the gift tax) must be "discounted" by the cost of waiting. The longer the donee must wait, the lower the gift tax value of the asset placed in trust and therefore the lower the cost of the gift. With discount rates that fluctuate from month to month, there can be wide swings in gift tax cost. For instance, if the IRC Section 7520 rate is 6.0%, the taxable gift in the example below would be $111,679 (.558395 x $200,000). At a 4.0% rate it would be $135,113 (.675564 x $200,000). (See Appendix B for valuation tables.)

    b. The federal estate tax doesn't reach a property interest unless the decedent owned it when he died or unless he held a "string," a property right strong enough to cause it to be pulled back into his estate. In a GRAT, GRUT, or QPRT, once the grantor lives longer than the specified term, he neither owns the property in the trust nor any rights thereto. It therefore escapes estate taxation.

2. GRATs, GRUTs, and QPRTs are the closest thing to a "no lose" situation; it is a "what have we got to lose?" technique.

    a. If the client doesn't use a GRAT, GRUT, or QPRT and purchases property in his sole name, the property and any growth on the property will be in his estate.

    b. If the client who sets up a GRAT, GRUT, or QPRT dies during the specified term, the result is that the property plus any appreciation will be includable in his estate (the same result as if the client had done nothing).

WHAT ARE THE DISADVANTAGES?

The downside risks, costs, or disadvantages of a GRAT, GRUT, and QPRT include:

1. Attorney fees and the other transaction costs, such as appraisal fees and property titling costs of establishing the trust.

2. Lost opportunity cost. The GRAT, GRUT, or QPRT is an irrevocable trust. So, once assets are placed into the trust, the grantor is precluded from taking other planning measures. If the grantor has used up a sizable part of the unified credit to offset the gift of the remainder interest in the GRAT, GRUT, or QPRT, then the grantor is not in a position to make large gifts of other assets that may substantially appreciate in value. If the grantor dies during the term, the gamble will have been lost. This may be especially true in light of EGTRRA 2001 which limits the amount a person can give tax free during life to $1,000,000, but which allows the limit on the amount that can be transferred tax free at death to rise to $3,500,000 by 2009.

3. If the grantor does die during the specified trust term, his executor may be liable for tax on the includable assets – but the property itself might not be available to pay that tax. (Solutions to this issue are discussed further below.)

HOW IT IS DONE – AN EXAMPLE

Assume a widow in a 48% gift tax bracket. Assume the IRC Section 7520 rate is 5.0%. She places her $200,000 personal residence into an irrevocable trust. The trust provides that she will live in the personal residence for a 10 year term. At the end of that time, the personal residence will pass to her children.

The present value of her right to live in the personal residence for 10 years is $77,217 (.386087 x $200,000). (See Appendix B for valuation tables.) Since the entire value of the personal residence placed in trust is $200,000 and the income interest retained by the grantor is $77,217, the value of the future interest gift being made at that point to the remainder person is the difference, $122,783. This entire amount ($122,783) is a taxable gift, because the gift tax annual exclusion is allowed only for gifts of a present interest. Of course, $1,000,000 can be sheltered by the gift tax unified credit equivalent, which means that the widow will pay no gift tax. Assuming the unified credit has already been used and a 48% gift tax rate, the gift tax would be $58,936. [Clients considering making taxable gifts in excess of the unified credit equivalent should be advised that EGTRRA 2001 has increased the estate tax unified credit equivalents and

lowers the gift and estate tax rates for 2002 to 2010, and repeals the estate tax for one year in 2010.]

If the $200,000 property appreciates at an after-tax rate of 5%, the property will be worth $325,779 by the end of the 10 year term.

Should the widow die before the term expires, the trust assets would be included in her estate at their values as of her date of death. So there would be no federal death tax savings.

But if the widow survived the 10 year period (no matter by how short a period of time), none of the trust assets would be in her estate. At a 50% estate tax rate, the savings would be approximately $103,954 [(50% x $325,779) - $58,936]. If the estate tax were discounted to reflect that it would be payable 10 years later than the gift tax, then the savings, on a time value of money basis, would be less than that shown. For example, at a 5% discount rate, the savings would be $41,064, on a time value of money basis [or (50% x $200,000) - $58,936, since a 5% growth rate was also used]. Furthermore, because the property would not pass through probate, probate costs on $325,779 would be avoided.

GRATs and GRUTs can provide similar gift, estate, and generation-skipping transfer tax discounts. A married couple could each establish GRATs and GRUTs (or split gifts – see Chapter 22) so as to utilize both spouse's unified credits and marginal gift and estate tax brackets.

WHAT ARE THE TAX IMPLICATIONS?

1. If the grantor outlives the specified term, none of the trust's assets should be included in the grantor's estate. This is because the grantor has retained no interest in trust assets at death. IRC Section 2036 (retained life estates) applies only if the grantor retained the right to possess or enjoy the property or the income it produces (a) for life, or (b) for a period not ascertainable without reference to the grantor's death, or (c) for any period which does not, in fact, end before the grantor's death.

2. The gift to the remainder person is a gift of a future interest. It therefore cannot qualify for the gift tax annual exclusion.

3. If the grantor lives beyond the specified term, there should be no further transfer tax since the gift was complete upon the funding of the trust.

4. The taxable portion of post-'76 gifts is considered an "adjusted taxable gift." Because the entire present value of the gift to the remainder person is taxable, that amount is considered an adjusted taxable gift. This will push up the rate at which the other assets in the grantor's estate, if any, will be taxed.

   But a rapidly growing asset will have been transferred at an extremely low transfer tax cost. This results in a significant "leveraging of the unified credit."

   Perhaps more importantly, 100% of post-gift appreciation in the property's value escapes estate, gift, and generation-skipping transfer tax. This makes a GRAT, GRUT, or QPRT an excellent "estate freezing" device with respect to post-transfer appreciation.

5. At the grantor's death beyond the specified term of years, no step-up in basis for the property will be allowed. Instead, basis is fractionalized.[2] At the time the trust is created, the grantor retains a percentage of his basis equal to the ratio of the present value of his term interest to the value of the entire property. In the example above, the grantor-widow would retain about 39% of the basis. The remainder person would therefore receive about 61% of the basis. So if the widow's original basis in the example above was $100,000, the donee's basis would be $61,913 (.613913 x $100,000).

   This would obviously result in a substantial gain if the remainder person disposes of the property. But the income tax rate on the gain will probably be well below the federal estate tax and GST tax rates that could have been imposed had the property been included in the widow's estate. Furthermore, the potential for significant tax deferral exists. If the $200,000 personal residence had been retained by the widow, an estate tax would have been due on it 9 months after her death. But if a QPRT is used, income tax (probably at a much lower rate) could be deferred for much longer. In fact, income tax would be imposed only if and when the remainder person disposes of the property.

6. If the grantor dies before the specified term expires, the date of death value of the property will be includable in the grantor's gross estate.[3] EGTRRA 2001 repeals the estate tax for one year in 2010. [It is possible, although uncertain, that the value of a GRAT or GRUT included in the grantor's estate could be less than 100% of the value of the property in the trust.] If there is an estate tax inclusion, (a) there would be no adjusted taxable gift[4], and (b) the unified credit utilized in making the gift would be restored to the estate. Note that if the spouse of the grantor "split the gift," the unified credit of the nongrantor spouse would not be restored. This could be solved if both spouses in fact are grantors. In other words, have each spouse create a separate GRAT or GRUT.

   It is appropriate for a beneficiary to purchase insurance on the life of the grantor and carry that life insurance during the period of time in which the death of the grantor would cause estate tax inclusion. The insurance proceeds, received estate tax free, could then be used to purchase assets from the grantor's estate and thereby provide the estate with the liquidity to pay the estate tax.

7. If appreciated property is transferred to a GRAT, GRUT or QPRT, the tax on any gain will eventually be paid by (a) the grantor, or (b) the trust, or (c) the beneficiaries. Having taxes paid by the grantor may not, however, be a disadvantage, since the purpose of the trust is to "defund" the grantor's estate and shift as much wealth as possible to the remainder person with minimal gift taxes.

8. GRITs, GRATs, and GRUTS are generally subject to IRC Section 2702.

Section 2702

In valuing a transfer in trust to or for the benefit of a member of the transferor's family, Section 2702(a) provides that all retained interests in trusts that are not "qualified interests" are valued at zero. The amount of any gift is then determined by subtracting from the value of the property the value of the retained interest.[5] The valuation of retained interests in trust under Section 2702 specifically does not apply to incomplete gifts (determined without regard to whether there is consideration); personal residence trusts (see heading below); charitable remainder annuity trusts and pooled income funds; charitable lead trusts (if the only interest other than the remainder or a qualified annuity or unitrust interest is the charitable lead interest); and certain charitable remainder unitrusts (if the CRUT provides for simple unitrust payments; or in the case of a CRUT with a lesser of trust income or the unitrust amount provision, the grantor and/or the grantor's spouse are the only noncharitable beneficiaries).

Section 2702 also does not apply to assignment of remainder interests in trusts if the only retained interest is distribution of income in the sole discretion of an independent trustee, as defined in IRC Section 674(c), and certain property settlement agreements.[6]

The following definitions apply under Section 2702:

1. A member of the family includes the spouse of an individual, the ancestor or lineal descendant of an individual or the individual's spouse, the brother or sister of an individual, and the spouse of any such person.[7]

2. An applicable family member includes the spouse of an individual, the ancestor of an individual or the individual's spouse, and the spouse of any such person.[8]

3. A transfer in trust includes a transfer to a new trust or an existing trust or an assignment of an interest in an existing trust, but not a transfer resulting from exercise of a power of appointment that would not constitute a taxable gift (e.g., lapse of "Crummey" power which does not exceed "5 or 5" limitation); or a disclaimer.[9]

4. A retained interest is one held by the same individual both before and after the transfer to the trust.[10]

Qualified interests are valued under IRC Section 7520 (i.e., at approximately 120% of the applicable federal midterm interest rate under IRC Section 1274(d)(1) for the month into which the valuation falls).

A qualified interest is:

1. a qualified annuity interest,

2. a qualified unitrust, or

3. a qualified remainder interest.[11]

Qualified Annuity Interests (GRATs)

A qualified annuity interest is an irrevocable right to receive a fixed amount at least annually, payable to or for the benefit of the holder of the term interest (i.e., the transferor or an applicable family member). A withdrawal right, whether or not cumulative, does not qualify, and neither does the issuance of a note or other debt instrument.[12]

The annuity payment can be a fixed dollar amount or a fixed percentage of the initial value of the trust.[13] Income in excess of the fixed amount can be distributable to the transferor, but is not considered in valuing the retained interest.[14] Subsequent contributions are prohibited. If the annuity is based on a percentage of the value of the trust, there must be a provision to adjust for incorrect valuation similar to the rules of Treas. Reg. §1.664-2(a)(1)(iii).[15] Payment can be made after the close of the taxable year of the trust if made by the filing date for the trust income tax returns, determined without regard to extensions. The annuity can be based on a fixed dollar amount or percentage of the value of the trust, and cannot vary except to the extent the amount (or percentage) in any year does not exceed 120% of the amount (or percentage) from the preceding year.[16]

Qualified Unitrust Interests (GRUTs)

A qualified unitrust interest is an irrevocable right to an annual payment of a fixed percentage of the net fair market value of the trust assets, to be determined annually.[17] Rules similar to those applicable to annuity trusts also apply here. Combinations of annuity and unitrust payments are not permitted. However, the trust may permit payment of the greater of an annuity or unitrust amount, to be valued at the higher value.[18]

As to both annuity and unitrust transfers, any payments to other persons are prohibited; the term of the trust must be stated either as a period of years or the term holder's life, or the shorter of the two; successive term interests for the same individual are permitted; and there must be no provision for commutation of any interest.[19] The transferor can retain a reversionary interest in either the GRAT or GRUT, contingent upon death during the trust term, but the reversion is valued at zero for gift tax purposes.

Qualified Remainder Interests

A qualified remainder interest is the right to receive all or a fractional share of the trust on termination of all or a fractional share of the trust, and includes a reversion. It must be non-contingent, i.e., payable to the beneficiary or the beneficiary's estate in all events. All other payments must be annuity or unitrust payments, with no provision for distributions of income in excess of the annuity or unitrust amount. The right to receive a pecuniary amount or the original value of the corpus does not qualify.[20]

The retention of a remainder interest is a relatively rare estate planning technique, because any increase in the value of the transferred property is included in the transferor's taxable estate, and unless the remainder (reversion) is valued at less than 5% of the value of the transferred property, the grantor will be taxed on the income in any case.[21]

Personal Residence Trusts (PRTs)

A grantor retained income trust can still be utilized effectively where the transferor transfers an interest in a personal residence to a trust and the transferor retains the right to use the property for residential purposes for a term of years. Section 2702 carves out an exception for a personal residence trust. The regulations require such a trust to be limited to holding a single residence, or a fractional interest in a residence – in no case can the term holder hold interests in trust in more than two residences.[22]

The residence may not be occupied by any person other than the grantor, a spouse or dependent; must be available at all times for such use; and cannot be sold or used for any other purposes. The property must be either the principal residence or another residence as described in IRC Section 280A(d)(1), without regard to IRC Section 280A(d)(2) (i.e., use as a residence for personal purposes for a number of days that exceeds the greater of 14 days or 10% of the number of days it is rented), or an undivided fractional interest in either.

The residence may include appurtenant structures and adjacent land reasonably appropriate for residential purposes, may be subject to a mortgage, but does not include any personal property, such as furnishings. Residential use includes activities described in IRC Sections 280A(c)(1) or 280A(c)(4) (i.e., limited use for business or day care if only secondary); and excludes providing transient lodging and substantial services (i.e., a hotel or bed and breakfast).

Interests owned by spouses in a residence, including community interests, can be transferred to the same trust so long as only the spouses hold the term interest. If there is an involuntary conversion, such as destruction of the residence by fire, or its condemnation, the trust can hold the proceeds of such a conversion, such as insurance proceeds or a condemnation award, so long as there is a qualified replacement under IRC Section 1033. However, both the proceeds of the involuntary conversion and any income from those proceeds must be invested in a new residence within two years of when the proceeds were received.

Qualified Personal Residence Trust (QPRTs)

Recognizing the lack of statutory guidance for the implementation of the personal residence trust, the regulations carve out a safe harbor called a qualified personal residence trust.[23] The terms are not as restrictive as the personal residence trust, but do contain provisions substantially the same as applicable to personal residence trusts. However, while the regulations seem to require that no assets other than an interest in a personal residence (or the proceeds of an involuntary conversion) can ever be held in a personal residence trust, and the interest in the residence cannot be sold during the term of the trust, the qualified personal residence trust permits both under limited circumstances. It is conceivable this trust could have income. If it does, it must be distributed to the term holder; no distributions can be made to any other person.

The qualified personal residence trust must prohibit the holding of any property other than the personal residence, and contain the following provisions:

1. No distributions to other persons are permitted.

2. Cash can be held for the initial purchase of the residence within three months, or purchase of a replacement residence within three months of the date the cash is added to the trust.

3. Cash can also be held for up to six months for payment of trust expenses, including mortgage payments, and for improvements.

4. If the property is sold or insurance proceeds are received, a two year replacement period is permitted. Excess cash must be distributed at least quarterly or at the termination of the trust to the term holder.

5. If the property is no longer used as a personal residence, the trust must terminate and its assets must be distributed to the term holder within 30 days, unless it is converted into a qualified annuity trust.

In the case of a qualified personal residence trust, it is possible to sell a residence, reinvest only part of the proceeds in a new residence, and convert the rest to an annuity. The governing instrument must prohibit the commutation (prepayment) of the term interest.

The IRS has issued a sample qualified personal residence trust document.[24] However, many practitioners feel the form is lacking, particularly since it does not provide for the retention of a reversion right in the event the grantor dies before the end of the term.

Subsequent Transfers of Retained Interests

A reduction of taxable gifts or adjusted taxable gifts is permitted if the individual subsequently transfers an interest in a trust that was valued under Section 2702. The amount of the reduction is the lesser of the increase in taxable gifts resulting from the application of Section 2702, or the increase in the transferor's subsequent taxable gifts, or taxable estate, which results from the subsequent transfer.[25] The rule applies to testamentary transfers only if a term interest in the trust is included in the transferor's taxable estate solely by reason of the operation of IRC Section 2033 or a remainder interest is included in the transferor's taxable estate, and such interest was valued under Section 2702. Where spouses have split gifts, the adjustment is allocated one-half to each spouse, but one spouse may assign this adjustment to the other.

IMPLICATIONS AND ISSUES IN COMMUNITY PROPERTY STATES

If husband and wife transfer community property to a GRAT or GRUT, each may reserve the right to the payment for the trust term as to his or her respective community interest. It would apparently be possible for them to retain a joint payment for the term. If either dies during the term, the value of his or her community interest in the trust would be included in his or her taxable estate, either in whole or in part. If either or both spouses survive the term, his or her community interest in the trust should not be included in his or her estate. Note that in the case of the personal residence trust and qualified personal residence trust, the spouses can transfer community interests in one or two personal residences to the trust and retain the right to live in the residence for its term.

QUESTIONS AND ANSWERS

Question – Assume a husband makes a large transfer to a GRAT, GRUT, or QPRT. To reduce the potential gift tax on the value of the remainder person's interest, his wife consents to "split" the gift and use her unified credit to reduce or eliminate the gift tax. If the husband dies before the specified term expires, will the wife's unified credit be restored?

Answer – No. Although the husband's unified credit is restored if he dies within the specified income term, his wife's unified credit is not restored. A potential solution to this inequity is for the husband to make a gift to his wife. She then could make her own actual contribution to the GRAT, GRUT, and QPRT. (Obviously, the IRS could consider this a step transaction, but this logic presumes that the gift to the wife (assuming the facts indicate it was an outright and unconditional gift) was per se a transfer to an agent of the husband. This presumption is at odds with the trend of constitutional and even tax law, i.e., recognition of a female as an independent person and the trend of antipathy to sexual bias.)

Question – What are the best assets to place into a GRAT or GRUT?

Answer – Assets that possess substantial appreciation potential are the best assets to place into a GRAT or GRUT.

Question – Can the IRS revalue a transfer to a GRAT, GRUT, or QPRT many years after the GRAT, GRUT, or QPRT is funded?

Answer – A gift made after August 5, 1997, cannot be revalued for estate or gift tax purposes if the gift was adequately disclosed on a gift tax return and the gift tax statute of limitations (generally, three years) has passed.[26] Therefore, a gift tax return with an adequate disclosure of valuation should be filed with respect to a transfer to a GRAT, GRUT, or QPRT to start the statute of limitations with respect to valuation of the gift.

Question – Is there an "escape mechanism" that could redirect the remainder interest if the grantor dies during the term? For instance, is there a way to provide that if the grantor's estate has to include GRAT, GRUT, or QPRT assets, funds in the trust return to the grantor's estate rather than going to the remainder person?

Answer – A reversion to the grantor (or better yet to a revocable trust he established during his lifetime to avoid probate), conditioned on his death within the specified term, would create the funds to pay the estate tax. However, the value of a contingent reversion will not reduce the value of the taxable gift to the remainder person in the case of a GRAT or GRUT subject to IRC Section 2702.

An as yet unproven technique offered by some estate planning practitioners is the use of a guaranteed GRAT. It involves the sale of the reversion interest simultaneously with the creation of the GRAT. Again, it is too early to tell if this technique will be approved by the IRS.

Question – Is there a cutoff age after which the GRAT, GRUT, or QPRT no longer is mathematically logical?

Answer – Since the GRAT, GRUT, and QPRT are "little to lose – a lot to gain" tools, even clients in their 80s may want to use a such a trust. For instance, assuming an IRC Section 7520 rate of 5.0%, the value of the income interest retained in a five year QPRT is .216474 of the principal. Some clients, especially those who are in very good health, may want to gamble with a GRAT, GRUT, or QPRT. For example, if the 80-year-old client opted for a ten year term, the value of the income interest jumps to .386087 of the funds placed in the QPRT (and therefore the taxable gift to the remainder person drops accordingly). (See Appendix B for valuation tables.)

For clients with a slightly lower risk tolerance, consider staggered terms. For instance, an 80-year-old client could transfer some property into a five year GRAT or GRUT and other property into a ten year GRAT or GRUT.

Question – Are there problems with using closely held stock with a GRAT or GRUT?

Answer – The major problem with using a GRAT or GRUT which holds closely held stock or other similarly hard-to-value assets concerns valuation. If the asset is not properly valued and/or not properly disclosed to the IRS, there is a risk of having to pay additional gift tax, penalties, and interest, or of using up more of the unified credit.

Question – Are there special provisions that should be inserted into a GRAT, GRUT, or QPRT?

Answer – It is extremely important to document the "completeness" of the transfer at the date the trust is funded. Specifically, the trust must provide that the donor has given up all dominion and control over the property.

The grantor must specifically give up any power to revoke the gift of the remainder. The trust should also forbid the grantor to change any beneficial interests in the remainder. Therefore, the grantor can retain no power of appointment (other than

possibly a power contingent on the grantor dying during the trust term).

The grantor should generally not be named as trustee (especially after the grantor's retained interest ends). An unrelated, independent trustee should be selected.

The trust should specifically deny the grantor any control over the manner or time in which the beneficiaries will enjoy the trust corpus (otherwise, that corpus will be pulled back into the grantor's estate).

Question – How should clients be advised who are concerned that if they transfer their personal residence into a trust for a term, and still want to live there at the end of the term, they will be unable to do so?

Answer – This is a concern to many clients, and there are planning ideas to help. A PRT or QPRT must prohibit the grantor or the grantor's spouse from repurchasing the personal residence from the trust.[27] However, one method to accomplish this goal is for the grantor to lease the residence from either the trust or the remainder person after the initial term of the PRT or QPRT. The IRS has privately ruled that if the residence is leased at fair market value, the grantor would not retain any economic benefit in the property. The IRS concluded that if the grantor survived the initial term of the trust and continued to live in the residence until death, leasing the residence for fair market value rent, the interest in the property transferred to the trust would not be includable in the grantor's gross estate under IRC Section 2036.[28]

Question – Can the QPRT be effectively used for a vacation home?

Answer – Possibly the most popular use of the QPRT is for the so-called second or vacation home. Under the facts of one ruling[29], grantor and spouse jointly own two vacation homes that could be successfully transferred to a QPRT. They intend to retitle them so that each spouse owns one property, then each will transfer his or her vacation home to a QPRT until the death of that grantor or a term of ten years. Income, if any, will be distributed to each grantor, and each will have the right to live in his or her residence. If the residences are sold, an annuity will be paid during the remainder of the term. If a grantor survives, the property will remain in trust until the surviving grantor dies. However, income will be accumulated until the death of the surviving spouse and then distributed to children. There is a reversion if the grantor dies during the trust term.

Question – Can stock in an S corporation be placed into a GRAT or GRUT?

Answer – Under usual circumstances, a GRAT or GRUT does not qualify to hold S stock because not all of the trust income is payable to the beneficiary. See Chapter 46. However, because any trust as to which the grantor is treated as the owner for income tax purposes can hold S corporation stock, the solution has been to make the GRAT or GRUT "defective" for income tax purposes (i.e., taxable under the grantor trust rules). See Chapter 27. There are many examples of this technique in private letter rulings.[30]

Question – Assume a grantor age 60 established a GRAT for a term of 15 years, but with a provision that should she die before the end of the term, it will terminate at her death. The value of the property placed in the trust is $500,000, the annuity payout rate is 6%, and the IRC Section 7520 rate is 5.0%. What is the amount of the gift? What would the amount be if the gift was for a 15 year term certain?

Answer – See Figures 26.1 and 26.2.

ASRS: Sec. 55, ¶58.2.

Figure 26.1

GRANTOR RETAINED ANNUITY TRUST			
(Term With Reversion - Table 90CM)			
Transfer to Trust:	$500,000	Annuity Payment:	$30,000
Age:	60	Term of Years:	15
Frequency of Payments:	Annual	Payments:	End of Period
Section 7520 Interest Rate:	5.0%		
Check Exhaustion of Trust Fund			
Ann. Factor (15 years, 5.0%):	10.3797	Adj. Factor (Annual, 5.0%):	1.0000
Annuity Test Value:	$311,391	Special Factors	Not Required
Valuation			
Ann. Factor (60, 15, 5.0%):	9.2583	Adj. Factor (Annual, 5.0%):	1.0000
Annuity Value:	$277,749	Remainder Value:	$222,251

Source: Trust Calculator (part of *The Ultimate Trust Resource*, a National Underwriter Company publication)

Figure 26.2

GRANTOR RETAINED ANNUITY TRUST			
(Term Certain)			
Transfer to Trust:	$500,000	Annuity Payment:	$30,000
Term of Years:	15	Frequency of Payments:	Annual
Payments:	End of Period	Section 7520 Interest Rate:	5.0%
Check Exhaustion of Trust Fund			
Ann. Factor (15 years, 5.0%):	10.3797	Adj. Factor (Annual, 5.0%):	1.0000
Annuity Test Value:	$311,391	Special Factors:	Not Required
Valuation			
Ann. Factor (15 years, 5.0%):	10.3797	Adj. Factor (Annual, 5.0%):	1.0000
Annuity Value:	$311,391	Remainder Value:	$188,609

Source: Trust Calculator (part of *The Ultimate Trust Resource*, a National Underwriter Company publication)

CHAPTER ENDNOTES

1. *Est. of Barlow v. Comm.*, 55 TC 666 (1971), acq. 1972 CB 1.
2. *Hunter v. Comm.*, 44 TC 109 (1965); Rev. Rul. 77-413, 1977-2 CB 298; Treas. Reg. §1.61-6(a).
3. IRC Secs. 2036(a)(1), 2039; *Est. of Fry v. Comm.*, 9 TC 503 (1947); FSA 200036012.
4. IRC Sec. 2001(b); Treas. Reg. §25.2702-6(a).
5. Treas. Reg. §25.2702-1(b).
6. Treas. Reg. §25.2702-1(c).
7. IRC Secs. 2702(e), 2704(c)(2).
8. IRC Secs. 2702(a)(1), 2701(e)(2).
9. Treas. Reg. §25.2702-2(a)(2).
10. Treas. Reg. §25.2702-2(a)(3).
11. IRC Sec. 2702(b); Treas. Reg. §25.2702-2(a)(5).
12. Treas. Reg. §25.2702-3(b)(1)(i).
13. Treas. Reg. §25.2702-3(b)(1)(ii).
14. Treas. Reg. §25.2702-3(b)(1)(iii).
15. Treas. Reg. §25.2702-3(b)(2).
16. Treas. Reg. §25.2702-3(b)(1)(ii).
17. Treas. Reg. §25.2702-3(c)(1). The trust assets are to be valued in accordance with Treas. Reg. §25.2522(c)-3(c)(2)(vii).
18. Treas. Reg. §25.2702-3(d).
19. Treas. Reg. §25.2702-3(d)(3).
20. Treas. Reg. 25.2702-3(f).
21. IRC Sec. 673.
22. Treas. Regs. §§25.2702-5(a), 25.2702-5(b).
23. Treas. Reg. §25.2702-5(c).
24. Rev. Proc. 2003-42, 2003-23 IRB 998.
25. Treas. Reg. §25.2702-6(a).
26. IRC Secs. 2001(f), 6501(c)(9); Treas. Reg. §301.6501(c)-1(f)(2).
27. Treas. Regs. §§25.2702-5(b)(1), 25.2702-5(c)(9).
28. Let. Ruls. 9433016, 9735012, 9723030.
29. Let. Rul. 9441039.
30. Let. Ruls. 9416009, 9444033.

Chapter 27

DEFECTIVE TRUST

WHAT IS IT?

An intentionally "defective" trust is an irrevocable trust with the following characteristics:

1. Transfers of property to the trust are completed gifts for federal gift tax purposes.

2. The trust assets will not be included in the taxable estate of the grantor or grantors.

3. The income of the trust is taxed to the grantor, who is treated as the "owner" of the trust for federal income tax purposes.

Such a trust is created by intentionally violating one or more of the grantor trust rules found in IRC Sections 671 to 677. Under IRC Section 671, trust income or deductions will be attributed to the grantor of the trust if the grantor is treated as the owner of the trust under the provisions of IRC Sections 672 to 677. These rules are discussed in Chapter 19 in connection with the Income Taxation of Trusts and Estates.

The grantor trust rules were enacted to prevent taxpayers from using trusts to shift income tax liabilities to a lower bracket taxpayer while retaining control or beneficial enjoyment of the trust property. Thus, a violation of the grantor trust rules was traditionally viewed negatively in that the grantor of the trust was, for income tax purposes, the owner of the trust assets, and was personally responsible for all items of income (ordinary income and capital gains) attributable to the trust assets. This personal responsibility existed whether or not the income and/or principal was actually distributed to the grantor.

The use of intentionally defective grantor trusts has become increasingly popular as an estate planning technique. Since the estate tax inclusion rules are applied separately from the income tax rules, unique opportunities are available to shift assets to a succeeding generation at no transfer or income tax cost and to otherwise reduce the grantor's estate.

WHEN IS THE USE OF SUCH A DEVICE INDICATED?

Defective trusts are particularly useful when the grantor wishes to remove an appreciating asset from his estate without making a gift. A gift may be undesirable for many reasons – *e.g.*, the grantor's gift tax unified credit equivalent (applicable exclusion) amount may not be sufficient to cover the value of the gift, the grantor may desire to retain a stream of income, etc.

By using a defective trust, the appreciating assets can be sold to the trust in exchange for an installment note without a gift being made.[1] In addition, the grantor will not recognize any taxable gain on the sale of the appreciating asset to the trust since the grantor and the trust are treated as one for income tax purposes.[2] Alternatively, the grantor can create a grantor retained annuity trust (GRAT), a grantor retained unitrust (GRUT), or a qualified personal residence trust (QPRT), all of which are grantor trusts. See Chapter 26.

Grantor trusts can also be used to hold stock in a Subchapter S corporation. In this case, it is particularly important that the grantor be treated as the owner of both the income and corpus of the entire trust. This is often more favorable than making an election for the trust to be treated as a qualified subchapter S Trust (QSST).

In addition, because the grantor pays the income taxes incurred by the trust, the assets held in the trust grow, in essence, tax free. In addition, by paying the income tax on the income that will pass to the beneficiaries, the grantor is reducing his estate without making a taxable gift to the beneficiary. However, it is possible the IRS will challenge this conclusion. In a letter ruling,[3] the IRS held that if the trust does not contain a clause directing the trustee to reimburse the grantor for any income tax the grantor pays on trust income not distributed to the grantor, the payment of the income tax by the grantor is a taxable gift! Note the following language:

> "If there were not a reimbursement provision, an additional gift to a remainderperson would occur when the grantor paid tax on any income

that would otherwise be payable from the corpus of the trust."

Although the IRS subsequently revised this ruling to remove the quoted language,[4] the potential for argument still exists. In addition, at least one private letter ruling indicates that the IRS will require such a reimbursement provision in order for a favorable ruling on a GRAT (which is a type of grantor trust).[5]

Taxing income to the grantor rather than the trust will almost always result in a substantial income tax savings because of the compressed tax rates applied to trusts. Consider the following income tax rates for estates and trusts in 2004:

Taxable income not over $1,950	15%
Over $1,950 but not over $4,600	$292.50 + 25% of excess
Over $4,600 but not over $7,000	$955 + 28% of excess
Over $7,000 but not over $9,550	$1,627 + 33% of excess
Over $9,550	$2,468.50 + 35% of excess

Conversely, if the grantor is in a higher income tax bracket than the trust beneficiary, there could be paid higher income taxes than if the income were taxed to the beneficiary. Of course, if the grantor's estate is reduced by the payment, the estate tax savings may justify this technique.

In the case of a personal residence trust, if the grantor is treated as the owner and the residence is sold, the benefits of IRC Section 121 (the $250,000 gain exclusion, $500,000 for certain married taxpayers) may be applied to exclude gain from the sale of the residence. Note that the trust must be defective as to both income and corpus.

Where a GRAT or GRUT is involved, it is possible that the trust may not generate sufficient income or cash flow to make the annuity or unitrust payments. The GRAT or GRUT distribution may be "in kind" (i.e., of the trust assets), without any income tax consequences to the trust.

A defective trust may facilitate the transfer of installment notes to the trust without accelerating the gain.[6] This technique may be used to set up an income tax deduction for transfers to charitable lead trusts.[7]

Additionally, if a residence is owned by a defective grantor trust, payments of rent by the grantor may not be taxable gifts. This may be one way to fund an insurance trust that makes premium payments without making gifts to the trust.

Since the grantor is treated as the owner of the trust assets for income tax purposes, he can sell assets to the

trust without incurring taxable gain. In addition, interest payments from an installment sale to the trust will not be treated as taxable income to the grantor.[8]

WHAT ARE THE REQUIREMENTS?

The trust is irrevocable. Either the grantor or a trustee that is not adverse retains certain powers. The grantor can retain the power in a nonfiduciary capacity to remove trust assets from the trust and substitute other assets of equal value. This apparently has no adverse estate tax consequences to the grantor. Note that the IRS has refused to rule on this in all cases, because it is a question of fact whether or not the grantor is acting in a nonfiduciary capacity.

A nonadverse party, acting in a fiduciary capacity, can be granted certain powers. One of these, which triggers the grantor trust rules of IRC Section 674, is to add beneficiaries other than afterborn children, so long as the grantor does not control this decision. In one private ruling[9], a trust provided that the trustee could, in its discretion, add as beneficiaries persons who were lineal descendants of the parents of the grantor. This brought the trust under the provisions of IRC Section 674, making it a grantor trust, eligible to hold S corporation stock.

In the case of an installment sale to an intentionally defective grantor trust, it is important that the assets that are the subject of the sale not be the sole source of the payments on the installment note. Thus, prior to the sale, the grantor should make a gift to the trust of cash or assets worth somewhere between 10% and 20% of the value of the asset being sold.[10] This can help to avoid an argument by the IRS that the grantor retained an interest in the asset that is includable in the grantor's estate under IRC Section 2036. If the trust is a generation-skipping or dynasty trust, the grantor can allocate some of his generation-skipping exemption to this initial gift so that the purchased asset will be excluded from the beneficiary's estate.

The trust beneficiary should *not* have any Crummey withdrawal right over the initial gift so as to avoid any argument that the beneficiary, rather than the grantor, is the owner of the assets for income tax purposes.[11]

It is also important that adequate interest be charged on the installment note so as to avoid any gift component. No gift should be deemed to have been made if the asset is sold at fair market value and the applicable federal rate of interest is used.

HOW IT IS DONE – AN EXAMPLE

Example 1. Francis Osborne owns all of the stock in a corporation that is electing to be taxed under Subchapter S of the Internal Revenue Code. He would like to make a gift of several shares of nonvoting common stock in trust for his children, but he also wants to retain a substantial part of the income stream from that stock for a period of years. It is explained to him about the possible use of a grantor retained annuity trust (GRAT) for a term of years. However, a GRAT is not a qualified shareholder in an S corporation, since there is no guarantee that all of the trust income would be paid to the grantor. The annuity could be more or less than that amount.

It is proposed that the trust contain a provision that Francis has the power, at any time during the term of the trust, to remove the trust assets and substitute other assets of equal value. Under IRC Section 675(4), if this power is exercisable in a nonfiduciary capacity, the trust will be classified as a grantor trust. Since S corporation stock can be held in a grantor trust, the S election will not be lost during the grantor's lifetime. Further, if the grantor does elect to swap trust assets, or repurchase assets from the trust at fair market value, such a swap or purchase will have no income tax consequences to either the trust or to Francis.

Example 2. George establishes an intentionally defective grantor trust for the benefit of his children, Sam and Dorothy. George owns a business that he expects will significantly increase in value over the next 10 years. He desires to sell this business to the defective trust in order to remove the anticipated increase in value from his estate, but does not wish to incur any income tax consequences on the sale.

George obtains an appraisal of the business and, thereafter, makes a gift of 20% of this value to the trust to serve as seed money for the anticipated purchase. George then sells the business, at its appraised fair market value, to the defective trust in exchange for a 20-year promissory note. Depending upon George's need (or desire) for income, the note can be structured to be interest-only (at the current AFR) with a balloon payment at the end of the term or principal and interest can be amortized over the 20-year term. The income produced by the initial gift and the purchased business will be used to make the note payments.

During the term of the note, George receives a stream of income that is not taxable to him. At the end of the term, neither the business (at its increased value) nor the promissory note will be included in George's estate. If, however, George dies before the note is paid off, the value of the promissory note at the time of his death will be included in his estate. In addition, because the trust's grantor trust status would terminate at George's death, the IRS *may* argue that the sale occurred at the time of death and that gain is taxable to George (on his final return) or to his estate.

WHAT ARE THE TAX IMPLICATIONS?

The following is a summary of the income tax rules pertaining to grantor trusts:

1. IRC Section 672 contains important definitions relating to adverse and nonadverse parties, and related and subordinate parties. Under the remaining sections, whether the grantor is treated as the owner of the trust may depend on whether certain powers are conferred on persons fitting these categories.

2. IRC Section 673 imposes the grantor trust rules where the grantor retains a reversionary interest in the trust, that is, a right to some future benefits.

3. IRC Section 674 covers the retention of control over the enjoyment of the trust by the grantor or certain other persons. It is one of the most complex provisions of the Internal Revenue Code.

4. IRC Section 675 treats the grantor as the owner of the trust if the grantor retains certain administrative powers over it. It is the provision most used in defective trust planning.

5. IRC Section 676 provides that the grantor is treated as the owner of the trust if the grantor can revoke it.

6. IRC Section 677 imposes the grantor trust rules where the grantor or grantor's spouse retains beneficial enjoyment of the trust, or its income is used to pay premiums on life insurance on the grantor or the grantor's spouse.

Note that the grantor could be the owner of only a portion of the trust, all or part of the trust income, or all or part of the trust corpus. Also note that, as a general rule, the grantor trust provisions apply if certain powers are retained by the spouse of the grantor.

Many grantor retained powers that cause the grantor to be treated as the owner for income tax purposes will also cause the trust to be included in the grantor's taxable estate, WHICH SHOULD BE AVOIDED. For example, the trust will be included in the grantor's taxable estate if:

1. The grantor retains a reversionary interest that is valued at more than 5% of the trust corpus.[12] Even where the reversionary interest is valued at over 5% of the value of the trust, determined at date of death, IRC Section 2037 will not apply if beneficiaries could have received distribution of trust assets without surviving the grantor.

2. The grantor personally retains control over the enjoyment of the trust.[13]

3. The grantor retains certain administrative powers, such as the power to vote stock transferred to the trust.[14]

4. The grantor retains the income.[15]

However, many powers can be granted to a nonadverse party other than the grantor (including a spouse, but that is *not* recommended) that will cause the grantor to be treated as the owner of the trust for income tax purposes. A nonadverse party is someone other than an adverse party, defined as a person with a substantial interest in the trust that would be adversely affected by the exercise or non-exercise of the power.[16]

There are special rules for related or subordinate parties who are presumed subservient to the wishes of the grantor. Related or subordinate parties are the grantor's spouse, mother, father, issue, brother, sister, an employee of the grantor, an employee of a corporation where the stock of the grantor and the trust is significant from the standpoint of voting control, or a subordinate employee of a corporation in which the grantor is an executive.[17]

Under IRC Section 674(c), certain powers granted to an independent trustee who is nonadverse do not trigger these rules; an independent trustee consists of a trustee or trustees, none of whom are the grantor or grantor's spouse, and no more than half of whom are related or subordinate and subservient to the grantor.

In creating defective trusts, the following are powers most frequently granted to a trustee who is someone other than the grantor but is a nonadverse party:

1. Powers to control beneficial enjoyment of the trust under IRC Section 674(a), but note the exceptions for certain powers under IRC Section 674(b), and exception for powers of an independent trustee under IRC Section 674(c).

2. Certain administrative powers under IRC Section 675, including the power to deal with the trust for less than full consideration, the power to borrow from the trust under certain circumstances, the power, in a nonfiduciary capacity, to vote or control investments where the trust includes stock where voting control held by the grantor and trust is significant, and the power to remove assets and substitute assets of equal value. Note that if the grantor retains the power in a nonfiduciary capacity to remove assets and replace them with assets of equal value, the grantor is treated as the owner for income tax purposes, but should not be for gift or estate tax purposes.

3. The power to revoke the trust in favor of the grantor under IRC Section 676 or to distribute income to the grantor under IRC Section 677. However, since this may subject the trust to the grantor's creditors, it is not recommended.

4. The power to apply income to the payment of premiums on life insurance on the grantor or grantor's spouse under IRC Section 677(a)(3).

Grantor trust status may be terminated by a number of actions, including renunciation of the power by which the grantor is treated as the owner, the death of the grantor, etc. Termination of grantor trust status *may* also result in the recognition of gain by the grantor.[18]

In an installment sale situation, upon the grantor's death, the value of the promissory note will generally be included in the grant's estate.

IMPLICATIONS AND ISSUES IN COMMUNITY PROPERTY STATES

Where assets transferred to defective trusts are community assets, the planner should be aware of the fact that the "grantor" of such a trust will be each spouse as to his or her community interest. For example, if a nonadverse trustee is used, be certain that person is nonadverse as to both spouses. If the grantor retains the power to remove and replace assets, consider the fact that if only one spouse has that power, the grantor trust rule might not apply to the other spouse as to his or her community interest.

In general, the grantor trust rules apply to powers retained by either spouse, and this may not be a serious problem. However, it would be wise to consider this aspect, and also the potential impact of a divorce on the defective trust plan.

As noted previously, grantor trust status is normally terminated by death. In the case of community property, however, grantor trust status will continue with respect to the portion of the trust contributed by the surviving spouse.

QUESTIONS AND ANSWERS

Question – Will the IRS attack the use of the defective trust?

Answer – Based on private letter ruling 9444033, it appears the IRS will attack the use of the defective trust, probably arguing that the payment of the income tax by the grantor on trust income distributed to the other beneficiaries is an additional gift to the trust beneficiaries. However, at least one court has held that the payment of income tax on the income of an irrevocable trust is not a gift.[19]

Question – Can the defective trust be used in connection with irrevocable life insurance trusts where trust income is to be used to pay insurance premiums?

Answer – Under IRC Section 677, the use or possible use of trust income to pay life insurance premiums will cause the grantor trust rules to apply to the trust. This would enable the client to transfer income-producing property to the irrevocable life insurance trust, which then acquires the life insurance, using the income from the property to pay the premiums. Since the payment of the premiums is not deductible, the effect is that the income will be taxed to the grantor. If properly planned, this will remove both the life insurance proceeds and the income-producing property from the grantor's estate. Note that the IRS will not presently rule on the income tax consequences of this technique.

Question – Can the defective trust concept be used to shift the income taxation of trust income to beneficiaries?

Answer – If trust beneficiaries are given a general power of appointment over a trust, they will be taxed on its income under IRC Section 678 whether or not they exercise that power. The beneficiaries may well be in a lower income tax bracket than the trust. This could also be considered where the beneficiaries are minors. However, if they are under 14, consideration must be given to the imposition of the "kiddie tax," under which the income would be taxed at the rates of the parent.

It should be noted that, although a beneficial withdrawal right to trust principal that is equal to the greater of $5,000 or 5% of the trust corpus will not be a taxable lapse if unexercised, such a right is likely to constitute a general power of appointment for purposes of IRC Section 678. Thus, the gift of $5,000 to a Crummey-type trust may result in the beneficiary being treated as the grantor of the trust corpus.

CHAPTER ENDNOTES

1. It is extremely important that the fair market value be accurately determined so as to avoid any argument that a gift was made.
2. IRC Secs. 674, 675, 677; Rev. Rul. 85-13, 1985-1 CB 184.
3. Let. Rul. 9444033.
4. PLR 9543049.
5. PLR 9838017.
6. Rul. 74-613, 1974-2 CB 153.
7. IRC Sec. 170(f)(2)(B).
8. See footnote 2.
9. Let. Rul. 9301020.
10. Byrle M. Abbin, *[S]he Loves Me, [S]he Loves Me Not – Responding to Succession Planning Needs Through a Three-Dimensional Analysis of Considerations to Be Applied In Selecting From the Cafeteria of Techniques*, 31 U. of Miami Inst. On Est. Plan., Ch. 13 (1997) (setting forth IRS's informal representation that assets equal to 10% of purchase price should provide adequate security for the payment of the acquisition indebtedness). Some practitioners feel that 20% will provide a better defense.
11. IRC Sec. 678(a)(1).
12. IRC Secs. 673, 2037(a)(2).
13. IRC Secs. 674, 2036, 2038.
14. IRC Secs. 675, 2036(b).
15. IRC Secs. 677, 2036(a).
16. IRC Sec. 672.
17. IRC Sec. 672(c).
18. See Treas. Reg. §1.1001-2(c), Example 5; *Madorin v. Comm.*, 84 TC 667 (1985).
19. *Hogle v. Comm.*, 165 F.2d 352 (10th Cir. 1947).

Chapter 28

REVOCABLE TRUST

WHAT IS IT?

An *inter vivos* (living) trust is a relationship, created during the lifetime of the grantor (the person establishing the trust), in which one party (the trustee) holds property for the benefit of another (the beneficiary).

It can be established for a limited period of time, last until the occurrence or nonoccurrence of a specific event, or it can continue after the death of the grantor.

A revocable living trust is one created by the grantor during lifetime in which during his lifetime the grantor retains the right to revoke the trust, change its terms, or regain possession of the property in the trust.

A revocable trust becomes irrevocable when the grantor, during his lifetime, relinquishes title to property placed in the trust and gives up all right to revoke, amend, alter, or terminate the trust, or when the grantor dies.

WHEN IS THE USE OF SUCH A DEVICE INDICATED?

1. Where the grantor wishes someone else to accept management responsibility for all or a portion of the grantor's property.

2. Where the grantor wishes to assure continuity of management and income flow of a business or other assets in the event of death or disability.

3. Where the grantor wishes to protect against his own legal incompetency or physical incapacity, or the incompetency or incapacity (physical, mental, or legal) of beneficiaries.

4. Where the grantor desires privacy in the handling and administration of his assets during lifetime and at death.

5. Where the grantor wishes to minimize estate administration costs and delay at death by avoiding probate.

6. Where the client would like to see the trust (and the trustee) in operation.

7. Where the client wishes to avoid ancillary administration of assets situated in other states by placing title in the trustee.

8. Where the client would like to reduce the potential for an election against, or a contest of, the will.

9. Where the client would like to select the state law under which the provisions of the dispositive document will be governed.

WHAT ARE THE REQUIREMENTS?

1. In order for a trust to exist, there must be trust property (also known as trust principal, *res* or corpus).

2. There must be the following parties, although in some jurisdictions it is possible for the same individual to hold all these positions:

    (a) a "grantor," sometimes referred to as a "settlor," or "trustor"–any person who transfers property to and dictates the terms of a trust;

    (b) a trustee–a party to whom property is transferred by the grantor, who receives legal title to the property placed in the trust, and who generally manages and distributes income according to the terms of a formal written agreement (called a trust instrument) between the grantor and the trustee;

    (c) a beneficiary–a party for whose benefit the trust is created and who will receive the direct or indirect benefit of the use of income from and/or principal of the trust property, as follows:

        (1) income beneficiary–the beneficiary who receives income, generally for life or for a fixed period of years or until the occurrence or nonoccurrence of a particular event;

(2) remainder person–the ultimate beneficiary of trust property, who can also be the income beneficiary.

3. The grantor and trustee must be legally competent.

HOW IT IS DONE – EXAMPLES

Russ Miller, a successful real estate broker, feels that if his wife survives him, she will be able to handle the assets in his estate and properly manage them. However, he is afraid that if his spouse predeceases him, his children will be unable to properly manage the assets left to them. His estate is not subject to significant estate taxes.

Russ makes his life insurance proceeds and/or other assets payable to his wife, if she survives him. However, if Russ's wife predeceases him, those assets are payable to a trust Russ set up during life. This type of inter vivos trust is revocable since Russ can always revoke the trust and repossess the property or change the terms of the trust. Often, such a trust is designed as a "contingent," or "step up," or "stand by" trust, since it will take effect only in the event of the contingency that the grantor's wife predeceases him.

Under different circumstances or to meet different objectives, an irrevocable living trust would be indicated. For example, if Russ were in a high income tax bracket, as well as a high estate tax bracket, he might consider transferring assets to an irrevocable trust for the benefit of his wife or children. The trust could accumulate income during Russ's life or distribute that income to, or use it for the benefit of, his children (but not for Russ's own benefit). At Russ's death, the trust could provide income to his wife for life and at her death, provide income and eventually principal for his children. However, the tax rates for income retained by a trust have been substantially compressed so that in 2004 the highest federal rate of 35% (which applies to individuals at a level of $319,100 of income) applies to trusts at a $9,550 level.

As another example, Philip and Kay Martin, living in a community property state, have decided to avoid the costs, delays, and publicity attendant to probates and also to avoid the possibility for conservatorship by putting their assets during their lifetime into a revocable trust. With a medium-sized estate they decide to use the marital deduction provisions described in Chapter 24 in order to have each of them be able to take advantage of the unified credit.

The insurance on Philip's wife was arranged so that the revocable trust is both the owner of the trust and the beneficiary of the insurance. Philip and Kay each have a will that has the two major functions of (1) naming a guardian for their children and (2) "pouring over" to the trust any assets that they neglected to place in the trust during their lifetime. At the death of either Philip or Kay the trust becomes irrevocable and the mechanism described in Chapter 24 to reduce federal and state death taxes comes into play.

As long as Philip and Kay are competent, each has the right to be able to remove their share of community property from the trust. In some community property states, however, both spouses will need to consent to such withdrawals. Most well drafted trusts for circumstances such as the Martins have three "pockets" or subtrusts: one for the separate property of the husband; one for the separate property of the wife; and one for community property. In this fashion, the revocable trust can still maintain the beneficial ownership of the property as the clients may desire.

WHAT ARE THE TAX IMPLICATIONS?

1. For federal income tax purposes, all income is taxed to the grantor at the grantor's tax rate, since he is considered the owner of the trust corpus.[1]

2. No gift tax is generated by establishing or funding a revocable trust since the gift is not completed until the trust becomes irrevocable.[2]

3. Since the grantor has not irrevocably disposed of any assets, the entire trust corpus will be included in the grantor's estate for federal estate tax purposes.[3] EGTRRA 2001 repeals the estate tax for one year in 2010.

ISSUES AND IMPLICATIONS IN COMMUNITY PROPERTY STATES

In dealing with community property, the inter vivos trust would have two grantors, the husband and the wife. For a revocable trust, where the grantors intend to retain the beneficial ownership of the property, care must be taken to ensure that accidental gifts under state gift tax law are not made by giving either spouse ownership rights over the other spouse's half of the property. The unlimited gift tax marital deduction eliminates a federal gift tax problem on interspousal gifts. Thus, if the trust is revoked, the property should be clearly indicated as being returned to the husband and wife, as co-owners, and not to one spouse or the other.

Is the character of community property altered by a transfer to a revocable trust that does not have separate subtrusts for separate property of each spouse and for community property? If the transfer is simply by husband and wife to trustee, and each retains a right to revoke, and the instrument specifically provides that the character of the property remains community in the trust and also if it is withdrawn from the trust, and state law recognizes the ability of the parties to achieve the intended result, the character of the property will remain unchanged. This means that, upon the death of the first spouse, the decedent's one-half and the surviving spouse's one-half interest in the trust will receive a new basis equal to fair market value at death or the alternate valuation date, and only the decedent's one-half of the property in the trust will be included in his estate. [EGTRRA 2001 repeals the estate tax for one year in 2010, and stepped-up basis is replaced by a modified carryover basis for property acquired from decedents dying in 2010.] There will be no gift at the time the trust is created and there will be no gift upon the death of the first spouse unless, at that time, the trust becomes irrevocable. This is avoided by language that divides the trust into two or three trusts upon the death of either of the donors with the formulas described in Chapter 24 coming into play to optimize the "use it or lose it" type of effective deduction provided by the unified credit. This type of revocable trust is used extensively in community property states to deal both with community property and to deal with separate property assets of the spouses.

Much care must be taken in determining the source and nature of title holding of property before taking the position that it is community property, as one may when the property is transferred to a trust that indicates that it is held as community property. Taxable gifts under state law may result if the property is the separate property of either spouse or is joint tenancy real property originally acquired with the separate property of one spouse. Although the unlimited marital deduction for federal gift tax purposes reduces the gift tax risks,[4] there still may be state gift tax implications. In addition, it could well inspire litigation in the event of a dissolution if there was not a clear intent between the parties that a gift take place.

Where insurance has been purchased with community property (and therefore belongs one-half to each spouse), care must be taken that the terms of a trust, becoming irrevocable at the death of the insured, do not result in a taxable gift by the surviving spouse of all or part of the survivor's half interest in the insurance proceeds. Such gifts are usually to the remainder person(s) of the trust and are not subject to the marital deduction.

Where the clients have come to the point where the non-insured spouse does not require the financial benefit of the life insurance policy, such policies are often given to irrevocable life insurance trusts as described in Chapter 31, noting that the insured spouse must live three years past the date of that gift in order for the transfer to be effective. More and more frequently now spouses are planning for dealing with estate tax by the purchase of survivorship policies that will never be owned by their revocable trusts but that would be owned from the beginning by an irrevocable trust to which they make gifts to fund the annual premiums.

Great care must be taken in drafting the provisions regarding the division of property at the death of one community property owning spouse so as to avoid unintended gifts by the surviving spouse. At times, such trusts may be intended to benefit the survivor more if he agrees to have his property also be managed and distributed according to the terms of the trust. Such "election" provisions may also result in gifts by the surviving spouse and, if used, should be drafted carefully by an experienced estate planner.

The marital deduction rules make it important that all inter vivos trusts be examined carefully and revisions considered to take advantage of the very important provisions which make it possible to have completely tax-free interspousal transfers. Chapter 24, on the marital deduction, reviews this in more detail.

Community property and separate property states generally have similar rules as to how long property can be held in trust and as to other trust law matters. However, property rights are different as to separate and community property, and estate plans involving trusts must be reviewed and probably revised when one moves from a separate property state to a community property state and vice versa.

QUESTIONS AND ANSWERS

Question – Why, if there can be no federal income or estate tax savings, are revocable trusts so appealing?

Answer – There is a substantial difference in planning practice between the northeastern part of the United States, where revocable trusts are less popular, and the West Coast and Florida, where revocable trusts are fairly popular. In some of the southern states and some of the midwestern states, the revocable trust is gradually becoming more popular.

There are two major arguments for the use of revocable trusts–probate and potential conservatorship savings and estate tax savings. In some states, the probate costs are relatively low and the argument for the use of revocable trusts for avoiding probate is not as strong. However, in some states, the costs of probate can be substantial with the fees often set by statutory formula. However, some costs may be reduced or eliminated if a family member is involved and agrees to serve with no fee.

Whether probate is avoided or not, there will be additional costs incurred in terms of dealing with estate tax returns for larger estates and in some cases for dealing with income tax matters. However, the probate costs are typically the area of focus.

There has been some criticism of books and presentations that emphasize the use of trusts to avoid probate. And, while there may be times where it is helpful to have the court supervise the distribution of assets, practitioners find this a less frequent occurrence. The printed forms and/or web page materials that are provided for "do it yourself trusts" are, generally, not useful (and can even be harmful) since planning for clients must be individualized and based upon their particular goals, estates, and circumstances. Otherwise, avoiding probate can be a substantial benefit in many circumstances.

Another area of concern for those persons who decide to use revocable trusts is that if they are unable to function, the assets maintained in their own name (as opposed to being in a revocable trust) will require the appointment of a conservator or guardian by state court and a continuing proceeding and annual charges for the maintenance of the conservatorship or guardianship. By having a revocable trust, the potential for guardianship or conservatorship is avoided since the trustee would take over the management of the assets if the trustor is incompetent.

The other major reason for the use of the revocable trust is the optimum use of the various credits and deductions available under the estate tax laws. As the laws become more complicated, formulas have been developed to optimize the available unified credit.

The same revocable trust that is used to avoid probate and potential conservatorship, as well as to reduce estate taxes, has the separate function of protecting the assets after the death of the spouse for the benefit of the children. Thus, the revocable trust usually has provisions for the trust continuing on for the children at the death of both spouses.

Where there has been good planning, the trust may take advantage of the rules relating to the generation-skipping tax and provide for one or more generations to have the use, control and benefit of property from parents that will not be subject to estate tax at their deaths. The amount that the parents can protect in this manner ranges from $3,000,000 in 2004 to $7,000,000 in 2009 (i.e., two times the GST exemption). This concept is discussed in Chapter 18 relating to generation-skipping transfers.

However, the creation of a revocable trust is only the beginning. It is necessary to actually transfer the title of assets to the trust in order to be able to avoid probate. In complicated estates, there may be more costs in the transfer of assets to the trust than in drafting it, but that is very unusual.

As long as the grantors are the trustees, no separate income tax return is required to be filed for the trust. Furthermore, a revocable trust is a grantor trust and income is generally taxable to the grantor. Thus the revocable trust has little impact upon income tax planning or income taxation of the grantors until one of them dies and the trust becomes irrevocable.

Although the revocable trust is recognized as a valuable estate planning tool, in many circumstances there are still many attorneys who, for various reasons, prefer to have their clients' assets go through probate.

Question – What is a "Pour-over Trust?"

Answer – As its name implies, a pour-over trust is one into which assets can be "poured" or funneled from the client's will, life insurance, pension or profit sharing plan, or other employee benefit plan.[5] This type of revocable trust is set up by the client during life and serves as a receptacle for any asset the client would like to pour into it. This unification is particularly useful if the client owns property in more than one state since it may save heirs a great deal of aggravation in addition to the cost savings inherent in avoiding multiple probates. Almost all states have laws regarding the validity of pour-overs to trusts established during the client's lifetime.

Question – What is a "Contingent Trust?"

Answer – A contingent trust (also known as a step up or standby trust) is one that takes over to manage and invest assets if and when the client is no longer able to do so. A contingent trust is triggered upon the occurrence of one or more specified contingencies such as the client's physical, mental, or emotional incapacity. It may also be triggered by the client upon an extended trip. Such a trust works well when coordinated with a durable power of attorney (see Chapter 56) and can help avoid the need for cumbersome and expensive probate proceedings. The client could appoint himself as trustee. The trust would provide that the grantor (client) would be succeeded by a corporate fiduciary and/or another person if the grantor becomes incompetent. Typically, this would be the same trustee designated to serve upon the client's death.

Incapacity could be defined in a number of ways – as broadly or as narrowly as the client desires. Quite often, the step up trustee takes over (a) upon the decision of a third party such as a child or friend, or (b) upon the trustee's decision that incapacity has occurred but only after a determination of incompetency by one or more specified doctors, or (c) upon a decision solely by the trustee that the grantor is incompetent, or (d) upon a judicial proceeding of incompetency, or (e) upon the determination of an independent arbitrator.

Question – When is a revocable trust funded?

Answer – Funding of a revocable trust can occur at the establishment of the trust or at any later date although most states require at least a token funding at the creation of the trust. The holder of a durable power of attorney may be authorized to make transfers of assets or shift the title to property to a previously established revocable trust. In some cases, courts have allowed such transfers even where not specifically authorized by the terms of the durable power although specific authorization is, of course, preferable. This court assistance is most likely where the dispositive terms of the revocable trust track closely with the terms of the client's will.

Question – What provisions should a trust contain if it is designed to provide property management during the grantor's incompetency?

Answer – The trust should (1) provide for income distribution to or for the grantor's benefit, (2) authorize that trust assets could be distributed to others to implement or continue a gift program (within the limits of the gift tax annual exclusion) by a duly-appointed agent, (3) specify that any pledges already made to a qualified charity be satisfied, (4) state that the management of a business interest be delegated to certain family members (this may be particularly important if the family-owned business deduction, see Chapter 42, is to be claimed).

Relatively recently, a number of states, including California, have adopted the Uniform Prudent Investor Act (UPIA). This act is based upon the idea that all trustees should be required to follow the investment concept known as the "Modern Portfolio Theory," a concept that is beyond many trustees.

The new law also requires substantial diversification and recognizes that inflation is a risk. As a result, it is no longer proper for a trustee acting under the rules imposed by this law to invest solely in fixed income assets such as government bonds. The diversification rules are such that, in addition to diversifying the types of assets, it is also necessary to diversify the investments so as to benefit both the current income beneficiary and the possible future beneficiaries (the remainder).

Thus, a trustee for a client whose trust becomes irrevocable or for a surviving spouse cannot really invest for the benefit of the current beneficiary but must invest in the stock market or some other equity investment to provide growth for future generations. Many trustees object strenuously to these rules being imposed but in many states they have been imposed upon all trusts, both those in existence and those created after the date of the enactment of the law.

Many practitioners now are providing for their trusts to be exempt from the rules of the UPIA so as to give the trustee much more flexibility to benefit the current beneficiary as opposed to having to invest so as to benefit the future beneficiaries. The law may be helpful in some circumstances and the law, for the first time in some state jurisdictions, does permit the shifting away from the trustee the responsibility for investments so that an investment manager or financial planner may be engaged to manage the assets and thus assume responsibility for them. As people become more aware of the law, substantial new opportunities may be coming for investment managers and financial planners.

Question – When does a revocable trust become irrevocable?

Answer – A revocable trust becomes irrevocable upon the earlier of the death of the grantor or when the grantor gives up the right to revoke. Generally, a grantor lacks the power to revoke a trust during incompetency. It is possible to specify that as soon as the client is deemed to be incompetent the trust becomes irrevocable. This would block a person acting under a durable power of attorney from changing the plan of disposition in the revocable trust. Note that the irrevocability of a trust may trigger adverse gift tax implications. A taxable gift can be made when a client parts with dominion and control over property. But immediate gift taxation can be blocked. The client could retain a life income in the trust's assets and delay taxation on the gift of the remainder interest (the portion going at his death to the ultimate beneficiaries of the trust) by the reservation of a testamentary power of appointment over that remainder interest. This should work even if the grantor is mentally incompetent since it is assumed that he may regain competency at any time before death.

Question – What happens to the assets in a revocable trust when a client dies?

Answer – Assuming a trust is funded at the time of a client's death, assets can be paid directly and immediately to the named beneficiaries and the trust can be terminated. Alternatively, the trust can be continued. However, it should be recognized that if there is any potential estate tax due, the trustee is individually responsible for payment of any estate tax if assets have been transferred out of the trust and there are not sufficient assets left to pay the estate tax. For this reason, in trusts where there may be any potential estate tax due, the trustee may require the retention of a certain amount of assets to deal with any potential estate tax.

The trust, which is now irrevocable, can serve as a receptacle to receive assets poured over into it. It can then continue to exist until its purpose or term has been completed. A third possibility is that the assets in the trust can be consolidated with another trust.

Assets in the trust at the grantor's death are subject to federal estate tax that will be based, not on the value of the assets when contributed to the trust, but on the value as of the date of death. EGTRRA 2001 repeals the estate tax for one year in 2010.

More and more in recent years, planners have been suggesting steps to reduce the value for transfer tax purposes (estate tax and gift tax) of the assets held. In some cases, the family limited partnership, discussed in Chapter 43, is a tool by which the value of the assets can be significantly reduced. Additionally, a number of actuarial and charitable programs can reduce the value for transfer tax purposes. However, the financial well being of the client may preclude many of the latter concepts since they do prohibit the client's access to the principal in many cases.

Question – What is the easiest way to shift joint property into a revocable trust?

Answer – For most couples the most effective way may be to create a single revocable trust which has subtrusts for each of the separate property of the husband, separate property of the wife, and for community property. By having only one trust as opposed to two trusts, it is much easier to do planning for estate tax minimization. To the extent that either spouse has separate property or an interest in property held in tenancy in common, those would be held in the subtrust for the person's separate property.

In some circumstances, it may be appropriate for the spouses to each have a separate revocable trust, but that practice has been declining in recent years. It is possible for the clients to convert property to trust property by merely naming it in the trust. However, even though this can result in the property being controlled by the trust, in most states it is also necessary to go to the probate court in order to actually have the title of the property transferred to the trust in a way that will be accepted by title companies. The result in this circumstance is that a failure to actually transfer the title during lifetime results in a much more expensive legal process to have the probate court assume the responsibility to transfer the assets. It also leaves room for doubt or possible argument that is not present if there are actual recorded deeds or other indicia of title that clearly show the transfer to the trust.

Question – What factors should be considered in selecting a trustee?

Answer – A trustee should possess business judgment (even if there is no business), honesty, and integrity.

The trustee must be able and willing to exercise a high degree of care over trust property and avoid (however tempting) investments or acts that are likely to result in losses.

A trustee must have legal capacity to contract. This precludes the appointment of a minor or incompetent adult. Geographical considerations contraindicate an individual who lives a considerable distance from the client or his heirs.

The type and size of assets to be placed into the trust, as well as the client's goals, are important considerations in selecting a trustee. Obviously, if the client's primary asset is a business, the trustee will have much more responsibility and must have higher and broader competence than if the trust's assets consisted mainly of cash.

Investment skill is necessary. Under the "prudent person" rule, a trustee will be liable to the beneficiary for losses unless he exercises the same care and skill that a person of ordinary prudence would exercise in dealing with his own property. But the Uniform Probate Code, now in effect in some form in most states, raises this standard for professional trustees by providing: "If the trustee has greater skill than that of a man of ordinary prudence, he is under a duty to exercise such skill."

Because a trustee must examine and review the trust periodically, administrative and legal skills and knowledge are important. Accountings must be made to the client and eventually to the other beneficiaries. All parties must be advised accurately on the tax and other legal effects. Provisions in the trust must, from time to time, be interpreted.

Question – Does a family member, close friend, or business associate make a good trustee?

Answer – There are significant advantages and disadvantages to naming a family member or business associate as trustee. A nonprofessional trustee is indicated where the minimum fee charged by local professional fiduciaries is higher than it's feasible to pay.

Is it appropriate for a family member, a close friend, or a business associate to serve as trustee? The obvious advantage is that such a person may have a working knowledge of the client, the family, and the finances and business. But selection of a person as trustee must also consider conflicts of interest and ethical problems. For instance, how will a trustee who is also a beneficiary react when faced with a choice that favors him at the expense of other beneficiaries or that favors other beneficiaries at his expense? Will the trustee favor other beneficiaries at his own expense? Will the fees charged by a family member or business associate as trustee be understood and accepted without resentment or will it cause conflict? Will the trustee's "hard choices" be injurious to family relationships? Is the trustee likely to show favoritism or be easily persuaded?

Can an untrained individual deal with the legal, tax, and investment functions of being a trustee? Even though a trustee is legally entitled to hire agents to serve as investment counselors, accountants, and attorneys to assist on special problems, the trustee remains responsible for the ultimate decisions. Would an untrained individual know whom to call? Would the trustee know if the advice he is receiving is both legally and practically correct? Does the trustee understand that he is personally liable for unpaid federal estate taxes if a distribution is made to beneficiaries before the estate tax liability is fully paid (even if the trust provides for immediate distributions from the trust on the grantor's death)? If a distribution is made that can't be recovered, the trustee will be personally liable to the extent remaining trust assets are insufficient to pay the estate's estate tax liability.

Question – When is a corporate trustee indicated?

Answer – A corporate fiduciary (with or without individuals as co-trustees) is clearly indicated where it is likely that the trust will span more than one generation. Corporate fiduciaries are also indicated where the amount placed into the trust is large and/or will require skillful and constant attention. If there is likelihood of family conflict, corporate fiduciaries can make decisions on a more objective disinterested basis than family members.

Question – What role does state law play in the choice of trustee?

Answer – A trust will be invalid if it does not meet state law requirements. Planners should be aware of two potential problems: (1) the Doctrine of Merger and (2) The Passive Trust theory.

In some states, when the same person is both trustee and beneficiary, the trust ceases to exist as a separate entity. Legal title to the property (held by the trustee) merges with the equitable (beneficial) title (held by the beneficiary). The result is that if the sole beneficiary of the trust is also the sole trustee, the beneficiary becomes the owner of the total rights in the trust assets. This is known as a "fee simple" or "fee simple absolute." The trust, as such, ceases to exist. However, in many states the same person may be both trustee and beneficiary.

A second potential problem occurs in the case of a so-called "passive trust." This is a trust that gives the trustee no meaningful duties to perform and gives the beneficiary unfettered enjoyment and management control of assets. The result is a merger of the legal title and the equitable title; the trust ceases to exist. Either through operation of law or through judicial action, where the trustee's duties are purely ministerial and all significant authority and decision making are placed in the hands of the beneficiary, the beneficiary receives total title to the property that was in the trust.

Question – What is the effect of a revocable trust on creditors?

Answer – The ability of a revocable trust to protect assets from the claims of the client's creditors will depend on state law and the provisions of the trust document. As a general rule, if the grantor has retained the right to trust assets or the right to alter, amend, revoke, or terminate the trust, there will be little if any protection from the claims of creditors. In the typical revocable living trust, the client retains too many rights over the trust assets to put those assets beyond the reach of creditors.

Question – Are there advantages to making the trust the beneficiary of qualified plan benefits?

Answer – First, naming a revocable trust as beneficiary of qualified pension or profit sharing plan or IRA or HR-10 payments helps to unify the administration of the estate and achieve the client's objectives. Second, a trust serves as a means of deferring the distribution of assets to beneficiaries who may not be ready or able to handle large sums of money. Third, a trust enables the sprinkling of capital and the spraying of income to those beneficiaries who need or deserve it the most or who are in the lowest tax brackets. Fourth, payment of qualified plan benefits to a trustee makes it possible for the trustee to make certain advantageous tax elections on behalf of the estate.

In addition, under new regulations, if the trust qualifies as a "designated beneficiary," it is possible to defer the payments from the plan over the life expectancy of the beneficiary of the trust. This allows a longer period for the plan assets to continue to grow on a tax-deferred basis. There are, however, certain strict requirements that must be met in order for a trust to qualify as a designated beneficiary. Also, the spouse of the participant cannot elect to be treated as the owner of plan proceeds if a trust is named beneficiary. These requirements are discussed in more detail in Chapter 51. If the trust does not qualify, the plan proceeds will have to be paid out either (1) over the participant's remaining life expectancy if the participant died after reaching age 70½, or (2) no later than the end of the fifth year after the year of the participant's death if the participant died before reaching age 70½. While a longer period of tax deferral may not be possible if the trust does not qualify, in some cases it is still more beneficial to name the trust as the beneficiary rather than individual persons.

Question – Can a revocable trust safely hold the stock of an S corporation?

Answer – To be eligible to elect the "pass through" taxation similar to a partnership, a corporation must meet stringent requirements. The only trusts which qualify as eligible shareholders of S corporations (see Chapter 46) are:

1. Voting trusts

2. A trust receiving stock under a will (but only for the first 2 years after the stock is transferred to the trust)

3. IRC Section 678 trusts (relating to trusts where a person other than the grantor is treated as the owner)

4. Grantor trusts (which includes revocable living trusts over which the grantor has retained all powers or to whom income is taxable under IRC Sections 671-677, and for 2 years after the grantor's death)

5. A qualified subchapter S trust (QSST)

6. An electing small business trust (ESBT)

If any other type of trust owns stock in an S corporation, the S election is automatically nullified.

The result is that the corporation would be taxed as a regular corporation and the pass through of income or deductions would be denied.

Question – Are there situations in which a revocable living trust is contra-indicated?

Answer – Yes. A revocable living trust may not make sense if there is no specific reason to set it up other than to save probate and administration costs – and the certain immediately payable present value cost of drafting the trust and maintaining it will exceed the future possible savings. A revocable living trust is not indicated where the client is not likely to follow through with the retitling of property and the other prerequisites and operating procedures to assure the continued validity of the trust and to assure it will be legally recognized when the client dies. Stock in a professional corporation may not be able to be transferred to a revocable trust because of the prohibition against ownership by anyone other than a professional. If IRC Section 1244 stock is held by a revocable living trust, it may not qualify for ordinary loss treatment. The deduction allowed to estates for the amount of income permanently set aside for charitable purposes is not allowed to trusts. A living trust is not necessary if the client's estate is modest, the mortgage paid off, and there is no reason to keep probate proceedings private, and the executor of the estate is a family member who will probably waive executor's fees and the client lives in a state where the attorney fees are modest. Finally, a revocable trust is not indicated if a less complex less expensive durable power of attorney can satisfy the need. For instance, a broadly drawn durable power of attorney will enable the holder to do many of the same ministerial tasks (such as preparing and filing tax returns) as the trustee of a trust.

Question – Are there disadvantages in putting investment real estate in a revocable trust?

Answer – There may be several. The impact on real property taxes must be considered. Some states have provisions for reassessment of real property for property tax purposes if it is transferred. If highly appreciated property is transferred to a revocable trust, this could result in a costly reassessment. Some states, such as California, exempt property transferred to a revocable trust from reassessment. Also, it should be determined whether or not the transfer will accelerate the payment of any mortgage or deed of trust on the property under so-called "acceleration" provisions in the note or mortgage. Again, many transactions are exempt.

Finally, great care should be taken to determine if the real property is presently generating losses or will be expected to do so after the death of the owner. Under IRC Section 469, losses from various activities, including some rental real estate activities, are characterized as passive losses, not deductible except under limited circumstances. However, Section 469(i) allows deduction for losses of up to $25,000 per year if the owner is actively participating in the management of the property. Section 469(i)(4) permits continued deduction of such losses for two years after the death of the owner by the owner's estate. It is generally assumed the use of the term "estate" could not be extended to cover revocable trusts. The safer course is to allow such property to pass through an estate, which after two years could distribute it to the trust under pour-over provisions discussed above.

Question – What is an "administrative" trust?

Answer – Practitioners generally use this term to refer to the revocable trust immediately after the death of the grantor where it is to be further divided into separate trusts, such as the marital deduction and bypass trusts discussed in Chapter 24. Since the actual funding of such separate trusts may take months or even years, most practitioners believe the revocable trust continues to be a separate trust entity for a period commencing with the death of the grantor and ending on the date any separate trusts are finally funded. Unfortunately, many living trust documents fail to indicate what to do with that trust during the interim period, which could have important tax consequences.

Question – If the grantor of a revocable trust is contemplating making gifts from the trust assets, is it better for the grantor to direct the trustee to make the gifts directly, or for the grantor to remove the assets from the trust and make the gifts directly?

Answer – Prior to TRA '97, there was a danger that a transfer from a revocable trust within three years of death might be subject to an IRS attack under IRC Section 2035. It should no longer matter whether the transfer is made directly by the grantor or indirectly through the Trustee.

Question – Will the use of revocable trusts present any problems if the grantor or husband and wife grantors are seeking public assistance for medical care?

Answer – The requirements for federal and state assistance for medical care, generally called "Medicaid," are discussed in Chapter 55. As noted in that chapter, the use of revocable trusts could have an adverse effect on the eligibility of the grantors for such assistance.

CHAPTER ENDNOTES

1. IRC Sec. 671.
2. *Burnet v. Guggenheim*, 288 U.S. 280 (1933).
3. IRC Sec. 2038.
4. IRC Sec. 2523.
5. It should be noted that retirement plans payable to a trust might not permit distributions to be "stretched-out" over the lifetimes of the beneficiaries. See Reg. §1.401(a)(9)-4.

Chapter 29

TAX BASIS REVOCABLE TRUST

WHAT IS IT?

Basically, the tax basis revocable trust is a revocable living trust discussed in Chapter 28. However, this form of the revocable trust is structured to achieve a step up in the income tax basis of property owned by either spouse on the death of either spouse. This is accomplished by using a general power of appointment in tandem with a marital deduction so that all of the property owned by the spouses will pass through the taxable estate of the first spouse to die. [However, see the final Question and Answer for a decedent dying in 2010.]

The tax basis revocable trust is a fairly recent development. There is little authority regarding use of this technique to obtain a step up in basis.

WHEN IS THE USE OF SUCH A DEVICE INDICATED?

This device may be considered in a variety of scenarios where one or both spouses own appreciated property. It is probably most advantageous where the combined estates of both spouses will be less than the available exemption equivalent provided by the unified credit (generally, a total of $3,000,000 in 2004). It will also be most advantageous where one spouse owns considerably more appreciated property than the other.

WHAT ARE THE REQUIREMENTS?

This technique starts with the establishment of either one revocable trust by both spouses, or separate revocable trusts by each spouse. In one such trust that was the subject of a private letter ruling,[1] a husband and wife created a joint revocable trust. Under its terms, the wife was given a general power of appointment over the assets transferred to the trust by the husband. She died without exercising that power. For federal estate tax purposes, the fact that she had that power at the date of her death resulted in inclusion of the husband's property in her taxable estate.[2] Since that was true, its income tax basis would be adjusted to fair market value at the date of her death.[3]

Since the wife in this example did not exercise her general power of appointment over the property of the husband, he can still revoke the trust. As a result, the estate of the wife can claim a federal estate tax marital deduction for the value of the property passing to the husband as the surviving spouse.[4] In other words, the husband ends up with the same property he had before, but with a brand new income tax basis.

However, the IRS held that the property in question did not receive a new income tax basis at the death of the wife. It held that the provisions of IRC Section 1014(e) would be applicable. Under that section, if property is transferred from one spouse to another within one year of the death of the transferee spouse, and at the death of that spouse is distributed to the transferor spouse, there is no basis adjustment. Under the facts of the ruling, the property had been transferred to the trust within one year of her death. The result may have been positive, however, had the transferee spouse lived for longer than one year after receipt of the gift.

An obvious drawback to this arrangement, in addition to the possible rejection of it by the IRS, is that the donee spouse may in fact exercise the power of appointment. This technique should be considered only in the case of very stable marriages.

The proponents of the technique seek to minimize this disadvantage by using one or two revocable trusts in which the general power of appointment is limited to appointment of the assets by the nonowner spouse to the creditors of the nonowner spouse. Further, the general power of appointment given to the donee spouse may be limited to a testamentary power, i.e., a power only exercisable by a will or other document at death. Further, the impact of the power may be further limited by restricting it to only certain assets, generally the ones that either have or that are most likely to appreciate in value.

HOW IT IS DONE – AN EXAMPLE

James and Martha Edwards, husband and wife, who live in a common law state, create a joint revocable trust. Under its terms, either spouse can revoke the trust while alive. If it is revoked, any assets contributed to the trust by either spouse will be returned to that spouse. Upon the death of either spouse, the deceased spouse has the power to direct the payment of any of his or her debts and taxes from assets contributed to the trust by the surviving spouse.

Assume the only contributions to the trust are separate assets of James worth $500,000, with an income tax basis of $100,000. Martha dies more than one year after the transfer. Since she has a general power of appointment over the trust, i.e., a power to appoint to her creditors, the property in the trust will be included in her taxable estate and presumably its income tax basis will be adjusted to its fair market value, $500,000.

Will the property also be included in the taxable estate of James on his subsequent death? That depends on the terms of the trust. If he can still revoke the trust, it will. If he cannot revoke the trust, but the assets are transferred to a trust that qualifies as a QTIP trust (see Chapter 24), it will be if the estate of Martha elected the marital deduction.

Assuming in this case James has no other substantial assets, there may be little estate tax risk on his subsequent death. If there is, it can be solved by a qualified disclaimer by James (assuming he can disclaim, see below), or in the case of the QTIP trust, by making no QTIP election or a partial QTIP election when Martha dies.

WHAT ARE THE TAX IMPLICATIONS?

This device is entirely tax motivated. As discussed above, it requires that the revocable trust or trusts grant the spouse who does not own the property a power of appointment over it that will qualify as a general power of appointment for federal estate tax purposes. It assumes that this power will not be exercised and that since the surviving spouse, who is really the owner of the property, has a power to revoke the trust, the estate of the nonowner spouse will obtain a full marital deduction for the property.

What if the owner spouse is the first to die? Since the owner spouse has a power to revoke the trust, all of the property is included in the taxable estate of the owner spouse.[5] As a result, the property will obtain a new income tax basis. If the surviving nonowner spouse has a general power of appointment over the property, it should qualify for the marital deduction.[6] The problem is that in that case it will all also be taxed in the estate of the surviving nonowner spouse. As a result, this tech-

nique requires the use of qualified disclaimers, discussed in Chapter 11.

The disclaimer should be available on the death of either spouse. For example, assume the nonowner spouse dies first, and does not exercise his or her general power of appointment. The owner spouse can revoke the trust, therefore the trust assets will all become part of his or her estate. The owner spouse may be able to disclaim enough of the property to assure the use of the available estate tax unified credit exemption equivalent of the nonowner spouse, as much as $1,500,000 in 2004. That part of the property could then pass either directly to children or other family members, or to a trust for the benefit of the family. If this is effective, that part of the property will not be included in the estate of the owner spouse and will not be subject to estate taxation.

Insofar as the authors are aware, the IRS has not ruled on whether or not the disclaimer would be effective in the foregoing situation. In effect, the owner is disclaiming an interest in property he or she already owns, not generally permitted under the disclaimer rules. However, since the IRS has conceded, in at least one private ruling, that the property passes first through the taxable estate of the nonowner spouse, the surviving owner spouse should have a disclaimer power.

The other use of the disclaimer here is in the event the owner spouse is the first to die. Since the surviving nonowner spouse has a general power of appointment over the trust, it would all pass through his or her taxable estate. The surviving nonowner spouse may disclaim a sufficient part of the property to take advantage of the available unified credit of the predeceased spouse, avoiding estate taxation to that extent. Again, the disclaimed property could pass to children, other family members, or in trust.

IMPLICATIONS AND ISSUES IN COMMUNITY PROPERTY STATES

Under applicable provisions of the Internal Revenue Code,[7] upon the death of either spouse, all of the community property owned by the spouses receives a new income tax basis equal to fair market value on the death of either spouse. Therefore, to the extent the property is community in nature, the tax basis revocable trust is not necessary. In fact, the tax basis revocable trust is often recommended as a way to achieve the same tax basis that would result if the property were community property.

Where either spouse owns separate property in a community property state, the tax basis revocable trust may be proposed as method of obtaining the income tax basis adjustment on the death of either spouse. Depending on state law, that result could also be obtained by converting the separate property to community property, which of course confers equal ownership on both spouses.

For decedents dying in 2010, an increased basis is not available merely because property was subject to a power of appointment, although a limited increase in basis may still be available for community property. See the final Question and Answer.

QUESTIONS AND ANSWERS

Question – Are the intended tax results of the tax basis revocable trust assured?

Answer – The only ruling on the tax consequences of this device, described above, denied the stepped up basis in trust assets on the death of the nonowner spouse. The rationale for that ruling is a statutory provision that only applies where property is transferred from one spouse to the other, the donee spouse dies, and the property is retransferred to the donor. That will not be the usual planning situation.

Also, as noted above, there may be some question as to the availability of a disclaimer by the owner spouse following the death of the nonowner spouse, on the theory that one cannot disclaim property he or she already owns. However, since that property passes first through the estate of another person, the disclaimer should be available. It should be noted that the IRS now concedes that where an individual places property in joint tenancy with another person, either joint tenant could have partitioned the property at will while both tenants were alive, and the other person is the first to die, the transferor can disclaim the survivorship interest in the transferee's half of the joint tenancy.

Question – What are the advantages and disadvantages of joint trusts or separate trusts?

Answer – The joint trust is most commonly used for smaller estates where the federal estate tax is not a major factor, or where only one spouse is contributing property to the trust. Where the federal estate tax and/or contributions by both spouses are involved, many practitioners prefer the use of separate trusts.

In this scenario, each spouse contributes property to a separate trust, and retains the power to revoke it during his or her lifetime, as well as income and other benefits. After the death of the first spouse, the surviving spouse is the beneficiary of both trusts for life, and they are both structured to qualify as QTIP trusts. As in the case of the joint trust, the deceased spouse has a power to appoint appreciated assets in the survivor's trust to creditors to create a general power of appointment. Also, the surviving spouse may have a power of revocation over the trusts. The use of disclaimers and QTIP election described above will apply here.

Question – How does EGTRRA 2001 affect the use of this technique?

Answer – EGTRRA 2001 repeals the estate tax for one year in 2010. Along with repeal of the estate tax, a modified carryover basis replaces a step-up in basis for property acquired from a decedent dying in 2010.[8] For purposes of the modified carryover rules, a decedent is not treated as the owner of property merely by reason of a power of appointment. Therefore, a step-up in basis cannot be allocated to property subject to a power of appointment of a powerholder who dies in 2010.

CHAPTER ENDNOTES

1. Let. Rul. 9308002.
2. IRC Sec. 2041(a)(2).
3. IRC Sec. 1014(a).
4. IRC Sec. 2056.
5. IRC Secs. 2036, 2038.
6. IRC Sec. 2056(b).
7. IRC Sec. 1014(b)(6).
8. IRC Sec. 1022.

Part 6:

LIFE INSURANCE

Chapter 30

LIFE INSURANCE

WHAT IS IT?

Life insurance is a contract under which for a stipulated consideration (a premium), one party (the insurer) agrees to pay the other (the insured), or his or her beneficiary, a defined amount upon the occurrence of death or some other specified event. In essence, life insurance is a contract under which economic protection is provided against the risk of cessation of income due to the insured's death. This definition of life insurance includes accidental death benefits under health insurance policies, whole life, endowment, universal, variable, and term life insurance policies. It encompasses both personally-owned and business-owned policies and includes group coverage as well as individually purchased plans.

WHEN IS THE USE OF SUCH A DEVICE INDICATED?

1. Life insurance is an important estate planning tool to provide cash for the payment of estate and inheritance taxes, debts, administrative costs, and other estate expenses. The Economic Growth and Tax Relief Reconciliation Act of 2001 repeals the estate tax for one year in 2010.

2. Life insurance will provide an income for family expenses.

3. Life insurance can be used for special needs such as the payment of college expenses, mortgage balances, or other large capital needs.

4. Life insurance is often used as a credit-building tool; lending institutions and other creditors often use life insurance on a debtor's life as security.

5. Life insurance provides a way to pay federal estate taxes at a "discount." For example, if an individual purchases a $100,000 policy and dies within the first year of a contract (after having paid $1,500 in premiums), $100,000 worth of taxes can be paid at a cost of only $1,500. The difference can be roughly thought of as a discount. Furthermore, properly arranged life insurance owned by a third party who is also named beneficiary can be used to pay estate settlement costs with no probate cost, no inheritance or other state death taxes, no income taxes, no transfer fees, and no federal estate taxes.

6. Life insurance can be used as the "funding" mechanism for business continuation agreements.

7. Life insurance can be used by a corporation to finance certain corporate obligations such as nonqualified deferred compensation or salary continuation, as well as be used as key person insurance to indemnify the corporation for the lost services of a key person.

8. Life insurance can be used to fund a charitable gift. (See Chapter 32.)

9. Life insurance can be used to supplement an individual's retirement program.

WHAT ARE THE VARIOUS TYPES OF LIFE INSURANCE?

Term Insurance

Under this type of insurance the insured must die before the term expires for which benefits are to be paid. If the insured survives to the expiration of the "term," the insurance protection terminates. Initially, the cash outlay for insurance protection is relatively low so that the policyowner receives the maximum short term protection for the minimum cash outlay.

There are basically five types of term insurance:

1. *Annual renewable term.* This type of policy is renewable each year (regardless of the insured's physical condition) at an increasing premium.

2. *Convertible term.* This type of policy may be exchanged without evidence of insurability, i.e., without the insured proving that he is physi-

cally and otherwise in a standard class of risks, for a whole life, universal life, variable life, or endowment type of policy.

3. *Decreasing term.* A familiar kind of decreasing term is often called "mortgage" insurance. The death benefit decreases over the specified period of time, but the premium generally remains level.

4. *Level term.* Here the death benefit remains the same for the entire term of the policy. Generally the premium also remains level. Common term periods are 5, 10, 15, 20, and 30 years.

5. *Re-entry term.* This type of policy provides a guaranteed term premium for an initial premium but allows the insured to re-qualify or re-enter after the initial period, if his or her health remains good. Re-entry can occur typically after a five- or ten-year period. If the insured does not re-qualify, the rates remain at the guaranteed rates, which are much higher than the re-entry rates.

Whole Life Insurance

The major characteristics of whole life insurance are: (a) the premium for a whole life insurance contract is guaranteed to remain level throughout the life of the contract; and (b) because of the "reserve" the insurance company needs to maintain a level premium when the insured reaches older ages, "cash value" builds up within the contract (this cash value increases annually and can be borrowed by the policyowner or taken as surrender proceeds).

There are basically two types of whole life insurance. The first type is known as straight whole life, while the second is known as limited payment life. The difference is basically that under a limited payment life policy, premiums are "compressed," i.e., they are payable over a shorter period of time, whereas in a straight whole life policy premiums are payable for the lifetime of the insured. For example, if a male age 35 purchased a $100,000 straight life policy, the "face amount" (death benefit) would be $100,000. If he purchased a $100,000 20-payment life policy at the same age, the death benefit would be the same and the protection would be provided for as long as the policyowner wanted to keep the policy in force, i.e., it could be kept in force for the insured's life. But because premiums would be compressed into a much smaller period of time (20 annual payments), they would be considerably higher under the limited payment type of plan.

There is another variety of whole life—modified life. A modified life insurance policy typically provides a given amount of insurance at unusually low premium rates for an initial period (e.g., five years) after issue and then the premium is correspondingly higher for the remainder of the premium period. Modified plans generally have a lower initial cash value than a corresponding face amount of typical straight life would have.

Riders, such as waiver of premium (waives premium if insured is disabled for a period of at least six months) and accidental death and dismemberment (doubles the death benefit if death is by accidental means), may be added to the basic contract.

Endowment Insurance

The primary characteristic of endowment insurance is that such a plan pays the face amount (e.g., $100,000) at the sooner of the time of "endowment" (the maturity of the contract, e.g., age 65) or at the insured's death. Endowment policies are basically purchased as a means of forced savings because the protection element is relatively minimal. Various types of endowment policies are often found in pension plans or personal savings programs. Since the cash value builds up tax free under an endowment policy, such plans are often utilized by individuals in high income tax brackets. Generally speaking as a result of changes to the tax code in 1984, endowment contracts no longer qualify as life insurance.

Universal Life Insurance

A universal life policy is interest sensitive life insurance in which the investment, expense, and mortality elements are separately and specifically defined. A contract owner selects a death benefit level. The death benefit may be one that increases over time, coinciding with the increased cash value of the policy (death benefit option II), or, alternatively, the death benefit can remain level regardless of the underlying value changes (death benefit option I). From the premium that is paid, the insurer then deducts a "load" for contractually defined expenses. The remaining premium is then credited toward the contract owner's cash values. Mortality charges are deducted. Interest earned on the remaining cash is then credited at rates based on current investment earnings. (Specific design features will vary from company to company depending on marketing policies and product objectives.) Under this configuration, increased interest rates result in higher cash value levels while increased expense loads and increased mortality charges result in lower cash values. Typically, there is a minimum contractual guarantee as to the interest credited, such as 4 or 4.5%. Mortality costs also have a guarantee through a maximum premium charge for the "pure" cost of the death benefit; however, most companies charge rates lower than the contractually allowed maximum.

There is no such thing as a predetermined "standard" universal life plan; each contract owner selects the level of premium and death benefit desired as well as the length of premium paying period. Significant flexibility in premium payments is possible. Usually a stated minimum premium must be paid the first policy year. But after that the contract owner can vary the amount, the payment date, or frequency of subsequent premiums. (Depending on the amount of the initial premium, additional premiums or premium increases may be limited to stated minimum or maximum levels.) "Stop and go" features allow the discontinuance as well as subsequent resumption of premium payments at any time. As long as there is enough cash value to pay the expense (loading) charges and mortality costs, the policy will remain in force. If the cash value falls below that level, the policy will terminate.

Gross premiums are reduced by specified expense charges (as well as mortality costs) to determine the universal life policy's cash value. Expense loads run between 5 and 10% of the gross premium and are charged year after year. Additionally, because of greater first year acquisition costs, an extra first year expense may be levied. (This may be factored into the policy as a "per policy" amount, an amount per $1,000 of death benefits, or as a percentage of first year mortality charges.) Some companies may spread out the additional first year expenses by increasing the annual percentage of gross premium charges on some minimum amount of cumulative premium and set a lower percentage charge on premiums in excess of that stated minimum amount. Alternatively, rather than increasing expense charges, many insurers are recovering expense and surrender costs through "surrender charges." Upon surrender, the contract owner receives an amount reduced by a surrender charge, generally a percentage of the cash (or accumulated) value. Generally, the longer the policy is held the less is taken out. Most surrender charges are applicable for 15 years or less.

Similar to traditional policies, riders such as waiver of premium or accidental death and dismemberment may be added to the basic contract.

Also similar to traditional life insurance, loans can be taken against cash values subject to an interest charge. Unlike most traditional whole life policies, there is the ability to make partial withdrawals of cash values while the insured is alive. Since withdrawals are not loans, no interest charges are incurred.

Variable Life Insurance

A variable life insurance policy resembles a traditional whole life policy with two major distinctions. Both the death benefit payable upon death and the surrender value payable during life are not guaranteed, but can increase or decrease depending upon the investment performance of the assets underlying the policy. The death benefit, however, generally, cannot decrease below the initial face amount of the policy, as long as all required premiums have been paid. With variable life, you trade the cash surrender value guarantee for the potential of investment growth by directing the overall strategy of your policy's investment program.

The policyowner, not the insurance company, allocates the premium, after certain deductions are made, to a particular sub-account held by the insurance company. Among the types of sub-accounts that may be offered are a money market type account, a growth stock account, a bond account, a balanced fund account, and a real estate account. And, depending on the insurance company, the choices may be changed several times a year. The death benefit typically will be adjusted once a year, whereas, the cash value will be adjusted on a daily basis. Premiums are fixed and always remain the same. Since both the surrender value and death benefit can vary, the product is known as variable life.

Among the charges that are deducted from the premium before any investment is made in a sub-account are administrative and sales expenses, any state premium taxes, and the cost for the mortality element.

Variable life enjoys the same favorable income tax treatment as other life insurance policies. Earnings from the investments are currently income tax deferred. In other words, there is no tax on the internal buildup of cash values until such values are realized by way of surrender, and then only if the surrender value exceeds the policyholder's cost basis, unless the policy is classified as a modified endowment contract (see question below). Death benefits, regardless of growth, pass income tax free.

Should a policyholder wish to have access to his cash values and not surrender the policy, he can borrow up to a designated percentage of the cash value (e.g., 90%). Interest, typically, is charged on these loans.

Similar to traditional policies, riders such as waiver of premium or accidental death and dismemberment may be added to the basic contract.

Unlike some other types of insurance, the sale of a variable life insurance product must be accompanied by or preceded by a prospectus approved by the Securities and Exchange Commission, as variable life is treated as a security. It can be sold by only agents registered as broker-dealers with the National Association of Securities Dealers (NASD).

Variable Universal Life Insurance

Variable universal life is a combination of universal life insurance and variable life insurance. It is like universal life with flexible premiums, adjustable death benefits, policy loan, and partial withdrawal privileges. However, unlike universal life and like variable life, the owner of the life contract and not the insurer decides where the premiums are invested. The alternative accounts where the premiums can be invested are similar to those in the variable life product described above.

Like variable life, variable universal life is a product subject to the rules of the Securities and Exchange Commission and, therefore, requires a prospectus be given to a prospective client before a sale can be made.

Survivorship Life Insurance

Survivorship life insurance, sometimes called joint and survivor life or second-to-die life, is a type of life insurance policy that insures two or more people. The policy may be either a whole life, term, universal, or variable type of policy. The death benefit under a survivorship policy is not realized until the last of two or more insured individuals dies. At that time the full death benefit is payable to the named beneficiary. Although there are several variations of this type of insurance, some of the policies that are of the whole life variety insure two individuals and provide for an increase in cash values upon the "first death," and, if the policies are participating (dividend paying), also provide for increased dividends. Depending upon the company, the premiums may continue until the survivor's subsequent death or, through a special option, the policy may be paid up at the "first death" and no further premiums would be required.

The policy can insure any two insureds as long as there is an insurable interest. Its use is typically confined to husband-wife, parent-child, or two related business people, such as business owners or key employees. The policy can be considered a very effective tool, relieving the federal estate tax burden of those couples who will be subject to that tax and have elected to take maximum advantage of the marital deduction, so that although there will not be any federal estate tax due upon the first spouse's death, there will be tax due at the survivor's death.

The policy may be owned by any party that could own any of the other traditional types of life insurance policy, including an irrevocable trust. There is no requirement that there be joint owners, despite the fact that there are two insured individuals.

First-to-Die Life Insurance

First-to-die insurance is a life insurance policy that insures two or more people. The policy may be a whole life, term, universal, or variable life type of policy. The death benefit is realized when the first of any of the insureds dies, at which time the death benefit is payable to the named beneficiary. Some policies, through a rider, allow the survivor to continue coverage if he or she desires after the first insured dies.

The policy can be used in either business or personal planning, where there is a need for coverage only until the death of one of the two insured parties. Using a single first-to-die policy to insure multiple parties usually costs less in premiums than the purchase of two separate policies.

Single Premium Whole Life Insurance

Single premium whole life insurance is a type of limited pay life insurance policy. Unlike traditional whole life policies, however, where premiums are due generally until age 90 or 100, a single premium whole life policy, as the name implies, requires only one premium.

The policyholder purchases a paid-up policy with just one payment rather than paying premiums year after year. For example, a $25,000 single premium might buy a 55-year-old man $75,000 worth of insurance coverage.

Single premium life offers some of the traditional tax advantages that regular whole life policies afford:

1. The money contributed to the policy builds up tax deferred through policy cash values.

2. The policyholder can borrow those cash values from the policy. Such a loan may trigger income tax consequences if the policy is classified as a modified endowment contract as it typically would be.

3. The proceeds from the policy (the face value, as distinct from the cash surrender value) at the death of the insured go to the beneficiaries completely income tax free and without probate.

4. One of the main characteristics of this type of insurance is that the policy develops immediate cash values. Interest is generally credited based upon some type of "new money" approach, and may be tied into short- or long-term investments of the particular insurance company. The values that the policy develops can be availed of either through a surrender of the policy or through a policy loan. Some companies allow the policyholder to borrow these values at no interest cost or at a nominal interest cost to the policyholder. For example, if a policyholder borrows $10,000, the insurance company might charge him 8% interest, but that is not his true cost. The company would credit his cash value account with the 8% interest he paid or 7% or 6% depending upon the company. Thus, the true interest cost to borrow would be anywhere from 0% to 2%. The policyholder need never pay back the loan. However, if the contract is classified as a modified endowment contract, borrowing from the policy will likely result in income tax consequences. Outstanding loans will reduce the death benefit, and interest on the loan is generally not income tax deductible.

WHAT ARE THE VARIOUS FEATURES OF A LIFE INSURANCE POLICY?

The professional should be familiar with the particular life insurance policy's ownership provisions, dividend provisions, and various additional benefits such as the accidental death benefit, disability waiver of premium, and guaranteed insurability, which is often called insurance of insurability.

The basic ownership rights are the right to name and change the beneficiary, the right to cash in a policy, the right to receive dividends, the right to borrow against policy cash values or to make partial withdrawals, and the right to dispose of some or all of the policy ownership rights mentioned above. An unconditional sale or gift of all ownership rights in a life insurance policy is known as an "absolute" assignment. When a policy is pledged as collateral for a loan, the assignment is known as a "collateral" assignment.

Dividend provisions are particularly important. Basically, a dividend is a refund of part of the premiums that the insured has paid to a life insurance company and is the result of the insured's participation in the business fortunes of the policy class to which he or she belongs. The size of the dividend is based on the relative amount of favorable mortality, interest, and "loading" (business cost) experience of the insurance company.

The policyowner can:

1. take dividends in the form of cash;

2. use dividends to reduce premiums;

3. buy paid-up additional insurance (each dividend buys a small single premium policy in addition to the basic plan; no physical examination is required; and this additional insurance is purchased without sales charges or other costs);

4. leave the dividend with the company to earn (taxable) interest;

5. purchase one-year term insurance equal to the cash value of the policy;

6. use dividends to "vanish the premiums" on the policy at an earlier than expected date;

7. use some combination of the above dividend options.

Dividends are generally not available on universal or variable policies.

A number of additional benefits can be added (usually by a "rider") to a life insurance policy. For example, an accidental death benefit, for a small extra premium, will be paid in addition to the basic death benefit if death occurs in an accident before a specified age. (Typically, the basic death benefit is doubled.)

A second additional benefit that can be added is known as "disability waiver of premium." Under this useful benefit, premiums are waived (taken over by the insurance company) after the insured is totally disabled for a period of six months. Generally, most companies will refund any premiums paid during the first six months of disability. Cash values on a whole life policy will continue to grow.

A third additional benefit that can be added and may be advisable when the insured is young is known as "guaranteed insurability" or "insurance of insurability." This benefit allows the insured to purchase additional life insurance at certain specified future dates without evidence of insurability. On the option date, the insured can exercise all, part, or none of the option to purchase additional insurance; but the options are non-cumulative. The rates for the new insurance are those applicable for the age in the year during which the option is exercised. In other words, if an insured waits until he is 35 to exercise an option, he pays the most favorable rates for males age 35.

WHAT ARE THE TAX IMPLICATIONS?

Taxation of Death Benefits

1. Generally, proceeds payable by reason of the insured's death are exempt from income tax.[1] Such death benefit payments are, therefore, excludable from the gross income of the beneficiary. For the possible effect of the alternative minimum tax on proceeds received by a regular C corporation, see Chapter 40.

2. Where death proceeds are held by the insurance company and the beneficiary receives only the interest (this is known as an "interest only" option), the principal amount, when received, is exempt from income taxes. However, the annual interest earnings are taxable at ordinary income rates to the beneficiary.[2]

3. When the beneficiary chooses to receive death proceeds under a life income or under another settlement option under which payments will be made in installments, the annual interest produced by the death proceeds is taxable to the beneficiary. The balance is recoverable income tax free.[3]

4. As mentioned, generally insurance proceeds paid by reason of the insured's death are excludable from the recipient's gross income. However, where, prior to death a policy or an interest in a policy had been sold or otherwise transferred for valuable consider-

ation, the death proceeds will be exempt only to the extent of: (1) the consideration paid by the transferee; (2) the net premiums paid by the transferee after the transfer; and (3) for contracts issued after June 8, 1997, interest paid or accrued by the transferee on indebtedness with respect to a contract if the interest is not allowable as a deduction under IRC Section 264(a)(4). The balance of the death proceeds is taxed at ordinary income rates. This is known as the "transfer for value" rule.[4]

Example: Rod Ross purchases a $25,000 policy on his own life. He pays four $500 annual premiums. Then he sells the policy to his son for $2,000. His son now owns a $25,000 policy on Rod's life for which he paid $2,000. Assume that Rod's son pays six additional $500 annual premiums ($3,000) and then Rod dies. At the time of Rod's death, his son would have paid a total of $5,000 for the policy ($2,000 for the policy itself plus $3,000 in premiums). When he receives the $25,000 of proceeds, only his cost, $5,000, will be excludable from income. The remaining $20,000 will be entirely subject to income tax.

The "transfer for value" rule does not apply if the sale or transfer is to (a) the insured, (b) a partner of the insured, (c) a partnership in which the insured is a partner, (d) a corporation in which the insured is a stockholder or officer, or (e) if the transferee's basis is determined in whole or in part by the transferor's basis; slightly oversimplified, if the transfer does not result in a tax basis change. For example, where a policy owned by a partnership is transferred along with other assets to a newly-formed corporation as part of a tax free incorporation or where one corporation transfers a policy to another corporation pursuant to a tax free merger or reorganization, the policy does not become subject to the transfer for value rule.[5]

Transfers between spouses made after July 18, 1984 (or December 31, 1983, if the spouses elect) or incident to a divorce, even if for value, come within an exception to the transfer for value rule.[6]

5. The proceeds of a life insurance policy are generally subject to the federal estate tax. (EGTRRA 2001 repeals the estate tax for one year in 2010.) Life insurance on the life of a decedent will be includable in the decedent's gross estate (1) if the proceeds are payable

to or for the benefit of his or her estate or, (2) if, at the time of death, the insured possessed any incidents of ownership in the policy (such as the right to change the beneficiary, the right to surrender the policy, or the right to obtain a policy loan);[7] or (3) where the policy is transferred as a gift by the decedent within three years of his death.[8] Also, the fair market value of a policy (generally the sum of the cash value plus unearned premiums) owned on another person's life is includable in the owner's gross estate.[9]

6. Gifts of life insurance policies or gifts of premium payments may be subject to the federal gift tax. The value of the gift is based on the fair market value of the insurance policy at the time of the gift or, in the case of premium payments, the cash amount of the premiums.[10] The gift tax value of a policy can generally be obtained from the insurance company and is measured differently depending upon the type of policy, i.e., term, whole life, etc.

Taxation of Premiums and Dividends

1. Premiums for personally owned life insurance are not deductible for income tax purposes. They are considered nondeductible personal expenses unless (a) premiums constitute alimony payments, under certain circumstances[11] or (b) premiums are paid on a policy irrevocably assigned to a charity and the insured does not reserve the right to surrender the policy for cash.[12]

2. Life insurance companies generally allow a discount if the premiums are paid one or more years in advance of the due date. The yearly interest increment earned on these pre-paid premiums is currently taxable to the policyowner.[13]

3. Dividends paid on participating policies are not taxable income (unless they exceed the cost basis in the contract).[14] This is consistent with the definition discussed above, i.e., life insurance policy dividends are generally considered to be a partial return of premiums. However, if dividends are left on deposit with the insurance company and accumulate interest, any interest on the accumulated dividends is taxable to the policyowner at ordinary income rates.[15] Dividends that are used to purchase paid-up additional insurance or one-year term insurance create no income tax liability. They are considered as if they were dividends paid in cash (a return of capital) and then used to buy single premium insurance.

Taxation of Living Benefits

1. Where the policyowner receives a lump sum cash settlement in excess of the cost of the contract, the difference is considered ordinary income and is taxable in the year the contract matures or is surrendered.[16] The "cost" of the contract is measured by the total premiums paid (excluding premiums paid for accidental death benefits or waiver of premium).[17] The dividend option selected will affect the actual cost or total premiums. For example, if dividends are accumulated or applied to purchase paid-up additional insurance, then the cost of the contract would be the gross premiums paid by the policyowner. However, if dividends are not accumulated or not used to purchase paid-up additional insurance, then the net premiums (gross premiums less dividends received in cash or applied to reduce policy premiums) paid determine the cost of the contract.

2. Often, rather than taking a lump sum, a policyowner will choose to take living benefits of a policy under a "settlement option." Proceeds placed under settlement options (other than the interest option) are taxed under the "annuity rules" of Section 72 of the Internal Revenue Code. Basically, these rules are designed so that the annuitant will not be taxed on the portion of the annuity income that is considered to be a return of premium payments.

   The portion of the annuity income that is considered to be gain is taxable; therefore, each payment is divided into two parts: (1) a nontaxable return of cost, and (2) taxable income.

   To determine which portion of each payment is excludable from gross income and which portion is taxable income, an exclusion ratio or percentage is found. The exclusion ratio is the ratio that the total investment in the contract bears to the total expected return; to find the percentage of each annual payment that is income tax free, divide the investment in the contract (cost) by the expected return.[18] The expected return is the annual payment multiplied by the recipient's life expectancy. (See Table V in Figure 30.1 for multiples representing life expectancy.) The exclusion ratio is then multiplied by each year's total annuity payments to yield the tax-free portion of total payments received during the year. The balance of the payments is taxable as ordinary income.

3. Provided the policy is not classified as a modified endowment contract, only cash distributions and not policy loans can cause current income taxation

Figure 30.1

	TABLE V — ORDINARY LIFE ANNUITIES ONE LIFE — EXPECTED RETURN MULTIPLES				
Age	**Multiple**	**Age**	**Multiple**	**Age**	**Multiple**
5	76.6	42	40.6	79	10.0
6	75.6	43	39.6	80	9.5
7	74.7	44	38.7	81	8.9
8	73.7	45	37.7	82	8.4
9	72.7	46	36.8	83	7.9
10	71.7	47	35.9	84	7.4
11	70.7	48	34.9	85	6.9
12	69.7	49	34.0	86	6.5
13	68.8	50	33.1	87	6.1
14	67.8	51	32.2	88	5.7
15	66.8	52	31.3	89	5.3
16	65.8	53	30.4	90	5.0
17	64.8	54	29.5	91	4.7
18	63.9	55	28.6	92	4.4
19	62.9	56	27.7	93	4.1
20	61.9	57	26.8	94	3.9
21	60.9	58	25.9	95	3.7
22	59.9	59	25.0	96	3.4
23	59.0	60	24.2	97	3.2
24	58.0	61	23.3	98	3.0
25	57.0	62	22.5	99	2.8
26	56.0	63	21.6	100	2.7
27	55.1	64	20.8	101	2.5
28	54.1	65	20.0	102	2.3
29	53.1	66	19.2	103	2.1
30	52.2	67	18.4	104	1.9
31	51.2	68	17.6	105	1.8
32	50.2	69	16.8	106	1.6
33	49.3	70	16.0	107	1.4
34	48.3	71	15.3	108	1.3
35	47.3	72	14.6	109	1.1
36	46.4	73	13.9	110	1.0
37	45.4	74	13.2	111	.9
38	44.4	75	12.5	112	.8
39	43.5	76	11.9	113	.7
40	42.5	77	11.2	114	.6
41	41.5	78	10.6	115	.5

to the recipient. Where a policyholder reduces the death benefit of a universal life policy, either by switching from an Option II death benefit (increasing death benefit) to an Option I death benefit (level death benefit), or by making a partial surrender, which reduces the face amount of the policy, a new calculation of the policy for the definitional test of life insurance must occur. If the policy has too much cash (after the death benefit reduction), above the maximum allowable under the definitional rules of IRC Section 7702, the excess must be "forced out" as a distribution.

If the force-out of the cash occurs in years 1 through 5, the policy (after the reduction in the face amount) must meet the guideline premium limitation/cash value corridor test to avoid the forced out distribution from being currently taxed as income to the extent there is a built-in gain in the policy at that time. If the policy after the reduction in face amount meets this test, the cash distributed would be considered a return of basis under the FIFO taxation rules (first in, first out). Only if the amount received exceeded the policyholder's basis would the gain be taxable to the recipient.

If the distribution occurs in policy years 6 through 15, the policy after reduction must meet the corridor percentage limits of Code section 7702. To the extent the cash value exceeds the required amount under this test and is forced out, it is taxable as income to the policyholder to the extent there is a gain in the policy.

For years after the 15th year, the policyholder is taxed on a FIFO basis (no income tax until basis is exceeded).

Provided the policy is not a modified endowment contract, in any year that a cash withdrawal is made and the definitional tests are still met after the withdrawal, any cash withdrawn is taxable only to the extent the amount received in that year and in all previous years exceeds the premiums paid into the contract, i.e., to the extent there is a gain in the contract.[19]

4. How are distributions such as cash withdrawals or policy loans taxable to the recipient if the policy is classified as a modified endowment contract? A modified endowment contract is one which meets the requirements of IRC Section 7702 (regarding what is a life insurance contract), was entered into on or after June 22, 1988 and fails to meet the seven pay test of IRC Section 7702A(b). If a policy falls into this category, distributions from the policy will be taxed less favorably than if the seven pay test is met.

A policy fails the seven pay test if the cumulative amount paid at any time during the first seven years of the contract exceeds the net level premiums that would have been paid during the first seven years if the contract provided for paid-up future benefits. If a material change in the policy's benefits occurs, a new seven year period for testing must begin.

Distributions, including policy loans, from modified endowment contracts are taxed as income first at the time received to the extent that the cash value of the contract immediately before the payment exceeds the investment in the contract, and recovery of basis second, much like distributions from annuity contracts are taxed. Additionally, a penalty tax of 10% applies to distribution amounts included in income unless the taxpayer has become disabled, or reached age 59½ or the distribution is part of a series of substantially equal payments made over the taxpayer's life.

With some exceptions, life insurance policies issued on or before June 21, 1988 are grandfathered and not required to comply with the seven pay test.

ISSUES AND IMPLICATIONS IN COMMUNITY PROPERTY STATES

Where community property funds are used to purchase an insurance policy and there has been no agreement otherwise affecting the ownership of the policy, the policy will be owned by the community–and therefore belongs one-half to each spouse.

Thus, if a policy on the husband is community property and the beneficiary is someone other than the spouse, a transfer subject to gift tax will occur when the insured dies and the proceeds are payable to that third person. The amount of the gift will be the wife's one-half interest in the proceeds.

For this reason, careful estate planners note the ownership and beneficiary designations of insurance policies to be able to consider any gift tax problems that may exist. Even payment to a trust of which the surviving spouse is the income beneficiary can result in a gift if the surviving spouse does not have a power under the trust to determine to whom the remainder interest is payable at his or her death. The amount of the gift would be the actuarial value (per IRS regulations in cases of normal health circumstances of the life tenant) of the remainder interest at the time of the transfer to trust, in the surviving spouse's half of the insurance proceeds.

The main problem in *acquiring* an insurance policy as the separate property of the non-insured spouse is the presumption in most community property states that property acquired during marriage is community property unless proven otherwise. This means that sufficient documentation of the separate property status of the policy must exist so as to overcome the community property presumption. The first step to indicate that an insurance policy is the separate property of one spouse is to name that spouse as owner of the policy. However, more evidence is usually necessary to overcome the presumption, and this requirement varies from state to state.

After the initial acquisition of a new policy as the separate property of one of the spouses or after the conversion of an existing policy into the separate policy of one spouse, the question arises as to what must be done in the future to retain the separate property status of the policy. The answer is dependent upon two different theories found in community property states that deal with the classification of interests in life insurance policies. These theories are known as the "premium tracing" doctrine and the "inception of title" doctrine.

At least two community property states, California and Washington, follow the "premium tracing" doctrine, which states that the classification of the policy as separate or community property depends on the proportion of premium payments made from separate or community funds. Under this doctrine, the classification of the policy is not constant. Therefore, if the policy is initially acquired as separate property, but 10% of the premiums are paid with community funds, absent any documentation taken to ensure the separate status of the policy, 10% of the proceeds would be community property. Therefore, each spouse would be treated as owning one-half of the 10%.

Under the "inception of title" doctrine, which is followed in at least two community property states, Louisiana and Texas, the policy's ownership does not vary depending on whether premiums are paid with separate or community funds. However, where community funds are used to pay premiums, in the absence of documentation to the contrary, the non-owner spouse will have a right of reimbursement to the extent of one-half of the community funds used to pay the premiums. This right of reimbursement may cause that portion of the proceeds to be includable in the insured spouse's estate.

Therefore, when an insured in a community property state wants to transfer his or her ownership in life insurance policies to his or her spouse, in addition to the transfer by written notification to the insurance company, it is wise to also sign a written waiver waiving any further community interest in the policy.

To effect such a waiver of interest, presently and for the future, it is usually best to use the form of "Community Property Waiver" provided by the insurance company. If no such form is available, you may consider using the type of form illustrated at Figure 30.2. It is recommended that such a written waiver contain the following minimum information: (1) a clear identification of the life insurance policy(ies) involved; (2) a statement indicating the parties' intent that the policy(ies) be held as separate property of one spouse; (3) a clear relinquishment by the other spouse of any community property interest in the policy; (4) and a statement that the payment of any future premiums with community funds shall be treated as a gift of the non-owner-spouse's community interest in those funds to the owner-spouse.

In most cases, even though the insured may be shown on the policy as "Owner" or otherwise indicated as owning the policy, the policy will be considered as community property of the two spouses in the absence of any evidence that there was an agreement between the spouses that it would be separate property.

A prenuptial agreement can be effective in most states to overcome presumptions of community property and to provide that future premium payments from community property funds will not vest in the community any ownership in the policies on the life of the insured. In view of the increasing frequency of divorce and remarriage, the use prenuptial agreements is encouraged by most estate planners to avoid subsequent confusion and possible lawsuits related to the ownership of insurance policies.

One type of insurance policy that remains the separate property of the insured, in spite of having premiums paid with community property earnings, is National Service Life Insurance and Servicemen's Group Life Insurance. These policies, made available by the federal government for persons in the service, have been determined to be incapable of transfer of ownership away from the insured on the basis of federal policy. In some cases, however, the courts of California in divorce and dissolution cases have frustrated the announced federal intent by awarding community prop-

Figure 30.2

> ## WAIVER OF COMMUNITY PROPERTY RIGHTS
>
> The undersigned hereby declares that __he intends to transfer to h____ spouse, _____, certain policies of life insurance, and that upon said transfer, all rights, privileges and incidents of ownership under any policies so transferred shall be the separate property of said spouse and the undersigned hereby waives any and all community property interest to which __he may, but for this waiver, hereafter be entitled under the community property laws of California or any other state, province or country.
>
> The undersigned consents to the use of community property funds h____ self and h____ spouse for the payment of any or all premiums and does further agree and declare that any future premium payments on the policies made with community funds shall constitute a gift from the undersigned to h____ said spouse to the extent of h____ interest in the community funds so applied.
>
> Any interest the undersigned may have, now or in the future, as a designated payee of the policies is not affected by this waiver.
>
> This instrument is executed in consideration of natural love and affection and shall be binding upon my heirs, executors, administrators and assigns, and is executed with the intent and knowledge that any interested parties may hence forth act in reliance thereon.
>
> Dated _____
>
>
> _____
> Signature
>
>
> WITNESSED BY:
>
> _____

erty of equal value to the non-insured spouse. However, the federal policy prevents the transfer of such NSLI policies for purposes of planning for reduction of federal estate taxes. However, only one-half of the proceeds is includable in the insured's gross estate for federal estate tax purposes where the premiums have been paid with community property.

QUESTIONS AND ANSWERS

Question – Are the annual increases in cash values for permanent insurance policies subject to income taxation?

Answer – No. Although several attempts have been made to tax the inside build-up of cash values, to date none have been successful.

Question – If a policy has an accidental death and dismemberment (double indemnity) rider providing for a doubling of the death benefit in the event of an accidental death, are the proceeds subject to income tax?

Answer – No. They are generally considered proceeds payable by reason of an insured's death and, under IRC Section 101, the proceeds are received income tax free.

Question – What is "split dollar" life insurance, how does it work, and what are its advantages?

Answer – Split dollar life insurance is an arrangement, typically between an employer and an employee (it can also be used between relatives such as a father and son or grandfather and grandson), under which the cash values, death benefits, and cost (premiums) may be split between the parties.

Under the classical arrangement, the employer pays that part of the annual premium that equals the current year's increase in the cash surrender value of the policy. The employee pays the balance, if any, of the premium. Under another version of split dollar, known as an "employer pay all" plan, the corporation pays the entire premium and the employee pays no portion of the premium. This provides an incentive to key employees, a way by which an employer can reward key individuals on a selective basis, and a means to provide stockholder-employees with substantial insurance at a minimal outlay.

In the event of the insured employee's death the corporation typically gets back the cash value or premiums paid by the corporation as a death benefit and the insured employee's beneficiary receives the balance of the proceeds. The result of the arrangement is for the employer to have an increasing death benefit and for the employee's beneficiary to have a decreasing death benefit. To maintain the insured-employee's death benefit on a level basis, dividends can be used to purchase an amount of term insurance equal to the cash surrender value of the contract; or, if a universal life policy is used, the death benefit can be increasing.

Furthermore, intrafamily split dollar would enable a son-in-law to purchase insurance on his life that he otherwise might not be able to afford. This way, a father can provide additional financial security for his daughter.

Split dollar can also be used between a corporation and its employee-stockholders. The corporation could split the premium dollars in such a way that the employee-stockholders could be able to afford sizable policies on each others' lives.

Split dollar thus provides an attractive incentive plan. It can be entirely selective. No Internal Revenue Service approval is necessary, although there is some income tax cost to the employee (see below). The split dollar arrangement used creatively can solve a number of estate and business planning problems.

A split dollar plan of insurance can be established as either a collateral assignment type or as an endorsement type arrangement. The collateral assignment method involves either the insured or a third party as the original owner of the contract. The owner then collaterally assigns the policy to the corporation to secure the corporation's interest in the policy.

The endorsement method involves the corporation as the owner of the contract and accordingly it has all policy rights including the right to borrow against the policy. Under this method, the employer endorses out or gives to the insured the right to designate the beneficiary of the pure term insurance protection.

It is possible that a split dollar plan can be arranged so that the death benefit passing to the beneficiary of a majority shareholder will be estate tax free. If the shareholder's spouse—or an irrevocable trust for the benefit of his beneficiaries or any third party—purchases a policy on his life, and then enters into a split dollar agreement with the corporation that prohibits the corporation from taking any action with respect to the policy that might endanger the policyowner's interest, the death benefit can be excludable. Chances of success in keeping the net amount at risk out of a controlling shareholder's estate are significantly increased if the corporation has no rights to policy values except at the insured's death. The corporation's right at that time should be limited to a recovery of the death proceeds equal to its contributions. The collateral assignment method of split dollar should be used to further evidence the limitation of the corporation's rights.[20]

Early in 2001, the Internal Revenue Service started revising the tax treatment of split dollar plans. It issued Notice 2001-10 followed by Notice 2002-8 as well as two sets of proposed regulations before adopting final split dollar regulations effective for split dollar plans entered into after September 17, 2003 or for existing plans that are "materially modified" after that date.[21]

The final regulations create two mutually exclusive tax regimes for split dollar life insurance plans based on who is named as policy owner of the life insurance contract: the economic benefit regime (for endorsement arrangements, wherein the employer is the owner of the insurance policy), and the loan regime (for collateral assignment arrangements wherein the employee is the owner of the insurance policy).

Under the economic benefit regime, if the employer is the owner, the employer's premium payments will be considered as providing taxable economic benefits to the non-owner (typically an employee), which include the value of the current life insurance protection, the amount of cash value to which the employee has "current access," and the value of any other economic benefits.

The measure of the life insurance protection for new plans is currently determined by using a published premium table that the IRS provided in Notice 2001-10 (see Figure 30.4) that results in a higher taxable income to the non-owner than was the case in the past. Note that for plans entered into prior to September 18th 2003, use of the old methods for reporting the economic benefit to the employee – the lesser of PS 58 or the insurer's lowest published term rates are generally allowed, except that for plans entered into after January 28th 2002 and before September 18th 2003, the insurer's lowest term rates would have to meet certain criteria, i.e., the insurer makes those rates generally available as sold through its normal distribution channel.

Where the employee is a non-owner of the policy, he must also report as income any cash value to which he has current or future access (to the extent that the amount was not taken into account in a prior year). This means a non-owner will be taxed on the annual increasing cash value to which he has current access.

The other regime for taxing split dollar is the loan method. Under the loan regime the employee is the owner of the life insurance policy (a collateral assignment plan). The employer's premium payments are treated as a series of loans from the employer to the employee, which, unless the employee is required to pay the employer a market rate of interest on the loan, will be treated under the below market loan rules. Under these rules the employer is deemed to have paid the employee an amount equal to the "forgone interest" which is taxable to the employee, and the employee is deemed to have repaid a like amount to the employer as interest. Whether interest is sufficient or not is made by reference to the applicable federal rate. The consequences of having a below market loan depend on whether the loan is a demand loan or a term loan. (For more information on below market loans see Chapter 37.)

Question – What is a "key person" life insurance policy and how is it taxed?

Answer – A key person life insurance policy is a policy owned by a business that insures the life of a particularly valuable employee for the benefit of a business. It is a good estate planning tool because it provides protection to offset financial loss to a business occurring by reason of the premature death of a valuable employee. Therefore, an employer might want to insure a key person and thereby stabilize and maximize the value of the business interest. Even more common is the situation where the business owner is the key to the success of the business. If the business is to be continued, it should consider insuring the business owner's life.

The business should be the premium payor, owner, and beneficiary of the policy. Proceeds, when received, could be used to offset reduced profits and help pay for the replacement of the key individual.

Premiums are not deductible by the corporation or other business entity, but proceeds, when received, will be free of income tax[22] with the possible exception of a corporate level alternative minimum tax.

For federal estate tax purposes, if the insured is a stockholder, the death proceeds will be considered in determining the value of the decedent's stock interest.[23] Even, where the insured is the controlling stockholder, as long as the corporation is the beneficiary, or the proceeds are paid for the benefit of the corporation (for example, to a corporate creditor), the insurance proceeds will not be separately taxable (as insurance) in the insured's estate.[24] So if the business owner controls only 60% of the business, only 60% of the insurance–enhanced value of the corporate stock will be includable in his estate for federal estate tax purposes. Note that if the death proceeds are payable to a personal beneficiary of an insured controlling shareholder (one who owns more than 50% of the corporation's stock) the proceeds will be fully includable as life insurance in his estate. (Note that EGTRRA 2001 repeals the estate tax for one year in 2010.)

Question – How is group life insurance taxed and how can it be used for estate planning purposes?

Answer – Group life insurance is a life insurance benefit provided by an employer for the benefit of its employees and is one of the most effective tools the stockholder-employee of a closely held corporation has for planning his or her personal estate. Likewise, it is extremely useful in planning the estate of an executive or other common law employee. The primary objective of group life insurance is to provide financial security for the employee's family.

Figure 30.3

"P.S. 58" RATES					
(For tax years ending before 2002)					

ONE YEAR TERM PREMIUMS FOR $1,000 OF LIFE INSURANCE PROTECTION

Age	Premium	Age	Premium	Age	Premium
15	$ 1.27	37	$ 3.63	59	$ 19.08
16	1.38	38	3.87	60	20.73
17	1.48	39	4.14	61	22.53
18	1.52	40	4.42	62	24.50
19	1.56	41	4.73	63	26.63
20	1.61	42	5.07	64	28.98
21	1.67	43	5.44	65	31.51
22	1.73	44	5.85	66	34.28
23	1.79	45	6.30	67	37.31
24	1.86	46	6.78	68	40.59
25	1.93	47	7.32	69	44.17
26	2.02	48	7.89	70	48.06
27	2.11	49	8.53	71	52.29
28	2.20	50	9.22	72	56.89
29	2.31	51	9.97	73	61.89
30	2.43	52	10.79	74	67.33
31	2.57	53	11.69	75	73.23
32	2.70	54	12.67	76	79.63
33	2.86	55	13.74	77	86.57
34	3.02	56	14.91	78	94.09
35	3.21	57	16.18	79	102.23
36	3.41	58	17.56	80	111.04
				81	120.57

Generally, the premium payor is the business, although many plans are contributory, where the employee pays a portion of the premium. The insured or a third party is given a certificate evidencing the insurance. The beneficiary can be anyone (including a trust) designated by the covered employee.

For estate tax purposes, the proceeds of a group life insurance policy are includable in the gross estate of the employee. However, these proceeds can usually be removed from the insured's estate with little or no gift tax cost by an absolute assignment of all incidents of ownership. If a policy is assigned within three years of the insured's death, the entire proceeds will be includable in the gross estate.[25] (Note that EGTRRA 2001 repeals the estate tax for one year in 2010.)

The annual gift where a policy has been assigned by the employee to a third party is apparently equal to the lesser of premium payments made by the employer or the value measured by the government Table I, below. However, the higher of premiums paid or the Table I rates is used for key employees in a discriminatory plan.[26]

Group life insurance premiums paid by the corporation are fully deductible as business expenses, subject to the limitation that they are reasonable compensation after considering all other compensation paid that employee.[27] Furthermore, employer-paid premiums are not considered taxable income to the covered employees to the extent the death benefit does not exceed $50,000 (this amount may be lower in some states).[28] The exception to this rule is that if a plan discriminates in favor of key employees, those employees must include in income the cost of their full coverage, including the first $50,000 of coverage. The cost of the coverage is the higher of the actual cost or the Table I rates shown

Figure 30.4

	TABLE 2001 (generally for use after 2000)				
INTERIM TABLE OF ONE-YEAR TERM PREMIUMS FOR $1,000 OF LIFE INSURANCE PROTECTION					
Attained Age	Section 79 Extended and Interpolated Annual Rates	Attained Age	Section 79 Extended and Interpolated Annual Rates	Attained Age	Section 79 Extended and Interpolated Annual Rates
0	$0.70	34	$0.98	67	$15.20
1	0.41	35	0.99	68	16.92
2	0.27	36	1.01	69	18.70
3	0.19	37	1.04	70	20.62
4	0.13	38	1.06	71	22.72
5	0.13	39	1.07	72	25.07
6	0.14	40	1.10	73	27.57
7	0.15	41	1.13	74	30.18
8	0.16	42	1.20	75	33.05
9	0.16	43	1.29	76	36.33
10	0.16	44	1.40	77	40.17
11	0.19	45	1.53	78	44.33
12	0.24	46	1.67	79	49.23
13	0.28	47	1.83	80	54.56
14	0.33	48	1.98	81	60.51
15	0.38	49	2.13	82	66.74
16	0.52	50	2.30	83	73.07
17	0.57	51	2.52	84	80.35
18	0.59	52	2.81	85	88.76
19	0.61	53	3.20	86	99.16
20	0.62	54	3.65	87	110.40
21	0.62	55	4.15	88	121.85
22	0.64	56	4.68	89	133.40
23	0.66	57	5.20	90	144.30
24	0.68	58	5.66	91	155.80
25	0.71	59	6.06	92	168.75
26	0.73	60	6.51	93	186.44
27	0.76	61	7.11	94	206.70
28	0.80	62	7.96	95	228.35
29	0.83	63	9.08	96	250.01
30	0.87	64	10.41	97	265.09
31	0.90	65	11.90	98	270.11
32	0.93	66	13.51	99	281.05
33	0.96				

below. The cost of any coverage that exceeds $50,000 of protection is taxable income to the employee. The value of this additional income is measured by the government table shown below.[29] If the employee contributes toward the cost of the insurance, his contribution can be used to offset his tax liability.

When the proceeds of group life insurance are received by the insured employee's family, they are not subject to income taxation.[30]

Question – What is a salary increase or "selective" pension plan?

"TABLE I" RATES FOR GROUP TERM INSURANCE

5-year age bracket	Cost per $1,000 of insurance for 1-month period
Under 25	$ .05
25 to 29	.06
30 to 34	.08
35 to 39	.09
40 to 44	.10
45 to 49	.15
50 to 54	.23
55 to 59	.43
60 to 64	.66
65 to 69	1.27
70 and above	2.06

NOTE
1. Age of the employee is attained age on the last day of the employee's taxable year.

Answer – A salary increase pension plan (some call this a "Section 162" plan) is an excellent way to: (1) provide benefits where group insurance is either unavailable or inadequate; (2) supplement the benefits of a qualified corporate pension or profit-sharing plan; (3) reward and hold key personnel; (4) provide estate liquidity for corporate executives; and (5) replace part or all of group term life insurance in excess of $50,000.

The corporation pays the premiums on a whole life, universal life, or variable life type policy insuring the selected employee. That employee is named as owner of the policy and designates his own personal beneficiary.

For estate tax purposes, since the policy is owned by the employee who has the right to name the beneficiary, the proceeds will be includable in the employee's gross estate.

The business is able to deduct premiums paid under a "salary increase" pension plan since the premiums are considered additional compensation. The employee must report as ordinary income the amount of premiums paid by the employer under such a plan. When the death proceeds are paid to the insured's personal beneficiary, under this type of plan, they are not subject to income tax.

Advantages of a salary increase plan using life insurance include:

1. Internal Revenue Service approval is not required.

2. The plan is simple and may be established by the mere signing of an application, ac-

ceptance by the insurer of evidence of insurability, and payment of the appropriate premium.

3. The employer is free to choose the employees to include in the plan and no minimum or maximum number of lives must be covered.

4. The employer can decide how much coverage to provide.

5. The cost of the plan is deductible by the employer.

6. The employee owns and has all rights to the insurance policy.

7. Dividends can be used to reduce the premium outlay or to offset the tax cost of the plan.

8. Cash values of the policy may be used without disqualifying the plan or incurring any tax penalties, provided that the policy is not classified as a modified endowment contract. (Interest will be charged on any policy loans.)

9. The plan may be discontinued at any time.

Question – Can a person achieve estate tax reduction by giving away the ownership of a policy on his life?

Answer – To the extent that one transfers away all of the incidents of ownership and the policy is not payable directly or indirectly to his estate, then the policy will not be included in his estate for federal estate tax purposes, providing that he survives three years past the date of transfer. (Note that EGTRRA 2001 repeals the estate tax for one year in 2010.)

Although a gift of insurance made more than three years before death can be effective in reducing the insured's estate for estate tax purposes, it also reduces the ownership rights of an insured during his lifetime, as many insureds have found upon dissolution of a marriage.

Transfer of insurance is subject to gift tax and, therefore, one must also consider the value of the policy when making a gift.

Question – Can interest that is paid on funds borrowed to purchase or carry a life insurance contract be deducted on an individual's income tax return?

Answer – The general rule is that a deduction is not allowed for interest paid on indebtedness incurred to purchase or carry life insurance if the insurance is purchased pursuant to a plan that contemplates the systematic direct or indirect borrowing of part or all of the increase in the cash surrender value of such contract. There are four exceptions to this general rule:

1. *Trade or business exception*–If the indebtedness is incurred in connection with the taxpayer's trade or business, the interest deduction will not be denied.

2. *$100 a year exception*–The interest deduction will be allowed if the interest on the loan is less than $100 a year.

3. *The seven-year exception*–An interest deduction will be allowed in spite of the general rule where at least four of the annual premiums due during the first seven years of the contract are paid by means other than direct or indirect borrowing. Therefore, if a policyholder pays *any* four full years' premiums out of the first seven years' premiums due, the interest deduction on policy loans, including interest on loans made during the first seven years, will be allowed.

4. *The unforeseen event exception*–An interest deduction will be allowed if the indebtedness is incurred as the result of an unforeseen substantial loss of income or unforeseen substantial increase in the taxpayer's financial obligations.[31]

However, even if a personally owned policy comes within one of the four just mentioned exceptions to the general rule, none of the interest has been allowed as a deduction of personal interest since 1990.

For insurance loans on policies owned by a taxpayer (corporation or other entity) carrying on any trade or business, a deduction will not be allowed for interest on any indebtedness with respect to one or more life insurance policies covering the life of any individual who is a "key person" (an officer or 20% owner of the business), in any trade or business carried on by the taxpayer, to the extent the loans aggregate more than $50,000 per insured. If you are not a "key employee" interest is not deductible for policy loans even if less than $50,000. However, for a policy owned by a taxpayer purchased on or before June 20, 1986, if the policy otherwise qualifies for an income tax deduction by coming within one of the four exceptions, interest will continue to be fully tax deductible.[32]

Several changes were made by both the 1996 and 1997 tax Acts regarding the deductibility of policy loan interest for company owned life policies. The general rule of IRC Section 264 states that no deduction will be allowed for interest paid or accrued on any indebtedness with respect to one or more life insurance policies owned by the taxpayer covering the life of any individual. For interest in policy loans for "key employees" however, there is an exception from the general disallowance rule and there can be an allowable deduction if the general rules regarding policy interest deductibility are met.

Furthermore, the Taxpayer Relief Act of 1997 added a new IRC Section 264(f) that generally provides that no deduction will be allowed for the part of the taxpayer's interest expense that is "allocable to unborrowed policy cash values." The portion which is "allocable to unborrowed policy cash values" is an amount that bears the same ratio to the interest expense as the taxpayer's average unborrowed policy cash values of life insurance policies and annuity and endowment contracts issued after June 8, 1997 bears to the sum of: (1) in the case of assets that are life policies or annuity or endowment contracts, the average unborrowed policy cash values; and (2) in the case of assets of the taxpayer that do not fall into this category, the average adjusted bases of such assets.

"Unborrowed policy cash value" is defined as the excess of the cash surrender value of a policy or contract (determined without regard to surrender charges) over the amount of the loan with respect to the policy or contract.

Question – What are the reasons life insurance is often purchased by the trustee of a pension and/or profit-sharing plan?

Answer – Among others, the premium (including any additional rating charge) becomes deductible (as part of the corporation's contribution). The dividend structure of a policy within a pension or profit-sharing plan is generally more favorable than dividends paid on policies owned outside the plan. The death benefit in excess of policy cash value is income tax free, and is, generally exempt from the claims of creditors. With some of the newer type policies, such as universal or variable life, favorable returns can also be achieved.

Question – If an individual exchanges one life insurance policy for another life insurance policy (e.g., whole life to universal life), are there income tax consequences?

Answer – The Internal Revenue Code provides that an exchange of one life insurance policy for another life insurance policy, whether with the same company or a different company, is a nontaxable exchange if the policies are on the same insured. If no cash or other property is received on the exchange, gain is not recognized. If there is an outstanding loan on the original policy that is not paid off, the amount of any loan assumed by the other party is treated as money received on the exchange and will be taxable to the extent the original policy is in a taxable gain position unless the new policy is subject to the same indebtedness.[33]

Question – Is the interest earned on a prepaid premium deposit account taxable as ordinary income to the policyholder?

Answer – Yes. The increase in value of a prepaid deposit account is taxable as income in the year it is applied to the payment of premiums or is made available for withdrawal, whichever occurs first. The amount of income is reportable to the IRS by the insurance company. Any amount reported will increase the basis of the contract.[34]

Question – How can you determine the financial strength of a life insurance company?

Answer – In addition to looking at the annual financial reports of each company, there are a number of independent rating services that rate the insurance companies. These ratings can be obtained from the particular rating services. Among the companies who provide ratings are: (1) A.M. Best Company; (2) Standard & Poor's Corporation; (3) Moody's Investors Services; (4) Fitch, Inc. (formed by the merger of Fitch IBCA and Duff & Phelps); and (5) Weiss Research.

Rating services look at the underlying essentials of companies, such as surplus, mortality experience, investments, and expenses. They then assign a letter rating to the company. The top two ratings assigned by the above-mentioned rating services are: A.M. Best Company – A++ and A+; Standard &

Poor's – AAA and AA+; Moody's Investors Services – Aaa and Aa1; Fitch, Inc. – AAA and AA; and Weiss Research – A+ and A.

Question – What is a viatical settlement?

Answer – A viatical settlement is the sale of a life insurance policy by a terminally ill person to a business that specializes in these transactions (viatical settlement companies). People with limited life expectancies oftentimes face financial difficulties. Viatical settlements allow these people to sell their life insurance policies and use the proceeds to help improve their financial situation.

The proceeds from a viatical settlement will generally be treated as an amount paid under the life insurance contract by reason of the insured's death and will not be includable in income.[35]

Question – Are life insurance benefits received by a terminally ill or chronically ill individual as an advancement of the death benefit by the insurance company, taxable as income to the recipient?

Answer – Any amount received under a life insurance contract on the life of a terminally ill insured or a chronically ill insured will be treated as an amount paid by reason of the death of the insured. In other words, amounts of this nature received after 1996 will be income tax free.

However, amounts paid to a chronically ill individual are subject to the same limitations that apply to long-term care benefits, which were added to the Internal Revenue Code in Section 7702B(d). Generally, in 2004 this is a $230 (adjusted for inflation) per day limitation. Accelerated death benefits paid to terminally ill individuals are not subject to this limit.

There are several special rules that apply to chronically ill insureds. Generally, the tax treatment outlined above will not apply to any payment received for any period unless the payment is for costs incurred by the payee (who has not been compensated by insurance or otherwise) for qualified long-term care services provided to the insured for the period. Additionally, the terms of the contract under which the payments are made must comply with several other requirements.

A terminally ill individual is a person who has been certified by a physician as having an illness or physical condition that can reasonably be expected to result in death within 24 months following the certification. A chronically ill individual is a person who is not terminally ill and who has been certified as being unable to perform, without substantial assistance, at least two activities of daily living for at least 90 days or a person with a similar level of disability. Further, a person may be considered chronically ill if he requires substantial supervision to protect himself from threats to his health and safety due to severe cognitive impairment and this condition has been certified by a health care practitioner within the previous 12 months.

The rules outlined above do not apply to any amount paid to any taxpayer other than the insured if the taxpayer has an insurable interest in the life of the insured because the insured is a director, officer or employee of the taxpayer or if the insured is financially interested in any trade or business of the taxpayer.[36]

CHAPTER ENDNOTES

1.   IRC Sec. 101(a).
2.   IRC Sec. 101(c).
3.   IRC Sec. 101(d)(1)(A), Treas. Reg. §1.101-4(a)(1)(i).
4.   IRC Sec. 101(a)(2).
5.   IRC Sec. 101(a)(2).
6.   IRC Sec. 1041.
7.   IRC Sec. 2042.
8.   IRC Sec. 2035.
9.   IRC Sec. 2033.
10. Treas. Reg. §25.2512-6.
11. *Carmichael*; 14 TC 1356 (1950), *Est. of Hart*, 11 TC 16 (1948).
12. See *Hunton*, 1 TC 821 (1943); *Behrend*, 23 BTA 1037 (1931), acq. X-2 CB 5.
13. Rev. Rul. 65-199, 1965-2 CB 20.
14. IRC Sec. 72(e)(1)(B); Treas. Reg. §1.72-11(b)(1).
15. Treas. Reg. §1.61-7(d).
16. IRC Sec. 72(e); Treas. Reg. §1.72-11(d).
17. IRC Sec. 72(c)(1); Rev. Rul. 55-349, 1955-1 CB 232.
18. See Treas. Reg. §1.72-4.
19. IRC Secs. 7702(e), 7702(f).
20. Rev Rul. 82-145, 1982-2 CB 213; Rev. Rul. 76-274, 1976-2 CB 278.
21. TD 9092; Rev. Rul. 2003-105, 2003-40 IRB. 696.
22. IRC Sec. 101.
23. Treas. Reg. §20.2031-2(f).
24. Treas. Reg. §20.2042-1(c)(6).
25. IRC Sec. 2035; Rev. Rul. 69-54, 1969-1 CB 221 as modified by Rev. Rul. 72-307, 1972-1 CB 307 and Rev. Rul. 84-031, 1984-2 CB 194.
26. See Rev. Rul. 84-147, 1984-2 CB 201.
27. IRC Sec. 162(a); Treas. Reg. §1.264-1.
28. IRC Sec. 79.
29. Treas. Reg. §1.79-3.
30. IRC Sec. 101.
31. IRC Sec. 264.
32. IRC Sec. 264.
33. IRC Sec. 1035(a).
34. See Rev. Rul. 65-199, 1965-2 CB 20, and Rev. Rul. 66-120, 1966-1 CB 14.
35   IRC Sec. 101(g).
36. IRC Sec. 101(g).

Chapter 31

IRREVOCABLE LIFE INSURANCE TRUST

WHAT IS IT?

An irrevocable life insurance trust is, as the name implies, a vehicle for holding life insurance policies. The primary goal of such a trust is to shift the ownership of the policies from the insured's generation to a lower generation in order to remove the policy proceeds from taxation at the death of the insured and/or his spouse. In that way, the family can have a fund of cash that can be used to loan money to or purchase assets from a decedent's estate, thereby creating liquidity in the estate for payment of death taxes, without the funds causing additional death taxes at the death of the insured.

This result can be achieved by giving policies or cash to purchase policies outright to the children or successor generation, as well as by gifts into trust. However, the benefit of using a trust is that a trustee can be chosen who understands the goal of providing liquidity for payment of taxes, and in that way there is more certainty that the proceeds will be used for the intended purpose.

Where the life insurance continues to require payment of premiums after the gift, a typical irrevocable life insurance trust plan will call for the insured to make annual gifts to the trust to cover the premium payments. In order to make those gifts qualify as a "present interest gift" and therefore come within the annual exclusion ($11,000 in 2004) from gift tax, the trust often will have a "Crummey" withdrawal power in the beneficiaries (usually the children).

With a Crummey withdrawal power, each time a contribution is made to the trust, the beneficiary has a temporary right to demand withdrawal from the trust. If the demand right is not exercised, the annual transfer for that year remains in the trust for management by the trustee. If the demand is made, the trustee must deliver the funds to the beneficiary. However, the beneficiary generally will recognize that such a withdrawal may affect the grantor's decision as to future transfers to that trust and the beneficiary may therefore not make a demand. Once the withdrawal right lapses, the trustee is then free to use the monies that were contributed to pay the premiums on the life insurance policies.

The name "Crummey trust" comes from the name of a party to a lawsuit, *Crummey v. Comm.*, 397 F.2d 82 (9th Cir. 1968).

WHEN IS THE USE OF SUCH A DEVICE INDICATED?

A life insurance trust can be used to good advantage whenever an individual (or a couple) faces a death tax in his or her generation, and wishes to provide liquidity for payment of those taxes with existing life insurance, or insurance to be purchased, without subjecting the proceeds themselves to depletion by death taxes.

In addition, gifts of life insurance generally are valued for gift tax purposes at the "interpolated terminal reserve value," which is usually close to the cash surrender value for a reasonably healthy individual. The face value of the policy is often many times greater than this gift tax value. In such cases, making gifts of life insurance policies is a way to "leverage" the donor's gift tax annual exclusions, unified credit, and/or generation-skipping exclusion, by making gifts of policies that have a low current "gift value" in relation to their value at the insured's death.

Specifically, a trust is indicated where the donor does not have confidence that the recipients of the gifts will cooperate in retaining the policies or their proceeds and making them available to the donor's estate for payment of taxes, or where the gifts are made to minor or other beneficiaries, who do not have the capacity or judgment to manage the policies/proceeds.

Where the insured's spouse is an owner or co-owner of the policy, this type of trust is indicated only where the spouse feels comfortable with giving up the use and benefit of the proceeds, since the donor cannot retain any income or other rights over the policies or proceeds and still have the property not taxed at the donor's death.

WHAT ARE THE REQUIREMENTS?

Requirements for Life Insurance Gift Trust

1. The donor(s) must create a trust vehicle to receive the insurance gift (or to receive cash with which to purchase a new policy) that has terms that will achieve the donor's goals both with respect to the availability of funds with which to pay taxes as well as appropriate terms for managing the assets for the beneficiaries both before and after the insured's death.

2. The donor(s) must then actually transfer the policy to the trust by signing an irrevocable assignment of the policy to the trustee of the trust, or by making a cash gift to the trust to enable the trustee to purchase a new policy.

3. The insured or proposed insured must be in reasonable health in order to avoid the policy being valued at a much greater value for gift tax purposes.

Requirements for Crummey Withdrawal Power

1. Each time a contribution is made to a Crummey trust, the beneficiary must have a right to demand withdrawal of an amount equal to the value of the gift. Frequently, the withdrawal right may be dependent upon the donor also specifying that the withdrawal right will apply to the gift, e.g., "This gift is made subject to the right of withdrawal provided in…." This permits one trust to be able to receive both annual exclusion "Crummey gifts" as well as other gifts that the donor can be assured will not be removed by the beneficiary.

   However, in order for the annual exclusion to be permitted, the withdrawal right cannot be illusory. Implicit in every Crummey trust is the notion that the beneficiary will not exercise the right to withdraw and the gifts to the trust will remain in the trust until termination. However, the right to withdraw must be real and legally possible.

   The exclusion is allowed under a number of circumstances that may be surprising. An example is a gift in trust in which the beneficiary given the right to withdraw (through his guardian) is an infant.

2. For an adult beneficiary to have an effective demand right, he must have effective notice of the demand right.[1] The IRS rulings have emphasized the importance of giving effective notice of the annual trust contributions that are subject to withdrawal, at least to adult beneficiaries. In several cases, the IRS has implied that notice may be necessary even for minor beneficiaries.[2] Although this notice is typically made in writing to have evidence that the requirement was met, it seems that even oral notice is adequate.

   It is the safest course of action to give notice of each transfer subject to the withdrawal power. According to the IRS, a "once only" notice is not sufficient.

3. In order for the demand right to be effective, an adequate amount of time must be allowed for the exercise of the power of withdrawal, especially if the exercise of the power would require a step such as appointing a guardian for a minor beneficiary. The IRS has not drawn a clear line between reasonable and unreasonable time limits. However, the IRS has disapproved a three-day period as not a sufficient duration,[3] but Crummey withdrawal periods of as little as thirty days after an addition to the trust have been deemed effective.[4]

4. An important feature of a Crummey trust is that it allows the grantor to make gifts that qualify for the annual exclusion from gift tax under IRC Section 2503. In order to qualify for the annual exclusion, a gift must be one of a "present interest." (A beneficiary must receive the immediate, unfettered, and ascertainable right to use, possess, or enjoy the money or other property placed into the trust for that year.) A "future interest" does not qualify. When a trust has no provisions for a current withdrawal of the gift, at least a portion of each gift is a future interest. It is the right of the beneficiary to withdraw the transferred asset that meets the requirement to make the gift eligible for the annual exclusion.

5. The beneficiary of a Crummey trust must be able to actually receive property if he exercises a demand right. The gift will be eligible for the annual exclusion only to the extent the trust has assets sufficient to satisfy the beneficiary's demand rights.[5]

6. Where a beneficiary is a minor, and is therefore unable to make an effective withdrawal, he will be deemed to have a present interest in the gift if a guardian can make a legally effective demand on his behalf.

7. The IRS has taken the position that the annual exclusion is available only where the beneficiary is a "primary" beneficiary with a substantial interest in the trust other than the withdrawal power. However, the Tax Court has held that invasion powers held by grandchildren were eligible for the annual exclusion where a trust was created for children and the only other interests held by the grandchildren were contingent on the death of their parents before the trust was distributed.[6]

The IRS continues to attack naked Crummey powers, powers given to persons who have little or no interest in the trust other than the Crummey powers and who are given the powers merely to increase the number of annual exclusions. According to the IRS, there is no intent to make a present interest gift by the grantor where the holder of a power who has no interest in income or principal does not make a withdrawal; the failure to make a withdrawal implies collusion, or intimidation by the trust's grantor.

HOW IS IT DONE?

Harry and Donna Bradley would like to make gifts that will qualify for the annual exclusion to each of their two children and four grandchildren. Their annual exclusion amount for gifts to these donees would be $132,000 per year. (The husband and wife can give $11,000 (in 2004) apiece to each of the six individuals.) However, the Bradleys would prefer not to make outright gifts, especially not to the grandchildren.

The Bradleys would, instead, prefer to have a trust that would continue until their youngest child reaches the age of 35. At that time, the trust would be distributed equally to the children and grandchildren. They decide that the trust will not make any distributions of current income.

An irrevocable life insurance trust would meet all the Bradleys' requirements. The trust they create can have all the desired terms plus Crummey powers of withdrawal in all of the children and grandchildren. Separate shares are required if the trust is to be exempt from generation-skipping tax.

ISSUES AND IMPLICATIONS IN COMMUNITY PROPERTY STATES

1. A couple owning community property can give $22,000 (in 2004) per recipient without any need for gift splitting because each spouse owns half the community property.

2. Because of the nature of community property (the fact that each spouse owns a one-half interest in each community asset), it is unusual in a community property state for a Crummey irrevocable insurance trust that benefits the surviving spouse as to the entire trust to be created.

In a separate property jurisdiction, the typical terms of such a trust might provide that at the death of the insured spouse (e.g., the husband) the proceeds of an insurance policy (purchased with funds given by the husband) will benefit the wife in the form of a life interest in the proceeds. After her death, the proceeds would be available to be lent to her estate (or to purchase assets from her estate) to provide funds to pay estate taxes then due.

In a community property state, on the other hand, the wife usually is the grantor as to one-half of the gifts used to pay the insurance premium, and it would not be appropriate to give the wife a life interest in the entire policy proceeds, for that would be a transfer with a retained interest, includable in the wife's estate as to the one-half purchased with her share of the community property gift.

Even in a community property state, one spouse may have separate property already, or a "split" of community property can be achieved to produce separate property. With a trust funded by such separate property gifts, the other spouse can have a life estate in all of the policy proceeds without making them subject to estate tax in her estate. Such planning must, however, be carefully undertaken.

WHAT ARE THE GIFT TAX AND ESTATE TAX IMPLICATIONS?

1. The gift of a life insurance policy is subject to gift tax, usually based on the policy's "interpolated terminal reserve value," usually close to the cash surrender value. However, where the insured is currently uninsurable or is even just in poor health, the policy may have a much greater value.

2. For the grantor/donor, a Crummey withdrawal power is an effective way to make a gift that qualifies for the annual exclusion from gift tax while avoiding the early distribution requirements of other forms of gifts that permit the donor to take advantage of

the $11,000 (in 2004) per donee per year exclusion from gift tax. The Crummey withdrawal power can make both cash gifts and gifts of the policies themselves qualify for the annual exclusion.

3. However, a second gift tax aspect arises when the beneficiary permits a lapse of his power to remove from the trust the contribution made by the grantor. This lapse of the withdrawal right was not often a problem when annual gifts from each donor were limited to $3,000, since IRC Section 2514(e) excludes from gift tax gifts that result from lapse of a power to withdraw assets from the trust up to the greater each year of $5,000 or 5% of the trust corpus. If each of two grantors gave $2,500 for a total of $5,000, the *de minimis* protection of Section 2514(e) kept the lapse of the beneficiary's power from being a gift subject to gift tax.

   However, Section 2514(e) no longer provided sufficient protection when the annual exclusion amount was increased to $10,000 in 1981, at which time gifts in excess of $5,000 began to be made to Crummey trusts. Unless the trust was quite large, even the 5% aspect of this so-called "five or five" rule did not give enough protection, and the lapse of the withdrawal power to the extent it exceeded the greater of $5,000 or 5% of trust corpus caused a taxable gift by the power holder to the remainder persons of the trust. Since the (possibly unknown) remainder persons did not have a power to withdraw the gift from the trust, the beneficiary made a future interest gift, which did not qualify for the annual exclusion.

4. This taxable gift by the Crummey trust beneficiary has two negative aspects. One is that the beneficiary had made a transfer subject to gift tax and would use up some of his unified transfer credit or have an actual gift tax to pay.

   The other negative aspect is that, since the beneficiary usually had some continuing right in the trust (e.g., a life estate), the property subject to the lapsed power would be included in his estate for estate tax purposes as a transfer in which an interest had been retained.[7]

   The gift tax problem resulting from the lapse of a power relating to trust property in excess of $5,000 or 5% of the trust corpus can be resolved through good tax planning. By reserving in the beneficiary a power that keeps the lapse from being a completed gift (e.g., the power to direct where the trust property

will go upon lapse of the withdrawal power), no gift tax is due. However, the estate tax problem is not avoided and the technically incomplete gift is included in the beneficiary's taxable estate. Since most Crummey trusts are intended to be paid out during the beneficiary's lifetime, this is not a great problem for most people.

5. Many trusts will direct the trustee to keep separate those portions of the property over which a withdrawal right has lapsed that are within the "five or five" rule from those portions that exceed the "five or five" limit. The portion within the "five or five" rule can avoid estate tax at the death of the beneficiary. (See Questions and Answers concerning the generation-skipping transfer tax.) The other portion (amounts in excess of the "five or five" limit) will be subject to estate tax at the death of the beneficiary who retains the power of appointment over the gift (in order to avoid the gift tax upon lapse). Careful record keeping is important if a portion of the trust is intended to pass free of both estate tax and generation-skipping transfer tax at the death of the beneficiary.

6. Regardless of how much of the gift is within or in excess of the "five or five" rule, the portion of the trust over which the beneficiary has a right of withdrawal at his death (e.g., the amount subject to the Crummey withdrawal where the withdrawal period had not lapsed) is included in his estate for estate tax purposes. This is because the beneficiary had the power to appoint (or transfer out) the property to himself and thus had a "general power of appointment" as described in IRC Section 2041. If the beneficiary lives past the point at which the removal power terminates, then the property that was subject to the withdrawal power can no longer be taken out and thus may escape taxation in the beneficiary's estate.

7. The primary goal of the life insurance trust is to remove the life insurance from the donor's taxable estate for death tax purposes. However, where the donor makes a gift of a life insurance policy and then dies within three years of making the gift, the value of the proceeds will be brought back into the donor's estate.[8] However, if an irrevocable life insurance trust purchases a new policy, the insured/donor never holds any incidents of ownership in the policy and the proceeds are not payable to the insured's estate, the insurance proceeds are not included in the insured's estate even if the insured dies within three years of the purchase by the trust.[9]

For this reason, it is often better to structure the life insurance trust so that only cash gifts are made to the trust, and those cash gifts are used to purchase the desired insurance on the donor(s).

8. EGTRRA 2001 repeals the estate tax and the generation-skipping transfer tax for one year in 2010.

QUESTIONS AND ANSWERS

Question – Is there a way to avoid the three-year rule and still give an insurance policy?

Answer – There is really no simple way that is effective. Some people have given money to the trust and then let the trust purchase the policy from the insured. This triggers the "transfer for value" rule. Policy proceeds will then be taxed as ordinary income to the extent that they exceed the purchase price of the policy. However, if the trust and the insured are legitimate partners in a partnership, the sale may qualify for an exception to the "transfer for value" rule. If there is real concern about the three-year rule, a much simpler solution is to purchase an additional term insurance rider equal to the potential estate tax.

Question – How does one avoid the three-year rule and still give an insurance gift?

Answer – Where the donor is still insurable, it may be that buying a new policy can actually be advantageous since some newer policies give a higher effective rate of return. If this is the case, then the donor can give money to the trust and then let the trustee buy the policy. As long as the trustee is not required to purchase insurance with the funds contributed by the grantor and there is no other basis for saying that the grantor's gift of cash was really a gift of an insurance policy, the transfers within three years of death rule can be avoided.

Question – If a person wants to cash in an insurance policy and buy a new one, are there any income tax aspects to the transaction?

Answer – Yes, to the extent that the insurance policy sale results in receiving more dollars than had been paid in net premiums, the "cashing in" of the policy can result in any gain being taxed as ordinary income.

Question – The generation-skipping tax applies to current gifts to grandchildren. Is it possible to draft a Crummey trust that will be able to avoid such a tax?

Answer – Yes, if separate shares are created. The annual exclusion is available for gift tax purposes with respect to all power holders who have a beneficial interest in the trust. However, a nontaxable gift which is a direct skip to a trust for the benefit of an individual has an inclusion ratio of zero (i.e., it is not subject to generation-skipping transfer tax) only if (1) during the life of such individual no portion of the trust corpus or income may be distributed to or for the benefit of any other person, and (2) the trust would be included in such individual's estate if such individual were to die before the trust terminated. A Crummey power can be used in conjunction with each such separate share to create an annual exclusion for generation-skipping transfer tax purposes. In addition, if the GST annual exclusion is not available, the trust could be protected from the GST tax by allocating GST exemption to the trust.

Question – What is the maximum number of annual exclusion gifts that can be made with a Crummey withdrawal power?

Answer – This is an area in which there has been a great deal of speculation. Some Crummey trusts have included withdrawal powers for individuals who have no beneficial interest in the trust other than the right to withdraw. Theoretically, an annual exclusion would be available for each individual with a withdrawal power.

However, the IRS has disallowed a number of exclusions where the beneficiaries' interests included only the withdrawal power. The IRS indicated that annual exclusions will be allowed only for gifts to beneficiaries who hold other beneficial interests in the trust or who have actually exercised their powers. However, the IRS has been unsuccessful in disallowing annual exclusions for persons with contingent interests in a trust.

It is prudent to include withdrawal powers only for individuals who have a beneficial interest in the trust. The number of annual exclusions available should therefore be limited to the persons who have some rights in the trust other than merely a power to withdraw.

Question – If a beneficiary of a Crummey trust does not exercise the withdrawal power, he is considered to have made a gift to the remainder persons of the trust. Since part of this gift may be taxable, how is it determined what is subject to gift tax and what is not?

Answer – For those older trusts in which only gifts of $5,000 or less to the trust were envisioned, there is often no continuing power in the beneficiary to affect the disposition of the gifts after they come into the trust. In this circumstance, any amounts subject to the Crummey withdrawal power in excess of $5,000 will be subject to a taxable gift upon lapse of the power. The exception to this is that if the total trust principal at the time of the gift is in excess of $100,000, then the alternate exception of 5% of the trust corpus under IRC Section 2514(e) would apply and that is the amount that would not be subject to gift tax.

Question – What should be done with an older trust that relies only on the "five or five" power to avoid a gift by the beneficiary because of the lapse of the withdrawal and as to which the donors now wish to make larger gifts?

Answer – Many practitioners are looking for ways to abandon such older trusts. Some wise practitioners included a provision for some third person to have a power to "kick out" assets. Many persons are arranging to have such a power exercised so that they may start out fresh with a new trust with more effective terms.

In some other cases, some grantors are buying from the trusts insurance policies on their lives (particularly when they cannot get new coverage) and making gifts of those policies to new Crummey trusts.

Question – How should the beneficiaries be notified of the annual withdrawal right?

Answer – The basic requirement is that actual notice must be made in a timely manner. In order to show compliance, it may be best to give written notice to all beneficiaries (and to the natural guardian of any minor) at least 30 days before the end of the withdrawal period (which is typically December 31).

Question – Is it sufficient if the beneficiaries are just given notice at the time the trust is created?

Answer – Not according to the IRS. It appears that a "once only" notice will not be adequate even if the notice indicates that later contributions will give rise to additional withdrawal rights in future years.

Question – Can a donee of a Crummey Trust have multiple demand rights no one of which exceeds the greater of $5,000 or 5% of principal and avoid the gift tax problems and estate tax problems when such powers lapse?

Answer – No. A donee is allowed only a single $5,000 or 5% limitation for lapsed withdrawal rights during a calendar year. Thus, where a donor made a $5,000 gift to each of two Crummey Trusts, the donee was required to aggregate the two gifts (as if they were made to the same trust) for purposes of the $5,000 or 5% limitation.[10]

Question – If a grantor of a Crummey Trust retains the right to replace the trustee with someone other than himself, will such a right cause the trust to be includable in his estate for estate tax purposes?

Answer – The IRS takes the position that a grantor's retention of the power to remove a trustee without cause and replace him with another trustee is tantamount to the grantor's retention of the trustee's powers, even though the grantor could not name himself as trustee.[11] Therefore, if the trustee had powers or ownership rights over the trust property which if held by the grantor would cause the property to be includable in the grantor's estate, the trust property will be includable in the grantor's estate. For purposes of IRC Section 2036 (retained life estates) and IRC Section 2038 (revocable transfers), but not IRC Section 2042 (life insurance), the IRS states that it will not include property in a grantor's estate because of the retained power to replace a trustee with an independent corporate trustee.[12] A later ruling determined that the right to replace a trustee for cause with someone other than the insured / grantor was not an incident of ownership.[13]

Question – Is it possible to use a Crummey trust to benefit my children and avoid both gift tax now and generation-skipping tax at my children's deaths using only annual exclusion gifts?

Answer – Generally, no. In order to obtain the annual exclusion for generation-skipping transfer tax purposes, separate trusts (or shares of trusts) must be used. Such separate trusts must benefit only one individual, and consequently, could not benefit both children and grandchildren.

If such separate shares are not created, a Crummey trust could use the gift tax annual exclusion in conjunction with allocations of the GST exemption to protect the trust from gift tax and generation-skipping transfer tax. Of course, any Crummey power that has not lapsed before a child's death would cause the property subject to the power to be includable in the child's estate.

Question – Would it ever be better to have a life insurance trust without a Crummey withdrawal power?

Answer – Yes. Except as noted above, gifts subject to the Crummey power cannot pass through the donees' generation without incurring either an estate tax or a generation-skipping tax. However, gifts of life insurance or cash to purchase or maintain insurance can pass tax free through the next generation if the donors make the gifts utilizing their unified credits (or make the gifts subject to gift tax if their unified credits have been used up), and allocate some of their generation-skipping exemptions to the gifts. Each donor has a generation-skipping exemption which can be allocated either to transfers to grandchildren or to trusts which may ultimately pass to grandchildren (e.g., a trust benefiting a child that passes to grandchildren at the child's death).

In the same way that gifts of life insurance can effectively "leverage" the benefits of the donor's unified credit, such gifts can "leverage" the benefits of the generation-skipping exemption because the donor need allocate only enough exemption to cover the "gift" value of the policy as opposed to the face value of the policy.

Question – Can the donor be the trustee of the Crummey trust?

Answer – It is possible in certain very restricted circumstances to have the donor act as trustee where there is no life insurance on the donor-trustee's life. However, this requires a severe restriction of powers of the trustee. It is far better to have both no opportunity for the IRS to attack the transfer as being one that is included in the donor's estate and also to avoid subjecting property to management under very restricted circumstances. The more flexibility that can be given to a competent trustee, the better the trustee can manage the property.

Question – What impact did EGTRRA 2001 have on irrevocable life insurance trusts?

Answer – There were several changes that may have an impact on life insurance trusts. The top estate and gift tax rate, as well as the generation-skipping transfer tax rate, have been reduced to 48% in 2004, 47% in 2005, 46% in 2006, 45% in 2007 to 2009, and 35% (gift tax only) in 2010. The gift tax unified credit equivalent (applicable exclusion) increased to $1,000,000 in 2002 and later years. The estate tax unified credit equivalent (applicable exclusion) has increased to $1,500,000 from 2004 to 2005, $2,000,000 from 2006 to 2008, and $3,500,000 in 2009. The generation-skipping transfer tax exemption is increased to equal the estate tax unified credit equivalent from 2004 to 2009. The estate tax and the generation-skipping transfer tax are repealed for one year in 2010. In 2011, all taxes revert to as they existed prior to EGTRRA 2001.

Although, the unified credit and GST exemption are increasing, some estates (those in excess of the exempted amounts) will still incur a tax liability. For those estates, irrevocable life insurance trusts will still be needed in order to provide liquidity to pay the tax due.

In terms of relative dollars, minimal protection is provided for a number of years because the largest increase in the exemption amount does not occur until 2009. In addition, the estate tax and generation-skipping transfer tax revert to as they existed prior to EGTRRA 2001 in 2011. Since one's date of death is not foreseeable, it would not be wise to count on the increased exemption to eliminate or reduce estate taxes that may be due.

Also, in conjunction with repeal of the estate tax and the generation-skipping transfer tax for one year in 2010, the unlimited step-up in basis is replaced with a modified carryover basis (with a partial step-up). Beneficiaries of property that has not been stepped-up will incur a tax upon sale of the property. Therefore, irrevocable life insurance trusts will also be needed to pay the income tax liability associated with such sales.

Question – What amount of gifts can be transferred to an irrevocable life insurance trust using the annual exclusion?

Answer – In 2004, the annual exclusion is $11,000. After 1998, the $10,000 annual exclusion for gifts is indexed annually for inflation, rounded down to the next lowest multiple of $1,000.

Inflation increases should be used, when available, to help donors make slightly larger gifts under the gift tax annual exclusion. It should also be used by individuals who have already exhausted their entire GSTT exemption. Crummey withdrawal powers should be drafted by referring to "the maximum amount allowable for the year as an exclusion under IRC Section 2503(b)" rather than to a fixed amount.

This indexing may eventually enable the payment of larger gift tax free life insurance premiums without the need to pay additional gift tax. One of the most powerful of all estate planning tools is a systematically used annual gift program that is started as early as possible and continued for life coupled with an irrevocable life insurance trust.

Question – What type of life insurance is best to put into an irrevocable life insurance trust?

Answer – The best type of product to put in such a trust is one that matches the objectives and circumstances of the parties involved. Since the main purpose of many, if not most, life insurance trusts is to provide for estate liquidity to help pay estate taxes and other death related expense at some future indeterminate date, some form of permanent insurance is usually preferable. Among the types of permanent insurance that can be placed in trust are whole life, universal life, or variable life insurance. Policies can be on the life of a single insured or can be of the survivorship type, wherein two parties, typically husband and wife, are insured and the policy pays the death benefit only after both parties die.

For those circumstances where it can be accurately predicted how long the need will be and that the coverage won't run out before the need does, term insurance can be appropriate.

CHAPTER ENDNOTES

1. Rev. Rul. 81-7, 1981-1 CB 474; Let. Ruls. 7946007, 7947066.

2. Let. Rul. 8019038.

3. Rev. Rul. 81-7, 1981-1 CB 474.

4. Let. Ruls. 8103074, 8006048, 8004172.

5. Let. Rul. 8103074.

6. TAMs 8727003, 914008; *Est. of Cristofani v. Comm.*, 97 TC 74 (1991), acq. in result 1992-2 CB 1.

7. IRC Sec. 2036.

8. IRC Sec. 2035.

9. *Est. of Leder v. Comm.*, 90-1 USTC ¶60,001 (10th Cir. 1989); *Est. of Headrick v. Comm.*, 90-2 USTC ¶60,049 (6th Cir. 1990); *Est. of Perry v. Comm.*, 91-1 USTC ¶60,064 (5th Cir. 1991); AOD 1991-012.

10. Rev. Rul. 85-88, 1985-2 CB 201.

11. TAM 8922003.

12. Rev. Rul. 95-58, 1955-2 CB 191.

13. Let. Rul. 9832039.

Part 7:

CHARITABLE GIVING

Chapter 32

CHARITABLE CONTRIBUTIONS

WHAT IS IT?

A charitable contribution is a gratuitous transfer of property to a charitable, religious, scientific, educational, or other specified organization. If the donee of the gift falls within one of the categories designated by law, a charitable deduction may be taken for income, gift, or estate tax purposes.

Charitable contributions have tax value, therefore, because they can result in a current income tax deduction, may reduce federal estate taxes, and can be made free of gift tax. From the charity's point of view, charitable contributions are also tax favored – the charity itself pays no tax upon receipt of either a lifetime gift or a bequest and, generally, no income tax is paid by the qualified charity on income earned by the charity on donated property. (This topic is covered in more detail in *The Tools and Techniques of Charitable Planning*.)

WHEN IS THE USE OF SUCH A DEVICE INDICATED?

1. When the donor wishes, for non-tax reasons, to benefit the charity.

2. When the donor wishes to reduce income or estate taxes by taking advantage of the deductions allowed for such gifts.

3. When the donor would like to achieve both motives described above.

WHAT ARE THE REQUIREMENTS?

1. Charitable contributions are deductible only if they are made to organizations that are "qualified." Examples of "qualified" organizations include non-profit schools and hospitals, churches and synagogues, the United Way, Community Chest, United Cerebral Palsy, YMCA, YMHA, The American Red Cross, the Boy Scouts, Campfire Boys and Girls, and the American Heart Association.

A donee will be considered qualified only if it meets three conditions: (1) it must be operated exclusively for religious, charitable, scientific, literary, or educational purposes; or to foster national or international amateur sports competition, or to prevent cruelty to children or animals; (2) no part of the organization's earnings can benefit any private shareholder or similar individual; (3) the organization cannot be one disqualified for tax exemption because it attempts to influence legislation or participates in, publishes or distributes statements for, or intervenes in, any political campaign on behalf of any candidate seeking public office. The Internal Revenue Service publishes a list of qualified charities in IRS Publication 78, which can be viewed on the IRS Website: http://www.irs.gov/bus_info/eo/eosearch.

It is important to note that the statutory descriptions of qualified charities for federal income tax purposes are not exactly the same as the descriptions of qualified charities for federal estate or gift tax purposes. One basic distinction is that for income tax purposes the donee must be a domestic organization, whereas the donee for estate tax charitable deduction purposes can be a foreign or a domestic charity. (Be certain to check the rules under all applicable Code sections.) Generally, the income tax deduction is available for contributions to churches, educational organizations, hospitals and medical research organizations, governmental units, and various other organizations and support organizations described in Internal Revenue Code Section 170(c). The client or practitioner should ascertain whether a potential donee is qualified under the Code. If it is not listed in IRS Publication 78, it is wise to request a copy of a determination letter from the IRS indicating that the charity does or does not qualify.

2. The second requirement necessary for a charitable contribution deduction is that property must be the subject of the gift. Therefore, the value of a taxpayer's time or services, even if contributed to a qualified charity, is not deductible. For example, if a carpenter spent 10 hours building chairs for his church, he

could not deduct his normal hourly wage as a charitable contribution. However, he could deduct the cost of materials he purchased and used in producing the finished product.

Likewise, a taxpayer who donates the use of his property to a charity has not made a contribution of property. So the rent-free use of an office, or even an office building, no matter how valuable the rent-free use of the facility might be, will not be considered a charitable contribution any more than a contribution of personal services.

3. A third requirement for a charitable contribution deduction is that there must be a contribution to the charity in excess of the value received by the donor. In some cases the donor will receive a benefit in conjunction with his charitable gift. Such a contribution is deductible only to the extent that the value of the contributed property exceeds any consideration or benefit to the donor. For example, the individual might donate cash to a charity. The charity in turn might pay the donor (and perhaps his survivors) an annuity income for life. Only the difference between the contribution made and the value of the annuity would be deductible (see Chapter 33). What the donor receives in return must be both incidental *and* insubstantial in relation to the gift made.

There must be intent to make a charitable gift rather than a bargain, regardless of how favorable that bargain is to the charity. Charitable intent is a *sine qua non* (i.e., an indispensable condition) to deductibility.

4. The fourth requirement that must be met for a deduction to be allowed is that the gift to charity must actually be paid in cash or other property before the close of the tax year in question. Typically, therefore, even an accrual basis taxpayer must actually pay cash or contribute other property before the close of the tax year in order to receive a deduction.

5. A charitable contribution at death will be deductible regardless of whether it is made by will, by the terms of a life insurance policy, or by gift during the decedent's lifetime in such a manner that the gift will be includable in his gross estate. But in order to be deductible, the transfer must be made by the decedent, as distinguished from a transfer made by his estate or beneficiaries. Therefore, a deduction would not be allowed for a bequest to charity if the bequest requires the approval of a third party.

6. Where the lifetime transfer or bequest to charity is a gift of a "partial interest" (i.e., where the gift will be split between noncharitable and charitable beneficiaries), strict rules apply. Generally, if a charity's interest in the transfer of property is a remainder interest (i.e., the charity receives what remains after the noncharitable income beneficiaries have received income for a specified time), a transfer in trust will qualify *only* if it is an annuity trust, unitrust, or a pooled income fund. (These terms are defined and described in Chapter 33.)

7. A qualified appraisal (Form 8283) must accompany a tax return showing donations of property valued at over $5,000. Who can be an appraiser? An individual is qualified to be an appraiser for tax purposes only if (1) he holds himself out to the public as an appraiser, (2) is qualified to appraise the particular type of property in question, and (3) understands that an overstatement of value may lead to the imposition of penalties. The appraisal may not be made by the donor, the organization receiving the contribution, any person from whom the property was acquired, or certain related individuals or entities. Generally, a separate appraisal must be made for each item of property unless similar items are donated in the same year. Partnerships donating property valued at over $5,000 must provide a copy of the appraisal to every partner who receives a proportionate share of the deduction.

In addition, in the case of charitable contributions of art valued at more than $5,000, the taxpayer may request a "Statement of Value" from the IRS to substantiate the gift for income tax purposes. The request must be accompanied by a copy of the appraisal, a completed appraisal summary, and the user fee ($2,500 for the first three pieces of art).

While the appraisal requirement does not apply to gifts of publicly traded securities, it does apply to non-publicly traded securities worth more than $10,000. Note there are severe penalties for overvaluation of charitable gifts.

In the case of all contributions, including cash, a charitable deduction is not allowed for any contribution of $250 or more unless the donor also obtains contemporaneous written acknowledgement that includes: (1) the amount of money, or a description of the property contributed; (2) whether the organization gave any goods or services to the taxpayer in return for the contribution; (3) a description and good faith estimate of the value of the goods and services; and (4) a statement that the goods and services provided consisted solely of intangible religious benefits. Canceled checks, alone, are not sufficient in such cases.

In addition, no charitable deduction is allowed for a non-cash contribution unless the taxpayer attaches Form 8283 to his tax return showing the required information (on Part A).

All donors must keep canceled checks, receipts, or other reliable written records. These documents must show the name of the donee, the date of the contribution, and the amount of the gift. The safest approach is to make the records at the same time the gift is made and have the recipient charity sign a receipt.

HOW IT IS DONE – AN EXAMPLE

A gift to charity is probably one of the simplest estate planning techniques. During lifetime, such a gift can be accomplished merely by writing a check, assigning stock, transferring life insurance policies, signing a deed to real estate, or conveying property to charity in any other standard outright manner. Likewise, at death, gifts to charity can be made by will, by life insurance contract, by employee benefit contract (i.e., the death benefits from a pension plan can be paid to charity), or by trust. Generally, lifetime gifts to charity yield both higher tax and nontax rewards.

WHAT ARE THE TAX IMPLICATIONS?

1. A charitable contribution to a qualified charity reduces current income taxes (assuming the donor itemizes deductions).

2. No federal gift tax is payable on a gift to a qualified charity regardless of the size of the gift.

3. Gifts to qualified charities can reduce the federal estate tax, with the amount of the deduction limited only by the value of the gift (i.e., the donor's entire estate can be left to charity and a deduction will be allowed for the entire gift).

4. The charity itself will pay no tax upon the receipt of either a lifetime gift or a bequest.

5. Generally, no income tax will be payable by a qualified charity on income earned by donated property.

6. If an otherwise deductible charitable contribution to a college or university entitles the donor to purchase tickets for athletic events, 80% of the contribution will be deductible.

7. For federal income tax purposes, there are percentage limitations on the amount that can be claimed as a charitable contribution deduction; these depend on, among other things, the type of property transferred. (The percentage limitations are discussed, below, in the Questions and Answers section, and are also displayed in Figure 32.1.)

For tax purposes, potential charitable donees will be classified either as a private foundation or a public charity. The percentage limitations discussed below are those generally applicable to public charities. There are stricter percentage limitations on deductions for contributions to most private foundations.

Any organization that is classified as a charity under Internal Revenue Code section 501(c)(3) is deemed a private foundation *unless* it is: a church; an educational organization with a regular curriculum, faculty, and student body; a hospital; a governmental unit; or certain other publicly supported institutions and support organizations.

In view of the importance of the income tax charitable contribution deduction and the percentage limitations, it is important for the advisor to determine not only whether the charitable recipient is a qualified charity, but also whether it is a private foundation, and if so, what type of private foundation.

ISSUES AND IMPLICATIONS IN COMMUNITY PROPERTY STATES

Because of the equal ownership aspect of community property between a husband and wife, care must be exercised in the creation of a charitable trust that benefits both parties, since a taxable transfer may occur.

Example: If community property is used to fund a trust that benefits only one of the spouses, there has been a gift by the other spouse. Conversely, if the separate property of one of the spouses is used to fund a trust that provides for a lifetime benefit for both spouses, there is a recognized gift to the non-contributing spouse.

After 1981, the availability of the unlimited marital deduction for federal gift tax purposes eliminates prior concerns as to federal gift tax (see Chapter 24). However, some states still have some form of gift tax, and only some of those states have an unlimited gift tax marital deduction. Therefore, state gift tax can still be a problem in these circumstances. However, if community property is used to fund a trust that provides a lifetime benefit for *both* spouses, there will be no gift tax consequences.

It is possible for community property to be "split," creating separate interests for each spouse, which could then be used to fund separate charitable trusts, each involving life interests of only the spouse making the gift. Or, one spouse can make a gift with her half of the "split" funds, and the other spouse can use the funds for his own purposes or to pay their joint income tax liability. In order for community property to be "split," an agreement between the parties must be made to that effect. A "split" is essentially a transmutation of community property to separate property; such transmutations must be in writing in some states (e.g., California).

Under the community property laws in many states, a valid contribution of community property cannot be made to a charity by one spouse without the consent of the other spouse. This consent should be obtained before the close of the tax year for which the deduction will be claimed; otherwise the IRS may argue the contribution was not complete and is not deductible.

Generally, the same income, estate and gift tax advantages that are available for gifts of separate property will be available in situations where community property is the subject of a charitable contribution.

QUESTIONS AND ANSWERS

Question – How do you calculate the tax savings and after-tax cost of a charitable contribution?

Answer – The tax savings and after-tax cost can be found as follows:

> Tax Savings = Amount of deductible gift x Effective tax bracket

---

Example: A $2,000 gift by a taxpayer in a 40% (federal and state) income tax bracket equals

$800 in tax savings. Stated another way, the out-of-pocket cost of the gift equals:

> Amount contributed — Tax savings

For instance, the $2,000 gift above less the $800 in income tax savings equals the out-of-pocket cost of the gift, $1,200.

Question – How do you determine the amount of an income tax charitable deduction?

Answer – The amount of a charitable contribution deduction that will be allowed for income tax purposes depends on the five following factors, which will be discussed in detail below:

1. *The type of property given away.*

    (a) Rent-free occupancy;

    (b) Cash;

    (c) Long-term capital gain property;

    (d) Ordinary income property;

    (e) Tangible personal property where the use of that property by the donee is *related* to the exempt functions of the donee; and tangible personal property where the use of that property is *unrelated* to the exempt purposes of the donee;

    (f) Future interests in property.

    (The various types of property listed above will be discussed in detail in the following question.)

2. *The identity of the donee.* Generally, contributions to publicly supported domestic organizations – so-called "public charities"– are more favorably treated than contributions to foreign organizations or to most private foundations. Cash contributions to public charities, for example, are fully deductible up to 50% of a donor's contribution base (i.e., adjusted gross income computed without regard to any net operating loss carryback to the taxable year). The deduction for an individual's contributions to most nonpublic (private) charities, regardless of the type of property given away, is limited to the lesser of (a) 30% of the taxpayer's contribution base, or (b) 50% of his contribution base minus

the amount of charitable contribution deductions allowed for contributions to the public-type charities.[1] For example, if a wealthy individual donates property worth 40% of his contribution base (AGI) to a public charity such as the Boy Scouts, his contributions to "30% charities" (private charities) are deductible up to only 10% of his contribution base.[2] The limitation for gifts of capital gain property to private foundations is the lesser of 20% *or* the unused portion of the 30% limitation. Donations to individuals or to foreign charities (except where allowed by treaty) are not deductible.

3. *The identity of the donor.* Deductions for individuals are limited to specified percentages of their contribution base. An individual must itemize deductions in order to claim an income tax charitable contribution deduction. A corporation is limited to a deduction based on a percentage of its taxable income.[3]

4. *The amount of property given away.* Both individuals and corporations can carry over excess contributions (i.e., contributions above their deductible limit) for up to five years.[4]

5. *The place where the contribution is to be used.* As mentioned above, gifts made to United States charities are treated more favorably than gifts to most foreign charities.

Question – How does the type of property interest given to charity affect the income tax limitation on deductions? What is the effect of a contribution of a partial interest in property to charity?

Answer – Generally, a charitable contribution of less than a donor's entire interest in property is not deductible. Gifts of a partial interest in property are deductible only in four very narrowly defined situations:

1. The first is a gift of an undivided portion of the donor's entire interest in property.[5] For example, if Jesse Verr, a successful businessman, gave his original Ramlo sculpture to the Philadelphia Museum of Art, but agreed with the museum that he could keep it as long as he or his wife lived, no current deduction would be allowed. However, if Jesse gave an undivided one-half interest in the sculpture (i.e., if he gave the museum an immediate, absolute, and complete right of ownership, for display purposes or otherwise, for one-half of each year), he

would likely be successful in obtaining a current deduction.[6]

2. The second situation involves a gift of a remainder interest in a personal residence or farm.[7] If Robin Lynn Kay gives her home or her farm to a qualified organization with the stipulation that she may live there for life, she may take a current income tax deduction for the value of the future gift. This assumes, of course, that the gift is irrevocable.

3. The third circumstance in which a charitable contribution of less than the donor's entire interest could generate a deduction is where the donor makes a gift to a qualified charitable organization of a remainder interest in real property granted solely for conservation purposes.[8]

4. Finally, a gift of a partial interest would be deductible if transferred in trust. This exception allows a charitable deduction for transfers of property in trust even if the taxpayer transfers less than his entire interest. The deduction is allowed to the same extent that a deduction would be allowed had the same property been transferred directly to the charitable organization rather than in trust.

The chart at Figure 32.1 and the discussion that follows illustrate how each type of property influences the limitation on the deduction for an individual who itemizes deductions.

(A) Rent-Free Occupancy

Contributions of a mere right to use property (such as a rent-free lease to the Boy Scouts) are not deductible.[9] This is the situation because to be deductible, contributions must be made in cash or other property. The mere right to use property is considered neither cash nor other property. The IRS considers a contribution of the right to use property as a contribution of less than the donor's entire interest in the property.

(B) Cash

Where the property is cash (as in a gift of any other type of property), it is necessary to ask, "Who is the donee?" If the donee is a publicly supported charity, the deduction ceiling (column 3) is 50% of the individual taxpayer's contribution base (generally, adjusted gross income).[10] A corporation's de-

Figure 32.1

CHARITABLE CONTRIBUTION DEDUCTION LIMITATIONS						
		PERCENTAGE LIMITATION				
		INDIVIDUAL AS DONOR	*CORP. AS DONOR*			
Type of Property N(1)	*Donee†* (2)	*Adjusted Gross Income*** (3)	*Taxable Income* (4)	*Individual Carryover* (5)	*Corporation Carryover* (6)	*TAX TREATMENT* (7)
(A) Rent-Free Occupancy or Services	—	—	—	—	—	No Deduction
(B) Cash	Public	50%	10%	5 yrs.	5 yrs.	Full Deduction
(C) Long-Term Capital Gain Property (except for tangible personal property)	Public	30% *	10%	5 yrs.	5 yrs.	Full Deduction for Fair Market Value
(D) Ordinary Income Property	Public	50%	10%	5 yrs.	5 yrs.	Deduction Limited to Basis††
(E) Tangible Personal Property (L.T.C.G. Property)						
(1) Use-Related	Public	30% *	10%	5 yrs.	5 yrs.	Full Deduction for Fair Market Value
(2) Use-Unrelated to Exempt Purposes of Donee	Public	50%	10%	5 yrs.	5 yrs.	Deduction Limited to Adjusted Basis
(F) Future Interests in Property*						

*   See detailed discussion in text.
** With certain adjustments.
†   Regardless of the type of property given, the deduction for an individual's contributions to private charities is limited to the lesser of (a) 30 percent of the taxpayer's "contribution base" (roughly the same as adjusted gross income) or (b) 50 percent of the contribution base less any charitable contribution deduction allowed for contributions to public-type charities.
†† There is an important exception. The deduction for corporate donors (other than S corporations) has a higher limit, basis plus one-half of appreciation in value, where the property is to be used by the donee solely for the care of the ill, the needy, or infants. (See the text below).

duction is limited to 10% of its taxable income (with certain adjustments).[11] Regardless of the type of property given, a corporation can always take a current deduction of up to 10% of its taxable income (column 4). Likewise, regardless of the identity of the donee, a corporation may carry over excess contributions for up to five years (column 6).

Contributions by individuals to "public" charities in excess of the deductible limit for the taxable year may also be carried over (column 5) for a period of up to five years.[12] In other words, excess contributions are not wasted and can be used as itemized deductions in future years. For example, if Scott Jeffries contributed $20,000 in cash to a synagogue, but his contribution base was only $36,000, he could currently deduct only 50% of his contribution base, $18,000. He could, however, carry over the $2,000 excess ($20,000 contribution minus $18,000) to the following year. (A 5-year carryover is also provided for excess contributions to private foundations.)

A full deduction, up to 50% of the contribution base of individuals who itemize deductions (or 10% of taxable income for corporations), is allowed for gifts of cash (column 7).[13]

(C) Long-Term Capital Gain Property

"Long-term capital gain property" is property that would have produced a long-term capital gain (held for more than one year) on the date of the gift had it been sold rather than donated to charity.

Long-term capital gain property can be divided into two types:

The first type consists of intangible personal property and all real property. A gift of Xerox stock purchased 11 years ago at $100 a share, now worth $400 a share, would be considered intangible personal long-term capital gain property. Appreciated land held the requisite "long-term" period would be an example of real property that is properly classified as long-term capital gain property.

The second type of long-term capital gain property is tangible personal property, such as a car, a painting, sculpture, an antique, or jewelry. Tangible personal property will be discussed in Section E.

Where intangible long-term capital gain property, such as stock held for the requisite period, is given to a "public" donee (column 2), an individual's deduction may not exceed 30% of his contribution base (column 3).[14] If his gift exceeds this percentage limitation, he may carry over the disallowed portion of the deduction for up to five succeeding years (column 5). The full fair market value of the gift is deductible (column 7).[15]

Example: Suppose Nick Catrini donates stock worth $25,000 to the United Way. The stock cost $12,000 when he purchased it four years ago. If his adjusted gross income is $50,000, his maximum deduction for the contribution is $15,000 (30% of $50,000). He will be able to carry over the $10,000 balance and apply that as a 30%-type deduction against future years' income.

The deduction for contributions of long-term capital gain property is doubly advantageous. First, a person saves the taxes on his potential profit; in the above example, Nick saves the tax on a $13,000 long-term capital gain. Second, he gets a deduction for the full fair market value of the gift; here it will be $25,000.

Contributions of certain publicly traded stock to private foundations share the same advantages as similar gifts to public charities. Generally, a gift of publicly traded stock (which if sold, would result in a long-term capital gain) made to a private foundation is deductible at its full fair market value provided that the amount of stock does not exceed 10% in value of all the outstanding stock of the corporation.[16]

There is an election the taxpayer may want to make in certain situations. The 30% limitation can be increased to 50% if the donor is willing to reduce the value of his gift by his potential gain.[17] The election can be extremely important for a taxpayer whose income fluctuates widely from year to year. It is of particular value when the amount of appreciation is small. For example, the value of a gift of

long-term capital gain property with a basis of $980 and a fair market value of $1,000 would be reduced by only $20. In this way, the taxpayer could qualify for the higher 50% limitation at the expense of losing only a very small portion of his deduction.

(D) Ordinary Income Property

"Ordinary income property" is an asset that would have generated ordinary income (rather than capital gain) on the date of contribution had it been sold at its fair market value rather than contributed.[18] Ordinary income property includes: (a) capital assets held less than the requisite long-term period at the time contributed; (b) Section 306 stock (i.e., stock acquired in a nontaxable corporate transaction that is treated as ordinary income if sold); (c) works of art, books, letters, and musical compositions, but only if given by the person who created or prepared them or for whom they were prepared; and (d) a taxpayer's stock in trade and inventory (which would result in ordinary income if sold).[19]

Ordinary income property given to a public charity (column 2) by an individual is deductible subject to a 50% of contribution base ceiling. However, a taxpayer's deduction is generally limited to his basis (cost) for the property (column 7).[20] For example, if a famous painter donated one of his paintings worth $25,000 to an art museum, his deduction would be limited to his cost for producing the painting. This means that only the cost for canvas, paint, etc., would be deductible. No deduction would be allowed for the value of his time and talent.

A similar situation occurs in the case of Tony Molino, who owned his National Motors stock for 4 months (i.e., a sale would have resulted in short-term capital gain). He purchased the stock at a cost of $12,000 and gave it to Villanova Law School when it was worth $25,000. Therefore, since the property is considered ordinary income property, only his cost (basis) is deductible. Tony will be limited to a charitable deduction of $12,000 even though the property had a fair market value of $25,000 at the time of the gift.

An exception to this rule is provided for certain ordinary income property, such as inventory, given by a corporation to a public charity, or a private operating foundation for use in its exempt purpose for the care of the ill, the needy, or infants (e.g., a contribution of medical supplies to the Red Cross).[21] In situations where this requirement can be met, the allowable deduction for contributions of appreciated ordinary income property is limited to (a) the donor's basis plus (b) one-half the potential gain in the property (but in no event can this deduction exceed twice the basis).[22]

Example: Assume a pharmaceutical corporation donates $11,000 worth of medicine (inventory) to a charity that performs services for ill and infirm individuals. If the basis to the corporation was $5,000, it may deduct $8,000 — its $5,000 basis plus one-half of the $6,000 potential gain.

Gifts of substantially appreciated ordinary income property should be avoided if possible. Capital assets should be held for the requisite long-term period if that will make it long-term capital gain property (i.e., deductible at full fair market value), or left to charity by will so that a full estate tax deduction can be obtained. Alternatively, ordinary income property could be left to the donor's children by will. The stepped-up basis they would receive in the property after the donor's death would enable them to obtain a larger income tax deduction then if they were to give the property to charity.[23]

(E) Tangible Personal Property

Tangible personal property (which would have produced capital gain if sold) includes cars, jewelry, sculpture, art works, books, etc., but only if created or produced by a person other than the donor.[24] With respect to this type of property, a distinction must be made between (a) gifts that will be used by the donee charity in such a manner that the use of the gift is related to the exempt purposes of the donee ("use related" gifts) and (b) gifts that will not be used by the charity in a manner related to the exempt purposes of the donee ("use unrelated" gifts).

An example might be the contribution of a stamp collection to an educational institution. If the stamp collection is placed in the donee organization's library for display and study by students, the use of the donated property is related to the educational purposes constituting the basis of the charitable organization's tax exemption. However, if the stamps were sold, even if the proceeds were used by the organization for educational purposes, the use of the property would be an unrelated use.

Example: Jeff Green has a $10,000 contribution base. He contributes a collection of whaling harpoons to the Cape May County Historical Museum for display purposes. The collection cost him $2,000, but on the date of contribution it was worth $10,000. The type of property contributed is tangible personal property. The donee is a public charity and the gift is "use related" to the exempt purposes of the Museum. Therefore, for the year of contribution, he can deduct up to 30% of his contribution base (AGI), $10,000. This figure is $3,000. In addition, because the full $10,000 contribution is deductible, he will be able to carry over the remaining $7,000 for up to five years (subject to the 30% rule each year).

If the gift is "use unrelated" (i.e., made to a donee whose direct use of the asset is unrelated to the charitable function of the donee), the deductible amount is limited to the donor's basis in the property. This is true for corporations as well as individuals.[25]

(F) Future Interests in Property

A "future interest" is any interest or right that will vest in possession or enjoyment at some time in the future. The term "future interest" includes situations where a donor purports to give tangible personal property to a charitable organization, but has made a written or oral agreement with the organization reserving to a noncharitable beneficiary (himself or a member of his immediate family) the right to use, possess, or enjoy the property. For example, suppose Robin Lynn donates a genuine Mellor photograph to an art museum, but arranges with the museum to keep the photograph in her home as long as she lives. The museum has a future interest in the photograph.

One of the basic general rules governing charitable deductions is that contributions must be: (a) actually paid; (b) paid in cash or other property; and (c) paid before the close of the tax year. Furthermore, generally no deductions are allowed for an outright contribution of less than the donor's entire interest in property.

Since the benefit to the museum – and consequently to the public – was deferred in the gift of the Mellor photograph, no current tax deduction would be allowed. The implication is that a deduction will not be allowed until the charity receives actual possession or enjoyment of the work of art. The gift of tangible personal property must be complete in the sense that all interests and rights to the possession and enjoyment of the property must "vest" in the charity. This means that a transfer of a future interest in property to a charity is not deductible until all intervening interests in and rights to possession held by the donor or certain related persons or organizations have expired, or unless the gift is in the form of a future interest in trust that meets the requirements discussed in Chapter 33.

Charitable remainder interests are a form of future interest in which an income interest is either retained by the donor or is given by the donor to another person. At the death of the income beneficiary, the principal goes to a designated charity. An example would be a gift to X for life where the "remainder" (i.e., the principal at the death of X) goes to charity (the "remainder person") upon the death of X (the income beneficiary). A gift "to X for life, remainder to Villanova School of Law" would be considered a gift of a future interest to the law school. Charitable remainder trusts are discussed in more depth in Chapter 33.

Question – Why are stocks and bonds often used for charitable gifts?

Answer – Securities such as listed stocks, mutual funds, or bonds are often selected as the subject of a charitable gift because:

(a) they are transferable with minimal cost or delay;

(b) as mentioned above, appreciated securities can often be transferred without causing the donor to realize gain on the appreciation and still yield a current deduction measured by the fair market value of the gift;

(c) if securities selling below their cost are sold, the net proceeds can be donated; this "sale-gift" procedure can lower the donor's tax;

(d) the donor's spendable income is often increased, rather than decreased, by the contribution;

(e) a lifetime gift removes appreciating property from an individual's estate

and, thus, may lower death taxes and administration expenses; and

(f) the gift is easily valued and documented.

Question – What is a bargain sale and how is it used for charitable purposes?

Answer – The bargain sale is a device used to minimize the out-of-pocket cost of a charitable gift. Prior to the Tax Reform Act of 1969, an individual could sell appreciated property to a charity at his cost. The donor would receive an amount equal to his investment. In addition, he would obtain a charitable deduction for the appreciation in the property with no tax on his portion.

Under current law, a taxpayer may have to recognize a taxable gain on the bargain sale because he must allocate his cost basis between the part of the property he sold to the charity and the part he donated.[26] This means the donor pays tax on his pro rata share of the appreciation.

Example: Suppose a donor sells property he has owned for several years to his favorite charity. On the date of the sale the property was worth $10,000. The sale price is the same as the donor's cost, $4,000. The gift amounts to 6/10 (60%) of the property, so he is deemed to have given the charity 60% of his $4,000 cost basis, $2,400. This leaves the donor only the difference, $1,600 of cost basis, to apply against the $4,000 he received. His long-term capital gain is therefore $2,400.

The $6,000 gift ($10,000 - $4,000) saves the donor $2,100 in taxes if he is in a 35% marginal tax bracket. He also has recovered his $4,000 investment, so his total "recovery" is $6,100. Since the maximum capital gain rate for assets held more than 12 months is 15%, his tax will be 15% of $2,400, or $360. The net return is $5,740 ($6,100 - $360), and the charity is enriched by $6,000.

Question – How can a gift of closely held stock be used to generate a charitable contribution deduction?

Answer – Several court decisions opened the door to another charitable contribution deduction tool: the use of closely held stock. The idea is to enable the owner of a closely-held corporation to siphon funds from his business free of income tax by making a charitable contribution of his personally owned stock, followed by an unrelated redemption of that stock by the corporation.[27] If used properly, the technique may reduce or eliminate the threat of an accumulated earnings tax problem, generate a current income tax deduction for the donor (with no loss of control), and provide cash for the donor's favorite charity with no out-of-pocket outlay.

It works like this. First, the stockholder donates some of his stock to the charitable organization. He receives a charitable deduction measured by the present value of the stock contributed. Then the corporation redeems the stock from the charity. (Had the corporation redeemed the stock directly from the donor, dividend treatment would probably have resulted.)

One use of this device involved a closely held corporation whose controlling shareholder gave a school about 200 shares of his corporation's stock each year. He took an annual deduction for the present value of the gifts, about $25,000.

The terms of the gift provided that the university could not dispose of the shares without first offering them to the corporation at their book value. The corporation was not required to purchase the stock, but did have 60 days in which to purchase any stock offered to it. Within a year or two after the shares were received by the school, they were offered to the corporation, which always purchased them. The proceeds of these redemptions were then invested by the school.

It appears that the key elements to the success of this device are the fact that the gifts were, in fact, complete and irrevocable, and that there was no formal or informal agreement that the university would offer the stock for redemption or that it would be redeemed. This avoided the obvious IRS attack that the corporation's redemptions from the charity were in essence redemptions from the donor and, thus, should have been taxed as ordinary income to the donor.[28]

Retention of substantial rights in the stock given to charity, such as voting rights, will result in disallowance of the deduction because the entire interest in the property will not have been transferred.[29] Furthermore, the stock will be included in the gross estate of the donor.

Question – Why is life insurance a good way to make charitable contributions?

Answer – Life insurance, like any other type of property, can be, and often is, the subject of a gift. In fact, life insurance is a favored means of making charitable contributions for a number of reasons.

First, the death benefit going to charity is guaranteed as long as premiums are paid. This means that the charity will receive an amount that is fixed in value and not subject to the potential downside risks of securities.

Second, life insurance provides an "amplified" gift that can be purchased on the installment plan. Through a relatively small annual cost (premium), a large benefit can be provided for the charity. A large gift can be made without impairing or diluting the control of a family business interest or other investments. Assets earmarked for the donor-insured's family can thus be kept intact.

Third, life insurance is a self-completing gift. If the donor lives, cash values, which can be used by the charity currently, grow constantly from year to year. If the donor becomes disabled and the policy contains a waiver-of-premium feature, the policy will remain in full force, guaranteeing the ultimate death benefit to the charity as well as the same cash values and dividend build-up that would have been earned had the insured not become disabled. Even if death occurs after only one deposit, the charity is assured of its full gift.

Fourth, the death proceeds can be received by the designated charity free of federal income and estate taxes, probate and administrative costs and delays, brokerage fees, and other transfer costs. Thus, the charity, in fact, receives "one hundred cent" dollars. This prompt cash payment should be compared with the payment of a gift to a selected charity under the terms of an individual's will. In that case, probate delays of up to several years are not uncommon.

Fifth, because of the contractual nature of the life insurance policy, large gifts to charity are not subject to attack by disgruntled heirs.

Finally, a substantial gift may be made with no attendant publicity (i.e., confidentially) because the life insurance proceeds to be paid to charity can be arranged so that they will not be part of the decedent's probate estate. Of course, publicity may be given if desired.

Warning: In Private Letter Ruling 9110016, the Service denied a charitable deduction for premiums paid on a life insurance policy assigned to a charity on the grounds that since the charity had no insurable interest (under New York law) in the insured, payment of the proceeds to the charity could violate state law. If so, it was determined that the proceeds would be included in the insured's estate and, thus, subject to federal estate tax. Subsequent to the Service's treatment of the matter, New York amended its insurable interest statute to give charities an insurable interest in donors' lives. The Service responded to New York's amendment by issuing Letter Ruling 9147040, which revoked Letter Ruling 9110016. Most states now have insurable interest statutes giving charities an insurable interest in the lives of their contributors. Some states require the charity to be the owner and irrevocable beneficiary while others allow the insured to be the initial owner if a subsequent transfer to the charity is made. A complete list of every state's insurable interest law is available at http://www.leimbergservices.com.

Question – How is the gift of a life insurance policy valued?

Answer – Since the bundle of rights in a life insurance policy can be considered equivalent to property, a gift of a life insurance policy is valued according to the same general tax rules as any other gift of property.

If a life insurance policy were sold at a gain, the gain would be taxed at ordinary income rates; therefore, a gift of life insurance is a gift of ordinary income property. Assuming the value of the policy (i.e., the interpolated terminal reserve plus unearned premium on the date of the sale) exceeds the policyholder's net premium payments, the deduction for a gift of a policy is generally limited to the policyholder's basis (cost) – in other words, his net premium payments.

Example: Suppose an individual assigns a policy on his life to the College for Financial Planning. His charitable contribution deduction is limited to his basis (i.e., his cost in the contract) or the value of the policy, if lower. If the individual paid net premiums of $15,000, but the policy had a value of $18,000, his charitable contribution deduction would be limited to $15,000.

If there had been no gain upon a sale of the policy, the value of the donated policy would then be equal to its replacement cost at the date of the gift. In other words, if the total net premiums paid exceeds the value of the policy when the individual assigns it (i.e., the policy would not give rise to a gain if sold), the deduction would be limited to the lower of the two, its replacement cost.

The amount of the deduction is dependent on the replacement cost of the policy. This differs depending on whether the policy in question is (1) a single premium or paid-up policy, (2) a premium-paying policy, or (3) a newly issued policy. The insurance company in question will generally calculate the exact value on IRS Form 712 upon request.

The replacement cost of a single premium or paid-up policy is the single premium the same insurer would charge for a policy of the same amount at the insured's attained age (increased by the value of any dividend credits and reduced by the amount of any loans outstanding).

The replacement cost of a premium-paying policy is the policy's interpolated terminal reserve plus any unearned premium at the date of the gift (again, taking into consideration any dividend credits and outstanding loans).

The replacement cost of a newly issued policy is the gross premium paid by the insured.

A gift of a life insurance policy to charity must, of course, satisfy local requisites of a valid gift. In most states, this means that the donor must have intended to make a present gift of the policy and that he delivered it, actually or constructively, to the charitable donee. An absolute assignment is the most straightforward way of effectuating the transfer.

Question – Is it possible to obtain a charitable deduction for premium payments if a charity owns a life insurance policy on the donor's life?

Answer – Premium payments are considered gifts of cash and are, therefore, fully and currently deductible as charitable contributions if the charity owns the policy outright.

The donor should send his check directly to the charity and have it pay the premium to the life insurance company in order to assure the most favorable tax results. The canceled check will serve as proof of (1) the fact that a gift was made to the charity, (2) the date the gift was made, and (3) the amount of the gift. It will also assure the donor of a full deduction up to 50% of his contribution base.

When an "indirect" gift is made to a charity, the annual deduction limit is lowered to 30% of the taxpayer's contribution base. A gift in trust is one such example. Another example of an indirect gift is where premiums on a policy owned by a charity are remitted directly to the life insurance company instead of to the charity itself.

If the gift to the charity exceeds $250, a statement will be required from the charitable organization showing the amount of money contributed and whether the charity gave any goods or services in return for the contribution.

Question – How could life insurance enable a charity to convince a donor to make an immediate gift of land or other property?

Answer – Life insurance can serve as a means of enabling a donor to make a large current gift. For example, assume that an individual is 50 years old, a widower, and has three children. His gross estate is about $1 million. One of his assets is a parcel of land with a basis and fair market value of about $200,000. He wants to perpetuate the memory of his late wife through a memorial scholarship fund, but at the same time he does not want to deprive his children of a significant part of his estate.

He can satisfy his overall objective through an immediate gift coupled with the purchase of life insurance to replace the gifted property. Assuming his income is taxed at a marginal combined federal and state rate of 40%, the arrangement would work like this:

He would contribute the $200,000 parcel of land to his favorite charity immediately. Since the gift is an outright contribution, it will be currently deductible up to 30% of his contribution base. (If his income is not high enough to allow him to deduct the entire $200,000 in one year, he could carry over the excess and deduct it against his next five years' income.) The $200,000 charitable contribution would result in $80,000 of tax savings, since he is in a 40% combined federal and state income tax bracket. He can take this $80,000 that otherwise would have been used to pay taxes and instead make annual gifts of up to $11,000 each to his children. They in turn could purchase a policy on his life and name themselves as owners and beneficiaries.

The chart at Figure 32.2 compares a charitable bequest of the $200,000 parcel of land by will to an immediate lifetime charitable gift of the property coupled with the purchase of life insurance to replace the gifted land. Although the federal estate tax is the same in either situation, the heirs receive $100,000 more by the lifetime gift/insurance purchase technique. Assume death occurs in 2004.

The premium on a $100,000 whole life policy for a male age 50 is only about $3,000 a year, so it will take about 27 years before the premiums equal his

Figure 32.2

	BEQUEST OF PROPERTY BY WILL	LIFETIME GIFT OF PROPERTY		BEQUEST OF PROPERTY BY WILL		LIFETIME GIFT OF PROPERTY
Gross Estate	$2,300,000	$2,100,000	Gross Estate	$2,300,000		$2,100,000
		less	Estate Tax (after unified credit)	273,000	less	273,000
Charitable Bequest by Will	200,000	0		2,027,000		1,827,000
Taxable Estate (Tentative Tax Base)	$ 2,100,000	$2,100,000	Charitable Bequest by Will	200,000	less	0
				1,827,000		1,827,000
					plus	
			New Life Insurance	0		100,000
			Passing to Heirs	1,827,000		1,927,000
			Advantage of Lifetime Gift		$100,000	

$80,000 tax savings. Meanwhile, the charity owns the land immediately, and he has provided his children with everything they would have received even if he made no gift. In fact, properly arranged, the policy proceeds will be received free of income tax, estate tax, inheritance tax, and probate costs. Thus, his children could be in better financial condition than if he had waited to make the gift.

Question – Can a donor obtain a charitable deduction if he splits policy death benefits between a charity and a family member?

Answer – A life insurance policy can be split into two parts, the protection element and the policy cash value. The protection element, often called the net amount at risk, is the difference between the face amount of the policy and its cash (surrender) value. By splitting the proceeds of a policy between a donor's family and a charity, a donor can provide additional protection for the benefit of his family and at the same time make a meaningful gift to charity.

Note that if a donor attempts to "split dollar" the charitable gift (i.e., to name his personal beneficiary as the recipient of the policy's pure death benefit (the amount at risk), but make the charity the owner of the cash value), the Service will disallow a deduction for the gift.[30]

Question – Can group term life insurance be used for charitable contributions?

Answer – Currently, employees must include the cost of group term life insurance coverage over $50,000 in their taxable income. The tax on this economic benefit must be paid with after-tax dollars, which has the effect of reducing the spendable income of the employee.

However, by naming a charity as the beneficiary of group insurance coverage over $50,000, the employee can provide for a gift to charity and at the same time avoid the tax on the economic benefit.

Example: A 63-year-old executive who is taxed at a combined federal and state marginal rate of 40% who had $140,000 of coverage would save 40% of $59.40 per month ($712.80) annually, or $285.12 annually (based on $140,000 of coverage *minus* $50,000 tax-free coverage, resulting in $90,000 taxable coverage; and 90 (per $1,000 of coverage) x .66 (cost of $1,000 of protection for

a 1-month period for an individual aged 63) equals $59.40). See Chapter 30.

ASRS: Secs. 52, ¶1000; 53, ¶20.5(h); 54, ¶¶31, 44.5(d); 55, ¶¶46, 57.10; and 49, ¶¶400.6(c), 400.12(d).

CHAPTER ENDNOTES

1.   IRC Sec. 170(b)(1)(B).

2.   Treas. Reg. §1.170A-8(f).

3.   IRC Secs. 170(b)(2), 170(d)(2)(A); Treas. Reg. §1.170A-11.

4.   IRC Sec. 170(b)(1)(B).

5.   IRC Sec. 170(f)(3)(B)(ii). *See also,* Rev. Rul. 58-260, 1958-1 CB 126; Treas. Reg. §1.170A-7(a).

6.   Treas. Reg. §1.170A-7(b)(1).

7.   IRC Sec. 170(f)(3)(B)(i).

8.   IRC Secs. 170(f)(3)(B)(iii), 170(h); Treas. Reg. §1.170A-7(b)(5).

9.   IRC Sec. 170(f)(3)(A); Treas. Reg. §1.170A-7(a).

10. IRC Sec. 170(b)(1)(A).

11. IRC Secs. 170(b)(2), 170(d)(2).

12. IRC Secs. 170(d)(1), 170(b)(1)(B), 170(b)(1)(D)(ii); Treas. Reg. §1.170A-10(a).

13. IRC Secs. 170(b)(1), 170(b)(2); Treas. Regs. §§1.170A-8(b), 1.170A-11.

14. IRC Sec. 170(b)(1)(C)(i).

15. IRC Sec. 170(b)(1)(C)(ii).

16. IRC Sec. 170(e)(5).

17. IRC Sec. 170(b)(1)(C)(iii); Treas. Reg. §1.170A-8(d)(2).

18. IRC Sec. 170(e)(i).

19. IRC Sec. 1221.

20. IRC Sec. 170(e)(1)(A); Sen. Rep. P.L. 91-171 (12060).

21. IRC Sec. 170(e)(3).

22. IRC Sec. 170(e)(3)(B).

23. Under EGTRRA 2001, a modified carryover basis regime replaces stepped-up basis for one year for property acquired from a decedent dying in 2010.

24. IRC Sec. 170(e)(1)(B)(i); Treas. Reg. §1.170A-4.

25. IRC Sec. 170(e)(1)(B)(i).

26. Treas. Reg. §1.1011-2.

27. Note that the basic planning principle in these cases (i.e., that the redemption by a corporation of closely-held stock from a charity will not be considered a dividend to the individual who donated the stock to the charity in the absence of a prearranged plan) is still useful. *Grove v. Comm.,* 490 F.2d 241 (2nd Cir. 1973); *Dewitt v. U.S.,* 503 F.2d 1406 (Ct. Cl. 1974); *Carrington v. Comm.,* 476 F.2d 704 (5th Cir. 1973). Although both *Grove* and *Carrington* were decided after 1969, they were decided on the basis of pre-1969 Tax Reform Act law. This is why the retention of a life income by the donor did not cause a loss of the charitable deduction. But under present law, a retention of the life income produced by the donated stock or by the proceeds of a sale of such stock would make the contribution a gift of "less than the donor's entire interest in the contributed property." Such a gift would not

qualify for a charitable deduction. See Letter Ruling 8123069 where the Service held that appreciated securities used for the redemption of all stock held by the charity would not cause dividend consequences.

28. *Palmer v. Comm.*, 62 TC 684 (1974), *aff'd on other grounds*, 523 F.2d 1308 (8th Cir. 1975), *acq.* 1978-1 CB 2. *See also* TAM 8623007, reaching the same conclusion as *Palmer* on "materially identical" facts. *But see* TAM 8552009, where controlling shareholders, H and W, gave nonvoting common stock shares in a family corporation to a qualified charitable trust. The shares were subject to a stock restriction agreement that would not allow the trust to sell the stock to anyone outside the stockholder group without first offering it to the corporation and the other authorized shareholders at a value contained in the agreement. The donors claimed a fair market value for the stock on their income tax return for the year of the gift of $18 million, and later had the corporation redeem the stock from the trust for the same amount. The IRS refused to apply the rationale of the *Palmer* case, above, claiming that the fair market value of the stock at the time of the gift was $32 million and at the time of the redemption was $36 million, and that the gift and the redemption were part of the taxpayers' plan to use the trust as a conduit to make a gift to the remaining stockholders, their descendants, by increasing the value of their descendants' shares and correspondingly decreasing the value of H's and W's shares. The Service characterized the transaction as a redemption by the corporation from H and W of all the ostensibly donated stock, followed by a gift of the proceeds to their descendants.

29. Rev. Rul. 81-282, 1981-2 CB 78.

30. IRC Sec. 170(f)(10).

Chapter 33

CHARITABLE SPLIT INTEREST TRUSTS

WHAT IS IT?

With the exception of pooled income funds and wealth replacement trusts, discussed below, this section deals with charitable split interest trusts that have both charitable and noncharitable beneficiaries.

A distinction must be made between trusts established solely for the benefit of charity (which are deductible without meeting the requirements below), and trusts that have both charitable and noncharitable beneficiaries. Deductions for contributions to this second type of trust are measured by the present value of the ultimate gift to charity. If the charity receives annuity or unitrust payments for a specified term and the corpus then goes to the donor's family or some other noncharitable beneficiary, the trust is referred to as a charitable lead trust, where the charity receives the "lead interest" (discussed in more detail below.) But if noncharitable beneficiaries receive annuity or unitrust payments for a specified period (e.g., "for 10 years" or "for life") and afterwards the charity receives the remaining corpus, the trust is called a charitable remainder trust, where the charity receives the "remainder interest."

Gifts of a remainder interest in trust generally are deductible only if made in one of three ways: (1) a "fixed annuity" trust; (2) a "unitrust;" or (3) a "pooled income fund."[1]

These three permissible forms of trust are an outgrowth of congressional concern over potential abuses of gifts of a remainder interest in trust to charity. For example, suppose Mr. and Mrs. W are a financially secure but childless couple. Mr. W might leave his property to his wife in trust. Mrs. W, according to the terms of the trust, would receive the income for life if she survived her husband. At her death, the principal in the trust would pass to a designated charity. Mr. W would take a current charitable contribution deduction for the present value of the gift that the charity would receive at the death of the income beneficiary. To counteract inflation and provide for contingencies, a clause might be inserted in the trust agreement authorizing an invasion of principal for Mrs. W's benefit.

The potential for abuse was that the principal in the trust was often invested in securities that produced an extremely high income but at the cost of a correspondingly high risk. This situation naturally worked to the detriment of the charitable remainder beneficiary. In addition, the ability of the trustee to make substantial invasions of the principal of the trust further increased the likelihood that little, if any, of the original contribution would be received by the charity. The result was a decrease in the value of the charity's remainder interest.

For these reasons, rules were designed to prevent a taxpayer from receiving a current charitable contribution deduction for a gift to charity of a remainder interest in trust which may be substantially in excess of the amount the charity may ultimately receive (because the assumptions used in calculating the value of the remainder interest had little relation to the actual investment policies of the trust).

Pursuant to these rules, deductions are basically limited to situations where the trust specifies: (a) a *fixed* annual *amount* that is to be paid to the noncharitable income beneficiary (i.e., an annuity trust); (b) the amount the income beneficiary will receive in terms of a *fixed percentage* of the value of the trust assets ascertained each year (i.e., a unitrust); or (c) that property contributed by a number of donors is commingled with property transferred by other donors, and each beneficiary of an income interest will receive income determined by the rate of return earned by the trust for such year (i.e., a pooled income fund).[2]

A charitable lead annuity trust or unitrust, which is essentially the reverse of the charitable remainder trust, provides that a fixed annual payment, either in the form of an annuity or a unitrust percentage, is made to one or more qualified charities during the term of the trust. At the end of that term, the property is usually transferred either to the donor or members of the donor's family.[3]

A "wealth replacement trust" (discussed below) is often used in conjunction with a charitable remainder trust to replace the loss of value to the family of the donor of the trust assets passing to a charitable remainder trust.

WHEN IS THE USE OF SUCH A DEVICE INDICATED?

A primary function of a charitable split interest trust is to provide either a present (remainder) or future (lead) economic benefit to the donor or other members of the family, or both, with a present or future transfer to charity which qualifies for income, estate, and gift tax charitable deductions. Refer to the extended discussion of these deductions in Chapter 32.

However, in the case of charitable remainder trusts, particularly the charitable remainder unitrust, and a primary motivation for using the trust is often the transfer of substantially appreciated property by the donor, which will then be sold by the trust. A charitable remainder trust is exempt from federal income tax (unless it has unrelated business taxable income, discussed later) and, therefore, will not be taxed on the gain. The trustee will then reinvest the proceeds from the sale to generate a high income yield. The retained annuity or unitrust interest of the donor (and/or the family of the donor) will be based on the pre-tax value of the property transferred to the trust. In other words, the donor can receive payments on the entire value of the fund, with no reduction for tax on the built-in gain on the transferred assets.

A principal drawback to this plan is the loss of the value of the trust assets to the family of the donor. This leads to the concept of the "wealth replacement trust," generally an irrevocable life insurance trust. The idea is that the additional income that otherwise would be paid to the donor by using this device can instead be used to pay premiums on insurance on the donor's life held in such a trust, which ultimately is distributed to the family to replace the "wealth" (i.e., the value of the assets in the charitable remainder trust). Additionally, the pre-contribution gain recognized in a sale by a NIMCRUT (defined later) will be treated as principal for purposes of distribution income to the noncharitable beneficiaries.

WHAT ARE THE REQUIREMENTS?

A charitable remainder annuity trust (CRAT) is a trust designed to permit payment of a fixed amount annually to a noncharitable beneficiary with the remainder going to charity.[4]

Using a basic charitable remainder annuity trust, the donor transfers money or securities to a trust that pays him a fixed dollar amount each year for life. If the income of the trust is insufficient to meet the required annual payment, the difference is paid from capital gains or principal. If the income is greater than the amount required in any given year, the excess income is reinvested in the trust. The income tax deduction is computed in the year funds are irrevocably placed in trust and is measured by the present value of the charity's right to receive the trust assets upon the death of the annuity beneficiary (or at the end of the term of years).

The value of the remainder interest is determined by a combination of the term of the trust or the beneficiary's age, the amount payable to the beneficiary, and the appropriate monthly IRC Section 7520 rate.

In order to qualify for income (and estate and gift) tax deductions, a charitable remainder annuity trust must meet a number of tests.[5] The primary requirements are these:

1. A fixed amount or fixed percentage of the initial value of the trust must be payable to the noncharitable beneficiary.

2. The annuity percentage must not be less than 5% nor more than 50% of the initial fair market value of all the property transferred in trust.

3. The specified amount must be paid at least annually to the noncharitable beneficiary out of income and/or principal.

4. The trust must be irrevocable and not subject to a power by either the donor, the trustee, or the beneficiary to invade, alter, or amend the trust.

5. The trust must be for the benefit of one or more persons (at least one of which is not an organization described in IRC Section 170 (c)) who must be living at the time of the transfer in trust, and their interests must consist of either a life estate or a term of years not exceeding 20 years.

6. The entire remainder must go to charity.

7. The value of the remainder must equal at least 10% of the initial fair market value of all assets transferred to trust.

If all the necessary tests are met, the donor of a charitable remainder annuity trust will be entitled to an income tax deduction equal to the value of the remainder interest, assuming his contribution base is sufficient to utilize the full amount of the deduction. (See Chapter 32 for discussion of the calculation of income tax deductions for charitable gifts).

A charitable remainder unitrust (CRUT), like a charitable remainder annuity trust, is basically designed to permit payment of a periodic sum to a noncharitable beneficiary with a remainder to charity.[6] The key distinction is in how the periodic sum is computed.

Example: A donor irrevocably transfers money or securities to a trustee. In return, the trustee agrees to pay the donor (or other beneficiary) a unitrust amount from the property for life. The donor also requires that if he predeceases his spouse, she in turn will receive a unitrust amount from the donated property for life. The donor will receive payments based on a fixed percentage of the fair market value of the assets placed in trust. The assets will be revalued each year.

In order to qualify for income, gift, and estate tax deductions, the structure of a charitable remainder unitrust must conform to guidelines set forth in the Internal Revenue Code.[7] These include:

1. A fixed percentage of the net fair market value of the principal, revalued annually, must be payable to the noncharitable beneficiary.

2. The percentage payable to the noncharitable beneficiary must not be less than 5% nor more than 50% of the annual value.

3. The unitrust may provide that the noncharitable beneficiary can receive the *lesser* of: (1) the specified fixed percentage; or (2) the trust income for the year, *plus* any excess trust income to the extent of any deficiency in the prior years (by reason of the distribution being limited to the amount of trust income in such years).

4. The noncharitable income beneficiaries must be living at the time of transfer in trust, and their interests must be for a life estate *or* a term of years not exceeding 20 years.

5. The entire remainder must go to charity.

6. The value of the remainder must equal at least 10% of the net fair market value of the assets transferred to trust.

An income tax deduction, if allowed at all, is permitted in the year that funds are irrevocably placed in trust. The deduction is measured by the present value at the date of the gift of the charity's right to eventually receive the unitrust's assets, subject to percentage limitations (discussed in Chapter 32). The portion of the deduction disallowed may generally be carried forward for five years (see Chapter 32).

A variation of the CRUT is one in which the payment to the beneficiary is limited to the lower of the set percentage *or* the actual income of the trust. Usually, there is also a provision to "makeup" for any occasion when the income is less than the set percentage. This net income with makeup CRUT (NIMCRUT) has been used a great deal for several years. Such NIMCRUTs have been used as an alternative to qualified pension plans by investing in assets that produced little or no income in the early years (while the donor's income is high), and then converting to high income investments in years after the donor's retirement.

A CRUT with a lesser of trust income or the unitrust amount provision may be subject to IRC Section 2702 (see Chapter 26) if (1) the grantor retains an interest in the CRUT, (2) the CRUT has more than one noncharitable beneficiary, and (3) at least one of the noncharitable beneficiaries is other than the grantor or the grantor's U.S. citizen spouse. However, Section 2702 would not apply if there are only two consecutive noncharitable beneficiary interests and the grantor holds the second interest. If Section 2702 applies, the gift to the noncharitable beneficiary by the grantor would generally be valued as equal to the value of the property transferred to the trust reduced only by the value of the charity's remainder interest; interests retained by the grantor would be valued at zero.[8]

A pooled income fund (PIF) is a trust generally created and maintained by a public charity rather than a private donor, which meets the requirements explained below.

The basic requirements are these:

1. The donor must contribute an irrevocable, vested remainder interest to the charitable organization that maintains the fund.

2. The property transferred by each donor must be commingled with the property transferred by other donors.

3. The fund cannot invest in tax-exempt securities.

4. No donor or income beneficiary can be a trustee.

5. The donor must retain for himself (or one or more named income beneficiaries) a life income interest.

6. Each income beneficiary must be entitled to and receive a pro rata share of the income, annually, based upon the rate of return earned by the fund.

If these tests are met, the donor will generally be entitled to an income, gift, or estate tax deduction.[9]

In order to deal with the fact that the assets in a charitable remainder trust will go to charity and not to the family, a "wealth replacement trust" is often used in conjunction with a CRT. A wealth replacement trust is usually an irrevocable life insurance trust that will benefit the remaining family members. Premium payments are usually funded by the income tax savings from the charitable deduction for creating the CRT, and the increase in income from reinvestment of the sales proceeds from the assets that were transferred to the CRT.

As stated above, a charitable lead trust (CLT) is essentially the reverse of a charitable remainder trust. It is an income tax device that enables a taxpayer to reduce the tax burden of an unusually high income year. If certain requirements are met, the taxpayer will be allowed a current deduction for the value of the annuity or unitrust interest given to a charity in trust with the remainder either going to a noncharitable beneficiary, or going back to the donor. The cost of the large current deduction is that the donor is taxed on the trust income each year under the "grantor trust" provisions (see Chapter 19). This means that the grantor *must* be treated as the owner of such interest under IRC Section 671 in order to obtain a current income tax deduction. Also, the charity must receive either a guaranteed annuity or a fixed percentage of the annual net fair market value of the trust assets.[10]

If for some reason the taxpayer is no longer taxed on the annual income of the trust, there will be a partial recapture of the previously allowed deduction, which must be reported by the taxpayer as income in that year. For example, if the individual contributes the income for five years but dies within three years of this contribution, recapture would be triggered. His income for the year of his death would have to include a recaptured portion of the excess deduction that he took at the time the trust was established.[11]

An alternative income tax plan is one in which the CLT is not a grantor trust and there is no deduction at the time of transfer to the CLT. This plan is often used where the goal is to avoid percentage limitations on gifts to charities, and to avoid the amount going to charity from the CLT each year being treated as income to the donor.

Alternatively, the transfer can be made at death, in which case there is no income tax deduction, but there is a step-up in income tax basis of the assets going into the trust.[12]

Another use of the CLT is to permit the transfer of assets to the next generation at a very low transfer tax value (a portion of such value having been given to charity).

The CLT works like this: The donor transfers income-producing property to a trust. The trust in turn will provide the charity with a guaranteed annuity (i.e., a charitable lead annuity trust), *or* annual payments equal to a fixed percentage of the fair market value of the trust property as annually recomputed (i.e., a charitable lead unitrust). At the end of the specified period, the property would be returned to the donor, or go to a noncharitable beneficiary of the donor's choice.

As long as the donor has a reversionary interest in the income or the principal of the trust that is greater than 5%, or is otherwise considered the owner of the income or principal under the grantor trust rules (see Chapter 19), he can take an immediate deduction at the inception of the trust. The deduction is based on the present value of the charity's future rights to annuity or unitrust payments and is subject to the percentage limitations described in Chapter 32.

A lead trust structured in such a way ensures that the income from the property held in trust, while payable to the charity, is includable in the donor's income. The donor does not receive an income tax charitable contributions deduction each year of the trust for the income payable to the charity, but does receive a charitable contributions deduction in the year the trust is funded for the present value of the payments the charity is to receive over the ensuing years. The donor would not receive this deduction unless he was considered the owner of the annuity or unitrust amount (as described in IRC Section 170(f)(2)(B)).

QUESTIONS AND ANSWERS

Question – What factors should be examined in deciding between an annuity trust and a unitrust?

Answer – The choice between an annuity trust and a unitrust involves a number of considerations. An annuity trust is indicated where simplicity in administration is desired since there is no need for an annual revaluation. (At least 5% of the initial fair market value of the trust property must be distributed in the case of an annuity trust, whereas if a unitrust is used, there must be a distribution of at least 5% of the trust's fair market value as redetermined each year.) Furthermore, depending on payout rate, and age of the annuitant, the annuity trust may yield a larger charitable contribution deduction. Generally, if the payout is greater than the current valuation table interest rate, the unitrust will produce a larger value for the remainder interest than would the annuity trust.

There are, however, a number of disadvantages of an annuity trust when compared with a unitrust. First, inflation may cause a fixed annuity to lose some of its value. Of course, the unitrust may, under adverse circumstances, also fail the income beneficiary. If investment results are poor, the life income beneficiary may experience an absolute loss of income. This will result in both an inflation loss and a

diminution of the dollar amount of his annual payment. On the other hand, if the trustee of the unitrust is skillful, he may be able to enhance the value of the principal fund and, consequently, the dollar amount of the annual payment.

A second disadvantage of the annuity trust is caused by regulations providing that the governing instrument in the case of an annuity trust must prohibit any additional contributions from being made.[13] This is probably done to confine the trust to a single valuation date. It therefore becomes impossible to pour over future testamentary bequests into the trust or to have other grantors make inter vivos additions to the already created trust, rather than having to set up new trusts for the same purpose. Conversely, regulations specifically permit additional contributions to unitrusts if the governing instruments contain provisions regarding the effect of such an addition upon valuation and the unitrust amount payable.[14] If trust income is less than the required percentage payment in a unitrust, the liquidity problem could be avoided if the noncharitable beneficiary is willing to forgive all or a part of any particular year's payment, an act tantamount to a contribution to the trust.

A third disadvantage of an annuity trust is that the specified annuity must be paid each year regardless of whether there is sufficient trust income.

Figure 33.1

CHARITABLE REMAINDER ANNUITY TRUST			
(One Life - Table 90CM)			
Transfer to Trust:	$100,000	Annuity Payment:	$5,200
Age:	55	Frequency of Payments:	Annual
Payments:	End of Period	Section 7520 Interest Rate:	5.0%
Check Possibility Charity Will Not Receive Interest			
Annuity Factor Exhaustion:	19.2308	Years to Exhaust Trust:	67
Mortality L(122):	0	Mortality L(55):	89658
Possibility:	0%	5% or Less Possibility Test Passed	
Check Exhaustion of Trust Fund			
Ann. Factor (55 years, 5.0%):	18.6335	Adj. Factor (Annual, 5.0%):	1.0000
Annuity Test Value:	$96,894	Special Factors	Not Required
Valuation			
Ann. Factor (Age 55, 5.0%):	13.1173	Adj. Factor (Annual, 5.0%):	1.0000
Annuity Value:	$68,210	Charitable Contribution:	$31,790

Source: Trust Calculator (part of *The Ultimate Trust Resource*, a National Underwriter Company publication)

If the corpus of the trust were real property, such as an apartment house, and if rents were to fall below the specified annuity plus expenses, the trustee would have to borrow against the property or sell it to make the required payments. However, if the trust instrument so provides a unitrust, can limit its payout to the income beneficiary to the actual trust income. In later years, if trust income exceeds the percentage regularly distributable, the deficiency could be made up by excess distributions. This is referred to as a "net income with makeup unitrust" (NIMCRUT).

Question – A client is considering transferring $100,000 to a trust that will pay him $5,000 a year for life, with a remainder to charity. How will his charitable contribution be determined?

Answer – The client's deduction would depend on his age at his nearest birthday. As Figure 33.1 illustrates (arbitrarily assuming a 5.0% Section 7520 rate), a 55-year-old donor would receive a $31,790 deduction. A 65-year-old would receive a $45,145 deduction for the same contribution.[15]

Question – Assuming the same facts, how would the result be different if the client were to transfer $100,000 to a charitable remainder unitrust, retain-ing an annual payment equal to 5% of the value of the trust each year?

Answer – The donor would receive $5,000 the first year. If the value of the trust had increased to $120,000 a year later, the donor would receive 5%, $6,000, and so on each year. If the income of the unitrust were insufficient in a given year to pay the stated per-centage, capital gains or principal could be used (but need not be, if the trust so provides) to make up the deficit.

Question – A 67 year old donor places $250,000 in a charitable remainder unitrust, retaining a payment equal to 9% of the annual value of the trust, pay-ments to be made quarterly at the end of each period. What is the total income tax deduction available to the donor?

Answer – Assuming the use of a 5.0% Section 7520 rate, the donor's deduction would be $77,540. The com-putation is illustrated in Figure 33.2.

Question – How can a charitable remainder trust be used to generate estate tax savings?

Answer – The estate tax deduction created by the use of a qualified charitable remainder trust is measured

Figure 33.2

CHARITABLE REMAINDER UNITRUST	
(One Life - Table 90CM)	
Transfer to Trust: $250,000	Unitrust Payout Rate: 9.0%
Age: 67	Frequency of Payments: Quarterly
Months Until First Payment: 3	Section 7520 Interest Rate: 5.0%
Adjusted Payout Rate Factor (Quarterly, 3 months, 5.0%):	.970057
Adjusted Payout Rate [9.0% x .970057]:	8.731%
One Life Unitrust Remainder Factor (Age 67, 8.6%):	.31464
One Life Unitrust Remainder Factor (Age 67, 8.8%):	.30780
Difference [.31464 - .30780]:	.00684
Interpolation Adjustment (8.731%):	.00448
Unitrust Remainder Factor [.31464 - .00448]:	.31016
Charitable Contribution [$250,000 x .31016]:	$77,540
Unitrust Interest [$250,000 - $77,540]:	$172,460
Source: Trust Calculator (part of *The Ultimate Trust Resource*, a National Underwriter Company publication)	

Figure 33.3

	ESTATE TAX SAVINGS USING A CHARITABLE REMAINDER TRUST (assume death occurs in 2004)	
	Without Charitable Trust	With Charitable Trust
Adjusted Gross Estate	$2,000,000	$2,000,000
Charitable Contribution		200,000
Taxable Estate (Tentative Tax Base)	$2,000,000	$1,800,000
Estate Tax Before Unified Credit	$ 780,800	$ 690,800
Unified Credit	555,800	555,800
Estate Tax after Unified Credit	$ 225,000	$ 135,000
Net Cost of $200,000 Charitable Contribution Is $110,000 ($200,000 - $90,000)		$90,000 Estate Tax Savings

by the value of the remainder interest that will pass to charity, using the same tables applied in connection with trusts created during life.

Figure 33.3 shows the federal estate tax savings possible through an inter vivos charitable remainder trust. The "without charitable trust" column shows the results for a widow who makes no provisions for a charitable remainder trust (or outright donation). In this situation her taxable estate is $2,000,000. If the same individual created a charitable remainder trust, which generated a $200,000 deduction, her taxable estate would be reduced considerably. In addition, a current income tax deduction would have been obtained for the value of the remainder interest of the property donated.

Question – A client, who is 68 years of age, has been approached by her alma mater with a request that she make a sizeable contribution. She would like to transfer $100,000 to the university, but believes she will need the income generated by that amount to live on the rest of her life. The university maintains a pooled income fund that is producing an annual return of 6%. What would be her total charitable deduction?

Answer – As illustrated in Figure 33.4, the client would be able to deduct $46,020.

Question – A client is a physician with a large annual income from her practice. She has reached the maximum limits on her qualified retirement plan, and is seeking a method to invest in such a way that she can accumulate funds tax-free for her retirement. Could a charitable remainder trust be of any use to her?

Answer – The client may want to consider what is sometimes called the "net income" charitable

Figure 33.4

POOLED INCOME FUND (One Life - Table 90CM)	
Transfer to Trust:	$100,000
Rate of Return:	6.0%
Age:	68
One Life Remainder Factor (Age 68, 6.0%):	.46020
Charitable Contribution ($100,000 x .46020):	$46,020
Source: Trust Calculator (part of *The Ultimate Trust Resource*, a National Underwriter Company publication)	

remainder unitrust. As noted in the text, this is a trust in which the annual payment is the lesser of the fixed unitrust percentage or the actual income generated by the trust.

An optional provision in such a trust is called the "makeup" provision. Under that provision, if the actual unitrust payment in any year based on the income is less than the unitrust percentage, the net difference is carried over to later years, so that in any subsequent year in which the net income exceeds the unitrust percentage, the amount carried over can be paid (so long as the total does not exceed the actual income).

Assume the physician in this example contributes $20,000 per year to such a trust, and the trustee invests in maximum growth, minimum income investments. Assume the unitrust percentage is 6%, and the actual income is in the range of 2 to 3%. The trustee would distribute only the actual income for the next several years, during which the donor will build up a substantial carryover credit. When the physician is ready to retire, the trustee changes the investments to maximum growth, and is now able to pay the entire amount of income to the donor because of the makeup provision. This plan functions much the same as a deferred annuity.

Again, life insurance may be a key element in such a plan. It can function as a wealth replacement vehicle in the manner just described. It can also be used as a hedge against the premature death of the client. In other words, since the purpose of this technique is to provide for retirement, there will be a substantial economic loss if the client dies before retirement, or early into retirement.

Question – If an appreciated asset is transferred to a charitable remainder trust, does the donor, the annuity or unitrust beneficiary, or the charity pay an income tax or capital gains tax if that asset is sold by the trust and the proceeds are reinvested?

Answer – None of the parties to a charitable remainder trust would have any income tax liability on the sale because charitable remainder trusts are exempt from income tax (except in years when they have unrelated business income). Therefore, a charitable remainder trust can accumulate, free of income or capital gains tax, any income in excess of that needed to satisfy noncharitable beneficiaries' annuity or unitrust obligations.

This fact would also allow the donor to receive a greater income than he otherwise would be able to, since if he sold the asset without transferring it to the trust, he would have to pay income or capital gains taxes.

However, when distributions are made from the trust to the noncharitable annuity or unitrust beneficiary, part of the distributions may be taxed to the beneficiary as ordinary income or capital gain from sale of the asset by the trust.

Question – How can a charitable lead trust be used for estate tax savings?

Answer – A charitable lead trust can be used for purposes of estate tax savings. As explained above, property is placed in the trust. A fixed amount of the income the property produces is paid annually to a charity for a specified period of time (this is the "front-end" or "lead" period). At the end of that period, full ownership of the property and the income it produces passes to noncharitable beneficiaries, such as the children or grandchildren of the trust's grantor.

When property is placed in the trust by bequest, an estate tax deduction is allowed for the actuarial value of the front-end annuity interest. As illustrated in Figure 33.5, a $747,732 estate tax deduction would be allowed (arbitrarily assuming a 5.0% Section 7520 rate) if a client left a $1,000,000 bequest in trust to pay $60,000 a year to The American College for 20 years. Stated another way, the deduction could remove about 75% of the trust property from the taxable estate. Furthermore, the property would go intact to the donor's family after 20 years. And, by properly combining the annuity payout level and the duration of the annuity period, it might be possible to eliminate an even greater amount of estate tax. For example, an annuity payout of $80,000 for 20 years would result in a deduction of $996,976 (arbitrarily assuming a 5.0% Section 7520 rate). Furthermore, those same remainder beneficiaries could be named as trustees and, therefore, control the property they someday will own.

Question – What is a wealth replacement trust?

Answer – A "wealth replacement trust" (sometimes called an asset replacement trust) is an irrevocable life insurance trust, which is used in conjunction with a charitable remainder trust, to replace the

Figure 33.5

CHARITABLE LEAD ANNUITY TRUST			
(Term Certain)			
Transfer to Trust:	$1,000,000	Annuity Payment:	$60,000
Term of Years:	20	Frequency of Payments:	Annual
Payments:	End of Period	Section 7520 Interest Rate:	5.0%
Check Exhaustion of Trust Fund			
Ann. Factor (20 years, 5.0%):	12.4622	Adj. Factor (Annual, 5.0%):	1.0000
Annuity Test Value:	$747,732	Special Factors	Not Required
Valuation			
Ann. Factor (20 years, 5.0%):	12.4622	Adj. Factor (Annual, 5.0%):	1.0000
Charitable Contribution:	$747,732	Remainder Value:	$252,268

Source: Trust Calculator (part of *The Ultimate Trust Resource*, a National Underwriter Company publication)

assets the heirs of the donor of a charitable remainder trust would be losing, because the assets would be passing to the charity after the noncharitable income beneficiaries' death.

Example: Assume a client, who is in a 48% federal estate tax bracket (in 2004), transfers $1,000,000 worth of appreciated stock to a charitable remainder annuity trust, retaining a 6% annuity interest for himself. After his death, the assets pass to a charity of his choice. Had he not created the trust, his heirs would have inherited $520,000 ($480,000 would have been the federal estate tax). Therefore, to replace the amount his heirs would have been disinherited by, he created an irrevocable life insurance trust, which can purchase insurance on his life.

Because the client receives immediate tax benefits upon establishing a charitable remainder trust (through an income tax deduction), and because the client would have an increased cash flow with the trust (since the trust paid no income tax on the sale of the assets, which could be reinvested at a potentially higher yield), the funding for the premium on the life insurance policy held in irrevocable life insurance trust can, in many cases, be achieved between the tax savings and the increased cash flow without any additional outlays by the client.

Question – A client has a sizeable block of stock in a company that he started and has since taken public. He is now able to sell that stock. However, the stock has an income tax basis of $100,000 and a current market value of $1,100,000. How might he use the wealth replacement trust concept? Assume a 10% investment return.

Answer – Under current capital gain rates for assets held for more than 12 months, the client would pay federal income tax of $150,000 ($1,100,000 - $100,000 basis = $1,000,000; $1,000,000 x 15%), and would be left with $950,000 ($1,100,000 - $150,000). If that amount were reinvested at 10%, he would have an annual yield of $95,000. Assume, instead, that the client transfers the stock to a charitable remainder annuity trust, in which he retains a 10% annual annuity. The trustee sells the stock, pays no income tax, and pays the client an annual annuity of $110,000 per year for life, which is $15,000 per year more than if the client had simply sold the stock and reinvested the proceeds.

However, the client's family will lose a potential inheritance of $1,100,000, *plus* the future growth in that investment (but *minus* the federal and state death taxes that would have to be paid on that amount). Assuming the investment would double in value by the time the client dies (based on the client's life expectancy and an anticipated growth rate of the property), his net loss of wealth would be $1,900,000 (2 x $950,000) *minus* federal estate tax of $912,000 (assume 48% x $1,900,000), or $988,000.

If the client is insurable, the client could replace this lost wealth by purchasing approximately $988,000 in life insurance, which would be owned either directly by his potential heirs or by an irrevocable trust for their benefit. If the annual premiums for such insurance were less than $15,000, the transaction would produce a net economic savings to the client.

CHAPTER ENDNOTES

1. IRC Secs. 170(f)(2)(A), 664(d). But see the discussion of gifts of a partial interest in Chapter 32 for an exception.

2. IRC Sec. 170(f)(2)(A).

3. IRC Sec. 170(f)(2)(B).

4. IRC Secs. 664(d)(1), 2055(e)(3); Treas. Reg. §20.2055-2(a).

5. IRC Secs. 170(f)(2)(A), 664(d)(1).

6. IRC Sec. 664(d)(2).

7. IRC Sec. 664(d)(2).

8. Treas.Reg. §25.2702-1(c)(3).

9. IRC Sec. 642(c)(5). To calculate the deduction for a contribution to a pooled income fund: (1) take the highest rate of return for the previous three years, (2) look to Valuation Table S in Appendix B for that rate, (3) find the proper age of the donor, (4) proceed to column 4 to find the appropriate remainder factor, and (5) multiply the factor by the amount contributed to obtain the deduction.

10. Treas. Reg. §1.170A-6(c).

11. Treas. Reg. §1.170A-6(c)(4).

12. Under EGTRRA 2001, a modified carryover basis regime replaces stepped-up basis for one year for property acquired from a decedent dying in 2010.

13. Treas. Reg. §1.664-2(b).

14. Treas. Reg. §1.664-3(b).

15. The computation of these amounts and all like amounts referred to hereafter involve the following steps:

For both annuity trust and unitrust computations, age is determined as of the individual's nearest birthday. Treas. Regs. §§20.2031-7A(d)(1)(ii), 1.664-4(e)(5).

In the case of an annuity trust, go to Valuation Table S (reproduced in Appendix B) to determine the value of an annuity at the given age. Arbitrarily assuming a Section 7520 rate of 5.0%, in the case of a person age 55 this is 13.1173. Also, the principal sum is $100,000 and the annual annuity payout is $5,200. The value of the annuity equals $68,210 ($5,200 x 13.1173). The value of the remainder is $31,790 ($100,000 - $68,210).

In the case of the unitrust, go to IRS Publication 1458, Table U(1). The value of a remainder interest after a 5% unitrust payout at age 67 is .32836. This factor applied to the principal sum of $100,000 is $32,836, the deduction allowed. (The actual payout rate may require adjustment under Table F, also found in Publication 1458, to reflect the number of months by which the valuation date precedes the first payment.)

It is interesting to note that the value of a charitable remainder interest of a residence in the hands of a noncharitable tenant may be greater for gift tax than for income tax purposes because no deduction for depreciation is required for gift tax purposes. Rev. Rul. 76-473, 1976-2 CB 306. For relevant decisions regarding the federal estate tax deduction for charitable remainders, see Rev. Rul. 76-543, 1976-2 CB 287, as amplified by Rev. Rul. 77-169, 1977-1 CB 286, and distinguished by Rev. Rul. 83-158, 1983-2 CB 159; Rev. Rul. 76-545, 1976-2 CB 289, as clarified by Rev. Rul. 82-97, 1982-1 CB 194; Rev. Rul. 76-546, 1976-2 CB 290; Rev. Rul. 77-385, 1977-2 CB 331; Rev. Rul. 87-37, 1987-1 CB 295.

Chapter 34

CONSERVATION EASEMENT EXCLUSION

WHAT IS IT?

The Taxpayer Relief Act of 1997 (TRA '97) introduced a significant incentive to private U.S. landowners to preserve undeveloped land. Through the addition of new IRC Section 2031(c), the law now provides for an estate tax exclusion related to the value of land that is subject to a donated qualified conservation easement.

Prior to TRA '97, donors of conservation easements that fulfilled the requirements of IRC Section 170(h) could claim an income tax deduction equal to the value of the easement. Taxpayers who made an inter vivos or testamentary gift of such an easement were also entitled to account for the effect of the gift on fair market value of their land through the estate tax appraisal, although the IRC did not expressly provide for an estate tax deduction for such transfers. Section 2031(c) does not amend pre-TRA '97 law, but rather, provides a new benefit for taxpayers, in the form of an exclusion, if, in general, the requirements of Section 170(h) are also met.

The value of the Section 2031(c) exclusion is limited to $500,000. In general, qualification for the exclusion is dependent on meeting geographical and ownership criteria, and on specific requirements for the grant of the easement. Within these limitations, the estate may deduct the lesser of $500,000 or 40 percent of the value of the land subject to a qualified conservation easement, reduced by 2 percent for every 1 percent that the easement represents less than 30 percent of the value of the land, to zero if the value is 10 percent or less of such land.[1] The values taken into account are such values as of the date of the contribution of the qualified conservation easement.

WHEN IS THE USE OF SUCH A DEVICE INDICATED?

1. When the land meets the specified geographical requirements.

2. When the land has been owned by the decedent or a family member for at least three years immediately prior to decedent's death.

3. When the easement is contributed on or before the due date (including extensions) for filing an estate tax return, and no interests are retained, except as allowed under the IRC.

WHAT ARE THE REQUIREMENTS?

1. As of the decedent's date of death, the land must be located in the United States or its possessions. The Economic Growth and Tax Relief Reconciliation Act of 2001 made this technique more appealing by eliminating the requirement that the land must be (a) in or within 25 miles of a metropolitan area, or (b) in or within 25 miles of a national park or wilderness area, or (c) in or within 10 miles of an Urban National Forest.[2]

2. The land must have been continuously owned by the decedent, or a member of the decedent's family, during the three years immediately preceding the decedent's death.[3]

3. The land must be subject to a "qualified conservation easement," which is a "qualified conservation contribution … of a qualified real property interest," as generally defined in Section 170(h).[4]

4. The contribution must be made to a qualified organization and used exclusively for conservation purposes.[5] In general, an organization is qualified to receive such a contribution if it is a federal, state or local agency, or a charity qualifying under IRC section 501(c)(3).[6]

5. A real property interest is qualified if it is a restriction granted in perpetuity on the use which may be made of the property.[7]

6. A "conservation purpose" includes preservation of land for public recreation or education, protection of a natural habitat of fish, wildlife, or plants, or the preservation of open space, including farmland and forestland.[8] The preservation of historically important land or certified historic structures, although referenced under Section 170(h)(4), is not a conser-

vation purpose under Section 2031(c).[9] The conservation purpose must be protected in perpetuity to be treated as exclusive.[10]

7. The donor may not retain rights to develop the easement for commercial purposes (other than farming).[11]

8. The applicable percentage of the value of the land subject to a qualified conservation easement that may be excluded from the decedent's gross estate is equal to the lesser of $500,000 or 40 percent of the value of such land, reduced by 2 percent for each 1 percent (or fraction thereof) by which the value of the easement is less than 30 percent of the value of the land.[12]

9. The election to take the exclusion under Section 2031(c) must be made on the estate tax return, and, once made, is irrevocable.[13]

HOW IT IS DONE – AN EXAMPLE

Mary Peshel inherited a ranch in the backcountry located next to a national park. The ranch had been in the family for 40 years. At the time of her death in 2004, the ranch was worth $1,000,000, without regard to the easement, which she gave shortly prior to her death.

Mary had conveyed a qualifying easement worth $250,000 (25 percent of the property value) for use by the Friends of the Earth organization, reducing the net value of the property to $750,000. Friends of the Earth qualifies as a publicly supported charity under IRC Section 501(c)(3). A right was retained to operate the property only for ranching and farming, keeping back no development rights.

Since only 25 percent of the value was conveyed, the 40 percent exclusion percentage is reduced by 2 percent for each 1 percent that the easement is below 30 percent of the value of the entire property. The reduction equals 10 percent [(30% - 25%) x 2%)]. This results in a 30 percent exclusion (40 percent less the 10 percent reduction), and the estate benefits from an estate tax exclusion for $225,000 (30 percent of $750,000). This is less than the $500,000 exclusion limit. Thus, Mary's estate will exclude $225,000 under Section 2031(c).

WHAT ARE THE TAX IMPLICATIONS?

1. The decedent's gross estate is reduced by the qualified conservation easement exclusion.

2. The basis in the property subject to the qualified conservation easement exclusion is not stepped-up for income tax purposes with respect to the exclusion.

QUESTIONS AND ANSWERS

Question – Does it matter when the easement was donated?

Answer – Generally, no. The exclusion election is available after the death of the decedent, but is calculated based on the date of transfer of the easement (although an easement donated after death must be made within a certain period after death, see below).

Question – May a married couple both use the exclusion for separate transfers of easements in the same property?

Answer – Yes. The exclusion is applied to a decedent's gross estate, without regard to the individual property, so that a married couple may exclude up to $1 million for gifts of easements in one property.

Question – May an executor or trustee donate land subject to a qualified conservation easement and make a post-mortem election under Section 2031(c), even though the decedent made no provision during his lifetime for such transfer?

Answer – Yes. Under Section 2031(c)(8)(A)(iii), an executor or trustee may make the necessary election and donate the easement.

Question – May an executor or trustee take remedial action after the death of the decedent to qualify an easement under Section 2031 that would not otherwise qualify for the exclusion?

Answer – Yes. Section 2031(c)(8)(A)(iii) also presents an opportunity for the executor or trustee to correct defects that might prevent an easement that was transferred inter vivos from qualifying for the exclusion. Thus, to the extent that an easement is not qualified, an executor or trustee may donate an interest that will qualify for the exclusion, since an executor or trustee are qualified persons under the IRC.

Question – Will the decedent's heirs receive a full stepped-up basis in land subject to a qualified conservation easement?

Figure 34.1

1.	Gross Value of Ranch Prior to Easement		$1,000,000
2.	Fair Market Value of Ranch After Gift of Easement		$ 750,000
3.	Basis of Ranch at Mary's death	$100,000	
4.	Value of Exclusion to Mary's Estate	$225,000	
5.	Percentage of Gross Value Represented By Exclusion Amount (line 4 divided by line 2)	30%	
6.	Carryover Basis (line 3 multiplied by line 5)	$ 30,000	
7.	Stepped-Up Basis (line 2 multiplied by 70%)	$525,000	
8.	TOTAL ADJUSTED BASIS (line 6 plus line 7)		$ 555,000

Answer – No. The portion of basis equal to that fraction of the value of the land represented by the qualified conservation easement receives a carryover basis.[14] For example, using the illustration provided in the preceding section, the exclusion allowed to Mary's estate represented 30 percent of the estate tax value of the ranch. Thus, 30 percent of the basis in the ranch would be carried over to Mary's heirs, and added to 70 percent of the fair market value at death (representing the step-up), to arrive at the adjusted basis. Figure 34.1 illustrates the steps necessary to calculate the heirs' basis in Mary's ranch, assuming that at Mary's death, the property had a basis of $100,000 and a fair market value of $750,000 after the gift of the easement.

Thus, the conservation easement excluded from the gross estate does not receive a basis stepped-up to fair market value (even in years before 2010). However, even for estates in the lowest marginal estate tax bracket (45% in 2004), the election should be beneficial, to the extent that the capital gains tax is lower.

Question – What type of development rights would disqualify an estate under Section 2031(c), should they be retained?

Answer – Section 2031(c)(5)(D) defines a development right as "any right to use the land subject to the qualified conservation easement in which such right is retained for any commercial purpose which is not subordinate to and directly supportive of the use of such land as a farm for farming purposes (within the meaning of section 2032A(e)(5))." Thus, a donor must carefully assess whether he will, even inad-vertently, retain rights to the easement that may fall under this broad definition, and counsel should use caution in drafting easements until regulations and judicial decisions become available for guidance.

Question – Will an executor or trustee be able to "save" the exclusion, if the decedent (or any other party) retained development rights in the easement?

Answer – Yes. Section 2031(c)(5)(B) provides that, if those persons with an interest in the land execute an agreement to extinguish some or all development rights on or before the filing date of the estate tax return, the exclusion shall be allowed to the extent that such rights were terminated. In addition, the IRC allows a donor to provide flexibility to heirs, since such an agreement need not be implemented until the earlier of two years after the decedent's death, or the sale of the land. Thus, where commercial development may prove more profitable than the value to the estate of the exclusion, the donor may wish to retain commercial development rights when creating the easement. If the agreement is not implemented within the proscribed period, an additional tax will be due, equal to the tax saved by the exclusion.

Question – Will recreational use of a commercial nature on the easement prevent qualification for the exclusion?

Answer – Yes, if it is more than a de minimis use for a commercial recreational activity. Congressional intent in this area was to prevent the nominal preservation of land that would be used for large commercial enterprises, such as golf courses or ski resorts. Committee Reports indicate that it was also intended to provide exceptions to leased use for hunting and fishing. However, in the absence of regulations, a donor should carefully consider any type of commercial use before relying on qualification for the exclusion.

Question – Does land that is subject to indebtedness qualify for the exclusion?

Answer – No. To the extent that property is debt-financed, and such debt is "acquisition indebtedness," as defined under Section 2031(c)(4), the exclusion shall not apply.

ASRS: Sec. 54, ¶44.2A.

CHAPTER ENDNOTES

1. IRC Sec. 2031(c)(1).
2. IRC Sec. 2031(c)(8)(A)(i).
3. IRC Sec. 2031(c)(8)(A)(ii).
4. IRC Sec. 2031(c)(8)(B).
5. IRC Sec. 170(h)(1).
6. IRC Sec. 170(h)(3).
7. IRC Sec. 170(h)(2).
8. IRC Sec. 170(h)(4).
9. IRC Sec. 2031(c)(8)(B).
10. IRC Sec. 170(h)(5)(A).
11. IRC Sec. 2031(c)(5).
12. IRC Sec. 2031(c)(2).
13. IRC Sec. 2031(c)(6).
14. IRC Sec. 1014(a)(4).

Part 8:

INTRAFAMILY AND OTHER
BUSINESS TRANSFERS TECHNIQUES

Chapter 35

INSTALLMENT SALES AND SCINS

WHAT IS IT?

The installment sale is a device for spreading out the taxable gain and thereby deferring the income tax on gain from the sale of property. The key ingredient in an installment sale is that at least one payment will be received by the seller after the taxable year in which the sale occurs.

The self-cancelling installment note, or SCIN, is a variation of the installment sale, a hybrid between an installment sale and a private annuity (see Chapter 36). It is not a statutory device and its taxation is covered by interpretation of statutes by the courts, the IRS and taxpayers. When it is used, the note contains a provision under which the balance of any payments due at the date of death are automatically canceled, with language such as the following:

> "Unless sooner paid, all sums due hereunder, whether principal or interest, shall be deemed canceled and extinguished as though paid upon the death of (Seller)."

It must be provided, however, that the term of the SCIN will be less than the life expectancy (actual) of the seller; otherwise, it will be taxed as a private annuity.

The uses of an installment sale or SCIN for estate planning purposes, as explained in this chapter, are based on the federal estate tax as in effect for years beginning before January 1, 2010, or after December 31, 2010. The Economic Growth and Tax Relief Reconciliation Act of 2001 (EGTRRA 2001) increases the exemption equivalent of the estate tax unified credit each year over a 9-year period, then repeals the estate tax for one year in 2010. For years beginning after December 31, 2010, the provisions of EGTRRA 2001 sunset (or expire), and absent other action by Congress, the estate tax unified credit would presumably revert to $1,000,000.

WHEN IS THE USE OF SUCH A DEVICE INDICATED?

1. An installment sale is indicated when a taxpayer wants to sell property to another individual who may not have enough capital to purchase the property outright. The installment sale provides a way, for example, for employees with minimal capital to buy out a business owner who, in return for allowing a long-term payout, may receive a higher price for his business. This device is often used to create a market for a business where none previously existed.

2. An installment sale is indicated where an individual in a high income tax bracket holds substantially appreciated real estate or securities (other than marketable securities). In certain cases, all or a portion of the tax on a sale of such property can be spread over the period of installments.[1]

   One of the big advantages of the installment sale with respect to certain property is that the taxable gain is prorated over the payment period. This means that the seller will pay the tax due only as actual payments from the sale are received. The seller may be able to shift most of the profit from a high income (high tax) year to a year or years in which he or she is in a lower bracket.

3. The installment sale permits more flexibility than the private annuity, an alternative. The agreement can be made to begin or end whenever the parties involved desire. This eliminates the need to follow a rigid schedule of payments such as is found in a private annuity.

4. An installment sale can be an effective estate freezing device where the sale is between family members and involves rapidly appreciating closely held stock, real estate, or other assets. Used in this manner, the installment sale may serve to freeze the size of an estate subsequent to the sale and thus stabilize the value of the seller's estate for federal estate tax purposes and shift future appreciation to a younger generation. An installment sale to a grandchild at full fair market value, for example, will avoid the generation-skipping transfer tax.

5. A SCIN is appropriate in instances where the seller desires to retain a payment stream that will not

continue beyond his or her death and may end at an earlier date. Unlike a private annuity, the SCIN allows the buyer to depreciate assets based on the purchase price paid and to deduct the portion of payments attributable to interest expense.

6. A SCIN is appropriate where the tax benefits attributable to excluding the unpaid principal from a taxable estate exceed the income tax cost that results from the buyer paying a premium for the cancellation at death feature.

WHAT ARE THE REQUIREMENTS?

1. A seller of property can defer as much or as little as desired using an installment sale and payments can be set to fit the seller's business or financial needs. The amount of payment received in the year of the sale is irrelevant. A sale for $1,000,000 can qualify even if $500,000 is paid in the year of the sale and the remaining $500,000 (plus interest on the unpaid balance) is paid over the next five years.

    Conversely, since a SCIN is a hybrid between an installment sale and private annuity, its requirements are still being determined. The IRS has stated its position as to when it will accept a SCIN.[2] Of importance is the requirement that the term of a SCIN not extend beyond the seller's life expectancy.

2. No payment has to be made in the year of the sale. The only requirement is that at least one payment must be made in a taxable year *after* the year of sale.[3] This means the owner of property can contract to have payments made at the time when it is most advantageous or least disadvantageous. For example, the parties could agree that the entire purchase price for payment of a $1,000,000 parcel of land will be paid five years after the sale.

3. No minimum sale price is required.

4. Installment sale treatment is automatic unless the taxpayer elects *not* to have installment treatment apply.[4] A SCIN is treated as a private annuity if the term extends beyond the seller's life expectancy.

5. A sale can be made on an installment basis even though the selling price is contingent.[5]

6. Installment reporting is not available for sales of marketable securities.[6]

HOW IT IS DONE – AN EXAMPLE

An individual would like to sell property she now owns. Her accountant has explained that a high tax on the inherent gain in the property could consume a substantial portion of her profit. If she receives all of the sale proceeds in the year of sale, the result is that her entire profit will be taxed in one year. So she would like to find a way to reduce or minimize the impact of taxes, or defer those taxes.

The installment sale is a possible solution to that problem. By taking advantage of the installment sale provisions of the Internal Revenue Code, she may be able to save a great deal of money.[7] Under an installment sale, the title to the property passes immediately from the seller to the buyer. But the distinguishing feature of an installment sale is that the seller does *not* receive a lump sum payment outright. Instead, the seller typically receives the sale price in installments spread out over two or more tax years (although a lump sum payment in a later year will qualify for installment reporting).

Example: If Mrs. Murphey sold land that cost her $50,000 and received $100,000, she would have a $50,000 gain reportable all in the year of the sale. But if she sells it for $100,000 and agrees to accept $10,000 a year for 10 years (plus appropriate interest on the unpaid balance), she will not have to report the $50,000 gain in the year of the sale. Instead, since her ratio of gross profit ($50,000) to contract price ($100,000) is 50%, she will report $5,000, 50% of each $10,000 payment she receives, as capital gain. (Interest has been ignored here for simplicity.)

To compute the payment, use a hand held financial calculator or computer program. You need to tell the calculator or computer the:

(1) interest rate (for semiannual divide annual rate by two);

(2) number of periods (for semiannual multiply years by two);

(3) amount to be repaid.

The result will be the annual (or other payment period) payment necessary. For example, to compute the semiannual payment where property worth $100,000 is sold over a 10-year period and the interest rate is 9%, input 4.5 (the annual interest rate divided by two) and

Figure 35.1

TAXATION OF SELLER UNDER INSTALLMENT SALE	
A. Recovery of basis (cost element)	Tax free
B. Gain element	Capital gain or ordinary income
C. Interest income	Ordinary income

	Computing Tax Free, Gain, and Interest Elements of an Installment Payment	
STEP 1	Segregate interest from payment principal	
STEP 2	Compute portion of principal payment which is gain	$\dfrac{\text{Total gain}}{\text{Sales price}}$ x principal payment
STEP 3	Compute portion of principal payment which is a return of capital	Principal payment - gain (Step 2)

press the i (interest) button, input 20 (two payments a year for 10 years) and press the *N* (number of periods) button, and input the present value of the loan, $100,000. Then press the PV (present value) button. Then press PMT to compute the $7,687.61 outlay.

The rule used to compute the annual gain above is:

Income is realized on each annual payment received in the same proportion that the gross profit (selling price less seller's adjusted basis) bears to the total contract price (amount to be received by the seller).

If the sale results in a loss, the installment method may not be used. The loss deduction must be taken in the tax year of the sale.[8]

More technically, for income tax purposes, the installments must be broken into three parts: (1) a return of capital; (2) profit; and (3) interest income.

Interest is segregated from principal payments and taxed as ordinary income. The profit percentage (basically the gain, or difference between the sale price and adjusted basis, expressed as a percentage of the total contract price, exclusive of interest) is applied to each installment payment of principal in order to determine the amount of each payment that is gain. The balance is considered a tax-free return of the seller's basis. (See Figure 35.1.)

What if the agreement does not specify an interest charge, or the amount is unreasonably low? This often occurs in intrafamily transactions. These types of sales will be taxed according to what is known as the "un-stated interest" rule. Under this rule, the Internal Revenue Service is allowed to "impute" interest (a legal fiction in which all the parties to the transaction are treated as if interest was paid at a statutory rate, compounded semiannually) unless the parties have agreed to at least a "safe harbor" rate of return on the unpaid balance.[9] In other words, a portion of the deferred payments will be treated as interest to both the buyer and the seller. For all tax purposes, from the buyer's perspective that part of a payment that is considered interest does not increase the basis of the property received; however, the buyer may be allowed an interest deduction. For additional details, see Chapter 37.

For SCINs, a premium is required to reflect the possibility that the seller will die during the term of the SCIN. Because the unpaid principal is forgiven upon an early death, the present value of expected payments will be less than the purchase price unless an adjustment is made. The adjustment is made by increasing the payments under the SCIN so that actuarially the present value of payments equals the purchase price.

There may be some flexibility to increase SCIN payments by either raising the interest rate or principal due on the rate. If the interest rate is increased, the buyer may take greater interest expense deductions. If the principal is increased, the buyer will have a higher base for taking depreciation deductions.

The following rules should be considered: Interest will not be deductible if it is considered "personal." Generally, this means the interest deduction will be denied unless the debt was properly allocable to:

(1) investment purposes (if the property or stock to be purchased is investment property, the interest deduction will generally be allowed, but only to the extent of the buyer's investment income);

(2) the conduct of a trade or business (other than the trade or business of performing services as an employee), in which case the interest would be deductible without limit;

(3) part of the computation of income or loss from a passive investment activity;

(4) estate or generation-skipping transfer taxes in installments under Internal Revenue Code Sections 6166 or 6161 (there is no limit on the amount of interest deduction in this case, but no deductions are allowed for interest paid in installments under Section 6166 for decedents dying after 1997); or

(5) a debt secured by property that at the time the interest is paid or accrued is a qualified residence (this is called "qualified residence interest" and is generally deductible only if the residence in question is the taxpayer's principal residence or a second residence). This deduction is limited to interest on a maximum of $1,000,000 of "acquisition indebtedness" and up to $100,000 of "home equity indebtedness."

Imputed interest is considered only for purposes of the income tax; it does not directly affect the terms of the sale. The imputed interest rules are extremely difficult and will not be discussed at length. The following rules of thumb should be helpful in planning the interest rates that should be built into an installment sale:

(1) There will be no imputed interest problem unless the installment sale contract (a) does not state *any* interest on the unpaid balance, or (b) the specified interest rate is less than the "applicable federal rate" (AFR), except as noted below.

(2) Certain sales of family land to family members require only that the interest rate assumed by the parties be 6%, compounded semiannually, or greater if the transaction is for $500,000 or less. The AFR is applied to amounts over $500,000.

(3) If the selling price is under $4,381,300 in 2004 ($4,280,800 in 2003), interest will be imputed at the lower of (a) 9%, compounded semiannu-

ally, or (b) the applicable federal rate. The selling price under which either rate applies is adjusted annually for inflation.[10]

WHAT ARE THE TAX IMPLICATIONS OF THE INSTALLMENT SALE?

1. Many of the income tax ramifications have been mentioned above. Note also that depreciation recapture as well as any investment tax credit recapture is reportable in full in the year of the sale, even if no proceeds from the sale are received in that year.

   Stock or securities that are traded on an established securities market do not qualify for installment treatment; all payments to be received are treated as received in the year of disposition.

   In addition, installment treatment is generally not allowed for sales of depreciable property to a controlled entity, such as a more than 50% owned partnership or corporation, or trust benefiting the seller or the seller's spouse. All payments to be received are treated as received in the year of disposition.

2. An installment sale will remove the property in question from the transferor-seller's estate, but the present value of any installments due at the seller's death must be included.[11] For instance, if at the date the seller died 10 annual payments remained on an installment sale, and each payment (made at the end of the year) to the estate or its heirs were $12,000, using a 5.0% AFR assumption, $92,660, the present value of the 10-year stream of payments remaining would be includable in the seller's gross estate ($12,000 x 7.7217 term certain annuity factor for 5% and 10 years from Appendix B). However, the installment sale is still a valuable estate planning tool since it removes the future appreciation on the property from the transferor-seller's estate without any gift tax implications. For instance, at a 10% growth rate, property worth $500,000 when sold in exchange for 10 annual payments would be worth $1,296,871 when the payout was complete.

   Additionally, a great deal of the cash proceeds of the sale may be removed from the seller's estate, gift tax free, by maximizing the use of the annual exclusion. After receiving payments, the seller could then give back–at his or her whim–all or a portion of the amounts paid.

3. For federal gift tax purposes, there is a split of authority in the courts as to whether the interest rate charged on the family installment sale must be equal to the prevailing market rate, the applicable federal rate, the special rates applicable to sales of farm land under $500,000, or the 9% rate specified in the case of sales under $4,381,300 (in 2004) that are charged for *income* tax purposes. (See the related discussion in Chapter 37.) The Tax Court has held in two separate cases that if a rate lower than the prevailing market rate is used, there will be a taxable gift measured by the difference between the fair market value of the property sold and the discounted present value of the installment note that is based on the lower interest rate used for sales of land (6%).[12] However, in one of these cases on appeal, the Court of Appeals for the Seventh Circuit reversed the Tax Court decision and held that the use of rates specified for income tax purposes would also control for gift tax purposes.[13] Conversely, in the other case on appeal, the Court of Appeals for the Eighth Circuit sustained the Tax Court's position on the issue and held that the income tax rate does not control for gift tax purposes.[14] The Supreme Court has refused to review the Eighth Circuit Court's decision.

It should be noted that the sales in both of the above cases arose before the adoption of applicable federal rates of interest, and it would seem that these federal rates should eliminate the gift tax problem. However, the law is unclear on what would happen if the federal rates were lower than prevailing market rates.

4. If the seller should die, the remaining payments are "income in respect of a decedent." (See the Questions and Answers, below.) As a result, the estate, or other testamentary beneficiary of the installments due would report the payments in the same way that the decedent would have reported them had he lived.[15] In other words, the allocation of the payments (return of capital, gain, or interest) is not affected by reporting on the installment basis.

There is no step-up in basis at death; however, the testamentary beneficiary of the installments would be entitled to an offsetting income tax deduction to the extent of the estate tax attributable to the installment sale balance that was taxed in the estate.[16]

5. It is important to note the effect of an installment sale on the property's basis for purposes of computing gains and losses and in order to compute the depreciation deduction available to the transferee-buyer. In the case of an installment sale, the transferee-buyer has a new income tax basis for the property, its fair market value at the date of the sale (i.e., the purchase price).[17] The transferee's basis is stepped-up, not carried over, for depreciation purposes.

One result of this stepped-up basis is that (subject to the "second disposition" rules discussed below) a lower bracket family member purchasing the property can sell the property transferred and reinvest the sale proceeds in more liquid or higher yielding assets and probably pay much less in tax on the sale than the transferor-seller would otherwise have had to pay.

An increased basis is of particular advantage in the case of high value, low basis property such as highly appreciated real estate. For example, if the transferor-seller bought undeveloped, non-income-producing land 10 years ago for $10,000 and it is now worth $100,000, he could sell it to his son for its $100,000 fair market value. After holding the land for at least two years (see below), the son could then sell it and purchase mutual funds or other income-producing securities with the proceeds of the sale. If the son received $105,000 for the land, his gain would be only the difference between his $100,000 cost and the amount realized on the sale, $105,000 (i.e., his total gain would be $5,000). He does not have to pay tax on the $90,000 gain his father would have been subject to had he sold the land. The advantage is compounded if the son is in a lower tax bracket than his father.

The overall tax savings is even more dramatic if the father is in a relatively high income tax bracket at the time of the sale but is about to retire. Future payments from son to father spread out the profit and defer taxes. Since the father may be in a lower tax bracket after retirement, less of his profits will be lost in the form of taxes.

6. Special rules apply to installment sales to related parties. For example, certain "second dispositions" (resales) by a related party purchaser trigger recognition of gain *by the initial seller*. In essence, this rule, stated in more detail below, provides that the original seller's gain on an installment sale will be accelerated if a trustee or other purchaser related to the seller resells the asset within two years of the installment sale.

7. Generally, interest paid by the purchaser on the unpaid balance will be deductible in full only if the debt is properly allocable to investment purposes (and then only to the extent of investment income) or to business purposes.

Special Rules for Disposition of Property Between Related Parties

Technically, there are three "related party" rules: one applicable to second dispositions of installment sale property by a related purchaser; a second that applies only to installment sales of depreciable property between "closely related" entities; and a third applicable to forgiveness or cancellation of installment debt between related parties. The term "related party" for purposes of these rules, includes brothers and sisters, spouses, ancestors, and lineal descendants, as well as many other related entities.[18]

"Second disposition" rule: The rule for "second dispositions" of installment sale property is as follows: If a related party (defined below) disposes of the property he has purchased in an installment sale (in other words if a "second disposition" occurs) before the initial seller (the person who made the "first disposition") has received all the payments he is due under the installment sale, then the amount realized on the second disposition is treated as received – at the time of the second disposition – by the initial seller.[19] For instance, if a mother sells appreciated land to her daughter, and the daughter immediately resells the land, the mother must report the gain.

Fortunately, the gain reportable is limited. Gain, based on her profit percentage, is reportable by the mother only to the extent the daughter receives more in the second disposition than she has already paid her mother. So the initial seller's gain would be accelerated only to the extent additional cash or other property flows into the related group because of the "second disposition."

Although there are no regulations that illustrate mathematically how the second disposition rules apply, it should be as follows:

1. When the related person disposes of the property (the second disposition) before the person making the first disposition receives all payments due from that sale, the first seller is treated as having received the amount actually received by the second (related) seller at the time of the second disposition. For example, assume Herb Cheezman bought land for $500,000 and sold it to his son Stephen for $600,000. Assume also that Stephen agreed to pay $60,000 a year for 10 years. (For simplicity, interest is ignored.) In the second year Stephen sells the land to a third party for $1,000,000. Herb is treated as having received $1,000,000 in the second year.

2. There is a limit, however, on the amount Herb must report.

The person making the first disposition (Herb) reports only the amount by which the *lesser of*

(A)	*(1)*	the total amount realized with respect to the second disposition by the close of the tax year, (in this example it is $1,000,000) *or*	
	(2)	the total contract price for the first disposition (in our example, $600,000)	$600,000

exceeds the total of

(B)	*(1)*	the sum of payments actually received with respect to the first disposition (Herb reeived $60,000 x 2 years, or $120,000) *plus*	
	(2)	the aggregate sum treated (under the related party — second disposition rules) as received with respect to the first disposition for prior taxable years (here $0)	120,000

So, in this example, Herb would report gain of $480,000

Of course, Stephen would be required to recognize his gain on the sale (i.e., the second disposition) — $1,000,000 (amount realized) minus $600,000 (Stephen's cost basis), or $400,000.

3. Where a second disposition results in recognition of gain to the first seller (Herb), subsequent payments actually received by the first seller from the related purchaser (Stephen) will be tax free until they have equalled the amount realized as a result of the second disposition.

There are limited exceptions to the "second disposition" rule. If the second disposition occurs more than two years after the date of the first sale, the rule will not apply (unless the sale was of stock or securities).[20] So, if Stephen waited two years and one month before he sold the land, Herb would not realize any gain as a result of Stephen's disposition. Stephen, of course, would have to report gain based on the difference between the amount he realizes on the sale (assume $1,000,000) and his basis (cost) of $600,000. Note that there is *no* 2-year exception for sales of stock or securities. Thus, if Herb sold his son Stephen *stock* instead of land, the time period for the "second disposition" rule is unlimited, and Herb will recognize gain on any subsequent disposition by Stephen, to the extent that Herb has not received all payments due on the sale. (Installment reporting is unavailable for sales of publicly traded stock or securities occurring after 1986.) This rule also will not apply if the second disposition results from the death of either party or from an involuntary conversion.

Rule for sales of depreciable property: A sale of depreciable property between related entities may not be reported on the installment method, unless it can be shown that avoidance of income tax was not a principal purpose.[21] This rule, unlike the other two "related party" rules, applies only to related entities, such as a corporation and an individual who owns more than 50% of its outstanding stock.

In addition to this rule, there is a special rule for *all* installment sales of depreciable property, regardless of whether the buyer and seller are related. Generally, that rule (described below) requires recapture of certain depreciation deductions claimed by the seller.

Rule for cancellation of debt: If an installment sale between related parties is canceled or payment is forgiven, the *seller* must recognize gain to the extent that the fair market value on the date of cancellation (or the face amount, if less) exceeds the seller's basis in the obligation.[22] "Related party" has the same meaning for purposes of this rule as for the "second disposition" rule.

Special Depreciable Property Rule

The installment sale reporting method generally does not apply to any portion of the sales price that is attributable to the prior depreciation deductions on personal property, such as equipment, or the prior depreciation deductions on certain commercial real property that was placed in service after 1981, but before 1986, and depreciated using an accelerated method of depreciation (faster than the straight line method). In addition, the installment sale reporting method does not apply to the portion of the prior depreciation deductions on residential and certain commercial real property that are in excess of the amount that would have been deducted if the taxpayer had used the hypothetical straight-line method.

These amounts, which are not subject to the installment sale reporting method because of the depreciation deductions (so-called depreciation recapture), must be reported by the seller in the year of the sale up to the amount of the seller's gain — even if any other gain is reported on the installment basis as payments are received.[23]

Since depreciation recapture must be reported in the year the property is sold, that amount can be added to the seller's basis. It therefore has the effect of reducing the reportable income that must be realized each year.

For instance, Charles Plotnick sells tangible personal property to Nick Martin for $70,000, to be paid in three installments. Interest is paid on the unpaid balance at current rates. Assume this is 9%. Also assume that the property originally cost $90,000, but has an adjusted basis of $50,000 at the time of the sale because Charles has taken depreciation deductions totaling $40,000.

Charles must "recapture" his depreciation up to the amount of his gain (the $20,000 difference between the sale price of $70,000 and his adjusted basis of $50,000). Since he must include the $20,000 of recaptured deductions as income in the year of the sale, he can increase his basis by $20,000 (from $50,000 to $70,000). Since he now has a 100% basis, he will realize no gain as payments are received.

Payments, exclusive of interest, should be $23,333, which is tax-free as a recovery of basis. But what if Charles sold the property for $110,000? The gain would be $60,000 (the $110,000 amount realized minus his adjusted basis of $50,000). The entire $40,000 he previously deducted as depreciation must now be recaptured. Since he must report $40,000, he can add that amount to his $50,000 basis. Thus, it now totals $90,000. Each payment, exclusive of interest, is $36,667 ($110,000 ÷ 3). Of this, $30,000 will be a tax-free recovery of basis, and the $6,667 balance will be gain.

Note, however, that installment treatment is not allowed for sales of depreciable property to a controlled entity, such as a more than 50% owned partnership or corporation, or a trust benefiting the seller or the seller's spouse. All payments to be received are treated as received in the year of disposition.

WHAT ARE THE TAX IMPLICATIONS OF THE SCIN?

All of the tax rules applicable to the installment sale apply to the self-cancelling installment note. However, there are additional factors to consider.

The Tax Court has held that in the case of installment sales from decedent to his children, with a provision that in the event decedent died before payments were completed, the balance would be canceled, the installment sale results in realization of taxable gain reported in the decedent's final return.[24] This decision was based on Code section 453B, which provides that where an installment note is canceled or becomes unenforceable, this is treated as a taxable disposition of the note. On appeal, the Court of Appeals for the Eighth Circuit reversed the Tax Court decision, but only by holding that the gain would be fully taxable to the decedent's estate as income in respect of a decedent, not as income on the decedent's final income tax return.[25]

In GCM 39503, the IRS set forth the circumstances under which a SCIN will be treated as an installment note and under which circumstances it will have income tax consequences as if it were a private annuity.

Note that for gift tax purposes, the actual value of the SCIN received by the seller is not equal to its face value, because the risk of death is a factor that clearly affects the value of the note. If this is not considered, the transaction will be treated as a bargain sale, with gift tax consequences to the seller). If the selling price is increased to include the consideration of the risk of death, and the seller lives to receive all payments, the seller will have to report gain in excess of the actual gain that would have been realized had the property been sold at fair market value. An alternative is to use a higher interest rate, but this will result in a larger amount of ordinary income compared to an increase in the principal amount.[26]

What are the estate tax consequences of the SCIN? The Tax Court has held that since the balance of the note is canceled at the death of the seller, there is nothing to include in his or her estate.[27] The IRS agrees, at least in part.

HOW LIFE INSURANCE CAN ENHANCE THIS PLANNING TOOL

Where an individual (or business) transfers property to someone else in return for installment payments, the seller will often purchase insurance on the life (or lives) of the transferee(s) to protect against the potential cessation of payments at the death of the transferee(s). The seller should consider owning, paying premiums on, and being the beneficiary of the policy (the agreed-upon amount of payments made by the purchaser of the property could be increased to provide enough cash to make premium payments).

After the installment sale agreement is signed, the transferee-buyer receives title to the property. This means that the asset itself, as well as any appreciation from the date of the transfer, will be included in the transferee's estate. To provide the liquidity necessary to pay taxes and other death expenses, life insurance is often purchased on the transferee's life by the transferee's spouse, adult children, or on behalf of the transferee's spouse and children by the trustee of an irrevocable trust. The spouse, adult child, or trustee would be the owner, premium payer, and beneficiary of the policy proceeds. In intrafamily transfers, the transferor-seller often will make a gift to the policyholder of enough cash to pay premiums on the insured's life.

A third use of life insurance for improving the benefits of an installment sale is to assure that the transferee's family has enough cash at his or her death to make the promised installment payments. (Since the property will be in the transferee's estate after the sale, its inclusion could generate substantial estate and inheritance tax problems. This, in turn, creates a need for cash to pay increased death costs and, thus, drains the estate of cash to make installment payments.)

However, if the transferee's spouse purchases the appropriate amount of insurance on his life, there will be no need to sell or liquidate the transferred asset (perhaps closely held corporate stock) in order to make the agreed upon installment payments. The insurance proceeds can be used to pay death costs, make installment payments, or both.

IMPLICATIONS AND ISSUES IN COMMUNITY PROPERTY STATES

Installment sales by married individuals in community property states often involve real property. In such situations, it is important to ascertain whether the interest in real property is community property. Both spouses should join in any conveyance of community real property. If one spouse does not join in the conveyance of community real property, he or she may be able to void the sale for a specified period (e.g., one year from the date of recording of the deed in California). This statute of limitations applies only to land standing in the name of the transferor spouse alone. If the land stands in the name of both spouses, an attempt by either spouse to transfer complete title would be void with respect to the interest of the other spouse. Certain sales made to parties, in good faith, who are not aware of the marriage relationship may be incontestable, but such controversies should be avoided.

A purchaser of personal property should also ascertain whether any community property rights are involved. California does not require the written consent of each spouse in connection with the sale of community personal property if the property is sold for "valuable consideration." However, as an exception, neither spouse can sell, convey, or encumber the furniture, furnishings, or fittings of the home or wearing apparel of the other spouse or minor children without the written consent of the other spouse.

Problems could arise as a result of recent cases regarding joint property rights of non-marital partners. Some courts have found implied agreements between non-married individuals to treat their property similarly to community property. Caution should be exercised if property is purchased from an individual involved in such a relationship. It may be advisable to ask the partner who may have a claim to convey title to any interest he or she may have in the property.

Another possibility to consider is the separate sale of each spouse's interest. One spouse could sell his or her interest outright and recognize all of his or her capital gain immediately, while the other spouse could sell his or her interest on the installment method and spread out his or her capital gain. This can reduce capital gain taxes while effectively allowing a greater amount of the sale price to be received in the year of the sale.

If undivided interests are sold at a discount, the amount of capital gains will be less, thereby creating estate tax savings and lower installment payments.

QUESTIONS AND ANSWERS

Question – How can the related party rules be avoided?

Answer – For property other than marketable securities, the related purchaser could hold the property for at least a 2-year period after the sale (to the extent that the special depreciable property rule does not apply). The installment obligation could be structured so that no payments need to be made until after the 2-year holding period has lapsed. If the related party was going to sell the property to raise cash to make installment payments, as an alternative the related party could use the property as collateral for a loan to provide the funds needed to make installment payments. (Note, however, that the loan must be bona fide, and the debtor must continue to bear the economic risk of loss.)

A private annuity could be used instead of an installment sale to avoid all three related party rules. Since the installment sale rules do not deal with private annuity arrangements, the transferee should be free to dispose of the transferred property at any time without accelerating the recognition of gain to the transferor.

In any installment sale to a related party, the risk of illiquidity of the initial seller in the event of a second disposition by the new owner should be considered. How can this potential problem be overcome? Perhaps the seller might insist on an acceleration clause. This would give the seller the right to demand additional cash payments if the property subject to the installment sale is disposed of before the 2-year waiting period has been met.

It probably would not be advisable to impose formal restrictions on the related purchaser's ability to dispose of the property. Likewise, it probably is not wise to give the seller a legal right to insist that the purchaser must lend him funds to pay a tax imposed on a second disposition. Such contractual restrictions or requirements could be viewed by the IRS as evidence that the entire transaction lacked economic substance.

Question – What type of security can the seller of property under an installment sale require without being taxed on his entire gain in the year of the sale?

Answer – A third party can guarantee payment in the event the buyer defaults. For example, a standby letter of credit that is used as security for a deferred payment sale will not be treated as a payment received on the installment obligation.[28]

But third party notes or other third party obligations that are transferable or marketable prior to default by the installment buyer will be treated as payments to the seller (and therefore taxable in the year received).[29]

Typically, the IRS and the courts will deem funds placed in an escrow account to secure the interest of the seller to be constructively received—and, therefore, currently taxable in the year of the sale. However, this result is not certain. No presumption of tax avoidance arises merely because the seller requested an installment payout or merely because the buyer was at all times willing to pay the entire purchase price in a lump sum.

The seller is more likely to be successful in avoiding current taxation of escrowed funds if (1) the arrangement serves a legitimate business purpose, and (2) the seller continues to look to the contractual obligation of the buyer for payment. An example would be where the escrow arrangement was negotiated in a manner that provided that payments from the escrow account were contingent on the seller's continued adherence to his agreement not to compete. This type of agreement would probably not result in constructive receipt by the seller even if he could control the investment of the money in the escrow account.

Question – What are the income and estate tax implications when the holder of an installment obligation dies?

Answer – The right to receive payments under the obligation is treated as income in respect of a decedent. Thus, payments on the installment obligation are taxable income to the person or entity that receives those payments as they are received. Payments are taxed in the same manner as they would have been taxed had the seller lived and received payment himself.

For estate tax purposes, the present value of the installment obligation is also includable in the decedent's gross estate. But to reduce the harshness of double taxation, a deduction from income is allowed to the recipient based on the federal estate taxes paid by the decedent's estate attributable to the inclusion of the installment obligation. This is called the Section 691 (income in respect of a decedent) deduction.

Question – Is there a problem in arranging an installment sale of property with an existing mortgage on it?

Answer – Yes. Where property subject to an existing mortgage is sold and the purchaser assumes or takes the property subject to that mortgage, any debt in excess of the seller's tax basis (cost) will be considered a payment received by the seller in the year of the sale. Any mortgage encumbering the property will be treated as assumed or taken subject to, even though title to the property does not pass in the year of sale and even though the seller remains responsible for payment of the mortgage (as in a "wrap-around" mortgage).[30]

Question – Does the "second disposition" rule mean there are no advantages to a transfer of property (which is not within the special depreciable property rule) from an individual to an irrevocable trust established for his family in return for installment payments or SCIN payments?

Answer – Many advantages still exist, including the following:

(1) Taxation on the gain can be spread over a larger number of years (assuming the trust does not dispose of the property within two years, and assuming the trust does not benefit the seller or the seller's spouse if the property is depreciable to the trust). This could lower the applicable total rate.

(2) The family of the seller is more secure from the claims of his creditors.

(3) No gift tax is incurred on the transfer if the property is sold to the trust at its fair market value.

(4) The trust may have little or no gain on the resale of the asset since it takes as its basis the full purchase price it agreed to pay. (Of course, the property may appreciate or decline in value during the two years it must be held in order to avoid accelerating the initial seller's gain.) The amount of gain to the buyer will be reduced if a SCIN having a premium on principal is used.

(5) None of the assets of the trust, or income, will be includable in the original owner's estate if the trust is irrevocable and the seller maintains no control. (The present value of future payments remaining on the note would, however, be includable if he died within the installment period. This, in turn, could cause a serious lack of liquidity. Conversely, the payments due on a SCIN are canceled at death and excluded from the seller's estate, but liquidity is needed for any income tax due at death.)

To obtain this favorable treatment, it is important that:

(1) the trustee be completely independent and that the grantor maintain no control over the trustee's actions;

(2) there be no prearrangement between the parties requiring the trustee to resell the property;

(3) the original owner not have a stake in the resale by the trust (i.e., the amount he receives cannot be dependent on the amount the trustee receives);

(4) there be a motive–other than tax savings–for the arrangement; and

(5) the "2-year holding rule" be met.

Question – Must there be any down payment in the year of sale to qualify for the installment method of reporting?

Answer – No. There is no requirement that there be any payment in the year of sale. The only requirement of this type is that at least one payment be made in the taxable year *after* the year in which the property was sold. However, some practitioners believe that if a trust created by the seller or a related party is the buyer, the buyer should have additional assets to make the payments, or a guaranty of the note be given, so as to avoid possible inclusion of the sold asset in the seller's estate.

Question – Will a bequest of an installment obligation to the obligor avoid tax recognition of the untaxed gain by the seller?

Answer – The installment obligation rules cannot be circumvented by cancelling the obligation during the seller's lifetime. Likewise, when an installment seller dies holding an installment obligation, the gain is not forgiven. Instead, gain is reportable by the seller's estate–or the recipient of the obligation–as payments are made. The amount of gain and the character of income realized are the same as the deceased seller would have reported had he or she lived. (Note that death itself does not trigger an acceleration of gain; tax is due only if payments are actually or constructively received or if the obligation is sold.)

Under prior law, it had been argued that if an installment obligation was bequeathed to the purchaser of the property, the interests of the obligor and the obligee "merged." Under this theory, there would be no gain realized because the estate would never realize the unpaid balance.

Current tax law accelerates the unrealized gain when the seller makes a bequest of the obligation to the buyer or his estate cancels the debt. Gain or loss will be recognized to the extent the fair market value of the obligation exceeds the obligation holder's basis. (Where the decedent-seller and the purchaser are related, the fair market value of the obligation cannot be less than its face amount.)

If a person forgives an installment obligation in his will, the cancellation is treated as a transfer of the obligation by the decedent's estate. The estate will report the accelerated gain. If a trust or some party other than the decedent held the obligation, the cancellation will be treated as a transfer by that person immediately after the decedent's death.

An installment obligation that becomes unenforceable at the seller's death is treated as if it were canceled in favor of the obligor.

Question – What is the tax effect where the seller cancels a buyer's obligation to make installments?

Answer – If a seller cancels a buyer's installment obligation (or it becomes unenforceable), the cancellation will be treated as a "disposition" of the obligation. This means the seller must report gain (or loss). The gain (or loss) is measured by the difference between the fair market value of the obligation at the time of its disposition and its basis.

Note that if the seller and buyer are considered "related persons," the fair market value of the obligation will be considered as not less than the face value. For instance, mom sells her summer home in Avalon to her daughter in an installment sale. Mom's basis in the home was $11,000. Her daughter will pay the purchase price, $55,000, in five equal annual $11,000 installments. (Interest is ignored for simplicity.) If mom immediately cancels the daughter's obligation, mom must report gain. Her gain is the difference between the value of what is owed to her, $55,000, and her $11,000 basis. She is also liable for any gift tax on the gift.

A solution would seem to be for mom to forgive – at her whim, and on a year-by-year basis – all or a portion of each $11,000 payment as it is paid. Her daughter should write a check for the full $11,000 to her. Then, without a prearranged or legally binding plan, mom can write her daughter, son-in-law, and each of her grandchildren, checks of $11,000 or under, all of which would be gift tax-free (and she could double the amount of each check if her husband joined in on a "split" gift). Mom will recognize gain of $8,800 each of the five years, rather than $44,000 in the year of sale.

Question – How is gain computed under the installment sale rules where the sale price is not fixed or determinable?

Answer – Often, the price at which property will change hands depends on some contingency. For example, Susan Harmon may sell her stock in the SH Corporation, a closely held business, to her son Mark in return for installment payments. But rather than selling at a specific dollar price, the amount may be set as a percentage of the gross profits of the business for each of the next 10 years. The parties may – or may not – put a maximum dollar amount on the selling price.

Installment sale treatment is available even when the actual price cannot be determined with precision. If there is a stated maximum selling price, the seller (in this example Susan) can recover basis by means of a "gross profit ratio."[31] This ratio is multiplied by the installment payment (exclusive of interest) to determine the portion of the payment that is gain.

$$\frac{\text{gross profit (realized or to be realized)}}{\text{total contract price (assume this is maximum selling price)}} \times \text{installment payment}$$

(The maximum selling price is defined as the largest price that could be paid assuming all contingencies, formulas, etc., operate in the seller's favor.) The seller then reports income on a pro rata basis (and recovers his basis over the scheduled payment period in equal annual increments) with respect to each installment payment.

Later, if it is found that the contingency will not be met (and therefore the seller will not actually receive the "maximum" selling price) a recomputation of the seller's income is allowed. The seller may report reduced income (not only in the adjustment year, but in all subsequent years). If as a result of the recomputation, the seller does not recover his or her

entire income tax basis for the property sold, the amount of basis will be deductible as a loss.[32]

If the sale price is indefinite and no maximum selling price can be determined – but the obligation is payable over a fixed period of time – the seller's basis would be recoverable ratably over that fixed period.[33]

If neither selling price nor payment period can be ascertained with certainty in advance, the arrangement will be closely scrutinized to determine whether there has been a sale or whether the payments, in economic effect, are merely in the nature of rent or royalty income. If it is determined that there has been a sale, the seller's basis will be recovered over 15 years commencing with the date of sale. Any basis not recovered in that time may be carried forward to succeeding years until recovered in full.

Generally, if in any year payments received are less than the basis allocated to that year, the excess basis must be reallocated over the balance of the 15-year period. (A period other than 15 years may be used or required where it is shown that a substantial and inappropriate deferral or acceleration of the recovery of the seller's basis would otherwise result.)[34]

The effect of the contingency sale price rules allowing installment reporting is that taxpayers have little justification for treating transactions as "open." (In open transactions, a taxpayer can recover his entire cost before reporting any gain, rather than reporting gain ratably.) This "cost recovery" method is available only in rare and extraordinary cases involving sales for a contingent price where it is impossible to value a purchaser's obligation to pay a contingent price.

Special rules apply with respect to contingent installment payments for sales of depreciable property to a controlled entity, such as a more than 50% owned partnership or corporation. The rules are:

(1) The seller's basis is recovered ratably in annual increments if (a) the installment sale is to a controlled entity, and (b) it is impossible to reasonably ascertain the fair market value.

(2) All noncontingent payments plus the fair market value of contingent payments must be reported in the year of the sale. For instance, assume Tom Miller sells depre-

ciable property to a corporation he controls for no down payment and 10% of the net profits from the business for the next 10 years. Assume the fair market value of the promise can be reasonably ascertained to be $200,000. Tom would have to include $200,000 in income in the year of the sale ($0 noncontingent payments plus $200,000 fair market value of contingent payments).

(3) The purchaser of the property may not increase his basis in the property by any amount before such time as the seller includes the amount in income.[35]

Question – How soon does a taxpayer have to elect to report payments in installments?

Answer – No election is necessary. Installment sale treatment is automatic for qualifying sales unless an election is made specifying installment sale treatment is *not* to apply. Although the temporary regulations are not specific as to how such an election is to be made, reporting the entire gain in gross income for the taxable year in which the sale occurs (on or before the due date for filing the tax return – including extensions) will operate as an election that installment sale reporting is not to apply.[36] Once a valid election out of the installment method has been made, it may not be revoked except under very limited circumstances. The Service has provided guidance in the form of a revenue ruling concerning when it will grant permission to make a late election out of the installment method.[37]

Question – When might it be a good idea to forego the installment method of reporting a gain, even though a sale was made on the installment basis?

Answer – If a taxpayer has unrelated losses, he might wish to offset those losses with the gain from the installment sale. He may have unusually low income or high deductions for the year. Thus, he or she would report the full gain in the year of sale even though the sale was an installment sale.

Question – When is interest payable on the unpaid balance of an installment sale deductible by the buyer?

Answer – Interest is deductible only in the period in which that interest is properly allocable. Regardless of how the parties have formed the agreement, the IRS will treat the interest as "constant" (whether the

taxpayer is on the cash or accrual method). The Service allocates the interest over the term of the contract. The net effect is that the parties must determine the effective interest on a compound interest basis and use that effective rate to compute the amount of any allowable interest deduction.

This rule limits both the interest deduction and the interest income to the amount of interest that accrues economically. The compounding period used in determining the effective rate of interest will probably be the same as that called for in the parties' agreement.

Question – When will a taxpayer be subject to the interest surcharge for installment sales in excess of $150,000?

Answer – There is a special interest surcharge imposed on certain installment obligations in which the sale price exceeds $150,000 and the aggregate deferred payments for such sales during the taxable year exceed $5,000,000. There are three exceptions to the application of the surcharge: (1) property used or produced in the trade or business of farming; (2) timeshares and residential lots; and (3) personal use property.[38]

CHAPTER ENDNOTES

1. IRC Sec. 453.
2. See Rev. Rul. 86-72, 1 CB 253; GCM 39503 (5-7-86).
3. IRC Sec. 453(b).
4. IRC Sec. 453(d).
5. IRC Sec. 453(j); Treas. Reg. §15A.453-1(c).
6. IRC Sec. 453(k)(2).
7. IRC Sec. 453.
8. Rev. Rul. 70-430, 1970-2 CB 51.
9. IRC Sec. 483.
10. IRC Sec. 1274A; Rev. Rul. 2003-119, 2003-47 IRB 1094; Rev. Rul. 2002-79, 2002-2 CB 908.
11. IRC Sec. 2033; Treas. Reg. §20.2033-1.
12. *Ballard v. Comm.*, TC Memo 1987-128; *Krabbenhoft v. Comm.*, 94 TC 887 (1990).
13. *Ballard v. Comm.*, 854 F.2d 185 (7th Cir. 1988).
14. *Krabbenhoft v. Comm.*, 939 F.2d 529 (8th Cir. 1991), *cert. denied*, 502 U.S. 1072 (1991).
15. Treas. Reg. §1.691(a)-3.
16. Treas. Reg. §1.691(c)-1.
17. *Ballard*; IRC Sec. 1012.
18. See IRC Secs. 453(f)(1), 318(a), 267(b).

19. IRC Sec. 453(e)(1).
20. IRC Sec. 453(e)(2).
21. IRC Sec. 453(g).
22. IRC Sec. 453B(f).
23. See IRC Sec. 453(i).
24. *Est. of Frane v. Comm.*, 98 TC 341 (1992).
25. *Est. of Frane v. Comm.*, 998 F.2d 567 (8th Cir. 1993).
26. GCM 39503 (5-7-86).
27. *Est. of Moss v. Comm.*, 74 TC 1239 (1980), *acq. in result*, 1981-1 CB 2.
28. Treas. Reg. §15A.453-1(b)(3).
29. Treas. Reg. §15A.453-1(e).
30. Treas. Reg. §15A.453-1(b)(3)(ii).
31. Temp. Treas. Reg. §15A.453-1(c)(2).
32. Treas. Reg. §15A.453-1(c)(2), Example (5).
33. Treas. Reg. §15A.453-1(c)(3).
34. Treas. Reg. §15A.453-1(c)(4).
35. IRC Sec. 453(g)(1).
36. Treas. Reg. §15A.453-1(d)(3).
37. Rev. Rul. 90-46, 1990-1 CB 107.
38. IRC Sec. 453A(b).

Chapter 36

PRIVATE ANNUITY

WHAT IS IT?

A private annuity is an arrangement between two parties, neither of whom is an insurance company. The transferor (annuitant) conveys complete ownership of property to a transferee (obligor, the party obligated to make payments to the person who has transferred the property). The transferee, in turn, promises to make periodic payments to the transferor for a period of time. Usually, this period of time is the transferor's life or, in some cases, the transferor's life plus the life of his or her spouse.

There are basically two types of private annuities: (1) the single life annuity under which payments cease at the death of the annuitant; and (2) the joint and last survivor annuity, in which payments continue until the death of the last survivor, e.g., payments continue as long as either the husband or wife is alive. Generally, since payments under this type of arrangement will continue for a longer period of time than payments under a single life annuity, the amount paid each year will be less than that payable under a single life annuity.

WHEN IS THE USE OF SUCH A DEVICE INDICATED?

1. When a client would like to "spread" gains. For example, the client owns low tax basis property. He needs cash and wants to sell a particular asset but wants to avoid "bunching" gains into a single tax year. Generally, such a client will be in a high income tax bracket. A private annuity will enable him to spread his gain (and therefore defer tax) over a number of years. Private annuities have become a more valuable deferral tool since the attractiveness of installment sales has generally declined over the past several years.

2. When a client wishes to retire and shift control of a business to a family member or to a key employee. For example, assume Ed Staller is the sole shareholder of a closely held corporation. Ed has no heir other than his wife. He has two key employees in the business who are capable of managing it. Ed would

like to sell them the business but he is concerned about adequate income upon his retirement. Presently, his business does not provide pension, profit-sharing, or nonqualified deferred compensation benefits. The key employees tell Ed they would like to buy the business but cannot afford to pay Ed in a lump sum. Ed could sell all of his stock to the two key employees and in return they could promise to pay him an income for his life (and perhaps for his wife's life). This should yield a higher income than if he sold the business in an installment sale. The income would be based on the fair market value of the business.

3. When a client desires to remove a sizable asset, such as a business, from his or her estate for estate tax purposes. [EGTRRA 2001 repeals the estate tax for one year for 2010.] For example, Abe Marks is the sole shareholder of a closely-held real estate corporation. He has two daughters who are presently working in the business. He could sell the business to his daughters in return for their agreement to pay an annuity for his life only. This will result in a reduction in Abe's estate (and thus save estate taxes) because the value of the business will be removed from his estate for federal estate tax purposes. At Abe's death, annuity payments cease and neither the close corporation stock nor the promised payments will be included in his estate.

The daughter's income tax basis in the stock, *after Abe's death*, will be the amount of annuity payments they made to him during his lifetime. Until Abe's death, their basis will be the greater of the amount they paid him or the amount paid plus the present value of all the future payments that will be paid if Abe lives to his life expectancy. Initially, the transferee's basis is equal to the fair market value of the property transferred–assuming no gift is built into the transaction.

4. When a client owns a large parcel of non-income producing property but is desirous of making it income producing. For example, the client is a widow. Her married son is currently providing $700 a month to support her. The widow owns real

estate that is currently not producing any income, but because of its choice location, is increasing substantially in value. It is expected that the full appreciation in the property will occur over the next 10 years.

A possible solution is for her son to discontinue gifts to his mother and, instead, his mother could transfer the real estate to him in exchange for a monthly lifetime income (say, $750 a month, assuming the present value of the land will support this payment). This will minimize the widow's estate, substantially reduce estate taxes at her death, and, at the same time, give her financial independence. The son becomes the immediate owner of the real estate. The growth in value (and increase in gross estate for tax purposes) will occur in the son's hands and not further increase his mother's estate.

5. When the client's estate is very large and the major or sole heir is a grandchild (or other individual two or more generations below that of the client). Because the private annuity is a sale and not a gift, it will not be subject to the generation-skipping transfer tax. [EGTRRA 2001 repeals the generation-skipping transfer tax for one year for 2010.]

6. Where the purchaser's objective is to bar others from obtaining the property in question but he cannot afford to pay for the asset in a lump sum outright purchase.

WHAT ARE THE REQUIREMENTS?

1. Any type of property can be used. For example, it is possible to transfer a home, undeveloped real estate, stocks, or a business interest. Preferably, the property transferred will be income producing, rapidly appreciating, and will not be subject to depreciation or investment credit recapture or to indebtedness.

2. It is important to ascertain immediately the ability of the obligor to make annuity payments. If the transferee (the obligor) has substantial independent income, then almost any asset can serve as the property to be sold. But, if the transferee has little or no other income, then the property sold should be either income producing or at least should be of a type that the obligor can easily and quickly resell or borrow against.[1]

3. It is extremely important that the obligor's promise be unsecured. If the promise of the obligor is se-

cured, a taxable event will occur immediately on a transfer.[2] This means the annuitant will pay tax on the full amount of the gain. The gain is the difference between the amount realized (the present value of the right to the promised payments) and the transferor's adjusted basis in the property.

4. The transferee (obligor) should be a person not regularly engaged in issuing private annuities.[3] Generally, the obligor would be the natural object of the transferor's (annuitant's) bounty. For example, most private annuities are made between parents and children. The device may also be useful for transfers between employers and trusted key employees.

5. The annuity amount must be determined by measuring the fair market value of the property. An appraisal by independent court-recognized appraisal experts shortly before the execution of the private annuity is suggested.

6. A client should be in a high estate tax bracket and should be desirous of reducing his or her estate and providing himself or herself with a lifetime income.

7. An agreement with a trust or corporation that has very few other assets may be attacked by the IRS as a sham.

8. Payments must be completely contingent on the life (or lives) of the transferor(s).

HOW IT IS DONE – EXAMPLES

George Gargas is 65 years old. He owns farmland with a fair market value of $1,000,000. His basis is only $100,000. He would like to remove the land from his estate and have his son, Bill, own it. He does not, however, want to pay any gift taxes on the transfer.

A private annuity agreement would be drawn stating that the farmland was sold to Bill in return for Bill's promise to pay his father an income for life. At age 65, the father's life expectancy (expected return multiple) is 19.5 years (20 years - 0.5 frequency of payment adjustment, see Table V in Appendix B).

Assume the annuity agreement was signed in a month when the IRC Section 7520 discount rate was 5.0%. The annual annuity generated by property worth $1,000,000 is $94,796. This is arrived at by dividing the fair market value of the property transferred by the present value factor for an annuity at the appropriate age (10.5490 – see single life table for 5.0% interest rate in Appendix B).

Figure 36.1

TAXATION OF SELLER UNDER PRIVATE ANNUITY	
A. Recovery of Basis (cost) Element	Tax Free
B. Gain Element	Capital gain
C. Income Element	Ordinary income

General Formula for Computing Annual Payment — Tax Free, Gain and Ordinary Income Elements	
STEP 1. Compute Annual Payment	$$\frac{\text{FMV of Property Transferred}}{\text{Present Value of Annuity Factor}}$$
STEP 2. Compute Exclusion Ratio	$$\frac{\text{Seller's Cost Basis}}{\text{expected return}}$$ $$\overline{\text{(annual payment } \times \text{ life expectancy)}}$$
STEP 3. Compute Excludable Amount (until total basis recovered)	Exclusion ratio × Annual Annuity
STEP 4. Compute Gain Element (until total gain recognized)	$$\frac{\text{Present value of annuity minus property's basis}}{\text{life expectancy of annuitant}}$$
STEP 5. Compute Ordinary Income Element	Annual Payment minus sum of (a) excludable amount and (b) gain amount

Note that the private annuity payments are significantly impacted by upward or downward changes in the Section 7520 rate, the federal discount rate published by the IRS once a month in a revenue ruling. The Section 7520 rate can be found at www.nationalunderwriter.com/taxfactsfx.

Out of the $94,796 he receives each year, Bill's father can exclude a portion ($5,119) from income. Assuming the annuity starting date is after 1986, Bill's father could exclude $5,119 each year *only* until his basis is recovered.

The exclusion ratio is determined by dividing the father's $100,000 basis in the property by his $1,848,522 expected return ($94,796 annual payment x 19.5 expected return multiple). The excludable amount is then found by multiplying this exclusion ratio ($100,000/$1,848,522) by the $94,796 annual payment.

Total capital gain to be recognized equals $900,000 ($1,000,000 fair market value - $100,000 adjusted basis). Gain from each annuity payment equals $46,154 ($900,000 ÷ 19.5 expected return multiple).

The balance of each payment, $43,523 [($94,796 – ($5,119 + $46,154)], is taxable as ordinary income.

Once the basis is recovered and the total capital gain included in income, the full amount of the annuity payment is treated as ordinary income.

WHAT ARE THE TAX IMPLICATIONS?

1. For federal estate tax purposes, where the annuity ceases at the death of the transferor, the value of the property sold to the transferee-obligor in return for his promise to pay the annuity is excludable from the annuitant-transferor's estate. [EGTRRA 2001 repeals the estate tax for one year for 2010.] This is because property sold by a decedent for full and adequate consideration before death is not taxable in his estate.[4]

Likewise, the value of the promised payment will be excludable. This is because the selling price in a private annuity arrangement is an annuity that will expire (in the case of a single life annuity) upon the annuitant's death.

Note that this is not the case with a joint and survivor annuity. In a joint and last survivor annuity, payments will continue until the death of the last survivor. So if the spouse of the transferor-annuitant is the other annuitant and the spouse survives, the present value of future payments to her will be includable in the transferor-annuitant's estate (assuming he was sole owner of the property that was transferred in return for the joint and survivor annuity payments).[5] However, because of the unlimited estate tax marital deduction, there would be no federal estate tax.

2. Each annuity payment made by the transferee-obligor to the transferor-annuitant is treated partially as a tax-free return of capital, partially as a capital gain and the balance as ordinary income.[6] If the annuity starting date is after 1986, once the transferor-annuitant has recovered his basis, the entire payment will be taxed as ordinary income. The obligor is not allowed a deduction for any payments made to the annuitant.[7]

3. There will be no gift if the annual payments made by the obligor to the annuitant are actuarially determined to be equal to the fair market value of the property sold. However, if the value of the promise made by the transferee-obligor is less than the value of the property transferred, the difference will constitute a gift by the annuitant-transferor.[8] (If the annuity were a joint and survivor annuity, the value of the survivor annuity would be a gift from the transferor to the survivor. Since it would be a gift of a future interest, it would not qualify for the gift tax annual exclusion.[9] If the donee were the transferor's spouse, the gift may qualify for the gift tax marital deduction.[10])

Example: Assuming a 5.0% Section 7520 rate, the government valuation tables indicate an annuity valuation factor of 10.5490 for a person age 65 (see Appendix B). If such an individual transfers property with a fair market value of $1,000,000, a fair exchange would be a life annuity of $94,796 per year ($1,000,000 divided by 10.5490). But if annuity payments were actually set at, say, $85,000 per year, which has a present value of about $899,665 ($85,000 x 10.5490), the difference, $100,335 ($1,000,000 - $899,665), would constitute a gift from the transferor to the transferee in the year the agreement was signed.

---

4. The transferee receives a "temporary basis" in the property equal to the value for calculation of the annuity. This provides a means for immediately increasing the basis for depreciation or depletion and can be a very significant benefit. The same basis is available for resale of the property, leaving little, if any, gain to be then taxed.

However, upon the transferor's death, the basis is adjusted to what the transferee actually paid in annuity payments. If he has retained the property, the only concern for imposition of income tax at the transferor's death would be his having depreciated the property below the basis as adjusted at such death. In that event, he would realize ordinary income to the extent of the difference between the adjusted basis at death and the basis after depreciation. On the other hand, if the transferee had sold the property at a gain based on the "temporary basis" amount, and if the adjusted basis at the transferor's death is less than the temporary basis, the difference between the temporary basis and the adjusted basis will be immediately taxed to the transferee.

5. The income tax treatment of unsecured private annuities is based on the following principles:

First, gain is equal to the difference between the present value of the annuity promised and the transferor's basis. Second, that gain should be reported ratably over a period of years measured by the life expectancy of the annuitant. (See Steps 2 through 4 in Figure 36.1, and the example in "How It Is Done," above.) Third, the transferor's "investment in the contract" is the transferor's basis in the property. Fourth, a portion of each annuity payment payable to the transferor is treated as (a) return of basis, (b) capital gain, and (c) ordinary income.

Here are the steps in computing the transferor's tax treatment:

a. Determine the value of the promised annuity by using the appropriate IRS annuity valuation tables (see Appendix B).

b. Compute the excludable amount. An exclusion ratio is found. This is a formula that can be applied against each annuity payment to determine the portion recoverable income tax free as basis. This is done by dividing the transferor's investment in the contract by "expected return," i.e., the annual payment is multiplied by the transferor's life expectancy (expected return multiple) measured by IRS life expectancy annuity (IRC Section 72) tables. This exclusion ratio is applied to each payment received by the transferor to determine the income tax free portion that is recovery of basis. As noted above, once the transferor has recovered his total basis, this portion will be taxed as ordinary income.

c. Determine the portion of each payment that is taxable at capital gain rates. Total gain is the difference between the value of the annuity (annual payment multiplied by the present value annuity factor) and the transferor's basis. This gain is then divided by the transferor's life expectancy to determine the portion of each payment that is capital gain. As noted above, once the transferor has recovered his total capital gain, this portion will be taxed as ordinary income.

d. Determine the ordinary income portion. This is simply the difference between each payment and the sum of the portion of each payment that is tax free recovery of basis plus the portion of each payment that is capital gain. As noted above, once the transferor has recovered his total basis and recognized his total gain, the entire payment will be taxed as ordinary income.

If a private annuity is "secured" or collateralized in any way, the transferor must immediately recognize income on the entire gain.

HOW CAN LIFE INSURANCE ENHANCE THIS TOOL?

The obligation of the transferee must be unsecured. This means that no specific assets are set aside to protect the transferor in case the transferee defaults. But at the death of the transferee-obligor, the obligation passes to his or her estate. The question then arises as to how to eliminate or minimize the possible hardships on the transferee's family and heirs. (The estate of the transferee will still have to continue promised payments for as long as the transferor-annuitant lives.)

Looking at the same problem from another viewpoint, how does one avoid disrupting the financial security of the transferor-annuitant in case the transferee dies before the transferor? Perhaps the best answer is life insurance. Life insurance can be obtained on the life of the transferee-obligor. It might be owned by and payable to the obligor's spouse (or irrevocable trust for her benefit).

There should be no formal connection between the life insurance and the private annuity; otherwise, the obligation of the transferee might be considered "secured." When the income and estate tax free insurance proceeds are received, the spouse will have cash to (a) continue payments to the transferor, and (b) pay estate taxes caused by the inclusion of the private annuity property in the transferee's estate.[11]

Occasionally, there is another reason that life insurance may be useful in conjunction with a private annuity. Assume a widow owns a business and has two adult sons and two adult daughters. How can she transfer the business to her sons but at the same time avoid disinheriting her daughters if she does not have considerable other assets?

Life insurance can be used to "equalize" the inheritance. The widow would sell the business to her sons in return for a private annuity. The daughters could be named owners, premium payors, and beneficiaries of a policy (or policies) on their mother's life. Annual gifts by the widow to the daughters could be used to provide premium payments. The widow could obtain the cash to give to her daughters from the private annuity income. When the widow died, each daughter could receive–in the form of tax-free life insurance proceeds–an amount equivalent to what she would have received if the business were divided in four equal shares. (Actually, since the sons are paying their mother for the business, the amount the daughters are to receive might be considerably less than half the value of the business.)

IMPLICATIONS AND ISSUES IN COMMUNITY PROPERTY STATES

In a community property jurisdiction, since the property is owned one-half by each spouse, the practitioner can either arrange a private annuity sale on a joint and survivor annuity basis, or on the basis of a separate annuity contract for each community half of the husband and wife, respectively. If the joint and survivor annuity is used, the total amount payable to the husband and wife is somewhat lower at the beginning than would be the total paid under separate annuities, but the payment remains constant at the death of the first spouse to die. Under the separate annuity approach, at the death of one spouse, the payments to that spouse cease, and the survivor does not have any benefit continuing under the decedent's annuity.

There are implications in community property states also from the standpoint of the purchaser of the property under a private annuity contract. A typical arrangement is to have a private annuity contract between the parents and a child (rather than a child and his spouse). However, it is unlikely that the property acquired by the child will generate sufficient income to make the private annuity payments. If the child uses his earnings to make up the shortfall, the child's spouse could either be acquiring a community property interest in the property purchased, or could be making a gift to the child as each annuity payment is made. Consideration should be given to this aspect before the annuity contract is entered into.

QUESTIONS AND ANSWERS

Question – What are the alternatives to a private annuity?

Answer – One alternative to a private annuity is the installment sale. However, if the seller were to die shortly after the sale took place, the death tax results would differ substantially. Since an installment sale is often evidenced by a series of notes, the present value of those notes would be includable in the estate of the seller. But under the private annuity arrangement where payments are to cease on the death of the annuitant, the entire amount of the transferred property could be excluded from the estate of the annuitant at his or her death.

Another disadvantage of an installment sale is that an installment note bearing interest would cause a sizable portion of each payment in the early years to be considered interest to the seller. Where the subject of the sale is publicly traded stock, the installment sale would not defer taxation. The cost of an installment sale is in many cases higher since investment interest is deductible only to the extent of investment income if the asset sold was considered an investment.

Question – What basis does the transferee have in the property he now owns?

Answer – In the case of a private annuity, the transferee-obligor has, as his new tax basis, the fair market value of the property, which is the actuarial value of future payments (temporary basis).[12] It is because his basis is the fair market value of the property at the time the agreement is executed that the private annuity is so useful. The new owner can immediately sell the property and reinvest the proceeds in more liquid or higher yielding assets. He does not have to worry about tax on gains that the transferor-annuitant would otherwise have had to face. The

basis is "stepped-up," not carried over, for purposes of determining the tax on gain if the property is sold or depreciated. This would enable a fully depreciated property (such as an apartment or office building) to receive a new (fair market value) basis for depreciation by the transferee.[13] (But be aware of potential recapture problems where accelerated depreciation has been used by the transferor.)

Question – What happens to the transferee's basis if the annuitant dies prematurely?

Answer – The transferee may have to readjust his temporary basis or report a gain. If the annuitant dies before the length of his life expectancy according to government tables, the transferee-obligor must make a downward adjustment to his basis for the property. His basis becomes the amount of payments he actually has made. However, if he had sold the property before the annuitant's death, adjustments are made to reflect the reduced basis in light of previously recognized gain or loss.[14]

Question – Can the property that will be the subject of the private annuity be placed in escrow as security for the private annuity?

Answer – Not if tax deferral is desired. A promise to pay a private annuity in return for an appreciated security or other asset does not cause the transferor-annuitant to realize an immediate gain for only one reason– the value of the buyer's promise to pay is deemed to be too contingent to value. In other words, the favorable annuity rules have been allowed in private annuity situations only because of the uncertainty as to whether or not the person agreeing to make payments will actually be able to make them.

Where there is any type of security that will be activated to protect the transferor in the event of the transferee's default, a completed sale for tax purposes occurs. This makes the entire gain element taxable immediately rather than taxable ratably over the annuity period.

Question – Can the private annuity be used in situations other than between family members?

Answer – Yes. One possible use for a private annuity involves stock redemptions. For example, assume a corporation is owned and operated by an elderly widow and her son-in-law. Each owns 50 percent of the corporation's stock. The corporation's financial health is strong. The widow would like to retire but needs the assurance of a steady income. The son-in-law is in a high income tax bracket but is personally "cash poor."

The corporation could purchase the widow's stock in return for the corporation's promise to pay her an income for life. The transaction would give the son-in-law 100 percent ownership of the corporation. No gift tax would be payable assuming the amount of the annual annuity payment was derived from the appropriate government tables and as the result of an arm's length transaction.

If the son-in-law had no primary and unconditional personal obligation to purchase the stock, the use of corporate dollars to effect the redemption will not result in a dividend to him. The widow should receive "sale or exchange" treatment if the redemption completely eliminates her interest (attribution rules do not cause problems in this factual situation, but extreme care should be taken before a redemption of stock is effected in any family-owned corporation).

Question – In a previous example in which a 65-year old individual transferred property worth $1,000,000 in return for an annuity of $94,796 per year, the annuitant's expected return in that example was $1,848,522. If the individual lived for the full 19.5-year life expectancy, how can it be said that he saved federal estate taxes by transferring property worth $1,000,000?

Answer – The property transferred is the fair market value of the property on the date of the transfer, which in this example occurs 19.5 years prior to the annuitant's death, according to life expectancy tables. Assuming that the fair market value of the property continues to increase at a net rate of 7 percent per year, on the projected date of the annuitant's death in 19.5 years, the fair market value of the property would be $3,740,965.

The entire $1,848,522 of expected return would not be included in the annuitant's estate since a portion of that amount must be used by the transferor-annuitant to pay his capital gains and ordinary income taxes. The annuitant could make sizable gifts to decrease the net amount of cash realized as a result of receiving the annuity payments. In addition, the annuitant will likely spend the majority of the annuity payments.

The key to success is to select property that has a high probability of significantly growing in value at a rate that exceeds the Section 7520 rate in the month the agreement is signed.

Question – What happens if the annuitant outlives his life expectancy?

Answer – The transferee must continue to make the annuity payments and such payments continue for the life of the annuitant. This is one of the risks involved in a private annuity; the actual amount to be paid by the transferee may exceed the expected return (the annual payments multiplied by the annuitant's life expectancy).

If an annuitant outlives his life expectancy (and thus has recognized total gain), the portion previously treated as capital gain is thereafter treated as ordinary income. Also, where the annuity starting date is after 1986, IRC Section 72(b) provides that if an annuitant outlives his life expectancy (and thus has recovered his basis) the remaining payments will be taxed entirely as ordinary income.

Question – In arranging a private annuity transaction, is it wise to tie the annuity payments to the income generated by the transferred property?

Answer – No. If this is done, the property may be brought back into the transferor's estate at death as a transfer with a retained life estate under IRC Section 2036.[15]

Question – Can a joint and survivor private annuity be designed?

Answer – Yes. Since the advent of an unlimited estate tax marital deduction for transfers between spouses, the joint and survivor annuity has become a more attractive planning technique. It has the advantage of providing security for the surviving spouse with no additional federal estate tax cost at either spouse's death (but may trigger state death taxes since some states do not have an unlimited marital deduction). At the time of the exchange, the gift of the survivor annuity may qualify for the gift tax marital deduction as qualified terminable interest property.[16] A second advantage is that the amount payable by the transferee each year is less than it would be in a single life private annuity. This makes it easier for a purchaser to meet annual obligations under the private annuity.

Example: Assume a client age 60, a spouse age 62, property with a fair market value of $1,000,000, and a 5.0% Section 7520 federal discount rate. The annual payment would be $72,133 for a joint and survivor private annuity. This is $22,663 less than the $94,796 payment for a single life annuity for a 60-year-old client.

Question – Will the use of a trust automatically cause the loss of the tax benefits of the private annuity?

Answer – No, but it is likely that the IRS will treat property for annuity exchanges involving trusts as if the transaction created a grantor trust rather than a sale. Therefore, all the income of the trust would, if the IRS were successful, be taxed to the seller (grantor, according to the IRS) as owner.

But this harsh result is neither automatic nor certain. The Ninth Circuit Court of Appeals checks to see if annuity payments are tied to the income of the trust, how payments are calculated, and what role the taxpayer takes in trust investment decisions. Case law[17] indicates that client success is most likely where (1) payment is computed by dividing the fair market value of the property by the appropriate annuity factor determined from the government's own tables, (2) the trust is obligated to pay the annuity without regard to the value of the property held in the trust or the income produced by trust assets, and (3) the grantor holds no powers to manage the trust or control the trustee.

The Tax Court has indicated that the annuity may lack substance where the transferor-annuitant retains too much control, the trustee is not independent, and there is a tie between the annuity payments and the income produced by the transferred property.[18] In another decision[19], the Tax Court considered the following factors:

1. The relationship between the creation of the trust and the transfer of property to it.

2. The relationship between the income from the property and the annuity payments.

3. The degree of control the annuitant exercises over the property.

4. The nature and extent of the annuitant's continuing interest in the property.

5. The source of the annuity payment.

6. The arm's length nature of the annuity-sale.

Question – May the valuation tables used in the IRS regulations always be relied upon in structuring a private annuity transaction?

Answer – The IRS and the courts have indicated that the valuation tables may not be used where there is substantial evidence that the annuitant has a very short life expectancy. In general, the courts and the IRS have taken the position that the tables must be used unless death is "imminent."[20] However, the courts seemed to limit this to situations where the annuitant was not expected to live over a year.[21] More recently, the IRS has sought a broader rule, and has had success in at least one case.[22]

The standard valuation tables are not to be used where an individual is terminally ill (a person with an incurable illness or other deteriorating physical condition and at least a 50% probability of dying within one year). However, if such an individual survives for 18 months after the transaction, the individual is presumed not to have been terminally ill at the time of the transaction unless the opposite is proved with clear and convincing evidence.[23]

As a rule of thumb, practitioners should consider a private annuity when the life expectancy of the client exceeds two years. Perhaps the best objective third party evidence of life expectancy is the acceptance of the individual as an insured by an insurance company. If an insurer will accept the risk, regardless of the "rating" (additional premium charged by the insurance company to place the insured in the risk category appropriate under the circumstances known to the insurer), the issuance of the policy is almost perfect documentation that life expectancy at that time exceeded two years.

ASRS: Sec. 51.

CHAPTER ENDNOTES

1. Where a sale is made to children through a private annuity, they or the trustee representing them should have a source of capital or income – other than solely the income from the transferred property – from which to make required payments, otherwise the IRS could argue that the seller's income is in reality inextricably tied to the success of the enterprise. See *Lazarus v. Comm.*, 513 F.2d 824 (9th Cir. 1975), aff'g 58 TC 854 (1972), acq. 1973-2 CB 2.

2. *Comm., v. Kann*, 174 F.2d 357 (3rd Cir. 1949); *Lloyd v. Comm.*, 33 BTA 905 (1936) acq., 1950-2 CB 3; *Est. of Bell v. Comm.*, 60 TC 469 (1973); *212 Corp. v. Comm.*, 70 TC 788 (1978).

3. Rev. Rul. 62-136, 1962-2 CB 12.

4. IRC Sec. 2033; *Fidelity-Philadelphia Trust Co. v. Smith*, 356 US 274 (1958).

5.   IRC Secs. 2039(a), 2039(b).

6.   IRC Sec. 72; Rev. Rul. 69-74, 1969-1 CB 43.

7.   *F. A. Gillespie & Sons Co. v. Comm.*, 154 F.2d 913 (10th Cir. 1946) (cert. den., reh. den.); *Steinbach Kresge Co. v. Sturgess*, 33 F. Supp. 897 (D.C., N.J., 1940).

8.   IRC Sec. 2512(b). To value an annuity, see Appendix B.

9.   Treas. Reg. §25.2503-3(c), Example (2); Rev. Rul. 70-514, 1970-2 CB 198; Let. Rul. 8811017.

10. IRC Sec. 2523(f)(6).

11. IRC Sec. 2033.

12. Rev. Rul. 55-119, 1955-1 CB 352.

13. Rev. Rul. 55-119, 1955-1 CB 352.

14. Rev. Rul. 55-119, 1955-1 CB 352.

15. *Lazarus v. Comm.*, 513 F.2d 824 (9th Cir. 1975).

16. IRC Sec. 2523(f)(6).

17. *LaFarge v. Comm.*, 689 F.2d 845 (9th Cir. 1982), aff'g in part and rev'g in part 73 TC 40 (1979); *Stern v. Comm.*, 84-2 USTC ¶9949 (9th Cir. 1984), rev'g and remanding 77 TC 614 (1981); *Est. of Fabric v. Comm.*, 83 TC 932 (1984).

18. See, for example, *Weigl v. Comm.*, 84 TC 1192 (1985).

19. *Stern v. Comm.*, 84-2 USTC ¶9949 (9th Cir. 1984), rev'g and remanding 77 TC 614 (1981).

20. *Est. of Fabric v. Comm.*, 83 TC 932 (1984); *Est. of Jennings* 10 TC 323 (1948).

21. *Est. of Fabric*, 83 TC 932 (1984).

22. *Est. of McLendon*, TC Memo 1993-459; Let. Rul. 9504004.

23. Treas. Reg. §20.7520-3(b)(3).

Chapter 37

INTEREST–FREE AND BELOW MARKET RATE LOANS

WHAT IS IT?

An interest-free or below market rate loan involves the lending of money to a party who is either not required to pay interest or who is required to pay a rate of interest below what is currently being charged in the marketplace.

Most interest-free (or below market rate) loans are made by a corporation to a nonshareholder employee or from a parent to a child or other family member. The economic advantage of an interest-free (or below market rate) loan lies in the borrower's ability to use either the funds or the interest from the funds.

There are few, if any, tax advantages to an interest-free or below market rate loan, due to the denial of all personal (consumer) interest deductions, and limitation of investment interest deductions to investment income. There are, however, many economic and other reasons that interest-free and below market rate loans are viable planning techniques.

WHEN IS THE USE OF SUCH A DEVICE INDICATED?

1. To reduce the estate of the lender to the extent the loan limits future growth in the value of assets and shifts economic wealth to the borrower.

2. As a corporate fringe benefit to enable an employee to purchase a home, provide for a child's college education, purchase stock of the employer-corporation, pay life insurance premiums, or pay medical bills.

3. Transfers of income through interest-free or below market rate loans can be used to support parents, provide support for children in school, or to help them purchase a home or business.

WHAT ARE THE REQUIREMENTS?

1. The transaction must constitute a bona fide debt (preferably in writing).

2. If the parties maintain books or records of account, the debt should be entered.

3. There should be a provision in the debt instrument (assuming a no-interest loan is desired) expressly precluding interest or, in the case of a below market rate loan, stating the interest to be charged.

In order to assure that a loan from a corporation to its employee is not construed as compensation income, the loan must conform to the following requirements:

1. The arrangement must constitute a bona fide debt (preferably a written note containing a reasonable repayment schedule or a note payable on demand).

2. A demonstrated intent to repay must be evidenced by an agreement between the parties. This is especially important where the loan is to a majority shareholder-employee. Otherwise, the IRS could claim that the "loan" is in fact a disguised dividend.

3. The amount of the loan must be reasonable in relation to the salary of the employee.

It is advisable to avoid situations where the corporation borrows money to make interest-free loans to shareholders. The IRS is likely to treat such a transaction as if the real loan was made between the lender and the shareholder. Following that reasoning, interest actually paid by the corporation to the lender could be treated as if the corporation paid a dividend to the shareholder who then paid interest to the lender. This attack is especially likely if the shareholder personally guaranteed the loan to the corporation.[1]

HOW IT IS DONE – EXAMPLES

Example 1: Your client, Maxine Grayboyes, is a key singer in the industrial productions corporation called, "Off Broad Street." To enable her daughter to purchase a new home, Maxine advances to her daughter, interest-free, $150,000.

Example 2: Terry Halpern is the owner of "Show Time," a magazine devoted to promoting show business and informing people who work for television, radio, theater groups, and other entertainment vehicles about news and current events. In order to promote a more favorable press image for herself Farrah Fawcelips lent Terry $4,000,000 at 2% interest for eight years. The best deal Terry could have gotten from a local bank would have been 6%.

While interest income will be imputed to the lender in each of these cases (see TAX IMPLICATIONS, below), the nontax advantages of the lender making the funds available to the borrower may be significant.

Example 3: Rich Marino is the President and one-third shareholder of the Bumpy Road Paving Company, Incorporated. Substantial interest-free loans were made by the corporation to him and his brothers, Larry and Tony, who are also shareholders. In order to make these loans, the Bumpy Road Paving Company had to carry interest-bearing obligations to third parties. In other words, suppliers to Bumpy Road Paving extended substantial amounts of credit. Rick, Larry, and Tony personally guaranteed these obligations. In this situation, the substance of the transaction is that Bumpy Road Paving is acting as the agent of the three individual taxpayers. It is as if Bumpy Road Paving, on behalf of Rick, Larry, and Tony, obtained loans and then paid interest to the creditors on behalf of the three shareholders. In essence, every time the Bumpy Road Paving Company paid interest, those payments (to the extent allocable to its interest-free loans to the shareholders) actually discharged the personal obligations of the shareholders. To the extent that these actual payments were, in fact, made, the taxpayers are deemed to have received dividend income and made an interest payment.[2]

WHAT ARE THE TAX IMPLICATIONS?

1. Loans with no interest or a below market rate of interest generally are recharacterized for tax purposes as loans bearing a market rate of interest accompanied by a payment or payments of interest from the lender to the borrower. These phantom payments (the difference between what should have been charged and what in fact was charged for the use of the money lent) are then subject to the general rules for interest deductions. Additionally, the phantom payment from the lender will be characterized as *compensation* from a business to an employee, as a *dividend* from the corporation to its shareholder, or as a *gift* from the shareholders of the corporation to the borrower or from a parent to a child. Such a gift may also be subject to the gift tax.

   Since personal interest is not deductible, interest-free or below market loans will often result in taxable income to the borrower, to the extent of the excess between what the borrower should be paying and what he, in fact, pays. Still, the interest-free or below market loan is appealing, not as a tax shifting device, but as an economically viable tool for accomplishing personal and business objectives.

2. Unless the transaction between a corporation and an employee (or an employee-shareholder) is a bona fide loan, the entire loan may be treated as additional salary or as a disguised dividend.

3. For a more detailed discussion of personal loans and tax issues, see QUESTIONS AND ANSWERS, below.

IMPLICATIONS AND ISSUES IN COMMUNITY PROPERTY STATES

As discussed in Chapter 22, relating to gifts (which should be reviewed in conjunction with this section), some states impose gift taxes on interspousal gifts. The following are some of the potential problem areas which might arise:

If the money lent is the separate property of one spouse (e.g., that spouse having inherited the funds) a gift can occur between the lending spouse if the demand note is made in favor of both spouses. The amount of the gift would be one-half of the value of the note (presumably the face amount of the note).

A similar gift may be found if the money lent is community property and the demand note received in exchange for the funds names only one spouse. It may be possible to show successfully that the named spouse was holding the note as trustee for the community and a gift avoided, but it creates the opportunity for the taxing authorities to claim that a gift was made and thus creates exposure to either gift tax, legal expense, or both, in dealing with the problem created.

Another unintended gift could occur if the money were lent to one spouse and then used to purchase assets in the names of both spouses.

An accidental gift may also result from the repayment of the loan. If the loan is made to one spouse and is used to make investments in the name of that spouse, the liability belongs entirely to that spouse. The use of community funds or the separate property of the non-borrowing spouse to repay the loan provides the basis for a taxable gift to be recognized.

If the note is called by the lender and the borrower does not have the funds to repay and his spouse or the community does, then a gift can be avoided by the borrower giving to the spouse (or the community) a note for the amount of funds used to repay his obligation.

These problems can be avoided by careful attention to the source of funds for loans and the manner in which investments or repayments are made.

QUESTIONS AND ANSWERS

Question – How can a loan to a key employee be structured in order to tie that employee into the business?

Answer – By making the loan callable upon separation from service or payable in the event of the employee's preretirement death, the corporation can protect its interest. The employee could protect his own estate by purchasing life insurance in the amount of the loan.

Question – How is "forgone interest" calculated?

Answer – Tax law creates a fiction; for income and gift tax purposes the tax law treats interest-free and below market loans as if a specified level of interest was charged and paid–even if it was not. In other words, interest is imputed on interest-free loans and on other below market rate loans. The amount subjected to gift and income taxation in most cases is the difference between (a) the "applicable federal rate" and (b) the interest actually payable (if any) under the agreement between the parties. This difference is the "forgone interest."[3]

Under this legal fiction, the borrower is treated as paying the forgone interest to the lender and therefore may take an income tax deduction for the "payment" (but only to the extent the borrower is

deemed to have investment income if the interest is considered investment interest; no deduction is allowed for personal interest). The lender will be treated as having received the forgone interest and therefore must report the income "received."

Question – What are the implications of a loan that is treated as a gift?

Answer – If a loan is considered a gift, the lender is treated as if he or she made a gift to the borrower in the amount of the "forgone interest." This gift may not qualify for the annual $11,000 (in 2004) gift exclusion. (See the discussion of term and demand loans below.)

Question – What are the implications if a loan is not a gift?

Answer – The tax characterization of a loan which is not a gift depends on the relationship between the parties. In any case, the IRS will treat the lender as having made a transfer to the borrower in the amount of the "forgone interest."

The Service will generally treat forgone interest as a dividend when the borrower is solely a shareholder (nondeductible by the corporation, taxable to the shareholder (although maybe at preferred rates), as interest paid by the shareholder, and taxable to the corporation as interest income).

If the borrower is solely an employee, the lender will have interest income to the extent of the forgone interest and a corresponding deduction for compensation paid (if reasonable). The borrower will have compensation income, but a deduction for the forgone interest may be denied or limited (see paragraph 1 under "WHAT ARE THE TAX IMPLICATIONS," above).

Question – How will interest-free or below market rate loans to shareholder-employees be treated?

Answer – The forgone interest will generally be treated as a dividend.

Question – How is the taxable amount computed?

Answer – That depends on two factors: (1) Is gift tax or income tax involved (or both)? (2) Is the loan a demand loan or a term loan (including loans with indefinite maturities)?

Demand loans are loans payable in full at any time on the demand of the lender. The amount subject to (both gift and income) tax is the "forgone interest." This forgone interest is measured by the applicable statutory rate specified during each calendar year the loan remains outstanding. This means that from year to year the rate will change. It also means that the interest income is reportable one year at a time.

A term loan is defined as any loan which is not a demand loan. The treatment of these loans depends on whether the loan is a "gift loan" or not. A gift loan is a below market loan where the lender intends to make a gift to the borrower in the amount of the forgone interest.

How much interest is forgone in the case of a term loan? Essentially, the foregone interest amount is the present value of the interest that should have been charged, minus the amount from the present value of the interest that was, in fact, charged. The difference is the taxable amount. In calculating present values, the statutory discount rate applicable at the time the loan is made must be used.

If the term loan is not a gift loan (for example, when it is "compensation-related," that is, a loan between an employer and an employee or between an independent contractor and the person for whom he performs services), the taxable amount is the present value of the forgone interest for the entire term of the loan. The borrower is deemed to be paying that interest while the lender is deemed to be receiving the interest and is therefore taxed on it. Taxation in the case of a non-gift term loan is at a level rate for each year of the loan.[4] (Withholding is not required by an employer on the deemed payment made to an employee arising from a demand or term loan.)

If the term loan is a gift loan, the amount subject to taxation is determined in the same way as a non-gift loan. But for gift tax purposes, the entire present value of forgone interest is subject to gift tax in the year of the loan. For income tax purposes, each year's forgone interest is taxed on a year by year basis.

If the loan is a term loan, the statutory interest rate affixed to the forgone interest amount will be the applicable federal rate in effect as of the day the loan was made. With respect to a demand loan, the interest rate will change each year as the applicable federal rates change.

Question – Are there transactions that will be treated as interest-free or below market rate loans even though they appear to be something else?

Answer – Yes. Congress was concerned with all transactions that in effect were tax avoidance or significant tax-shifting schemes. Therefore, many situations which do not look like loans will invoke the below market rules. For example, assume a local country club requires its members to pay a refundable, non-interest-bearing deposit as part of their membership fee. In essence, the member is paying part of the fee with the income that the club earns on the deposit. The IRS could easily apply the rules described above.

Question – Are there any exceptions or limitations to the interest-free and below market rate loan rules?

Answer – There are a number of important exceptions:

(1) A loan made from one individual to another, from a corporation to an employee or independent contractor, or from a corporation to a shareholder is exempt from both gift and income tax rules described above if the outstanding balance on the total of all loans made to that person from the lender does not exceed $10,000. This is known as the "$10,000 and under de minimus rule."[5]

This protection will not apply if the loan is a gift loan and the loan proceeds are used in connection with income producing property. Furthermore, for term loans that are not gift loans, once the outstanding balance exceeds $10,000, the exception no longer applies, even if the outstanding balance is later reduced below $10,000.[6] Finally, if the loan is a "compensation-related" loan or a "corporate-shareholder" loan (any loan between a corporation and any shareholder), the protection will not apply if federal tax avoidance is a principal purpose for the loan.

(2) The second exception to the general rules governing interest-free and below market rate loans is the "$100,000 and under" rule. This rule provides that where gift loans are made directly between individuals and the outstanding balances due on the aggregate of the loans made to that person by the lender do not exceed $100,000, the law limits the amount of the "forgone" interest.

The limit is the lower of (a) the statutory rate or (b) the borrower's net investment income for the year. If the borrower does not earn more than $1,000 in the year, the law treats the parties as if there were no forgone interest.

The $100,000 and under rule applies only if federal tax avoidance is not a principal purpose of the loan.[7]

(3) The third exception to the general rules governing interest-free and below market rate loans is for any below market loan made by a lender to a qualified continuing care facility pursuant to a continuing care contract if the lender (or his spouse) attains age 65 before the close of such year. This exception applies to the extent that the aggregate amount of the loan, added to the aggregate outstanding amount of all other previous loans between the lender (or his spouse) and any qualified continuing care facility, does not exceed a specified amount, which is indexed for inflation. As it appears in the statute, the amount is $90,000; in 2004, the amount is $154,500 as indexed.[8]

ASRS: Sec. 53, ¶20.3(a); Sec. 55, ¶57.5(b); Sec. 63, ¶150

CHAPTER ENDNOTES

1. *Creel v. Comm.*, 72 TC 1173 (1979).

2. *Creel v. Comm.*, above 72 TC 1173 (1979). For other cases on interest-free loans see *Saunders v. U.S.*, 294 F. Supp. 1276, 1282, (D. Hawaii 1968), *rev'd on other grounds*, 450 F.2d 1047 (9th Cir. 1971); *Joseph Lupowitz Sons, Inc. v. Comm.*, 497 F.2d 862 (3rd Cir. 1974); *Lisle v. Comm.*, TC Memo 1976-140; *Suttle v. Comm.*, TC Memo 1978-393; *Zager v. Comm.*, 72 TC 1009 (1979), *aff'd*, 649 F.2d 1133 (5th Cir. 1981); *Martin v. Comm.*, TC Memo 1979-469; *Williams v. Comm.*, TC Memo 1978-306; *Dolese v. U.S.*, 79-2 USTC ¶9540 (10th Cir. 1979).

3. IRC Sec. 7872(e).

4. IRC Secs. 7872(b)(2), 1272(a)(1).

5. IRC Sec. 7872(c)(2),(3); Prop. Reg. §1.7872-8(b)(3).

6. IRC Sec. 7872(f)(10).

7. IRC Sec. 7872(d)(1).

8. IRC Sec. 7872(g)(1),(2); Rev. Rul. 2003-118, 2003-47 IRB 1095.

Chapter 38

SPLIT INTEREST PURCHASE OF PROPERTY (Split)

WHAT IS IT?

A "Split" is an arrangement under which two parties agree to purchase an asset. One party (usually a parent) purchases a life estate (the right to receive the income from the property or the right to use, possess, and enjoy the property itself for as long as the life tenant lives). The second party (usually a son or daughter or grandchild of the life tenant) purchases a remainder interest (the right to the property, whatever it is worth, when the first party's interest terminates. If the first party purchased a life interest, by definition his interest terminates when he dies). Each party to the Split pays the actuarial value of the interest purchased.

The adoption of IRC Section 2702 has considerably reduced and limited the attractiveness of Splits between related persons. However, Splits between unrelated persons are not subject to Section 2702.

WHEN IS THE USE OF SUCH A DEVICE INDICATED?

1. When a client would like to improve current income. If a Split is used to purchase income producing investment property, the client's income is enhanced by the return provided on the remainder person's investment.

2. When it is important to keep property within a family, but the client wants to enjoy it or needs to use it or receive its income for life, a Split may be strong protection against a will contest or an election against the will. Split property passes by contract and should not be part of the probate estate. So generally a disgruntled heir would have no right to property purchased through a Split. Likewise, a Split offers protection against the claims of a client's creditors and, because it does not pass through probate, it affords the parties privacy.

3. When it is desirable to avoid ancillary administration, the Split is useful since at the termination of the first party's interest, the remainder person automatically by contract becomes full and complete owner of the property. This means the cost of multiple state probates is avoided.

4. Splits are indicated where federal gift and estate taxes are not a major consideration or will be of relatively minor importance in the overall plan. In some limited circumstances, there may still be some transfer tax advantages using a Split.

5. When the parties are unrelated (as defined in IRC Section 2702). For example, an unmarried couple should be able to create a Split that is not subject to Section 2702.

WHAT ARE THE REQUIREMENTS?

Ownership of the property is bifurcated into two parts: a "term" interest, which may be either the right to receive stipulated payments from the property for a term of years, or life, or in a very limited situation, the right to use the property for that period. The second part is the "remainder" interest, which will pass to the other joint owner when the term interest expires.

Both the term holder and the remainder holder pay their proportionate part of the purchase price for the property based on government valuation tables setting an actuarial value for the term interest and the remainder interest. It is essential that the purchaser of the term interest furnish no part of the consideration for the purchase of the remainder interest.[1]

Because the term holder and remainder holder are co-owners of the property, it cannot be sold without the consent of both parties. Because, under most circumstances, the term holder is limited to a fixed dollar payment from the property, the term holder will apparently have no other rights in it. In the limited situations where the term holder can retain full possession and enjoyment of the property for the term, the term holder should have all of the legal rights of a joint tenant in the property. The exact nature of the rights of the term holder and the remainder holder is dependent on state law.

HOW IT IS DONE–AN EXAMPLE

An about-to-be-separated 50 year old father wishes to invest in a painting or in some unimproved real estate. He wants his daughter to receive the painting or unimproved real estate at his death. He has used none of his annual exclusion or unified credit. He wants to begin to shift wealth to his daughter who is a financially successful women's clothing designer. If he purchases the painting or unimproved real estate in his own name, he knows that it could be lost in litigation with his wife. He expects the painting or unimproved real estate to appreciate considerably each year.

The father purchases a life estate (or term interest) in the painting or unimproved real estate. He must pay an amount equal to the present value of what the painting or unimproved real estate could be rented for over his lifetime (or term interest). The daughter pays the balance using her own money. The daughter receives the appreciated property when her father dies (or at the end of the term interest). Comparable rental values may be extremely difficult to obtain; failure to do so could lead to adverse gift tax results.

Alternatively, the father could purchase property with his daughter and retain an annuity or unitrust interest in the property for life (or for a term). The daughter would receive the hopefully appreciated property when her father dies (or at the end of the term interest). The father would pay the actuarial value of his annuity or unitrust interest and his daughter would pay the actuarial value of her remainder interest based upon government valuation tables.

WHAT ARE THE TAX IMPLICATIONS?

Section 2702

For federal gift tax purposes, joint purchases of property by related parties are treated as transfers to a trust under the provisions of IRC Section 2702 (discussed in more detail in Chapter 26), and the person or persons who acquire term interests in the property in a transaction or series of transactions shall be treated as having acquired the entire property and then having transferred the other interests to the other persons in exchange for any consideration provided by such other persons.[2] Any term interest in property, such as a life estate or term of years, but not co-ownership, such as tenancy in common or joint tenancy, is treated as if held in trust under Section 2702.[3] A leasehold is not a term interest if for full and adequate consideration where a good faith attempt is made to determine fair rental value.[4]

In the case of a joint purchase, the amount considered transferred by an individual to family members for this purpose shall not exceed the actual consideration furnished by that individual for the property.[5]

As a result of the limitations imposed on the joint purchase under Section 2702, the technique will have disastrous gift tax consequences if the term holder purchases an income interest in the property. Under Section 2702, that income interest is valued at zero for federal gift tax purposes. The term holder will be treated as if he made a gift to the remainder person, equal to the fair market value of the property less the actual consideration paid by the remainder person for the remainder interest. However, the amount of the gift is limited to the actual consideration paid by the term holder.

Retained Annuity or Unitrust Interests

The unfortunate results just described can be avoided if, instead of retaining the income for the term, the term holder retains a fixed annuity payment or percentage payments based on the annual valuation of the property under the same conditions described in Chapter 26 for GRATs and GRUTs, which are devices that serve as exceptions to the rules under Section 2702. If the consideration paid by the term holder is exactly equal to the actuarial value of the annuity or unitrust payments, there would be no taxable gift of the remainder, because the value of the annuity or unitrust payments would be subtracted in arriving at the taxable gift, as would the consideration paid by the remainder person.

The Tangible Property Exception

Section 2702 does preserve the traditional form of Split in certain limited circumstances. The nonexercise of rights under a term interest in tangible property, such as a painting or unimproved real property which does not have a substantial effect on the value of the remainder interest, is not valued at zero, but at the amount a third party would pay for the term interest (e.g., the right to possess the painting for life).[6] This means that it is possible to arrange for the split purchase of a work of art, or unimproved real estate, with the term holder acquiring the right to use the property for the term, or life, and the remainder to someone else.

However the valuation of a term interest in tangible property is valued under a willing buyer-willing seller test, not under actuarial tables.[7] This means that to avoid a taxable gift, the term holder would have to prove that what he paid for the term interest in the tangible property is the same as what an unrelated person would pay for the same interest in an arm's length transaction. The difficulties of proving this are tremendous. Comparable sales or rentals are given greater weight in valuation than appraisals in most cases.

The tangible property exception rule applies to property for which no allowance for depreciation or depletion would be allowable, and as to which the failure to exercise any rights with respect to the property will not affect its value. There is a de minimis rule for depreciation of certain improvements.

A conversion of the term interest into some other property right (other than a qualified annuity trust) is treated as a gift transfer of the retained term interest determined at the date of original transfer. Any alteration or improvement of the property that so alters its character that it would not qualify under this rule is treated as a conversion of the property under this rule. If the property is converted, it is possible to switch to a qualified annuity trust described in Chapter 26.

Planning Implications

While the pros and cons of grantor retained interest transfers generally apply here, there is an important difference. Section 2702 is a gift tax provision, and should not apply in determining whether or not the joint purchase has estate tax consequences. If the term holder pays full and adequate consideration for the term interest, whether it be in the form of an annuity or unitrust payment, or the use of qualified tangible property, then the death of the term holder should have no federal estate tax consequences. Unlike a GRIT, GRAT, or GRUT, the term can be for the life of the term holder. The retained interest should not result in inclusion of the value of the property in the term holder's estate because the term holder did not "transfer" the remainder interest, and IRC Section 2036(a), which applies to transfers in which the transferor retains income or other interests for life, should not be applicable (but see "QUESTIONS AND ANSWERS," below). The joint acquisition of income producing property could be a very useful technique for certain clients.

ISSUES AND IMPLICATIONS IN COMMUNITY PROPERTY STATES

The situation here is analogous to the transfer of community property to a grantor retained annuity trust or unitrust discussed in Chapter 26. If community funds are used to purchase the term interest, presumably the retained interest will either be paid jointly to the transferors or each will receive one-half of the required payment for the term.

QUESTIONS AND ANSWERS

Question – Can a personal residence trust and joint purchase be combined?

Answer – The personal residence trust and qualified personal residence trust, or QPRT, are discussed in Chapter 26. Many commentators have suggested that a personal residence could be acquired through a joint purchase, and then placed in a personal residence trust.

Under a typical scenario, parent and children would locate residential property which parent wishes to occupy as a personal residence for a term of years. Parent would purchase the term interest in the property, paying full fair market value based upon the actuarial value of a term interest, and the children would purchase the remainder interest, also paying full fair market value but based upon the actuarial value of a remainder interest. Under the joint purchase rule of IRC Section 2702, the effect would be a gift from parent to children, because the term interest would be valued at zero for federal gift tax purposes.

However, if the residence is purchased via a joint purchase trust agreement containing the requirements of a personal residence trust, it can be argued that under the statutory exception described above,[8] the full value of the term interest would be an offset for federal gift tax purposes, and the result is no taxable gift. Further, if the parent dies during the term, it can also be argued that there was no retained interest in the residence which would result in its inclusion in the parent's taxable estate under IRC Section 2036(a), arguing that that section cannot apply since the parent paid "full and adequate consideration" for the value of the term interest.

If the transaction is not structured and maintained properly, however, the entire value of the property could be included in the estate of the term holder. In a letter ruling, the IRS brought the entire property back into the estate of the term holder because the term holder furnished all the consideration with which the remainder holder purchased his interest.[9]

Also, if a jointly purchased property is sold and the joint purchase trust is converted to a GRAT, the IRS may bring the value of the property back into the grantor's estate under IRC Section 2039. In Letter Ruling 9412036, the parties unsuccessfully attempted to create a split-purchase grantor retained unitrust that would provide one parent a unitrust for life followed by a unitrust for the other parent for life. In purchasing property to be held in trust, the parents would pay the part of the purchase price equal to their actuarial interests in the trust. There would also be a right of first refusal should any of the interest holders seek to sell their interests. The trust failed to contain required provisions relating to commutation of interests and adjustments for incorrect valuations, so it did not qualify under IRC Section 2702.

However, the ruling went even further and held that the property would be includable in a parent's estate under either IRC Sections 2036 or 2039. Under Section 2036, the amount includable would be equal to the lesser of (1) the original value of the parent's transferred share of property held in the trust reduced by the original value of the income interest attributable to transfers to the trust by others, or (2) an amount which would yield the unitrust payment at the parent's death. Under Section 2039, a parent's estate would include that portion of the date of death value of the property that is proportionate to the decedent's share of all trust contributions.

Question – Should the split-purchase technique be completely abandoned?

Answer – In the right situations, the joint or split purchase may still be very useful. Unlike the GRAT or GRUT, the gift in this case is limited to what the term holder pays for the life or term interest, not the entire value of the property. Therefore, even if the term holder retains an income interest valued at zero under the statute, the gift will still be limited to the actuarial value of the income interest (assuming that is what the term holder pays for the term interest), not 100% of the value of the property, as in the case of a GRIT. In other cases, there could be no gift at all.

If the term holder pays full fair market value for the income interest, annuity interest, or unitrust interest, there should be nothing to include in the term holder's estate at death under IRC Section 2036(a), because the term holder never transferred an interest for federal estate tax purposes. However, as noted above, if the transaction is not properly structured, the IRS will apparently take the opposite position on this issue.

CHAPTER ENDNOTES

1. TAM 9206006.
2. IRC Sec. 2702(c)(2).
3. Treas. Reg. §25.2702-4(a).
4. Treas. Reg. §25.2702-4(b).
5. Treas. Reg. §25.2702-4(c).
6. IRC Sec. 2702(c)(4).
7. Treas. Reg. §25.2702-2(c).
8. IRC Sec. 2702(a)(3)(A)(ii).
9. TAM 9206006.

Chapter 39

SALE (GIFT) – LEASEBACK

WHAT IS IT?

A sale-leaseback involves one party selling property (or in the case of a gift-leaseback, giving property) to another party and then leasing back the same property. This type of transaction is usually intended to secure one or more of a number of income and/or estate tax advantages.

WHEN IS THE USE OF SUCH A DEVICE INDICATED?

1. When a client's problem is cash flow; his corporation is "rich" in assets, but is "poor" in cash. The sale of a selected corporate asset and the immediate leaseback of that asset can generate cash without a loss of the use of that asset.

2. When a client earns a large amount of income and is, therefore, in a high income tax bracket. He wants to divert highly taxed income to a member of his family in a lower tax bracket. The hoped-for result is the netting of more after-tax income within the family unit.

3. When a client owns property that is rapidly appreciating and would like to save estate taxes on that future growth.

4. When a client would like to find an alternative to financing business property through a mortgage. Sale-leasebacks have been called "off balance sheet" financing because the lease obligation will often appear as a footnote on the balance sheet rather than as a liability. This should have the effect of increasing his credit standing and ability to borrow money.

WHAT ARE THE REQUIREMENTS?

1. The transaction must have validity to avoid litigation and conflict with the Internal Revenue Service. There must actually be a completed and irrevocable sale (or gift) and a legally enforceable lease agreement.

2. In the case of a sale, the transaction must represent a necessary business operation and not one designed solely and merely to shift income tax responsibility.

3. The terms of the transaction, and especially the amount of the lease payment, must be arrived at in an arm's length, bona fide manner. Any rent or lease amount should be reasonable.

4. If a trustee is involved, the trustee should, in fact, be independent from the grantor of the trust. When the term of the trust is over, trust corpus should not return to the grantor.

5. Under the kiddie tax rules (see Chapter 22), to successfully shift taxation to the bracket of a child, that child must be age 14 or over.

   The following factors should be considered: (a) Are the lease provisions, especially payments, strictly observed? (b) Does the lessee pay the entire amount of the promised rent? (c) Is the rent reasonable? (d) Was the sale price equivalent to the fair market value of the property?[1]

   A positive answer to these questions is necessary for a successful shift of income tax burdens and the attainment of a rental deduction by the lessee.

   If a trust is used, these questions should be asked: (a) Is the trust temporary? (b) Will the property revert to the grantor at the end of a given period (reversionary interest trust)? (c) Is the trust or trustee controlled by the grantor?[2]

   A positive answer to any of these questions will result in taxation of income to the grantor.

   The danger factors noted above are particularly important where the transactions are between related parties such as (1) a corporation and its stockholders; (2) husbands and wives; (3) parents and children; (4) grantors using relatives as trustees to create benefits for dependents; (5) affiliated corporations with common stockholders; and (6) taxpayers and foundations created by them.

HOW IT IS DONE – EXAMPLES

Your client, Dennis Raihall, is the president of the Son Ray Corporation. He explains to you that the business is in need of cash. It is on the verge of a break-through in its production process that could double corporate earnings, but it needs money to pay for expensive retooling.

The corporation has a number of valuable assets. One of these assets is selected and sold to the LeClair Corporation. The LeClair Corporation pays Son Ray Corporation the fair market value of the asset and now owns it. Since Son Ray Corporation still needs the asset in its business, it arranges to lease it back from the LeClair Corporation for a reasonable rental price. (It is important that the shareholders of the two corporations are not the same individuals.)

There are a number of types of assets the Son Ray Corporation could have sold: trucks, cars, machinery, equipment, fixtures, office buildings, apartment houses, and other types of real property. Furthermore, professional equipment such as computers, X-ray machines, etc., are all possibilities. (CAVEAT: Beware of depreciation and investment credit recapture on the sale. Note that gain is both realized and recognized on the corporate level if an appreciated asset is sold.[3]) It is important to make certain that the proposed sale-leaseback is not prohibited by a loan agreement with the firm's bank.

The after-tax proceeds of the sale will give the Son Ray Corporation additional cash and increase its working capital. Assets continue in operation just as they did before the sale. The basic difference is that instead of Son Ray carrying that particular item on its books as an asset, it now leases the property and pays rent for its use. Son Ray will now have the use of a large sum of cash, the after tax proceeds of the sale, which can be used to generate additional profits.

Suppose that Son Ray Corporation owned a factory it built more than 10 years ago at a cost of $200,000. The market value of the property is currently $250,000 (land $50,000, building, $200,000). The Son Ray Corporation has decided not to mortgage the property because the rate of interest it would have to pay is very high, it would not be able to write off payments of principal, and it feels that it could obtain more cash through a sale. Another reason it chose not to mortgage the property was that such a debt would adversely affect its credit standing and ability to borrow additional funds.

The property could be sold for $250,000 and leased back for 10 years with additional options at an annual rental of $30,000. Only the profit on the sale (net proceeds less adjusted basis) would be subject to tax. If an accelerated method of depreciation had been used, deductions taken in prior years may have to be recaptured and reported as additional income received on the sale. Son Ray Corporation now has the balance of the after tax sale proceeds to develop the process that may double overall corporate earnings. Also, the rent paid to the buyer will be a tax deductible expense (with a greater deduction than prior depreciation amounts).

Another way the leaseback arrangement is often utilized is in intrafamily transfers. For example, a client, Mary Jo Kopeznsky, a highly compensated physician, complains about the high income tax burden she faces every year. She wants to know how she can maximize her family income by minimizing her overall tax burden.

She could transfer (as a gift) business property she owns (such as expensive medical equipment or a professional office building she owns and shares with a number of other professionals) to an irrevocable inter vivos trust established for her 14 year old daughter. The trustee could be a bank or other independent fiduciary. The trust, at a reasonable rental, leases the building back to Doctor Kopeznsky. This means the doctor does not have to move out of her building or lose the use of her equipment. Her daughter is immediately benefited. It is extremely important that there be no preconceived agreement with the trustee as to the amount of rental to be paid or the terms of the lease.

The trust could either distribute the rental income each year to the doctor's daughter or accumulate it for later distribution to her. For example, when her daughter reaches age 18 (and in many states is no longer a minor), trust income or principal might be distributed each year and paid outright and unconditionally to the daughter. If the daughter chose to, she could use the money to pay for her own college education. If, under the applicable state law a parent is not obligated to provide a college education for an adult child, none of the income will be taxable to the high tax bracket mother, even if it is paid directly to the daughter's college. Moreover, the property would be owned outside the reach of the doctor's creditors, an additional benefit.

WHAT ARE THE TAX IMPLICATIONS?

1. In the case of a sale and leaseback, the corporation that sells an asset must pay tax on any gain realized just as in the case of any other sale. Likewise, just as any partnership or corporation that rents property

is allowed to take a tax deduction for the cost of the rental, when a sale-leaseback occurs, the fair rental paid by the seller for the use of its previously owned property is completely deductible as an ordinary and necessary business expense.[4]

2. In the case of a gift-leaseback, proper care will enable the donor to receive a double benefit. First, the donor will obtain a business tax deduction for payments of rent. Then, when the rental income is paid to the trust (assuming it is a nongrantor trust), it will generally be taxed to the trust (as long as it is accumulated) or to the donor's child or other trust beneficiary.[5] Ordinarily, the tax bracket of the beneficiary or the trust will be lower than the donor's. The tax savings can provide an excellent means of establishing a college education fund. When income is paid to a minor below age 14, the child will be taxed, but at the parent's top bracket, to the extent the payment exceeds $1,600 (as indexed for 2004). Therefore, a recipient child must be 14 or older for the income shift to work.

3. By making an irrevocable gift of an asset (except life insurance transferred by the insured within three years of death), future growth is removed from the client's estate at no additional estate tax cost.

4. There may be gift tax implications if there is an outright gift or if the sales price is less than the property's fair market value.

5. Cost recovery and interest deductions may offset a significant portion of the income from the lease. The lessee will be able to completely deduct the lease payments as an ordinary and necessary business expense. In the case of a sale-leaseback, the lessee would have to report interest income. If the lessee-user acquires the property and subsequently disposes of it, he will be subject to the recapture rules relating to cost recovery deductions, just as if he had been the owner of the property all along.

6. Where the property is sold to family members, and the installment payments are closely geared to the rental paid by the seller under the leaseback, the IRS will contend, and the courts will probably agree, that this is really a transfer with a retained life estate under IRC section 2036(a). This will certainly be the case where the lease is in effect for life. See *Est. of Maxwell*,[6] where a mother sold the property to a son on an installment sale, then forgave the payments on the sales price except the interest on the installment note, which was almost exactly the same as the rent she paid. She was in her 80s and had cancer

when she sold the property. Although the property here was a personal residence, the same rationale could extend to business assets.

IMPLICATIONS AND ISSUES IN COMMUNITY PROPERTY STATES

With respect to the sale-leaseback, two aspects are present. Initially, if the sale price is later found to be less than what was the then fair market value, the amount of the gift (undervaluation) is spread between both spouses if the asset was community property. However, some states' gift taxes have a much lower threshold than federal gift taxes, as to current cash tax payments, and consideration may be given to filing, in the year of the sale-leaseback, a gift tax return based on some other gift, thus possibly starting any statute of limitation periods to begin to run as to any subsequent imposition of a gift tax deficiency, including interest and penalties. The filing of a federal gift tax return should be considered to start the running of the statute of limitations if the risk of an audit is not significant.

The second concern is making sure that valid legal title has passed. The California statutory scheme, for example, grants the right to the management and control of community property to either spouse, with certain exceptions. With respect to the lease, mortgage, or transfer of real property, both spouses must join in executing the conveying instrument, and practitioners should obtain both signatures for any transfer (including the gift) of any asset.

QUESTIONS AND ANSWERS

Question – In the case of a gift-leaseback, what are the basic prerequisites?

Answer – Where a donor transfers an office building or other income producing assets to a trust for a child and then leases it back:

(1) The donor cannot retain substantially the same control over the property as he or she did before the gift was made.

(2) The leaseback must be in writing and must provide for a reasonable rental (get an appraisal).

(3) The leaseback, as distinguished from the gift in trust, must have a bona fide business purpose.[7]

(4) The trust must have an independent trustee unrelated to the grantor.[8]

(5) Title to the property should be in the trust or the child and should be recorded.

Question – What does the Internal Revenue Service look at in the case of sale-leaseback between related parties?

Answer – Basically, the Internal Revenue Service is trying to determine whether the transaction is genuine or merely structured as a sale. If the transaction is, in reality, a disguised loan, at best only part of the "rental" payments will be deductible because they will be considered payments of interest and principal. Only the interest portion can be taken as a tax deduction.[9] Assuming the interest is considered "investment interest," it will be deductible, but only to the extent the taxpayer has investment income. Interest will be deductible without limit if it is considered "business interest." The characterization will be determined case by case, based on the facts and circumstances.

Alternatively, if the transaction is considered a sale, the seller-lessee has to pay a tax on any gain realized and recapture accelerated depreciation. If the property is leased for business purposes, he will be able to deduct his payment under the lease as rent.

The buyer-lessor also would be concerned with the distinction. In the case of a bona fide sale, the buyer-lessor may take depreciation or cost recovery deductions to the extent of the portion of the purchase price that is allocable to buildings or improvements and be entitled to a deduction for all expenses relating to the maintenance and operation of the property.[10] However, if the Internal Revenue Service treats the transaction as a loan, the buyer will not be entitled to these deductions. This is because the buyer will be considered as a mere mortgagee rather than as owner of the property.

If the transaction is considered a sale, the next question is whether or not the sale price is equal to the fair market value of the property. If the sale price is less than the fair market value of the property transferred, the difference may be considered a gift. This may result in a gift tax being imposed on the seller-lessee.

An adjustment clause might be used to require an additional payment to the seller if the IRS revalues the property at a higher price. However, it is questionable whether an adjustment clause can be used to avoid gift tax.

Question – How can the transaction be structured to minimize an Internal Revenue Service challenge that the arrangement is in reality a loan?

Answer – If possible, the transaction should be structured so that it falls within the following safe harbor: (1) the lessor must be a corporation other than an S corporation, (2) the lessor must have a minimum "at risk" investment of 10% of the adjusted basis of the property at all times, (3) the term of the lease, including extensions, must not exceed certain limits, (4) the property must be leased within three months of its acquisition or, in the case of a sale-leaseback, it must be purchased by the lessor within three months of the lessee's acquisition for a price not in excess of the adjusted basis of the property in the hands of the lessee.

If the safe harbor test cannot be utilized, then the transaction should have economic reality. In this regard, all the significant burdens and benefits of ownership should be transferred to the new owner. The parties should assume their obligations as lessee and lessor, respectively. The sale price of the property should be fair and reasonable in light of current market conditions and sales of comparable properties. Financial arrangements must be reasonable. The IRS has indicated it will litigate two party gift and leaseback cases (i.e., the lessee is the donor, or an S corporation or partnership).

The transaction should not force a "buy-back." If there is a compulsory repurchase option, the seller is in virtually the same position he would have been in had he mortgaged the property rather than selling it and leasing it back. If a buy-back provision is included, the terms must be arranged and the amount of the purchase price computed as a result of arm's length bargaining. (For related parties, consider IRC section 2703.)

The buyer must receive the benefit of any appreciation in value. A final factor generally examined is the application of rent toward the repurchase price. The rental price paid by the lessee should be realistic. It should closely approximate rentals for comparable property and comparable facilities. If part of the rent is to be applied to a repurchase price, the Internal Revenue Service might claim that such payments are in reality disguised payments of interest rather than payments for the use of the property.[11]

Question – What is the primary economic disadvantage to funding through a sale-leaseback rather than a mortgage?

Answer – The primary drawback to funding through a sale-leaseback is the loss of the residual value of the property at the termination of the lease. This drawback can be minimized through a repurchase option or option(s) to renew the lease over the expected life of the property.

Question – What terms should be specified in the lease that may help sustain an equal bargaining position between the donor and the trustee?

Answer – The following should be helpful:

A. Set rent at current market rates (obtain at least one outside appraisal expert's opinion).

B. Provide for a single year lease term that must be renegotiated each year.

C. Place the property on the open market for lease (the higher the rental the grantor actually pays, the greater the overall tax shift). Note, however, that to the extent rents are deemed "excessive," they might be disallowed as deductions.

D. Provide that lease payments are made "as a condition to the continued use or possession of the premises."

E. Trustee should establish–and strictly enforce–a payment schedule. (Where payments were made randomly, in different amounts, at the client's convenience, and not according to a schedule determined by the trustee, it was held that the grantor failed to relinquish total control over trust property.)

Question – In what situations will the grantor be taxed on trust income?

Answer – The grantor will be taxed on trust income:

1. if he or his spouse has retained a reversionary interest;

2. if he or his spouse retains power to control beneficial enjoyment;

3. if he or his spouse retains certain administrative powers;

4. if he or his spouse retains the power to revoke the trust;

5. if the income is used to pay support and maintenance to a person whom the grantor or his spouse is legally obligated to support;

6. if the income can be distributed or accumulated to the grantor or his spouse without the approval of an adverse party.

Note that avoiding these situations does not per se assure a rental deduction. These situations concern only the issue of "Is there a valid trust?" and "To whom is the income taxable?" Although the two issues are concurrently operative, they are treated by the IRS as mutually exclusive.

One possible solution is to have someone other than the client or his spouse fund the trust. For instance, the client's parents could put cash into an irrevocable trust for the client's children. A loan to the trust from relatives or a third party, such as a bank, could be used to fund the purchase. The trust could use that cash to purchase assets owned solely by the client in his own name. The trust could then lease the assets to the client's corporation.

Question – What are the best types of property to use in a gift-leaseback?

Answer – The best types of property are *tangible* assets used in the client's trade, business, or profession, such as: land, depreciated buildings (beware of recapture), office equipment (such as computers, word processors, photocopiers), library, trucks and machinery, and other tangibles and office accoutrements needed in business.

Question – Will *cash* work in a gift-leaseback?

Answer – A client *could* fund the trust with cash. The trustee could then acquire new equipment and lease it to the grantor or the grantor's corporation or purchase equipment from the grantor and then lease it back. (Note that some authorities feel the "transfer of cash" method is more vulnerable to IRS attack than the "transfer of property" method where the cash is used to buy property already owned by the grantor.)

Question – Is geographical location of the taxpayer a consideration in planning a transfer and leaseback arrangement?

Answer – It is with respect to your client's chances of prevailing in litigation with the IRS. The chart at Figure 39.1, "Your Odds in the Circuits," lets you see at a glance where the outlook is favorable, unfavorable, or chancy.

ASRS: Sec. 51, ¶220.

CHAPTER ENDNOTES

1. See Rev. Rul. 55-540, 1955-2 CB 39; Rev. Proc. 75-21, 1975-1 CB 715, as modified by Rev. Proc. 79-48, 1979-2 CB 529; *Est. of Franklin*, 64 TC 752 (1975); *Narver v. Comm.*, 76 TC 53 (1980); *Hager v. Comm.*, 76 TC 759 (1981).

2. See *Oakes v. Comm.*, 44 TC 524 (1965); *Audano v. U.S.*, 428 F.2d 251 (5th Cir., 1970).

3. IRC Secs. 1245, 1250.

4. IRC Sec. 162. Can a sale-leaseback result in a deductible loss? Yes, says the Tax Court, if there is a bona fide sale and not an exchange of like-kind property. But, in the favorable case of *Leslie, Co. v. Comm.*, 64 TC 247 (1975), the IRS has non-acquiesced. Nonacq. 1978-2 CB 1.

5. IRC Secs. 641, 652, 662.

6. 3 F.3d 591 (2nd Cir. 1993), aff'g 98 TC 584 (1992).

7. *Van Zandt v. Comm.*, 341 F.2d 440 (5th Cir. 1965) aff'g. 40 TC 824, cert. den. 382 U.S. 814.

8. *Oakes v. Comm.*, 44 TC 524 (1965).

9. See Rev. Rul. 55-540, 1955-2 CB 39. In *Serbousek v. Comm.*, TC Memo 1977-105, the Tax Court allowed a rent deduction on a gift-leaseback of a medical building. In that case a taxpayer (1) gave up all beneficial control over the property; (2) paid a reasonable rent; (3) had a business purpose for the lease (he needed the building for his practice); and (4) retained no equity in the property during the lease period. See also *Lerner v. Comm.*, 71 TC 290 (1978), acq. in result 1984-1 CB 1. *May v. Comm.*, 76 TC 7 (1981).

   For an example of how *not* to arrange a gift-leaseback, see *Frank Lyon Co. v. U.S.*, 38 AFTR 2d 76-5019 (8th Cir. 1976); *Hilton v. Comm.*, 74 TC 305 (1980).

10. IRC Secs. 167, 168, 162; Treas. Reg. §1.162-4.

11. See Rev. Rul. 55-540, 1955-2 CB 39; Rev. Proc. 75-21, 1975-1 CB 715, as modified by Rev. Proc. 79-48, 1979-2 CB 529. See also AOD 1984-037.

Figure 39.1

YOUR ODDS IN THE CIRCUITS		
Second, Eighth and Ninth Circuits	**Third and Seventh Circuits**	**Fourth Circuit**
New York, Vermont, Connecticut, North Dakota, South Dakota, Nebraska, Minnesota, Iowa, Missouri, Arkansas/Montana, Washington, Oregon, Idaho, Nevada, California, Arizona, Alaska, Hawaii, and Guam	Pennsylvania, New Jersey, Delaware and the Virgin Islands/ Wisconsin, Illinois, and Indiana	West Virginia, Virginia, Maryland, North Carolina, South Carolina
Courts should side with the taxpayer if 1. Taxpayer doesn't maintain control over property (satisfied by independent trust). 2. Rental payments are reasonable and terms of rent reduced to writing. 3. Leaseback has a business purpose.	Courts will side with taxpayer if Eighth and Ninth Circuit tests are met.	Courts are tougher here than in Eighth, Ninth, Third and Seventh Circuits, and deduction still possible where grantor gives up control and title to property is placed in valid irrevocable trust.
See *Quinlivan v. Comm.*, 599 F.2d 269 (8th Cir. 1979); *Brooke v. Comm.*, 468 F.2d 1155 (9th Cir. 1972); *Rosenfeld v. Comm.*, 83-1 USTC ¶9341 (2nd Cir. 1983).	See *Brown v. Comm.*, 180 F.2d 926 (3rd Cir. 1950); see also *S. Kemp v. Comm.*, 168 F.2d 598 (7th Cir. 1948).	See *Perry v. U.S.*, 520 F.2d 235 (4th Cir. 1975), cert. den.

Fifth Circuit	**Circuits That Have Not Ruled on Gift Leasebacks**
Mississippi, Louisiana, Texas	All others
Taxpayers have consistently failed in attempts to obtain rental deductions. (This court looks at the purpose of the arrangement as well as the arrangement itself and this Circuit has demanded that the taxpayer show a business reason for *both* the leaseback and the gift itself.) But this court has not held that all intra-family trust leasebacks are economic nullities nor has it held that "economic reality" was unattainable with trust leasebacks. It appears that the Fifth Circuit is placing undue weight on the origin of the trustee's title in the property a factor which is not otherwise considered relevant in cases dealing with rental payment deductability.	Taxpayers likely to face litigation but likelihood of success is highest if 1. independent trustee used 2. arm's length lease signed after negotiation with trustee 3. duration of trust exceeds length of lease
See *Van Zandt v. Comm.*, 341 F.2d 440 (5th Cir. 1965), cert. den. See also *Butler*, 65 T.C. 327 (1975).	Although there are cases on gift leasebacks in these circuits (cited below), none of these met all the tests set forth by the Tax Court, so it is not known how an Appeals Court in one of these circuits would react to a properly structured arrangement. See *Duffy v. U.S.*, 487 F.2d 282 (6th Cir. 1973)

Chapter 40

BUY–SELL (BUSINESS CONTINUATION) AGREEMENT

WHAT IS IT?

A business continuation agreement is an arrangement for the disposition of a business interest in the event of the owner's death, disability, retirement, or upon withdrawal from the business at some earlier time. Business continuation agreements can take a number of forms:

(1) an agreement between the business itself and the individual owners (either a corporate stock redemption agreement or partnership liquidation agreement), frequently called an "entity" plan;

(2) an agreement between the individual owners (a cross-purchase or "criss-cross" agreement);

(3) an agreement between the individual owners and key person, family member, or outside individual (a "third-party" business buy-out agreement); or

(4) a hybrid combination of the foregoing, such as the "wait and see" buy-sell discussed below.

In the case of corporations, the most common types of business continuation agreements are stock redemption plans (often called stock retirement plans), or shareholder cross-purchase plans. The distinguishing feature of the redemption agreement is that the corporation itself agrees to purchase (redeem) the stock of the withdrawing or deceased shareholder. In a cross-purchase plan the individuals agree between or among themselves to purchase the interest of a withdrawing or deceased shareholder.

In the case of a partnership, an agreement similar to the corporate stock redemption plan is the partnership liquidation agreement, where the partnership in effect purchases the interest of the deceased or withdrawing partner by distributing assets in liquidation of the partner's interest, or the partners agree to a cross-purchase similar to the corporate cross-purchase plan.

WHEN IS THE USE OF SUCH A DEVICE INDICATED?

1. When a guaranteed market must be created for the sale of a business interest in the event of death, disability, or retirement.

2. When it is necessary or desirable to "peg" the value of the business for federal and state death tax purposes.

3. When a shareholder or partner would be unable or unwilling to continue running the business with the family of a deceased co-owner.

4. When the business involves a high amount of financial risk for the family of a deceased owner and it is desirable to convert the business interest into cash at the owner's death.

5. When it is necessary or desirable to prevent all or part of the business from falling into the hands of "outsiders."

   This could include a buyout of an owner's interest in the event of a divorce, disability, or insolvency, if there is a danger a business interest would be transferred to a former spouse or creditors.

6. Where it is desirable to lend certainty to the disposition of a family closely-held business. Rather than relying on will provisions of a parent to transfer the business interest, a binding buy-sell agreement between parent and child could be used. However, under IRC Section 2703, this has become exceedingly difficult.

7. When state law restricts the parties who can own an interest in the entity. An example is a professional corporation or association. State law might allow only licensed practitioners in that field, doctors for instance, to own the stock. In such a case, an heir or beneficiary of one of the doctors could not be an owner of an interest in the firm. A buy-sell agreement would be a legal and practical necessity.

WHAT ARE THE REQUIREMENTS?

A written agreement is drawn stating the parties to the agreement, purchase price, terms, and funding arrangements. The agreement typically obligates the retiring (or disabled) owner (or owner's estate) to sell the business either (a) to the business itself, (b) to the surviving owner(s), (c) to a third party non-owner, or (d) to a combination of parties.

Occasionally the agreement combines the types of obligations. For example, the agreement may give the other owners the option to purchase the stock or partnership interest, but provide that if they fail to exercise that option, the interest must be redeemed or liquidated by the corporation or partnership. Conversely, the agreement may provide that if the entity cannot purchase the interest, the remaining owners have either an obligation or option to do so. Such agreements must be carefully drafted to avoid a situation in which the entity discharges an obligation of the other owners to purchase the interest, which could have adverse tax consequences to the other owners. For example, if the shareholders under the agreement are obligated to buy the stock of a deceased shareholder, and the corporation redeems the stock, the amount of the obligation of which the remaining shareholders are relieved could be considered a taxable dividend to them.

The buy-sell agreement specifies the event triggering the respective obligations. Generally that event is death, disability, or retirement of the owner. However, as already indicated, it could (and usually should) include divorce, insolvency, or bankruptcy, and could also include such events as loss of a professional license by an owner or conviction of an owner of a state or federal crime. Valuation may be based on several factors, including book value, asset value, formula value, or some agreed amount.

"Funding" pertains to how the promises under the agreement will be financed. Generally, in a redemption or liquidation agreement, the business will purchase, own, pay premiums, and be the beneficiary of life (and often disability income) insurance on each person who owns an interest in the business.

In the case of a cross-purchase agreement, the prospective buyer (each business associate) purchases, owns, pays for, and is a beneficiary of a life and disability income insurance policy on the other owners.

HOW IT IS DONE – AN EXAMPLE

Stock Redemption Plan

Herb and Steve are equal stockholders in a business valued at $5,000,000. The business purchases $2,500,000 of life insurance on both men.

At Herb's death, his stock passes to his estate. The life insurance proceeds on Herb's life are paid to the business. Then the business pays the agreed upon amount or formula price to Herb's estate according to the agreement. In return for the cash, Herb's executor transfers the stock to the business. Steve, therefore, ends up with ownership of all the outstanding voting stock (the stock owned by the business itself is not entitled to vote).

Under the buy-sell agreement, should Herb become totally disabled prior to retirement, he would receive his full salary for one year. At the end of a year of total disability, Herb's interest would be sold to the business. The business would pay at least $250,000 (10% x $2,500,000) as a down payment to Herb. The business would also issue Herb a 10-year note (secured by his stock which is placed in an escrow account) for the remaining value of the stock. The business would pay interest on the note. The rate would be the safe harbor rate needed to avoid the unstated interest rules. In order to help pay off the note, the business would apply for, pay for, and name itself beneficiary of a disability income insurance policy.

In the event Herb retired, he would sell his stock to the business. The business would pay Herb at least $250,000 (10% x $2,500,000) as a down payment, plus it would give Herb a 10-year note (secured by his stock) for the remaining amount. The business would pay interest on the note at the safe harbor rate needed to avoid the unstated interest rules. The cash value of the life insurance policy on Herb's life could be used to help finance the down payment. One limiting factor, in general, is that in many states, the corporation can redeem its stock only to the extent it has earned surplus.

Cross-Purchase Agreement

Assume Herb and Steve are equal stockholders in a business valued at $5,000,000. Herb purchases a $2,500,000 life insurance policy and a disability income policy on Steve's life. Steve purchases policies in equal amounts on Herb's life.

Assuming Herb dies first, his stock passes to his estate. The insurance proceeds on Herb's life are paid directly to Steve. Steve then pays cash to Herb's estate according to the cross-purchase agreement. In return for the cash, Herb's executor transfers stock to Steve. Therefore, Steve becomes the sole owner of the corporation.

In the event of Herb's disability, he receives his full salary for one year assuming he is totally disabled. At that time, Herb must sell his business interest to Steve. Steve will pay at least $250,000 (10% x $2,500,000) as a down payment to Herb. Steve will also give Herb a 10-year note (secured by his stock) for the balance. Steve will pay interest on the note at the safe harbor rate needed to avoid the unstated interest rules. During this time, Steve will be receiving income from the disability income insurance policy purchased on Herb's life that can be used to pay off the note.

At Herb's retirement or departure from the firm prior to normal retirement Herb will sell his stock to Steve. Steve will pay at least $250,000 (10% x $2,500,000) as a down payment to Herb. Steve will also give Herb a 10-year note (secured by his stock) for the balance. Steve will pay interest on the note at the safe harbor rate needed to avoid the unstated interest rules. Steve can use the cash value of the policy he owns on Herb's life to help provide the down payment.

WHAT ARE THE TAX IMPLICATIONS?

Stock Redemption Agreements

1. Assuming the corporation is owner and beneficiary of the policy(ies), the value of the insurance on the decedent's life will not be includable (as insurance proceeds per se) in his gross estate for federal estate tax purposes. However, the insurance proceeds will be considered in valuing the decedent's interest in the business unless there is a valid arm's length agreement fixing the price for federal estate tax purposes and the proceeds are excluded from the purchase price under the terms of the agreement.[1]

    The buy-sell agreement will generally establish the value of the business for federal estate tax purposes if: (1) the estate is obligated to sell at the decedent-shareholder's death, or the estate is obligated to offer the decedent's shares at his death at the agreement price; (2) the agreement prohibits the shareholder from disposing of his interest during his lifetime without first offering it to the corpo-

ration at no more than the contract price; (3) the price was fair and adequate at the time the agreement was made and resulted from a bona fide arm's length transaction between the parties; and (4) the price was fixed by the terms of the agreement, or, preferably, the agreement contained a formula for determining the price.[2] Where the shareholders or partners are related, or the "natural objects of the bounty" of each other, there are additional requirements, discussed later under the heading "Family Business Enterprises."

2. Life insurance or disability income premiums used to fund the agreement are not deductible by the corporation.[3] On the other hand, death proceeds (or disability income proceeds) will be received by the corporation income tax free regardless of amount.[4] (But see the discussion later on the corporate alternative minimum tax). Premiums paid by the corporation will not be taxable income to its shareholders.

3. The biggest potential problem in a corporate stock redemption agreement is the possibility that the redemption will be treated as a dividend distribution. The Internal Revenue Code states the general rule that, no matter how the parties label a transaction, a distribution of money or property in redemption of stock by a corporation will generally be treated as a dividend (resulting in subjecting the entire distribution to income taxation to the extent of the corporation's earnings and profits). Fortunately, the seller can often avoid this treatment and can usually have the transaction treated as a capital gain if the distribution or redemption meets certain exceptions to the general rule.

    The most common exception is that a redemption of all of a shareholder's stock (a complete termination of his interest) will not be treated as a dividend. For example, Herb and Steve, unrelated parties, own all of the stock in a closely held corporation. Herb dies and his stock passes to his estate. The corporation redeems (buys back) all of Herb's stock from his estate. The result is a total redemption. The distribution will not be subjected to dividend treatment because Herb's estate has given up all control, share of future profits, and share of future assets in the event of a sale or liquidation of the corporation, i.e., Herb's estate has completely terminated its interest.

    Unfortunately, this favorable tax treatment can be complicated or even thwarted by what is known as "constructive ownership" (attribution) rules.[5]

Essentially, the basic constructive ownership rules work as follows:

a. The "estate/beneficiary" attribution rule. Under this rule, stock owned by a beneficiary of an estate is considered constructively (treated for tax purposes as if it were actually) owned by the estate.[6] A redemption of all the stock actually owned by the estate (without a simultaneous redemption of stock owned by a beneficiary) may be considered a partial redemption and may be taxable to the estate as a dividend. The estate is still considered a stockholder because it is deemed to own stock actually owned by the beneficiary.

Example: Herb and Steve are father and son. Herb owns 75% of the stock while Steve owns the remaining 25%. Steve is a beneficiary under Herb's will. If the corporation redeems only Herb's stock from his executor, the entire amount paid by the corporation for the stock may be treated and taxed as a dividend (to the extent of corporate earnings and profits) because the redemption is *deemed* to be of less than all the stock owned directly or indirectly by the estate. After the redemption, the estate is considered to own *all* the outstanding shares of the corporation because Steve's stock is attributed to (deemed to be owned by) Herb's estate.

In other words, Herb's estate constructively owns the shares actually owned by Herb's son. (It may be possible to avoid the estate/beneficiary attribution rule by "eliminating the beneficiary." If, before the redemption takes place, the son has received all the property to which he is entitled from the estate, no longer has a claim against the estate, and no liabilities of the estate can be assessed against him as a beneficiary, his stock will not be attributed to the estate because he will no longer be considered a beneficiary.)

b. The "family/trust/corporation" attribution rule. Under this rule, an individual is considered to own the stock owned directly or indirectly by or for the individual's spouse, children, grandchildren, and parents. Stock owned by certain other parties and entities is also attributed to and from each party or entity in determining whether all the stock has been redeemed.[7] These other parties include:

(i) With certain exceptions, a trust and its beneficiaries.

(ii) A partnership and its partners.

(iii) A corporation and over-50% shareholders.

There is also the possibility of an incomplete termination as a result of stock being attributed through a double linking, first from a close family member to an estate beneficiary and then through the estate beneficiary to the estate.

Example: Herb owns 1,000 shares in a closely held corporation. His son, Steve, owns the remaining 500 shares. Herb's widow is the sole beneficiary under Herb's will. Even if the corporation immediately redeems Herb's entire 1,000 shares at his death, the redemption will be treated as less than a complete redemption and therefore may become subject to dividend treatment because Steve's 500 shares are attributed to (treated as if owned by) his mother under the family attribution rules. Then the shares she is deemed to own are in turn considered to be owned by Herb's estate under the estate/beneficiary attribution rules. So even after all the shares Herb actually owned are purchased by the corporation from Herb's estate, his estate is still constructive owner of all the outstanding stock of the corporation. Steve's shares are traced to his mother and from her to Herb's estate.

There is an important exception to the family attribution rule. Under certain circumstances, it may be possible to "waive" the family attribution rule (but not the estate or entity rules) and therefore break the "chain" between family members. This "10-year waiver rule" works as follows: In essence, the family attribution rules will not be applied if, immediately following the redemption, the stockholder whose stock is redeemed has no interest in the corporation (except as creditor) and agrees not to acquire an interest for 10 years following the redemption, other than by bequest or inheritance.[8]

One of the difficulties of implementing a redemption of a family member coupled with a waiver of family attribution is the unwillingness of a key person, often a founder of the business, to completely disassociate from it. The cases are clear that the key person cannot safely function in any capacity (other than creditor), even as a consultant.

In the example discussed above, Herb's executor would sell Herb's stock to the corporation. Herb's widow would notify the IRS of her election to waive attribution between her son, Steve, and herself. Because she doesn't own any stock personally and because she has "waived" her right to receive any stock except by bequest or inheritance, when the corporation redeems the stock held by the estate's executor, there is no attribution from Steve to her and then from her to the estate. Therefore, the redemption results in a complete termination of the estate's interest. The proceeds of the redemption, therefore, are not subject to dividend treatment.

Entities such as a corporation, trust, or estate may waive the constructive ownership and break the fictional ownership linkage from a family member who actually owns stock to a beneficiary who does not (but is deemed to own it). The individual who is deemed to own stock must join in the waiver. After the redemption, neither the entity nor the beneficiary may hold an interest in the corporation. They must agree not to acquire such an interest for at least 10 years. They must also agree to notify the IRS if they do acquire such an interest. There is joint and several liability in the event either the entity or the waiving family members acquires a prohibited interest within the 10-year period. The statute of limitations remains open during that time for the IRS to levy on any deficiency.

As noted above, it is important to note that an entity may break the fictional linkage only between family members; it may not waive "entity" attribution, the constructive ownership between a beneficiary and an entity. For example, assume 30% of the stock of a corporation is owned by a trust. Its beneficiaries, Michael, David, and Danny Green, own no stock personally. Debbie Green, the trust beneficiaries' mother, owns 52% of the corporation's stock. The remaining stock is held by unrelated employees of the corporation.

Assume the trust sells all of its stock back to the corporation. The redemption is still not complete because the trust's beneficiaries, Michael, David, and Danny, are deemed to own stock owned by their mother through the "family" attribution rule. The stock they are deemed to own is then attributed from them to the trust through the entity attribution rule. So the redemption of stock from the trust would be less than complete. But if the trust and all three brothers waive attribution and break the link

connecting the mother's stock to the sons, the redemption would be complete. But what if one or more of the sons actually owned stock in the corporation? In that case the trust could break the link from Debbie Green to her children (the family attribution) but not the link between the children and itself (the entity attribution).

4. A purchase (either through stock redemption or cross-purchase) of a decedent-shareholder's interest generally means that the estate of a decedent will not realize any taxable gain for income tax purposes. The stock purchased from the estate obtains a "stepped-up basis," i.e., a new "cost" in the executor's hands equal to its value for federal estate tax purposes.[9] (EGTRRA 2001 replaces this step-up in basis with a modified carryover basis for one year for property received from a decedent dying in 2010.) Because the purchaser generally pays a price equal to the value of the stock at the applicable federal estate tax valuation date, there is not any gain realized by the estate; the amount paid for the stock equals the basis of the stock in the hands of the executor.

Example: on January 1st Herb and Steve, who are unrelated, each invested $50,000 in a corporation that is worth $500,000 ($250,000 each) at Herb's death. If the corporation paid Herb's estate $250,000 in complete redemption of his stock, there would be no income tax consequences to his estate because the estate's basis in the stock is "stepped up" from $50,000 to $250,000 (the value for death tax purposes) and this was the amount received by the estate under the redemption. The "amount realized" ($250,000) by the estate did not exceed the estate's basis ($250,000) and so there is no taxable gain.

Note that the surviving shareholder (Steve) does not receive an increase in basis for income tax purposes since the corporation is redeeming Herb's stock. In a cross purchase arrangement, if Steve had purchased Herb's stock from his estate, Steve would receive an increase in basis by the amount of the price paid. This is an important reason to consider a cross purchase rather than stock redemption arrangement.

5. Congress was concerned corporations would be able to report large profits for financial accounting purposes but report little profit (and therefore pay little or no tax) for income tax purposes. So it imposed a revenue raising measure called the corporate alternative minimum tax (AMT). This is based

on a variety of adjustments to the taxable income of the corporation to arrive at an amount defined as alternative minimum taxable income (AMTI).[10]

For tax years beginning after 1997, this AMT does not apply to "small corporations." These are defined as corporations that had average gross receipts of less than $5,000,000 for the previous three years. A corporation that meets the $5,000,000 gross receipts test will continue to be treated as a small corporation as long as its average gross receipts do not exceed $7,500,000.[11]

Note that a corporation that does not qualify as a small corporation for 1997 (or for its first tax year, if it was formed after 1996) will never be eligible for small corporation treatment. A corporation that fails to meet the $7,500,000 gross receipts test becomes subject to the corporate AMT only with respect to preferences and adjustments that relate to transactions and investments entered into after the corporation loses its status as a small corporation. The cost of protection from the AMT afforded to small corporations is that the alternative minimum tax credit allowable to a small corporation is limited. Generally, the corporation's regular tax liability (reduced by applicable credits) used to calculate the credit is reduced by 25% of the amount that such liability exceeds $25,000.

Roughly speaking, "C" (regular) corporations that do not qualify as small corporations must pay AMT at a 20% rate on an amount equal to 75% of the excess of certain earnings and profits (technically called "adjusted current earnings," or "ACE.") over alternative minimum taxable income.

Here's a simplified example of how this extremely complex law works with respect to

A. Death Benefits from corporate owned life insurance:

Step 1:	State the total death benefit	$_____
Step 2:	State the cash value	$_____
Step 3:	Subtract to find the Net Amount at Risk	$_____
Step 4:	Multiply Step 3 Result by	.75
	Amount Taxable	$_____
Step 5:	Multiply by AMT rate	.20
	Alternative Minimum Tax	$_____

For instance, if a C corporation receives $1,200,000 of (otherwise income tax free) life insurance proceeds at the death of its key person, assuming the cash surrender value of the policy was $200,000 the day before the key person's death, the net amount at risk would be $1,000,000. Because only 75% is taxable, $750,000 (.75 x $1,000,000) would be exposed to tax at a 20% rate. This means the net alternative minimum tax is $150,000 (.20 x $750,000).

The amount necessary before the AMT to net a "target amount" can be computed by multiplying the target amount by 118%. For example, suppose the target amount is $1,000,000. To net this much after any possible AMT, the corporation should purchase $1,180,000 ($1,000,000 x 118%). Using the five step formula above, out of $1,180,000, $885,000 would be subject to the AMT. The AMT, at a 20% rate, would be $177,000. The net result, $1,003,000, is just slightly more than the $1,000,000 target amount. (To be precise, multiply the target amount by 117.7%).

It is important to understand that the AMT is truly an alternative tax, not an additional tax. Once the total AMT is computed, as in the above example, that amount is compared to the "regular" tax on the corporate income for the year in question. The alternative amount is paid only if it is higher than the regular tax.

Keep in mind that payments of AMT are more like prepayments of a future tax than a separate tax; what a corporation pays as an AMT can be used in future tax years as a dollar for dollar reduction (credit) against the corporation's regular income tax liability (but not below the alternative minimum tax in any given year).

B. Cash Values

The inside buildup on a corporate owned life insurance policy is included in adjusted current earnings (ACE). Therefore, to the extent the policy cash value increase exceeds the premium paid in a given year, exposure to the AMT goes up.

C. Premiums

A deduction for AMT purposes is allowed for the portion of any premium that is attributable to insurance coverage. Therefore, to the extent the premium paid is greater in a given year than the policy's cash value increase, exposure to the AMT goes down.

The bottom line is no surprise: both (otherwise income tax free) death benefits and the (otherwise income tax free) inside buildup in a life insurance contract are includable in the amount upon which the corporate AMT is based.

So what advice should be given to clients?

First, tell clients that the corporation needs the insurance, "BUY IT! Buy enough – after the AMT – to meet the need!" There is no question that even considering a "worst case" scenario, there is no more cost effective means of creating surplus to protect both the corporation and its creditors in the event of a key employee's death than corporate owned life insurance. Likewise, in most cases nonqualified deferred compensation and corporate debt reduction should be funded with corporate owned insurance "grossed up" enough to net the target amount.

Second, where it is possible and appropriate in the opinion of the firm's advisers to purchase necessary life insurance outside the corporation, do so. Other factors being equal, buy-sell agreements of family-owned businesses and most closely–held corporations should typically be set up on a cross purchase basis.

Third, remember that this tax does not impact S corporations, LLCs, FLPs, regulated investment companies, real estate investment trusts, real estate mortgage investment conduits, or financial asset securitization investment trusts.

Fourth, no AMT is imposed until the corporate exemption of $40,000 is used up. (This exemption is reduced by 25% of the amount by which alternative minimum taxable income exceeds $150,000, but not less than zero). Therefore, small amounts of tax preference in a given year will typically have no effect.

Finally, remember that most family-owned and closely-held corporations will be "small corporations" and thus exempt from the AMT.

Cross–Purchase Agreements

1. The value of life insurance owned on a decedent-shareholder's life by a surviving co-shareholder will not be included in the decedent's estate for federal estate tax purposes. This is because the decedent-shareholder insured has no incidents of ownership in the policy his co-shareholder owns. However, the value of life insurance the decedent owned at the time of death on the lives of co-shareholders will be includable.[12] (Generally, the includable amount is equivalent to the policy's interpolated terminal reserve plus unearned premiums but may be much higher if the insured is terminally ill or severely ill and old at the time of the owner-co-shareholder's death.)

    As with the stock redemption agreement a properly drawn cross-purchase agreement will, generally, be effective in helping to establish the value of the business for federal estate tax purposes providing: (1) the estate is obligated to sell at the decedent-shareholder's death, or the estate is obligated to offer the decedent's shares at his death at the agreement price; (2) there is a lifetime "first offer" provision prohibiting a shareholder from disposing of his stock interest without first offering it to the other shareholders at no more than the contract price; (3) the price was fair and adequate when made and resulted from a bona fide arm's length transaction; and (4) the price is fixed by the terms of the agreement or the agreement contains a formula or method for determining the price. (Where there are family members involved, see discussion below on Family Business Enterprises).

2. Life insurance or disability income premiums paid to fund the agreement are not deductible by the co-shareholders. The death proceeds or disability benefits will be received by the respective co-shareholders income tax free. There will be no AMT regardless of the size of the policy.

3. Assuming the corporation does not directly or indirectly take over the buying shareholder's liability once it becomes fixed, there is no possibility under a cross-purchase agreement that "redemptions" will be treated as dividends and no potential attribution problems because there are no redemptions; there should be no transaction between the corporation and its shareholders in a cross-purchase agreement. By definition, in a cross-purchase plan the entire transaction is between the co-shareholders.

4. Under a cross-purchase agreement, if the price paid for the stock is more than its basis (cost) in the selling shareholder's hands, the difference is usually taxable at capital gain rates. Under a stock redemption, the distribution for the stock is generally treated as a dividend unless certain exceptions apply.

5. Under a cross-purchase agreement, the surviving shareholder has the advantage of increasing his basis in the company for income tax purposes by the amount of money he or she pays for the stock. This is not available under a stock redemption. This will result in a reduced gain, in the event of a subsequent lifetime sale, to the surviving shareholders.

6. Where more than one shareholder is involved, the implications of the transfer for value rule, see Question below, must be analyzed if there are life insurance policies that could be transferred among the shareholders or from the corporation to the shareholders.

Business Continuation Plans for S Corporations

Where the entity or cross-purchase plan is structured for a corporation electing to be taxed under subchapter S of the Internal Revenue Code, there are additional issues that must be considered. The tax characteristics of S corporations are discussed in Chapter 46.

Most practitioners favor the cross-purchase plan for an S corporation. There is some concern that a stock redemption plan under which the corporation will purchase stock of shareholders would create a second class of stock, which would disqualify the corporation for the S election. However, rulings and regulations indicate the IRS will rarely take this position. More practical reasons for preferring the cross-purchase plan include the fact that any life insurance owned by the corporation to fund a stock redemption agreement is really paid for with shareholder dollars, because the dollars used to pay premiums are dollars taxed to the shareholders. Also, the impact of the life insurance premiums and proceeds on the income tax basis of the shareholders' stock is unclear. If the S corporation has corporate earnings and profits accumulated before the S election is made, the insurance may affect the amount the corporation can distribute to shareholders without dividend consequences. The impact of life insurance on S corporation shareholders is discussed further in Chapter 46.

On the other hand, life insurance in an S corporation, no matter how large, does not trigger alternative minimum tax problems. A stock redemption decreases any of the S corporation's earnings and profits, which could someday give rise to dividends. And because most S corporations have little or no earnings and profits, all the complex dividend issues under the redemption-family attribution rules are generally not

an issue, because a redemption cannot create a taxable dividend if there are no earnings and profits.

In structuring a buy-sell agreement for an S corporation, note that corporate profit and loss is allocated on a daily basis to all shareholders, including a deceased shareholder, to the date of death, or a selling shareholder to date of sale. An election can be made to actually close the tax year on the date of death or sale and allocate income or loss between two tax years. The agreement should spell out which approach is to be used. Remember that a shareholder's pro rata share of corporate profit or loss will increase or decrease the income tax basis of the shareholder's stock, which would have an impact on the gain or loss realized on the sale.

One of the purposes of a buy-sell agreement in an S corporation is to prevent the stock from falling into the hands of a disqualifying shareholder, such as a trust that cannot own S stock or a nonresident alien. The agreement should be structured so that the sale is complete before any such disqualifying transfer is made and should specifically bar sales to any disqualifying party.

Business Continuation Plans for Partnerships

Partnership buyouts present several different problems and solutions. Unlike a corporation, if more than 50% of the total partnership capital *and* profits are sold within a 12-month period, the partnership is dissolved under IRC Section 708. However, the regulations under Section 708 indicate that if the interest of a partner is liquidated rather than sold, there is no dissolution even if that interest exceeds 50%. If the buyout does terminate the partnership, it is treated as having made a pro rata liquidating distribution of all of its assets to the partners, which are then treated as re-contributed to the partnership. Both functional transactions are generally tax free.

If a partnership buy-sell agreement involves the sale of a partnership interest to other partners (or even a third person, such as an employee), any gain or loss realized by the selling partner is treated as a gain from sale or exchange of a capital asset, except to the extent it is attributable to so-called "hot assets" as defined in IRC Section 741 (generally, unrealized receivables and inventory items). Note that in the case of a sale of a deceased partner's interest, the stepped-up basis at death will eliminate most of this gain, except that attributable to items of income in respect of a decedent owned by the partnership. The purchaser acquires the cost basis in the partnership interest under IRC Section 742, and in addition, may seek to adjust the basis of the partnership assets to reflect the purchase price under IRC Sections 743(b) and 754.

Consideration should always be given to the use of a liquidation plan that meets the requirements of IRC Section 736, so that part of the payment can take the form of a tax-deductible guaranteed payment that can be spread over a period of several years. Under that section, payments in *complete* liquidation of a retiring or deceased partner's interest are broken into two categories, 736(b) payments and 736(a) payments.

Section 736(b) payments are those made in exchange for a deceased partner's interest in partnership property, including goodwill if specified as such in the agreement, and will result in taxable gain to the selling partner only if cash received, including relief from liabilities, exceeds the basis of the partner's interest in the partnership.

Section 736(a) payments made to successors of a deceased partner are classified as guaranteed payments, or represent an interest in future partnership income. Either way, they are tax-deductible to the partnership and taxable income to the recipient. Payments for receivables are always characterized as 736(a) payments. Payments for goodwill can be 736(a) payments unless the partnership agreement specifies they are for goodwill.

In summary, liquidation plans prevent termination of the partnership because the over 50% sale rule will not apply, so long as there are at least two partners remaining after the liquidation is complete. Part of the liquidation payment can be made tax deductible to the remaining partners, and payments for goodwill can specifically be made tax deductible by bringing them under Section 736(a).

However, the use of guaranteed payments under Section 736(a) has been severely curtailed in the case of partnership agreements entered into after January 4, 1993. Section 736(b) has been amended to provide that payments for unrealized receivables and goodwill of the partnership cannot be characterized as guaranteed payments under Section 736(a) unless capital is not a material income producing factor for the partnership, and the partner who is retiring or deceased is (or was) a general partner. This rule will not apply to partners retiring under an agreement that was binding on the parties on January 4, 1993. This change effectively limits the use of Section 736(a) guaranteed payments to service partnerships, such as professional practices.

If life insurance is used to provide funding in the case of the liquidation plan, the insurance is owned by the partnership and used to make liquidation payments. The IRS could argue that each partner has incidents of ownership in the policy on his life because of his management rights as partner. However, the IRS has taken this position only where the insurance proceeds were payable to a party outside the partnership.[13]

Note that the receipt of the insurance proceeds increases the income tax basis of the partnership interests of all partners, including the interest owned by the decedent. It may be possible to change this by a provision in the partnership agreement.

Where insurance on the life of each partner is owned by other partners under a cross-purchase plan, the policies can be transferred between the partnership and partners without fear of the transfer for value rule under IRC Section 101(a)(2)(B). This is because there is an exception to the transfer for value rule if the transferee is either a partnership in which the insured is a partner or a partner of the insured. If an LLC is taxed as a partnership, the same exception should apply.

Cross ownership should not be the basis for an IRS claim that each partner has incidents of ownership in the policy on his life owned by the other partner by reason of the agreement.[14]

Family Business Enterprises

IRC Section 2703, applicable to options or agreements created or substantially modified after October 8, 1990, raises a host of additional problems in planning business continuation agreements for family businesses. It provides that any restrictions that result from options or agreements permitting *any* person to acquire any property at less than fair market value, or any such restriction on the right to sell or use the property, are disregarded in valuing that property. However, there is an exception for options, agreements, etc., that meet the following three tests:

- They are bona fide business arrangements;

- They are not devices to transfer property to the decedent's family or the natural objects of the decedent's bounty for less than full and adequate consideration; and

- The terms are comparable to similar arrangements entered into by persons in arm's length transactions.

While the first two requirements are not really new, the third requirement, establishing that the terms and conditions of the agreement are comparable to others entered into by unrelated persons, is very difficult to meet in most planning situations. Such agreements simply do not exist, or if they do, generally, they are not available for comparison. Both the congressional committee reports and the regulations under Section 2703 indicate that there are four factors in such agreements:

- the present fair market value of the property or business,

- its expected value at the date of exercise of rights under the agreement,

- adequacy of any consideration offered for the option or agreement, and

- the expected terms of the agreement.

According to the congressional committee reports, the third test is not met simply by showing isolated comparables but requires a demonstration of the general practices of unrelated parties. Expert testimony would be evidence of such practice. In unusual cases where comparables are difficult to find because the taxpayer owns a unique business, the taxpayer can use comparables from other businesses.

The Senate report also emphasizes that the law does not alter other preexisting requirements for buy-sell agreements, such as a requirement of lifetime restrictions if the agreement is to be binding at death.

According to the regulations, the restrictive agreement will meet the requirements of the statute to control valuation if it is a binding agreement and if more than 50% of the value of the property or business is owned by persons who are not family members (or natural objects of the transferor's bounty).

However, the use of the term "natural objects of the transferor's bounty" is broadly defined and means that the provisions of Section 2703 may apply even where the shareholders are unrelated. The final regulations do not say this, but they do say that members of the family include persons described in IRC Section 2701, covered in Chapter 58, and other persons who are natural objects of the transferor's bounty. The preamble to the final regulations also states that natural objects of bounty may include persons not "related by blood or marriage."

Similar arrangements among unrelated parties in the same business are generally comparable, if they consider the term of the agreement, present and anticipated fair market value of the property, and adequacy of consideration. General business practice of unrelated parties is comparable, but again, isolated comparables are insufficient, and if two or more valuation methods are generally used, the fact that the agreement falls within one of them is not sufficient. It is important to note that the requirement of finding comparable buy-sell agreements, which is very difficult in most cases, appears to have been replaced in the regulations by a requirement of proof that unrelated persons dealing at arm's length would have entered into the same agreement. Thus, in setting the terms of a business continuation agreement where family members are involved, remember to consider the four key factors – present and anticipated future value of the business, the expected term of the agreement, and consideration. Obtain evidence and expert opinions to establish that the terms and conditions of this buy-sell agreement would be acceptable to unrelated persons. Under no circumstances set arbitrary prices or values, such as, for example, a price based on the face value of the life insurance, and consider a provision for periodic review and adjustment of the price, or preferably, a formula.

If a business continuation agreement was in place before the effective date of Section 2703, it is not covered unless it is substantially modified thereafter. The following are not substantial modifications:

- a modification required by the instrument;

- a discretionary modification containing a right or restriction that does not change the right or restriction, or results in only a de minimis change;

- a modification of a capitalization rate tied to a market rate; or

- a modification to a price that more adequately reflects fair market value.

The following are considered substantial modifications:

- failure to update an agreement that by its terms requires periodic updating; and

- the addition of a family member to the agreement, unless mandated by the terms of the agreement, or unless the new family member is assigned to a generation no lower than that of existing parties to the agreement (generation assignment is determined under the generation-skipping rules, discussed in Chapter 18).

IMPLICATIONS AND ISSUES IN COMMUNITY PROPERTY STATES

Several problems can arise in connection with buy-sell agreements as a result of community property rights. If all or part of the stock is subject to a buy-sell agreement, careful planning is required (1) to protect against the risk that the shareholder's spouse may predecease the seller and leave the spouse's community property interest in the stock to third parties, (2) to protect against attachment by creditors of the shareholder's spouse, and (3) to protect the agreement from attachment by the stockholder's spouse if the spouse survives the stockholder and seeks to claim his community property interest in the stock free of the agreement. If all or part of the stockholder's interest is quasi-community property, care should be taken to protect against the spouse's claim, if the spouse survives the stockholder, that the spouse is entitled to a community property interest in the stock free of the agreement. Appropriate written consents should be obtained in the above situations.

The impact of divorce in a community property state must be considered. If a spouse who is not active in the business should receive stock in the closely held corporation, or a partnership interest, as part of the property settlement, this may not be covered by the buy-sell agreement.

Consideration should be given to making provisions in the buy-sell agreement for such an eventuality. One solution is to grant the remaining shareholders or partners, particularly the other spouse in the divorce action, a right to purchase the interest of the soon-to-be ex-spouse. Alternatively, the corporation or partnership could have at least an option to purchase the interest. If the spouses are all made parties to such an agreement, great care must be taken to assure these provisions are fair, or else they may be unenforceable.

It is important to determine the nature of the interest held by the stockholder, not only for purposes of determining whether consents need to be obtained and wills reviewed, but also to evaluate the tax consequences. If all of the stock is community property, the community property interest of the stockholder's spouse will be included in the spouse's estate if the spouse predeceases the stockholder, and will be excluded from the stockholder's estate if the stockholder dies first. If all of the stock is the separate property of the stockholder, it will be included in the stockholder's estate only (unless the stockholder passes the stock to the spouse and then dies). If all of the stock is quasi-community property, the stockholder's spouse will have no interest if the spouse dies first, and the full value of the stock will be in the stockholder's estate for federal estate tax purposes.

The basis of property acquired from a decedent is subject to a peculiar set of rules.

Generally, the basis of property acquired from a decedent is the fair market value of the property at the date of the decedent's death. (EGTRRA 2001 replaces the step-up in basis with a modified carryover basis for one year for property received from a decedent dying in 2010.) IRC Section 1014 defines which property is deemed "acquired from a decedent" and therefore subject to these special basis rules. Generally, Section 1014 applies to all property includable in the gross estate.

The surviving spouse is deemed to have acquired her one-half share of the community property from the decedent spouse. This gives the surviving spouse a new basis even though her one-half of the community property was not included or taxed in the decedent spouse's estate. The new basis for the surviving spouse's one-half will therefore be equal to the fair market value of the property at date of death. This rule operates, however, only if the decedent's one-half is fully included in the gross estate.[15] If the property's fair market value is greater than its adjusted income tax basis, the basis will receive a "step-up" free of income taxes. If the fair market value is less than the adjusted basis, the new basis will actually be a "step-down."

This "step-up" or "step-down" in basis for both spouses' halves of the community property does not apply to property held as joint tenancy or tenancy in common property. Even though the original nature of the property was community property (e.g., a spouse's earnings in a community property state), taking the title as joint tenants or tenants in common will change its nature so that it no longer has the attributes of community property. However, in most states with community property laws, it is possible to re-establish the property as community property by an agreement between the spouses without actually changing the recorded title to the property.

The ability of the surviving spouse to sell immediately the entire community interest of corporate stock, either under a buy-sell contract to other shareholders or to redeem some or all of it within the scope of IRC Section 303 (avoiding dividend treatment), can often be the most significant estate planning step taken by husband and wife shareholders in community property states.

Problems can occur when attempting to determine whether stock held by a married person in a community property state is community property. A portion of the stock can be separate property and a portion community property. A common example is a man who owns a business prior to marriage.

Let us examine the setting in which this issue frequently arises. Assume that Mr. Jones owns all of the stock in Jones Manufacturing Company, Inc. The company was incorporated prior to his marriage to Mrs. Jones. At the time of the marriage, the company was worth $100,000. However, during the marriage the value of the company appreciates rapidly. If Mr. Jones dies, will the stock in the company, or, in the alternative, the appreciation in value of the stock, be deemed his separate property or will it be community property?

Court decisions characterizing appreciation in closely-held businesses arise in only three settings: (1) a claim by a creditor that the business should be made available for the payment of a debt, (2) divorce and the division of property pursuant to divorce, and (3) the death of one of the spouses.

Most states use some form of an "apportionment rule" to characterize the increase in value of closely-held business interests during marriage which were originally held as a spouse's separate property. Under the apportionment rule, if one of the spouses invests separate property in a business and conducts that business during the marriage, the resulting projects or increases in value of the business will be apportioned or allocated between the community estate and the spouse's separate estate according to the amount attributable to the spouse's personal efforts on the one hand (inuring to the benefit of the community), and to the capital improvement on the other (inuring to the benefit of the spouse's separate estate).

The possibility of creating such a community property interest in a corporation originally held as the separate property of one spouse can be determined only by a court in the absence of a written agreement. Thus, it is advisable for the spouses to agree, in writing, on the nature of their interests and the proportion of community and separate property.

There are other possible combinations of interest, such as combinations of community property and quasi-community property, combinations of separate property and quasi-community property, or combinations of all three types of property. In any event, the exact nature of stock ownership and their respective proportions should be identified and agreed upon in writing. In many situations it may be advisable to incorporate the property agreement into the buy-sell agreement.

QUESTIONS AND ANSWERS

Question – Under what situations would a business buy-out by a third party be indicated?

Answer – There are certain situations in which an owner of a business interest is either unwilling or unable to enter into a conventional stock redemption or cross-purchase agreement. Usually, such a business owner will have problems such as estate liquidity or lack of management skills or interest by members of his family, or desires the value of the business to be "pegged" for federal estate tax purposes.

A typical example is where an individual has a wife and three children, only one of whom he desires or expects to be able to take over the business. He would like to treat his children as equally as possible. One way he could do this is by entering into a buy-sell agreement with the one child he expects to take over the business. That child will take over the business through the buy-sell agreement. The funds paid by that child to the decedent's executor in return for the business interest could provide the client's widow and remaining children with cash for their living needs and estate settlement costs.

The client could create a trust for the other children. That trust could be funded by life insurance to help "equalize" the estate.

Another example is where two individuals are in business together but, at the death of one, the other wants a child who presently owns no stock to come into the business. In other words, the agreement can be structured to require a sale to and purchase by someone who presently owns no interest in the business. This could be a relative, employee, or competitor.

Question – What are some of the various methods of establishing the purchase price of a business?

Answer – The purchase price to be paid for the stock of a shareholder may be set by a variety of methods.

One method is to provide for the exact purchase price in advance with the further provision that the parties may change the price at any time upon mutual agreement.

Another method of fixing the price is to use book value based on the company's financial statements.

A third method of valuation is a formula approach. Formula valuation methods are often used to take into account net profits and, to some degree, goodwill. An example would be straight capitalization of the average net profits of the business at a definite rate. For instance, as the NumberCruncher illustration below shows, at a 12% rate, a business producing average net after-tax profits of $100,000 would be worth about $833,333 using this approach ($100,000 divided by .12). A 50% interest in such a business would be worth $416,667, half of $833,333. Combinations of these three methods can also be used. (See Chapter 57 on Valuation Planning.)

CAPITALIZATION OF INCOME

INPUT: CAPITALIZATION RATE 0.120
INPUT: ADJUSTED EARNINGS $100,000

EXPECTED RATE OF RETURN	VALUE OF ASSET OR BUSINESS
0.08	$1,250,000
0.09	$1,111,111
0.10	$1,000,000
0.11	$909,091
0.12	$833,333
0.13	$769,231
0.14	$714,286
0.15	$666,667
0.16	$625,000
0.17	$588,235

Question – What is the goodwill method of valuation and how is it applied?

Answer – A closely-held business should (and often does) produce an income in excess of the amount that could be expected from the mere employment of the capital its shareholders have invested. That additional amount of income is derived from an intangible value in the business, a value in excess of the total value of the tangible assets. This is called "goodwill."

By capitalizing this "earnings attributable to intangibles," i.e., by dividing the additional profits generated by the firm's goodwill by an appropriate rate, it is possible to estimate goodwill value. If this amount is then added to book (net tangible asset) value, an estimated total business value can be found.

Some of the elements that may comprise a firm's goodwill include:

(1) location of the business,

(2) reputation of the business,

(3) public recognition of the company's name,

(4) list of customers and prospects owned by the business,

(5) management effectiveness and depth,

(6) sales, operations, and accounting skills,

(7) employee morale,

(8) position of the business relative to competitors,

(9) other factors that generate income in excess of that amount which could be expected after multiplying the value of tangible assets by a reasonable rate of return.

Note that goodwill does not include the portion of profits attributable to the corporation's ownership of patents, copyrights, formulas, or trademarks, even though they are intangible, since these are all specifically identifiable.

Goodwill, as is the case with other valuation formulas and procedures, should be used only as a guideline along with other valuation methods and not as the sole determinate of value. Goodwill has minimal relevance to the valuation of most investment companies since they usually do not have large amounts of intangibles. Officially, the IRS does not give strong credibility to goodwill (although the IRS still insists that goodwill must be taken into account in the valuation process). It can still serve as a guideline. The NumberCruncher illustration below shows the operation of this method.

GOODWILL VALUATION

Average Annual Earnings:	$100,000
Estimated Capitalization Rate:	0.2000
Average Annual Asset Value:	$500,000
Rate of Return on Tangible Assets:	16.000%

Option	Return on Tangible Assets	Earn from Tangible Assets	Earn from Intangible Assets	Goodwill Value	Total Business Value
1	16.000%	$80,000	$20,000	$100,000	$600,000
2	17.000%	$85,000	$15,000	$75,000	$575,000
3	18.000%	$90,000	$10,000	$50,000	$550,000
4	19.000%	$95,000	$5,000	$25,000	$525,000
5	20.000%	$100,000	$0	$0	$500,000

Question – What can be done if one of the persons involved in a business continuation agreement is uninsurable?

Answer – First, planners should remember that few individuals are truly uninsurable. Almost all individuals, except those in "exceptionally" ill health or in an exceedingly dangerous occupation, can obtain life insurance, albeit at a rate higher than the rate the standard insured would pay. Life insurance may be used for the insurable stockholders, and for the uninsurable stockholders, a sinking fund method should be used to at least accumulate enough money for a down payment. Often an amount equivalent to the appropriate insurance premium on the uninsurable person's life (given that person's age) is deposited into some type of segregated reserve account. Such an account might be invested in bonds, mutual funds, a fixed or variable annuity, or merely left in a savings account until the death of the uninsurable.

Typically, the agreement will provide that installment payments covering the remainder of the purchase price can be spread over a relatively long period of time.

Several life insurance companies are offering guaranteed issue type contracts even on those stockholder-employees previously thought to be uninsurable as long as the stockholder-employee is actively at work full time. One type of policy provides that if a death occurs during a certain initial period of time, e.g. three years, only premiums paid plus interest are payable as a death benefit. After the initial period the full death benefit is payable. A second type policy provides for a graded death benefit, i.e., one that increases over a period of time to the full death benefit.

Question – Will an agreement giving a surviving stockholder or the corporation an *option* to buy the deceased shareholder's stock usually fix the value of a business interest for federal estate tax purposes?

Answer – Yes, if there is a "first offer" provision and the price was fair and adequate when made. (A "first offer" provision requires the selling shareholder [or his executor] to offer the interest to the specified purchaser at an agreed upon price [fixed or set by formula] both during lifetime and after death before offering it to others.) Although the estate must be either obligated to sell at death or obligated to offer at death at the agreement price, the survivor(s) or the corporation need not be obligated to buy. An option in their hands would be sufficient. However, agreements involving substantially only family members may be determined not to be made at arm's length and therefore not effective in pegging the value for federal estate tax purposes. (See discussion above – Family Business Enterprises).

Question – Assume that there are three stockholders of a corporation and all stockholders have entered into a cross-purchase agreement. One of the stockholders dies and the other two stockholders purchase the decedent's stock using the life insurance proceeds under which the decedent was the insured and the remaining two stockholders were the policyowners and beneficiaries.

The decedent's personal representative now owns an insurance policy on the life of each of the surviving shareholders. They purchase their respective policies from the personal representative. Are there any potential tax problems?

Answer – No. This situation brings into play the "transfer-for-value" rule. This tax trap creates an exception to the general rule that the proceeds of an insurance policy are exempt from federal income tax.

The transfer-for-value rule provides that if insurance policies are transferred for value (consideration in money or money's worth has been given for such transfer) then the owner-beneficiary of that policy will have taxable income when the insured dies. The difference between the proceeds of the policy and the sum of (a) the value paid and (b) the premiums paid by the new owner-beneficiary after receipt of the policy will be taxable as ordinary income.

There are exceptions to the transfer-for-value rule where the transfer for value is made:

(1) to the insured (as is the case here),

(2) to a corporation in which the insured is an officer or stockholder,

(3) to a partner of the insured,

(4) to a partnership in which the insured is a partner,

(5) where the new owner's basis (cost) is determined in whole or in part by reference to the transferor's basis, or

(6) where a transfer of a policy or an interest in a policy is made between spouses or between spouses incident to a divorce. For instance, if a divorce decree requires one spouse to transfer a policy to another, the transfer will be considered a nontaxable event that results in a carryover basis in the policy and avoids the transfer-for-value tax trap.

Question – Assume that there is a stock redemption agreement funded by life insurance. The amount of the life insurance on the date of the death of one of the stockholders exceeds the corporate obligation under the redemption agreement. Are there any tax consequences?

Answer – The proceeds of corporate-owned life insurance will generally not be taxable to the corporation when it receives the same (except for potential exposure to a corporate level alternative minimum tax). However, the earnings and profits of the corporation will be increased by the amount of the proceeds and then reduced when a portion of the proceeds is used to redeem the shares of stock.

If the entire amount of the proceeds has not been used to redeem a decedent-shareholder's interest, there will be a permanent increase in corporate earnings and profits, which means that there should be additional dollars available for the payment of dividends; because of this, the potential exists for imposition of the accumulated earnings tax penalty, as well as dividend treatment on any distribution made by the corporation to its shareholders.

Question – Assume that the parties enter into either a redemption agreement or a cross-purchase agreement. Should anything be done to protect their rights with respect to a possible transfer to third parties?

Answer – The stock certificates owned by the parties to either the redemption agreement or the cross-purchase agreement should bear a legend (stamp) indicating a restriction on the ability to transfer those shares of stock as a result of the redemption or cross-purchase agreement.

Question – Why is a cross-purchase plan often preferred over a stock redemption arrangement?

Answer – Where a corporation purchases the stock of a withdrawing, disabled, or deceased stockholder, the surviving shareholders cannot increase their basis (cost for purposes of determining gain) by the amount paid. For example, assume Steve, Roberta, and Lee each own an interest in the SRL Corporation worth $100,000. Each invested $10,000 in 1977 when the corporation was formed. If Lee dies and the corporation (pursuant to a fully funded buy-sell agreement) pays his executor $100,000 for his stock, Steve's basis and Roberta's basis remain at $10,000. But if Steve and Roberta had been the purchasers and had each *personally* paid $50,000 to Lee's executor, their individual basis would have increased by that $50,000 amount. The distinction is important because, in this simplified example, the taxable gain on a future sale of Steve's stock or Roberta's stock could be as much as $50,000 less using a cross-purchase arrangement.

It is important to recognize, however, that this does not mean a cross-purchase plan will always be better than a stock redemption. In some cases, a stock redemption will be preferred:

(1) The basis increase may be higher when a stock redemption is used if

(a) surviving shareholders intend to retain the stock they own until death, and

(b) there is high appreciation in the value of the stock.

(2) Shareholders will often prefer, for both psychological and cash flow reasons, that corporate dollars be used to pay premiums.

(3) Premium payments by a corporation may be indicated when the corporation is in a lower income tax bracket than the individual shareholders.

(4) Where there are more than 3 shareholders involved, administrative inconvenience and cost generally make corporate-owned life insurance preferable over the multiplicity of policies required in a cross-purchase arrangement. For example, if there were 5 shareholders, 20 separate policies would be required. (The formula for determining the number of policies is N x (N - 1) with N being the number of shareholders.)

Other factors to consider in deciding between a cross-purchase and stock redemption include:

(1) possibility of dividend treatment because of constructive ownership (attribution) rules in family-owned corporations;

(2) state law restrictions on a corporation's right to purchase its own stock in the absence of sufficient surplus;

(3) transfer-for-value problems at the death of a shareholder if estate-owned policies are transferred to individuals other than the insureds;

(4) stock ownership desired after the purchase occurs;

(5) premium outlay differences due to differences in age and ownership interests between shareholders; or

(6) possible alternative minimum tax problems where life insurance is used to fund a stock redemption and the corporation is not "small" and therefore not exempt from the alternative minimum tax.

Question – Is there a solution to the dilemma of the cross-purchase vs. stock redemption decision?

Answer – One technique that may avoid or minimize problems inherent in a buy-sell of either the cross-purchase or the stock redemption type is the "Wait and See" (also known as the "option") approach.

Under a "Wait and See" type agreement, the estate of a deceased shareholder is bound to sell at an agreed-upon price or according to a predetermined formula, but the parties *wait* a specified length of time after the death of a shareholder to *see* if – and see to what extent – a cross-purchase or stock redemption or combination (perhaps even coordinated with an IRC Section 303 stock redemption) should be used.

The suggested method is for the corporation to have a first option to purchase any or all of a deceased shareholder's interest. Surviving shareholders have a secondary option to purchase any or all stock remaining. If, at this point, some stock still remains in the executor's hands, the corporation is *required* to purchase the entire balance.

Life insurance could be purchased by the corporation, by the surviving shareholders, or by both. (The corporation might, for example, purchase permanent life insurance while the shareholders might purchase term insurance.) If the corporation is owner and beneficiary of the insurance it can apply proceeds directly to the extent a stock redemption is indicated or make loans to the extent necessary to shareholders who will be purchasing stock on an individual basis. If life insurance is owned by and payable to shareholders on an individual basis, they could apply proceeds directly to the extent a cross-purchase is indicated or make loans or capital contributions to the corporation to enable it to effect a stock redemption.

The "Wait and See" approach provides an infinite variety of options and a maximum in planning flexibility.

Question – If a cross-purchase agreement funded with life insurance is changed to a stock redemption agreement, and the insurance that was owned by the individuals on each other is transferred to the corporation, will there be any income tax consequences as relates to the insurance?

Answer – No. Changing insurance from a cross-purchase agreement to a stock redemption agreement will not violate the transfer-for-value rule, because policies can be transferred from a stockholder to a corporation of which the insured is a stockholder. This will qualify as an exception to the transfer-for-value rule. Note, however, that the reverse, i.e., change from a stock redemption to a cross-purchase, will be a violation of the transfer-for-value rule if insurance is transferred from the corporation to a stockholder other than the insured.

Question – Can a buy-sell agreement "peg" the value of a business interest for federal gift tax purposes?

Answer – Although an agreement will probably not be controlling for federal gift tax purposes, it should carry strong evidentiary weight as to the business value and will be considered along with other relevant factors. An agreement will probably be successful in establishing value if:

(1) the price (or formula) is reasonable at the time the agreement is signed;

(2) the agreement is negotiated by parties knowledgeable of relevant facts and at arm's length;

(3) the price (or formula) agreed upon is as binding during lifetime as at death, i.e., the lifetime price permitted cannot be higher than the sale price at a shareholder's death; and

(4) the price is fixed by the terms of the agreement or the agreement contains a formula or method for determining price.

Where family members own at least 50% of the business, additional requirements will probably apply. See discussion above – Family Business Enterprises.

Question – What is the advantage of using a trustee in a buy-sell agreement?

Answer – Potential difficulty can be avoided through use of a trustee in carrying out the terms of the agreement. Prior to death of one of the parties to the agreement there are many duties to be performed. The trustee can obtain the premiums on insurance used to fund the agreement from the appropriate parties and can pay the premiums when they become due. The trustee can also serve as custodian of the policies subject to the agreement.

After death of a party to the agreement, the trustee will receive proceeds of the insurance on the life of the deceased business owner. The trustee can then act as a disinterested middleman in paying the purchase price for the decedent's business interest to the legal representative of the decedent's estate and in transferring the business interest to the purchaser.

Question – What is the potential tax trap in using a trusteed buy-sell approach?

Answer – Note that although the law is not entirely clear, the use of a trustee will probably not eliminate a transfer for value problem as to life insurance acquired by the trustee. For example, assume a corporation has three equal shareholders who enter into a cross-purchase plan. A trustee is named to act under the agreement and purchases insurance on all three shareholders to fund the agreement. After the death of the first shareholder, the agreement continues for the remaining two shareholders. The authors believe that the shift of economic interests in the insurance policies on the remaining shareholders will constitute a transfer for value. This is not a problem in a partnership buy-sell. In fact, if shareholders in a buy-sell are also partners in an unrelated business, even though there is a transfer of an interest in a policy and even if there is valuable consideration, the insurance may still be income tax free at death because of the "partnership safe harbor" to the transfer for value rules, discussed below.

Question – Is it possible to be certain the price established in a business continuation agreement involving family members will establish the estate tax value of the interest of a deceased partner or shareholder?

Answer – No. Assuring that values in a family buy-sell agreement will be accepted by the IRS and the courts has become much more difficult since the adoption of IRC Section 2703. Because related persons are by definition not dealing at arm's length in establishing the terms and price of their business continuation agreement, the price may not determine value for tax purposes unless it can be shown that the terms and price of the agreement could have been obtained in a fair bargain among unrelated parties in the same business dealing with each other at arm's length.[16] This standard, which is from the regulations, appears to be more demanding than the one Congress intended, which mandates a showing that the agreement could have been obtained in a hypothetical arm's length agreement.[17]

Careful planning, however, should increase the likelihood that the agreement will be able to "peg" values. Using a formula approach, rather than a stated dollar value, has a better chance of accomplishing this goal.

Question – Four shareholders in a closely held corporation want to enter into a cross purchase plan to acquire the stock of a deceased shareholder, fully funded with life insurance. You have explained to them the problems that will occur upon the death of any shareholder under the transfer for value rule if economic interests in the insurance policies on the remaining shareholders are shifted so that the agreement may remain in effect. Can you offer any solutions to this problem?

Answer – Other than canceling existing policies and acquiring new ones, there appear to be two other techniques to deal with this problem. The first is to have all of the remaining shareholders transfer their interests in policies on the other shareholder to the corporation, and substitute a stock redemption plan for the cross purchase plan. Since they are all shareholders in the corporation, the transfer of the policies to it falls within a safe harbor exception to the transfer for value rule.

Another solution, which has been the subject of a series of private letter rulings, is to consider the establishment of a partnership among all of the shareholders. As discussed above, transfers of policies among partners is one of the safe harbor exceptions to the transfer for value rule. Frequently the shareholders are involved in other business or investment activities, such as the ownership of property leased to the corporation, which could be the basis for the formation of a partnership. One private letter ruling held that the mere ownership of the life insurance policies would be a sufficient business or investment activity to justify formation of a partnership. However, cautious practitioners should not rely on this ruling, and advise the parties that they should carry out some other business or investment activity in such a partnership to assure its validity.

Question – Are the costs involved in a stock redemption deductible to the corporation?

Answer – No. Tax law prohibits a deduction for the costs involved in a stock redemption.[18] This prohibition applies even if the purchase of the interest is necessary to save the corporation's business life. The purchase of a corporation's own stock is a capital transaction and no deduction is allowed for either the purchase price or the expenses associated with the purchase.

Question – If and when repeal of the estate tax becomes a reality, will the purchase of a business interest at an owner's death trigger an income taxable event?

Answer – That's quite possible. Assuming estate tax repeal becomes a reality in 2010 and remain permanent, it will probably be accompanied by a modified carryover basis regime. Under the modified carryover basis regime, the estate's basis would be carried over from the decedent except to the extent that stepped-up basis is allocated to the business interest. Stepped-up basis could be allocated for up to $1,300,000 of property received from a decedent. An additional $3,000,000 of stepped-up basis could be allocated to property received by a surviving spouse.

To the extent that the purchase price exceeds the estate's basis, the estate will realize a capital gain. Payment of that income tax, unlike the estate tax, cannot be deferred.

ASRS: Secs. 40-43.

CHAPTER ENDNOTES

1. IRC Sec. 2042; See *Newell v. Comm.*, 66 F.2d 102 (7th Cir. 1933).
2. Treas. Reg. §20.2031-2(h); *May v. McGowan*, 194 F.2d 396 (2nd Cir. 1952); *Comm. v. Child's Est.*, 147 F.2d 368 (3rd Cir. 1945); *Est. of Mitchell*, 37 BTA 1 (1938). See also Rev. Rul. 59-60, 1959-1 CB 237.
3. IRC Sec. 264(a)(1).
4. IRC Sec. 101(a)(1).
5. IRC Secs. 302(c)(1), 318.
6. IRC Sec. 318(a)(3).
7. IRC Secs. 318(a)(1), 318(a)(2).
8. IRC Sec. 302(c)(2).
9. IRC Sec. 1014.
10. IRC Secs. 55, 56.
11. IRC Sec. 55(e).
12. IRC Secs. 2042, 2033.
13. Rev. Rul. 83-147, 1983-2 CB 158.
14. See *Est. of Infante*, TC Memo 1970-206.
15. IRC Sec. 1014(b)(6).
16. Treas. Reg. §25.2703-1(b)(4).
17. *Explanation of Revenue Provisions for Inclusion in Fiscal Year 1991 Budget Reconciliation Package as Approved by Committee 10/13/90*, Senate Finance Committee, 101st Cong., 2nd Sess., 136 Cong. Rec. S 15679, S 15683.
18. IRC Sec. 162(k).

Chapter 41

SECTION 303 STOCK REDEMPTION

WHAT IS IT?

IRC Section 303 allows a corporation to make a distribution in redemption of a portion of the stock of a decedent that will not be taxed as a dividend. A Section 303 partial redemption can provide cash and/or other property from the corporation without resulting in dividend treatment and provides cash for the decedent shareholder's executor to use to pay death taxes and other expenses.

WHEN IS THE USE OF SUCH A DEVICE INDICATED?

1. When there is a desire to keep control of a closely-held or family corporation within the decedent-shareholder's family after death.

2. When the corporation's stock is a major estate asset and a forced sale or liquidation of the business in order to pay death taxes and other costs is a threat.

3. Where a tax-favored withdrawal of funds from the corporation at the death of the stockholder would be useful.

4. When a redemption of IRC Section 306 stock is desirable.

WHAT ARE THE REQUIREMENTS?

1. The redeemed stock must be included in the decedent's gross estate for federal estate tax purposes.[1]

2. The value for federal estate tax purposes of all stock of the corporation that is included in determining the value of the decedent's gross estate must be *more than* 35% of the excess of (1) the value of the gross estate over (2) the sum allowable as a deduction under IRC Sections 2053 (estate expenses, indebtedness, and taxes) and 2054 (losses).[2]

3. Only an amount equal to the total of (a) all estate, inheritance, legacy, and succession taxes (including generation-skipping transfer taxes) and interest thereon imposed by reason of decedent's death, and (b) funeral and administration expenses (whether or not claimed as a deduction on the federal estate tax return) can be redeemed and receive favorable income tax treatment (i.e., avoid dividend treatment). Any excess will be taxed under the rules of IRC Section 302.[3] This means any balance may be taxed as a dividend to the "seller," the executor or heir from whom the stock is being redeemed, or the balance may qualify for favorable tax treatment (no realization of taxable gain due to the stepped-up basis of the stock upon the decedent's death) if within the purview of IRC Section 302.

4. A redemption under Section 303 will qualify for favorable tax treatment only to the extent that the interest of a shareholder whose stock is redeemed is reduced either directly or indirectly through a binding obligation to contribute toward the payment of the decedent's administration expenses and death taxes.[4]

In a hypothetical situation, assume the gross estate is $1,250,000; administrative and funeral costs are $250,000, and there are no other deductible expenses. To qualify for a Section 303 redemption, the value of the stock in question must *exceed* $350,000 (i.e., must be more than 35% of ($1,250,000 – $250,000)).

HOW IT IS DONE – AN EXAMPLE

The Section 303 stock redemption is relatively simple. The corporation redeems stock from the party who receives it at the death of the decedent-stockholder in question. Usually, the recipient of the stock will be the decedent-shareholder's personal representative, that is, the decedent's executor or administrator. Sometimes the seller will be a direct heir, surviving spouse, or trustee of an irrevocable trust created by the decedent. The redemption is protected under Section 303, however, only if it is from a stockholder who is obligated to pay death taxes, funeral, or administration expenses or whose share of the decedent's estate is reduced by these expenses.

Figure 41.1

DETERMINATION OF WHETHER ESTATE QUALIFIES FOR SECTION 303 STOCK REDEMPTION	
FEDERAL ESTATE TAX VALUE OF CORPORATE STOCK IN GROSS ESTATE	(1) $1,200,000
GROSS ESTATE LESS ALLOWABLE DEDUCTIONS	(2) $2,000,000
35% OF GROSS ESTATE LESS ALLOWABLE DEDUCTIONS	(3) $700,000
QUALIFIES IF (1) IS GREATER THAN (3)	
REDEMPTION UNDER SECTION 303 PROTECTED TO EXTENT OF	
FUNERAL AND ADMINISTRATION EXPENSES	$90,000
FEDERAL ESTATE AND GENERATION-SKIPPING TAXES	$200,100
STATE DEATH TAXES	$24,900
GENERATION-SKIPPING TRANSFER TAXES	$0
INTEREST COLLECTED AS PART OF ABOVE TAXES	$0
MAXIMUM ALLOWABLE SECTION 303 REDEMPTION	$315,000

Courtesy of NumberCruncher Software.

Stock may not be redeemed from any stockholder who acquired his stock by purchase or gift (if the donor was not the decedent).[5] For example, if a father wills stock to his son and his son later sells or gives the stock to his brother, the brother's stock is not eligible for a Section 303 stock redemption in the father's estate. Also, Section 303 is not applicable where stock is redeemed from a stockholder who has acquired the stock from the executor in satisfaction of a specific monetary bequest.[6]

Without adequate prior planning, there may be insufficient funds in the corporation to effect a Section 303 redemption. Generally speaking, cash will be needed if the main purpose of a Section 303 redemption is to provide liquidity. Although the corporation could borrow the money to pay for the stock, the ability of the business to obtain large amounts of cash may be uncertain and the terms and conditions of the loan may be prohibitive. A method of funding that will guarantee the necessary cash on the insured's death is the purchase of life insurance on the stockholder by the corporation.

The life insurance used to fund the Section 303 redemption should be a typical key person policy. The corporation should be the applicant, owner, premium payor, and beneficiary. (In the case of an uninsurable stockholder, a sinking fund can be established by using fixed or variable annuities, mutual funds, or other securities.)

Example: Assume Aaron, a widower who dies in 2004, owns 75% of a corporation. His son Joshua owns the remaining 25%. Aaron's stock is valued at $1,200,000. His gross estate less allowable deductions under IRC Sections 2053 and 2054 is $2,000,000. Assume he has minimal estate liquidity. The family corporation is in the 34% federal income tax bracket. Aaron is in a combined federal and state 30% income tax bracket. The corporation would purchase $315,000 of life insurance on Aaron's life. (This assumes Aaron's estate and inheritance taxes and other death related expenses will approximate $315,000.)

Step 1: At Aaron's death, his stock will pass to his estate. *Step 2:* The corporation then receives the insurance proceeds on Aaron's life. *Step 3:* The corporation uses the life insurance proceeds to pay Aaron's estate for stock qualifying for the Section 303 redemption. *Step 4:* The estate transfers $315,000 worth of stock to the corporation. *Step 5:* Aaron's estate uses the cash to pay federal and state death taxes and administrative and funeral expenses.

WHAT ARE THE TAX IMPLICATIONS?

1. The amount paid to the estate should not be treated as a dividend distribution. Instead, it will be treated as the "exchange price" for the stock and will generally result in no gain being recognized at all by the estate if the basis for the stock has been "stepped-up" by reason of being included in the shareholder's estate, unless the stock was a gift to the decedent within one year of his death and the property passes from the donee-decedent back to the donor or the donor's spouse.[7] [EGTRRA 2001 replaces stepped-up basis with a modified carryover basis for one year for property acquired from decedents dying in 2010.] However, to the extent the price paid to the estate exceeds the estate's basis, the estate will pay a tax on any such gain.

   Under the step-up-in-basis rules, a Section 303 redemption typically results in no adverse income tax consequences to the shareholder from whom the corporation made the redemption (generally the executor of the estate).

   The favorable treatment occurs because the basis of the stock in the executor's hands (say $10 a share) is "stepped up" to the stock's fair market value for federal estate tax purposes (say $26 a share) and the $26 a share price paid to the executor by the corporation to redeem the stock is generally equal to the stock's basis, i.e., the $26 a share fair market value for federal estate tax purposes. Thus, the amount realized on the "sale" is exactly equal to the seller's basis and there is no taxable gain for income tax purposes. In some cases the value per share paid by the corporation is greater than the value of the stock per share for federal estate tax purposes; when that happens, a capital gain results.

2. The insurance premiums paid on the life of the insured stockholder are not income tax deductible by the corporation.[8]

3. When the proceeds of the key person life insurance are paid to the corporation at the death of the stockholder, they will be received free of federal income taxes (with the possible exception of any corporate level alternative minimum tax).[9]

4. Section 303 redemptions are specifically exempt from attribution (constructive ownership) problems, helping to make redemptions from family corporations possible without the threat of dividend treatment.

IMPLICATIONS AND ISSUES IN COMMUNITY PROPERTY STATES

In order to qualify (aggregate) an ownership interest in two or more corporations for purposes of meeting the "more than 35% of adjusted gross estate" test, there must be at least 20% in value of each corporation included in the decedent's estate. In determining the 20% stock ownership by decedent, the surviving spouse's half of stock constituting community property may be included by treating it as if it had been included in determining the value of the gross estate of the decedent.

QUESTIONS AND ANSWERS

Question – Is cash the only property that may be distributed by the corporation?

Answer – No. If the need for liquidity exists, cash is generally the most practical type of property, but Section 303 does not require that the corporation make its purchase of the decedent's stock in cash. The corporation can distribute property "in kind." For instance, the corporation might distribute income-producing assets such as rental property (e.g., an apartment house, office building, or parking lot) in return for the stock it receives. Unfortunately, the corporation would recognize gain on the distribution of the appreciated property, and could also have taxable income in the event of recapture of depreciation,[10] liability in excess of basis,[11] and the excess of the fair market value distributed over the adjusted basis.[12]

The corporation can also issue notes to pay for the stock. The redemption rules will be met when the notes are delivered, not when they are actually paid. However, the notes should have a fairly short maturity (5 years or less).

Stock of the corporation making the distribution does not qualify as "property."[13]

Question – Do the funds received in the redemption have to be used to pay estate settlement costs?

Answer – No, the funds received in the redemption do not have to be used directly to pay estate settlement costs. Sometimes, an estate will already have sufficient cash. The estate's settlement costs (exclusive of debts) only serve as a measure of the amount which can be redeemed. As long as the requirements for Section 303 are met, the corporation can redeem the permitted number of shares regardless of whether or not the executor actually needs the cash for liquidity purposes. Similarly, money or property received by the seller does not actually have to be used to pay estate settlement costs.

Question – Is an agreement necessary for Section 303 redemptions?

Answer – Generally, an agreement is unnecessary in the case where the executor will acquire the controlling interest in the corporation. However, an agreement would be advantageous to a minority stockholder. This would provide assurance that his estate will benefit from a Section 303 redemption. (Quite often, however, a complete redemption is preferable to a partial redemption. This is particularly true in the case of the death of a minority shareholder because of the relatively weak voting control position the survivors of such a shareholder will have.) Specific permission should be granted by the stockholder in his will allowing his or her executor to effect the redemption.

Question – Can a Section 303 stock redemption be done without a majority stockholder's losing control?

Answer – It is possible to complete a Section 303 stock redemption without losing corporate control or diluting stock interest. Where there is a nonvoting class of stock outstanding, it is permissible for the corporation to redeem only the nonvoting stock.[14]

Generally, only one class of stock (common) is outstanding. There are two or perhaps three ways to accomplish the 303 redemption without creating voting or control problems. Recapitalization is the first method. If a corporation has only one class of stock outstanding, a shareholder may exchange a portion of his or her voting common stock for nonvoting preferred stock of equal value. The new

preferred stock is then redeemed under Section 303. This creates no adverse effect on the voting control of the corporation.

A second method of overcoming voting and control problems is the issuance of a preferred stock dividend prior to the death of a decedent-stockholder. A preferred stock dividend is declared on the common stock. This entails no recapitalization and, normally, the dividend is tax free. Then the preferred stock is redeemed pursuant to Section 303.

A third possible means of taking money out of a closely held corporation through Section 303 without a relative loss of control was suggested by a ruling that allowed the company to issue a stock dividend of nonvoting stock and to redeem the newly issued stock from the estate without creating a taxable distribution. The approval for such a stock dividend followed by a redemption should be obtained from corporate shareholders.[15]

Question – How is it possible to improve the chances of meeting Section 303 tests?

Answer – Lifetime gifts of personal insurance or other property (except the stock in question) to the surviving shareholder's family may reduce the gross estate of the stockholder (but only to the extent such gifts are not made within three years of the stockholder's death). Gifts of assets within three years of death are brought back into the gross estate under IRC Section 2035 for purposes of Section 303 and its tests.

A sale by the stockholder to the corporation of a personally owned life insurance policy on the stockholder's life or a contribution to the capital of the corporation should make qualification for a Section 303 redemption easier. This is because the stockholder's gross estate may not be significantly changed. The value of his business interest relative to his personal estate should be increased. (This may also make it easier to qualify for an installment payout of estate taxes attributable to the business.) Another technique to accomplish the same result is the purchase by the corporation of new key person insurance coverage.

Question – Can a Section 303 redemption be effected at any time?

Answer – The proceeds must be received after the decedent's death and no later than: (1) three years and 90 days from the due date of the federal estate tax return; or (2) 60 days after a tax court decision in a contest of estate tax liability has become final; or (3) the time permitted for the payment of estate tax installments where the executor has elected and the estate qualifies for a deferred payment of estate taxes attributable to the business under IRC Section 6166 (up to 14 years).

However, where a distribution is made more than four years after the decedent's death, the amount of protected distribution is limited to the lesser of: (a) the amount of taxes, funeral, and administrative expenses remaining unpaid at that time, or (b) the taxes and expenses that are actually paid within one year of the Section 303 payment to the stockholder.

Question – If there is more than one class of stock outstanding, can the aggregate value of all classes be taken into account in meeting the "more than 35%" test?

Answer – Yes, all classes of stock can be added together in meeting the "more than 35%" test regardless of which class of stock is being redeemed.[16]

Question – May stock of two or more corporations be aggregated for purposes of meeting the "more than 35% of adjusted gross estate" tests?

Answer – Only if 20% or more in value of the outstanding stock of *each* corporation is included in the decedent's gross estate.[17]

Question – Are the constructive ownership (attribution) rules a problem?

Answer – No, to the extent that stock is redeemed under Section 303, these rules can be ignored.

Question – Assume the executor needs cash quickly and before an IRS audit a Section 303 redemption takes place. At the audit of the estate tax return: (a) the IRS increases the valuation on the stock; (b) the IRS decreases the valuation; or (c) for some other reason the redemption does not qualify under Section 303. How can dividend treatment be avoided?

Answer – Arrange for the first contingency by providing that the purchase price and the number of shares redeemed will be adjusted so that the corporation will pay no more, and no less, than the value of the stock as finally determined for federal estate tax purposes. Alternatively, a contingency agreement

that voids the purchase and sale could be arranged in the event that the "more than 35%" test is not met.

Question – Can the corporation redeem stock other than that held by the executor at the time of the stockholder's death?

Answer – Yes, subject to the limitations discussed directly above; if for any reason stock was included in the decedent-stockholder's gross estate, it can be redeemed even if it is in the hands of someone other than the estate's executor at the time of the redemption.[18] For example, if a mother purchased stock with her own funds and held it jointly with her daughter when she died, the entire value of the stock would be in the mother's estate but the daughter would become the owner of the stock. A Section 303 redemption would be permissible to the extent the daughter's interest had to bear a portion of her mother's estate's taxes and estate settlement costs. The corporation could purchase (redeem) the stock directly from the daughter.

Likewise (subject to the limitation discussed above regarding an obligation for taxes and expenses), where the stock transferred is considered included in the decedent's estate because of a transfer with a retained life estate, a transfer taking effect at death or a revocable transfer,[19] the corporation could purchase the stock under Section 303 from the new owner. The same result occurs where the stock is placed into a revocable trust. Because the stock would be included in the decedent-stockholder's estate, a redemption from the trustee would be allowed (again, assuming the share of the estate going into the trust bears a direct or indirect burden to pay death taxes or administration costs or is reduced by such amounts).

Question – Will life insurance owned by the corporation to fund the Section 303 redemption cause or aggravate an accumulated earnings tax problem?

Answer – In general, if in any tax year the corporation's taxable income is retained for the purpose of paying insurance premiums (or for any other purpose) in excess of the amount of the $250,000 accumulated earnings credit ($150,000 in the case of certain personal service corporations), the corporation should be prepared to show that such excess retentions are necessary to meet reasonable needs of the business; such excess retentions that are beyond reasonable business needs may attract the tax. Where an uncommitted key individual life insurance policy (of the appropriate amount and type) is used to shift the risk of the loss of a key person's services, it will generally not cause or aggravate an accumulated earnings tax problem.

Likewise, even though death proceeds do increase earnings and profits (to the extent they exceed premiums paid), they should not, per se, cause or aggravate an accumulated earnings tax problem. Term, whole life, or a similar low cash value policy should be used. Furthermore, the redemption should be effected, wherever possible, in the same fiscal year that death occurs.

Note: The statute provides that "the reasonable needs of the business" include the "Section 303 redemption needs of the business." However, the Internal Revenue Service's position is that this provision applies only to amounts accumulated in the year of death and thereafter.

Many authorities suggest that a third party – such as an irrevocable trust – own the life insurance. At the shareholder's death, the proceeds would be paid to the policyowner who could then make a fully secured loan to the corporation. The corporation could then redeem the stock under Section 303. The three advantages of this technique are: (1) the insurance proceeds don't "swell" the value of the corporation for estate tax purposes; (2) cash values cannot trigger an accumulated earnings tax problem; and (3) neither cash values nor death proceeds can trigger an alternative minimum tax problem.

Question – If closely held stock is left to a specific legatee under the terms of a deceased stockholder's will, and there is a provision in the will that states that estate and inheritance taxes will be paid out of the residue of the estate, can there be a Section 303 redemption?

Answer – No. There cannot be a Section 303 redemption because the specific legatee will not bear any portion of paying the taxes. The redemption will qualify under Section 303 only to the extent that the interest of the redeemed shareholder is reduced directly or through a binding obligation to contribute to the payment of death taxes or funeral or administration costs.

Question – Can stock of an S corporation qualify for Section 303?

Answer – Yes. Stock of any corporation, including an S corporation, may qualify under Section 303.[20] In addition, any class of stock, common, preferred, voting or non-voting may be redeemed if otherwise qualifying for a Section 303 redemption.

Question – If the executor elects to take an income tax deduction on the estate's income tax return for funeral and administration expenses, rather than deduct such expenses on the estate tax return, does this have any impact on the amount qualifying for redemption under Section 303?

Answer – No. The fact that the executor deducts funeral and administrative expenses on the income tax return of the estate will not reduce the amount of stock that can be redeemed.

ASRS: Sec. 43.

CHAPTER ENDNOTES

1. IRC Sec. 303(a).
2. IRC Sec. 303(b)(2)(A).
3. IRC Sec. 303(a).
4. IRC Sec. 303(b)(3).
5. Treas. Reg. §1.303-2(f).
6. Treas. Reg. §1.303-2(f).
7. Treas. Reg. §1.303-1; IRC Sec. 1014(e).
8. IRC Sec. 264(a)(1).
9. IRC Sec. 101(a)(1).
10. IRC Secs. 1245, 1250.
11. IRC Sec. 311(b)(2).
12. IRC Sec. 311(b)(1)(B).
13. Rev. Rul. 65-289, 1965-2 CB 86; IRC Secs. 303(a), 317.
14. Treas. Reg. §1.303-2(c)(1).
15. Rev. Rul. 87-132, 1987-2 CB 82.
16. Treas. Reg. §1.303-2(c)(1).
17. IRC Sec. 303(b)(2)(B).
18. Treas. Reg. §1.303-1.
19. IRC Secs. 2036-2038.
20. Let. Rul. 9009041.

Chapter 42

FAMILY–OWNED BUSINESS DEDUCTION

WHAT IS IT?

The Economic Growth and Tax Relief Reconciliation Act of 2001 (EGTRRA 2001) repealed the family-owned business deduction[1] for 2004 to 2009, as the estate tax unified credit exemption equivalent increased above $1,300,000. EGTRRA 2001 also repeals the estate tax for one year in 2010. The family-owned business deduction returns in 2011, along with the estate tax.

For decedents dying in 1998 to 2003 or after 2010, the deduction is available for up to $675,000 of qualified family-owned business (QFOB) interests.[2] The family-owned business deduction applies only to the estate tax. If the deduction is taken, then the estate tax unified credit exemption equivalent (applicable exclusion) is equal to the lesser of the regular unified credit exemption equivalent or $1,300,000 minus the deduction. The benefit of the deduction is generally recaptured if qualified heirs dispose of the interest or fail to materially participate in the business within ten years after decedent's death.

When available, this provision can be a very real benefit to owners of small and medium businesses. Because of the numerous requirements for qualification for this benefit, careful planning must be done for the estate.

WHEN IS THE USE OF SUCH A DEVICE INDICATED?

1. When a substantial portion of the estate will consist of an interest in a family-owned business; and

2. When the decedent or decedent's family has materially participated in the business for five of the eight years preceding decedent's death; and

3. When the intention is to pass the business on to "qualified heirs," who will continue to operate it for ten years following the decedent's death.

WHAT ARE THE REQUIREMENTS?

1. Decedent must die in 1998 to 2003 or after 2010.

2. The decedent must have been a U.S. citizen or resident at death.[3]

3. The executor must elect the application of IRC section 2057 and file an agreement with the estate tax return, which provides for the payment of additional estate tax upon the occurrence of certain recapture events within ten years of the decedent's death, and prior to the death of the qualified heir.[4]

4. The value of all qualified business interests, plus certain gifts made of such interests, must exceed 50% of the adjusted gross estate.[5]

5. A qualified family-owned business interest is defined as either: (a) a proprietorship, or (b) an interest in an entity carrying on a trade or business.[6]

6. In the case of an interest in a trade or business, 50% of the entity must be owned by the decedent and decedent's family, or 70% by two families, or 90% by three families. In the case of the 70% and 90% tests, the decedent and decedent's family must own at least 30% of the entity.[7] Interests held by entities, including trusts, are subject to special attribution rules.[8] The decedent or decedent's family must have materially participated in the business.

7. A qualified family-owned business interest does not include: (a) a business whose principal place of business is outside the U.S.; (b) any business whose stock or securities was readily tradable within three years of the decedent's death; (c) any business if, during the tax year including the date of the decedent's death, more than 35% of adjusted gross income of the business was personal holding company income; (d) that portion of a business interest attributable to certain assets which produce personal holding company income, or foreign personal holding company income; or (e) that portion of a business interest attributable to excess working capital.

8. The qualified family-owned business interest must pass to a "qualified heir." This classification includes not only members of the decedent's family but also any individual who was actually employed

Figure 42.1

ADJUSTMENTS TO BUSINESS VALUE			
1. Value of Qualified Family-Owned Business Interest			$1,400,000
2. Plus: Gifted Business Interests			40,000
3. Less: Total Debts		($72,000)	
4. Subtract from Total Debts (line 3):			
Residence debt (to the extent deductible under IRC §163(h)(3))	$60,000		
Qualified educational / medical expense debt	0		
Other debts ($10,000 cap)	10,000	70,000	
5. Total Debt Adjustment (line 3 minus item 4)			(2,000)
Adjusted Value of Qualified Family-Owned Business Interest			1,438,000

Figure 42.2

GROSS ESTATE FOR QUALIFIED FAMILY-OWNED BUSINESS PURPOSES		
Gross Estate (including business)		$1,800,000
Less: Usual Deductions (debts, administration, etc.)		(100,000)
Adjusted Assets		1,700,000
Plus: Gifts		
i. Gifted business interests	$40,000	
ii. Gifts to spouse within 10 years of death	0	
iii. Non-business gifts over $10,000 within 3 years of death	0	40,000
Gross Estate for Qualified Family-Owned Business Purposes		1,740,000

Figure 42.3

CALCULATING ELIGIBILITY FOR THE DEDUCTION	
50% Gross Estate (Gross Estate from Figure 42.2)	$ 870,000
(if less than next line, estate is eligible)	
Adjusted Qualified Family-Owned Business Interest (from Figure 42.1)	1,438,000
Maximum Deduction	675,000
Actual Deduction	675,000
(lesser of Adjusted Qualified Family-Owned Business Interest, or Maximum Deduction amount)	

in the trade or business for at least 10 years prior to the decedent's death.

9. After qualifying for the deduction, certain "recapture events" must be avoided within ten years after the decedent's death, but before the death of the qualified heir(s), or an additional estate tax will become payable. These events include: (a) the failure by the heir or his family to materially participate in the business for at least five years out of any eight year period; (b) the disposition of the business, other than to a family member or through a qualified conservation contribution; or (c) loss of

U.S. citizenship by the heir (although a transfer into a qualified trust may be made in this event).

HOW IT IS DONE – AN EXAMPLE

Although the calculation of the qualified family-owned business deduction itself is reasonably simple, the determination of a decedent's eligibility is not as obvious. As noted above, adjustments must first be made to the value of the qualified family-owned business interest and to the gross estate, before calculating whether the adjusted value of the interest exceeds the 50% threshold of the adjusted gross estate. Assuming qualification, the availability of the deduction will then be limited to the lesser of $675,000 or the actual value of the adjusted qualified family-owned business interest.

Qualification for the family-owned business deduction is best illustrated through an example. Charles is single, and has two children. Charles owns and operates a dried fruits business, Nuts-4-U, Inc., which he manages and in which he participates on a full-time basis. The business is incorporated, and he and his children are the only shareholders. Charles died in 2003, leaving a gross estate of $1.8 million. Charles bequeathed his stock in the corporation equally to both children. The children are "qualified heirs" under the statute.

At his death, Charles was liable under an unsecured note to his brother, in the amount of $12,000. He also owned his home, and owed $60,000 under a mortgage at his death.

Charles made gifts of stock in Nuts-4-U, Inc. to both children in 1997 and 1999, within his annual exclusion amount, totaling $40,000 in fair market value as of his death. The value of Charles' interest in Nuts-4-U, Inc. was $1.4 million at his death.

Figure 42.1 illustrates the calculation that determines the adjusted value of Charles' interest in the business. Certain debts and expenses reduce the adjusted value.

Figure 42.2 illustrates the means by which the adjusted value of Charles' gross estate is calculated. Certain excluded gifts, including gifts of qualified family-owned business interests made within the annual exclusion, are brought back into the estate for purposes of calculating eligibility.[9]

As Figure 42.3 illustrates, once the values of the estate and the business interest have been established, determining eligibility for the deduction and the amount of the deduction is relatively straightforward. The actual amount of the deduction to the estate is also illustrated in Figure 42.3.

WHAT ARE THE TAX IMPLICATIONS?

1. The decedent's taxable estate is reduced by the qualified family-owned business interest deduction.

2. The benefit of the deduction is generally recaptured if qualified heirs dispose of the interest or fail to materially participate in the business within ten years after decedent's death.

IMPLICATIONS AND ISSUES IN COMMUNITY PROPERTY STATES

Since an important consideration in qualifying for the deduction involves determining the percentage of the business owned by the decedent, the question arises whether a surviving spouse's community property interest in the business is also included in this calculation. Under the IRC, interests owned by the decedent's family members are included in the calculation.[10] Thus, this attribution test results in the inclusion of a surviving spouse's interest for purposes of the 50% ownership test, whether that spouse's interest is community or separate property.

QUESTIONS AND ANSWERS

Question – Who is liable for the possible recapture of the estate tax deduction following the decedent's death?

Answer – In the event that a qualified family-owned business interest is not held for the required period following the decedent/transferor's death, the qualified heir who is responsible for triggering the recapture (generally through sale of his interest to a non-qualified heir) must pay his own proportionate share of the tax. Moreover, this responsibility will carry over to any transferee-qualified heir during the recapture period. Such transferees must also sign a new recapture agreement with the IRS. Any additional tax liability accrued as the result of a recapture event is due six months following such event.

Question – If the decedent failed to meet the material participation test with respect to the qualified family-owned business interest, but had owned a family business prior to the enterprise for which the deduction is sought, can the decedent's participation in the prior business be "tacked on" for purposes of the test?

Answer – Yes. Tacking by the estate of the decedent's material participation in a family business is allowed, where the family business for which the deduction is sought was acquired through an IRC section 1031 or 1033 tax-free exchange.

Question – Is a trust for a qualified heir eligible to receive a qualified family-owned business interest?

Answer – Yes. Section 2057 references the rules under IRC section 2032A(g). It appears that all successive trust beneficiaries must be qualified heirs.[11]

Additionally, under the special use valuation rules, a power in the trustee to divest a qualified heir of his interest, in favor of a disqualified heir, would bar an election under that IRC section. Thus, in anticipation of the future application of those rules to qualification under Section 2057, the conservative estate planner may consider providing that the trustee has no power to transfer qualified family-owned business interests to a disqualified heir. Moreover, considering the recent introduction of Section 2057, the trustee should also be given the power to amend a trust that holds a qualified family-owned business interest to comply with the section.

Question – Should trust documents make special provision for the allocation of a qualified family-owned business interest, following the death of the first spouse?

Answer – Yes. Since the new law provides for a deduction, allocation of the qualified family-owned business interest, which is nontaxable property, to a "Bypass" trust, or trust holding the decedent's unified credit exclusion equivalent amount, will not waste the decedent's credit.

ASRS: Sec. 54, ¶44.5(e).

CHAPTER ENDNOTES

1. IRC Sec. 2057.
2. IRC Sec. 2057(a)(2).
3. IRC Sec. 2057(b)(1)(A).
4. IRC Secs. 2057(b)(1)(B), 2057(h).
5. IRC Sec. 2057(b)(1)(C).
6. IRC Sec. 2057(e).
7. IRC Sec. 2057(e)(1)(B).
8. IRC Sec. 2057(e)(3)(A).
9. IRC Sec. 2057(c).
10. IRC Sec. 2057(e)(1)(B)(i).
11. IRC Sec. 2057(i)(3)(L).

Chapter 43

FAMILY LIMITED PARTNERSHIPS

Note: A checklist of issues to consider when choosing an entity, such as a proprietorship, partnership, limited liability company (LLC), C corporation, or S corporation, appears at the end of Chapter 47 as Figure 47.3.

WHAT IS IT?

A family partnership is a partnership that exists between members of a family (defined for income tax purposes as including only an individual's spouse, ancestors, lineal descendants, and any trusts established primarily for the benefit of such persons).[1] If a partnership among family members is a genuine partnership, it will be treated tax-wise the same as any other partnership and the same rules will apply.

The family partnership is a technique frequently used as a means of shifting the income tax burden from parents to children or other family members. However, the benefit of shifting income to children under age 14 has been substantially eliminated. For children under age 14, unearned income in excess of $1,600 (as indexed for 2004) generally will be taxed at the parent's top marginal rate under the "Kiddie Tax" rules.

Although family partnerships have sometimes been attacked by the IRS as being mere tax avoidance schemes that should not be recognized for tax purposes, if the rules for establishing and operating such partnerships are carefully followed, the IRS currently recognizes the validity of this income shifting device.[2] Although the IRS has asserted that a taxable gift can arise upon the contribution of capital to a family limited partnership, this argument was rejected where the partnership agreement allocated income and expenses on a pro rata basis based on the partners' contributions to the partnership. The court stated there cannot be a gift on formation where each investor's interest is proportional to the capital contributed.[3]

Two major forms of family partnerships commonly used are the general partnership and the limited partnership.

The general partnership is an entity under which all partners have a voice in management (by percent-age vote) but are personally liable for all of the debts and other liabilities of the general partnership. This very negative aspect often makes the general partnership entity unsuitable for family wealth preservation and has prompted the use of the limited partnership for the majority of family activities for which a partnership is appropriate.

One benefit of a general partnership is that, in some circumstances, the partners may share in the losses generated by the partnership for income tax purposes. This is much more difficult for limited partners due to the passage of various "anti-tax shelter" laws which restrict the sharing of losses among partners in limited partnerships.

A family limited partnership (FLP) is a limited liability entity created under state law. Family limited partnerships are so named because ownership of partnership interests typically is limited to members of the same family unit. Since the limited partnership form is most frequently used for the majority of family activities, this chapter will deal mainly with that form of doing business or holding assets.

Ownership rights in the FLP are governed by state law as modified by the FLP agreement. Most states have adopted the Uniform Limited Partnership Act (ULPA) or some modified version thereof. Although there may be slight differences in the statutory partnership rules from one state to another, there generally is a high degree of uniformity among the states.

Upon formation, family members contribute property in return for an ownership interest in the capital and profits of the FLP. The partners designate a general partner (or general partners) who will be given management responsibility and who will assume personal liability for debts and other liabilities that are not satisfied from the assets of the FLP. Conversely, in return for giving up their rights of management and control over the assets of the FLP, the personal liability of the limited partners generally is limited to the amount of capital that they contribute.

Although an underlying purpose of most FLPs is to manage family assets and to plan for the transfer of such assets from parents to children, many parents are not willing to part with control over their assets when the FLP is created. In some cases, the parents simply desire to continue managing their property and in other cases, the children lack the maturity or business skills required to manage the assets. In the latter case, an FLP usually provides the parents with the time and opportunity to educate their children about managing their assets.

Although a thorough understanding of partnership law is essential to preparing an effective limited partnership agreement, the concepts underlying FLPs are not difficult to comprehend and an FLP can be easily integrated into an estate plan.

WHEN IS THE USE OF SUCH A DEVICE INDICATED?

Family limited partnerships are often used to fractionalize the ownership of business assets or real estate to take advantage of valuation discounts (see Chapters 57 and 58) which significantly reduce transfer taxes. In most cases, an FLP will be used to facilitate the making of gifts of limited partner interests from parents to children and other family members without divesting control from the parents. In other cases, an FLP will be used to ensure continuous ownership of assets within the family unit for several generations.

Until most recently, FLPs were used primarily as a means of (1) shifting the income tax burden from parents to children or other family members or (2) to "freeze" the value of assets by shifting future growth in various assets to other family members. Although these uses have been somewhat curtailed by the passage of the Kiddie Tax and the enactment of IRC Section 2701, the many other benefits provided by the FLP have made it a valuable tool in developing a comprehensive estate plan.

With greater frequency, many practitioners are coming to recognize the many tax and non-tax benefits that an FLP can provide. An FLP would be an appropriate device in the following circumstances:

1. To reduce the value of an estate for transfer tax (e.g., estate, gift, and generation-skipping) purposes. EGTRRA 2001 repeals the estate tax and the generation-skipping transfer tax for one year in 2010.

    Because control of the assets of an FLP is centralized in the general partner(s), a limited partner often experiences an immediate decrease in the value of his interest compared to the value of the

property contributed to the FLP. This decrease in value results because of the lack of control and marketability that accompany ownership of a limited partnership interest and the inherent inability of a limited partner to access the capital and profits of the FLP.

It is well accepted that value often appears and disappears in an FLP. Value can appear in the form of a control premium that attaches to the right to manage assets or to liquidate assets into cash. Value can also disappear due to the giving up of management rights and exchange of assets in return for an unmarketable ownership interest.

Past cases demonstrate that the value of FLP interests typically will be reduced by valuation discounts falling within the 30% to 35% range. Under these circumstances, a married couple with a taxable estate of $4,000,000 in 2004 could use an FLP to reduce the value of their estate to a point where little or no estate tax is owed.

2. When it is desired to shift the income tax burden from a parent who is in a high income tax bracket to a child or other relative who is in a lower income tax bracket, thus providing intra-family income splitting and tax saving.

    Use of an FLP can facilitate parents shifting income to their children, with the income taxed at the child's lower income tax bracket. This will increase the family's cash flow. Although the gradual narrowing of the federal income tax rate brackets for individuals (the maximum rate is currently 35%) and enactment of the Kiddie Tax has reduced the effects of income shifting, substantial income tax savings can still be achieved in the majority of cases. (Example 1 at the end of this chapter presents an illustration of the income shifting context in the case of a family business.)

3. Where it is desirable to conduct a family business in a form other than a sole proprietorship or a corporation.

    In selecting a choice of business entity, the use of a corporation may cause tax problems that would not exist if the business were instead operated as an FLP. For example, subchapter C corporations are subject to personal holding company rules, the accumulated earnings tax, and unreasonable compensation problems, while subchapter S corporations are restricted as to who and how many persons may be shareholders. Similarly, placing a sole proprietorship business into a trust may result in the trust taxed by the IRS as a corporation, which is usually a very bad result. FLPs generally offer flexibility in income taxation compared to these other forms of businesses. (A summary of some of the differences in these business entity forms is provided at the end of this chapter).

4. Where a parent desires to maintain control over assets that will be transferred to younger generations through gifts of limited partner interests.

One of the major benefits of an FLP is the ability to retain control over assets without having to own a majority of the interests of the FLP. This permits parents to transfer their assets to an FLP and then give or sell a majority interest (50% or more) to the children while retaining control over the assets. Such control can be achieved by retaining as little as a 1% general partner interest in the FLP. Although the children may hold a majority interest in the FLP, the control over the assets remains in the hands of the general partner.

Use of an FLP can also permit the parents to implement a succession plan for the ownership, management and control of assets so that undesired beneficiaries do not gain access to the assets.

5. Where it is desirable to protect assets from creditors of the partners.

If a family member is in a high risk profession, such as a doctor or engineer who is vulnerable to lawsuits, an FLP may be effective to shield personal assets by placing them in the hands of other family members, away from the reach of future creditors. In most cases, a judgment creditor will be unable to attach partnership assets to satisfy a debt of an individual partner.

However, although the asset protection features of an FLP (discussed below) may discourage a creditor from aggressively seeking satisfaction of the debt from the partnership assets, the use of an FLP as an asset protection device may also prevent the assets from being reached by the partner since a judgment creditor has the right to attach the partner's interest in the FLP or attach any assets that are distributed by the FLP to the partner. This characteristic may cause a stalemate between the partner and creditor and encourage settlement of the debt at an amount that is favorable to both parties.

Protecting assets may also present a number of ethical issues for the practitioner since certain transfers can be attacked as fraudulent conveyances. For these reasons, extreme care and consideration should accompany the use of an FLP for any such purpose.

6. When retention of ownership of assets within the family unit is desired.

By including in the FLP agreement a right of first refusal for transfers of partnership interests, the partners can virtually guarantee that outside persons will not acquire ownership interests in the FLP. Also, by limiting the rights of a transferee partner to that of an "assignee" (who lacks voting rights) the ability of a partner to sell his interest is likely to be severely impaired, thereby achieving the intended goal of maintaining immediate family ownership.

7. Where a parent desires to protect assets, which are to be transferred to younger generations, from being dissipated through mismanagement or divorce.

A parent who makes gifts of property to his children runs the risk that the child will cause the gift to be unwisely managed or lost to a spouse or creditor. These pitfalls can be avoided by placing the assets into an FLP instead and transferring a limited partner interest to the child. In this case, the parent may retain control over the assets until the child is mature and has achieved sufficient financial acumen to manage the property.

Similarly, because a divorce action can result in the court awarding the spouse a share of the limited partner interest, it may be worthwhile for the parent to transfer the interest to the child in trust to be held for the child's lifetime, thereby defeating the rights of the spouse.

8. Where flexibility in setting the rules for managing property is desired.

Unlike an irrevocable trust, an FLP can be amended by vote of a given percentage of partnership interests. This results in a parent being able to easily change the governing rules that apply to the partnership if the parent maintains the necessary percentage ownership interest to amend the agreement.

9. To simplify ownership of assets.

Use of an FLP may allow for cost savings through consolidation of ownership into one entity. Such consolidation may result in diversification of money managers and reduced investment adviser fees. By pooling family assets, the FLP may obtain advantages in terms of diversification and size of investment that cannot be achieved individually by the partners.

Further, by giving the general partner discretion to reinvest partnership profits over the long-term, the FLP can carry out an investment strategy that focuses on long-term benefits to the partners. In situations where generation-skipping trusts are used to hold FLP interests during the lifetime of a beneficiary, the death of the beneficiary will not pose a threat to the continued operation of the FLP since the FLP provides for continuity of ownership and estate tax will not be due on the FLP interest held in a generation-skipping trust (to the extent the assets and estate tax "skip" the child).

10. To ease the distribution of assets at death among family members without having to remove the assets from the partnership.

Upon the death of a parent, assets may remain in the partnership and only partnership interests are transferred to the heirs (to the extent permitted under the Limited Partnership Agreement), thereby enabling the partnership operations to remain intact.

11. To avoid out-of-state probate costs.

Since FLP interests are personal property, they should not be included for probate purposes in those states in which the partnership owns property. Such interests are subject to probate only in the domiciliary state of the partner.

12. To discourage family members from fighting over FLP assets and to provide a forum for the resolution of disputes among family members if and when such disputes arise.

Unlike trusts, an FLP agreement may require binding arbitration of disputes among the partners for all issues relating to partnership assets. Further, the FLP agreement may be drafted so that the losing partner must pay the court fees of the prevailing party, thereby reducing the likelihood and cost of litigation among the partners.

WHAT ARE THE REQUIREMENTS?

Because state law governs the formation of partnerships, it is necessary to refer to the applicable law of the state in which the partnership is formed to determine the various procedural aspects of forming a limited partnership. In general, the following requirements will need to be met in order to create a limited partnership that will be respected for state law purposes.

1. A written agreement setting forth the rights and duties of the partners. If no written agreement exists, the terms of the partnership may be difficult to prove if claimed to be different than under applicable state law.

2. Filing a certificate of limited partnership and obtaining all necessary business licenses and registrations.

3. Obtaining a separate tax identification number for the partnership.

4. Transferring title of all contributed assets into the name of the partnership and opening new accounts in the name of the partnership.

5. Amending contracts to show the partnership as the real party in interest (e.g., adding the partnership as an additional insured on liability insurance policies).

6. Avoiding commingling of partnership assets with those assets of the individual partners or using partnership assets for personal business of the partners.

7. Filing annual state and federal income tax returns and allocating partnership income to the partners.

8. Paying annual state franchise taxes, if applicable, and making any other filings required under state law.

PROVIDING MANAGEMENT AND CONTROL

Control over assets contributed to an FLP is achieved by retaining ownership of the general partner interest (or the managing partner interest in cases where the FLP has multiple general partners). In most instances, the most important decision to be made in creating an FLP is who to name as the general partners since they will exercise exclusive control over the partnership business operations and determine if, when, and how much of the partnership income is to be distributed to the partners.

For estate planning purposes, it may be advisable for the partners to implement a succession plan for management. This may be achieved by designating a non-managing general partner who will succeed in the duties of management and control upon vacancy of the general partner's interest.

For most FLPs, possible general partners include one or both parents, either individually or as trustee of a family living trust, an S corporation or limited liability company controlled by one or more persons, or mature and financially experienced children or grandchildren (individually or using trusts for their benefit). It is not recommended that children be given management powers over their parents' assets unless the parents expressly desire to relinquish control and the child has sufficient experience and maturity in managing property.

Even though much of the value of the FLP may be given away by transferring limited partner interests to the children, the general partners maintain control of the assets in the FLP even though they retain only a small percentage ownership interest. For this reason, many practitioners recommend use of an FLP for parents who desire to maintain control of their assets while having transferred away most of the assets' economic benefits.

The general partner should have the necessary willingness, knowledge, and experience to do the following:

1. Manage and invest partnership assets.

2. Make decisions as to distributions of partnership income and/or assets.

3. File income tax returns on behalf of the partnership and understand the income tax law.

4. Furnish annual partnership income tax information (Schedule K-1) to the partners.

5. Make necessary filings with the state's Secretary of State.

6. Give or withhold consent to transfers of partnership interests and amendment of the FLP agreement.

ENSURING FAMILY OWNERSHIP

Continuous family ownership of the FLP is guaranteed by restricting each partner's ability to sell or otherwise transfer his interest to non-family members. Because most FLPs are used by parents to transfer partnership interests to their children at reduced transfer tax values, the existence of rights of first refusal, buy-sell provisions, or other restrictions on transfer are of paramount concern and require considerable attention. However, much care must be exercised in drafting the partnership agreement in order to avoid the transfer tax pitfalls of Chapter 14 of the IRC (see Chapter 57).

In almost all instances, the FLP agreement should prohibit the partners from selling or transferring their interests in a manner that is disruptive to the continuation of the family asset arrangement plan or disruptive to family harmony. To achieve this result, the FLP agreement typically will provide the partners a right of first refusal to deal with a circumstance where another partner wishes to sell, or otherwise transfer, his interest to a non-family member. In such cases, the non-selling partners will usually have the right to purchase the interest of the selling partner for cash or with an unsecured long-term promissory note which bears an interest rate favorable to the buyer (but note that the restriction should not constitute "financial detriment" to any donee partner and such restriction should also satisfy the requirements of IRC Sections 2703 and 2704). Only if the non-selling partners fail to exercise their purchase rights may the interest then be sold to the non-family member.

If the family members do not wish for the new partner to possess any voting rights, then the agreement should permit them to treat the new partner as a mere assignee who is entitled to receive only income distributions and a proportionate share of partnership income, expenses, deductions and credits. This mechanism provides the family members with protection from the influence of undesired active partners, enhances continued family ownership, and does not disrupt good asset management.

REDUCING TRANSFER TAXES

For individuals having substantial wealth, another important benefit of implementing an FLP is the reduction of values for transfer tax purposes.

As a general rule, the value of an FLP interest is worth less than direct ownership of the same percentage interest in the underlying assets of the FLP. Put another way, the sum of all of the FLP interests combined does not equal the sum of the assets themselves. This is because ownership of a limited partner interest in an FLP does not convey any rights of management or control over the underlying assets and the FLP agreement prohibits the partners from freely transferring their interests to non-family members. Accordingly, transfer tax values are reduced by the application of discounts (determined by appraisal) to reflect these restrictions.

Because FLPs may be used to transfer partnership interests to lower generation family members, reduced transfer tax values allow for (1) shifting a greater amount of partnership interests by percentage from parents to subsequent generations and (2) lower overall estate tax liability on those interests retained by a deceased partner. For the majority of FLPs, combined discounts in the range of 25% to 35% are typically achieved.

Despite the reduction in value of FLP interests, the real income production and growth potential of the FLP's assets remain available to the partners since control remains within the family unit.

SECURING VALUATION DISCOUNTS

A *discount for lack of control* is routinely applied in establishing estate and gift tax values of minority limited partner interests (see Chapter 57 for a detailed discussion of discounts to FLP interests). This discount reflects the inability of a limited partner to control the operations of the FLP and to invest its assets in a manner that is of the greatest benefit to the limited partner.

Because management and investment decisions (including the decision as to when to distribute partnership income) are outside the control and influence of the limited partners, the value of a limited partner's interest is reduced to reflect such lack of control. Typical discounts for lack of control (minority interest) generally range between 20% and 30%.

A *discount for lack of marketability* is also applied to the value of privately-held limited partnership interests that do not offer a readily available market for trading. Such a discount reflects the fact that a partner who contributes assets to an FLP in return for a limited partnership interest generally will have difficulty in finding a buyer (if one exists).

Factors that typically influence the amount of the discount for lack of marketability include the nature of

the FLP's asset mix (e.g., real property, securities, equipment, etc.), the availability and accuracy of information relating to the FLP and its owners, the existence of transfer restrictions against ownership interests, the willingness of the partners to accept new partners, whether income is currently distributed to the partners, and the expected date on which capital contributions will be returned to the partners.

Whereas an understood purpose of most family limited partnerships is to maintain ownership of assets for the benefit of members of one or more selected families, marketability outside the family group is generally disfavored.

The inclusion of rights of first refusal and other transfer restrictions in the FLP agreement will also reduce the marketability of an FLP interest for transfer tax valuation purposes (provided that the requirements of IRC Section 2703 are satisfied), further reducing values for estate tax and gift tax purposes. Based upon the number and severity of the transfer restrictions and the factors stated above, lack of marketability discounts may reach as high as 30% or more.

A discount for built-in capital gains tax may also apply to the value of privately-held limited partnership interests if the tax basis of the assets owned by the partnership is demonstrably lower than the current fair market value of such assets, thereby signifying future potential capital gains tax liability. To the extent that the net asset value of the partnership is subject to inherent gains tax liability, consideration should be allowed for valuation purposes.[4]

Additionally, in determining the value of an interest in an FLP, consideration should always be given as to whether the interest can be liquidated through the enforcement of withdrawal rights. If the partnership agreement or state law does not confer upon the limited partner any right to withdraw capital, then the limited partner's investment may remain in the partnership until expiration of the partnership term (often 35-50 years in length) or longer if the partners elect to amend the limited partnership agreement and continue the term of the partnership. In such case, the limited partner's interest is said to be "locked-in" to maintaining his investment in the partnership and a *lock-in discount* is appropriate.

In determining whether a lock-in discount is applicable, IRC Section 2704(b) must be reviewed. This section is discussed in greater detail in Chapter 57.

PROTECTING ASSETS

Family limited partnerships provide a limited degree of asset protection to the partners since assets of the FLP generally cannot be attached to satisfy personal debts of the partners. Under the Uniform Limited Partnership Act, the remedy of a personal creditor is to obtain a "charging order" from a court against the interest of the limited partner. The charging order entitles the creditor to receive the distributions that would normally be paid to the limited partner until the debt is fully paid.

A charging order does not give the creditor any voting rights in FLP matters and the creditor cannot be assured that the general partner will elect to pay out the FLP income to the partners. Furthermore, the IRS in Revenue Ruling 77-137 has indicated that even though the general partner does not pay out any income to the creditor and other partners, the responsibility for paying the income tax attributable to the attached limited partner's interest will fall upon the creditor.[5]

Notwithstanding the negative aspects of a charging order, a debtor partner is not necessarily guaranteed access to FLP assets if the judgment creditor is insistent upon collecting its debt. The judgment creditor may quietly wait for the partnership to distribute assets to the debtor partner in hope of attaching the assets immediately after distribution. For this reason, the use of an FLP by itself as an asset protection device is not a guaranteed means of avoiding creditor liability.

Additionally, in view of the surge in popularity of the use of FLPs and the emphasis placed on their asset protection features, it is possible that future courts may be reluctant to continue such asset protection for partnerships in which substantially all of the interests are owned by one person or family, or the assets of the partnership are mainly liquid in nature (e.g., marketable securities, cash, etc.).

INCOME TAX ASPECTS

IRC Section 704(e) was enacted to prevent taxpayers from using family partnerships as a means of splitting family income and circumventing the progressive tax rate structure of the federal income tax. In order for a donee-partner of an FLP to be recognized as a partner for income tax purposes, the following three factors must be satisfied:

(a) Capital must be a material income-producing factor. This means that the FLP's business must require substantial inventories or substantial investment in plant, machinery or other equipment, as contrasted with a personal service corporation.[6]

(b) A donee or purchaser of a capital interest in a partnership is not recognized as a partner unless such interest is acquired in a bona fide transaction, not a mere sham for tax avoidance or evasion purposes, and the donee or purchaser is the "real owner" of such interest.[7]

(c) The donee's distributive share must be included in his gross income, except to the extent that such distributive share is determined without allowance of reasonable compensation to a donor partner for services rendered to the partnership and except to the extent that the portion of such distributive share attributable to donated capitol is proportionately greater than the share of the donor attributable to the donor's capital.[8]

The validity of an FLP for income tax purposes is dependent upon the donee partner's "owning" a capital interest. The IRC does not define exactly what constitutes "ownership" of a capital interest. However, the regulations state that a transferee of a partnership interest must be the "real owner" of the capital interest and have dominion and control over that interest.

As provided in the IRS regulations, there are four types of retained controls (i.e., powers retained by a donor of an FLP) that are of particular importance in showing that a donee lacks true ownership of his interest. If the donee is not the real owner of his capital interest, then the income attributable to the capital interest will be taxable to the donor. These controls include:

(a) The donor's retaining control of the distribution of income or restricting the amount of such distributions.

(b) The donor's limiting the right of a donee partner to dispose of his interest without financial detriment.

(c) The donor's retaining control of assets that are essential to the partnership business.

(d) The donor's retaining management powers which are inconsistent with normal partnership relations.[9]

The cases that have discussed whether a donee is a real owner stress the importance of receiving current distributions of income.[10]

Because partnership agreements frequently limit the ability of a partner to transfer or liquidate his interest, it is important that the partner be able to dispose of the interest "without financial detriment." This test is aimed at determining whether the partner has control over the current benefits of the interest. The term "financial detriment" is interpreted as requiring that the partner be able to realize the fair market value of the interest. Thus, the regulations indicate that a partnership agreement that requires a partner first offer his interest to the partnership (or partners) at the same price as that of any bona fide offer from an outside party will not be considered as imposing a financial detriment upon the interest of a donee partner.

The regulations under Section 704(e) allow a donor to retain management or voting control over a family partnership if the retention is of a manner that is common in ordinary business relationships.[11] However, the donor's retention of control is directly related to the donee's ability to dispose of the interest without financial detriment. Generally, the donee will not be deemed to possess this right unless he is both independent of the donor and has sufficient maturity and understanding of his rights to exercise his right to withdraw his capital interest from the partnership. Thus, FLP interests that are transferred to minors should be held either by a guardian or in trust.

In addition to these direct controls, an examination of several indirect controls may determine if a donee partner is a real owner of his capital interest. As provided in the regulations, the following factors are to be examined:

(a) Whether the donee participates in the management of the business.

(b) Whether there have been income distributions to the donee partner.

(c) Whether the donee partner is held out to the public as a partner.

(d) Whether the partnership has complied with local laws regarding use of fictitious names and other business registration statutes.

(e) Control of business bank accounts.

(f) Whether the donee's rights in distributions of partnership property and profits have been recognized.

(g) Whether the donee's interest is recognized in insurance policies, leases, and other business contracts and in litigation affecting business.

(h) The existence of written agreements, records, memoranda, which establish the partnership and partners' rights.

(i) Whether the partnership has filed income tax returns.[12]

Assuming that a FLP satisfies the requirements of Section 704(e), a number of valuable income tax benefits may be provided to the partners. Among these benefits are the following:

1. Pass through of items of income, expense, credit, and deduction to the partners.

2. Achieving a "step-up" in income tax basis in FLP assets for interests received from a deceased partner (or upon purchase by a new partner) if an election is made by the general partner under IRC Section 754.

3. Withdrawal of assets without recognition of taxable gain (unlike corporate ownership).

4. Income shifting to family members.

5. No income tax gain on contribution of assets to the FLP or upon dissolution of the FLP in most cases.

These income tax benefits make FLPs extremely attractive in planning for income tax responsibilities of the partners. If properly structured, the FLP will not increase income taxes and may even reduce income taxes in some cases.

Other tax implications exist in operating an FLP. In general, the following rules will apply:

1. A reasonable allocation of partnership income must be made to any donor partner (which includes a parent who has sold a partnership interest to a family member) to recognize the value of his services to the FLP in order for the family partnership rules of Section 704(e) to be satisfied.

   Where interests of family members are acquired by gift and/or intra-family sale, a mandatory allocation of the FLP's profits in proportion to capital contributed, after due allowance has been made for the donor's services, must be made. For example, assume father and son are each 50% partners in an FLP that has a net income of $100,000. Father is paid $20,000 as reasonable compensation for his services. The remaining $80,000 would be taxed $40,000 each to father and son. This would be in addition to the father's reporting $20,000 of income for his services to the FLP.

If a contributing partner acquires capital from an independent source and not by an intra-family gift or purchase, the mandatory allocations described above will not apply and profit and loss may be allocated in a different manner.

2. Unless an election is made by the FLP to be taxed as a corporation, the partnership itself does not pay federal income taxes since it is a passthrough entity.

However, a federal income tax return (Form 1065) must be filed showing each partner's allocable share of income, expenses, deductions, and credits. Each partner must pay income taxes based upon his share of partnership income.

3. Generally, no gain or loss is realized when property is contributed to the FLP.

However, IRC Section 721 should be examined in order to ensure that the FLP is not classified as an "investment company" which would cause income tax on gains to be owed due to the formation of the partnership. The rules for determining whether an FLP is an investment company are the same rules found under IRC Section 351. Under these rules, an investment company exists if 80% or more of the entity's capital is comprised of marketable securities and diversification of assets among the partners has occurred.[13] In making contributions to an FLP, the basis of the FLP in the contributed assets is the same basis the property had in the hands of the contributing partners.

4. Gifts of FLP interests are subject to gift tax and will likely raise questions concerning the value of the transferred interest.

The regulations state that the same principles that apply in valuing stock in corporations apply to valuing interests in an FLP. The fair market value at the date of gift will be the value for gift tax purposes.[14]

In valuing interests in a family limited partnership, regulations set forth requirements for pro-

viding "adequate disclosure" to the IRS, in order to commence running of the gift tax statute of limitations.[15] The following is a synopsis of these requirements:

a. *Non-gift transactions*

- same information as required for adequate disclosure of a gift

- explanation describing why the transfer was not subject to the gift tax

b. *Gift transactions*

- description of the transferred property and any consideration received

- identity of and relationship between the transferor and transferee

- if property transferred in trust, the trust's tax identification number and a brief description of the terms of the trust or a copy of the trust

- detailed description of the method used to determine the FMV of the property transferred

- any restrictions on the property or discounts taken

c. *Securities*

- recitation of exchange

- CUSIP number

- mean between the highest and lowest quoted selling price on the valuation date

d. *Transfer of an interest in an entity* (e.g., FLP or LLC)

- description of any discount claimed in valuing the interest or any assets of the entity

- if the value of the entity is determined based on the net value of the assets

- a statement regarding the FMV of 100% of the entity without regard to any discounts in valuing the entity or assets owned by the entity

- the pro rata portion of the entity subject to transfer

- a description of how the fair market value of the transferred interest is determined

- if 100% of the value of the entity is not disclosed, the taxpayer bears the burden of demonstrating that the FMV of the entity is properly determined by a method other than a method based on the net value of the assets held by the entity

- if the entity owns an interest in another non-actively traded entity, the same information must be provided for that entity if the information is relevant and material in determining the value of the interest

e. *Submission of appraisals*

- prepared by an appraiser who is an individual who holds himself out as an appraiser

- the appraiser must be qualified to make appraisals of the type of property being valued

- the appraiser must not be the donor, the donee, or a member of the family or any person employed by the donor, the donee, or a member of the family

f. *Appraisal contains*

- date of the transfer

- date on which property appraised

- purpose of appraisal

- description of the property

- description of appraisal process employed

- description of assumptions, hypothetical conditions, and any limiting conditions and restrictions

- information considered in determining the appraised value

- appraisal procedures followed and reasoning that supports analyses, opinions, and conclusions

- valuation method utilized

- specific basis for the valuation

5. Increased scrutiny for estate, gift, and generation-skipping transfer tax purposes of transaction involving FLP and valuation discounts.

IMPLICATIONS AND ISSUES IN COMMUNITY PROPERTY STATES

In Arizona, California, Nevada, New Mexico, and Washington, the income from separate property of one spouse is separate property income. In Texas, Louisiana, Idaho, and Wisconsin, the income from the separate property of one spouse is community property income. It is in the former group of states where the FLP may require extra vigilance if it is owned prior to marriage, is given or inherited, or is separate property of a spouse for whatever reason. In these instances, it is necessary to make a distinction between the earnings of the manager (which is probably community property) and the income received from ownership of the partnership interest (which is separate property).

Using the separate property income from the FLP to purchase items that are taken in the names of both spouses creates a taxable gift (with the exception of real property taken as joint tenants). Thus, if the partner-spouse receives $80,000 in income from an FLP that was owned prior to marriage, over and above his wages from the FLP, and if he uses the $80,000 to buy stock in both his and his spouse's names, he will have made a gift of $40,000 taxable to the spouse. For transfers after 1981, this does not create a federal gift tax problem because of the unlimited marital deduction that applies to both separate property and community property (see Chapter 24). Depending upon state gift tax law, however, it may still create a gift tax problem.

Another frequently encountered problem in an FLP in community property states is the failure to designate in the agreement whether the FLP interest is separate property or community property. This failure is a great source of comfort and fees to litigation attorneys in divorce proceedings. This is rather important in view of the high rate of divorce.

DETRIMENTS

As exists with the formation of any entity, use of an FLP also has some detriments. For example, the following issues will generally be encountered:

1. The FLP will be required to pay applicable minimum franchise tax fees in most states in which it does business.

2. The FLP must file annual income tax returns and keep separate accounting records.

3. In states with restrictions on real property tax increases, great care should be taken in contributing real property to the FLP and in transferring partnership interests so that the property tax assessment on the property is not adversely changed.

4. The cost of formation and transferring title of assets into the FLP.

For the most part, the detriments that accompany the use of an FLP are heavily outweighed by its benefits and the decision to implement an FLP should not be materially affected by these issues.

COMPARING FLPs WITH OTHER BUSINESS ENTITIES

The differences between FLPs and other business entities can be significant in determining which entity would best suit a particular business need. Figure 43.1 provides a brief review of the differences between an FLP, C corporation, S corporation, and a limited liability company taxed as a partnership. More detailed explanations concerning these different types of business entities are discussed elsewhere in this book. (See Chapter 47 on Incorporation, Chapter 44 on Limited Liability Companies, and Chapter 46 on S Corporations.)

HOW IS IT DONE – EXAMPLES

1. Mark Ciarelli, a successful businessman, is married and has two children, Irv and Eric. He presently is the sole owner of an unincorporated manufacturing business (Pierz Enterprises) in which both personal services and capital are material income producing factors. The net profits from the business for last year were approximately $200,000, before Mark's salary. Mark files a joint return with his wife, Judy. His wife and children do not have an income of their own. Mark pays himself a salary of $1,000 per week. The net profit of the business after salary was actu-

Figure 43.1

	S Corp.	C Corp.	FLP	LLC
Limited Liability	All Owners	All Owners	Limited Partners	All Owners
Income Tax Levels	Single	Double	Single	Single
Capital Ownership Restrictions	Yes	No	No	No
Limits on Classes of Capital	Yes	No	No	No
Basis Adjustments	Outside Only	Outside Only	Outside and Inside	Outside and Inside
All Members Vote	Yes	Yes	No	Yes
Federal Tax Election Required	Yes	No	No	No
Distributions on Liquidation Taxable	Yes	Yes	No	No

ally $148,000. Because Mark is unincorporated, both the $52,000 salary and the $148,000 net profit are taxable to him.

Mark can minimize his income tax burden by "splitting" the income with his children through an FLP. He could transfer a 30% interest in the business assets directly to Irv and Eric, with each child receiving a 15% interest. If Irv and Eric were minors, these interests could be placed in trust for their benefit. A gift tax return would be filed and gift tax paid to the extent that Mark's (and Judy's) gift tax unified credit has been used up. An FLP agreement could be drafted and Irv and Eric could transfer their 15% interests to the FLP. Mark could continue to run the business and would have to pay himself a salary of $52,000 per year. However, the balance of the FLP income would be divided 70% to Mark, 15% to Irv, and 15% to Eric.

This planning would cause Mark to receive $103,600 in addition to his salary and Irv and Eric would each receive $22,200 of annual income. These amounts would be taxable to each partner. The net result is that Mark will have shifted $44,400 of income each year to his children. This income will be taxed at the children's lower income tax brackets (if they are over the age of 14), thus generating an immediate income tax saving. Further, if the business continues to grow, 30% of the future appreciation will accrue to Irv and Eric and not to Mark, thereby reducing Mark's estate.

2. John and Robin Scott are each age 70. They have four children and six grandchildren and their estate consists of the following assets held in their family living trust:

Asset	Value
Marketable Securities	$1,500,000
Apartment Complex	$1,000,000
Other Real Estate	$1,500,000
Residence	$ 500,000
Total	$4,500,000

During the year, John and Robin meet with their attorney and agree to implement an FLP to maintain ownership of their property in the family. The securities, apartment, and other real estate (but not the residence) are contributed to an FLP, constituting a total value of partnership assets of $4,000,000.

In return for their capital contributions, Mr. and Mrs. Scott each receive a 1% general partner interest and the Scott Family Trust receives a 98% limited partner interest. The FLP agreement gives the general partners the discretion to accumulate partnership income for future business needs and restricts the partners' ability to transfer their interests to persons outside the Scott family.

At the end of the year, the Scotts implement a gift program in which they each transfer a 6.25% limited partner interest to each of their four children, thereby transferring away a total of 50% of the partnership and $2,000,000 of the underlying asset value. An appraiser is hired to determine the value of the gifts of limited partner interests and concludes that a combined 40% discount for lack of control, lack of marketability, and lock-in status is appropriate for the limited partner gifts.

After applying this discount to the proportionate value of FLP assets, Mr. and Mrs. Scott were found to have each given limited partner interests worth $150,000 to each child for a total gift by each of $600,000. Because the gift tax unified credit of each of them is fully intact, no cash payment of gift tax is required. At the end of the year, ownership of the Scott FLP is as follows:

	General Partner	Limited Partner
John Scott	1.00%	0.00%
Robin Scott	1.00%	0.00%
Scott Family Trust	0.00%	48.00%
Child No. 1	0.00%	12.50%
Child No. 2	0.00%	12.50%
Child No. 3	0.00%	12.50%
Child No. 4	0.00%	12.50%
Totals	2.00%	98.00%

In the next year and each year thereafter, the Scotts make annual gifts of limited partner interests worth $10,000 to each of the four children and six grandchildren. The same 40% discount to value is applied to the gifts. During the next ten years, the assets in Scott FLP grow at a 5% annual rate. During this period, Mr. and Mrs. Scott continue to make annual exclusion gifts of $10,000 to the children and grandchildren and significantly reduce their ownership interests in the FLP while remaining in control as the general partners.

At the end of the tenth year, John is struck with a sudden illness and dies. At that time, the underlying value of the FLP assets is $6,205,313 and ownership is as follows:

	General Partner	Limited Partner
John Scott	1.00%	0.00%
Robin Scott	1.00%	0.00%
Scott Family Trust	0.00%	18.40%
Child No. 1	0.00%	15.46%
Child No. 2	0.00%	15.46%
Child No. 3	0.00%	15.46%
Child No. 4	0.00%	15.46%
Grandchild No. 1	0.00%	2.96%
Grandchild No. 2	0.00%	2.96%
Grandchild No. 3	0.00%	2.96%
Grandchild No. 4	0.00%	2.96%
Grandchild No. 5	0.00%	2.96%
Grandchild No. 6	0.00%	2.96%
Totals	2.00%	98.00%

In determining the value of the FLP interests includable in John's estate, a 25% discount was applied to the general partner interest and a 40% discount was applied to the limited partner interest on the estate tax return. As shown on the return, the estate tax value of Mr. Scott's interest in the FLP after adding back his $600,000 in gifts in prior years is as follows:

	Value
General Partner (1.00%)	$ 46,540
Limited Partner (9.20%)	$342,533
Total	$389,073
Prior Taxable Gifts	$600,000
Total Gifts and Interests	$989,073

Had the Scotts chosen not to form their FLP and if no discounts to value were applied on the estate tax return, the value of John's one-half interest in the apartments, real estate, and marketable securities would have been $3,102,657 at his death. However, by implementing a gift program using an FLP, his taxable estate was reduced by $2,113,584 and, assuming a 48% tax rate, $1,014,520 in estate tax was saved.

QUESTIONS AND ANSWERS

Question – Can a minor hold a partnership interest directly?

Answer – Yes. A minor will be recognized as a bona fide partner if it is determined that he is competent to manage his own property and to participate in the FLP activities. This requires that the minor possess sufficient maturity and experience to assume dominion and control over the interest transferred to him. Ordinarily, however, a minor will not be deemed to possess the requisite maturity and experience. Therefore, as a practical matter, an FLP interest should not be transferred directly to a minor.

If a minor's interest is transferred to a fiduciary, such as a court-appointed guardian whose conduct is subject to judicial supervision, the minor will be recognized as a partner. Similarly, if an FLP interest is transferred in trust for the benefit of a minor to an independent trustee, this will also permit the minor to own an interest in the FLP.

Question – Parent and children create an FLP to hold and operate a farm. The parent transfers interests in the farm partnership by gift to the children, who are limited partners. The parent is the sole general partner, lives in a farm house on the property, operates the farm, and takes most of the partnership profits as salary. Is this a valid FLP for estate tax purposes?

Answer – The IRS will likely assert that the parent has retained the enjoyment of the entire farm for his life and seek to include 100% of the value of the farm in the parent's taxable estate under IRC Section 2036(a). The IRS reached this conclusion in Letter Ruling 7824005, where the parent lived on the property and received income in the form of salary although she did not manage the property. Compare Letter Ruling 9131006 where the FLP was recognized although the parent retained a great deal of control over it.

It is recommended that a person who uses assets of the FLP for non-business purposes should enter into a lease agreement and pay a reasonable market rent for the used property. The payment of rent is consistent with the FLP's business purpose of owning assets for the purpose of making a profit. A failure to pay reasonable rental rates could be construed as a retention of the enjoyment of FLP assets and create adverse estate tax results.

Question – Do gifts of interests in an FLP qualify for the gift tax annual exclusion?

Answer – The IRS has ruled that such gifts do qualify where there is no substantial restriction under the

FLP agreement on the rights of the donee partners to dispose of their interests in the FLP. However, if the partnership agreement attempts to prohibit assignment, there will be a problem.[16] In addition, advisors and practitioners should be aware that the IRS has recently taken the position that gifts of membership interests in a family LLC were not gifts of present interests and therefore did not qualify for the gift tax annual exclusion. This position was upheld by the Tax Court and the Seventh Circuit in *Hackl v. Comm.*[17] Though many practitioners believe that the Tax Court and the Seventh Circuit reached the wrong decision in *Hackl*, it is very important that advisors and practitioner be familiar with *Hackl*, and that gifts of FLP interests be structured to qualify as present interests in order to ensure that such gifts qualify for the gift tax annual exclusion.

Question – When a partner dies, is there any change in the income tax basis of partnership assets?

Answer – Generally, under IRC Section 1014, the income tax basis of a decedent's assets is adjusted to the value of such assets for federal estate tax purposes, typically their fair market value as of the date of death. (EGTRRA 2001 changes the step-up in basis to a modified carryover basis, for decedents dying in 2010.) Where the estate owns an FLP interest, this basis adjustment will apply to the basis of the FLP interest. Also, if the general partner makes a timely election under IRC Section 754, the basis of the assets owned by the FLP will be adjusted to reflect the date of death values according to IRC Section 743(b). If assets have appreciated in value, this adjustment will be advantageous only to the interest of the deceased partner who will receive a date of death basis in the FLP assets.

Question – What are some helpful hints for operating an FLP?

Answer – Helpful hints include:

1. There should be a written FLP agreement setting forth the rights of the partners.

2. Accurate business records should be kept.

3. The donor (general partner) should receive reasonable compensation for his services.

4. Distributions to the donee partners should not be used to discharge parental support obligations.

5. If minors are partners and their interests are held in trust, the trustee should be an independent trustee and not subject to the direct or indirect control of the donor.

6. Assets should be transferred into the name of the partnership.

Question – Can a family partnership be funded solely by contributing marketable securities?

Answer – To date, family partnerships holding such assets have not been invalidated. IRC Section 7701(a)(2) defines a partnership as including a "syndicate, group, pool, joint venture, or other unincorporated organization, through or by means of which any business, financial operation, or venture is carried on, and which is not, within the meaning of this title, a trust or estate or a corporation." Those practitioners who advocate the creation of family partnerships solely to hold marketable securities often point to this statute as partial authority for their position. However, the attempt of the Service in promulgating Treas. Reg. §1.704-2 and retraction of Examples (5) and (6) (the latter of which was to be used to attack certain "paper shuffling" partnerships) suggests that the Service may attack such entities in the future. Where the transferred assets include large amounts of publicly traded securities, watch out for the investment company rules, discussed above, which could result in gain or loss on the transfer.

The Tax Court has upheld the use of a FLP as a vehicle for owning primarily marketable securities. In a couple of cases, the IRS attacked the use of a FLP as a vehicle for applying valuation discounts to the interests of the decedent, but still allowed discounts.[18]

Question – How does the IRS determine whether an entity should be taxed as a partnership?

Answer – Effective January 1, 1997, business entities other than corporations or trusts can elect their tax classification (under the so-called "Check-the-Box" regulations). If the entity has at least two members, it can be classified either as a partnership or an association taxable as a corporation. An election will be effective on the date specified by the entity on the IRS Form 8832 or the date filed if no date is specified on the IRS Form 8832 (the effective date specified on IRS Form 8832 cannot be more that 75 days prior to the date on which the election is filed and cannot be more than 12 months after the date on which the election is filed).[19] After that period, the election is effective on the date the election is made. A copy of the election must be included with the entity's first tax return. If the entity with two or more members fails to file an election, the default classification would be a partnership.[20]

Question – How does a state determine whether an entity should be taxed as a partnership for state tax purposes?

Answer – Prior to enactment of the Check-the-Box regulations noted in the preceding answer, the IRS and states determined the tax classification of an entity based upon the number of corporate characteristics it possessed. Since enactment of the federal Check-the-Box regulations, many states have conformed their state law to the new federal classification regulations. California elected to follow federal entity classification for state income tax purposes, beginning January 1, 1998.[21]

If a state does not follow the federal check-the-box regulations, then the state may treat a family partnership as an association taxable as a corporation for state tax purposes if three or more of the following characteristics are determined to exist in the partnership.

1. Centralized management;

2. Free transferability of interests;

3. Continuity of life; and

4. Limited liability.

The drafter of the partnership agreement in such a state should be careful in assuring that the partnership lacks at least two of the above characteristics. For FLPs, the agreement is usually drafted so that free transferability of interests and continuity of life are lacking.

Question – What are guaranteed payments and are they significant in the family limited partnership?

Answer – Guaranteed payments are payments for services or the use of capital, often made to senior partners, under IRC Section 707(c). If these are determined without regard to partnership income, they will be treated as payments to unrelated persons, which will generally be taxable income to the recipient and deductible by the partnership if they

are reasonable, ordinary, and necessary. They provide a method of making cash flow available to senior family members on a tax deductible basis. Note, however, they may be subject to the self-employment tax.

Question – What action should be taken in structuring a family limited partnership to avoid the special valuation rules of IRC Section 2701?

Answer – Gifts of interests in a family limited partnership may be required to be valued under the artificial valuation rules of Section 2701, which are discussed in Chapter 57. Section 2701 will apply if the senior family members retain interests that are defined as "applicable retained interests." These partnership interests resemble preferred stock in that they confer preferential distribution rights, or have a fixed liquidation value.

A so-called "vertical slice" in the entity is not covered by this section. For example, if the transferor, each family member, and each applicable family member hold substantially the same interest before and after the transfer, Section 2701 does not apply. Similarly, it does not apply if the interests transferred are of the same class proportionately as the interests retained. Differences only in voting rights, or in the case of partnerships, differences in management and liability, are generally considered proportionate.

The key to avoiding Section 2701 is to structure the partnership so that each partner will share proportionately in capital, income, losses, and distributions. For examples, see Letter Rulings 9427023 and 9451050.

Question – Are there any problems in transferring stock in a closely held corporation to a family limited partnership?

Answer – If voting stock in a controlled corporation as defined in IRC Section 2036(b) is transferred to a family partnership and the transferor votes the stock as a general partner, this would appear to be an indirect retained voting power over the stock, resulting in its inclusion in the transferor's taxable estate. It would be better to limit transfers of stock to nonvoting shares. Note that control under this statute is broadly defined, and includes any corporation in which the transferor and family members own a 20% interest.

Question – Can life insurance be transferred to a family limited partnership?

Answer – The family partnership may be an excellent vehicle for holding life insurance, functioning in a manner similar to an irrevocable insurance trust as discussed in Chapter 31. However, if the only function of the partnership is to hold life insurance policies, there are serious questions. Under both general legal principles and tax law, a valid partnership is supposed to engage in some business or financial activity. At least one private letter ruling has held that ownership of life insurance with investment characteristics is sufficient.[22] However, caution indicates the partnership should be engaged in some other business or investment activity in addition to holding life insurance.[23]

Question – What are the potential IRS attacks against FLPs?

Answer – The IRS has made several attacks against FLPs. However, some of the theories underlying these IRS attacks have been rejected by the courts. In creating and administering a FLP, it is very important to be familiar with and understand the arguments the IRS has made, and is continuing to make, against FLPs and the manner in which the courts have dealt with such arguments. Below is a list of several arguments the IRS has made against particular FLPs, with citations to some of the cases in which the arguments have been litigated. It is not an exhaustive list of IRS arguments against FLPs or cases dealing with FLPs, and should not serve as a substitute for reading the cases cited.

1. The FLP should be disregarded because it lacks a valid business purpose and/or economic substance.[24]

2. On formation of the FLP, the founding partners made a gift to the other partners of the difference between the fair market value of the assets transferred to the partnership and the discounted value of the partnership interests.[25]

3. All of the assets of the FLP should be included in the estate of a decedent under Section 2036(a)(1), because the decedent retained the possession or enjoyment of, or the right to withdraw income from, such assets.[26]

4. All of the assets of the FLP should be included in the estate of the decedent under Section 2036(a)(2), because the decedent retained the right, either alone or in conjunction with any person, to designate the persons who shall possess or enjoy the property or its income (e.g., the ability, either alone or in conjunction with the other partners, to dissolve the partnership).[27]

A discussion of strategies for minimizing the potential for a successful IRS attack is beyond the scope of this chapter.[28]

ASRS: Sec. 42.

CHAPTER ENDNOTES

1. IRC Sec. 704(e)(3).

2. Treas. Reg. §1.704-1(e) sets forth additional requirements in order for a family partnership to be acknowledged for income tax purposes. Although the Service's attempt at applying the scope of these regulations to estate, gift, and generation-skipping taxes has generally failed, it is likely that the Service will continue to look for ways to challenge family partnerships that substantially reduce transfer taxes.

3. *Church v. U.S.*, 2000-1 USTC ¶60,369 (W.D. Tex. 2000).

4. *Est. of Davis v. Comm.*, 110 TC 530 (1998).

5. Rev. Rul. 77-137, 1977-1 CB 178.

6. IRC Sec. 704(e)(1).

7. Treas. Reg. §1.704-1(e)(1)(iii).

8. IRC Sec. 704(e)(2); Treas. Reg. §1.704-1(e)(1)(ii).

9. Treas. Regs. §§1.704-1(e)(2)(ii)(a), 1.704-1(e)(2)(ii)(d).

10. See, e.g. *Payton v. U.S.*, 425 F.2d 1324 (5th Cir. 1970); *Kuney v. U.S.*, 448 F.2d 22 (9th Cir. 1971).

11. See Treas. Reg. §1.704-1(e)(2)(ii)(d).

12. See Treas. Reg. §1.704-1(e)(2)(vi).

13. See Treas. Reg. §1.351-1(c) for rules pertaining to what constitutes diversification of investment securities.

14. See Treas. Regs. §§25.2512-2, 25.2512-3. See also Rev. Rul. 59-60, 1959-1 CB 237.

15. Treas. Reg. §301.6501(c)-1(f).

16. See TAMs 199944003 (present interests) and 9751003 (future interests).

17. *Hackl v. Comm.*, 118 TC 279 (2002), *aff'd* 335 F.3d 664 (7th Cir. 2003).

18. See, e.g. *Knight v. Comm.*, 115 TC 506 (2000).

19. Treas. Reg. §301.7701-3(c)(1)(iii).

20. Treas. Reg. §301.7701-3.

21. Cal. Rev. & Tax. Code §23038(b)(2).

22. Rev. Rul. 9309021.

23. See Let. Rul. 200017051.

24. See, e.g., Est. of *Strangi v. Comm.*, 115 TC 478 (2000), *aff'd in part and rem'd in part*, 293 F.3d 279 (5th Cir. 2002), *on remand*, TC Memo. 2003-145; *Knight v. Comm.*, 115 TC 506 (2000); *Church v. United States*, 2000-1 USTC ¶60,369 (W.D. Tex. 2000), *aff'd without published opinion* 268 F.3d 1063 (5th Cir. 2001); *Est. of Harper v. Comm.*, TC Memo 2002-121.

25. See, e.g., Est. of *Strangi v. Comm.*, 115 TC 478 (2000), *aff'd in part and rem'd in part*, 293 F.3d 279 (5th Cir. 2002), *on remand*, TC Memo. 2003-145; *Knight v. Comm.*, 115 TC 506 (2000).

26. See, e.g., *Est. of Schauerhammer v. Comm.*, TC Memo 1997-242; *Est. of Reichardt v. Comm.*, 114 TC 144 (2000); *Est. of Harper v. Comm.*, TC Memo 2002-121; *Est. of Thompson v. Comm.*, TC Memo 2002-246; *Kimbell v. U.S.*, 2003-1 USTC ¶60,455 (N.D. Tex. 2003); Strangi, supra.

27. See, e.g., *Est. of Strangi v. Comm.*, 115 TC 478 (2000), *aff'd in part and rem'd in part*, 293 F.3d 279 (5th Cir. 2002), *on remand*, TC Memo 2003-145; *Kimbell v. U.S.*, 2003-1 USTC ¶60,455 (N.D. Tex. 2003).

28. For a discussion of such strategies, see Steve Leimberg's Estate Planning Newsletter Nos. 550, 575, 589, and 595 (www.leimbergservices.com); and Blattmahr and Gans, "Avoiding the *Strangi II* Legacy for Old and New Partnership," Tax Notes, September 1, 2003.

Chapter 44

LIMITED LIABILITY COMPANIES

WHAT IS IT?

The limited liability company (LLC) is a relatively new form of business organization which is intended to obtain for investors, called members, the same advantages of limited liability as in the corporate form of business, while at the same time avoiding corporation income tax rules. All 50 states and the District of Columbia have adopted LLC statutes, although these statutes may vary widely from state to state.

As noted above, the LLC is used to obtain the advantages of limited liability for investors and participants (i.e., they cannot be liable for debts of the entity beyond their investment), while being classified as a partnership for federal income tax purposes. The result is avoidance of corporate double tax on income, and in many situations, avoidance of any tax on liquidation. The impact of double taxation of income of normal ("C") corporations is discussed in connection with the S corporation in Chapter 46.

Another significant reason for the use of the LLC is that any losses incurred by the entity will be passed through and deductible by the members under the partnership rules, provided the LLC is classified as a partnership for income tax purposes. No such passthrough is permitted in the case of a C corporation.

It is helpful to compare the LLC to the S Corporation. Both are formed to avoid double taxation and permit the passthrough of losses to shareholders. However, as discussed in Chapter 46, the use of the S corporation is severely restricted. The number of shareholders is limited to 75. Only individuals, estates, and certain trusts qualify as shareholders. The passthrough of losses to shareholders is generally limited to the income tax basis of their stock plus any loans they have made to the corporation. In the case of partnerships and LLCs, any debt of the entity is also considered in determining how much loss partners or members may deduct. Only voting and nonvoting common stock may be issued in an S corporation, while there are no limitations on classes of memberships in an LLC.

From the estate planning standpoint, a major advantage of either the partnership, or an LLC classified as a partnership, over a C or S corporation is that upon the death of a partner or member, the partnership or LLC may elect to adjust the basis of its assets to fair market value to the extent of the decedent's interest.[1]

The LLC may also be considered an alternate to the family limited partnership, discussed in Chapter 43. The transfer of family business, real estate, or other investments to a family partnership has become a major estate planning technique. It would appear the LLC would function just as well in many cases, with the advantage that no family member needs to function as a "general" partner and assume liability for debts of the entity. However, as covered in the Questions and Answers section below, there are potential problems with the use of an LLC in this situation.

In most jurisdictions, the LLC, or its counterpart the limited liability partnership (LLP), may also be used as a form of organization for a professional practice. The advantage is that while a professional will remain liable for his own errors or omissions in the practice or business, he can avoid liability for the acts of any of the other owners. In an ordinary professional partnership, each partner may be held liable for the errors or omissions of any other partner.

WHAT ARE THE REQUIREMENTS?

The content of LLC statutes varies widely. Most statutes borrow heavily from the Uniform Limited Partnership Act (ULPA) discussed in Chapter 43. These statutes were drafted to ensure that the LLC would be classified as a partnership for federal income tax purposes based on the entity classification regulations that were in effect prior to the current Check-the-Box regulations. Some statutes were drafted so that it was a certainty the LLC would be classified as a partnership for federal tax purposes, while others permitted the entity, by adopting flexible provisions, to be classified either as a partnership or corporation. The former are generally called "bulletproof" statutes; the latter "flexible" statutes. The "Check-the-Box" rules discussed below eliminate much – but not all – of the uncertainty with respect to LLCs.

While it is impossible to generalize on the various statutes, the following will be found, with variations, in all of them:

1. There are articles of organization that set forth the purposes for which the entity is formed, and provides that the entity can generally exercise the same powers as a partnership or corporation.

2. The participants are called members. There generally must be at least two members, but some states permit LLCs with only one member. Various other entities such as corporations, partnerships, trusts, and estates, can be members.

3. There are provisions for capital contributions similar to partnerships.

4. The key to management is an operating agreement, which governs management of the entity. The LLC may have officers, like a corporation, if specified in the operating agreement. The agreement also provides that the entity may be managed either by delegation to "Managers," who are elected in somewhat the same manner as a Board of Directors, or retained by all of the members. Unlike partnerships, voting in an LLC is generally in proportion to capital contributions. However, it may be based on profit participation.

5. Allocation of profits and losses and distributions to members is generally covered by the operating agreement. Under most, if not all, statutes it is possible to have different classes of members who participate differently in profits, losses, and distributions.

6. Assignment of interests in the LLC generally follows the pattern of the limited partnership, with some unique characteristics. A complete assignment of an interest generally means the assignor is no longer a member. The assignee does not automatically become a member, and is only entitled to receive distributions that would otherwise be made to the member. There may be a provision for admission of an assignee as a member based on a vote of the members or member-managers.

7. The dissolution of the entity, which also has considerable tax consequence, normally will occur upon the unanimous consent of the members, or if the LLC is formed for a fixed term,

upon the expiration of that term. However, under most statutes, events such as death, disability, voluntary withdrawal, expulsion, or bankruptcy of a member results in automatic dissolution, unless the business is continued either by unanimous consent or majority vote of members.

8. Many of the legal requirements can be altered under many state statutes by provisions in the operating agreement or a separate business continuation agreement.

HOW IT IS DONE – AN EXAMPLE

Ten unrelated investors are considering establishing a joint venture to acquire and develop mining property in a western state. This is an extremely risky operation, but if it is successful, there will be large profits. If it is not successful, they would experience large losses. Also, the mining operation may result in considerable liability to its owners, both for debts incurred in the operations, and potential damages to adjacent property or injuries to workers. While some insurance is available to cover these risks, it is not enough.

These investors could form an S corporation, assuming they are all qualified shareholders, and achieve limited liability and direct passthrough of profits and most losses. However, they find the S corporation structure too limiting. Under their proposed agreement, different participants would share in profits and losses unequally, and an S corporation can have only voting and nonvoting stock, with no special allocation of profits and losses. They cannot use a general partnership, because they would all be personally liable for claims and lawsuits. They cannot use a limited partnership, because no participant is willing to assume the liabilities of a general partner.

The LLC would allow all members to achieve limited liability and to participate in the venture or delegate management, would create different classes of ownership and participation, and would allow a direct passthrough of either profits or losses.

WHAT ARE THE TAX IMPLICATIONS?

The key to the use of the LLC is, almost always, the classification of the entity as a partnership for federal income tax purposes. In the past, great effort was made to structure the LLC so that it had no more than two of the four corporate characteristics set forth in the regulations.[2]

These are limited liability, centralized management, free transferability of interests, and continuity of life. However, because of an incredible number of cases on this issue, so called "Check-the-Box" regulations were issued to eliminate much of the uncertainty. To properly classify an entity, it is necessary to ask three questions:

1. Is there an entity separate and apart from its owners? If so,

2. Is that entity a trust – or is it a business entity? If it is a business entity, then

3. Is the entity – per se – a corporation? If "no," then it can elect its classification for federal tax purposes – merely by checking a box.

The regulations state that federal tax law and not state law determines whether or not an organization will be recognized as an entity separate from its owners.[3] A joint undertaking merely to share expenses will not be sufficient to be considered a separate entity - nor will mere co-ownership of property that is maintained, kept in repair, and rented or leased. On the other hand, the co-owners of an apartment building who provide services to tenants, directly or through an agent, have a separate entity. A joint venture or other contractual arrangement may also create a separate entity for tax purposes if the participants carry on a trade, business, financial operation, or venture and divide the profits.[4] It appears that the level of activity is the key factor.

An entity will be considered a business entity if it is not a trust (a trust has no associates or business objective[5]), or is subject to a special tax regime. Once considered a business entity, it will then be treated as (a) a corporation, (b) a partnership, or (c) a sole proprietorship.

"Per se" corporations include: (a) business entities incorporated under federal or state statutes where the statute describes or refers to the entity as incorporated or as a corporation; (b) associations; (c) joint stock companies; (d) insurance companies; (e) state chartered banks insured by the FDIC; (f) business entities owned by a state or one of its political subdivisions; (g) business entities taxed as corporations under certain IRC provisions; or (h) certain foreign entities.[6] A partnership is a business entity that is not a corporation and that has at least two members. (A business entity that is not a corporation but which has only one member is not considered an entity separate from its owner.[7])

The following chart summarizes the Check-the-Box regulations, effective January 1, 1997[8]:

TYPE OF ENTITY	TREATMENT
Corporation Under State Law or Publicly Traded Entity	Always Taxed as Corporation
Two or More Members (Partnership, Limited Partnership, LLC, LLP)	Taxed as Partnership Unless it Affirmatively Elects to be Taxed as Corporation
Single Member Unincorporated Association (e.g., 1 Person LLC)	Taxed as Sole Proprietorship Unless it Affirmatively Elects to be Taxed as Corporation

These rules make it possible – without risk of being considered a corporation for federal income tax purposes – for a partnership or LLC to have officers and a board of managers, permanent life, freely transferable certificates, and even limited liability. The election to change classification from the default in the chart above is made by the eligible entity by filing Form 8832, Entity Classification Election, within the first 75 days after the year to which it applies.

Does a mere checking of a box eliminate all problems and uncertainty? Probably not. Nor is it clear that if the only asset in the entity is life insurance that the IRS will recognize the entity as a partnership merely because a box was checked – especially if the entity would not qualify as a partnership under state law. Until the IRS rules in this area, caution is advised, especially if the LLC or partnership holds only life insurance or marketable securities.

COMMUNITY PROPERTY CONSIDERATIONS

In a community property state, the investment in an LLC may be of cash or property which is characterized as community or marital property under state law. If so, the membership interest itself will probably also be classified as community property, even though only one spouse is listed as the member.

Where the membership carries voting or management rights, this classification may be material as to the rights of the spouse of a member to participate in either a vote or management. While state law may vary on this point, some states, such as California, generally restrict the voting or management to the spouse who is designated as the member. If this is not true in a particular jurisdiction, it may be necessary to make the spouses parties to the operating agreement to clear up voting and management rights.

In the event of death of either the member or nonmember spouse, or a divorce, the rights in the membership may be divided to reflect the rights of the spouses under state community property laws. It would appear a nonmember spouse who is assigned an interest in the membership would not have the full rights of a member, but would be treated as an assignee of an interest as described in the foregoing discussion. However, this will again depend on the law of the particular state.

QUESTIONS AND ANSWERS

Question – Will the LLC replace the family limited partnership as an estate planning tool for family business and investments?

Answer – In most family limited partnerships, discussed in Chapter 43, the entity is formed by parents or members of a senior generation who transfer business or investment assets to a partnership in which they retain general partnership interests. They then make gifts of limited partnership interests to children or younger generation members.

One drawback of the family limited partnership is the fact that senior generation members, by acting as general partners, assume personal liability for any debts or obligations of the venture. The LLC could be used in this setting and has the great advantage of allowing the senior family members to avoid personal liability. They may still retain management of the business or investments by providing in the articles or operating agreement that they will be the managing members.

A major problem with the use of the LLC in place of the family limited partnership is that, under state law, the entity will dissolve on the death, withdrawal, etc., of any member for any reason. This would permit transferees to force a dissolution of the entity, unless there is either a unanimous or majority vote, depending on state law, of the remaining members to continue the entity. Many senior family members would not be willing to confer that power on the younger generation. In a family limited partnership, only the withdrawal of the last remaining general partner will trigger a dissolution.

Question – Referring to the preceding question, is there any way of achieving limited liability for the senior family members in the family limited partnership?

Answer – The IRS has issued several rulings, five holding that the general partner in a limited partnership could be a corporation, and in particular, an S corporation. Note that under those rulings, the corporation must have at least a one percent interest in the partnership, and should have some substantial assets. Thus, the senior family members could form a corporation which they control to act as general partner, and will generally be successful in avoiding personal liability. It seems likely they could also use an LLC as the general partner in the family limited partnership.

Question – If the LLC is used as a vehicle for the transfer of family business or investments, what will be the impact on the valuation of transfers of membership interests for federal gift tax purposes?

Answer – As discussed in Chapter 43, one of the reasons for the use of family limited partnerships as a vehicle for gifts is the ability to claim valuation adjustments or discounts to reflect the fact that the transferred limited partnership interests are not marketable, represent minority interests, have no right to participate in control of the entity, and most important, cannot force a dissolution of the entity. In the case of the LLC, the withdrawal of a member for any reason, as noted above, will result in dissolution of the entity. This provided the IRS with a good argument that valuation discounts should be reduced or eliminated, since the transferee members are in a position, by withdrawing from the LLC, to realize the net asset value of their interests in the LLC. It may be possible under a state LLC statute to modify the right of transferee members to withdraw from the LLC. Prior to the Check-the-Box rules, this would create the risk of the entity being classified as a corporation for federal tax purposes, but it should not present a problem under current regulations.

However, even if there is no issue of whether the entity will be taxed as a corporation or a partnership, there is still a major problem. Under IRC section 2704(b), any restriction on the rights of the members to force a liquidation of the LLC which are greater than those imposed by state law will be ignored in valuing their interests. Since the so-called "default" rule under most state LLC statutes is that the entity will dissolve if a membership interest terminates for any reason, that rule can only be modified by a contrary agreement among the members. The IRS will likely characterize this as a restriction which will be ignored under Section

2704(b) for valuation purposes. It will instead value the transferred interests on the assumption that those members can force a dissolution of the LLC and reach the underlying assets, thus negating the argument that a valuation discount should be allowed. Only a change in underlying state law will eliminate this problem.

As of this writing, some states have begun to modify their LLC statutes to avoid the so-called "default" rules of Section 2704(b). In particular, Arizona has limited the value of the interest of a family member who withdraws from an LLC, and Colorado has restricted the rights of members who withdraw to receive the full liquidation value of their interests in the LLC.

Question – Will a family LLC be subject to special scrutiny under the same rules applicable to family partnerships?

Answer – If the LLC is classified as a partnership for federal income tax purposes, it will likely be subject to the special restrictions on family partnerships under IRC section 704(e). These are discussed in Chapter 43. Basically, the allocation of income to transferee partners will not be recognized for federal income tax purposes if capital is not a material factor in producing the income, substantial capital interests are not transferred, or the managing transferor family members are not adequately compensated for their services. In addition, the regulations under Section 704(e) provide the allocation of income to transferees will not be recognized if the transferors retain too much control over the transferred interests.

Question – Is the LLC a better alternative for unrelated individuals entering into new ventures or investments?

Answer – Aside from the special problems of family businesses, the LLC will probably be the entity of choice for a variety of new business enterprises, particularly those that involve a degree of risk, or are likely to generate losses.

Like the S corporation, the participating members in the LLC may fully participate in the management and operation of the venture without exposure to personal liability. Examples include real estate, investments in mineral rights, and oil and gas. It should be noted, however, that there is always some possible exposure to liability, as in the case of share-holders in a corporation, if the entity is undercapitalized or used in an abusive manner, or if the members sign as individuals on business loans. However, the entity is not subject to the limitations which apply to S corporations, discussed above.

There are some drawbacks that must be considered. If the business operates in more than one state, the issue will be whether or not it will be recognized as an LLC in a state other than the one in which it was formed. If it is not, the members may be subject to personal liability for debts incurred in the other state. There is a statute that provides for recognition of so-called "foreign" LLCs, but it has not been adopted by all states. There are also unresolved issues on the application of self employment taxes on members of the LLC, although the IRS has now provided some guidance in this area.[9]

Question – Will the LLC become the entity of choice for professional practices?

Answer – In the states that permit its use for professional practices, it has already become the entity of choice. Most of the major accounting firms have already been reformed as LLCs or LLPs, as have many of the major law firms. What is good for the large professional firms is probably also good for small professional practices.

ASRS: Sec. 42, ¶100.

CHAPTER ENDNOTES

1. IRC Secs. 743(b), 754. For a useful and detailed discussion of the LLC, see Commito, *Working with LLCs and FLPs*, National Underwriter Company (2d ed. 2000).

2. Treas. Reg. §§301.7701-1, 301.7701-2, as in effect prior to January 1, 1997.

3. Treas. Reg. §301.7701-1(a).

4. Treas. Reg. §301.7701-1(a)(2).

5. Treas. Reg. §301.7701-1(b).

6. Treas. Reg. §301.7701-2(b).

7. Treas. Reg. §301.7701-2(c)(2)(i).

8. TD 8697 and Notice 97-1, 1997-1 CB 348, which makes obsolete prior rules under IRC section 7701.

9. Prop. Treas. Reg. §1.1402(a)-2(h). However, Section 935 of the Taxpayer Relief Act of 1997, aimed at Prop. Treas. Reg. §1.1402(a)-2(h), states that no temporary or final regulations with respect to the definition of a limited partner for self employment tax purposes may be issued or made effective before July 1, 1998. Even though this provision has expired, it is unlikely the IRS will issue regulations in this area until it is sure it has the support of the Congress.

Chapter 45

PERSONAL HOLDING COMPANY

WHAT IS IT?

A personal holding company is a corporation that meets two particular tests (and is not specifically excluded from such status).[1] These two tests are: (1) a stock ownership test; and (2) an income test. Both tests must be met in the same taxable year so that it is possible for a corporation to attain personal holding company status in one year and not in the next.

The stock ownership test works like this: The corporation meets the stock ownership requirements if more than 50% in value of its outstanding stock is owned directly or indirectly by or for not more than five individuals at any time during the last half of the taxable year.[2] The second test, the income test, is sometimes referred to as the 60% test. If the stock ownership test has been met and at least 60% or more of the corporation's adjusted ordinary gross income is personal holding company income (generally, dividends, interest, certain royalties, rents, or amounts received in return for a certain type of personal services), the corporation will be classified as a personal holding company.[3]

Prior to enactment of the Jobs and Growth Tax Relief Reconciliation Act of 2003 (JGTRRA), the personal holding company provisions imposed a tax at the highest individual income tax rate, separate and in addition to the existing corporate tax on specifically defined undistributed income of personal holding companies. However, under JGTRRA, the personal holding company tax was reduced and, for tax years beginning after 2002, the personal holding company tax is imposed at the rate of 15% of the undistributed personal holding company income, in addition to the regular corporate income tax and the minimum tax on certain tax preference items.[4] The reduced 15% personal holding company tax is currently scheduled to sunset and will not apply in taxable years beginning after 2008.

Care should be exercised in the use of personal holding companies based on the repeal of the *General Utilities* doctrine by the Tax Reform Act of 1986. If assets in the corporation appreciate, generally there will be two taxes created, one at the corporate level (upon a sale of the assets or liquidation of the corporation) and one at the shareholder level (upon a liquidation of the corporation or dividend distribution).

WHEN IS THE USE OF SUCH A DEVICE INDICATED?

1. Where an individual has a large estate consisting of highly appreciated and readily marketable securities and wants to reduce federal estate taxes attributable to those assets.

2. Where an individual would like to reduce the value of his estate through court approved methods for discounts.

3. Where it is desired to achieve gift and estate tax savings for appreciated assets while retaining economic control and flexibility in making economic decisions. However, the planner should give careful consideration to other entities that can achieve the same result without double tax problems. These include, the family partnership, discussed in Chapter 43, the limited liability company, discussed in Chapter 44, and the S corporation, discussed in Chapter 46. In the case of the S corporation, its assets may consist entirely of passive investments, such as marketable securities, without triggering a corporate level tax so long as it has no corporate earnings and profits. Generally, if an S corporation has earnings and profits it will be from when it was a C corporation.

WHAT ARE THE REQUIREMENTS?

A corporation is formed by an individual who owns a substantial amount of appreciated property. The individual transfers a portfolio of common stock of various companies to a newly formed closely held corporation in return for its stock. This transfer can be accomplished without recognition of any gain. The transfer of assets to a corporation in exchange for its stock will not be a taxable event if the transferor controls 80% of the voting power and 80% of each class of stock immediately after the transfer.[5]

The individual transferring this stock will have a basis (cost for purposes of determining gain or loss) in the new stock equal to the basis in the property transferred to the corporation.[6] Likewise, the corporation will receive the stock transferred to it with the same basis this property had in the individual's hands.[7]

HOW IT IS DONE – EXAMPLES

Denise Lopez, a wealthy investor, purchased shares of Gro-Quick, a closely held corporation, many years ago. These shares are now worth 10 times what she paid for them and are continuing to appreciate rapidly. If Denise retains the stock, the shares will be includable in her estate. If she gives them away, she will incur a sizable gift tax. (The taxable portion of any gifts will be considered adjusted taxable gifts and therefore increase the rate at which the taxable estate will be taxed.) Furthermore, some of her beneficiaries are minor children and she does not want to make outright gifts. However, she does not want to use a trust because of certain administrative problems associated with a trust.

Denise forms a corporation and retains 100% of its stock. The stock she transfers to the corporation has a fair market value of $1,000,000. The corporation is capitalized as follows: $800,000 (fair market value) of non-voting common stock is issued to Denise. In addition, she receives $200,000 worth of voting common stock. (The breakdown is arbitrary and can be varied according to the particular situation.)

Since one of Denise's main objectives is to maintain control while making gifts to limit future appreciation in the value of her estate, she retains the voting stock and begins a gift program with the non-voting common. She gives, over a period of years, the $800,000 worth of non-voting common stock to family members. This enables her to continue to direct and control the investment program. Because of the gift tax unified credit equivalent or applicable exclusion amount ($1,000,000) and the annual exclusions ($11,000 per donee per year, in 2004) the transfer can be made with little or no gift tax cost. Because the non-voting common stock represents most of the right to the financial growth of the business (80%), substantial future appreciation is removed from Denise's estate. For example, if the underlying assets double in value after the gift of the common stock, 80% of that appreciation is realized in the hands of the donees rather than in Denise's hands.

In the case of family corporations, the use of common and preferred stock in either capitalizing or recapitalizing the entity, followed by a transfer of shares to other family members by gift or sale, may and probably will create a gift tax valuation problem under IRC section 2701 or a gift, estate, or generation-skipping transfer tax problem if restrictions on certain classes of stock lapse

under IRC section 2704. These issues are covered in detail in Chapter 22.

An additional benefit of using a corporation to hold significant assets is the fact that the corporate stock may be worth less than the value of the assets in the corporation. Courts have consistently allowed discounts of 15% and more (in one case as much as 55%) on the theory that stock of a personal holding company is less attractive to an investor than a similar stock listed on an exchange with ready access to the investing public.

Example: A gift of 100 shares of AT&T is worth more than a gift of shares representing a 10% interest in a personal holding company whose only assets are 1,000 shares of AT&T. It is this fact – that an investment in a personal holding company is less desirable than in the underlying shares because the underlying assets can be easily traded in the market while shares in the personal holding company cannot – that is the primary reason for the discount from the net asset value of the underlying shares. (See Figure 45.1, which illustrates the percentage, discounts allowed in a number of personal holding company cases.) Thus, in the example above, Denise's $1,000,000 portfolio may be valued for estate purposes at considerably less than the $1,000,000 that the underlying assets are worth. (The value of a gift of less than a controlling interest would be further reduced because of the lack of voting control.)

WHAT ARE THE TAX IMPLICATIONS?

1. As mentioned above, substantial estate and gift tax savings may be possible through "discounts" in the valuation process. (See list of cases in Figure 45.1.)

2. The individual forming the personal holding company can perform bona fide services for it and receive a salary. Assuming the salary paid is reasonable, the individual will be taxed at a maximum rate of 35% for the tax years 2003 through 2010, on compensation and that amount will be fully deductible by the corporation. Any "excess" compensation (compensation deemed unreasonable) would be subject to tax at the corporate level (nondeductible) and then taxed at the individual level. Operating expenses may even generate a net operating loss. (Local and state franchise taxes should be considered.)

Figure 45.1

PERSONAL HOLDING COMPANY CASES INVOLVING ESTATE TAX DISCOUNTS

Case	Company & Holdings	Shs. to be Valued	Total Shares	Discount Allowed
Celia Waterman 20 TCM 281 (1960)	*Maxcell Corp.* (Apt bldgs)	299	571	30.8%
Lida E. Tompkins Est. 20 TCM 1763 (1961)	*H Street Building Corp.* (Gen'l real estate business, building, contracting and construction)	186	650	32.8%
Drybrough v. U.S. 60 TCM 645 (W.D. Ky 1962)	(5 separate real estate holding companies)			35.0%
Harry S. Leyman 40 TC 100 (1963)	*Leyman Corp.* (Real estate, 2 Buick agencies, parking garages)	2,309	9,400	36.7%
Hamm v. Comm. 325 F.2d 934 (8th Cir. 1963)	*United Properties, Inc.* (Commercial real estate and 10 closely held subsidiaries)	263N	1,000	27.2%
Gregg Maxcy Est. 28 TCM 783 (1969) Rev'd on appeal, 441 F.2d 192 (5th Cir. 1971)	*Maxcy Securities, Inc.* (Citrus grove, restaurant, mortgages (1) and accounts receivable (2))	164 86	174 174	15.0% 25.0%
Heckscher v. Comm. 63 TC 485 (1975)	*Anaheim Realty Co.* (Undeveloped Florida real estate and securities)	2,500	108,675	48.3%
Lloyd R. Smith Est. 9 TCM 907 (1950)	*Smith Investment Co.* (Stock of A O Smith Corp)	408	1,860	22.1%
Bishop Tr. Co. Ltd. v. U.S. 501 USTC ¶10,764 (DC Hawaii 1950)	*Henry P. Baldwin Ltd.* (Stock listed on Honolulu Exchange)	1,861	15,000	32.8%
Goss v. Fitzpatrick 97 F. Supp. 765 (D.C. Conn. 1951)	*Alden M. Young Co.* (Marketable securities; some real estate)	1,900	13,518	42.9%
Clarence J. Grootematt, Est. 79,049 (P-H)	*Greendale Land Co.* (development and sale of real estate)	40	400	25.0%
Ernest A. Oberting Est. TC Memo 1984-407	*Warrior Oil Co.* (percent interest in Indonesian oil contracts)	45	225	65.0%
Estate of Cotchett TC Memo 1974-31	*Eddy Investment Co.* (cash and marketable securities)	20,692	103,621	34.0%
Estate of Hayes TC Memo 1973-236	*DuQuoin Coca Cola* (farm land, dairy business, soft drink bottling business)	930	5,952	25.0%

3. The taxable income of the corporation can be lowered further by providing a working stockholder and working members of his family with various fringe benefits. These include a qualified pension or profit-sharing plan. Furthermore, some medical expenses may be deductible. These expenses must be reasonable in view of the services performed by the employee shareholder.

4. A capital loss of a corporation can be carried back up to three years to offset prior capital gain income while individuals are not allowed a carryback of losses.

5. There is, of course, a substantial disadvantage if a personal holding company is not properly handled. As in any corporation, there is the potential for double taxation (the first incident when the corporation sells securities and again when the shareholder receives the proceeds or other property as a dividend or on the liquidation of the corporation). However, the potential for double taxation can be minimized or eliminated by carefully controlling the type of investments and expenses incurred.

The other problem is the imposition of state capital stock or franchise tax on the value of the personal holding company stock or on the net income remaining in the corporation each year.

HOW CAN LIFE INSURANCE ENHANCE THIS TOOL?

It is possible to transfer to a personal holding company, in addition to other assets, life insurance policies. Thus, an individual would transfer existing life insurance policies (term, whole life, or endowment) having little present value as compared with their face amounts to the personal holding company in exchange for voting common stock. (Alternatively, the company could purchase insurance on the life of the holder of the voting stock.) By then giving non-voting common stock in the holding company to the donee-family members (alternatively, the corporation could sell those family members stock for cash or other property), most of the eventual appreciation due to the death value of the life insurance can be transferred out of the donor-owner's estate.

Because the decedent's executor will have voting control over the personal holding company by virtue of his ownership of the personal holding company voting common stock, that individual could direct the corporation to make an IRC section 303 stock redemption, thus providing estate liquidity.

IMPLICATIONS AND ISSUES IN COMMUNITY PROPERTY STATES

The particular form of property ownership between spouses holding an interest in a corporation classified as a personal holding company has no particular bearing on meeting the stock ownership test, by virtue of the family attribution rules.[8] That is, the ownership interest of one's spouse will be attributed back, regardless of whether the spouse's interest is community or separate property.

However, for estate planning purposes, a community property form of ownership is advantageous, as compared to joint tenancy or tenancy in common, because of the "step-up" in the tax basis of both halves of the community property on the death of one spouse. EGTRRA 2001 replaces the step-up in basis with a modified carryover basis for one year for property received from decedents dying in 2010.

Of particular importance to estate planners when dealing with a personal holding company is the classification of the income produced by the enterprise, because, in order to meet the 60% test, a significant amount of the income must be classified as personal holding company income (i.e., dividends, interest, rents, etc.).

If the stock ownership is community property, then, absent an agreement to the contrary, the income will also be community property. However, as noted in Chapter 43 on Family Limited Partnerships, in some community property states, if the stock ownership is separate property, this does not necessarily mean that the income produced, or any accretion in value, will also be separate property.

As previously discussed in Chapter 40, if an increase in the value of separate property is attributable to the ability or activity of either spouse, for which the community has not been sufficiently rewarded (e.g., by an appropriate salary), at least a portion of that increase may well be determined to be community property (thereby reducing the gross estate of the original owner-spouse).

In addition, the income produced may be classified as both community and separate property. If one of the spouses invests separate property in a business and conducts that business during marriage, without adequate reward to the community for the spouse's efforts, the resulting profits may be community and separate property in proportion to the amounts attributable to the personal efforts and to capital investment, respectively.

In such circumstance, depending on which spouse dies first, it may be important to be able to show that the profits from, and appreciation in value of, the business are from one (or both) spouse's efforts, rather than merely a natural enhancement in value, in order to spread the increased value between the two estates, and to provide a "step-up" in basis for both halves of the community property at the first death. If the spouse who originally owned the business dies first, then the entire business will receive a "stepped-up" basis regardless of the amount of community property effort.

QUESTIONS AND ANSWERS

Question – How can stock be shifted to children and grandchildren without incurring gift tax costs if the children do not have cash or other property to purchase the stock?

Answer – The parent of a child can lend money directly to his children or their custodian or to an irrevocable trust established for their benefit, or guarantee a loan between the child and a third party, such as a bank.[9] The child (or trust) can then purchase stock directly from the corporation for cash. The child could obtain cash to pay back the loan if the personal holding company declares dividends on the common stock. Income shifting from parent to child – and therefore income tax savings – is possible if the child is age 14 or older.

Question – Assuming that personal holding company status is – at some date – considered onerous, how can such classification be avoided?

Answer – As mentioned above, there are two tests – both of which must be met – before a corporation will be classified as a personal holding company. The first requires that five or fewer shareholders own more than 50% of the value of the stock at some time during the last six months of the taxable year. This test can be sidestepped by distributing ownership of shares to unrelated parties or by issuing a second class of stock to unrelated parties in order to dilute ownership value.

The second test requires that personal holding company income be greater than or equal to 60% of adjusted ordinary gross income. To avoid this test, property that produces personal holding company income, such as rental property, can be transferred out of the corporation (with potential tax consequences). Conversely, by producing income (active

as opposed to passive) within the corporation, the 60% test can be avoided.

Furthermore, expenses related to adjusted ordinary gross income can be deferred into future periods or a depreciation method can be selected to maximize adjusted ordinary gross income. Finally, if there is a potential personal holding company liability, cash dividends can be paid out during the tax year, post year-end dividends can be paid, consent dividend procedures can be used, deficiency dividend procedures can be used and, as a final alternative, the corporation can be liquidated.

However, the lack of a capital gains deduction upon a sale or exchange or liquidation makes the liquidation alternative more expensive. In addition, gain from appreciated property that the corporation distributes will be taxed at the corporate level. If the corporation does not have any earnings and profits (or declares a dividend to eliminate any), it can elect S corporation status and avoid any personal holding company tax regardless of the level of passive income. This is because S corporations are not subject to tax under Chapter 1 of the Internal Revenue Code.[10] Such an election may bring into play the built-in gain rules.[11]

Question – Is the personal holding company technique a "sure fire" way to obtain an estate or gift tax valuation discount?

Answer – Not every personal holding company will result in an estate or gift tax discount. In one case, the value of stock in two personal holding companies that were owned by the decedent was not reduced by a lack of marketability discount.[12] The court held that the proper estate tax value was the net asset value of the companies less the cost involved in liquidating them. Note that the result occurred because the decedent owned 100% of both companies and therefore had the unqualified right to liquidate them at any time. Note also that all the assets in both companies were cash or marketable securities, and that neither corporation had any significant liabilities. Planners should use this case as a "how not to do it" guideline.

CHAPTER ENDNOTES

1. IRC section 542(c) contains 10 types of business entities that are specifically excluded from personal holding company status, such as tax-exempt corporations, banks, and life insurance companies.

2. IRC Sec. 542(a)(2). The ownership test pertains to value and not to the number of outstanding shares. Under constructive ownership rules an individual is deemed to own all the stock directly or indirectly owned by or for his brothers and sisters, spouse, ancestors, and lineal descendants. Likewise, stock owned directly or indirectly by or for a corporation, partnership, estate, or trust is considered as being owned proportionately by its shareholders, partners, or beneficiaries. IRC Sec. 544(a).

3. IRC Sec. 542(a)(1). "Adjusted ordinary gross income" is essentially gross income less gains from sales or other dispositions of capital assets and IRC section 1231 property, and further reduced by depreciation, certain taxes, interest, and rents attributable to income from certain rents and royalties. IRC Sec. 543(b).

4. IRC Sec. 541.

5. IRC Secs. 351, 368(c); Treas. Reg. §1.351-1(a).

6. IRC Sec. 358(a).

7. IRC Sec. 362(a).

8. IRC Sec. 544(a)(2).

9. TRA '84 severely limited the utility of interest-free loans. See IRC section 7872 and Chapter 37 of this book. Also, note the IRS position in PLR 9113009 that a guarantee, for less than full and adequate consideration, is a completed gift for gift tax purpose. (This ruling was withdrawn by the IRS in PLR 9409018 without comment on the taxable gift issue.)

10. IRC Sec. 1363.

11. IRC Sec. 1374.

12. *Est. of Jephson v. Comm.*, 87 TC 297 (1986).

Chapter 46

S CORPORATION

Note: A checklist of issues to consider when choosing an entity, such as a proprietorship, partnership, limited liability company (LLC), C corporation, or S corporation, appears at the end of Chapter 47 as Figure 47.3.

WHAT IS IT?

An "S" corporation is a corporation that has made an election to have its income, deductions, capital gains and losses, charitable contributions, and credits passed through to its shareholders. To a great extent an S corporation is treated for tax purposes similarly to a partnership.

WHEN IS THE USE OF SUCH A DEVICE INDICATED?

1. When a client (currently a sole proprietor or partnership) is entering a new, high risk business, and would like the legal protection against creditors offered by corporate status, but wants to be able to personally deduct losses of the business enterprise if the venture fails. (This same goal can be achieved to a limited degree through the use of IRC Section 1244 stock in a normal corporation.)

   An "S" election enables corporate losses to be passed through the corporation and deducted on the tax returns of the individual shareholders (but only to the extent of the adjusted basis of their stock in the corporation and loans made to the corporation).[1] Thus, losses of an S corporation may be used to offset income earned outside of the business.

2. Where the business, although not inherently risky, has a period of loss during the first years of starting up, the client may elect S corporation status for the early loss years. When the business begins to make a profit, the election may be terminated and future profits taxed to the corporation. The method and other effects of the termination should be carefully planned.

3. When the stockholder(s) would like to take out all corporate income without the normal double taxa-tion on corporate earnings and such payments could not be justified as reasonable compensation. In other words, when S corporation status has been elected, generally there is no tax at the corporate level; typically, income earned by the S corporation is taxed only once, to the individual shareholders, regardless of the amount of income or the services performed, if any, by the shareholders.

Double taxation has always been a problem when income is earned and then accumulated in a regular ("C") corporation. Double taxation under current law is even more onerous than in the past. There are four reasons:

a. Corporate tax rates can sometimes exceed individual rates. This is particularly true in the case of professional service corporations, which are taxed at a flat rate of 35% on every dollar of taxable income. No "run up the brackets" is allowed to these corporations.

b. Distributions of the cash proceeds of a sale of appreciated property (assets with a fair market value in excess of their tax basis) of a regular ("C") corporation upon its liquidation, or even distributions of the appreciated property itself, will trigger tax both at the corporate and shareholder levels. (Under prior law, the "built-in gains" in corporate assets usually escaped taxation on the corporate level when the assets were sold or distributed in a liquidation or IRC Section 303 distribution even if the corporation had not made an S election. This is no longer true following the repeal of the *General Utilities* doctrine.)

c. Corporate gains on capital assets are not eligible for a lower capital gains rate. These gains are generally taxed at the corporation's regular tax rate.

d. The net proceeds of the gain already taxed at the corporate level are again taxed when distributed to shareholders.

The double taxation problem suffered by regular corporations' shareholders year after year can be alleviated, or in some cases even eliminated, by an increase in shareholders' salaries (thus reducing corporate taxable income).

But this ploy will not work with the potentially huge tax at the time a corporation is liquidated. First, the tax may be many times the normal "doubletax." Second, it is difficult to justify proportionately large salaries in the year the corporation is going out of business. With the loss of the ability to income average, the ultimate tax on a final liquidation could absorb the work product of years of hard work.

4. When the nontax benefits of incorporation are desired, but the individual shareholders are in lower tax brackets than the corporation and they would like the advantage of the tax savings that can be obtained by having the income earned by the corporation taxed directly to them as individuals.

5. Where it is desired to spread income among a number of family members, an S corporation is a useful device. By giving stock, the tax on corporate earnings may be shifted to a large number of relatively low tax bracket individuals and taxed at their brackets rather than at the client's bracket (provided they are age 14 or over).

6. When avoidance of the AMT (alternative minimum tax) is desirable.

7. When avoidance of the accumulated earnings tax is desirable.

WHAT ARE THE REQUIREMENTS?

1. The corporation must be a domestic corporation.[2] This means it must be created or organized in the U.S. or one of its states.

2. It must have no more than 75 shareholders.[3]

3. Shareholders must be individuals, estates, or certain types of trusts. Nonresident aliens may not be shareholders.[4] In tax years beginning after December 31, 1997, a tax-exempt organization such as a qualified retirement plan trust or a charitable organization (501(c)(3)) may be a shareholder in an S corporation. The qualified tax exempt shareholder is counted as only one shareholder for purposes of determining the number of shareholders.

4. The corporation can have only one class of stock.[5] That means each share must confer equal rights to distribution and liquidation proceeds. However, it is possible to provide for differences in voting rights among shares of common stock. For instance, there can safely be a "Class A" and a "Class B" voting stock with different terms or powers, so long as both classes confer equal rights to distribution and liquidation proceeds. Similarly, bona fide buy-sell agreements, agreements restricting transferability of shares, and redemption agreements will not be held to constitute a second class of stock so long as they are not entered into to circumvent the one-class-of-stock requirement and do not establish a purchase price that is significantly in excess of or below the fair market value of the stock.

A "straight debt instrument" is not considered, for these purposes, a second class of stock. A "straight debt instrument" means a written unconditional promise to pay on demand or on a specified date a sum certain in money so long as: (a) the interest rate (and payment dates) are not contingent on the corporate profits, the discretion of the corporation, or other similar factors, (b) the instrument is not convertible into stock, *and* (c) the creditor is a person, estate or trust eligible to hold S corporation stock, or a person actively and regularly engaged in the business of lending money.[6] This favorable treatment is not lost merely because the interest rate is dependent upon the prime rate (or a similar factor not related to the debtor corporation).

HOW IT IS DONE – AN EXAMPLE

There are five equal shareholders in the ABC Corporation, which is currently earning profits of $100,000 per year. The federal corporate tax on $100,000 is $22,250. This means the amount that could be distributed to the corporation's shareholders if $77,750 ($100,000 - $22,250). Each shareholder's share is $15,550 ($77,750 ÷ 5). In 2003 the top dividend tax rate for most dividends was reduced to 15%. Each shareholder pays tax of $2,333 (15% x $15,550) on the dividend. The aggregate taxes on all five individual's dividends will be $11,665. In total, the taxes paid are $33,915 ($22,250 of corporate tax plus $11,665 of tax on dividends).

Now assume the corporation has elected "S" status. The election, of course, does not change corporate profits, which are still $100,000. However, the $100,000 is now passed directly through to the shareholders (the character of the income also is passed through) and there is no corporate tax to pay. The net profits subject to distribution are $100,000. Dividing that figure by five, each shareholder's share is $20,000. Assuming each owner has a personal income tax rate of 31%, his or her tax is $6,200 each. The total personal income taxes for all shareholders on the $100,000 profit are $31,000 ($100,000 x 31%).

Taxes Before S Election	Taxes After S Election
$33,915	$31,000

The S election saves $2,915 annually in this case. It should be noted that whether there is an advantage depends on relative tax rates. For example, with corporate income of $50,000 and the same individual income tax rate of 31%, the C corporation scenario tax would be $13,875 [($50,000 x 15%) + ($50,000 x 85%) x 15%] and the S corporation scenario tax would be $15,500 ($50,000 x 31%).

WHAT ARE THE TAX IMPLICATIONS?

1. S corporations and their shareholders are taxed under essentially the same rules that apply to partnerships and their partners. Generally, the S corporation does not pay federal income tax. Its income (or loss) is passed through directly to its shareholders and therefore avoids the double tax on corporate earnings.[7]

2. Essentially, taxable income of an S corporation is computed as follows:

Any income that could affect the individual tax liability of a shareholder is passed directly through the corporation to the shareholders. Likewise, any loss, deduction, or credit that could affect the liability of a shareholder is passed through just as if the entity were a partnership. Even tax exempt income such as municipal bond interest or life insurance proceeds is passed through as tax exempt income.

Shareholders must report or deduct all these "separately treated" items in proportion to their shareholdings. In other words, a 10% shareholder would be required to report 10% of the corporation's income, but would be entitled to 10% of any corporate earned deductions or credits.

Typical separately treated items include (1) gains and losses from corporate sales or exchanges of capital assets, and (2) charitable contributions (the corporation's contributions are passed through to shareholders who add them to their own personal contributions in determining the charitable contribution deduction on their own personal returns).

3. Tax exempt interest received by an S corporation retains its tax exempt character and increases the

Figure 46.1

TAX PAYABLE BY ENTITY OR SOLE SHAREHOLDER
C CORPORATION v. S CORPORATION

The chart below compares the tax payable by an entity owned by a sole shareholder who operates as a "C" corporation with the tax the same individual would pay in 2004 if the corporation had elected S corporation status. It is assumed the shareholder files jointly, that the S corporation income is exactly equal to his or her taxable income, and the shareholder does not take earnings and profits out of the C corportion (which would increase the total tax payable in the C corporation scenario because of the additional tax at the shareholder level and swing the advantage to the S election much more quickly than is apparent in the chart).

Taxable Income	Tax as a C Corporation	Tax as an S Corporation
$25,000	$ 3,750	$ 3,035
50,000	7,500	6,785
100,000	22,250	18,475
150,000	41,750	31,958
200,000	61,250	47,026
500,000	170,000	149,643
750,000	255,000	237,143
1,000,000	340,000	324,643
2,000,000	680,000	674,643

shareholders' basis. If the interest is subsequently distributed, it is not taxable but reduces the shareholders' basis.

4. Amounts passed through as credits are passed through on a per-share per-day basis and are claimed by the shareholders on their personal returns.

5. Allowances for depletion with respect to oil and gas wells are separately computed for each shareholder. Each shareholder must keep records of his basis in each well, and adjust the basis for any depletion taken.

6. Net operating loss is deductible by a shareholder as an ordinary loss in computing adjusted gross income. If it exceeds the shareholder's other income, it can be carried back for two years and then carried forward for up to 20 years. The amount of loss that can be passed through in a given year is limited to the sum of (a) the basis of the shareholder's S corporation stock and (b) the basis of loans he has made to the corporation. However, losses in excess of this sum can be carried forward indefinitely until the shareholder has a restored basis in the stock or debt.

The corporation's remaining (the nonseparately computed) income, if any, is taxable to the shareholders. Each shareholder reports on Schedule E of his Form 1040 his pro rata share. Likewise, each shareholder must report his pro rata share of corporate preference items.

All this income must be reported by a shareholder in his taxable year in which, or with which, the corporation's tax year ends. (S corporations must use a calendar year for tax accounting purposes, unless a business reason is established for using a fiscal year period, so the tax year of most S corporations ends on December 31.) In the case of a deceased shareholder, pro rata shares of income attributable to the portion of the corporation's tax year prior to his death are reportable on the final return. Income earned in the balance of the year is reported on the estate's income tax return or on the return of the beneficiary who received the stock.

The pro rata shares are determined on a day by day per-share basis. This per-share per-day method of prorating income liability also applies where S corporation stock is sold or given away.

There are two circumstances where an S corporation may pay tax at the maximum corporate rate, currently 35%.

The first situation is where the S corporation has earnings and profits, (derived either while it was a C corporation or due to an acquisition of a C corporation), and now has passive investment income. Passive investment income includes such items as rents, royalties, dividends, and interest. The tax is based on the passive investment income for the year in excess of 25% of the corporation's gross receipts.[8]

The second situation occurs where a corporation converts from a C to an S corporation and had appreciated assets at the time of the conversion. The so-called "built in" gain on such assets will be taxed at the corporate level if the appreciated assets are sold within 10 years.[9] Thus, it is important to determine the value of corporate assets when an S election is made, if the corporation was previously taxed as a C corporation.

IMPLICATIONS AND ISSUES IN COMMUNITY PROPERTY STATES

A husband and wife, shareholders of community property stock in an S corporation, both must give their consent to the corporation's election to have its earnings taxed to the shareholders. If retention of the S corporation election is desirable, in a situation where an individual is purchasing shares with community property funds, a contract should be entered into with both that individual and his spouse whereby they would agree not to refuse to consent to the election.

The same concern discussed in Chapter 43, dealing with earnings from a separate property investment, should also be considered.

As noted, husband and wife holding stock as community property are counted as only one shareholder. Additionally, community property stock, because half is owned by each spouse, can be more easily given within the scope of the annual exclusion without the necessity of filing a gift tax return.

QUESTIONS AND ANSWERS

Question – When must an election to be taxed as an S corporation be made by an existing C corporation?

Answer – An "S" election may be made (a) at any time during the entire taxable year prior to the election year, or (b) on or before the 15th day of the 3rd month of the election year. Elections made after that date are treated as made for the next tax year.[10] For instance, for an election to be effective in 2004, a corporation must file the election sometime between January 1, 2003 and March 15, 2004.

An effective election presupposes both that all eligibility requirements are met and that the proper consent from shareholders has been obtained. It is possible to obtain an extension of time to file in certain cases even if a shareholder fails to consent in time.

All shareholders on the day the election is made must consent (on IRS Form 2553 or on a separate consent document). Minors can sign the consent even without legal or natural guardians (or such individuals may consent on behalf of a minor who is unable to act). A decedent's personal representative (executor or administrator) signs on behalf of an estate holding S corporation stock.

Question – Under what circumstances can the S election be terminated?

Answer – An election of an S corporation will terminate under any of the following circumstances:[11]

(a) Shareholders holding more than 50% of the corporation's stock consent to revoke the election. There is no official form; the corporation files a statement with the IRS revoking the election. The termination is effective for the entire taxable year if the revocation is filed on or before the 15th day of the third month of the taxable year; otherwise, the revocation is effective on the first day of the following taxable year. The entrance of a new stockholder cannot revoke an election unless that person owns more than 50% of the corporation's stock and that person revokes the election; if no revocation occurs, new shareholders are bound by the same rules that apply to other shareholders.

(b) The corporation fails to satisfy any of the four qualification requirements discussed above under the heading "What Are the Requirements?" The termination is effective on the day the disqualifying event occurs. For instance, the election ends if the limit on the number of shareholders is exceeded or shares are transferred to an ineligible party. Therefore, a transfer of even one share of S corporation stock to a partnership, corporation, nonresident alien, or

nonqualifying trust terminates an election. Likewise, if a second class of stock is issued the election would terminate.

(c) Certain passive income exceeds 25% of the corporation's gross receipts for three consecutive tax years and the corporation has accumulated earnings and profits (either from its days as a C corporation or due to a corporate acquisition) at the end of each such year.

Question – If an S election is terminated, how soon may a new election be made?

Answer – Once terminated, an S election cannot be made again for five years unless the Commissioner of Internal Revenue consents.[12] The IRS may waive the effect of an inadvertent termination for any period if the corporation (a) corrects the event that created the termination in a timely manner and (b) agrees, together with all its shareholders, to make such adjustments as may be required by the IRS with respect to such period.[13]

Question – How is life insurance owned by an S corporation taxed?

Answer – Key person life insurance premiums are nondeductible. Death proceeds are received income tax free by the corporation and are not subject to either an accumulated earnings tax or an alternative minimum tax. When the proceeds are distributed to the corporation's shareholders, they will be treated in the same manner as any other distributions of separately treated items, i.e., it retains its character as tax free income. If a policy is surrendered during the insured's lifetime or the policy matures, any gain is taxable directly to the corporation's shareholders.

Most advisors recommend that insurance that is indicated be owned on a personal basis. This is because shareholders in an S corporation are currently taxed on corporate income used to purchase nondeductible items such as corporate life insurance, even if there is no actual distribution of cash to pay that tax. For instance, if a corporation pays a $10,000 premium, shareholders of an S corporation are taxed on $10,000 even though they do not receive it.

The corporation should pay a deductible bonus to each shareholder, which, after tax, would be sufficient to pay premiums on the appropriate amounts of insurance.

Question – Can an S corporation set up a nonqualified deferred compensation plan?

Answer – An S corporation can establish a deferred compensation plan. But the tax advantage enjoyed by a conventional corporation is not available. This is because shareholders are taxed directly and immediately on the current taxable income of the corporation, whether or not that income is distributed. Because premiums are not deductible, the outlay for life insurance that is used to finance the corporation's obligation under the deferred compensation plan is immediately taxable to the individual shareholders. A corporation with a $50,000 gross income, $30,000 of deductible expenses, and which pays $5,000 in key person insurance premiums has only $15,000 available for distribution. Yet shareholders are taxed as if they had received $20,000.

Question – How are S corporations treated for fringe benefit purposes?

Answer – S corporations generally will be treated as partnerships for purposes of plan eligibility and taxation of "employee fringe benefits." All shareholders owning more than 2% of the stock will be considered partners.[14]

The result is that most shareholder-employees would not be "employees" for purposes of favorable IRC Section 79 group term, medical reimbursement, or other coverage. This results generally in taxation of the more-than-2% shareholder-employees.

Question – Is an outright gift the best way to shift income to a minor child age 14 or older through an S corporation?

Answer – An outright gift of S corporation stock to a minor makes it impossible to exercise any rights with the stock unless a court-appointed guardian is obtained. This is usually expensive, inconvenient, and typically involves a great deal of administrative inflexibility.

An alternative to an outright gift to a minor is a gift to a custodian under the appropriate Uniform Gifts to Minors Act (UGMA). Unfortunately, this device has its limitations.

First, once the minor reaches age 21 (18 in some states), shares must be distributed. Many clients feel that this age is an inappropriate time to distribute

large amounts of money or securities. Most individuals are unwilling to allow a donee-child to obtain unlimited ownership and control at that time.

A second possible problem is that if the minor dies prior to the age at which the shares must be distributed under applicable local law, the likelihood is great that the shares will be returned to the donor through the operation of state intestacy statutes.

The third potential problem is that the custodian may die or become unable to act. Under the Uniform Gifts to Minors Act it is possible that the custodian could name a successor. (Such a successor may be named by the donor when the UGMA account is established or the custodian may name his or her own successor.) Lacking advance preparations, court proceedings may have to be instituted in order to name a successor custodian; a procedure that would entail costs and delays.

Gifts to a minor in trust should be considered as an alternative to custodianship. Additionally, gifts of non-voting stock should be considered if it is desired that the minor (guardian) not participate in business decisions.

Question – Can a trust be a shareholder of an S corporation?

Answer – A trust can be a shareholder of an S corporation, but only if (a) the grantor or other individual is treated for income tax purposes as the owner of the trust property under IRC Sections 671 to 678 (a so-called "grantor trust"); (b) such a grantor trust continues after the grantor's death (limited to a period of two years after death); (c) the trust receives the stock under a will (a so-called "testamentary trust") and it holds S corporation stock only up to a maximum of two years after the stock is transferred to the trust; (d) the trust was created primarily to vote stock (a so-called "voting trust"); (e) the trust is a qualified subchapter S trust (QSST); or (f) the trust is an electing small business trust (ESBT).[15]

Question – What is a grantor trust?

Answer – A grantor trust, one in which the grantor is treated as if he owned trust property for income tax purposes, is eligible to own stock in an S corporation. A grantor trust can hold S corporation stock regardless of whether it is revocable. In fact such a trust can continue as an S corporation shareholder even after the death of the grantor (but only for a limited period of up to 2 years). Thus, revocable living trusts may own stock in an S corporation.

The disadvantage of the grantor trust as a receptacle for S corporation stock is obvious: its income will be taxed to the grantor (and therefore the ability to shift the tax on income is lost).

Question – What is a Section 678 trust?

Answer – A Section 678 trust is another alternative to outright and UGMA gifts to a minor. "A nongrantor-owner trust" is an eligible S corporation stock shareholder. The criterion for favorable tax treatment under this type of trust (IRC Section 678 governs, and therefore these nongrantor-owner trusts have come to be called "Section 678 trusts") is that the beneficiary must have unrestricted power "exercisable solely by himself to vest the corpus or the income therefrom in himself." In other words, the beneficiary will be taxed on the income from the S corporation held by the trust if he has the right to take both income and corpus whenever he wants. There must be no restrictions on the beneficiary's right to exercise a withdrawal power.

A Section 678 trust can be created by a parent or grandparent who transfers S corporation stock to it for the benefit of a minor. The minor would be given an unrestricted power to withdraw income or corpus for his own benefit.

Question – What is a qualified subchapter S trust (QSST)?

Answer – A qualified subchapter S trust (QSST) is one type of trust that is eligible to hold S corporation stock.[16] Specifically, a QSST is defined in the Internal Revenue Code as one that:

1. owns stock in one or more S corporations (and may hold other types of assets)

2. actually distributes all of its income to one individual (who must be a United States resident or United States citizen)

3. has trust terms requiring that:

    (a) there can be only one beneficiary at any given time

    (b) if corpus is distributed during the term of the trust, it can be distributed only to the individual who is at that time the current income beneficiary

    (c) if an income beneficiary dies, the income interest itself will end at that death or upon the earlier termination of the trust

    (d) if the trust ends before the income beneficiary dies, all the assets of the trust must be distributed to that income beneficiary

4. requires an election to be made by the income beneficiary (or the income beneficiary's legal representative) to have the QSST qualify as such. (Once that election is made, it is irrevocable and can be revoked only if the IRS consents.) That election must be made by each income beneficiary as he or she becomes one. Separate elections must be made if the stock of more than one S corporation is held in the trust.

If the requirements described above are met, the income beneficiary of a QSST (which can be set up during the grantor's lifetime or by will) is treated as the owner of the stock. The consequence is that any income, as well as any gains or losses, passes directly from the S corporation to the beneficiary, not to the trust.

What are the advantages of a QSST? A gift of S corporation stock can be made to a minor through the trust without incurring the disadvantages of outright ownership. This enables an individual to split income among family members while at the same time eliminating the gift from inclusion in his gross estate. So both income shifting and wealth transfers are possible through the QSST.

Unlike a custodianship, a QSST can continue beyond age 18 (or 21) and can last as long as the grantor directs it to last. This means that if the minor dies before the trust terminates, the trust can continue for the lives of a number of successive income beneficiaries and does not need to force trust assets into the estate of the deceased income beneficiary.

Question – What is an electing small business trust (ESBT)?

Answer – An electing small business trust (ESBT) is another type of trust that can hold stock in an S corporation.[17] An ESBT may have as its beneficiaries, individuals, estates, or certain charitable organizations that are eligible to be S corporation shareholders. Each potential current beneficiary is counted as a shareholder for purposes of the 75 shareholder limitation. Trusts exempt from the income tax, QSSTs, and charitable remainder trusts may not be ESBTs. An interest in an ESBT may not be obtained by purchase. An ESBT is taxed at the highest income tax rate for individuals.

Question – How are gifts to a trust qualifying as an S corporation shareholder taxed for gift tax purposes?

Answer – From a gift standpoint, if no inappropriate powers are retained by the trustor(s), a contribution to a trust will be considered a complete gift. Such gifts can qualify for the gift tax annual exclusion either by meeting the requirements of IRC Section 2503(c) or by including a Crummey withdrawal power.

Question – Will the property in a trust qualifying as an S corporation shareholder be includable in the gross estate of a beneficiary?

Answer – In the case of a grantor trust, the trust will be includable in the grantor's gross estate if the grantor holds certain interests at death or transfers such interests within three years of death. In general, these include interests such as a retained life estate, a reversion, a revocable transfer, or certain interests in an annuity or in life insurance. Actually, inclusion of a trust in a grantor's estate can occur whether or not the trust is treated as a grantor trust for income tax purposes.

In the case of a Section 678 trust, the beneficiary must be given a general power of appointment (the power of withdrawal) over all or a portion of the trust. Property subject to that power at the time of the beneficiary's death will be includable in his or her estate. If the beneficiary exercises or releases a power of appointment in such a way that the property would have been includable in the estate of the beneficiary if the beneficiary were treated as owner of the property, as described in the preceding paragraph, the property would also be includable in the beneficiary's estate. A lapse of a power that is no more than the greater of $5,000 or 5% of the property from which the power is exercisable is not treated as a release.

In the case of a QSST beneficiary, if trust assets are distributed to the beneficiary at death, the trust is includable in his or her gross estate.

A beneficiary of an ESBT need not be given any interest that would cause the trust to be includable in the beneficiary's estate.

Question – How can a client transfer ownership of a business through an S corporation and at the same time shift income?

Answer – An S corporation is an ideal vehicle to shift both wealth and income to other family members. For instance, assume a doctor, as a sideline, establishes a laboratory or dispensary. He could incorporate the business as an S corporation and give all the shares of the newly formed business to his children (all of whom are 14 or older).

The business would pay no income taxes at the corporate level. The children would pay income taxes on their share of the company's profits (which would otherwise have been taxed to their higher bracket father). If the children were transferred shares through a defective grantor trust, the grantor would pay the income tax while the beneficiaries would receive nontaxable distributions.

The best type of business for wealth and income shifting purposes is one in which the client performs no services (or the services are only incidental). If the client performs significant services or services that generate all the corporation's income, the IRS is likely to attribute earnings to the client and tax him accordingly. For instance, if the doctor, as a sideline, gives medical lectures for a fee, the S corporation will not be able to shift the tax on income it receives as compensation for his lectures to his children.

Conversely, if income from a passive investment (such as S corporation income from a laboratory run by a person unrelated to the doctor) is channeled to an age 14 or older child, income (and therefore tax) can be shifted without challenge.

It is important to follow formalities. For instance, stock-owning children or their guardians should be invited to shareholder meetings.

Question – How have recent tax law changes affected the popularity of S corporations?

Answer – Recent tax law changes have significantly increased the number of S elections for eligible corporations. Reasons an S election is more valuable than ever include:

1. The corporate-level exclusion on gains for distributions of property at liquidation was repealed. Therefore, the liquidation of a regular ("C") corporation will often result in gain at the corporate level and then again at the shareholder level. This will seldom occur in an S corporation liquidation.

2. A flat tax rate of 35% is imposed on all taxable income of personal service C corporations. But corporations electing S corporation treatment are generally not subject to any tax at the corporate level, and their shareholders – even professional shareholders – remain entitled to the "run through the brackets" starting with rates as low as 10%.

Although the S election is not available for all businesses and is, likewise, not appropriate for every circumstance, a substantial number of closely held corporations can benefit from these tax advantages.

Question – What are the disadvantages of S corporation status?

Answer – Among the drawbacks to S corporation status are that an S corporation:

(1) cannot accumulate earnings and profits for capital needs at lower corporate brackets;

(2) is limited in its ability to use carryovers (such as, net operating losses or investment tax credits);

(3) is restricted in the fringe benefits it can offer its shareholder-employees (although the tax law doesn't prohibit the S corporation from offering the benefit, because the shareholder-employee is taxable and the benefit may be nondeductible by the corporation, the cost of many fringes is prohibitive);

(4) is not appropriate as a holding vehicle for certain real estate or other investments;

(5) at death, assets in the corporation do not receive a step-up in basis, although the decedent's basis in the stock does get stepped-up. [EGTTRA 2001 replaces a stepped-up basis with a modified carryover basis for one year for property acquired from a decedent dying in 2010.]

Additionally, shareholders of an S corporation are prohibited from borrowing from their retirement plans (and will likely have to pay back all loans from such plans before an S election becomes effective).

Question – What is the impact of state law on the decision to elect S corporation treatment?

Answer – A decision to elect S corporation status must consider state tax laws:

(1) Some states do not recognize the S corporation's status for state income tax purposes. There are a number of jurisdictions that do not currently allow corporate income to be passed through directly to shareholders as it is under federal law. This means the corporation will have to pay tax at the corporate level.

(2) States tax "passed-through" income at their own rates. Therefore, the reduction of federal tax rates on individuals has not, in many cases, been carried through at the state level.

(3) If the federal income tax base of individuals is used at the state level for computing the state income tax and itemized deductions of a shareholder, an S election may increase the shareholder's state taxable income.

(4) Nonresident shareholders of S corporations typically must pay income tax to the state where the S corporation does business. But if the S corporation is "doing business" in several states, the multiple tax preparations and payments could be burdensome.

(5) Some states require both a federal and a separate state S corporation election. This increases costs and administrative burdens as well as the possibility for unintentional loss of S corporation status. The IRS may not recognize for federal purposes a corporation that was not recognized as such for state purposes.

Question – How does the corporate alternative minimum tax (AMT) affect corporations that have elected S corporation status?

Answer – A corporate alternative minimum tax applies to "C" (regular) corporations. Generally, this tax does not apply to S corporations. This means an S election may result in significant tax saving.

Question – Do the passive loss rules affect S corporations?

Answer – If a shareholder does not materially participate in the business, losses from the business would be considered "passive." They can therefore be used only to offset passive income of the shareholder. Likewise, income received by such a shareholder from the business should be considered "passive" and should therefore offset any passive losses from other investments of the shareholder.

Question – Will the pro-rata allocation of income to shareholders in a family S corporation always be allowed for federal income tax purposes?

Answer – Not necessarily. Following rules based on those applicable to family partnerships, discussed in Chapter 43, the allocation of S corporation income to family members may be disregarded if the income is not derived from capital, the transferor family members are not adequately compensated

for their services, or the transferor family members retain too much control over the transferred stock.[18]

ASRS: Secs 43; 53, ¶22.5; 59, ¶490.4(b).

CHAPTER ENDNOTES

1. IRC Sec. 1366(d); Treas. Reg. §1.1363-1.
2. IRC Sec. 1361(b)(1).
3. IRC Sec. 1361(b)(1)(A).
4. IRC Secs. 1361(b)(1)(B), 1361(b)(1)(C).
5. IRC Sec. 1361(b)(1)(D).
6. IRC 1361(c)(5)(B).
7. IRC Secs. 1363, 1366, 1368.
8. IRC Sec. 1375.
9. IRC Sec. 1374.
10. IRC Sec. 1362(b).
11. IRC Sec. 1362(d).
12. IRC Sec. 1362(g); Treas. Reg. §1.1362-5(a).
13. IRC Sec. 1362(f).
14. IRC Sec. 1372.
15. IRC Secs. 1361(b)(1)(B), 1361(c)(2), 1361(d), 1361(e).
16. IRC Sec. 1361(d).
17. IRC Sec. 1361(e).
18. IRC Sec. 1366(e).

Chapter 47

INCORPORATION

Note: This discussion deals with the general treatment of corporations. In the case of corporations that have elected special status under Subchapter S, different rules may apply (see Chapter 46). A checklist of issues to consider when choosing an entity, such as a proprietorship, partnership, limited liability company (LLC), C corporation, or S corporation, appears at the end of this chapter as Figure 47.3.

WHAT IS IT?

For federal tax purposes a business entity with two or more owners is classified as a corporation or partnership. A business entity with only one owner may elect to be classified as a corporation or elect to be treated as a sole proprietorship. Under regulations, an organization that is incorporated under Federal or state law is treated as a corporation for tax purposes and is not eligible to elect a different classification under the so-called "Check-the-Box" rules.[1]

In addition, the "Check-the-Box" rules generally permit unincorporated organizations to elect to be treated as associations taxable as corporations for federal tax purposes without regard to the number of corporate characteristics (limited liability, continuity of life, centralized management, and free transferability of interest) they possess.

Under the regulations the term "corporation" means:

(1) A business entity organized under a federal or state statute, if the statute describes or refers to the entity as incorporated or as a corporation, body corporate, or body politic;

(2) An association;

(3) A business entity organized under a state statute, if the statute describes or refers to the entity as a joint-stock company or joint-stock association;

(4) An insurance company;

(5) Certain state-chartered business entities conducting banking activities;

(6) A business entity wholly owned by a state or a political subdivision of a state;

(7) A business entity that is taxable as a corporation under a provision of the Internal Revenue Code other than Section 7701(a)(3); and

(8) Certain foreign entities.

All entities included in the above list are classified as corporations for income tax purposes. An entity not on the above list with two or more owners may elect to be taxed as a corporation or as a partnership for income tax purposes. In addition, an entity not on the above list with only one owner may also elect to be taxed as a corporation or as a sole proprietorship.[2]

WHEN IS THE USE OF SUCH A DEVICE INDICATED?

1. When the individual owners desire limited liability. A corporation, not its individual shareholders, is responsible for corporate obligations.

2. When the individual owners desire a relatively simple and inexpensive means of transferring ownership. It is relatively easy to provide for a new owner's entrance and an existing owner's exit merely by endorsing shares of stock. This is especially important in making gifts to minors.

3. When the individual owners desire to take advantage of the wide range of fringe benefits that the corporation can provide. These benefits are, within limits, tax deductible by the corporation and generally not currently taxable to the employee – including shareholder-employees. These fringe benefits may include:

   • pension/profit-sharing plans,

   • group life insurance,

   • group health insurance,

   • disability income coverage,

- medical reimbursement plans,

- cafeteria plans, and

- auto and travel costs.

4. When other tax-oriented advantages are desired. For instance, assuming a corporation does not need to pay out substantial dividends, the overall tax result may be lower federal income taxes than if the enterprise were run in the form of a sole proprietorship or partnership. It might be easiest to illustrate this point by comparing partnership with corporate tax treatment. If a partnership were formed, owners would be taxed on all the income earned as partners at their individual rates (which may be higher than the applicable corporate rate) – even if they did not actually withdraw all partnership earnings from the firm. However, as stockholder-employees, they would be taxed only on salaries (assuming no dividend had to be paid). A lower federal income tax may result under the corporate form as compared to the partnership form.

Because the corporation's tax rate may be lower than the individual's tax rate, this income splitting can yield a lower overall current tax. This is especially true on the first $50,000 of corporate income, which is taxed at only a 15% rate.

However, it may be more expensive tax-wise to be a corporation when it comes down to selling the business. Under the rules, there may be two taxes as a result of a corporate sale of assets (followed by liquidation) instead of one tax when the seller is a proprietorship or partnership. Thus, if the corpora-

tion has assets that are likely to appreciate, the income-splitting benefit may be more than offset by the additional taxes at liquidation.

The rates on corporate taxable income (Corporate Tax Table), including worksheets for computing the tax, are shown below:[3]

CORPORATE TAX TABLE

Taxable Income	Base Amount	Base Tax Owed	% on Excess
0	50,000	0	15
50,000	75,000	7,500	25
75,000	100,000	13,750	34
100,000	335,000	22,250	39
335,000	10,000,000	113,900	34
10,000,000	15,000,000	3,400,000	35
15,000,000	18,333,333	5,150,000	38
18,333,333	....	6,416,667	35

CORPORATE TAX CALCULATING WORKSHEET

	Example
Step 1: List Taxable Income	$200,000
Step 2: List Base Tax	22,250
Step 3: Compute "Excess" Over Base Amount	$100,000
Step 4: List % on "Excess"	.39
Step 5: Multiply Step 3 x Step 4	39,000
Step 6: Total Steps 2 and 5	61,250

Figure 47.1 compares the tax payable by various taxpayers on $100,000 of taxable income based on 2004 rates.

Figure 47.1

TAX COMPARISON — 2004					
	TAXABLE INCOME	TAX	NET INCOME	MARGINAL RATE (%)	OVERALL RATE (%)
CORPORATE*	$100,000	$22,250	$77,750	34	22
PERSONAL SERVICE CORPORATION	$100,000	$35,000	$65,000	35	35
JOINT	$100,000	$18,475	$81,525	25	18
SINGLE	$100,000	$22,627	$77,373	28	23
SEPARATE	$100,000	$23,513	$76,487	33	24
HEAD/HOUSEHOLD	$100,000	$20,600	$79,400	25	21
TRUST/ESTATE	$100,000	$34,125	$65,875	35	34

*Not a personal service corporation.

Note that personal service corporations are taxed at a flat rate of 35 percent.[4] The term "qualified personal service corporation" means one in which (a) substantially all of the activities involve the performance of services in the fields of health, law, engineering, architecture, accounting, actuarial science, performing arts, or consulting, and (b) substantially all of the stock of which is held by employees, retirees, their estates, or persons acquiring stock due to the death of an employee or retiree (but only for a two-year period following the death).[5]

A corporation can generally declare and pay dividends – as well as salaries – in such a manner as to avoid a "bunching" of income at the entity level in those years when personal income is highest. On the other hand, if the business were established in the partnership form, the owners would have little control over the receipt and taxation of income. This ability to "time" income is important because, if income can be timed, the ultimate taxes payable can be lowered.

5. When the estate owner wants to entice family members into the business by giving them a stake in the business without giving them control or the ability to bind the corporation with their actions.

6. When privacy is desired. The transfer of stock in a closely held corporation is not generally a matter of public record. This makes it possible to shield family financial affairs from public scrutiny.

7. When continuity of operation is important. A corporation may, within limits, legally continue its business with little or no hindrance from the probate court. This makes it possible for corporate officers to make major decisions regarding property that the client has contributed to the corporation without the necessity or delay of the judicial process, and with little or no publicity.

8. When gift tax savings are desired. The transfer of a minority interest in a closely held business may result in a discounted value for gift tax purposes. In other words, transfers of property (via its stock "wrapper") can sometimes be made at discounted values for gift tax purposes.

9. When estate tax savings are desired. Transfers of stock reduce the donor's estate by (1) shifting appreciation in value from donor to donee and (2) shifting income on stock (dividends) to the donee. The stock that is ultimately included in the donor's estate may itself be a minority interest and may therefore (or because of lack of marketability) be valued at a discount.

Disadvantages of the Corporate Form

1. There are a number of additional expenses associated with forming and maintaining a corporation (e.g., attorney fees, accounting fees, corporate supplies, state incorporation fees, and the ongoing expenses of maintaining the corporate form).

2. While some types of income passed through to shareholders are taxed only once (e.g., salaries), dividends are subject to both corporate and shareholder levels of tax.

3. At one time, a corporation could avoid recognizing a gain upon a liquidation or sale (followed by a liquidation) of the business. There was generally only one tax at the shareholder level (except for certain recaptures, receivables, etc.).

For example, under the prior rules, if a shareholder invested $10,000 in a corporation and the corporation invested the cash in a piece of land that was worth $100,000 after 10 years, upon liquidation the corporation would give the land to the shareholder, and the shareholder would receive a $100,000 value in exchange for turning in the stock that cost him $10,000. This would result in a $90,000 capital gain. The corporation generally would not recognize any gain and was not taxed on any excess of value over the cost the corporation had in the land.

A 1986 tax act abolished the *General Utilities* doctrine that made that possible. Now, upon liquidation, the corporation is treated as having "sold" the corporate assets and is taxed on the excess value of the assets over the corporation's basis in the assets. If the corporation has only a $10,000 income tax basis in the land and the land is worth $100,000, then the corporation first must recognize a $90,000 gain. Whatever is left after the corporation pays the tax will come out to the shareholder in the liquidation and the shareholder is then taxed on that receipt, resulting in two taxes to pay.

4. Corporations demand a more complex organizational structure and may have to contend with additional complex issues (e.g., personal holding company tax, accumulated earnings tax, dividend treatment, and collapsible corporation rules).

5. Personal service corporations are taxed at a flat rate of 35 percent from the very first dollar. This 35 percent tax eliminates the benefit of the "run up the brackets" for doctors, lawyers, accountants, architects, and other professionals who practice in the corporate form. If the corporation "zeroes out" its taxable income through reasonable salary payments to employee shareholders, there will be no taxable income upon which the IRS can impose the 35 percent tax. But this makes it more likely that the IRS will soon try to disallow deductions for salary payments in a personal service corporation under the "reasonableness" test. In other words, the IRS has a strong incentive to claim that payments made as compensation should be recharacterized as nondeductible dividends to shareholder employees. If the IRS is successful with such an attack, the corporation will then be taxed at 35 percent – and then the same dollars will again be taxed to the shareholders upon receipt. One way out of the 35 percent tax trap is to elect S corporation treatment.

HOW IT IS DONE – AN EXAMPLE

Stevens, Roberts, and Lee are engineers who feel they can develop a relatively inexpensive process for manufacturing an aircraft safety component that is in great demand for new jet airliners.

Stevens is a sole proprietor currently engaged in producing aircraft parts. Roberts, a young man who has a post-graduate degree in business administration and an undergraduate degree in engineering, has worked for Stevens for a number of years. He first started as an engineer and almost by accident moved into the firm's sales division. Robert's sales efforts have been so successful that Stevens would like to offer him an interest in a new business venture.

Lee is slightly older than Stevens or Roberts. He is a well-known and highly respected authority in the area of aircraft safety parts. He does quite a bit of consulting work for both government and private enterprise. He met Stevens and Roberts on such a consulting project, and the three men have become good friends. Lee is quite wealthy, and he is interested in keeping both his money and his mind at work.

All three men have something to contribute to a corporation. In return they will want to participate in the control and profits of the business while it is running, or in a distribution of the assets of the business if the corporation's life ends. In other words, they will expect "shares" of the corporation. Assume Stevens will contribute his business (his sole proprietorship). Lee will contribute cash or securities. Roberts wants to contribute his services and a small amount of cash in return for his stock.

Assuming this were the case, here is what might happen: If Lee decides that his contribution to the capital of the corporation will be cash, the stock he receives will normally have a value at the time of the exchange equal to the cash. For example, if he transfers $10,000 of cash to the corporation, he will ordinarily receive back stock with a fair market value of $10,000. Because the value of the stock he receives is no more or less than the value of the cash he transfers to the corporation, he realized neither a gain nor a loss. If he later sells his stock, the cash he paid will determine the basis of his stock. If he realizes $21,000 on the sale of the stock, his gain would be $11,000, the difference between his basis for the stock ($10,000) and the amount he realizes on the sale ($21,000).

Absent provisions in the tax law to the contrary, if any of the three contributed appreciated property to the corporation in return for its stock, a taxable gain would result. But there is an important exception to that general rule.

The exception was designed to encourage the formation of a new corporation. It enables a taxpayer to transfer appreciated property, or even a going business, into a new corporation without the transferor recognizing income on the appreciation at the very time when his other expenses – the expenses involved in the organization and operation of the corporation – are the highest. The exception provides that even if the transferor "realizes" a gain when he transfers appreciated property to his new corporation, he does not have to "recognize" gain for tax purposes.[6]

This exception is conditioned on meeting certain basic requirements. The rule is that where a person or persons transfer *property* to a corporation (a) solely in exchange for the corporation's own stock, and (b) the transferor(s) control the corporation immediately after the transfer, no gain will be recognized on the appreciated business or securities contributed to the new corporation. Control generally means ownership of 80 percent or more of the corporation's stock.[7]

Stock can be received in exchange for appreciated assets without the recognition of gain. However, any securities received are treated as "boot." Gain is recognized to the extent of the lesser of the amount of gain inherent in the assets transferred or the amount of "boot" received.

The tax free exchange for stock is similar to the theory making a like-kind exchange tax free. The transferor who receives stock in exchange for his property has really maintained an interest in the original property. It has merely changed form and now has the physical identity of "stock." This "continuity of interest" concept is a key to nonrecognition of the gain on the appreciated property transferred. (It is important to recognize, however, that for the purposes of corporate law, a shareholder has an undivided interest [shared with all other shareholders] in all corporate property, but that his rights in any specific corporate property [even though originally transferred by him to the corporation in a tax-free exchange] are extremely limited.)

Example: Suppose Stevens, who is now operating as a sole proprietor, decides to transfer his going business to the new corporation. If his basis for the sole proprietorship is $10,000, and the fair market value of his business is $50,000 at the time he transfers it to the new corporation, he would probably receive $50,000 worth of stock.

Under the general rule for taxing sales and exchanges, he would realize a $40,000 gain. However, the nonrecognition provision provides that because he received only stock and through that stock controlled the corporation (just as he previously controlled his sole proprietorship), what has happened is really only a substitution of stock certificates for his former physical possession of the property.

This rule is logical because to realize gain there must be a taxable event, which usually occurs in the form of a sale, exchange, or other disposition of property. Although technically there may be a sale (a transfer of property in return for money or a promise to pay money) or exchange (a transfer of property in return for other property or services), there has been no exchange in substance. Stevens, in the example, has not disposed of his property. He has merely received certificates that evidence that he changed the form of ownership in the original property. This would apply no matter how many people transfer property to the corporation. As long as it was done collectively, if the taxpayers transferring property to the corporation still have both (a)

control and (b) interest in the property they originally owned, they would not have to recognize any gain on receipt of the new corporation's stock. Thus, Stevens would not have to recognize the $40,000 gain until and unless he later sells his stock.

Under the assumed facts, if Roberts were to receive stock in the new corporation in exchange for his services, the value of the stock would be currently taxable to him, as stock issued for services is not considered as issued for "property." If Roberts' stock was issued solely for services, it will not be counted in determining whether the transferors of property control the corporation after the exchange.

In addition, if the property that is contributed is subject to liabilities in excess of basis, gain will be recognized to the extent of such excess.

IMPLICATIONS AND ISSUES IN COMMUNITY PROPERTY STATES

Stock purchased by an investor in a corporation will take on the character of the assets used to purchase the stock. Thus, if an individual transfers $1,000 to a corporation in return for stock and that $1,000 consists of community property earnings, the stock itself will be community property. Of course, this result could be altered by a written agreement between the spouse and the investor to treat the stock as property other than community property, or by titling the stock in some other fashion, e.g., as joint tenancy or as the separate property of one spouse.

Upon divorce or death of the stockholder, the community property interest of the spouse will become important. It will be necessary to determine what portion of the stock is community property. As discussed in Chapter 40, a common problem is the situation where a person owned all or most of the stock of a corporation prior to marriage, the person works full time for the corporation, and the value of the corporation increases significantly. A portion of the increase in value of the person's stock may be community property to the extent the increase is attributable to his or her insufficiently rewarded hard work during the marriage, and a portion will be separate property to the extent the increase is the result of the natural increase or earnings of the original stock. The method of valuation cannot be predicted with certainty.

One question that often arises in community property states is the power to manage and control the community property. Until 1975, California law provided that the husband had the management and control over the community property. Under a revision of the community property laws, both spouses now have management power and control over community property. (Similar changes have occurred in the laws of other community property states.) This has implications in connection with the management and control over a corporation. California law provides that a spouse who is operating or managing a business or an interest in a business that is community personal property has the sole management and control of the business or interest. Thus, if an individual owns all the stock in a manufacturing corporation and that individual is also the manager of the business, or a substantial participant in the management of the business, the individual's spouse will not be able to exercise equal control in regard to the management of that business. This allows people to choose business associates and manage a business without regard to the effect of community property laws.

QUESTIONS AND ANSWERS

Question – Why do stockholders often finance business needs by lending money to their corporations rather than by increasing their equity (stock) interest?

Answer – One of the key advantages of operating a business in the corporate form is that many different types of ownership interests in corporations can be created. The interests of any particular investor can be met by creating a security that fits his special needs and desires. This factor facilitates the acquisition of capital. Suppose that in order to acquire working capital and capital for long-term planning the corporation issued bonds. These are written obligations to repay a definite sum of money on a definite date, usually at least 10, and more often 29 or more, years from the date the bond was issued.

Bonds are a favored means of raising corporate capital. One reason for this is that a corporation will obtain a deduction for the interest paid on the indebtedness, but no deduction is allowed for dividends paid on either preferred or common stock. As long as a corporation can earn money at a higher rate (with the cash raised by issuing the bond) than it costs the corporation (in interest necessary to "service the debt"), it usually makes sense for the corporation to borrow money. This is known as "leverage."

Issuance of the bonds generally creates no tax liability to either the corporation or the bondholder. This is because the corporation has merely borrowed money and agreed to return it. Conversely, the bondholders have merely loaned money. When the bond "matures," the principal becomes payable and the bondholders are entitled to a tax-free return of their capital investment. In contrast, the return of equity is a taxable dividend, unless the return can qualify as a stock redemption (which is not a dividend).

A distribution by a corporation with respect to its stock is considered a return on the shareholders' investment and is taxable as a dividend to the extent of corporate earnings and profits – unless the distribution can qualify as a "sale" or "exchange," in which case only the gain in excess of basis is taxable.

Any money bondholders receive in the form of interest, and any money they receive at the maturity of their bonds in excess of their capital investment will be taxed at ordinary income rates. Receiving money in excess of capital investment can occur when bonds are purchased at a discount but are paid off at face value. (When bonds are *issued* at a discount by the issuing corporation, a bondholder must include a ratable portion of the discount in income each year as the bond matures. For example, if a bond with a par value of $1,000 was issued for $800 and is payable in 10 years, the $200 discount would be included in the taxpayer's income at the rate of $20 a year.)

Another reason bonds are often favored over an increase in equity is that the accumulation of earnings and profits within the corporation to pay debt obligations can be justified more readily than accumulating income to redeem stock. This helps avoid an additional tax on an unreasonable income accumulation.

Question – What is "thin capitalization"?

Answer – Because the interest paid on corporate indebtedness is deductible, the cost of borrowing money through long-term corporate debt is substantially reduced. However, some shareholders attempt to overdo it – they contribute almost no equity investment and characterize almost their entire contribution as debt owed to them by the corporation. This is known as "thin capitalization," because the capital investment is "thin" in relation to the debt, but the "debt" is really disguised stock.

Once the form of the "debt" is disregarded by the IRS and the substance is treated appropriately, corporate deductions for "interest" payments to shareholders are disallowed. Second, receipt of "interest" payments by shareholder-creditors are reclassified and treated as dividends. Third, when the corporation pays off its "debt" to the shareholders, the payments may be taxed as dividends. This means that instead of treating the amount received as a tax-free repayment of a debt, the shareholder-creditor must report some or all of the distribution as income. Finally, money that the corporation purportedly was accumulating to pay off the "debt" may be subject to the accumulated earnings tax (which is discussed below). Also, a debt that is reclassified as stock could cause a termination of a Subchapter S election, because a Subchapter S corporation is allowed to have only one class of stock.

To determine if a security should be classified as debt rather than equity, the courts usually examine a number of factors such as: Was there an intention by shareholders to enforce payment of the debt? Was there a debt instrument and did it give the shareholders management or voting rights (like stock)? What was the ratio of debt to equity? A general rule of thumb, subject to variation depending upon the industry, is that if the amount of debt exceeds shareholders' equity by more than four to one, the corporation is thinly capitalized. Basically, the court would examine all the factors relevant to determining if a "loan" by shareholders was in reality more like an ownership interest (stock) than a debtor-creditor relationship.[8]

Keep in mind that, while bonds are a tax-favored means of obtaining corporate funds, frequently a corporation does not want to become obligated to make fixed payments for interest and debt amortization. To avoid a cash flow problem, therefore, corporations often finance long-term operations or investments by common stock, which entail no obligation to pay dividends or preferred stock on which dividend payments can frequently be avoided.

Question – How is a corporation taxed?

Answer – A corporation is taxed as an entity separate from its shareholders. A 15 percent rate is applied to the first $50,000 of corporate taxable income, a 25 percent rate applies to the next $25,000, a 34 percent rate is levied on the next $25,000, 39 percent on the next $235,000, then 34 percent on the next $9,665,000, then 35 percent on the next $5,000,000, then 38 percent on the next $3,333,333, then 35 percent on any additional taxable income.

The 39 percent tax on income between $100,000 and $335,000 includes a 5 percent add-on tax that is designed to phase out the graduated rates below 34 percent.

The 38 percent rate on income between $15,000,000 and $18,333,333 includes a 3 percent add-on tax that is designed to phase out the graduated rates below 35 percent.

Example: A corporation with $100,000 of taxable income would pay a tax of $22,250 ($50,000 x 15%, plus 25% of $25,000, plus 34% of $25,000). A corporation with $500,000 of taxable income would pay a tax of $170,000 (34% of $500,000). Corporations, like individuals, are liable for a number of other state and local taxes as well. The corporation reports its federal income tax on IRS Form 1120.

Graphically, the return might look like the illustration at Figure 47.2.

Gross income includes such items as profit from sales and receipts from services. It also includes gains on sales or exchanges, income from rent, royalties, interest, and dividends.

A corporation is entitled to two types of deductions; ordinary deductions and special deductions. Ordinary deductions include compensation of officers and salaries, bonuses, rent payments, charitable contributions, repair expenses, interest paid on indebtedness, casualty losses, deductions for depreciation and amortization of research and experimental costs, advertising, and corporate contributions to pension and profit-sharing plans. A corporation also receives a carryover deduction for a net operating loss.

"Special" deductions include a "dividends received" deduction. Prior law allowed a corporation that owned less than 80 percent of the stock of another corporation to deduct 80 percent of the dividends received. Under current law, there are now three rules:

(1) If the recipient corporation owns less than 20 percent of the voting power and value of stock of the issuing corporation, the 80 percent dividends received deduction is reduced to 70 percent of the amount of the dividend.

Figure 47.2

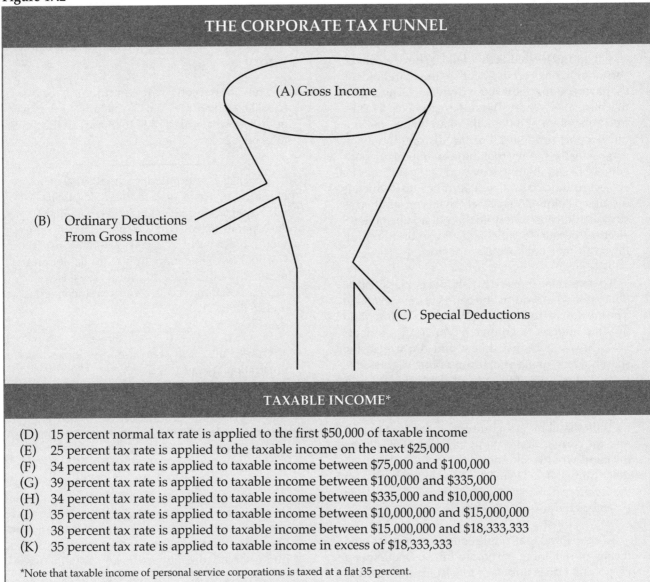

THE CORPORATE TAX FUNNEL

(A) Gross Income

(B)   Ordinary Deductions
From Gross Income

(C) Special Deductions

TAXABLE INCOME*

(D)   15 percent normal tax rate is applied to the first $50,000 of taxable income
(E)   25 percent tax rate is applied to the taxable income on the next $25,000
(F)   34 percent tax rate is applied to taxable income between $75,000 and $100,000
(G)   39 percent tax rate is applied to taxable income between $100,000 and $335,000
(H)   34 percent tax rate is applied to taxable income between $335,000 and $10,000,000
(I)   35 percent tax rate is applied to taxable income between $10,000,000 and $15,000,000
(J)   38 percent tax rate is applied to taxable income between $15,000,000 and $18,333,333
(K)   35 percent tax rate is applied to taxable income in excess of $18,333,333

*Note that taxable income of personal service corporations is taxed at a flat 35 percent.

(2)   If the recipient corporation holds 20 percent or more (up to 80 percent) of the stock of the issuing corporation, the 80 percent dividends received deduction remains at 80 percent.

(3)   If the recipient corporation owns 80 percent or more of the stock of the issuing corporation, a 100 percent deduction may apply to dividends received.[9]

The bottom line is that a closely held corporation that holds the stock of a publicly held corporation will likely be entitled to deduct 70 percent of every dollar it receives in the form of dividends on the stock it holds. It therefore will pay a top tax of 39 percent on 30 percent of each dividend dollar, an effective rate of only 11.7 percent.

A corporation may also elect to amortize its organizational cost over five or more years.[10] This would also be considered a special deduction.

Taxable income is what is left after taking ordinary and special deductions. It is the amount to which the various percentage tax rates are applied. Certain credits are then directly applied against this tax, such as corporate overpayments of tax in previous years, payments for estimated taxes (paid on a quarterly basis), and credit on certain foreign taxes paid.

Question – Many business and estate planning tools are corporate fringe benefits that are deductible to the extent reasonable (as well as ordinary and necessary). What is meant by "reasonable"?

Answer – A corporation is entitled to a deduction for salaries or any other compensation for personal services, but only if the services are actually rendered and the amount paid as compensation for those services is considered "reasonable." Reasonable means only that amount which would ordinarily be paid for similar services by other corporations under similar circumstances.

This reasonableness test is imposed most frequently on closely held corporations because of the large degree of coincidence of executive and shareholder interest. It is designed to prevent the shareholders from draining off corporate profits in the disguise of tax-deductible salaries. Corporate profits are usually paid out in the form of dividends that are taxable to the shareholders, but nondeductible by the corporation. The portion of the salary considered unreasonable is usually classified as a disguised dividend and, to that extent, the corporation's deduction is disallowed. However, even though that amount may not be deducted by the corporation, it is still taxable as a dividend to the shareholder-recipient.

Reasonableness is a question of determining the amount that would ordinarily be paid for like services by like enterprises under similar circumstances. Generally, where an executive employee does not own or have options to purchase stock, arm's length bargaining as to the amount of salary is assumed. One element that could be considered in determining reasonableness is the fact that a given individual was not adequately compensated in prior years. Thus, if high compensation in the current year can be attributed to services rendered in prior years, the total current salary might be considered reasonable.

However, the amount of cash compensation is not the only relevant factor. Corporate contributions to pension and profit-sharing plans are considered business expenses and are allowed as deductions as long as the total amount of all forms of compensation paid on behalf of an individual does not exceed a reasonable total.

Some of the other indirect forms of compensation may be: premiums for life insurance, hospitalization, medical care, and salary continuation plans. Costs of these plans, although generally deductible by the corporation, often do not result in taxable income to the individual. Because the corporation is a separate and distinct tax entity, and because working shareholders would be considered salaried employees, they would be eligible for these forms of indirect compensations. This is true even if in addition to being employees, they are also officers, directors, and shareholders of the corporation.

An employee may exclude from gross income the following fringe benefits: (1) a "no-additional-cost service" (e.g., free stand-by flights to airline employees); (2) "qualified employee discounts" (e.g., discounts on the selling price of qualified property or services of the employer); (3) certain working condition fringes (e.g., employer paid subscriptions to business periodicals); and (4) "de minimus" fringes such as typing of personal letters by the company secretary or the personal use of company copying machines.[11]

In order for the "no-additional-cost services" and the "qualified employee discounts" to be excluded from income of officers, owners and highly compensated employees, they must be provided to employees on a nondiscriminatory basis.

Question – What is the accumulated earnings tax?

Answer – One of the easiest and most common means of financing growth is to accumulate earnings and plow them back into the corporation to purchase new machinery, buildings, and other necessary capital assets. These "plowed-back" earnings and profits begin to add up very quickly. Because the corporate tax rate may be lower than the rate of tax upon the incomes of individual shareholders, they may attempt to use the corporation as a vehicle for reducing taxes by having the corporation retain earnings rather than make taxable distributions in the form of nondeductible dividends.

If a corporation reasonably allows earnings to accumulate in order to fund current or anticipated needs or projects that the corporation has planned, there should not be a problem. However, once earnings are allowed to accumulate beyond the reasonable needs of the business, those earnings may be subject to an additional tax, the accumulated earnings tax.[12]

The accumulated earnings tax is imposed on every corporation that is formed or used for the purpose of avoiding personal income tax with respect to its shareholders by permitting earnings and profits to accumulate instead of being distributed. The purpose of the tax is to discourage the use of a corporation as an accumulation vehicle to shelter its individual stockholders from taxation at personal income tax rates. As a regulative device, the accumulated earnings tax was designed to force the distribution of retained earnings at the point where they no longer serve a legitimate business purpose. Without such a tax on improper accumulations, stockholders could arrange to have dividends paid in years when their incomes were low or they could indefinitely accumulate earnings and profits inside the corporation until the corporation was liquidated.

An accumulated earnings credit of $250,000 ($150,000 in the case of personal service corporations) is allowed that will be presumed to be for the reasonable business needs of the corporation.[13] A controlled group of corporations is allowed one accumulated earnings credit, not one per corporation. Thus, if a corporation begins to accumulate amounts in excess of $250,000, it should be prepared to show a bona fide business reason for not distributing these earnings in the form of dividends.

The accumulated earnings tax is designed to tax only earnings retained beyond the reasonable needs of the business. The question then becomes: "What reasonable needs would a corporation have for accumulating profits?" The regulations state that working capital needs and capital for building expansion or for the replacement of plant or equipment are among the needs that would allow a business to properly accumulate earnings.[14] In addition to these needs, a sinking fund to retire corporate bonds at maturity has often been found to be a reasonable need to accumulate cash. In other cases, funds set aside to acquire minority interests or quarreling stockholders' interests were also deemed to be retained for reasonable business needs. The term "reasonable needs of the business" includes the IRC Section 303 redemption needs of the business (see Chapter 41), although specific protection from the tax (within limits) is provided only in the corporation tax year in which the stockholder dies and in subsequent years.[15] The reasonableness of accumulations in years prior to a year in which the shareholder dies is to be determined solely upon the facts and circumstances existing at the times the accumulations occur.[16]

The accumulated earnings tax rate is 15 percent (in 2004) on all "accumulated taxable income."

The tax, if applicable, is imposed only on "accumulated taxable income"; an amount that is derived from the taxable income of the corporation for the particular year in question. Thus, the tax does not apply to all of the accumulated earnings and profits of the corporation, but only to the accumulated taxable income of the year or years as to which the tax is asserted.

This tax on a corporation's accumulated taxable income is payable in addition to the regular tax payable by the firm. "Accumulated taxable income" generally means the corporation's taxable income for the year in question with certain adjustments (such as a reduction for federal income taxes paid) minus the sum of (a) distributions from current earnings and profits that the shareholders have reported as ordinary income (dividends paid), (b) amounts from earnings and profits that the shareholders have reported as dividends even though no actual distribution was made (disguised dividends), and (c) the accumulated earnings credit.

In determining whether or not the current year's accumulated taxable income has been retained for the reasonable needs of the business, the availability of prior years' accumulated earnings must also be considered. If past years' accumulations are sufficient to meet current needs (i.e., this year's business needs) there is no justification for accumulating current earnings.

Question – Will corporate-owned cash value life insurance purchased for key person, split dollar, or deferred compensation financing cause an accumulated earnings tax problem?

Answer – That depends on whether or not the insurance answers a valid corporate business need. There must also be a close correlation between the type of policy and amount of death benefit and the alleged corporate need. Generally, hedging against the loss of a key employee's service because of unexpected death is considered to be a reasonable business need.[17]

Key person life insurance is insurance that is owned by the corporation insuring the life of a key employee. The purpose of such a policy is to provide a fund at the employee's death that will compensate the corporation for the financial loss resulting from the unavailability of the employee to render services to the corporation. Often, key person insurance death proceeds are also used to help in finding and compensating a suitable replacement.

Therefore, the purchase of life insurance and the earnings used to pay policy premiums should not, per se, be subject to the penalty tax. The point is that it is not the amount, but the purpose of the accumulation, that is important.

The same question often arises as to the effect of a split dollar plan. If a corporation attempts to prevent taxation of income to shareholders by accumulating its earnings rather than distributing them, the existence or nonexistence of a split dollar policy will not, by itself, deter the imposition of the tax penalty provided by the law. Conversely, the existence of a split dollar policy will not, per se, incur the accumulations tax penalty if the corporation is not, in fact, accumulating earnings beyond the reasonable needs of the business.

This provision exists to deter tax evasion and not to prevent a business from operating in a normal businesslike manner. The same principle applies in cases where the corporation has obligated itself to make pre-retirement death benefits to a key executive under a deferred compensation agreement. An accumulation of corporate earnings to meet obligations under such an agreement is generally considered a reasonable business need (just as the funds accumulated to retire an outstanding corporate bond would be considered reasonable).

A third area where this question often arises is the use of accumulated earnings to provide surplus cash for the redemption of stock. In this case, if the redemption is to be utilized to shift partial or complete control to the remaining shareholders without depleting their personal funds (as for example, where, by shareholder agreement, the corporation will retire shares on the death of a shareholder), it is doubtful that accumulations to reach this result would be found to be a reasonable need. However, if a business purpose can be found, such as an accumulation to purchase the shares of a dissenting minority, then the accumulation may be found to be reasonable.[18] The primary purpose must be a corporate, rather than an individual, benefit from the stock redemption.

Question – What is the personal holding company tax?

Answer – IRC Section 541 imposes a 15% (in 2004) tax on companies classified as personal holding companies. The tax applies to undistributed personal holding company income and is designed to discourage the use of corporations as "incorporated pocket-

books" wherein income from securities, real property, or personal talents is taxed at corporate rates rather than individual rates.

To be classified as a personal holding company, the corporation must meet both of the following tests: (1) at any time during the last half of the taxable year more than 50% of the value of its stock is owned by five or fewer individuals, and (2) at least 60% of its "adjusted ordinary gross income" is "personal holding company income."[19] Personal holding company income consists of (1) passive income, such as rents, royalties, dividends, and interest, and (2) income from personal service contracts under which the corporation is to furnish personal services but the corporation does not have the right to select the individual who will perform the services, and the individual selected by the client owns directly or indirectly 25% or more of the stock in the corporation.[20]

For more on personal holding companies, see Chapter 45.

Question – What problems may a "personal service corporation" with only one significant customer face from the Internal Revenue Service where the primary purpose of incorporating was to obtain tax benefits?

Answer – IRC Section 269A specifically authorizes the IRS to reallocate between an employee-owner of a "personal service corporation" (defined as a corporation whose principal activity is the performance of personal services, with such services substantially performed by employee-owners) and the "personal service corporation" all income, deductions, credits, exclusions and other allowances to the extent necessary to prevent tax avoidance or evasion or to reflect clearly the income of the "personal service corporation" or any of its employee-owners. The authority to reallocate applies only in the event that substantially all of the services of the "personal service corporation" are performed for or on behalf of one other corporation, partnership or other entity and the "personal service corporation" was formed for the principal purpose of avoiding or evading federal income tax by reducing the income of the employee-owner or by securing for him a significant tax benefit not otherwise available. The typical corporation affected by this law is a corporate partner in a partnership of personal service corporations.

The potential impact of Section 269A has been greatly reduced by the parity created between corporate and Keogh plans, because the tax benefits of a corporate qualified plan are now available to non-corporate entities.

Question – What is the corporate alternative minimum tax (AMT) and how does it affect corporate owned life insurance?

Answer – The corporate AMT is the excess, if any, of a tentative minimum tax over the regular corporate income tax.[21] Life insurance proceeds and inside buildup on a life insurance contract are among the tax "preferences" added to a corporation's ordinary taxable income to determine its alternative minimum taxable income (AMTI) and, therefore, its alternative minimum tax.

Certain small corporations are exempt from the AMT. In general, a small corporation is defined as one that had average gross receipts of $5,000,000 or less for the three-taxable-year period that ended with the first tax year after 1996. After this initial test, applicable for tax year 1997, in order to continue to qualify, the three-taxable-year average is raised to $7,500,000. It is important to note that if a corporation does not qualify under the 1997 test of $5,000,000, it can never qualify later, even if it is able to meet the three-taxable-year average gross receipts test of $7,500,000.[22]

To determine a corporation's alternative minimum tax, the corporation must first compute a "tentative alternative minimum taxable income" (TAMTI) equal to its regular taxable income plus certain disallowed deductions. The corporation must then compute its "adjusted current earnings" (ACE). The ACE adjustment is designed to approximate the corporation's pre-tax net book income as measured for financial accounting purposes and is calculated by beginning with AMTI, adding earnings and profits income items (including life insurance proceeds and inside buildup on a life insurance contract), subtracting certain deductible items, and recalculating certain depreciation deductions. The corporation then increases or decreases its TAMTI by 75% of the amount by which ACE exceeds or falls short of TAMTI to arrive at the final alternative minimum taxable income. The tax itself is a flat 20% of AMTI. A corporation receives a $40,000 exemption that is reduced by 25% of the amount by which AMTI exceeds $150,000 (thus phasing out completely at $310,000).[23]

The AMT can be considered a prepayment of the corporation's regular tax because a credit is allowed that reduces the regular tax of the corporation in future years. This credit is equal to the amount by which the AMT exceeds the regular tax. The amount of AMT credit that may be taken in a subsequent year may not exceed the amount by which that year's regular tax exceeds the AMT.[24]

Example: A calendar year corporation has ACE of $400 in 2001, $300 in 2002, and $200 in 2003. Unadjusted AMTI is $300 for each of those years. In 2001, ACE exceeds unadjusted AMTI by $100, 75 percent of which ($75) must be included as an additional item of AMTI. In 2003, unadjusted AMTI exceeds ACE by $100, creating a potential negative adjustment to AMTI of $75. As the aggregate increases to AMTI for prior years equals $75 (the amount added to alternative minimum tax in 2001) and there are no aggregated reductions, the full amount of the potential negative adjustment will reduce AMTI for 2003.

Aside from affecting a corporation's ACE adjustment, corporate-owned life insurance is taxed as follows:

- The premiums are not tax deductible.

- The annual premium reduces earnings and profits to the extent the premium exceeds the annual increase in the cash surrender value of the policy. If the increase exceeds the premium, then that difference will increase earnings and profits.

- The insurance proceeds are income tax free (for regular corporate purposes).

- Upon receipt of the policy proceeds, earnings and profits are increased by the excess of the amount received over the cash surrender value of the policy at the close of the immediately preceding taxable year.

There are several ways of dealing with the AMT. The easiest is merely to make up the difference through additional life insurance coverage. The following calculation shows how to determine the approximate amount of additional life insurance necessary to compensate the corporation for the effect of the AMT:

Step 1: State the face amount
before the AMT tax: $1,000,000

Step 2: Divide the face amount by .85: $1,176,471

This amount, $1,176,471, is (roughly) the before-AMT amount necessary for the corporation to net $1,000,000 after the AMT. Conservative planners will round up this amount.

Another alternative to the purchase of more life insurance is an S corporation election. Had the same business elected S status with no taxable income, there would be no tax at either the corporate or individual level.

ASRS: Sec. 43.

CHAPTER ENDNOTES

1.   Treas. Reg. §301.7701-2(b).
2.   Treas. Reg. §301.7701-3(a).
3.   IRC Sec. 11(b)(1).
4.   IRC Sec. 11(b)(2).
5.   IRC Sec. 448(d)(2).
6.   IRC Sec. 351.
7.   IRC Sec. 368(c); Treas. Reg. §1.351-1(a)(1).
8.   IRC Sec. 385.
9.   IRC Sec. 243.
10. IRC Sec. 248.
11. IRC Sec. 132.
12. IRC Secs. 531, 532.
13. IRC Sec. 535(c).
14. Treas. Reg. §1.537-2.
15. IRC Secs. 537(a)(2), 537(b)(1).
16. Treas. Reg. §1.537-1(e)(3).
17. *Bradford-Robinson Printing Co. v. Comm.*, 1 AFTR 2d 1278 (D. Colo. 1957).
18. *Gazette Publishing Co. v. Self*, 103 F. Supp. 779 (E.D. Ark. 1952).
19. IRC Sec. 542.
20. IRC Sec. 543.
21. IRC Sec. 55(a).
22. IRC Sec. 55(e).
23. IRC Secs. 55, 56, 57.
24. IRC Sec. 53.

Figure 47.3

CHOOSING AN ENTITY — A CHECKLIST OF ISSUES TO CONSIDER	

PROPRIETORSHIP

(1) One person owner _____
(2) Few employees _____
(3) Relatively low income _____
(4) Relatively low start up costs _____
(5) No double tax on business earnings _____
(6) Not possible to "time" or "split" income _____
(7) Administration of estate difficult _____
(8) Valuation freezing techniques not available _____
(9) Should not be operated as part of a trust _____
(10) No shield against personal liability _____
(11) Income reportable on owner's individual income tax return _____
(12) Funds in Keogh plan generally not safe from creditors _____
(13) Generally may avoid franchise tax imposed by many states on operating as a corporation _____
(14) Self employment (payroll) tax now equal to total of employer and employee federal payroll tax _____

PARTNERSHIP & LLC

(1) Sharing of net profits _____
(2) Presence of loss sharing _____
(3) Pass through of losses _____
(4) Avoidance of double taxation on profits _____
(5) Relatively low start up costs _____
(6) Relatively economical operation costs _____
(7) Taxable years must match those of partners or members _____
(8) No restrictions on who can invest or number of investors _____
(9) Easy to convert to another form of entity _____
(10) No accumulated earnings tax _____
(11) No personal holding company tax _____
(12) Unlimited personal liability unless limited partnership or LLC used to protect limited partners or members _____
(13) Subject to "at risk" limitations _____
(14) Losses not deductible in excess of basis _____
(15) Interest deduction limits at personal level _____
(16) Equity received for services creates income _____
(17) On contribution of encumbered property, generally, only liabilities assumed by other partners or members in excess of contributing partner's basis is taxable _____
(18) Income splitting — wealth shifting potential _____
(19) IRS can reallocate income if member of family renders services without reasonable compensation _____
(20) Partners who render services are treated as employees for certain fringe benefit purposes but tax law typically precludes nontaxable fringe benefits for most partners or members _____
(21) Separate income tax return required _____
(22) Funds in Keogh plan generally not safe from creditors of partner _____
(23) Franchise tax imposed on partnerships or LLCs by some states _____

Figure 47.3 (continued)

CORPORATIONS — "C"

(1) Limited liability to creditors if capital is adequate and corporate amenities observed _____

(2) Shareholder-employees can exclude certain fringe benefits from income _____

(3) Income taxed at corporate level subject to tax again at shareholder level on payment of dividend or on liquidation _____

(4) Reasonableness of compensation an issue _____

(5) Accumulated earnings and alternative minimum tax liability _____

(6) Losses trapped at corporate level _____

(7) Passive loss rules avoided at corporate level (except for certain closely-held C corporations and personal service corporations) and deductions at corporate rates _____

(8) Flexibility in terms of numbers of shareholders _____

(9) Can have more than one class of stock _____

(10) Stock can be used as compensation _____

(11) Ability to form subsidiaries _____

(12) Must be adequately capitalized _____

(13) Decision making centralized through management structure _____

(14) Possible to retain earnings without tax at personal level but taxed at corporate level _____

(15) Dividends received deduction _____

(16) Low federal income tax rate on first $75,000 of income _____

(17) 35 percent flat rate on certain professional service corporations _____

(18) Subject to double taxation upon liquidation _____

(19) Separate income tax returns required _____

(20) Franchise tax imposed by many states _____

(21) Non-calendar fiscal year end may be chosen by regular corporations, permitting some shift of income from one year to next by timing of salaries — not for personal service corporations in many circumstances _____

(22) Possible for employees to borrow up to $50,000 from their accounts in corporate retirement plans _____

(23) Employees' funds in corporate retirement plans generally safe from creditors _____

CORPORATION — "S" — DIFFERENCES FROM "C" CORPORATION

(1) Restrictions on who can hold stock _____

(2) Limits on number of investors _____

(3) Only one class of stock (common) allowed _____

(4) Only limited subsidiaries permissible _____

(5) Some states do not recognize pass through of income or losses _____

(6) Limited liability as with "C" corporation _____

(7) Decision making centralized through management structure _____

(8) Pass through of income, losses, and credits _____

(9) Difficult to do estate planning since certain trusts cannot own S stock _____

(10) Limits on type of business an S corporation can be _____

(11) Potential for accidental or nonvoluntary termination of S election _____

(12) Limits on employee benefits for owners _____

Part 9:

PLANNING FOR EMPLOYEE
BENEFITS AND RETIREMENTS

Chapter 48

DEFERRED COMPENSATION (NONQUALIFIED)

WHAT IS IT?

Nonqualified deferred compensation is an arrangement whereby an employer promises to pay an employee in the future for services rendered currently. The plan is generally set up to provide for the employee's salary to be continued over a period of years after retirement or other termination of employment.

These payments are referred to as "deferred" compensation because they represent compensation earned currently but which will not be paid to the person who earned that money until a future date or event. The term "nonqualified" refers to the fact that the plan does not attempt to meet the stringent coverage and contribution requirements necessary to obtain government approval and the very favorable tax treatment available only to qualified retirement plans.

WHEN IS THE USE OF SUCH A DEVICE INDICATED?

1. When a business does not have a government approved ("qualified") retirement plan to offer key employees and would like to provide those key employees with retirement benefits.

2. Where a business has a qualified retirement plan, but would like to provide additional retirement benefits for certain key people over and above those permissible under a qualified plan.

3. Where a highly paid employee or executive would like to defer the taxation on income from peak earning years to a future date when he might be in a lower income tax bracket (usually at retirement).

4. When an executive or other highly paid individual would like to use his employer to, in effect, provide a forced savings program for him and to use such a savings program as a retirement plan.

5. When the corporate rates at the top brackets are lower than individual rates at the top bracket, deferred compensation becomes more attractive

and the deferral of both income to the employee and the deduction to the employer makes more sense.

6. When there are stringent limitations on the maximum benefits under qualified plans, the use of nonqualified plans will be stimulated.

7. When an employer would like the ability to pick and choose who will be covered and would like to determine on a person-by-person basis the benefit levels and terms and conditions of coverage.

WHAT ARE THE REQUIREMENTS?

1. In order to successfully defer income tax, an agreement should contain a contingency that may cause the employee to forfeit rights to future payments. As long as an employee's rights are forfeitable, there can be no constructive receipt of income under the agreement.[1]

2. Even if an employee's rights are nonforfeitable, he will not be deemed to have constructive receipt of income if the agreement is entered into before the employee earns the compensation in question and the employer's promise to pay is not secured in any way. This means that the agreement cannot be formally funded (no interest in a trust or escrow fund or in a specific asset can be given to the employee) without causing the money to be immediately taxable.[2]

However, it is permissible for a corporation to finance its obligation under the agreement by purchasing a life insurance contract, annuities, mutual funds, securities, or a combination of these investment media, without adverse tax consequences to the employee. The assets that will be used to finance the employer's obligation to the employee must remain the unrestricted property of the corporation (subject to the claims of the corporation's creditors). The employee must be given no interest or specific rights in the monies that the corporation sets aside to meet its obligation under the agreement.[3]

The Internal Revenue Service has permitted the establishment of so-called "Rabbi Trusts" in conjunction with certain plans of deferred compensation. These trusts enable an employer to transfer funds to an irrevocable grantor trust that satisfies certain criteria (including the requirement that the trust assets remain subject to the claims of the employer's general creditors in the event of insolvency).[4] Although such a trust can provide some protection from loss of benefits (for example, in the event of a hostile takeover), its real benefit is more psychological, since in the event of employer insolvency or bankruptcy the assets held in trust must be available to the employer's general creditors.[5] (This topic is covered in more detail in *The Tools and Techniques of Employee Benefit and Retirement Planning*.)

HOW IT IS DONE—AN EXAMPLE

The selected employee enters into an employment contract with his employer. The contract stipulates that specific payments will be made to the employee or the employee's beneficiaries in the event of death, disability, or retirement. This creates a direct enforceable obligation; the employer must provide the agreed upon benefits. In return for this promise, the selected employee agrees to continue in the service of the company.

The agreement will sometimes obligate the employee to (1) refrain from engaging in any competitive business after retirement; and (2) remain available for consultation purposes after retirement.

Often, the employer will purchase life insurance (alone or in combination with other savings vehicles, such as a fixed or variable annuity or a mutual fund) to provide the required benefits. The business will apply for and own the policy (or other security) on the life of the employee. The business will pay the premiums and be named the policy beneficiary. The business will completely control and own the policy (as well as any other asset used to finance the employer's obligation under the agreement).

The purpose of the life insurance policy is to provide funds necessary to pay retirement benefits called for under the contract. Policy cash values can be used for this purpose. Alternatively, the policy can be held by the corporation until the employee's death, and the employee can be paid the agreed upon deferred compensation out of other corporate assets. Should the employee die prior to retirement, the corporation will receive the life insurance and then can use it to provide death benefit payments to the employee's family.

Example: The Krauss Corporation is in the 34% federal and state income tax brackets. The corporation enters into a nonqualified deferred compensation agreement with its president, Robert P. Krauss, who is 45 years old. Krauss agrees to defer a $5,000 annual salary increase. Instead of receiving the $5,000 salary increase currently, the after-tax cost of this raise ($3,300) is applied on Krauss' behalf as the annual premium for a life insurance policy on his life.

The Krauss Corporation then agrees to provide retirement and death benefits as follows: (1) if Krauss dies before retirement, $5,000 a year will be paid to his widow for a period equal to the number of years he was covered under the plan; and (2) if he remains with the corporation until retirement at age 65, he will receive $10,000 a year for 10 years, in addition to any other fringe benefits to which he may be entitled.

Because the Krauss Corporation is in a 34% marginal tax bracket (including state income taxes), each $1,000 of benefit payments made to its president (or his widow) would actually cost only $660. Retirement benefits could be paid out of current earnings and the corporation could continue the insurance policy in force until the tax-free death proceeds are received. Alternatively, the cash values of the policy could be used to finance the corporation's obligation under the contract.

Assume for this example that a premium of $3,300 would purchase approximately $185,000 of life insurance (whole life) for a male age 45. If Krauss died at age 50 after five years' worth of premium payments, the corporation would receive $185,000 of tax free policy proceeds[6] (in addition to dividends and perhaps interest); it would have paid $16,500 in premiums; it is obligated to pay a total of $25,000 ($5,000 a year for five years) to Bob's widow, but its after-tax cost for making such payments is only $16,500 (66% x $25,000). This results in a net gain to the corporation of approximately $152,000 ($185,000 insurance proceeds less $16,500 of premiums and less $16,500 of after-tax cost of such payments).

If Bob Krauss' death occurs at age 75, the corporation receives over $325,000 in death proceeds and dividends; it has paid $66,000 in premiums; it has made lifetime payments of $100,000 ($10,000 a year for 10 years) so its net after-tax-deduction cost for those deferred compensation payments has been $66,000 ($100,000 minus $100,000 x 34% tax). This results in a net gain to the corporation of approximately $193,000 ($325,000 insurance proceeds minus $66,000 premiums, minus $66,000 cost of deferred compensation payments).

WHAT ARE THE TAX IMPLICATIONS?

The Employer's Tax Position

1. If life insurance is purchased, premiums paid by the employer are not tax deductible. The life insurance policy is considered an asset of the employer and is, therefore, carried on the books of the employer as such. Therefore, no tax deduction is allowed for payment of the premiums.[7] (Nor is a current deduction allowed for any other informal funding vehicle.)

2. When the executive reaches retirement age, the employer, as owner of the policy, may choose one of the settlement options available under the policy to fulfill its obligation under the plan. In this case, a portion of each installment payment received by the employer would be taxable under the annuity rules.[8] However, if the policy is surrendered and a lump sum payment is received, that portion which exceeds the employer's cost (the net premiums the employer has paid) is treated as ordinary income.[9]

3. At the employee's death, the entire policy proceeds receivable by the employer are generally income tax free.[10] (See paragraph 5 of "What Are The Tax Implications?" in Chapter 40 for the possible alternative minimum tax on proceeds received by a regular C corporation that does not qualify as "small.") If the employee dies before retirement, these proceeds can be used to pay his or her family the agreed-upon benefits. If the employee lives beyond retirement and begins to receive deferred compensation, the employer, rather than surrendering the policy at this time, may choose to make benefit payments out of current or accumulated earnings. Therefore, the employer can continue the policy in force until the employee dies. At that time, the death proceeds would be received by the corporation on an income tax free basis.

4. When the benefits are paid by the employer under the deferred compensation plan, either to the employee (after retiring) or to his or her family (on death before retirement), payments by the corporation are deductible, assuming that benefits constitute reasonable additional compensation.[11]

5. Deferred amounts will be considered to be wages and will be subject to social security tax in the year in which services are performed unless they are subject to a substantial risk of forfeiture, in which case the deferred amounts will be subject to social security tax when there is no longer a substantial risk of forfeiture. Similar rules apply to FUTA (the Federal Unemployment Tax).[12]

All nonqualified deferred compensation taken into account as wages for social security tax purposes is subject to the Medicare hospital insurance (HI) portion of the social security tax.[13] Whether such nonqualified deferred compensation will also be taxed under the old age, survivors, and disability insurance (OASDI) portion of the social security tax will depend upon whether the participant's other earnings for the year at issue equal or exceed that year's OASDI taxable wage base.

The Employee's Tax Position

1. During employment, the employee is not taxed on amounts set aside by the employer to meet its financial obligation. Therefore, if a life insurance policy is purchased on the life of the employee, assuming it is part of the general assets of the employer and is not specifically earmarked for the purpose of carrying out the liabilities under the deferred compensation agreement, premiums paid by the employer will not be taxable to the employee.[14] This same principle applies to the employer's purchase of an annuity, mutual fund, or other savings vehicle to finance its obligation.

2. Benefits received from the deferred compensation plan by the employee (or his family) are taxable at ordinary income rates as received; however, the tax liability may be reduced because benefit payments typically commence at retirement. Yet, while some individuals will be in a lower income tax bracket at retirement, others will not be. For the year 2004,

there are effectively six individual income tax brackets. In the case of married individuals filing joint returns, these will be as follows:

Taxable Income			Tax on Lower Amount	Tax Rate on Excess
$ -0-	to	$14,300	$ -0-	10%
14,300	to	58,100	1,430.00	15%
58,100	to	117,250	8,000.00	25%
117,250	to	178,650	22,787.50	28%
178,650	to	319,100	39,979.50	33%
319,100	to	......	86,328.00	35%

3. The commuted value of benefit payments remaining at a covered employee's death will be included in the employee's gross estate for federal estate tax purposes. Therefore, the present value of the future income promised to the employee's spouse will be taxable in the employee's estate.[15] This is "income in respect of a decedent" (IRC Section 691 Income) and an income tax deduction will be allowed to the recipient of such income for the additional federal estate tax attributable to the inclusion of the deferred compensation.[16]

But because of the unlimited federal estate tax marital deduction, if the death benefit is payable to the employee's surviving spouse in a qualifying manner, no estate tax will be incurred when the employee dies. (Therefore, no deduction for income in respect of a decedent will be allowed.)

The federal estate tax is scheduled to be repealed for one year in 2010 as a result of the Economic Growth and Tax Relief Reconciliation Act of 2001.

4. As pointed out in paragraph 5 of "The Employer's Tax Position," above, deferred amounts are generally considered wages for social security tax purposes in the year in which services are performed or, if later, when they are no longer subject to a substantial risk of forfeiture.[17] Because all wages are now subject to the HI portion of the social security tax, nonqualified deferred compensation counted as wages will be taxed under at least the HI portion of the social security tax.[18] Whether nonqualified deferred compensation counted as wages will also be taxed under the OASDI portion of the social security tax will depend upon whether the participant's other earnings for the year at issue equal or exceed that year's OASDI taxable wage base.

IMPLICATIONS AND ISSUES IN COMMUNITY PROPERTY STATES

As stated previously (see general discussion in Introduction), the earnings of a resident husband or wife are generally treated as community property in the nine community property states. This can cause some problems in the context of nonqualified deferred compensation. A spouse may enter into a deferred compensation arrangement with his or her employer. The deferred amount would be community property if paid currently. If the spouses obtain a divorce or one of the spouses dies, it may be necessary to determine the present value of the deferred amount in order to divide the community assets.

Whether, as regards forfeitable nonqualified deferred compensation rights, there is "property" subject to division in divorce or at death is a preliminary problem, although not one of as much importance now as it was previously under the former reasoning that only "vested" rights could be "property" subject to division. Under the extreme view, there was "property" only if the rights had fully matured and payments were either being presently received or there was a non-forfeitable right to immediate payment. The generally accepted current analysis establishes that there is "property" subject to division even though there is no certainty that compensation will ever be received.

A useful classification of nonqualified deferred compensation rights and pension rights has been suggested: (1) "vested and matured"–a nonforfeitable right to immediate payment; (2) "vested and unmatured"–a nonforfeitable right to payment at some future time, even though the right might terminate on a participant's death prior to retirement; (3) "contingent"– a nonvested accrued right and the contractual right to continue in the plan with, probably, a reasonable expectation of acquiring vested benefits within a relatively short time; and (4) "mere expectancy."

While forfeitable deferred compensation has been treated as a "mere expectancy" and thus of no value in a division of community property, at least one community property state, California, has abandoned this approach in the context of deferred compensation. California courts hold that the present value of deferred compensation can be determined. The fact that the deferred compensation obligation is unsecured and not formally funded would be a significant factor in reducing value. If the benefits are forfeitable, additional reductions in value are appropriate. In many circumstances, it may be appropriate to order a division of deferred compensation as it is paid, rather than requiring a current division. Thus, the spouse who did not earn the deferred compensation may not be paid. He or she presumably would receive a greater amount if the deferred benefit was actually paid (as opposed to 50% of a current value discounted for risk factors).

Another aspect commented on elsewhere in *Tools and Techniques*, which also relates to all community property planning, is the danger of signing a so-called "community property agreement," which makes all property owned by both spouses the community property of both of them.

Example: Dr. Lee Stein, an employee who worked for a national corporation while he was a resident of a separate property state, accrued a substantial deferred compensation benefit. If Lee then moves to a community property state, the deferred compensation benefit already accrued is still his separate property (specifically, "quasi-community property"); if he then signs an agreement making all property of his wife, Rhonda, and himself community property, he will be making a taxable gift to Rhonda.

Because of the nature of the gift, it may be that even the $11,000 (as indexed for inflation in 2004) gift tax annual exclusion will not be available (since Rhonda may not be able to dispose of her newly received interest). On the other hand, the transfer should qualify for the unlimited marital deduction; however, the long range tax implications of that deduction should be fully understood (see Chapter 24). Moreover, state gift tax laws should still be considered.

Therefore, one should be very careful in entering into such agreements without receiving competent advice from an attorney knowledgeable in both property law and taxation.

QUESTIONS AND ANSWERS

Question – Can a nonqualified deferred compensation plan provide a disability benefit?

Answer – Yes. A plan may be set up to include a disability benefit. There are several ways of providing disability benefits: (1) a disability income policy can be purchased along with the other assets used to finance the employer's obligation under the plan; (2) a disability waiver of premium benefit attached to the life insurance policy will enable the company to cover its liability in the event that the employee becomes totally disabled; (3) a combination of these methods can be used. The second approach works like this:

Example: If Bob Krauss, in the example above, became disabled, the money normally set aside for premium payments ($3,300 a year) would not have to be paid since premiums would be waived. The Krauss Corporation would have $5,000 to pay out to the employee since his salary continuation payments by the corporation would be deductible.

Generally, wage continuation payments and disability retirement income payments are fully includable in an employee's gross income. However, under IRC Section 22, an employee who is under the age of 65, is retired on disability, and is considered totally and permanently disabled may be entitled to a tax credit for disability retirement income.

Question – What effect does ERISA (the Employee Retirement Income Security Act of 1974) have on unfunded nonqualified deferred compensation plans?

Answer – Very little, if the plans fit into certain "safe harbors." For example, unfunded plans maintained primarily for the purpose of providing deferred compensation for a select group of management or highly compensated employees (often referred to as "top hat" plans) are exempt from almost all ERISA requirements. They are subject to easily complied with reporting requirements, and are subject to administrative and enforcement provisions– including the obligation to provide a claims procedure. (To the extent such a deferred compensation plan is also considered an employee welfare benefit plan for ERISA purposes, it may also be subject to at least some fiduciary responsibility requirements, although this is not clear.) Thus, such plans are not subject to ERISA requirements as to participation, vesting, nondiscrimination, minimum funding, and (at least to the extent they are not employee welfare benefit plans) fiduciary responsibility rules.[19]

The employer can comply with the reporting requirement by (1) filing within 120 days of the adoption of the plan a simple written statement (a letter will do) with the Secretary of Labor, including

(a) the employer's name and address, (b) the employer's IRS identification number, (c) a declaration that the employer maintains a plan primarily for the purpose of providing deferred compensation to a select group of management or highly compensated employees, and (d) a statement of the number of such plans and the number of employees in each plan; and (2) providing plan documents upon request to the Secretary of Labor.

Question – What is the earliest date the corporation can take a deduction for unfunded deferred compensation payments?

Answer – Generally, a corporation cannot take a deduction until it actually makes payments to the employee (or a deceased employee's beneficiary), regardless of whether the corporation is on a cash or accrual basis of accounting.[20]

Question – Can directors' fees be deferred through an unfunded deferred compensation agreement?

Answer – Yes. Individual nonqualified deferred compensation agreements can be made with independent contractors, directors, and even employees of other business organizations.[21] Also, tax-exempt organizations can establish nonqualified deferred compensation plans.[22]

Question – If a corporation finances its obligation under a deferred compensation agreement with corporate owned annuity contracts, are there any current adverse tax consequences to the employee or to the employer-corporation?

Answer – There are no current tax consequences to the employee so long as the annuity remains the asset of the corporation and the employee has no interest in the annuity. However, for contributions made after February 28, 1986 to annuity contracts held by a "nonnatural person," such as a corporation, "the income on the contract" for the tax year of the policyholder is generally treated as ordinary income received by the contract owner for that year.[23]

Question – What is a secular trust?

Answer – A secular trust is an irrevocable trust used to formally fund and protect nonqualified deferred compensation. Funds placed in a secular trust are not subject to the claims of the employer's creditors. Thus, a secular trust can protect deferred compensation from an employer's bankruptcy or insolvency.

There are two principal types of secular trusts: employer-funded trusts and employee-funded trusts. The employer can make contributions to an employee-funded trust, but the arrangement is structured in such a way that the employee is considered to have constructively received the amounts before they are given to the trust.

Generally, use of a secular trust causes immediate or accelerated taxation to the employee and provides an immediate or accelerated deduction to the employer.[24] Employers may "gross up" participants to help them pay their taxes.

The secular trust became popular in the years after the Tax Reform Act of 1986 (TRA '86), when the top corporate income tax rate bracket (34% before OBRA '93) was higher than the top individual income tax rate bracket and the top individual rate bracket was relatively low (28% after TRA '86, 31% after the Omnibus Budget Reconciliation Act of 1990). However, the imposition in OBRA '93 of brackets of 36% and 39.6% marginal rates on individuals curtailed the use of this device, since most employees who are candidates for this planning are in their highest income tax brackets while employed, and may be in lower brackets when deferred benefits are received. Note, the highest individual tax rate is 35% as of 2004.

Question – What is the impact of deferred compensation plans that allow an employee to make a "phantom" investment of the deferred amounts, or that provide for interest to be credited on the deferred amounts?

Answer – Such arrangements are often considered as a hedge against inflation or to offset the erosion in the value of the deferred benefit equal to a fixed dollar amount payable at the end of several years. Both plans present problems. If the employee is permitted to make a hypothetical investment of the funds, the employer will be put to the cost of record keeping for hypothetical gains, losses, dividends, etc., and will be faced with a problem of accounting for the actual cost of the benefit.[25]

The use of hypothetical interest is more feasible. It could be based on something like a cost of living adjustment, or an average rate of inflation, such as 3%. It seems clear that such interest or other adjustment should be treated as part of the total deferred compensation, with no deduction to the employer or taxation to the employee until paid or made available to the employee.[26]

Question – Where an employer has entered into a deferred compensation plan that provides for accrual of additional benefits based on the passage of time, could these additional amounts be deducted by the employer before they are paid or made available to the employee on the theory that they are interest?

Answer – The answer is apparently no, since the 9th Circuit Court of Appeals reversed a 1993 decision allowing such an interest deduction and now holds that there is no deduction for such amounts until they are includable in employee income.[27]

Question – Under what circumstances is income and tax deferral not appropriate?

Answer – Although tax deferral is generally beneficial, it can be counterproductive if an employee's tax rate increases by the time the compensation is actually received. In the current environment of constantly changing tax policy, fluctuating federal and state deficits, and economic uncertainty, predicting future tax rates can be difficult if not impossible.

Therefore, the critical issue for many employees and employers who are contemplating the use of nonqualified deferred compensation arrangements is whether deferral is a sound financial tactic. That is, will employees be better off with the deferred compensation arrangement than they would be if compensation were paid currently?

Clearly, if tax rates do not rise, a highly compensated employee will almost always be better off deferring some of his or her compensation until a later date. However, if tax rates do rise, an employee will be better off deferring the compensation to a later date only if the compensation is deferred for a sufficient period of time – the break even period.

Specifically, if compensation is deferred and tax rates do rise, the employee will be taxed in a future tax year at a higher tax rate on the entire amount, including the interest credited on the account. If compensation is not deferred, he or she will pay tax at the current lower tax rate immediately and therefore have less available for investment.

The tradeoff is between: (1) the current lower tax rate, which must be paid immediately and which reduces the amount available for investment; and (2) the higher future tax rate, which must be paid later and which allows the entire before-tax amount to earn interest.

If the period of time is sufficiently long, the benefit of earning interest on the before-tax amount of deferred compensation will exceed the cost of the higher tax rate that is applied to the whole amount when it is ultimately received.

The NumberCruncher illustration that follows shows the years to break even under various assumptions.

Amount to be Deferred:	$20,000
Current Tax Rate:	35%
Number of Years Compensation will be Deferred:	20
Assumed Future Tax Rate:	33%
Assumed Before Tax Rate of Return:	6%
Current After-Tax Value of Compensation:	$19,500

After-Tax Accumulation in 20 Years

If Tax Rate Decrease Occurs:	Early	Middle	Late
With Deferred Comp. Plan:	$64,463	$64,463	$64,463
Without Deferred Comp. Plan:	$42,892	$42,399	$41,913
Gain From Deferring Comp.:	$21,571	$22,064	$22,550
Years to Break Even:	0	0	0

Note that when the retirement tax rate is higher than the before retirement tax rate, it will take a number of years to break even by deferring compensation as this second NumberCruncher illustration demonstrates:

Amount to be Deferred:	$30,000
Current Tax Rate:	33%
Number of Years Compensation will be Deferred:	20
Assumed Future Tax Rate:	35%
Assumed Before Tax Rate of Return:	6%
Current After-Tax Value of Compensation:	$20,100

After-Tax Accumulation in 20 Years

If Tax Rate Decrease Occurs:	Early	Middle	Late
With Deferred Comp. Plan:	$62,539	$62,539	$62,539
Without Deferred Comp. Plan:	$43,202	$43,704	$44,211
Gain From Deferring Comp.:	$19,337	$18,835	$18,328
Years to Break Even:	2	2	2

Question – Are there securities issues with respect to nonqualified plans?

Answer – It appears that, subject to certain exceptions noted below, the IRS will require the registration of all nonqualified deferred compensation plans as "securities" if the plan involves employee contributions. The key is whether the employees making the contributions have "investment motives" (i.e., the plan involves investments in underlying securities whose return is credited to the employee) or "tax deferral" motives (i.e., primarily to save income taxes). An investment-motivated plan will be considered a security and must be registered; however, a deferral-motivated plan will not be considered a security and will not need to be registered.

If a NQDC plan is required to register as a security with the SEC, the failure to register the plan may have tax implications. A participant in a plan that has not registered with the SEC, and is required to do so, may be able to rescind the deferral of compensation; however, such a right to rescind could cause the participant to be in constructive receipt of the deferred amounts.

NQDC plans provide an employer with the ability to: (1) create a retirement plan for specified individuals; (2) select who will be covered; and (3) determine the terms and conditions of that coverage. Although many of these plans were previously financed by crediting the amounts deferred with a given interest rate, more and more frequently these plans are financed through a combination of variable life insurance (to finance a death benefit) and equities such as mutual funds or other equity-type assets. Additionally, although most NQDC plans in the past covered only a select group of high level executives or other key employees, recently plans have become much more broad based.

The key registration exemptions that would apply to most small corporation plans are for:

(a) Securities offered and sold only to persons resident within a single state, and where the issuer is doing business in that state. This is commonly called the "intrastate exemption."

(b) Small offerings. This is commonly called the "small offering" exemption.

(c) Nonpublic offerings. This is commonly called the "nonpublic offering" exemption.

There is a "Regulation D, Rule 505" and "506" safe harbor, which encompasses the later two exemptions and works like this:

(1) Offers and sales of securities with a total offering price of $5,000,000 or less in which there are no more than 35 purchasers and which meet certain other rules will be protected from registration requirements.

(2) Offers and sales of securities which do not involve more than 35 purchasers are protected from registration requirements – regardless of the dollar amount of the offering – if every purchaser who is not considered an "accredited investor" is considered capable of evaluating the merits and risks of the prospective investment.

The SEC has left businesses in a state of uncertainty on this issue, since each case will be measured on its own facts and circumstances.[28] This may have a chilling effect upon the creation of new NQDC plans. Few companies will set up plans covering a large number of employees, and most "smaller companies" that set up plans for a dozen or so key executives will be able to fall within the safe harbor exemptions described above–and therefore avoid the cost and aggravation of SEC registration. Many plans, however, involving a very large number of covered individuals or large amounts of money, may have to register. Certainly, employers cannot ignore this issue and should obtain competent legal advice.

Question – What methods are available to informally fund deferred compensation obligations?

Answer – In the "pay-as-you-go" approach, the employer uses working capital as needed to make any benefit payments, and there is no advance "funding."

With the "sinking fund" approach, a certain amount of assets are set aside to fund the obligations under the deferred compensation plan.

Since neither one of these approaches protects either the employer or the employee in event of a premature death, corporations will very often turn to corporate owned life insurance (COLI) to finance both the retirement and pre-retirement obligations under the plan.

Finally, a combination of the above approaches can be used.

ASRS: Sec. 64

CHAPTER ENDNOTES

1. See Regs. §§1.451-1, 1.451-2.

2. See Rev. Rul. 60-31, 1960-1 CB 174, as modified by Rev. Rul. 70-435, 1970-2 CB 100. See also Let. Rul. 8439012, under which an executive's deferred compensation was placed in a trusteed bank account, but his rights were only those of an unsecured

general creditor of the company. No income was recognized by the executive as a result of the company's placing the money in the trust account. See also *Oates v. Comm.*, 18 TC 570, *aff'd*, 207 F.2d 711 (7th Cir. 1953), *acq.*, 1960-1 CB 5.

3. See, e.g., Rev. Rul. 72-25, 1972-1 CB 127; Rev. Rul. 68-99, 1968-1 CB 193.

4. See Rev. Proc. 92-64, 1992-2 CB 422, including model form of the trust. Also see Rev. Proc. 92-65, 1992-2 CB 428.

5. See, e.g., *Goodman v. Resolution Trust Corp.*, 7 F.3d 1123 (4th Cir. 1993).

6. See paragraph 5 of "What Are The Tax Implications?" in Chapter 40 for possible alternative minimum tax on proceeds received by a regular C corporation.

7. IRC Sec. 264(a)(1).

8. See generally, IRC Sec. 72.

9. IRC Sec. 72(e); Treas. Reg. §1.72-11(d)(1).

10. IRC Sec. 101(a)(1).

11. See IRC Secs. 404(a)(5), 162(a)(1), 212. Note that publicly held corporations generally cannot deduct compensation in excess of $1 million per tax year to certain top level executives. See IRC Sec. 162(m).

12. IRC Secs. 3121(v)(2)(B), 3306(r)(2)(B). See also Notice 94-96, 1994-2 CB 564. Final regulations became effective January 29, 1999 and are applicable to amounts deferred and benefits paid on or after January 1, 2000. Treas. Regs. §§31.3121(v)(2)-1, 31.3306(r)(2)-1(a).

13. See IRC Sec. 3121(a)(1).

14. Rev. Rul. 68-99, 1968-1 CB 193. See also Rev. Rul. 72-25, 1972-1 CB 127 (annuity contracts).

15. IRC Sec. 2039(a); *Goodman v. Granger*, 243 F.2d 264 (3rd Cir. 1957), *cert. denied*, 355 U.S. 835 (1957).

16. IRC Sec. 691(c). The income tax deduction for the additional federal estate tax generated by the inclusion of the IRD is as follows:

Federal estate tax payable (with net IRC Sec. 691 income included in the gross estate

Minus

Federal estate tax payable (with no IRC Sec. 691 income included in gross estate)

Equals

Portion of Federal Estate Tax attributable to IRC Sec. 691 items

Note the planning implication of this computation: To the extent that no estate tax is generated by IRD, no income tax deduction will be allowed. So, if deferred compensation payments are made to a surviving spouse (or to a marital trust on such spouse's behalf), to the extent that they qualify for the marital deduction, the IRC Section 691 income tax deduction is lost.

17. See note 12, above. Self-employed individuals pay social security taxes through self-employment (SECA) taxes rather than through FICA taxes. Nonqualified deferred compensation of self-employed individuals is usually counted for SECA purposes when it is includable in income for income tax purposes. See IRC Sec. 1402(a); Treas. Reg. §1.1402(a)-1(c). (As with the FICA tax, there is no wage base cap for the hospital insurance portion of the SECA tax. See IRC Sec. 1402(b)(1)). So, deferred compensation of self-employed individuals is generally counted for SECA purposes when paid (or constructively received, if earlier). As an exception to this rule, corporate directors who deferred receipt of fees for

services performed in tax years beginning on or after January 1, 1988, but before 1991 were required to include the deferred fees for SECA purposes in the year(s) in which the services were performed. IRC Sec. 1402(a); see also Let. Rul. 8819012.

18. See note 13, above.

19. See ERISA Secs. 201(1), 201(2), 301(a)(1), 301(a)(3), 401(a)(1), 503, 4021(a), 4021(b)(6); Labor Regs. §§2520.104-23, 2520.104-24, 2560.503-1(a), 2560.503-1(b).

20. See IRC Secs. 404(a)(5), 404(d). The weight of authority even holds that an accrual basis taxpayer cannot take a current deduction for amounts credited as "interest" on unfunded deferred compensation; the deduction for such amounts must be postponed until such amounts are includable in employee income. See the seventh and eighth Questions and Answers in this chapter and the authorities cited in notes 27 and 28.

21. See Rev. Rul. 71-419, 1971-2 CB 220.

22. See, generally, IRC Sec. 457.

23. IRC Sec. 72(u).

24. The full picture of the taxation of employees participating in secular trusts is much more complex than this. For the rules applicable to participants in employer-funded secular trusts, see IRC Sec. 402(b); Regs. §§1.402(b)-1(a), 1.402(b)-1(b); Let. Ruls. 9502030, 9417013, 9302017, 9212024, 9212019, 9207010, 9206009. For the rules applicable to employees participating in employee-funded secular trusts, see Let. Ruls. 9450004, 9437011, 9337016, 9328007, 9322011, 9316018, 9316008, 9235044, 9031031, 8843021, 8841023. For more on the employer's deduction in the context of an employer-funded secular trust, see Treas. Reg. §1.404(a)-12(b)(1); Let. Ruls. 9502030, 9417013, 9302017, 9212024, 9212019, 9207010, 9206009. For more on the employer's deduction in the context of an employee-funded secular trust, see Let. Ruls. 9450004, 9437011, 9337016, 9328007, 9322011, 9316018, 9316008, 9235044, 9031031, 8843021, 8841023.

25. The ground rules governing employee direction of investments in nonqualified deferred compensation plans are not entirely clear. To avoid accelerated taxation, plans probably should not allow employees to control the actual investment of funds. In other words, plans allowing employee input into the actual investment of funds probably should provide that the asset holder (for example, the employer, or the trustee of a rabbi trust) need not follow the employee's wishes. Whether plans that allow participants to select hypothetical investments also should provide that the employee's investment wishes need not be followed is not clear. See generally Let. Ruls. 9517019, 9505012, 9504007, 9452035, 9332038, 9122019, 8952037, 8903088, 8834015, 8804057, 8804023, 8648011, 8607022, 8507028; Tax Mgmt. (BNA), U.S. Income Series, Portfolio #385-3rd (Deferred Compensation Arrangements), V.D.1; AALU *Washington Report*, Bulletins Nos. 94-107 (12/19/94) and 94-46 (5/13/94).

Plans allowing employee input into the actual investment of funds may also want to limit the employee's investment choices to broad categories of investments (such as stocks, bonds, or money market instruments) rather than allowing the employee to choose more specific investments. Compare Rev. Rul. 82-54, 1982-1 CB 11 (annuity policyholders who could direct investment of annuity fund among several mutual funds representing different, broad investment strategies would not control individual investment decisions and for tax purposes would not be considered to own the mutual fund shares). Whether plans permitting employees to select hypothetical investments should similarly limit choices is not clear.

26. See *Albertson's, Inc. v. Comm.*, 95 TC 415 (1990) (divided court) ("interest" credited on unfunded deferred compensation is really additional deferred compensation that cannot be deducted until includable in employee income), *aff'd on other grounds*, 42 F.3d 537, 94-2 USTC ¶50,619 (9th Cir. 1994); TAM 8619006 (same); see also Notice 94-38, 1994-1 CB 350 (amounts credited as interest on unfunded deferred compensation are deductible when includable in employee income); Let. Rul. 9201019 (amounts credited as interest on unfunded deferred compensation are includable in employee income when paid or made available).

27. *Albertson's Inc. v. Comm.*, 42 F.3d 537, 94-2 USTC ¶50,619 (9th Cir. 1994), *vacating in part* 12 F.3d 1529 (9th Cir. 1993), *aff'g in part* 95 TC 415 (1990) (divided court), *en banc rehearing denied*, (9th Cir. 1995), *cert denied*, 516 U.S. 807 (1995); see also Notice 94-38, 1994-1 CB 350; Let. Rul. 9201019; TAM 8619006.

28. In 1995, several companies set up such plans and, to be safe, requested "no action" letters from the SEC. One such company was Merrill Lynch, whose plan covered about 2,000 brokers. The SEC responded negatively by refusing Merrill Lynch's request. Merrill Lynch then registered its plan with the SEC–and a number of other companies followed by registering their own plans. The Employee Benefits Committee of the American Bar Association Section on Taxation requested clarification from the SEC. At a 1997 meeting of the Committee, an SEC spokesperson stated that the SEC considered all NQDC plans (with certain exceptions discussed in the text above) as "registerable" and that it would be issuing a formal statement on its position.

Chapter 49

EMPLOYEE STOCK OWNERSHIP PLAN

WHAT IS IT?

An employee stock ownership plan ("ESOP") is a type of qualified retirement plan that must invest its assets primarily in the employer's securities. ESOPs are essentially qualified stock bonus plans, but differ in that a stock bonus plan is not required to invest in employer securities. Additionally, an employer may lend funds or the use of its credit facilities to an ESOP, but not to a stock bonus plan, to facilitate the purchase of employer securities.[1]

A formal designation must be made to set up an ESOP, and a trust must be established. The ESOP plan trust is usually called an employer stock ownership trust or ESOT, and it may qualify as a tax-exempt employee trust.

An ESOP trust may be a shareholder of an S corporation; however, the potential for flagrant abuses of this "tax loophole" were largely eliminated in 2001. (For additional details, see the questions and answers later in this chapter as to S corporation ESOPs.)

There are significant advantages to both the employer and the employee that can be derived from the ESOP, and it can offer significant benefits for business owners in need of an exit strategy. Favorable tax treatment has made ESOPs even more attractive for many small employers.

WHEN IS THE USE OF SUCH A DEVICE INDICATED?

1. When a shareholder who is a substantial owner of a closely-held business would like to shift his investment, on a tax-deferred basis, into publicly traded securities. Tax-free rollover of the proceeds received from the sale of a business to an ESOP may be available if the proceeds are invested in another business. This rollover provision is intended to encourage employee stock ownership (see discussion of mechanics under "What Are the Tax Implications," below).

2. When an employer would like to obtain an income tax deduction with little or no cash outlay. A current deduction is allowed (within limits) for both employer contributions of cash and for contributions of stock (including stock of the employer company) or other property contributed to the ESOP.[2] A contribution of an employer's stock generates a deduction equal to its fair market value. The sizable deduction reduces cash flow out of the corporation in profit years and in loss years, a carry-back is created which might result in a tax refund to the corporation.[3]

3. When an employer wants to create a market for its stock. An ESOP may be able to purchase treasury stock or authorized but unissued stock, as well as stock owned by individual shareholders, without causing a loss of corporate control by majority shareholders. (But note that if a defined contribution plan–other than a profit sharing plan–is established by an employer whose stock is not readily tradable on an established market and employer stock constitutes more than 10% of the plan's assets, participating employees must be entitled to exercise voting rights of stock allocated to their account on certain major corporate matters.)

4. When a corporation faces an accumulated earnings threat. An ESOP can be used to take cash out of a corporation and thus reduce the potential for an accumulated earnings tax problem. The reduction in taxable income of the corporation due to deductible contributions lessens the pressure on a corporation to pay dividends. Certain dividends may be subject to lower income tax rates to the recipient, but they are nondeductible by the corporation.

5. When an employer is seeking a way to motivate and compensate long service employees. Since the ultimate value of an employee's ESOP interest is directly related to the value of the employee's stock, increased productivity and corporate growth become an employee concern. ESOPs also provide a means for employees (including shareholder-employees) to supplement Social Security as well as other corporate-provided retirement benefits.

6. When shareholders with large amounts of corporate stock in their estate want liquidity, the stock may be

sold to the ESOP in exchange for cash, thus providing the liquidity to pay taxes and other debts.

7. When a corporation desires to make payment of premiums for life insurance on key employees from deductible contributions. In appropriate cases, life insurance payments on key employees, who are also shareholders, may be shifted to the ESOP from the corporation, and these premium payments, which are otherwise not deductible to the corporation, effectively become deductible contributions to the ESOP. The insurance policy is an investment of the ESOP and may be the source of liquidity to buy the shareholder's stock at his death.

8. When an employer is seeking a means for financing corporate growth through the use of untaxed dollars. By selling rather than contributing stock to the ESOP, an employer can obtain a large amount of cash. Conversely, if the corporation had borrowed cash from a bank to finance corporate expansion, only interest payments on the loan would be deductible. The principal would have to be repaid with "expensive" (nondeductible) dollars. On the other hand, the corporation will get a deduction for the dollars it then contributes to the ESOP. The ESOP receives these free of tax and uses them (without reduction for income taxes) to repay the bank loan.

WHAT ARE THE REQUIREMENTS?

1. ESOPs meeting certain requirements may distribute benefits in the form of employer stock *or* cash. Participants must be given the right to receive employer stock if they so desire, unless the employer's charter or by-laws restrict the ownership of substantially all outstanding employer stock to employees and/or the ESOP. (See the questions and answers related to S corporations later in this chapter.) If ownership is so restricted, a participant need not be given the right to receive employer stock. The participant must then be given the right to receive his benefit in cash.

If employer stock is distributed, participants must be given a "put" option for a limited time, which allows them to purchase the stock from the employer at its fair market value. The put option requirement does not apply to a bank which maintains an ESOP if the bank is prohibited by law from redeeming or buying its own stock and participants are given the right to receive their benefits in cash. It appears that an ESOP with no cash distribution option (which would

not be typical) is required to give a put option to participants only with respect to employer stock acquired by the plan after December 31, 1979 or acquired with proceeds of a loan obtained from or guaranteed by a disqualified person (unless the stock is readily tradable on an established securities market).[4]

2. The plan must meet the same requirements as apply to other qualified plans, with respect to coverage, nondiscrimination in contributions, nonforfeitability on termination, rules regarding forfeitures, and rules relative to the source of contributions.[5] IRS regulations do not allow an ESOP to be integrated with Social Security.[6] Certain ESOPs in existence on November 1, 1977, that were integrated with Social Security were "grandfathered" and may be able to continue to use those provisions. As is the case for all qualified retirement plans, an ESOP must be in writing.[7]

3. The trust must be for the exclusive benefit of the employees and their beneficiaries (e.g., the ESOP is not meant as a means of bailing out financially troubled employers).[8]

4. The trust must be a United States trust and not a foreign trust.

5. The cost of employer stock purchased by the trustee must not exceed its fair market value. An independent appraisal is required for ESOP transactions unless the securities are publicly traded on a national securities exchange.[9]

6. Participants must be entitled to vote employer stock that has been allocated to their accounts if the stock is registered under the Securities Exchange Act of 1934. If the employer's stock is not readily tradable on an established market and more than 10% of the plan's assets are invested in employer stock, the plan must give participants voting rights on major corporate issues (generally those involving the approval or disapproval of any corporate merger or consolidation, recapitalization, reclassification, liquidation, dissolution, sale of substantially all assets of a trade or business, or similar transactions).[10]

7. Participants who have completed 10 years of participation in the ESOP must be given the opportunity to diversify 25% of their account balances beginning at age 55 and an additional 25% at age 60.[11]

8. Generally, the plan must provide that, if the participant elects (and if the required spousal consent

is properly given), the distribution of a participant's account balance will commence within one year after the plan year (1) in which he separates from service by reason of attainment of normal retirement age, disability, or death, or (2) which is the fifth plan year following the plan year in which he otherwise separates from service.[12]

9. The plan must insure that, in the case of certain "qualified sales" (after October 22, 1986) of employer securities by a participant (under Code section 1042) or executor (under former Code section 2057) to the ESOP, no portion of the assets of the plan attributable to the securities purchased by the plan may accrue or be allocated during the nonallocation period for the benefit of (1) the taxpayer who made the election under Section 1042 (or the decedent whose executor made the election under former Section 2057), (2) any individual who is a member of the family (brother, sister, spouse, ancestor, lineal descendant) of the taxpayer or decedent, or (3) any person who owns, or is considered as owning under the attribution rules of Section 318(a), more than 25% (by number or value) of any class of outstanding stock of the employer or any corporation which is a member of the same controlled group of corporations as is the employer.[13]

10. An ESOP can own stock in an S corporation, so long as the plan provides that no portion of the assets of the plan attributable to the employer securities accrue to the benefit of a "disqualified person" in a "nonallocation year." In basic terms, a "disqualified person" includes (1) an officer or director (or an individual having powers or responsibilities similar to those of an officer or director); (2) a person who owns 10% or more of the stock in the employer's S corporation; and (3) a highly compensated employee earning 10% or more of the yearly wages of an employer.[14]

HOW IT IS DONE – EXAMPLES

A corporate client has been consistently earning $200,000 per year. The corporation has no pension or profit-sharing plan. The employees are eager to see some type of deferred compensation program instituted. Because of an expansion program, the corporation periodically is in a cash-poor position. The schedule below shows the amount of the increase in corporate working capital by comparing an ESOP with a profit-sharing plan and with no deferred compensation plan.

From the comparison, it is clear that establishing an ESOP gives the greatest increase in working capital.

Another corporate client needs a new building that will cost approximately $250,000. The only available loans require an amortization of the $250,000 at the rate of $50,000 per year over five years, plus interest on the unpaid balance. Using the schedule set forth below, if the corporation established a profit-sharing plan, only $66,000 would be left after taxes on $200,000 of earnings in order to amortize the principal debt and pay the interest. Clearly, this would not be enough money. If the corporation had no plan, sufficient monies would be available to amortize the debt and pay the interest although the net worth increase after such payments would be rather small. If an ESOP were established, the ESOP could borrow the $250,000 from the bank (the loan may have to be guaranteed by the corporation) and the ESOP would immediately purchase $250,000 of capital stock from the corporation. The corporation's net working capital would be immediately increased by $250,000. The corporation would then make contributions to the ESOP on an annual basis and the ESOP would repay the bank.

	No Plan	Profit Sharing Plan	ESOP
Earnings Before Tax	$200,000	$200,000	$200,000
Contributions (15% x $600,000 of compensation eligible for coverage)	0	90,000	90,000
Taxable Income	$200,000	$110,000	$110,000
Tax (assume combined federal and state bracket is 40%)	80,000	44,000	44,000
Net Earnings After Taxes	$120,000	$ 66,000	$ 66,000
Net Worth Increase: Net Earnings After Taxes	$120,000	$ 66,000	$ 66,000
Cash from Sale of Capital Stock to ESOP	0	0	90,000
Increase in Working Capital	$120,000	$ 66,000	$156,000

For loans made prior to August 21, 1996 for an ESOP to purchase or refinance employer securities, one-half of the interest received by a lender is exempt from income tax provided certain conditions are met.[15] Although lenders may no longer exclude such interest for post-August 20, 1996 loans, the exclusion is still available for loans made under a binding written contract prior to June 10, 1996, or for certain refinancing loans, provided the loans meet the requirements of former Code section 133.

A third example of the use of an ESOP is a situation where a majority of the stock of a closely held corporation is owned by one individual, and his wife and/or children own the balance of the stock. The stock represents a part of the individual's estate, but not more than 35% of his adjusted gross estate and, therefore, not enough to qualify for a redemption under section 303 of the Internal Revenue Code. Additionally, the spouse and/or the children, also shareholders, are beneficiaries of the estate and therefore a redemption of the stock by the corporation would constitute a dividend to the estate (by reason of the attribution rules of section 318 of the Code). Also, consider that the corporation may not have sufficient funds to redeem all the shares of stock and certainly any partial redemption would also constitute a dividend.

The creation of an ESOP would establish an entity that could purchase all or any portion of the stock owned by the estate and not create dividend consequences to the estate. Such a purchase would indirectly give rise to a deduction for the corporation, a deduction it could not take if the purchase were made directly from the estate. (Although such a transaction has been given approval by the Internal Revenue Service in at least one private letter ruling, it would be advisable to obtain a favorable ruling in advance of a sale.) The Internal Revenue Service has stringent requirements that must be met for an advance ruling. These requirements are updated annually.[16]

A fourth example of the use of an ESOP involves the conversion of premiums on nondeductible key individual life insurance into a tax deduction. Assume that a corporation is owned by two or more stockholders equally and the stockholders desire to have a buy-sell agreement (either an entity or cross purchase type) funded by life insurance so that on the death of any one stockholder there will be sufficient monies to purchase or redeem the shares of stock of the decedent and permit the company to continue in business. Payments of the life insurance premiums are normally nondeductible.

If, however, the company established an ESOP and the investment committee directed the ESOP to purchase key individual insurance on the lives of all of the stockholders, then upon the death of any stockholder, the trust (as the beneficiary of the life insurance policy) would be entitled to the proceeds. The trust would then be able to use the proceeds and negotiate with the personal representative of the deceased stockholder for the purchase of the shares of stock, at the then fair market value of those shares on the date of the decedent's death. Consideration must be given to the possibility

that the ESOP would not be able to acquire the stock, which then would leave the life insurance proceeds in the plan. An alternative may be to have the corporation continue to own the policies and contribute enough stock to the plan each year to offset the insurance premium tax cost.

Final regulations prohibit an ESOP from buying life insurance with the proceeds of a loan obtained from or guaranteed by a disqualified person. In addition, a leveraged ESOP must not obligate itself to purchase stock at an indefinite future time (although it can be given an option to acquire stock).[17]

WHAT ARE THE TAX IMPLICATIONS?

A corporation is allowed a deduction (within limits) for contributions made to the ESOP even if it had no profits during the year the contribution was made.[18] The excess deduction might therefore generate a net operating loss carryback with a resulting tax refund.

Generally, an employer can generally deduct a contribution to a single ESOP of up to 25% of the total compensation paid to all participants in the plan. (For plan years beginning before January 1, 2002, the limit was 15%.[19]) If the employer contributes less than the deductible amount, the difference between the amount that was actually contributed and the amount that could have been deducted may be carried forward and used to increase the deduction limit in future years.[20] In years before 2002, employers often combined ESOP of the stock bonus type with a money purchase pension plan to increase the annual deduction to 25% of plan participants' compensation.[21]

Special deduction rules apply to C corporation plans that have incurred debt to purchase employer stock (i.e., leveraged C corporation ESOPs). An employer may contribute as much as 25% (whether before 2002 or after 2001) of covered compensation to a single ESOP where the contributions are applied to make principal payments on the loan. Additional unlimited deductions are allowed for employer contributions used to pay interest on the loan.[22] However, these provisions are not available for S corporation ESOPs. In addition, limitations on allocations to employee accounts (which apply if more than one-third of contributions are allocated to certain key employees) may limit the availability of these special deduction limits in some circumstances.[23]

The employer does not have to make the contribution to the ESOP in stock of the employer. The contribution may be made in cash, any other property, or employer stock. However, a contribution of property may result in a prohibited transaction or other problems that should be carefully examined. Any one of the three contribution media, alone or in combination with the others, can create a deduction to the corporation equal to the cash and the fair market value of the assets being transferred.

If the corporation transfers assets to the ESOP that have appreciated in value, the gain will constitute income to the corporation.[24] For example, if the corporation bought stock, which grew from $3 to $8 a share, a contribution of that stock would result in a $5 per share gain. This rule applies to any transfer of property with the exception of cash and stock of the employer.

The corporation is allowed a special deduction for cash dividends paid with respect to stock held on the dividend record date by an ESOP, provided the dividends (a) are paid directly in cash to participants or their beneficiaries, or (b) are paid indirectly to them through the plan within 90 days after the close of the plan year, or (c) are used to make payments on a loan incurred to purchase qualifying employer securities.[25] For shares acquired by an ESOP after August 4, 1989, a deduction is allowed under (c) only if the dividends are paid on shares purchased with the loan proceeds.

A corporation is also generally permitted a deduction for dividends paid to the plan (or paid out to participants or beneficiaries) and reinvested in qualifying employer securities, if so elected by the participants or their beneficiaries.[26]

A major income tax benefit is available to an individual who sells stock to an ESOP and replaces it with within certain time limits. Under Section 1042, recognition of gain may be deferred on the sale of closely held stock to an ESOP if: (1) the sale would qualify for long-term capital gain treatment, (2) after the sale the ESOP owns at least 30% of the total value of the employer securities, (3) within a 15-month period (beginning three months prior to the day of sale) "qualified replacement securities" are purchased, and (4) the taxpayer held the shares for three years or longer. "Qualified replacement securities" generally means stock or bonds issued by a domestic corporation which, for the taxable year of issuance, does not have passive investment income of more than 25% of gross receipts. If the cost of the replacement securities is less than the amount of the deferred gain, the difference is currently taxable.

Although it is possible for a shareholder to obtain beneficial nonrecognition of gain on the sale of stock to

an ESOP under Code section 1042, there is a pitfall to avoid. With respect to sales of securities after October 22, 1986, if there is a prohibited accrual or allocation (see paragraph (9) under "What are the Requirements," above), a penalty tax equal to 50% of the amount of the prohibited accrual or allocation will be levied against the employer sponsoring the plan.[27] In addition, the amount of any prohibited accrual or allocation will be treated as if distributed to the individual involved and taxed as such.[28] Up to 5% of the securities purchased by the ESOP in the Section 1042 transaction can be allocated to the benefit of lineal descendants of the seller without creating any adverse tax consequences.[29]

Furthermore, if an ESOP has made an investment in stock of an S corporation, allocations to a person who directly owns 10% or more of the S corporation stock (or owns 20% or more indirectly with members of his family) may result in significant penalties. Thus, for smaller corporations, a purchase of S corporation stock after March 14, 2001 must be very carefully considered.[30]

Assuming none of the penalties described above apply, employer contributions are not currently taxable to participating employees. ESOP trust assets grow tax free, even if an employee's rights become nonforfeitable. An employee pays no tax until a distribution is made to him (see the discussion of the tax treatment of distributions in Chapter 52).

IMPLICATIONS AND ISSUES IN COMMUNITY PROPERTY STATES

Benefits from qualified plans (pension/profit sharing plans, HR-10 plans and ESOPs) and IRAs are generally held to be community property to the extent contributions are made by or on behalf of a married employee who is a resident of one of the community property states (enumerated in the discussion of community property in the "Introduction") during the period of employment.

This rule, while relatively simple to state, can present significant problems when applied to specific situations. The major areas of difficulty are divorce and death of an employee.

It was unclear after the enactment of the Employee Retirement Income Security Act of 1974 (ERISA) whether community property laws continued to apply to qualified plan benefits. Some argued that ERISA "preempted" state community property laws. Others argued that award of a part of an employee's qualified plan benefits to his spouse was an assignment or alienation of benefits prohibited by ERISA. If the courts had followed these latter arguments, spouses in community property states would no longer be entitled to the 50% of qualified plan benefits that they had prior to ERISA. Many courts faced with the issue determined that ERISA did not supersede state community property laws. However, in a landmark 1997 case, the U.S. Supreme Court held in a 5-4 decision that a deceased spouse may not make a bequest of her community property interest in her participant spouse's undistributed qualified plan benefits.[31] Writing for the majority, Justice Kennedy upheld ERISA's prohibition on the assignment or alienation of benefits, thus preempting state community property law. Nonetheless, it is generally accepted that a non-participant spouse personally retains a valid community property interest in qualified plan benefits, as discussed in this chapter and Chapter 52.

A spouse's community property interest in his spouse's qualified plan benefits is included in his gross estate if he or she predeceased the spouse with the qualified plan benefits. Estate taxes apply even though the surviving spouse may have no immediate access to the benefit to provide funds to pay the tax. Unfortunate situations also arise where the appraised "value" of the deceased spouse's community property interest is much greater than the benefit actually received from the plan; for example, when the surviving spouse is less than 100% vested and terminates employment soon after his spouse's death. However, most such benefits go to the surviving spouse and thus are eligible for the marital deduction and no federal death tax is due.

However, if any employee with qualified plan benefits predeceases his spouse, and benefits are paid to a beneficiary other than the surviving spouse, the surviving spouse may be treated as making a gift of 50% of the benefits payable to other beneficiaries (to the extent the benefits were community property). Thus, it may be found that the surviving spouse has made a taxable gift where the participant has directed both community property interests in the benefit to other beneficiaries. However, with the significant rights given to non-participant spouses by the Retirement Equity Act of 1984, it became difficult to have significant plan proceeds distributed without the spouse's permission. Such accidental and unintended taxable gifts can be a problem for persons not aware of the possible trap.

A question arises as to whether a spouse's consent to the designation of a trust as a beneficiary of the employee's plan benefits is a transfer with a retained life estate under Section 2038 of the Internal Revenue Code.

If the spouse is a lifetime beneficiary of the trust, care must be exercised to minimize the possibility that the IRS will claim that the spouse's community property share of plan benefits remaining in the trust is subject to federal estate tax at the spouse's death.

The community property states have adopted varying positions to deal with the problem of valuing qualified plan benefits for purposes of division in a divorce. Prior to 1976, for example, California courts divided only *vested* qualified plan benefits, holding that non-vested benefits were "mere expectancies." However, a 1976 decision of the California Supreme Court overruled that position and held that *non-vested* qualified plan benefits were community property assets subject to division in a divorce proceeding. The benefits can be valued using actuarial methods. The court, recognizing that unfairness may result if the benefit does not actually "vest," stated that it may be appropriate in certain situations to divide benefit payments as they are received (rather than fixing a lump sum value at the time of the divorce). Thus, each spouse would share the risk that the full benefit would fail to fully vest.

QUESTIONS AND ANSWERS

Question – How should employer stock be valued?

Answer – If the employer's stock is not readily tradable on an established market, an independent appraisal is necessary annually to establish the value of the stock for contribution purposes (if the corporation contributes its stock) or for purposes of determining a proper purchase price (if the ESOP purchases stock from the corporation or from any third party stockholder). This valuation is always subject to scrutiny by the Internal Revenue Service and the Department of Labor.

Question – If there are no stock purchases or stock contributions during the year, is an annual appraisal still necessary?

Answer – An annual appraisal is probably still necessary in order to meet the reporting requirements established by ERISA with respect to the current value of the plan assets and the ERISA requirement that the value of a participant's account be determined annually. This information would have to be submitted to the Department of Labor, and current value probably could not be determined without such an appraisal. If there is a purchase of employer stock by the ESOP trust, the value of the stock must be ascertained at the time of purchase. If an ESOP were to pay a price greater than the fair market value of the employer's stock, the investment would be considered improper and might result in a disqualification of the plan.

Question – Are there any provisions of ERISA that do not apply to an ESOP?

Answer – ERISA treats the ESOP as an individual account plan. An individual account plan escapes that part of the ERISA reporting provisions that requires a statement of an actuary and is also exempt from paying plan termination insurance premiums to the Pension Benefit Guaranty Corporation.

Question – Can an ESOP allow voluntary nondeductible employee contributions?

Answer – Voluntary nondeductible contributions can be made to an ESOP, as well as to qualified pension, profit-sharing, or stock bonus plans. These contributions will be deemed annual additions for maximum contribution (i.e., Section 415) purposes and thus, will have the impact of reducing the maximum employer contribution. The contributions will also have to pass a special nondiscrimination test.[32]

Provisions allowing voluntary nondeductible contributions to an ESOP should be approached with caution. Voluntary contributions to an ESOP should not be invested in employer stock unless the employer has complied with applicable federal and state securities requirements.

Question – What is the tax treatment of a distribution of employer stock to a plan participant?

Answer – If employer stock is paid to a plan participant in a lump sum distribution (as that term is defined in the Internal Revenue Code), any unrealized appreciation on that stock that is not attributable to deductible employee voluntary contributions will not be taxed to the participant until the participant sells the stock.[33]

This unrealized appreciation will be treated as long-term capital gain when the stock is sold. Any appreciation after distribution will be treated as long- or short-term capital gain depending on whether the participant has held the stock for the requisite holding period following the date of distribution. The cash portion and that portion of the lump sum distribution that is an amount equal to the employer contributions used to purchase stock may, under some circumstances, be taxed to the participant at the time of distribution.

———————

Example: if the individual receives an ESOP distribution of $30,000 cash and employer stock worth $100,000 on the distribution date and if the employer had contributed an amount equal to $75,000 which was used to purchase that stock, then the $25,000 gain will not be taxed to the participant until the securities are sold. But at the date of distribution, the $105,000 will be taxed under the lump sum distribution rules in effect at the time of distribution.

———————

Amounts attributable to deductible employee contributions are not considered part of a lump sum distribution and are taxed as ordinary income on receipt; any net unrealized appreciation on employer securities attributable to deductible employee contributions is taxed upon distribution of the securities, whether or not they are sold.[34]

If the participant or beneficiary of a participant does not take a lump sum distribution of the cash or employer securities but instead receives the employer securities over a period in excess of one taxable year of the recipient (or beneficiary), the entire amount attributable to the employer contribution, deductible employee contributions, and any subsequent appreciation on employer stock will be taxed at the ordinary income rate in effect at the time of distribution.[35]

If the employee has made any nondeductible contributions to the ESOP, any unrealized appreciation in the employer stock that is attributable to such contributions will escape taxation until the participant sells the securities. At that time, the gain will be taxed.[36]

Question – A participant in an ESOP retires. He receives a distribution of employer stock. Is he under any obligation to sell the stock to the ESOP?

Answer – It seems clear that no prearranged enforceable agreement can exist between the participants of the plan and the ESOP requiring that the participants, upon receipt of the stock distribution from the ESOP, sell those securities back to the ESOP. (ESOPs are allowed by law in order to encourage employers to place capital stock in the hands of employees. An agreement binding the employee to sell the stock back defeats this intent.) Regulations specifically prohibit a "call" option on employer stock acquired with the proceeds of a loan obtained from or guaranteed by a disqualified person.[37]

However, the IRS has permitted an ESOP to retain a "right of first refusal" on employer stock that is not publicly traded. In other words, if the participant wants to sell the employer stock distributed to him to a third party, he must first offer it to the employer or the ESOP.[38]

It is possible to have a large number of stockholders with minimal interests in a company as a result of employer-stock distributions from the ESOP. All of these "small" stockholders are entitled to certain information and have certain rights under ERISA, state corporate laws, and state and federal securities laws. This factor can be a deterrent to establishing ESOPs.

Question – Can an ESOP purchase life insurance on the life of a key employee of the corporation?

Answer – The ESOP can purchase life insurance, commonly referred to as "key person" life insurance, on the life of an important employee of the corporation. The ESOP can use monies contributed to it by the corporation to pay the premiums, provided, however, that the amount of dollars used for the purchase of such insurance is limited to ensure that the ESOP meets the requirements of investing primarily in qualifying employer securities. On the death of the insured, the ESOP would be the beneficiary of the life insurance and could then use the proceeds for the purchase of shares of stock from the insured, thereby providing a market for the insured's stock as well as liquidity in the insured's estate.

Question – Can an ESOP purchase life insurance and make the proceeds payable to the beneficiaries of employees participating in the ESOP?

Answer – An ESOP may provide life insurance for its participants so long as the insurance is deemed "incidental." The plan will generally meet this requirement if the premiums for any participant do not exceed 25% of the amount allocated to his or her ESOP account.

Question – If a shareholder makes a sale of "qualified securities" to the ESOP, can the replacement securities be transferred to a revocable trust or other form of grantor trust?

Answer – The IRS has ruled that such a transfer will not result in a recapture of the gain rolled over, and that any purchases of stock by the trust will be deemed purchases by the grantor.[39]

Question – Assume that there is only one key person in a corporation and that key person owns 100% of the stock of the corporation. Is an ESOP an appropriate estate planning tool to use if there is no one in management who wishes to, or who is capable of continuing the business?

Answer – The ESOP sometimes does not present an appropriate estate planning tool in this situation because the obligation to continue the business would be on the trustee of the ESOP. It can be very difficult to find a trustee willing to take the responsibility for operating the business. However, this problem can be avoided by finding another company (possibly a competitor) or person who will want to acquire the corporation at the stockholder's death.

Question – Can an ESOP be used to purchase the majority of the stock of a corporation from present owners?

Answer – There is no problem with a transfer of ownership from present stockholders to employees through an ESOP purchase of the present owners' stock.

Question – A man entitled to $50,000 from an ESOP dies having designated his adult son as the beneficiary of his plan benefits. Assume the funds are community property, and that the wife did not consent to the beneficiary designation. Can the wife be deprived of her 50% share of the pension benefits by her husband's action? If she did consent, has she made a taxable gift to her son of $25,000?

Answer – Certain restrictions are imposed on a married participant's ability to name a beneficiary for plan death benefits other than the surviving spouse. Generally, unless the surviving spouse is designated as the sole beneficiary, a qualified plan is required to pay plan benefits in the form of a "qualified preretirement survivor annuity" for participants who die prior to reaching retirement age and in the form of a "qualified joint and survivor annuity" for married participants who die after reaching retirement age (see Chapter 52).

With respect to the community property rights, in most community property states, the wife cannot be deprived of her community property interest by her husband's unilateral action of naming their son as the sole beneficiary. Thus, she is entitled to $25,000 from the plan. If the plan has already paid the funds to the son, the plan could be liable to the wife. Thus, it is important for plans to verify the existence or nonexistence of community property rights before distributing benefits. If the wife consented to the designation of the son as beneficiary, however, she would have no claim. It may be found that the surviving spouse has made a taxable gift to the son.

Question – Can an employer make contributions in excess of the annual additions limit to pay interest on a loan obtained by an ESOP to buy employer stock?

Answer – Employer contributions applied to pay loan interest, and forfeitures of fully leveraged (loaned) employer stock owned by the ESOP are disregarded for purposes of the annual additions limit on contributions to a participant's account in the ESOP; however, this rule applies only if deductible contributions allocated to "highly compensated employees" (as defined in Code section 414(q) – see Chapter 52), are not more than one-third of the total contributions.[40] Furthermore, this applies only to C corporation ESOPs, not S corporations.[41]

Question – What types of employer stock qualify as "employer securities" for purposes of an ESOP?

Answer – An ESOP must be designed to invest primarily in "employer securities." Shares of common stock of an employer that are readily tradable on an established securities market are "employer securities." If the employer has no stock that is publicly traded, "employer securities" are shares of common stock issued by the employer with a combination of voting power and dividend rights equal or greater than the classes of common stock of the employer with the greatest voting power and dividend rights. Noncallable preferred stock can be "employer securities" if the preferred stock is convertible at any time into common stock meeting the above requirements, and the conversion price is reasonable.[42]

Question – Are pre-age 59½ distributions from ESOPs assessed a 10% excise tax?

Answer – Generally, yes, with the exception of certain dividends paid on ESOP stock.[43] Certain pre-1990

ESOP distributions were exempt from the early distribution excise tax, but that exception was repealed by TAMRA '88. Some legislators have proposed reinstating the ESOP exception to the early withdrawal penalty, since current law requires an ESOP to distribute benefits to terminated employees without regard to age. Some have argued that it is improper to subject a mandatory distribution to a penalty tax.

Question – Can an S corporation implement an ESOP?

Answer – Yes. The Small Business Job Protection Act of 1996 (SBJPA '96) provided that certain trusts (i.e., including an ESOP trust) may be a shareholder in an S corporation in tax years beginning after 1997. Furthermore, the Taxpayer Relief Act of 1997 (TRA '97) provided that an ESOP established by an S corporation is not required to grant participants the right to receive distributions in the form of employer stock, provided that distributions will otherwise be made in cash equivalent to the fair market value of the stock.[44] The 1997 provision was enacted to prevent inadvertent termination of S corporation status where ESOP participants could demand distributions in the form of stock, thus causing the total number of shareholders to exceed the 75 shareholder limit permitted for corporations maintaining an S election.

Under EGTRRA 2001, provisions generally effective for plan years ending after March 14, 2001 are designed to restrict the allocations that can be made to owners in small S corporation ESOPs. Generally, an allocation under the plan to a person who owns 10% directly, or 20% indirectly (or more), of the S corporation may result in a 50% excise tax against the plan, an additional 50% excise tax on certain shares of the S corporation, and current income taxation of the allocation. The new rules are intended to limit perceived abuses of the ESOP provisions by S corporations designed primarily to benefit highly compensated employees.[45]

Question – How will S corporation income be treated in the hands of an ESOP?

Answer – S corporation income is not treated as unrelated business taxable income ("UBTI").[46] Prior to the legislative protection enacted by TRA '97, ESOP participants were technically subject to the unrelated business income tax on their proportionate share of items of S corporation income. This protection extends to S corporation income or loss on employer securities.

Question – In general, does an ESOP provide much in the way of tax benefits?

Answer – Yes. ESOPs are presently one of the most effective tax minimization techniques available under the Internal Revenue Code! The arguments of former Senator Russell Long still prevail to the effect that employers should be given significant tax incentives to persuade them to make their employees owners of the business.

ASRS: Sec. 59, ¶270.1.1.

CHAPTER ENDNOTES

1. See IRC Secs. 401, 4975(e)(7); ERISA Secs. 407(d)(1), (5) and (6); 408(e).
2. See IRC Secs. 404(a)(3), 404(a)(9).
3. IRC Sec. 172.
4. IRC Secs. 4975(e)(7), 409(h)(1)(B).
5. See generally, IRC Sec. 401(a).
6. Treas. Reg. §1.401(l)-1(a)(4).
7. ERISA Sec. 402(a)(1).
8. IRC Sec. 401(a).
9. ERISA Sec. 408(e); IRC Sec. 401(a)(28)(C).
10. IRC Sec. 401(a)(22). This rule applies to employer stock acquired after December 31, 1979.
11. IRC Sec. 401(a)(28)(B). This applies only to stock acquired after December 31, 1986.
12. IRC Sec. 409(o). This rule applies only with respect to distributions attributable to stock acquired after December 31, 1986,
13. IRC Sec. 409(n).
14. See IRC Sec. 4975(e)(2)(H).
15. IRC Sec. 133, prior to repeal by SBJPA '96.
16. See, e.g., Rev. Proc. 2004-4, 2004-1 IRB 125.
17. See Treas. Regs. §§54.4975-7, 54.4975-11.
18. Treas. Reg. §1.401-1(b)(iii).
19. IRC Sec. 404(a)(3)(A)(i)(I), as amended by EGTRRA 2001. It should be noted that all provisions of EGTRRA 2001 are scheduled to sunset (expire) for years beginning after December 31, 2010.
20. IRC Sec. 404(a)(3)(A)(ii). Special rules apply to unused pre-1987 contribution carryforwards. See IRC Sec. 404(a)(3)(A)(v).
21. IRC Sec. 404(a)(7).
22. IRC Sec. 404(a)(9).
23. IRC Sec. 415(c)(6).
24. Rev. Rul. 73-345, 1973-2 CB 11.
25. IRC Sec. 404(k).
26. IRC Sec. 404(k)(2)(A). This rule applies to tax years beginning after 2001.
27. IRC Sec. 4979A.
28. IRC Sec. 409(n)(2).
29. IRC Sec. 409(n)(3)(A).
30. See IRC Secs. 409(p), 4979A. See the question, "Can an S corporation implement an ESOP?" under the Questions and Answers, for additional information.
31. *Boggs v. Boggs*, 117 S.Ct. 1754 (1997).
32. IRC Sec. 401(m).
33. IRC Sec. 402(e)(4)(B).
34. IRC Sec. 402(e)(4)(A).
35. IRC Sec. 402(e)(4)(A).
36. IRC Sec. 402(e)(4)(A).
37. Treas. Reg. §54.4975-7(b)(4).
38. Treas. Reg. §54.4975-7(b)(9).
39. Let. Rul. 9141046.
40. IRC Sec. 415(c)(6).
41. IRC Sec. 404(a)(9)(C).
42. IRC Secs. 4975(e)(8), 409(l).
43. See IRC Sec. 72(t)(2)(A)(vi).
44. IRC Sec. 1361(c)(6), IRC Sec. 409(h)(2)(B).
45. IRC Secs. 409(p), 4979A. For ESOPs established after March 14, 2001, and ESOPs that in effect on or before March 14, 2001 for which an S election was not in effect on that date, the new rules apply for plan years ending after March 14, 2001. For any other ESOPs, the amendments generally apply to plan years beginning after 2004.
46. IRC Sec. 512(e)(3).

Chapter 50

HR-10 (KEOGH) RETIREMENT PLAN FOR THE SELF-EMPLOYED

WHAT IS IT?

Under an HR-10 (Keogh) plan, a self-employed individual (this term includes a sole proprietor and partners who have earned income) is allowed to take a tax deduction for money he sets aside to provide for retirement. The HR-10 plan is also a means of providing retirement security for employees working for the self-employed individual.

WHEN IS THE USE OF SUCH A DEVICE INDICATED?

1. When there is a desire on the part of the self-employed individual to provide personal retirement funds.

2. When there is a desire on the part of the self-employed individual to provide financial security for the retirement of his or her employees.

3. When the self-employed individual would like to defer tax on otherwise currently taxable income.

WHAT ARE THE REQUIREMENTS?

1. HR-10 eligibility rules are the same as those for corporate plans. Full time employees who are below age 21 or who have less than one year of service may be excluded from coverage. However, a plan may require two years of service if there is 100% immediate vesting for each participant. A year of service generally means a 12-month period during which the employee has worked at least 1,000 hours.[1]

   Likewise, an HR-10 plan must meet the minimum participation, coverage and nondiscrimination rules applicable to corporate qualified plans.[2] See the discussion in Chapter 52 under "Eligibility."

2. HR-10 plans must meet the minimum vesting standards applicable to regular corporate plans. Vesting refers to the nonforfeitability of employer contributions for covered employees. Full vesting is required after five years or after seven years under an accelerated graduated vesting schedule.[3] Faster vesting is required for top-heavy plans and for the match portion of traditional 401(k) plans.[4]

3. An HR-10 plan must be in writing.[5] The plan can be described in an individually drafted trust instrument or in a master or prototype plan. A "master plan" refers to a standardized form of plan, with or without a trust, administered by an insurance company or bank acting as the funding medium for purposes of providing benefits on a standardized basis. In a master plan, the sponsoring organization both funds the benefits and administers the plan.

   A "prototype plan" refers to a standardized form of plan which is made available by the sponsoring organization for use without change by a self-employed individual who wishes to adopt such a plan. A prototype plan will not be administered by the sponsoring organization. The employer (the self-employed individual) administers the plan. Internal Revenue Service approval of the plan is generally sought by the sponsoring organization.

   An HR-10 plan is not required to have an institutional trustee, such as a bank or insured credit union. Thus, the owner-employee maintaining the plan can be the trustee.

4. In addition to the creation of a written instrument, the owner-employee must make a contribution in order to bring the plan into being.

   In addition to the above requirements, there are a number of others that an HR-10 plan must meet in order to be "qualified" under section 401(a) of the Internal Revenue Code. The advantages of being "qualified" are many, including a current deduction for contributions to the plan and deferred taxation of benefits until distribution.

HOW IT IS DONE – AN EXAMPLE

Your client, Marvin Gimpel, is a druggist. He has four full-time employees. Marvin's earned income is $80,000 a year. All his employees have more than one year of service and have attained age 21. Two of his assistants earn $20,000 each, and two other clerks earn $10,000 a year each, a total of $60,000.

Marvin establishes an HR-10 plan. The plan calls for contributions of 10% of his earned income to be used to provide a pension for him and contributions of 10% of each employee's earnings to provide for their retirements. Since his employees' total salary is $60,000, he would contribute $6,000 for his employees, or 10% of the $60,000 of salary.

Marvin could deduct this entire amount. After making the contribution, however, his own earned income drops to $74,000 ($80,000 minus his $6,000 contribution). However, his earned income would drop further because it is computed after taking into account amounts contributed by the self-employed individual to the HR-10 plan for himself, as well as for his common law employees.[6] Thus, a formula is needed to determine how much he can contribute on his behalf, since one cannot know what the contribution will be until after one knows how much the earned income is for the self-employed individual, and one does not know what the earned income is until one knows what the contribution will be. This calculation is further complicated by the deduction for one-half of the self-employment tax permitted for self-employed individuals.[7] Both calculations are explained at the question and answer on "earned income," below.

WHAT ARE THE TAX IMPLICATIONS?

1. Contributions made on behalf of an owner-employee to an HR-10 plan are deductible from gross income on the owner-employee's federal income tax return.[8] Although substantial parity has been established between HR-10 plans and corporate qualified plans for federal tax purposes, some states may still allow a lower deduction for contributions to an HR-10 plan.

2. The deductible deposits made by an employer are not currently taxable either to the employer himself or to a participating employee. No tax will be paid until benefits are actually received.[9]

3. Income earned by assets in the plan accumulates tax-free.[10]

4. A lump-sum distribution receives basically the same tax treatment that a similar distribution would receive from a corporate-sponsored qualified plan.[11]

5. Plan benefits are subject to estate tax to the same extent as any other asset.[12]

6. The maximum contribution allowed to a defined contribution plan on behalf of a self-employed individual is limited to the lesser of (a) 100% of earned income, or (b) $41,000 (in 2004, as indexed).[13] This is known as the annual additions limit, or the Section 415 limit.

    The annual additions limit does not apply to *defined benefit* HR-10 plans; they are subject to a separate Section 415 limit based on the benefit promised by the plan. Contributions to defined benefit plans are based on actuarial calculations designed to accumulate a reserve large enough to pay the retirement benefits provided by the plan. A defined benefit HR-10 plan based on retirement as early as age 62 can be funded to provide an annual retirement benefit of the lesser of 100% of the participant's average compensation for his highest paid three years of participation or $165,000 (as indexed for 2004).[14] This limit is indexed for inflation in increments of $5,000. If retirement benefits are to commence prior to age 62, the limit is reduced.[15]

7. An owner-employee may make nondeductible voluntary contributions (like a common law employee), in addition to his deductible contribution. All such contributions are counted for purposes of the annual additions limitation and must conform to the special nondiscrimination test provided in Code section 401(m).

8. The deduction limits on contributions to HR-10 plans depend on the type of plan. In the case of defined contribution plans, the deductible amount is 25% of total compensation of plan participants (earned income in the case of the self-employed individual).[16] (For plan years beginning prior to 2002, the deduction amount for profit sharing plans was limited to 15% of total compensation, and a higher limit of 25% applied to defined contribution *pension* plans, such as money purchase pensions.[17]) In the case of a defined benefit plan, the amount that is deductible is the amount actuarially determined to be necessary to pay for the benefits promised.[18] In no event, however, can amounts in excess of the Section 415 limits (discussed in paragraph 6, above) be deducted.[19]

9. There is a 10% annual nondeductible excise tax on "excess" contributions (i.e., contributions above the deductible limits mentioned above) made to the plan until the excess is eliminated, subject to certain exceptions.[20]

10. A 10% penalty tax is imposed on distributions before the participant attains age 59½, with certain exceptions (death, divorce, disability, payments made over the participant's life, and extraordinary medical expenses).[21] In the case of a SIMPLE IRA plan, the penalty is increased to 25% during the first two years of participation.

IMPLICATIONS AND ISSUES IN COMMUNITY PROPERTY STATES

The benefit accumulated in an HR-10 plan for an employee who was married during his participation in the plan while a resident of a community property state belongs equally to the employee and his or her spouse. The employee and spouse can, however, change the normal effect of community property laws by an agreement, such as a pre-nuptial agreement, to the effect that all earnings of the individual will be community property but that contributions to a qualified retirement plan for the employee's benefit will be solely the employee's property. However, the joint and survivor annuity rules of Section 401(a)(11) limit the ability of a married participant to solely retain plan benefits without the consent of the participant's spouse (see Chapter 52).

Another frequent issue concerns individuals moving from common law to community property states. For instance, assume a married employee was a resident of a non-community property state for 10 years. He and his wife then moved to California where they resided for five years. Contributions were made to an HR-10 plan each year on his behalf throughout the 15-year period. What is the status of ownership of benefits accumulated in the plan over the fifteen-year period? The answer is that a portion of the benefits will be community property. Depending on the circumstances, a court may determine the community property portion on the basis of the "contributions made" or the "time" method.

The "contributions made" method would divide the benefits in the proportion of contributions made after moving to the community property state, plus earnings, to the total amount in the plan. The "time" method would divide benefits on the basis of proportionate years of participation in the plan (i.e., one-third of the benefits would be community property).

Each method has advantages and disadvantages. If annual contributions for the employee were greater in the years in which he lived in a community property state, the "time" method would cause more of the benefits to be separate property than the "contributions made" method. Other methods of dividing community property HR-10 benefits could be used where appropriate.

The non-community property portion of the HR-10 benefit would be the separate property of the employee. In the event of a divorce or the death of the employee, California law provides that certain separate property of the employee will be treated as community property for purposes of division on divorce or the employee's death. This separate property is referred to as quasi-community property. Generally, quasi-community property is personal property, wherever situated, and real property situated in California, which would have been community property had the owner acquired it in California. For all purposes other than division on divorce or the employee's death, the benefits remain the employee's separate property. Thus, if the employee's wife predeceases him, her estate would not have any rights to any part of the separate property portion of the HR-10 benefits.

QUESTIONS AND ANSWERS

Question – What is meant by the term "earned income"?

Answer – Earned income is, generally, net earnings derived from a self-employed individual's business as a result of personal efforts or personal service rendered, as distinguished from investment income. Therefore, inactive owners, such as limited partners, whose income is derived solely from an investment made in the partnership, have no earned income from the firm.

Generally, the entire net earnings received by a self-employed individual who is an attorney, an accountant, a physician, or other professional, is considered as earned income. However, for purposes of determining earned income, net earnings must be adjusted. Adjusted net earnings means gross earnings less all allowable business deductions, allowable deductions under Code sections 62 and 404 pertaining to contributions to a qualified plan, and the deduction for one-half of the self-employed individual's self-employment tax.[22] The allowable deductions for HR-10 contributions include not only the deductions for common law employees but deductions for self-employed individuals as well.

If deductions for self-employed individuals must be taken into account before determining such self-employed individual's "earned income," a complex situation presents itself. One cannot determine a self-employed individual's earned income until the allowable contribution for him is known. The allowable contribution cannot be determined until his earned income is known. In some cases, an interdependent variable formula will be needed to determine the proper deductible contribution. Added to this complexity is the fact that the IRS has ruled that self-employment tax must be computed and the deduction for one-half of the self-employment tax must be taken before determining the HR-10 contribution.[23]

Self-employment tax is determined by subtracting 7.65% from the self-employed individual's net earnings. In 2004, net earnings up to $87,900 are subject to 12.4% OASDI tax and all net earnings are subject to 2.9% for hospital insurance tax. One-half of the self-employment tax is then subtracted from net earnings (i.e., 6.2% OASDI and 1.45% HI). The resulting figure is the base amount used to determine the self-employed individual's HR-10 contribution.[24]

Determining the HR-10 contribution is relatively simple when there are no employees. For example, if the self-employed individual's net earnings (after deducting one-half of self-employment tax) are $60,000, multiply that amount by 20% to obtain the maximum contribution allowable on his behalf. The figure arrived at is $12,000. That is the same figure computed by multiplying his $48,000 earned income ($60,000 - $12,000) by 25%.

Calculating the self-employed individual's maximum contribution is not difficult even if there are employees. For instance, assume a payroll of $10,000 for other employees. If that amount is multiplied by 25%, a $2,500 contribution must be made on behalf of those employees. This drops the $60,000 base for determining the self-employed individual's contribution in the example above down to $57,500. If $57,500 is then multiplied by 20%, a contribution of $11,500 is arrived at. This is the same as if his earned income of $46,000 ($57,500 - $11,500) was multiplied by 25%.

Question – Can an individual who is a full-time corporate employee but who conducts independent consulting work or "moonlights" and receives fees make contributions based on self-employment income?

Answer – Yes. For example, Sel Horvitz, a practicing attorney who teaches three days a week at a local law school and who is participating in the school's tax deferred annuity plan, can still set up an HR-10 plan for himself based on the income earned in private practice. However, there are overall "all plans" limits, which may not be exceeded. In 2004, Sel can also contribute to a traditional or Roth IRA up to a maximum of $3,000 (plus catch-up amounts if he is age 50 or over), or 100% of his compensation, whichever is lower.[25] However, the availability of a tax deduction for his traditional IRA contributions will depend in part on whether his income falls within the limits discussed in Chapter 51.[26] Tax deferred compounding of traditional IRA contributions still occurs, even if the contribution to the IRA is not deductible.[27]

Question – Under what circumstances can benefits be paid from an HR-10 plan?

Answer – A 10% early distribution penalty is imposed on distributions before the participant attains age 59½, with certain exceptions (death, divorce, disability, payments made over the participant's life, and deductible medical expenses).[28]

In addition, an HR-10 plan generally *must* begin distributing benefits by April 1 of the year following the year the employee attains age 70½; however, as with all corporate qualified plans, the plan may delay distributions until April 1 of the year following the year an employee retires, provided he is not a more-than-5% owner.[29] (See Chapter 52 for other distribution requirements.)

Question – What is a lump sum distribution?

Answer – A distribution will be considered to be made in a "lump sum" if (a) it is made within one taxable year of the recipient, (b) it consists of the balance of the employee's account, and (c) it occurs under one of the following circumstances:

1. On account of the death of an employee or self-employed person.

2. After the disability of a self-employed person.

3. After a self-employed individual or any other employee attains age 59½ (even if employment has not yet terminated).[30]

Question – How may contributions be invested?

Answer – HR-10 plan funds can be invested in life insurance contracts (subject to limitations), mutual funds, variable annuities, government bonds, savings accounts, securities, real estate, etc., or a combination of these funding media.

Question – Can pre-retirement death benefits be provided under an HR-10 plan?

Answer – Yes. Immediate and substantial death benefits can be made available through life insurance to beneficiaries of the self-employed individual and other plan participants. These benefits will be received income tax free and can be coordinated with the personal life insurance programs of the participants. (Note, however, that the cash value portion of the death benefit will be subject to income tax.)[31]

Question – If life insurance is used in a plan and paid for by employer contributions to the plan, is any of the premium taxable to the employee?

Answer – The cost of pure insurance is taxable as a current economic benefit. For common law employees the amount the covered person must include is based on government tables.[32] The cost of insurance for a self-employed person is not a deductible contribution. (Pure insurance is the difference between the face amount of the policy, i.e., the death benefit, and the policy's cash value.)[33]

For example, if a $1,000 premium is paid for an ordinary life insurance policy and $150 of the premium represents the cost of pure life insurance, an employee is taxed currently on $150, and a self-employed individual cannot deduct the $150.

Any deductible employee contributions that are applied toward the purchase of life insurance will be treated as a distribution in the year so applied.[34]

Question – Many HR-10 plans are "defined contribution plans," that is, the pension benefit at retirement will be whatever a specified contribution, plus appreciation on the contributions, will earn. Are there other types of plans?

Answer – Yes. There are two general types of plans: defined contribution plans and defined benefit plans. A defined contribution plan can be a profit sharing plan, as described above, or a pension plan (e.g., a money purchase plan) in which a definitely determinable benefit is provided to employees, generally at retirement. In a profit sharing plan,

contributions are based on a formula that is applied to the earned income (the profits) of the self-employed individual. A defined contribution pension plan, such as a money purchase plan, provides for fixed (required) contributions that are used to purchase a retirement benefit.

A defined benefit plan is the alternative to a defined contribution plan. Under a defined benefit plan, a predetermined (i.e., defined) annual retirement benefit is funded on an annual basis. A defined benefit formula may have some advantages for the self-employed person over a defined contribution formula. First, contributions are not subject to the annual additions limit (see item (6) under "What are the Tax Implications" above for the Section 415 limit for defined benefit plans). Second, the proportionate contribution for other employees may be lower than in a defined contribution plan, especially if the other employees are younger than the self-employed person.

Question – In an HR-10 plan, may employees below a certain age be excluded from coverage?

Answer – Yes, an HR-10 plan may require the same eligibility requirements as a corporate qualified plan (see "Eligibility," at Chapter 52).

Question – What must a sole proprietor or partnership do to set up an HR-10 plan?

Answer – To set up an HR-10 defined contribution or defined benefit plan, a plan that meets the applicable requirements for tax qualification must be adopted on or before the last day of the proprietor's or partnership's tax year. Employees must be informed in writing of the plan and contributions must be made within the period required for filing the sole proprietor's or partnership's income tax return (including extensions). In contrast, a simplified employee pension (SEP) may be adopted after the end of the plan year, but before the due date (including extensions) of the sole proprietor's or partnership's income tax return.

Question – If a self-employed individual contributes less than the maximum amount allowed in any one year, can he make catch-up contributions in the next tax year?

Answer – Generally, no. The deduction for contributions to an HR-10 plan for self-employed individuals is allowed only on a year-to-year basis. The law has no provisions allowing the carryover of an unused deduction for HR-10 contributions. Thus, if the amount contributed in a given year was less than the amount allowable, the self-employed individual cannot make it up and deduct more than the allowable amount in the following year.[35] Similarly, a self-employed individual who contributes less than the amount permitted under Section 415 may not carry over unused amounts.

Certain elective deferral plans (e.g., 401(k) plans, SIMPLE IRAs, SAR-SEPs) may provide for catch-up contributions for individuals who have reached age 50 by the end of the plan year.[36]

Question – Can an excess contribution be made to an HR-10 plan without penalty?

Answer – No. Contributions exceeding the deductible limit are subject to an excise tax equal to 10% of the nondeductible contribution each year until the excess is eliminated.[37]

Question – Can a loan be made from an HR-10 plan to a self-employed person without it being treated as a taxable distribution?

Answer – Yes.[38] Within certain limits a loan from an HR-10 plan that must be repaid within five years will not be considered a taxable distribution, provide it does not exceed the lesser of $50,000 or one-half of the employee's nonforfeitable accrued benefit under the plan. (However, a loan of up to $10,000 can be permitted, even if it is more than half the employee's accrued benefit.) The $50,000 limit is reduced by the highest outstanding loan balance during the prior 12-month period.[39] This effectively prohibits "rollovers" of loans in excess of $25,000.

The loan must bear a reasonable rate of interest, be adequately secured, provide a reasonable repayment schedule, and be made available on a basis that does not discriminate in favor of highly compensated employees. The 5-year repayment rule does not apply to loans used for residential mortgages.[40] A loan in excess of these prescribed limits would be treated as a taxable distribution.

In years prior to 2002, loans to "owner-employees" were included in the definition of prohibited transactions, and thus were unavailable.[41]

Question – What is a "top heavy" HR-10 plan? Of what significance is the term?

Answer – Any plan is a "top heavy" plan if as of the determination date (generally, the last day of the preceding plan year or last day of a new plan's first year) the present value of the aggregate accrued benefits of "key employees" in a defined benefit plan or the account balances of "key employees" in a defined contribution plan exceed 60% of the aggregate accrued benefits or account balances of all employees.[42] Under this definition, most HR-10 plans will be considered "top heavy."

Generally, a key employee is any employee-participant who, at any time during the plan year is an officer earning more than $130,000, a more than 5% owner, or a more than 1% owner earning more than $150,000 a year.[43] In years beginning before January 1, 2002, "key employees" included any officer earning more than 50% of the Section 415 dollar limit, any employee owning one of the ten largest interests in the employer, and anyone who met the definition (as then in effect) during a 4-year lookback period.

If a plan is considered "top heavy" certain additional requirements must be met. These include:

(1) Rapid vesting–A top heavy plan must provide for vesting under one of two alternative schedules. One schedule provides that any employee with three years of service must be 100% vested. The other alternative provides a 6-year graduated schedule beginning after two years of service.

(2) Minimum non-integrated contribution or benefit for non-key employees–For a defined contribution plan, the employer generally must contribute for a non-key employee an amount equal to at least 3% of that participant's compensation. However, if the key employee uses a percentage for himself that is lower, that percentage may be used.

For a defined benefit plan, the benefit for a non-key employee which must be accrued is at least 2% of the employee's average annual compensation multiplied by the employee's years of service with the employer in which a top heavy plan year ends. The minimum benefit, however, need not exceed 20% of such annual compensation. Years of service before January 1, 1984 need not be counted.

SIMPLE IRAs, SIMPLE 401(k) plans and safe harbor 401(k) plans, are generally exempt from the top heavy requirements.[44] Furthermore, the vesting, minimum benefits and limits on compensation requirements do not apply to any employee who is represented by a collective bargaining unit where evidence exists that retirement benefits were the subject of good faith bargaining.

Question – Can plans covering self-employed individuals be integrated with Social Security?

Answer – Yes, an HR-10 plan may be integrated under the same rules that apply to corporate plans. (The terminology used in the regulations refers to "permitted disparity" instead of integration.) For example, in the case of defined contribution plans, the contribution rate (%) that applies to compensation above the taxable wage base may not exceed the contribution rate (%) that applies to compensation below the taxable wage base by more than the *lesser of* (1) the rate applied to compensation below the wage base or (2) 5.7% points (or, if greater, the rate of social security tax attributable to old-age insurance).[45] Thus, if the plan provides for contributions of 10% of pay in excess of the wage base, it would be properly integrated if it provided for contributions of at least 5% on pay below the wage base.

Question – Are Keogh plans subject to the survivor annuity rules under Code Section 417?

Answer – Yes; the survivor annuity requirements apply to any defined benefit or defined contribution plan, which would include an HR-10 plan. This means that in the event a married owner-employee retires, the retirement income must be in the form of a qualified joint and survivor annuity, unless the spouse has consented to an alternate form of distribution. If the owner-employee dies leaving a surviving spouse, there must be a qualified survivor annuity for the surviving spouse. This requirement may be waived; see the discussion in Chapter 52.

CHAPTER ENDNOTES

1. IRC Sec. 410(a).
2. IRC Secs. 401(a)(4), 410(b), 401(a)(26).
3. IRC Sec. 411(a)(2).
4. See IRC Sec. 416(b) and IRC Sec. 411(a) (12). It is important to remember that all provisions of EGTRRA 2001 sunset (or expire) for years beginning after December 31, 2010. The schedule for employer matching contributions or top heavy plans is three years for cliff (full) vesting, or graduated vesting over 3-7 years (at the rate of 20% each year) or faster. The rule requiring faster vesting for matching contributions to traditional 401(k) plans applies for years beginning after 2001.
5. IRC Sec. 402(a)(1).
6. IRC Sec. 401(c)(2)(A).
7. IRC Sec. 164(f).
8. IRC Sec. 62(a)(6). Contributions on behalf of common law employees are deductible under Sec. 404(a).
9. IRC Sec. 402(a); Treas. Reg. §1.402(a)-1(a)(1)(i).
10. IRC Sec. 501(a).
11. IRC Sec. 402(d).
12. IRC Sec. 2039. In years beginning before 1985, certain plan benefits were subject to an estate tax exclusion. The Tax Reform Act of 1984 contained a provision which permitted individuals who were both in pay status and had made an irrevocable election as to the form of benefit distribution to continue to have the benefit of the estate tax exclusion (the unlimited exclusion for participants in pay status prior to January 1, 1983, or the $100,000 exclusion for participants in pay status prior to January 1, 1985). The Tax Reform Act of 1986 somewhat liberalized the grandfathering provisions by providing that the participant no longer needed to have been in pay status as of the applicable date. The participant needed only to have separated from service prior to the applicable date and not to have made any change in the form of benefit to be paid.
13. IRC Sec. 415(c)(1)(A).
14. IRC Sec. 415(b).
15. IRC Sec. 415(b)(2)(C).
16. IRC Sec. 404(a)(3)(A).
17. IRC Sec. 404(a)(3)(A).
18. IRC Sec. 404(a)(1)(A).
19. IRC Sec. 404(j).
20. IRC Sec. 4972.
21. IRC Sec. 72(t).
22. IRC Sec. 401(c)(2)(A).
23. GCM 39807.
24. See IRS Pub. 560, "Retirement Plans for the Self-Employed."
25. See IRC Sec. 219(b).
26. IRC Sec. 219(g).
27. IRC Sec. 408(o).
28. IRC Sec. 72(t).
29. IRC Sec. 401(a)(9).
30. IRC Sec. 402(d)(4)(A).
31. IRC Sec. 72(m)(3)(C).
32. Treas. Regs. §§1.402(a)-1(a)(3); 1.72-16. For guidance explaining the replacement of the P.S. 58 rates with the Table 2001 rates, see Notice 2001-10, 2001-1 CB 459. For additional details, see the questions and answers for Chapter 30.
33. IRC Sec. 404(e).
34. IRC Sec. 72(o)(3).
35. IRC Sec. 404(a)(3)(A).
36. See IRC Sec. 414(v).
37. IRC Sec. 4972.
38. See IRC Sec. 4975(f)(6). This rule applies for years beginning after 2001; prior to 2002, plan loans were not permitted for self-employed individuals.
39. IRC Sec. 72(p)(2)(A).
40. IRC Sec. 72(p)(2)(B).
41. IRC Sec. 4975(d)(1). Under certain circumstances, an administrative exemption could be obtained from the Department of Labor for a loan to an owner-employee. See ERISA Sec. 408(d).
42. IRC Sec. 416(g).
43. IRC Sec. 416(i).
44. See IRC Sec. 416(g).
45. IRC Sec. 401(l).

Chapter 51

INDIVIDUAL RETIREMENT PLANS (and SEPs)

WHAT IS A TRADITIONAL IRA?

Any individual who is not participating in a qualified private or governmental pension plan, profit-sharing plan, HR-10 plan, or tax sheltered annuity can set up a traditional individual retirement account (IRA) and take a deduction from gross income equal to the lesser of: (1) $3,000 (for 2004) or (2) 100% of compensation includable in his gross income for the taxable year.[1] For years 2005-2007, the limit is $4,000. For 2008-2010, it is $5,000. Also, the $5,000 amount will be indexed for inflation in increments of $500 for years beginning after 2008. Additionally, taxpayers who have attained the age of 50 can make an additional $500 contribution each year through 2005. Beginning in 2006, they can make additional contributions of $1,000.[2]

If an individual or his spouse is actively participating in a qualified plan or tax sheltered annuity, the maximum annual contribution may be made to an IRA, subject to certain limitations. The tax deduction for this contribution to an IRA is allowed in full to the extent that the taxpayer's adjusted gross income ("AGI") does not exceed an applicable threshold. These thresholds vary according to the taxpayer's filing status and the tax year.[3] The thresholds are as follows:

AGI Threshold

Tax Year	Single Returns	Joint Returns
2004	45,000	65,000
2005	50,000	70,000
2006	50,000	75,000
2007 and thereafter	50,000	80,000

The threshold remains zero for married individuals filing a separate return. For non-active participants with an active participant spouse, the deduction begins to phase out when AGI exceeds $150,000. For a taxpayer who exceeds these thresholds, the maximum deduction is reduced by the following formula

$$\text{Maximum annual contribution} \times \frac{\text{AGI minus AGI Threshold}}{\$10,000}$$

Example: In 2004, Sarah's AGI is $47,000. Sarah is unmarried, and is an active participant in a qualified retirement plan. The applicable threshold for 2004 is $45,000. If Sarah contributes $3,000 to her IRA for taxable year 2004, her deduction is reduced by $600 [$3,000 x (($47,000 - $45,000) ÷ $10,000)]. Thus, Sarah may claim a deduction on her return for 2004 of $2,400 ($3,000 - $600).

For married individuals filing a joint return *after* 2006, the denominator of the ratio in the formula above is increased to $20,000. All taxpayers may continue to make a nondeductible IRA contribution of up to the lesser of the dollar limit or 100% of compensation, to the extent that contributions to all IRA accounts (including Roth IRAs, discussed below) do not exceed the maximum annual limit in total.

For married individuals filing a joint return, if only one spouse is a participant in an employer-sponsored plan, the limit on deductible IRA contributions applies only to the participant spouse. The non-participant spouse may be eligible to make a deductible IRA contribution. However, the deductible IRA contribution limit begins to phase out for the non-participant spouse if the couple's adjusted gross income is above $150,000. It is eliminated at $160,000. In other words, the threshold in the previous ratio is $150,000 and the denominator is $10,000. Note that in this situation, the $10,000 amount is *not* increased to $20,000 for tax years beginning after 2006.

Example: Jill is a participant in her employer's retirement plan, but her husband, Jack, is not. They file a joint return in 2004 showing adjusted gross income of $125,000. Jack, as a non-participant in his employer's retirement plan, can make a deductible $3,000 contribution to his IRA (because Jack and Jill's adjusted gross income is under $150,000). However, Jill cannot make a deductible contribution to her IRA because their combined adjusted gross income exceeds the threshold for 2004, discussed above, for a deductible contribution by an active participant filing a joint return.

Example: The facts are the same as above, except that Jack and Jill's combined 2004 adjusted gross income is $200,000. Neither Jack nor Jill can make a deductible IRA contribution. Jack cannot make a deductible contribution, even though he does not participate in his employer's retirement plan, because Jack and Jill's 2004 adjusted gross income exceeds $160,000.

An individual may make a deductible contribution to a spousal IRA for a spouse with less taxable compensation than the individual.[4] Such an individual may deduct the lesser of: (1) the maximum annual limit; or (2) 100% of the spouse's compensation for the taxable year plus 100% of the individual's compensation for the taxable year, less any IRA deductions taken by the individual, less any nondeductible contributions made by the individual, and less any Roth IRA contributions for the individual. The effect of this is to potentially allow a couple with one non-working spouse to contribute and deduct up to twice the maximum annual limit into two traditional IRAs (for example, in 2004, $3,000 could be contributed to one IRA and another $3,000 to a spousal IRA). Simplified employee pensions (SEPs) and SIMPLE IRAs are discussed below in the question and answer section.

ROLLOVERS

The Internal Revenue Code also allows certain individuals receiving certain distributions from a qualified plan (including pension, profit-sharing, stock bonus, or annuity plans) or a tax deferred annuity to "roll over" the distribution within 60 days to an IRA without incurring income tax on the distribution. This tax-free rollover treatment is available to individuals who receive most types of distributions from a qualified plan or tax deferred annuity. Distributions of accumulated deductible employee contributions which were made to such qualified plans or tax deferred annuities may also be rolled over tax free to an IRA (or in some cases even to another qualified employer plan–if such plan permits). No rollover is permitted for benefits attributable to nondeductible employee contributions made by the individual to the qualified plan in years prior to 2002.

EGTRRA 2001 increased the portability of retirement plan assets. Any part of the taxable portion of a distribu-

tion received after 2001 from a qualified retirement plan, tax sheltered annuity, or eligible Section 457 governmental plan can be rolled over without incurring income tax to an IRA or to any of the above listed plans.[5] Also after-tax contributions will be allowed to be rolled over into an IRA.[6] There are exceptions to this general rule allowing rollover treatment. No tax-free rollover is permitted if the distribution is a required minimum distribution, is part of a series of substantially equal payments made over the life expectancy of the plan participant or the joint life expectancies of the participant and his or her beneficiary, or over a period of ten or more years. Additionally, hardship distributions generally will not be eligible for tax-free rollover treatment.[7]

Further, any qualified plan, tax sheltered annuity, or eligible Section 457 governmental plan must allow its participants to elect to have any distribution that is eligible for rollover treatment handled by means of a direct rollover, i.e., a trustee-to-trustee transfer. If this method is not elected, but rather the funds are distributed to the individual participant, a mandatory income tax withholding of 20% must be made. The participant cannot elect out of withholding from such a distribution. This mandatory 20% withholding applies even if the participant receiving the distribution rolls the funds over within 60 days.[8]

Individuals who receive a distribution which includes property can make a bona fide sale of the property and roll over, within the usual 60-day period, all or part of the proceeds to an IRA. It is not necessary to roll over the actual property received.

The spouse of a deceased IRA holder may be able to roll over a distribution received after the deceased spouse's death to an IRA. This is discussed in the question and answer section of this chapter.

WHAT IS A ROTH IRA?

TRA '97 created a new type of IRA called the "Roth IRA."[9] With a Roth IRA, contributions are not deductible but, if certain requirements are met, withdrawals from a Roth IRA may be entirely tax free.

Annual contributions to a Roth IRA may be made up to the lesser of $3,000 (for 2004) or 100% of compensation includable in gross income for the taxable year, reduced by any contributions made to a traditional IRA for that year on the individual's own behalf. For years 2005-2007, the limit is $4,000. For 2008-2010, the limit is $5,000. Also, the $5,000 amount will be indexed for inflation in increments of $500 for years beginning after 2008. Additionally, taxpayers age 50 and above can make additional contributions of $500 for each year through 2005 and additional contributions of $1,000 beginning in 2006. (Contributions to a SIMPLE IRA or a SEP are not taken into account for the maximum annual contribution limit. Additionally, SIMPLE IRAs and SEPs, discussed later in this chapter, may not be designated as Roth IRAs.) Unlike traditional IRAs, contributions can be made after reaching age 70½ so long as the combined earnings of the taxpayer(s) for the year are greater than the combined Roth IRA contributions. Distributions are not required to begin until after death.

If AGI exceeds certain limits, a contribution to a Roth IRA cannot be made for that year. For single taxpayers, the maximum contribution is reduced by: the maximum annual contribution available multiplied by the ratio that the excess of the taxpayer's AGI over $95,000 bears to $15,000. Thus, for single taxpayers, no contributions can be made to a Roth IRA if AGI is more than $110,000 and the amount that may be contributed is reduced proportionately if AGI is between $95,000 and $110,000. For taxpayers filing a joint return, the maximum contribution is reduced by: the maximum annual contribution multiplied by the ratio that the excess of the taxpayer's AGI over $150,000 bears to $10,000. Thus, for joint filers, no contributions can be made to a Roth IRA if AGI is more than $160,000 and the amount that may be contributed is reduced proportionately if AGI is between $150,000 and $160,000. For married taxpayers filing a separate return, the maximum contribution is reduced by: the maximum annual contribution multiplied by the ratio that the excess of the taxpayer's AGI over $0 bears to $10,000. Thus, for married taxpayers filing separately, no contributions can be made to a Roth IRA if AGI is more than $10,000 and the amount that may be contributed is reduced proportionately if AGI is between $0 and $10,000.

The rules on allowable Roth IRA contributions apply without regard to a taxpayer's active participation in a qualified retirement plan. For some clients, the permitted "rollover" of a traditional IRA to a Roth IRA (discussed further in this chapter) may be desirable.

WHAT IS AN ESA?

A non-deductible contribution of up to $2,000 per child in 2004 can be made to a Coverdell Education Savings Account (ESA, formerly known as an Education IRA) to pay qualified education expenses, subject to limits based on AGI.[10] EGTRRA 2001 expanded qualified

education expenses to include elementary and secondary school expenses. (An individual may claim a Hope Scholarship Credit or Lifetime Learning Credit for the same taxable year as amounts distributed from an ESA on behalf of the same student are excluded as long as there are sufficient qualified education expenses to cover both.) An ESA must be designated as such at the time of its creation and is generally exempt from income tax. The designated beneficiary does not include in his or her income either contributions to, or earnings on, an ESA.

The ESA contribution must be made in cash and be made on or before the date on which the designated beneficiary reaches age 18, and total no more than $2,000 per year per beneficiary (except for rollover contributions). The annual contribution per beneficiary is available in full only if the contributor's AGI is $95,000 or less for single taxpayers and is phased out ratably if AGI is between $95,00 and $110,000 for single taxpayers. The phaseout range is between $190,000 and $220,000 for married taxpayers filing jointly.

Contributions must be made by the due date for filing the contributor's income tax return for that year. Thus, contributions to an ESA can be made until April 15 of the following year.

There is an excise tax for excess contributions to an ESA. The excess contribution is the amount of any contribution over the maximum annual limit. The excess contribution tax does not apply if the contribution is returned before the due date of the contributor's income tax return for the taxable year. Excess contributions from previous taxable years, to the extent not corrected, will continue to be taxed as excess contributions in subsequent years.

If a beneficiary's qualified education expenses equal or exceed the total ESA distributions for the taxable year, the distributions are entirely excludable from income. However, if distributions exceed qualified education expenses, only a pro-rata amount is excludable. Amounts includable in income may also be subject to a 10% premature distribution penalty.

WHEN IS THE USE OF SUCH A DEVICE INDICATED?

1. The use of a traditional IRA is indicated when the married client or his spouse is covered under a qualified plan and does not make in excess of the AGI amount at which deductible contributions to an IRA are not permitted. Even if the contribution is

not tax deductible under the above limits, the earnings will accumulate income tax-free, although in such cases, it is likely to be more beneficial to make non-deductible contributions to a Roth IRA rather than a traditional IRA. Additionally, the client should be receiving an income which is not needed by the family to maintain its current standard of living, and which could be put aside for retirement.

2. A traditional IRA is indicated where neither the client nor spouse is covered under a qualified plan, but both work. If the client and spouse are both working, each can have his or her own traditional IRA and contribute up to the maximum based on his or her respective income assuming both otherwise qualify.

3. A traditional IRA is also indicated where the client is not covered under a plan, has earned income, is married, and his or her spouse has no income from employment.

4. A rollover IRA may also be indicated where an individual has received a distribution from a qualified plan, tax sheltered annuity, or an eligible Section 457 governmental plan and seeks to avoid current taxation on all or a part of the distribution.

5. The client may be an employer who does not have any type of qualified retirement plan and would like to establish a plan covering only himself.

6. A Roth IRA is indicated where the client would not otherwise qualify for a deduction for contributing to a traditional IRA. Alternatively, where a client anticipates a reduced need to access IRA funds during retirement, a Roth IRA may be preferred, since the mandatory distribution rules of traditional IRAs (requiring traditional IRAs to be distributed after age 70½ over the participant's lifetime) do not apply to Roth IRAs. Thus, funds can continue to accumulate tax free in a Roth IRA through retirement, preserving more benefits for the heirs.

7. Clients anticipating that they will be in a high marginal tax bracket following retirement may benefit more from the tax-free withdrawal benefit of the Roth IRA than from the initial deduction associated with traditional IRAs. Factors to be considered include the clients' tax bracket at the time of the contribution, the length of time until anticipated distributions begin, the estimated return on invested assets, and estimated post-retirement income.

WHAT ARE THE REQUIREMENTS?

1. An individual can set aside retirement savings in a variable premium annuity contract, a regular fixed rate annuity contract, or a trusteed or custodial account with a bank, savings and loan, or credit union. Also, it is possible to split total contributions into more than one IRA. For example, a part of the permissible contribution could go into a variable premium annuity contract and the balance could be placed into a trusteed bank account.[11]

2. Three parties can make deposits to a traditional IRA. These are the employee, the employee's employer, or the employee's union. Generally, anyone can contribute to an ESA.

3. Annual contributions must be made in cash. Contributions of other property are not permissible (except in the case of "rollovers").[12]

4. The plan must be established and the contribution made within the taxable year for which a deduction is allowed or before the due date (not including extensions) for filing the individual's tax returns for that taxable year. For most taxpayers, contributions to a traditional or Roth IRA, or to an ESA, must, therefore, be made by April 15th of the following year.

5. Traditional IRAs must begin to pay a participant's benefit by the April 1st following the calendar year in which the participant reaches age 70½. This is called the required beginning date or RBD. ESAs must be distributed within 30 days after the date on which the designated beneficiary attains age 30. The earnings on such distributed balances may be includable in income and subject to the 10% penalty tax. Any amount remaining in the ESA at the end of the 30-day period will be deemed to be distributed.

6. For traditional IRAs, if the IRA owner dies *before* beginning distributions (i.e., the required beginning date), there are two basic alternatives. If there is a designated beneficiary, payments are made over the life expectancy of the beneficiary. If there is no designated beneficiary, payments must be paid out within five years of the IRA owner's death. If the sole beneficiary is the IRA owner's spouse, distributions may be made over the remaining life expectancy of the spouse beginning at the later of the end of the calendar year immediately following the calendar year in which the owner died or the end of the calendar year in which the owner would have attained age 70½. The spouse may also roll over the

balance to the spouse's own IRA or elect to treat the decedent's IRA as the spouse's own.

If the IRA owner dies *on or after* the required beginning date, there are two alternatives. If there is a designated beneficiary, payment is made over the life expectancy of the beneficiary. If there is no designated beneficiary, payments shall be made over the remaining life expectancy of the IRA owner immediately before his or her death. If the sole designated beneficiary is the IRA owner's spouse, distribution cam be made over the remaining life expectancy of the spouse beginning with the calendar year immediately following the calendar year in which the IRA owner died. The spouse may also roll over the balance to the spouses's own IRA or elect to treat the decedent's IRA as the spouses's own IRA.[13]

Generally, Roth IRAs follow the rules above for IRA owners dying before the required beginning date. Roth IRAs do not have a lifetime required beginning date.

ESAs must be distributed within 30 days of the death of the beneficiary. If the ESA is distributed to the surviving spouse or family member of the designated beneficiary, it will be treated as if the spouse or family member is the designated beneficiary, provided the surviving spouse or family member has not yet attained age 30. Any balance remaining in the ESA at the end of the 30-day period following the designated beneficiary's death will be deemed distributed.

HOW IT IS DONE – AN EXAMPLE

The IRA should be relatively easy to establish. Banks and insurance companies provide prototype plans. The IRS also provides prototype trusteed and custodial plans. Once an IRA is established all that need be done is to make contributions.

Tax savings could be substantial. For example, a $3,000 annual deductible contribution to a traditional IRA by an individual in a 15% bracket would save $450 a year in taxes. A partner in a partnership who did not care to include any other employees in the plan could establish an IRA for himself without having to cover other employees. If the partner's tax bracket were 25%, a $3,000 annual deductible IRA contribution would save $750 a year in taxes.

Similarly, a Roth IRA can be a powerful tax saving device. The exact benefit will depend upon whether, in the absence of establishing a Roth IRA, the client would have paid tax at ordinary income rates (such as would be the case on most distributions from traditional IRAs), or at capital gains rates (which would apply if the client had invested in an asset outside of a retirement plan which qualified for capital gains treatment).

WHAT ARE THE TAX IMPLICATIONS?

1. Money set aside in a traditional IRA is currently deductible from gross income up to the limits specified.[14]

2. The earnings of the IRA account, between the time contributions are deposited and the time distributions are received accumulate tax free.[15]

3. An individual generally must be at least 59½ years old to receive a traditional IRA payment without tax penalty. The nondeductible penalty tax on a "premature distribution" is 10% of the amount of the distribution that is includable in income. Under some circumstances, the total value of the assets of the account may be deemed to be distributed.[16] (An example of this would be where an individual borrows against his IRA.) So, if your client received (or is deemed to have received) a total distribution at age 53 and his account is worth $5,000 at that time, he must pay a $500 nondeductible tax in addition to the regular income tax on the $5,000 distribution. The 10% penalty tax also applies to a taxable distribution from a Roth IRA.

The exceptions to this rule include withdrawals due to death or disability, and withdrawals taken in the form of a series of periodic payments which meet certain requirements.

In addition, the 10% early withdrawal penalty tax does not apply to a "qualified first-time homebuyer distribution." Distributions for this purpose cannot total more than $10,000 during the taxpayer's lifetime. A withdrawal qualifies as a first-time home buyer distribution if it is used within 120 days to pay the "qualified acquisition costs" of the "principal residence" of the first-time home buyer. Qualified acquisition costs include funds used for reasonable settlement, financing or other closing costs. The buyer can be a spouse, or any child, grandchild or ancestor of the IRA participant. A "first-time home buyer" must not have had an ownership interest in a principal residence during the two-year period ending with the date the contract of sale is entered into, or the date when construction begins. Thus, a "first-time home buyer" under these rules does not necessarily mean a person buying a home for the first time.

Furthermore, the 10% early distribution tax does not apply to withdrawals used to pay "qualified higher education expenses." Of course, the withdrawal will be subject to income tax under the rules applicable to traditional and Roth IRA withdrawals. These expenses include tuition at an eligible post-secondary educational institution, as well as room and board, fees, books, supplies and equipment required for enrollment or attendance. Expenses for graduate level courses are also covered. Qualifying recipients include the IRA participant, the participant's spouse, children, the spouse's children, grandchildren or spouse's grandchildren.

4. Upon distribution of the funds accumulated in a traditional IRA account, the client will be taxed at ordinary income tax rates.[17] Lump sum distribution tax treatment is not available for distributions from IRAs.

5. A "qualified distribution" from a Roth IRA is not taxable. A distribution is a "qualified distribution" if it is not made within the five-year period starting with the first taxable year for which the individual or the individual's spouse made a contribution to a Roth IRA established for the individual, and it is made at or after age 59½ or in the event of death, disability or for first-time homebuyer expenses.[18] Since assets must be held in a Roth IRA for five tax years before they can be withdrawn in a tax-free distribution, it appears that the waiting period includes the calendar year for which the contribution is made, even if the contribution is not made until the due date of the income tax return in the following year.

Unlike traditional IRAs, there is not a requirement to begin distributions from a Roth IRA at age 70½. However, the traditional IRA minimum distribution rules apply to the beneficiary of a Roth IRA following the death of the IRA participant. Thus, a beneficiary can continue to shelter the Roth IRA earnings from income tax, subject to minimum distribution requirements.

Withdrawals from Roth IRAs that do not meet the requirements for qualified distributions are includable in income only to the extent that the withdrawal (plus any earlier withdrawals) exceed the total of contributions made to the Roth IRA. These non-qualified distributions from Roth IRAs are treated as made first from contributions other than rollover contributions, then from qualified rollover contributions and finally, from any earnings on the contributions. All of an individual's Roth IRAs are aggregated for this purpose.

IMPLICATIONS AND ISSUES IN COMMUNITY PROPERTY STATES

The division of community property interests in qualified plan benefits is becoming an increasingly important factor in divorce proceedings in community property states. In many situations the spouses' respective retirement benefits are their largest assets.

IRAs will undoubtedly be the subject of controversy in many divorce proceedings. To some extent, however, the division of an interest in an IRA should be less difficult than dividing an interest in a qualified corporate plan. All benefits in an IRA must be nonforfeitable. Thus, the problems of valuing nonvested benefits will not be present.

In many cases, each spouse will have his or her own IRA. If the contributions to each IRA were similar, each spouse could agree to keep his own IRA in a divorce settlement. If only one spouse has an IRA or one IRA contains substantially more assets than the other spouse's IRA or spouses with equal IRAs or IRA subaccounts cannot agree to divide their IRA interests equally, significant problems could arise. A spouse may find he or she is obligated to divide an interest in his or her IRA with the other spouse. The obligated spouse may not have sufficient assets outside of the IRA to provide the other spouse with the value of his or her interest. Thus, the obligated spouse may seek a distribution from the IRA to provide funds to settle with his or her spouse. If, however, the spouse with the IRA is under age 59½ and not disabled, the spouse will incur a 10% "premature distribution" tax as well as be subject to ordinary income tax on the distribution he or she received (or is deemed to receive). To avoid this undesirable result, the spouses could agree to divide the assets of the IRA after the spouse with the IRA attains age 59½. If an agreement cannot be reached, the spouse with the IRA may be able to persuade a court to postpone division of the IRA until he or she attains age 59½.

An exception provided by the Employee Retirement Income Security Act of 1974 (ERISA) could eliminate the undesirable consequences described above. ERISA provides that the transfer of an individual's interest in an

IRA to his or her former spouse under a divorce decree or under a written instrument in connection with the divorce is not a taxable distribution. Thereafter, the IRA will be treated as that of the other spouse. This exception appears to apply only to the transfer of the spouse's entire interest in an IRA. Transfers of partial interests may cause the "premature distribution" tax and ordinary income tax to be imposed.

The tax consequences above should be considered when dividing community property IRA or qualified plan interests. Courts have taken varying approaches to consideration of tax aspects in division of retirement benefits. Some are unwilling to consider tax consequences when dividing retirement benefits. Others, however, have held that tax considerations should be taken into account when dividing retirement benefits in divorce proceedings.

QUESTIONS AND ANSWERS

Question – What does it mean to be an "active participant" in a qualified plan for purposes of the traditional IRA contribution limitations?

Answer – An individual is considered an "active participant" for a taxable year if the individual is covered by (1) a qualified pension, profit-sharing or stock bonus plan, (2) a qualified annuity plan, (3) a tax sheltered annuity plan, (4) a simplified employee pension plan, (5) a government sponsored plan, or (6) an employee only contributory plan exempt from tax under IRC Section 501(c)(18).[19] The rules vary depending on whether the plan is a defined benefit pension plan or a defined contribution plan.

1. *Defined benefit pension plan.* An individual is an active participant as long as he is not excluded under the plan's eligibility provisions. Active participation exists even when the individual declines participation, fails to make mandatory contributions or fails to perform the minimum service required to accrue a benefit. The plan being in frozen status does not necessarily mean active participation does not exist.

2. *Defined contribution plan.* An individual is an active participant if employer contributions, employee contributions, or forfeitures are added to the individual's account.[20]

Question – Can a client borrow from his IRA account?

Answer – No. Borrowing will create a forfeiture of the IRA's tax qualification. Your client will be deemed to have received all the assets in his or her account and must pay ordinary income tax to the extent includable in income.[21] In addition, if the client is neither disabled nor 59½ years old at that time, unless another exception applies, there will also be a 10% nondeductible "premature distribution" tax.

Question – How long can an individual wait before beginning to receive distributions from a traditional IRA?

Answer – Distributions do not have to be made until April 1 following the calendar year in which a client reaches age 70½ (of course, payments can begin as early as age 59½ without penalty).[22]

Question – If an individual chooses a particular investment vehicle for his IRA, but later changes his mind, is a shift to another type of investment allowed?

Answer – Yes. It is possible to liquidate an IRA investment and reinvest the proceeds within 60 days in another investment on a tax-free basis. For example, if your client originally purchased mutual funds but later wanted to split his investment between mutual funds and a flexible premium annuity, the change can be made without incurring adverse income tax consequences. This tax-free reinvestment of funds can occur only once each year.

It is also possible to initiate a trustee-to-trustee transfer at any time without restrictions. For example, an individual may choose to move an IRA account from a bank to a brokerage. So long as the transaction is completed between the two institutions (i.e., the check or securities are not payable to the IRA participant, but to the new brokerage), it will not count as a rollover, nor will any tax consequences result.

Of course, the investment vehicle itself (e.g., Certificate of Deposit, bond, stock, fund, etc.) may be liquidated within a "master" IRA account, and the funds reinvested in the same master account, without regards to either the 60-day rollover or trustee-to-trustee rules. Such transactions are commonplace within most brokerage accounts, if the brokerage firm and IRA custodian offer multiple investment choices.

Question – Can an IRA invest in gold coins or stamps?

Answer – If an IRA acquires collectibles, the cost of such collectibles shall be regarded as a current taxable distribution to the IRA owner. A collectible is defined as any work of art, any rug or antique, any metal or gem, any stamp or coin, any alcoholic beverage, or any other tangible personal property specified by the IRS. However, an exception to this rule is permitted for IRA investments in gold or silver coins issued by the United States or any coins minted by a state. An exception is also allowed for gold, silver, platinum or palladium bullion. Certain platinum coins are also excluded.[23]

Question – A partner owning more than 10% of the partnership's capital was a participant in his partnership HR-10 plan. He left the partnership and received the distribution of his retirement plan monies. Can he use a "rollover" traditional IRA? Secondly, assuming he can establish a "rollover" IRA, several years later when he is employed by a corporation which has a retirement plan, can he make a contribution from the "rollover" IRA into the corporate retirement plan?

Answer – The partner can roll over the distribution into a "rollover" IRA, and he may roll over those monies from the "rollover" IRA into another qualified plan.[24] However, in order to preserve capital gains and special averaging treatment for a qualified plan distribution, the money from the qualified plan cannot be commingled with money from other sources.

Note that distributions received are subject to a mandatory 20% income tax withholding unless a direct rollover is used.

Question – Can an existing traditional IRA be rolled over into a Roth IRA?

Answer – Yes. If a taxpayer's AGI is $100,000 or less, a traditional IRA may be rolled over (excluding married taxpayers filing separately), in whole or in part, to a Roth IRA.[25] For purposes of calculating AGI, the rollover is excluded. For tax years beginning in 2005, any amounts included in gross income due to certain required minimum distributions will not be taken into account for purposes of the $100,000 AGI limitation. (Note that generally, if a taxpayer has rolled over funds from a traditional IRA to a Roth IRA during the taxable year, and later discovers his AGI is in excess of $100,000, the taxpayer has until the due date for filing his return (including extensions) to correct such a conversion without penalty, to the extent all earnings and income allocable to the conversion are also transferred back to the original

IRA, and no deduction was allowed with respect to the original conversion.)

The rollover must be completed within 60 days after the distribution, as with the regular rollover rules. Distributions from the traditional IRA are subject to income tax. The 10% premature withdrawal penalty is waived for rollovers from traditional to Roth IRAs. For 1998 rollovers only, income incurred as a result of such rollovers was included in income ratably over 4 years, including tax year 1998, unless the taxpayed elects otherwise. To the extent the taxpayer withdrew amounts attributable to such rollovers within the 4-year period, the inclusion of the amounts in income were accelerated. If the taxpayer died prior to the end of the 4-year period, the remaining contributions were includable in the taxpayer's gross income in the year of death, unless the sole beneficiary of the beneficiary of the Roth IRA was the surviving spouse, in which case, the spouse could elect to continue to defer the inclusion of the contributions over the same 4-year period. Note that if a portion of a distribution is properly allocated to a qualified rollover contribution, and such distribution is made within the 5-year period beginning with the year the contribution was made, then the 10% penalty tax for early distributions applies as if such portion of the distribution was includable in gross income.

Question – Should I withdraw funds from a converted Roth IRA to pay the taxes due?

Answer – No. Taxes should be paid out of other funds.

Question – What is a SEP?

Answer – A simplified employee pension ("SEP") is a type of IRA or annuity established by an employer, to which the employer can contribute on the employees' behalf, and where contributions are only made according to a predetermined formula.

Question – How much can be contributed annually to a SEP?

Answer – The dollar limit on contributions to SEPs is the lesser of $41,000, for 2004, or 25% of employee compensation (up to $205,000 for 2004) without regards to the employer contribution. The employee excludes the contribution from gross income up to the same limits.

Employee elective deferrals are no longer allowed, with the exception that a SEP maintained by an employer of no more than 25 employees (for the year prior to the tax year in question) that allowed for elective employee salary reduction as of December 31, 1996, may qualify to continue offering elective deferrals. If permitted, such employee deferrals cannot exceed $13,000 in 2004. Elective deferrals in excess of the annual limit will be included in gross income.[26] Additionally, taxpayers 50 and over can make catch-up contributions of $3,000 in 2004, with catch-up contributions gradually increasing to $5,000 in 2006.

Question – What are the requirements for a SEP?

Answer – The essential requirements are

1. The employer (can be a corporation, partnership, or sole proprietorship) must make a contribution to the plan for each employee age 21 or older who has worked for the employer during at least 3 of the last 5 years. An employer need not contribute on behalf of any employee for a calendar year in which the employee's compensation was less than $450, as indexed in 2004.[27] In the case of elective deferral SEPs, the employer must have had 25 or fewer eligible employees during the prior taxable year, and at least 50% must have elected to contribute to the SEP.[28]

2. The employer's contribution cannot discriminate in favor of employees who are "highly compensated." It is possible to exclude nonparticipating union employees with respect to whom there is good faith bargaining on retirement benefits and nonresident aliens in considering whether or not contributions are discriminatory in favor of any member of the prohibited class. A special nondiscrimination test is applicable to salary reduction SEPs. Employer contributions may be made for an employee who has reached age 70½, unlike the situation with an IRA.

3. A limited disparity between the contribution percentages applicable to compensation above and below the social security wage base is permitted. (This is also referred to as "integration.") An elective deferral SEP may not be integrated. Integration is not permitted for a year in which the employer also maintains an integrated pension, profit sharing, or stock bonus plan or tax deferred annuity.

4. The employee must own the IRA account or annuity. That means 100% immediate vesting

for all employees. The employer cannot restrict the employee's right to keep or withdraw money contributed to the SEP.

5. The SEP has to be in writing. It must spell out

   (a) what an employee has to do to "get a piece of the action" and

   (b) how the "pie is to be sliced," i.e., the manner in which the amount allocated is to be computed.

Question – Can a person participating in some other employer-sponsored plan also be covered by a SEP? Can a person covered by a SEP take a deduction for an IRA contribution?

Answer – Participants in simplified employee pension plans are permitted to participate in other employer qualified plans. Any contribution by an employer to a SEP must be aggregated with other contributions by that employer to other qualified plans for purposes of the overall limit on contributions or benefits. A participant can take a deduction for an IRA contribution, under the limits discussed above. Participation in a SEP is treated as active participation for purposes of the traditional IRA deduction limitations.

Question – How long does an employer have to make a contribution to a SEP (and deduct it)?

Answer – In general, the employer must make contributions no later than the tax filing deadline, plus extensions. If the employer elects a calendar year, contributions are deductible for the tax year in which the calendar year ends. In fact, the plan itself need not be established until such dates.

Question – What is a model SEP? What is a non-model SEP?

Answer – To establish a SEP, there must be a written agreement. IRS has issued Form 5305 – SEP, Simplified Employee Pension – Individual Retirement Accounts Contribution Agreement for those employers wishing to have a pre-approved IRS agreement. Plans using the IRS form are called model SEPs, while plans using other agreements are called non-model SEPs. Employers who currently maintain any other qualified plan cannot use a model SEP, but, rather they must use a non-model SEP.

Question – May a divorced spouse make and deduct contributions to a spousal IRA?

Answer – A divorced or legally separated person can make an IRA contribution from taxable alimony or separation payments he or she receives during the year.

Question – May an alternate payee roll over a distribution to an IRA or a qualified plan if made pursuant to a Qualified Domestic Relations Order?

Answer – If an alternate payee who is the spouse or former spouse of the participant receives a distribution by reason of a Qualified Domestic Relations Order, the rollover rules apply to the alternate payee as if the alternate payee were the participant.[29] Thus, the alternate payee has 60 days in which to roll over any portion of an eligible rollover distribution without the distribution becoming includable in income.[30] Generally, such a rollover must be handled as a direct rollover to avoid a mandatory income tax withholding rate of 20%.[31]

Question – Are there special rules for "inherited" IRAs acquired by someone other than a surviving spouse?

Answer – Yes. Inherited IRAs acquired by someone other than a surviving spouse cannot be "rolled over" tax-free and cannot receive tax-free rollovers from other qualified plans or IRAs. No income tax deduction is allowed for amounts contributed to an inherited IRA.

Question – May a contribution be made to a traditional IRA even though it is not deductible?

Answer – Yes. Designated nondeductible contributions may be made on behalf of an individual to an IRA even though he participates in a qualified pension or profit sharing plan. These contributions are intended to provide a tax incentive for retirement savings, and the tax on the earnings on the nondeductible contributions is deferred until withdrawn. The nondeductible limit is the excess of:

(a) the lesser of the maximum annual limit or 100% of compensation over

(b) the amount allowable as a deduction for IRA contributions by active participants.[32]

Question – When may a surviving spouse roll over a distribution received from a qualified plan or IRA of a deceased spouse?

Answer – A surviving spouse can roll over all or part of a distribution from a qualified plan or IRA of the deceased spouse to an IRA.[33] If this is done, the IRA of the deceased spouse is treated as if the surviving spouse was the original participant. Thus, the rules pertaining to rollovers discussed in this chapter are applicable. A surviving spouse may also make a rollover to another qualified plan in which the spouse is a participant.

Since it is possible the surviving spouse already has an IRA, or will create one after the rollover, it is a good idea not to commingle the funds from the rollover with the separate IRA funds of the surviving spouse.

Where the deceased spouse's IRA or qualified plan benefit is transferred to a trust in which the surviving spouse is a beneficiary, there is no right to roll over the distribution even if the spouse is the sole beneficiary of the trust.[34]

Question – What is a SIMPLE plan?

Answer – A "savings incentive match plan for employees" (SIMPLE) has the following major features:

- The plans are available only to employers with 100 or fewer employees (only employees with at least $5000 in compensation for the prior year are counted) during any two preceding years.

- The plans are available only to employers who do not sponsor another qualified plan 403(b) plan, or SEP.

- Contributions can be made to each employee's IRA or to a 401(k) account for the employee. In effect, there are thus two types of SIMPLE plans – those that include the 401(k) requirements, and those funded through IRAs.

- Employees who earned at least $5,000 from the employer in the preceding two years, and are reasonably expected to earn at least $5,000 in the current year, can contribute (through salary reductions) up to $9,000, as indexed for 2004. The limit is $10,000 in 2005. Additionally, tax-payers age 50 and above will be allowed catch-up contributions of $1,500 in 2004, increasing by $500 every year until it reaches $2,500 in 2006.

- The plans require an employer contribution equal to either

a) a dollar for dollar matching contribution of up to three percent of the employee's compensation (the employer can elect a lower percentage, not less than one percent, in not more than two out of any five years), or

b) a nonelective contribution of two percent of compensation for all eligible employees earning at least $5,000 (whether or not they elect salary reductions).

The new SIMPLE plans are somewhat simpler to administer and explain than the SARSEPs available under prior law, and SIMPLE IRAs are available to a broader range of employees (up to 100 employees instead of 25). However, SIMPLE IRAs may be less beneficial to employees than SARSEPs because of the lower elective deferral and catch-up contribution limits applicable to SIMPLE IRAs. Also, from the employer viewpoint, contributions to SIMPLE IRAs are less flexible than for SARSEPs.[35]

ASRS: Sec. 62.

CHAPTER ENDNOTES

1. Technically, the initials IRA have a more limited connotation but will be used here to denote any type of individual retirement savings plan.
2. Sec. 219(b).
3. Sec. 219(g).
4. IRC Sec. 219(c).
5. Sec. 402(c)(8)(B).
6. Sec. 402(c)(2).
7. Sec. 402(c)(4).
8. Sec. 3405(c).
9. Sec. 408A.
10. Sec. 530.
11. Secs. 408(a); 408(b).
12. Sec. 408(a)(1).
13. For the regulations regarding required minimum distributions, see Treas. Reg. §1.408-8.
14. Sec. 219(a).
15. Sec. 408(e)(1).
16. Secs. 72(t), 408(e)(2), 408(e)(3).
17. Sec. 408(d).
18. Sec. 408A(d).
19. Sec. 219(g)(5).
20. 87-16, 1987-1 CB 446.
21. IRC Sec. 408(e)(3).
22. Secs. 408(a)(6); 408(b)(3).
23. Sec. 408(m).
24. Sec. 408(d)(3)(A).
25. Sec. 408A(c)(3)(B).
26. Sec. 402(g).
27. Sec. 408(k)(2).
28. Sec. 408(k)(6).
29. Sec. 402(e)(1).
30. Sec. 402(c)(1).
31. Sec. 3405(c)(1).
32. Sec. 408(o)(2)(A).
33. Sec. 402(c)(9).
34. Treas. Reg. 1.408-8, A-5.
35. Sec. 408(p).

Chapter 52

PROFIT SHARING/401 (k)/PENSION PLAN

WHAT IS IT?

A profit sharing plan, as its name implies, is a retirement plan for sharing employer profits with employees. A profit sharing plan need not provide a definite, predetermined formula for determining the amount of profits to be shared. However, there must be a definite formula for allocating these profits to each participant. But absent a definite contribution formula, an employer must make recurring and substantial contributions to a profit sharing plan.[1]

A pension plan is a retirement plan established and maintained by an employer to provide a *definitely determinable benefit* for the employer's employees and their beneficiaries. The primary purpose of a pension plan must be to provide benefits for the employees upon their retirement because of age or disability.

A 401(k) plan, also known as a cash or deferred arrangement (CODA), is actually a feature that is part of a profit sharing plan, stock bonus plan, and, in some cases which are beyond the scope of this book, a money purchase pension plan. CODAs provide an employee an option to choose whether his employer should pay a certain amount to him in cash or contribute that amount to a qualified profit sharing or stock bonus plan on his behalf. A plan that contains a 401(k) feature generally must include the customary provisions required of all defined contribution plans. For additional information on 401(k) plans, see the questions and answers at the end of this chapter.

WHEN IS THE USE OF SUCH A DEVICE INDICATED?

1. When your client would like to be sure of a steady, adequate, and secure personal retirement income.

2. When your client would like to set aside money for retirement on a tax deductible basis.

3. When your client wants to reward long-service employees and provide for their economic welfare after retirement.

4. When your client would like to put his or her business in a better competitive position for attracting, retaining, and eventually retiring personnel.

5. When your client's corporation is about to run into an accumulated earnings tax problem. The corporation may need to "siphon off" some of its earnings and profits and reduce or eliminate the threat of a penalty tax on unreasonably accumulated earnings.

6. When your client has employees who would like to defer compensation on an elective, pre-tax basis to a qualified retirement plan.

WHAT ARE THE REQUIREMENTS?

1. The plan must be for the exclusive benefit of employees or their beneficiaries.[2]

2. The primary purpose of the plan must be to offer employees a retirement benefit (or, in the case of a profit sharing plan, provide employees with a share in the company's profits).

3. The plan provisions must set forth, in writing, a description of the plan and details of the plan.[3] Furthermore, details of the plan must be communicated to employees.

4. The plan must be permanent. This means the plan must contain no set termination date.

5. The plan must not discriminate in favor of highly-compensated employees. Plans that are "top heavy," that is, plans that provide more than 60% of aggregate accumulated benefits or account balances for current key employees, must meet more stringent vesting, minimum benefit, and other rules.

6. The plan must meet minimum age and service standards, minimum coverage requirements and, in the case of defined benefit plans, a minimum participation test.

7. The plan must meet minimum vesting standards and provide for benefits or contributions that do not exceed the Section 415 limits.

8. Distributions generally must begin to *all* partici- pants by the April 1 following the year of attaining age 70H; however, (1) employees who are not more- than-5% owners and (2) participants in governmen- tal or church plans, generally need not begin distri- butions until April 1 of the year following the year they retire, if that is later.[4]

9. Although traditional 401(k) plans are entitled to favorable tax treatment, they must meet certain special qualification requirements in addition to the regular plan qualification requirements. These spe- cial qualification requirements are as follows:

   (a) The plan must permit the employees to elect either to have the employer make a contribu- tion on his behalf or to receive an equivalent amount in cash.

   (b) Unlike a typical profit sharing or stock bonus plan, a 401(k) plan cannot allow employees to receive a distribution of funds held in the plan which are attributable to elective deferrals merely because of the lapse of a fixed number of years or the completion of a specified period of participation.[5]

   (c) The employee's rights to benefits derived from elective contributions, as well as from qualified matching and qualified nonelective contribu- tions used to satisfy the ADP (actual deferral percentage) test, are nonforfeitable.[6]

   (d) The employer cannot condition the availability of any other benefit (except employer matching contributions) on whether an employee elects to make elective contributions under the CODA or to receive cash in lieu thereof.[7]

   (e) The plan must meet special nondiscrimination tests with respect to the amount of elective con- tributions made to the plan each year. See QUES- TIONS AND ANSWERS for more details.

   (f) Unlike a typical profit sharing or stock bonus plan, the CODA cannot require, as a condition of participation, that an employee complete more than one year of service for the employer maintaining the plan.

   (g) The amount of the elective contributions made to the plan on behalf of a participant cannot exceed $13,000 (in 2004). This amount is sched- uled to increase by $1,000 each year until it reaches $15,000 in 2006.[8] Thereafter, the limit will be indexed for inflation.

   (h) Participants who have reached age 50 by the end of the plan year may make catch-up elective deferrals. (However, the total amount of a participant's elective deferrals may not exceed 100% of compensation for the year.) The catch- up amount is $3,000 in 2004, increasing by $1,000 each year until it reaches $5,000 in 2006. There- after, the limit will be indexed for inflation.[9]

The requirements for pension and profit sharing plans listed above are not exhaustive. For example, other requirements may include meeting minimum stan- dards on participation, coverage, and funding.[10]

There are two basic types of qualified retirement plans. The first is known as a fixed or defined benefit plan. Here, definitely determinable retirement benefits are computed using a pre-determined benefit formula established when the plan is created. Each employee is promised a specific amount of retirement benefits. The amount of the employer's contribution to fund that benefit is based on an actuarial determination of the cost of benefits promised. In other words, contributions are based on benefits and the limits on contributions are based on the benefit they will produce.

A money purchase pension plan, which is a type of defined contribution plan, bases the retirement benefit upon an employer's commitment to make an annual contribution. Benefits are directly dependent upon the length of time an employee participates in the plan and the amount of money contributed on his behalf each year (plus interest and appreciation on such funds). In a money purchase pension plan, therefore, the employer is not obligated to provide a specific amount of retire- ment benefits, but is required to make the specified amount of contributions.

A profit sharing plan is an arrangement by which an employer shares a portion of corporate profits with employees. Contributions can be made even if there are no profits. It is a type of defined contribution plan. For all defined contribution plans, the limits on annual contributions to the plans are based on the employee's salary, which directly limits the contributions. There is no limit to the benefits produced by the plan.

The corporation can distribute these payments cur- rently in the form of cash bonuses, or profits can be shared on a deferred basis through contributions to a profit sharing plan.

In deferred profit sharing, contributions are made into an irrevocable trust. Funds then accumulate and are dis- tributed to participants, usually as a retirement benefit, at some later date. Under a profit sharing plan, participants can also receive benefits in the event of a termination other than retirement, such as death, layoff, or disability.

One important advantage of a profit sharing plan is that the employer need not make a contribution in years in which no profits are earned. (However, a substantial amount of contribution flexibility can also be made possible in a well-designed pension plan.)

A traditional 401(k) plan may stand on its own (e.g., permit only elective contributions) or it may permit other types of employer contributions and/or employee contributions. The key feature of a cash or deferred arrangement is that an employee can elect to have the employer make an elective contribution on his behalf in the form of a compensation reduction agreement under which the employee elects to reduce cash compensation and to have the employer contribute such amount to the plan on the employee's behalf. In some cases, the employer may agree to make a matching contribution based on the employee's contribution (e.g. 50 cents from the employer for every dollar put in by the employee from his or her compensation).

The comments that follow explain the basic principles of eligibility, vesting, contributions, actuarial assumptions, death benefits, retirement age, and Social Security integration for qualified plans in general. There are also special rules for "top heavy" plans, see below.

Eligibility

A qualified corporate retirement plan may not impose an age or service requirement that would exclude any full-time employee who has attained age 21, or who has completed one year of service, whichever is later.[11] If there is 100% immediate vesting, a two-year waiting period is permitted.[12]

A plan must be nondiscriminatory in its coverage of employees. (It is permissible to favor rank and file employees.) A plan will qualify if it benefits at least 70% of the nonhighly compensated employees, or benefits a percentage of nonhighly compensated employees which is at least 70% of the percentage of highly compensated employees benefiting under the plan.[13] Alternatively, a plan will qualify if it does not discriminate in favor of highly compensated employees and the average benefit percentage for the nonhighly compensated employees is at least 70% of the average benefit percentage for the highly compensated employees.[14] Additionally, a defined benefit plan must cover, on each day of the plan

year, the lesser of 50 employees or 40% or more of all employees of the employer.[15]

A plan may exclude part-time and seasonal employees (those employees who work less than 1,000 hours in a 12-month period).[16] Also, a collective bargaining unit may be excluded if the union prefers not to be covered under a plan and the decision is made as the result of good-faith bargaining.[17]

Vesting

Minimum vesting standards must be met by all plans. Vesting refers to nonforfeitability of benefits by covered employees. The general rule is that the benefits attributable to employee contributions must always be 100% vested.[18] Likewise, with respect to a 401(k) plan, an employee's rights to benefits derived from elective contributions, as well as from qualified matching and qualified nonelective contributions used to satisfy the actual deferral percentage (ADP) test, must be 100% vested at all times.[19]

Full vesting is required under one of the following schedules: for 401(k) matching contributions and for top heavy plans, after (a) three years, or (b) six years under a graduated vesting schedule. For all other plans, vesting must take place no later than (c) after five years or (d) after seven years under a graduated vesting schedule.[20] The following chart shows the required vesting percentages under each method at various years of service:

Years of Service	(a)	(b)	(c)	(d)
1	0%	0%	0%	0%
2	0	20	0	0
3	100	40	0	20
4		60	0	40
5		80	100	60
6		100		80
7				100

A plan must take into account all years of service (generally 1,000 hours in a plan year) completed after the employee attains age 18 for vesting purposes.

Contributions and Benefits

The law imposes certain limitations on contributions and benefits.

Defined Contribution Plans

Defined contribution type plans include money purchase pension plans, profit sharing plans, stock bonus plans, 401(k) plans, ESOPs, thrift plans, and target or assumed benefit plans.

Defined contribution plans are subject to an annual additions limit equal to the lesser of (a) 100% of compensation or (b) $41,000 (in 2004, as indexed).[21]

An employer who sponsors a profit sharing plan is permitted a maximum deduction of up to 25% of the total compensation of plan participants. (For plan years beginning prior to January 1, 2002, the employer deduction was limited to 15% of total compensation in the case of a profit sharing plan.[22]) Furthermore, elective deferrals are not counted toward the maximum deduction limit. In addition, total compensation in a 401(k) plan is determined before subtracting any elective deferrals.[23]

Employees are typically not required to contribute their own funds as a condition of plan participation but plans can provide for voluntary contributions. Thrift plans commonly do require employees to contribute and require the employer to make matching contributions.

Defined contribution plans may be integrated with Social Security based on the Social Security tax (excluding hospital premium) for the current year.

Disabled plan participants (other than a disabled employee who is highly compensated) can receive the benefit of an employer contribution to a defined contribution plan based on the annualized compensation of the employee during his last year of employment. All such contributions must be immediately 100% vested.[24]

Defined Benefit Plans

A defined benefit plan is a plan which provides a fixed or determinable benefit such as 40% of an employee's final three years average salary or 1% times final three years average salary times number of years of plan participation or service with the employer.

The maximum normal retirement benefit for a defined benefit plan, based on retirement no earlier than age 62, is the lesser of (a) 100% of the highest three consecutive years of average compensation while actively participating in the plan, or (b) $165,000 (in 2004,

as indexed).[25] The limitation is increased for retirement after age 65 and decreased for retirement before age 62.[26] These limits are based on the annual payment which, with interest compounded until the retirement date of the employee, will create a fund sufficient to provide the described benefit to the employee for his actuarial life expectancy. The benefit must be reduced pro-rata if the employee has fewer than 10 years of plan participation with the employer.[27]

A $10,000 minimum annual benefit may always be provided for an employee who has never been covered by a defined contribution plan maintained by the employer regardless of the rules mentioned above.[28] But this amount must be reduced pro-rata if the employee has served the employer for less than 10 years at retirement.[29]

All the limits above must be actuarially reduced to reflect any post retirement death benefits except in the case of a qualified joint and survivor annuity.[30]

Further reductions must be made in the limits described above if an employee retires before age 62.[31] If retirement benefits are to commence prior to age 62, the limit is reduced to the actuarial equivalent of a $165,000 benefit at age 62. If retirement benefits commence after age 65, the limit is increased to the actuarial equivalent of a $165,000 benefit at age 65. For this purpose, the interest rate assumption must be not greater than the lesser of 5% or the rate specified in the plan.[32]

Furthermore, the limit must be reduced if the normal form of retirement is something other than a nonrefund life annuity.[33] All of the dollar limits described above are subject to the annual cost-of-living changes.

Target or Assumed Benefit Plan

A target or assumed benefit plan is a hybrid between a defined contribution and defined benefit plan in which a "target benefit" is established under the plan for each participant, such as 50% of an employee's five highest years average salary.

Once the "target benefit" is found, contributions necessary to attain that goal are then actuarially determined based on a conservative interest assumption, such as 5% or 6%, and the age of the participant. The plan then becomes a money purchase plan.

The maximum annual addition to the account of a participant in a target benefit plan cannot exceed the lesser of (a) 100% of salary or (b) $41,000 (in 2004, as indexed).[34]

Each participant's account is credited with any investment earnings or gains and losses. This means the actual retirement benefit of a participant under a target benefit plan can be more or less than the actual target itself.

Deduction of Contributions

In a defined benefit pension plan, an employer can contribute and deduct the amount necessary to pay for the benefits promised. Technically stated, the employer may pay and deduct the plan's "normal cost" plus any amount necessary to amortize liability for benefits earned through the past service of employees. Past service (simplified, past service is the cost of financing benefits credited for past services) liability can be amortized over as few as 10 years (but no more than 30 years).[35]

Generally, the deductible contributions referred to above can be made up to the plan's full funding limitation. The full funding limitation is essentially the amount by which the lesser of (1) in plan years beginning before 2004, an applicable percentage of current liability (see below), or (2) the accrued liability under the plan, exceeds the value of the plan's assets.[36]

For plan years beginning in:	The applicable percentage is:
2002	165
2003	170

An employer sponsoring a profit sharing plan may contribute and deduct a maximum of 25% of the total compensation of plan participants (without carry-forwards). A $100,000 covered payroll would therefore yield the right to a $25,000 deductible contribution.[37]

Where the employee is utilizing both a pension and profit sharing plan, the maximum deductible contribution for both plans is the greater of 25% of the compensation of covered employees or the contribution required to fund the minimum funding standard. This deduction limitation also applies to combinations of defined benefit and money purchase plans.[38]

Prior to 1987, employees could deduct "qualified voluntary employee contributions" made to the plan up to a maximum of $2,000 per taxable year or, if less, 100% of compensation. The plan had to contain special provisions allowing these contributions.[39] Qualified voluntary employee contributions (made prior to 1987) must be accounted for separately, although separate investment will not be required. No loans to participants or investments in life insurance contracts should be made with plan assets attributable to deductible employee contributions or such action will be considered a distribution.[40]

Since a CODA must be part of a profit sharing or stock bonus plan, the limitation on the employer's tax-deductible contributions to such a plan is 25% of the participants' total compensation.[41] Furthermore, for purposes of the limitation on annual additions, elective contributions made under a qualified CODA are not considered employer contributions.[42]

Employers may also permit employees to make voluntary contributions to a separate account or annuity, referred to as a "deemed IRA." If certain requirements for a traditional or Roth IRA are met, then the account or annuity will be treated as a traditional or Roth IRA, not as a qualified plan.[43]

Actuarial Assumptions

In a defined or fixed benefit pension plan, a conservative estimate should be made as to the rate of return of funds invested in assets other than life insurance. Interest rate assumptions of 5% to 7% are typical. Any actual return in excess of the amount assumed must be used to reduce the employer's future contributions.

After challenging the use of rates as low as 5% or 6% for a number of years, the IRS backed down on its position that such rates were too conservative. The Tax Court and several circuit courts had sided with the employers in several such cases, noting that Congress intended actuaries to be "afforded a range of latitude in establishing a mix of reasonable assumptions, and that only if such assumptions are 'substantially unreasonable' should they be challenged and changed retroactively."[44]

In a money purchase plan, the investment experience directly affects the amount a participant will have at retirement. Normally, earnings are allocated to the participant's account in proportion to his or her account balance.

In a profit sharing plan, the investment experience directly affects the amount in a participant's account. Gains and losses must be allocated proportionately to each individual. Typically, such allocations are made in proportion to the account balances of each participant. At retirement a participant may have more or less than was contributed, depending on the investment experience of the plan.

In the event an employee terminates, under a defined benefit plan the portion of a terminated participant's nonvested account is used to reduce future employer contributions.[45] However, in a profit sharing plan, the funds in a terminated participant's nonvested account (forfeitures) can be allocated among the accounts of remaining participants on the same basis as the following year's contribution, or can be used to reduce future employer contributions, depending upon what provisions have been made in the plan.[46] Generally, forfeitures under all defined contribution plans, including money purchase plans, may also be used to increase participants' account balances.[47]

Mortality is an important actuarial assumption. In a fixed benefit pension plan, if life insurance is included in the plan, the investment account is generally not used to provide the death benefit. Instead, the investment account that would have gone to the deceased employee had he or she lived is used to reduce future employer contributions to the plan. If life insurance is included in the plan, death proceeds generally go to the employee's beneficiary.

In either a money purchase pension plan or a profit sharing plan, the total funds in a participant's account are paid to a beneficiary as a death benefit. This includes the life insurance proceeds as well as any other investments.

Retirement Age

Generally, plans will make provision for normal, early, and late retirement age. Usually, normal retirement age will be age 65.

Mandatory retirement is generally prohibited. Exceptions exist for certain top executives and for good faith occupational requirements.

Employers are required to accrue additional benefits or pay the actuarial equivalent of normal retirement benefits to employees who choose to work beyond normal retirement age. It is unlawful to eliminate the accrual of further benefit credits to an employee's retirement account after the employee attains normal retirement age.[48]

It is also unlawful to exclude an employee from participation in a pension plan even though his age is within five years of the age set for normal retirement. Allowance is made, however, for the extension of the normal retirement date for any such late-age-hired person.[49] Most pension plans state that the normal retirement age of participants who are over age 55 at the time they enter the plan is five years from the date of entering the plan.

Early retirement benefits are generally available under a defined benefit plan at an actuarially reduced amount. In a money purchase plan, the amount of a pension that can be provided with the participant's vested share is what he or she will receive at early retirement. Under a profit sharing plan, in the case of early retirement, the amount accumulated in a participant's account will be paid generally as a lump sum or as monthly income.

The IRS has challenged the use of retirement ages under age 65 in small defined benefit plans; however, it backed down on this issue. The Tax Court and several circuit courts had sided with the employers in litigation of some of these cases. (See the discussion above, under "Actuarial Assumptions" with regard to IRS challenges to the use of low interest rates.)

Social Security Integration

Generally speaking, the benefit structure of Social Security can be viewed as discriminating against the higher-paid employee, which usually includes the key shareholders and highly-paid management. Social Security benefits replace, relatively speaking, a higher percentage of the lower-paid employee's pre-retirement income. In essence, the business owner is already providing a base pension through contributions to the Social Security system.

Integration of a retirement plan with Social Security allows an employer to coordinate the benefits provided by Social Security with those provided by the employer's retirement plan. Through integration, the two benefits combined produce roughly the same proportionate benefit for higher-paid employees as for lower-paid employees. (The Internal Revenue Code and the IRS refer to integration as "permitted disparity.")

Example: In the case of a money purchase or profit sharing plan, the contribution rate (%) that applies to compensation above the taxable wage base may not exceed the contribution rate

(%) that applies to compensation below the taxable wage base by more than the *lesser of* (1) the rate applied to compensation below the wage base or (2) 5.7% points (or, if greater, the rate of Social Security tax attributable to old-age insurance).[50] Thus, if the plan provides for contributions of 10% of pay in excess of the wage base, it would be properly integrated if it provided for contributions of at least 5% on pay below the wage base.

It is also possible to integrate a defined benefit pension plan. But here integration is on the basis of benefits rather than contributions.

Top Heavy Plans

Plans which are considered "top heavy" must meet the basic qualification requirements of other qualified plans and, in addition, meet the following requirements: (1) implement one of two alternative rapid vesting schedules; (2) provide minimum nonintegrated contributions or benefits for plan participants who are non-key employees; and (3) reduce the aggregate limit on contributions and benefits for some key employees.[51]

A plan is considered "top heavy" when more than 60% of its aggregate accumulated benefits or account balances is provided to key employees. An employee's status and whether or not a plan is top heavy is determined on a year by year basis. The determination is made on the last day of the preceding plan year for existing plans and on the last day of the first plan year for new plans.[52]

A key employee is any employee-participant who, at any time during the plan year is an officer earning more than $130,000, a more than 5% owner, or a more than 1% owner earning more than $150,000 a year (as indexed for 2004).[53]

Special rules apply for smaller employers: If the business (or aggregated group of businesses) has fewer than 500 employees, only 10% will be considered officers, but if the business has fewer than 30 employees, at least three officers must be counted.

Each additional qualification requirement will be discussed below.

Vesting

A top heavy plan must meet one of two special vesting rules. The first is a three-year 100% vesting rule. Under this rule an employee who is at least 21 years old and who has completed at least three years of service with the employer (or employers) maintaining the plan must be given a nonforfeitable right to 100% of his accrued benefit derived from employer contributions. The second is a 6-year graded vesting rule. This provides 20% vesting at the end of the second year of service and 20% in each succeeding year. Full vesting must be attained by the end of the 6-year period.[54]

Six-year graded vesting

Years of service	Nonforfeitable percentage
2	20
3	40
4	60
5	80
6 or more	100

Contributions and Benefits

Special limitations on contributions and benefits are imposed if the plan is considered top heavy.[55] Minimum benefits under defined benefit plans must be provided to non-key employees. The benefit accrued during a top heavy year must be at least 2% of average pay for the highest five years for each year of service in which a top heavy plan year ends, up to a total of 20% of average pay.

In the case of top heavy defined contribution plans, in each year the plan is top heavy, non-key employees must receive minimum contributions of at least 3% of compensation. But if the plan provides the contribution rate of less than 3% for all participants, then instead of the 3% contribution rate, the highest contribution rate percentage on behalf of any key employee can be used (counting only the first $205,000 of compensation for plan years beginning in 2004).

In determining benefits under a top heavy plan, only the first $205,000 of compensation (for plan years beginning in 2004) can be counted, as is the case in non-top heavy plans.[56] The $205,000 limit is indexed for inflation. Social Security benefits or contributions cannot be counted against the required minimum benefits or contributions.

HOW IT IS DONE – AN EXAMPLE

There are basically three ways an employer places funds into a retirement plan. The first is known as a "fully-insured" plan. Here, the employer places contributions into a funding vehicle of an insurance company, such as a retirement income life insurance contract. The funds usually receive a guarantee as to principal, minimum rate of interest, and annuity purchase rate (the "rate of exchange" at which pension funds can be changed into lifetime payment guarantees). It is the simplest method of investing pension monies.

The second type of investment vehicle is known as the "split funded" plan. Here, the employer places contributions into a trust fund. The trust fund splits contributions into two parts: part of the funds are placed in fixed assets, annuities, and/or life insurance, while the remainder is invested in other investments for diversification. There are principal, interest, and annuity purchase rate guarantees for the funds invested with the insurance company. However, frequently funds invested otherwise have no guarantees of principal or interest, but they may have the advantage of appreciation if invested in equities.

The third type of funding vehicle is known as uninsured. This type of funding implies that the employer contributions are invested solely by investments including equities. Contributions are made by the employer to a trust fund. There are no guarantees as to principal or interest although funds may be applied to buy a guaranteed annuity at normal retirement age. This funding method involves the highest risk because there are no guarantees made by a third party, but in return for the extra risk, this method offers the greatest potential appreciation (or depending upon how the plan is arranged, the lowest possible employer cost).

All three arrangements have advantages and disadvantages. For example, the fully-insured plan guarantees the principal, interest, annuity purchase rates, and expenses. It is the easiest plan to install and administer. The cost and effort of compliance with the Employee Retirement Income Security Act (ERISA) is relatively minimal. A disadvantage is that the growth of dollars in the plan is fixed, and so there is no chance for an equity-type appreciation of funds.

The split funded plan combines guarantees with the possibility of appreciation. The funds invested in insurance contracts obtain guarantees on principal and interest earnings, expense costs, and annuity rates. The side fund is usually invested in growth-oriented securities. Of course, since the side fund is invested in equities, the possibility exists that depreciation in the value of the securities will result in lower benefits for employees (or higher costs for the employer).

The main advantage of a full equity funded approach is that all funds have the possibility of appreciation. If the investment manager is successful, the result will be either reduced cost for the employer or increased benefits for the employees, depending on the type of plan utilized. The disadvantage of this arrangement is that there are no guarantees applied to the funds. Also, if an insurance company is not used, the employer or the plan must pay directly for actuarial, administrative, and investment expenses. The cost of hiring private actuarial and administrative services will be higher for small employers in most cases than if an insurer's services were utilized.

WHAT ARE THE INCOME TAX IMPLICATIONS?

1. Within the limits mentioned above, employer contributions to these plans are fully deductible for income tax purposes.[57]

2. Earnings on plan assets accumulate income tax free.[58]

3. Distributions made in the form of a lump sum distribution are included as ordinary income to the employee in the year paid. Certain amounts may be subject to 10-year averaging, in the case of a taxpayer who attained age 50 before January 1, 1986. In any event, special averaging cannot be used for the portion of a taxable distribution attributable to deductible employee contributions. Payment of such amounts can be distributed in a different tax year from the balance of the lump sum payment without jeopardizing any special averaging treatment that may still be available. See the table in Appendix D for the federal tax consequences of a lump-sum distribution based on the use of special averaging.

4. Before distribution is made, an employee generally does not have to include an employer's contribution in gross income, even if rights to the benefits in the plan are fully nonforfeitable. Benefits payable under a qualified retirement plan–including deductible employee contributions and earnings on those contributions–are taxed only when paid to a participant or beneficiary and are not taxed if merely "made available."[59]

However, if life insurance protection is provided under the plan, an employee is considered to have received a distribution each year (a current economic benefit) equal to the portion of the employer's contributions or trust earnings that have been applied during the year to provide pure insurance on the employee's life. This is the so-called "Table 2001 cost."[60] The employee includes this as income just as if he or she had received a bonus in that amount; however, such costs will be recovered income tax free when benefits are received under the contract. (If life insurance is purchased with deductible employee contributions, the amount spent is treated as a distribution.[61])

When an employee first becomes eligible to receive benefits, those benefits do not have to be paid and immediately rolled over into an IRA to avoid current income taxation. If the plan allows, they can be left in the plan and are not taxed until paid (but if paid to a child or creditor of the employee, they are treated as if paid to the employee).

The plan must place some limits on this deferral of receipt of benefits. Distributions generally must begin by April 1 of the year following the year the participant reaches age 70½ (see item (8) under "What are the Requirements" above). The plan must provide that the entire interest of the participant will be distributed over one of the following permissible periods: (1) the life of the participant; (2) the lives of the participant and his or her "designated beneficiary"; (3) a period not extending beyond the life expectancy of the participant; or (4) a period not extending beyond the life expectancy of the participant and his or her "designated beneficiary." Under regulations issued in 2003, a "Uniform Distribution Period" is used to determine the participant's lifetime distributions, regardless of who is named as the beneficiary.[62] However, the amount required to be distributed will be somewhat less if the designated beneficiary is the participant's spouse and is more than 10 years younger than the participant.[63] A designated beneficiary is generally any individual designated by the participant to receive the balance of his or her benefits remaining at the participant's death.

5. An employee who retires and receives periodic payments from the retirement plan is taxed on the receipt of such payments in accordance with the annuity rules, which vary depending on the annuity starting date.

Effective for annuity starting dates that are later than November 18, 1996, a table is set forth in the Code for determining the excludable portion of each monthly payment from such an annuity. The excludable portion of an annuity subject to this provision is determined by dividing the employee's investment in the contract by the number of anticipated payments based on the age of the annuitant, as follows[64]:

Age on annuity starting date	Number of anticipated payments
Not more than 55	360
More than 55 but not more than 60	310
More than 60 but not more than 65	260
More than 65 but not more than 70	210
More than 70	160

In the case of annuity starting dates after December 31, 1997, a separate table is provided for annuities payable over two or more lives. The excludable portion of such an annuity is determined by dividing the employee's investment in the contract by the number of anticipated payments based on the age of the annuitant, as follows[65]:

If the combined ages of the annuitants are:	Number of payments
Not more than 110	410
More than 110 but not more than 120	360
More than 120 but not more than 130	310
More than 130 but not more than 140	260
More than 140	210

For annuity starting dates beginning after July 1, 1986 and before November 19, 1996, an exclusion ratio is used to determine the taxable portion of the annuity payouts. The exclusion ratio is the ratio of the employee's "investment in the contract" (cost) to the employee's "expected return," expressed as follows:

$$\frac{\text{Investment In Contract}}{\text{Expected Return}}$$

The employee's cost or "investment in contract" is essentially his nondeductible contributions. Where life insurance is included in the plan, it also includes the total of all one year term insurance costs that have been reported as taxable income. The "expected return" is the annual payment the employee will receive multiplied by the employee's life expectancy (see Table V, One Life-Expected Return Multiples in Appendix D). (Adjustments must be made for payouts made over differing time periods or where minimum payout guarantees are present.) Once the fraction is determined, it is multiplied by the annual payment. The product is the amount not subject to taxation. The balance of each payment is taxable as ordinary income.[66] A simplified safe harbor method for taxing annuity payments (see IRS Pub. 575) is available for individuals whose annuity starting date is after July 1, 1986.[67]

Distributions of deductible employee contributions are generally taxed under a pro-rata recovery rule.[68]

6. Distributions before the participant attains age 59½ are subject to a 10% penalty tax with certain exceptions (death, divorce, disability, payments made over the participant's life starting from separation from service, and medical expenses).[69] The penalty is increased to 25% in the case of distributions from a SIMPLE IRA during the first two years of participation in the plan.

7. A beneficiary receiving death benefits from a qualified retirement plan is taxed on the amount received for income tax purposes under either the lump sum or annuity rules. However, voluntary employee contributions that were deductible are not allowed the relief granted lump-sum distributions and are includable in ordinary income.[70] In computing the amount of taxable income the beneficiary must report as a result of the distribution, if the distribution is made in a lump sum and if any portion of the distribution consists of life insurance proceeds for which the employee paid the insurance costs or reported this Table 2001 cost as taxable income on his return, then the difference between the face amount of the insurance contract and the insurance contract cash value (this difference is called the "pure insurance") passes to the beneficiary free of income tax.[71] Thus, the beneficiary treats only the cash value portion of any death benefit plus any other cash distributions from the plan as income subject to tax.

If, on the other hand, the employee did not pay the insurance cost of the life insurance contract or did not report the cost of such insurance as taxable income, the portion of the insurance proceeds consisting of pure insurance (as defined above) will be considered taxable income to the beneficiary.

8. If the plan participant suffers permanent loss or loss of use of a member or function of the body, or permanent disfigurement, it may be possible for him or her to receive benefits under a qualified plan free of income tax under Code section 105(c). In order for the payment to qualify, the plan must provide 100% vesting of benefits if the participant ceases employment due to total and permanent disability, and must also include statutory language from Section 105(c) to establish the dual purpose of the plan (i.e., a retirement plan and an "accident and health" plan).

Code section 105 applies to amounts received under "Accident and Health Plans." A minority of courts have found that a qualified plan can serve a dual function of providing retirement benefits and disability benefits. To the extent benefits are provided due to the participant's disability, they may be income tax free if the requirements of Section 105(c) are satisfied.

Section 105(c)(2) requires that the disability payment be computed by taking the nature of the injury into account in determining the benefit without regard to the period the employee is absent from work. This requirement may be difficult to satisfy in most pension plan contexts. However, a provision giving the committee discretion to determine disability benefits with reference to the nature of the injury may enable the disabled participant to overcome this hurdle.

WHAT ARE THE ESTATE TAX IMPLICATIONS?

The entire value of a qualified plan death benefit is subject to inclusion in the decedent's gross estate for federal estate tax purposes. However, only high-income plan participants will actually be subject to estate tax. First, there is a substantial unified credit applicable to the estate tax, which essentially eliminates estate taxes for gross estates of less than $1,500,000 for 2004 and 2005; $2,000,000 for 2006, 2007, and 2008; and $3,500,000 for 2009. In 2010, the estate tax is repealed for a year. Finally, in 2011, the exemption equivalent of the unified credit reverts to $1,000,000.[72] In addition, the unlimited marital deduction for federal estate tax purposes defers federal estate tax on property transferred at death to a spouse in a qualifying manner until the death of the second spouse.[73]

Avoiding federal estate tax can be significant if the estate is relatively large, the participant is single, or, for whatever reason, the participant is unwilling to pay the death benefit to the spouse. In each of these situations, the marital deduction would not be available. Also, even when the death benefit is payable to a spouse, federal estate tax is merely delayed and is not really avoided; a spouse is often about the same age as the decedent, and thus within a few years much of the property transferred to the spouse is potentially subject to federal estate tax at the surviving spouse's death.

Only a limited exclusion is available from the federal estate tax for retirement plan distributions payable at an employee's death. The Tax Reform Act of 1984 contained a provision that permitted individuals who were both in pay status and had made an irrevocable election as to the form of benefit distribution to continue to have the benefit of the estate tax exclusion (the unlimited exclusion for participants in pay status prior to January 1, 1983, or the $100,000 exclusion for participants in pay status prior to January 1, 1985). TRA '86 somewhat liberalized the grandfathering provisions by providing that the participant no longer needs to be in pay status as of the applicable date. The participant needs only to have separated from service prior to the applicable date and not to have made any change in the form of benefit to be paid prior to death.

State inheritance tax laws covering distributions from qualified pension and profit sharing plans vary widely. In Pennsylvania, for example, death benefits are excludable from inheritance taxes as long as such amounts are not available to pay death taxes and other estate expenses (i.e., payments will be state death tax free if payable to a named beneficiary other than the decedent-employee's estate). On the other hand, New Jersey, a neighboring state, taxes retirement plan death benefits payable to any beneficiary other than the deceased employee's spouse, regardless of the manner in which benefits are paid.

IMPLICATIONS AND ISSUES IN COMMUNITY PROPERTY STATES

Many community property implications and issues have been discussed in previous chapters. Some additional tax implications should also be mentioned.

Generally, for purposes of divorce, the community property laws are recognized; however, there will be a substantial difference in rights in the event of the prior death of the nonparticipant spouse. Generally, if the participant spouse is married, the required form of distribution on the death of either spouse is in the form of a survivor annuity for the surviving spouse. Where the participant spouse is the first to die, this means the surviving spouse will receive the required annuity regardless of the community nature of the qualified plan benefit.

Further, where the nonparticipant spouse is the first to die, one court[74] has held that his or her community interest in a pension plan in effect passes to the surviving participant spouse regardless of any direction of the deceased spouse, or any contrary provisions in the will of the deceased spouse. In effect, the required survivor rights supersede state community property laws.

This position was affirmed in a landmark 1997 case,[75] where the U.S. Supreme Court held in a 5-4 decision that a deceased spouse may not make a bequest of her community property interest in her participant spouse's undistributed qualified plan benefits, as further discussed in Chapter 49.

Note that the survivor annuity rule does not apply to distributions from IRAs, SIMPLE IRAs, or Simplified Employee Pensions, as discussed in Chapter 51, and that the survivor annuity may be waived, as discussed at the end of this chapter.

QUESTIONS AND ANSWERS

Question – Who is a fiduciary and what are the fiduciary responsibility rules established by ERISA?

Answer – A fiduciary is a person who (a) exercises any discretionary authority or discretionary control respecting management of the plan or exercises any authority or control respecting management or disposition of assets; (b) renders investment advice for a fee or other compensation, direct or indirect, with respect to any monies or other property of the plan, or has any authority or responsibility to do so; or (c) has any discretionary authority or discretionary responsibility in the administration of the plan.[76] The term "fiduciary" also includes persons named by a fiduciary to carry out fiduciary responsibilities (other than trustee responsibilities) under the plan. ERISA established rules governing the conduct of fiduciaries and other persons dealing with the plan. The Department of Labor administers certain provisions that pertain to rules and remedies similar to those under traditional trust law governing the conduct of fiduciaries.

Specifically, these fiduciary responsibility rules relate to plan administration, provide general standards of conduct for fiduciaries, and make certain transactions "prohibited transactions" in which plan fiduciaries may not engage.[77] Other provisions that are enforced by the Treasury Department impose an excise tax on certain persons who violate the prohibited transaction rules.[78]

Basically, ERISA requires each fiduciary of a plan to act with the care, skill, prudence, and diligence under the circumstances then prevailing that a prudent person acting in a like capacity and familiar with such matters would use in conducting an enterprise of like character and with like aims.

Furthermore, ERISA requires that a qualified retirement plan be for the exclusive benefit of the plan's employees and their beneficiaries.[79] Under the "exclusive benefit" umbrella:

1. the cost of plan assets must not exceed fair market value at the time of purchase;

2. assets should bring a fair return commensurate with the prevailing rate;

3. the plan should maintain sufficient liquidity to permit distributions; and

4. the safeguards and diversity that would be adhered to by a prudent investor must be present.

Question – How does plan termination insurance work?

Answer – ERISA established, within the Department of Labor, a public corporation named the Pension Benefit Guaranty Corporation (PBGC). The PBGC is a federal insurance company that provides mandatory plan termination insurance to protect the benefit rights of workers whose defined benefit pension plans go out of existence. As one of its main duties, the corporation administers plan termination insurance for defined benefit pension plans, up to specified limits.[80]

Premiums for PBGC coverage are $19.00 per participant, plus an additional amount, calculated by dividing the plan's unfunded vested benefits as of the end of the preceding plan year by the number of plan participants at that time. The additional premium is equal to $9.00 per thousand (or fraction thereof) of the plan's unfunded vested benefits as of the end of the preceding plan year. For plan years beginning before July 1, 1994, the aggregate increase in the premium for a participant due to the additional premium could not exceed $53.00. This cap was phased out for plan years beginning after June 30, 1994.[81]

Question – Can a pension plan make a loan to a participant or plan beneficiary?

Answer – Yes, if the loan is made in accordance with specific provisions in the plan governing such loans, a reasonable charge is made for the use of plan assets, and the loan is adequately secured. Loans must be available to all participants on a reasonably equivalent basis.[82]

Plan loans can also be offered from HR-10 plans to owner employees, such as partners, S corporation shareholders, and sole proprietors. (In plan years prior to 2002, such loans constituted "prohibited transactions"; therefore, they could not be made without specific Department of Labor approval.[83])

Limits are imposed on tax-free participant borrowing from qualified plans, from tax sheltered annuities, and from plans (qualified and nonqualified) of federal, state, and local governments and their agencies and instrumentalities.

Certain loan transactions are treated as distributions. Loan transactions include: (1) the direct or indirect receipt of a loan, and (2) the assignment (or agreement to assign) or the pledging (or agreement to pledge) of any portion of an employee's interest in a plan.[84]

The following rules and exceptions apply to plan loans:

1. *Loan agreement.* The plan loan must be evidenced by a legally enforceable agreement, specifying the date, amount and term of the loan;[85]

2. *Term requirement and dollar limitation.* The term of the loan must be no longer than five years.[86] Loans which are to be repaid within five years are taxed as distributions only to the extent that the amount of the loan (together with any other outstanding loans the employee has made from plans with the same employer) exceeds the lesser of (a) $50,000 reduced by the highest outstanding

loan balance during the prior 12 months, or (b) half of the employee's vested benefits under the employer plans from which he has borrowed (or $10,000, if greater).[87] If the loan exceeds the dollar limitation, a distribution of the amount in excess of the dollar limit is deemed to occur when the loan is made.[88]

3. *Loans that do not have to be repaid within five years* are fully taxable as distributions. Whether or not a loan must be repaid within five years is ascertained as of the date the loan is made.

4. *Repayment*. The loan agreement must specify the amount and terms of the loan and the repayment schedule. Failure to make a repayment of a plan loan installment when it is due will generally result in a deemed distribution, unless payment is made within specified "cure" (grace) periods.[89]

Some loans of five years or less may be subsequently extended. The loan balance at the time of the extension is considered a distribution at that time. If repayment under a "5-year-or-less" loan is not made (so at the end of five years, the participant still owes the plan money), any remaining amounts due are considered plan distributions.

"More-than-5-year" loans are not converted to "5-year-or-less" loans or in any other way favorably treated merely because they are repaid in five years or less (regardless of the reason for the early repayments).

Exception 1: *Housing loans*. A loan of more than five years generally is not treated as a distribution to the extent that it is used by the plan participant to purchase the participant's principal residence.[90]

Exception 2: *Certain mortgage loans*. Where plan trustees invest a specific percentage or amount of plan assets in residential mortgages or in other types of mortgage investments, such investments are not considered loans as long as the amount lent does not exceed the fair market value of the property the loan was used to purchase. Loans to officers, directors, or owners (or their beneficiaries) are not protected under this exception.

Question – What are the reporting and disclosure requirements of ERISA?

Answer – In general, every plan that is not specifically exempted must file certain reports each year. The annual report for plans with 100 or more participants must include an audited financial statement. Annual reports of defined benefit plans must contain a certified actuarial report. If the plan terminates, additional special reports are required.

The number of participants covered by a plan has no effect on the reporting and disclosure requirements–an annual report must be filed regardless of how many or how few participants are covered. However, where a plan contains less than 100 participants, a simplified report may be authorized.

Furthermore, certain information must be provided to plan participants and beneficiaries. They must be given a summary of the plan written in a manner understandable by the average participant or beneficiary (i.e., a Summary Plan Description). Furthermore, beneficiaries and participants can request a status report once a year showing total benefits accrued and nonforfeitable pension benefit rights. Employees who have terminated employment during the plan year must also be given a statement of their deferred vested rights in the plan. Many of these documents become public information and can be inspected.[91]

Failure to meet the reporting and disclosure requirements can result in serious civil and/or criminal penalties, which include fines and imprisonment.

Question – What is a target benefit pension plan?

Answer – It is a retirement plan under which the required contribution is initially based upon an assumed retirement benefit for each participant, but under which the actual retirement benefit received is based upon the market value of the assets in the individual participant's account at the time of retirement.

Question – What is an age-weighted profit sharing plan?

Answer – Under traditional profit sharing plan arrangements, employer contributions are generally allocated each year to employees either in proportion to relative compensation or in proportion to relative compensation together with integration with Social Security benefits. However, an employer may maintain a qualified profit sharing plan in which the participant's age is taken into account when allocating the employer's contribution.[92] The result is that somewhat larger allocations (as a percentage of pay) are provided to older employees than to younger employees. Nonetheless, the allocations must satisfy either a "minimum allocation gateway" (e.g., generally 5% of compensation for NHCEs or one-third of that provided to HCEs) or "broadly available allocation rates" must be used.[93]

Question – What limitations are imposed on a qualified retirement plan regarding the purchase of ordinary life insurance?

Answer – In a profit sharing plan, less than 50% of the aggregate employer contributions and forfeitures allocated to each participant's account can be used to purchase ordinary life insurance. If insurance may be purchased only with funds that have been accumulated in the plan for two or more years, the 50% rule does not apply.[94] In addition to this requirement, a profit sharing plan must require the trustee at or before retirement either (a) to convert the policies into cash, or (b) to distribute the policies to the employee. A money-purchase plan has the same "less than 50%" rule with regard to the purchase of ordinary life insurance.

Life insurance is a permissible purchase in a defined benefit pension plan if it meets either of two tests. The first test is essentially the same as the money-purchase plan test. The alternative test is the "100 to 1" test whereby the insurance is permissible if the insurance amount does not exceed 100 times the expected monthly retirement benefit.[95] For example, if the projected monthly benefit is $1,000, the life insurance cannot exceed $100,000.

Question – What is a thrift and savings plan?

Answer – The major characteristic of a thrift and savings plan is that employee-participants must contribute some percentage of compensation to the plan. The employer matches contributions of employees according to some formula. For example, an employer may match each dollar of employee contribution with more or less than $1 of employer contribution. A thrift and savings plan can be tax qualified or can be informal.

A tax qualified thrift and savings plan will result in a current employer deduction for contributions to the plan and, yet, employees will not be currently taxed on employer contributions. Both employer and employee contributions will grow tax-free within the plan. When distributions from a qualified thrift and savings plan are made, they are subject to the same rules applicable to other qualified retirement plans. Typically, a thrift and savings plan will require employees to contribute a percentage of compensation in order to participate. It is important when incorporating thrift and savings features in a plan that such required contributions meet a special nondiscrimination test.[96] All contributions are counted for purposes of the annual additions limitation.

Question – Can a qualified pension or profit sharing plan provide for voluntary deductible employee contributions?

Answer – No. Prior to 1987, anyone who had earned income, regardless of whether he was an active participant in a qualified plan, could establish an IRA. A voluntary deductible contribution of up to $2,000 could be made to an employer's plan (if the plan so provided), to an IRA, or as a combination split in any proportion between the two.[97]

Voluntary *nondeductible* employee contributions to qualified pension, profit sharing, or stock bonus plans are allowed, providing they meet a special nondiscrimination test.[98] Also, 100% of employee contributions, whether voluntary or mandatory, will be included in the annual addition for purposes of the dollar limitation. Accordingly, both employer and employee contributions to a defined contribution plan count toward the $41,000/100% (in 2004) limitation.[99]

Question – What is a cash or deferred arrangement (or 401(k) plan) and is it subject to current taxation?

Answer – Under a 401(k) plan, an employee can elect to have the employer make an elective contribution to the plan on the employee's behalf or to receive an equivalent amount in cash.[100]

To the extent the employee elects to receive cash, the cash payment will be subject to all payroll taxes currently. If the employee elects to have the employer make an elective contribution, such contributed amount will not be subject to income tax, but it will be subject to Social Security taxes and the Federal

Unemployment Taxes Act (FUTA).[101] Of course, amounts contributed in excess of the elective deferral limit of $13,000 (in 2004), are subject to income tax as well.[102] The $13,000 limitation is scheduled to increase by $1,000 each year until it reaches $15,000 in 2006.

A 401(k) plan may also allow special catch-up contributions by participants who have reached age 50 by the close of the plan year. The elective deferral limit for such individuals is increased by the lesser of (a) an "applicable dollar amount," or (b) the amount of the participant's compensation, reduced by any other elective deferrals of the participant for the year. The applicable dollar amounts are $3,000 in 2004, $4,000 in 2005, and $5,000 for plan years beginning in 2006 and thereafter.[103]

Question – What special nondiscrimination tests apply to 401(k) plans?

Answer – In order to meet the nondiscrimination requirement, qualified 401(k) plans must either satisfy the actual deferral percentage (ADP) test, adopt a SIMPLE 401(k) plan (see below) or meet the requirements for an alternative safe harbor, as described below.

The ADP test is designed to limit the extent to which elective contributions made on behalf of highly compensated employees may exceed the elective contributions made on behalf of nonhighly compensated employees.[104]

The amount of elective deferrals to be credited to a participant's account for any plan year must satisfy the following tests.

If the nonhighly compensated group contributes an average of:	The highly compensated group may contribute an average of:
Under 2% of compensation.	2 times the rate of the nonhighly compensated group.
Between 2-8% of compensation.	2% of pay more than the non-highly compensated group.
Over 8% of compensation.	1¼ times the rate of the nonhighly compensated group.

The ADP test can be performed by comparing the ADP of highly compensated employees for a plan year to the ADP of nonhighly compensated employees for either the same plan year (current year testing) *or* the preceding plan year (prior year testing).[105]

Question – What is a safe harbor 401(k) plan?

Answer – A safe harbor 401(k) plan is one that meets the nondiscrimination requirement by satisfying an alternative safe harbor set forth in Section 401(k)(12) in place of the traditional ADP test. Under the safe harbor, the plan will be considered nondiscriminatory if (a) the employer satisfies a matching contribution requirement for nonhighly compensated employees (100% of the employee contribution up to 3% of compensation, plus 50% from 3% to 5% of compensation) and certain design requirements, including 100% vesting; *or* (b) the employer makes a nonelective (nonmatching) contribution for all eligible nonhighly compensated employees equal to at least 3% of compensation.[106]

Question – What is a SIMPLE 401(k) plan?

Answer – A SIMPLE 401(k) plan is a cash or deferred arrangement that satisfies the nondiscrimination requirement by meeting special requirements set forth in Section 401(k)(11). Among these requirements are that: (a) the employer must have 100 or fewer employees (only employees with at least $5,000 in compensation for the preceding year are counted) on any day in the year; (b) employees must be eligible to make elective salary reductions contributions for the year of up to $9,000 (for plan years beginning in 2004) annually; (c) the employer is required to make a contribution equal to either (i) a dollar for dollar matching contribution up to 3% of the employee's compensation, or (ii) 2% of compensation for all eligible employees earning at least $5,000 (whether or not they elect salary reductions); (d) the employer may not maintain any other plan (e.g., qualified plan, SEP, 403(a) annuity, 403(b) tax-sheltered annuity) that covers any of the same employees as the SIMPLE 401(k) plan; and (e) all contributions to the SIMPLE 401(k) plan must be nonforfeitable. SIMPLE 401(k) plans are not subject to the top-heavy requirements, nor to separate nondiscrimination testing; however, they are subject to the other qualification, administrative and ERISA requirements that apply to a qualified Section 401(k) plan.[107]

Question – What are excess contributions to a 401(k) plan?

Answer – An excess contribution is the excess of the elective contributions (including qualified nonelective and matching contributions that are treated as elective contributions) made on behalf of highly compensated employees for the plan year over the maximum amount permitted under the ADP test for such plan year.[108]

Question – How can excess contributions be corrected?

Answer – A 401(k) plan will not fail the ADP test for any plan year, and thus will maintain its qualified status if: (1) the amount of excess contributions for such plan year, along with any income attributable thereto, is returned to highly compensated employees within 12 months after the close of the applicable plan year; or (2) the highly compensated employee elects to recharacterize the excess amount contributed as an after-tax voluntary contribution.[109]

Question – What happens if a 401(k) plan fails to correct excess contributions?

Answer – A 10% excise tax is imposed on the employer unless the excess contributions are corrected within 2½ months after the end of the plan year for which they were made.[110] If excess contributions are not corrected before the end of the plan year following the plan year for which the excess contributions were made, the plan will fail to qualify for the plan year for which the excess contributions were made and for all subsequent plan years during which the excess contributions remain in the plan.[111]

Question – Are there any measures that can be taken to assure compliance with the special nondiscrimination tests for 401(k) plans?

Answer – Yes. The plan may limit the amount subject to deferral and, if necessary, provide for a minimum level of nonelective employer contributions. For example, if a profit sharing plan provides for nonelective employer contributions of 2% of compensation, which are nonforfeitable and subject to appropriate distribution restrictions, and if eligible employees are limited to deferring an additional 2% of compensation, the nondiscrimination tests will be satisfied in all cases. An alternative would be to make the cash-or-deferred election irrevocable for the entire plan year.

Question – Are there any restrictions on the distribution of elective contributions?

Answer – Yes. A 401(k) plan must provide that amounts attributable to elective contributions may not be distributed before the occurrence of one of the following events:

1. The participant's retirement, death, disability, or other termination of service;

2. The termination of the plan without the establishment of a successor defined contribution plan;

3. The sale of the business or subsidiary;

4. The participant's attainment of age 59½, or

5. The participant's financial hardship.[112]

Question – What constitutes "financial hardship" for purposes of permissible distributions?

Answer –For a distribution to be considered as having been made on account of financial hardship it must be made due to an immediate and heavy financial need of the employee and it must be necessary to satisfy that need. The determination of the existence of the immediate and heavy financial need must be made in accordance with nondiscriminatory and objective standards set forth in the plan.

Question – What amounts from the plan may be distributed on account of a financial hardship?

Answer – A distribution that is made due to hardship must be limited to the distributable amount. The "distributable amount" is equal to the employee's total elective contributions as of the date of distribution, reduced by the amount of previous distributions on account of hardship.

Question – What are some examples of permissible hardship distributions?

Answer – A distribution is treated as being made on account of immediate and heavy financial need if it is for:

1. The payment of expenses for medical care that were either previously incurred by, or are necessary for the medical care of, the employee or the employee's spouse or dependents;

2. The costs directly related to the purchase, excluding mortgage payments, of the employee's principal residence;

3. The payment of tuition, related educational fees and room and board for the next 12 months of post-secondary education for the employee, his spouse, children, or dependents; and

4. The payment of amounts necessary to prevent the eviction of the employee from his principal residence or to prevent foreclosure on the mortgage on the employee's principal residence.

The IRS has the authority to expand the above list of expenses found under the regulations, through the issuance of revenue rulings, notices and other documents of general applicability, rather than on an individual basis.[113]

Question – What are examples of distributions that are not treated as necessary to satisfy an immediate and heavy financial need?

Answer – Distributions are not treated as necessary to satisfy an immediate and heavy financial need of an employee:

1. To the extent the amount of the distribution is in excess of the amount required to relieve the financial need. The amount of the immediate and heavy financial need may include amounts necessary to pay federal, state or local income taxes or penalties reasonably anticipated to result from the distribution; and

2. To the extent the need may be relieved from other sources that are reasonably available to the employee, referred to as an "employee resource." For example, a vacation home owned by the employee and his spouse is treated as an employee resource. However, property held in an irrevocable trust for the benefit of the employee's children is not treated as an employee resource.

Question – What are the advantages of life insurance in a qualified retirement plan?

Answer – There are a number of advantages. These include (1) protection against the premature death of a participant, (2) securing the right to use guaranteed annuity rates at a future retirement date, (3) assurance that insurance can be purchased

at original age rates when the participant retires or terminates employment, and (4) in a profit sharing plan providing key person insurance on the lives of corporate officers or valuable employees for the benefit of the trust and its participants.

Question – Can a qualified pension or profit sharing plan provide any protection from the claims of creditors?

Answer – Yes. ERISA provides that a pension, profit sharing, or HR-10 plan will not be qualified unless it provides that benefits provided under the plan may not be assigned or alienated, voluntarily or involuntarily. An exception to this rule exists for assignments used to secure plan loans to a participant and voluntary and revocable assignments that do not exceed 10% of any benefit payment to a participant, unless the assignment is made for purposes of defraying plan administrative costs.[114]

It has generally been accepted in the non-bankruptcy context that the anti-alienation provision protects pension interests from the reach of creditors. The Supreme Court has recently ruled that the anti-alienation provision also protects a debtor's interest in his qualified pension plan from the reach of his creditors in bankruptcy.[115]

In addition, the creation, assignment, or recognition of a right to any benefit payable from a plan under a "qualified domestic relations order" (QDRO) is not treated as a prohibited assignment or alienation under ERISA or the Internal Revenue Code, thus allowing enforcement of state QDROs.[116] All qualified retirement plans are required to provide for the payment of benefits in accordance with the terms of any QDRO.

The term "domestic relations order" means a judgment, decree, or order (including approval of a property settlement agreement) which relates to the provision of child support, alimony payments, or marital property rights to a spouse, former spouse, child or other dependent of a participant, and is made pursuant to state domestic relations law. To be *qualified*, a domestic relations order must (1) create or recognize the existence of an alternate payee's right to receive all or a portion of the benefits payable with respect to a participant under a plan; (2) clearly specify certain facts (e.g., name and address of participant and alternate payee, amount of benefits to be paid and the number of payments); and (3) not alter the amount or form of benefits under a plan. The term "alternate payee" means any spouse, former spouse, child or other dependent of a participant who is recognized by a domestic relations order as having a right to receive all, or a portion of, a participant's benefits under a plan.[117]

A QDRO can require benefits to be paid to an alternate payee at the participant's earliest retirement age under the plan without regard to whether the participant has separated from service or retired.

Question – When does an employee become subject to tax on benefits accruing in a qualified plan?

Answer – An employee or beneficiary of a qualified plan will not be taxed until benefits are received from the plan. For example, even though a participant in a profit sharing plan has the unrestricted right to make withdrawals of employer or deductible employee contributions, or the earnings on nondeductible employee contributions, there will be no current tax based on constructive receipt. This increases the appeal of making voluntary contributions to qualified plans even when such contributions are nondeductible.

Question – Are there any restrictions on pension or profit sharing plan investments in "collectibles"?

Answer – Yes. Investment in "collectibles" by an individually directed account under a qualified plan is treated as a current taxable distribution. Collectibles are defined as (1) art, (2) rugs or antiques, (3) metals or gems, (4) stamps or coins, (5) alcoholic beverages, or (6) any other tangible personal property designated as a "collectible" by the Secretary of the Treasury.[118]

Question – Is a qualified plan required to provide a participant's surviving spouse survivor benefits?

Answer – Yes. A participant's surviving spouse must be provided "automatic survivor benefits."[119] Defined benefit plans and defined contribution plans are required to provide automatic survivor benefits (1) in the form of a "qualified joint and survivor annuity," to a vested participant who receives a plan distribution for reasons other than the participant's death (i.e., termination of employment, retirement or disability); and (2) in the form of a "qualified pre-retirement survivor annuity" to a vested participant who dies before reaching the "annuity starting date" under the plan and who has a surviving spouse.

For automatic survivor coverage purposes, a vested participant means a participant who has a nonforfeitable right to any portion of the accrued benefit or account balance, whether or not the participant is still employed by the employer. The term "annuity starting date" means the first day of the first period for which an amount is payable as an annuity (or, in the case of a non-annuity benefit, the first day on which all events have occurred entitling the participant to the benefit).[120]

The automatic survivor coverage rules do not apply to a profit sharing or stock bonus plan if (a) the plan provides that the participant's vested account balance will be paid to his or her surviving spouse (or to a designated beneficiary if there is no surviving spouse or if the surviving spouse gives the proper consent); (b) the participant does not elect payment of benefits in the form of a life annuity; and (c) with respect to the participant, the plan is not a transferee of a plan required to provide automatic survivor benefits.[121]

A "qualified joint and survivor annuity" is an annuity for the life of the participant with a survivor annuity for the life of the spouse that is not less than 50% (and not greater than 100%) of the amount that is payable during the joint lives of the participant and spouse, and that is the actuarial equivalent of a single life annuity for the life of the participant.[122]

A "qualified pre-retirement survivor annuity" is an annuity for the life of the surviving spouse of the participant with payments to the surviving spouse which are not less than the payments that would have been made under the qualified joint and survivor annuity (or the actuarial equivalent thereof), under the rules set forth in Code section 417(c).

A qualified joint and survivor annuity and a qualified pre-retirement survivor annuity need not be provided by a plan unless the participant and the surviving spouse have been married throughout the one-year period ending on the earlier of the participant's retirement, disability or the date of the participant's death.[123]

A plan participant may elect not to receive the qualified joint and survivor annuity and/or the qualified pre-retirement survivor annuity at any time during an applicable election period and to receive benefits in another form offered under the plan. The participant is permitted to revoke any such election during the applicable election period.

The applicable election period, in the case of a qualified joint and survivor annuity, is the 90-day period ending on the annuity starting date. The applicable election, in the case of a qualified pre-retirement survivor annuity, is a period beginning on the first day of the plan year in which the participant attains age 35 and ending on the date of the participant's death. If the participant separates from service, the applicable election period begins not later than the date of separation.[124]

An election by the participant not to take survivor coverage is effective only if the participant's spouse consents in writing, the consent is witnessed by a plan representative or a notary public, and the spouse's consent acknowledges the effect of the election. Spousal consent is not required if it is established (to the satisfaction of a plan representative) that there is no spouse or that the spouse cannot be located.[125]

Question – Will a plan participant on a 1-year leave of absence from work due to a maternity/paternity reason incur a "break-in-service" and therefore cease to participate in the plan?

Answer – No. An employee who is on a leave of absence for maternity/paternity reasons will not incur a 1-year break-in-service for purposes of participation or vesting in the year in which a break would otherwise occur.[126] Maternity/paternity reasons include pregnancy, childbirth, adoption or child caring immediately after childbirth or adoption.

Question – Are there any other taxes that may affect a qualified plan or its participants?

Answer – Generally, there are four other taxes affecting retirement plans (which have not been discussed elsewhere). The taxes are as follows:

1. A 20% nondeductible excise tax is imposed on the amount of any "employer reversion" from a qualified plan if (a) a significant amount of the reversion is used to fund benefits in a replacement plan, (b) a significant amount is used to increased the benefits of participants under the terminating plan, or (c) the employer is in bankruptcy. Otherwise, the tax is 50%.[127] Liability for this tax rests on the employer. An "employer reversion" is the amount of cash and the fair market value of other property received (directly or indirectly) by an employer from a qualified

plan. Certain mistaken excess payments may be excluded.

2. There is a 50% nondeductible excise tax for the failure to make a minimum required distribution from the plan. The tax is equal to 50% of the amount by which the minimum required distribution exceeds the actual amount distributed during the taxable year. The tax is imposed on the payee. A "waiver" is allowed for "reasonable error" if steps are being taken to pay out the balance due.[128]

3. An additional penalty tax applies in cases where there is an underpayment of tax due to an overstatement of pension liabilities. The amount of the penalty depends on the amount of the overstatement: 20% for overstatements of 200% or more but less than 400% of the correct amount of liabilities and 40% for overstatements of 400% or more.[129]

4. There is a 50% excise tax on prohibited allocations of employer securities acquired in a transaction involving the tax-deferred sale to an ESOP.[130]

Question – Where a beneficiary designation for a pension plan names the surviving spouse as primary beneficiary, but with an alternate gift to a Family Trust in the event of the death of the surviving spouse before the passage of a reasonable time following the participant's death (e.g., 90 days), or in the event of a disclaimer by the surviving spouse, are there any concerns over restrictions created by the Retirement Equity Act of 1984?

Answer – REA '84 generally provides that all benefits from pension and profit sharing plans, with some exceptions, must be in the form of annuities. If the participant has died, then the general provision under REA '84 is that there be an annuity for the lifetime of the survivor as to at least one-half of the property. Whether the transfer can be made to a trust in lieu of the surviving spouse is something that has been questioned by a number of practitioners. Indeed, *The REA Book* says that the requirements of the Act cannot be met by naming an irrevocable trust as sole beneficiary even though the surviving spouse is the sole beneficiary of the trust and the benefits payable under the trust meet the survivor annuity benefit requirements of the Act.[131]

If the surviving spouse dies, then it may be that REA '84 no longer applies, and any normal transfer can be made and property can go to a trust outright as opposed to being in an annuity form.

On the other hand, the Act seems to lay out clearly the rule that any transfer outside the normal REA '84 rules must be done only on the basis of a written exception being made by the participant and a particular form of written waiver by the surviving spouse of any annuity rights. There have been suggestions that payments by pension plans administrators to trusts without such a formal written request and written waiver might cause the trust to be disqualified.

This is an area of the law in which a pension law expert should be consulted on beneficiary designations involving large amounts.

The beneficiary designation form reproduced at Figure 52.1 (3 pages) at the end of this chapter is used by Ralph Gano Miller in his California practice and contains language designed to overcome the problems inherent in the law as it presently reads.

Question – What are the gift and estate tax consequences of joint and survivor annuities and survivor annuities to a spouse?

Answer – These annuity payments automatically qualify for the gift and estate tax marital deduction so long as no payments can be made to anyone other than a spouse until the death of the surviving spouse. This is true even though there could be payments or distributions to another person after the death of both spouses.

Note that in the case of the estate tax marital deduction, the executor of the estate of the first spouse to die can elect out of the marital deduction.

Question – Can a life insurance trust be created within a qualified retirement plan?

Answer – Many commentators believe it can, although there is no authority on this point. The plan would provide for the creation of a separate trust, which is in effect an irrevocable life insurance trust. As discussed in Chapter 31, it is structured so that the insured has no control over the trust, and the policy proceeds cannot be distributed to the insured or his or her estate. The premiums are paid through the plan.

This technique has not been tested, and may run into problems where there is a surviving spouse, because of the survivor annuity rules. Also, some issues have been raised as to whether there could be a problem with a prohibited transaction. Finally, it must be remembered that the growth and income from investments in qualified plans is tax free until retirement, and since the inside build-up of value in life insurance policies is generally also tax free, it may be better to maintain insurance outside of qualified plans.

Question – If a distribution from a qualified plan is made to a surviving spouse on the death of the participant, can he or she roll this over into an individual retirement account (IRA)?

Answer – A spousal rollover is permitted as to all or part of such a distribution, and the distribution will not be subject to income tax to the extent it is rolled over. Spousal rollovers are discussed in Chapter 18.

ASRS: Sec. 59.

CHAPTER ENDNOTES

1. Treas. Reg. §1.401-1(b)(2).
2. IRC Sec. 401(a).
3. IRC Sec. 402(a)(1).
4. IRC Sec. 401(a)(9).
5. IRC Sec. 401(k)(2)(B)(ii).
6. IRC Secs. 401(k)(2)(C), 401(k)(3)(D).
7. IRC Sec. 401(k)(4)(A).
8. IRC Sec. 402(g); IRC Sec. 401(a)(30). It is important to note that all provisions of EGTRRA 2001 are scheduled to sunset, or expire, for years beginning after December 31, 2010.
9. IRC Sec. 414(v).
10. IRC Sec. 401(a).
11. IRC Sec. 410(a)(1).
12. IRC Sec. 410(a)(1)(B).
13. IRC Sec. 410(b)(1).
14. IRC Sec. 410(b)(2).
15. IRC Sec. 401(a)(26). In years beginning before 1997, this provision applied to all qualified plans.
16. IRC Secs. 410(a)(1)(A), 410(a)(3)(A).
17. IRC Sec. 410(b)(3)(A).
18. IRC Sec. 411(a)(1).
19. IRC Secs. 401(k)(2)(C), 401(k)(3)(D).
20. IRC Sec. 411(a)(2).
21. IRC Secs. 415(c)(1), 415(d)(1).
22. IRC Sec. 404(a)(3)(A).
23. IRC Sec. 404(n).
24. IRC Sec. 415(c)(3)(C).
25. IRC Sec. 415(b)(1).
26. IRC Secs. 415(b)(2)(C), 415(b)(2)(D).
27. IRC Sec. 415(b)(5)(A).
28. IRC Sec. 415(b)(4).

29. IRC Sec. 415(b)(5)(B).

30. IRC Sec. 415(b)(2)(B).

31. IRC Sec. 415(b)(2)(C).

32. IRC Sec. 415(b)(2)(D).

33. IRC Secs. 415(b)(2)(B); 415(b)(2)(E)(ii).

34. IRC Sec. 415(c)(1).

35. IRC Sec. 404(a)(1).

36. IRC Sec. 412(c)(7).

37. IRC Sec. 404(a)(3). Pre-1987 unused contribution carryforwards may still be available.

38. IRC Sec. 404(a)(7).

39. IRC Sec. 219(e).

40. IRC Sec. 72(o)(3).

41. IRC Sec. 404(a)(3).

42. IRC Sec. 404(n).

43. IRC Sec. 408(q).

44. *Vinson & Elkins v. Comm.*, 93-2 USTC ¶50,632 (5th Cir. 1993); *Rhoades, McKee & Boer v. U.S.*, 93-2 USTC ¶50,425 (W.D.MI 1993); *Wachtell, Lipton, Rosen & Katz v. Comm.*, TC Memo 1992-392, aff'd 94-1 USTC ¶50,272 (2d Cir. 1994).

45. Treas. Reg. §1.401-7.

46. Treas. Reg. §1.401-4(a)(1)(iii).

47. IRC Sec. 401(a)(8).

48. IRC Secs. 411(b)(1)(H), 411(b)(2).

49. IRC Sec. 411(a)(8).

50. IRC Sec. 401(l).

51. IRC Sec. 416.

52. IRC Sec. 416(g).

53. IRC Sec. 416(i)(1).

54. IRC Sec. 416(b).

55. IRC Sec. 416(c).

56. IRC Sec. 401(a)(17).

57. IRC Secs. 404(a)(1), 404(a)(3).

58. IRC Sec. 501(a).

59. IRC Sec. 402(a).

60. Notice 2001-10, 2001-1 CB 459, revoking Rev. Rul. 55-747, 1955-2 CB 228, which set forth "P.S. 58" rates; see also Treas. Reg. §1.72-16(b).

61. IRC Sec. 72(o)(3).

62. IRC Sec. 401(a)(9)(A); see Treas. Reg. §1.401(a)(9)-9.

63. Treas. Reg. §1.401(a)(9)-5(a)(4).

64. IRC Sec. 72(d)(1)(B)(iii).

65. IRC Sec. 72(d)(1)(B)(iv).

66. IRC Sec. 72(b).

67. Notice 88-118, 1988-2 CB 450.

68. IRC Sec. 72(e)(8).

69. IRC Sec. 72(t).

70. IRC Sec. 402(d)(4)(A), prior to repeal after 1999 by SBJPA '96.

71. See Notice 2001-10, 2001-1 CB 459, revoking Rev. Rul. 55-747, 1955-2 CB 228; Treas. Reg. §1.72-16(c).

72. IRC Sec. 2010(c).

73. IRC Secs. 2001(c), 2010(a), 2505(a), 6018(a).

74. *Ablamis v. Roper*, 937 F.2d 1450 (9th Cir. 1991).

75. *Boggs v. Boggs*, 117 S.Ct. 1754 (1997).

76. ERISA Sec. 3(21)(A).

77. ERISA Sec. 406(a)(1)(D).

78. IRC Sec. 4975(a).

79. ERISA Sec. 404(a)(1).

80. ERISA Sec. 4022(b)(3); PBGC Reg. §2621. App. A.

81. ERISA Secs. 4006(a)(3)(A)(i) and 4006(a)(3)(E).

82. ERISA Sec. 408(b)(1); Labor Reg. §2550.408(b)-1.

83. IRC Sec. 4975(f)(6), ERISA Sec. 408(d).

84. IRC Sec. 72(p)(1).

85. Treas. Reg. §1.72(p)-1, A-3 (b).

86. IRC Sec. 72(p)(2)(B)(i).

87. IRC Sec. 72(p)(2)(A).

88. Treas. Reg. §1.72(p)-1, A-4 (a).

89. See Treas. Regs. §§1.72(p)-1, A-3 (b), 1.72(p)-1, A-10.

90. IRC Sec. 72(p)(2)(B)(ii).

91. ERISA Secs. 101-105.

92. Treas. Reg. §1.401(a)(4)-2(b)(4).

93. See Treas. Reg. §1.401(a)(4)-8(b)(1).

94. Rev. Rul. 61-164, 1961-2 CB 99; Rev. Rul. 66-143, 1966-1 CB 79.

95. See e.g., Rev. Rul. 60-83, 1960-1 CB 157.

96. IRC Sec. 401(m).

97. IRC Sec. 219(e).

98. IRC Sec. 401(m).

99. IRC Sec. 415(c)(2)(B).

100. IRC Sec. 401(k)(2(A).

101. IRC Secs. 402(g), 3121(v).

102. IRC Sec. 402(g).

103. IRC Sec. 414(v).

104. IRC Sec. 401(k)(3).

105. IRC Sec. 401(k)(3)(A); see also Notice 98-1, 1998-1 CB 327.

106. IRC Sec. 401(k)(12).

107. IRC Sec. 401(k)(11).

108. IRC Sec. 401(k)(8)(B).

109. IRC Sec. 401(k)(8)(A).

110. IRC Sec. 4979.

111. IRC Sec. 401(k)(8).

112. IRC Sec. 401(k)(2)(B).

113. Treas. Reg. §1.401(k)-1(d)(2)(iv).

114. ERISA Sec. 206(d).

115. *Patterson v. Shumate*, 112 S.Ct. 2242 (1992).

116. IRC Sec. 401(a)(13)(B).

117. IRC Sec. 414(p).

118. IRC Sec. 408(m).

119. IRC Secs. 401(a)(11), 417.

120. IRC Sec. 417(f)(2).

121. IRC Sec. 401(a)(11)(B).

122. IRC Sec. 417(b).

123. IRC Sec. 417(d).

124. IRC Sec. 417(a)(6).

125. IRC Sec. 417(a)(2).

126. IRC Secs. 410(a)(5)(E), 411(a)(6)(E).

127. IRC Sec. 4980.

128. IRC Sec. 4974.

129. IRC Sec. 6662(f).

130. IRC Sec. 4979A.

131. Wilf, et al., *The REA Book* (REA Publishing Company: Philadelphia, 1987), Qs I.54 and I.55. Q. I.67 also addresses the question of the surviving spouse's disclaimer of annuity benefits required under REA, pointing out that such a disclaimer may be a prohibited assignment or alienation, in which event payment pursuant to the disclaimer could subject the plan administrator to fiduciary liability and could endanger the qualified status of the plan.

Figure 52.1

DESIGNATION OF BENEFICIARY FOR

_____

_____

_____   _____
Employee's Name   Employee's Soc. Security No.

1. I hereby designate the following, in the order of priority indicated, as the beneficiary to whom (or to which) any such benefit shall be distributed at the death of the participant:

   A. To _____, my spouse, or if my spouse is not then living, or if my spouse disclaims such benefit (as provided in Paragraph 6 below), then in accordance with Paragraph B below.

   B. To the Trustees of the _____, dated _____, hereinafter called the "Family Trust", to be held, managed, administered and distributed according to the terms and provisions thereof.

2. If at the time of death, none of the above beneficiaries survive me or are in existence, then this Plan and Trust share shall be distributed as then provided in the Plan and Trust Agreement.

3. I reserve the right to revoke or change the designation or any of them shown above, but such revocation or change shall be in writing directed to the Committee, and no such revocation or change shall be effective unless and until received by the Committee.

4. Rights of the designated beneficiaries shall be subject to the terms and conditions of the Plan and Trust Agreement and all rules and regulations formulated thereunder.

5. Payment of any credits or funds in the Trust Account to the beneficiary or beneficiaries designated herein shall be a full and complete release and discharge of the Trustee, the Committee and the Employer to the extent of such payment.

6. Disclaimer may be by any method which is effective under the laws of the State of California or by written transfer of the right to receive the death benefit, provided that such transfer meets the requirements of Section 2518(c)(3) of the Internal Revenue Code as is from time to time amended.

7. Any voluntary contribution account benefits shall be distributed according to the terms of this direction and shall be treated as completely separate benefits for the purposes of disclaimer.

8. This beneficiary designation shall not be construed in any way as a revocation of any election I have made pursuant to Section 242(b)(2) of the Tax Equity and Financial Responsibility Act of 1982 (P.L. 97-248) 1982-2 CB 462.

Dated _____

                                                           _____
                                                           Participant

[See Spousal Consent Over]

Figure 52.1 (cont'd)

TO BE EXECUTED IN THE PRESENCE OF A NOTARY PUBLIC

SPOUSE'S CONSENT TO BENEFICIARY DESIGNATION

CAVEAT: THIS BENEFICIARY DESIGNATION MAY NO LONGER BE VALID ONCE THE PARTICIPANT HAS REACHED HIS OR HER "ANNUITY STARTING DATE" as defined in Section 417 of the Internal Revenue Code if the participant elects a distribution in a form other than a qualified joint and survivor annuity unless the participant's spouse at that time properly completes the consent form shown on page 3 hereto.

I, the spouse of the above-named participant, hereby consent to the above Beneficiary Designation, which names an individual(s) or entity other than myself as primary beneficiary of the benefits payable to the participant in the event of his or her death under the Plan. I hereby waive any rights I may have under federal or state law to receive benefits under the Plan in the form of a qualified pre-retirement survivor annuity and acknowledge that I am not to be the direct recipient of any benefits the Plan provides to a participant's "primary beneficiary" (a spouse may be the indirect beneficiary of such benefits in certain circumstances — such as designation of a family trust as primary beneficiary). I further acknowledge that I am familiar with the financial and legal consequences of my consent to my spouse's election to waive a qualified pre-retirement survivor annuity form of benefit.

By my signature below, I am also consenting to any change by my spouse in designation of beneficiary following the date of this consent.

Dated: _____   _____
                                                        Spouse's Signature

THE SPOUSE'S SIGNATURE MUST BE WITNESSED BY A NOTARY PUBLIC!

STATE OF CALIFORNIA   )
                       : ss.
COUNTY OF SAN DIEGO   )

On this _____ day of _____, _____, before me, a Notary Public in and for said County and State, personally appeared _____, personally known to me or proved to me on the basis of satisfactory evidence to be the person described in and whose name is subscribed to the foregoing instrument, and executed such instrument before me.

WITNESS my hand and official seal.

_____
                        Notary Public

The Plan Committee hereby accepts the foregoing beneficiary designation.

Dated _____   By _____

Figure 52.1 (cont'd)

SPOUSE'S CONSENT TO BENEFICIARY DESIGNATION

(REQUIRED TO BE COMPLETED IN THE NINETY (90) DAY PERIOD PRIOR TO EITHER (1) THE BEGINNING OF RECEIPT OF ANNUITY PAYMENTS; OR (2) IN THE CASE OF NON-ANNUITY BENEFITS, THE FIRST DAY ON WHICH ALL EVENTS HAVE OCCURRED WHICH ENTITLE THE PARTICIPANT TO RECEIVE BENEFITS)

I, the spouse of the above named participant, hereby consent to the above Beneficiary Designation, which names an individual(s) or entity other than myself as primary beneficiary of the benefits payable to the participant in the event of his or her death following his or her election to waive the Qualified Joint and Survivor Annuity form of distribution under the Plan.

I understand that by consenting to my spouse's election to receive benefits in a form other than a Qualified Joint and Survivor Annuity, I am waiving my right to receive a survivor annuity under the Plan and am hereby consent to payment of any death benefits provided by the Plan to the beneficiary designated above by my spouse. I further represent that I have received as much financial information from the Plan and my spouse as I deemed necessary to consent to my spouse's designation of such beneficiary.

By my signature below, I am also consenting to any change by my spouse in designation of beneficiary following the date of this consent.

Dated _____   Name: _____

                                       Address: _____

                                                  _____

                                                  _____

THE SPOUSE'S SIGNATURE MUST BE WITNESSED BY A NOTARY PUBLIC!

STATE OF CALIFORNIA)

  : ss.

COUNTY OF SAN DIEGO)

On this _____ day of _____, _____, before me, a Notary Public in and for said County and State, personally appeared _____, personally known to me or proved to me on the basis of satisfactory evidence to be the person described in and whose name is subscribed to the foregoing instrument, and executed such instrument before me.

WITNESS my hand and official seal.

_____
Notary Public

Chapter 53

SURVIVOR'S INCOME BENEFIT PLAN

WHAT IS IT?

A "Survivor's Income Benefit" (SIB) plan (often called a "Death Benefit Only" or DBO plan) is an agreement between a corporation and an employee. The corporation agrees that if the employee dies before retirement, it will pay a specified amount (or an amount determinable by a specified formula) to the employee's spouse or another designated class of beneficiaries, such as the employee's children. Typically, the amount may be a multiple of salary, such as two, three, or five times the average base pay in the three years preceding death.[1]

A Survivor's Income Benefit Plan should not provide for or be linked in any way with a plan that provides any kind of post-retirement annuity benefits.

WHEN IS THE USE OF SUCH A DEVICE INDICATED?

1. When additional income is desired for the family of an individual in a high estate tax bracket.

2. When an employer would like to provide a selected employee or employees with an impressive fringe benefit over and above that provided under a qualified retirement plan.

3. When a client presently covered under a split dollar arrangement is experiencing rapidly-increasing economic benefit (also known as "Table 2001") costs, has run into Sarbanes-Oxley issues, or the split-dollar arrangement has been terminated.[2] The split dollar plan could be converted into a survivor's income benefit plan so that the security could be continued without the income tax burden.

4. When a corporation would like to provide an immediate death benefit for the family of a young employee, which could later be coupled (by changing the SIB at retirement to a nonqualified deferred compensation plan) with a retirement benefit.

HOW IT IS DONE – AN EXAMPLE

Nina Wasserman is a 35-year-old senior executive of Ship Shape Model Corporation (SSM). In order to encourage her to give her ultimate effort for SSM, the corporation makes a legally binding promise to her that, "If Nina should die while an executive of SSM, SSM will pay her children, Ross and Michelle, a death benefit equal to three times the average annual base compensation she received for the three years prior to her death–up to a maximum of $500,000. The payments will be made in equal annual installments over a 10-year period." In this example, assume payments would be $50,000 a year. Assume also that SSM is in a 40% combined federal and state corporate tax bracket.

SSM could finance its obligation by purchasing a $500,000 life insurance policy on Nina's life. The policy would be owned by and payable to SSM. At Nina's death, SSM could use the cash proceeds to purchase $500,000 worth of tax-free municipal bonds. Assuming the bonds earned 8%, the net income from the bonds would be $40,000 a year. This means corporate cash inflow would be $40,000. Outflow, after the corporation's $20,000 tax deduction (40% of $50,000) would be $30,000 ($50,000 - $20,000). Its net positive inflow each year would therefore be $10,000. In 10 years, the corporation could add $100,000 to its surplus. At the end of the payout period, SSM would have $500,000 worth of bonds, and would have accumulated $10,000 a year for 10 years. At 8%, this $10,000 annual amount would grow to $156,455 by the end of the 10th year. This would probably be enough to reimburse the business for its costs, the use of its money, and any administrative expenses it may have incurred.

WHAT ARE THE TAX IMPLICATIONS?

The Employer's Tax Position

1. The premiums that the corporation pays on the life insurance policy covering the insured employee are not deductible.[3]

2. Life insurance proceeds received by the corporation at the employee's death are income tax free.[4] Proceeds may be subject to the corporate alternative minimum tax (AMT) as an adjustment for adjusted current earnings. But, at worst, this possible tax on

proceeds will generally not exceed 15% with respect to the adjustment for adjusted current earnings. Generally, the full amount of AMT liability may be carried forward as a credit.[5]

3. Payments made by the corporation to the designated beneficiaries are deductible if and to the extent that (a) such payments represent reasonable compensation for services that the employee rendered, and (b) the plan serves a valid business (as opposed to a shareholder) purpose.[6]

The Employee's Tax Position

1. If the plan is properly drafted, under most circumstances, none of the death benefit of an SIB plan will be includable in the covered employee's estate (see the Q&A section below).

2. Payment of premiums by the corporate employer will not be income to the employee.

3. The IRS, reversing an earlier position, now agrees with the Tax Court that when the taxpayer and his employer enter into a DBO plan, there is no taxable gift to the beneficiary, either at the time when the plan is entered into, or upon the death of the employee.[7]

The Beneficiary's Tax Position

Payments received from the corporation by beneficiaries will be treated the same as salary (i.e., each payment will be taxed as deferred salary).

IMPLICATIONS AND ISSUES IN COMMUNITY PROPERTY STATES

In community property states, it may be necessary to determine whether the employee's spouse has any community property interest in the survivor's income benefit. This becomes important upon the divorce of the employee and the spouse. As previously stated, if a survivor's income benefit plan is properly drafted, none of the death benefits should be includable in the employee's estate for federal estate tax purposes, although state laws may vary on this issue. This is because courts have consistently found that the decedent had no interest in the payments at the time of his death.

This may also be the case upon a divorce after an employee has entered into a survivor's income benefit plan. As of the date of the divorce, the employee would have no interest which could be includable in his estate, and thus there may not be any interest to be divided in a divorce proceeding.

However, many courts and the IRS generally have found that the employer's promise to pay a death benefit to a specified beneficiary in return for the employee's promise to continue working is a transfer by the employee of a property right. Community property states typically provide that a spouse may not make a gift of community personal property or dispose of community personal property without a valuable consideration, unless he or she obtains the written consent of the other spouse. The employee's employment, by its very nature in a community property state, is generating a community property interest in the spouse through salary and other employment benefits.

In a divorce proceeding, although an employee may be performing some services in return for the employer's promise to pay a stated amount to a named beneficiary at the time of the divorce proceeding, it does not follow that there are current property interests which can be divided equally between the spouses. The employee has no current right to any benefit, nor is there any assurance that he will ever have a named beneficiary to receive a benefit. The survivor's income benefit is subject to many contingencies, among them the employee's continuing to work for the employer. Assuming the employee's spouse is the beneficiary of the survivor's income benefit plan, the spouse has obtained a benefit during the term of the marriage (i.e., if the employee were to die during the marriage, the spouse would receive the survivor's income benefit).

If the employee's spouse contends that there is an interest which can be valued and divided upon a divorce, the question of whether any value can be attributed to the survivor's income benefit may be solved differently in the various community property states. California, for example, has found that a non-vested benefit from a pension plan is not a mere expectancy, but is a contingent property right. Although we are not familiar with any case actually valuing a survivor's income benefit under this theory, it may be possible that California courts would attempt to value the survivor's income benefit and divide that value in the divorce proceedings. The value would probably be very low because of the substantial discounts for the many contingencies involved in this type of an arrangement.

As one can imagine, severe problems of valuation and the proportion of benefits to be paid to a former spouse could arise in the event that the employee were to remarry and continue working for the same employer. What portion of the survivor's income benefit is attributable to the employee's employment while married to his first spouse and what portion is attributable to the portion of his employment while married to his second spouse? With vexing problems like this, coupled with the employee's lack of any right to a benefit prior to his death, it is likely that a court will put little or no value on the survivor's income benefit plan in the event of a divorce.

In most instances, the employee's spouse will be his or her beneficiary under the survivor's income benefit plan. In this instance, upon the employee's death, there will be no controversy over the community property issue, unless the employee was previously married. In the event of a divorce, the community property issue may arise, even though the spouse is designated as the beneficiary, but the result is quite uncertain.

QUESTIONS AND ANSWERS

Question – What circumstances would cause death benefits to be includable in the employee's estate?

Answer – The employer's promise of the employer to pay a death benefit to the specified beneficiary in return for the employee's promise to continue working has been considered to constitute a transfer by the employee of a property right.

If the agreement gives the employee the right to change the beneficiary, that retention of the power to designate who will enjoy the "transfer" will result in inclusion of the present value of the stream of payments in the employee's estate.[8]

If the beneficiary's right to receive the death benefit is conditioned upon surviving the employee and the employee retained a right to direct the disposition of the property (for example, where the death benefit is payable to the employee's spouse, but if the spouse does not survive the employee, the death benefit is payable to the employee's estate), that reversionary interest may cause inclusion.[9]

If the beneficiary is a revocable trust established by the employee, the right to alter, amend, or revoke the transfer by changing the terms of the trust would cause inclusion.[10] Another problem relates to an employee who is also a controlling (more than 50%) shareholder. Does such an individual, by virtue of his or her voting power, have the right to alter, amend, revoke, or terminate the agreement? The Tax Court has held that the answer is "yes."[11]

If the employee already has post-retirement annuity benefits, such as a nonqualified deferred compensation agreement that pays a retirement benefit, the IRS could claim that the pre-retirement survivor's death benefit and the post-retirement deferred salary plans should be considered as one plan. This would cause the present value of the death benefit to be treated, for estate tax purposes, as if it were a joint and survivor annuity; the present value of the death benefit would be includable in the deceased employee's estate.[12]

If the death benefit is payable to a trust over which the employee had a general power of appointment, the IRS might argue that he had a power of appointment over the death proceeds.[13]

If the death benefit is funded with life insurance on the employee's life and the employee owned the policy or had veto rights over any change in the beneficiary, the IRS would probably attempt to include the policy proceeds, because of the employee's incidents of ownership.[14]

EGTRRA 2001 repeals the federal estate tax for one year in 2010.

Question – If proceeds are payable to the employee's spouse, will they qualify for the unlimited marital deduction?

Answer – Yes. If, for any reason, the IRS successfully maintains that the SIB generated a taxable transfer (either during life or at death), there should be no adverse gift or estate tax consequence if the spouse of the employee is named an outright beneficiary. It is also possible that the employer could pay SIB payments to a "QTIP" (Qualified Terminable Interest Property) trust established by the employee (see Chapter 31). This would secure the marital deduction– if one were needed–and, in any case, assure that the principal would pass to the party designated by the decedent upon the surviving spouse's death.

However, if the SIB were not included in the employee's estate for tax purposes, the payment could not result in a marital deduction.

Question – Is a DBO plan a "funded" plan for ERISA purposes?

Answer – Although the *Dependahl* case[15] stated that DBOs did not qualify for various exemptions from ERISA, at first impression it appeared that the court improperly interpreted both the facts and ERISA in its desire to assist employees who seemed to have been terminated for malicious and unjustifiable reasons. The company involved in this case sent a letter each year to the executives covered by its DBO plan. Those letters advised the participants of the annual status of "their" insurance policies. The obvious implication is that the participants could look to the policies for their families' security under the DBO plan. This fact was not contained in the Court's opinion, and may well have been the key reason the Court reached the conclusion the plan was "funded" for ERISA purposes.

Subsequent to the *Dependahl* case, the Department of Labor issued an Advisory Opinion, which states that life insurance is not considered a "plan asset" if:

1. It is owned by and payable to the corporation;

2. It is under the total control of the corporation;

3. It is subject to the claims of the corporation's creditors;

4. No participant has a preferred claim against the policies;

5. The policies are not formally tied to the plan; and

6. There will be no representation to any participant or beneficiary that the policies would be used solely to provide plan benefits or represent security for the payment of benefits or that plan benefits would be limited by the amount of the insurance proceeds received by the corporation.[16]

In light of *Dependahl* and the Department of Labor Advisory Opinion, the use of the phrase "to fund" (or "to informally fund") should be avoided in discussing the use of life insurance policies to support the plan in any documentation associated with the plan (e.g., corporate resolutions, plan document, SEC annual report disclosure statements). It is probably safest to purchase and own insurance (and to reflect this ownership in a corporate resolution) as key employee coverage.

Part of the corporate resolution authorizing the plan and the purchase of the supporting policies might better read as follows:

RESOLVED: that in order for the X-ON Corporation to support its financial obligations under the Death Benefit Only plan and to insure itself against all other financial losses which would be incurred in the event of a pre- or postretirement death of *(Name of Executive)*, the vice-president of the Corporation is hereby authorized to enter into a contract of *(Description of Life Insurance Contract)* life insurance with the _____ Life Insurance Company for coverage of $___ insuring the life of *(Name of Key Executive)*.

Question – Is a voluntary DBO plan the answer to the estate tax question?

Answer – If a death benefit is not made under a contract or plan but is purely voluntary on the employer's part, it will not be includable in the employee's estate.[17] An employer could adopt a program that is something less than a legally binding commitment giving rise to "hopes and expectancies, not enforceable obligations with respect to a death benefit."

Voluntary benefits are not includable in the employee's estate because neither the employee nor the employee's beneficiary possessed any right to compel the employer to pay the benefit, and therefore there was no transfer.

The problem here is a practical one. The benefit provides no peace of mind–nor financial security in an economic sense–except to the extent that the employee can rely on the willingness and ability of the employer to pay a substantial sum of money after the employee's death.

Question – What is the formula for a successful DBO plan?

Answer – An employer may offer a plan under which benefits are payable only to "eligible beneficiaries." This class would be determined by the employer and might include spouses and/or children of employees. No benefit would be payable if the employee is not survived by an eligible beneficiary. The employee would have no right to select or change the beneficiary.

ASRS: Sec. 64.

CHAPTER ENDNOTES

1. Some insurance carriers offer a coverage known as group survivors' income benefit insurance, commonly written as a supplement to group life insurance. Under this coverage, the

employee has no choice of beneficiary, benefits are paid only if there is a survivor who qualifies, and a lump-sum payment of the commuted value of benefits is not available.

2. Current life insurance protection provided under a qualified plan may be valued by using government 1-year term premium rates. For many years, "P.S. 58" rates were used to calculate the value of the protection. Rev. Rul. 55-747, 1955-2 CB 228. The IRS has now revoked Rev. Rul. 55-747, and will accept the use of P.S. 58 rates only for tax years ending before 2002. The IRS has issued "Table 2001" generally for use in determining the value of life insurance protection after 2000. Notice 2001-10, 2001-5 IRB 459. See Chapter 30.

3. IRC Sec. 264(a)(1).

4. IRC Sec. 101(a).

5. See, generally, IRC Secs. 55-59.

6. IRC Sec. 162(a)(1).

7. See *Est. of DiMarco*, 87 TC 653 (1986), acq. in result 1990-2 CB 1.

8. IRC Sec. 2036; Rev. Rul. 76-304, 1976-2 CB 269.

9. IRC Sec. 2037; *Est. of Fried v. Comm.*, 54 TC 805 (1970), aff'd., 445 F.2d 979 (2nd Cir. 1971), cert. den., 404 US 1016 (1972); Rev. Rul. 78-15, 1978-1 CB 289.

10. IRC Sec. 2038.

11. *Est. of Levin*, 90 TC 723 (1988).

12. IRC Sec. 2039; *Est. of Fusz v. Comm.*, 46 TC 214 (1966), acq. 1967-2 CB 2.

13. IRC Sec. 2041.

14. IRC Sec. 2042.

15. *Dependahl v. Falstaff Brewing Corp.*, 491 F. Supp. 1188 (E.D. Mo. 1980), aff'd in part, 653 F.2d 1208 (8th Cir.), cert. den.; see also *Belka v. Rowe Furniture Corp.*, 571 F. Supp. 1249 (D. Md. 1983), where the court found a plan to be exempt from ERISA funding requirements where less than 5% of total employees were participants, and where participants' compensation averaged $55,000.

16. DOL Ad. Op. 81-11A.

17. *Courtney v. U.S.*, 84-2 USTC ¶13,580 (N.D. Ohio, 1984).

Chapter 54

HEALTH REIMBURSEMENT ARRANGEMENT

∎

WHAT IS IT?

A health reimbursement arrangement (sometimes referred to as an HRA) is an arrangement provided by an employer (including a professional corporations) to reimburse one or more employees for dental expenses, cosmetic surgery, and other medical expenses which are not covered under a medical plan available to all employees. Typically, an HRA reimburses employees for medical expenses incurred by the employee, his or her spouse, and dependents.

An HRA is used (1) as a substitute for health insurance; (2) as a supplement to provide payments for medical expenses not covered under the company's health insurance plan (such as dental expenses or cosmetic surgery); or (3) to pay for medical expenses in excess of the limits in the company's health insurance plan (including deductibles and coinsurance).

The objective–from a tax standpoint–of a health reimbursement arrangement is to provide benefits on a tax-free basis to the employee. A corresponding objective is to make such payments tax deductible by the employer.

WHEN IS THE USE OF SUCH A DEVICE INDICATED?

A health reimbursement arrangement is particularly useful in the following situations:

1. Where a corporation is closely held and family members are the primary or only employees. The health reimbursement arrangement makes otherwise nondeductible medical expenses deductible.

2. In a professional corporation, where the only employee is a professional in a high income tax bracket, or where there are few other employees and they are receiving relatively smaller salaries. The health reimbursement arrangement makes what might otherwise be nondeductible medical expense payments deductible.

3. Where an employer would like to provide significant (and tax favored) benefits to

employees beyond those provided by the basic medical coverage already in force.

WHAT ARE THE REQUIREMENTS?

Aside from "insured" plans (see the last Q&A below), a health reimbursement arrangement that reimburses an employee for medical expenses incurred for the care of the employee and/or his family must be *non*discriminatory.[1] A plan may be considered discriminatory in either (or both) of two ways. A plan may be considered to discriminate as to: (1) coverage; or (2) operation.[2]

Generally speaking, the penalty for a plan which is considered discriminatory is that all or part of the reimbursements to highly compensated employees will be included in their income.[3] Rank and file employees, however, will remain entitled to the income tax exclusion even if the plan is considered discriminatory.

As to coverage, a plan must benefit 70% or more of all employees. Alternatively, if 70% of all employees are eligible to be covered, 80% of those individuals must in fact participate in coverage.[4] There is a second alternative: An employer might be able to satisfy nondiscrimination requirements by setting up and covering classes of employees in a manner that does not discriminate in favor of highly compensated employees or their families.[5] Since this is not a definite mathematically determinable test, the IRS will determine, on a case by case basis, whether there has been discrimination.

Highly compensated employees–for purposes of discrimination–are defined as (1) the five highest paid officers; (2) shareholders holding more than 10% of the outstanding stock value of the corporation; and (3) the highest paid 25% of all employees.[6]

If a plan discriminates in coverage, a fraction of payments received will be includable in income.[7] That fraction is:

$$\frac{\text{Amount reimbursed to all participating } \textit{highly compensated} \text{ employees}}{\textit{Total} \text{ amount reimbursed to } \textit{all} \text{ employees under the plan}} \times \begin{array}{l}\text{Payment received by given highly compensated employee}\end{array}$$

Inclusion, in other words, depends on the proportion of total payments that went to highly compensated employees. This percentage will then be multiplied by each highly compensated employee's reimbursement.

Example: SRL Corporation's plan fails the coverage requirements. The corporation paid out $10,000 in medical reimbursements, $2,500 of which went to highly compensated employees. $2,000 of that went to Ed Staller, a company vice president. Ed must include $500 in income

$$\frac{\$2,500}{\$10,000} \times 2,000 = 1/4 \times \$2,000 = \$500$$

A plan would be considered *discriminatory in operation* if highly compensated employees are eligible to receive greater benefits than other employees. This means benefit levels cannot be based on a percentage or proportion of compensation. This is known as the "dollar for dollar" discrimination rule. It is applicable to eligible benefits, rather than amounts actually paid. (The mere fact that highly compensated employees happen to submit more claims than other employees will not, *per se*, make the plan discriminatory.)

If the plan discriminates in operation (e.g., a highly compensated employee is eligible for twice the benefit available to nonhighly compensated employees), the recipient highly compensated employee will have to include the entire amount of excess reimbursement actually received in income–whether or not coverage requirements are met.

Example: Dayton Coles, president of the State College Coal Company, received a $1,000 reimbursement for dental coverage, a benefit provided only for him and his family. The entire $1,000 is includable in Dayton's income.

HOW IT IS DONE

Example 1

Powers, Inc. maintains a self-insured health reimbursement arrangement covering all of its employees, which is operated on the calendar year.

However, the plan provides limitations on the maximum benefits subject to reimbursement. Those limitations are $5,000 for officers, and $1,000 for all other participants.

During the 2004 plan year, James Powers, one of the five highest paid officers, received reimbursements in the amount of $3,000. Since the same amount of benefits provided for the highly compensated individuals is not provided for all other participants, the plan is deemed to be discriminatory in operation. Thus, James Powers received an excess reimbursement of $2,000 ($3,000 - $1,000), the amount by which his reimbursement exceeded the reimbursement benefit available to nonhighly compensated employees. This $2,000 will be includable in James Powers' gross income for 2004, his tax year in which the plan year ended.

It is not currently certain, but it is the authors' opinion that a member of the prohibited class must also include in income for the year the $1,000 reimbursement amount as well.[8]

Example 2

Western Industries, Inc. maintains a self-insured medical reimbursement plan for its employees. Benefits subject to reimbursement under this plan are the same for all plan participants. However, of the 100 employees in the company, only 10 (six of whom are stockholders) are eligible to participate. Therefore, the plan discriminates as to coverage (eligibility). During the plan year ending in 2004, Jordan Thomas, a highly compensated individual, was hospitalized for surgery, and accrued medical expenses of $4,500, which were reimbursed to him under the plan. During the plan year, the corporation's medical plan paid a total of $50,000 in benefits, $30,000 of which were payments to highly compensated individuals. The amount of excess reimbursement that will be included in the income of Jordan Thomas in 2004 is $2,700. That amount is calculated as follows:

$$\frac{\$30,000}{\$50,000} \times \$4,500 = \$2,700$$

IMPLICATIONS AND ISSUES IN COMMUNITY PROPERTY STATES

No significant difference exists with regard to the application of the rules regarding health reimbursement arrangements in community property states.

QUESTIONS AND ANSWERS

Question – Is a ruling or advance determination letter required?

Answer – No. While no advance rulings are required, as in the case of a qualified pension or profit-sharing plan, it is expected that advance rulings will be available.

Question – If an amount is considered an excess reimbursement and subject to inclusion in the income of the highly compensated individual, *when* is that amount included?

Answer – The amount of the excess reimbursement is included in the income of the highly compensated individual for that individual's taxable year within which the plan's year ends. Thus, if an HRA has a plan year end of June 30, and the highly compensated individual receives an excess reimbursement on November 1, 2004, he will include that amount in his gross income in his 2005 taxable year, because the applicable plan year ends June 30, 2005.

Question – May benefits under an HRA be calculated as a percentage of the participant's compensation?

Answer – Generally, no. If a plan covers employees who are highly compensated individuals in addition to rank and file employees, and the type or amount of benefits subject to reimbursement under the plan is in proportion to the employee's compensation, the plan will be deemed to discriminate as to benefits.[9]

Question – What are "medical benefits" for purposes of an HRA?

Answer – Generally, the medical expenses which will be considered "medical benefits" subject to this nondiscrimination provision are the same expenses that would result in itemized medical expense deductions from an individual's personal income.

Certain "diagnostic procedures" are not subject to the discriminatory plan rules. Medical diagnostic procedures include routine medical examinations, blood tests, and x-rays. They do not, however, include expenses incurred for the treatment, cure, or testing of a known illness or disability, or the treatment or testing for a physical injury, complaint, or specific symptom of bodily malfunction.

Question – If an employer has an insured health reimbursement arrangement, but that plan has a deductible portion, which the employer, pursuant to a plan, agrees to pay, will such payment be subject to the discriminatory medical reimbursement plan rules?

Answer – Yes. The regulations state that the nondiscrimination rules apply to a self-insured portion of an employer's medical plan or arrangement, even if the plan is in part underwritten by insurance. Thus, if an employer's medical plan reimburses employees for the deductible amounts under the insured portions, such reimbursement is subject to the medical expense nondiscrimination rules. However, a plan that reimburses employees for premiums paid under an insured plan is not subject to these rules.[10]

Question – Is it possible to exclude any employees from coverage under a health reimbursement arrangement?

Answer – Yes. The "don't have to be covered" class includes (1) employees with fewer than three years of service; (2) employees under age 25; (3) part-time employees whose customary weekly employment is for fewer than 35 hours; (4) seasonal employees whose customary annual employment is for fewer than nine months; (5) certain union employees who are engaged in collective bargaining units (but only if accident and health benefits were the subject of good-faith bargaining).

Question – The law currently exempts "insured" plans. What is meant by an insured plan?

Answer – Where accident and health insurance benefits are provided by an insurance company, the nondiscrimination tests do not apply. An insured plan is one in which risk has been shifted to and accepted by an insurer.[11]

Example: The Quickbucks Corporation buys a policy from Fastpay Life, a licensed insurance company, which provides an exact reimbursement of 100% of an employee's medical expenses. The premium for such a policy is equal to the amount of the expenses reimbursed, plus a certain percentage (presumably to provide for the administration costs).

This arrangement appears to be an attempt to avoid the intent of Congress when it excluded insured plans (i.e., Congress felt that underwriting considerations generally preclude or effectively limit abuses in insured plans, so that the nondiscrimination rules were not necessary with respect to them). The plan purchased by the Quickbucks Corporation is not what Congress meant by an "insured" plan, since there is no shifting of the risk to an insurer.

Here's a similar arrangement that also claims to be an insured plan–but probably is *not* what Congress intended:

Example: The Lotsamoney Corporation buys a policy from Livelong Life, a licensed insurance company, which provides for a complete reimbursement of all medical expenses. The premium is level. At the time of the employee's termination of employment, for any reason whatsoever, any amount of premium which has been paid by the employer and has not been used or needed to reimburse an employee is refunded to the employer. The premium is set high enough so that it is likely to provide a refund to the employer.

This second arrangement does shift some risk–but perhaps not enough to be a legitimate plan of insurance. Both arrangements are more like self-insured than insured plans.

CHAPTER ENDNOTES

1. IRC Sec. 105(h).
2. IRC Sec. 105(h)(2).
3. IRC Sec. 105(h)(1).
4. IRC Sec. 105(h)(3)(A)(i).
5. IRC Sec. 105(h)(3)(A)(ii).
6. IRC Sec. 105(h)(5).
7. IRC Sec. 105(h)(7)(B).
8. A strict reading of IRC Sec. 105(h)(7)(A) indicates that the entire amount paid to or on behalf of a member of the prohibited group would be fully taxable. In the example above, this means that the $1,000 amount available to all employees would not be excludable.

   An interpretation of the Senate Finance Committee reports would lead to the conclusion that if there is a benefit that is available to a broad cross-section of employees, but the plan discriminates in some other fashion (whether in providing additional benefits, or in not meeting the coverage tests), then the member of the prohibited class must take into income for the year *some* of the money that he has received under the benefit. For this, we must go to the fraction.

   In the above example, assume that, while James Powers is the only member of the prohibited group to receive an excess reimbursement during the year, amounts reimbursed to officers (including Powers), *within the $1,000 limit applicable to non-officers*, total $4,000 for the year. Assume further that amounts reimbursed to officers and non-officers alike, within the $1,000 limit, total $10,000 for the year. This means that the percentage received by members of the prohibited class amounts to 40% of the amount received with respect to benefits that are available to the cross-section. In the example, the highly compensated employee received $3,000. Therefore, he receives $2,000 in ordinary income (because that is a benefit not available to the cross-section), plus 40% of the first $1,000 he received (the benefit available to all employees).

   In this way, the statute effectively penalizes members of the prohibited class because the plan was discriminatory, even with respect to benefits that are available to a broad cross-section of all employees.
9. Treas. Reg. §1.105-11(c)(3)(i).
10. Treas. Reg. §1.105-11(b)(2).
11. The IRS has issued Treas. Reg. §1.105-11(b)(1)(ii), to be used in determining what constitutes an insured medical plan. This regulation specifically states that a "plan underwritten by a policy of insurance or a prepaid health care plan *that does not involve the shifting of risk to an unrelated third party* is considered self-insured for purposes of this section" (emphasis added). Thus, a plan which has been underwritten by a policy of insurance that contains no shifting of risk, or merely provides administrative or bookkeeping services, will be considered self-insured under this section.

    However, a regular health insurance program, with risk shifted to the insurance company, is not affected.

Part 10:

INCAPACITY PLANNING

Chapter 55

ELDERLY AND DISABLED (PLANNING FOR)

WHAT IS IT?

Planning for the elderly and disabled focuses on clients or their dependents who, by reason of age or disability, or both, require specific health care and financial planning. Several other chapters in this book deal with aspects of this area of planning. For example, durable powers of attorney and durable powers of attorney for health care, discussed in Chapter 56, are particularly important for persons who fall within these definitions. So are revocable trusts, discussed in Chapter 28, which are often used for management of the assets of persons who are unable to manage their own affairs.

Unlike many other tools and techniques discussed in this book, the practice in this area requires the practitioner to deal with a variety of personal problems and decisions of the client or dependent. These range from health care decisions to who will care for these persons if they are unable to care for themselves, and even where they will live. Planning for these types of individuals is time sensitive and opportunities available currently may be foreclosed quickly. This makes time of the essence in making preparations, in drafting, and in having these documents properly executed, witnessed, and notarized.

WHEN IS THE USE OF SUCH A DEVICE INDICATED?

This planning should always be undertaken where, by reason of age or health, there is a real possibility the individual will become mentally or physically incapacitated with age or deteriorating health. In many cases, the need for this planning will be speculative, as most elderly and disabled persons are able to function without special assistance.

However, this chapter also covers the problems of medical care for clients who are not disabled, in the sense they have suffered no loss of their capacity to manage their own affairs and make their own decisions. It also discusses the problems of support for persons who are unable to support themselves.

WHAT ARE THE REQUIREMENTS?

The planning scenarios for elderly and disabled persons include the following:

1. Provision for management of the financial affairs of the client or dependent in the event they are unable to do so themselves. This employs such techniques as durable powers of attorney, revocable living trusts, and nominations of persons the individual would want to serve as a guardian or conservator in the event he needs someone to manage his affairs.

2. Providing for support of individuals who, due to age and/or health, are no longer self supporting and have not accumulated sufficient assets to provide for their cost of living.

3. Planning for long-term health care, including possible institutional care.

4. Protecting property from claims of the state or federal government for reimbursement of health care costs.

5. Planning for the drastically changing tax results that are directly dependent on the year of the client's death. For instance, an 80 year old client who dies in 2009 (or in 2011 or later) may suffer an incredibly larger loss to estate tax than if she dies in 2010, due to changes made by EGTRRA 2001.

WHAT ARE THE TAX IMPLICATIONS?

Aside from the concerns raised by the fifth requirement above, planning in this area is not particularly tax driven. However, there are some special tax benefits available to the elderly that should not be overlooked. While income and self employment taxes are not dependent upon age, persons over 65 and those who are blind are entitled to an increase in their standard deduction in filing their income tax returns.[1] Widows and widowers may use joint income tax returns for two years following the death of the spouse.[2] Taxpayers who are supporting dependent family members may be entitled to additional dependency exemptions on their income tax returns. These include parents and grandparents, among others.[3] There is a dependent care credit available for certain employment related expenses.[4]

Taxpayers (of any age) who sell their personal residences are entitled to an exclusion once every two years for up to $250,000 ($500,000 if married filing jointly) of the gain realized on the sale.[5]

IMPLICATIONS AND ISSUES IN COMMUNITY PROPERTY STATES

As a general rule, each spouse has a legal duty to support the other spouse, and both community and separate property can be reached to provide for such support. In addition, community assets can be reached to pay the debts and obligations of either spouse incurred during marriage.

If one spouse becomes incompetent, the law may vary on the right of the other spouse to manage community assets. The other spouse may be able to take over complete management, or may in some circumstances be required to share management with a guardian or conservator for the incompetent spouse.

QUESTIONS AND ANSWERS

Long-term Care Planning

Question – How can a client plan for long-term care expenses?

Answer – Long-term care includes a continuum of services from nursing home care to assisted living to home health care to adult day care. Although a large portion of the overall cost for long-term care is paid by federal programs, the restrictions and uncertainty of these benefits makes reliance on government assistance unwise. Proper planning for long-term care involves either self-insurance – if retirement assets and income are sufficient – or the purchase of a long-term care insurance contract.

Long-term care insurance contracts vary with respect to benefit amounts, elimination (waiting) periods, maximum benefit amounts, inflation protection, and benefit triggers. It is important to choose a combination of policy features that meets a client's

needs for protection while remaining affordable enough for the client to maintain the policy in effect until it may be needed.

The cost of long-term care in a nursing home and the client's ability to pay a portion of that cost generally determine the benefit amount needed from a long-term care insurance policy. The benefit amount is usually stated in terms of a maximum daily benefit amount. It is also important to factor in the long-term impact of inflation on the real value of a daily benefit amount. A one-year stay in a nursing home in 1996 cost $30,000 on average. By 2002, the average was over $60,000. By 2030, a year in a nursing home could cost well over $200,000. Inflation protection riders typically provide an annual inflation adjustment, typically a 5% increase, to the daily benefit amount. This adjustment may be "simple," based on the original daily benefit amount, or "compounded," based on each prior year's adjusted benefit amount.

Benefits offered by a "qualified long-term care insurance contract" – a contract that meets certain federal statutory requirements – are generally not includable in income.[6] However, there is a limit on the amount of qualified long-term care benefits that may be excluded from income. Generally, if the total periodic long-term care payments received from all policies and any periodic payments received that are treated as paid by reason of the death of the insured (under IRC Section 101(g)) exceed a daily limitation, the excess must be included in income. The daily limitation is equal to the greater of the dollar amount limitation or the actual costs incurred for qualified long-term care services provided for the insured. For 2004, the dollar amount limitation is $230 per day. It is adjusted for inflation annually.

Question – What is an accelerated death benefit or a viatical settlement?

Answer – Several years ago, partially in response to the growing number of persons with AIDS, some life insurance companies began offering persons with terminal illnesses or long-term medical care needs an "accelerated death benefit," the opportunity to receive a portion of the death proceeds from their life insurance policies prior to the insured person's actual death.

Generally, any amount received under a life insurance contract on the life of a terminally ill insured or a chronically ill insured will be treated as an amount paid by reason of the death of the insured.[7] Amounts received under a life insurance contract by reason of the death of the insured are not includable in gross income. Thus, an accelerated death benefit meeting these requirements will generally be received free of income tax.

However, amounts paid to a chronically ill individual are subject to the same limitations that apply to long-term care benefits ($230 per day in 2004). Accelerated death benefits paid to terminally ill individuals are not subject to this limit.

A terminally-ill individual is a person who has been certified by a physician as having an illness or physical condition that can reasonably be expected to result in death within 24 months following the certification. A chronically ill individual is a person who is not terminally ill and who has been certified as being unable to perform, without substantial assistance, at least two activities of daily living (ADLs) for at least 90 days or a person with a similar level of disability. Further, a person may be considered chronically ill if he requires substantial supervision to protect himself from threats to his health and safety due to severe cognitive impairment and this condition has been certified by a health care practitioner within the previous 12 months. The activities of daily living are: (1) eating; (2) toileting; (3) transferring; (4) bathing; (5) dressing; and (6) continence.

There is one exception to this general rule of non-includability for accelerated death benefits. The rules outlined above do not apply to any amount paid to any taxpayer other than the insured if the taxpayer has an insurable interest in the life of the insured because the insured is a director, officer or employee of the taxpayer or if the insured is financially interested in any trade or business of the taxpayer.

A viatical settlement is the sale or assignment of any portion of the death benefit under a life insurance contract on the life of a terminally or chronically ill insured to a viatical settlement provider. In a viatical settlement, the amount paid for the sale or assignment will be treated as an amount paid under the life insurance contract by reason of the insured's death. In other words, such an amount will not be included in income. A viatical settlement provider is defined as "any person regularly engaged in the trade or business of purchasing, or taking assignments of, life insurance contracts on the lives of insureds" who are terminally or chronically ill provided that certain licensing and other requirements, discussed below, are met.

Question – What federal programs are available to assist in providing health care for the elderly and disabled?

Answer – Government assistance programs include the following:

1. Social security disability benefits where an individual is unable to engage in gainful employment by reason of medically established mental or physical impairment. This impairment must be expected to last until death, or continuously over a period of at least 12 months.

2. Supplemental security income, often called SSI, which provides for needy persons who are elderly, blind, or otherwise disabled.

3. Medicare, which provides medical benefits on the basis of the age of the person, without regard to need.

4. Medicaid, which provides medical assistance regardless of age to the needy.

Question – In general, what are the eligibility requirements for Medicare?

Answer – Taxpayers who are 65 and eligible for social security, or who are 65 and whose spouses are eligible for social security, are eligible for Medicare. Part A of Medicare provides hospital insurance at no cost except for deductible and coinsurance amounts that must be paid by the patient. Part A also provides limited coverage for care in a skilled nursing facility, a hospice, or post-hospital home health services. Part B of Medicare primarily covers physician's services, and is voluntary. Premiums are required under Part B. Certain individuals over 65 who are not covered by Part A may elect voluntary coverage by paying premiums if they are enrolled in Part B. Certain disabled persons under 65 can also be eligible for Medicare benefits.

Question – What is medigap insurance?

Answer – "Medigap" is a generic name for health insurance which covers some or all of the expenses not covered by either Part A or Part B of Medicare.

Question – What is Medicaid?

Answer – Medicaid is a joint federal and state program that provides assistance for health care to certain aged, disabled, or blind individuals. The intent is to provide help to needy individuals. In some cases, this is integrated with the requirements for supplemental security income (SSI) mentioned above. Many states impose an income cap based on SSI requirements. The tests here are largely dependent on state law. There are also special requirements for nursing home benefits.

Question – For purposes of Medicaid, what are "resources," and how do they affect eligibility?

Answer – Resources refer to assets owned by an individual or available to an individual. If these exceed a certain dollar value, that individual will be ineligible for various benefits, particularly nursing home care. These generally include assets owned by the spouse of the individual. In addition, the income of the individual and spouse are also available resources.

Question – Does the individual's personal residence count as an asset for purposes of Medicaid eligibility?

Answer – This depends on state law. For example, in California, the residence is exempt if the individual is in a nursing home six months or less, because the individual is presumed to intend to return to it.

Question – Can individuals transfer assets so that they will not be counted as resources for purposes of Medicaid?

Answer – Congress has imposed and continues to impose strict limits on transfers of assets to achieve Medicaid eligibility. For example, the value of any assets transferred within 36 months before the individual makes an application for Medicaid will be considered an available resource.[8] The penalties are in the form of denial of Medicaid benefits for a period of months depending on the value of the property transferred. There are exceptions, including one for transfers to children who are "caretakers" for their parent. There are other exceptions for transfers to spouses, minor children, trusts for disabled children, etc. Check the law for the effective dates of this look-back period.

In general, for assets transferred to trusts, the look-back period is 60 months from the date the individual makes a Medicaid application or the date the individual enters a nursing home. Assets transferred to trusts within 60 months prior to these dates are considered an available resource.[9] This includes trusts, other than trusts created by will, created by

the individual, his spouse, and certain third persons, such as conservators and trustees. The purpose for which the trust was created is not relevant.

Assets in a revocable trust are presumed available resources, regardless of when the trust was created. Further, if any assets are transferred from the revocable trust to another individual within the 60-month period, that is also a transfer subject to the 60-month look-back period. Note that if the individual who created the trust personally removes the assets and personally transfers them by gift, the 36-month rather than the 60-month look-back period will apply.

Assets in an irrevocable trust are also deemed to be available resources if payment could be made to the individual from the trust. There are various exemptions, and the statutes are confusing as to the extent of availability. However, it appears the 60-month rather than the 36-month look-back period applies in this situation.

Question – May an individual or his spouse waive or forfeit pension rights to become eligible for Medicaid?

Answer – No. Any waiver of pension income, inheritances, or damage claims, as in personal injury suits, is ineffective.

Question – Will amounts paid to family members who are furnishing personal care for an individual be counted as resources?

Answer – While reasonable payments for personal care are not viewed as gifts for Medicaid purposes, payment for past services are viewed with suspicion.

Question – If an individual transfers property by gift, but retains a life estate, what amount will be treated as an available resource?

Answer – According to the federal government, the actuarial value of the life estate, based on the life expectancy of the individual, is subtracted from the value of the property, and the remainder is considered the gift of an available resource.[10]

Question – If an individual purchases a life annuity, will that be subject to the look back gift rules?

Answer – If the annuity is "actuarially sound," based on the life expectancy of the individual, it will not be deemed a partial gift.

Question – Will the transfer of a personal residence to either a revocable or irrevocable trust trigger the look-back rules?

Answer – No. Since the personal residence is an excluded asset under the Medicaid rules, the transfer is not subject to the rule. However, the federal government takes the position[11] that it is a resource. As noted above, the personal residence is often an exempt asset.

Question – Three adult children are contributing equally to the support of their elderly parent. May any of them claim her as a dependent?

Answer – Since no child is furnishing over one half of the parent's support, none of them can claim her as a dependent unless they sign a multiple support agreement. Essentially, this is an agreement that one of the children will claim the mother as a dependent, and the others will not.

Question – When one spouse is in a nursing home, to what extent are the assets of the other spouse protected from claims for reimbursement for public assistance or counted as available resources of the institutionalized spouse?

Answer – The law permits the other spouse, who is called the "community" spouse, to retain assets of a certain value. The amount varies from state to state. In this regard, revocable trusts, discussed in Chapter 28, may cause substantial problems. If the trust language permits the use of trust assets for the support of the institutionalized spouse, the trust will be considered an available resource. Further, the community spouse may not be able to claim any exemption for the trust assets since they are not in his name. The revocable trust should contain specific language dealing with these issues.

Question – What is a special needs trust?

Answer – A special needs trust is one established by clients who have children who are under a disability and are receiving supplemental social security (SSI) benefits, or other forms of state or federal assistance. They are intended to permit the parents to furnish some economic benefits to their children without disqualifying them for public assistance. The device may also be used to provide for elderly persons who are disabled, such as a parent.

The purpose of the special needs trust is to permit payments by the trustee to cover needs of the dis-

abled person which do not affect his eligibility for public assistance. The special needs trust should not be geared to the basics, such as food, clothing, shelter, and in particular, medical care.

The guidelines for what assets may be considered available resources to the disabled person are found in the Program Operational Manual, commonly referred to as POM, which is used by government representatives. If the assets in the trust are available for the basic needs of the disabled person, they may result in denial of public assistance, or the appropriate government agency may even seek to compel reimbursement of public assistance payments from the trust assets.

On the other hand, property held in such a trust does not count as a resource of the disabled person if access to the trust assets is restricted. In general, such trusts should follow a discretionary or protective trust format used for asset protection, but must be even more restrictive. For example, if the trust provided that the trustee could use trust assets only for the "support" of the disabled person, it would count as an available resource.

Such trusts should specifically provide that the trustee may not make any payments that cover items provided by public assistance programs. The trust must be irrevocable and an independent trustee is preferred. It may be part of the basic estate plan of the parents, either in a will or living trust that takes effect at death. While the trust could be created irrevocably while the parents are alive, this is generally discouraged. It may have gift tax consequences, and government officials must be informed whenever the disabled person becomes the beneficiary of an irrevocable trust.

To guard against attacks from the providers of public assistance, these trusts may provide for contingent beneficiaries, such as other children, who could become the exclusive beneficiaries of the trust if such an attack is launched. The trust may also have a destruct clause, providing that if the providers do attempt to reach it, or use it to disqualify the disabled person, it will terminate and be distributed entirely to contingent beneficiaries, such as the other children.

Question – Can a client who wishes to qualify for Medicaid create a form of special needs trust for his own benefit?

Answer – Both state and federal law provide that if the individual or spouse transfers assets to an irrevocable trust for the benefit of the individual, all of its assets are deemed available resources.[12] However, this will not apply to trusts created by third persons, such as children, which should be structured as special needs trusts.

Disability Planning

Question – What is disability income insurance?

Answer – Disability income insurance provides coverage for lost earnings suffered during the period of a disability that prevents a client from working. Disability policies typically pay benefits equal to a substantial percentage (50 to 70 percent) of regular earnings, providing enough income for a reasonable standard of living.

Disability income policies differ with respect to the elimination (waiting) period, the benefit period, and the definition of disability an insured must meet to qualify for benefits. Some policies only pay benefits if an insured is unable to perform any gainful employment; other policies may pay benefits if an insured is unable to perform the duties of his particular profession. Policies may pay benefits for life or to a specific age.

The benefits paid by disability income policies are tax-free to the extent the policy premiums were paid by the individual with after-tax dollars.[13] Benefits attributable to policy premiums paid by an employer are fully includable in gross income. Under an individual policy, the premiums paid in the current year are taken into account. Under a group policy, the employee's contributions for the last three years, if known, are considered.

For self-employed individuals or professionals, a disability income policy that pays a percentage of net business income without taking into account on-going business expenses may not be sufficient. For example, a business owner may bring in monthly revenue of $10,000, which pays for $5,000 in monthly business expenses and provides $5,000 in monthly take-home pay. A disability income policy that pays 60% or $3,000 per month in tax-free benefits may adequately provide for living expenses, but does not account for any on-going business expenses.

Business overhead expense policies (also called business continuation coverage) are available to fill the gap. Business expense policies pay on a reim-bursement basis for actual expenses incurred. These expenses may include fringe benefits paid for by the business for the benefit of the business owner. Business expense policies generally have short elimination periods and offer an open-ended benefit period with a maximum dollar benefit. The policies are generally intended to last for shorter periods, from 6 months up to 3 years. After longer periods, presumably, a business will be sold or wrapped up.

Question – In general, what are the eligibility requirements for social security disability benefits?

Answer – An individual who is unable to engage in any substantial gainful activity by reason of a medically determinable physical or mental impairment may be entitled to social security disability benefits if he:

1. is under age 65;

2. has been disabled for 12 months, is expected to be disabled for at least 12 months, or has a disability which is expected to result in death;

3. is "fully insured" under social security (see below);

4. has worked under social security for at least 5 of the 10 years (20 out of 40 quarters) just before becoming disabled, or if disability begins before age 31 but after age 24, for at least one-half of the quarters after reaching age 21 and before becoming disabled (but not less than six);

5. files an application for disability benefits; and

6. completes a 5-month waiting period or is exempt from the waiting period.

A person is "fully insured" under social security if he has 10 years (40 quarters) of employment under social security or if he has worked under social security for as many quarters as there are years since he reached age 21 and before the year in which he became disabled.

Incapacity Planning

Question – What is a Living Will? What is a Do Not Resuscitate Declaration?

Answer – A Living Will, also called an Advance Directive or a Natural Death Declaration, enables an individual to direct in advance what kind of health care he desires or rejects in the event he becomes so ill he cannot at the time communicate his desires with respect to life-sustaining medical treatment. Usually, the point of a living will is to express an individual's desire not to receive life-sustaining treatment if he is in a terminal condition. A more positive view is that the living will enables an individual to choose what kind of medical care he wants or does not want under given circumstances he describes. Many states have statutory living will forms (a form of living will designed by a state legislature) designed for use specifically in terminal illness situations.

A Do Not Resuscitate Declaration (DNR) authorizes health care providers to withhold CPR or other measures to restart a patient's heart or breathing. Unlike a Living Will, a DNR is appropriate only for a small group of people who are in the final stages of a terminal illness or who are suffering from a serious condition such that they do not want to receive emergency treatment.

A durable power of attorney for health care (DPAHC), if it is so drafted, can be both an advance directive as to health care and a proxy directive. While the living will is usually concerned only with directives concerning the withdrawal or withholding of life-sustaining medical treatment in the event of a terminal illness, the DPAHC can address itself to any range of health decisions desired by the principal. For general information on the power of attorney, see Chapter 56.

In the absence of either a living will or a DPAHC, an incapacitated patient's desires with respect to life-sustaining treatment may be determined and communicated by a court-appointed surrogate or guardian. Once a guardian is appointed, he is the sole advocate for the patient's wishes as they were conveyed to others by the patient prior to incapacity. Because there is no hard evidence as to an incapacitated patient's desires in the absence of a living will or DPAHC, the patient's wishes may sometimes go unfulfilled due to the high standard of proof required by most states in these types of cases.

Question – What is a guardianship or a conservatorship?

Answer – Guardianship is a fiduciary relationship created by the law for the purpose of enabling one person, the guardian, to manage the person or estate, or both, of another person, the ward, when the law has determined that the ward is incapable of managing his person or estate himself. Wards fall into two general categories: (1) minors, and (2) adults who have been legally adjudged incompetent to act for themselves.

The term "guardian" is used to refer both to the guardian of the person of the ward and to the guardian of the ward's property. The guardian of the person takes custody of the ward, looks after his personal needs, and in general performs the duties performed by parents of a minor (except the duty of support). The guardian of a ward's property, sometimes known as a conservator, a curator, or a committee, is charged with the responsibility of investing and managing the estate of the ward. One who is appointed a guardian, without any further words of limitation, is held to serve in both guardianship capacities. In this discussion, the term "guardian," without further description, should be taken to refer to a guardian serving in both capacities. A guardian of the property merely will be referred to as a conservator.

Unlike a trustee, a guardian does not take title to the ward's property. Title to the ward's property remains in the ward; the guardian takes custody and control of the ward's property as an officer of the court under whose supervision he acts. While a trustee derives his powers from the trust instrument, a guardian derives his powers from the law.

The court normally having jurisdiction to appoint a guardian is the court in the state of the ward's domicile that has jurisdiction of probate matters. Since a guardian's powers at common law do not extend outside the state in which the guardian is appointed, and since a guardian functions as an officer of the court that appointed him, courts are reluctant to appoint as guardians anyone not a resident within the jurisdiction of the court.

Some states have statutes requiring guardians appointed within the state to be residents of the state. Sometimes, therefore, an ancillary conservator of the estate will be appointed in the state (outside the ward's domicile) where the ward owns property. In many cases, however, the state (outside the ward's domicile) where the ward actually resides or where his property is located will, as a matter of comity, recognize the authority of the guardian appointed by the state of the ward's domicile. But "full faith and credit" requirements of the U.S. Constitution do not appear to hold much sway in guardianship;

if a local court thinks the welfare of the ward requires appointment of a local guardian, such action is likely to be taken whether or not a guardian was appointed in the state of the ward's domicile. Some courts will, if necessary, and if statutes permit, appoint nonresident guardians.

CHAPTER ENDNOTES

1. IRC Sec. 63.
2. IRC Sec. 2.
3. IRC Secs. 151, 152.
4. IRC Sec. 21.
5. IRC Sec. 121.
6. IRC Sec. 7702B.
7. IRC Sec. 101.
8. 42 USC Sec. 1396p(c)(1)(B)(i).
9. Id.
10. Transmittal No. 64, State Medicaid Manual, November, 1994.
11. Id.
12. 42 USC Sec. 1396A(k).
13. Treas. Reg. §1.105-1.

Chapter 56

DURABLE POWER OF ATTORNEY

WHAT IS IT?

A power of attorney is a written document that enables an individual, the "principal," to designate another person or persons as his "attorney-in-fact," that is, to act on the principal's behalf. The scope of the power can be severely limited ("only to pay my utility bills") or quite broad ("all the legal powers I myself have, including but not limited to the following –").

A "durable" power of attorney is a power of attorney that is not terminated by subsequent disability or incapacity of the principal. At this date, all states have recognized some form of durable power of attorney. The vast majority of such states have either enacted in total the durable power of attorney provisions of the Uniform Probate Code (U.P.C.) or have drafted their own statutes in conformity with the provisions of the U.P.C.

The definition of a durable power of attorney, according to the Uniform Probate Code, is:

"A durable power of attorney is a power of attorney by which a principal designates another his attorney in fact in writing and the writing contains the words 'This power of attorney shall not be affected by subsequent disability or incapacity of the principal, or lapse of time,' or 'This power of attorney shall become effective upon the disability or incapacity of the principal,' or similar words showing the intent of the principal that the authority conferred shall be exercisable notwithstanding the principal's subsequent disability or incapacity, and, unless it states a time of termination, notwithstanding the lapse of time since the execution of the instrument."

WHEN IS THE USE OF SUCH A DEVICE INDICATED?

1. When the principal is elderly and there is a significant chance that he will become senile. The use of a broadly drawn durable power of attorney may negate the necessity of petitioning the local court for appointment of a guardian or conservator to handle the principal's assets.

2. When an individual is suffering from a physical disability or illness, the effect of which could lead to a permanent or long term incapacity.

3. In all situations where an individual desires to provide for the continuity of the management of his or her assets in the event he or she is unable to manage such assets for either a short or long duration of time because of physical or mental incapacity. The durable power of attorney permits the individual, when competent, to make a determination of who will handle his or her affairs.

4. As a temporary and expedient substitute for a living revocable trust. The trust device is more burdensome and possibly much more costly than the durable power of attorney.

5. As an addition to the revocable living trust, to provide flexibility.

6. To avoid the necessity of legal proceedings to establish a legal guardianship or conservatorship for an individual who may face short or long term incapacity.

WHAT ARE THE REQUIREMENTS?

1. The principal (the one giving the power) must be of legal age and competent at the time the power is given.

2. The attorney in fact (the one receiving the power) must be of legal age at the time the power is exercised.

3. To be effective in the event of disability, the power of attorney must include the words "this power of attorney shall not be affected by subsequent disability or incapacity of the principal" or "this power of attorney shall become effective upon the disability or incapacity of the principal" or similar words showing the principal's intent that the authority conferred shall be exercisable regardless of whether or not he or she subsequently becomes disabled or incapacitated.

HOW IS IT DONE?

Assume your client, Joe Mozino, a widower, is on his deathbed on December 28. He could make annual exclusion gifts for this year and if he's alive four days later on January 1 he could make another round of gifts. None of these gifts would be includable in his estate for federal estate tax purposes.

The problem is, he may be mentally competent to act–and physically able–on the 28th of December. But if he becomes either physically or mentally incompetent after that date, the estate tax savings he is legally entitled to will be lost unless someone is entitled by state law to act (specifically to make gifts) on his behalf. Joe could name his son, Andrew, his attorney-in-fact and give him the power (in addition to other powers) to make gifts on his behalf. Andrew could draw checks on Joe's account to each of the donees (just as if Joe drew the checks).

An example of a broadly drawn durable power of attorney appears at Figure 56.1.

WHAT ARE THE TAX IMPLICATIONS?

The holder of the durable power of attorney, if the power is broadly drawn, can be given: (1) the right to execute on behalf of the principal all tax returns including income and gift tax returns; (2) the power to make gifts on behalf of the principal (thereby possibly reducing the principal's estate for federal estate tax purposes) and (3) the right to elect to treat gifts made by the competent spouse as split between the competent spouse and the incompetent principal for federal gift tax purposes. Other nontax powers that can be given under a power of attorney include the right to buy or sell real estate, the right to invest in stocks, bonds or other securities, or the right to sue on behalf of the principal.

ISSUES AND IMPLICATIONS IN COMMUNITY PROPERTY STATES

Because community property is owned equally by both husband and wife, many transactions require the signature of both spouses in order to be effective. Particularly in situations where the couple has a community property proprietorship business, the incapacity of one spouse could seriously affect the stability and viability of the business.

Incapacity of one spouse could also prevent the sale of securities or the sale of or even borrowing against real or other property. Because of presumptions of community property status in many instances, title companies and others concerned with the completeness of title transfer usually require the signature (personally or by exercise of a power of attorney) of both spouses even though the property is in the name of only one spouse.

In many cases, a wife will give a power of attorney to her husband if he is the primary manager of the property for the sake of convenience of management. However, consideration should also be given to providing a method of dealing with both halves of the property if either the husband or the wife should suffer any incapacity.

It should be noted that while all states authorize some form of durable power, not all states have adopted the Uniform Durable Power of Attorney provisions.

Some community property states, such as California, provide that if one spouse is legally incompetent, the other spouse will succeed to management of the community property, with court approval required for some transactions. If the attorney-in-fact is not the spouse, there could be serious conflicts between the competent spouse and the attorney-in-fact pertaining to management and investment of community property.

QUESTIONS AND ANSWERS

Question – How broad can a durable power of attorney be written?

Answer – The extent of the powers conferred by the principal upon the attorney-in-fact are limited only by the desires of the principal. The example of a broad general power of attorney shown in Figure 56.1 is an attempt by a principal to confer upon the attorney-in-fact the right to act to the same extent the principal could have acted if the principal were present and able to act.

Question – What is the duration of a durable power of attorney?

Answer – The durable power of attorney, once properly executed, continues until revoked by the principal or until it terminates by its terms on the death of the principal. However, as a practical matter, many insurance companies and financial institutions generally decline to recognize any power of attorney that has been executed more than six months before the date it is presented for use. The obvious purpose of this "rule of convenience" is to make certain that the power of attorney is still in full force and effect.

Figure 56.1

POWER OF ATTORNEY

KNOW ALL MEN BY THESE PRESENTS, that I, Brett A. Rosenbloom, of Delaware County, Pennsylvania, hereby revoke any general power of attorney that I have heretofore given to any person, and by these Presents do constitute, make and appoint my brother, Eric J. Rosenbloom, of Delaware County, Pennsylvania, my true and lawful attorney.

1. To ask, demand, sue for, recover and receive all sums of money, debts, goods, merchandise, chattels, effects and things of whatsoever nature or description which are now or hereafter shall be or become owing, due, payable, or belonging to me in or by any right whatsoever, and upon receipt thereof, to make, sign, execute and deliver such receipts, releases or other discharges for the same, respectively, as he shall think fit.

2. To deposit any moneys which may come into his hands as such attorney with any bank or bankers, either in my or his own name, and any of such money or any other money to which I am entitled which now is or shall be so deposited to withdraw as he shall think fit; to sign mutual savings bank and federal savings and loan association withdrawal orders; to sign and endorse checks payable to my order and to draw, accept, make, endorse, discount, or otherwise deal with any bills of exchange, checks, promissory notes or other commercial or mercantile instruments; to borrow any sum or sums of money on such terms and with such security as he may think fit and for that purpose to execute all notes or other instruments which may be necessary or proper; and to have access to any and all safe deposit boxes registered in my name.

3. To sell, assign, transfer and dispose of any and all stocks, bonds (including U.S. Savings Bonds), loans, mortgages or other securities registered in my name; and to collect and receipt for all interest and dividends due and payable to me.

4. To invest in my name in any stock, shares, bonds, securities or other property, real or personal, as to vary such investments as he, in his sole discretion, may deem best; and to vote at meetings of shareholders or other meetings of any corporation or company and to execute any proxies or other instruments in connection therewith.

5. To enter into and upon my real estate, and to let, manage, and improve the same or any part thereof, and to repair or otherwise improve or alter, and to insure any buildings thereon; to sell, either at public or private sale or exchange any part or parts of my real estate or personal property for such consideration and upon such terms as he shall think fit, and to execute and deliver good and sufficient deeds or other instruments for the conveyance or transfer of the same, with such covenants of warranty or otherwise as he shall see fit, and to give good and effectual receipts for all or any part of the purchase price or other consideration; and to mortgage my real estate and in connection therewith to execute bonds and warrants and all other necessary instruments and documents.

6. To contract with any person for leasing for such periods, at such rents and subject to such conditions as he shall see fit, all or any of my said real estate; to give notice to quit to any tenant or occupier thereof; and to receive and recover from all tenants and occupiers thereof or of any part thereof all rents, arrears of rent, and sums of money which now are or shall hereafter become due and payable in respect thereof; and also on non-payment thereof or of any part thereof to take all necessary or proper means and proceedings for determining the tenancy or occupation of such tenants or occupiers, and for ejecting the tenants or occupiers and recovering the possession thereof.

7. To commence, prosecute, discontinue or defend all actions or other legal proceedings pertaining to me or my estate or any part thereof; to settle, compromise, or submit to arbitration any debt, demand or other right or matter due me or concerning my estate as he, in his sole discretion, shall deem best and

Figure 56.1 (cont'd)

for such purpose to execute and deliver such releases, discharges or other instruments as he may deem necessary and advisable; and to satisfy mortgages, including the execution of a good and sufficient release, or other discharge of such mortgage.

8. To execute, acknowledge and file all Federal, State and Local tax returns of every kind and nature, including without limitation, income, gift and property tax returns.

9. To engage, employ and dismiss any agents, clerks, servants or other persons as he, in his sole discretion, shall deem necessary and advisable.

10. To convey and transfer any of my property to trustees who shall hold the same for my benefit and/or the benefit of my children and other members of my immediate family upon such trust terms and conditions as to my attorney shall deem desirable.

11. To make gifts to my wife and/or issue upon such terms and conditions as he in his discretion shall determine.

12. In general, to do all other acts, deeds and matters whatsoever in or about my estate, property and affairs as fully and effectually to all intents and purposes as I could do in my own proper person if personally present, giving to my said attorney power to make and substitute under him an attorney or attorneys for all the purposes herein described, hereby ratifying and confirming all that the said attorney or substitute or substitutes shall do therein by virtue of these Presents.

13. In addition to the powers and discretion herein specially given and conferred upon my attorney, and notwithstanding any usage or custom to the contrary, to have the full power, right and authority to do, perform and to cause to be done and performed all such acts, deeds and matters in connection with my property and estate as he, in his sole discretion, shall deem reasonable , necessary and proper, as fully, effectually and absolutely as if he were the absolute owner and possessor thereof.

14. In the event of my disability or incompetency, from whatever cause, this power of attorney shall not thereby be revoked.

IN WITNESS WHEREOF, I have hereunto set my hand and seal this   day of
          , 20

_____(SEAL)
BRETT A. ROSENBLOOM

STATE OF PENNSYLVANIA:
          ss.
COUNTY OF DELAWARE

Before me, the undersigned, a Notary Public within and for the County of Delaware, Commonwealth of Pennsylvania, personally appeared Brett A. Rosenbloom, known to me to be the person whose name is subscribed to the within instrument, and acknowledged that he executed the same for the purposes therein contained.

IN WITNESS WHEREOF, I have hereunto set my hand and official seal this   day of
          , 20

_____
Notary Public

However, the six month rule suggested above should not be applicable to a durable power of attorney. The durable power of attorney by its very nature is designed to cover the situation where the principal becomes incompetent. If, in fact, the principal is incompetent, it would be impossible for the attorney to obtain a freshly dated power of attorney.

Question – Can there be more than one attorney-in-fact under a durable power of attorney?

Answer – Yes; however, caution must be taken in drafting the power of attorney. If the power of attorney merely names John Doe and Mary Roe as the holders of the power, then both must act together in order for the power to be operable. If, however, the power is in favor of, "John Doe *or* Mary Roe, either of them to act in place of the principal," then each person can act independently.

Furthermore, the power of attorney can provide for successor attorneys-in-fact in the event of the primary attorney's death or inability to serve.

Question – Does a power of attorney terminate upon disability?

Answer – A power of attorney that is not a durable power of attorney terminates upon disability. However, actions taken by the attorney-in-fact when he or she is unaware of the principal's disability are binding upon the principal.

A durable power of attorney by its very definition survives and continues and is not affected by subsequent disability or incapacity of the principal.

Question – Does the death of the principal terminate a durable power of attorney?

Answer – Yes. The death of the principal terminates a power of attorney whether or not it is durable. However, as in the case of a power of attorney that is not durable, the durable power of attorney permits the attorney-in-fact who has no notice of the death of his principal to continue to act according to and under the power until the attorney-in-fact learns of the death of the principal.

Question – What is the relationship between the attorney-in-fact under a durable power of attorney and a court appointed guardian for the incompetent?

Answer – The durable power of attorney continues in operation after the appointment of a guardian for the incompetent. However, the guardian of the incompetent appointed by the Court has the same rights as the principal and can terminate the durable power of attorney on behalf of his ward, the incompetent.

Question – What is a "springing" power of attorney?

Answer – Four-fifths of the states recognize a particular form of durable power of attorney known as the springing power. The typical durable power of attorney takes effect upon execution. Clients who are reluctant to grant another person wide powers to act at a time when the principal is capable of acting may prefer to use a springing power. A springing power does not become effective until the occurrence of a specified event such as physical or mental incapacity or disappearance.

Some states define the contingencies under which the springing power becomes effective by statute, while other states require that the contingencies be specified in the instrument. All states require that the instrument name the person or persons who are to determine whether the contingency has occurred. For instance, if the contingency is incapacity, a doctor or group of doctors should be named to make such a determination. The attorney-in-fact may be the person making the determination. Obviously, alternate individuals should be named in case the person originally named is no longer able to make such a determination.

As with all tools and techniques, there are costs and downsides. The major drawback of a springing power is the potential difficulty in determining whether the contingency has occurred. There may be family disputes over whether a disability has in fact triggered the springing power. This puts a premium on clear and precise language in the instrument defining the contingency and creating an objective mechanism for determining whether it has actually occurred. An even greater potential problem is the reluctance on the part of banks, hospitals, and other organizations to accept a document granting broad powers over property if that document was executed a number of years prior to the date when it "springs." Financial institutions quite often raise the problem of "staleness," even though there is nothing in state law suggesting that the mere passage of time dates a power. For this reason, all powers of attorney should be revised every three years or less. Although banks and other financial institutions should honor a power of attorney, it is good practice to check to see if that institution has its own specific power of attorney form or wording.

Question – What is a durable power of attorney for health care?

Answer – A durable power of attorney for health care is a document in which the principal confers upon the attorney in fact the power to make health care decisions for the principal in the event the principal is not legally competent. The extent of the permissible powers varies according to state law. In general, the principal authorizes the attorney-in-fact to consent to medical treatment, including surgical procedures. One of the most important and controversial aspects of this document is the extent to which it authorizes the attorney-in-fact to terminate treatment or even terminate life support where the principal is terminally ill or is in what is called "a persistent vegetative state," meaning the principal is in a permanent coma and the best medical opinion is that he or she will never recover.

In some states, the durable power of attorney for health care is a separate legal document, and requires more formality in execution than the durable power for management of property requires. In other states, the two powers are combined in a single document.

Question – Can the attorney-in-fact make gifts on behalf of the principal?

Answer – This is the one area involving the use of durable powers that has resulted in the most tax controversy. In the usual situation, the principal is elderly and/or seriously ill, and is not legally competent. The attorney-in-fact proposes to make a series of gifts that fall within the annual exclusion ($11,000 in 2004) discussed in Chapter 22 to reduce the principal's taxable estate. The IRS has success-

fully argued that unless gift giving is clearly authorized in the power of attorney itself, or under state law pertaining to the durable powers, the gifts are incomplete for federal tax purposes and still included in the taxable estate of the principal.[1]

Note that if the durable power of attorney is drafted to permit the attorney-in-fact to make gifts, consideration should be given to whether or not the power holder can make gifts to himself or herself. Bear in mind that the attorney-in-fact is often a close family member. If that person can make gifts to himself or herself, this power could be deemed a general power of appointment for federal tax purposes, and the failure to exercise the power could be a taxable gift.

Question – Does the attorney-in-fact under the durable power assume the same legal liabilities and responsibilities as a trustee?

Answer – The law in this area is unclear, but it is safe to assume the attorney in fact assumes at least some of the potential liability and duties of a trustee. This includes possible claims the attorney in fact made imprudent investments, or failed to protect the best interests of the principal. A person who is being considered for such an appointment should be fully informed of his or her potential liabilities.

Question – Who can serve as attorney-in-fact?

Answer – Any trusted person, such as a spouse, relative, or friend. It need not be an attorney. It is a good idea to have an alternative attorney-in-fact to serve if the first choice cannot serve for whatever reason.

CHAPTER ENDNOTES

1. *Est. of Casey v. Comm.*, 91-2 USTC ¶60,091 (4th Cir. 1991); TAMs 9347003, 9342003.

Part 11:

VALUATION ISSUES

Chapter 57

VALUATION PLANNING

WHAT IS IT?

Valuation planning describes any technique used to affect the valuation of property or business interests for gift, estate, or generation-skipping transfer tax purposes. Since the basis for valuation of assets for these purposes is fair market value, which is defined in regulations as what a willing buyer would pay a willing seller, it may be possible to undertake planning moves that can actually reduce the value of the property, and thus reduce federal transfer taxes.

EGTRRA 2001 repeals the estate tax and the generation-skipping transfer tax for one year in 2010.

WHAT ARE THE REQUIREMENTS

The client transfers undivided interests in property to other family members, thus reducing the value of the interests in the same property retained by the client. In fact, since the transferred interests represent less than 100% ownership of the property, even the transferred interests have a lower value. By fractionalizing the ownership of the property or business interests through transfers to family members, the client reduces the value of the property or business interests for gift and estate tax purposes.

HOW IT IS DONE – AN EXAMPLE

Client owns 100% of the stock in a closely held corporation, which is engaged in real estate development. He transfers 20% stock interests to each of his three children, either outright or in trust. Since the transferred interests are minority interests, the value of the stock for gift tax purposes may be reduced to reflect the lack of control over the corporation.[1] Further, since the client now owns 40% rather than 100% of the business, the value of his interest may also be reduced, since he is no longer able to sell the entire business unless his children agree.

WHAT ARE THE TAX IMPLICATIONS?

Introduction

Valuing property for federal gift, estate, and generation-skipping transfer tax purposes is a most complex and often uncertain process. Frequently, the taxpayer's valuation has differed widely from the value established by the Internal Revenue Service. Courts will then be asked to resolve the valuation question.

Thus, value is a variable upon which reasonable minds can and will continue to differ. But value is not determined by a mere flip of the coin. The use of careful and thorough appraisals by qualified experts, documentation of sales of similar property recently sold, and well drawn arm's length restrictive agreements (such as a buy-sell arrangement) have proved effective tools in substantiating favorable values.

General Valuation Rules

The regulations under IRC Section 2031 discuss factors to recognize to value items includable in the gross estate for federal estate tax purposes.[2] Under the regulations, value is fair market value, "the price at which the property would change hands between a willing buyer and a willing seller, neither being under any compulsion to buy or to sell and both having reasonable knowledge of relevant facts." Thus, the value a particular person would place on property may vary greatly from the measure of worth placed on that same item by the government. In fact, it is neither necessary that there be an established market for an item, nor that there be the "willing buyer and seller" spoken of in the regulations. In the absence of an actual sale, the value is based on a hypothetical sale.

Generally, when an organized market does in fact exist, the market price will prevail. The ignorance of a material fact by the buying public or its inability to properly assess the significance of certain events does not form a basis for reducing the price indicated on the organized market. The contrary result applies in the absence of an established market. A purchase or sale is not regarded as determinative of value in situations in which one of the parties was ignorant of a material fact.

The following external factors have had varying effects on the probative value of sales: (a) the frequency of sales (the courts tend to disregard isolated or sporadic sales); (b) the relationship between the buyer and the seller (it is unusual for sales between parents and children or employers and employees to be given great weight in the light of their almost definitional unequal bargaining positions); (c) offers to purchase or sell (offers as opposed to options present little evidence of value).

Not only should all the factors affecting value be considered, but there should be sound reasoning for the relative weight given to each one.

Determining Value

The Internal Revenue Service would likely consider all the facts and circumstances that a hypothetical buyer and seller would consider. The derived price at which the property would have changed hands between parties "X" and "Y" thus determines the Service's valuation. By this rule, a forced sale–or a sale outside of regular business channels–would not be determinative of the value.[3] Thus, generally, the Service's position is that the price at which the item or a comparable item would have been sold at retail is determinative.

Value is basically a question of fact in those situations where there is an established market for identical property. But valuation problems become essentially problems of evidential proof (and often, opinion) where:

1. There are different markets for the same property, such as in the case of a property with both wholesale and retail markets.

2. The appraisal of the worth must be made on the basis of comparison with somewhat similar property (which properties should be selected?; how comparable is it?). What is derived is at best an opinion based upon fact.

3. The property in question is unique, such as a patent or copyright. Here, the data must be analyzed (is the examiner capable of making an adequate analysis?), and an opinion must be formulated as to how much the potential anticipated benefits are worth.

Since, in practice, valuation problems are frequently viewed by the Service and the courts as problems of negotiation and compromise, the appraiser's object should be to derive a fair and sound value that, if litigated, would be sustained by the court. Evidence and proof secured in the form of expert advice through appraisal, promptly after death, would likely have a greater probative value than evidence obtained at a later date. (As to the valuation of specific types of property, one must turn to the regulations, rulings and court decisions.)

Date Assets are Valued

Generally, federal estate taxes are based either on the fair market value of the transferred property as of the date the decedent died or the value of the property six months after the date of the decedent's death (alternate valuation date).[4] Once selected for valuation purposes – date of death or alternate valuation – such date applies to all assets in the estate.

If the alternate valuation date is selected and if the property is distributed, sold, exchanged, or otherwise disposed of within six months of the decedent's death, it will be valued as of that date, not the six month date.[5] Certain types of property diminish in value as time goes on; for example, the present value of an annuity reduces each time a payment is made. Any such property interest or estate whose value is affected by the mere passing of time is valued as of the date the decedent died.[6]

Valuation of Real Property

Because of the uniqueness of land, the value of any real property as of a given date may be subject to widely differing opinions. Absent a market for such property, the greater of (a) the highest price available or (b) the salvage value will control. Where there is a market for real property, the basic factors that affect valuation are:

1. The nature and condition of the property, its physical qualities and defects, and the adequacy or inadequacy of its improvements.

2. The size, shape, and location of the property.

3. The actual and potential use of the property and how the trends of development and economic conditions (such as population growth) affect it.

4. How suitable the property is for its actual or intended use.

5. Zoning restrictions.

6. Size, age, and condition of the buildings (degree of deterioration and obsolescence).

7. The market value of other properties in the area in which the property is located.

8. The value of net income received from the property. Rentals are often capitalized and then adjusted for depreciation. (See discussion of capitalization of income, below.) The same principle can be applied to gross rents. This method, however, must be adjusted to account for operating costs.

9. The value accepted by state probate courts for purposes of state death taxes, if based on appraisals made by qualified real estate experts.

10. Prices at which comparable property in the same area was sold at a time near the applicable valuation date (providing it was an arm's length transaction for the best price obtainable). Usually more than one "comparable property" sale will be used, especially where the property to be valued is a personal residence or undeveloped acreage.

11. How much, taking depreciation into account, would it cost to duplicate the property? The cost or value of land would have to be separated from the total value. The cost of reproducing the building, using present cost figures, would have to be estimated, and then the loss in value due to depreciation would have to be subtracted from the total of the other two figures.

12. Unusual facts.

In the event of a sale of real property within a reasonable period of time after the decedent's death, in such a manner as to insure the highest possible price, the amount received will usually be accepted as its value. Unaccepted offers to purchase the property will also be considered. What of a sale at auction? Usually, this price will be accepted only if it appears that there was no other method that would have obtained a higher price.

Land does not have to produce income or have an active market to attain substantial value. Where lands are in or adjacent to a settled community, owners frequently hold such lands in anticipation of realizing their true value from future sales. For example, a home at the edge of an expanding shopping center might be worth far more to the shopping center developer than it would to a potential buyer in the residential market.

Special Valuation of Certain Farm and Business Real Property

An executor may elect to value qualifying real property on the basis of its actual "special" use rather than its "highest and best" use. This rule, especially useful where the price of farmland is artificially increased by, or has not kept up with, the price per acre of encroaching housing developments, enables the executor to value the farmland at its value for farming purposes. The maximum reduction of the decedent's gross estate under this provision is $850,000 (as indexed for 2004).

The following are the qualification requirements:

1. On the date of the decedent's death, the property must be involved in a "qualified use." That term is defined by IRC Section 2032A(b)(2) as use as a farm for farming purposes or in a trade or business other than farming.

2. The value of the qualified property (less debts or unpaid mortgages) in the decedent's estate must equal at least 50% of the decedent's gross estate (less debts or unpaid mortgages).

3. At least 25% of the gross estate (less debts and unpaid mortgages on all property in the gross estate) must be qualified farm or closely held business real property.

4. Such property must pass to a "qualified heir." This term is defined at IRC Section 2032A(e) to include the decedent's immediate family plus his ancestors or lineal descendants, his spouse or the spouse of a descendant, or a lineal descendant of a grandparent. A legally adopted child of an individual shall be treated as the child of such individual by blood.

5. The real property must have been owned by the decedent or a member of his family and used as a farm or in a closely held business for an aggregate of five years or more of the eight year

Figure 57.1

SECTION 2032A SPECIAL USE VALUATION WORKSHEET

(1) Year of Death .... _____

(2) FMV of Gross Estate[1] .... $_____

(3) Debt on Property Includable in Gross Estate[2] .... ($_____)

(4) Adjusted Value of Gross Estate [(2) - (3)] .... $_____

(5) FMV of Qualified Use Property[1, 3] .... $_____

(6) Debt on Qualified Use Property[2] .... ($_____)

(7) Adjusted Value of Qualified Use Property [(5) - (6)] .... $_____

(8) 50% of Adjusted Value of Gross Estate [(4) x 50%] .... $_____

If amount of (8) is more than amount of (7), estate is not eligible for special use valuation – STOP.

(9) FMV of Qualified Use Real Property[1, 4] .... $_____

(10) Debt on Qualified Use Real Property[2] .... ($_____)

(11) Adjusted Value of Qualified Use Real Property [(9) - (10)] .... $_____

(12) 25% of Adjusted Value of Gross Estate [(4) x 25%] .... $_____

If amount of (12) is no more than amount of (11), estate is eligible for special use valuation. If not, STOP.

(13) FMV of Qualified Real Property[1, 5] .... $_____

(14) Debt on Qualified Real Property[2] .... ($_____)

(15) Adjusted Value of Qualified Real Property [(13) - (14)] .... $_____

Amount of (15) must be no less than amount of (12).

(16) FMV of Qualified Real Property [(13)] .... $_____

(17) Tentative Special Use Value of Qualified Real Property .... ($_____)

(18) Tentative Value Reduction [(16) - (17)] .... $_____

(19) Statutory Maximum Special Use Reduction As Indexed .... $_____

(20) FMV of Qualified Real Property [(16)] .... $_____

(21) Reduction in Value [Lesser of (18) or (19)] .... ($_____)

(22) Special Use Value [(20) - (21)] .... $_____

Source: *Advanced Sales Reference Service* (a National Underwriter Company publication).

INSTRUCTIONS FOR SECTION 2032A
SPECIAL USE VALUATION WORKSHEET

Definitions

Qualified use means use of the property in farming or other trade or business.

Qualified heir means a member of the decedent's family who acquired the property from the decedent.

Member of the family means, with respect to an individual: (a) the spouse of the individual; (b) an ancestor of the individual; (c) a lineal descendent of the individual, or of the spouse or parent of the individual; or (d) the spouse of a lineal descendant listed in (c).

Figure 57.1 (cont'd)

Notes

1 Fair market value (FMV) determined without regard to special use valuation.

2 Where the value of the property has not been reduced by the debt on the property.

3 Real or personal property includable in decedent's estate which: (a) on the date of the decedent's death, was being used for a qualified use by the decedent or family member; and (b) was acquired from or passed from the decedent to a qualified heir.

4 Real property includable in decedent's estate which: (a) was acquired from or passed from the decedent to a qualified heir; (b) was owned by the decedent or family member and used for a qualified use by the decedent or family member for 5 of the last 8 years prior to the decedent's death; and (c) was used in the qualified use in which the decedent or family member materially participated in 5 years out of the 8 years immediately preceding the decedent's death (or retirement or disability).

5 Real property includable in decedent's estate which: (a) is located in the United States; (b) was acquired from or passed from the decedent to a qualified heir; (c) on the date of the decedent's death, was being used for a qualified use by the decedent or family member; (d) was owned by the decedent or family member and used for a qualified use by the decedent or family member for 5 of the last 8 years prior to the decedent's death; (e) was used in the qualified use in which the decedent or family member materially participated in 5 years out of the 8 years immediately preceding the decedent's death (or retirement or disability); and (f) is designated in the Section 2032A election and recapture agreement.

Some of the real property on line 9 may not be eligible for special use valuation because it does not meet requirements (a), (c), and (f) for real property on line 13.

Indeed, with regard to (f), special use valuation can be elected for less than all of the real property that would otherwise be eligible. However, if the election is made, the election must be made for enough real property so that the adjusted value of such property [line 15] is not less than 25% of the adjusted value of the gross estate [line 12].

---

period ending on the date of the decedent's death. During this period the decedent or a member of his family must have been a material participant in the operation of the farm or other business.

If the above conditions are met, the property qualifies for the special valuation rule.

Then if the executor elects to apply IRC Section 2032A, the farm method of valuing land is generally determined as follows:

A. Average annual gross cash rental for comparable land.

B. Average annual state and local real estate taxes for such comparable land.

C. Average annual effective interest rate for all new Farm Credit Bank Loans.

Formula: $\dfrac{A-B}{C}$ = value for section 2032A purposes.

This formula provides that the income that is to be capitalized is the average annual gross cash rental income (for five years prior to the decedent's death) less the average annual state and local real estate taxes (for the same five year period) for that comparable land.

"Comparable land" is (1) land used for farming purposes and (2) must also be located in the same vicinity as the farmland to be valued. If there is no comparable land, or if the executor chooses to have the farm valued in the manner of a qualifying closely held business, other factors are applied.

The executor may not use cash rentals from the farm to be valued. The rentals used from comparable farmland must have been the result of arm's length bargaining.

The capitalization rate, the average annual effective interest rate on new Farm Credit Bank loans, is the average billing rate charged on new agricultural loans to farmers in the farm credit district in which the qualified property is located. These amounts are published by the IRS according to the Farm Credit Bank district in which property is located. A reproduction of the relevant parts of the latest ruling on this topic follows.

In order to determine the special use value of a farm under the formula method the average annual effective interest rates on new Farm Credit Bank loans to be used for estates of decedents dying in 2003 are as follows:

Farm Credit Bank District in Which Property is Located	Interest Rates Year of Death 2004
Columbia	9.18%
Omaha\Spokane	7.23%
Sacramento	6.92%
St. Paul	7.36%
Springfield	7.26%
Texas	7.19%
Wichita	7.44%

These are the states within each Farm Credit Bank district:

District	States
Columbia	Delaware, District of Columbia, Florida, Georgia, Maryland, North Carolina, Pennsylvania, South Carolina, Virginia, West Virginia.
Omaha/Spokane	Alaska, Idaho, Iowa, Montana, Nebraska, Oregon, South Dakota, Washington, Wyoming.
Sacramento	Arizona, California, Hawaii, Nevada,Utah.
St. Paul	Arkansas, Illinois, Indiana, Kentucky, Michigan, Minnesota, Missouri, North Dakota, Ohio, Tennessee, Wisconsin.
Springfield	Connecticut, Maine, Massachusetts, New Hampshire, New Jersey, New York, Rhode Island, Vermont.
Texas	Alabama, Louisiana, Mississippi, Texas.
Wichita	Colorado, Kansas, New Mexico, Oklahoma.

The following example assumes an average annual gross cash rental for comparable land of $84,000, average annual state and local real estate taxes for such comparable land of $4,000, and a capitalization rate of 9.18%.

$$\frac{A-B}{C} = \text{value for section 2032A purposes.}$$

$$\frac{\$84,000 - \$4,000}{9.18\%} = \$871,460$$

If there is no comparable land, or if the executor elects to have the farm valued in the manner of a qualifying closely held business, then the following factors shall apply.

1. The capitalization of income that the property can be expected to yield for farming or closely held business purposes over a reasonable period of time under prudent management using traditional cropping patterns for the area, taking into account soil capacity, terrain configuration, and other factors.

2. The capitalization of the fair rental value of the land for farmland or closely held business purposes.

3. Assessed land values in a state that provides a differential or use value assessment law for farmland or real estate owned by a closely held business.

4. Comparable sales of other farms or closely held business land in the same geographical area far enough removed from a metropolitan or resort area so that nonagricultural use is not a significant factor in the sales price.

5. Any other factor that fairly values the farm or closely held business value of the property.

If a farm or a closely held business qualified for the special valuation rules and its value so determined is used for federal estate tax purposes, then an additional estate tax will be imposed if within 10 years after the decedent's death and before the death of the qualified heir, the qualified heir who receives such property disposes of any interest in that property, other than to a qualified family member, or ceases to use that property in the manner in which it was used to qualify for this special tax treatment.

Generally, the additional tax imposed shall be the excess of the tax that would have been imposed on the property if it was valued at its best use over the tax imposed because the property was valued at its "qualified use" value.

If the additional tax is imposed, it is due six months after the date of the disposition of the property or the cessation of its use as a farm or as part of the closely held business. The qualified heir who received such property is personally liable for the additional tax imposed.

Valuation of Life Insurance

Proceeds of life insurance on the life of the decedent receivable by or for the benefit of his estate will be taxed in the insured decedent's estate.[7] In addition, where the decedent held incidents of ownership, such ownership will invoke taxation.[8] The amount includable is the amount receivable by the beneficiary. This includes dividends and premium refunds. In determining how much is includable, no distinction is made between an ordinary life policy, a term policy, group insurance, or an accidental death benefit.

If a settlement option is elected, the amount that would have been payable as a lump sum is the amount includable. If the policy did not provide for a lump sum payment, the amount includable is the commuted amount used by the insurance company to compute the settlement option payments.

The value of an unmatured policy owned by a decedent on the life of another is included in the policy owner's gross estate where he predeceases the insured.

1. If a new policy is involved, the gross premium paid would be the value.

2. If the policy is paid-up or a single premium policy, its value is its replacement cost, that is, the single premium which that company would have charged for a comparable contract of equal face value on the life of a person who was the insured's age (at the time the decedent-policyholder died).

3. If the policy is an established whole life policy, the value is found by adding any unearned portion of the last premium to the interpolated terminal reserve.

4. If the policy is a term policy, the value is the unused premium.

Valuation of U.S. Government Bonds

Series E bonds are valued at their redemption price (market value) as of the date of death since they are neither negotiable nor transferable and the only definitely ascertainable value is the amount at which the Treasury will redeem them.

Valuation of Household and Personal Effects

The general rule for valuing household property and personal effects such as watches, rings, etc., is: the "willing buyer-willing seller" rule. A room by room itemization is typical, especially where household goods include articles of artistic or intrinsic value such as jewelry, furs, silverware, paintings, engravings, antiques, books, statuary, oriental rugs, or coin or stamp collections.

In other than community property states, "household goods" and like personalty acquired by and used by husband and wife during marriage are generally presumed to be the property of the husband. Therefore, in the absence of sufficient evidence to rebut this presumption, household goods and personal effects would be includable in the husband's estate.

Valuation of Annuities, Life Estates, Terms for Years, Remainders, and Reversions

Commercial annuities (annuities under contracts issued by companies regularly engaged in their sale) are valued by reference to the price at which the company issues comparable contracts. A retirement income policy, from the point in time that there is no longer an insurance element, is treated as a contract for the payment of an annuity.

Where the annuity is noncommercial, such as a private annuity, the present value of future payments determines its fair market value. Likewise, for gift and estate tax purposes, the fair market value of life estates, terms for years, remainders, and reversions is their present value.

An annuity is defined as a systematic liquidation of principal and interest. Payments might be made for the life of the annuitant (life annuity) or over a period of years (term certain).

A life estate is a disposition of property in which the primary beneficiary receives distributions of only income. Payments might be made for the life of the recipient or could be based on the life of a third party, but the income beneficiary of a life estate receives no right to enjoy the principal. In other words, a life estate is the right of a person for his life, or for the life of another person, to receive the income from or the use of certain property. An example would be, "I give my home to my wife for life." The wife's interest would be a life estate. At her death, the property would go to some other party, called a "remainderperson," or revert to the grantor.

In the case of a term certain arrangement, the present value of income for a given number of years is found in a like manner.

A remainder (the beneficiary gets the principal after a third party has enjoyed the income for life, or for a given period of time) is actuarially equivalent to a "reversion." An example of a remainder would be "to my son John, for life, remainder to Mary." Instead of coming back to the grantor (a reversion), the property "remains" away from the grantor and goes instead to Mary. Mary is said to have a remainder interest. An example of a reversion is where the principal (after a given beneficiary has enjoyed an income for life or for a given period) "reverts" to the grantor. If the grantor dies before the person enjoying the lifetime interest, his right to "will" that reversion to his heirs, who will some day receive the principal, is valued under the same rules as annuities, remainders, and life estates.

Annuities, life estates, reversions, remainders, and terms for years are valued according to a discount rate that changes monthly.

The first step in valuing an annuity based on a life (or on the joint lives of two or more people), a life estate, or a reversion or remainder based on a life (or joint lives) is to convert one of the unknowns (the length of the lifetime involved) to a known (life expectancy). This is done by means of a mortality table, which, based on a study of the longevities of a large number of people over a selected period of time, indicates the expectancy of life (in years) for a mythical individual who represents the average experience at each age of life.

The second step is to determine a proper discount interest rate (the second unknown that should be attributed to the interest being valued). When that interest rate is determined, a valuation table can be constructed which converts the two factors to be applied, life expectancy and the rate of interest, into one factor to be applied to the amount of the periodic payment, to determine the present worth or value of the property interest.

The valuation tables in Appendix B (Tables B and S) are used to do term and life computations. A more detailed explanation for use for the tables can be found there.

Valuation must be based on an interest rate (rounded to the nearest 2/10ths of one percent) equal to 120% of the federal midterm rate in effect for the month in which the valuation date falls.

Two qualifications need to be added to this explanation of the law respecting valuation. First, these valuation provisions do not apply to interests valued with respect to qualified plans (including tax sheltered annuities and IRAs) or in other situations specified in Treasury regulations. Second, if an income, estate, or gift tax charitable contribution is allowable for any part of the property transferred, the taxpayer may elect to use the discount rate for either of the two months preceding the month in which the valuation date falls. However, if a transfer of more than one interest in the same property is made with respect to which the taxpayer could use the same interest rate, such interest rate is to be used with respect to each such interest.[9]

Valuation of Listed Stocks

Where a stock has an established market and quotations are available to value the stock as of the date in question, the fair market value per share on the applicable valuation date governs for both gift and estate tax purposes.

The FMV is based on selling prices when there is a market for the stock or bond. This would be the mean between the highest and lowest quoted selling price on the valuation date. If there were no sales on the valuation date, but there were sales on dates within a reasonable period both before and after the valuation date, the FMV is determined by taking a weighted average of the means between the highest and lowest sales on the nearest date before and the nearest date after the valuation. The average is then weighted inversely by the respective number of trading days between the selling date and the valuation date.

Where there is a large block of stock that could not be marketed in an orderly manner, the block might depress the market because it could not be converted to cash as readily as could a few shares. Therefore, selling prices and bid and asked prices may not reflect fair market value. Sometimes it may be necessary to value this type of stock as if it were closely held and not actively traded. If this can be established, a reasonable modification of the normal basis for determining FMV can be made. In some cases, a "blockage" discount is determined by the effect that block would have had on the market if it were sold over a reasonable period of time and in a prudent manner.[10] A similar situation occurs where sales at or near the date of death are few or of a sporadic nature and may not indicate a fair market value.[11]

The converse of the "blockage" situation above is where the block of stock to be valued represents a controlling interest (either actual or effective) in a going business. Here, the price of normally traded shares may have little relation to the true value of the controlling lot. The large block could have the effect of increasing value because of its element of control.

Valuation of Corporate Bonds

The valuation of bonds is similar to that of listed common stock. The means of the selling prices on or near the applicable valuation date, or, if there were no sales, the means of bona fide asked prices weighted inversely to the number of trading days from the valuation date will determine the fair market value of the bonds.

In the absence of sales or bid and asked prices, the value must be determined by:

(1) Ascertaining the soundness of the security.

(2) Comparing the interest yield on the bond in question to yields on similar bonds.

(3) Examining the date of maturity.

(4) Comparing prices for listed bonds of corporations engaged in similar types of business.

(5) Checking the extent to which the bond is secured.

(6) Weighing all other relevant factors including the opinion of experts, the good will of the business, the industry's economic outlook, the company's position in the industry and its management.

Valuation of Interests in Closely Held Corporations

There are at least seven situations in which the estate planner must value a business or professional practice. Valuation plays a critical role when a planner needs to:

- plan for a client's estate liquidity

- establish a price for buy-sell purposes (should a buy-out be necessitated by death, disability or other health problems, retirement, or lifetime termination of relationship) (e.g., sale of an interest in the business or practice to a third party)

- properly recognize the business's or practice's worth in a client's prenuptial or postnuptial agreement

- apportion assets in a marital dissolution

- ascertain the worth of the business or practice as loan collateral

- perform a "fiscal checkup" to test the financial health of a client's business or practice, detect adverse financial trends, or uncover opportunities (for instance, a doctor might find that patients are getting older and the business or practice should try to attract younger people or can profitably move into a new area of specialty)

- prepare an estate or gift tax valuation

In the settlement of many estates, the valuation of closely held corporate stock can be a most difficult, time-consuming, and costly problem, especially when a confrontation arises between the executor and the Internal Revenue Service. But careful use of a properly drafted restrictive business agreement can help alleviate and control the problem (subject to the requirements of IRC Sections 2701 to 2704).

What exactly is "closely held stock"? Various criteria have been used to define such stock. Some of these are: (a) the number of stockholders; (b) restrictions imposed on a shareholder's ability to transfer the stock; (c) absence of exchange listing or regular quotation in the "over-the-counter" market; (d) an irregular, limited history of sales or exchanges.

For general purposes, however, stock can be considered "closely held" where there is some question as to whether its value can be found solely by reference to an established market. The problem of valuing closely held stock is compounded because, by definition, such stock is seldom traded.

The relevant Internal Revenue Code sections and regulations[12] are of little help. They are so vague and general that their application to a specific valuation question is of minimal planning value.

Valuing Stock and Partnership Interests for Estate Planning Purposes

Copyright 1988 by Stephan R. Leimberg. Reproduced with permission from NumberCruncher Software.

Basic factors to consider. The fair market value of a closely held corporation or partnership is determined in the same manner as stock in a professional practice. Reg. §20.2031-3; Rev. Rul. 80-202, 1980-2 CB 363. In determining the value of a closely held business, Rev. Rul. 59-60, 1959-1 CB 237, the master guideline for valuing all businesses, requires that eight factors must be considered:

- *Nature of the business and the history of the enterprise from its inception.* This factor measures the risk, stability, depth of management of the business, and the diversity of its operations. With respect to the valuation of a professional practice, the appraiser should review the stability of the practice's financial history, its growth patterns, changes in ownership, market share, marketing approach, and "product" breakdown. For example, is this a law practice that does 70% negligence and personal injury work, 20% financial and estate planning, and 10% real estate? Significant events should be emphasized and events not likely to recur should be eliminated.

- *Economic outlook in general and for the specific industry in particular.* Here, the appraiser must evaluate the "industry" outlook and the position of the practitioner with reference to his competition. The appraiser should consider the cyclical nature of the practitioner's business, the direction of the national economy, and any unique elements in the professional's practice position.

- *Book value of the stock and the financial condition of the business.* The appraiser here must consider the asset value of the professional's practice. Note that the professional's statements are historical-cost based; they should be adjusted to reflect fair market value. Depreciation as recorded under generally accepted accounting principles need not bear any relationship to economic depreciation and the true net value of the assets under consideration.

- *Earnings capacity of the company.* The earnings of a professional practice have been held by many valuation authorities to be the essence of its fair market value, since "everyone knows that the value of shares in a … company depends chiefly on what it will earn." (Judge Learned Hand in *Borg v. Int'l*

Silver, 11 F.2d 147 (1925).) What is at issue is earnings *capacity*, future income potential, not net income. Adjustments should be made for salaries, travel, and entertainment expenses, nonrecurring items, and potential legal and tax liabilities. In a corporate setting, note that loans to shareholders may represent disguised dividends; loans from shareholders may represent equity rather than debt.

- *Dividend paying capacity.* The emphasis again is on *capacity*, not actual payout. With the professional corporation, the appraiser should focus on cash flow projections and relate dividend capacity to earnings capacity, with due consideration for the need to reinvest in the professional's practice.

- *Goodwill or intangible values.* Goodwill has been extensively discussed above. In its simplest form, goodwill is the excess earnings of the practice over the normal return on tangible assets. Note that the normal return should be the "fair rate of return" earned by comparable practitioners. Tangible assets should be valued at their fair market value rather than at historically based book value.

- *Sales of the stock and the size of the block to be valued.* Here, recent sales are most important. Has the interest in the practice been sold to insiders? What percentage of the practice has been sold? Have there been any recent events since the sale that would affect significantly the value of the practice?

- *The market price of stock of corporations engaged in the same or a similar line of business having their stock traded in a free and open market.* This factor is extremely difficult to apply to professional practices. Few professional practices exist as public corporations. Those that do rarely are comparable to closely held professional practices. A publicly held practice by definition has a value premium for marketability.

The following discussion summarizes four often-used approaches to business valuation: (1) book value, (2) comparable company, (3) capitalization of income, and (4) going concern value.

(1) Book Value

Book value (essentially assets minus liabilities) is a particularly good place to begin the process of valuing a closely held corporation in each of the following situations:

1. Where the business in question is primarily an asset holding company–such as an investment company.

2. Where the company is in the real estate development business and assets are the major profit making factor.

3. Where one person is the sole or major driving force since such businesses are typically worth only their liquidation value upon the death, disability, or termination of employment of such a person.

4. Where the liquidation of the corporation is in process or imminent at the valuation date. The impact of sacrifice sales and capital gains taxation must often be considered since the true value of a liquidating business is only the amount available to shareholders after all expenses and taxes.

5. Where the business is highly competitive but only marginally profitable. Past profits thus become an unreliable tool to measure potential future earnings.

6. Where the assets or the business itself is relatively new.

7. Where some form of merger is likely to occur with another firm.

8. Where the business is experiencing large deficits.

Book value must be adjusted since the assets of most businesses are usually carried on the company's books at historical cost rather than fair market value.

Adjustments are recommended in the following cases:

1. When assets are valued at cost. For instance, the primary assets of a closely held investment company consist of marketable securities. These are typically carried on the company's books at cost. Likewise, land is an asset most companies will carry at cost but which may be worth considerably more on the open market. The result is a book value that bears little or no relationship to the true present worth of the business.

2. When assets have been depreciated at a rate in excess of their true decline in economic value. A good example is the operating company (one which produces or sells products or services to the public) that has purchased machinery or equipment originally costing $1,000,000 but which, on the company's books, has been depreciated down to $300,000. The equipment may be worth a lot more or a lot less than either its cost or the $300,000 figure at which it is presently carried.

3. When items such as potential lawsuits or unfavorable long-term leases have not been shown in the footnotes of the firm's balance sheet.

4. When one or more assets with significant economic value have been completely "written off"–thus reflecting a book value far below the price which they should realistically bring.

5. When the business has carried assets such as franchises and goodwill on the books at a nominal cost.

6. When the business experiences difficulty in collecting its accounts receivable.

7. When the firm's inventory includes goods that are either obsolete or for some other reason are not readily marketable.

8. Where the working capital or liquidity position of the business is poor (low current assets relative to current liabilities).

9. Where the firm is burdened with a substantial amount of long-term indebtedness.

10. Where the retained earnings are high only because they have been accumulated over a long period of time. Such a business may have poor current earnings and the outlook for increased earnings in the future may be dim.

After the adjustments described above have been made, the value of any other class of stock with a priority as to dividends, voting rights, or preference to assets in the event of a sale or liquidation must be subtracted. For example, the owner of common stock can't realize the value of the assets until owners of preferred stock have been satisfied.

Once the adjusted book value has been determined for the entire business, it is then necessary to divide the book value by the number of shares outstanding to determine the value per share.

Book value should rarely be used as the only means of valuing a closely held business. It should be used in conjunction with or as a means of testing the relevancy of the capitalization of earnings and other methods. (Be sure not to "double count" an asset when combining two or more methods).

Book value should not be used when capital plays a minor role in profit making or where you are valuing the stock of a party who does not have the voting power to force liquidation, since in that case book values have little relevance.

Book Value Calculation

Input: "Adjusted" Asset Value of
Common Stock $500,000

Input: Total Adjusted Liabilities $100,000

Input: Par Value of Preferred Stock $50,000
Total Deductions $150,000
Adjusted Book Value of Entire
Business $350,000

Input: Number of Common Shares
Outstanding 1,000
Value Per Share of Common Stock $350.00

(2) Valuation By Reference To Comparable (Traded Securities) Companies

A business can sometimes be valued by reference to the value of a comparable company if the stock of that second company is listed, and actively traded, on a securities exchange or on the over-the-counter (OTC) market.

The price per share of the publicly traded stock is divided by its earnings per share. The resulting ratio is then applied to the earnings per share of the business to be valued in order to arrive at the market value per share.

Comparable traded securities research should start with federal government publications such as the *Standard Industrial Classification* manual (which categorizes industries), the *S.E.C. Directory of Companies Required to File Annual Reports* (which, as its name implies, lists companies which must file reports under various S.E.C. acts), the U.S. Department of Commerce, *Census*

of Business (which is a compilation of statistics and ratios on various businesses), Dun & Bradstreet's *Dun's Review* (which gives key operating and financial ratios), Moody's *Investors Service and Manual* (which provides a detailed description of many publicly held corporations), and Standard & Poor's *Corporation Records* (which provides financial and operating ratios for many corporations).

Be sure to check trade magazines for the industry in question. Many associations also provide detailed information for members of their industry.

In searching for comparable companies, look for similarities in product line, service, size, marketing and geographic area, growth, profitability, overhead, and competitive position. Examine balance sheets and income statements (use the ratios template) to compare ratios and trends. Seldom, if ever, will a perfect match be found and many adjustments may have to be made even after a "close fit" is found.

This technique has a number of shortcomings: first, it is difficult to use. Second, an enormous expenditure of time and effort is required to compile accurate and adequate information concerning the business to be valued, the comparable business or businesses, and then to analyze and evaluate the data.

The larger the closely held business, the more likely this approach will be appropriate since the size, corporate capital structure, earnings, liabilities, rate of growth, and diversification are more likely to be comparable to a publicly traded company.

Value Per Share of Closely Held Stock

Input: Per Share Market Price of Similar
Publicly Traded Company $45.00

Input: Earnings Per Share of Similar
Publicly Traded Company $4.50

Input: Earnings Per Share of Business
to be Valued $14.00
Computed Price/Earnings Ratio 10.00
Equivalent Capitalization Rate 0.10
Value Per Share of Closely
Held Business $140.00

(3) Capitalization of Income

No formula exists that applies to all assets and that will be accepted by both the IRS and the courts. Converting the projected flow of income from a business or asset

Figure 57.2

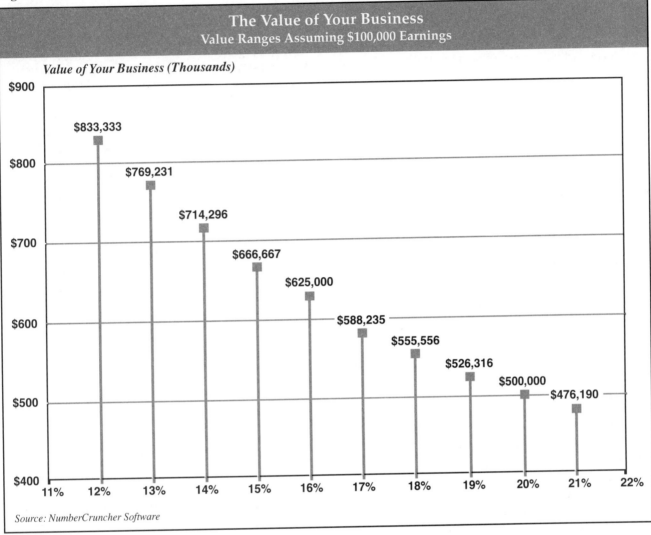

The Value of Your Business
Value Ranges Assuming $100,000 Earnings

Value of Your Business (Thousands)

- $833,333
- $769,231
- $714,296
- $666,667
- $625,000
- $588,235
- $555,556
- $526,316
- $500,000
- $476,190

Source: NumberCruncher Software

into its present value, i.e., "capitalizing the income," provides a simple, reasonably accurate, and commonly accepted way of estimating fair market value.

The concept of income capitalization is simple: determine what amount of income is realistic and proper under the circumstances and then apply a capitalization rate that meets the same criterion. In essence the capitalization rate is the desired rate of return; the rate of return an investor would be willing to accept for the given level of risk. A high risk investment would equate to a high capitalization rate (which in turn results in a lower value). The asset or business is then presumed to be worth the result when adjusted earnings are divided by the capitalization rate.

The graph at Figure 57.2 illustrates the valuation of a business generating adjusted earnings of $100,000 a year using ten different capitalization rates.

Transforming theory into practice is often complex and frustrating. The brief comments below, pertaining to "adjusting" the earnings and selecting the appropriate rate of return may help:

(A) Adjustments to income (in the case of a business, use five year average after-tax profits):

(1) Add back excessive salaries

(2) Reduce earnings if salaries were too low

(3) Add back bonuses paid to stockholder-employees

(4) Add back excessive rents paid to shareholders

(5) Reduce earnings where rents paid to shareholders were below what was reasonable in the market

(6) Eliminate nonrecurring income or expense items

(7) Adjust for excessive depreciation

(8) Adjust earnings for major changes in accounting procedures, widely fluctuating or cyclical profits, or abnormally inflated (or deflated) earnings.

(9) If there has been a strong upward or downward earnings trend, "weight the average" to obtain a more realistic appraisal of the company's prospects.

(B) Determine the capitalization rate (this is the amount that is divided into adjusted earnings). The result is the same as multiplying the reciprocal of the rate, (the result of dividing the number one by 5). In other words, you obtain the same result by multiplying $100,000 of income by 5 as you do if you divide the income by .20.

In deciding on a capitalization rate, consider the following:

(1) A smaller capitalization rate will result in a higher value. A higher capitalization rate results in a lower value. You can check this by examining the value of a business with an adjusted after tax income of $50,000 a year capitalized at 6% (that is, divided by .06), $833,333 and comparing the result with one capitalized at 15% (i.e., divided by .15), $333,333.

(2) Stable businesses with large capital asset bases and established goodwill should be less risky investments and you should use a lower capitalization rate than if you were valuing a small business with little capital, financial history, or management depth.

Assign a high capitalization rate to a personal business that depends on the presence of only one or two key people. An investor purchasing this type of business would want a high rate of return as a reward for that risk. (Another way to say the same thing is that such an investor would not make the investment unless a rapid return of capital through a high income stream was expected.)

Comparison Chart

	"MULTIPLIER" (MULTIPLY THIS TIMES EARNINGS)	OR	CAPITALIZA- TION RATE (DIVIDE THIS INTO EARNINGS)
LOW	28.6	=	3.5 %
RISK	25	=	4 %
	20	=	5 %
	16.67	=	6 %
	14.29	=	7 %
	12.5	=	8 %
	11.11	=	9 %
	10	=	10 %
	9.09	=	11 %
	8.33	=	12 %
	7.69	=	13 %
	7.14	=	14 %
	6.67	=	15 %
	6.25	=	16 %
	5.88	=	17 %
	5.56	=	18 %
	5.26	=	19 %
	5	=	20 %
	4	=	25 %
HIGH	3.33	=	30 %
RISK	2.86	=	35 %

It is important to note that there are no "correct" or "official" rates. Even the IRS uses different rates at different times and under different circumstances. It is for this reason that the capitalization of income template provides ten automatic options (which you can change to provide an infinite number of variations).

(4) Valuation of a Business As a "Going Concern"

A closely held business should (and often does) produce an income in excess of the amount that could be expected from the mere employment of the capital its shareholders have invested. That additional amount of income is derived from an intangible value in the business, a value in excess of the total value of the tangible assets.

By capitalizing this "earnings attributable to intangibles," i.e., by dividing the additional profits generated by the firm's goodwill, by an appropriate rate, it is possible to estimate goodwill value. If this amount is then added to book (net tangible asset) value, the total business value can be found.

Some of the elements that may comprise a firm's goodwill include:

(1) Location of the business

(2) Reputation of the business

(3) Public recognition of the company's name

(4) Lists of customers and prospects owned by the business

(5) Management effectiveness and depth

(6) Sales, operations, and accounting skills

(7) Employee morale

(8) Position of the business relative to competitors

(9) Other factors that generate income in excess of that amount which could be expected after multiplying the value of tangible assets by a reasonable rate of return.

Note that goodwill does not include the portion of profits attributable to the corporation's ownership of patents, copyrights, formulas, or trademarks, even though they are intangible, since these are all specifically identifiable.

Goodwill, as in the case with other valuation formulas and procedures, should be used only as a guideline and not as the sole determinate of value. Goodwill has minimal relevance to the valuation of most investment companies since they usually do not have large amounts of intangibles. Officially the IRS does not give strong credibility to goodwill (although the service still insists that goodwill must be taken into account in the valuation process).

Going Concern Value

Input:	Average Annual Earnings	$100,000
Input:	Average Annual Asset Value	$500,000
Input:	Estimated Capitalization Rate	0.200
Input:	Rate of Return on Tangible Assets	0.16

Option	Return On Tangible Assets	Earn From Tangible Assets	Earn From Intangible Assets	Goodwill Value	Total Business Value
1	0.160	$80,000	$20,000	$100,000	$600,000
2	0.170	$85,000	$15,000	$75,000	$575,000
3	0.180	$90,000	$10,000	$50,000	$550,000
4	0.190	$95,000	$5,000	$25,000	$525,000
5	0.200	$100,000	$0	$0	$500,000

A reduction in value is often allowed because the shares being valued represent a "minority" interest in the business. Courts tend to aggregate the lack of marketability inherent in a closely held corporation with the minority interest principle although the "minority interest" discount arises because such shares have no power to force dividends, compel liquidation, or to control corporate policy. This in turn limits the potential market for such stock to the remaining (and usually controlling) shareholders and reduces the price at which such shares would be purchased.

Conversely, where the shares in question represent a "controlling" interest, the IRS will generally attempt to increase the stock's value. "The size of the block of stock itself is a relevant factor to be considered. Although it is true that a minority interest in an unlisted corporation's stock is more difficult to sell than a similar block of listed stock, it is equally true that control of a corporation, either actual or in effect, representing as it does an added element of value, may justify a higher value for a specific block of stock."

Discount For Loss of Key Employee

Both the IRS and the courts have long recognized that the loss of a manager, scientist, salesperson, or other key individual will almost always have a serious effect on the earning power and sometimes on the very stability of a business. Although the principle applies in publicly-held businesses, it is particularly true in a closely held corporation where profits are dependent on the ability, initiative, judgment, or business connections of a single person or small group of owner-employees. A discount in valuation may therefore be appropriate. (This same concept may also be used in determining the amount of key employee insurance a corporation should own.)

There is no universally recognized and accepted formula for computing the economic effect of the loss of a key person. One used in several court cases utilizes a discount approach: a percentage discount is taken from the going-concern value of the business.

Some authorities feel that if the business will survive the death of the key employee, and in time a competent successor can be found, a discount factor of from 15% to 20% should be used. Where the business is likely to fail, or be placed in serious jeopardy upon the death (or disability) of the key employee, a discount of from 25% to 45% is more appropriate. The exact discount factor should be arrived at through consultation with the officers of the company and the firm's accounting and legal advisers.

Some questions that should be answered in the process of determining the factor (or range of factors) to be used include:

(1) How long will it take for a new person to reach the efficiency of the key individual?

(2) How much will it cost to locate and situate a replacement? Will the new employee demand more salary? How much will it cost to train the new person?

(3) What mistakes is a replacement likely to make during the "break in" period and how much are those mistakes likely to cost the company?

(4) What proportion of the firm's current net profits are attributable to the key employee?

(5) Is the employee engaged in any projects that, if left unfinished at death or disability, would prove costly to the business? How costly? Would a potentially profitable project have to be abandoned or would a productive department have to be closed?

(6) Would the employee's death result in the loss of clientele or personnel attracted to the business because of his personality, social contacts, or unique skills, talents, or managerial ability?

(7) What effect would the key employee's death have on the firm's credit standing?

(8) What proportion of the firm's actual loss is it willing to self insure, if any?

Key Employee Valuation

Input: Fair Market Value of Business
with Key Employee $750,000

Input: Discount Percent (%) without
Employee ....

Discount Percent	Value W/O Key Employee	Value of Key Employee
0.16	$630,000	$120,000
0.17	$622,500	$127,500
0.18	$615,000	$135,000
0.19	$607,500	$142,500
0.20	$600,000	$150,000
0.21	$592,500	$157,500
0.22	$585,000	$165,000
0.23	$577,500	$172,500
0.24	$570,000	$180,000

There are a number of ways–other than the approach used in the template–to value a key person's contribution to a corporation's profits. One way is to measure the number of working years remaining to the executive (say 10). Estimate the annual loss of earnings attributable to that person (say $30,000 per year). Then discount (see present value templates) the value of that annual loss (for example, at 10%). This will result in the present value of the key person's services, about $113,000.

Alternatively, the goodwill template could be adjusted to measure the goodwill produced through the efforts of the management team and this total would then further be apportioned (perhaps by relative salaries) among the key employees.

For instance, assume a firm had an average annual asset value of $450,000 and an average annual earnings after taxes of $75,000. If 10% were thought to be a fair rate of return on tangibles, then $45,000 ($450,000 x .10) of the $75,000 would be attributable to tangibles. The remaining $30,000 would be attributable to goodwill. Assume 60% of this, $18,000, could reasonably be allocated to management. If it takes five years to replace the entire management team, then $18,000 should be multiplied by five, or a total of $90,000. If the executive in question drew 80% of the total salaries of the management team, then that person's worth would approximate $72,000 ($90,000 x .80).

Most shareholders of closely held corporations restrict the marketability of co-shareholder's stock through "purchase options" or mandatory buy-sell agreements. If the terms of such agreement definitely fix the values of the shares in question, it is not necessary to examine either book value or earnings. The price fixed in the restrictive agreement will serve as the shares' market value, but to "peg" the value of such stock for federal estate tax purposes:

1. The agreement as to per share value must be made at arm's length and must have been fair and adequate at the time the agreement was executed.

2. The agreement must be binding during the lifetime of the stockholder; that is, he must be obligated to offer the stock to the corporation or other shareholders (a "first offer" commitment) at the specified offer price before offering it to an outsider if he wishes to dispose of his stock during his lifetime.

3. The agreement must be "binding" at death–his executor must be legally obligated to sell the shares to the corporation at the price fixed by the agreement. Furthermore, the price stated in the agreement must either be fixed (e.g., fixed dollar price or book value on the repurchase date) or determinable according to the formula.

4. The agreement must not be a "testamentary device" to transfer value to the natural objects of the decedent's bounty.

The Treasury believes that taxpayers in general tend to keep values low and therefore restrictions which tend to limit the value of family owned closely held stock will be closely scrutinized to determine whether the agreement is a bona fide arm's length business arrangement and not just a device to pass the decedent's shares for less than adequate consideration. See discussion of IRC Section 2703 in Chapter 40.

Valuing a Professional Practice

This section explains why estate planners must be able to value professional practices and discusses

- how a professional practice differs from a typical business, and why these differences are important

- considerations in valuing goodwill

- how to value a professional's stock for buy-sell purposes

- a shortcut approach to valuing a professional practice

- how to use the "prior transactions," "capitalization of billings," and "excess earnings" valuation methods

- rough rules of thumb

A Complex Task

Valuation of a manufacturing business is difficult enough; the valuation of a professional practice, with its many intangible factors, is more complex still. Productivity, goodwill, and the multitude of other factors that affect a professional practice are difficult to quantify. Rules of thumb may differ widely from one appraiser to another and from one group of professionals to another. Some variables may have greater weight for some buyers than for others. For example, a young doctor seeking to purchase a practice may wish to buy one for about the same costs he'd incur if starting from scratch. Conversely, many hospitals purchase the practices of retiring staff physicians to help insure that the practice will continue to fill hospital beds. The hospital might pay more for the practice if the doctor typically referred patients to it, or if the practice might otherwise be sold to a competing hospital.

The questions asked and the methods used differ depending on the purpose of the valuation and the type of practice in question. For instance, valuations for divorce, one of the most common reasons a professional practice is valued, will emphasize the practitioner's age and health, experience, length of practice, financial success, skills, and reputation. The value of the goodwill these factors might generate could be more important to the divorce court than the factors leading to strong marketability, which would be important for estate tax purposes. Factors established by statute and case law, which tend to vary widely from state to state, must also be taken into account. For example, some states give more weight than others to minority interests or lack of marketability discounts with reference to professional corporations.

Why a Professional Practice is Different

A professional practice differs from other businesses mainly because of:

Expertise. The expertise – or, more important, the *perceived* expertise – of the professionals involved is of paramount importance in determining the fees that can be charged and the income that can be earned from the practice. The education, training, and experience a professional brings to his practice, and the "consumer's" dependence on the delivery of the practitioner's services, are extremely important economic factors that must be considered in determining value. For example, a patient needing brain surgery typically does not shop for a bargain price.

Entry barriers. Higher education, licensing, and certification requirements all serve to slow or limit entrants into professional practice. If, for any reason, licensing or certification is lost, the practitioner can no longer practice. If a professional dies or is permanently disabled, his family members cannot continue to operate the practice unless they are duly licensed and certified in the same profession.

Professional goodwill. Reputation and recommendations are the life blood of the professional practice. Although some professionals obtain significant business from "walk-in" traffic due to location or advertisement, most depend mainly on referrals from peers and the recommendation of present clients to bring in new business. This is particularly true with respect to specialists. For this reason, trust, respect, and "liking" of the practitioner – by peers as well as patients or clients – are crucial to the success of the practice.

Nontransferability. Substitution may be difficult or impossible. Professional skills are to some extent unique and not interchangeable. Consider the relationship between psychiatrist and patient: If the psychiatrist is ill for three weeks and unable to work, an attorney-spouse can't "run the store."

Continuing education. In most professions, information becomes outdated, and the professional must engage in continuous education. This may be through formal course work or by keeping up with professional journals and magazines.

Why The Differences Are Important

Most businesses have as part of their value an asset called "goodwill." This can be defined as the quantified expectation of future profits from some source other than mere dollars at work. For instance, if a firm enjoys $80,000 of earnings on a $60,000 capital investment that can reasonably be expected to return 20% ($12,000) at a given risk level, then $68,000 of income ($80,000-$12,000) is attributable to something other than capital. This business-oriented goodwill is an asset of the business that generates value over and above the entity's net asset value.

In a professional practice there are two types of goodwill: business-oriented (stemming from the entity) *and* professional (originating from the individual).

Business-oriented goodwill is attributable to the elements of a professional practice that are similar to those of a regular business: location, operating systems, staff, and patient or client base. Business-oriented goodwill can have significant transferable value, value that can be sold to another licensed practitioner.

Professional goodwill, on the other hand, depends on the unique characteristics of the particular practitioner. At the professional's death, disability, or retirement, that portion of the practice income attributable to professional goodwill will generally leave with the individual. Much of this personal goodwill, however, can be transferred in a sale to another practitioner by creating a well-organized transition in which the departing professional lends credibility to the entering professional.

Valuing Business–Oriented Goodwill and Future Income Flow

Although many sources are available to provide information for valuing a practice's transferable business-oriented goodwill and its likely future earnings, the most accurate source will typically be the firm's own CPA. The CPA should examine ten factors.

Projected earnings. Projected earnings are normally an extension of past earnings. Financial statements and tax returns (specifically income statements, balance sheets, and cash flow statements) should be examined and adjusted to determine:

- *The level of gross income.* Net income figures may be misleading, since principals may be taking profits in the form of perquisites and benefits as well as salaries. The CPA should determine how salaries compare to the "norm" for services performed. Are they too high? Alternatively, if they are lower than comparable payments to similar professionals, does this indicate cash flow or earnings problems?

- *Earnings trend.* At least five years should be reviewed. Measure each year's amount as a percent of a "base" year. A business "trending up" indicates the likely presence of growing goodwill. However, the CPA must also consider whether there are unusual or nonrecurring factors that artificially inflate or deflate income. Large pension contributions, malpractice claims, fees or court costs, and salary structures should be studied particularly carefully. The inability of one or more professionals to work during the period examined would obviously have a strong impact on earnings. Did the professional, out of choice, work 40 hours a week or only 20?

Competition. An increased demand for established practices is typically reflected in an increase in prices.

This has occurred in a number of professions due, in large part, to the increase in the number of newly licensed professionals – e.g., dentistry. An appraiser must also consider the number of other practitioners in the area, how thoroughly their practices saturate the market, and the price trend for services similar to those being valued.

Size of patient or client base. The greater the number of satisfied current patients or clients, the greater the likelihood that a large number of referrals will be made to the practice. More emphasis should be given to this factor when selling the entire practice than when valuing the practice for purposes of appointing assets in a divorce or legal separation. The distribution of the client base should also be evaluated. Consider whether the clients are repeaters, recent additions, referrals from prior clients, young or old, etc. How many patients or clients are seen each day?

Payment sources. How the professional is paid greatly influences both the level and the stability of the practice's income. Measure how likely the practice is to be paid for services rendered, and how soon. Government programs typically pay less per procedure than the usual fee; so the source of payment may also indicate how much will be paid. Questions that should be asked by an appraiser include:

- Is the practice dependent on any particular group of patients or clients for a significant portion of its income?

- What percentage of patients pay bills through private insurance, Medicare, Medicaid, other sources?

- What is the aging of the professional's accounts receivable? Are monthly bills paid in 30, 60, 90 days, etc.? (This is a good indication of the financing needs and efficiency of the practice's collection procedures.)

Practitioner's workload. Income figures alone do not tell how many hours it took to generate a given level of profit. A practice that took 40 hours of work to generate a given amount of earnings is worth more than one that took 70 hours to develop the same earnings. Factors that must be considered in this area include:

- Is the practice a "personal" type or "mass production" type? How much time spent with the patient or client was due merely to the practitioner's work style?

- Does the practitioner spend time on administrative or other problems that could be handled more efficiently and at lower cost by an office manager or other staff?

Fee structure. A great deal can be ascertained by examining the practice's fee structure. A professional who has been consistently and *successfully* charging above-average fees probably has developed significant professional goodwill. If fees are average or below average, perhaps there is an uncovered problem or a potential to increase revenues. An appraiser should ascertain:

- How do this practitioner's fees compare with fees charged in the community by other practitioners of similar reputation and skill?

- When was the last time fees were raised?

- How often have fees been raised in the last five years, and for what reasons?

- Was there measurable resistance to the last increase in fees (a significant drop-off in then current or prospective patients or clients)? Would there be a sizable loss of patients or clients if a fee increase was instituted? How large an increase would the market bear?

- Is billing computerized and how well is the system working?

Staff strength. Second only to the principal(s) in importance to the value of a professional practice is the quality and depth of the staff. Staff includes nonowner professionals (who may or may not carry clientele away if they leave), paraprofessionals, and clerical employees. Questions that should be asked by an appraiser in this area are:

- How long have the various individuals been with the practice; would they be likely to stay if the owner-professional(s) were to die or the practice were sold? What patients or clients (or essential skills) would nonowners take with them if they left? What costs would be involved in recruiting replacements and training them?

- What duties do the nonowners in the practice perform? What percentage of the total practice can be performed without the owner-professional?

Figure 57.3

Worksheet for Valuing a Physician's Practice
WORKSHEET ASSUMPTIONS

ACCOUNTS RECEIVABLE. Sellers sometimes exclude accounts receivable from the sale of the practice to keep the sales price down or to simplify the process; the selling professional collects the revenue from the receivables and the buyer doesn't have to worry about the collectibility or the trouble of collection. Conversely, the purchaser may want a practice with accounts receivable to maintain contact with the patients or clients (similar to purchasing a customer list).

Bills outstanding for more than one year are considered uncollectible; those that have been turned over to collection agencies are not considered as part of accounts receivable. Accounts receivable within 30 days of billing are considered worth between 80% and 90% of their face value. Between 30 and 60 days, the value drops to between 50% and 80%; while in most practices, accounts receivable are worth little after 60 days, *unless* a government agency or private insurer will pay the claim.

Practice point. It is important to view accounts receivable in perspective. Has the professional been "cleaning out" his accounts receivable and living off previous work he's now collecting for? Has he imposed fee increases which create the impression of a constant level of patient volume which is in reality decreasing? Has the professional done a good job of collecting and reporting accounts receivable? In many cases, poor bookkeeping or collection procedures understate the true value of the practice. For instance, a practice may be building its patient volume but, because of inefficiencies or poor pricing of services, hasn't generated a representative cash flow.

BUILDINGS/LAND. The fair market value of the real estate owned by the practice must be used rather than the book value.

EQUIPMENT/FURNISHINGS. A potential purchaser views equipment as capital that will have to be replaced. Equipment depreciates rapidly, partially due to wear and partially to obsolescence caused by the introduction of more effective or efficient (less labor intensive) or easier to use technology.

Some appraisal experts suggest that each item be priced between original cost and present book value. This worksheet suggests that equipment less than five years old be listed at 40% of its cost and older equipment at about 20% of cost. Where appropriate, use an actual fair market value appraisal; for example, certain furniture-say, an antique desk-may have value in excess of its original cost.

DRUGS/SUPPLIES. Most physicians have at least a two-month supply of drugs and other supplies. Divide the annual supply cost by six. Unused disposables are typically worth their cost less 10% to 20%, although a buyer may not choose to use what is currently in inventory, further reducing the practice value.

GOODWILL. Various methods of determining goodwill are discussed throughout this reading. The worksheet rule of thumb-25% of annual gross-can be used as an alternative to another commonly used guideline, $3 to $5 per record of regularly seen patients. Note that these are "quick guess" guidelines; they should not substitute for appropriate financial analysis and evaluation.

Value of Accounts Receivable

	Age	*Percent of Face Value*	*Example*	*Your Figure*
Input:	0-30 days	80-90%	$ 20,000	$_____
Input:	31-60 days	50-60%	50,000	_____
Input:	61 days or more	0 unless insurance	5,000	_____

Buildings and Land

Input:	Market value of building and land	1,000,000	_____

Equipment and Furnishings

	Age	*Percent of Face Value*		
Input:	Less than 5 years	40% of cost	$ 30,000	_____
Input:	5 years or more	20% of cost	4,000	_____
Input:	Drugs, supplies (last 2 month's bills)		12,000	_____
Input:	Cash and market value of invested securities		10,000	_____
Input:	Goodwill (25% of annual gross)		200,000	_____
	Total estimate of practice assets		$1,331,000	$_____

Liabilities

Input:	Balance owed on equipment and furnishings	$ 5,000	_____
Input:	Salaries, bonuses, severance pay due	60,000	_____
Input:	Taxes due	40,000	_____
Input:	Accounts payable	23,000	_____
Input:	Insurance premiums due	70,000	_____
Input:	Mortgage balance	80,000	_____
Input:	Other liabilities	3,000	_____
	Total estimate of practice liabilities	$ 281,000	_____
	Total estimate of practice assets	$1,331,000	_____
	Total estimate of practice liabilities	281,000	_____
	Estimate of value practice	$1,050,000	_____

- How well are nonowners compensated compared to similar employees in similar practices?

- Are there enforceable employment contracts, covenants not to compete, or special fringe benefits that would tie key employees to the practice even if new ownership takes over?

Location of the practice. In general, practices located in economically vibrant and growing communities are more valuable than those in unattractive and depressed areas, but this is not always true. For example, a dentist may have a higher volume of business in an area where preventive tooth care has not been stressed; a criminal attorney may have more potential business in the inner city than in a suburb.

Ironically, a practice producing a high income isn't necessarily more valuable in a community where there is a shortage of professionals; it would be relatively easy for a new practitioner to take advantage of the demand. Conversely, in a community saturated by and long-settled with professionals, start-up time and expense would be high for a new practitioner; so the value of an established practice with a full appointment book and a well-trained staff would therefore be higher.

Physical and mental health of the professional. Particularly in marital distribution situations, the professional's health is a dominant valuation factor. Significant professional goodwill may exist if the professional is in good health and can repeat or improve upon his past earnings record. But what if past earnings were generated by years of 80-hour weeks that are no longer feasible? A surgeon who has a blood-pressure problem, or worse yet, an alcohol or other drug problem, may not be capable of sustaining the workload that "built the business."

Age of the professional. Age is another factor that should be given great weight in a valuation for divorce or separation purposes. Age, aside from its tangential relationship to health, can be used to indicate how long a past flow of earnings can reasonably be projected into the future. Although it is logical to project the earnings of a young practitioner for a longer time than a practitioner only a few years from retirement, an appraiser must consider that the earnings of a younger practitioner are lower and less certain.

Shortcut approach to buy-sell valuations. Since nonprofessionals cannot generally hold stock in a professional corporation and since most states require

that such stock be bought back by the corporation or its surviving shareholders within a relatively short period of time after the transfer of interest, it is essential that a fully funded buy-sell agreement be utilized to protect the interests of all parties. Quite often the parties to such an agreement are unwilling to hire an independent appraiser to value their stock according to the appropriate sophisticated methods. For this reason, a quick and relatively inexpensive method of determining value is often desired, such as the "one times annual net income" formula all too often used for solo private practices.

Although there is no universal rule or perfect formula for arriving at a price, the simplified worksheet shown in Figure 57.3 provides a quick way to "guesstimate" the worth of a physician's practice; it can be easily modified to apply to other professional practices.

Warning: Remember that the guidelines in the worksheet are only that; they will vary depending on the circumstances. Be sure to review the list of assumptions accompanying the worksheet. Note that a solo practice is almost always worth less than one where two or more professionals work together. This is why many practitioners bring in one or more associates well before they retire and negotiate a buyout that will effect a long and smooth transition period. This worksheet should be considered only a starting place for a full valuation.

Valuation Methods

Prior transactions method. Perhaps the most reliable method of valuing a practice, when it is available, is to ascertain the price it sold for in a previous transaction. This assumes, of course, that there was a recent sale or exchange and that it was at arm's length. Consideration should also be given to the magnitude of prior transactions – e.g., the purchase of greater than 50% of a practice creates a control premium, whereas the purchase of less than a 50% interest should involve a minority discount.

Capitalization of billings method. A practice can be valued by dividing the net income by the cost of capital. For example, using this formula, if the practice produced an adjusted net income after the owner's salary of $100,000, and it was assumed that capital should be "costed" at 20% (i.e., a buyer with a similar risk opportunity would demand a 20% return on his investment), the practice would be worth $500,000 ($100,000 divided by 20%).

Another traditional way of arriving at a practice value is by using a multiple of gross billings. The formula for determining the multiple to use is: net income percentage divided by capitalization rate equals percentage of billing factor. For example, assume the firm in our prior example billed $500,000 during the year. Since its adjusted net income was $100,000, its net income percentage on billings was 20% ($100,000 ÷ by $500,000). Given the 20% capitalization rate, its value is $500,000, or 100% of billings (20% ÷ 20% = 1 or 100%). If the same firm billed only $400,000 but still netted $100,000 (a percentage of billing factor of 25%), it would be worth *more* than 100% of the billings. Using the formula, we get a 125% multiple: 25% ÷ by 20% = 1.25 or 125%. Thus, the practice's value, on these facts, would still be $500,000 (i.e., $400,000 x 125%).

Excess earnings method. This is another simple, widely-used – and often court-blessed – method of quantifying the value of intangible assets. Essentially, earnings (pretax, *including* the professional owner's salary and fringe benefits) are adjusted as discussed above. Then the earnings in excess of that which is earned by similar professionals in similar types of practices are computed and that excess is "capitalized" (divided by a percentage to arrive at the capital it would take to produce it annually). The result is the estimated value of the goodwill in the practice. This would be added to the fair market value of tangible assets to arrive at a total value.

For example, assume Doctor Know's average compensation for the last five years – after appropriate adjustments and weighting for its upward trend – was $180,000, but that similar physicians earned only $120,000 during the same period. This indicated that the difference, about $60,000 a year, is due to something other than return on tangible assets.

Excess earnings for most professional practices are capitalized at rates between 20% and 100%. The wide variation is a result of varying risk levels and differing ages of the professionals in question; the median capitalization rate is 33⅓%. Here are the goodwill values of Doctor Know's practice at various capitalization rates:

Rate	Adjusted Excess	Value
20%	$60,000	$300,000
25%	$60,000	$240,000
33%	$60,000	$180,000
50%	$60,000	$120,000
100%	$60,000	$ 60,000

This brings up the question asked at the beginning of the discussion on valuations of businesses: what is meant by a "capitalization rate" and how does the appraiser know what capitalization rate to use? The capitalization rate is the projected cost of capital. But there is no fixed and certain answer to the question of "What is the right rate to use?" A good appraiser will consider such things as (1) how many more productive years the professional has, (2) where on the income-producing cycle the professional was as of the valuation date (highest income-producing years for most professionals occur between ages 45 and 55), and (3) changes in the profession, the economy, and in government regulation. For instance, skyrocketing malpractice costs are rapidly changing the practicing environment, causing many professionals to drastically change the way they work.

Most appraisers working with professional corporations will be conservative and use relatively high capitalization rates, 50% to 100% (meaning a low multiplier). *Reason:* It is more difficult to maintain "excess earnings" than earnings produced by passive income investments and, further, total earnings have been used as a base. If pretax earnings after reduction for owner's compensation and benefits is used as the base, a 20% or 40% capitalization rate (and thus a higher multiple) would be more appropriate. The table below sets out various capitalization rates and their related multipliers for determining value using the excess earnings method.

Capitalization Rate/Value

Capitalization Rate	Value (multiply adjusted excess by this rate)
3.5%	28.57/1
4.0%	25.00/1
5.0%	20.00/1
6.0%	16.67/1
7.0%	14.29/1
8.0%	12.50/1
9.0%	11.11/1
10.0%	10.00/1
11.0%	9.09/1
12.0%	8.33/1
13.0%	7.69/1
14.0%	7.14/1
15.0%	6.67/1
16.0%	6.25/1
17.0%	5.88/1
18.0%	5.56/1
19.0%	5.26/1
20.0%	5.00/1
25.0%	4.00/1
30.0%	3.33/1

Caveat: As is the case with any valuation method, the excess earnings concept has its limitations. Goodwill can be understated, because even a practice without excess earnings may have considerable worth as a going concern. On the other hand, goodwill can be overstated, because the excess earnings method does not consider whether or not the practice is marketable. Third, many subjective judgments are required (such as the appropriate weight to give the trend of earnings, the adjustments to make to earnings, and the capitalization rate to use).

Rough Rules of Thumb for Valuations

Almost all tax practitioners and financial planners use rules of thumb (often called SWAGs, scientific wild asset guesses) that they've developed as the byproduct of practical experience. SWAGs lie between calculations and pure conjecture and serve as starting places in the valuation process, later to be abandoned or modified. They can also be used where more precise methods are deemed impractical. The following rough rules of thumb are suggested for valuing various professions:

- *Medical:* Net asset value plus 20% to 40% of annual revenue for goodwill (referral practices would be worth less, continuing client base practices worth more).

- *Veterinary:* Net asset value plus 60% to 90% of annual revenue for goodwill.

- *Legal:* Because client's files can't be sold (lawyers are ethically precluded from selling their law practices), personal goodwill typically does not enter into the valuation process. Therefore, net asset value is often the major value determinant. In the case of distribution upon divorce, if there is a buy-sell agreement, the price set in the agreement is usually considered merely an indication of value and is certainly rebuttable. Remember that work-in-progress fees are not reflected in the records of a law firm. So, even if the firm's accounting records are accurate and nonfraudulent, a firm that takes no retainers and sends no bills, but has many contingent fee arrangements, can easily be undervalued. Conversely, fees contingent on events that may not occur must be discounted.

- *Accounting:* Net asset value plus a goodwill payment of from 80% to 130% of annual revenue (paid out over time). Another common method uses 20% of projected fees for five years, discounted for both attrition and the time value of money. According to the CPA Handbook, a third commonly used formula is 40% of gross receipts for the prior three years and a percentage of average annual fees as follows: 100% for clients served over four years, 75% for clients served from three to four years, 50% for clients served from two to three years, and 25% for clients served from one to two years.

- *Dental:* Net asset value plus 30% to 40% of annual revenues for goodwill.

- *Engineering/Architecture:* Net asset value plus 25% to 50% of annual revenues for goodwill (firms with few continuing clients would, of course, have little if any goodwill).

Data Needed in the Valuation Process

Valuation experts should review each of the following:

- Last five years' profit and loss statements and balance sheets (certified financial statements by an independent CPA firm are preferable). Five years is a common time frame because it (1) minimizes the possibility of "valuation planning," (2) covers a complete business cycle, (3) examines good as well as bad times, (4) permits discounting or elimination of "aberration years," and (5) illustrates the stability and trend of profits. Graphs are particularly useful in identifying and illustrating aberration years or the direction and velocity of a profit trend.

- Last five years' federal income tax returns.

- Any business leases.

- Last five years' fee schedules.

- Brochures on the firm.

- Articles of incorporation and by-laws, and minutes of board of directors' meetings for the last five years.

- Last five years' appointment books.

- State employment research data (particularly information from state professional licensing department).

- Demographic and practice economics information available from state or county professional societies (such as the state or local medical or bar association).

- Studies published in professional journals such as the American Medical Association's "Socioeconomic Characteristics of Medical Practice" (published annually), or by the American Bar Association, or in private publications such as "Medical Economics," or, for the legal profession, "Corporate Law Department Surveys and Survey of Law Firm Economics" (Altman-Weil Management Consultants, Inc., published annually) and "Compensation of Attorneys" (Steven Langer and Associates).

Qualified appraisers are designated by several appraisal groups: (1) the American Society of Appraisers, (2) the Appraisal Institute, (3) the Certified Valuation Appraisers, and (4) the International Business Appraisers.

PLANNING FOR VALUATION DISCOUNTS IN CLOSELY HELD AND FAMILY BUSINESSES

Various other circumstances have substantial impact on the valuation of business, including restrictive agreements, such as cross purchase or redemption plans, and partnership liquidation agreements. IRC Section 2703 (see Chapter 40) will have a substantial impact on the use of such agreements in many closely held businesses.

Lower valuation for the business interest may result where it does not fully participate in the future growth of the business, i.e., preferred stock and "frozen" partnership interests (see Chapter 58), and long-term installment sales (see Chapter 35).

A failure to undertake proper valuation planning for the family business will leave the estate at the mercy of the IRS, and may make it impossible to retain the enterprise. To be really effective, any plan must contain the following elements:

1. A present transfer of interests in the business from family members in the older generation to those in younger generations, either by sale, gift or both.

2. A shift of all or part of the future growth of the enterprise to the younger generation.

3. The owners of the family business should seriously consider taking full use of their unified credit and even their GST tax exemption during life through transfers of interests in family businesses.

For a good example, see TAM 9131006, where decedent created a family partnership to engage in real estate operations and transferred mostly limited partnership interests to 4 children and 14 grandchildren, with one general partnership interest to a son, all covered by the $10,000 annual exclusion. No gift tax returns were filed, and all income was allocated to the decedent for a management fee. Held – no gift or estate tax consequences, profits were to be allocated proportionately to the partners, and all limited partnership interests were transferable, subject to a right of first refusal.

On the other hand, retention of value in the estates of the older generation may facilitate stock redemptions, particularly under IRC Section 303 (Chapter 41); deferred payment of tax under IRC Section 6166 (Chapter 16), and special use valuation for real property under IRC Section 2032A.

Regardless of the difficulties, the conclusion is inescapable that lifetime transfers of interests in family business enterprises are almost essential to planning for succession.

The two most common discounts available for family and closely held businesses are the discounts for lack of marketability and for a minority interest. Similarly, an additional discount may be appropriate to reflect those instances in which a limited partner cannot withdraw from the partnership and is locked in to his investment (i.e., a "lock-in" discount). Also, other discounts may be applied to reflect built in capital gains or key management personnel.

Minority Interest Discounts

The cases have been liberal in permitting substantial discounts in value based on the fact that the decedent's interest in the business is a fractional or minority interest.[13] In some instances, value may be increased to reflect a control premium.

The minority interest discount principle refers to the fact that the owner of less than a majority interest in an enterprise cannot by himself control day-to-day or long range managerial decisions, impact future earnings, control efforts for growth potential, establish executive compensation, or get at the corporate assets through liquidation. Because the owner of a minority interest lacks these benefits of control over the business an acquiror of a minority interest will pay less for that interest, on a pro-rata basis, than if he were acquiring a controlling interest in the business. In instances where the owner lacks the ability to exercise control over the operations of the enterprise, the owner's interest may be worth significantly less than its "liquidation" value.

For many years, the Service was uncomfortable with the idea that minority interests owned among family members could be valued at a discount even though the collective ownership of the individual family members gave the family control of the corporation. In 1981, the Service issued Revenue Ruling 81-253, 1981-2 CB 187, which stated that no minority interest discount would be allowed for intrafamily transfers of shares of stock in a corporation controlled by the family in the absence of discord among the family members (the concept is commonly referred to as the "family attribution" principle.) However, after experiencing a long line of cases in which the family attribution principle was rejected,[14] the Service announced its abandonment of the family attribution principle in Revenue Ruling 93-12, 1993-1 CB 202.

In determining the size of the minority interest discount to be applied, each case must take into consideration all relevant facts and circumstances.[15] The amount of discount applied in other cases is not normally a determinant as to the proper discount to be applied in a given case.[16] The reference to prior cases and articles discussing discounts is appropriate for demonstrating the existence of a discount, but will not be given any weight for proving the magnitude of discount in a specific case.

A crucial factor in establishing the minority interest discount is the bundle of rights that are possessed by the owner of the corporate or partnership interest. Such rights will be set forth by both a combination of applicable state law, corporate articles and bylaws, partnership agreement, or other rights and restrictions agreed to by the parties. An appraiser who conducts an examination of ownership rights must disregard any provision that constitutes an "applicable restriction" under IRC Section 2704(b) and the attorney may have a duty to inform the appraiser of those rights which fall within this definition.

Thus, restrictive provisions that are drafted into an agreement should be carefully considered before being implemented.

While the courts, Service and taxpayers all agree that a minority interest is worth less than a controlling interest on a pro-rata basis, the issue now is not whether a minority interest discount is allowable, but rather the amount of the minority interest discount.

The primary source of data utilized by business appraisers to determine discounts for minority interests in operating entities comes from acquisitions of controlling interests in the public marketplace. This data is utilized because the applicable minority interest discount can be calculated as the inverse of the control premium paid by an investor who acquires various rights that are otherwise unavailable to the minority interest. A number of comprehensive sources that accumulate such information are readily available to the public. Two well-known sources of control premium data are *Mergerstat Review* and *Mergerstat Control Premium Study*.

In determining minority interest discounts for privately-held real estate concerns, a different source of empirical data is often utilized. With the decision in *Estate of Berg v. Commissioner*,[17] the Tax Court has specified that a permissible approach for determining minority interest discounts for interests in real estate companies is the "REIT Approach." This approach involves an analysis of publicly traded real estate entities (including real estate investment trusts or "REITS") that report the aggregate appraised values of their real estate holdings.

Advanced estate planners and appraisers are quick to point out that the use of REIT data may be inapplicable for valuing smaller less diverse corporations and partnerships. They argue that the relatively larger size of the typical publicly traded REIT makes such an entity incomparable for discount purposes. This observation is supported by the recent trend of many REITs in 1994 to trade at premiums rather than discounts.

A better means of gauging the discount for family limited partnerships and corporations that are of relatively small capitalization (under $25,000,000) may be achieved by making comparison to smaller privately owned limited partnerships traded on the "secondary" market. These entities typically have partnership agreements which contain similar restrictions to those found in family limited partnerships and usually maintain a less diverse asset base that the typical REIT. Discounts for such entities generally are higher than found in REITs. Data on the trading of such interests is now available through a number of sources.[18]

Lack Of Marketability Discounts

The lack of marketability principle is well documented and is based on the fact that stock in a closely held business enterprise is less attractive and more difficult to sell than publicly traded stock.[19] Lack of marketability discounts relate to the inherent lack of flexibility in getting in and out of investments with no ready market. Where an active trading market does not exist, then other factors may be used as valuation benchmarks, and the lack of marketability discount becomes operative and applicable.

The Service issued Revenue Ruling 77-287, 1977-2 CB 319, in order to provide information and guidance to taxpayers, Service personnel, and others concerned with the valuation, for federal tax purposes, of securities that cannot be immediately resold because they are restricted from resale pursuant to federal securities laws. In valuing restricted securities, Revenue Ruling 77-287 states that the following documents and facts should be reviewed:

1. A copy of any declaration of trust, trust agreement, and any other agreements relating to the shares of restricted stock;

2. A copy of any document showing any offers to buy or sell or indications of interest in buying or selling the restricted shares;

3. The latest prospectus of the company;

4. Annual reports of the company for 3 to 5 years preceding the valuation date;

5. The trading prices and trading volumes of the related class of traded securities one month preceding the valuation date;

6. The relationship of the parties to the agreements concerning the restricted stock, such as whether they are members of the immediate family or perhaps whether they are officers or directors of the company; and

7. Whether the interest being valued represents a majority or minority ownership.

Of recent importance is the Tax Court's opinion on marketability discounts in *Mandelbaum v. Comm.*, TC Memo 1995-255. This case appears to be an extension of the Tax Court's heightened level of scrutiny in *Estate of Berg*, TC Memo 1991-279. The sole issue of the case involved the size of the discount for lack of marketability on gifts of privately owned stock in a corporation that was involved mainly in the women's apparel industry. The Tax Court expressed its displeasure with the appraisal reports and testimony of the experts for both the taxpayer and the Service, and stated that the magnitude of the lack of marketability discount should be based, among other things, upon the following factors:

1. Comparison of sales prices for private versus public stock.

2. Financial statement analysis.

3. Company's dividend paying policy.

4. Nature of company, position in the industry, economic outlook.

5. Quality of the company's management.

6. Amount of control in transferred interest.

7. Restrictions (if any) on transfer of interest.

8. Holding period for the interest.

9. Redemption policy of company, as shown historically.

10. Costs associated with public offering.

This case again makes clear the need for property specific analysis in valuing corporations and other entities. The Tax Court's message is clear that a subject entity's value must be determined based upon a comprehensive review of its circumstances relative to the circumstances of other entities that are being offered for comparison.

The amount of published research data on lack of marketability discounts continues to increase. However, the appraisal profession has been unable to agree upon the method for quantifying lack of marketability discounts. On the one hand, there have been the following studies pertaining to restricted stocks:

Study	Mean Discount
SEC Institutional Investor Study (1966-1969)	24%
Gelman Study (1968-1970)	33%
Trout Study (1968-1972)	33%
Maroney Study	36%
Maher Study (1969-1973)	35%
Standard Research Consultants Study (1978-1982)	45%
Willamette Management Associates Studies (1975-1985)	42%-47%
Silber Study (1981-1988)	34%
FMV Opinions, Inc. Study (1979-1992)	23%
Management Planning Study (1980-1992)	27%
Johnson Study (1991-1995)	20%
Columbia Financial Advisors Study (1996-1997)	21%
Columbia Financial Advisors Study (1997-1998)	13%

Lock-In Discount

For partnerships, consideration should always be given as to whether the interest can be liquidated through the enforcement of withdrawal rights. In some states, if the partnership agreement does not provide a time for when capital will be returned, a limited partner is given the right to withdraw from the partnership no sooner than six months after giving notice to the general partner. In other states, applicable state law prohibits the return of capital to a limited partner except upon the occurrence of certain events specified in the partnership agreement (e.g., upon expiration of the partnership term). California recently amended its limited partnership act to remove withdrawal rights unless specified in the partnership agreement.

If the partnership agreement or state law does not confer upon the limited partner any right to withdraw capital, then the interest may remain in the partnership until expiration of the partnership term (often 35-50 years in length). In such case, the limited partner is "locked-in" to maintaining his investment in the partnership and a lock-in discount is appropriate.

In determining whether a lock-in discount is applicable, IRC Section 2704(b) must be reviewed. Under this section, a lock-in discount may not exist for federal tax purposes if it constitutes an "applicable restriction" under state law (see discussion below). In such case, the limited partner may be locked in to the partnership under the partnership agreement but prevented by Section 2704(b) from considering the effect of the withdrawal restriction if such restriction is more stringent that applicable state law.

Other Discounts

In valuing interests in corporations that hold investment assets (e.g., real property, marketable securities, coins, etc.) consideration should be given as to whether there are potential capital gains that will be taxed at the corporate level.[20] It should be noted, however, that a discount for built-in-gains tax is not automatic.[21]

Chapter 14

Effective October 8, 1990, Chapter 14 of the Internal Revenue Code must be considered in valuing interests in corporations and partnerships. Chapter 14 presents valuation rules for determining the value of interests in corporations and partnerships that are controlled by family members (generally where more than 50% of value is held by the family). The application of these statutes can result in a gift even though no wealth is actually transferred to other family members (e.g., IRC Section 2701's use of the subtraction method for valuing applicable retained interests) and cause certain restrictive provisions in an agreement to be disregarded for transfer tax purposes (e.g., IRC Section 2704(b)'s disregard of "applicable restrictions").

Section 2701 applies to valuation of corporate and partnership interests designed for estate freeze purposes. In instances where there are capital interests that have a preference as to income distributions, the valuation of transfers (including recapitalizations) among family members may result in gift tax. In instances in which there are no preferences as to capital ownership, Section 2701 generally does not apply.

IRC Section 2702 applies to interests in trusts (e.g., GRITs, GRATs and GRUTs, split interest purchases) and does not require consideration in valuing a closely held business.

IRC Section 2703 applies to "any option, agreement, or other right to acquire or use the property at a price less than the fair market value of the property (without regard to such option, agreement or right) or any restriction on the right to sell or use such property." Thus, a right or restriction contained in a partnership agreement, articles of incorporation, corporate bylaws, shareholders' agreement, or any other agreement will fall subject to Section 2703. Similarly, a right or restriction may be implicit in the capital structure of an entity.[22] Such rights and restrictions will have no effect for valuation purposes unless the following three conditions exist: (1) there is a bona fide business purpose, (2) the agreement is not a testamentary device to transfer property to members of the decedent's family for less than full and adequate consideration in money or money's worth, and (3) the terms are comparable to similar arrangements entered into by persons in arm's length transactions.

Recent attempt by the IRS to extend Section 2703 to disallow discounts for investment partnerships when a decedent died shortly after its formation evidence an adverse position by the IRS on the use of investment partnerships for discount purposes (see TAMs 9736004, 9730004, 9725002, 9719006). Notwithstanding such attacks, many practitioners believe the IRS position on this issue is unfounded and will continue to be defeated in the courts upon presentment. See, e.g., *Church v. U.S.*, 2000-1 USTC ¶60,369 (W.D. Tex. 2000).

IRC Section 2704 applies to lapsed voting and liquidation rights in a corporation or partnership if the individual holding such right immediately before the lapse and members of such individual's family hold, both before and after the lapse, control of the entity. If lapsed voting or liquidation rights exist, then the amount of the transfer is determined by the value of the interest before the lapse minus the value after the lapse.

A voting right means a right to vote with respect to any matter of the entity. In the case of a partnership, the right of the general partner to participate in partnership management is a voting right.[23] A liquidation right is defined as a right or ability to compel the entity to acquire all or a portion of the holder's equity interest in the entity, including by reason of aggregate voting power, whether or not its exercise would result in the complete liquidation of the entity.[24] A lapse of a voting right occurs at the time a presently exercisable voting right is restricted or eliminated, while a lapse of a liquidation right occurs at the time a presently exercisable liquidation right is restricted or eliminated. However, a transfer of an interest that results in a lapse of a liquidation right is not subject to Section 2704 if the rights with respect to the transferred interest are not restricted or eliminated.

Additionally, Section 2704 allows for the value of property to be determined without consideration of any "applicable restrictions." An applicable restriction is defined as any restriction

1. that effectively limits the ability of the corporation or partnership to liquidate.

2. with respect to which either of the following applies

   a. The restriction lapses, in whole or in part, after the transfer [of an interest in the corporation or partnership to (or for the benefit of) a member of the transferor's family], or

   b. The transferor or any member of the transferor's family, either alone or collectively, has the right after such transfer to remove, in whole or in part, the restriction.

Excepted from the definition of applicable restrictions are any commercially reasonable restriction which arises as part of any financing by the corporation or partnership with a person who is not related to the transferor or transferee, or a member of the family of either, or any restriction imposed, or required to be imposed, by any federal or state law. An example of an applicable restriction is where a partnership agreement requires unanimous vote to liquidate where state law imposes a less stringent requirement (e.g., unanimous consent of the general partners and a majority of limited partners).

As discussed above, a lock-in discount may be negated by Section 2704(b) if the lock-in discount is created by an applicable restriction.

Fractional Interest Discounts

The courts have long recognized that the value of a fractional interest in real property may be less than the pro-rata value of the same real property if held as a full fee simple.[25] Among the factors cited by the courts in justifying the application of a discount to the pro-rata value of a fractional interest in real property are the following:

1. The owner of a fractional interest will have greater difficulty in finding a ready market for the sale of the interest due to the fact that a buyer of the interest will have to share ownership with another;

2. The owner of a fractional interest cannot sell the fee interest in the property or lease the property without the consent of the holder of the remaining interest(s);

3. The owner of a fractional interest by himself generally cannot obtain a loan from normal

sources of credit secured by only a partial interest in the real property;

4. The owner of a fractional interest may not have the right to exclusive use of the property so as to put it to its highest and best use;

5. An action by an owner of a fractional interest to partition real property does not guaranty that the partitioning co-owner will receive property whose utility is equal to that of the entire parcel from which the partition took place;

6. The cost of bringing an action to partition real property is often substantial and a fee interest in a portion of the property received may be worth less than the proportionate share of the whole property or the sales proceeds (if the property may not be fairly partitioned) may not equal the property's fair market value; and

7. The existence of an undivided fractional interest is a legal matter affecting title to real property and often cannot be solved without obtaining legal counsel and commencing legal proceedings at significant cost.

For these reasons, many courts have allowed a discount to the proportionate value of real property in order to arrive at the value a willing purchaser would be willing to pay for an undivided fractional interest in real property.[26] If the taxpayer asserts that a discount from the proportionate value of the entire property is warranted, the taxpayer must prove that a willing buyer would purchase the property and a willing seller would sell the property at a price that is less than its proportionate value. Generally, the taxpayer may satisfy this burden by using expert opinion testimony of competent and experienced real estate brokers or appraisers, backed by records of actual sales of fractional interests in the same or similar property.[27]

The IRS valuation manual acknowledges the allowance by courts of decreases in value for partial ownership. The Guide states that the extent of ownership rights in each case is to be determined under state law. Although the IRS Valuation Manual states that the fractional interest discount is generally based on the cost of dividing the land (e.g., survey costs, court costs, legal fees, etc.) the following other factors must be considered:

1. Size of the fractional interest.

2. Number of owners.

3. Size of tract and likelihood of partition.

4. Use of land.

5. Access to financing.

Whereas co-owners are free to contract with one another and impose restrictions upon their ownership rights, one means of negating the IRS' "cost of partition" argument is through the use of a Coÿ-DOwnership Agreement in which each co-owner agrees to waive his right to partition the subject property. Such waivers serve a legitimate business purpose of keeping the property in the immediate family for future generations. It should be kept in mind that a Co-Ownership Agreement is likely to invoke the requirements of IRC Section 2703 and will not have any effect for federal tax purposes unless the three requirements for the safe harbor are met.

In *Est. of Barge v. Comm.*, TC Memo 1997-188, the Tax Court applied a discounted net cash flow approach to value an undivided 25% interest in timberland gifted by the donor. The court's analysis reviewed the following factors: (1) time in years to partition; (2) required rate of return; (3) estimated value upon partition date; (4) estimated annual income; and (5) estimated partition costs. The result produced a 26% discount to the otherwise proportionate value of the interest.

Using Fractional Interests With Family Partnerships

Another advanced planning technique is to reduce asset values by applying multiple discounts. This concept is referred to as "double discounting" and permits the use of fractional interests with a family limited partnership to gain the benefits of all four discounts (i.e., fractional interest discount, minority interest discount, lack of marketability discount, and lock-in discount).

Under this planning, the family limited partnership will own less than 100% of the real property. Usually, the remaining interest in the property will be owned outside the partnership by children or grandchildren. Ownership of such undivided interests in the form of a generation-skipping trust is often desirable since the income from the fractional interest can be distributed to the child or grandchild and used to pay expenses of education or other expenses (e.g., music lessons, art, dance, travel to Europe) that are not legal obligations of the parents. The use of a Co-Ownership Agreement to waive the right to partition or cause a forced sale should be included in this planning in order to prevent the child or grandchild from attempting to liquidate its fractional interest.

Although this technique theoretically reduces the value of partnership interests, it can be enhanced by providing empirical data that quantifies the magnitude of last value. To date, the authors are aware of no specific studies that quantify the amount of discount by this planning.

Avoiding Pitfalls

In planning for discounted asset values, watch out for the problem created by *Estate of Smith*, 94 TC 872 (1990), holding that for purposes of computing adjusted taxable gifts on the federal estate return, the value of all lifetime gifts may be reconsidered, even if a gift tax return was filed and the statute of limitations has run. While additional gift tax cannot be collected, this could force the taxable estate into a higher bracket and alter marital deduction gifts.

Gifts made after August 5, 1997 are no longer revalued for estate tax purposes if the gift tax statute of limitations has run and an appropriate gift tax return has been filed. However, this may very well increase the likelihood of having a gift tax audit because the IRS may no longer revalue such gifts on the estate tax return.

Also, do no overlook *Estate of Murphy*, TC Memo 1990-472, where 18 days before death decedent transferred less than 1% to each of two children to bring her percentage below 50%, and her estate claimed a minority discount. The Tax Court allowed a discount for lack of marketability, but rejected the minority discount, noting that decedent gave up control on paper, but not in reality.

Note that the cases indicate that courts are closely examining the approach used by experts in valuing business interests, and the qualifications of the appraisers. In *Estate of Campbell*, TC Memo 1991-615, the court emphasized the importance of evaluating both earnings and net asset values in arriving at the actual value, and allowed a substantial discount. In *Estate of Berg*, TC Memo 1991-279, a 60% discount in the value of closely held stock was claimed to represent both minority and lack of marketability discounts. The

appraisal was by petitioner's CPA, Mr. Whalen, an experienced practitioner who had served on the faculty of several universities and had testified as an expert witness in several cases on lack of marketability and minority discounts, but as the court noted, with no formal education as an appraiser. The court said: "we find the appraisal by Whalen, who is not a certified appraiser, unpersuasive for two reasons. First, he relies on *Estate of Andrews v. Commissioner*, supra, which does not support petitioner's position. The only other support for Whalen's appraisal is two articles by H. Calvin Coolidge." Although the underpayment penalty that was assessed was later reversed by the Eighth Circuit, this case is a good example of why a formal appraisal should always be commissioned.

Control And The Swing Vote Issue

It is well established that if the business interest being valued is a controlling interest, then a premium must be added to the valuation to reflect control. Recently, the IRS has applied this concept to situations where the transfers to individual family members were of minority interests, but they could collectively exercise control over the business entity. A donor owned 100% of the stock in a family corporation. He transferred 30% to each of 3 children, and 5% to his spouse. The gifts were valued at net asset value less a 25% discount for minority interest and lack of marketability.

In Letter Ruling 9436005, the IRS held that even though each gift is valued separately under Revenue Ruling 93-12, 1993-1 CB 202, since the blocks were transferred simultaneously, each had a "swing vote" characteristic, meaning that the owner of any 30% block could join with the owner of any other 30% block to exercise control, and that characteristic affected the value of the gift, citing *Estate of Winkler*, TC Memo 1989-231. The IRS pointed out that had the gifts been sequential, the first 30% would not have the swing vote characteristic, but the second would. Further, the transfer of the second 30% would increase the value of the first 30%, and would be an indirect gift. The same would occur on the transfer of the third 30% block.

Costs Of Liquidation As A Valuation Factor

Where valuation of interests in corporations is based on the value of the underlying assets of the corporation, should that value be discounted for a hypothetical income tax that would be incurred if the corporation were liquidated to reach the assets? The IRS steadfastly denies such a discount is available.

The Partition Theory

The IRS has also ruled that when valuing undivided interests in property, rather than permitting discounts, the property should be valued under the "partition" theory. Under that theory, the value of the property in question is reduced by the hypothetical costs of a legal action to partition it. For example, in the case of an undivided one half interest in a farm, the valuation would start with 100% of the value of the farm, then subtract the legal costs of partitioning it into two farms of equal value, and dividing the result by two.

In what appears to be a blow to the IRS theory of valuation of undivided interests in property based on the cost of partition rather than fractional discounts, the Tax Court has held a fractional interest discount in excess of partition costs is appropriate for a decedent's interest in a farm. In *Estate of Cervin*, TC Memo 1994-550, the court held the farm could not be easily partitioned and a homestead could not be easily sold. In finding higher discounts, the court did not really reject the partition theory, other than with respect to homestead property. It concluded that a partition would involve substantial costs and fees, and the ability of the co-owners to agree on relative values. In other words, it used a discount rather than hypothetical costs of partition. It also rejected reliance by the estate's experts on case decisions and articles, indicating that it is up to the court, not the appraiser, to evaluate the significance of such authorities! A similar discount approach was applied in *Estate of Barge v. Comm.*, TC Memo 1997-188, in finding a discount based on a number of factors, not just the cost of partition.

The erosion of the Service's cost-to-partition theory is observed by TAM 9718004, where the Service recognized fractional interest discounts are not always limited to partition costs. Also, the IRS Valuation Training for Appeals Officers course book states that an appropriate discount for a fractional interest is based on several factors, including: (1) the size of the fractional interest (lower interest indicates a larger discount, (2i) the number of owners (higher number of owners indicates a larger discount), (3) the size of the tract and ability to partition (smaller tract indicates a larger discount), (4) the use of the land (less productive indicates a larger discount), (5) the number of owners (more owners indicates a larger discount), and (6) the availability of financing (no financing indicates a larger discount.)

Obtaining Valuation Discounts

First, be reasonable about discounts. Back justifications up–in writing–with an independent qualified third party appraisal that would hold up in court. File that analysis with the gift tax return to start the statute of limitations clock. More importantly, make sure the appraisal satisfies the adequate disclosure provisions of IRC Sec. 6501(c).

Second, give the entity a business or investment purpose self-evident from its ongoing activities. An entity must be able to show that the reason for its existence is more than a mere attempt to obtain a gift tax valuation discount. Build in and document a business or investment reason for the partnership to exist–other than to save estate tax. Meet state law requirements for the type of entity claimed. The stronger business and investment reasons there are, the more likely the gift and estate tax discounts will be sustained.

Third, the owner must–in reality–treat the entity as separate from himself. In other words, as far as the IRS is concerned, an entity that is the alter ego of the founder isn't an entity. Where the parties intend that nothing of substance will change–except the level of federal transfer tax–expect an IRS challenge. If the IRS can disregard the entity, most if not all of the underlying reason for the discount vanishes.

Fourth, time really is money. Deathbed family limited partnerships (FLPs) are an invitation to litigation. So create a FLP before it's needed to save estate taxes.

Conclusion

The valuation of all business and property interests is an art, not a science. Many variables must be considered and evaluated. The quality of evaluation will be, in part, a function of the appraiser's skill in applying experienced judgment and subjectivity to the objective facts that are gathered. Increasingly, the value of assets must be made within the proper legal framework, and must be supported by a review of all factors, not just those that favor or disfavor a taxpayer.

References

Valuing Small Business and Professional Practices, Pratt et al, McGraw-Hill, is an excellent text in the business valuation area. Other helpful references are:

Valuing a Business: The Analysis and Appraisal of Closely-Held Companies, Pratt et al, McGraw-Hill.

Advanced Sales Reference Service, The National Underwriter Company.

"Present Value Analysis in Estate Planning after ERTA," *CLU Journal*, May 1985, 52.

The Professional Handbook of Business Valuation, Addison-Wesley Publishing Co.

Qualitative Business Valuation: A Mathematical Approach for Today's Professionals, Abrams, McGraw-Hill.

CHAPTER ENDNOTES

1. See TAM 9436005 where IRA held a control premium should apply to a minority interest claiming it was a "swing vote" that might act in concert with other related shareholders.

2. See Treas. Reg. §25.2512-1 for use of fair market value for gift tax purposes.

3. Treas. Regs. §§20.2031-1(b); 25.2512-1.

4. IRC Secs. 2031(a), 2032(a)(2).

5. IRC Sec. 2032(a)(1).

6. IRC Sec. 2032(a)(3).

7. IRC Sec. 2042(1).

8. IRC Sec. 2042(2).

9. IRC Sec. 7520.

10. See *Est. of Smith*, 57 TC 650 (1972), acq. 1974-2 CB 4.

11. Treas. Reg. §20.2031-2(e).

12. IRC Secs. 2031, 2512. Treas. Regs. §§20.2031-1(b), 20.2031-2(b), 20.2031-2(f), 25.2512-2.

13. See, e.g., *Gallun v. Comm.*, 33 TCM 1316 (1974); *Kirkpatrick v. Comm.*, 34 TCM 1490 (1975); *Est. of Thalheimer v. Comm.*, 33 TCM 877 (1974); *Northern Trust Co.*, 87 TC 349 (1986).

14. See, e.g., *Est. of Bright v. U.S.*, 81-2 USTC ¶13,436 (5th Cir. 1981) (community property interest in stock of one spouse not attributed to other spouse to produce a control premium); *Propstra v. U.S.*, 82-2 USTC ¶13,475 (9th Cir. 1982) (fractional interest discount allowed for decedent's community property interest in real property); *Est. of Lee*, 69 TC 860 (1978), nonacq. 1980-1 CB 2 (fractional interest discount allowed for community stock ownership); and *Est. of Andrews*, 79 TC 938 (1982) (discounts permitted for stock in corporation owned by siblings).

15. *Northern Trust Co. v. Comm.*, 87 TC 349, 384 (1986); See also Treas. Reg. §20.2031-2(f).

16. *LeFrak v. Comm.*, 66 TCM 1297 (1993).

17. 61 TCM 2949 (1991).

18. The Partnership Spectrum published by Partnership Profiles, Inc. of Dallas, Texas publishes limited partnership trading data for many partnerships on a bi-monthly basis.

19. *Central Trust Co. v. U.S.*, 62-2 USTC ¶12,092; *Messing v. Comm.*, 48 TC 502 (1967), acq. 1968-1 CB 2.

20. See *Est. of Jameson v. Comm.*, TC Memo 1999-43; *Est. of Simplot*, 2001-1 USTC ¶60,405 (9th Cir. 2001); *Est. of Davis*, 110 TC 530 (1998); *Eisenberg v. Comm.*, 155 F.3d 50 (2nd Cir. 1998).

21. In *Jones v. Comm.*, 116 TC 121 (2001), a built-in-gains discount was disallowed for a family limited partnership because the court assumed that a limited partner could transfer a fair market basis to the buyer through an adjustment under IRC Sec. 754.

22. Treas. Reg. §25.2703-(3).

23. Treas. Reg. §25.2704-1(a)(2)(iv).

24. Treas. Reg. §25.2704-1(a)(2)(v).

25. See *Est. of Youle*, 56 TCM 1594; *Est. of Wildman*, 58 TCM 1006; *Est. of Whitehead*, 33 TCM 253 (1974); *Mooneyham v. Comm.*, 61 TCM 2445 (1991).

26. See *Est. of Anderson v. Comm.*, 56 TCM 78 (1988) (discount of 20% allowed to value of undivided one-half community property interest); *Mooneyham v. Comm.*, 61 TCM 2445 (1991) (discount of 15% allowed to undivided one-half interest in real property owned as tenants-in-common by brother and sister); *Est. of Wildman v. Comm.*, 58 TCM 1006 (1989) (discount of 15% allowed to value of undivided one-fifth interest in real property owned as tenants-in-common); *Est. of Feuchter v. Comm.*, 63 TCM 2104 (1992) (partnership owning undivided one-half interest in three tracts of land allowed 15% discount); *Est. of Baggett v. Comm.*, 62 TCM 333 (1991) (decedent's undivided 25% interest in real property discounted 35% to reflect fractional interest); *Est. of Pillsbury v. Comm.*, 64 TCM 284 (1992) (15% discount applied to undivided 77% and 23% fractional interests held in trust).

27. *Stewart*, 31 BTA 201 (1934).

Chapter 58

FREEZING TECHNIQUES – CORPORATIONS AND PARTNERSHIPS

WHAT IS IT?

In the most fundamental sense, an estate freeze is any planning device where the owner of property attempts to freeze the present value of his estate and shift the future growth to successors, generally the next generation. It may also involve the retention of some form of income stream or cash flow from the property.

This definition of an estate freeze is so broad it includes a variety of techniques, including installment sales of property (see Chapter 35), a variety of gift planning techniques (see Chapter 22), and buy-sell agreements (see Chapter 40). As generally used, the term has been more limited to cover structuring of family businesses and investments in such a way that the original owners retain much of the present value and control, and some source of revenue, while the growth is shifted. The usual vehicle is the family limited partnership (see Chapter 43), or limited liability company (see Chapter 44), or corporation (see Chapters 46 and 47).

In the case of the family corporation, the senior generation typically retains control through the use of voting preferred stock that has a fixed liquidation value, usually par value. Either by forming a new corporation or recapitalizing an existing one, one or more classes of common stock are created, which may be nonvoting or at least have limited voting rights. All or part of this common stock is sold or given to the next generation.

The counterpart in the case of the partnership is the formation or restructuring of an existing partnership in such a way that the senior family members retain partnership interests that control the management of the business or investments, from which they receive preferred profit distributions, but which have a fixed liquidation value. Thus, the retained partnership interests resemble preferred stock in a corporation. The remaining partnership interests may then, like the common stock in the case of a corporation, be sold or given to the next generation.

WHEN IS THE USE OF SUCH A DEVICE INDICATED?

Where a family business is involved, the freeze has been an important planning tool to assure retention of the enterprise in the family at minimum tax cost. The same may apply to family investments, particularly real estate. It will only be used where there is a desire to perpetuate the business or investment in the family.

WHAT ARE THE REQUIREMENTS?

As discussed above, a business entity, either a corporation or a partnership, must be created or altered to structure this form of a freeze. The retained stock or partnership interests of the senior generation must have a limited liquidation value, since that is what makes it impossible for the value of those interests to grow. The retention of preferred dividends or profit distributions is not essential, but adds to the value of the retained interest, which in turn reduces the value of the interests transferred to the next generation. Since the transfer of interests may and probably will have gift tax implications, the value of the retained interests is very important.

HOW IT IS DONE – AN EXAMPLE

Client owns 100 percent of the common stock in Acme Corporation, a manufacturing concern. It has been valued at $1,000,000. He wants to bring his two children into the business, give them an incentive to work there by giving them an equity stake in the enterprise, and minimize his own gift and estate taxes.

Client recapitalizes the corporation with $1,000,000 par value preferred stock with an 8 percent cumulative preferred dividend and common stock. The preferred stock is voting, and in the event of corporate liquidation, the preferred shareholders can receive only par value for it. The common stock is then transferred by gift or sale to the children.

WHAT ARE THE TAX IMPLICATIONS?

1. IRC Section 2701, titled "Special valuation rules in case of transfers of certain interests in corporations or partnerships" (applicable to transactions entered into after October 8, 1990), focuses on the valuation of retained senior interests in such entities in determining the extent of taxable gifts of other junior interests in the same entity. It also deals with the transfer tax treatment of the retained interests, and how those retained interests will be valued for subsequent transfers during life or at death.

2. Also to be considered in this area is IRC Section 2704, providing in general that most lapsing restrictions on transferred interests in businesses created after October 8, 1990 will be ignored in valuing the interest for transfer tax purposes, or the lapse itself will trigger a transfer tax. This involves situations in which restrictions are imposed on the value of retained stock or partnership interests, which depress the value of those interests. After the owner dies, these restrictions either lapse or can be readily removed by family members.

Section 2701

How Retained Interests Are Valued for Gift Tax Purposes

For the purposes of determining whether or not the transfer of interests in partnerships or corporations to family members are gifts, and the value of the gifts, any retained interest in the partnership or corporation must be valued under IRC Section 2701, unless it falls within an exception.

The assumption under the statute is that the value of the residual interests transferred to "family members," in this case corporate stock or partnership interests, will be valued by subtracting from the total value of the entire corporation or partnership the value of any retained interests that have preferred rights, adjusted to reflect the proportionate interest of the transferor in the business entity.

For purposes of Section 2701, "family members" are the transferor's spouse, lineal descendant of the transferor or spouse, and the spouse of any descendant.[1]

Covered transfers include contributions to capital, redemptions, and other changes in capital structure, as well as any transfer that increases the property owned by or the value of the applicable retained interest (defined below) of the transferor or applicable family member, including transfers to a start up entity.[2] A sale is covered by these valuation rules if there is an applicable retained interest (e.g., the sale of common stock in the entity for its full fair market value where the transferor retains preferred stock).[3]

Example: Transferor owns 100% of the common stock of a corporation worth $1,000,000. He recapitalizes, taking voting preferred stock with a par value of $1,000,000 and paying a cumulative preferred dividend of 8%, and made a gift of the nonvoting common stock to his children. The gift is valued at $1,000,000 less the value of the preferred stock.

According to Section 2701(b), what is valued under the statute is an "applicable retained interest," which is:

1. A "distribution right," if immediately after the transfer the transferor and "applicable family members" "control" the entity; or

2. Liquidation, put, call, or conversion rights.

A distribution right is defined as a right to distributions from a corporation with respect to its stock or a partnership with respect to a partnership interest, except:

1. Rights in connection with "junior equity interests," defined as common stock or partnership interests under which rights to income and capital are junior to all other equity interests.[4]

2. "Liquidation, put, call, or conversion rights," defined as any such right, or similar right, that affects the value of the transferred interest.[5] However, the term does not include any right that must be exercised at a specific time at a specific amount.

3. Rights to guaranteed payments from a partnership defined in IRC Section 707(c), which are certain payments determined without regard to partnership income.[6]

"Control" means at least a 50 percent interest in a corporation by vote or value of the corporate stock, or at least 50 percent of the capital or profits in a partnership, or the holding of any partnership interest as a general partner. Control includes interests held by "applicable family members." It also includes attribution through entities and interests held by brothers or sisters or lineal descendants of an individual.[7]

An "applicable family member" means the transferor's spouse, ancestor of the transferor or transferor's spouse, or the spouse of an ancestor.[8]

According to the regulations, applicable retained interests include extraordinary payment rights and distribution rights in a controlled entity.[9] As noted, guaranteed payments from a partnership covered by IRC Section 707(c), and possibly other rights to distributions under IRC Section 707, are excluded from Section 2701. Also excluded from this definition are any right to distributions of the same class as the transferred interests.

Extraordinary payment rights are retained put, call, conversion rights, and rights to compel liquidation, or similar rights.[10] A right falls within this definition only if it affects the value of the transferred interest.

Certain rights, such as the right to mandatory payments fixed as to time and amount are neither extraordinary payment rights nor distribution rights.[11] Thus, mandatory redemption rights (e.g., a requirement that preferred stock be redeemed at a fixed price at a time certain) are not covered. A right to participate in a liquidation is not covered unless the transferor, family members, and applicable family members can compel liquidation.

Nonlapsing conversion rights in a corporation (i.e., the right to convert an equity interest into a fixed percentage of shares of the transferred interest except for nonlapsing differences in voting rights) are not covered.[12] Similar rights in a partnership are also not covered (e.g., where all rights in partnership interests are the same except for nonlapsing differences in management rights and limitation of liability).

If the transferor retains both a qualified payment right and an extraordinary right, the value of all rights is determined by assuming the extraordinary right is exercised in such a way as to produce the lowest possible valuation.[13] The special valuation rules do not apply to the transfer of any interest for which market quotations are readily available on the date of transfer from an established securities market,[14] and the following retained interests are specifically excluded from these special valuation rules:

1. An interest that can be valued on an established securities market.

2. An interest that is of the same class as the transferred interest.

3. An interest that is proportionately the same as the transferred interest, except for nonlapsing differences in voting rights or in the case of a partnership, nonlapsing differences in management and limitations on liability unless the transferor or applicable family member can alter the liability of the transferee.

The valuation of the applicable retained interest is zero, except to the extent it consists of the right to receive a "qualified payment."[15] Qualified payments are any periodic dividend on cumulative preferred stock, any comparable payment from a partnership interest, or any other payment where an irrevocable election is made to treat other payments, such as noncumulative preferred dividends, as qualified payments. Further, an irrevocable election can be made out of qualified payment status, in which case the distribution right will apparently be valued at zero. The right to a qualified payment is to be valued at fair market value (i.e., what a willing buyer would pay a willing seller for it).

The rules of Section 2701 are complex. Possibly the following summary of how the section works will be helpful:

Section 2701 applies to an interest in a corporation or partnership transferred to a family member where the transferor or "applicable family member" retains a certain interest in the enterprise classified as an "applicable retained interest." If the section applies, the gift resulting from the transfer is determined by subtracting from the value of the entire entity the value of any interests senior to those transferred.

The applicable retained interest consists of the following:

1. An "extraordinary payment right" (i.e., a discretionary liquidation, put, call, conversion, or similar right, valued at zero).

2. A distribution right, also valued at zero unless it is a "qualified payment" right.

3. A qualified payment right, generally a fixed-rate cumulative payment, or a payment which the transferor elects to treat as such a payment, valued as if the rights valued at zero do not exist, but otherwise without regard to Section 2701.

If an extraordinary payment right is held in conjunction with a qualified payment right, the rights are valued on the assumption they will be exercised in such a way as to produce the lowest possible value.

The Minimum Value Rule

Since the value of the gift under the above rules is determined by subtracting the value of the retained qualified payment from the value of the entire entity, it is possible the result could be a small amount where the value of the qualified payment is large. However, regardless of the results of the subtraction method, the minimum value that can be assigned to the transfer of a junior equity interest is 10 percent of the total value of all equity interests in the partnership or corporation, plus the total indebtedness of the entity to the transferor, or applicable family member.[16]

Transfer Taxation of Cumulative Unpaid Distributions

If the corporation or partnership fails to make the required cumulative distributions, or noncumulative distributions the transferor has elected to treat as cumulative distributions, then upon the occurrence of a "taxable event," the taxable gifts or estate of the transferor will be increased by the value of such unpaid distributions. This value will be determined on the assumption all payments are made when due, then compounded as if reinvested at the same discount rate used in valuing the retained interest, less actual distributions paid, based on the date actually paid, but with a 4 year grace period for late payment.

The total amount subject to tax cannot exceed the transferor's proportionate interest in the excess value of all junior interests in the entity at the applicable date of the taxable event over the value of all such transfers at the original date of transfer. In other words, the additional amount subject to federal transfer tax is limited to the actual growth in the enterprise that was shifted.

A taxable event is the death of the transferor if the applicable retained interest is included in his or her estate, or the transfer of such applicable retained interest. Also, the transferor can elect to treat late payment as a taxable event.[17]

Where the transfer is to a spouse and is not taxable because of the marital deduction or because the transfer was for full and adequate consideration, the above rules will not apply, but the spouse will inherit the tax consequences on a subsequent taxable event.[18] Applicable family members other than the transferor are subject to the same taxable event rule with respect to their retained interests, and if the applicable retained interest is transferred to an applicable family member, such applicable family member is subject to the same rules as to distributions accumulating after the transfer.[19]

Qualified payments can be made in the form of debt instruments if they are for not more than 4 years and compound interest at a rate no less than the appropriate discount rate is payable from the due date of the payment.[20]

It is important to note that the value of the unpaid distribution is added to the taxable estate or taxable gifts of the transferor along with the value of the retained corporate stock or partnership interest. According to the regulations, the amount subject to transfer tax will be reduced by any amount subject to transfer tax with respect to the same rights to prevent double taxation.

Value of the Retained Frozen Interests for Purposes of Subsequent Transfers

Section 2701 only deals with the value of the retained interest for purposes of valuation of a transferred interest at the time of the transfer of the transferred interest. Apparently, the retained preferred stock or partnership interests would be valued under normal rules for purposes of any subsequent transfers. This means any retained put, call, conversion or liquidation rights valued at zero under Section 2701 will subsequently be valued when the retained interest is transferred. The result is clearly double taxation, since an interest that was valued at zero when retained is subsequently valued at fair market value when the transferor dies or transfers the retained interest.

To avoid this result, there is an adjustment to the decedent's adjusted taxable gifts by reducing them to reflect the amount by which decedent's taxable gifts were increased due to Section 2701 over the increase in the estate or adjusted taxable gifts attributable to inclusion of the applicable retained interest in the estate. The adjustment may also be available to the transferor's spouse.[21]

Is the Freeze a Viable Planning Alternative?

Although a corporate or partnership freeze through the use of common and preferred stock or partnership interests is now available, many commentators believe it has less utility than in the past. In order to avoid a zero valuation for retained interests, it will be necessary to make distributions with respect to the retained interests. The income tax will be paid now, while the estate tax is deferred, often until the death of a surviving spouse. Note that the use of the freeze eliminates qualification for the S election, since preferred stock is involved. However, if the entity is a partnership, particularly one with a good cash flow, the freeze may make a great deal more sense – the maximum individual federal income tax rate has been decreased to 35%.

If the qualified payments are not made, the resulting inclusion of accumulated distributions in the transferor's taxable gifts or estate could easily exceed the value of the retained interest for federal gift tax purposes.

Example: Assume the applicable discount rate is 10%, and the retained dividend is 8%. Based on the assumption that the present value of the annual dividend is its fair market value, as required by the regulations, the value of the retained interest is 80% of the value of the transferred property. Thus, if the business is valued at $1,000,000, the retained interest is valued at $800,000, the gift at $200,000.

However, if the dividends are not paid for 10 years, and the grace period does not apply, the amount of the cumulative unpaid distributions subject to federal gift or estate tax under Section 2701(d)(1) would be approximately $1,275,000.

Note: The amount included in the taxable transfers of the transferor cannot exceed the actual growth in the business.

If a freeze is contemplated, can the amount of the taxable transfer be reduced by discounts? The Congressional Committee Reports acknowledge that all existing discounts are preserved, which means it is possible to argue that the value of the transferred interest for federal gift tax purposes must be reduced to reflect discounts for minority interests, lack of marketability, etc.

The regulations under Section 2701 recognize the existence of such discounts, and set forth a four step method to value the taxable gift, taking into account such discounts, as follows:

1. Determine the fair market value of all family-held interests in the entity.

2. Subtract all senior equity interests held by the family other than applicable retained interests held by the transferor or applicable family members, with a pro-rata adjustment for any control premium, followed by the subtraction of the value of all applicable retained interests held by the transferor and applicable family members.

3. Allocate the remaining value among the transferred interests and any other family-held junior (or subordinate) interests.

4. Reduce value for consideration received, and for any minority or similar discounts (presumably including a discount for lack of marketability), determined by subtracting the fair market value of the family-held interests (determined as if voting rights were held by one person who had no other interest in the entity other than the family-held interests of the same class) from the value of the transferred interest determined without regard to Section 2701.

Note that if the transfer is to a grantor retained interest trust (i.e., a GRAT or GRUT, see Chapter 26), any reduction in the value of the transfer under IRC Section 2702 will also be subtracted to determine the net taxable gift.

Alternatives to the Freeze

If the transferor retains common stock or partnership interests, and transfers the preferred interests, Section 2701 does not apply. This is sometimes called a "reverse" freeze. When the transferor dies, the value of the common stock will reflect growth, but should be substantially discounted in value because of the burden of the preferred stock with its prior claim to dividends and liquidation proceeds.

Consider the use of a variety of other techniques to freeze growth. This includes installment sales of business interests to family members (see Chapter 35), use of the private annuity (see Chapter 36), and premortem stock redemptions or partnership liquidations of interests of senior family members, giving them a cash flow and transferring the growth in the value of the enterprise to the next generation. Under some circumstances, if the transferor receives a debt instrument issued by a family partnership or corporation, the IRS may seek to treat it as retained preferred stock. See Example 1, Senate Committee Report (OBRA '90), referring to "convertible debt" and treating it as retained preferred stock.

Section 2704

IRC Section 2704 deals with the transfer tax consequences of lapsing rights, and provides that property in general will be valued without regard to lapsing restrictions. As a result, the lapse of a voting or liquidation right in a family controlled corporation will have transfer tax consequences.

Example: If parent and child control a corporation, and parent's stock has a voting right that lapses at parent's death, parent's stock is valued for federal estate tax purposes as if that right were nonlapsing.[22]

Section 2704 applies if the individual holding such right and members of the family control the corporation, as control is defined in Section 2701(b)(2). However, in this case, "family member" includes the spouse of the individual, ancestors and lineal descendants of the individual or spouse, brothers and sisters of the individual, and spouses of any of them.[23]

Under the regulations, the taxable transfer is measured by the reduction in value of all interests in the entity owned by the holder immediately before the lapse unless attributable to other causes. The lapse of the right is deemed to be a transfer subject to transfer tax, at date of lapse, based on the difference between the values of all interests in the entity held by the individual before the lapse and after the lapse.[24] This provision is so broad that any shift of equity or growth could be deemed a lapse, and any contingency that results in lapse of payment, voting, or other rights could have transfer tax consequences.

A voting right is defined as the right to vote on any matter, and in the case of a partnership, includes the rights of management held by general partners.[25] A liquidation right is the right to compel the entity to acquire all or a portion of the holder's interest, including a right arising solely by reason of the fact the holder owns sufficient voting rights to compel liquidation.[26]

A lapse occurs whenever a presently exercisable right is restricted or eliminated. However, a transfer with respect to a liquidation right is not a lapse of a liquidation right unless the transfer eliminates the right of that individual to compel liquidation of an interest other than the interest conferring the power.

Example: D, who owns 84% of the voting common stock of corporation, gives 14% each to three children. Even though this reduces D's voting rights to 42%, and D loses control, this is not a lapse covered by the statute because the voting rights have only been transferred, not eliminated.

Example: Assume D is both the general and a limited partner in a family partnership. As general partner, D can compel liquidation. If D transfers her general partnership interest, she can no longer compel liquidation, but since the successor general partner has the same voting rights, there is no lapse as to D's rights as a general partner. However, there is a lapse as to D's rights as a limited partner, since D has lost the power to compel liquidation of the limited partnership interest, which was an interest other than the interest conferring the power.

A lapse of rights in a retained interest valued under Section 2701 is not subject to Section 2704.[27] Nor is the inability of the family to liquidate after the transfer where the holder could have liquidated before the transfer.[28] If the lapsed right may be restored upon the occurrence of a future event not within the control of the family, there is no lapse so long as the right could be restored.[29]

A voting or liquidation right may arise by state law, corporate charter or bylaws, an agreement, or in any other manner. Similarly, a lapse may occur by reason of state law, corporate charter or by-laws, agreement, or any other means. However, if the lapse is caused only by a change in state law, it is not subject to Section 2704.[30]

In addition, an "applicable restriction," which is any restriction that effectively limits the ability of the corporation or partnership to liquidate, is to be disregarded if the transferor and family members control the entity, and the restriction either lapses after the transfer or can be removed by the transferor or family members, individually or collectively.[31] However, the term does not include a commercially reasonable restriction imposed in connection with financing if furnished as either a debt or equity contribution by an unrelated person (as defined by IRC Section 267(b), excluding banks as defined by IRC Section 581) for trade or business operations.[32]

An "applicable restriction" is a limitation on liquidation of an entity that is more restrictive than state law. It is only a restriction if it will either lapse or can be removed by the transferor, transferor's estate, or members of the family. Any buy-sell agreement, option, or restriction covered by IRC Section 2703 (see Chapter 40), is not subject to Section 2704.[33]

Example: D owns all of the preferred stock of corporation, and can compel liquidation after 10

---

years. All common stock is owned by D's children. If D transfers the preferred stock to the children, it is valued without regard to the restriction on liquidation (i.e., as if the right to compel liquidation was immediately exercisable).

The IRS has applied Section 2704(b) to disregard liquidation restrictions imposed by a family limited partnership agreement when valuating a partnership interest held by a decedent. The partnership was created on the decedent's deathbed and the partnership agreement's liquidation provisions were more restrictive than state law.[34] However, the courts have held that restrictions imposed by state law in a partnership are not applicable restrictions.[35]

IMPLICATIONS AND ISSUES IN COMMUNITY PROPERTY STATES

In a community property state, the business or investment assets may be co-owned by both husband and wife as community property. If so, both must participate in the transaction, and the preferred stock or partnership interests will be held by them as community property. If the common stock or partnership interests are transferred to the children by gift, they may be separate property of the children, depending on state law. However, it is possible that the spouses of the children will obtain a community interest in the transferred property; particularly, if they purchase the stock, its status as community or separate property will depend on what assets they use to pay for it. Thus, the use of trusts to acquire the stock may minimize or eliminate this potential problem.

QUESTIONS AND ANSWERS

Question – Client owns 100% of the common stock of X Corporation, which has been valued at $1,000,000. It has been suggested that he recapitalize the corporation to create voting preferred stock with a par and liquidation value of $1,000,000, and a noncumulative preferred dividend of 8% per annum, and nonvoting nopar common stock. He would then transfer the common stock to his children. What are the gift tax consequences?

Answer – Under Section 2701, unless an election is made, the gift will be $1,000,000. The transaction falls within Section 2701, assuming none of the interests involved have a readily ascertainable market value.

The common stock is being transferred to "family members," children of the transferor. The transferor has an "applicable retained interest," the preferred stock. It consists of a "distribution right," i.e., the right to the preferred dividend, and a "liquidation right." Under Section 2701, the liquidation right is valued at zero. The distribution right is also valued at zero unless it is a "qualified payment." Since a qualified payment is the right to a fixed cumulative preferred dividend, this dividend is not a qualified payment. As a result, under the "subtraction" method required by Section 2701, the gift is the entire value of the enterprise, $1,000,000, less the value of the applicable retained interest, zero.

However, the transferor could elect to treat the noncumulative dividend as if it were cumulative. If so, it is a qualified payment and can be valued and subtracted from the value of the enterprise to determine the taxable gift. The regulations indicate the qualified payment is to be valued under general valuation principals, that is, at fair market value.

Question – In 1991, parent transferred undivided interests in the family farm, which was worth $1,000,000, to her children, and simultaneously, parent and children formed a family partnership into which they transferred their respective interests in the property. Parent, who was the general partner, received a capital interest of $1,000,000, and is entitled to an annual distribution of partnership profits of up to $80,000 before any profits are distributed to children. This right to distributions is cumulative, and if not made in one year, carries over to the next. If the partnership liquidates, the parent will receive the first $1,000,000 in liquidation proceeds, and any additional proceeds will be distributed to the children. The children receive limited partnership interests and are entitled to share in any partnership profits and liquidation proceeds not distributed to the parent.

Ten years later, parent dies. No partnership distributions were ever made to parent. Under the terms of the decedent's will, her partnership interest, and all rights to distributions, passes to her surviving spouse outright. The farm was worth $1,500,000 at date of death. What are the estate tax consequences?

Answer – The initial formation of the partnership was covered by Section 2701, and the gift tax on the transfers of interests in the farm to the children would be computed by subtracting from the value of the farm in 1991 the value of the right to partnership distributions, which would be "qualified payments."

However, since the qualified payments were never made, they constitute "cumulative unpaid distributions" under the statute. When a "taxable event" occurs, in this case the death of the parent, the value of those unpaid distributions is subject to the applicable federal transfer tax, in this case the federal estate tax. However, since the right to the payments passes to the surviving spouse, the tax will be deferred until the surviving spouse either dies or otherwise transfers the interest.

Note several other points. The maximum amount that could have been taxed in the estate would have been the total growth of the enterprise, $500,000. Also, since there is a four year grace period during which qualified payments can be made to avoid the transfer tax at death, the full unpaid amount may not be subject to tax. When the partnership was formed, parent could have elected to value the qualified payment at zero and pay gift tax on the full value of the farm, $1,000,000. If she had done so, there would be no additional tax on the cumulative unpaid amounts.

Also note that the decedent's estate would in any case include the value of her capital interest in the partnership, arguably worth at least $1,000,000, and her right to unpaid distributions, since those are valuable property rights owned by her estate. The regulations indicate there will be no double tax on the unpaid distributions.

Question – A family corporation is owned equally by two shareholders, parent and child. In 1991, the corporation is recapitalized, with parent and child each receiving voting preferred stock with a fixed liquidation value and a cumulative preferred dividend, and the child also receiving nonvoting common stock. The child then makes a gift of the nonvoting common stock to grandchild. Assume the preferred stock issued to the parent was equal to the full value of his interest in the corporation. What are the potential transfer tax consequences, if any, to the parent?

Answer – The parent did not make a taxable transfer when the corporation was recapitalized, since he received full value for his interest in the business and made no gift to the grandchild. However, since parent is an "applicable family member," he or his estate may be vulnerable to a later transfer tax.

In computing the taxable gift to grandchild under the subtraction method, the child may subtract from the value of the corporation the right to all "qualified payments," in this case, the right to cumulative preferred dividends held by both the parent and child. If this is done, the parent is subject to the rules for transfer tax on cumulative unpaid distributions, i.e., if the corporation does not pay the dividends, there will be a gift or estate tax to parent on a lifetime or deathtime transfer of his preferred stock. As a result, even though the parent was not even a party to the taxable gift, he or his estate can incur a substantial transfer tax liability.

Note that the parent can avoid this result if he elects not to have his right to the preferred dividend treated as a qualified payment. If he does so, the child cannot subtract its value for gift tax purposes, and there would be no later transfer tax to the parent under the cumulative unpaid distribution rules.

Question – Client proposes to form a family partnership to operate a business enterprise. He will retain a general partnership interest and a limited partnership interest, and sell limited partnership interests to his children for their full value. All partners will participate proportionately in partnership profits and the proceeds of liquidation. Will either Section 2701 or 2704 apply to him?

Answer – Since the facts indicate all partners will share proportionately in both profits and growth, the gift tax consequences of these transactions are not subject to the provisions of Section 2701.[36] As a result, since client sold interests to his children for their full value, there are no gift tax consequences. Note that limitations affecting liability and management do not bring the transaction under Section 2701, unless there is a provision for lapse of voting rights and management rights, or the transferor or applicable family member can alter the liability of the transferee partners. Such was not the case here.

However, if client dies or transfers his general partnership interest, he loses the power to compel liquidation of the partnership. Under Section 2704, this would be treated as a lapse of his power to compel liquidation of his limited partnership interest, subject to gift tax if he makes a lifetime transfer of his general partnership interest, or estate tax on his death.

ASRS: Sec. 51 ¶200; Sec. 55 ¶58.

CHAPTER ENDNOTES

1. IRC Sec. 2701(e)(1).
2. Treas. Reg. §25.2701-1(b)(2).
3. Treas. Reg. §25.2701-1(b)(1).
4. IRC Sec. 2701(a)(4)(B)(i).
5. IRC Sec. 2701(c)(2).
6. IRC Sec. 2701(c)(1)(B).
7. IRC Secs. 2701(b)(2), 2701(e)(3).
8. IRC Sec. 2701(e)(2).
9. Treas. Reg. §25.2701-2(b)(1).
10. Treas. Reg. §25.2701-2(b)(2).
11. Treas. Reg. §25.2701-2(b)(4).
12. IRC Sec. 2701(c)(2)(C).
13. IRC Reg. §25.2701-2(a)(3).
14. IRC Sec. 2701(a)(1).
15. IRC Sec. 2701(a)(3)(A).
16. IRC Sec. 2701(a)(4).
17. IRC Sec. 2701(d).
18. IRC Sec. 2701(d)(3)(B).
19. IRC Sec. 2701(d)(4).
20. Treas. Reg. §25.2701-4(c)(5).
21. Treas. Reg. §25.2701-5.
22. Treas. Reg. §25.2704-1(f)(Ex. 1).
23. IRC Sec. 2704(c).
24. Treas. Reg. §25.2704-1(d).
25. Treas. Reg. §25.2704-1(a)(2)(iv).
26. Treas. Reg. §25.2704-1(a)(2)(v).
27. Treas. Reg. §25.2704-1(c)(2)(ii).
28. Treas. Reg. §25.2704-1(c)(2)(i).
29. Treas. Reg. §25.2704-1(a)(3).
30. Treas. Regs. §§25.2704-1(c)(2)(i)(B); 25.2704-1(c)(2)(iii).
31. IRC Sec. 2704(b).
32. Treas. Reg. §25.2704-2(b).
33. Treas. Reg. §25.2704-2(b).
34. TAMs 9723009, 9725002, 973003, 9735003.
35. *Knight v. Comm.*, 115 TC 506 (2000); *Est. of Stranghi v. Comm.*, 115 TC 478 (2000).
36. See *Church v. U.S.*, 2001-1 USTC ¶60,369 (W.D. Tex. 2000).

APPENDICES

Appendix A

TAX RATES AND CREDITS

Income Tax Rate Schedules

	Taxable Years Beginning in 2004
STANDARD DEDUCTION:	
Married, filing jointly	$9,700
Married, filing separately	4,850
Head of Household	7,150
Single	4,850
PERSONAL EXEMPTION*:	$3,100

*Subject to phase out at higher levels of taxable income.

SCHEDULE X — SINGLE INDIVIDUALS
Taxable Years Beginning in 2004

Taxable Income			Tax on Lower Amount	Tax Rate on Excess
$ -0-	to	$ 7,150	$ -0-	10.0%
7,150	to	29,050	715	15.0%
29,050	to	70,350	4,000	25.0%
70,350	to	146,750	14,325	28.0%
146,750	to	319,100	35,717	33.0%
319,100	to	......	92,592	35.0%

SCHEDULE Y-1 — JOINT RETURNS AND SURVIVNG SPOUSES
Taxable Years Beginning in 2004

Taxable Income			Tax on Lower Amount	Tax Rate on Excess
$ -0-	to	$14,300	$ -0-	10.0%
14,300	to	58,100	1,430	15.0%
58,100	to	117,250	8,000	25.0%
117,250	to	178,650	22,788	28.0%
178,650	to	319,100	39,980	33.0%
319,100	to	......	86,328	35.0%

SCHEDULE Y-2 — MARRIED FILING SEPARATELY
Taxable Years Beginning in 2004

Taxable Income			Tax on Lower Amount	Tax Rate on Excess
$ -0-	to	$7,150	$ -0-	10.0%
7,150	to	29,050	715	15.0%
29,050	to	58,625	4,000	25.0%
58,625	to	89,325	11,394	28.0%
89,325	to	159,550	19,990	33.0%
159,550	to	......	43,164	35.0%

SCHEDULE Z — HEAD OF HOUSEHOLD
Taxable Years Beginning in 2004

Taxable Income			Tax on Lower Amount	Tax Rate on Excess
$ -0-	to	$10,200	$ -0-	10.0%
10,200	to	38,900	1,020	15.0%
38,900	to	100,500	5,325	25.0%
100,500	to	162,700	20,725	28.0%
162,700	to	319,100	38,141	33.0%
319,100	to	......	89,753	35.0%

TAX RATE SCHEDULE FOR ESTATES AND TRUSTS
Taxable Years Beginning in 2004

Taxable Income			Tax on Lower Amount	Tax Rate on Excess
$ -0-	to	$1,950	$ -0-	15.0%
1,950	to	4,600	292	25.0%
4,600	to	7,000	955	28.0%
7,000	to	9,550	1,627	33.0%
9,550	to	......	2,468	35.0%

TAX RATE SCHEDULE FOR CORPORATIONS‡
Taxable Years Beginning in 2004

Taxable Income			Tax on Lower Amount	Tax Rate on Excess
$ -0-	to	$ 50,000	$ -0-	15%
50,000	to	75,000	7,500	25%
75,000	to	100,000	13,750	34%
100,000	to	335,000	22,250	39% *
335,000	to	10,000,000	113,900	34%
10,000,000	to	15,000,000	3,400,000	35%
15,000,000	to	18,333,333	5,150,000	38%**
18,333,333	to	......	6,416,667	35%

REDUCTION IN INCOME TAX RATES (JGTRRA 2003)

2002	10.0%	15.0%	27.0%	30.0%	35.0%	38.6%
2003-2010	10.0%	15.0%	25.0%	28.0%	33.0%	35.0%
2011	10.0%	15.0%	28.0%	31.0%	36.0%	39.6%

‡ Personal Service Corporations are taxed at a flat rate of 35%.

* A 5% surtax is imposed on income above $100,000 until the benefit of the 15 and 25% tax rates has been canceled. Thus, taxable income from $100,000 to $335,000 is taxed at the rate of 39%.

** Corporations with taxable income over $15,000,000 are subject to an additional tax of the lesser of 3% of the excess over $15,000,000 or $100,000. Thus, taxable income exceeding $18,333,333 is taxed at 35%. See Ann. 93-133, 1993-32 IRB 12.

LUMP SUM DISTRIBUTIONS

10 Yr. Averaging*

Net Lump Sum Taxable Amount	Tax	Effective Tax Rate
$ 10,000	$ 550	.06
20,000	1,100	.06
30,000	2,521	.08
40,000	4,187	.10
50,000	5,874	.12
75,000	10,305	.14
100,000	14,471	.14
150,000	24,570	.16
200,000	36,922	.18
250,000	50,770	.20
300,000	66,330	.22
500,000	143,682	.29
1,000,000	382,210	.38
2,000,000	882,210	.44
3,000,000	1,382,210	.46
4,000,000	1,882,210	.47
5,000,000	2,382,210	.48

* Amount of tax and effective tax rates rounded.

Income averaging for lump sum distributions is discussed in more detail in Chapter 52.

Gift and Estate Tax Rate Schedules

2003 GIFT AND ESTATE TAX TABLE

Taxable Gift/Estate		Tax on	Rate on
From	To	Col. 1	Excess
$0	$10,000	$0	18%
10,000	20,000	1,800	20%
20,000	40,000	3,800	22%
40,000	60,000	8,200	24%
60,000	80,000	13,000	26%
80,000	10,0000	18,200	28%
100,000	150,000	23,800	30%
150,000	250,000	38,800	32%
250,000	500,000	70,800	34%
500,000	750,000	155,800	37%
750,000	1,000,000	248,300	39%
1,000,000	1,250,000	345,800	41%
1,250,000	1,500,000	448,300	43%
1,500,000	2,000,000	555,800	45%
2,000,000	....	780,800	49%

2004 GIFT AND ESTATE TAX TABLE

Taxable Gift/Estate		Tax on	Rate on
From	To	Col. 1	Excess
$0	$10,000	$0	18%
10,000	20,000	1,800	20%
20,000	40,000	3,800	22%
40,000	60,000	8,200	24%
60,000	80,000	13,000	26%
80,000	10,0000	18,200	28%
100,000	150,000	23,800	30%
150,000	250,000	38,800	32%
250,000	500,000	70,800	34%
500,000	750,000	155,800	37%
750,000	1,000,000	248,300	39%
1,000,000	1,250,000	345,800	41%
1,250,000	1,500,000	448,300	43%
1,500,000	2,000,000	555,800	45%
2,000,000	....	780,800	48%

2005 GIFT AND ESTATE TAX TABLE

Taxable Gift/Estate		Tax on	Rate on
From	To	Col. 1	Excess
$0	$10,000	$0	18%
10,000	20,000	1,800	20%
20,000	40,000	3,800	22%
40,000	60,000	8,200	24%
60,000	80,000	13,000	26%
80,000	10,0000	18,200	28%
100,000	150,000	23,800	30%
150,000	250,000	38,800	32%
250,000	500,000	70,800	34%
500,000	750,000	155,800	37%
750,000	1,000,000	248,300	39%
1,000,000	1,250,000	345,800	41%
1,250,000	1,500,000	448,300	43%
1,500,000	2,000,000	555,800	45%
2,000,000	....	780,800	47%

2006 GIFT AND ESTATE TAX TABLE

Taxable Gift/Estate		Tax on	Rate on
From	To	Col. 1	Excess
$0	$10,000	$0	18%
10,000	20,000	1,800	20%
20,000	40,000	3,800	22%
40,000	60,000	8,200	24%
60,000	80,000	13,000	26%
80,000	10,0000	18,200	28%
100,000	150,000	23,800	30%
150,000	250,000	38,800	32%
250,000	500,000	70,800	34%
500,000	750,000	155,800	37%
750,000	1,000,000	248,300	39%
1,000,000	1,250,000	345,800	41%
1,250,000	1,500,000	448,300	43%
1,500,000	2,000,000	555,800	45%
2,000,000	....	780,800	46%

Gift and Estate Tax Rate Schedules (cont'd)

2007 - 2009 GIFT AND ESTATE TAX TABLE

Taxable Gift/Estate		Tax on	Rate on
From	To	Col. 1	Excess
$0	$10,000	$0	18%
10,000	20,000	1,800	20%
20,000	40,000	3,800	22%
40,000	60,000	8,200	24%
60,000	80,000	13,000	26%
80,000	10,0000	18,200	28%
100,000	150,000	23,800	30%
150,000	250,000	38,800	32%
250,000	500,000	70,800	34%
500,000	750,000	155,800	37%
750,000	1,000,000	248,300	39%
1,000,000	1,250,000	345,800	41%
1,250,000	1,500,000	448,300	43%
1,500,000	....	555,800	45%

2010 GIFT TAX ONLY TABLE

Taxable Gift		Tax on	Rate on
From	To	Col. 1	Excess
$0	$10,000	$0	18%
10,000	20,000	1,800	20%
20,000	40,000	3,800	22%
40,000	60,000	8,200	24%
60,000	80,000	13,000	26%
80,000	10,0000	18,200	28%
100,000	150,000	23,800	30%
150,000	250,000	38,800	32%
250,000	500,000	70,800	34%
500,000	....	155,800	35%

2011 GIFT AND ESTATE TAX TABLE

Taxable Gift/Estate		Tax on	Rate on
From	To	Col. 1	Excess
$0	$10,000	$0	18%
10,000	20,000	1,800	20%
20,000	40,000	3,800	22%
40,000	60,000	8,200	24%
60,000	80,000	13,000	26%
80,000	10,0000	18,200	28%
100,000	150,000	23,800	30%
150,000	250,000	38,800	32%
250,000	500,000	70,800	34%
500,000	750,000	155,800	37%
750,000	1,000,000	248,300	39%
1,000,000	1,250,000	345,800	41%
1,250,000	1,500,000	448,300	43%
1,500,000	2,000,000	555,800	45%
2,500,000	3,000,000	1,025,800	53%
3,000,000	10,000,000	1,290,800	55%
10,000,000	17,184,000	5,140,800	60%
17,184,000	....	9,451,200	55%

Unified Credit

GIFT TAX UNIFIED CREDIT		
Year	Exemption Equivalent	Unified Credit
2001	$675,000	$220,550
2002-2009	$1,000,000	$345,800
2010	$1,000,000	$330,800
2011	$1,000,000	$345,800

ESTATE TAX UNIFIED CREDIT		
Year	Exemption Equivalent	Unified Credit
2001	$675,000	$220,550
2002-2003	$1,000,000	$345,800
2004-2005	$1,500,000	$555,800
2006-2008	$2,000,000	$780,800
2009	$3,500,000	$1,455,800
2010	NA	NA
2011	$1,000,000	$345,800

Maximum Credit Table for State Death Taxes

The amount of any state death taxes paid may be subtracted from the federal estate tax as determined under the preceding tables, provided, however, that the maximum to be subtracted may not exceed the maximum determined under the following table:

MAXIMUM STATE DEATH TAX CREDIT*			
Taxable Estate		Credit on	Rate on
From	To	Column 1	Excess
$0	$100,000	$0	0%
$100,000	$150,000	$0	0.8%
$150,000	$200,000	$400	1.6%
$200,000	$300,000	$1,200	2.4%
$300,000	$500,000	$3,600	3.2%
$500,000	$700,000	$10,000	4.0%
$700,000	$900,000	$18,000	4.8%
$900,000	$1,100,000	$27,600	5.6%
$1,100,000	$1,600,000	$38,800	6.4%
$1,600,000	$2,100,000	$70,800	7.2%
$2,100,000	$2,600,000	$106,800	8.0%
$2,600,000	$3,100,000	$146,800	8.8%
$3,100,000	$3,600,000	$190,800	9.6%
$3,600,000	$4,100,000	$238,800	10.4%
$4,100,000	$5,100,000	$290,800	11.2%
$5,100,000	$6,100,000	$402,800	12.0%
$6,100,000	$7,100,000	$522,800	12.8%
$7,100,000	$8,100,000	$650,800	13.6%
$8,100,000	$9,100,000	$786,800	14.4%
$9,100,000	$10,100,000	$930,800	15.2%
$10,100,000	....	$1,082,800	16.0%

* This table resembles the table contained in IRC Section 2011(b), but it is not the same. The table in the Code is based on the *adjusted taxable estate*, defined as the taxable estate reduced by $60,000. This table is a modification of that table and can be used directly from the *taxable estate*.

The maximum state death credit calculated from the table is reduced by 25% for decedents dying in 2002, 50% for decedents dying in 2003, and 75% for decedents dying in 2004. Multiply the amount calculated above by 75% in 2002, 50% in 2003, and 25% in 2004. The state death tax credit is replaced by a deduction for state death taxes for 2005 to 2009. The federal estate tax is repealed for one year in 2010. The federal estate tax returns, along with the full state death tax credit, in 2011.

WORKING WITH THE IRS VALUATION TABLES

■

It is essential that an estate planner understand how to work with the IRS *Actuarial Values* volumes (IRS Pub. 1457 and IRS Pub. 1458)[1] if the planner uses any tool or technique involving annuities, life estates, remainders, and terms of years. These include GRATs, GRUTs, QPRTs, CRATs, CRUTs, CLTs, private annuities, and other tools and techniques. A portion of these actuarial/valuation tables are reproduced at the end of this article.

Specifically, an estate planner must understand the impact of mortality and interest assumptions and how to compute present values if a suggestion to a client or tax computation pertains to:

(1) valuing property for federal estate, gift, and generation-skipping transfer tax purposes (IRC Sections 2031, 2512, and 2624);

(2) valuing charitable contributions for income, gift, and estate tax purposes (IRC Sections 170, 641, 664, 2522, and 2055); and

(3) valuing amounts qualifying for the federal estate and gift tax marital deduction (IRC Sections 2056 and 2523).

Note that the rules explained below do not apply for purposes of (a) the pension and profit sharing rules provided in IRC Sections 401 to 409 and (b) "any other provision" specified by the IRS.[2]

THE VALUATION PROCESS

The Computational Rules. To make these time value of money computations, an interest rate (rounded to the nearest 2/10ths of one percent) based on 120% of the applicable federal midterm rate (computed from the average market yield of U.S. obligations) must be used for the month when the valuation is to be made.

Once the Section 7520 rate is set, it does not change. This rate can be found each month in a revenue ruling released by the IRS. Look for the table in the ruling that shows the rate under IRC Section 7520 for the coming month. The Section 7520 rate can also be found at www.nationalunderwriter.com/taxfactsfx.

Finding the Section 7520 rate is relatively simple; working with the number to compute the deduction for a charitable remainder trust or to make any other valuation is a much more difficult matter. Computer software can make the task easier.

"Date stamping" all illustrations involving time value of money sensitive concepts is recommended since the positive or negative results of a given concept can vary significantly from month to month. The importance of timely implementation of suggestions cannot be over-emphasized.

An important qualification in the application of these rules in charitable situations should be kept in mind: if an income, estate, or gift tax charitable contribution is allowable for any part of the property transferred, the taxpayer may elect to use either the month of transfer Section 7520 rate or the rate for either of the two months preceding the month in which the valuation date falls. In essence this provides an incredible three month choice not available in other circumstances. In fact if the client waits until toward the end of the month when the following month's Section 7520 rate is published, the client can choose among four month's rates.

DOING THE COMPUTATIONS:

For gift, estate, and generation-skipping transfer tax valuation purposes, the fair market value of remainder interests,[3] terms for years,[4] annuities,[5] and life estates[6] is the present value of future payments.

Remainders and Reversions

The following example illustrates how the values of remainders and reversions are computed under the rules:

Assume a client makes a transfer of $100,000 to an irrevocable trust. The income interest lasts for a term of 10 years. What is the gift tax value of the remainder portion of that gift? Assume that the Section 7520 rate is 6.0 percent. The present value of the gift can be determined directly by this process:

(1) Start with IRS Pub. 1457 (portions of the valuation tables are reproduced following this discussion of working with the tables).

(2) Go to Table B (Which shows the present worth of an annuity, an income interest, and a remainder interest for a term certain).

(3) Find the appropriate interest rate (6.0%) subtable of Table B.

(4) Go down the "Years" column to "10," and then across to the right under the "Remainder" column. The six-decimal-place factor is 0.558395.

(5) Multiplying 0.558395 by $100,000 produces a present value of $55,839.50.[7]

Income Interests

Using the same example as above, with the same assumptions, the value of the ten-year term certain income interest would be determined as follows:

(1) Go to the 6.0 percent subtable of Table B.

(2) Go down the "Years" column to "10," and then across to the right under the "Income Interest" column. The factor in this case is 0.441605. (Alternatively, subtract the remainder factor (0.558395) – found either by formula or from Table B – from 1.000000.)

The right to a stream of income from a trust that will last for ten years is worth roughly 44 cents for every dollar placed into the trust if money is presumed to be worth 6.0 percent per year. If $100,000 were placed into a trust lasting ten years, the present value of the income stream would be $44,160.50. Together with the $55,839.50 remainder, the two would be worth 100 percent of the original $100,000.

Annuities

Another example may be used to illustrate how term annuities are valued. Assume a client makes a gift of an annuity interest for a ten-year term. Assume again that the Section 7520 rate is 6.0 percent. The valuation factor is found once again in the 6.0 percent subtable of Table B in the same manner as above under the "Annuity" column.[8] The factor is 7.3601. To compute the present value of the annuity from the factor, multiply the annuity payable annually by the factor.

For instance, if the annuity payable was $10,000 a year (payable at the end of each year), the present value of payments to be made for ten years is $73,601 ($10,000 x 7.3601). This procedure can be used to compute term certain valuation factors for charitable lead and remainder annuity trusts for terms of years.

Because the annuity factors from Table B are based on the assumption annuity payments will be made once a year at the end of the year, these factors must be adjusted when payments are more frequently and/or at the beginning of each payment period.[9]

Life Estates and Annuities for Life

Tables S and R(2) in IRS Pub. 1457 provides practitioners with annuity, life estate, and remainder interest valuation factors for a single life and two lives, respectively, based on a wide range of rates and ages between 0 and 109. (Portions of these valuation tables are reproduced following this discussion of working with the tables.) At 6.0 percent, for example, the value of a single life estate is found by this process:

(1) Find the 6.0 percent page in Table S.

(2) Look in the "Age" column for the appropriate age, for example, 60.

(3) Follow the row to the right until finding the factor in the "Life Estate" column. With these assumptions, the life estate factor would be 0.64967.

The value of the life annuity factor can be found by looking in the "Annuity" column or it may be computed directly by dividing the life estate factor by the Section 7520 rate. Here it would be 0.64967/0.060 = 10.8279. [Due to rounding, Table S shows 10.8279 instead of 10.8278.]

SUMMARY AND SUGGESTIONS

Almost every time value of money or longevity sensitive estate and financial planning tool or technique has, to some extent, been affected by the monthly changing Section 7520 valuation rates. Illustrating the numerical advantages of a given concept is now more difficult because present and future monetary values will vary (sometimes considerably) from month to month and the certainty of accomplishing stated objectives has become less certain than ever.

Planners should "date stamp" all written proposals and suggestions to clients and impress upon them the importance of timely (but carefully planned) implementation of suggested tools and techniques. To avoid malpractice situations, planners should base illustrations on ranges of interest rates rather than making projections dependent on just one rate.

More attention must be paid by planners to the trend of interest rates and the impact of that trend on tools and techniques. Timing is essential since starting a tool or technique in one month rather than another may result in significant tax savings (or costs). The "wait and see" approach (waiting until the IRS publishes the Section 7520 rate) and selecting the optimum month for making a gift can, by itself, result in substantial valuation differences.

CHAPTER ENDNOTES

1. These two IRS volumes are available for a fee by writing to the Superintendent of Documents, United States Government Printing Office, Washington, DC, 20404; or online at www.irs.gov.

2. IRC Sec. 7520(b). With respect to a charitable remainder unitrust, although the stipulated percentage payout is the principal factor involved in calculating the client's deduction, the computation must also take into account the impact of the frequency of payout (monthly, quarterly, semiannually, etc.), and the number of months between the valuation date and the first required payout. These unitrust factors and an explanation of their use can be found in IRS Pub. 1458.

3. A remainder is the right to use, possess, and enjoy property when the prior owner's interest ends. A remainder interest is valued by subtracting the present value of any prior interest from the fair market value of the property.

   A reversion, which has the same monetary value as a remainder interest, is a future right the transferor of property has retained to use, possess, or enjoy the property in question. It is the fixed right to future possession that was never given away or sold.

4. An income interest for a term of years is a right – limited to a specific period of time – to the income from property or the right to use nonincome producing property. It is not dependent on some outside measurement such as the life of one or more persons.

5. An annuity is a systematic liquidation of principal and interest over a period of time. The length of the annuity can be set to last for a fixed number of years regardless of events. Alternatively, payments can take the form of a "life annuity" measured by the span of one or more lives. For instance, the payments can last for the life of a client or the lives of the client and his or her spouse.

6. A life estate is the right to use, possess, and enjoy property or the income it produces for the life of a specified person. That measuring life (using an age based on the individual's nearest birthday) can be the life of the holder of the life interest or may be measured by the life of some other person (an estate per autre vie). A life estate can also be payable for more than one life (for instance, the life estate can last for the lives of the client and his

or her spouse). The life income beneficiary receives no right to enjoy principal.

7. Remainder factors for a term certain may be computed directly without the use of Table B. In the text example the remainder factor is computed in the following manner:

   Step 1: Add 1 to the applicable interest rate (6.0 percent). Result: 1.060

   Step 2: Increase the result of Step 1 to the exponential power of the number of years in the term (10). Result: 1.790847

   Step 3: Divide the number 1 by the result of Step 2 to arrive at the remainder factor. Result: 0.558395. (IRS Notice 89-24 indicates that valuation factors for term interests must be computed to 6 decimal places.)

   Step 4: The result of Step 3 is then multiplied by the value of the principal placed into the trust to arrive at the gift, estate, or GST tax value of the remainder interest. So if $100,000 were placed into the trust, the remainder (or reversion) would have a value of $55,839.50, as indicated in the text.

8. Alternatively, the term annuity factor may be computed directly by dividing the "income factor" by the applicable interest rate (6.0% in this case). In this example, dividing 0.441605 by 6.0 percent results in an annuity factor of 7.3601.

   Although valuation factors for incomes and remainders for terms of years must be rounded to 6 decimal places according to Notice 89-24, valuation factors for annuities for terms of years are still rounded to 4 decimal places. Valuation factors for life estates and remainders that are based on life expectancy are rounded to 5 decimal places and for life annuities are rounded to 4 decimal places.

   Practitioners doing these computations by hand must take into account the sometimes significant differences these rounding conventions can make.

9. Certain adjustments must be made to the annuity factor if an annuity is paid more frequently than annually and/or is paid at the beginning rather than the end of each period. For instance, if payments are made weekly, monthly, quarterly, or semiannually, enjoyment of the annuity is to some extent accelerated as compared with annual payments that are assumed to be paid at the end of the year.

   The adjusted value is computed by multiplying the normal end-of-year factor by a second factor that converts the weekly, monthly, quarterly, or semiannual payments into amounts that are actuarially equivalent to a single payment at the end of the year. Likewise, if payments are based on a life expectancy but are payable at the beginning of weekly, monthly, quarterly, semiannual, or annual periods, certain adjustments must be made.

   Frequency adjustment factors are given in Annuity Adjustment Factors Table A and Table B for various interest rates and payment frequencies.

   The adjustment factors are applied in the following manner. The annual annuity factor, once found, is multiplied by the appropriate frequency adjustment factor. For example, the value of a 10-year term annuity of $5,000 paid at the end of each semiannual period (20 payments) would be derived by multiplying the $10,000 total annual payment by the annual factor of 7.3601 (computed on the basis of a 6.0 percent Section 7520 rate) and by 1.0148 (from Annuity Adjustment Factors Table A) to derive a value of $74,690 as compared to $73,601 when the payments are made at annual intervals.

   If an annuity is based on life expectancy and payments are made at the beginning of an interval, rather than the end, the value is determined by computing the value with payments that are made at the end of the interval plus one interval's payment. For example, a monthly annuity of $5,000 payable at the beginning of each month for the life of a 60 year old would be valued as follows if the interest rate were 6.0 percent. The single life annuity factor from Table S(6.0) is 10.8279. The total annual payment, $60,000, is multiplied by 10.8279 and by the monthly periodic adjustment factor from Annuity Adjustment Factors Table A, 1.0272. The result is $667,345. Finally this value must be adjusted for the fact that payments are at the beginning rather than the end of each month. To make this final adjustment,

simply add one monthly payment, $5,000, to $667,345 to derive the value of the annuity, $672,345.

IRS Pub. 1457 does not provide a table of adjustment factors for term annuities with payments that are made at the beginning of annual, semiannual, quarterly, monthly, or weekly intervals. Annuity Adjustment Factors Table B, reproduced from the *Advanced Sales Reference Service*, can be used where term annuity payments are made at the beginning of an interval. Simply multiply the total annual payment by the product of (1) the annual annuity factor multiplied by (2) the factor from the Annuity Adjustment Factors Table B.

VALUATION TABLES

TABLE 90CM

Age x	l(x)	Age x	l(x)	Age x	l(x)
0	100000	37	95969	74	62852
1	99064	38	95780	75	60449
2	98992	39	95581	76	57955
3	98944	40	95373	77	55373
4	98907	41	95156	78	52704
5	98877	42	94928	79	49943
6	98850	43	94687	80	47084
7	98826	44	94431	81	44129
8	98803	45	94154	82	41091
9	98783	46	93855	83	37994
10	98766	47	93528	84	34876
11	98750	48	93173	85	31770
12	98734	49	92787	86	28687
13	98713	50	92370	87	25638
14	98681	51	91918	88	22658
15	98635	52	91424	89	19783
16	98573	53	90885	90	17046
17	98497	54	90297	91	14466
18	98409	55	89658	92	12066
19	98314	56	88965	93	9884
20	98215	57	88214	94	7951
21	98113	58	87397	95	6282
22	98006	59	86506	96	4868
23	97896	60	85537	97	3694
24	97784	61	84490	98	2745
25	97671	62	83368	99	1999
26	97556	63	82169	100	1424
27	97441	64	80887	101	991
28	97322	65	79519	102	672
29	97199	66	78066	103	443
30	97070	67	76531	104	284
31	96934	68	74907	105	175
32	96791	69	73186	106	105
33	96642	70	71357	107	60
34	96485	71	69411	108	33
35	96322	72	67344	109	17
36	96150	73	65154	110	0

ANNUITY ADJUSTMENT FACTORS TABLE A*

FREQUENCY OF PAYMENTS

INTEREST RATE	ANNUALLY	SEMI ANNUALLY	QUARTERLY	MONTHLY	WEEKLY
3.0%	1.0000	1.0074	1.0112	1.0137	1.0146
3.2%	1.0000	1.0079	1.0119	1.0146	1.0156
3.4%	1.0000	1.0084	1.0127	1.0155	1.0166
3.6%	1.0000	1.0089	1.0134	1.0164	1.0175
3.8%	1.0000	1.0094	1.0141	1.0173	1.0185
4.0%	1.0000	1.0099	1.0149	1.0182	1.0195
4.2%	1.0000	1.0104	1.0156	1.0191	1.0205
4.4%	1.0000	1.0109	1.0164	1.0200	1.0214
4.6%	1.0000	1.0114	1.0171	1.0209	1.0224
4.8%	1.0000	1.0119	1.0178	1.0218	1.0234
5.0%	1.0000	1.0123	1.0186	1.0227	1.0243
5.2%	1.0000	1.0128	1.0193	1.0236	1.0253
5.4%	1.0000	1.0133	1.0200	1.0245	1.0262
5.6%	1.0000	1.0138	1.0208	1.0254	1.0272
5.8%	1.0000	1.0143	1.0215	1.0263	1.0282
6.0%	1.0000	1.0148	1.0222	1.0272	1.0291
6.2%	1.0000	1.0153	1.0230	1.0281	1.0301
6.4%	1.0000	1.0158	1.0237	1.0290	1.0311
6.6%	1.0000	1.0162	1.0244	1.0299	1.0320
6.8%	1.0000	1.0167	1.0252	1.0308	1.0330
7.0%	1.0000	1.0172	1.0259	1.0317	1.0339
7.2%	1.0000	1.0177	1.0266	1.0326	1.0349
7.4%	1.0000	1.0182	1.0273	1.0335	1.0358
7.6%	1.0000	1.0187	1.0281	1.0344	1.0368
7.8%	1.0000	1.0191	1.0288	1.0353	1.0378
8.0%	1.0000	1.0196	1.0295	1.0362	1.0387
8.2%	1.0000	1.0201	1.0302	1.0370	1.0397
8.4%	1.0000	1.0206	1.0310	1.0379	1.0406
8.6%	1.0000	1.0211	1.0317	1.0388	1.0416
8.8%	1.0000	1.0215	1.0324	1.0397	1.0425
9.0%	1.0000	1.0220	1.0331	1.0406	1.0435
9.2%	1.0000	1.0225	1.0339	1.0415	1.0444
9.4%	1.0000	1.0230	1.0346	1.0424	1.0454
9.6%	1.0000	1.0235	1.0353	1.0433	1.0463
9.8%	1.0000	1.0239	1.0360	1.0442	1.0473
10.0%	1.0000	1.0244	1.0368	1.0450	1.0482
10.2%	1.0000	1.0249	1.0375	1.0459	1.0492
10.4%	1.0000	1.0254	1.0382	1.0468	1.0501
10.6%	1.0000	1.0258	1.0389	1.0477	1.0511
10.8%	1.0000	1.0263	1.0396	1.0486	1.0520

*For use in calculating the value of an annuity payable at the end of each period or, if the term of the annuity is determined with respect to one or more lives, an annuity payable at the beginning of each period.

ANNUITY ADJUSTMENT FACTORS TABLE B*

FREQUENCY OF PAYMENTS

INTEREST RATE	ANNUALLY	SEMI ANNUALLY	QUARTERLY	MONTHLY	WEEKLY
3.0%	1.0300	1.0224	1.0187	1.0162	1.0152
3.2%	1.0320	1.0239	1.0199	1.0172	1.0162
3.4%	1.0340	1.0254	1.0212	1.0183	1.0172
3.6%	1.0360	1.0269	1.0224	1.0194	1.0182
3.8%	1.0380	1.0284	1.0236	1.0205	1.0192
4.0%	1.0400	1.0299	1.0249	1.0215	1.0203
4.2%	1.0420	1.0314	1.0261	1.0226	1.0213
4.4%	1.0440	1.0329	1.0274	1.0237	1.0223
4.6%	1.0460	1.0344	1.0286	1.0247	1.0233
4.8%	1.0480	1.0359	1.0298	1.0258	1.0243
5.0%	1.0500	1.0373	1.0311	1.0269	1.0253
5.2%	1.0520	1.0388	1.0323	1.0279	1.0263
5.4%	1.0540	1.0403	1.0335	1.0290	1.0273
5.6%	1.0560	1.0418	1.0348	1.0301	1.0283
5.8%	1.0580	1.0433	1.0360	1.0311	1.0293
6.0%	1.0600	1.0448	1.0372	1.0322	1.0303
6.2%	1.0620	1.0463	1.0385	1.0333	1.0313
6.4%	1.0640	1.0478	1.0397	1.0343	1.0323
6.6%	1.0660	1.0492	1.0409	1.0354	1.0333
6.8%	1.0680	1.0507	1.0422	1.0365	1.0343
7.0%	1.0700	1.0522	1.0434	1.0375	1.0353
7.2%	1.0720	1.0537	1.0446	1.0386	1.0363
7.4%	1.0740	1.0552	1.0458	1.0396	1.0373
7.6%	1.0760	1.0567	1.0471	1.0407	1.0383
7.8%	1.0780	1.0581	1.0483	1.0418	1.0393
8.0%	1.0800	1.0596	1.0495	1.0428	1.0403
8.2%	1.0820	1.0611	1.0507	1.0439	1.0413
8.4%	1.0840	1.0626	1.0520	1.0449	1.0422
8.6%	1.0860	1.0641	1.0532	1.0460	1.0432
8.8%	1.0880	1.0655	1.0544	1.0471	1.0442
9.0%	1.0900	1.0670	1.0556	1.0481	1.0452
9.2%	1.0920	1.0685	1.0569	1.0492	1.0462
9.4%	1.0940	1.0700	1.0581	1.0502	1.0472
9.6%	1.0960	1.0715	1.0593	1.0513	1.0482
9.8%	1.0980	1.0729	1.0605	1.0523	1.0492
10.0%	1.1000	1.0744	1.0618	1.0534	1.0502
10.2%	1.1020	1.0759	1.0630	1.0544	1.0512
10.4%	1.1040	1.0774	1.0642	1.0555	1.0521
10.6%	1.1060	1.0788	1.0654	1.0565	1.0531
10.8%	1.1080	1.0803	1.0666	1.0576	1.0541

*For use in calculating the value of a term certain annuity payable at the beginning of each period.

TABLE B
TERM CERTAIN FACTORS

INTEREST RATE

	3.4%				3.6%		
YEARS	ANNUITY	INCOME INTEREST	REMAINDER	YEARS	ANNUITY	INCOME INTEREST	REMAINDER
1	0.9671	.032882	.967118	1	0.9653	.034749	.965251
2	1.9024	.064683	.935317	2	1.8970	.068291	.931709
3	2.8070	.095438	.904562	3	2.7963	.100667	.899333
4	3.6818	.125182	.874818	4	3.6644	.131918	.868082
5	4.5279	.153948	.846052	5	4.5023	.162083	.837917
6	5.3461	.181767	.818233	6	5.3111	.191199	.808801
7	6.1374	.208673	.791327	7	6.0918	.219304	.780696
8	6.9027	.234693	.765307	8	6.8454	.246433	.753567
9	7.6429	.259858	.740142	9	7.5727	.272619	.727381
10	8.3587	.284195	.715805	10	8.2748	.297894	.702106
11	9.0509	.307732	.692268	11	8.9526	.322292	.677708
12	9.7205	.330495	.669505	12	9.6067	.345842	.654158
13	10.3679	.352510	.647490	13	10.2381	.368573	.631427
14	10.9941	.373801	.626199	14	10.8476	.390514	.609486
15	11.5998	.394392	.605608	15	11.4359	.411693	.588307
16	12.1854	.414305	.585695	16	12.0038	.432137	.567863
17	12.7519	.433564	.566436	17	12.5519	.451869	.548131
18	13.2997	.452190	.547810	18	13.0810	.470916	.529084
19	13.8295	.470203	.529797	19	13.5917	.489301	.510699
20	14.3419	.487623	.512377	20	14.0847	.507048	.492952
21	14.8374	.504471	.495529	21	14.5605	.524177	.475823
22	15.3166	.520765	.479235	22	15.0198	.540712	.459288
23	15.7801	.536524	.463476	23	15.4631	.556672	.443328
24	16.2283	.551764	.448236	24	15.8910	.572077	.427923
25	16.6618	.566503	.433497	25	16.3041	.586947	.413053
26	17.0811	.580757	.419243	26	16.7028	.601300	.398700
27	17.4865	.594542	.405458	27	17.0876	.615154	.384846
28	17.8787	.607875	.392125	28	17.4591	.628527	.371473
29	18.2579	.620769	.379231	29	17.8177	.641436	.358564
30	18.6247	.633238	.366762	30	18.1638	.653895	.346105
31	18.9794	.645298	.354702	31	18.4978	.665922	.334078
32	19.3224	.656962	.343038	32	18.8203	.677531	.322469
33	19.6542	.668241	.331759	33	19.1316	.688737	.311263
34	19.9750	.679150	.320850	34	19.4320	.699553	.300447
35	20.2853	.689700	.310300	35	19.7220	.709993	.290007
36	20.5854	.699904	.300096	36	20.0020	.720070	.279930
37	20.8756	.709772	.290228	37	20.2722	.729798	.270202
38	21.1563	.719315	.280685	38	20.5330	.739187	.260813
39	21.4278	.728544	.271456	39	20.7847	.748250	.251750
40	21.6903	.737470	.262530	40	21.0277	.756998	.243002
41	21.9442	.746103	.253897	41	21.2623	.765442	.234558
42	22.1897	.754451	.245549	42	21.4887	.773593	.226407
43	22.4272	.762526	.237474	43	21.7072	.781460	.218540
44	22.6569	.770334	.229666	44	21.9182	.789054	.210946
45	22.8790	.777886	.222114	45	22.1218	.796384	.203616
46	23.0938	.785190	.214810	46	22.3183	.803460	.196540
47	23.3016	.792253	.207747	47	22.5080	.810289	.189711
48	23.5025	.799084	.200916	48	22.6912	.816882	.183118
49	23.6968	.805691	.194309	49	22.8679	.823245	.176755
50	23.8847	.812080	.187920	50	23.0385	.829387	.170613

TABLE B
TERM CERTAIN FACTORS

INTEREST RATE

	3.8%				4.0%		
YEARS	ANNUITY	INCOME INTEREST	REMAINDER	YEARS	ANNUITY	INCOME INTEREST	REMAINDER
1	0.9634	.036609	.963391	1	0.9615	.038462	.961538
2	1.8915	.071878	.928122	2	1.8861	.075444	.924556
3	2.7857	.105855	.894145	3	2.7751	.111004	.888996
4	3.6471	.138589	.861411	4	3.6299	.145196	.854804
5	4.4769	.170124	.829876	5	4.4518	.178073	.821927
6	5.2764	.200505	.799495	6	5.2421	.209685	.790315
7	6.0467	.229773	.770227	7	6.0021	.240082	.759918
8	6.7887	.257970	.742030	8	6.7327	.269310	.730690
9	7.5036	.285135	.714865	9	7.4353	.297413	.702587
10	8.1923	.311306	.688694	10	8.1109	.324436	.675564
11	8.8557	.336518	.663482	11	8.7605	.350419	.649581
12	9.4949	.360807	.639193	12	9.3851	.375403	.624597
13	10.1107	.384207	.615793	13	9.9856	.399426	.600574
14	10.7040	.406751	.593249	14	10.5631	.422525	.577475
15	11.2755	.428469	.571531	15	11.1184	.444735	.555265
16	11.8261	.449392	.550608	16	11.6523	.466092	.533908
17	12.3566	.469549	.530451	17	12.1657	.486627	.513373
18	12.8676	.488969	.511031	18	12.6593	.506372	.493628
19	13.3599	.507677	.492323	19	13.1339	.525358	.474642
20	13.8342	.525700	.474300	20	13.5903	.543613	.456387
21	14.2912	.543064	.456936	21	14.0292	.561166	.438834
22	14.7314	.559792	.440208	22	14.4511	.578045	.421955
23	15.1555	.575907	.424093	23	14.8568	.594274	.405726
24	15.5640	.591433	.408567	24	15.2470	.609879	.390121
25	15.9576	.606390	.393610	25	15.6221	.624883	.375117
26	16.3368	.620800	.379200	26	15.9828	.639311	.360689
27	16.7021	.634682	.365318	27	16.3296	.653183	.346817
28	17.0541	.648056	.351944	28	16.6631	.666523	.333477
29	17.3932	.660940	.339060	29	16.9837	.679349	.320651
30	17.7198	.673352	.326648	30	17.2920	.691681	.308319
31	18.0345	.685311	.314689	31	17.5885	.703540	.296460
32	18.3377	.696831	.303169	32	17.8736	.714942	.285058
33	18.6297	.707930	.292070	33	18.1476	.725906	.274094
34	18.9111	.718622	.281378	34	18.4112	.736448	.263552
35	19.1822	.728923	.271077	35	18.6646	.746585	.253415
36	19.4433	.738847	.261153	36	18.9083	.756331	.243669
37	19.6949	.748407	.251593	37	19.1426	.765703	.234297
38	19.9373	.757618	.242382	38	19.3679	.774715	.225285
39	20.1708	.766491	.233509	39	19.5845	.783379	.216621
40	20.3958	.775040	.224960	40	19.7928	.791711	.208289
41	20.6125	.783275	.216725	41	19.9931	.799722	.200278
42	20.8213	.791209	.208791	42	20.1856	.807425	.192575
43	21.0224	.798853	.201147	43	20.3708	.814832	.185168
44	21.2162	.806217	.193783	44	20.5488	.821954	.178046
45	21.4029	.813311	.186689	45	20.7200	.828802	.171198
46	21.5828	.820145	.179855	46	20.8847	.835386	.164614
47	21.7560	.826730	.173270	47	21.0429	.841717	.158283
48	21.9230	.833073	.166927	48	21.1951	.847805	.152195
49	22.0838	.839184	.160816	49	21.3415	.853659	.146341
50	22.2387	.845071	.154929	50	21.4822	.859287	.140713

TABLE B
TERM CERTAIN FACTORS

INTEREST RATE

	4.2%				4.4%		
YEARS	ANNUITY	INCOME INTEREST	REMAINDER	YEARS	ANNUITY	INCOME INTEREST	REMAINDER
1	0.9597	.040307	.959693	1	0.9579	.042146	.957854
2	1.8807	.078990	.921010	2	1.8753	.082515	.917485
3	2.7646	.116113	.883887	3	2.7542	.121183	.878817
4	3.6129	.151740	.848260	4	3.5959	.158221	.841779
5	4.4269	.185931	.814069	5	4.4022	.193698	.806302
6	5.2082	.218743	.781257	6	5.1746	.227680	.772320
7	5.9579	.250234	.749766	7	5.9143	.260230	.739770
8	6.6775	.280455	.719545	8	6.6229	.291408	.708592
9	7.3680	.309457	.690543	9	7.3016	.321272	.678728
10	8.0307	.337291	.662709	10	7.9518	.349878	.650122
11	8.6667	.364003	.635997	11	8.5745	.377278	.622722
12	9.2771	.389638	.610362	12	9.1710	.403523	.596477
13	9.8629	.414240	.585760	13	9.7423	.428661	.571339
14	10.4250	.437850	.562150	14	10.2896	.452741	.547259
15	10.9645	.460509	.539491	15	10.8138	.475805	.524195
16	11.4822	.482254	.517746	16	11.3159	.497898	.502102
17	11.9791	.503123	.496877	17	11.7968	.519059	.480941
18	12.4560	.523151	.476849	18	12.2575	.539329	.460671
19	12.9136	.542371	.457629	19	12.6987	.558744	.441256
20	13.3528	.560817	.439183	20	13.1214	.577341	.422659
21	13.7743	.578519	.421481	21	13.5262	.595154	.404846
22	14.1788	.595508	.404492	22	13.9140	.612217	.387783
23	14.5669	.611812	.388188	23	14.2855	.628560	.371440
24	14.9395	.627458	.372542	24	14.6412	.644215	.355785
25	15.2970	.642474	.357526	25	14.9820	.659209	.340791
26	15.6401	.656885	.343115	26	15.3085	.673572	.326428
27	15.9694	.670715	.329285	27	15.6211	.687330	.312670
28	16.2854	.683988	.316012	28	15.9206	.700507	.299493
29	16.5887	.696725	.303275	29	16.2075	.713130	.286870
30	16.8797	.708949	.291051	30	16.4823	.725220	.274780
31	17.1591	.720681	.279319	31	16.7455	.736801	.263199
32	17.4271	.731939	.268061	32	16.9976	.747893	.252107
33	17.6844	.742744	.257256	33	17.2391	.758519	.241481
34	17.9313	.753113	.246887	34	17.4704	.768696	.231304
35	18.1682	.763065	.236935	35	17.6919	.778444	.221556
36	18.3956	.772615	.227385	36	17.9041	.787782	.212218
37	18.6138	.781780	.218220	37	18.1074	.796726	.203274
38	18.8232	.790576	.209424	38	18.3021	.805293	.194707
39	19.0242	.799017	.200983	39	18.4886	.813499	.186501
40	19.2171	.807118	.192882	40	18.6673	.821359	.178641
41	19.4022	.814893	.185107	41	18.8384	.828888	.171112
42	19.5799	.822354	.177646	42	19.0023	.836100	.163900
43	19.7503	.829514	.170486	43	19.1593	.843008	.156992
44	19.9140	.836386	.163614	44	19.3096	.849624	.150376
45	20.0710	.842981	.157019	45	19.4537	.855962	.144038
46	20.2217	.849310	.150690	46	19.5916	.862032	.137968
47	20.3663	.855384	.144616	47	19.7238	.867847	.132153
48	20.5051	.861213	.138787	48	19.8504	.873417	.126583
49	20.6383	.866807	.133193	49	19.9716	.878752	.121248
50	20.7661	.872176	.127824	50	20.0878	.883862	.116138

TABLE B
TERM CERTAIN FACTORS

INTEREST RATE

	4.6%				4.8%		
YEARS	ANNUITY	INCOME INTEREST	REMAINDER	YEARS	ANNUITY	INCOME INTEREST	REMAINDER
1	0.9560	.043977	.956023	1	0.9542	.045802	.954198
2	1.8700	.086020	.913980	2	1.8647	.089505	.910495
3	2.7438	.126214	.873786	3	2.7335	.131207	.868793
4	3.5791	.164641	.835359	4	3.5625	.170999	.829001
5	4.3778	.201377	.798623	5	4.3535	.208969	.791031
6	5.1413	.236499	.763501	6	5.1083	.245199	.754801
7	5.8712	.270075	.729925	7	5.8285	.279770	.720230
8	6.5690	.302175	.697825	8	6.5158	.312758	.687242
9	7.2362	.332863	.667137	9	7.1716	.344235	.655765
10	7.8740	.362202	.637798	10	7.7973	.374270	.625730
11	8.4837	.390250	.609750	11	8.3944	.402929	.597071
12	9.0666	.417065	.582935	12	8.9641	.430276	.569724
13	9.6239	.442701	.557299	13	9.5077	.456370	.543630
14	10.1567	.467210	.532790	14	10.0264	.481269	.518731
15	10.6661	.490640	.509360	15	10.5214	.505028	.494972
16	11.1530	.513040	.486960	16	10.9937	.527698	.472302
17	11.6186	.534455	.465545	17	11.4444	.549330	.450670
18	12.0637	.554929	.445071	18	11.8744	.569972	.430028
19	12.4892	.574502	.425498	19	12.2847	.589668	.410332
20	12.8960	.593214	.406786	20	12.6763	.608462	.391538
21	13.2848	.611103	.388897	21	13.0499	.626395	.373605
22	13.6566	.628206	.371794	22	13.4064	.643506	.356494
23	14.0121	.644556	.355444	23	13.7465	.659834	.340166
24	14.3519	.660187	.339813	24	14.0711	.675414	.324586
25	14.6768	.675131	.324869	25	14.3809	.690281	.309719
26	14.9873	.689418	.310582	26	14.6764	.704467	.295533
27	15.2843	.703077	.296923	27	14.9584	.718002	.281998
28	15.5681	.716134	.283866	28	15.2275	.730918	.269082
29	15.8395	.728618	.271382	29	15.4842	.743243	.256757
30	16.0990	.740553	.259447	30	15.7292	.755003	.244997
31	16.3470	.751962	.248038	31	15.9630	.766224	.233776
32	16.5841	.762870	.237130	32	16.1861	.776931	.223069
33	16.8108	.773298	.226702	33	16.3989	.787148	.212852
34	17.0276	.783268	.216732	34	16.6020	.796897	.203103
35	17.2348	.792799	.207201	35	16.7958	.806199	.193801
36	17.4329	.801911	.198089	36	16.9807	.815076	.184924
37	17.6222	.810623	.189377	37	17.1572	.823546	.176454
38	17.8033	.818951	.181049	38	17.3256	.831627	.168373
39	17.9764	.826913	.173087	39	17.4862	.839339	.160661
40	18.1418	.834525	.165475	40	17.6395	.846698	.153302
41	18.3000	.841802	.158198	41	17.7858	.853719	.146281
42	18.4513	.848759	.151241	42	17.9254	.860419	.139581
43	18.5959	.855410	.144590	43	18.0586	.866812	.133188
44	18.7341	.861769	.138231	44	18.1857	.872912	.127088
45	18.8663	.867848	.132152	45	18.3069	.878733	.121267
46	18.9926	.873660	.126340	46	18.4227	.884287	.115713
47	19.1134	.879216	.120784	47	18.5331	.889587	.110413
48	19.2289	.884527	.115473	48	18.6384	.894644	.105356
49	19.3392	.889605	.110395	49	18.7390	.899470	.100530
50	19.4448	.894460	.105540	50	18.8349	.904074	.095926

TABLE B
TERM CERTAIN FACTORS

INTEREST RATE

	5.0%				5.2%		
YEARS	ANNUITY	INCOME INTEREST	REMAINDER	YEARS	ANNUITY	INCOME INTEREST	REMAINDER
1	0.9524	.047619	.952381	1	0.9506	.049430	.950570
2	1.8594	.092971	.907029	2	1.8542	.096416	.903584
3	2.7232	.136162	.863838	3	2.7131	.141080	.858920
4	3.5460	.177298	.822702	4	3.5295	.183536	.816464
5	4.3295	.216474	.783526	5	4.3056	.223894	.776106
6	5.0757	.253785	.746215	6	5.0434	.262256	.737744
7	5.7864	.289319	.710681	7	5.7447	.298723	.701277
8	6.4632	.323161	.676839	8	6.4113	.333387	.666613
9	7.1078	.355391	.644609	9	7.0449	.366337	.633663
10	7.7217	.386087	.613913	10	7.6473	.397659	.602341
11	8.3064	.415321	.584679	11	8.2199	.427432	.572568
12	8.8633	.443163	.556837	12	8.7641	.455734	.544266
13	9.3936	.469679	.530321	13	9.2815	.482637	.517363
14	9.8986	.494932	.505068	14	9.7733	.508210	.491790
15	10.3797	.518983	.481017	15	10.2408	.532519	.467481
16	10.8378	.541888	.458112	16	10.6851	.555626	.444374
17	11.2741	.563703	.436297	17	11.1075	.577592	.422408
18	11.6896	.584479	.415521	18	11.5091	.598471	.401529
19	12.0853	.604266	.395734	19	11.8907	.618319	.381681
20	12.4622	.623111	.376889	20	12.2536	.637185	.362815
21	12.8212	.641058	.358942	21	12.5984	.655119	.344881
22	13.1630	.658150	.341850	22	12.9263	.672166	.327834
23	13.4886	.674429	.325571	23	13.2379	.688371	.311629
24	13.7986	.689932	.310068	24	13.5341	.703775	.296225
25	14.0939	.704697	.295303	25	13.8157	.718417	.281583
26	14.3752	.718759	.281241	26	14.0834	.732336	.267664
27	14.6430	.732152	.267848	27	14.3378	.745566	.254434
28	14.8981	.744906	.255094	28	14.5797	.758143	.241857
29	15.1411	.757054	.242946	29	14.8096	.770098	.229902
30	15.3725	.768623	.231377	30	15.0281	.781462	.218538
31	15.5928	.779641	.220359	31	15.2358	.792264	.207736
32	15.8027	.790134	.209866	32	15.4333	.802532	.197468
33	16.0025	.800127	.199873	33	15.6210	.812293	.187707
34	16.1929	.809645	.190355	34	15.7994	.821571	.178429
35	16.3742	.818710	.181290	35	15.9691	.830391	.169609
36	16.5469	.827343	.172657	36	16.1303	.838775	.161225
37	16.7113	.835564	.164436	37	16.2835	.846744	.153256
38	16.8679	.843395	.156605	38	16.4292	.854319	.145681
39	17.0170	.850852	.149148	39	16.5677	.861520	.138480
40	17.1591	.857954	.142046	40	16.6993	.868365	.131635
41	17.2944	.864718	.135282	41	16.8245	.874872	.125128
42	17.4232	.871160	.128840	42	16.9434	.881057	.118943
43	17.5459	.877296	.122704	43	17.0565	.886936	.113064
44	17.6628	.883139	.116861	44	17.1639	.892525	.107475
45	17.7741	.888703	.111297	45	17.2661	.897837	.102163
46	17.8801	.894003	.105997	46	17.3632	.902887	.097113
47	17.9810	.899051	.100949	47	17.4555	.907688	.092312
48	18.0772	.903858	.096142	48	17.5433	.912251	.087749
49	18.1687	.908436	.091564	49	17.6267	.916588	.083412
50	18.2559	.912796	.087204	50	17.7060	.920711	.079289

TABLE B
TERM CERTAIN FACTORS

INTEREST RATE

	5.4%				5.6%		
YEARS	ANNUITY	INCOME INTEREST	REMAINDER	YEARS	ANNUITY	INCOME INTEREST	REMAINDER
1	0.9488	.051233	.948767	1	0.9470	.053030	.946970
2	1.8489	.099842	.900158	2	1.8437	.103248	.896752
3	2.7030	.145960	.854040	3	2.6929	.150803	.849197
4	3.5132	.189715	.810285	4	3.4971	.195837	.804163
5	4.2820	.231229	.768771	5	4.2586	.238482	.761518
6	5.0114	.270616	.729384	6	4.9797	.278865	.721135
7	5.7034	.307985	.692015	7	5.6626	.317107	.682893
8	6.3600	.343439	.656561	8	6.3093	.353321	.646679
9	6.9829	.377077	.622923	9	6.9217	.387615	.612385
10	7.5739	.408991	.591009	10	7.5016	.420090	.579910
11	8.1346	.439271	.560729	11	8.0508	.450843	.549157
12	8.6666	.467999	.532001	12	8.5708	.479965	.520035
13	9.1714	.495255	.504745	13	9.0633	.507542	.492458
14	9.6503	.521115	.478885	14	9.5296	.533657	.466343
15	10.1046	.545650	.454350	15	9.9712	.558388	.441612
16	10.5357	.568928	.431072	16	10.3894	.581806	.418194
17	10.9447	.591013	.408987	17	10.7854	.603983	.396017
18	11.3327	.611967	.388033	18	11.1604	.624984	.375016
19	11.7009	.631847	.368153	19	11.5156	.644871	.355129
20	12.0502	.650709	.349291	20	11.8519	.663704	.336296
21	12.3816	.668604	.331396	21	12.1703	.681538	.318462
22	12.6960	.685583	.314417	22	12.4719	.698426	.301574
23	12.9943	.701691	.298309	23	12.7575	.714419	.285581
24	13.2773	.716975	.283025	24	13.0279	.729563	.270437
25	13.5458	.731475	.268525	25	13.2840	.743904	.256096
26	13.8006	.745232	.254768	26	13.5265	.757485	.242515
27	14.0423	.758285	.241715	27	13.7562	.770346	.229654
28	14.2716	.770669	.229331	28	13.9737	.782525	.217475
29	14.4892	.782418	.217582	29	14.1796	.794057	.205943
30	14.6957	.793566	.206434	30	14.3746	.804979	.195021
31	14.8915	.804142	.195858	31	14.5593	.815321	.184679
32	15.0773	.814177	.185823	32	14.7342	.825114	.174886
33	15.2536	.823697	.176303	33	14.8998	.834388	.165612
34	15.4209	.832730	.167270	34	15.0566	.843171	.156829
35	15.5796	.841299	.158701	35	15.2051	.851488	.148512
36	15.7302	.849430	.150570	36	15.3458	.859363	.140637
37	15.8730	.857144	.142856	37	15.4790	.866821	.133179
38	16.0086	.864463	.135537	38	15.6051	.873884	.126116
39	16.1372	.871407	.128593	39	15.7245	.880572	.119428
40	16.2592	.877996	.122004	40	15.8376	.886905	.113095
41	16.3749	.884246	.115754	41	15.9447	.892903	.107097
42	16.4848	.890177	.109823	42	16.0461	.898582	.101418
43	16.5890	.895803	.104197	43	16.1421	.903960	.096040
44	16.6878	.901142	.098858	44	16.2331	.909053	.090947
45	16.7816	.906207	.093793	45	16.3192	.913876	.086124
46	16.8706	.911012	.088988	46	16.4008	.918443	.081557
47	16.9550	.915571	.084429	47	16.4780	.922768	.077232
48	17.0351	.919897	.080103	48	16.5511	.926864	.073136
49	17.1111	.924001	.075999	49	16.6204	.930742	.069258
50	17.1832	.927894	.072106	50	16.6860	.934415	.065585

TABLE B
TERM CERTAIN FACTORS

INTEREST RATE

	5.8%				6.0%		
YEARS	ANNUITY	INCOME INTEREST	REMAINDER	YEARS	ANNUITY	INCOME INTEREST	REMAINDER
1	0.9452	.054820	.945180	1	0.9434	.056604	.943396
2	1.8385	.106636	.893364	2	1.8334	.110004	.889996
3	2.6829	.155610	.844390	3	2.6730	.160381	.839619
4	3.4810	.201900	.798100	4	3.4651	.207906	.792094
5	4.2354	.245652	.754348	5	4.2124	.252742	.747258
6	4.9484	.287006	.712994	6	4.9173	.295039	.704961
7	5.6223	.326092	.673908	7	5.5824	.334943	.665057
8	6.2592	.363036	.636964	8	6.2098	.372588	.627412
9	6.8613	.397955	.602045	9	6.8017	.408102	.591898
10	7.4303	.430959	.569041	10	7.3601	.441605	.558395
11	7.9682	.462154	.537846	11	7.8869	.473212	.526788
12	8.4765	.491639	.508361	12	8.3838	.503031	.496969
13	8.9570	.519508	.480492	13	8.8527	.531161	.468839
14	9.4112	.545849	.454151	14	9.2950	.557699	.442301
15	9.8404	.570745	.429255	15	9.7122	.582735	.417265
16	10.2462	.594277	.405723	16	10.1059	.606354	.393646
17	10.6296	.616519	.383481	17	10.4773	.628636	.371364
18	10.9921	.637542	.362458	18	10.8276	.649656	.350344
19	11.3347	.657412	.342588	19	11.1581	.669487	.330513
20	11.6585	.676193	.323807	20	11.4699	.688195	.311805
21	11.9646	.693944	.306056	21	11.7641	.705845	.294155
22	12.2538	.710722	.289278	22	12.0416	.722495	.277505
23	12.5272	.726580	.273420	23	12.3034	.738203	.261797
24	12.7857	.741569	.258431	24	12.5504	.753021	.246979
25	13.0299	.755737	.244263	25	12.7834	.767001	.232999
26	13.2608	.769127	.230873	26	13.0032	.780190	.219810
27	13.4790	.781784	.218216	27	13.2105	.792632	.207368
28	13.6853	.793747	.206253	28	13.4062	.804370	.195630
29	13.8802	.805053	.194947	29	13.5907	.815443	.184557
30	14.0645	.815740	.184260	30	13.7648	.825890	.174110
31	14.2386	.825842	.174158	31	13.9291	.835745	.164255
32	14.4033	.835389	.164611	32	14.0840	.845043	.154957
33	14.5588	.844413	.155587	33	14.2302	.853814	.146186
34	14.7059	.852942	.147058	34	14.3681	.862088	.137912
35	14.8449	.861004	.138996	35	14.4982	.869895	.130105
36	14.9763	.868624	.131376	36	14.6210	.877259	.122741
37	15.1004	.875826	.124174	37	14.7368	.884207	.115793
38	15.2178	.882633	.117367	38	14.8460	.890761	.109239
39	15.3287	.889067	.110933	39	14.9491	.896944	.103056
40	15.4336	.895149	.104851	40	15.0463	.902778	.097222
41	15.5327	.900897	.099103	41	15.1380	.908281	.091719
42	15.6264	.906330	.093670	42	15.2245	.913473	.086527
43	15.7149	.911465	.088535	43	15.3062	.918370	.081630
44	15.7986	.916318	.083682	44	15.3832	.922991	.077009
45	15.8777	.920906	.079094	45	15.4558	.927350	.072650
46	15.9524	.925242	.074758	46	15.5244	.931462	.068538
47	16.0231	.929340	.070660	47	15.5890	.935342	.064658
48	16.0899	.933214	.066786	48	15.6500	.939002	.060998
49	16.1530	.936875	.063125	49	15.7076	.942454	.057546
50	16.2127	.940335	.059665	50	15.7619	.945712	.054288

TABLE B
TERM CERTAIN FACTORS

INTEREST RATE

	6.2%				6.4%		
YEARS	ANNUITY	INCOME INTEREST	REMAINDER	YEARS	ANNUITY	INCOME INTEREST	REMAINDER
1	0.9416	.058380	.941620	1	0.9398	.060150	.939850
2	1.8283	.113353	.886647	2	1.8232	.116683	.883317
3	2.6632	.165115	.834885	3	2.6534	.169815	.830185
4	3.4493	.213856	.786144	4	3.4336	.219751	.780249
5	4.1895	.259752	.740248	5	4.1669	.266683	.733317
6	4.8866	.302968	.697032	6	4.8561	.310792	.689208
7	5.5429	.343661	.656339	7	5.5039	.352248	.647752
8	6.1609	.381978	.618022	8	6.1127	.391211	.608789
9	6.7429	.418058	.581942	9	6.6848	.427830	.572170
10	7.2908	.452032	.547968	10	7.2226	.462246	.537754
11	7.8068	.484023	.515977	11	7.7280	.494592	.505408
12	8.2927	.514146	.485854	12	8.2030	.524993	.475007
13	8.7502	.542510	.457490	13	8.6494	.553564	.446436
14	9.1809	.569219	.430781	14	9.0690	.580418	.419582
15	9.5866	.594368	.405632	15	9.4634	.605656	.394344
16	9.9685	.618049	.381951	16	9.8340	.629376	.370624
17	10.3282	.640347	.359653	17	10.1823	.651669	.348331
18	10.6668	.661344	.338656	18	10.5097	.672621	.327379
19	10.9857	.681115	.318885	19	10.8174	.692313	.307687
20	11.2860	.699732	.300268	20	11.1066	.710821	.289179
21	11.5687	.717261	.282739	21	11.3784	.728215	.271785
22	11.8350	.733768	.266232	22	11.6338	.744563	.255437
23	12.0857	.749311	.250689	23	11.8739	.759927	.240073
24	12.3217	.763946	.236054	24	12.0995	.774368	.225632
25	12.5440	.777727	.222273	25	12.3116	.787940	.212060
26	12.7533	.790703	.209297	26	12.5109	.800695	.199305
27	12.9504	.802922	.197078	27	12.6982	.812684	.187316
28	13.1359	.814428	.185572	28	12.8742	.823951	.176049
29	13.3107	.825261	.174739	29	13.0397	.834540	.165460
30	13.4752	.835463	.164537	30	13.1952	.844493	.155507
31	13.6301	.845068	.154932	31	13.3413	.853846	.146154
32	13.7760	.854113	.145887	32	13.4787	.862638	.137362
33	13.9134	.862630	.137370	33	13.6078	.870900	.129100
34	14.0427	.870650	.129350	34	13.7291	.878665	.121335
35	14.1645	.878202	.121798	35	13.8432	.885964	.114036
36	14.2792	.885312	.114688	36	13.9504	.892823	.107177
37	14.3872	.892008	.107992	37	14.0511	.899270	.100730
38	14.4889	.898312	.101688	38	14.1458	.905329	.094671
39	14.5847	.904249	.095751	39	14.2347	.911023	.088977
40	14.6748	.909839	.090161	40	14.3184	.916375	.083625
41	14.7597	.915103	.084897	41	14.3970	.921405	.078595
42	14.8397	.920059	.079941	42	14.4708	.926133	.073867
43	14.9149	.924726	.075274	43	14.5402	.930576	.069424
44	14.9858	.929120	.070880	44	14.6055	.934752	.065248
45	15.0526	.933258	.066742	45	14.6668	.938677	.061323
46	15.1154	.937155	.062845	46	14.7245	.942365	.057635
47	15.1746	.940824	.059176	47	14.7786	.945832	.054168
48	15.2303	.944278	.055722	48	14.8295	.949090	.050910
49	15.2828	.947531	.052469	49	14.8774	.952152	.047848
50	15.3322	.950595	.049405	50	14.9224	.955030	.044970

TABLE S (3.4)
SINGLE LIFE FACTORS BASED ON LIFE TABLE 90CM

3.4% INTEREST

AGE	ANNUITY	LIFE ESTATE	REMAINDER	AGE	ANNUITY	LIFE ESTATE	REMAINDER
0	26.38590	0.89712	0.10288	55	15.68940	0.53344	0.46656
1	26.53600	0.90223	0.09777	56	15.34540	0.52174	0.47826
2	26.45790	0.89957	0.10043	57	14.99790	0.50993	0.49007
3	26.37040	0.89660	0.10340	58	14.64820	0.49804	0.50196
4	26.27710	0.89342	0.10658	59	14.29700	0.48610	0.51390
5	26.17860	0.89007	0.10993	60	13.94490	0.47413	0.52587
6	26.07590	0.88658	0.11342	61	13.59160	0.46211	0.53789
7	25.96890	0.88294	0.11706	62	13.23610	0.45003	0.54997
8	25.85800	0.87917	0.12083	63	12.87850	0.43787	0.56213
9	25.74250	0.87524	0.12476	64	12.51950	0.42566	0.57434
10	25.62220	0.87116	0.12884	65	12.15930	0.41342	0.58658
11	25.49760	0.86692	0.13308	66	11.79740	0.40111	0.59889
12	25.36870	0.86254	0.13746	67	11.43320	0.38873	0.61127
13	25.23670	0.85805	0.14195	68	11.06730	0.37629	0.62371
14	25.10300	0.85350	0.14650	69	10.70100	0.36383	0.63617
15	24.96840	0.84893	0.15107	70	10.33560	0.35141	0.64859
16	24.83330	0.84433	0.15567	71	9.97260	0.33907	0.66093
17	24.69700	0.83970	0.16030	72	9.61280	0.32684	0.67316
18	24.55910	0.83501	0.16499	73	9.25700	0.31474	0.68526
19	24.41820	0.83022	0.16978	74	8.90400	0.30273	0.69727
20	24.27330	0.82529	0.17471	75	8.55280	0.29080	0.70920
21	24.12420	0.82022	0.17978	76	8.20270	0.27889	0.72111
22	23.97110	0.81502	0.18498	77	7.85370	0.26703	0.73297
23	23.81340	0.80966	0.19034	78	7.50670	0.25523	0.74477
24	23.65070	0.80412	0.19588	79	7.16340	0.24355	0.75645
25	23.48250	0.79841	0.20159	80	6.82630	0.23209	0.76791
26	23.30900	0.79251	0.20749	81	6.49760	0.22092	0.77908
27	23.12930	0.78640	0.21360	82	6.17820	0.21006	0.78994
28	22.94440	0.78011	0.21989	83	5.86830	0.19952	0.80048
29	22.75390	0.77363	0.22637	84	5.56560	0.18923	0.81077
30	22.55810	0.76698	0.23302	85	5.26850	0.17913	0.82087
31	22.35710	0.76014	0.23986	86	4.97940	0.16930	0.83070
32	22.15070	0.75312	0.24688	87	4.70150	0.15985	0.84015
33	21.93830	0.74590	0.25410	88	4.43500	0.15079	0.84921
34	21.72030	0.73849	0.26151	89	4.17960	0.14211	0.85789
35	21.49600	0.73086	0.26914	90	3.93530	0.13380	0.86620
36	21.26570	0.72303	0.27697	91	3.70570	0.12599	0.87401
37	21.02930	0.71500	0.28500	92	3.49440	0.11881	0.88119
38	20.78620	0.70673	0.29327	93	3.30040	0.11221	0.88779
39	20.53660	0.69825	0.30175	94	3.12070	0.10611	0.89389
40	20.28010	0.68952	0.31048	95	2.95130	0.10034	0.89966
41	20.01630	0.68055	0.31945	96	2.79280	0.09496	0.90504
42	19.74540	0.67134	0.32866	97	2.64670	0.08999	0.91001
43	19.46740	0.66189	0.33811	98	2.50990	0.08534	0.91466
44	19.18250	0.65221	0.34779	99	2.37710	0.08082	0.91918
45	18.89160	0.64231	0.35769	100	2.24860	0.07645	0.92355
46	18.59450	0.63221	0.36779	101	2.12250	0.07216	0.92784
47	18.29220	0.62194	0.37806	102	1.99910	0.06797	0.93203
48	17.98430	0.61147	0.38853	103	1.87710	0.06382	0.93618
49	17.67110	0.60082	0.39918	104	1.74760	0.05942	0.94058
50	17.35210	0.58997	0.41003	105	1.62110	0.05512	0.94488
51	17.02790	0.57895	0.42105	106	1.46030	0.04965	0.95035
52	16.69920	0.56777	0.43223	107	1.26740	0.04309	0.95691
53	16.36650	0.55646	0.44354	108	0.97360	0.03310	0.96690
54	16.02990	0.54502	0.45498	109	0.48360	0.01644	0.98356

TABLE S (3.6)
SINGLE LIFE FACTORS BASED ON LIFE TABLE 90CM

3.6% INTEREST

AGE	ANNUITY	LIFE ESTATE	REMAINDER	AGE	ANNUITY	LIFE ESTATE	REMAINDER
0	25.21860	0.90787	0.09213	55	15.32450	0.55168	0.44832
1	25.36850	0.91327	0.08673	56	14.99590	0.53985	0.46015
2	25.30060	0.91082	0.08918	57	14.66380	0.52790	0.47210
3	25.22390	0.90806	0.09194	58	14.32900	0.51584	0.48416
4	25.14150	0.90509	0.09491	59	13.99260	0.50373	0.49627
5	25.05440	0.90196	0.09804	60	13.65490	0.49158	0.50842
6	24.96330	0.89868	0.10132	61	13.31560	0.47936	0.52064
7	24.86810	0.89525	0.10475	62	12.97390	0.46706	0.53294
8	24.76920	0.89169	0.10831	63	12.62980	0.45467	0.54533
9	24.66600	0.88798	0.11202	64	12.28390	0.44222	0.55778
10	24.55830	0.88410	0.11590	65	11.93640	0.42971	0.57029
11	24.44640	0.88007	0.11993	66	11.58700	0.41713	0.58287
12	24.33050	0.87590	0.12410	67	11.23490	0.40446	0.59554
13	24.21170	0.87162	0.12838	68	10.88080	0.39171	0.60829
14	24.09130	0.86729	0.13271	69	10.52590	0.37893	0.62107
15	23.97000	0.86292	0.13708	70	10.17150	0.36617	0.63383
16	23.84820	0.85854	0.14146	71	9.81910	0.35349	0.64651
17	23.72540	0.85412	0.14588	72	9.46950	0.34090	0.65910
18	23.60110	0.84964	0.15036	73	9.12330	0.32844	0.67156
19	23.47390	0.84506	0.15494	74	8.77960	0.31607	0.68393
20	23.34290	0.84035	0.15965	75	8.43740	0.30375	0.69625
21	23.20790	0.83548	0.16452	76	8.09580	0.29145	0.70855
22	23.06910	0.83049	0.16951	77	7.75500	0.27918	0.72082
23	22.92590	0.82533	0.17467	78	7.41570	0.26697	0.73303
24	22.77780	0.82000	0.18000	79	7.07980	0.25487	0.74513
25	22.62450	0.81448	0.18552	80	6.74960	0.24299	0.75701
26	22.46610	0.80878	0.19122	81	6.42740	0.23139	0.76861
27	22.30170	0.80286	0.19714	82	6.11410	0.22011	0.77989
28	22.13220	0.79676	0.20324	83	5.80980	0.20915	0.79085
29	21.95740	0.79047	0.20953	84	5.51230	0.19844	0.80156
30	21.77740	0.78399	0.21601	85	5.22020	0.18793	0.81207
31	21.59230	0.77732	0.22268	86	4.93560	0.17768	0.82232
32	21.40200	0.77047	0.22953	87	4.66190	0.16783	0.83217
33	21.20590	0.76341	0.23659	88	4.39920	0.15837	0.84163
34	21.00420	0.75615	0.24385	89	4.14730	0.14930	0.85070
35	20.79630	0.74867	0.25133	90	3.90620	0.14062	0.85938
36	20.58260	0.74098	0.25902	91	3.67930	0.13246	0.86754
37	20.36290	0.73306	0.26694	92	3.47050	0.12494	0.87506
38	20.13660	0.72492	0.27508	93	3.27880	0.11804	0.88196
39	19.90390	0.71654	0.28346	94	3.10110	0.11164	0.88836
40	19.66430	0.70792	0.29208	95	2.93350	0.10561	0.89439
41	19.41760	0.69903	0.30097	96	2.77670	0.09996	0.90004
42	19.16370	0.68989	0.31011	97	2.63190	0.09475	0.90525
43	18.90290	0.68050	0.31950	98	2.49650	0.08987	0.91013
44	18.63510	0.67086	0.32914	99	2.36500	0.08514	0.91486
45	18.36130	0.66101	0.33899	100	2.23760	0.08055	0.91945
46	18.08130	0.65093	0.34907	101	2.11250	0.07605	0.92395
47	17.79600	0.64066	0.35934	102	1.99020	0.07165	0.92835
48	17.50500	0.63018	0.36982	103	1.86920	0.06729	0.93271
49	17.20850	0.61951	0.38049	104	1.74070	0.06266	0.93734
50	16.90630	0.60863	0.39137	105	1.61510	0.05814	0.94186
51	16.59860	0.59755	0.40245	106	1.45540	0.05240	0.94760
52	16.28630	0.58631	0.41369	107	1.26370	0.04549	0.95451
53	15.96970	0.57491	0.42509	108	0.97120	0.03496	0.96504
54	15.64910	0.56337	0.43663	109	0.48260	0.01737	0.98263

				TABLE S (3.8) SINGLE LIFE FACTORS BASED ON LIFE TABLE 90CM			
				3.8% INTEREST			
AGE	ANNUITY	LIFE ESTATE	REMAINDER	AGE	ANNUITY	LIFE ESTATE	REMAINDER
0	24.13740	0.91722	0.08278	55	14.97310	0.56898	0.43102
1	24.28660	0.92289	0.07711	56	14.65930	0.55705	0.44295
2	24.22750	0.92064	0.07936	57	14.34160	0.54498	0.45502
3	24.16010	0.91808	0.08192	58	14.02110	0.53280	0.46720
4	24.08730	0.91532	0.08468	59	13.69860	0.52055	0.47945
5	24.01010	0.91238	0.08762	60	13.37460	0.50823	0.49177
6	23.92910	0.90931	0.09069	61	13.04870	0.49585	0.50415
7	23.84440	0.90609	0.09391	62	12.72010	0.48336	0.51664
8	23.75610	0.90273	0.09727	63	12.38880	0.47077	0.52923
9	23.66370	0.89922	0.10078	64	12.05550	0.45811	0.54189
10	23.56710	0.89555	0.10445	65	11.72020	0.44537	0.55463
11	23.46650	0.89173	0.10827	66	11.38270	0.43254	0.56746
12	23.36210	0.88776	0.11224	67	11.04220	0.41960	0.58040
13	23.25490	0.88369	0.11631	68	10.69950	0.40658	0.59342
14	23.14630	0.87956	0.12044	69	10.35550	0.39351	0.60649
15	23.03680	0.87540	0.12460	70	10.01170	0.38044	0.61956
16	22.92690	0.87122	0.12878	71	9.66950	0.36744	0.63256
17	22.81610	0.86701	0.13299	72	9.32960	0.35453	0.64547
18	22.70390	0.86275	0.13725	73	8.99280	0.34173	0.65827
19	22.58890	0.85838	0.14162	74	8.65810	0.32901	0.67099
20	22.47040	0.85388	0.14612	75	8.32450	0.31633	0.68367
21	22.34800	0.84922	0.15078	76	7.99120	0.30367	0.69633
22	22.22200	0.84444	0.15556	77	7.65830	0.29102	0.70898
23	22.09180	0.83949	0.16051	78	7.32660	0.27841	0.72159
24	21.95700	0.83437	0.16563	79	6.99780	0.26592	0.73408
25	21.81710	0.82905	0.17095	80	6.67440	0.25363	0.74637
26	21.67230	0.82355	0.17645	81	6.35850	0.24162	0.75838
27	21.52180	0.81783	0.18217	82	6.05110	0.22994	0.77006
28	21.36630	0.81192	0.18808	83	5.75230	0.21859	0.78141
29	21.20570	0.80582	0.19418	84	5.46000	0.20748	0.79252
30	21.04010	0.79952	0.20048	85	5.17260	0.19656	0.80344
31	20.86960	0.79304	0.20696	86	4.89250	0.18592	0.81408
32	20.69390	0.78637	0.21363	87	4.62290	0.17567	0.82433
33	20.51260	0.77948	0.22052	88	4.36390	0.16583	0.83417
34	20.32590	0.77238	0.22762	89	4.11540	0.15638	0.84362
35	20.13310	0.76506	0.23494	90	3.87740	0.14734	0.85266
36	19.93470	0.75752	0.24248	91	3.65340	0.13883	0.86117
37	19.73030	0.74975	0.25025	92	3.44700	0.13099	0.86901
38	19.51950	0.74174	0.25826	93	3.25750	0.12379	0.87621
39	19.30230	0.73349	0.26651	94	3.08180	0.11711	0.88289
40	19.07840	0.72498	0.27502	95	2.91590	0.11081	0.88919
41	18.84740	0.71620	0.28380	96	2.76070	0.10491	0.89509
42	18.60940	0.70716	0.29284	97	2.61740	0.09946	0.90054
43	18.36450	0.69785	0.30215	98	2.48330	0.09436	0.90564
44	18.11270	0.68828	0.31172	99	2.35300	0.08941	0.91059
45	17.85480	0.67848	0.32152	100	2.22670	0.08461	0.91539
46	17.59070	0.66845	0.33155	101	2.10270	0.07990	0.92010
47	17.32120	0.65821	0.34179	102	1.98140	0.07529	0.92471
48	17.04600	0.64775	0.35225	103	1.86130	0.07073	0.92927
49	16.76530	0.63708	0.36292	104	1.73380	0.06588	0.93412
50	16.47870	0.62619	0.37381	105	1.60920	0.06115	0.93885
51	16.18660	0.61509	0.38491	106	1.45060	0.05512	0.94488
52	15.88970	0.60381	0.39619	107	1.26000	0.04788	0.95212
53	15.58840	0.59236	0.40764	108	0.96890	0.03682	0.96318
54	15.28290	0.58075	0.41925	109	0.48170	0.01830	0.98170

TABLE S (4.0)
SINGLE LIFE FACTORS BASED ON LIFE TABLE 90CM

4.0% INTEREST

AGE	ANNUITY	LIFE ESTATE	REMAINDER	AGE	ANNUITY	LIFE ESTATE	REMAINDER
0	23.13420	0.92537	0.07463	55	14.63470	0.58539	0.41461
1	23.28220	0.93129	0.06871	56	14.33480	0.57339	0.42661
2	23.23070	0.92923	0.07077	57	14.03080	0.56123	0.43877
3	23.17140	0.92686	0.07314	58	13.72380	0.54895	0.45105
4	23.10710	0.92429	0.07571	59	13.41460	0.53658	0.46342
5	23.03860	0.92154	0.07846	60	13.10360	0.52414	0.47586
6	22.96650	0.91866	0.08134	61	12.79040	0.51162	0.48838
7	22.89080	0.91563	0.08437	62	12.47430	0.49897	0.50103
8	22.81190	0.91248	0.08752	63	12.15530	0.48621	0.51379
9	22.72910	0.90916	0.09084	64	11.83390	0.47336	0.52664
10	22.64220	0.90569	0.09431	65	11.51040	0.46042	0.53958
11	22.55170	0.90207	0.09793	66	11.18430	0.44737	0.55263
12	22.45740	0.89830	0.10170	67	10.85500	0.43420	0.56580
13	22.36060	0.89442	0.10558	68	10.52310	0.42092	0.57908
14	22.26240	0.89050	0.10950	69	10.18960	0.40758	0.59242
15	22.16350	0.88654	0.11346	70	9.85600	0.39424	0.60576
16	22.06420	0.88257	0.11743	71	9.52360	0.38094	0.61906
17	21.96410	0.87856	0.12144	72	9.19320	0.36773	0.63227
18	21.86260	0.87450	0.12550	73	8.86550	0.35462	0.64538
19	21.75860	0.87034	0.12966	74	8.53950	0.34158	0.65842
20	21.65130	0.86605	0.13395	75	8.21420	0.32857	0.67143
21	21.54020	0.86161	0.13839	76	7.88890	0.31556	0.68444
22	21.42570	0.85703	0.14297	77	7.56370	0.30255	0.69745
23	21.30720	0.85229	0.14771	78	7.23930	0.28957	0.71043
24	21.18430	0.84737	0.15263	79	6.91750	0.27670	0.72330
25	21.05660	0.84226	0.15774	80	6.60060	0.26403	0.73597
26	20.92410	0.83696	0.16304	81	6.29080	0.25163	0.74837
27	20.78610	0.83145	0.16855	82	5.98920	0.23957	0.76043
28	20.64340	0.82574	0.17426	83	5.69580	0.22783	0.77217
29	20.49570	0.81983	0.18017	84	5.40850	0.21634	0.78366
30	20.34320	0.81373	0.18627	85	5.12580	0.20503	0.79497
31	20.18590	0.80744	0.19256	86	4.85000	0.19400	0.80600
32	20.02360	0.80094	0.19906	87	4.58450	0.18338	0.81662
33	19.85590	0.79423	0.20577	88	4.32910	0.17317	0.82683
34	19.68290	0.78732	0.21268	89	4.08390	0.16336	0.83664
35	19.50400	0.78016	0.21984	90	3.84900	0.15396	0.84604
36	19.31960	0.77278	0.22722	91	3.62770	0.14511	0.85489
37	19.12930	0.76517	0.23483	92	3.42380	0.13695	0.86305
38	18.93270	0.75731	0.24269	93	3.23640	0.12946	0.87054
39	18.73000	0.74920	0.25080	94	3.06260	0.12251	0.87749
40	18.52060	0.74082	0.25918	95	2.89850	0.11594	0.88406
41	18.30420	0.73217	0.26783	96	2.74480	0.10979	0.89021
42	18.08090	0.72324	0.27676	97	2.60300	0.10412	0.89588
43	17.85070	0.71403	0.28597	98	2.47010	0.09881	0.90119
44	17.61370	0.70455	0.29545	99	2.34100	0.09364	0.90636
45	17.37070	0.69483	0.30517	100	2.21590	0.08864	0.91136
46	17.12150	0.68486	0.31514	101	2.09300	0.08372	0.91628
47	16.86680	0.67467	0.32533	102	1.97260	0.07890	0.92110
48	16.60640	0.66426	0.33574	103	1.85350	0.07414	0.92586
49	16.34050	0.65362	0.34638	104	1.72700	0.06908	0.93092
50	16.06850	0.64274	0.35726	105	1.60340	0.06413	0.93587
51	15.79100	0.63164	0.36836	106	1.44580	0.05783	0.94217
52	15.50870	0.62035	0.37965	107	1.25640	0.05025	0.94975
53	15.22170	0.60887	0.39113	108	0.96660	0.03866	0.96134
54	14.93040	0.59722	0.40278	109	0.48080	0.01923	0.98077

TABLE S (4.2)
SINGLE LIFE FACTORS BASED ON LIFE TABLE 90CM

4.2% INTEREST

AGE	ANNUITY	LIFE ESTATE	REMAINDER	AGE	ANNUITY	LIFE ESTATE	REMAINDER
0	22.2019	0.93248	0.06752	55	14.3087	0.60097	0.39903
1	22.3483	0.93863	0.06137	56	14.0219	0.58892	0.41108
2	22.3035	0.93675	0.06325	57	13.7310	0.57670	0.42330
3	22.2512	0.93455	0.06545	58	13.4368	0.56434	0.43566
4	22.1943	0.93216	0.06784	59	13.1402	0.55189	0.44811
5	22.1333	0.92960	0.07040	60	12.8415	0.53934	0.46066
6	22.0691	0.92690	0.07310	61	12.5404	0.52670	0.47330
7	22.0014	0.92406	0.07594	62	12.2363	0.51392	0.48608
8	21.9307	0.92109	0.07891	63	11.9290	0.50102	0.49898
9	21.8563	0.91797	0.08203	64	11.6191	0.48800	0.51200
10	21.7781	0.91468	0.08532	65	11.3067	0.47488	0.52512
11	21.6964	0.91125	0.08875	66	10.9916	0.46165	0.53835
12	21.6112	0.90767	0.09233	67	10.6729	0.44826	0.55174
13	21.5236	0.90399	0.09601	68	10.3515	0.43476	0.56524
14	21.4347	0.90026	0.09974	69	10.0281	0.42118	0.57882
15	21.3451	0.89650	0.10350	70	9.7043	0.40758	0.59242
16	21.2553	0.89272	0.10728	71	9.3814	0.39402	0.60598
17	21.1647	0.88892	0.11108	72	9.0601	0.38052	0.61948
18	21.0729	0.88506	0.11494	73	8.7411	0.36713	0.63287
19	20.9787	0.88111	0.11889	74	8.4235	0.35379	0.64621
20	20.8813	0.87702	0.12298	75	8.1064	0.34047	0.65953
21	20.7805	0.87278	0.12722	76	7.7888	0.32713	0.67287
22	20.6763	0.86841	0.13159	77	7.4711	0.31378	0.68622
23	20.5684	0.86387	0.13613	78	7.1538	0.30046	0.69954
24	20.4562	0.85916	0.14084	79	6.8387	0.28722	0.71278
25	20.3395	0.85426	0.14574	80	6.5282	0.27419	0.72581
26	20.2181	0.84916	0.15084	81	6.2245	0.26143	0.73857
27	20.0916	0.84385	0.15615	82	5.9284	0.24899	0.75101
28	19.9604	0.83834	0.16166	83	5.6402	0.23689	0.76311
29	19.8244	0.83263	0.16737	84	5.3578	0.22503	0.77497
30	19.6838	0.82672	0.17328	85	5.0798	0.21335	0.78665
31	19.5386	0.82062	0.17938	86	4.8082	0.20195	0.79805
32	19.3886	0.81432	0.18568	87	4.5466	0.19096	0.80904
33	19.2333	0.80780	0.19220	88	4.2949	0.18038	0.81962
34	19.0729	0.80106	0.19894	89	4.0529	0.17022	0.82978
35	18.9067	0.79408	0.20592	90	3.8210	0.16048	0.83952
36	18.7352	0.78688	0.21312	91	3.6024	0.15130	0.84870
37	18.5579	0.77943	0.22057	92	3.4009	0.14284	0.85716
38	18.3745	0.77173	0.22827	93	3.2156	0.13506	0.86494
39	18.1851	0.76377	0.23623	94	3.0437	0.12784	0.87216
40	17.9891	0.75554	0.24446	95	2.8813	0.12102	0.87898
41	17.7862	0.74702	0.25298	96	2.7292	0.11463	0.88537
42	17.5766	0.73822	0.26178	97	2.5887	0.10873	0.89127
43	17.3601	0.72913	0.27087	98	2.4571	0.10320	0.89680
44	17.1369	0.71975	0.28025	99	2.3292	0.09783	0.90217
45	16.9078	0.71013	0.28987	100	2.2052	0.09262	0.90738
46	16.6724	0.70024	0.29976	101	2.0833	0.08750	0.91250
47	16.4316	0.69013	0.30987	102	1.9639	0.08249	0.91751
48	16.1851	0.67977	0.32023	103	1.8458	0.07753	0.92247
49	15.9330	0.66918	0.33082	104	1.7202	0.07225	0.92775
50	15.6748	0.65834	0.34166	105	1.5975	0.06710	0.93290
51	15.4110	0.64726	0.35274	106	1.4410	0.06052	0.93948
52	15.1424	0.63598	0.36402	107	1.2527	0.05261	0.94739
53	14.8690	0.62450	0.37550	108	0.9643	0.04050	0.95950
54	14.5911	0.61283	0.38717	109	0.4798	0.02015	0.97985

		TABLE S (4.4)						
		SINGLE LIFE FACTORS BASED ON LIFE TABLE 90CM						
		4.4% INTEREST						

AGE	ANNUITY	LIFE ESTATE	REMAINDER	AGE	ANNUITY	LIFE ESTATE	REMAINDER
0	21.3340	0.93870	0.06130	55	13.9945	0.61576	0.38424
1	21.4784	0.94505	0.05495	56	13.7202	0.60369	0.39631
2	21.4394	0.94333	0.05667	57	13.4415	0.59143	0.40857
3	21.3934	0.94131	0.05869	58	13.1595	0.57902	0.42098
4	21.3428	0.93908	0.06092	59	12.8748	0.56649	0.43351
5	21.2885	0.93669	0.06331	60	12.5879	0.55387	0.44613
6	21.2312	0.93417	0.06583	61	12.2985	0.54113	0.45887
7	21.1706	0.93151	0.06849	62	12.0057	0.52825	0.47175
8	21.1071	0.92871	0.07129	63	11.7095	0.51522	0.48478
9	21.0402	0.92577	0.07423	64	11.4106	0.50207	0.49793
10	20.9697	0.92266	0.07734	65	11.1090	0.48879	0.51121
11	20.8958	0.91941	0.08059	66	10.8043	0.47539	0.52461
12	20.8187	0.91602	0.08398	67	10.4959	0.46182	0.53818
13	20.7392	0.91252	0.08748	68	10.1845	0.44812	0.55188
14	20.6586	0.90898	0.09102	69	9.8709	0.43432	0.56568
15	20.5774	0.90540	0.09460	70	9.5565	0.42049	0.57951
16	20.4960	0.90182	0.09818	71	9.2427	0.40668	0.59332
17	20.4139	0.89821	0.10179	72	8.9302	0.39293	0.60707
18	20.3308	0.89455	0.10545	73	8.6197	0.37927	0.62073
19	20.2453	0.89079	0.10921	74	8.3102	0.36565	0.63435
20	20.1569	0.88690	0.11310	75	8.0009	0.35204	0.64796
21	20.0652	0.88287	0.11713	76	7.6909	0.33840	0.66160
22	19.9704	0.87870	0.12130	77	7.3803	0.32474	0.67526
23	19.8719	0.87437	0.12563	78	7.0700	0.31108	0.68892
24	19.7695	0.86986	0.13014	79	6.7614	0.29750	0.70250
25	19.6627	0.86516	0.13484	80	6.4572	0.28412	0.71588
26	19.5514	0.86026	0.13974	81	6.1593	0.27101	0.72899
27	19.4352	0.85515	0.14485	82	5.8687	0.25822	0.74178
28	19.3145	0.84984	0.15016	83	5.5856	0.24577	0.75423
29	19.1893	0.84433	0.15567	84	5.3080	0.23355	0.76645
30	19.0595	0.83862	0.16138	85	5.0344	0.22152	0.77848
31	18.9254	0.83272	0.16728	86	4.7671	0.20975	0.79025
32	18.7865	0.82661	0.17339	87	4.5092	0.19841	0.80159
33	18.6426	0.82028	0.17972	88	4.2611	0.18749	0.81251
34	18.4938	0.81373	0.18627	89	4.0224	0.17698	0.82302
35	18.3393	0.80693	0.19307	90	3.7933	0.16691	0.83309
36	18.1796	0.79990	0.20010	91	3.5774	0.15740	0.84260
37	18.0143	0.79263	0.20737	92	3.3782	0.14864	0.85136
38	17.8431	0.78510	0.21490	93	3.1950	0.14058	0.85942
39	17.6659	0.77730	0.22270	94	3.0250	0.13310	0.86690
40	17.4824	0.76922	0.23078	95	2.8643	0.12603	0.87397
41	17.2921	0.76085	0.23915	96	2.7137	0.11940	0.88060
42	17.0951	0.75218	0.24782	97	2.5746	0.11328	0.88672
43	16.8914	0.74322	0.25678	98	2.4443	0.10755	0.89245
44	16.6811	0.73397	0.26603	99	2.3175	0.10197	0.89803
45	16.4648	0.72445	0.27555	100	2.1946	0.09656	0.90344
46	16.2425	0.71467	0.28533	101	2.0737	0.09124	0.90876
47	16.0147	0.70465	0.29535	102	1.9554	0.08604	0.91396
48	15.7811	0.69437	0.30563	103	1.8382	0.08088	0.91912
49	15.5419	0.68385	0.31615	104	1.7135	0.07540	0.92460
50	15.2968	0.67306	0.32694	105	1.5917	0.07004	0.92996
51	15.0459	0.66202	0.33798	106	1.4363	0.06320	0.93680
52	14.7901	0.65076	0.34924	107	1.2491	0.05496	0.94504
53	14.5295	0.63930	0.36070	108	0.9620	0.04233	0.95767
54	14.2643	0.62763	0.37237	109	0.4789	0.02107	0.97893

TABLE S (4.6)
SINGLE LIFE FACTORS BASED ON LIFE TABLE 90CM

4.6% INTEREST

AGE	ANNUITY	LIFE ESTATE	REMAINDER	AGE	ANNUITY	LIFE ESTATE	REMAINDER
0	20.5247	0.94414	0.05586	55	13.6915	0.62981	0.37019
1	20.6670	0.95068	0.04932	56	13.4290	0.61773	0.38227
2	20.6330	0.94912	0.05088	57	13.1621	0.60545	0.39455
3	20.5923	0.94725	0.05275	58	12.8915	0.59301	0.40699
4	20.5475	0.94518	0.05482	59	12.6183	0.58044	0.41956
5	20.4990	0.94295	0.05705	60	12.3426	0.56776	0.43224
6	20.4477	0.94059	0.05941	61	12.0641	0.55495	0.44505
7	20.3934	0.93809	0.06191	62	11.7822	0.54198	0.45802
8	20.3363	0.93547	0.06453	63	11.4967	0.52885	0.47115
9	20.2760	0.93269	0.06731	64	11.2082	0.51558	0.48442
10	20.2122	0.92976	0.07024	65	10.9169	0.50218	0.49782
11	20.1453	0.92669	0.07331	66	10.6223	0.48863	0.51137
12	20.0754	0.92347	0.07653	67	10.3238	0.47489	0.52511
13	20.0032	0.92015	0.07985	68	10.0219	0.46101	0.53899
14	19.9300	0.91678	0.08322	69	9.7177	0.44701	0.55299
15	19.8562	0.91339	0.08661	70	9.4124	0.43297	0.56703
16	19.7824	0.90999	0.09001	71	9.1074	0.41894	0.58106
17	19.7079	0.90656	0.09344	72	8.8034	0.40496	0.59504
18	19.6325	0.90309	0.09691	73	8.5011	0.39105	0.60895
19	19.5549	0.89953	0.10047	74	8.1995	0.37718	0.62282
20	19.4746	0.89583	0.10417	75	7.8977	0.36329	0.63671
21	19.3911	0.89199	0.10801	76	7.5950	0.34937	0.65063
22	19.3046	0.88801	0.11199	77	7.2915	0.33541	0.66459
23	19.2148	0.88388	0.11612	78	6.9878	0.32144	0.67856
24	19.1211	0.87957	0.12043	79	6.6857	0.30754	0.69246
25	19.0232	0.87507	0.12493	80	6.3875	0.29383	0.70617
26	18.9212	0.87037	0.12963	81	6.0952	0.28038	0.71962
27	18.8143	0.86546	0.13454	82	5.8100	0.26726	0.73274
28	18.7032	0.86035	0.13965	83	5.5319	0.25447	0.74553
29	18.5877	0.85503	0.14497	84	5.2590	0.24191	0.75809
30	18.4679	0.84952	0.15048	85	4.9898	0.22953	0.77047
31	18.3438	0.84382	0.15618	86	4.7265	0.21742	0.78258
32	18.2153	0.83790	0.16210	87	4.4725	0.20573	0.79427
33	18.0818	0.83176	0.16824	88	4.2277	0.19448	0.80552
34	17.9435	0.82540	0.17460	89	3.9922	0.18364	0.81636
35	17.7998	0.81879	0.18121	90	3.7660	0.17324	0.82676
36	17.6510	0.81195	0.18805	91	3.5527	0.16342	0.83658
37	17.4968	0.80486	0.19514	92	3.3558	0.15437	0.84563
38	17.3368	0.79749	0.20251	93	3.1747	0.14604	0.85396
39	17.1710	0.78987	0.21013	94	3.0065	0.13830	0.86170
40	16.9990	0.78195	0.21805	95	2.8475	0.13098	0.86902
41	16.8204	0.77374	0.22626	96	2.6984	0.12413	0.87587
42	16.6351	0.76522	0.23478	97	2.5606	0.11779	0.88221
43	16.4434	0.75640	0.24360	98	2.4315	0.11185	0.88815
44	16.2450	0.74727	0.25273	99	2.3059	0.10607	0.89393
45	16.0408	0.73788	0.26212	100	2.1841	0.10047	0.89953
46	15.8306	0.72821	0.27179	101	2.0642	0.09496	0.90504
47	15.6149	0.71829	0.28171	102	1.9468	0.08955	0.91045
48	15.3935	0.70810	0.29190	103	1.8306	0.08421	0.91579
49	15.1665	0.69766	0.30234	104	1.7069	0.07852	0.92148
50	14.9336	0.68694	0.31306	105	1.5860	0.07296	0.92704
51	14.6949	0.67596	0.32404	106	1.4316	0.06585	0.93415
52	14.4512	0.66475	0.33525	107	1.2455	0.05729	0.94271
53	14.2026	0.65332	0.34668	108	0.9597	0.04415	0.95585
54	13.9494	0.64167	0.35833	109	0.4780	0.02199	0.97801

TABLE S (4.8)
SINGLE LIFE FACTORS BASED ON LIFE TABLE 90CM

4.8% INTEREST

AGE	ANNUITY	LIFE ESTATE	REMAINDER	AGE	ANNUITY	LIFE ESTATE	REMAINDER
0	19.7689	0.94891	0.05109	55	13.3993	0.64317	0.35683
1	19.9088	0.95562	0.04438	56	13.1480	0.63110	0.36890
2	19.8792	0.95420	0.04580	57	12.8921	0.61882	0.38118
3	19.8433	0.95248	0.04752	58	12.6325	0.60636	0.39364
4	19.8034	0.95056	0.04944	59	12.3701	0.59377	0.40623
5	19.7601	0.94848	0.05152	60	12.1051	0.58104	0.41896
6	19.7141	0.94628	0.05372	61	11.8371	0.56818	0.43182
7	19.6653	0.94393	0.05607	62	11.5655	0.55515	0.44485
8	19.6139	0.94147	0.05853	63	11.2903	0.54193	0.45807
9	19.5594	0.93885	0.06115	64	11.0118	0.52857	0.47143
10	19.5017	0.93608	0.06392	65	10.7303	0.51505	0.48495
11	19.4410	0.93317	0.06683	66	10.4454	0.50138	0.49862
12	19.3774	0.93011	0.06989	67	10.1563	0.48750	0.51250
13	19.3117	0.92696	0.07304	68	9.8637	0.47346	0.52654
14	19.2451	0.92376	0.07624	69	9.5685	0.45929	0.54071
15	19.1780	0.92054	0.07946	70	9.2720	0.44505	0.55495
16	19.1109	0.91732	0.08268	71	8.9754	0.43082	0.56918
17	19.0433	0.91408	0.08592	72	8.6796	0.41662	0.58338
18	18.9748	0.91079	0.08921	73	8.3852	0.40249	0.59751
19	18.9043	0.90741	0.09259	74	8.0912	0.38838	0.61162
20	18.8312	0.90390	0.09610	75	7.7968	0.37425	0.62575
21	18.7550	0.90024	0.09976	76	7.5011	0.36005	0.63995
22	18.6762	0.89646	0.10354	77	7.2044	0.34581	0.65419
23	18.5941	0.89252	0.10748	78	6.9073	0.33155	0.66845
24	18.5083	0.88840	0.11160	79	6.6114	0.31735	0.68265
25	18.4186	0.88409	0.11591	80	6.3191	0.30332	0.69668
26	18.3249	0.87959	0.12041	81	6.0324	0.28955	0.71045
27	18.2265	0.87487	0.12513	82	5.7524	0.27611	0.72389
28	18.1242	0.86996	0.13004	83	5.4791	0.26300	0.73700
29	18.0175	0.86484	0.13516	84	5.2108	0.25012	0.74988
30	17.9068	0.85953	0.14047	85	4.9459	0.23740	0.76260
31	17.7919	0.85401	0.14599	86	4.6866	0.22496	0.77504
32	17.6728	0.84829	0.15171	87	4.4362	0.21294	0.78706
33	17.5488	0.84234	0.15766	88	4.1949	0.20135	0.79865
34	17.4203	0.83617	0.16383	89	3.9624	0.19020	0.80980
35	17.2865	0.82975	0.17025	90	3.7391	0.17948	0.82052
36	17.1478	0.82309	0.17691	91	3.5283	0.16936	0.83064
37	17.0038	0.81618	0.18382	92	3.3337	0.16002	0.83998
38	16.8542	0.80900	0.19100	93	3.1546	0.15142	0.84858
39	16.6989	0.80155	0.19845	94	2.9882	0.14343	0.85657
40	16.5376	0.79380	0.20620	95	2.8308	0.13588	0.86412
41	16.3697	0.78575	0.21425	96	2.6832	0.12879	0.87121
42	16.1955	0.77738	0.22262	97	2.5468	0.12225	0.87775
43	16.0148	0.76871	0.23129	98	2.4189	0.11611	0.88389
44	15.8277	0.75973	0.24027	99	2.2945	0.11013	0.88987
45	15.6347	0.75047	0.24953	100	2.1736	0.10433	0.89567
46	15.4358	0.74092	0.25908	101	2.0548	0.09863	0.90137
47	15.2315	0.73111	0.26889	102	1.9384	0.09304	0.90696
48	15.0215	0.72103	0.27897	103	1.8230	0.08751	0.91249
49	14.8060	0.71069	0.28931	104	1.7003	0.08161	0.91839
50	14.5845	0.70005	0.29995	105	1.5803	0.07585	0.92415
51	14.3572	0.68915	0.31085	106	1.4269	0.06849	0.93151
52	14.1250	0.67800	0.32200	107	1.2420	0.05961	0.94039
53	13.8878	0.66661	0.33339	108	0.9574	0.04596	0.95404
54	13.6459	0.65500	0.34500	109	0.4771	0.02290	0.97710

TABLE S (5.0)
SINGLE LIFE FACTORS BASED ON LIFE TABLE 90CM

5.0% INTEREST

AGE	ANNUITY	LIFE ESTATE	REMAINDER	AGE	ANNUITY	LIFE ESTATE	REMAINDER
0	19.0619	0.95309	0.04691	55	13.1173	0.65587	0.34413
1	19.1994	0.95997	0.04003	56	12.8766	0.64383	0.35617
2	19.1736	0.95868	0.04132	57	12.6313	0.63156	0.36844
3	19.1418	0.95709	0.04291	58	12.3821	0.61911	0.38089
4	19.1063	0.95531	0.04469	59	12.1300	0.60650	0.39350
5	19.0675	0.95338	0.04662	60	11.8751	0.59376	0.40624
6	19.0262	0.95131	0.04869	61	11.6172	0.58086	0.41914
7	18.9823	0.94911	0.05089	62	11.3555	0.56777	0.43223
8	18.9359	0.94679	0.05321	63	11.0899	0.55450	0.44550
9	18.8866	0.94433	0.05567	64	10.8211	0.54105	0.45895
10	18.8343	0.94171	0.05829	65	10.5490	0.52745	0.47255
11	18.7791	0.93896	0.06104	66	10.2733	0.51366	0.48634
12	18.7212	0.93606	0.06394	67	9.9933	0.49966	0.50034
13	18.6613	0.93307	0.06693	68	9.7096	0.48548	0.51452
14	18.6006	0.93003	0.06997	69	9.4231	0.47115	0.52885
15	18.5395	0.92697	0.07303	70	9.1350	0.45675	0.54325
16	18.4784	0.92392	0.07608	71	8.8466	0.44233	0.55767
17	18.4169	0.92084	0.07916	72	8.5587	0.42794	0.57206
18	18.3546	0.91773	0.08227	73	8.2719	0.41360	0.58640
19	18.2904	0.91452	0.08548	74	7.9853	0.39927	0.60073
20	18.2238	0.91119	0.08881	75	7.6980	0.38490	0.61510
21	18.1544	0.90772	0.09228	76	7.4093	0.37046	0.62954
22	18.0824	0.90412	0.09588	77	7.1192	0.35596	0.64404
23	18.0072	0.90036	0.09964	78	6.8283	0.34142	0.65858
24	17.9287	0.89643	0.10357	79	6.5385	0.32692	0.67308
25	17.8463	0.89232	0.10768	80	6.2519	0.31260	0.68740
26	17.7601	0.88801	0.11199	81	5.9706	0.29853	0.70147
27	17.6696	0.88348	0.11652	82	5.6957	0.28478	0.71522
28	17.5751	0.87876	0.12124	83	5.4272	0.27136	0.72864
29	17.4766	0.87383	0.12617	84	5.1633	0.25817	0.74183
30	17.3741	0.86871	0.13129	85	4.9026	0.24513	0.75487
31	17.2678	0.86339	0.13661	86	4.6473	0.23236	0.76764
32	17.1572	0.85786	0.14214	87	4.4005	0.22002	0.77998
33	17.0420	0.85210	0.14790	88	4.1625	0.20812	0.79188
34	16.9225	0.84612	0.15388	89	3.9331	0.19665	0.80335
35	16.7978	0.83989	0.16011	90	3.7125	0.18563	0.81437
36	16.6683	0.83342	0.16658	91	3.5042	0.17521	0.82479
37	16.5338	0.82669	0.17331	92	3.3119	0.16559	0.83441
38	16.3938	0.81969	0.18031	93	3.1347	0.15674	0.84326
39	16.2483	0.81241	0.18759	94	2.9701	0.14851	0.85149
40	16.0968	0.80484	0.19516	95	2.8144	0.14072	0.85928
41	15.9391	0.79695	0.20305	96	2.6682	0.13341	0.86659
42	15.7750	0.78875	0.21125	97	2.5331	0.12665	0.87335
43	15.6046	0.78023	0.21977	98	2.4064	0.12032	0.87968
44	15.4279	0.77140	0.22860	99	2.2831	0.11415	0.88585
45	15.2455	0.76228	0.23772	100	2.1633	0.10817	0.89183
46	15.0572	0.75286	0.24714	101	2.0455	0.10228	0.89772
47	14.8636	0.74318	0.25682	102	1.9300	0.09650	0.90350
48	14.6643	0.73322	0.26678	103	1.8156	0.09078	0.90922
49	14.4595	0.72298	0.27702	104	1.6937	0.08468	0.91532
50	14.2488	0.71244	0.28756	105	1.5746	0.07873	0.92127
51	14.0323	0.70162	0.29838	106	1.4223	0.07111	0.92889
52	13.8109	0.69054	0.30946	107	1.2384	0.06192	0.93808
53	13.5844	0.67922	0.32078	108	0.9551	0.04776	0.95224
54	13.3533	0.66766	0.33234	109	0.4762	0.02381	0.97619

TABLE S (5.2)
SINGLE LIFE FACTORS BASED ON LIFE TABLE 90CM

5.2% INTEREST

AGE	ANNUITY	LIFE ESTATE	REMAINDER	AGE	ANNUITY	LIFE ESTATE	REMAINDER
0	18.3996	0.95678	0.04322	55	12.8451	0.66795	0.33205
1	18.5345	0.96380	0.03620	56	12.6144	0.65595	0.34405
2	18.5121	0.96263	0.03737	57	12.3791	0.64371	0.35629
3	18.4840	0.96117	0.03883	58	12.1399	0.63127	0.36873
4	18.4522	0.95952	0.04048	59	11.8976	0.61867	0.38133
5	18.4175	0.95771	0.04229	60	11.6524	0.60592	0.39408
6	18.3803	0.95578	0.04422	61	11.4040	0.59301	0.40699
7	18.3407	0.95372	0.04628	62	11.1517	0.57989	0.42011
8	18.2988	0.95154	0.04846	63	10.8955	0.56657	0.43343
9	18.2541	0.94921	0.05079	64	10.6358	0.55306	0.44694
10	18.2066	0.94674	0.05326	65	10.3728	0.53938	0.46062
11	18.1563	0.94413	0.05587	66	10.1059	0.52551	0.47449
12	18.1035	0.94138	0.05862	67	9.8347	0.51140	0.48860
13	18.0488	0.93854	0.06146	68	9.5595	0.49709	0.50291
14	17.9933	0.93565	0.06435	69	9.2813	0.48263	0.51737
15	17.9376	0.93275	0.06725	70	9.0014	0.46807	0.53193
16	17.8819	0.92986	0.07014	71	8.7210	0.45349	0.54651
17	17.8259	0.92694	0.07306	72	8.4407	0.43892	0.56108
18	17.7691	0.92399	0.07601	73	8.1613	0.42439	0.57561
19	17.7107	0.92096	0.07904	74	7.8818	0.40985	0.59015
20	17.6499	0.91780	0.08220	75	7.6014	0.39527	0.60473
21	17.5865	0.91450	0.08550	76	7.3193	0.38060	0.61940
22	17.5207	0.91107	0.08893	77	7.0356	0.36585	0.63415
23	17.4519	0.90750	0.09250	78	6.7510	0.35105	0.64895
24	17.3798	0.90375	0.09625	79	6.4670	0.33628	0.66372
25	17.3042	0.89982	0.10018	80	6.1860	0.32167	0.67833
26	17.2249	0.89569	0.10431	81	5.9100	0.30732	0.69268
27	17.1413	0.89135	0.10865	82	5.6400	0.29328	0.70672
28	17.0541	0.88681	0.11319	83	5.3762	0.27956	0.72044
29	16.9630	0.88208	0.11792	84	5.1166	0.26607	0.73393
30	16.8681	0.87714	0.12286	85	4.8601	0.25272	0.74728
31	16.7695	0.87201	0.12799	86	4.6085	0.23964	0.76036
32	16.6668	0.86667	0.13333	87	4.3653	0.22699	0.77301
33	16.5598	0.86111	0.13889	88	4.1305	0.21479	0.78521
34	16.4484	0.85532	0.14468	89	3.9041	0.20301	0.79699
35	16.3321	0.84927	0.15073	90	3.6863	0.19169	0.80831
36	16.2113	0.84299	0.15701	91	3.4805	0.18098	0.81902
37	16.0855	0.83644	0.16356	92	3.2903	0.17109	0.82891
38	15.9543	0.82962	0.17038	93	3.1151	0.16199	0.83801
39	15.8178	0.82253	0.17747	94	2.9523	0.15352	0.84648
40	15.6756	0.81513	0.18487	95	2.7981	0.14550	0.85450
41	15.5272	0.80741	0.19259	96	2.6533	0.13797	0.86203
42	15.3726	0.79938	0.20062	97	2.5195	0.13102	0.86898
43	15.2119	0.79102	0.20898	98	2.3940	0.12449	0.87551
44	15.0449	0.78234	0.21766	99	2.2718	0.11813	0.88187
45	14.8723	0.77336	0.22664	100	2.1531	0.11196	0.88804
46	14.6940	0.76409	0.23591	101	2.0362	0.10588	0.89412
47	14.5103	0.75454	0.24546	102	1.9217	0.09993	0.90007
48	14.3211	0.74470	0.25530	103	1.8081	0.09402	0.90598
49	14.1264	0.73457	0.26543	104	1.6872	0.08773	0.91227
50	13.9258	0.72414	0.27586	105	1.5690	0.08159	0.91841
51	13.7196	0.71342	0.28658	106	1.4176	0.07372	0.92628
52	13.5083	0.70243	0.29757	107	1.2349	0.06421	0.93579
53	13.2920	0.69118	0.30882	108	0.9529	0.04955	0.95045
54	13.0710	0.67969	0.32031	109	0.4753	0.02471	0.97529

TABLE S (5.4)
SINGLE LIFE FACTORS BASED ON LIFE TABLE 90CM

5.4% INTEREST

AGE	ANNUITY	LIFE ESTATE	REMAINDER	AGE	ANNUITY	LIFE ESTATE	REMAINDER
0	17.7782	0.96002	0.03998	55	12.5823	0.67944	0.32056
1	17.9106	0.96717	0.03283	56	12.3611	0.66750	0.33250
2	17.8911	0.96612	0.03388	57	12.1353	0.65531	0.34469
3	17.8661	0.96477	0.03523	58	11.9055	0.64290	0.35710
4	17.8378	0.96324	0.03676	59	11.6725	0.63032	0.36968
5	17.8066	0.96155	0.03845	60	11.4365	0.61757	0.38243
6	17.7731	0.95975	0.04025	61	11.1973	0.60465	0.39535
7	17.7373	0.95781	0.04219	62	10.9540	0.59152	0.40848
8	17.6993	0.95576	0.04424	63	10.7067	0.57816	0.42184
9	17.6588	0.95357	0.04643	64	10.4558	0.56461	0.43539
10	17.6155	0.95123	0.04877	65	10.2014	0.55088	0.44912
11	17.5696	0.94876	0.05124	66	9.9431	0.53693	0.46307
12	17.5213	0.94615	0.05385	67	9.6802	0.52273	0.47727
13	17.4713	0.94345	0.05655	68	9.4133	0.50832	0.49168
14	17.4205	0.94071	0.05929	69	9.1432	0.49373	0.50627
15	17.3696	0.93796	0.06204	70	8.8711	0.47904	0.52096
16	17.3187	0.93521	0.06479	71	8.5983	0.46431	0.53569
17	17.2676	0.93245	0.06755	72	8.3254	0.44957	0.55043
18	17.2159	0.92966	0.07034	73	8.0531	0.43487	0.56513
19	17.1626	0.92678	0.07322	74	7.7806	0.42015	0.57985
20	17.1071	0.92378	0.07622	75	7.5068	0.40537	0.59463
21	17.0491	0.92065	0.07935	76	7.2312	0.39048	0.60952
22	16.9889	0.91740	0.08260	77	6.9537	0.37550	0.62450
23	16.9258	0.91399	0.08601	78	6.6751	0.36045	0.63955
24	16.8597	0.91042	0.08958	79	6.3968	0.34543	0.65457
25	16.7901	0.90666	0.09334	80	6.1213	0.33055	0.66945
26	16.7170	0.90272	0.09728	81	5.8504	0.31592	0.68408
27	16.6399	0.89856	0.10144	82	5.5852	0.30160	0.69840
28	16.5593	0.89420	0.10580	83	5.3259	0.28760	0.71240
29	16.4750	0.88965	0.11035	84	5.0707	0.27382	0.72618
30	16.3870	0.88490	0.11510	85	4.8181	0.26018	0.73982
31	16.2955	0.87996	0.12004	86	4.5704	0.24680	0.75320
32	16.2001	0.87480	0.12520	87	4.3306	0.23385	0.76615
33	16.1004	0.86942	0.13058	88	4.0990	0.22135	0.77865
34	15.9967	0.86382	0.13618	89	3.8755	0.20928	0.79072
35	15.8882	0.85796	0.14204	90	3.6604	0.19766	0.80234
36	15.7752	0.85186	0.14814	91	3.4570	0.18668	0.81332
37	15.6575	0.84550	0.15450	92	3.2689	0.17652	0.82348
38	15.5345	0.83887	0.16113	93	3.0957	0.16717	0.83283
39	15.4065	0.83195	0.16805	94	2.9346	0.15847	0.84153
40	15.2727	0.82473	0.17527	95	2.7820	0.15023	0.84977
41	15.1330	0.81718	0.18282	96	2.6386	0.14249	0.85751
42	14.9873	0.80931	0.19069	97	2.5061	0.13533	0.86467
43	14.8356	0.80112	0.19888	98	2.3818	0.12862	0.87138
44	14.6777	0.79260	0.20740	99	2.2606	0.12207	0.87793
45	14.5144	0.78378	0.21622	100	2.1429	0.11572	0.88428
46	14.3453	0.77464	0.22536	101	2.0271	0.10946	0.89054
47	14.1710	0.76524	0.23476	102	1.9134	0.10332	0.89668
48	13.9913	0.75553	0.24447	103	1.8008	0.09724	0.90276
49	13.8061	0.74553	0.25447	104	1.6807	0.09076	0.90924
50	13.6150	0.73521	0.26479	105	1.5634	0.08442	0.91558
51	13.4184	0.72459	0.27541	106	1.4130	0.07630	0.92370
52	13.2167	0.71370	0.28630	107	1.2313	0.06649	0.93351
53	13.0100	0.70254	0.29746	108	0.9506	0.05133	0.94867
54	12.7986	0.69112	0.30888	109	0.4744	0.02562	0.97438

		TABLE S (5.6)					
		SINGLE LIFE FACTORS BASED ON LIFE TABLE 90CM					
		5.6% INTEREST					
AGE	ANNUITY	LIFE ESTATE	REMAINDER	AGE	ANNUITY	LIFE ESTATE	REMAINDER
0	17.1944	0.96289	0.03711	55	12.3284	0.69039	0.30961
1	17.3242	0.97015	0.02985	56	12.1163	0.67851	0.32149
2	17.3073	0.96921	0.03079	57	11.8995	0.66637	0.33363
3	17.2851	0.96797	0.03203	58	11.6787	0.65400	0.34600
4	17.2597	0.96654	0.03346	59	11.4545	0.64145	0.35855
5	17.2316	0.96497	0.03503	60	11.2273	0.62873	0.37127
6	17.2014	0.96328	0.03672	61	10.9968	0.61582	0.38418
7	17.1690	0.96146	0.03854	62	10.7622	0.60268	0.39732
8	17.1346	0.95954	0.04046	63	10.5234	0.58931	0.41069
9	17.0977	0.95747	0.04253	64	10.2809	0.57573	0.42427
10	17.0582	0.95526	0.04474	65	10.0348	0.56195	0.43805
11	17.0162	0.95291	0.04709	66	9.7847	0.54794	0.45206
12	16.9720	0.95043	0.04957	67	9.5299	0.53367	0.46633
13	16.9261	0.94786	0.05214	68	9.2709	0.51917	0.48083
14	16.8796	0.94526	0.05474	69	9.0085	0.50448	0.49552
15	16.8330	0.94265	0.05735	70	8.7440	0.48966	0.51034
16	16.7865	0.94004	0.05996	71	8.4785	0.47480	0.52520
17	16.7398	0.93743	0.06257	72	8.2128	0.45991	0.54009
18	16.6926	0.93479	0.06521	73	7.9474	0.44505	0.55495
19	16.6439	0.93206	0.06794	74	7.6815	0.43016	0.56984
20	16.5932	0.92922	0.07078	75	7.4142	0.41520	0.58480
21	16.5401	0.92625	0.07375	76	7.1449	0.40011	0.59989
22	16.4849	0.92315	0.07685	77	6.8735	0.38491	0.61509
23	16.4270	0.91991	0.08009	78	6.6006	0.36964	0.63036
24	16.3663	0.91651	0.08349	79	6.3280	0.35437	0.64563
25	16.3022	0.91292	0.08708	80	6.0577	0.33923	0.66077
26	16.2348	0.90915	0.09085	81	5.7918	0.32434	0.67566
27	16.1636	0.90516	0.09484	82	5.5314	0.30976	0.69024
28	16.0890	0.90099	0.09901	83	5.2765	0.29549	0.70451
29	16.0109	0.89661	0.10339	84	5.0255	0.28143	0.71857
30	15.9293	0.89204	0.10796	85	4.7769	0.26750	0.73250
31	15.8442	0.88728	0.11272	86	4.5327	0.25383	0.74617
32	15.7555	0.88231	0.11769	87	4.2964	0.24060	0.75940
33	15.6627	0.87711	0.12289	88	4.0679	0.22780	0.77220
34	15.5659	0.87169	0.12831	89	3.8473	0.21545	0.78455
35	15.4645	0.86601	0.13399	90	3.6348	0.20355	0.79645
36	15.3589	0.86010	0.13990	91	3.4338	0.19229	0.80771
37	15.2486	0.85392	0.14608	92	3.2479	0.18188	0.81812
38	15.1333	0.84747	0.15253	93	3.0765	0.17229	0.82771
39	15.0130	0.84073	0.15927	94	2.9171	0.16336	0.83664
40	14.8872	0.83369	0.16631	95	2.7660	0.15490	0.84510
41	14.7556	0.82632	0.17368	96	2.6241	0.14695	0.85305
42	14.6182	0.81862	0.18138	97	2.4928	0.13960	0.86040
43	14.4748	0.81059	0.18941	98	2.3696	0.13270	0.86730
44	14.3255	0.80223	0.19777	99	2.2496	0.12598	0.87402
45	14.1707	0.79356	0.20644	100	2.1329	0.11944	0.88056
46	14.0104	0.78458	0.21542	101	2.0180	0.11301	0.88699
47	13.8449	0.77532	0.22468	102	1.9052	0.10669	0.89331
48	13.6741	0.76575	0.23425	103	1.7935	0.10043	0.89957
49	13.4978	0.75588	0.24412	104	1.6743	0.09376	0.90624
50	13.3158	0.74568	0.25432	105	1.5578	0.08724	0.91276
51	13.1281	0.73518	0.26482	106	1.4085	0.07887	0.92113
52	12.9355	0.72439	0.27561	107	1.2279	0.06876	0.93124
53	12.7380	0.71333	0.28667	108	0.9484	0.05311	0.94689
54	12.5356	0.70199	0.29801	109	0.4735	0.02652	0.97348

				TABLE S (5.8) SINGLE LIFE FACTORS BASED ON LIFE TABLE 90CM				
				5.8% INTEREST				
AGE	ANNUITY	LIFE ESTATE	REMAINDER	AGE	ANNUITY	LIFE ESTATE	REMAINDER
0	16.6452	0.96542	0.03458	55	12.0830	0.70082	0.29918
1	16.7723	0.97279	0.02721	56	11.8796	0.68901	0.31099
2	16.7576	0.97194	0.02806	57	11.6713	0.67694	0.32306
3	16.7379	0.97080	0.02920	58	11.4590	0.66462	0.33538
4	16.7152	0.96948	0.03052	59	11.2433	0.65211	0.34789
5	16.6899	0.96801	0.03199	60	11.0246	0.63942	0.36058
6	16.6626	0.96643	0.03357	61	10.8023	0.62653	0.37347
7	16.6331	0.96472	0.03528	62	10.5759	0.61340	0.38660
8	16.6018	0.96291	0.03709	63	10.3453	0.60003	0.39997
9	16.5682	0.96096	0.03904	64	10.1109	0.58643	0.41357
10	16.5321	0.95886	0.04114	65	9.8728	0.57262	0.42738
11	16.4937	0.95664	0.04336	66	9.6305	0.55857	0.44143
12	16.4531	0.95428	0.04572	67	9.3834	0.54424	0.45576
13	16.4110	0.95184	0.04816	68	9.1320	0.52966	0.47034
14	16.3683	0.94936	0.05064	69	8.8771	0.51487	0.48513
15	16.3255	0.94688	0.05312	70	8.6199	0.49996	0.50004
16	16.2829	0.94441	0.05559	71	8.3615	0.48497	0.51503
17	16.2402	0.94193	0.05807	72	8.1027	0.46996	0.53004
18	16.1971	0.93943	0.06057	73	7.8440	0.45495	0.54505
19	16.1526	0.93685	0.06315	74	7.5846	0.43991	0.56009
20	16.1062	0.93416	0.06584	75	7.3236	0.42477	0.57523
21	16.0575	0.93134	0.06866	76	7.0603	0.40950	0.59050
22	16.0068	0.92840	0.07160	77	6.7948	0.39410	0.60590
23	15.9537	0.92532	0.07468	78	6.5276	0.37860	0.62140
24	15.8978	0.92207	0.07793	79	6.2604	0.36310	0.63690
25	15.8387	0.91865	0.08135	80	5.9953	0.34773	0.65227
26	15.7765	0.91504	0.08496	81	5.7343	0.33259	0.66741
27	15.7107	0.91122	0.08878	82	5.4785	0.31775	0.68225
28	15.6416	0.90721	0.09279	83	5.2280	0.30322	0.69678
29	15.5692	0.90301	0.09699	84	4.9810	0.28890	0.71110
30	15.4934	0.89862	0.10138	85	4.7362	0.27470	0.72530
31	15.4143	0.89403	0.10597	86	4.4957	0.26075	0.73925
32	15.3317	0.88924	0.11076	87	4.2626	0.24723	0.75277
33	15.2452	0.88422	0.11578	88	4.0372	0.23416	0.76584
34	15.1548	0.87898	0.12102	89	3.8195	0.22153	0.77847
35	15.0601	0.87348	0.12652	90	3.6096	0.20936	0.79064
36	14.9612	0.86775	0.13225	91	3.4109	0.19783	0.80217
37	14.8578	0.86175	0.13825	92	3.2270	0.18717	0.81283
38	14.7496	0.85548	0.14452	93	3.0576	0.17734	0.82266
39	14.6365	0.84892	0.15108	94	2.8998	0.16819	0.83181
40	14.5182	0.84205	0.15795	95	2.7502	0.15951	0.84049
41	14.3941	0.83486	0.16514	96	2.6097	0.15136	0.84864
42	14.2643	0.82733	0.17267	97	2.4797	0.14382	0.85618
43	14.1288	0.81947	0.18053	98	2.3576	0.13674	0.86326
44	13.9874	0.81127	0.18873	99	2.2386	0.12984	0.87016
45	13.8408	0.80276	0.19724	100	2.1229	0.12313	0.87687
46	13.6886	0.79394	0.20606	101	2.0090	0.11652	0.88348
47	13.5314	0.78482	0.21518	102	1.8971	0.11003	0.88997
48	13.3689	0.77540	0.22460	103	1.7862	0.10360	0.89640
49	13.2010	0.76566	0.23434	104	1.6679	0.09674	0.90326
50	13.0275	0.75559	0.24441	105	1.5523	0.09003	0.90997
51	12.8484	0.74521	0.25479	106	1.4039	0.08143	0.91857
52	12.6644	0.73453	0.26547	107	1.2244	0.07101	0.92899
53	12.4754	0.72357	0.27643	108	0.9462	0.05488	0.94512
54	12.2817	0.71234	0.28766	109	0.4726	0.02741	0.97259

TABLE S (6.0)
SINGLE LIFE FACTORS BASED ON LIFE TABLE 90CM

6.0% INTEREST

AGE	ANNUITY	LIFE ESTATE	REMAINDER	AGE	ANNUITY	LIFE ESTATE	REMAINDER
0	16.1278	0.96767	0.03233	55	11.8459	0.71075	0.28925
1	16.2522	0.97513	0.02487	56	11.6505	0.69903	0.30097
2	16.2395	0.97437	0.02563	57	11.4505	0.68703	0.31297
3	16.2220	0.97332	0.02668	58	11.2463	0.67478	0.32522
4	16.2016	0.97209	0.02791	59	11.0387	0.66232	0.33768
5	16.1787	0.97072	0.02928	60	10.8279	0.64967	0.35033
6	16.1540	0.96924	0.03076	61	10.6136	0.63682	0.36318
7	16.1273	0.96764	0.03236	62	10.3951	0.62371	0.37629
8	16.0988	0.96593	0.03407	63	10.1723	0.61034	0.38966
9	16.0680	0.96408	0.03592	64	9.9456	0.59674	0.40326
10	16.0350	0.96210	0.03790	65	9.7151	0.58291	0.41709
11	15.9997	0.95998	0.04002	66	9.4804	0.56882	0.43118
12	15.9624	0.95774	0.04226	67	9.2407	0.55444	0.44556
13	15.9236	0.95542	0.04458	68	8.9967	0.53980	0.46020
14	15.8844	0.95306	0.04694	69	8.7490	0.52494	0.47506
15	15.8450	0.95070	0.04930	70	8.4988	0.50993	0.49007
16	15.8060	0.94836	0.05164	71	8.2473	0.49484	0.50516
17	15.7669	0.94601	0.05399	72	7.9951	0.47971	0.52029
18	15.7274	0.94364	0.05636	73	7.7429	0.46457	0.53543
19	15.6867	0.94120	0.05880	74	7.4898	0.44939	0.55061
20	15.6441	0.93865	0.06135	75	7.2349	0.43409	0.56591
21	15.5995	0.93597	0.06403	76	6.9775	0.41865	0.58135
22	15.5530	0.93318	0.06682	77	6.7177	0.40306	0.59694
23	15.5041	0.93025	0.06975	78	6.4560	0.38736	0.61264
24	15.4526	0.92716	0.07284	79	6.1941	0.37164	0.62836
25	15.3981	0.92389	0.07611	80	5.9340	0.35604	0.64396
26	15.3407	0.92044	0.07956	81	5.6778	0.34067	0.65933
27	15.2797	0.91678	0.08322	82	5.4265	0.32559	0.67441
28	15.2157	0.91294	0.08706	83	5.1801	0.31081	0.68919
29	15.1484	0.90891	0.09109	84	4.9372	0.29623	0.70377
30	15.0780	0.90468	0.09532	85	4.6961	0.28177	0.71823
31	15.0044	0.90026	0.09974	86	4.4592	0.26755	0.73245
32	14.9274	0.89565	0.10435	87	4.2294	0.25376	0.74624
33	14.8467	0.89080	0.10920	88	4.0070	0.24042	0.75958
34	14.7623	0.88574	0.11426	89	3.7920	0.22752	0.77248
35	14.6737	0.88042	0.11958	90	3.5847	0.21508	0.78492
36	14.5810	0.87486	0.12514	91	3.3882	0.20329	0.79671
37	14.4841	0.86904	0.13096	92	3.2065	0.19239	0.80761
38	14.3824	0.86295	0.13705	93	3.0388	0.18233	0.81767
39	14.2761	0.85656	0.14344	94	2.8827	0.17296	0.82704
40	14.1646	0.84987	0.15013	95	2.7346	0.16408	0.83592
41	14.0475	0.84285	0.15715	96	2.5955	0.15573	0.84427
42	13.9249	0.83550	0.16450	97	2.4666	0.14800	0.85200
43	13.7967	0.82780	0.17220	98	2.3457	0.14074	0.85926
44	13.6628	0.81977	0.18023	99	2.2278	0.13367	0.86633
45	13.5237	0.81142	0.18858	100	2.1130	0.12678	0.87322
46	13.3792	0.80275	0.19725	101	2.0000	0.12000	0.88000
47	13.2298	0.79379	0.20621	102	1.8890	0.11334	0.88666
48	13.0751	0.78451	0.21549	103	1.7790	0.10674	0.89326
49	12.9152	0.77491	0.22509	104	1.6616	0.09969	0.90031
50	12.7497	0.76498	0.23502	105	1.5468	0.09281	0.90719
51	12.5787	0.75472	0.24528	106	1.3994	0.08396	0.91604
52	12.4027	0.74416	0.25584	107	1.2209	0.07325	0.92675
53	12.2219	0.73331	0.26669	108	0.9439	0.05664	0.94336
54	12.0363	0.72218	0.27782	109	0.4717	0.02830	0.97170

TABLE S (6.2)
SINGLE LIFE FACTORS BASED ON LIFE TABLE 90CM

6.2% INTEREST

AGE	ANNUITY	LIFE ESTATE	REMAINDER	AGE	ANNUITY	LIFE ESTATE	REMAINDER
0	15.6396	0.96966	0.03034	55	11.6165	0.72022	0.27978
1	15.7615	0.97721	0.02279	56	11.4290	0.70860	0.29140
2	15.7505	0.97653	0.02347	57	11.2366	0.69667	0.30333
3	15.7349	0.97556	0.02444	58	11.0402	0.68449	0.31551
4	15.7165	0.97442	0.02558	59	10.8403	0.67210	0.32790
5	15.6959	0.97314	0.02686	60	10.6371	0.65950	0.34050
6	15.6734	0.97175	0.02825	61	10.4304	0.64669	0.35331
7	15.6491	0.97024	0.02976	62	10.2195	0.63361	0.36639
8	15.6231	0.96863	0.03137	63	10.0041	0.62026	0.37974
9	15.5950	0.96689	0.03311	64	9.7849	0.60666	0.39334
10	15.5646	0.96501	0.03499	65	9.5617	0.59282	0.40718
11	15.5322	0.96300	0.03700	66	9.3342	0.57872	0.42128
12	15.4978	0.96087	0.03913	67	9.1017	0.56431	0.43569
13	15.4621	0.95865	0.04135	68	8.8648	0.54962	0.45038
14	15.4259	0.95641	0.04359	69	8.6240	0.53469	0.46531
15	15.3897	0.95416	0.04584	70	8.3806	0.51960	0.48040
16	15.3538	0.95194	0.04806	71	8.1357	0.50442	0.49558
17	15.3180	0.94971	0.05029	72	7.8900	0.48918	0.51082
18	15.2818	0.94747	0.05253	73	7.6440	0.47393	0.52607
19	15.2445	0.94516	0.05484	74	7.3970	0.45861	0.54139
20	15.2054	0.94274	0.05726	75	7.1480	0.44317	0.55683
21	15.1644	0.94020	0.05980	76	6.8963	0.42757	0.57243
22	15.1217	0.93754	0.06246	77	6.6421	0.41181	0.58819
23	15.0767	0.93476	0.06524	78	6.3858	0.39592	0.60408
24	15.0292	0.93181	0.06819	79	6.1290	0.37999	0.62001
25	14.9789	0.92869	0.07131	80	5.8738	0.36418	0.63582
26	14.9258	0.92540	0.07460	81	5.6222	0.34858	0.65142
27	14.8693	0.92190	0.07810	82	5.3753	0.33327	0.66673
28	14.8099	0.91821	0.08179	83	5.1331	0.31825	0.68175
29	14.7474	0.91434	0.08566	84	4.8940	0.30343	0.69657
30	14.6819	0.91027	0.08973	85	4.6567	0.28872	0.71128
31	14.6133	0.90602	0.09398	86	4.4232	0.27424	0.72576
32	14.5415	0.90157	0.09843	87	4.1966	0.26019	0.73981
33	14.4661	0.89690	0.10310	88	3.9772	0.24658	0.75342
34	14.3872	0.89201	0.10799	89	3.7649	0.23342	0.76658
35	14.3042	0.88686	0.11314	90	3.5600	0.22072	0.77928
36	14.2174	0.88148	0.11852	91	3.3659	0.20869	0.79131
37	14.1264	0.87584	0.12416	92	3.1861	0.19754	0.80246
38	14.0308	0.86991	0.13009	93	3.0203	0.18726	0.81274
39	13.9307	0.86371	0.13629	94	2.8658	0.17768	0.82232
40	13.8256	0.85719	0.14281	95	2.7192	0.16859	0.83141
41	13.7151	0.85034	0.14966	96	2.5813	0.16004	0.83996
42	13.5993	0.84315	0.15685	97	2.4537	0.15213	0.84787
43	13.4779	0.83563	0.16437	98	2.3339	0.14470	0.85530
44	13.3510	0.82776	0.17224	99	2.2170	0.13745	0.86255
45	13.2190	0.81958	0.18042	100	2.1032	0.13040	0.86960
46	13.0817	0.81107	0.18893	101	1.9911	0.12345	0.87655
47	12.9396	0.80225	0.19775	102	1.8810	0.11662	0.88338
48	12.7923	0.79312	0.20688	103	1.7719	0.10985	0.89015
49	12.6399	0.78367	0.21633	104	1.6553	0.10263	0.89737
50	12.4819	0.77388	0.22612	105	1.5414	0.09557	0.90443
51	12.3185	0.76375	0.23625	106	1.3949	0.08649	0.91351
52	12.1502	0.75331	0.24669	107	1.2175	0.07548	0.92452
53	11.9771	0.74258	0.25742	108	0.9417	0.05839	0.94161
54	11.7992	0.73155	0.26845	109	0.4708	0.02919	0.97081

TABLE S (6.4)
SINGLE LIFE FACTORS BASED ON LIFE TABLE 90CM

6.4% INTEREST

AGE	ANNUITY	LIFE ESTATE	REMAINDER	AGE	ANNUITY	LIFE ESTATE	REMAINDER
0	15.1785	0.97143	0.02857	55	11.3947	0.72926	0.27074
1	15.2978	0.97906	0.02094	56	11.2145	0.71773	0.28227
2	15.2884	0.97845	0.02155	57	11.0295	0.70589	0.29411
3	15.2745	0.97757	0.02243	58	10.8404	0.69379	0.30621
4	15.2579	0.97651	0.02349	59	10.6479	0.68146	0.31854
5	15.2392	0.97531	0.02469	60	10.4520	0.66893	0.33107
6	15.2188	0.97400	0.02600	61	10.2526	0.65616	0.34384
7	15.1966	0.97258	0.02742	62	10.0488	0.64312	0.35688
8	15.1728	0.97106	0.02894	63	9.8407	0.62980	0.37020
9	15.1471	0.96941	0.03059	64	9.6285	0.61622	0.38378
10	15.1192	0.96763	0.03237	65	9.4124	0.60239	0.39761
11	15.0893	0.96572	0.03428	66	9.1918	0.58828	0.41172
12	15.0576	0.96368	0.03632	67	8.9663	0.57384	0.42616
13	15.0245	0.96157	0.03843	68	8.7361	0.55911	0.44089
14	14.9911	0.95943	0.04057	69	8.5020	0.54413	0.45587
15	14.9578	0.95730	0.04270	70	8.2652	0.52897	0.47103
16	14.9248	0.95518	0.04482	71	8.0267	0.51371	0.48629
17	14.8918	0.95308	0.04692	72	7.7872	0.49838	0.50162
18	14.8586	0.95095	0.04905	73	7.5473	0.48303	0.51697
19	14.8244	0.94876	0.05124	74	7.3061	0.46759	0.53241
20	14.7885	0.94646	0.05354	75	7.0628	0.45202	0.54798
21	14.7508	0.94405	0.05595	76	6.8167	0.43627	0.56373
22	14.7115	0.94153	0.05847	77	6.5679	0.42035	0.57965
23	14.6700	0.93888	0.06112	78	6.3168	0.40428	0.59572
24	14.6262	0.93608	0.06392	79	6.0650	0.38816	0.61184
25	14.5797	0.93310	0.06690	80	5.8147	0.37214	0.62786
26	14.5305	0.92995	0.07005	81	5.5676	0.35633	0.64367
27	14.4781	0.92660	0.07340	82	5.3250	0.34080	0.65920
28	14.4229	0.92307	0.07693	83	5.0868	0.32556	0.67444
29	14.3648	0.91935	0.08065	84	4.8516	0.31050	0.68950
30	14.3038	0.91544	0.08456	85	4.6178	0.29554	0.70446
31	14.2399	0.91135	0.08865	86	4.3877	0.28081	0.71919
32	14.1729	0.90706	0.09294	87	4.1642	0.26651	0.73349
33	14.1024	0.90255	0.09745	88	3.9477	0.25265	0.74735
34	14.0286	0.89783	0.10217	89	3.7382	0.23924	0.76076
35	13.9508	0.89285	0.10715	90	3.5357	0.22629	0.77371
36	13.8693	0.88764	0.11236	91	3.3438	0.21400	0.78600
37	13.7839	0.88217	0.11783	92	3.1660	0.20263	0.79737
38	13.6940	0.87641	0.12359	93	3.0019	0.19212	0.80788
39	13.5997	0.87038	0.12962	94	2.8490	0.18234	0.81766
40	13.5005	0.86403	0.13597	95	2.7039	0.17305	0.82695
41	13.3962	0.85736	0.14264	96	2.5674	0.16431	0.83569
42	13.2866	0.85034	0.14966	97	2.4410	0.15622	0.84378
43	13.1716	0.84298	0.15702	98	2.3222	0.14862	0.85138
44	13.0512	0.83528	0.16472	99	2.2063	0.14120	0.85880
45	12.9259	0.82726	0.17274	100	2.0935	0.13399	0.86601
46	12.7954	0.81891	0.18109	101	1.9823	0.12687	0.87313
47	12.6601	0.81025	0.18975	102	1.8731	0.11988	0.88012
48	12.5198	0.80127	0.19873	103	1.7648	0.11294	0.88706
49	12.3744	0.79196	0.20804	104	1.6490	0.10554	0.89446
50	12.2236	0.78231	0.21769	105	1.5360	0.09830	0.90170
51	12.0674	0.77231	0.22769	106	1.3905	0.08899	0.91101
52	11.9064	0.76201	0.23799	107	1.2140	0.07770	0.92230
53	11.7405	0.75139	0.24861	108	0.9395	0.06013	0.93987
54	11.5700	0.74048	0.25952	109	0.4699	0.03008	0.96992

1980 COMMISSIONERS STANDARD ORDINARY MORTALITY TABLE
(Life expectancy, years)

Age	Male	Female	Age	Male	Female	Age	Male	Female	Age	Male	Female
0	70.83	75.83	25	47.84	52.34	50	25.36	29.53	75	8.31	10.32
1	70.13	75.04	26	46.93	51.40	51	24.52	28.67	76	7.84	9.71
2	69.20	74.11	27	46.01	50.46	52	23.70	27.82	77	7.40	9.12
3	68.27	73.17	28	45.09	49.52	53	22.89	26.98	78	6.97	8.55
4	67.34	72.23	29	44.16	48.59	54	22.08	26.14	79	6.57	8.01
5	66.40	71.28	30	43.24	47.65	55	21.29	25.31	80	6.18	7.48
6	65.46	70.34	31	42.31	46.71	56	20.51	24.49	81	5.80	6.98
7	64.52	69.39	32	41.38	45.78	57	19.74	23.67	82	5.44	6.49
8	63.57	68.44	33	40.46	44.84	58	18.99	22.86	83	5.09	6.03
9	62.62	67.48	34	39.54	43.91	59	18.24	22.05	84	4.77	5.57
10	61.66	66.53	35	38.61	42.98	60	17.51	21.25	85	4.46	5.18
11	60.71	65.58	36	37.69	42.05	61	16.79	20.44	86	4.18	4.80
12	59.75	64.62	37	36.78	41.12	62	16.08	19.65	87	3.91	4.43
13	58.80	63.67	38	35.87	40.20	63	15.38	18.86	88	3.66	4.09
14	57.86	62.71	39	34.96	39.28	64	14.70	18.08	89	3.41	3.77
15	56.93	61.76	40	34.05	38.36	65	14.04	17.32	90	3.18	3.45
16	56.00	60.82	41	33.16	37.46	66	13.39	16.57	91	2.94	3.15
17	55.09	59.87	42	32.26	36.55	67	12.76	15.83	92	2.70	2.85
18	54.18	58.93	43	31.38	35.66	68	12.14	15.10	93	2.44	2.55
19	53.27	57.98	44	30.50	34.77	69	11.54	14.38	94	2.17	2.24
20	52.37	57.04	45	29.62	33.88	70	10.96	13.67	95	1.87	1.91
21	51.47	56.10	46	28.76	33.00	71	10.39	12.97	96	1.54	1.56
22	50.57	55.16	47	27.90	32.12	72	9.84	12.26	97	1.20	1.21
23	49.66	54.22	48	27.04	31.25	73	9.30	11.60	98	0.84	0.84
24	48.75	53.28	49	26.20	30.39	74	8.79	10.95	99	0.50	0.50

TABLE V – ORDINARY LIFE ANNUITIES – ONE LIFE – EXPECTED RETURN MULTIPLES

Age	Multiple	Age	Multiple	Age	Multiple
5	76.6	42	40.6	79	10.0
6	75.6	43	39.6	80	9.5
7	74.7	44	38.7	81	8.9
8	73.7	45	37.7	82	8.4
9	72.7	46	36.8	63	7.9
10	71.7	47	35.9	84	7.4
11	70.7	48	34.9	85	6.9
12	69.7	49	34.0	86	6.5
13	68.8	50	33.1	87	6.1
14	67.8	51	32.2	88	5.7
15	66.8	52	31.3	89	5.3
16	65.8	53	30.4	90	5.0
17	64.8	54	29.5	91	4.7
18	63.9	55	28.6	92	4.4
19	62.9	56	27.7	93	4.1
20	61.9	57	26.8	94	3.9
21	60.9	58	25.9	95	3.7
22	59.9	59	25.0	96	3.4
23	59.0	60	24.2	97	3.2
24	58.0	61	23.3	98	3.0
25	57.0	62	22.5	99	2.8
26	56.0	63	21.6	100	2.7
27	55.1	64	20.8	101	2.5
28	54.1	65	20.0	102	2.3
29	53.1	66	19.2	103	2.1
30	52.2	67	18.4	104	1.9
31	51.2	68	17.6	105	1.8
32	50.2	69	16.8	106	1.6
33	49.3	70	16.0	107	1.4
34	48.3	71	15.3	108	1.3
35	47.3	72	14.6	109	1.1
36	46.4	73	13.9	110	1.0
37	45.4	74	13.2	111	.9
38	44.4	75	12.5	112	.8
39	43.5	76	11.9	113	.7
40	42.5	77	11.2	114	.6
41	41.5	78	10.6	115	.5

Frequency of Payment Adjustment Table

If the number of whole months from the annuity starting date to the first payment date is	0-1	2	3	4	5	6	7	8	9	10	11	12
And payments under the contract are to be made:												
Annually	+0.5	+0.4	+0.3	+0.2	+0.1	0	0	-0.1	-0.2	-0.3	-0.4	-0.5
Semiannually	+ .2	+ .1	0	0	- .1	- .2	....	....	....	....	....	....
Quarterly	+ .1	0	- .1	....	....	....	....	....	....	....	....	....

FIGURING COMPOUND INTEREST AND ANNUITY VALUES

The two tables that follow on the next two pages enable the estate planner to make various projections in actual cases. They show the compound interest and annuity functions at interest rates of 5 and 10 percent.

There are three functions which can be used for compound interest computations:

1. Amount of $1 (what a dollar will be worth at some date in the future if the deposit is made immediately).

   Example. If $1,000 is invested today and grows at a rate of 10 percent per year compounded annually, it will be worth $1,948.72 in 7 years. (Go to Form A on the following page. Find 7th year. Look under "Amount of 1" column. The value is 1.948717 multiplied by $1,000.)

2. Amount of $1 per period (what a series of $1 deposits will be worth at some date in the future if the deposits are made at the end of each period).

   Example. If $1,000 is invested at the end of each year for 10 years and the return has been 10 percent interest compounded annually, the value of the fund is $15,937. (Go to Form A. Find 10 years. Look under the "Amount of 1 per Period" column. The value is 15.937425. Multiply this by $1,000.)

3. Sinking fund payment (how much you need to deposit at the end of each period to have a given sum of money at a specified point in the future).

   Example. You'll need $100,000 in 5 years to pay off a debt. If you can earn 10 percent compounded annually on your money, you must deposit $16,379.74 each year for 5 years. (Go to Form A. Find 5 years. Look under the "Sinking Fund Payment" column. The value is .1637974808. Multiply that figure by $100,000.)

There are three functions which enable annuity computations:

1. Present worth of $1 (the value of $1 today if it will not be received until some time in the future).

   Example. You are owed $1,000 and it will be paid to you in 10 years. Assuming a 5 percent interest rate, the present value of that debt is $613.91. (Go to Form B. Find 10 years. Look under the "Present Worth of 1" column. The value is 0.613913. Multiply that by $1,000.)

2. Present worth of $1 per period. (How much is a future stream of dollars–payable at the end of each year–worth today?)

   Example. Suppose you were to receive $1,000 at the end of each year for the next 20 years. Assuming 10 percent interest, that stream of dollars would be worth $8,513.56 today. (Go to Form A. Find 20 years. Look under the "Present Worth of 1 per Period" column. The value is 8.513564. Multiply that by $1,000.)

3. Periodic payment to amortize $1. (What mortgage payment must be made each year to pay off a given loan? In other words, you have a dollar now. What annuity do you have to pay each year–given a certain number of years–to pay off the loan?)

   Example. What is the annual payment needed to pay off a $100,000 loan over 10 years if a 10 percent interest rate is payable on the unpaid balance? Assuming payments are made annually at the end of each year and interest is compounded annually, the amount is $16,274.54. (Go to Form A. Find 10 years. Look under the "Periodic Payment to Amortize 1" column. The value is 0.1627453949. Multiply that by $100,000.)

There is one measurement function: total interest (how much interest is paid over a given period of time where a loan is amortized by regular periodic payments).

   Example. Assume you were going to borrow $100,000 over 10 years at 10 percent interest. The total interest you'd pay on such a loan is $62,745. (Go to Form A. Find 10 years. Look under the "Total Interest" column. The value is 0.627454. Multiply that by $100,000.)

FIGURING COMPOUND INTEREST AND ANNUITY VALUES 10 PERCENT

	Amount of 1	Amount of 1 Per Period	Sinking Fund Payment	Present Worth of 1	Present Worth of 1 Per Period	Periodic Payment to Amortize 1	Total Interest
	What a single $1 deposit grows to in the future. The deposit is made at the beginning of the first period.	What a series of $1 deposits grow to in the future. A deposit is made at the end of each period.	The amount to be deposited at the end of each period that grows to $1 in the future.	What $1 to be paid in the future is worth today. Value today of a single payment tomorrow.	What $1 to be paid at the end of each period is worth today. Value today of a series of payments tomorrow.	The mortgage payment to amortize a loan of $1. An annuity certain, payable at the end of each period worth $1 today.	The total interest paid over the term on a loan of $1. The loan is amortized by regular periodic payments.
YEARS							
1	1.100000	1.000000	1.0000000000	0.909091	0.909091	1.1000000000	0.100000
2	1.210000	2.100000	0.4761904762	0.826446	1.735537	0.5761904762	0.152381
3	1.331000	3.310000	0.3021148036	0.751315	2.486852	0.4021148036	0.206344
4	1.464100	4.641000	0.2154708037	0.683013	3.169865	0.3154708037	0.261883
5	1.610510	6.105100	0.1637974808	0.620921	3.790787	0.2637974808	0.318987
6	1.771561	7.715610	0.1296073804	0.564474	4.355261	0.2296073804	0.377644
7	1.948717	9.487171	0.1054054997	0.513158	4.868419	0.2054054997	0.437838
8	2.143589	11.435888	0.0874440176	0.466507	5.334926	0.1874440176	0.499552
9	2.357948	13.579477	0.0736405391	0.424098	5.759024	0.1736405391	0.562765
10	2.593742	15.937425	0.0627453949	0.385543	6.144567	0.1627453949	0.627454
11	2.853117	18.531167	0.0539631420	0.350494	6.495061	0.1539631420	0.693595
12	3.138428	21.384284	0.0467633151	0.318631	6.813692	0.1467633151	0.761160
13	3.452271	24.522712	0.0407785238	0.289664	7.103356	0.1407785238	0.830121
14	3.797498	27.974983	0.0357462232	0.263331	7.366687	0.1357462232	0.900447
15	4.177248	31.772482	0.0314737769	0.239392	7.606080	0.1314737769	0.972107
16	4.594973	35.949730	0.0278166207	0.217629	7.823709	0.1278166207	1.045066
17	5.054470	40.544703	0.0246641344	0.197845	8.021553	0.1246641344	1.119290
18	5.559917	45.599173	0.0219302222	0.179859	8.201412	0.1219302222	1.194744
19	6.115909	51.159090	0.0195468682	0.163508	8.364920	0.1195468682	1.271390
20	6.727500	57.274999	0.0174596248	0.148644	8.513564	0.1174596248	1.349192
21	7.400250	64.002499	0.0156243898	0.135131	8.648694	0.1156243898	1.428112
22	8.140275	71.402749	0.0140050630	0.122846	8.771540	0.1140050630	1.508111
23	8.954302	79.543024	0.0125718127	0.111678	8.883218	0.1125718127	1.589152
24	9.849733	88.497327	0.0112997764	0.101526	8.984744	0.1112997764	1.671195
25	10.834706	98.347059	0.0101680722	0.092296	9.077040	0.1101680722	1.754202
26	11.918177	109.181765	0.0091590386	0.083905	9.160945	0.1091590386	1.838135
27	13.109994	121.099942	0.0082576423	0.076278	9.237223	0.1082576423	1.922956
28	14.420994	134.209936	0.0074510132	0.069343	9.306567	0.1074510132	2.008628
29	15.863093	148.630930	0.0067280747	0.063039	9.369606	0.1067280747	2.095114
30	17.449402	164.494023	0.0060792483	0.057309	9.426914	0.1060792483	2.182377
31	19.194342	181.943425	0.0054962140	0.052099	9.479013	0.1054962140	2.270383
32	21.113777	201.137767	0.0049717167	0.047362	9.526376	0.1049717167	2.359095
33	23.225154	222.251544	0.0044994063	0.043057	9.569432	0.1044994063	2.448480
34	25.547670	245.476699	0.0040737064	0.039143	9.608575	0.1040737064	2.538506
35	28.102437	271.024368	0.0036897051	0.035584	9.644159	0.1036897051	2.629140

FIGURING COMPOUND INTEREST AND ANNUITY VALUES 5 PERCENT

	Amount of 1	Amount of 1 Per Period	Sinking Fund Payment	Present Worth of 1	Present Worth of 1 Per Period	Periodic Payment to Amortize 1	Total Interest
	What a single $1 deposit grows to in the future. The deposit is made at the beginning of the first period.	What a series of $1 deposits grow to in the future. A deposit is made at the end of each period.	The amount to be deposited at the end of each period that grows to $1 in the future.	What $1 to be paid in the future is worth today. Value today of a single payment tomorrow.	What $1 to be paid at the end of each period is worth today. Value today of a series of payments tomorrow.	The mortgage payment to amortize a loan of $1. An annuity certain, payable at the end of each period worth $1 today.	The total interest paid over the term on a loan of $1. The loan is amortized by regular periodic payments.
YEARS							
1	1.050000	1.000000	1.0000000000	0.952381	0.952381	1.0500000000	0.050000
2	1.102500	2.050000	0.4878048780	0.907029	1.859410	0.5378048780	0.075610
3	1.157625	3.152500	0.3172085646	0.863838	2.723248	0.3672085646	0.101626
4	1.215506	4.310125	0.2320118326	0.822702	3.545951	0.2820118326	0.128047
5	1.276282	5.525631	0.1809747981	0.783526	4.329477	0.2309747981	0.154874
6	1.340096	6.801913	0.1470174681	0.746215	5.075692	0.1970174681	0.182105
7	1.407100	8.142008	0.1228198184	0.710681	5.786373	0.1728198184	0.209739
8	1.477455	9.549109	0.1047218136	0.676839	6.463213	0.1547218136	0.237775
9	1.551328	11.026564	0.0906900800	0.644609	7.107822	0.1406900800	0.266211
10	1.628895	12.577893	0.0795045750	0.613913	7.721735	0.1295045750	0.295046
11	1.710339	14.206787	0.0703888915	0.584679	8.306414	0.1203888915	0.324278
12	1.795856	15.917127	0.0628254100	0.556837	8.863252	0.1128254100	0.353905
13	1.885649	17.712983	0.0564557652	0.530321	9.393573	0.1064557652	0.383925
14	1.979932	19.598632	0.0510239695	0.505068	9.898641	0.1010239695	0.414336
15	2.078928	21.578564	0.0463422876	0.481017	10.379658	0.0963422876	0.445134
16	2.182875	23.657492	0.0422699080	0.458112	10.837770	0.0922699080	0.476319
17	2.292018	25.840366	0.0386991417	0.436297	11.274066	0.0886991417	0.507885
18	2.406619	28.132385	0.0355462223	0.415521	11.689587	0.0855462223	0.539832
19	2.526950	30.539004	0.0327450104	0.395734	12.085321	0.0827450104	0.572155
20	2.653298	33.065954	0.0302425872	0.376889	12.462210	0.0802425872	0.604852
21	2.785963	35.719252	0.0279961071	0.358942	12.821153	0.0779961071	0.637918
22	2.925261	38.505214	0.0259705086	0.341850	13.163003	0.0759705086	0.671351
23	3.071524	41.430475	0.0241368219	0.325571	13.488574	0.0741368219	0.705147
24	3.225100	44.501999	0.0224709008	0.310068	13.798642	0.0724709008	0.739302
25	3.386355	47.727099	0.0209524573	0.295303	14.093945	0.0709524573	0.773811
26	3.555673	51.113454	0.0195643207	0.281241	14.375185	0.0695643207	0.808672
27	3.733456	54.669126	0.0182918599	0.267848	14.643034	0.0682918599	0.843880
28	3.920129	58.402583	0.0171225304	0.255094	14.898127	0.0671225304	0.879431
29	4.116136	62.322712	0.0160455149	0.242946	15.141074	0.0660455149	0.915320
30	4.321942	66.438848	0.0150514351	0.231377	15.372451	0.0650514351	0.951543
31	4.538039	70.760790	0.0141321204	0.220359	15.592811	0.0641321204	0.988096
32	4.764941	75.298829	0.0132804189	0.209866	15.802677	0.0632804189	1.024973
33	5.003189	80.063771	0.0124900437	0.199873	16.002549	0.0624900437	1.062171
34	5.253348	85.066959	0.0117554454	0.190355	16.192904	0.0617554454	1.099685
35	5.516015	90.320307	0.0110717072	0.181290	16.374194	0.0610717072	1.137510

ANATOMICAL GIFTS

WHY TALK ABOUT IT?

Perhaps one of the most emotionally charged issues that should be discussed between a planner and a client is the making of anatomical gifts.

One way or another, the issue must be faced. If a client wants to make a gift he should know how to do it. Conversely, if a client is strongly against a gift of one or more organs, as estate planners we have a duty to protect them against the violation of their desires by others after they die.

WHAT IS IT?

The Uniform Anatomical Gifts Act (UAGA) has been enacted in every state. The purpose of this Act is to encourage various types of organ donations and to avoid inconsistency among the various jurisdictions.

The UAGA provides that any person over 18 may donate his entire body or any one or more of its parts. The donee can be any hospital, physician, medical or dental school, or various organ banks or storage facilities. Organ gifts can be made for education, research, therapy, or transplants. These gifts become effective at death and can be made by will.

Many states have also modified the UAGA to allow minors within certain age groups (*e.g.*, 15 to 17 in California, 16 and over in Maine) to make such donations. In some states, the consent of the minor's parent or guardian will be needed.

HOW DOES IT WORK?

There are two ways a gift can be made under the UAGA. One is that the donor can designate a specific individual to receive the gift. For instance, the person might specify that one of his eyes be given to a blind sister. A hierarchy of donees can be established and various body parts can be specified to go to specific donees.

A second way the UAGA works is to allow persons other than the decedent to have the power to make the gift. In other words, various family members can donate a person's body or organs. If there is no actual knowledge that the decedent does not want to make an anatomical gift, his spouse, adult children, parents, and siblings can make a donation. The UAGA establishes a priority system of relatives starting with the deceased's spouse and moving down from closest to furthest relatives who can make, or refuse to allow, anatomical gifts. The gifts can be made by these third parties unless (1) there is actual knowledge that the decedent would not want to make an anatomical gift, or (2) unless someone in the same or higher "class" opposes the gift. Donations can be authorized by third parties either before or after an individual's death.

Because of the possibility that an ill-intentioned relative would use anatomical gifts to obtain postmortem revenge, a person's intention regarding such gifts should be clearly specified one way or the other.

WHAT ARE THE REQUIREMENTS?

The UAGA requires that gifts must be made in writing by the donor and attested to by at least two witnesses. The donor must be of sound mind at the time of the writing (although there is no procedure for proving legal capacity in a manner similar to that used in probate). When gifts are made by family members, a written document is not a legal requirement and a telegram or tape recording may satisfy statutory formalities.

Many states provide for the making of anatomical gifts by a telegraphic, recorded telephonic, or other recorded message in the donor's voice or by a donation card on a driver's license. But most authorities feel that because of the wide variety and the potential for problems with regard to revoking gifts made in such a way, it is better to either make or object to an anatomical gift through a document other than a driver's license and a method other than a recorded message.

A person wishing to donate a particular body part to an individual might use language such as: "I give my _____ to _____, if needed by him or her for purposes of transplantation or therapy." A general gift to an institution might be made using language such as: "I give my _____ to _____ for purposes of transplantation, therapy, study, or research."

WHEN IS THE CLIENT DEAD?

The Uniform Anatomical Gifts Act does not provide for a specific definition of death. Most states define death as a "total and irreversible loss of brain function" and require the opinion of at least two physicians. The UAGA forbids the physician who certifies death to participate in any organ removal or transplant procedures.

WHAT MUST THE ESTATE PLANNER DO TO MEET A CLIENT'S WISHES?

Regardless of the estate planner's personal feelings about anatomical gifts, the client's wishes should be honored. Likewise, regardless of the wishes of family members, the client's desires regarding anatomical gifts should be met if possible. Estate planners should explain to clients that a traditional funeral service is possible in most cases (check with local clergy) even if an entire body is left for medical research. This will alleviate a great deal of the tension regarding anatomical gifts. You might also point out that the anatomical gift is a "postself" device, a way to continue to have meaning beyond the event of your physical death.

Documents meeting the requirements of the Uniform Anatomical Gifts Act should be prepared separate and apart from the will. A codicil to the decedent's will would be useful to state the client's intentions regarding anatomical gifts in a way that does not disclose the other provisions of the will. Alternatively, the client's desires can be set forth in an Advance Health Care Directive or in a separate Anatomical Gift Donor Form. If at all possible the client should designate a specific donee such as a family member or medical institution (and there should be "backup" donees in case the primaries can't or won't accept the gift for any reason).

WHAT SHOULD THE ESTATE PLANNER DO WHERE A CLIENT FEELS STRONGLY ABOUT NOT MAKING AN ANATOMICAL DONATION?

If a client does not want a gift of his body parts to be made, such desires should be clearly and strongly expressed. Prepare a "nonconsent" document and if the client feels quite strongly about not wishing to make an anatomical gift, consider providing in the will that any bequests made to an individual who consents to an anatomical gift will be void.

A nonconsent document might provide that: "I do not wish to make anatomical gifts under any circumstances," or "I do not wish any body part be used for transplantation, therapy, study, or research."

The discussion of anatomical gifts is one more facet of the uncomfortable–but highly important–nontax aspects of estate planning. It's part of the process by which the estate planner learns not only to face facts but also to face a face.

Appendix D

INTERNET IN ESTATE PLANNING

ALL ADDRESSES START WITH http://www. UNLESS OTHERWISE NOTED.

Leimberg Information Services Inc.	leimbergservices.com
Tools and Techniques on the Web, plus more	nationalunderwriter.com/taxfactsfx
FindLaw	findlaw.com/01topics/31probate/index.html
Dan Evans, Esq.	evans-legal.com/dan/
The Internet Law Library	lawresearch.com/
Probate & Property Magazine	abanet.org/rppt/magazine.html
LawCrawler	lawcrawler.com/federal.html
Key Code Sections	tns.lcs.mit.edu/uscode/TITLE_26/Subtitle_B/toc.html
IRS	irs.ustreas.gov
State Probate Laws	law.cornell.edu/topics/state_statutes.html#probate
Uniform Probate Code	law.cornell.edu/uniform/probate.html
Dennis Kennedy, Esq.	estateplanninglinks.com
Layne Rushforth	rushforth.net
ABA Business Valuation	demaio.com/vcbv/
FRM, INC. Bus Valuation	frminc.net
American College of Trust & Estate Counsel	actec.org/
U.S. Trust	ustrust.com
Martindale-Hubble	martindale.com/
U.S. Government	findlaw.com/10fedgov/index.html
Current Legislation	(no www) http://thomas.loc.gov/
Research Institute of America	riahome.com
PhilanthroTec	ptec.com/

IRS	irs.ustreas.gov/prod/cover.html
Tax Analysts	taxanalysts.com
Internal Revenue Code	access.gpo.gov/uscode/uscmain.html
Government Printing Office	access.gpo.gov/su_docs/aces/aaces002.html
Internal Revenue Bulletins	irs.ustreas.gov/prod/bus_info/bullet.html
Tax Articles	dtonline.com
Tax Articles	ey.com/global/content.nsf/us/home

INDEX

Please send me the following : *(please indicate quantity)*

The Tools & Techniques of Estate Planning	_____ Book (#2850013) $74.95
The Tools & Techniques of Practice Management	_____ Book (#2690000) $74.95
The Tools & Techniques of Investment Planning	_____ Book (#2730000) $74.95
The Tools & Techniques of Income Tax Planning	_____ Book (#2740000) $74.95
The Tools & Techniques of Employee Benefit and Retirement Planning	_____ Book (#2710008) $52.95
The Tools & Techniques of Financial Planning	_____ Book (#2770006) $64.95
The Tools & Techniques of Life Insurance Planning	_____ Book (#2700002) $44.95
The Tools & Techniques of Charitable Planning	_____ Book (#2500000) $49.95
The Tools & Techniques Online Library	_____ 1 Year Subscription (TTLIB) $195.00

❏ Check enclosed*   Charge My ❏ AMEX ❏ MC ❏ VISA (check one) ❏ Bill me

*Make check payable to The National Underwriter Company. Please include the appropriate shipping & handling and any applicable sales tax.

Card # _____ CVV#** _____ Exp. Date _____

Signature _____

Name _____ Title _____

Company _____

Address _____

City _____ State _____ Zip+4 _____

Business Phone (_____) _____

E-mail _____

BB

**For Visa/MC, the three-digit CVV# is usually printed on the back of the card. For American Express, the four-digit CVV# is usually on the front of the card.

The **National Underwriter** Company
A Unit of Highline Media LLC

Please send me the following : *(please indicate quantity)*

The Tools & Techniques of Estate Planning	_____ Book (#2850013) $74.95
The Tools & Techniques of Practice Management	_____ Book (#2690000) $74.95
The Tools & Techniques of Investment Planning	_____ Book (#2730000) $74.95
The Tools & Techniques of Income Tax Planning	_____ Book (#2740000) $74.95
The Tools & Techniques of Employee Benefit and Retirement Planning	_____ Book (#2710008) $52.95
The Tools & Techniques of Financial Planning	_____ Book (#2770006) $64.95
The Tools & Techniques of Life Insurance Planning	_____ Book (#2700002) $44.95
The Tools & Techniques of Charitable Planning	_____ Book (#2500000) $49.95
The Tools & Techniques Online Library	_____ 1 Year Subscription (TTLIB) $195.00

❏ Check enclosed*   Charge My ❏ AMEX ❏ MC ❏ VISA (check one) ❏ Bill me

*Make check payable to The National Underwriter Company. Please include the appropriate shipping & handling and any applicable sales tax.

Card # _____ CVV#** _____ Exp. Date _____

Signature _____

Name _____ Title _____

Company _____

Address _____

City _____ State _____ Zip+4 _____

Business Phone (_____) _____

E-mail _____

BB

**For Visa/MC, the three-digit CVV# is usually printed on the back of the card. For American Express, the four-digit CVV# is usually on the front of the card.

The **National Underwriter** Company
A Unit of Highline Media LLC

Order the *Tools & Techniques Series* and other
titles by The National Underwriter Company.

Save 5% Instantly when you order online at
www.NationalUnderwriterStore.com.
Include code BB at checkout.

The **National Underwriter** Company
A Unit of Highline Media LLC

ORDERS DEPARTMENT
THE NATIONAL UNDERWRITER COMPANY
PO BOX 14448
CINCINNATI OH 45250-9786

ORDERS DEPARTMENT
THE NATIONAL UNDERWRITER COMPANY
PO BOX 14448
CINCINNATI OH 45250-9786